Handbook of Research on Modern Systems Analysis and Design Technologies and Applications

Mahbubur Rahman Syed
Minnesota State University, Mankato, USA

Sharifun Nessa Syed
Minnesota State University, Mankato, USA

T0345108

INFORMATION SCIENCE REFERENCE

Hershey · New York

Acquisitions Editor:	Kristin Klinger
Development Editor:	Kristin Roth
Senior Managing Editor:	Jennifer Neidig
Managing Editor:	Jamie Snavely
Assistant Managing Editor:	Carole Coulson
Copy Editor:	Ashlee Kunkel and Joy Langel
Typesetter:	Jeff Ash
Cover Design:	Lisa Tosheff
Printed at:	Yurchak Printing Inc.

Published in the United States of America by
Information Science Reference (an imprint of IGI Global)
701 E. Chocolate Avenue, Suite 200
Hershey PA 17033
Tel: 717-533-8845
Fax: 717-533-8661
E-mail: cust@igi-global.com
Web site: http://www.igi-global.com

and in the United Kingdom by
Information Science Reference (an imprint of IGI Global)
3 Henrietta Street
Covent Garden
London WC2E 8LU
Tel: 44 20 7240 0856
Fax: 44 20 7379 0609
Web site: http://www.eurospanbookstore.com

Library of Congress Cataloging-in-Publication Data

Handbook of research on modern systems analysis and design technologies and applications / Mahbubur Rahman Syed and Sharifun Nessa Syed.

     p. cm.

  Summary: "This book provides a compendium of terms, definitions, and explanations of concepts in various areas of systems and design, as well as a vast collection of cutting-edge research articles from the field's leading experts"--Provided by publisher.

  Includes bibliographical references and index.

  ISBN 978-1-59904-887-1 (hard cover) -- ISBN 978-1-59904-888-8 (ebook)

  1. System analysis--Handbooks, manuals, etc. 2. System design--Handbooks, manuals, etc. I. Syed, Mahbubur Rahman, 1952- II. Syed, Sharifun Nessa, 1954-

  T57.6.H3634 2008

  004.2'1--dc22

                              2008007571

British Cataloguing in Publication Data
A Cataloguing in Publication record for this book is available from the British Library.

All work contributed to this book set is original material. The views expressed in this book are those of the authors, but not necessarily of the publisher.

Editorial Advisory Board

List of Contributors

Table of Contents

Section I
System Development Methodologies

Section V
Object Oriented Development

Section VI
Design Applications

Section VII
Medical Applications

Section VIII
Educational Applications

Detailed Table of Contents

Section I
System Development Methodologies

Chapter I

    Tony C. Shan, Bank of America, USA
    Winnie W. Hua, CTS Inc., USA

Solutions architecting method (SAM) is defined as a methodical approach to dealing with the architecture complexity of enterprise information systems in IT solution designs. This comprehensive method consists of eight interconnected modules: framework for e-business architecture and technology, prescriptive artineering procedure, technology architecture planning, architecture stack and perspectives, rapid architecting process, architecture readiness maturity, generic application platform, and Tao of IT development & engineering. Collectively, these modules form a holistic discipline guiding the process of developing architected solutions in an enterprise computing environment. Several unconventional concepts and thinking styles are introduced in this overarching structure. This systematic method has been customized and adapted to be extensively applied in one form or another to develop various IT solutions across a broad range of industrial sectors. Reference solutions are presented and articulated to illustrate the exemplary implementations of some key elements in SAM. Best practice and lessons learned as well as future trends are discussed in the context.

Chapter II

    Vivienne Waller, Swinburne University of Technology, Australia
    Robert B. Johnston, University of Melbourne, Australia & University College Dublin, Ireland
    Simon K. Milton, University of Melbourne, Australia

This chapter presents a new high level methodology for the analysis and design of information systems specifically to support routine action at the operational level of organizations. The authors argue that traditional methods fail to adequately address the unique requirements of support for routine operational action. The main innovation of the methodology is the use of an action-centred approach derived from recent work on the nature of purposeful human action, and as such, emphasises both the information requirements for action and the dependence of action upon appropriately structured environments. A brief case study illustrates how using the methodology can sensitize the analyst to opportunities to increase human efficiency and effectiveness through lighter weight information systems.

Chapter III

This chapter introduces an assembly-based method engineering approach for constructing situational analysis and design methods. The approach is supported by a meta-modeling technique, based on UML activity and class diagrams. Both the method engineering approach and meta-modeling technique will be explained and illustrated by case studies. The first case study describes the use of the meta-modeling technique in the analysis of method evolution. The next case study describes the use of situational method engineering, supported by the proposed meta-modeling technique, in method construction. With this research, the authors hope to provide researchers in the information system development domain with a useful approach for analyzing, constructing, and adapting methods.

Chapter IV

Advances in GPS, personal locator technology, Internet and network technology, and the rapidly growing number of mobile personal devices are helping to drive the fast growth of mobile e-commerce, we refer to as m-commerce. A special case of m-commerce is enabled with location based services (LBS) where often the actual position of the terminal is used in the service provision. In this chapter, we concentrate on the analysis and design issues and techniques for the LBS. We give a brief introduction of LBS and its applications and present the most important user, system, and infrastructure requirements. We also present the architecture and database design issues in LBS systems and study the performance an LBS system and evaluate its properties.

The software engineering discipline has developed the concept of software process to guide development teams towards a high-quality end product that be delivered on-time and within the planned budget. Consequently, several software-systems development life-cycles (PM-SDLCs) have been theoretically formulated and empirically tested over the years. In this chapter, a conceptual research methodology is used to review the state of the art on the main PM-SDLCs formulated for software-intensive systems, with the aim to answer the following research questions: (a) What are the main characteristics that describe the PM-SDLCs?, (b) What are the common and unique characteristics of such PM-SDLCs?, and (c) What are the main benefits and limitations of PM-SDLCs from a viewpoint of a conceptual analysis? This research is motivated by a gap in the literature on comprehensive studies that describe and compare the main PM-SDLCs and organizes a view of the large variety of PM-SDLCs.

Francisco Alvarez, Autonomous University of Aguascalientes, Mexico
Rory O'Connor, Dublin City University, Ireland
Jorge Macias-Luévano, Autonomous University of Aguascalientes, Mexico

Requirements engineering is the process of discovering the purpose and implicit needs of a software system that will be developed and making explicit, complete, and non ambiguous their specification. Its relevance is based in that omission or mistakes generated during this phase and corrected in later phases of a system development lifecycle, will cause cost overruns and delays to the project, as well as incomplete software. This chapter, by using a conceptual research approach, reviews the literature for developing a review of types of requirements, and the processes, activities, and techniques used. Analysis and synthesis of such findings permit to posit a generic requirements engineering process. Implications, trends, and challenges are then reported. While its execution is being mandatory in most SDLCs, it is done partially. Furthermore, the emergence of advanced services-oriented technologies suggests further research for identifying what of the present knowledge is useful and what is needed. This research is an initial effort to synthesize accumulated knowledge.

Chapter VII
Massimo Magni, Bocconi University, Italy
Bernardino Provera, Bocconi University, Italy
Luigi Proserpio, Bocconi University, Italy

Improvisation is rapidly becoming an important issue for both scholars and practitioners. Organizations that operate in turbulent environments must learn to swiftly adapt and respond to such instability, especially in areas as innovation and new product development. In such contexts, traditional top-down, carefully-planned approaches to innovative projects may represent an obstacle to effectively dealing with environment uncertainty. Prior research on improvisation has focused considerable attention on the centrality of improvisation in individual and group outcomes, while less emphasis has been placed on how individual attitude toward improvisation is formed. In an attempt to fill this gap, we will theoretically analyze the antecedents of individual attitude toward improvisation, by looking at the information systems development (ISD) domain. In particular, the outcome of this chapter is the development of theoretical propositions which could be empirically tested in future research.

Chapter VIII
John Wang, Montclair State University, USA
James Yao, Montclair State University, USA
Qiyang Chen, Montclair State University, USA
Ruben Xing, Montclair State University, USA

Since their creation in the early 1960's, decision support systems (DSSs) have evolved over the past 4 decades and continue to do so today. Although DSSs have grown substantially since its inception, improvements still need to be made. New technology has emerged and will continue to do so and, consequently, DSSs need to keep pace with it. Also, knowledge needs to play a bigger role in the form of decision making. We first discuss design and analysis methods/techniques/issues related to DSSs. Then, the three possible ways to enhance DSSs will be explored.

Chapter IX
John Wang, Montclair State University, USA
James G.S. Yang, Montclair State University, USA
Jun Xia, Montclair State University, USA

In contrast to ongoing, functional work, a project is a temporary endeavor undertaken to achieve or create a unique product or service(s). The project management knowledge and practices are best described as component processes—initiating, planning, executing, controlling, and closing. We have taken a closer look at project management by reviewing the types of methodologies and tools that exist in business today. We observed the major existing risk factors facing project management practices. We also evaluated the unique issues in delivering projects brought about by globalization. As we were extracting the information, it became apparent that there should be measures taken related to the project management process that could alleviate the some major risk factors in some way.

Chapter X

Reuse helps to decrease development time, code errors, and code units. Therefore, it serves to improve quality and productivity frameworks in software development. The question is not HOW to make the code reusable, but WHICH amount of software components would be most beneficial, that is, cost-effective in terms of reuse, and WHAT method should be used to decide whether to make a component reusable or not. If we had unlimited time and resources, we could write any code unit in a reusable way. In other words, its reusability would be 100%. However, in real life, resources are limited and there are clear deadlines to be met. Given these constraints, decisions regarding reusability are not always straightforward. The current research focuses on decision-making rules for investing in reuse frameworks. It attempts to determine the parameters, which should be taken into account in decisions relating to degrees of reusability. Two new models are presented for decision-making relating to reusability: (i) a restricted model and (ii) a non-restricted model. Decisions made by using these models are then analyzed and discussed.

This chapter presents three alternatives for structuring static tables—those tables in which the collection of keys remains unchanged and in which the FIND operation is optimized. Each alternative provides performance guarantees for the FIND operation which can help those who design and/or implement systems achieve performance guarantees of their own. The chapter provides clear and concise algorithms for construction and/or usage and simple guidelines for choosing among the strategies. It is intended that this presentation will help inform system design decisions. It is further intended that this chapter will assist implementation activities for systems which make use of static tables.

Chapter XII

This chapter introduces the irreducibility principle within the context of computer science and software engineering disciplines. It argues that the evolution, analysis, and design of the application software, which represent higher level concepts, cannot be deduced from the underlying concepts, which are valid on a lower level of abstractions. We analyze two specific sweeping statements often observed in the software engineering community and highlight the presence of the reductionism approach being treated already in the philosophy. We draw an analogy between the irreducibility principle and this approach. Furthermore, we hope that deep understanding of the reductionism approach will assist in the correct application of software design principles.

Section II
Modeling Processes

Chapter XIII

Applications require short development cycles and constant interaction with customers. Requirement gathering has become an ongoing process, reflecting continuous changes in technology and market demands. System analysis and modeling that are made at the initial project stages are quickly abandoned and become outmoded. Model driven architecture (MDA), rapid application development (RAD), adaptive development, extreme programming (XP), and others have resulted in a shift from the traditional waterfall model. These methodologies attempt to respond to the needs, but do they really fulfill their objectives, which are essential to the success of software development? Unified modeling language (UML) was created by the convergence of several well-known modeling methodologies. Despite its popularity and the investments that have been made in UML tools, UML is not yet translatable into running code. Some of the problems that have been discovered have to do with the absence of action semantics language and its size. This chapter reviews and evaluates the UML evolution (UML2, xUML), providing criteria and requirements to evaluate UML and the xUML potential to raise levels of abstraction, flexibility, and productivity enhancement. At the same time, it pinpoints its liabilities that keep it from completely fulfilling the vision of software development through a continuous exactable modeling process, considered to be the future direction for modeling and implementation.

Chapter XIV

The main purpose of a corporate information system is the support of the company's business processes. The development of information systems is therefore typically preceded by an analysis of the business processes it is supposed to support. The tasks of analysing business processes and designing information systems are governed by two seemingly incompatible perspectives related to the interaction between human actors or inanimate agents (objects), respectively. As a consequence, the corresponding modeling languages also differ. DEMO (dynamic essential modeling of organization) is a typical language for modeling business processes, the UML is the predominant language for information systems modeling. We challenge the assumption of incompatibility of the perspectives by providing a framework for the integration of these languages.

Chapter XV

This chapter provides an overview of business process management and business process modeling. We approach business process management by giving a historical classification of seminal work, and define it by the help of the business process management life cycle. Business process models play an important role in this life cycle, in particular, if information systems are used for executing processes. We deduct a definition for business process modeling based on a discussion of modeling from a general information systems point of view. In the following, we detail business process modeling techniques, in particular, modeling languages and modeling procedures for business process modeling. Finally, we discuss some future trends with a focus on the business process execution language for Web services (BPEL), and conclude the chapter with a summary. The chapter aims to cover business process modeling in a comprehensive way such that academics and practitioners can use it as a reference for identifying more specialized works.

Section III
Agile Software Development

Chapter XVI

Q.N.N. Tran, University of Technology, Sydney, Australia
B. Henderson-Sellers, University of Technology, Sydney, Australia
I. Hawryszkiewycz, University of Technology, Sydney, Australia

The use of a situational method engineering approach to create agile methodologies is demonstrated. Although existing method bases are shown to be deficient, we take one of these (that of the OPEN process framework) and propose additional method fragments specific to agile methodologies. These are derived from a study of several of the existing agile methods, each fragment being created from the relevant powertype pattern as standardized in the Australian Standard methodology metamodel of AS 4651.

Chapter XVII

Q.N.N. Tran, University of Technology, Sydney, Australia
B. Henderson-Sellers, University of Technology, Sydney, Australia
I. Hawryszkiewycz, University of Technology, Sydney, Australia

Method fragments for work units and workflows are identified for the support of agile methodologies. Using one such situational method engineering approach, the OPEN process framework, we show how the full set of these newly identified agile method fragments, each created from the relevant powertype pattern as standardized in the Australian Standard methodology metamodel of AS 4651, can be used to recreate four of the currently available agile methods: XP, scrum, and two members of the crystal family—thus providing an initial validation of the approach and the specifically proposed method fragments for agile software development.

Section IV
System Design and Considerations

Chapter XVIII

Adir Even, Ben Gurion University of the Negev, Israel
G. Shankaranarayanan, Boston University School of Management, USA
Paul D. Berger, Bentley College, USA

This chapter introduces a novel perspective for designing and maintaining data resources. Data and the information systems that manage it, are critical organizational resources. Today the design and the maintenance of data management environments are driven primarily by technical and functional requirements. We suggest that economic considerations, such as the utility gained by the use of data resources and the costs involved in implementing and maintaining them, may significantly affect data management decisions. We propose an analytical framework for analyzing utility-cost tradeoffs and optimizing design. Its application is demonstrated for analyzing certain design decisions in a data warehouse environment. The analysis considers variability and inequality in the utility of data resources, and possible uncertainties with usage and implementation.

Chapter XIX

Kenneth J. Knapp, U. S. A. F. Academy, USA

To promote the development of inherently secure software, this chapter describes various strategies and techniques for integrating security requirements into the systems development life cycle (SDLC). For each major phase of the SDLC, recommendations are made to promote the development of secure information systems. In brief, developers should identify risks, document initial requirements early, and stress the importance of security during each phase of the SDLC. Security concerns are then offered for less traditional models of systems analysis and development. Before concluding, future trends are discussed. Practitioners who read this chapter will be better equipped to improve their methodological processes by addressing security requirements in their development efforts.

Chapter XX

Robert Z. Zheng, University of Utah, USA
Laura B. Dahl, University of Utah, USA
Jill Flygare, University of Utah, USA

This chapter focuses on the design of human-computer interface, particularly the software interface design, by examining the relationship between the functionality and features of the interface and the cognitive factors associated with the design of such interface. A design framework is proposed followed by an empirical study to validate some of the theoretical assumptions of the framework. The findings indicate that learners become more perceptually engaged when a multiple sensory-input interface is used. Our study also shows that building affective interaction at the perceptual level could significantly enhance learners' perceptual engagement which further leads them to cognitive engagement. Guidelines for designing an effective interface are proposed. The significance of the study is discussed with some suggestions for future study.

Chapter XXI

Mara Nikolaidou, Harokopio University of Athens, Greece
Nancy Alexopoulou, University of Athens, Greece

System design is an important phase of system engineering, determining system architecture to satisfy specific requirements. System design focuses on analyzing performance requirements, system modeling and prototyping, defining and optimizing system architecture, and studying system design tradeoffs and risks. Modern enterprise information systems (EIS) are distributed systems usually built on multitiered client server architectures, which can be modeled using well-known frameworks, such as Zachman enterprise architecture or open distributed processing reference model (RM-ODP). Both frameworks identify different system models, named views, corresponding to discrete stakeholder's perspectives, specific viewpoints, and could serve as a basis for model-based system design. The main focus of this chapter is to explore the potential of model-based design for enterprise information systems (EIS). To this end, the basic requirements for model-based EIS design are identified, while three alternative approaches are discussed based on the above requirements, namely, rational unified process for systems engineering (RUP SE), UML4ODP and EIS design framework.

Chapter XXII

Tagelsir Mohamed Gasmelseid, King Faisal University, Saudi Arabia

This chapter addresses the software engineering dimensions associated with the development of mobile and context-aware multiagent systems. It argues that despite the growing deployment of such systems in different application domains little has been done with regards to their analysis and design methodologies. The author argues that the introduction of mobility and context awareness raises three main challenges that deserve a paradigm shift: the challenge of information integrity, service availability on mobile devices, and the complexity of decision modeling. Because they reflect different operational and procedural dimensions, the author argues that the conventional software engineering practices used with intelligent systems that possess other agency qualities need to be "re-engineered." The chapter emphasizes that the envisioned methodology should reflect a thorough understanding of decision environments, domains representation, and organizational and decision-making structures. Furthermore, the chapter provides a description for the appropriate enablers necessary for integrated implementation.

Chapter XXIII

This chapter introduces and investigates the applicability of the multiagent paradigm for engineering and developing CSCW systems with the aim of advocating modern design dimensions and software engineering implications. It argues that the use of multiagent systems can significantly improve and enhance the functionalities of computer supported work systems. To meet such an objective, the chapter raises the importance of "revisiting" the context and domain of CSCW in accordance with the growing organizational transformations, situational shifts, and technological developments. While such changes are motivating group collaboration, the information systems that support them must be powerful. The author believes that because of their specific limitations and the continuous changes in the collaboration environment, there is an urgent importance of using thorough system-oriented approaches to address the way they evolve. Furthermore, the chapter draws a framework for the use of the multiagent paradigm to understand and deploy CSCW systems by adopting an integrated context of analysis that improves our general understanding about their potentials.

Section V
Object Oriented Development

This chapter describes the use of design patterns as reusable components in program design. The discussion includes the two core elements: the class diagram and examples implemented in code. The authors believe that although precanned patterns have been popular in the literature, it is the patterns that we personally create or adapt that are most useful. Only after gaining intimate familiarity with a particular class structure will we be able to use it in an application. In addition to the conventional treatment of class patterns, the discussion includes the notion of a class template. A template describes functionality and object relations within a single class, while patterns refer to structures of communicating and interacting classes. The class template fosters reusability by providing a guide in solving a specific implementation problem. The chapter includes several class templates that could be useful to the software developer.

This chapter presents a brief overview of the object/relational mapping service known as Hibernate. Based on work provided in the book Java Persistence with Hibernate, it is argued that the paradigm mismatch problem consists of five problems: the problem of granularity, the problem of subtypes, the problem of identity, the problem of associations, and the problem of data navigation. It is argued that Hibernate, if it is to be considered a successful object/relational mapping service, must solve the paradigm mismatch problem and, hence, each of the five problems noted above. A simplified version of an order entry system is presented together with the mapping files required to store persistent objects to a database. Examples are given for one-to-one, one-to-many, and many-to-many mappings. The distinction between value and entity types is explained and the mapping technique required for value types is introduced into the order entry system application. The n+1 selects problem is explained and a strategy for solving that problem using Hibernate's support for lazy, batch, and eager fetching strategies is discussed.

Section VI
Design Applications

People's demands are escalating with technology advances. Now, people are not happy with only text or voice messages, they like to see video as well. Video transmission through limited bandwidth, for example, an existing telephone line, requires an efficient video coding technique. Unfortunately, existing video coding standards have some limitations due to this demand. Recently, a pattern-based video coding technique has established its potentiality to improve the coding compared to the recent standard H.264 in the range of low bit rates. This chapter describes this technique with its background, features, recent developments, and future trends.

With the remarkable growth of Internet and multimedia applications, production and distribution of digital media has become exceedingly easy and affordable. Applications such as distance education, e-commerce, telemedicine, digital library, and live audio/video broadcast activities require distribution and sharing of digital multimedia contents. Consequently, maintaining the quality of service of the applications and the rights of the content owner as well as enforcing a viable business model among the producer, consumer, and distributor of digital contents has become an increasingly challenging task, leading to a contentious area called digital rights management (DRM). This chapter presents how digital watermarking (DWM) technology can addresses part of this DRM problem of secure distribution of digital contents

From the beginning, machine learning methodology, which is the origin of artificial intelligence, has been rapidly spreading in the different research communities with successful outcomes. This chapter aims to introduce for system analysers and designers a comparatively new statistical supervised machine learning algorithm called support vector machine (SVM). We explain two useful areas of SVM, that is, classification and regression, with basic mathematical formulation and simple demonstration to make easy the understanding of SVM. Prospects and challenges of future research in this emerging area are also described. Future research of SVM will provide improved and quality access to the users. Therefore, developing an automated SVM system with state-of-the-art technologies is of paramount importance, and hence, this chapter will link up an important step in the system analysis and design perspective to this evolving research arena.

Section VII
Medical Applications

This chapter focuses on hybrid data mining algorithms and their use in medical applications. It reviews existing data mining algorithms and presents a novel hybrid data mining approach, which takes advantage of intelligent and statistical modeling of data mining algorithms to extract meaningful patterns from medical data repositories. Various hybrid combinations of data mining algorithms are formulated and tested on a benchmark medical database. The chapter includes the experimental results with existing and new hybrid approaches to demonstrate the superiority of hybrid data mining algorithms over standard algorithms.

This chapter describes the application of machine learning techniques to solve biomedical problems in a variety of clinical domains. First, the concept of development and the main elements of a basic machine learning system for medical diagnostics are presented. This is followed by an introduction to the design of a diagnostic model for the identification of balance impairments in the elderly using human gait pattern, as well as a diagnostic model for predicating sleep apnoea syndrome from electrocardiogram recordings. Examples are presented using support vector machines (a machine learning technique) to build a reliable model that utilizes key indices of physiological measurements (gait/electrocardiography [ECG] signals). A number of recommendations have been proposed for choosing the right classifier model in designing a successful medical diagnostic system. The chapter concludes with a discussion of the importance of signal processing techniques and other future trends in enhancing the performance of a diagnostic system.

In this chapter we aim to promote an understanding of the complexity of healthcare as a setting for information systems and how this complexity influences the achievement of successful implementations. We define health informatics and examine its role as an enabler in the delivery of healthcare. Then we look at the knowledge commodity culture of healthcare, with the gold standard of systematic reviews and its hierarchy of evidence. We examine the different forms of quantitative and qualitative research that are most commonly found in healthcare and how they influence the requirements for health information systems. We also examine some domain-specific issues that must be considered by health information systems developers, including those around clinical decision support systems and clinical classification and coding systems. We conclude with a discussion of the challenges that must be balanced by the health systems implementer in delivering robust systems that support evidence-based healthcare processes.

Recent development in telecommunication and information technologies came up with several technology options for telemedicine applications in hospitals and for medics for quality healthcare to patients. The research trends therefore need to be addressed for the proper deployment of technologies in a clinical setting or in a telemedicine environment with the adaptive compromise of technology and suitability. In this chapter, along with a description of the research trends and system design issues concerned with telemedicine, a mobile telemedicine system architecture and design have been proposed. Other current telemedicine technology options and prospects and challenges of future research in this emerging area are also described to indicate the possible future research challenges. Research in telemedicine is a future to provide improved and quality access to the healthcare professionals and patients. Therefore, developing telemedicine systems with state-of-the-art technologies is of paramount importance and hence, this chapter would link up an important step in system analysis and design perspective to this evolving research arena.

Section VIII
Educational Applications

The recent advances in knowledge engineering entail us to represent knowledge associated with a course in an expressive yet computable format as a hierarchical prerequisite relation-based weighted ontology. A schema called the course concept dependency schema written in Web ontology language (OWL) is designed to represent the prerequisite concept dependency. The knowledge associated with educational resources, like the knowledge required for answering a particular test question correctly, can be mapped to subgraphs in the course ontology. A novel approach for selectively extracting these subgraphs is given and some interesting inferences are made by observing the clustering of knowledge associated with test questions. We argue that the difficulty of a question is not only dependent on the knowledge it tests but also the structure of the knowledge it tests. Some assessment parameters are defined to quantify these properties of the knowledge associated with a test question. It is observed that the parameters are very good indicators of question difficulty.

The process of designing a university curriculum in the information systems discipline needs to follow many of the same processes that professional systems analysts use. Of concern are the product, the stakeholders, the drivers, and the methods; indeed, an information systems curriculum is an information system. This chapter presents a case study of one small regional university's efforts to create an updated information systems curriculum addressing the challenges of curriculum development using the framework of the very systems analysis and design course content that the students are expected to learn. The chapter identifies each component of the information system curriculum and details the processes supporting each development step along the way, from problem identification to system operation and support. This case study presents a cohesive approach to dealing with the many pressures associated with information systems curriculum development and might be instructive for curriculum development in other disciplines as well.

This chapter reports on the design, development, and implementation of a hybrid introductory systems analysis and design (SAD) semester long course taught at the junior/senior level. Five online instructional modules that focus on student-centered, problem-based learning (PBL) were developed. Each module parallels and reinforces the classroom session content. The classroom "seat-time" saved by having students study and complete online materials provides the instructor and students with additional time for face-to-face and electronic discussions. To further encourage PBL throughout the semester, students use an iterative approach to the SAD life cycle to analyze, design, and implement a prototypic solution to a real world problem presented by the authentic client. The use of a learning management system allows the client to participate in the course throughout the semester regardless of the physical distance between the students and the client. Instructor experiences, hybrid module development strategies, and a summary of student and client feedback are included.

Preface

Methodical and well-planned analysis and design is a key factor in the successful development, implementation, and efficient use of any system. With explosive growth of computer-based systems in diverse application areas, appropriate and additional application-specific methods of analysis and design are emerging. New approaches are being developed and new ways of utilizing older and new techniques are being constantly reviewed. In such an ever-evolving environment the practitioners, educators, researchers, and professionals of a discipline need access to the most current information about the methodologies, concepts, issues, trends, tools, and techniques in systems analysis and design. The *Handbook of Research on Modern Systems Analysis and Design Technologies and Applications* will be a useful source for comprehensive coverage and definitions of related topics, providing evolution of systems analysis and design methodologies and practices with insight into the comparative study of general and application-specific analysis and design approaches.

This book has 35 chapters divided into eight broader areas:

- System development methodologies
- Modeling processes
- Agile software development
- System design and considerations
- Object oriented development
- Design applications
- Medical applications
- Educational applications

The following paragraphs are intended to put together the abstracts from the chapters in this book that will provide an overview of the topics covered.

System Development Methodologies: The ever-growing business needs in large organizations demand for complex, but flexible, scalable, extensible, and forward-thinking technical solutions. To effectively manage the architecture assets and design top-quality IT solutions in a diverse environment the highly structured methodologies are of critical importance to achieve an array of goals, such as separate concerns, divide responsibilities, encapsulate the complexity, utilize patterns, leverage best practices, control quality, ensure compliance, and establish execution processes. Chapter I discusses the solutions architecting method (SAM), which is defined as a methodical approach to dealing with the architecture complexity of enterprise information systems in IT solution designs. It consists of eight interconnected modules: framework for e-business architecture and technology, prescriptive artineering procedure, technology architecture planning, architecture stack and perspectives, rapid architecting process, architecture readiness maturity, generic application platform, and tao of IT development and engineering. Best practice and lessons learned as well as future trends are discussed in the context. Chapter II presents a new high level methodology for the analysis and design of information systems, specifically to support routine action at the operational level of organizations. A brief case study illustrates how using the methodology can sensitize the analyst to opportunities to increase human efficiency and effectiveness through lighter weight information systems. Chapter III introduces an assembly-based method engineering approach for constructing situational analysis and design methods. It is supported by a metamodelling technique, based on UML activity and class diagrams. Chapter IV focuses on the analysis and design issues and techniques for the location-based service (LBS). It also presents the architecture and database design issues in LBS systems and studies the performance of an LBS system and evaluates its properties. Chapter V aims to identify important research questions in PM-SDLC formulated for software-intensive systems. Chapter VI is an effort to synthesize accumulated knowledge through developing a review of the types of requirements, processes, activities, and techniques used in software systems development. Analysis and synthesis of such findings permit to posit a generic requirements engineering process. Chapter VII is an attempt to theoretically analyze the antecedents of individual attitude toward improvisation by looking at the information systems development domain, while Chapter VIII discusses design and analysis methods, techniques, and issues related to decision support systems (DSS). Chapter IX takes a closer look at project management, highlighting the major existing risk factors and some measures facing project management practices. It also evaluates the unique issues in delivering projects brought about by globalization. Chapter X focuses on decision-making rules for investing in reuse frameworks and attempts to determine the parameters that should be taken into account in decisions relating to degrees of reusability. Two new models, a restricted model and a nonrestricted model, used for decisions-making relating to reusability are presented, analyzed, and discussed. Chapter XI presents three alternatives for structuring static tables and provides algorithms for construction. It also provides simple guidelines for choosing among the strategies. Chapter XII argues that the evolution, analysis, and design of the application software representing higher level concepts cannot be deduced from the underlying concepts, which are valid on a lower level of abstractions.

Modeling Processes: Model driven architecture (MDA), rapid application development (RAD), adaptive development, extreme programming (XP), and others have resulted in a shift from the traditional waterfall model. Unified modeling language (UML) was created by the convergence of several well-known modeling methodologies. Chapter XIII reviews the UML evolution (UML2, xUML), and outlines criteria and requirements to evaluate UML and xUML. It discusses the potentials and limitations that impose restrictions on it to completely fulfill the vision of software development through a continuous exactable modeling process. Chapter XIV discusses the dynamic essential modelling of organization (DEMO), which is a typical language for modelling business processes and the UML, which is a predominant language for information systems modelling. It also challenges the assumption of their incompatibility by providing a framework for the integration of these languages. Chapter XV provides an overview of business process management and business process modeling in a comprehensive way such that academics and practitioners can use it as a reference for identifying more specialized works.

Agile Software Development: Agile development emphasizes the relationship and communality of software developers as opposed to a universally applicable methodology for software and systems development. Chapter XVI hypothesize that an agile method can be created from method fragments, once those fragments have been identified and appropriately documented. It identifies and documents the method fragments that conform to an underpinning metamodel (AS4651) and that support a range of agile methods, including XP, Crystal, Scrum, ASD, SDSM, and FDD. An important part of any such research is the validation phase. This is described in Chapter XVII, where four agile methods are recreated from the fragments in the newly enhanced OPEN process framework (OPF) method base.

System Design and Considerations: The design and the maintenance of data management environments are driven primarily by technical and functional requirements. Chapter XVIII suggests that economic considerations, such as the utility gained by the use of data resources and the costs involved in implementing and maintaining them, may significantly affect data management decisions, and accordingly proposes an analytical framework for analyzing utility-cost tradeoffs and optimizing design. Chapter XIX emphasizes identifying security risks and documentation requirements from the very early stage in the development life stage, which is vital for the design, use, and maintenance of data, and the information system that manages it. It argues that practitioners will be able to improve both the security and the overall quality of computerized information systems by paying attention toward improving security with automated tools, performing abuse cases, tracing security requirements, holding regular security reviews, conducting certification and accreditation, and developing security response processes.

Chapter XX focuses on the design aspects of human-computer interface by examining the relationship between the functionality and features of the interface and the cognitive factors associated with the design of such interface. It proposes a framework and guidelines for designing an effective interface. Chapter XXI explores the potential of model-based design for enterprise information systems (EIS) and identifies the basic requirements for model-based EIS design. It discusses the RUP SE, UML4ODP, and EIS design framework based on the above requirements.

The significant advances exhibited in the field of mobile and wireless information systems have resulted into a rapid proliferation of mobile information devices and considerable improvement in their capabilities. Chapter XXII addresses the software engineering dimensions associated with the development of mobile and context-aware multiagent systems, while Chapter XXIII introduces and investigates the applicability of the multiagent paradigm for engineering and developing CSCW systems with the aim of advocating modern design dimensions and software engineering implications.

Object Oriented Development and design patterns: Chapter XXIV describes the use of design patterns as reusable components in program design, while Chapter XXV introduces Hibernate, which is described as a powerful, high performance object/relational persistence and query service.

Design Applications: With the remarkable growth of the Internet and multimedia applications, the production, distribution, and transmission of digital media are gaining importance. With increasing demand of video, its transmission through limited bandwidth media requires efficient video coding techniques. Chapter XVI describes the background, features, recent developments, and future trends of a pattern-based video coding technique that has recently established its potentiality to improve coding compared to the standard H.264 in the range of low bit rates. Chapter XVII discusses the issue of secure distribution of digital contents maintaining the quality of service of the applications and the rights of the content owner as well as enforcing a viable business model among the producer, consumer, and distributor of digital contents. Chapter XVIII deals with the development of an automated support vector machine (SVM) system with state-of-the-art technologies.

Medical Applications: Chapters XXIX to XXXII discuss tools, design, and trends in medical applications development. The first chapter focuses on hybrid data mining algorithms and their use in medical applications. It includes experimental results with existing and new hybrid approaches to demonstrate the superiority of hybrid data mining algorithms over standard algorithms. The next chapter describes the application of machine learning techniques to solve biomedical problems in a variety of clinical domains. Chapter XXXI provides an understanding of the complexity of healthcare as a setting for information systems and how this complexity influences the achievement of successful implementations. It discusses the challenges that must be balanced by the health systems implementer in delivering robust systems that support evidence-based healthcare processes. The next chapter discusses research trends and system design issues of telemedicine and proposes a mobile telemedicine system architecture and design.

Educational Applications: Chapters XXXIII to XXXV introduce design and analysis concepts in educational applications. Chapter XXXIII discusses the "course concept dependency schema" using Web ontology language (OWL) to represent the prerequisite concept dependency. The next chapter argues that an information systems curriculum is an information system, and, as such, design of a university curriculum in the information systems discipline needs to follow many of the same processes that professional systems analysts use. The last chapter reports on the design, development, and implementation of a hybrid introductory systems analysis and design (SAD) course.

As is evident from the above collection of the abstracts, many different audiences can make use of this book. Contributions to this publication have been made by scholars from around the world with notable research portfolios and expertise. Provocative ideas from the methodologies, applications, case studies, and research questions in different chapters from different aspects will make it instrumental in providing researchers, scholars, students, and professionals access to current knowledge related to systems analysis. Even a casual reader may benefit from it by getting broader understanding of the design and analysis terminologies and concepts.

Mahbubur Rahman Syed
Sharifun Nessa Syed
Editors

Mahbubur Rahman Syed *is currently a professor of Information Systems and Technology at Minnesota State University, Mankato (MSU). He has about 25 years of experience in teaching, in industry, in research and in academic leadership in the field of computer science, engineering, information technology and systems. Earlier he worked in the Electrical and Computer Engineering Department at the North Dakota State University, in the School of Computing and Information Technology, Monash University in Australia, in the Department of Computer Science and Engineering in Bangladesh University of Engineering and Technology (BUET) in Bangladesh and Ganz Electric Works in Hungary. He was a founding member of the Department of Computer Science and Engineering at BUET and served as Head of the Department during 1986-92. He served as the general secretary of Bangladesh Computer Society and also as the General Secretary of BUET Teacher's Association. He received the UNESCO/ROS-TSCA '85 award for South and Central Asia region in the field of Informatics and Computer Applications in Scientific Research. He won several other awards. He has co-edited several books in the area of e-commerce, software agents, multimedia systems and networking. He guest edited the 2001 fall issue of IEEE multimedia. He has more than 100 papers published in journals and conference proceedings. He has been serving in different roles such as co-editor-in chief, associate editor, editorial review committee, member of several international journals. Syed has been involved in international professional activities including organizing conferences and serving as conference and program committee chair.*

Sharifun Nessa Syed *is currently teaching Management Information Systems as an adjunct in the Department of Management at Minnesota State University, Mankato. She also taught at other educational institutions that include the South Central Technical College in Mankato, Rasmussen College in Mankato and BRAC University in Bangladesh. She worked as a consultant in the Canadian International Development Authority (CIDA) in Dhaka. She also worked as an assistant chief in the Planning Commission of the Government of Bangladesh. She completed her masters degree in economics from Dhaka University in Bangladesh, Masters of Business from Monash University in Australia and Bachelors in Computer and Information Sciences from Minnesota State University, Mankato. She also completed a post graduate diploma in Urban and Regional Planning under a joint program between BUET (Bangladesh) and AIT (Bangkok, Thailand). She has publications in the area of IT, economic analysis, resource mobilization and administration.*

Acknowledgment

Many people deserve credit for the successful publication of this book. We express our sincere gratitude to each of the chapter authors in this book, who contributed and expanded all the ideas mentioned above and made their expertise available in bringing this book to fruition. Our sincere thanks to the many colleagues and authors who have contributed invaluable suggestions in their thorough reviews of each chapter. Support from colleagues and staff in our respective departments, that is, the Department of Information Systems and Technology and the Department of Management at Minnesota State University Mankato, helped sustain our continued interest. A special note of thanks goes to all staff at IGI Global, whose contribution throughout the whole process from inception of the initial idea to final publication has been invaluable.

Mahbubur Rahman Syed
Sharifun Nessa Syed
Editors

Section I
System Development Methodologies

Chapter I
Towards a Systematic Method for Solutions Architecting

Tony C. Shan
Bank of America, USA

Winnie W. Hua
CTS Inc., USA

ABSTRACT

Solutions architecting method (SAM) is defined as a methodical approach to dealing with the architecture complexity of enterprise information systems in IT solution designs. This comprehensive method consists of eight interconnected modules: framework for e-business architecture and technology, prescriptive artineering procedure, technology architecture planning, architecture stack and perspectives, rapid architecting process, architecture readiness maturity, generic application platform, and Tao of IT development & engineering. Collectively, these modules form a holistic discipline guiding the process of developing architected solutions in an enterprise computing environment. Several unconventional concepts and thinking styles are introduced in this overarching structure. This systematic method has been customized and adapted to be extensively applied in one form or another to develop various IT solutions across a broad range of industrial sectors. Reference solutions are presented and articulated to illustrate the exemplary implementations of some key elements in SAM. Best practice and lessons learned as well as future trends are discussed in the context.

INTRODUCTION

The e-business models in today's fast-paced on-demand business world mandate increasing flexibility of information systems applications. It is compulsory for the information technology (IT) group to provide a higher level of services at a lower cost for the business to compete and succeed in a glo-balized economy. The reality is that IT must build more complicated, flexible, scalable, extensible, and forward-thinking technical solutions, to satisfy the ever-growing business needs.

In large organizations like worldwide financial institutions, virtually hundreds, if not thousands of IT applications and systems have been built, acquired, or purchased through the years, to provide both external customers and internal employees with reliable electronic services, utilizing heterogeneous technologies and architectures to satisfy diverse functional requirements from different lines of business. In the financial services industry, the banking business processes generally involves different business divisions that address retail, commercial, investment, wealth management, treasury, and capital markets. In particular, services are delivered via different channels. To effectively manage the architecture assets and design top-quality IT solutions in such a diverse environment, a highly structured methodology is of critical importance to achieve an array of goals—separate concerns, divide responsibilities, encapsulate the complexity, utilize patterns, leverage best practices, control quality, ensure compliance, and establish execution processes.

BACKGROUND

The computing paradigm has gone through several generations of evolution in the last five decades: monolithic, client/server, multi-tier, structured methods, object-oriented, component-based, service-oriented, and event-driven model. The overall solution architecture has become increasingly complicated and thus hardly manageable through a traditional waterfall process. Previous work over the past few years has strived to address the complexity issue in the architecture design and process. A pioneer effort in this space was the Zachman framework (Zachman, 1987), which is a logical structure to classify and organize the descriptive representations of an enterprise computing environment, which are important to the development of the enterprise systems and the enterprise management. In a form of a two-dimensional matrix to symbolize the enterprise architecture environments, it has achieved a substantial level of penetration in the domain of business and information systems architecture as well as modeling. Though it is primarily used as a planning or problem-solving tool, it tends to implicitly align with data-driven and process-decomposition methods and processes, and it operates above and across the individual project level. A similar approach is taken in the extended enterprise

architecture framework (E2AF) (IEAD, 2004) with a scope of aspect areas containing business, information, system, and infrastructure in a 2-D matrix. Rational unified process (RUP) (Kruchten, 2003) overcomes these shortcomings by taking a use-case driven, object-oriented and component-based approach, using a standard notation—unified modeling language (UML). The concept of 4+1 views offers multi-perspective interpretations of the overall system structure. RUP is more process-oriented, and to some extent is a waterfall approach. RUP has little to address software maintenance and operations, and lacks a broad coverage of physical topology and development/testing tools. It generally operates at the individual project level. Enterprise unified process (EUP) (Nalbone, 2005) attempts to extend the RUP to cover the entire IT lifecycle. An open source unified process (OpenUP/Basic) is also under development in Eclipse (OpenUP, 2007).

Another heavyweight approach, the open group architecture framework (TOGAF) (Open Group, 2007), is a comprehensive framework with a set of supporting tools for developing an enterprise architecture to meet the business and information technology needs of an organization. The three core parts of TOGAF are architecture development method (ADM), enterprise architecture continuum, and resource base. The scope of TOGAF covers business process architecture, applications architecture, data architecture, and technology architecture.

All these approaches are heavyweight methodologies, which require a fairly steep learning curve to get started. On the other hand, model-driven architecture (MDA) (OMG, 2007) takes a lightweight approach. MDA aims to separate business logic or application logic from underlying platform technology. The core of MDA is the platform-independent model (PIM) and platform-specific model (PSM), which provide greater portability and interoperability as well as enhanced productivity and maintenance. The primary focus of MDA is on software modeling in the development life-cycle process.

Quite a few agile methods are available such as extreme programming (XP), dynamic systems development method (DSDM), agile modeling (AM), feature driven development (FDD), crystal, adaptive software development (ASD), scrum, and test-driven design (TDD). Agile methods typically fit well with small- or medium-size projects developed by highly-skilled people. It is noteworthy that in DSDM (DSDM, 2007) time is fixed for a project, and resources are fixed as far as possible. The consequence of these restrictions in DSDM is that the requirements have to be allowed to change.

In the business process management (BPM) space, the business process management initiative (BPMI) organization (BPMI, 2007) has been working to develop open, complete, and royalty free XML-based BPM standards such as business process modeling language (BPML), business process modeling notations (BPMN), and business process query language (BPQL), but there have been only a handful of implementations so far. The business process execution language (BPEL) is specified by the OASIS group and has been gradually endorsed by many vendors. The extended business modeling language (xBML) (Business Genetics, 2007) differs from other approaches in that it dissects the business into separate and distinct "atomic" dimensions and then reintegrates these individual elements to produce a representative model of the entire business process that supports the business purpose. This proprietary language is only used in the tools supported by the vendor. A lack of interoperability is a big challenge in the BPM space.

Other related work on enterprise architecture frameworks is largely tailored to particular domains. These are useful references when an IT group creates its own models for the organization. The C4ISR architecture framework (DoD, 1997) provides comprehensive architectural guidance for the various commands, services, and agencies within the United States Department of Defense, with the purpose of ensuring interoperability and cost effectiveness in military systems. The treasury enterprise architecture framework (TEAF) (Treasury Department, 2000) gives the direction and guidance to all bureaus and offices of the treasury department for structuring enterprise architecture. The federal enterprise architecture (FEA) framework (Federal Office, 2007) aims to guide the planning and development of enterprise architecture in U.S. federal agencies. The Purdue enterprise reference architecture (PERA) (Purdue University, 2007)

is aligned to computer integrated manufacturing. ISO/IEC 14252 (IEEE Standard 1003.0-1995) (IEEE, 2007) is built on open systems standards as an architectural framework. Aiming at standardizing the open distributed processing, the ISO reference model for open distributed processing (RM-ODP) (Putman, 2001) is a coordinating framework that integrates the support of distribution, interconnections, portability, and interoperability, with four elements and five viewpoints.

In recent publications on the architecture process, practices, planning, patterns, methods, and platforms, the majority of these studies (Shan, 2004; Wada, 2006; Shan, 2006) focus on the high level or specific layers of enterprise architecture.

A new architecting model is introduced in the next section, with the key artifacts and features of various modules described in the subsequent sections, followed by the future trends and conclusion sections.

COMPREHENSIVE APPROACH

As discussed in the foregoing section, most of the previous methods reveal the architectural aspects of an information systems application to some extent from a single viewpoint or limited perspectives. The necessity of a comprehensive approach to architecting the end-to-end IT solutions becomes more and more evident, demanding a systematic disciplined way. A highly structured method is thus designed in this chapter to meet this ever-evolving need, and present a detailed and holistic view of all architectural elements, components, knowledge, platforms, planning, practices, and their interrelationships. Design processes are established accordingly in this approach to facilitate the creation, organization, and management of the architecture assets and solutions at different levels in a large organization.

Design Philosophy

The following design principles and philosophies are applied in developing the disciplined method, partly adapted from TOGAF (Open Group, 2007) but significantly modified/expanded to tailor to the services-oriented architecting process.

1. **Business Principles**
   a. **Primacy of principles:** All groups and stakeholders within an organization must follow these principles of solutions architecting.
   b. **Maximize benefits:** Maximum benefits will be achieved to the entire organization at the corporate level.
   c. **Business continuity:** Business operations are not interrupted in spite of system changes.
   d. **Active engagement:** All stakeholders that participated in the process will accomplish business objectives.
   e. **Compliance with regulations:** The architecting processes comply with all relevant regulations, policies, and laws.
   f. **IT accountability:** The IT group accounts for owning and implementing IT solutions, platforms, infrastructure, and processes to ensure that the deliverables satisfy business requirements for functionality, quality, service levels, cost, and delivery timelines.
   g. **Innovations:** The stimulation and protection of the corporate innovations is enforced in the IT architecture, management, standardization, planning, and governance processes.

2. **Technical Principles**
   a. **Flexibility:** The technical model is agile and nimble to be adaptive in response to future business needs.
   b. **Responsive change management:** Modifications to the corporate architecture/infrastructure environment are planned and implemented in a phased approach.
   c. **Requirement scope control:** Manage scope creeping effective.
   d. **Iterative process:** Use incremental development method rather than a waterfall approach.
   e. **Technology standardization:** Technological diversity is controlled to minimize immature and proprietary solutions and products.
   f. **Interoperability:** Software, hardware, network, and infrastructure must conform to industry and corporate standards that promote compatibility for applications, services, communications, integration, data, security, and technology.

3. **Solution Principles**
   a. **Ease of use:** Solutions are user friendly, with the underlying technology transparent to users, so they can concentrate on tasks at hand.
   b. **Technology independence:** Technical solutions are independent of specific technology/platform selections and decision, ensuring portability on different technology platforms.
   c. **Common services and components:** Minimize the redundant development of similar functionalities to promote common service and components across the organization.

4. **Data Principles**
   a. **Data asset:** Data is a corporate asset that has value to the enterprise and is managed accordingly.
   b. **Data ownership:** Each data element owned by an entity accountable for the data quality.
   c. **Common vocabulary and metadata:** Data is defined consistently throughout the organization, following common business taxonomy, and the metadata are standardized and accessible for all relevant users.
   d. **Shared data:** Data is shared across lines of business for individual applications and systems to perform their duties.
   e. **Data access:** Authorized users can access relevant data to perform their functions.
   f. **Data security:** Data is protected from unauthorized access, disclosure, use, and distribution. Regulatory requirements are strictly enforced. Sensitive and proprietary information is also protected,

particularly in international business, to comply with regional rules and laws.

Architecting Method

The solutions architecting method (SAM) is designed in this chapter as a systematic approach to developing and managing architecture of IT solutions. It utilizes a variety of conventional and unconventional problem-solving techniques such as the divide-and-conquer, recursive decomposition, and strengths-weaknesses-opportunities-threats (SWOT) strategies to abstract concerns, separate responsibilities, and manage complexities at different levels and from various standpoints. *SAM* is a methodical way to develop IT solution architecture, organize and visualize the architectural artifacts, identify static architectural aspects, specify dynamic architectural behaviors, and further help verify and optimize the strategy, resources, process, systems, applications, tools, and technology. As illustrated in Figure 1, *SAM* comprises eight key modules:

- **Framework for e-business architecture and technology (FEAT):** A 4-pillar framework for solution architecture design and governance.
- **Prescriptive artineering procedure (PAP):** A prescriptive method to combine both art and engineering approaches to designing and developing IT solutions.
- **Technology architecture planning (TAP):** A systematic approach to construct the IT blueprint and roadmaps with strategic alignment and agility.
- **Architecture stack and perspectives (ASAP):** A multi-perspective pyramid model for architectural artifacts and views.
- **Rapid architecting process (RAP):** A multi-dimensional procedural approach to develop orthogonal models in IT solutions.
- **Architecture readiness maturity (ARM):** an analysis method to assess architecture lifecycle (review-refactoring-reengineering-rearchitecting) and levels of capability maturity.

- **Generic application platform (GAP):** A modular platform addressing prominent development facets as an IT solution baseline.
- **Tao of IT development & engineering (TIDE):** A holistic best-practice model as guidance to effective IT solution constructions.

SAM MODULES

The modules in the SAM model are articulated in great detail in the next few subsections.

Framework for E-business Architecture and Technology (FEAT)

The framework for e-business architecture and technology is a high-level service-oriented framework for architecting IT solutions, composed of 4 core pillars—d*esign methodology, systematic process, solution patterns,* and *integrated maturity & performance management,* as shown in Figure 2.

The *design methodology* pillar deals with the approaches used to dissect business requirements and design architectures of IT solutions. The *systematic process* pillar specifies the step-by-step procedures in planning, designing, and maintaining architectural assets. The *solution patterns* pillar covers architecture models, common platforms, and reference solutions. The *integrated maturity & performance management* pillar is with regard to managing and assessing the maturity and performance of the artifacts in the framework.

FEAT is a foundation of the core scope of *SAM.* The modules discussed in the subsequent sections all fall into this overarching framework. In the *design methodology* pillar, practical methods are defined to consolidate the key techniques used in various schools of methodologies and to migrate the existing approaches to the next level, combining the art, engineering, and science disciplines. Based on these methods, pragmatic processes are constructed in the *systematic process* pillar, to form a cookbook approach to executing the methods in a step-by-step procedure. The *solution patterns* pillar serves as a repository of best practices templates and standards. Anti-patterns are also cataloged to capture lessons learned and pitfalls to avoid in the solution design. The *integrated maturity & performance management* pillar bridges the system quality requirements with the overall architecture aspects. The quality attributes are measured qualitatively and, more importantly, quantitatively in a repeatable way.

Prescriptive Artineering Procedure (PAP)

The great majority of the architecting processes today are in the form of an art. UML provides a mechanism to document the key artifacts in the application development in a standardized way. However, UML is largely limited to the software part of an IT solution, primarily towards object-oriented analysis and design. Some research work has been conducted to extend the UML to support other architectural concepts, but there has been little standardization that combines these activities into a single extension. The current design and documentation of IT architecture are more or less free-form, using a wide variety of illustrative "box-and-line" diagrams and formats. Multiple efforts were funded by DARPA to develop architecture description languages (ADLs), but many of the ADLs are in the format of programming languages rather than specification languages. Portability and interoperability are the hurdles to overcome as no standardization exists to combine results from one description into another or to verify a representation in one language by recasting it in another language.

To make the matter worse, due to the lack of standards in architecture descriptions, there is no single standardized method to be applied to architect an IT solution. The consequence becomes twofold. First, almost every application has a "unique" architecture designed and documented in distinctive ways. The applications may generally be classified to categories at a very high level. Some common grouping criteria are: Java EE or .NET applications, Struts or JSF as the MVC framework, and Hibernate/Cayenne or Java Persistence API as object-relational mapping technology. Nonetheless, it is extremely hard to conduct apple-to-apple comparisons at this conceptual level. Second, the development procedures are to

Figure 1. Solutions architecting method

Figure 2. Framework for e-business architecture and technology

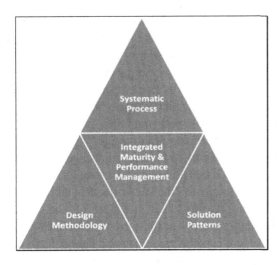

a large extent spontaneous and ad hoc, behind the perceptive rationale that each application development environment has its own "individual" needs. Making objective assessments and quantifying the effectiveness measurements of the development procedures are out of the question.

A prescriptive method is proposed, which is adapted and expanded from our previous work (Shan, 2006a), to standardize the solution development in both art and engineering approaches. The method is coined as prescriptive artineering procedure, which implies a combination of art and engineering disciplines in the design practice.

This comprehensive solution method is composed of the following key components, as shown in Figure 3:

- Service patterns
- Architecture process
- Hybrid design methodology
- Service-oriented enterprise model
- Service-oriented solution platform

The primary benefits of this pragmatic method are architecture abstraction, process standard, cross-application framework, and portfolio engineering.

The five components of this method address the primary focus areas in the solution design. The *service patterns* map the application requirements to a category in the problem domain for a pattern-based analysis and high-level modeling. The *architecture process* defines a multi-layer structure to abstract architecture complexity and cope with the architecture assets and responsibilities in a systematic manner. The *hybrid design methodology* provides a balanced approach to design a flexible and agile technical solution model. The *service-oriented enterprise model* presents a holistic view of the cross-portfolio and cross-application IT service model with service-oriented architecture (SOA), service-oriented process (SOP), service-oriented integration (SOI), and service-oriented management (SOM). The *service-oriented solution platform* offers a common baseline for all application solutions in a particular vertical market sector.

The hybrid design methodology utilizes both top-down and bottom-up approaches to take advantage of the benefits of the two schemes. The composite services & process layer is an important bridge between the two camps, as illustrated in Figure 4. Another key in this methodology is the mandatory deliverable of a platform-independent technical model, on which the platform-specific technical model is built and based, but not the opposite way around. In addition, existing applications can be service-enabled and migrated via pattern-based techniques—wrapping, decomposing, consolidating, and transforming, rather than being thrown away in order to transit to a SOA paradigm.

This comprehensive method has been successfully applied in the e-banking business domain to derive a service-oriented architecture model for the Internet-channel financial services space (Shan, 2004).

Technology Architecture Planning (TAP)

Figure 5 shows a triangle model for architecture planning. The simplicity of the model is its usefulness and strength of abstraction at a high level. The "as-is" element reveals the current architecture we have built or acquired. The "to-be" element represents the future architecture we wish to have. The third element is all of the people who have impacts on or are significantly affected by the architecture changes. The stakeholders include the business users, analysts, architects, developers, testers, system administrators, DBAs, subject matter experts, engineers, specialists, vendors, standards organizations, and legal entities. They may be for a change, be against it, be neutral, or not even know about it yet. Due to the different interests, relevant expertise, and roles played from various parties, there are conflicting forces and factors in the decision-making process. And it is not uncommon that wrong tools are inadvertently misused from time to time in investigating various aspects in different domains by different parties. It is, however, crucial to leverage appropriate tools to look into the details of the elements for analysis and synthesis. The analogy illustrated in the diagram demonstrates that, when evaluating the "to-be" element, a binocular is needed to see things in the distance, whereas a telescope must be used to observe things further far away. Likewise, in order to inspect greater details

of the "as-is" element, a microscope is necessary as a magnifying glass would not reveal the fine points at the level of granularity desired. Moreover, the internal structure may have to be disclosed via an X-ray or MRI image. The metaphor indicates that we need not only "do things right," but also "rely on right tools to help do things right."

There is a fourth element in the model—balanced approach, which is the architecture planning that balances the pros and cons, and resolves the conflicts with tradeoffs and compromises to lay out a reasonable path to the needed changes.

Based on this triangle model, a quadrant is constructed to identify the key artifacts in architecture planning, as illustrated in Figure 6. The "as-is" element is mapped to the current state assessment, which collects the input data and analyzes the existing environment. In the same way, the "to-be" element is mapped to the future state definition, which creates the future state vision. The future state specification serves as a blueprint of the desired form. The gap analysis is subsequently conducted to bridge the two states. A roadmap is thus defined to transit the current state to the future state in a

Figure 3. Prescriptive artineering procedure

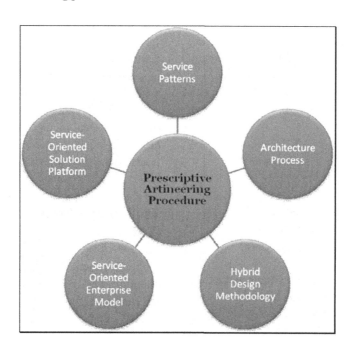

Figure 4. Hybrid design methodology

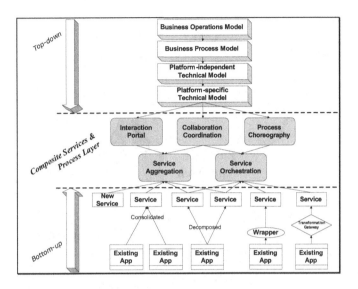

controlled manner. Usually, the changes are staged in multiple phases in an incremental fashion. Depending on the timeframe desired, the future state vision is typically strategic and targeted to the long term. However, tactical solutions are often needed to deliver required business functionalities in a short period of time. It is of vital importance to have the future state well defined, so that the strategic goals are not deserted when pragmatic approaches are crafted for the short-term goals.

This approach serves as a use-case driven pattern-based procedure for iterative architecture planning. Round-trip architecture engineering is enforced to articulate the multi-perspective views, using the industry standards on visual modeling and semantic ontology, such as UML, SysML/DSL, BPMN, BPEL, and OWL. Loosely-coupled interface and integration are imposed in the principle of design by contract. The 80-20 rule is leveraged in the use case drill-down for objective sizing and empirical estimation in the service-centered paradigm.

To provide better abstraction and individual agility, the solution domain is divided into two areas: business process domain and IT solution domain. The business process domain captures the information pertinent to the static structure on which the business runs—the business process, the

operations method, the dynamic process, the data requirements, and the usage scenarios. The IT solution domain describes the IT systems supporting and realizing the business process. The key artifacts in the IT solution domain are application domain pattern, conceptual architecture, architectural style, logical architecture, and technology model. The gap between the business model and IT model is daunting in almost every large organization. There have been constant conflicts in the alignment of IT models with business models due to the delivery schedule, resources, skillset, risks, and budgets. The strategy to alleviate this pain is to seamlessly integrate the models in these two areas. The engaging of end-to-end round-trip engineering principles with traceability and auditability is a necessity to make IT models nimble and adaptive.

A pragmatic procedure is further defined in Figure 7 to facilitate the current state evaluation and future state specification. There are eight steps in the procedure:

- Operations model
- Scope/functional analysis
- Use case model
- Business process flow
- Business data requirements

Figure 5. Triangle model for architecture planning

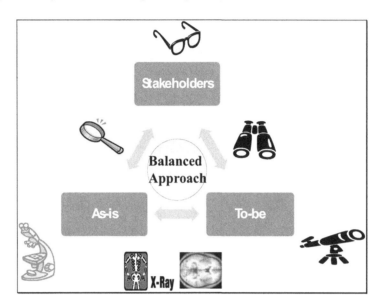

- Application/architecture pattern
- Conceptual model
- Technology model

Last but not the least, the SWOT technique is employed to conduct a thorough analysis on all major factors and options. The analysis reveals the requirement conflicts and design constraints as well as presumptions and limitations from a particular stakeholder's point of view. Focus on a single factor is meant to minimize risks only from that attribute perspective at a fine-grained level. This is often insufficient when a variety of conflicting attributes play an equivalently important role or have non-distinctive impacts in the system, so that a balance between these interacting attributes must be established. The outcome of the SWOT exercise is the key to the unbiased justification of tradeoffs in a balanced approach. The harmonious approach resolves the conflicts in local/individual attributes to reach a global optimization.

Architecture Stack and Perspectives (ASAP)

Various architectures have been used in application design practices, such as application architecture, data architecture, network architecture, and security architecture. The need for an organization scheme of multiple architectures within the enterprise is evidently indispensable as the scheme represents progressions from logical to physical, horizontal to vertical, generalized to specific, and an overall taxonomy. The architecture stack in the technology and information platform (TIP) model, shown in a pyramid shape in Figure 8, provides a consistent way to define and understand the generic rules, representations, and relationships in an enterprise information system. It represents taxonomy for classifying architecture artifacts as an aid to organizing reusable solution assets. It assists communication and understanding, within enterprises, between enterprises, and with vendor organizations. It has occurred frequently that IT professionals talk at cross-purposes when discussing architecture because they are referencing different points in the architecture stack at the same time without realizing it. The stack helps avoid these misunderstandings and miscommunications.

The generic architecture stack (GAS) in the TIP model comprises seven interrelated layers:

- Layer 1—enterprise business architecture
- Layer 2—enterprise technical architecture

Figure 6. Quadrant for architecture planning

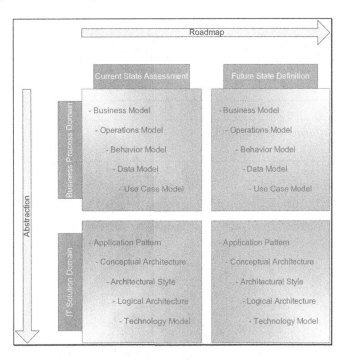

- Layer 3—cross business-line architecture
- Layer 4—channel specific architecture
- Layer 5—application solution architecture
- Layer 6—aspect-oriented architecture
- Layer 7—component technology architecture

The TIP model also provides multi-perspective views of the architecture assets in a large organization from both business and technical standpoints. The contextual spectrum is depicted in Figure 9, which contains four core parts: *process, abstraction, latitude,* and *maturity* (PALM). The *process* perspective covers operations, risk, financial, resources, estimation, planning, execution, policies, governance, compliance, organizational politics, and so forth. The *abstraction* perspective deals with what, why, who, where, when, which, and how (6W+1H). The *latitude* perspective includes principles, functional, logical, physical, interface, integration & interoperability, access & delivery, security, quality of services, patterns, standards, tools, skills, and the like. And the *maturity* perspective is about performance, metrics, competitive

assessment, scorecards, capacity maturity, benchmarks, service management, productivity, gap analysis, transition, and so on.

The abstraction perspective presents a high-level overview of the key artifacts for each architecture layer:

- What—definition of the architecture
- Why—value proposition and benefits
- Who—practitioners
- Where—usage scenarios and patterns
- When—time-based sequence and maturity
- Which—information and data dealt with
- How—approach and tools

Rapid Architecting Process (RAP)

The rapid architecting process (RAP) is designed based on the TIP model discussed in the preceding section. The focus of RAP is meta architecture, conceptual architecture, service architecture, systems architecture, information architecture, and software architecture, as shown in Figure 10. There are four dimensions defined in the process:

Figure 7. Technology architecture planning

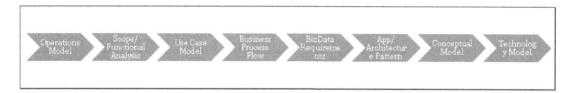

Figure 8. Technology and information platform

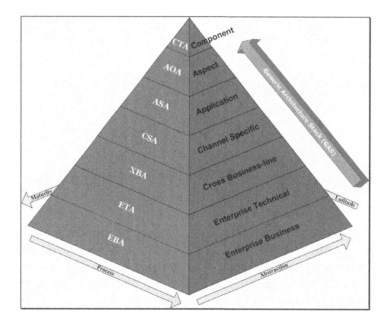

requirement analysis, specification, validation, and planning (RSVP). The requirement analysis is to identify the architectural requirements. The specification dimension is about designing the architecture based on the outcome of the analysis results and producing the architecture specifications. The validation dimension is for objective/subjective verification and certification of the architecture design completed. Lastly, the focus of the planning dimension is the generalization and optimization of the architectures in a domain and across portfolios.

Further, the process is broken down to eight interrelated steps:

- Step 1—meta-architecture
- Step 2—conceptual architecture
- Step 3—logical architecture

- Step 4—physical architecture
- Step 5—deployment architecture
- Step 6—data architecture
- Step 7—aspect-oriented architecture
- Step 8—component architecture

1. **Architecture requirement analysis:** The requirements of meta-architecture are architecture vision, principles, and trends, as well as the alignment of business and technology models. The conceptual architecture deals with modeling the system functionalities, identifying non-functional requirements, determining the service-level agreements, and analyzing the business process. The scope of the logical architecture is the overall IT system structure,

technology options and selection criteria, and application domain modeling. The physical architecture is about platform selection criteria, product mapping approach, capacity planning, and quality attribute analysis. The deployment architecture is with regard to the run-time environment to host the individual applications. The staging requirement of releases such as alpha and beta testing are in conjunction with various QA tests. A pilot may be required for large system rollout in the production environment. A recovery plan is important to provide business continuity in case of disasters. Data architecture handles the data and content requirements such as persistence, reporting, data integration, data quality, analytics, business intelligence, and data extract-transform-load. Aspect architecture treats crosscutting concerns as aspects in software using the architectural patterns. Component architecture is at the level of detailed design and implementation in application software. The analysis of the component needs helps identify reusable components and toolkits to

be leveraged, either commercial off-the-shelf (COTS) or open source.

2. **Architecture specification:** The meta-architecture specifies a number of key architecture artifacts across the application portfolio: architecture mission and vision, strategy, roadmap, methods, tools, frameworks, cross application architecture models, architectural patterns, business analysis patterns, and standards. The deliverables of the conceptual architecture design are use case diagram, use case specification, system scope, architecture constraints and assumptions, architecture risks, user interface specification, and service access specification (API and service interface). In the logical architecture, the design is specified via the architecture diagram, subsystem responsibilities and relationships, communication diagram, activity diagram, key technology selection, architecture layering, and interoperability. The physical architecture captures the platform selection, hardware model, system management, system backup and disaster recovery, scalability, high availability, authentication & authorization, security, and

Figure 9. Contextual spectrum in TIP model

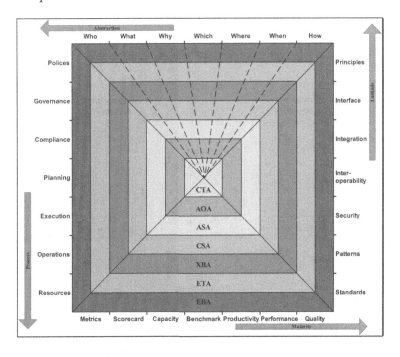

network requirement. The key elements in the deployment architecture are the network topology, hosting farm or hotel, deployable build models, development/test/production environments, configuration specification, deployment diagram, installation specification, user guide, and data center operations. The data architecture pertains to data model, storage, database engine, database schema, replication, data transfer, data backup, data caching, reporting, meta-data, query, workload priority, and access control. The aspect architecture specifies the application framework, design patterns, sequence diagram, collaboration diagram, performance tuning, session management, and open source products. Finally, the component architecture covers the component specification, CRC cards, class diagram, design patterns, technology, package, and open source utilities.

3. **Architecture validation:** The architectural artifacts as deliverables in the specification stage are verified, typically in a certification process. For meta-architecture, enterprise standards and polices are established, coupled with reference models and solution patterns. Prototype and proof-of-concept evaluations are used to justify the feasibility of new technologies and products. Best practice guidelines and development cookbooks are created as guiding documentation for the project teams. In the conceptual architecture, the business patterns and skeletal architecture are assessed to conduct the impact analysis. The focus of the logical architecture validation is on the architectural patterns, business rules, workflow, integration patterns, and reference models. A key decision justification in the physical architecture is build versus buy. Enterprise standards are checked with regard to the products used in the projects. In the deployment architecture, the deployment patterns should have been considered as the engineering implementation approaches. Data, aspect, and component related artifacts are validated in the respective architecture.

Figure 10. Rapid architecting process

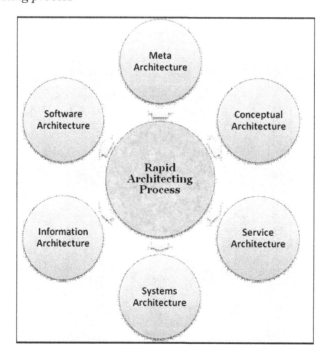

Last but not the least, the compliance with regulatory requirements and industry standards are investigated across all these architecture models.

4. **Architecture planning:** Architecture planning is for both individual application architecture and portfolio architecture. The granularity can be at the enterprise, CIO, channel, and business domain levels. Benchmarks are used to measure and track the maturity of architecture models. The planning emphasizes the architecture reusability and generalization, which lead to architectural styles and patterns for an enterprise computing environment. The TAP section presented earlier specifies a pragmatic method to conduct effective architecture planning.

Table 1 is a 2-D matrix, which summarizes the key artifacts in the RAP. The matrix serves as a blueprint of key activities defined in the architecting process. It may also be used to verify the deliverables produced in each individual architecting step.

Architecture Readiness Maturity (ARM)

An application architecture has a lifecycle, similar to a product lifecycle but at a different level. The relationship of the architecture lifecycle to system lifecycle is analogous to that of an engine to a car. Comprehensive assessment of the application architecture to identify the positioning of the architecture maturity in its lifecycle is decisively important.

A review-refactoring-reengineering-rearchitecting (R4) process is designed to facilitate a comprehensive technical analysis of the application and consequently recommend the next step in the lifecycle. Figure 11 illustrates this process model. The review course provides a complete technical assessment to clearly identify where an existing application stands in its lifecycle. Based on the review results, three methods are leveraged to revamp the application: refactoring, reengineering, and rearchitecting. Refactoring is useful to improve an application without dramatic structural changes. It

also helps reverse-engineer an application to recover the technical model, if not previously created in the forward engineering process, which is not uncommon in old applications that lacked disciplines in development. Reengineering is a valuable solution to migrate an application to next-generation technologies with no major architectural restructuring. It is sometimes the most cost-effective way to rebuild legacy systems. Rearchitecting is necessary if an application almost reaches the end of its lifecycle in terms of its technical model and architecture maturity. Replatforming usually falls in between reengineering and rearchitecting.

In addition, other techniques are complementary in assessing the architecture capability maturity, such as CMMi and six sigma. The capability maturity of a solution architecture can be rated to one of the five levels, similar to the CMMi model in principle:

*   Level 1—*ad-hoc*: No common format and deliverables are defined. The designers differ from each other drastically in their descriptions produced.
*   Level 2—*pattern-based*: Reference architecture is established as architectural models, which serve as templates for solution designs. Domain-specific patterns are identified.
*   Level 3—*standardized*: Industry standard methodologies are employed to specify a solution architecture, with an aid of modeling tools.
*   Level 4—*portfolio-based*: Connections and relationships of different architectures inside a domain and between the portfolios are identified and controlled. Management tools are leveraged to monitor the architectural assets and demands.
*   Level 5—*optimized*: The individual solution architecture and the architectural models within a domain are reconstructable, quantifiable, and consultable at run time, with iterative and adaptive generalization and optimization in a governable fashion.

The R4 process and the maturity levels are useful to assess the state of a particular application and/or

Table 1. RAP matrix

(RSVP)	Meta-Architecture	Conceptual Architecture	Logical Architecture	Physical Architecture	Deployment Architecture	Data Architecture	Aspect Architecture	Component Architecture	Construction execution
Architecture Requirements (analysis)	- Architecture principles - Architecture trends - Biz/Technology alignment - Architecture rationalization/simplification	- Functionality modeling - Non-functional requirements - SLA - Business process flow - System scope	- IT system structure - Technology options and selection - Application domain modeling	- Platform requirements - Product mappings - Network requirement - Quality attribute analysis	- Run-time environment - Staging - Pilot - Recovery time and point objectives - Release and backout plan	- Persistence requirement - Reports - ETL - BI - Data warehouse - Data mart - Risk data - OLTP/OLAP	- Crosscutting concerns - Application, software, hardware, network, infrastructure - Aspect patterns	- Detailed/Micro design - Service components - Process-service-component-object-method decomposition	- Requirement engineering - Lifecycle traceability - Integrated design environment - Constructs and assembly
Architecture Specification (modeling)	- Cross-app architecture - Roadmap - Architectural patterns - Business analysis patterns - Architecture methods - Architecture standards - Architecture frameworks - Modeling tools	- Use case diagram & specification - System context - Architecture constraints and assumptions - Architecture risks - User interface specification - Service access specification - Computation-independent	- Architecture diagram - Subsystem responsibilities and relationships - Communication diagram - Activity diagram - Key technology selections - Architecture layering - Interoperability	- Platform selection - Hardware model - System management - System backup and DR - Scalability - High availability - Authentication - Security - Capacity planning	- Network topology - Farm/Hotel - Build models - Configuration specification - DEV, TEST, UAT, PROD environments - Deployment diagram - Installation specification - User guide - Data centers	- Data model - Storage - DBMS - Database schema - Replication - Data transfer - Backup - Data caching - Reporting - Metadata - Query - Workload priority - Access control	- Application framework - Design patterns - Sequence diagram - Collaboration diagram - Performance tuning - Session management - Open source products - System & UI navigation	- Component specification - Service definitions - CRC cards - Class diagram - Design patterns - Technology - Package - Open source utilities - Libraries - Widgets - Toolkits - API	- Methodology - Development tools - Unit/Load testing tools - Configuration management - Code quality analysis - Automatic build/testing - Defect tracking - Coding style - Naming conventions
Architecture Validation (governance)	- Review - Prototype/POC - Reference models - Solution patterns - Best-practice guidelines - Cookbooks - Standards - Benchmarks	- Assessment - Impact analysis - Skeletal architecture - Business patterns - Industry standards - Notation standardization - Agility analysis	- Review - Architectural patterns - Business rules - Workflow - Integration patterns - SOA, BPM, ESB, WS - Biz process choreography	- Review - Enterprise standards - Compliance - Exception rationale - Reference models - Regulatory requirements - Build vs buy	- Review - Deployment patterns - Enterprise standards - Compliance - SSO and authorization - Encryption - Resource sharing	- Normalization - Data security - Data integrity - Transactional vs analytic - Data reuse - Data replication - Data quality - Data analysis - Data stream flow & audit	- Review - Enterprise standards - Compliance - Dependency injection - Annotations - Proxy - Industry standards - Reusable assets	- Review - Enterprise standards - Compliance - Open source asset repository - Interface - Component composition - Component orchestration	- SDLC - Common Application Platform (CAP) - Best practices - Lessons learned - Quality of services - Usability - Scorecard - Audit trail
Architecture Planning (vision)	- Architecture strategy - Domain/Channel architecture - Architecture reuse - Architecture optimization - Blueprint	- Process, Content, & Context - Architecture reuse - Architecture generalization	- Model alignment with biz process/architecture - Platform-independent & tech-agnostic	- Product lifecycle - Product roadmap - Architecture maturity - Longevity	- Data Center planning - Business Continuity - Technology recovery - Virtualization	- Reference data - Data integration & virtualization - Knowledge engineering - Data retention and archiving	- Common concerns - Patterns - Aspect-oriented design method - Inversion of control	- Component hierarchy - Maintainability - Conventions - Component catalog and repository	- Design process - Architecture refinement - Round-trip engineering - Stability - Reliability
	X-portfolio	*System level*					*Software level*		*Project level*

project architecture in its lifecycle. However, the objective maturity assessment of multiple architectural models at a domain level continues to be a challenge. Likewise, conducting apple-to-apple comparisons of architectures in different portfolios for simplification or rationalization is difficult, even though the practice recommendations and tools are emerging to address these issues in the application and project portfolio management space.

Generic Application Platform (GAP)

The generic application platform (GAP) forms a common baseline to implement service-oriented architecture, integration, process, and management in IT systems. It primarily focuses on architecture, hosting environment, application frameworks, components, tools, unit testing, build/deploy management, integration, methodology, system management, security, quality of services, and best practices. GAP consists of several units, as illustrated in Figure 12.

- **System environment:** The *logical architecture* module deals with application partitioning through multiple layers/tiers using architectural patterns. The *physical architecture* module covers system topology, performance optimization through intelligent load balancing, scalability via horizontal and vertical scaling, high availability through different redundancy and fail-over mechanisms, as well as clustering, disaster recovery, and network specifications. The *hardware model* module includes server brands and models, with CPU, memory, and disk space specifications. The *server software* module contains software products installed on Web, application, and database servers.
- **Application technology:** The *application framework* module has application frameworks, which are the foundation of application micro-structures. The *software components* module comprises the packages and toolkits used in software development. The *integration solutions* module handles data resource

integration. The *shared services* module is made of common services sharable across channels and lines of business.
- **Development lifecycle:** The *development tools* module is composed of tools used in modeling, development, profiling, defects tracking, configuration management, and code quality analysis. The *unit testing* module consists of standardized unit testing at component, application, and system levels. The *build & deployment* module focuses on the build process for deployment. The *process & methodology* module addresses the design approach and system development lifecycle.
- **Nonfunctional aspects:** The *system management* module concentrates on application and server level management. The *security solutions* module deals with security at the data, application, system, network, and data center levels. The *availability & scalability* module copes with the capacity planning, performance, and high availability. The *best practices* module includes the state-of-the-art solutions and industry-proven patterns.

Tao of IT Development and Engineering (TIDE)

The key components in SAM have been discussed in the foregoing sections, which covers the method, process, platform, and patterns. The Tao of IT development & engineering model introduced in this section is an overarching model of best practices utilizing the components discussed. The model consists of 20 functional blocks, each of which has a name of a word starting with the letter 'p'—*partition, path, patterns, people, performance, perspectives, philosophy, picture, plan, platform, policy, portfolio, power tools, practices, principles, problem solving, process, project management, protection,* and *prototyping*.

The goal of this best-practice approach is to enable competitive and effective development of IT solutions with wisdom, vision, strategy, and thought leadership. The key aspects in each module are listed in the functional blocks in Figure 13.

Figure 11. R4 process

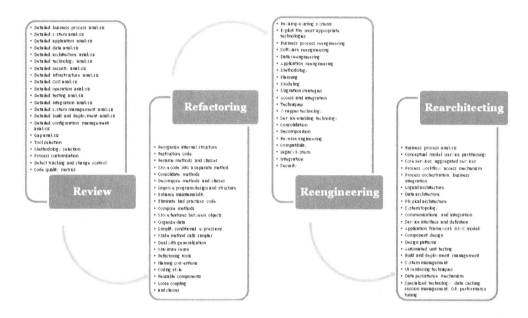

With regard to the *principles* module, though there are many different approaches to information systems development, there is a core set of design principles that are applied to guide how enterprise applications are designed and constructed. The design principles, in the neighborhood of hundreds in number, can be generally grouped into several categories: general, method, object, component, service, data, and infrastructure. In the object-oriented design, a few well-known principles give useful guidance to the interface and class design:

- **Open-closed principle:** Computing entities should be open for expansion, but closed for change.
- **Liskov substitution principle:** A reference to base types in a module must be replaceable by a reference to derived types without affecting the behaviors of the module. In other words, assuming that there is an instance obj2 of class X, for each instance obj1 of class Y as a subtype of X, the behavior of all programs P defined in terms of Y remains unchanged when obj1 is substituted for obj2.
- **Dependency inversion principle:** High level modules must be independent of low level modules. Abstractions must be independent of details. Conversely, details should rely on abstractions.
- **Interface segregation principle:** Clients should be forced to rely on only the interfaces that they use, no more and no less.
- **Design by contract principle:** Every method is defined with pre-conditions and post-conditions, whereas the pre-conditions specify the minimum requirements that must be satisfied in order for the method to execute successfully, and the post-conditions specify the results of a successful method execution. The contract is then formed between the method and the method caller.

As an example, the design by contract principle is widely applied in application integration design. It prescribes that precise and checkable interface specifications must be defined for the interacting components based on abstract data types, analogous to the conceptual metaphor of a business contract. In the object-oriented implementation, the principle imposes a certain obligation that a client module guarantees on entry to invoke the functionality, and it also guarantees a certain property on exit.

The use of this idiom has been extended to other fields beyond the object-oriented paradigm, such as Web services, where the Web services description language (WSDL) defines a standard binding interface between the service consumer and provider. Even in the code-first approach, WSDL provides a message-based XML language standard that is programming language independent. In addition to the input, output, and fault definitions, a WSDL schema specifies the endpoint address and transport protocol as well as custom data types.

FUTURE TRENDS

There are a plethora of architecture methods and frameworks developed in the last two decades.

Some of them have evolved and others have diminished to be consolidated or migrated to other forms. However, most of the prominent architecture methods and frameworks serve different purposes and focus on different domains with dissimilar scope and structures based on different principles and approaches. As a result, it may be difficult to directly apply these methods and frameworks into a domain portfolio. Consequently, there are generally three main streams on how to make use of the existing methods and frameworks. One approach is to customize a method or framework to be tailored to the needs in a specific segment. In this case, typically a heavyweight method or framework is selected as the baseline, which is further streamlined and customized to adapt to an individual domain. Another way is to combine several methods and

Figure 12. Generic application platform

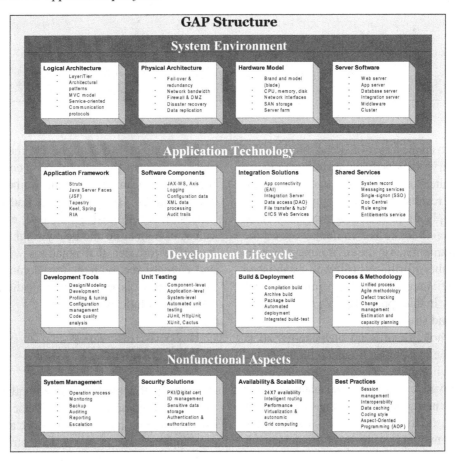

Figure 13. Tao of IT development & engineering

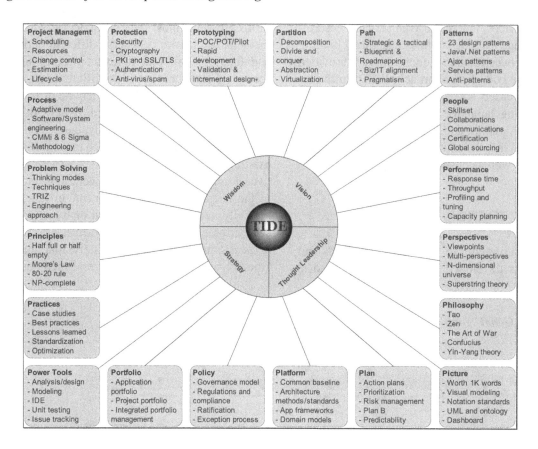

frameworks to create a best-of-breed solution. The constituents in various methods and frameworks are selectively united to formulate a compound process. This usually results in a hybrid approach in the real-world application. The other alternative is for an organization to create its own framework for the particular requirements in the environment. Nevertheless, a number of artifacts in the well-established methods and frameworks can be leveraged directly and indirectly in this approach, such as principles, techniques, and structures.

On the whole, there is no one-size-fits-all in this space. The existing architecture methods and frameworks will continue to grow and mature, incorporating innovative techniques and adapting to the latest advance in technologies. Brand-new methods and more holistic frameworks, like SAM designed in this work, may emerge to meet the new needs

in the architecture paradigm. On the other hand, convergence tends to take place to consolidate the methods and frameworks with similar capabilities and structures. Hybrid methods and frameworks possess more promising potential, exploiting the values of both agile and heavyweight approaches. It can be foreseen that notations will be unified and standardized, with the forthcoming round-trip engineering tools to fully automate the architecting process in solutions design.

CONCLUSION

Aiming to effectively organize and manage the architecture complexity and diverse business requirements in a large organization, a comprehensive approach is a necessity to abstract concerns, define responsibilities, and present a holistic view of the architectural aspects in a highly structured way. The solutions architecting method (SAM) is a methodical framework for architecting information systems applications. It defines the key artifacts in the design of solutions architecture.

The core constituent entities of *SAM* are *design methodology*, *systematic processes*, *solution patterns*, and *integrated maturity & performance managements*. The key modules related to these constituents are defined and articulated in the chapter: *prescriptive artineering procedure, technology architecture planning, architecture stack and perspectives, rapid architecting process, architecture readiness maturity,* and *generic application platform.* Additionally, a Tao of IT development & engineering model is designed as a best practice platform to make good use of these modules in the real-world project work.

Collectively, these modules form a holistic discipline guiding the process of developing architected solutions in an enterprise computing environment. Several unconventional concepts and thinking styles are utilized in this overarching framework.

This method has been extensively utilized directly or indirectly in developing various IT solutions in different industries such as finance/banking, telecommunications, and public sector. A few reference solutions have been presented to illustrate the exemplary implementations of the key elements in *SAM.*

REFERENCES

BPMI. (2007). *Business process management initiative.* Retrieved May 18, 2007, from http://www.bpmi.org

Business Genetics. (2007). *xBML methodology.* Retrieved May 18, 2007, from http://www.xbmlinnovations.com

DSDM. (2007). *Dynamic systems development method.* Retrieved May 18, 2007, from http://www.dsdm.org

DoD C4ISR Architecture Working Group. (1997). *C4ISR architecture framework* (Version 2).

Federal Office of Management and Budget. (2007). *Federal enterprise architecture framework.* Retrieved May 18, 2007, from http://www.whitehouse.gov/omb/egov/a-2-EAModelsNEW2.html

IEAD (Institute for Enterprise Architecture Developments). (2004). *Extended enterprise architecture framework.*

IEEE Standard 1003.0-1995. (2007). *IEEE guide to the POSIX open system environment.* Retrieved May 18, 2007, from http://standards.ieee.org/reading/ieee/std_public/description/posix/1003.0-1995_desc.html

Kruchten, P. (2003). *The rational unified process: An introduction* (3rd ed.). MA: Addison Wesley.

Nalbone, J., Vizdos, M., & Ambler, S. (2005). *The enterprise unified process: Extending the rational unified process.* New Jersey: Prentice Hall PTR.

OMG (Object Management Group). (2007). *Model driven architecture.* Retrieved May 18, 2007, from http://www.omg.org/mda

The Open Group. (2007). *The open group architecture framework.* Retrieved May 18, 2007, from http://www.opengroup.org/architecture/togaf8/index8.htm

OpenUP. (2007). *OpenUP/basic development process.* Retrieved May 18, 2007, from http://www.eclipse.org/epf/openup_component/openup_vision.php

Purdue University. (2007). *The Purdue enterprise reference architecture.* Retrieved May 18, 2007, from http://pera.net

Putman, J. R. (2001). *Architecting with RM-ODP.* New Jersey: Prentice Hall PTR.

Shan, T. C., & Hua, W. W. (2004). Building a service-oriented e-banking platform. In *Proceedings of 1st IEEE Conference on Services Computing* (pp. 237-244). China.

Shan, T. C., & Hua, W. W. (2006a). Service-oriented solution framework for Internet banking. *International Journal of Web Services Research, 3*(1), 29-48.

Shan, T. C., & Hua, W. W. (2006b). Solution architecture for N-tier applications. In *Proceedings of 3rd IEEE International Conference on Services Computing* (pp. 349-356). USA.

Treasury Department CIO Council. (2000). *Treasury enterprise architecture framework* (Version 1).

Wada, H., Suzuki, J., & Oba, K. (2006). Modeling non-functional aspects in service oriented architecture. In *Proceedings of 3rd IEEE International Conference on Services Computing* (pp. 222-229). USA.

Zachman, J. A. (1987). A framework for information systems architecture. *IBM Systems Journal, 26*(3), 276-295.

KEY TERMS

Architecture: The fundamental structure of a system and organization of its components, their relationships to each other, and to the environment, and the guiding principles and tenets for the design and evolution.

E2AF: Extended enterprise architecture framework, covering business, information, system, and infrastructure in a 2-D matrix.

Framework: A well-defined reusable structural and behavioral model in which applications can be organized and developed.

MDA: Model-driven architecture, an agile approach. MDA aims to separate business logic or application logic from the underlying platform technology.

RM-ODP: Reference model for open distributed processing, a coordinating framework for the standardization of open distributed processing in heterogeneous environments, with five viewpoints and eight transparencies.

RUP: Rational unified process, a use-case driven, object-oriented and component approach.

TOGAF: The open group architectural framework, a detailed framework with a set of supporting tools for developing an enterprise architecture, composed of architecture development method (ADM), enterprise architecture continuum, and TOGAF resource base.

Zachman Framework: A logical structure used to categorize and organize the descriptive representations of an enterprise IT environment, designed by John Zachman.

Chapter II
A Methodology for Situated Analysis and Design

Vivienne Waller
Swinburne University of Technology, Australia

Robert B. Johnston
University of Melbourne, Australia & University College Dublin, Ireland

Simon K. Milton
University of Melbourne, Australia

ABSTRACT

This chapter presents a new high level methodology for the analysis and design of information systems specifically to support routine action at the operational level of organizations. The authors argue that traditional methods fail to adequately address the unique requirements of support for routine operational action. The main innovation of the methodology is the use of an action-centred approach derived from recent work on the nature of purposeful human action, and as such, emphasises both the information requirements for action and the dependence of action upon appropriately structured environments. A brief case study illustrates how using the methodology can sensitize the analyst to opportunities to increase human efficiency and effectiveness through lighter weight information systems.

INTRODUCTION

Situated analysis and design focuses on providing information in support of routine action at the operational level in organizations. It is the outcome of applying the situational theory of action to the analysis and design of information systems (Johnston, Waller, & Milton, 2005; Milton, Johnston, Lederman, & Waller, 2005; Waller, Johnston, & Milton, 2006). A high level methodology for situated analysis and design was developed in a 3 year funded research project employing iterative theory development and testing by means of two system development case studies (Johnston et al., 2005; Waller et al., 2006) and one comparative experiment (Waller, Johnston, & Milton, 2008).

The methodology was designed specifically to address the problem of high failure rates and poor user acceptance of traditionally designed information systems at the operational level. We have argued in a previous publication that the heart of this problem lies in the implicit theory of action which informs information systems design. The traditional information systems analysis and design approach, manifested in methodologies such as SSADM (British Standards Institution, 1994), is informed by a deliberative theory of goal-directed action. The deliberative theory posits that an actor creates a mental model of the state of the world and that action invariably results from reasoning about this mental model. The traditional information system then supplies information about the state of the world to inform the actor's mental model (Johnston & Milton, 2002).

In other disciplines, there has been a move towards a situational theory of action, the idea that actors respond directly to structures in the environment in order to act appropriately. For example, work undertaken in artificial intelligence (Agre, 1997), situated cognition (Clancey, 1997; Lave & Wenger, 1991), animal behavior (Hendriks-Jansen, 1996), ecological psychology (Gibson, 1979; Heft, 2001), and situated action (Suchman, 1987) is based on this alternative theory of action.

The situated approach to systems design supplies the actor with information about action that enables routine action rather than deliberative action. Rather than attempting to represent the real world, the situated system informs actors when to do something and what to do without there being need for recourse to a representation of the state of the world; the information is located 'in' the world and can be observed directly. The purpose of this chapter is to provide a brief overview of the principles, concepts, and methods of situated information systems analysis and design. The approach is illustrated with a brief description of one of the system development cases conducted during its development.

BACKGROUND

Traditionally designed information systems are computerised models of the work system (Weber, 1997). While they provide support for managerial work such as decision making, accounting, planning, and standards production, they often do not effectively support routine operational activity, particularly in time-constrained routine environments. Estimates of failure rates are as high as 50% (Fortune and Peters, 2005). Analyses of why IS projects fail tend to focus on technical factors, such as the performance of the system, and organisational factors, such as the quality of project management, communication, management support, and user acceptance (Bostrom & Heinen, 1977; Ciborra & Schneider, 1992; Cannon, 1994; Gowan & Mathieu, 1996; Checkland & Holwell, 1998; Glass, 1998). In previous work (Johnston and Milton, 2002; Johnston et al., 2005), we have suggested a more fundamental reason for the failure of IS systems, specifically those designed to support real-time operations of the organisation. We have suggested that the problem lies with a misconceptualization of how the IS can best support these operations.

Whereas traditional systems analysis and design approaches aim to design a computerised model of the organization's work systems and processes, the situated systems methodology aims to identify ways that the environment of action can be restructured to enable new operational routines and to identify minimal informational cues that will enable actors to fluidly execute these new routines. With this aim in mind, the methodology proposes a radically different approach to analysing existing operational action systems, negotiating change, and designing new action systems that can be effectively routinized.

The key innovation of the new methodology is its use of an action-centred approach to information systems analysis and design. On the analysis side, this means resolving existing routinized action systems into a hierarchy of dependent actions and goals on the one hand, and on the other hand, identifying the environmental structures (physical, temporal, and organizational) upon which these actions depend. On the design side, an action-centred approach means simultaneously reconfiguring action environments for effective situated action and providing adequate information cues to actors about the action dependencies of redesigned action sequences.

Through focusing on routinizing action, situated analysis and design can improve the effectiveness and efficiency of action. In particular, systems developed using situated analysis and design should improve human efficiency in time-constrained environments. They do this by reducing the effort expended in searching for required information about the conditions of action and deliberating on possible courses of action. They can also be lightweight and more reliable than conventional systems. Because implementation issues are explicitly addressed in the design phase of the situated analysis and design methodology, these systems are more likely to be embraced by users. The methodology is directed to identifying the minimal information requirement that will allow reliable routine performance of work processes. As such, it does not commit to the form of information delivery; this could take various digital or non-digital forms.

Information systems analysis, design, and development methodologies are generally collections of procedures, techniques, tools, and documentation aids (Avison & Fitzgerald, 2003). The situated analysis and design methodology is an action-centered approach to conceptualizing information support for routine work. While outlining procedures and techniques, it does not prescribe the use of particular tools for representation or documentation aids (although the tools used need to have particular representational capabilities)

SITUATED ANALYSIS AND DESIGN

Situated analysis and design makes use of the following three properties of actions: (1) that actions are always situated in the environment, (2) that actions are multi-scale in nature, and (3) that actions are dependent on the execution of other actions for instantiation as part of the action system. The concepts needed to make use of these properties make up the conceptual toolkit of situated analysis and design.

Conceptual Toolkit of Situated Analysis and Design

Every action is conducted by an actor in time and space, making use of resources. The *action context* is the actor, location, time, and resources associated with an action. In other words, the action context is the particular dimensions of the environment in which a particular action occurs. The set of all the actions available to an actor (in a particular location, at a particular time, and with particular resources) is conceptualised as the *action possibility space*.

Structures are patterns in the environment which constrain or enable action. Physical structures include the way work spaces are organised and the arrangement of things. Organizational structures include roles and norms. Temporal structures include blocks of time reserved for particular types of action and times at which particular actions are to occur.

Actions are multi-scale in nature. This means that both actions and the action context can be specified at different levels of detail or grain-size. Another way of saying this is that an action can be expanded into a set of lower level actions that occur in valid particularisations of the context of the higher action. For example, the action of selling a house can be expanded into the actions of the vendor putting some possessions into storage, a real estate agent showing a house to prospective buyers, the auctioneer taking bids, and the vendor signing the contract.

The actions associated with attaining a goal can be arranged into an action abstraction hierarchy (Johansson, 1989). For any particular action, asking *why* that action is conducted moves one up the action abstraction hierarchy, emphasising the goal aspects of the action (for example, the possessions are put into storage in order to sell the home). Asking *how* that action is conducted moves one down the action abstraction hierarchy to more specific levels. The lower one goes down the action hierarchy, the more detail is specified about the action context (that is, details of actor, location, time and resources). In other words, the action becomes more situated in a specific practice. By the same process, the implementation details of the higher-level action become specified more precisely as a set of more detailed actions.

In any system of actions designed to achieve a particular purpose, there are actions which are dependent on the execution of other actions for instantiation in this action system. The term *action dependency* describes this type of relation between two actions.

APPLYING THE METHODOLOGY

Figure 1 is a schematic depiction of the three main steps involved in applying the situated analysis and design methodology. Conceptually, each triangle in Figure 1 represents a system of actions designed to achieve the goal(s) near the apex. The steps involved in applying the methodology are elaborated in the following sections.

ANALYSING THE EXISTING SYSTEM OF ACTIONS

The first triangle in Figure 1 depicts this stage of analysing the existing system of actions. Analysis involves both description and evaluation. The existing system of actions is described in order to identify what is currently being achieved; at the same time, the efficiency and effectiveness of the existing system of actions is evaluated against their purpose. There are three conceptually distinct aspects to the

Figure 1. Applying the situated analysis and design methodology

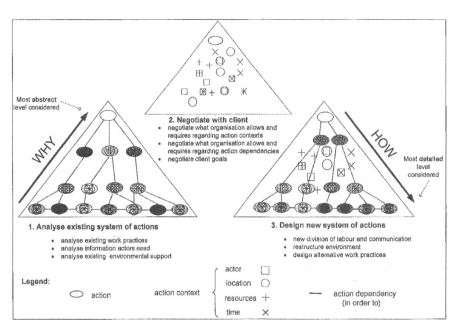

analysis of the existing system of actions: analysis of existing work practices, analysis of information actors need, and analysis of existing environmental support for action. In practice, these analyses may occur concurrently.

Analysing Existing Work Practices

In analysing existing work practices, one needs only to go down to that level of detail which makes sense to actors in describing what they do. The situated information system is only concerned with providing information about non-discretionary action. Those actions which are not to be routinized, (because, for example, they depend on an individual's judgement) are treated as a black box in the analysis.

A variety of modeling tools to describe action systems already exist, and the choice of tool for analysis is not important to the methodology. What is important is that the modeling tools and documentation aids used are able to represent the action context and action dependencies. The basic principle is that existing work practices need to be analysed in terms of actions and their context, that is, when and where and who does what with what. These actions also need to be described in terms of their action dependencies and the purpose of each action needs to be established.

Describing the action system in this way makes it possible to identify whether the sequence of actions (what), and division of labour, use of resources, timing, and location (how) is efficient in terms of human effort and time. This analysis assists in identifying whether any actions are redundant and whether there is a need for better coordination as well as making explicit exactly where any delays are occurring.

Analysing Actors' Information Needs

In a system of actions, in order to act at the right time, actors need to know that the actions on which their action is dependent have been successfully completed. Analysis of the action dependencies reveals what information actors need in order to act. The rule of thumb is to provide actors with the information that they need in the time and place in which they need it.

Analysing Existing Environmental Support

In analysing the action context, it becomes evident as to what extent existing environmental structures (physical, organizational, and temporal) support action. By paying attention to how the existing environmental structures enable or constrain action, the analyst can see what sort of environmental redesign will improve efficiency and effectiveness. Efficiency has three aspects: temporal efficiency, or the minimisation of the expenditure of time, human efficiency, or the minimisation of mental or physical effort, and economic efficiency, or the minimisation of financial cost (Bevan, 1995). Effectiveness means that the intended goals are achieved, completely and accurately (Agerfalk & Eriksson, 2006).

NEGOTIATIONS REGARDING THE NEW SYSTEM OF ACTIONS

In traditional information systems analysis and design under the waterfall model, a requirements analysis is conducted to determine client needs. In situated analysis and design, a negotiation phase occurs based around aspects of action; broadly, what is to be done and how it is to be done. This stakeholder negotiation differs from that which occurs in traditional information systems and design.

In any organization, choosing which actions are to be routinized is a matter of negotiation between stakeholders, and is not evident *a priori*. Any increase in efficiency or effectiveness needs to be weighed against the effects on actor satisfaction. For example, actors who gain satisfaction from relying on their professional skill and judgement to carry out particular actions, may not wish to see these actions routinized.

Negotiation of the Action Context and Action Dependencies

Organizational constraints are limitations on the action context and action dependencies; specifically, what is allowed and what is required by the organization. What is allowed by the organization can be understood as the set of actors, locations, times, and resources that can be associated with action. A subset of these contains what is required by the organization. What is required by the organization may reflect the organization's preferred way of operating or may be in response to outside pressures, such as legislation. The organization may have requirements regarding the action context. For example, in a health care context, the organization may require that certain actions be conducted by a particular type of actor, (e.g., doctor), a particular actor (e.g., Doctor Jones), in a particular type of location (e.g., sterile environment), a particular location (e.g., Ward 7), using a particular type of resource (e.g., expandable patient record) or particular resource (e.g., written patient record)—or any combination of these. The time may also be constrained. For example, operations that take more than 4 hours may have to be begun in the morning.

The organization may also have some requirements regarding action dependencies, for instance, regarding the order of actions. For example, the organization may require that treatment for a private patient does not commence until the level of health insurance cover is established.

However, some of what the organization allows or requires will be negotiable, especially as some of the perceived requirements will be simply the way things have always been done. It is only in the negotiation phase that the analyst can identify which constraints are 'hard' (Johnston et al., 2005); that is, those which the organization cannot or is unwilling to see changed. These 'hard' constraints are those constraints that necessarily govern aspects of any redesigned system; that is, they are not negotiable with the client. Thus, the 'hard' constraints contained in the second triangle in Figure 1 are also present in the third triangle depicting the new system of actions.

Negotiation of Client Goals

The client's goals for the system can be viewed as another type of 'hard' organizational constraint. Describing the existing system of actions includes establishing the purpose of existing work practices. In terms of Figure 1, it involves moving up the action abstraction hierarchy. The analyst makes a pragmatic decision to move up the action abstraction hierarchy until reaching those actions which the client considers are the goals. As well as describing the purpose of what is done, these higher-level actions become constraints on what is done.

As Figure 1 indicates, in the design phase, all organizational constraints that have been identified through negotiations as 'hard' are taken as given aspects of the new system of actions.

DESIGNING A NEW SYSTEM OF ACTIONS

Designing a new system of actions involves taking account of hard constraints identified in the previous stage and making use of the action possibilities of the mix of possible actors, locations, resources, and temporal ordering. This means moving down from the agreed goals, through the 'hard' context and dependency constraints and designing a new set of actions, dependencies, and contexts which satisfy the agreed goals. The action possibility space is also deliberately manipulated to constrain and enable particular actions. The purpose is to increase efficiency and effectiveness through routinization of action. Working within the 'hard' constraints, use may be made of the way that existing environmental structures enable or constrain action or the existing environmental structure may be changed in order to routinize the action.

Providing information to support routine action is also of key importance. Information is conveyed through representation of the possibility for action. This information assists actors not only to know *what* to do next but also gives them the required information that allows them to *do* the next thing. In designing a new system, the action system need only be specified with enough precision that actors know what they have to do.

The system redesign choices are directed to improving operational efficiency and effectiveness. Because the methodology is intended to support routine action, improvement in system efficiency and effectiveness will mainly be achieved by minimising human effort and time, and improving reliability. Particular emphasis is placed on eliminating unnecessary actions in search of information and improving action reliability by careful design of environmental structure.

APPLICATION CASE STUDY

The situated analysis and design methodology described was developed in a 3 year grant funded research project (Australian Research Council Grant, DP0451524). Based on an initial theoretical proposal (Johnston & Milton, 2002), the methodology was iteratively tested and refined through application in two real-world system analysis and design cases in contrasting organizational settings (Johnston et al., 2005; Waller et al., 2006). In each case, the current instantiation of the methodology was used to analyse the redesign of a dysfunctional operational system and to propose a more effective and better routinized alternative employing light weight digital information technology. While the research arrangement in each case did not include implementation of these systems by the researchers, management acceptance of the proposed systems was high. In addition, a case-based experiment was conducted in which an experienced but traditionally trained systems analyst separately repeated the analysis and design tasks for one of the case problems in a simulated setting. Systematic differences in approach and proposed solution confirmed

the potential of the new methodology to produce paradigmatically different proposals for this business problem (Waller et al., in press).

To illustrate the application of the approach and the insights it produces, we now present a brief account of the first case study conducted. Cabling Communications Pty Ltd (pseudonym), a workforce management services company, had an outsourcing contract with a larger telecommunications provider, Telco (pseudonym), and subcontracted the work it received to a team of 40 technicians working as independent contractors installing residential telecommunications equipment. Cabling managed the installation of 100-150 telecommunications products each day, and the disconnection of a roughly equivalent number. Cabling's management were interested in a redesigned system that would result in improved efficiency and effectiveness as well as cost savings to cabling, and which could be applied to any workforce management activities that cabling might undertake in the future.

A customer places an order with Telco for a telecommunications connection. Each installation requires a visit from a technician to the customer's house. Telco sends cabling details of the required work, one day in advance. The work is imported into a software package that represents each job as a dot on a map of the city and the router, a member of the centrally located cabling dispatch team uses this package to visually allocate the jobs to technicians according to their base region. Technicians receive a listing of jobs by e-mail the night before. Each installation technician routinely communicates with cabling's job dispatchers at least 10 times per day. Technicians may choose to communicate with dispatchers via SMS or phone. SMS messages arrive at a central dispatch inbox as e-mails. These messages are the data source for (partly) automated updates by the dispatchers of various central computerised systems provided by cabling for internal job status, inventory and management reporting, and by Telco for the actual network connection activation.

In keeping with the routine nature of the activity system being analysed, the researcher-analyst embedded herself in the work environment using a mixture of participatory observation techniques. The researcher first trained and worked as a dispatcher. Semi-structured interviews were also conducted with dispatchers, technicians, and warehouse staff, and their work was directly observed with the researcher asking questions about their activities as they worked. Of particular importance was the participant observation; the experience of actually working as a dispatcher enabled the researcher to obtain a deeper understanding of the system than the traditional systems analyst who relies largely on observation and questions. A version of the methodology described was used to analyse existing activity systems and identify opportunities for improvement.

The main area of dysfunction identified using the situated systems analysis approach was that daily coordination between field technicians and the central dispatchers in the course of connecting and provisioning the broadband connection were not effectively routinized. There were two problems here. Firstly, transcription of equipment ID numbers to SMS was time consuming and a source of error, a problem that suggested various technical solutions given that all equipment used was bar-coded. The second was more subtle. Dispatch responded to routine communications from technicians (phone calls and SMS) and non-routine phone calls from others in the order in which they arrived. This meant that dispatchers experienced downtime waiting for the phone to ring or an SMS to arrive, interspersed between periods of intense activity in which calls were received, notes made, and data entered manually into multiple systems without regard for priority.

Our proposal to cabling was that technicians upgrade to smartphones (converged mobile phone/PDA devices) which could transfer data via GPRS and which would be fitted with a separate barcode reader attachment (at the time, smartphones with built in barcode readers are just emerging). Rather than develop an application on the smartphone, we proposed that the smartphone browser act as a "thin client," accessing and updating secure information on the cabling Web server. This meant that the technician could access jobs from a home PC and print them out, just as under the current system. However, the technician could now execute the job activity reporting by accessing a cut-down Web page, displaying these jobs using the smartphone browser. Those transactions requiring an equipment ID number could be completed by scanning the barcode on the telecommunications equipment. Previously, the information for these transactions was manually entered into an SMS or read over the phone to a dispatcher who updated the various systems manually.

However, an important part of this solution was that it proposed that the SMS messages received by dispatch be routed into several queues based on transaction priority. This meant that dispatchers could now effectively balance their activity of updating the diverse central systems over peaks and trough of input activity. We conceived this part of the solution as a restructuring of the temporal organization of the dispatchers' work environment.

In a sense, using advanced mobile devices to take information systems to a mobile work force is an obvious move and a current trend in out-of-office technology. However, our action-oriented analysis approach allowed as to pinpoint the problem as involving *both* the need for very minimal, highly specific information transfer *and* the simultaneous restructuring of the dispatchers' action environment to allow the coordinated activity to be effectively routinized. It is just this ability of our analysis and design approach to sensitize the analyst to the opportunities to improve the effectiveness of routine aspects of work using light-weight information solutions and properly restructured work environments which we claim as its main benefit.

A conventionally oriented analyst could have been tempted to see the main problem as a lack of technical integration between the cabling systems, the Telco systems, and the technicians' mobile devices. This would be consistent with the traditional view that the job of information systems is to provide an integrated abstract model of the physical work system. However, given that cabling was not in a commercial position to affect the Telco system, we chose to interpret this as a solution constraint. Similarly, a technocentric analyst might be tempted to see job-scheduling as the change opportunity since resource allocation is a well trodden theory area, and novel GPS-based bidding systems exist to facilitate new approaches. It was because our approach allowed us to see that the current arrangement was largely optimal in terms of socio-cultural constraints and goals (incentives to technicians) that we were deflected from these technology-push approaches.

WHAT IS DIFFERENT ABOUT SITUATED ANALYSIS AND DESIGN?

Situated analysis and design has some points of similarity with other related methodologies, in particular, soft systems methodology (SSM), multiview, ETHICS, cognitive work analysis, and business process reengineering.

Checkland and Holwell (1998) have described SSM as "a set of principles of method rather than a precise method." Situated analysis and design also fits this description. Situated analysis and design shares with SSM a broad concern with providing information in support of action. However, whereas situated analysis and design is concerned with routine action, SSM is concerned with ill-defined problem situations. Although the terms appear similar, the 'activity systems' of SSM are quite different from the 'action systems' of situated analysis and design. The activity systems of SSM are conceptual and may bear little relation to actions in the real world (Checkland & Holwell, 1998). In contrast, the action systems of situated analysis and design are descriptive of the actions actually undertaken in the organization.

ETHICS (Mumford, 1983) entails a participatory design approach to systems analysis and design,

with particular attention to job satisfaction. Situated analysis and design shares with ETHICS an appreciation of the importance of implementation issues and the view that technology must be appropriate to the organization. The two approaches are not incompatible and it is conceivable that situated analysis and design could be conducted within an ETHICS framework. While ETHICS focuses on the organizational processes involved in systems analysis and design, situated analysis and design focuses on the analytic processes. In order to conduct situated analysis and design using an ETHICS framework, the situated analysis and design would be conducted using the organizational process of participatory design. Job satisfaction would be negotiated as a 'hard' constraint'.

Like situated analysis and design, multiview (Avison & Fitzgerald, 2003) also explicitly includes attention to implementation issues and the relationship between the social and the technical. However, it presupposes a computerised solution. Moreover, the analysis techniques used in multiview (both Multiview 1 and Multiview 2) are quite different from the situated analysis and design focus on situated action. Multiview 1 analyses information needs using conventional data flow and entity models while Multiview 2 uses object-oriented analysis.

Business process reengineering (Hammer, 1990) pays attention to performance measures other than direct cost saving. The situated analysis and design approach subsumes the approaches of business process reengineering in providing a more general conceptual framework to identify opportunities to improve the efficiency and effectiveness of action. However, business processes are not the same as actions. Business processes are commonly understood as a fixed sequence of well-defined activities that converts inputs to outputs (Melao & Pidd, 2000). According to this view, the world can be perceived as a succession of changing states; this is quite different from the situated analysis and design view of fluid actions occurring in the environment.

In some respects, the abstraction action hierarchy used in situated analysis and design is similar to that advocated in cognitive work analysis (Rasmussen & Pejtersen, 1995; Vicente, 1999). Both involve abstraction away from the details of existing work practices to goals in order to facilitate redesign. However, situated analysis and design is more explicitly centred around action and the intention of situated analysis and design is to support routine operational activity whereas cognitive, decision-making activity is typically the focus of cognitive work analysis. Cognitive work analysis involves reengineering the physical surroundings; no consideration is given to altering the organizational or temporal environment.

FUTURE TRENDS

Mobile communication technologies are particularly suitable for use in systems designed using the situated analysis and design approach. As well as enabling lightweight systems, they enable routine action by providing information to actors where and when they need it. Future increases in the technical capabilities of mobile communication technologies can be exploited in innovative practical applications of the situated analysis and design approach. Similarly, the development of ubiquitous computing (Prekop & Burnett, 2003) will enable even more innovative and lightweight situated systems.

CONCLUSION

The primary purpose of situated analysis and design is to support routine action, which is not explicitly considered in conventional IS methodologies. The situated system is designed to provide information about the action context and the action dependencies in order to enable fluid routine action without excessive dependence on deliberation. The action possibility space is manipulated to ensure that the action context is appropriate to the required action. The possibility for action is represented to inform the actor about satisfaction of the action dependencies.

Applying the situated analysis and design methodology can enable organizations to increase efficiency and effectiveness with a lightweight system that is acceptable to users. As well as increasing temporal efficiency, systems designed using situated analysis and design also aim to increase human efficiency; in particular, to reduce wasted human effort in search of information.

Situated systems can not replace traditional information systems; complete support for work systems should include both situated and traditional components. For example, interaction of actors with situated systems potentially provides a stream of high quality data for traditional systems that support managerial action. Because this data authentically captures the operational reality, it is of higher quality than that obtained through a mandated process of data entry conducted parallel to actual work. This not only increases the quality of decision making, it also reduces data collection costs and user resistance to these systems.

REFERENCES

Agerfalk, P., & Eriksson, O. (2006). Socio-instrumental usability: IT is all about social action. *Journal of Information Techology, 21*(1), 24-39.

Agre, P. (1997). *Computation and human experience*. Cambridge: Cambridge University Press.

Avison, D., & Fitzgerald, G. (2003). *Information systems development: Methodologies, techniques and tools*. England: McGraw Hill.

Bevan, N. (1995). Measuring usablity as quality of use. *Software Quality Journal, 4*(2), 115-150.

Bostrom, R. P., & Heinen, J. S. (1977). MIS problems and failures: A socio-technical perspective. *MIS Quarterly , 1*(1), 17-32.

British Standards Institution. (1994). *BS7738-1:1994 specification for information systems products using SSADM (structured systems analysis and design method)*. London.

Cannon, J. A. (1994). Why IT applications succeed or fail: The interaction of technical and organisational factors. *Industrial and Commercial Training, 26*(1), 10-15.

Checkland, P., & Holwell, S. (1998). *Information, systems and information systems—Making sense of the field.* Chichester: John Wiley and Sons.

Ciborra, C., & Schneider, L. (1992). Transforming the routines and contexts of management, work, and technology. In P. S. Adler (Ed.), *Technology and the future of work* (pp. 269-291). New York: Oxford University Press.

Clancey, W. J. (1997). *Situated cognition: on human knowledge and computer representation.* Cambridge: Cambridge University Press.

Fortune, J., & Peters, G. (2005). *Information systems: Achieving success by avoiding failure.* Chichester: John Wiley and Sons.

Gibson, J. (1979). *The ecological approach to visual perception.* Boston: Houghton Mifflin Company.

Glass, R. L. (1998). *Software runaways: Lessons learned from massive software project failures.* NJ: Prentice Hall.

Gowan, J. A., & Mathieu, R. G. (1996). Critical factors in information system development for a flexible manufacturing system. *Computers in Industry, 28*(3), 173-183.

Hammer, M. (1990). Reengineering work: Don't automate, obliterate. *Harvard Business Review, 68*(4), 104-112.

Heft, H. (2001). *Ecological psychology in context: James Gibson, Roger Barker, and the legacy of William James's radical empiricism.* New Jersey: Lawrence Erlbaum Associates.

Hendriks-Jansen. (1996). *Catching ourselves in the act: Situated activity, interactive emergence, evolution, and human thought.* Cambridge: The MIT Press.

Johansson, I. (1989). *Ontological investigations: An inquiry into the categories of nature, man and society.* London: Routledge.

Johnston, R. B., & Milton, S. K. (2002). The foundational role for theories of agency in understanding of information systems design [Special Issue]. *Australian Journal of Information Systems, 9*, 40-49.

Johnston, R. B., Waller, V., & Milton, S. (2005). Situated information systems: Supporting routine activity in organisations. *International Journal of Business Information Systems, 1*(1/2), 53 - 82.

Lave, J., & Wenger, E. (1991). *Situated learning: Legitimate peripheral participation.* Cambridge: Cambridge University Press.

Melao, N., & Pidd, M. (2000). A conceptual framework for understanding business processes and business process modelling. *Information Systems Journal, 10*(2), 105-129.

Milton, S. K., Johnston, R. B., Lederman, R., & Waller, V. (2005). *Developing a methodology for designing routine information systems based on the situational theory of action.* Paper presented at the Thirteenth European Conference on Information Systems, Regensburg, Germany.

Mumford, E. (1983). *Designing human systems for new technology: the ETHICS method.* Manchester: Manchester Business School.

Prekop, P., & Burnett, M. (2003). Activities, context and ubiquitous computing. *Computer Communications, 26*(11), 1168-1176.

Rasmussen, J., & Pejtersen, A. M. (1995). Virtual ecology of work. In J. Flach, P. Hancock, J. Caird, & K. Vicente (Eds.), *Global perspectives on the ecology of human-machine systems* (pp. 121-156). New Jersey: Lawrence Erlbaum Associates.

Suchman, L. A. (1987). *Plans and situated actions: the problem of human machine communication.* Cambridge: Cambridge University Press.

Vicente, K. (1999). *Cognitive work analysis: toward safe, productive, and healthy computer-based work.* Mahwah, NJ: Lawrence Erlbaum Associates.

Waller, V., Johnston, R. B., & Milton, S. (2006). Development of a situated information systems analysis and design methodology: a health care setting. In Z. Irani, O. D. Sarikas, J. Llopis, R. Gonzalez, & J. Gasco (Eds.), *CD-ROM/online proceedings of the European and Mediterranean Conference on Information Systems (EMCIS) 2006.* Costa Blanca, Alicante, Spain.

Waller, V., Johnston, R. B., & Milton, S. (2008). An empirical investigation of the epistemological assumptions underlying two IASAD approaches. *Journal of Enterprise Information Systems*, *28*(2), 125-138.

Weber, R. (1997). *Ontological foundations of information systems.* Melbourne: Coopers and Lybrand.

KEY TERMS

Action Abstraction Hierarchy: The actions associated with attaining a goal can be arranged into an action abstraction hierarchy (Johansson, 1989). For any particular action, asking *why* that action is conducted moves one up the action abstraction hierarchy to more abstract levels. Asking *how* that action is conducted moves one down the action abstraction hierarchy to more specific levels. At the bottom of the hierarchy are actions conducted by a specified actor using specified resources, at a specified time, in a specified location.

Action Context: The action context is the actor, location, time, and resources associated with an action. In other words, the action context is the particular dimensions of the environment in which a particular action occurs.

Action Dependency: An action dependency is the relation between two actions, whereby one action is dependent on the other action for instantiation as part an action system.

Action Possibility Space: A conceptualisation of the environment as a space of all possible actions. This term can be applied at the level of a specific actor in a particular time, place, and with particular resources at hand. It can also be applied to the more general level of the possible actions available to a type of actor with time, place, and resources unspecified.

Effectiveness: Effectiveness means that the intended goals are achieved, completely and accurately (Agerfalk & Eriksson, 2006).

Efficiency: Efficiency has three aspects: temporal efficiency, or the minimisation of the expenditure of time, human efficiency, or the minimisation of mental or physical effort, and economic efficiency, or the minimisation of financial cost (Bevan, 1995).

Environmental Structure: Recognisable patterns in the environment that constrain or enable action. Physical structures include the way work spaces are organised and the arrangement of things. Organisational structures include roles and norms. Temporal structures include blocks of time reserved for particular types of action and times at which particular actions are to occur.

Goal: A goal is understood as a more abstract level of specifying an action (answering the "why" question for those actions below it in the action abstraction hierarchy).

Routine Action: Routine action is characterised by the removal of discretion in the conduct of an action in one or more of the following aspects: what action is done, when the action is done, and how the action is done. This is removal of discretion at a meaningful grain size rather than complete removal of discretion.

Chapter III
Meta–Modeling for Situational Analysis and Design Methods

Inge van de Weerd
Utrecht University, The Netherlands

Sjaak Brinkkemper
Utrecht University, The Netherlands

ABSTRACT

This chapter introduces an assembly-based method engineering approach for constructing situational analysis and design methods. The approach is supported by a meta-modeling technique, based on UML activity and class diagrams. Both the method engineering approach and meta-modeling technique will be explained and illustrated by case studies. The first case study describes the use of the meta-modeling technique in the analysis of method evolution. The next case study describes the use of situational method engineering, supported by the proposed meta-modeling technique, in method construction. With this research, the authors hope to provide researchers in the information system development domain with a useful approach for analyzing, constructing, and adapting methods.

INTRODUCTION

Many methods for developing information systems (IS) exist. The complexity of the projects in which they are used varies, as well as the situational factors that influence these projects. Over the years, more methods will be developed, as the technology will continue to diversify and new ISs are being developed. However, often methods are too general and not fitted to the project at hand. A solution to this problem is situational method engineering to construct optimized methods for every systems analysis and design situation, by reusing parts, the so-called method fragments, of existing established methods.

In this chapter, an overview of current method engineering research is given. A general approach on situational method engineering is described, as well as a meta-modeling technique, which supports the process of situational method engineering. The technique will be illustrated in two examples. Finally, we describe our future research and conclusions.

BACKGROUND

No IS development method exists that is best in all situations. Therefore, to improve the effectiveness of a method, it should be engineered to the situation at hand, by taking into account the uniqueness of a project situation (Kumar & Welke, 1992). This is defined as "*method engineering*: the engineering discipline to design, construct and adapt methods, techniques and tools for the development of information systems" (Brinkkemper, 1996).

A special type of method engineering is situational method engineering. The term *situational method* is defined as "an information systems development method tuned to the situation of the project at hand" (Harmsen, Brinkkemper, & Oei, 1994). Situational method engineering is often used in combination with route maps, high-level method scenario's, which can be used to tune the method into situational methods (Van Slooten & Hodes, 1996). Different routes are used to represent the different situations: new IS development, COTS (commercial of the shelf) tool selection, re-engineering, and so forth.

Several situational method engineering approaches have been described in literature, by, for example, Brinkkemper (1996); Saeki (2003); Ralyté, Deneckère, and Rolland (2003); and Weerd, Brinkkemper, Souer, and Versendaal (2006). To execute the method engineering process, methods need to be described for which several modeling techniques have been proposed. Saeki (2003), for example, proposed the use of a meta-modeling technique, based on UML activity diagrams and class diagrams, for the purpose of attaching semantic information to artifacts and for measuring their quality using this information. In Rolland, Prakash, and Benjamin (1999) and Ralyté et al. (2003), a strategic process meta-model called Map is used to represent process models.

In all research on situational method engineering, several steps are followed in the process to develop a situational method. By comparing the different approaches, we could distinguish the following generic steps in a situational method engineering approach (Weerd et al., 2006):

- Analyze project situation and identify needs;
- Select candidate methods that meet one or more aspects of the identified needs;
- Analyze candidate methods and store relevant method fragments in a method base; and
- Select useful method fragments and assemble them in a situational method by using route map configuration to obtain situational methods.

The third and fourth steps are supported by a meta-modeling technique, especially developed for method engineering purposes. This technique, in which a so-called *process-deliverable diagram* (PDD) is built, is used in analyzing, storing, selecting, and assembling the method fragments. The meta-modeling technique is adopted from Saeki (2003), who proposed the use of a meta-modeling technique for the purpose of attaching semantic information to the artifacts and for measuring their quality using this information. In this research, the technique is used to reveal the relations between activities (the process of the method) and concepts (the deliverables produced in the process). We will elaborate on this in the next section.

PROCESS-DELIVERABLE DIAGRAMS

This section describes the technique used for modeling activities and artifacts of a certain process. As we are modeling methods and not the artifacts of an IS, this type of modeling is called meta-modeling. We express the meta-models of method in PDDs, which consist of two integrated diagrams. The process view on the left-hand side of the diagram is based on a UML activity diagram (OMG, 2003) and the deliverable view on the right-hand side of the diagram is based on a UML class diagram (OMG,

2003). In this chapter, first the left-hand side of the diagram is explained, then the right-hand side, and finally the integration of both diagrams.

The meta-modeling technique is explained, where notational explanation will be illustrated by an example in practice. Those examples are taken from a project to create a situational method for implementing Web-applications with a content management system (Weerd et al., 2006).

Meta-Process Modeling

Meta-process modeling is done by adapting the UML *activity diagram*. According to Booch, Rumbaugh, and Jacobson (1999), an activity diagram is "a diagram that shows the flow from activity to activity; activity diagrams address the dynamic view of a system." This diagram consists of activities and transitions. Activities can be decomposed into sub-activities, if necessary, and thereby creating a hierarchical activity decomposition. Transitions can be used to show the control flow from one activity to the next. A simple arrow depicts this. Four types of transitions exist: unordered, sequential, concurrent, and conditional activities.

Activity Types

We use different types of activities for several reasons. Firstly, activity types are used for scope definition. It may be interesting to know which processes exist adjacent to the process that is focused on. The details of this process are not interesting and are therefore not shown. Secondly, for purposes of clarity of the diagram, some processes are expanded elsewhere. Finally, in some cases the sub activities are not known or not relevant in the specific context.

The following activity types are specified (see Figure 1):

- **Standard activity:** An activity that contains no further (sub) activities. A standard activity is illustrated with a rounded rectangle.

- **Complex activity:** An activity that consists of a collection of (sub) activities. They are divided into:
  - **Open activity:** A complex activity whose (sub) activities are expanded. This expansion can be done in the same diagram or in another diagram. Therefore, we use two notational variants, which are:
    - ➤ A rounded rectangle, containing two ore more sub activities and
    - ➤ A rounded rectangle with a white shadow, to indicate that the activities are depicted elsewhere.
  - **Closed activity:** A complex activity whose (sub) activities are not expanded since it is not known or not relevant in the specific context.

In Figure 2 we give some examples of activity types. 'List features' is a standard activity that has no further sub activities. In case of 'describe candidate requirements,' the activity is open, since we find it interesting to describe its sub activities. 'Define use case' model is closed, since we are not interested in the details of this process. The naming conventions for activity names are that the names always consist of a verb and an object, except when the activity name is literally copied from a method source, such as a book. Activities for the highest level are excluded form this naming convention, since they usually get the name of a stage or phase.

In the following sections, the four activity transitions will be introduced and exemplified.

Sequential Activities

Sequential activities are activities that need to be carried out in a *predefined* order. The activities are connected with an arrow, implying that they have to be followed in that sequence, although the activity completion before the next can be started is *not* strictly enforced. Both activities and sub-activities can be modeled in a sequential way. In Figure 3

Figure 1. Activities types

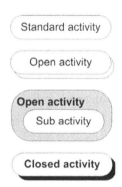

Figure 2. Example activity types

an activity diagram is illustrated with one activity and two sequential sub-activities. A special kind of sequential activities are the start and stop states, which are also illustrated in Figure 3.

In Figure 4 an example is illustrated. The example is taken from the requirements capturing workflow, of which the main activity, 'model users & domain,' consists of three activities that need to be carried out in a predefined order.

Unordered Activities

Unordered activities are used when sub-activities of an activity can be executed in any order, that is, they do not have a predefined execution sequence. Only sub-activities can be unordered. Unordered activities are represented as sub-activities without transitions within an activity, as is shown in Figure 5.

An activity may consist of sequential and unordered activities, which is modeled by dividing the main activity in different parts. In Figure 6 an example is taken from the requirements analysis workflow. The main activity, 'describe candidate requirements,' is divided into two parts. The first part is a sequential activity. The second part consists of four activities that do not need any sequence in order to be carried out correctly. Note that all unordered activities must be carried out before continuing to the next activity.

Concurrent Activities

Activities can occur concurrently. This is handled with forking and joining. By drawing the activities parallel in the diagram, connected with a synchronization bar, one can fork several activities. Later on these concurrent activities can join again by using the same synchronization bar. Both the concurrent execution of activities and sub-activities can be

Figure 3. Sequential activities

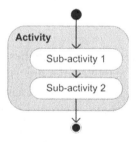

Figure 4. Example sequential activities

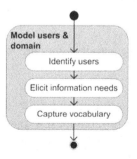

modeled. In the example of Figure 7, Activity 2 and Activity 3 are concurrent activities.

In Figure 8 a fragment of the requirements capturing process is depicted. Two activities, 'define actors' and 'defining use cases' are carried out concurrently. The reason for carrying out these activities concurrently is that definition of actors and of use cases influence each other to a high extend.

Conditional Activities

Conditional activities are activities that are only carried out if a predefined condition is met. This is graphically represented by using a branch. Branches are denoted with a diamond and can have incoming and outgoing transitions. Every outgoing transition has a guard expression, the condition, denoted with square bracket '[ ]'. This guard expression is actually a Boolean expression, used to make a choice which direction to go. Both activities and sub-activities can be modeled as conditional activities. In Figure

9, two conditional activities are illustrated.

In Figure 10, an example from a requirements analysis starts with studying the material. Based on this study, the decision is taken whether to do an extensive requirements elicitation session or not. The condition for not carrying out this requirements session is represented at the left of the branch, namely [requirements clear]. If this condition is not met, [else], the other arrow is followed.

Roles

In some methods it is explicitly stated by which individuals or organizational role the process is to be carried out. In this case, the role is indicated in the activity. In Figure 11, an activity with three sub activities is depicted. In the lower right corner, the role is positioned. Please note that the usage of roles is not restricted to activities, but, if necessary, can also be used in sub-activities.

Figure 7. Concurrent activities

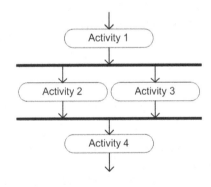

Figure 5. Unordered activities

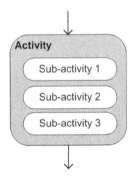

Figure 6. Example of unordered activities

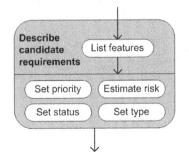

Figure 8. Example concurrent activities

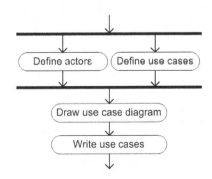

In Figure 12, the usage of roles is illustrated. The same example as in Figure 4 is used with the difference that the role, in this case 'consultant,' is indicated.

Meta-Deliverable Modeling

The deliverable side of the diagram consists of a *concept diagram*. This is basically an adjusted class diagram as described Booch et al. (1999). Important notions are concept, generalization, association, multiplicity and aggregation.

Concept Types

A concept is a simple version of a UML class. The class definition of Booch et al. (1999) is adopted to define a concept, namely: "a set of objects that share the same attributes, operations, relations, and semantics."

The following concept types are specified:

- **STANDARD CONCEPT:** A concept that contains no further concepts. A standard concept is visualized with a rectangle.
- **COMPLEX CONCEPT:** A concept that consists of an aggregate of other concepts. Complex concepts are divided into:
  - **OPEN CONCEPT:** A complex concept whose sub concepts are expanded. An open concept is visualized with a white shadow border. The aggregate structure may be shown in the same diagram or in a separate diagram.
  - **CLOSED CONCEPT:** A complex concept whose sub concepts are not expanded since it is not relevant in the specific context. A closed concept is visualized with a black shadow border.

Figure 11. Roles

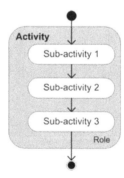

Figure 9. Conditional activities

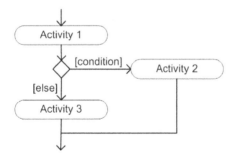

Figure 12. Example role

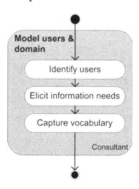

Figure 10. Example conditional activities

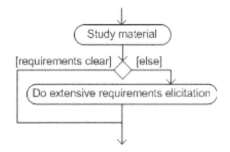

Similar as for activities, this usage of different concept types is introduced for clarity and scope definition.

In Figure 13, the three concept types that are used in the modeling technique are illustrated. Concepts are singular nouns and are always capitalized, not only in the diagram, but also when referring to them in the textual descriptions outside the diagram.

In Figure 14, all three concept types are exemplified. Part of the PDD of a requirements workflow is illustrated. The USE CASE MODEL is an open concept and consists of one or more ACTORS and one or more USE CASES. ACTOR is a standard concept, it contains no further sub-concepts. USE CASE, however, is a closed concept. A USE CASE consists of a description, a flow of events, conditions, special requirements, and so forth. Because in this case we decided it is unnecessary to reveal that information, the USE CASE is illustrated with a closed concept.

Generalization

Generalization is a way to express a relationship between a general concept and a more specific concept. Also, if necessary, one can indicate whether the groups of concepts that are identified are overlapping or disjoint, complete, or incomplete. Generalization is visualized by a solid arrow with an open arrowhead, pointing to the parent, as is illustrated in Figure 15.

In Figure 16, generalization is exemplified by showing the relationships between the different concepts described in the preceding paragraph. CONTROL FLOW and DATA FLOW are both a specific kind of FLOW. Also note the use of the *disjoint* (d) identifier. This implies that occurrence of one concept is incompatible with the occurrence of the other concept; that is, there are no CONTROL FLOWS that are also DATA FLOWS and vice versa. The second identifier we use is *overlapping* (o), which would indicate in this example that there may be occurrences that are CONTROL FLOWS or DATA FLOWS, but also occurrences that are

both. Finally, *categories* (c) mean that the disjoint concepts have no occurrences in common and that the decomposition is exhaustive. In the example, this would imply that every occurrence of flow is either a CONTROL FLOW or DATA FLOW. No other FLOWS exist, and there are no occurrences that are both CONTROL FLOW and DATA FLOW.

Association

An association is a structural relationship that specifies how concepts are connected to another. It can connect two concepts (binary association) or more than two concepts (n-ary association). An association is represented with an undirected solid line. To give a meaning to the association, a name and name direction can be provided. The name is in the form of an active verb and the name direction is represented by a triangle that points in the direction one needs to read. Association with a name and name direction is visualized in Figure 17.

In Figure 18, an example of a fragment is shown of the PDD of the requirements analysis in the Unified Process (Jacobson, Booch, & Rumbaugh, 1999). Because both concepts are not expanded

Figure 13. Standard, open and closed concepts

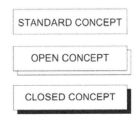

Figure 14. Example of standard, open and closed concepts

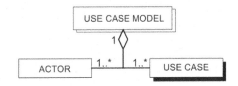

any further, although several sub concepts exist, the concepts are illustrated as closed concepts. The figure reads as "SURVEY DESCRIPTION describes USE CASE MODEL."

Multiplicity

Except name and name direction, an association has another characteristic. With *multiplicity*, one can state how many objects of a certain concept can be connected across an instance of an association. Multiplicity is visualized by using the following expressions: *1* for exactly one, *0..1* for one or zero, *0..** for zero or more, *1..** for one or more, or for example, *5* for an exact number. In Figure 19, association with multiplicity is visualized.

An example of multiplicity is represented in Figure 20. It is the same example as in Figure 18, only the multiplicity values are added. The figure reads as "exactly one SURVEY DESCRIPTION describes exactly one USE CASE MODEL." This implies in an IS project that a SURVEY DESCRIPTION will always be related to just one USE CASE MODEL and the other way round.

Aggregation

A special type of association is *aggregation*. Aggregation represents the relation between a concept (as a whole) containing other concepts (as parts). It can also be described as a 'has-a' or 'consists of' relationship. In Figure 21, an aggregation relationship between OPEN CONCEPT and STANDARD CONCEPT is illustrated. An OPEN CONCEPT consists of one or more STANDARD CONCEPTS and a STANDARD CONCEPT is part of one OPEN CONCEPT.

In Figure 22, aggregation is exemplified by a fragment of a requirements capture workflow. A USE CASE MODEL consists of one or more ACTORS and USE CASES.

Properties

Sometimes the need exists to assign properties to CONCEPTS. Properties are written in lower case, under the CONCEPT name, as is illustrated in Figure 23.

In Figure 24, an example of a CONCEPT with properties is visualized. DESIGN has seven properties, respectively: code, status, author, effective date, version, location, and application.

Process-Deliverable Diagram

The integration of both types of diagrams is quite straightforward. Activities are connected with a dotted arrow to the produced deliverables, as

Figure 15. Generalization

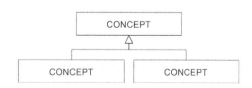

Figure 16. Example generalization

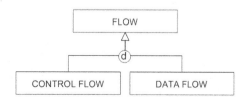

Figure 17. Association

Figure 18. Example association

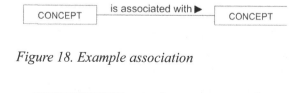

is demonstrated in Figure 25. Note that in UML class diagrams, dotted arrows are used to indicate dependency from one class on another. However, this construction is not used in PDDs. We have some extra remarks concerning the PDD. Firstly, all activities in Figure 25 result in deliverables. However, this is not compulsory. Secondly, it is possible for several activities to point to the same deliverable, see for example, sub-activity 2 and 3. Finally, we assume that all artifacts in the diagram are available to all roles.

Example of a Process-Deliverable Diagram

In Figure 26, an example of a PDD is illustrated. It concerns an example of drawing an object chart, as described in Brinkkemper, Saeki, and Harmsen (1999). This is an example of method assembly, in which an object model and Harel's state chart are integrated into object charts.

Notable is the use of an open concept: STATE TRANSITION DIAGRAM. This concept is open, since it is a complex concept, and should be expanded elsewhere. However, due to space limitations, this is omitted. The activities of 'drawing an object chart' are carried out by one person. Therefore, no roles are depicted in the diagram.

In Table 1, the activities and sub-activities, as well as their relations to the deliverables, which are depicted in the diagram, are described.

In Table 2, an excerpt if a concept table is shown. Every concept is provided with a description and a reference.

The process in Figure 26, where object model diagrams and state charts are amalgamated into object charts, is an example of situational method engineering for a project situation where is was required to model state charts for each class. Similarly, situational factors may require various kinds of adaptations of the method. Different analysis

Figure 21. Aggregation

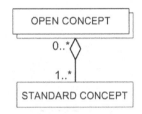

Figure 22. Example aggregation

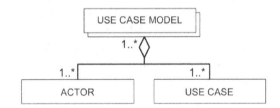

Figure 23. Properties

Figure 24. Example properties

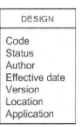

Figure 19. Multiplicity

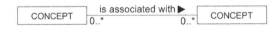

Figure 20. Example multiplicity

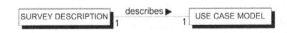

Figure 25. Process-deliverable diagram

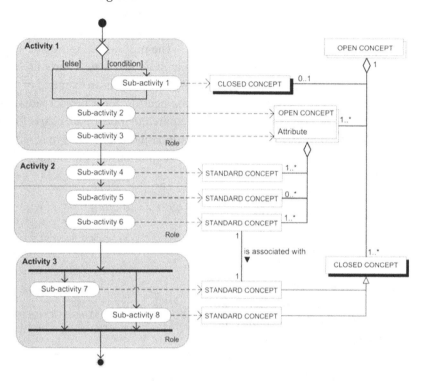

and design situations in a project give rise to a huge variety of method adaptations: in a simple project just one class diagram may be sufficient to analyze the object domain, whereas in a more complex project, various class diagrams, object models and state charts are required. To support the adaptations, PDDs are very instrumental as both modifications of activities as of concepts can be easily documented.

META-MODELING FOR METHOD EVOLUTION ANALYSIS

Introduction

PDDs can be used to analyze the method evolution of a company over the years. In Weerd, Brinkkemper, and Versendaal (2007), general method increments were deducted from literature and case studies. The resulting list of general method increments was then tested in a case study at Infor Global

Solutions (specifically the former Baan company business unit), a vendor of ERP (enterprise resource planning) software. The time period that is covered in the case study ranges from 1994 to 2006. We analyzed 13 snapshots of the evolution of the software development process at Baan, with emphasis on product management activities. An overview of these method increments is listed in Table 3.

In the next sections, we will illustrate two of these increments, namely increment #3 and increment #4.

Snapshot of Increment #3

In Figure 27, increment # 3 of the requirements management and release definition process a Baan is illustrated.

We can distinguish two main activities in the figure, namely 'requirements management' and 'release definition.' The first main activity consists of one sub activity, namely 'create requirement,' in which the REQUIREMENTS are created by the product

Figure 26. Example PDD—drawing an object chart

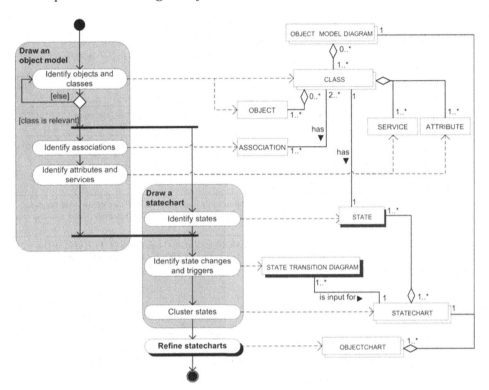

manager. The other main activity consists of three sub activities. Firstly, the product manager writes a first draft of the VERSION DEFINITION. Secondly, the product manager writes, if necessary, a CONCEPTUAL SOLUTION per REQUIREMENT. Finally, the VERSION DEFINITION is reviewed by the head of the research & development department. If he approves the VERSION DEFINITION, they can continue with the next activity. If he does not approve it, the product manager has to rewrite the VERSION DEFINITION. A more elaborated description of the activities and the concepts is provided in Table 4 and Table 5.

Note that the activity 'create conceptual solutions' and the concept CONCEPTUAL SOLUTION are both closed. This implies that they are both complex, that is, consisting of sub activities or concepts, respectively. In this work, it is not relevant to elaborate further on both elements. However, they are specified in Weerd et al. (2006).

Requirements Management and Release Definition Increment

In Figure 28, the snapshot of method increment #4 is depicted. Again, the snapshot consists of two main activities: 'requirements management' and 'release definition.' The first main activity now consists of three unordered sub activities: the product manager creates MARKET REQUIREMENTS, releases independent BUSINESS REQUIREMENTS, and he maintains the product line.

Notable in this part of the snapshot is the division between MARKET REQUIREMENTS and BUSINESS REQUIREMENTS. Natt och Dag et al. (2005) give a good elaboration of this separation. They state that MARKET REQUIREMENTS are expressions of the perceived market need, written in the form of a customer's wish. They change frequently, according to the market need changes. BUSINESS REQUIREMENTS, on the other hand, are written from the company's

Table 1. Activities and sub-activities in drawing an object chart

Activity	Sub-Activity	Description
Draw an object model	Identify objects and classes	Key phenomena that require data storage and manipulation in the IS are identified as OBJECTS. OBJECTS that share the same attributes and services are identified as a CLASS.
	Identify associations	Relationships between CLASSES are identified when instance OBJECTS of different CLASSES are to be related to each other in the IS.
	Identify attributes and services	For each CLASS, the descriptive ATTRIBUTES and the operational SERVICES are identified.
Draw a state chart	Identify states	Lifecycle statuses of OBJECTS that serve a process in the IS are to be identified as STATES. Similarly for CLASSES.
	Identify state changes and triggers	Events that trigger changes of a STATE and the conditions under which they occur are determined.
	Cluster states	STATES that are sub statuses of a higher level STATE are groups together in a cluster. Furthermore, state transitions between STATES are depicted resulting in a STATECHART.
Refine state charts		Based on the OBJECT MODEL DIAGRAM and the STATECHART, an OBJECTCHART is created by linking STATECHARTS to each CLASS.

Table 2. Excerpt of a concept table

Concept	Description
ASSOCIATION	An association specifies a semantic relationship that can occur between typed instances. It has at least two ends represented by properties, each of which is connected to the type of the end (OMG, 2004).
STATE	A state models a situation during which some (usually implicit) invariant condition holds (OMG, 2004).
OBJECTCHART	An extension of a State chart to model reactive systems from an object-oriented view (Brinkkemper, Saeki, & Harmsen, 1999).
…	

perspective. These requirements are those that find the company worthwhile to implement one of the following product releases. Both types of requirements are important. MARKET REQUIREMENTs for communicating with the customer and tracing which customer wishes actually get implemented in the product. PRODUCT REQUIREMENTs are important as a basis for release planning, for conducting feasibility studies, and for a functional description of the feature to be implemented. The separation of the two types ensures a solid basis for decision-making about future releases, as well as a clear tracing device which improves the communication with the customer (Natt och Dag et al., 2005).

The other change in the 'requirements management' activity is the insertion of an activity called 'maintain product line.' This activity is not further elaborated in this work, but globally, the product manager has to ensure that requirements are linked to themes and common components, in order to maintain a unambiguous product line. More information can be found in Weerd et al. (2006).

The rest of the snapshot is the same as the snapshot of increment # 4. Concluding, the contents of the 'requirements management' activity have been changed from one to three sub activities. Secondly, the REQUIREMENT concept has been split up into two new concepts: MARKET REQUIREMENT and BUSINESS REQUIREMENT. Finally, the concepts COMMON COMPONENT and THEME have been added. In Table 6 and Table 7, the activities and concepts are further specified.

Table 3. Overview of method increments at Baan

#	Increment	Date
0	Introduction requirements document	1994
1	Introduction design document	1996
2	Introduction version definition	May, 1998
3	Introduction conceptual solution	November, 1998,
4	Introduction requirements database, division market and business requirements, and introduction of product families	May, 1999
5	Introduction tracing sheet	July, 1999
6	Introduction product definition	March, 2000
7	Introduction customer commitment process	April, 2000
8	Introduction enhancement request process	May, 2000
9	Introduction roadmap process	September, 2000
10	Introduction process metrics	August, 2002
11	Removal of product families & customer commitment	May, 2003
12	Introduction customer voting process	November, 2004
13	Introduction master planning	October, 2006

Figure 27. Snapshot of increment #3

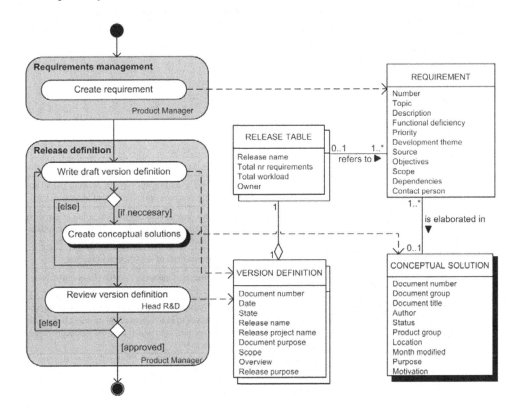

Table 4. Activity table of increment #3

Activity	Sub activity	Description
Requirements management	Create requirement	The product manager adds the REQUIREMENT and its properties to the requirements Excel sheet.
Release definition	Write draft version definition	The product manager writes a draft of the VERSION DEFINITION.
	Create conceptual solution	If necessary, the product manager elaborates on the requirements in a CONCEPTUAL SOLUTION.
	Review version definition	The head of the research & development department reviews the RELEASE DEFINITION. Either he approves it, in which case the process continues in a new activity, or he disapproves it, in which case the product manager rewrites the VERSION DEFINITION.

Table 5. Concept table of increment #3

Concept	Description
REQUIREMENT	A REQUIREMENT is a functional description of a new functionality that is to be implemented in the new release of a product.
RELEASE TABLE	The RELEASE TABLE is part of the VERSION DEFINITION, and lists the references to the REQUIRE-MENTS that are implemented in the new release.
VERSION DEFINITION	A document with the listing of REQUIREMENTS of the new release along with the needed personnel resources. (Natt och Dag, Regnell, Gervasi, & Brinkkemper, 2005)
CONCEPTUAL SOLUTION	A document with a sketch of the business solution for one preferred or more REQUIREMENTS. (Natt och Dag et al., 2005)

Table 6. Activity table of increment #4

Activity	Sub activity	Description
Requirements management	Create market requirement	The product manager adds a customer wish to the requirements database.
	Maintain product line	Requirements are structured according the THEME they relate to and the COM-MON COMPONENT that is affected, in order to maintain the product line.
	Create BR release independent	The product managers adds BUSINESS REQUIREMENTS to the requirements database, by linking MARKET REQUIREMENTS that cover the same subject and by describing the requirement from the company's perspective.
Release definition	Write draft version definition	The product manager writes a draft of the VERSION DEFINITION.
	Create conceptual solution	If necessary, the product manager elaborates on the requirements in a CONCEPTUAL SOLUTION.
	Review version definition	The head of the research & development department reviews the RELEASE DEFINITION. Either he approves it, in which case the process continues in a new activity, or he disapproves it, in which case the product manager rewrites the VERSION DEFINITION.

META-MODELING FOR METHOD CONSTRUCTION

Introduction

The meta-modeling example described in this section covers the assembly of a new method for implementing CMS-based Web applications. The research was carried out at GX creative online development, a Web technology company in the Netherlands. The company implements Web applications, using GX WebManager, a generic CMS-based Web application tool that enables people without a specific technological background in creating, maintaining, and integrating several dynamic Web sites and portals. In addition to their product, GX also provides a service, which is creating a Web application 'around' the CMS-based Web application. The development of this Web application is currently carried out by a proprietary method. However, the need existed to optimize this method in order to save time and money. Also, the need for a standardized Web application development method exists, which can be used by implementation partners of the company. At time of the research, no methods existed for implementing CMS-based Web applications. Development methods for conventional information systems, as well as for Web applications, do not cover the needs for this particular type of development. Therefore, we developed the GX Web engineering method (WEM).

Assembly-based method engineering

We applied an assembly-based situational method engineering approach to develop the new method, consisting of the following steps:

1. Analyze implementation situations and identify needs.

   Three implementation situations were identified, namely standard, complex, and migration situations. In Table 8, example needs are given for the standard and complex implementation situations.

2. Select candidate methods that meet one or more aspects of the identified needs.

   The candidate methods that were selected are: the unified software development process (UP), UML-based Web-engineering (UWE), and the proprietary company method (GX).

3. Analyze candidate methods and store relevant method fragments in a method base.

   We analyzed the methods by modeling them into PDDs. The method base was filled with four GX PDDs, 2 UP PDDs, and four UWE PDDs. In total, 10 process data diagrams were stored in the method base.

4. Assemble a new method from useful method fragments and use route map configuration to obtain situational methods.

   Based on the implementation situations needs, we chose the method fragments for the new method. The resulting method consists of three phases (acquisition, orientation, and definition) and three routes (standard, complex, and migration). The rest of the method (design, realization, and implementation) were subject to further research. In the next section, we will further elaborate on the resulting method.

Routemap of the Definition Phase

Instead of showing the entire PDD, we will depict the standard and complex routes in one diagram, to make clear what the differences are between the two implementation situations. Therefore, we omitted the data-side of the diagram, as can be seen in Figure 29. The main activities in the diagram are marked to indicate the original method. A checked pattern indicates that this method fragment originates from the proprietary method at GX; grey indicates that it is a UWE fragment; and, finally, white indicates a unified process origin. Note that the roles in this diagram are omitted, because all activities are handled by the same person, namely the consultant.

The main difference between the standard and complex route is, next to the extensive requirements

Table 7. Concept table of increment #4

Concept	Description
MARKET REQUIREMENT	A customer wish related to current or future markets, defined using the perspective and context of the user. (Natt och Dag et al., 2005)
BUSINESS REQUIREMENT	A generic customer wish to be covered by a product described in the vendor's perspective and context. (Natt och Dag et al., 2005)
RELEASE TABLE	The RELEASE TABLE is part of the VERSION DEFINITION, and lists the references to the REQUIREMENTS that are implemented in the new release.
COMMON COMPONENT	A software component that is shared by multiple products in the product line.
THEME	A predefined release THEME that is set by the board.
VERSION DEFINITION	A document with the listing of BUSINESS REQUIREMENTS of the new release along with the needed personnel resources. (Natt och Dag et al., 2005)
CONCEPTUAL SOLUTION	A document with a sketch of the business solution for one preferred or more BUSINESS REQUIREMENTS. (Natt och Dag et al., 2005)

Figure 28. Snapshot of increment #4

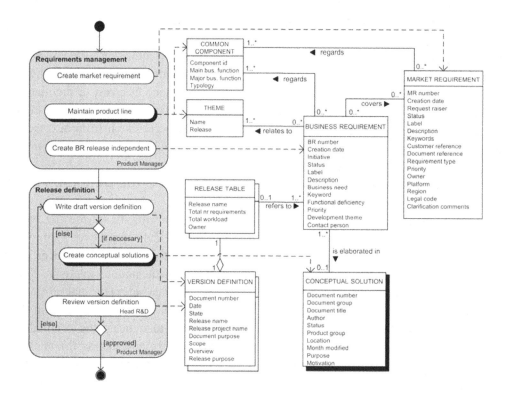

Table 8. Example implementation situation needs

Situation	Need
Standard & Complex	The method should deliver a requirements document that is understandable for the customer and informative for the stakeholders at GX.
Standard	Standard project often have a small budget. This implies that the amount of time for specifying the requirements is limited. Therefore, the method should make it possible to translate the requirements quickly into Web manager solutions.
Complex	A solution has to be found to the problem of changing requirements after the contract is signed. Although one can expect the requirements to change during the requirements analysis, the customer often does not understand that this affects the budget.

elicitation and validation, the use of use case modeling. In the complex route, this is used to describe the people who will interact with the Web application, as well as how they will interact with the system. In the standard route, this is partly handled in the user and domain modeling fragment and partly in the application modeling.

Method Implementation

WEM was developed with input of the requirements management workgroup. The goal of this workgroup was an overall improvement in the requirements process at GX. Members of the workgroup were consultants and project managers of GX and one external consultant. After validating the WEM method in an expert review and two case studies, the method was implemented in the company. Firstly, templates were written for every document that had to be delivered after completing a method stage. Secondly, explanations were provided with the templates. This information was then published on the intranet of the company and presented for the developers, consultant, architects, and project managers.

FUTURE TRENDS

History has proven that new types of information systems are conceived frequently. Emergent technologies for mobile systems, Web applications, and intelligent agent solutions have triggered innovative

IS applications. At the same time, new methods are developed to design and support these information systems. Existing method knowledge can play an important role, as parts of it can be reused in new project situations, and is codified into new methods. This has also happened when the well-known state transition diagrams where reused into UML (OMG, 2004) for the analysis and design phases of object-oriented IS.

The trend is to build method knowledge infrastructures, that is, a Web-enabled knowledge resource that can be accessed, shared, and enriched by all IS project workers. Those knowledge infrastructures can be open to anyone on the Internet, such as the open modeling language (Firesmith, Henderson-Sellers, & Graham, 1998), an object oriented modeling language.

Many large IT service companies have development methods on their corporate Internet, where every IS project on any location worldwide, can be executed according to the same method. Usually, these corporate methods are enriched by borrowing new concepts from the public ones on the Internet. In the future, more and more open method knowledge infrastructures for specific types of IS will be established and gradually expanded into full-blown environments to execute complete IS development projects. The facilities for situational method engineering to adapt the method to specific project circumstances are to be included. An example for the product software vendors is the product knowledge software infrastructure that enables product software companies to obtain a custom-made advice

Figure 29. Routemap of the definition phase in WEM

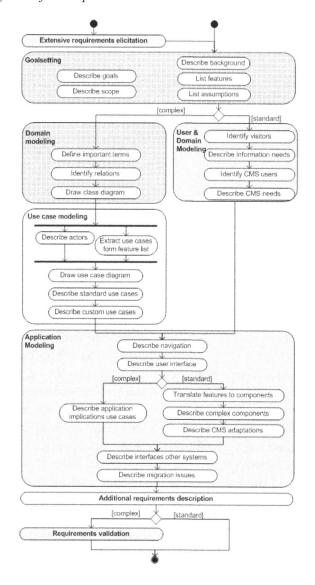

that helps them to mature their processes (Weerd et al., 2006).

CONCLUSION

PDDs have proven to be effective means for the meta-modeling of methods, especially for the analysis and design stages. The meta-modeling can serve different purposes: in the examples, two purposes are explained, namely method analysis or method construction. Other possible applications are method comparison and method adaptation. Providing the explicit description of the activities and concepts of a method in a PDD allows for a more formal addition of activities and deliverables. Method engineering tools for modeling and adapting methods will aid in the creation of high quality situational methods.

REFERENCES

Booch, G., Rumbaugh, J., & Jacobson, I. (1999). *The unified modeling language user guide.* Redwood City, CA: Addison Wesley Longman Publishing Co., Inc.

Brinkkemper, S. (1996). Method engineering: engineering of information systems development methods and tools. *Information and Software Technology, 38*(4), 275-280.

Brinkkemper, S., Saeki, M., & Harmsen, F. (1999). Meta-modelling based assembly techniques for situational method engineering. *Information Systems, 24*(3), 209-228.

Coleman, F., Hayes, F., & Bear, S. (1992). Introducing objectcharts or how to use statecharts on object-oriented design. *IEEE Trans Software Engineering, 18*(1), 9-18.

Firesmith, D., Henderson-Sellers, B. H., Graham, I., & Page-Jones, M. (1998). *Open modeling language (OML)—reference manual. SIGS reference library series.* Cambridge, etc.: Cambridge University Press.

Harmsen, F., Brinkkemper, S., & Oei, J. L. H. (1994). Situational method engineering for informational system project approaches. In *Proceedings of the IFIP WG8.1 Working Conference on Methods and Associated Tools for the IS Life Cycle* (pp. 169-194).

Jacobson, I., Booch, G., & Rumbaugh, J. (1999). *The unified software development process.* Redwood City, CA: Addison Wesley Longman Publishing Co., Inc.

Karlsson, F. (2002). *Bridging the gap between method for method configuration and situational method engineering.* Skövde, Sweden: Promote IT.

Natt och Dag, J., Regnell, B., Gervasi, V., & Brinkkemper, S. (2005). A linguistic-engineering approach to large-scale requirements management. *IEEE Software, 22*(1), 32-29.

Object Management Group. (2004). *UML 2.0 superstructure specification* (Technical Report ptc/04-10-02).

Ralyté, J., Deneckère, R., & Rolland, C. (2003). Towards a generic model for situational method engineering. *Lecture Notes in Computer Science, 2681*, 95.

Rolland, C., Prakash, N., & Benjamen, A. (1999). A multi-model view of process modelling. *Requirements Engineering, 4*(4), 169-187.

Saeki, M. (2003). Embedding metrics into information systems development methods: an application of method engineering technique. In *Proceedings of the 15th Conference on Advanced Information Systems Engineering* (pp. 374-389).

Weerd, I. van de, Brinkkemper, S., Souer, J., & Versendaal, J. (2006). A situational implementation method for Web-based content management system-applications: Method engineering and validation in practice [Accepted for a special issue]. *Software Process: Improvement and Practice.*

Weerd, I. van de, Brinkkemper, S., & Versendaal, J. (2006). *Incremental method evolution in requirements management: A case study at Baan 1994-2006* (Technical report UU-CS-2006-057). Institute of Computing and Information Sciences, Utrecht University.

Weerd, I. van de, Brinkkemper, S., & Versendaal, J. (2007). Concepts for incremental method evolution: Empirical exploration and validation in requirements management. *19th Conference on Advanced Information Systems Engineering.* Trondheim, Norway.

Weerd, I. van de, Versendaal, J., & Brinkkemper, S. (2006, June 5-6). A product software knowledge infrastructure for situational capability maturation:

Vision and case studies in product management. In *Proceedings of the Twelfth Working Conference on Requirements Engineering: Foundation for Software Quality (REFSQ'06)*. Luxembourg: Grand-Duchy of Luxembourg.

KEY TERMS

Activity: A process step that is used for capturing the process-view of a method.

Concept: A set of objects that share the same attributes, operations, relations, and semantics, used for capturing the deliverable-view of a method.

Method Engineering: The engineering discipline to design, construct, and adapt methods, techniques, and tools for the development of information systems.

Method Fragment: A coherent piece of an IS development method (Brinkkemper, 1996). Methods fragments are distinguished in process fragments, for modeling the development process, and product fragments, for modeling the structure of the products of the development process.

Process-Deliverable Diagram: A process-deliverable diagram (PDD) consists of two integrated diagrams. The left-hand side of the diagram is based on a UML activity diagram and the right-hand side of the diagram is based on a UML class diagram.

Route Map: A route map represents a predefined path of a method where method fragments are combined to form new situational methods.

Situational Method: An information systems development method tuned to the situation of the project at hand.

Chapter IV
Location–Based Service (LBS) System Analysis and Design

Yuni Xia
Indiana University Purdue University–Indianapolis, USA

Jonathan Munson
IBM T.J. Watson Research Center, USA

David Wood
IBM T.J. Watson Research Center, USA

Alan Cole
IBM T.J. Watson Research Center, USA

ABSTRACT

Advances in GPS, personal locator technology, Internet and network technology, and the rapidly growing number of mobile personal devices are helping to drive the fast growth of mobile e-commerce, we refer to as m-commerce. A special case of m-commerce is enabled with location based services (LBS) where often the actual position of the terminal is used in the service provision. In this chapter, we concentrate on the analysis and design issues and techniques for the LBS. We give a brief introduction of LBS and its applications and present the most important user, system, and infrastructure requirements. We also present the architecture and database design issues in LBS systems and study the performance an LBS system and evaluate its properties.

IINTRODUCTION

Location based services are services that are sensitive to and take advantage of the location of the service user. Any service that makes use of the location of the user can be called a location based service. The location of a person can be determined using a GPS receiver or other technologies, now available in many mobile phone platforms. This position-determination technology (PDT) is generally carried by the person, from which the location must be provided to the location-based service provider. Today, the location-based services are generally hosted in the network, which may pose performance and scalability issues..

The uptake of mobile phones with PDT capabilities continues to grow and most mobile phone users have a phone which can be traced with good accuracy and a lower cost. This new technology has given the LBS market a greater push. Location based services can be divided into four categories:

- Business to business
- Business to consumer
- Consumer to business
- Consumer to consumer

The business to business services include fleet tracking, courier tracking, and others. Business to consumer services include pushed ads based on the location, where a user will receive ads most relevant to the location. Consumer to business services include location based search, where a user is searching for the nearest restaurant, petrol pump, and so forth. A consumer to consumer service is the friend finder service where the user will be alerted if his friend is within a few meters (Jacob, 2007).

Location Based Services Examples

Typical location based services include:

- **Fleet tracking service:** Fleet tracking service can be used to locate and track moving vehicles. This can be very useful for fleet owners/individual vehicle owners. This enables them to pinpoint their vehicles on a map. Taxi fleets can use the location information to calculate the distance traveled, and use that for internal billing. Government can use this service for preventing misuse of government vehicles. Also, the tracker will help in finding the vehicle in case of a theft.
- **Courier tracking:** Courier or costly assets can be tagged with tracking devices so that the position of these can be monitored. In case of freight items, such tracking will allow the user to exactly know where his package is. This avoids manual intervention for data

entry and can speed up the handling process. Current freight tracking systems use passive components to track items.

- **Traffic alerts:** Traffic and weather alerts are among the most widely used location services. These alerts provide a traveling person with the latest traffic situation on the road ahead. It also delivers the latest weather updates for the subscriber's current region. Traffic radios are very popular in many countries, but location based traffic alerts can provide customer specific traffic alerts only when he needs an alert.
- **Location sensitive advertising:** LBS can be used to provide location sensitive advertising. Consider a scenario where a traveler gets a message about the nearest hotels as soon as he lands in an airport. In a shopping mall, the service can be used to push information about shops offering a discount. Everyone within a fixed distance from the mall will get the promotional message. This can increase sales and brand awareness.
- **Emergency assistance:** Emergency assistance is the most useful and life saving among all location based services. In case of an accident, a panic button can be pressed, which will send out the location information where the accident took place to nearest control center/ambulance/patrol car. This will help the police/paramedics to reach the accident scene earlier and save lives.
- **E911 services:** Location based services got a boost when the E-911 enhancements were suggested to the 911 system in the USA. E-911 specifies that all operators must provide the location of a 911 caller so that the emergency team can reach the spot faster. This brought about many technological and business changes. Mobile locating technology enables and improves E911 services with increased accuracy and faster query time.
- **Location based yellow page look up:** When you are traveling you will require many kinds

of information, like the nearest restaurant, medical shop, ATM counter, hospital, tourist places, and so forth. Such information can be provided location specific, if we know the traveler's location. The user can request for such services using his mobile and he will get the result in the mobile itself, either using SMS or GPRS.

- **Friend finder:** Friend finding services allows the user to keep track of his friends' locations. A user can query to find out where his friends are right now. This service has some implications on privacy, but still this is an interesting service. Alerts can be provided to users when his or her friends come within a specific distance.
- **Real-time dynamic routing and navigation service:** Electronic maps greatly benefit from knowing the location of a user. The information can be used to plot the location of the user. The map also can show real time direction tips to reach a destination. With a voice enabled LBS-navigation system, the device will give you directions, asking you to "turn right" or "turn left" when a deviation comes.
- **Child/pet tracking:** Tracking devices can be installed in collars or lockets and can be used to track children and pets. Software can be made in such a way that the users can set boundaries. When the child or the pet approaches the boundary or crosses it, the software can raise an alarm or can send an alert message informing the parent or owner.
- Location based billing: Location based billing can be used for promotional activities. The concept is that the billing tariff depends in part on the location of the user. Operators can club with other service providers to make maximum use of location based billing.
- **Games:** Location based games can be very attractive, especially to youth. Treasure hunts, urban combat games, and find me are some famous location based games (Jacob, 2007).

LBS System Components

LBS is an intersection of three technologies:

- New information and communication technologies (NICTS) such as the mobile telecommunication system and hand held devices;
- Internet; and
- Geographic information systems (GIS) with spatial databases.

LBS give the possibility of a two way communication and interaction. Therefore, the user tells the service provider his actual context, like the kind of information he needs, his preferences, and his position. This helps the provider of such location services to deliver information tailored to the user needs (Steiniger, Neun, & Edwardes, 2007).

If the user wants to use a location based service, different infrastructure elements are necessary. The basic components in LBS are:

- **Mobile devices:** A tool for the user to request the needed information. The results can be given by speech, using pictures, text, and so on. Possible devices are PDA's, mobile phones, laptops, and so on, but the device can also be a navigation unit of car or a toll box for road pricing in a truck.
- **Communication network:** The second component is the mobile network, which transfers the user data and service request from the mobile terminal to the service provider and then the requested information back to the user.
- **Positioning determination technology (PDT) component:** For the processing of a service, the user position usually has to be determined. The user position can be obtained either by using the mobile communication network or by using the global positioning system (GPS). Further possibilities to determine the position are WLAN stations, active badges, or radio beacons. The latter position-

ing methods can be especially used for indoor navigation, like in a museum. If the position is not determined automatically it can be also specified manually by the user.

- **Service and application provider:** The service provider offers a number of different services to the user and is responsible for the service request processing. Such services offer the calculation of the position, finding a route, searching yellow pages with respect to position, or searching specific information on objects of user interest (e.g., a bird in wild life park) and so forth.
- **Data and content provider:** Service providers will usually not store and maintain all the information which can be requested by users. Therefore, geographic base data and location information data will usually be requested from the maintaining authority (e.g., mapping agencies) or business and industry partners (e.g., yellow pages, traffic companies) (Steiniger, Neun, & Edwardes, 2007).

LOCATION BASED SERVICE REQUIREMENTS ANALYSIS

Besides the general requirements for m-commerce, location-based services are subject to a set of specific requirements. The requirements can be classified into the following categories: user (functional), usability, reliability, privacy, location infrastructure, and interoperability. These requirements cover some basic issues in location-based services (Tsalgatidou, Veijalainen, Markkula, Katasonov, & Hadjiefthymiades, 2003).

User Requirements: Functional Requirements

User requirements are formed on mobile user exceptions of a LBS. These requirements are the source for the functional requirements of an LBS application. Hermann and Heidmann analyzed a specific LBS application, namely location based fair guide. They conducted interviews with a set of potential users of such a system and a set of visitors of a book fair in order to investigate the user requirements empirically (Hermann & Heidmann, 2002). The list of features the interviewees considered indispensable includes browsing of spatial information (locations of facilities and exhibitors) connected with catalogue data, activity planning, and way finding. The same requirements apply, of course, to any LBS serving a visitor in an unfamiliar environment, whether it is a fair, museum, city, or country. Therefore, the main LBS functional requirements are the following:

- Browsing of spatial information, for example, in the form of a city map.
- **Navigation:** The user must be able to acquire directions and guidance for reaching a specific point of interest.
- Access to catalogue data, for example, names of restaurants and their description like menu, range of prices, opening hours, and so forth. Catalogue data must be spatially referenced so the facilities in the catalogue can be represented on the map and directions for reaching them can be acquired.
- **Location-based access:** The user must be able to access map and catalogue data based on his/her present location. If locating the user cannot be resolved automatically by the system, the user must be provided with the option of manually entering his/her location. The system should be able to handle such requests through geocoding procedures.
- **Personalized access:** The user must be able to specify the type of information s/he needs, for example, a map depicting just the street network or a map including various points of interest. A profile mechanism should also be provided so that the user does not have to input his preferences every time s/he uses the service.

- **Fast access:** The user must be able to run various queries, for example, for nearby restaurants or even for the nearby vegetarian restaurants that are opened after 9 p.m. As can be seen, the LBS user interface must deliver to the user various information including a static map image of the desired area, the location of the user, and possibly, locations of other mobile objects, descriptive information on points of interest, route information, and so forth. Clearly, all this information cannot be presented at once, so an implied requirement is that LBS must provide a set of alternative views:
- **Geographical view:** Graphical representation of a geographical area, usually in the form of a map.
- **View corresponding visual perceptions:** The view as the user could see it if s/he went to the place of interest. This view can be implemented with photographs or 3D modeling.
- **Geographical information view:** Textual description of points of interest enabling the user to browse through it.
- **Status view:** Description of the current state of the user in the form of picture, text of voice.
- **Context view:** Tied to information representation about close objects and the user possibilities in the current context.
- **Route view:** Graphical representation of a route from one point to another.
- **Logistic view:** Abstract route model, showing only intermediate and final points, but no specific distances and directions
- **Guidance view:** Turn-by-turn instruction for the user, usually in a text form and also possibly as voice.

Usability Requirements

Mobile computing environment has certain features that impose restrictions. The properties of mobile networks are: (relatively) low bandwidth, strong bandwidth variability, long latency, unpredictable disconnections, and communication autonomy.

The properties of mobile terminals are: small and low-resolution displays, limited input capabilities, limited computing power, limited power, and small memory size. The practical conditions, when and where the mobile devices are used, bring also additional restrictions. The using conditions cannot be expected to be constant, as usually is the case in "desktop" conditions. The mobile users are typically in very unstable environments, in varying conditions, where their cognitive capacity is demanded for other tasks as well. All these restrictions have to be taken very carefully into account when designing LBS. Some of the implied requirements are:

- Not very intensive use of mobile network and minimal volume of transmitted data;
- Possibility to offline operation; and
- User interface should be very simple and user friendly and the amount of presented information content limited and well specified.

Reliability Requirements

LBS are intended mainly for traveling people as a tool providing support in making decisions about where to go. Therefore, wrong information may mean wrong decisions, lost time and, as a result, client anger in the best case and a court examination in the worse case. Consider, for example, a case where LBS misled the user when he needed an urgent medical assistance. Reliability requirements can be divided into the following sub-requirements:

- **Data reliability:** The most important since LBS are built around spatial and catalogue data and incorrect or missed data can easily lead to problems.
- **Software reliability:** Applies to both server and client sides.
- **Appropriateness and precision of exploited algorithms and methods:** Depending on the task in hand, for example, user positioning precision may be sufficient or insufficient, calculating distances by straight line may be sufficient for some tasks but insufficient for

others (the road network thus must be taken into account).

Privacy Requirements

Privacy handling is a major issue in LBS deployment and provision and a critical success factor to the wide acceptance of this technology framework. The term privacy handling consolidates issues like ownership of location information, use of location information, disclosure to service providers, and so forth. Skepticism arises as to where and how privacy handling should take place within the LBS provision chain.

Existing proposals from operators and standardization bodies (e.g., OMA, 3GPP) specify a priority scheme whereby the core network elements (e.g., home location registers) have master control on location information. The provision/disclosure of such information to other entities (e.g., location servers, LBS serving nodes, ASPs) is subject to subscriber needs (e.g., registration information) and regulatory frameworks.

Location Infrastructure Requirements

Location-based service consists of roughly two phases, determining the position of the customer and providing service or contents based on the position. For the location method at least the following requirements can be listed:

- The method should provide good accuracy subject to the requirements of the application and the respective cost.
- The area where the mobile device can be located should be as large as possible; it should be possible to determine in advance where the device can be located; ideally, this should happen within the whole coverage area of mobile networks.
- The method should be fast: also in this respect, the applications have different demands, for

example, the emergency applications and car navigation systems have higher demands than "FIND restaurant"—type applications.

- The location method should not generate too much signaling load within the mobile network.
- The effects of adding location method support to a terminal and using it should be minimal, that is, it should not increase its size, weight, power consumption, or price.
- The location method should have a minimum impact on the mobile network in terms of complexity and cost.
- It should be possible to locate all mobile devices irrespective of their type and whether they are roaming or not.
- It should be possible to locate a large group of mobile devices at the same time.
- Consumer privacy must be ensured, by, for example, providing means for the consumer to turn off the locating feature of the terminal.

Service Interoperability Requirements

The interoperability should be assured on all levels of the system architecture. The LBS platform should be interoperable with several types of terminals (e.g., PDAs, GSM terminals) and positioning infrastructures (e.g., indoor, GPS). The platform should be able to handle different coordinate reference systems (e.g., WGS-84 and local systems) in order be able to utilize geographic data available in existing GIS databases. The seamless service provision when different infrastructures are visited by the user is also a requirement in the highly diversified modern telecomm landscape (Tsalgatidou et al., 2003).

LOCATION BASED SERVICE SYSTEM DESIGN

The work flow of LBS is shown as in Figure 1. Where mobile users need information service or the management center needs to track them, the embedded positioning device, that is, GPS provides current positioning information and transmits it to the center. The service requirements are analyzed by the GPS central GIS server to get results, which is transmitted to the mobile users. LBS generally include two processes. One is to collect the position; the other is to provide service according to user requirement (Hightower & Borriello, 2001; Chen, Zhang, Sun, & Luo, 2004)

LBS System Architecture Design

In this section, we will focus on the architecture design of location utility, which is a typical distributed LBS system developed for supporting a large class of applications that involve responding to the movements of large numbers of mobile users. Other architectures have been proposed in the literature (Agre, Akinyemi, Ji, Masuoka, & Thakkar, 2002); we choose to present the location utility architecture for the simplicity and efficiency. Location utility was proposed and developed by the IBM Watson Research Center. As shown in Figure 2, it consists of a control center (LUCC) and a set of local servers (LULS). This distributed architecture is proposed for the purpose of scalablity. Application rules/functions are distributed to all local server nodes, but each local server handles the subset of the users associated with the local node.

Let us take a simple example and see how this architecture works. Suppose there is a location based service that monitors a few restricted areas and sends alarms when an unauthorized person enters them. This service is first subscribed through the control center. The control center then identifies every local server whose cover region intersects with the restricted areas and the service is subscribed in these relevant local servers as well. The rule subscribed in each local server is:

If (!IsMemberOf(AuthorizedPersonnel)) and Position.ContainedInPolygonClass(RestrictedArea) sendAlarm()

This rule is evaluated at the local servers. When it is true, an alarm is sent to the control center and the control center will send an alarm to the application.

Local server nodes receive the raw subscriber position information from the positioning technology and evaluate the rules assigned to them. Rules that evaluate to true generate reports, which are sent to the application that subscribed to the rule. If the application subscribed to a rule through a local server directly, the report is forward to the application directly; if the application subscribed through the control center, the report is forwarded to the control center, which will in turn forward it to the application. To be able to evaluate rules that involve multiple subscribers, local server nodes may themselves subscribe to rules in other local servers. Where possible, local server nodes are deployed in alignment with the network infrastructure in order

Figure 1. LBS work flow

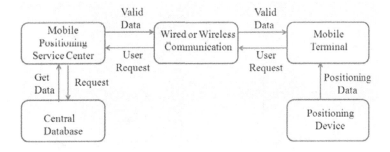

to take advantage of local information about the user presence.

A local server may not evaluate all rules distributed to it. Knowing which users it is currently serving and the geographic region it serves, a local server can, for some rules, decide that the rules can never evaluate to true, and "deactivate" them to reduce its own load. In short, rules that refer to geometries that lie outside a local server's service region and rules that refer to no specific subscribers currently not served by a local server, will not be evaluated by that local server. Because the set of subscribers served by a local server is dynamic, a rule's evaluation status is dynamic. A rule pertaining to a particular subscriber is activated in a local server node when the subscriber moves into the region covered by the node. Any subscriber resources attached to the subscriber are also moved to that local server.

The control center is the locus of control and management functions, and is the primary point of contact for applications to subscribe to rules and set up application resources. It also provides an interface for retrieving subscriber positions and any resources applications may have created for them. When an application subscribes to a rule through the control center, the control center records the subscription information and forwards the rule to all local server nodes. Reports from these rules are sent from the local server nodes to the control center, which aggregates them and forwards them to the application. Application resources set up through the control center are also forwarded to the local server nodes, but resources that have associated geometries are forwarded only to those local server nodes whose geographical domain intersects them. The control center maintains a table of control center information to enable this.

The application interface to the control center includes a function to immediately retrieve rule evaluation results, which will be retrieved from the local server nodes where they are maintained. For those rules that are evaluated at all local server nodes, all nodes will be requested to return the results. For those rules that are evaluated only at certain nodes, because they apply only to the domains of

Figure 2. Location-based service system architecture

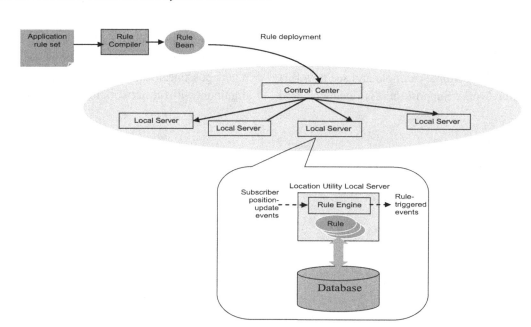

certain nodes, only those nodes will be requested to return the results.

When a subscriber moves from the region served by one local server to that of another, the resources that applications may have created for the subscriber must be transferred from one to the other. The control center must also be notified of the new serving local server. A detailed description of the system architecture and components can be found in Munson, Cole, Duri, and Wood (2003).

LBS Database Design

In this section, we present a data model for representing moving objects in database systems. It is called the moving objects spatio-temporal (MOST) data model (Sistla, Wolfson, Chamberlain, & Dao, 1997).

Existing database management systems (DBMSs) are not well equipped to handle continuously changing data, such as the position of moving objects. The reason for this is that in databases, data is assumed to be constant unless it is explicitly modified. For example, if the salary field is 30K, then this salary is assumed to hold (i.e., 30K is returned in response to queries) until explicitly updated. Thus, in order to represent moving objects (e.g., cars) in a database, and answer queries about their position (e.g., How far is the car with license plate RWW860 from the nearest hospital?), the car's position has to be continuously updated. This is unsatisfactory since either the position is updated very frequently (which would impose a serious performance and wireless-bandwidth overhead), or, the answer to queries is outdated. Furthermore, it is possible that due to disconnection, an object cannot continuously update its position. One common solution is to represent the position as a function of time; it changes as time passes, even without an explicit update (Saltenis, Jensen, Leutenegger, & Lopez, 2000; Tao, Papadias, & Sun, 2003). For example, the position of a car is given as a function of its motion vector (e.g., north, at 60 miles/hour). In other words, a higher level of data abstraction is considered, where an object's motion vector (rather than its position) is represented as an attribute of the object. Obviously, the motion vector of an object can change (thus it can be updated), but in most cases it does so less frequently than the position of the object.

A data model called moving objects spatio-temporal was proposed for databases with dynamic attributes, that is, attributes that change continuously as a function of time, without being explicitly updated. In other words, the answer to a query depends not only on the database contents, but also on the time at which the query is entered. Furthermore, we explain how to incorporate dynamic attributes in existing data models and what capabilities need to be added to existing query processing systems to deal with dynamic attributes. Clearly, the MOST model enables queries that refer to future values of dynamic attributes, namely future queries. For example, consider an air-traffic control application, and suppose that each object in the database represents an aircraft and its position. Then the query Q = "retrieve all the airplanes that will come within 30 miles of the airport in the next 10 minutes" can be answered in the MOST model.

Continuous queries are another topic that requires new consideration in our model. For example, suppose that there is a table called MOTELS giving for each motel its geographic-coordinates, room-price, and availability. Consider a moving car issuing a query such as "Display motels (with availability and cost) within a radius of 5 miles," and suppose that the query is continuous, that is, the car requests the answer to the query to be continuously updated. Observe that the answer changes with the car movement. When and how often should the query be reevaluated? Our query processing algorithm facilitates a single evaluation of the query; reevaluation has to occur only if the motion vector of the car changes.

A. Data Model

The traditional database model is as follows. A *database* is a set of object-classes. A special database object called *time* gives the current time at every instant; its domain is the set of natural numbers, and its value increases by one in each clock tick. An *object-class* is a set of attributes. For example, MOTELS is an object class with attributes name, location, number-of-rooms, price-per room, and so forth.

Some object-classes are designated as *spatial*. A spatial object class has three attributes called X.POSITION, Y.POSITION, and Z.POSITION, denoting the object's position in space. The spatial object classes have a set of spatial methods associated with them. Each such method takes spatial objects as arguments. Intuitively, these methods represent spatial relationships among the objects at a certain point in time, and they return true or false, indicating whether or not the relationship is satisfied at the time. For example, INSIDE(o,P) and OUTSIDE(o,P) are spatial relations. Each one of them takes as arguments a point-object o and a polygon-object P in a database state; and it indicates whether or not o is inside (outside) the polygon P in that state. Another example of a spatial relation is WITHIN-ASPHERE (r, o1, o2, ... on). Its first argument is a real number, and its remaining arguments are point-objects in the database. WITHIN-A-SPHERE indicates whether or not the point-objects can be enclosed within a sphere of radius r. There may also be methods that return an integer value. For example, the method DIST (o1, o2) takes as arguments two point-objects and returns the distance between the point-objects.

To model moving objects, the notion of a dynamic attribute was introduced.

B. Dynamic Attributes

Each attribute of an object-class is either static or dynamic. Intuitively, a static attribute of an object is an attribute in the traditional sense, that is, it changes only when an explicit update of the database occurs; in contrast, a dynamic attribute changes over time according to some given function, even if it is not explicitly updated. For example, consider a moving object whose position in a two dimensional space at any point in time is given by values of the x, y coordinates. Then each one of the object's coordinates is a dynamic attribute.

Formally, a *dynamic attribute* A is represented by three sub-attributes, A.value, A.updatetime, and A.function, where A.function is a function of a single variable that has value 0 at time 0. The *value* of a dynamic attribute depends on the time, and it is defined as follows. At time A.updatetime the value of A is A.value, and until the next update of A the value of A. At time A.time+t0 is given by A.value + A.function (t0). An explicit update of a dynamic attribute may change its value sub-attribute, or its function sub-attribute, or both sub-attributes.

In addition to querying the value of a dynamic attribute, a user can query each sub-attribute independently. Thus, the user can ask for the objects for which X.POSITION.function=5*t, that is, the objects whose speed in the x direction is 5.

There are two possible interpretations of A.updatetime, corresponding to valid-time and transaction-time. In the first interpretation, it is the time at which the update occurred in the real world system being modeled, for example, the time at which the vehicle changed its motion vector. In this case, along with the update, the sensor has to send to the database A.updatetime. In the second interpretation, A.updatetime is simply the time-stamp when the update was committed by the DBMS. In this chapter, it is assumed that the database is updated instantaneously, that is, the valid-time and transaction-time are equal.

When a dynamic attribute is queried, the answer returned by the DBMS consists of the value of the attribute at the time the query is entered. In this sense, our model is different than existing database systems, since, unless an attribute has been explicitly updated, a DBMS returns the same value for the attribute, independently of the time at which the query is posed. So, for example, in our model the answer to the query: "retrieve the current X position of object O" depends on the value of the dynamic attribute X.POSITION at the time at which the query is posed. In other words, the answer may be different for time-points t1 and t2, even though the database has not been explicitly updated between these two time-points (Sistla, Wolfson, Chamberlain, & Dao, 1997).

SYSTEM PERFORMANCE ANALYSIS AND PLANNING: A CASE STUDY

In this section, we present the results of some experiments to analyze the performance of the local server in location utility LBS systems. The execution time needed to process the most common requests or operations in local based services are measured and the most time consuming computations and operations are identified. The data obtained in these experiments will not only identify time consuming operations or potential bottlenecks so to optimize the system, but also provide reference for hardware selection, performance and capacity planning, and tailoring the various components to suit the complex needs of the application and the system.

This section also offers a quantitative way of finding the optimal cell size for deploying local servers for the local based services system. The model relates several factors such as local server processing capacity, control center capacity, mobile users' arrival and departure rate, and the traffic types. The goal of this work is to specify an approach of computing optimal coverage region for the local server that satisfies two criteria: (i) queries/services can be finished in timely way and (ii) the number of crossover or handoffs should not become overwhelming. It gives a set of basic results and offers an understanding of cell size tradeoffs in location-based service systems. It also provides a general guideline for choosing the covering range when deploying local based services local servers.

Performance Analysis Environment Setup

In all the experiments, a 2.4Ghz Pentium III machine with 1GB of memory is used. Due to the unavailability of actual object movement data, a synthetic dataset generated by the City Simulator is used. The City Simulator was developed by IBM Almaden Research Center to create dynamic spatial data simulating the motion of up to 1 million people. The data format generated by the City Simulator is as follows:

```
1, 0.037288, 530.8,164.0,18.0    cycle = 1
2, 0.074932, 299.4,143.6,24.0    cycle = 1
3, 0.096154, 312.6,805.0,5.3     cycle = 1
...
1, 29.926125, 529.2,164.0,18.0   cycle = 2
2, 29.957042, 299.4,143.6,24.0   cycle = 2
3, 29.978109, 312.2,804.4,5.3    cycle = 2
...
```

Each record contains a unique person ID, a time stamp, and the x,y,z coordinates. These data are stored in spatial position record (SPR) files. In the experiments, the LULS reads the SPRs of each object from SPR files, simulating the locations of users and the arrival of these events at the LULS. It is assumed that LULS has the latest locations of each object. In LULS, location services are expected to be implemented through rules or rule combinations. Take the example of the location-based advertising/promotion service, when a preferred customer enters the proximity of certain stores, coupons or advertisements will be sent to him/her. The query of finding such customers in LULS would be a rule combination as following:

IsMemberOf (PreferredCustomerClass) and ContainedInPolygonClass(StoreClass).

For the underlying database system, the IBM's DB2 relational database system with spatial extender is used. Resources such as polygons and points, which represent places of interest such as restaurants, hotels, gas stations, and other static locations of interest, are stored in the spatial database.

The notion of RPS (rule per second) was proposed to be the benchmark parameter that should be measured. This benchmark is similar to MIPS (million instructions per second) performance parameter for CPU and TPS (transactions per second) for database systems. To get RPS for different rules, the time needed to process each rule is measured.

Functions Measured

The following are the most common rules/operations for location-based services. All the rules here serve as the basic predicates or operations in the system. Complicated applications and services can be built based on them.

- **HasIdentity:** Test if the subscriber has the given identity ID.
- **HasValue:** Test if there is a variable with the give name. Both cases—when the variable exists and when it does not exist, are tested.
- **IsMemberOf(subscriberClass):** Test if the subscriber is a member of one or more of the given classes. To test this rule, a MembershipGenerator was developed for generating membership with specified size. Four memberships were generated, with size 100, 1K, 10K, and 100K respectively.
- **IsTrue/IsFalse:** IsTrue/IsFalse is the simplest rule. By measuring the time needed for processing these rules, we get an idea of the pure overhead of going through the rule evaluating process.
- **Logical rules:** Performs basic logic operations including AND, OR, NOT.
- **Relational:** Performs basic comparison operations including EQ (=), GE (>=), GT (>), LE (<=), LT (<), and NE (!=).
- DistanceFrom
    1. **DistanceFrom.Point:** Returns the great circle distance from the given subscriber position to the specified point.

2. **DistanceFrom.Subscriber:** Returns the great circle distance from the given subscriber position to the specified subscriber.

- **ContainedIn.Polygon:** Test if the subscriber position is contained in the given polygon. The polygon is a resource that stored in database.
- **ContainedIn.PolygonClass:** Test if the subscriber position is contained in the given set of polygons, which are referred to via a class identifier. To test ContainedIn.PolygonClass, a PolygonGenerator was developed for generating a number of uniformly distributed polygons with specified area size. These polygons can then be loaded into the database as one class.
- **WithinDistanceOf.Point:** Test if the subscriber position is within the given distance from the given point.
- **WithinDistanceOf.PointClass:** Test if the subscriber position is within the given distance from the given set of points, which are referred to via a class identifier. To test WithinDistanceOf.PointClass, a PointGenerator was developed for generating a number of uniformly distributed points within the specified space. These points are then loaded into the database as one class.
- **WithinDistanceOf.Subscriber:** Test if the subscriber position is within the given distance from the position of the given subscriber.
- **WithinDistanceOf.SubscriberClass:** Test if the subscriber position is within the given distance from the position of one or more of the given subscribers, referred to via a class identifier.

Execution Time

The process of measuring the execution_time is as following: the rules to be tested are subscribed into LULS, and then SPRS are fed in through a socket. The time needed to evaluate each rule is then measured.

The execution time for each rule/operation is shown in Table 1. As we can see from the table, the processing time of these rules varies significantly, ranging from 0.26ms to almost 300ms.

Generally speaking, there are two types of rules: rules that need access to the database, for example, ContainedIn.PolygonClass and WithinDistance. PointClass, and rules that do not need access to the database, such as HasIdentity. As shown in Table 1, rules that access the database usually take much more time than rules that do not. That is easy to understand since database operations tend to be I/O intensive and time consuming.

Performance Improvements

A. Use Spatial Index

Since rules that access the database take a much longer time than rules that do not, this indicates that database access is a costly operation. In order to improve the database performance, spatial indexes are used. DB2 spatial extender provides a grid index, which was used for measuring the process time of two rules: ContainedIn.Polygon-Class and WithinDistanceOf.PointClass. It showed that when the database has only a small number of geometries, like less than 1000 polygons or points, the index does not improve the performance or may even harm it. The reason is that with an index, the database may have to go through the index to reach the actual data, and the index access causes extra I/Os. However, as the number of geometries in the database gets larger, the index starts to show its benefit. The index can efficiently help with pruning and reduce the number of objects queries that need access. Therefore, the more geometries in the database, the more significant the index improvement is. Figure 3 shows that for 100,000 polygons, the processing time of ContainIn.PolygonClass without index is between 270 to 300ms, while with index; it takes only 47-50 ms. That is an over 5 times performance gain.

B. Reduce Communication Cost

The cost of communicating an SPR from the (simulated) positioning technology to an LULS was also evaluated. The processing time of each rule was measured both when SPRs were sent from another host and then read through a local socket, and when SPRs are simply read from a local file.

The execution times of these two approaches are shown in Table 2. For rules that access database and therefore take a long time, the performance does not differ much by using the two approaches. However, for simple rules that do not access database, reading SPRs from a file can be 20-30 times faster than reading SPR from a socket. The reason is that reading SPRs from a socket does take more time than reading from a file, but for rules that access a database and take a long time itself to execute; this performance gain is not obvious since database access cost dominates the overall cost. What is learned from this experiment is that the communication cost can be reduced, probably by exploiting some caching mechanism to store the incoming and outgoing data, so that the server does not waste precious CPU cycle waiting for the data to be read in or sent out.

Identify the Most Time Consuming Functions

To find out which operations or functions take the most time during the rule evaluation, Rational Quantify, a runtime analysis tool, was run to help developers identify performance bottlenecks and portions of code subject to performance optimization. Rational Quantify was run for both rules that access the database and that do not. Some representative results are shown in Tables 3 and 4.

It is shown that:

- For rules that do not access database, the largest amount of time is taken by JVM Garbage Collector. As show in Table 4, the system spent one third of the time doing garbage collection.

Table 1. Execution time of the functions

Process Time		
Rules	Parameters	Time(ms)
ContainedIn.Polygon	Area 10	3.6
	Area 100	3.7
	Area 1000	3.7
ContainedIn.PolygonClass	100 polygons	3-4
	1000 polygons	11-13
	10000 polygons	28-32
	100000 polygons	270-300
DistanceFrom	Point (PointConstant)	0.37
	Point (PointVariable)	9.1
	Subscriber (SubscriberID)	0.37
HasIdentity	SubscriberID	0.38
HasValue	-	1.6
IsMemberOf	100 members	0.37
	1000 members	0.41
	10000 members	0.56
	100000 members	0.61
IsTrue/IsFalse	-	0.26
Logical	-	0.26
Relational	-	0.33
WithinDistanceOf.Point	-	9.7
WithinDistanceOf.PointClass	100 points	3.2
	1000 points	7.4
	10000 points	25-30
	100000 points	170-200
WithinDistanceOf.Subscriber		0.26
WithinDistanceOf.SubscriberClass	100 members	4.7
	1000 members	5.8
	10000 members	13.7

- For rules that access the database, the largest amount of time is taken by database operations. Table 4 shows that database related operations take more than half of the time and Java Garbage Collector takes another quarter.

Both of these discoveries leave a great space for system optimization.

System Capacity Planning

Studying the execution time of each rule gives us an idea of the processing capability of an LULS. For example, give a certain number of subscribed users and rules and location update frequency, can an LULS process the entire load in time? Or for a given update frequency, how many subscribers or services can an LULS handle?

Let us suppose objects have a uniform update frequency and they update their locations every T

Figure 3. Effect of the index

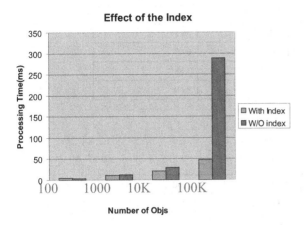

seconds and the number of objects in the LULS is n. Suppose the location update of object i result in K_i (i= 1,...n) rules to be revaluated (assume other rules are irrelevant) and the processing time of the rules are t_{ij}, (i = 1, ..., n; j = 1, ..., K_i). Then the total processing time needed for each cycle is $\sum_{i=1}^{n}\sum_{j=1}^{K_i}t_{ij}$. For the LULS to handle the load in time, $\sum_{i=1}^{n}\sum_{j=1}^{K_i}t_{ij}$ should to be less than T. By studying the user profiles (how many services a typical user would subscribe to and how complicated these services are) and distribution, it can be estimated that the maximum number of users each LULS can handle for an update frequency. When $\sum_{i=1}^{n}\sum_{j=1}^{K_i}t_{ij} > T$, system

administrators have to choose either evaluating rules at a lower frequency or do load shedding, which is a technique in data stream systems that discard some fraction of the unprocessed data in order for the system to continue to provide up-to-date query responses. Although both approaches could potentially harm the freshness of the queries, there are some heuristics that have been proposed earlier to maximize the accuracy.

OPTIMAL CELL SIZE FOR SERVER DEPLOYMENT

In order to achieve scalability, the system is designed in a distributed mode, where each local server covers a cell and handles the subscribers and applications related to that cell. A key issue in this environment is: what is the optimal cell size for deploying the local servers? Choosing the cell size or covering region of local servers suffers from two conflicting requirements. On the one hand, a small cell size is desirable since the smaller the cell is, the fewer the subscribers are in each cell and the faster the response to the location-based services could be. On the other hand, a large cell size is desirable since the smaller cell size can potentially result in a large number of crossovers between the cells. Each crossover requires a certain amount of overhead including rule migration, resources transferring, and rule activation or deactivations.

Table 2. Effect of the communication cost

SPR from Socket vs Local		
Rule	Socket	Local File
DistanceFrom.PointVariable	9.1	9.0
DistanceFrom.PointConstant	0.37	0.016
DistanceFrom.SubscriberID	0.37	0.015
IsTrue/IsFalse	0.26	0.010
HasIdentity	0.38	0.012
Logical	0.26	0.011
Relational	0.33	0.012

Table 3. Method time for the rule HasIdentity

Method&Calls	Method Time	Method time %
JVM Garbage Collector	7005.13	35.14
String.charAt	1321.40	6.63
LocalPerformanceTester.main	773.14	3.88
FloatingDecimal.readJavaFormatString	535.88	2.69

Table 4. Method time for the rule WithinDistanceOf

Method&Calls	Method Time	Method time %
DB2PreparedStatement.SQLExecute	61,816.39	47.04
JVM Garbage Collector	29,920.98	22.77
DB2ResultSet.SQLFreeStmtClose	12,434.50	9.46
FSRuleTable.processALL	1437.27	1.09
String.charAt	1348.51	1.03

Since the control center is involved in processing the handoffs, a large number of handoffs could make the control center become the bottleneck of the system. These conflicts are shown in Figure 4. By balancing these two factors, an approach was proposed to compute the optimal cell size for deploying the local servers.

Let us denote P(t) as the processing load of the local server during a time period t. Let α be the number of subscribed rules in the local server, λ be the subscribers' arrival rate and μ be the departure rate of subscribers, then $P(t) = K_1 \bullet \alpha \bullet t \bullet SPRrate + K_2 \bullet \beta \bullet t + K_3 \bullet \gamma \bullet t$.

The first part is the workload to handle all the subscribed rules in local server during the time t. Assume K_1 is the average cost of evaluating one rule and α is the number of subscribed rules, then $K_1 \bullet \alpha$ is the total cost of going through all rule evaluation once. $t \bullet SPRrate$ is the number of new position records received during this time period t. Since for each new SPR, local server needs go through all the rules, therefore, $K_1 \bullet \alpha \bullet t \bullet SPRrate$ is the cost of processing all the subscribed rules in local server during the time period t.

Besides processing the subscribed rules, the local server also has to process handoffs. Suppose K_2 is the cost of handling a subscriber arrival and K_3 is the cost of handling a subscriber leaving, β is the subscribers arrival rate and γ is the subscribers departure rate, then $K_2 \bullet \beta \bullet t + K_3 \bullet \gamma \bullet t$ is the total overhead to process arriving and departing users during this time segment. Since the control center is involved in handling handoffs, the time of waiting for the control center to process the handoffs should be measured. Assuming the arrival of events (handoffs) at the control center is a poisson distribution, the M/M/1 queuing model is used to compute the time taken by the control center. The average time of each event in the control center, including waiting time and service time, should be $\frac{1}{\mu - \lambda}$, where μ is the service rate and λ is the event arrival rate (Jose, Moreira, Rodrigues, & Davies, 2003). While μ is determined by the processing capacity of the control center, λ is highly related to the cell size. The smaller the cell is, the more handoff would occur. However, the exact relation between the cell size and the number of handoffs are determined by another factor—traffic.

According to Nanda (1993), with homogeneous traffic, the handoff rate is directly proportional to the total boundary length and it increases as the square-root of the increase in the cell density. An n^2 increase in the number of cells per unit area results in a handoff rate increase by a factor of n. With non-homogeneous traffic, traffic can be dominated by a few or just one traffic path; the increase in handoff rate is linear with the increase in cells per unit area. The optimal cell size for local servers in both cases is computed in the following sections.

Homogeneous Traffic

Under the assumptions that:

1. Mobile users are distributed uniformly in the region.
2. Direction of travel of mobile users is uniformly distributed over $[0, 2\pi)$,

the handoff rate is proportional to the total boundary length (Nanda,1993). Thus, for each cell the number of handoff rate is Kr, where r stands for the edge length of the cell. Suppose the space is divided into n^2 cells, $n = \frac{l}{r}$, l is the side length of the whole space and r is the side length of a cell.

The handoff rate of the whole space should be:

$$n^2 Kr = \frac{l^2}{r^2} Kr = K\frac{l^2}{r}.$$

The process load for each local server during time period t is:

$$P = K_1(c_1 r^2)(t.SPRrate) + (+c)(K_2 r)t = C_1 r^2 + (\frac{1}{\mu - \lambda} + c)C_2 r$$

λ is the events arrival rate, which is the handoff rate in the system, as computed before, $\lambda = K\frac{l^2}{r}$.

$$P = C_1 r^2 + (\frac{1}{\mu - \lambda} + c)C_2 r = C_1 r^2 + (\frac{1}{\mu - \frac{Kl^2}{r}} + c)C_2 r =$$

$$C_1 r^2 + \frac{C_2 r}{\mu - \frac{C_4}{r}} + cC_2 r = C_1 r^2 + \frac{C_2 r^2}{\mu r - C_4} + C_3 r = C_1 r^2 +$$

$$\frac{\frac{C_2}{\mu^2}(\mu r - C_4)(\mu r + C_4) + \frac{C_2 C_4^2}{\mu^2}}{\mu r - C_4} + C_3 r = C_1 r^2 + \frac{C_2}{\mu^2}(\mu r + C_4)$$

$$+ \frac{\frac{C_2 C_4^2}{\mu^2}}{\mu r - C_4} + C_3 r = C_1 r^2 + \frac{C_2}{\mu} r + \frac{C_2 C_4}{\mu^2} + \frac{\frac{C_2 C_4^2}{\mu^2}}{\mu r - C_4} + C_3 r$$

$$= C_1 r^2 + (\frac{C_2}{\mu} + C_3)r + \frac{C_2 C_4}{\mu^2} + \frac{\frac{C_2 C_4^2}{\mu^2}}{\mu r - C_4}$$

$$\frac{dP}{dr} = 2C_1 r + (\frac{C_2}{\mu} + C_3) - \frac{C_2 C_4^2}{\mu}(\mu r - C_4)^{-2}$$

Figure 4. Local server load

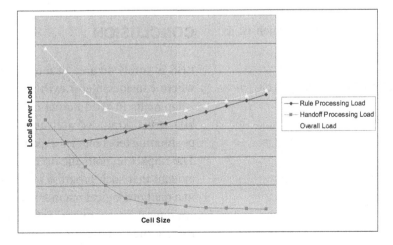

To get the minimum value of P let $\frac{dP}{dr} = 0$, then

$$2C_1r + (\frac{C_2}{\mu} + C_3)\frac{C_2 C_4^2}{\mu}(\mu r - C_4)^{-2} = 0.$$

This is a cubic equation that has general solutions, which is the optimal cell size. For the detailed solution, please refer to the appendix.

Non-Homogeneous Traffic

The result obtained in 3.1 is based on the assumption of the homogeneity of vehicular traffic. It applies to situations where each cell consists of a large number of traffic paths with random orientation. As cells get smaller, the traffic is no longer homogenous. The distinct paths in each cell, their orientation, and traffic flow become important. In this case, the increase in over handoff rate is linear with the increase in cell density (Nanda, 1993). Therefore, the handoff rate for each cell is basically a constant K. Suppose the space is divided into n^2 cells, $n = \frac{l}{r}$, l is the side length of the whole space and r is the side length of a cell. The handoff rate of the whole space should be $K\, n^2 = K\frac{l^2}{r^2}$.

Again, the process load for each local server during time period t is:

$$P = K_1(c_1 r^2)(t.SPRrate) +$$

$$(\frac{1}{\mu - \lambda} + c)\, K_2 t = C_1 r^2 + (\frac{1}{\mu - \lambda} + c)C_2$$

λ is the handoff rate in the system, which is, as computed before, $K\frac{l^2}{r^2}$.

$$P = C_1 r^2 + (\frac{1}{\mu - \lambda} + c)C_2 = C_1 r^2 + (\frac{1}{\mu - K(\frac{l}{r})^2} + c)C_2 =$$

$$C_1 r^2 + \frac{C_2}{\mu - \frac{Kl^2}{r^2}} + C_3 = C_1 r^2 + \frac{C_2 r^2}{\mu r^2 - Kl^2} + C_3 =$$

$$C_1 r^2 + \frac{\frac{C_2}{\mu}(\mu r^2 - Kl^2) + \frac{C_2^2 l^2}{\mu}}{\mu r^2 - Kl^2} + C_3 = C_1 r^2 + C_4 +$$

$$\frac{C_5}{\mu r^2 - Kl^2} + C_3$$

Take r^2 as a variable X, the above is $C_1 X + \frac{C_5}{\mu X - Kl^2} + (C_3 + C_4)$

$$\frac{dP}{dX} = C_1 - C_5\mu(\mu X - Kl^2)^{-2}$$

to get the minimum value of P, let $\frac{dP}{dr} = 0$, we get $(\mu X - Kl^2)^2 = \frac{C_5\mu}{C_1}(\mu X - Kl^2)$ should be larger than 0, for the reason that $(\mu X - Kl^2) = X(\mu - K\frac{l^2}{X})$ and X, which is r^2, is positive; and $\mu - K\frac{l^2}{X} = \mu - K(\frac{l}{X})^2$ is the process time of control center, which is also positive.

Therefore, $\mu X - Kl^2 = \sqrt{\frac{C_5\mu}{C_1}}$, which means X $= \frac{\sqrt{\frac{C_5\mu}{C_1}} + Kl^2}{\mu}$

Since $C_5 = \frac{C_2^2 l^2}{\mu}$, X $= \frac{\frac{C_2 L}{\sqrt{C_1}} + Kl^2}{\mu}$.

Hence, the optimal cell size is proportional to the handoff rate and to inverse of the control center service rate and the residents' rule processing overhead, that is, the higher the hand off rate is, the larger the cell should be. The more time needed to process the residents' subscription rules, the smaller the cell should be. The smaller the process rate of the control center is, the larger the cell should be.

CONCLUSION

LBS is surely an area of modern mobile services where considerable growth is observed. The developments in the Internet domain, wireless/mobile networking, as well as the proliferation of positioning technologies expedited such evolution. The impact on nomadic users is tremendous. It is evident that such progress needs to be addressed in a methodological manner and supported, where appropriate by coordinated standardization efforts. Requirements need to be reviewed and studied very carefully by all the involved actors. Their coverage—fulfillment by modern technological platforms, is also a very important issue. Our work is mainly moving along these lines. The analysis and design techniques, as presented in this chapter, shows that the technologies and issues involved in LBS deployment and provision cover a very wide spectrum including operating system capabilities, user interface design, positioning techniques, terminal technologies, network capabilities, and so forth. The meticulous mapping of these technical aspects to the identified requirements is a critical success factor for LBS.

REFERENCES

Agre, J., Akinyemi, A., Ji, L., Masuoka, R., & Thakkar, P. (2002). *A layered architecture for location-based services in wireless ad hoc networks.* Retrieved on August 15, 2007, from www.flacp. fujitsulabs.com/~rmasuoka/papers/200203-LocationProtocol7.doc

Chen, X., Zhang, F., Sun, M., & Luo, Y. (2004). System architecture of LBS based on spatial information integration. *Geoscience and Remote Sensing Symposium, IGARSS IEEE International, 4,* 2409-2411.

Hermann, F., & Heidmann, F. (2002). User requirement analysis and interface conception for a mobile, location-based fair guide. Mobile HCI, Lecture Notes in Computer Science, 2411, 388-392.

Hightower, J., & Borriello, G. (2001). Location systems for ubiquitous computing. *IEEE Computer, 34*(8), 57-66.

Jacob, K. (2007). *Location based services.* Retrieved on May 15, 2007, from http://www.kenneyjacob. com/2007/05/13/location-based-services/

Jose, R., Moreira, A., Rodrigues, H., & Davies, N. (2003). The AROUND architecture for dynamic location-based services. *Mobile Networks and Applications, 8*(4), 377-387.

Munson, J., Cole, A., Duri, S., & Wood, D. (2003). *Architectural specification of the location utility* (Version: 0.4). IBM report.

Nanda, S. (1993). Teletraffic models for urban and suburban microcells: Cell sizes and handoff rates. *IEEE Transaction of Vehicular Technology, 42*(4).

Saltenis, S., Jensen, C., Leutenegger, S., & Lopez, M. (2000). Indexing the positions of continuously moving objects. SIGMOD, 331-342.

Sistla, A. P., Wolfson, O., Chamberlain, S., & Dao, S. (1997). Modeling and querying moving objects. *ICDE,* 422-432

Steiniger, S., Neun, M., & Edwardes, A. (2007). *Foundations of location based services.* Retrieved August 26, 2007, from http://www.spatial.cs.umn. edu/CS8715/IM7_steiniger.pdf

Tao, Y., Papadias, D., & Sun, J. (2003). The TPR*-Tree: An optimized spatio-temporal access method for predictive queries. VLDB, 790-801.

Tsalgatidou, A., Veijalainen, J., Markkula, J., Katasonov, A., & Hadjiefthymiades, S. (2003). Mobile e-commerce and location-based services: Technology and requirements. *ScanGIS,* 1-14.

Virrantaus, K., Markkula, J., Garmash, A., & Terziyan, Y. V. (2001). Developing GIS-supported location- based services. In *Proceedings of the WGIS'2001—First International Workshop on Web Geographical Information Systems* (pp. 423-432). Kyoto, Japan.

Wolfson, O., Xu, B., Chamberlain, S., & Jiang, L. (1998). Moving objects databases: Issues and solutions. *Statistical and Scientific Database Management,* 111-122.

KEY TERMS

Location Based Services: Location based services are information services accessible with mobile devices through the mobile network and utilizing the ability to make use of the location of the mobile device (Virrantaus et al., 2001).

Location Based Access: the user can access map and catalogue data based on his/her present location. If locating the user cannot be resolved automatically by the system, the user must be provided with the option of manually entering his/her location. The system should be able to handle such requests through geocoding procedures.

Location Utility (LU): Location utility is a distributed LBS system proposed and developed by the IBM Watson Research Center. It is developed for supporting a large class of applications that involve responding to the movements of large numbers of mobile users. It consists of a control center (LUCC) and a set of local servers (LULS). This distributed architecture is proposed for the purpose of scalablity. Application rules/functions are distributed to all local server nodes, and each local server handles the subset of the users associated with the local node (Munson et al., 2003).

Location Utility Local Server (LULS): LULS nodes receive the raw subscriber position information from the positioning technology and evaluate the rules assigned to them. Rules that evaluate to true generate reports, which are sent to the application that subscribed to the rule. Where possible, local server nodes are deployed in alignment with the network infrastructure in order to take advantage of local information about the user presence (Munson et al., 2003).

Location Utility Control Center (LUCC): The LUCC is the locus of control and management functions, and is the primary point of contact for applications to subscribe to rules and set up application resources. It also provides an interface for retrieving subscriber positions and any resources applications may have created for them. When an application subscribes to a rule through the control center, the control center records the subscription information and forwards the rule to all local server nodes. Reports from these rules are sent from the local server nodes to the control center, which aggregates them and forwards them to the application (Munson et al., 2003).

Moving Objects Spatio-Temporal (MOST) Model: MOST model was proposed for databases with dynamic attributes, for example, the positions of moving objects. The dynamic attributes of objects can change continuously as a function of time, without being explicitly updated. Therefore, the answer to a query depends not only on the database contents, but also on the time at which the query is entered (Sistla et al., 1997).

Positioning Determination Technologies (PDT): PDT are technologies that exist for determining physical position. The user position can be obtained either by using the mobile communication network or by using the global positioning system (GPS). Further possibilities to determine the position are WLAN stations, active badges, or radio beacons. The latter positioning methods can be especially used for indoor navigation like in a museum.

Spatial Indexes: Spatial indexes are used by spatial databases to optimize spatial queries. Spatial indexes can effectively handle features such as how far two points differ and whether points fall within a spatial area of interest. Common spatial index methods include Grid, Quadtree, R-tree, and kd-tree.

APPENDIX

Find the General Solution to:

$$2C_1 r + (\frac{C_2}{\mu} + C_3) = \frac{C_2 C_4^2}{\mu}(\mu r - C_4)^{-2}$$

Take $\mu r - C_4 = X$, and let both side of the equation multiply by μX^2,

$$2C_1(X + C_4)X^2 + (C_2 + C_3 \mu)X^2 = C_2 C_4^2$$

$$2C_1 X^3 + (2C_1 C_4 + C_2 + C_3 \mu)X^2 - C_2 C_4^2 = 0$$

AX^3+BX^2-C=0

We apply the substitution X= Y-$\dfrac{B}{3A}$ to the cubic equation and obtain:

$$A(Y-\frac{B}{3A})^3 + B(Y-\frac{B}{3A})^2 + C = 0$$

$$AY^3 - \frac{B^2}{3A}Y + (C+\frac{2B^3}{27A^2}) = 0$$

We are left with solving a cubic equation of the form $y^3+Py=Q$. How to solve this equation had been discovered earlier by *Scipione dal Ferro*.

We will find *s* and *t* so that:

3st = P $\qquad\qquad\qquad\qquad$ (1)

s^3-t^3=Q $\qquad\qquad\qquad\qquad$ (2)

It turns out that $y=s$-t will be a solution. Let's check that: Replacing *A*, *B* and *y* as indicated transforms our equation into:

$(s$-$t)^3$+3st $(s$-$t)=s^3$-t^3.

This is true since we can simplify the left side by using the binomial formula to:

$(s^3$-3s^2t+3st^2-$t^3)$+$(3s^2t$-3$st^2)=s^3$-t^3.

Solving the first equation for *s* and substituting into (2) yields:

$$(\frac{P}{3t})^3 - t^3 = Q$$

Simplifying, this turns into the "tri-quadratic" equation:

$$t^6 + Ot^3 - \frac{P^3}{27} = 0$$

$$u^2 + Qu - \frac{P^3}{27} = 0$$

which using the substitution $u=t^3$ becomes the quadratic equation:

$$u^2 + Qu - \frac{P^3}{27} = 0$$

From this, we can find a value for *u* by the quadratic formula,

$$u = \frac{-Q \pm \sqrt{Q^2 - \dfrac{4P^3}{27}}}{2}$$

then obtain *t*,

$$t = \sqrt[3]{\frac{-Q \pm \sqrt{Q^2 - \dfrac{4P^3}{27}}}{2}}$$

By equation (2),

$$s^3 = Q + \frac{-Q \pm \sqrt{Q^2 - \dfrac{4P^3}{27}}}{2}$$

Y is the difference of *s* and *t*:

$$Y = \sqrt[3]{Q + \frac{-Q \pm \sqrt{Q^2 - \dfrac{4P^3}{27}}}{2}} - \sqrt[3]{\frac{-Q \pm \sqrt{Q^2 - \dfrac{4P^3}{27}}}{2}}$$

The solution to our original cubic equation is given by:

$$X = Y - \frac{B}{3A} =$$

$$\sqrt[3]{Q + \frac{-Q \pm \sqrt{Q^2 - \dfrac{4P^3}{27}}}{2}} - \sqrt[3]{\frac{-Q \pm \sqrt{Q^2 - \dfrac{4P^3}{27}}}{2}} - \frac{B}{3A}$$

Chapter V
Process Models of SDLCs:
Comparison and Evolution

Laura C. Rodríguez
Autonomous University of Aguascalientes, Mexico

Manuel Mora
Autonomous University of Aguascalientes, Mexico

Miguel Vargas Martin
University of Ontario Institute of Technology, Canada

Rory O'Connor
Dublin City University, Ireland

Francisco Alvarez
Autonomous University of Aguascalientes, Mexico

ABSTRACT

The software engineering discipline has developed the concept of software process to guide development teams towards a high-quality end product to be delivered on-time and within the planned budget. Consequently, several software-systems development life-cycles (PM-SDLCs) have been theoretically formulated and empirically tested over the years. In this chapter, a conceptual research methodology is used to review the state of the art on the main PM-SDLCs formulated for software-intensive systems, with the aim to answer the following research questions: (a) What are the main characteristics that describe the PM-SDLCs?, (b) What are the common and unique characteristics of such PM-SDLCs?, and (c) What are the main benefits and limitations of PM-SDLCs from a viewpoint of a conceptual analysis? This research is motivated by a gap in the literature on comprehensive studies that describe and compare the main PM-SDLCs and organizes a view of the large variety of PM-SDLCs.

INTRODUCTION

In order for a product to be developed, a development (formal, semi-formal, or informal) process is required. For the specific case of software artifacts, a software (development) process is a method of producing such artifacts. This process is usually denoted as **the software-systems development life-cycle.** To guide its execution under different design conditions, a set of process models have been also proposed: **process model of systems development life cycles** (PM-SDLCs). In general, the aim of each single process is "to facilitate the engineer doing the job well rather than to prevent them from doing it badly" (Tyrrel, 2000).

In the software engineering discipline, the concept of a software *process* has been developed to guide the development team on constructing a high-quality end product that be delivered on-time and within the planned budget. Consequently, several PM-SDLCs have been theoretically formulated and empirically tested over the years, and in general many have been an evolution of previous models. In some cases, the evolution is originated as a result of a major advance in information and communications technologies (ICT), and in other cases, as a result of more planned changes in the organizations' settings and their business environments.

In this chapter, we use a conceptual research methodology (Glass, Vessey, & Ramesh, 2002; Mora, 2004) to review the state of the art on the main PM-SDLCs formulated for software-intensive systems, with the aim to answer the following research questions: (a) What are the main characteristics that describe the PM-SDLCs?, (b) What are the common and the unique characteristics of such PM-SDLCs?, and (c) What are the main benefits and limitations of PM-SDLCs from a viewpoint of a conceptual analysis?

The conceptual research approach is widely used in the software engineering domain (Glass et al., 2002). According to Cournellis' ideas (2000)—quoted by Mora (2004)—this research method studies concepts, ideas, or constructs on empirical objects. This chapter uses the research

methodology process, described in Mora, 2004, that consists of the following phases: (1) formulation of the research problem; (2) analysis of related studies; (3) development of the conceptual artifact; and (4) validation of the conceptual artifact. The first phase and second phases are similar to other well-known research methods. In the third phase, two activities are conducted: the development of a general framework/model and the detailed development of this general framework/model. This third phase is a creativity-intensive process guided by the findings, contributions, and limitations found in the second phase and a set of preliminary proforms that are fixed through an iterative process (Andoh-Baidoo, White, & Kasper, 2004). Finally, in the last phase, the conceptual artifact's validation can be conducted using a panel of experts, a logical argument discourse, or/and a proof of concept developing a prototype or pilot survey. In this study, we used the first procedure with two internal academic experts and an expert practitioner in the development of SwE projects. Satisfactory average scores of 4.6 in a 5-point Likert scale of an instrument conceptual composed of eight items was achieved (Mora, 2004).

This research is motivated by the knowledge gap in the literature on comprehensive studies that describe and compare the main available PM-SDLCs. The research relevance can be considered high because the main objective of software engineering is the development of high-quality, on-time, and within budget software projects, which can only be delivered with the utilization of a systematic development process, as has been proven in other engineering disciplines. Therefore, this study contributes to organize the diverse and partial views of PM-SDLCs.

BACKGROUND

Software engineering, according to the *IEEE Standard Computer Dictionary* (1990) is the: " (1) Application of quantifiable approach, disciplined to the software development, operation and maintenance;

this is, the application of the software engineering and (2) The study of the approaches that refers the point 1 of this definition." In turn, systems engineering can be defined as "an interdisciplinary field and their means for achieving the realization of successful systems" (INCOSE, 2004). Finally, the information systems discipline is "the study of the administration, use and impact of information technologies with the consideration of technical, socio-economic, cultural and organizational aspects" (Lee, 2004). From a software-intensive system's developer perspective, the foundation knowledge upon PM-SDLCs and their related disciplines becomes critical.

The relevance of studying PM-SDLCs has been reported in numerous studies. Fuggetta (2000) suggests, for example, the need for investigating the software process, because this lead to the completion of the most successful software products. For Fuggetta, the concept of life cycle is directly related to the notion of software process. A life cycle defines the different stages of software-product life: "...a software lifecycle defines the skeleton and philosophy according to which the software process has to be carried out." A life cycle also defines the *software process* as "the coherent set of policies, organizational structures, technologies, procedures, and artifacts that are needed to conceive, develop, deploy, and maintain a software product."

In the domain of information systems, Avison and Fitzgerald (2003) observe the need to follow a development methodology: "... perhaps we are in danger of returning to the bad old days of the pre-methodology era and its lack of control, standards, and training." They define a development-systems methodology as the "...recommended collection of phases, procedures, rules, techniques, tools, documentation, management, and training used to develop a system." Further, they remark on the importance of the philosophy of the methodology, which is, all those assumptions that are not stated explicitly by the authors of a methodology, but, that ruled them out of being successful. For example, a methodology may not explicitly consider the size of projects, the environment, the technology or the organizational context. The authors finally suggest that the main reason for using a methodology is to get better products, improve the development process, and gain standards that ensure the quality of products.

Another relevant study (Sorensen, 1995) reports the concept of methodology as a model plus techniques. Under such premise, the author analyzes the models of Waterfall, Incremental, Spiral, and the techniques: Prototype[i], Cleanroom, and Object-oriented. Sorensen also suggests that a possible combination of method and techniques can be used. For example: waterfall method with prototyping and object-oriented techniques. Thus, if for each model there is a total of eight combinations (it could include the case where none technique used) of techniques that may be applied, then there are a total of 24 methodologies for the list of models and techniques reported by Sorensen (1995). With more models and techniques, the number of potential methodologies can be extensive.

The objective of software engineering is to build and maintain software-intensive systems under planned schedules, agreed functionality, and cost restrictions. Within the domain of software engineering, software process improvement (SPI) aims to improve the quality of development products and the productivity of software engineers. However, the existence of a large variety of PM-SDLCs obfuscates its understanding and practical usage. Furthermore, as PM-SDLCs have been posed in various disciplines—software engineering, systems engineering, and information systems—for academics and practitioners, this situation increases both learning curve and application complexity. While we support that an interdisciplinary development is worthy for scientific progress, we consider that a systematic view of the different proposals is required. Then, academics and practitioners could acquire a more shared mental model of the PM-SDLCs.

COMPARISON AND EVOLUTION OF PROCESS MODELS OF SDLCS

Well-Defined Software Process

Oktaba and Ibargüengoita (1998) have developed a general meta-model of software process (Figure 1), which provides a 'parsimonious' and 'engineering-based' mode to conceptualize a well-defined software process. In this model, a process is composed of the following elements: *phases, activities, artifacts, roles,* and *agents*; where a *software process* is the main concept that is being modeled; a *phase* is the highest-activity level of a process that is being modeled; and an *activity* is the execution of an useful work to deliver a main *artifact* or artifacts (e.g., pieces of the full software artifact, documents, components, data files, or codes). The concepts of *role* and *agent* complete this semi-formal definition. A *role* is a functional responsibility in the process that is assigned to an *agent*, which can be a human-being, a tool, or a combination of both. The class *software process* is made up of the several instances of the *phase* class. Figure 1 shows the meta-model using a class diagram notation.

An instance of a *process* class is composed of several instances of *phase* class. *Phase* class is re-lated with several instances of *activity* class. Under an operation of specialization, the authors report that the *phase* class can be specialized in *analysis, design, code and test,* and *installation* phases. Similarly, the *activity* class can be specialized in *production, control, technology,* and *communication* activities, and each one of these, in other specializations. The *activity* class is also related to at least an input *artifact* and an output one, represented by the instances of the *artifact* class. Specialization of *artifacts* is also feasible in the model. Finally, a many-to-many association between the *role* and *activity* classes and a one-to-many from *agent* and *role* classes are defined in the model. We use this meta-model as base for a conceptual framework to compare different process models. Under the consideration of each life cycle is an instance of the model; the comparative framework provides a theoretical base to develop instances for the generic classes of *phase, artifact,* and *role. Activity* and *agent* classes are not considered in this chapter.

Phases and Artifacts in the PM-SDLCs

It has been also reported (Fuggetta, 2000) that: *software applications are complex products that*

Figure 1. Well-defined software process model

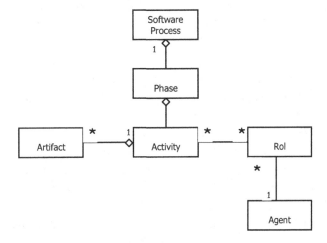

*are difficult to develop and test. Very often, software exhibits unexpected and undesired behaviors that may even cause severe problems and damages. For these reasons, researchers and practitioners have been paying increasing attention to understanding and improving the quality of the software being developed. The underlying assumption is that there is a direct correlation between the quality of the process and the quality of the developed software. The research area that deals with these issues is referred to using the term **software process**.*

The large diversity of PM-SDLCs suggests, then, that apparently none of the PM-SDLCs is sufficient for covering all needs to guarantee a successful development of software-intensive systems. This study, then develops a comparison of the main PM-SDLCs based on their historical evolution, and in terms of their component structure (e.g., based in the Oktaba & Ibargüengoitia meta-model, 1998) to help organize the available knowledge on these models. For this, the following specialization of *phases* was identified in the same study: *user conditions, business context pre-systematization, component identification, requirements, analysis, design, coding, test, implementation, postmortem analysis,* and *iteration decisions*. These activities constitute the generic life-cycle (proposed in this chapter) that includes all *activities* of the PM-SDLC under study. The phases are proposed by considering all activities that are part of each phase of each PM-SDLC under study.

The 13 PM-SDLCs analyzed are: waterfall (Royce, 1970), SADT (Dickover, McGowa, & Ross, 1977), prototyping (Naumann & Jenkins, 1982), structured cycle (Yourdon, 1993), spiral (Boehm, 1988), win-win spiral (Boehm & Rose, 1994; Egyed & Boehm, 1998), unified process (Rational Software Corporation, 1998), MBASE (Center for Software Engineering, 1997), component-based cycles (Aoyama, 1998; Brown & Wallnau, 1996), XP (Beck, 1999), PSP (Humphrey, 2000), TSP (McAndrews, 2000), and RAD (Cross, 2006). Table 1 shows the comparative *framework*, for the *phase* class of the 13 PM-SDLCs analyzed. A scheme of

three macro-phases (definition, development, and deployment) well-known in systems engineering is used to group the *phases* (Sage & Armstrong, 2000).

The symbol ♦ used in Table 1 indicates that the *phase* reported in the related row is part of the PM-SDLC reported in the corresponding column. No similar comparison was found in the literature. *Phases* are grouped by the general macro-phases: definition of the system, development of the system, and deployment of the system, a well-know systems engineering model. Table 1 contributes to organize comprehensively the phases reported of practically all public PM-SDLCs, and suggests from its analysis a set of generic phases.

The most relevant findings from Table 1 can be summarized as follows:

a. The set of common phases includes the **analysis, design, codification, testing,** and **implementation** phases (Note: the emergent agile-based systems approaches such as XP also support an engineering view of these phases);

b. The initial business and high-level systems *phases* (as part of the macro-phase definition of the system) are only part of some PM-SDLCs;

c. The iterative approach was disseminated by prototyping SDLC, but this was originally suggested in the Royce's[4] (1970) variant of the waterfall model. Later, was reinforced and extended by the spiral model; and

d. The *postmortem* phase, which appeared previous to year 2000, was indirectly suggested by MBASE and XP, and it is attributed mainly to PSP and TSP models.

It must be noted that the unique features are considered in the period of their formulation, then, some elements that were considered unique at once, later were incorporated to other models. Table 2 shows the comparative framework for the "*artifact*" component versus the several PM-SDLCs studied.

Table 1. Comparative framework for PM-SDLCs

Phases		Waterfall (1970)	SADT (1977)	Prototyping (1982)	Structured Cycle (1988)	Spiral (1988)	RAD (1991)	Win-Win Spiral (1994)	Unified Process (1998)	MBASE (1998)	Component-based cycles (1998)	XP (1999)	PSP (2000)	TSP (2000)
Definition	*User Conditions (Survey, Agreements, Stories)*				◆			◆		◆		◆		
	Business Context Pre-systematization				◆	◆	◆	◆	◆	◆	◆	◆	◆	
	Component Identification						◆				◆			
	Requirements	◆	◆	◆		◆	◆	◆	◆	◆				◆
	Analysis	◆	◆	◆	◆	◆	◆	◆	◆	◆	◆	◆		◆
Development	**Design**	◆	◆	◆	◆	◆	◆	◆	◆	◆	◆	◆	◆	◆
	Codification	◆	◆	◆	◆	◆	◆	◆	◆	◆	◆	◆	◆	◆
	Testing	◆	◆	◆	◆	◆	◆	◆	◆	◆	◆	◆	◆	◆
Deployment	**Implementation**	◆	◆	◆	◆	◆	◆	◆	◆	◆	◆	◆	◆	◆
	Postmortem Analysis									◆[2]		◆[3]	◆	◆
	Evolution/ Iteration Decisions			◆		◆		◆		◆		◆		

We propose a comparative specialization of **artifacts**. In this table, each number means the number of *artifacts* that are generated as equivalent to the *artifact* specialization proposed. Then, "1" implies that an *artifact* of the PM-SDLC (indicated in the column) is equivalent with one artifact of the *artifact* specialization proposed. For the cases of "2," "3," "4," and "5," they indicate that more of one *artifact* of the PM-SDLC (indicated in the column) corresponds to a unique *artifact* of the comparative specialization. A greater number of artifacts implies that the model aggregates more control or detail in the definition of such *artifacts*.

Due to space limitations, the specialization of *roles* is not reported here. However, we can report that in general, the *roles* of *agents-persons* have not suffered much variation, but the number of activities each one executes as well as the number of required agents has been increased. Additionally, the PM-SDLC descriptions usually do not report explicit information about *roles*.

From the previous tables and the conceptual analysis of each PM-SDLC, we identified a set of common, distinct, and unique features. Table 3 summarizes the common and distinct features, whereas the Table 4 summarizes the set of unique ones.

These distinct features remark the historic evolution and allow to establish a time-line evolution (based from Avison and Fitzgerald, 2004) of critical events of the PM-SDLCs that is shown in Table 5.

The time line (Table 5) shows how the several PM-SDLCs have been proposed since 1970s. The

Table 2. PM-SDLCs vs artifacts

Main Artifacts Delivered	Waterfall (1970)	SADT (1977)	Prototyping (1982)	Structured Cycle (1988)	Spiral (1988)	RAD (1991)	Win-Win Spiral (1994)	Unified Process (1998)	MBASE (1998)	Component-based cycles (1998)	XP (1999)	PSP (2000)	TSP (2000)
List of Stakeholders				1			1		1		1		
List of Functions				1									
List of Conditions							1		1				
Objectives, Constrains an Early Risks				4	1	1	1	5	1	1		1	
System Architecture						1			1	1			
Early Prototype					1	1	1		1				
Initial Operational Prototype					1		1						
Operational Concept					1		1	1	1			1	
Components						1				1			
Life Cycle Plan				1	3		3	3	4		1	2	
SRS	1	1	1		1		1						3
Design Specification	1			1									3
General View of the System	1	1			1		1						3
Database Design	1												
Subroutine Storage Allocations	1							2				1	
Subroutine Execution Times Allocations	1	1		3	1		1		1				3
Operational Procedures	1					1							
Prototype	1	1	1					1					
Risks			2					3	5				
Integrated System				1	1		1		1	1	1	1	2
Prototype Review	1												
Interface Design Specification	1												
Interface Design Document	1												
Test Planning	1												
Review of Critical Software	1												

continued on following page

Table 2. continued

Final Design Document	1												
Testing and Results Document	1	1		1									
Final Acceptance User's Document	1				1		1	1					
Converted System		3		1				1					
Operational User's Manual	1			1				2	2				
Implemented System			1	2	1	1	1	2		1	1	1	3
System's Evolution Analysis Document						1						5	

Table 3. Common and distinct features for PM-SDLCs

Common Features	Distinct Features
1. **Group of activities that are performed to identify stakeholders and the set of user requirements and conditions.** First, these activities were focused to collect and specify requirements and then they were extended to business modeling, system conceptual definition, based-scenarios analysis and design, stories construction, and in some cases the building of prototypes. 2. **Group of activities that are performed to define the scope of system** (negotiation of stakeholders' conditions; objectives, alternatives and restrictions determination; risk analysis). First, these activities were limited to objectives, alternatives and restrictions determination, and risk analysis was then integrated. 3. **Group of activities that are performed to define the system architecture** (system-requirements definition, architecture design and analysis). First, these were limited to system-requirements definition and analysis but system architecture was integrated later as a common feature. 4. **Group of activities that are performed to design, build, test, and implement the software artifact** (design, coding, test, implementation). 5. **Five models consider the development of a prototype** (waterfall[5], SADT, spiral, prototyping, and RAD). 6. **Four models include explicitly the elaboration of the user manual** (waterfall, a modern structured cycle, unified process, and MBASE).	1. **Non-iterative, iterative, and incremental approaches.** Some methodologies carry out several iterations by repetitions of the phases of the same manner in each iteration (iterative approach like **unified process**), while others PM-SDLC carry out several iterations executing the phases with distinct tasks in each iteration (incremental approach like **spiral**). Other ones do not utilize iteration (like **structured cycle**). 2. **Iteration/increment next-entry-condition.** Some models execute the next iterations/increment strictly depending on some condition that indicates the product has reached these objectives. Others execute it in a certain number of iterations/ increments, independently of the total fulfillment of the condition. 3. **Level of detail of the formulation of the PM-SDLC.** There are significant differences between the models regarding to the level of detail used to formulate/describe the tasks and the concept of a well-defined process that the software engineering claims. 4. **Sophistication of techniques and tools.** The most recent models suggest the utilization of techniques and tools for analysis, design, codification, testing, and implementation of more sophisticated models.

historic evolution is since the 1950s with code & fix, to the 2000s with MBASE, unified process, component-based, XP, PSP, and TSP. Hence, a relevant research purpose that emerges is to explore the next evolution stage.

FUTURE TRENDS

We can generalize the evolution in terms of advances in "technology" (that push advances in PM-SDLCs) or advances in "knowledge" (demanded for a better project management control in PM-SDLCs). The distinct elements shown in Table 4 were unique at the moment in which this PM-SDLC was proposed. Lately, such "unique" features were included in subsequent PM-SDLCs. Such repetition of elements from a PM-SDLC to a new PM-SDLC suggests how the models evolve and the need to use PM-SDLC to develop success software systems. The evolution of PM-SDLCs is a response to the advances in technology, and to the interest in reinforcing the project management control weaknesses of the previous PM-SDLCs. This evolution indicates the scientific advance and the need to accumulate the previous knowledge on PM-SDLC. The challenge is to cope with this evolution caused by the appearance of new technologies, but also incorporating the knowledge gained in the formulation and utilization of previous PM-SDLCs.

The evolution map (Figure 2, extended from Rodriguez, Mora, & Alvarez, 2007), summarizes the evolution based in the two aforementioned drivers (technological advances and knowledge

Table 4. Set of unique features of PM-SDLCs

PM-SDLC	Unique Elements
Waterfall	Execution of preview phases to the coding phase for the development of a system (e.g., requirements, analysis, and design phases).
SADT	A graphic-based model of the process that was strongly influenced by theory of systems and hierarchical models from systems engineering.
Prototyping	First to suggest the building of an operational first version of the system, deploying the prototype, and then executing iterations to evolve the prototype till to generate sufficient level-functionality for the users' needs.
Structured Cycle	An explicit control of documentation and users' training activities in the SDLC. Based on a "*top down*" and "*divide and conquer*" design approaches.
Spiral	Explicit consideration of risk analysis as a critical part of the software-system definition.
Win-Win Spiral	Augments the spiral model, with the concept of "***win-conditions***," to strengthen the first phase of the SDLC trying to include all of stakeholders' conditions. It also carries out business reconciliation between stakeholders on the conditions agreed in each iteration of development cycle.
Unified Process	Conceptualization of the SDLC in two time-dimensions (phases execution and tasks executions). The level of effort conducted in each tasks varies according to the phase performed. A most-to-least effort shift and vice versa usually occurs for the first and last tasks respectively.
Component-based Cycles	Explicit reutilization and building of software components as the fundamental design approach.
XP	Explicit utilization of: (a) stories to know the environment and users' needs, (b) the coding by pairs, (c) the need of a multi-role training by agents that participate in the development cycle, and (d) the lean-manufacturing design approach.
PSP	A systematic and explicit quality control of activities that a single person must perform under the concept of software engineering.
TSP	A systematic and explicit quality control of activities that a development team must perform in each development phase (*launch/relaunch*, inspection, and analysis *postmortem*).
RAD	Explicit utilization of: (a) scenarios based-analysis, (b) specification of components to maximize the reuse, (c) rapid development, and (d) frequent tests. It is highly related to the original prototyping model with the utilization of CASE tools to support fast development.

Table 5. PM-SDLCs time line of critical events

Pre-Methodology Era
Early software development was often done using the simple technique of ***Code & Fix*** (Boehm, 1988); prior to 1956, a basic model used in this early days of software development included two steps: (1) write some code and (2) fix the problems within the code.
Early Methodology Era
After 1956, the experience gained on the first large software projects led to the recognition of control problems and the development of a stage-wised model. This model stipulated that software products should be developed in successive stages (operational plan, operational, operational specifications, coding specifications, coding parameter testing, assembly testing, shakedown, and system evaluation, Boehm, 1988).
Methodology Era
In 1970 Royce proposes the ***waterfall*** model, that includes for first time in its internal structure the risks and the use of prototypes as well as the inclusion of users in the development process. According to Boehm (1998), it provides two primary enhancements to stage-wised: "(1) the recognition of the feedback loops between stages to minimize the expensive rework involved in feed back across many stages and (2) an initial incorporation of preliminary prototype in the phase "do it twice", in parallel with requirements analysis and design;" later in the 1970s, the ***SADT*** improves the ***waterfall*** model a more controlled development and the addition of several specifications and appears ***prototyping*** that develops the initial concept of preliminary design ("***do it twice***") of a program, originally reported in the ***waterfall*** model. Next, evolution state corresponds to the emergence of the ***structured cycle***, ***spiral***, ***RAD*** and ***win-win spiral*** models that mainly integrate the risk analysis to avoid the accumulation of problems and reviews until the final *phases*. All of them, except ***structured cycle***, incorporate the advantages of ***prototyping*** about the early view of a system.
Post-Methodology Era
A set of new models are developed: ***MBASE***, ***component-based***, ***XP***, ***PSP***, and ***TSP***, that are based in the re-utilization of components, CASE tools, and CMMI quality maturity frameworks, as well as the emergent agile systems-development paradigms. All of them with the aim to accelerate the development periods without sacrificing the quality dimension. According to the previous evolution period, planning activities are a fundamental part of these models.

gaps) and classifies the PM-SDLCs in terms of two industrial design philosophies: "specification rigor" and "agility."

In the evolution map (Figure 2), the arrows represent the time-line of models (Table 5) and it considers the era perspective for classifying them (Avison & Fitzgerald, 2004). Similar analysis to the evolution map in Figure 2 could be elaborated by using the findings and analysis reported in the previous section of this chapter. According to Rodriguez et Al. (2007): *...under this methodology chronological era perspective, it is interesting to note that every new era starts with a model with high or medium specification rigor level, except in the pre-methodology era. This evidence suggests that software engineering principles and foundations toward the specification rigor are pursued before agility attributes. However, the industrial pressure to reduce manufacturing or realizing time cycles keeping high-quality products, also suggest that a trade-off between specification rigor and agility must be balanced.*

Recent reports suggest that the next steps will lead to the development of service-oriented systems

(SOS), and thus a service-oriented software engineering (SOSE) discipline is emerging (Di Nitto et al, 2006; Arsanjani et al, 2006). PM-SDLCs for developing service-oriented systems are only now being formulated, with initial proposals considering the importance of systems requirements; business process models and their way for system specification and construction; tools for fast building and the new languages for specification and executing of business process based commonly in Web services. However, the initial analysis reveals that the evolution is being driven by technological factors (e.g., by the apparition of new development language and tool), and consequently, the risk to return at the initial characteristics of lack of rigor. This risk of return to past problems is caused by rapid changes in technology that have exceeded the methodologies' capabilities for engineering such systems efficiently and effectively. Thus, the new research question emerging from this continuous evolution is: "What elements of the existing PM-SDLCs can be used to define a new service-oriented PM-SDLC?" We claim this research is relevant because the benefits by the using of PM-SDLC to develop software-intensive

Figure 2. Map of PM-SDLC's evolution

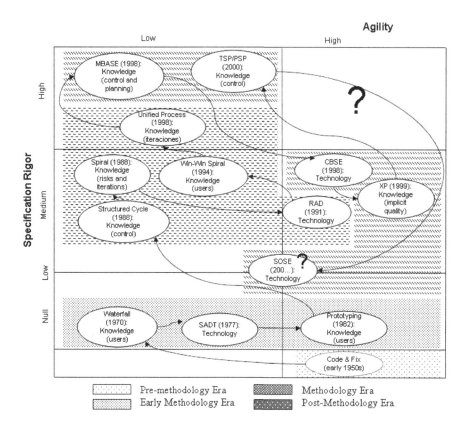

systems were evidenced through the self evolution of PM-SDLCs. The evolution map (Figure 2) shows a tentative placement for service-oriented PM-SDLC. Given an initial analysis, this new PM-SDLCs still cannot be classified in a single octant.

CONCLUSION

We can conclude, under the consideration of a well-defined SDLC process (Oktaba & Ibargüengoitia, 1998), that no model includes all the required components defined as part of a process model. Each process model has common and unique elements, and each PM-SDLC has its own benefits and limitations. The formulation of newer PM-SDLCs are all influenced by previous models. Main drivers to cre-

ate new process models are "technological" (to cope with the challenges of the new technologies) and "knowledge gaps" (to cope with the user's demands and organizational settings and environments for a better project management control). We can also identify that there is not a single unique PM-SDLC that could be applied in all cases. This implies that the application of a specific PM-SDLC will rely on the particular characteristics of the application under development, the organization's size, the technology used, and the developer's experience. The benefit of using a process model for the development of software-intensive systems has been proven and its rejection could lead to non successful products (Fuggetta, 2000).

This conceptual and comparative study of such models is useful to reveal some future trends and recommendations for the theory and praxis: (a) PM-SLDC formulations have improved from early periods, (b) all of them are still based in the first waterfall model and their iterative and feedback recommendations, (c) the comparative framework and findings suggest a comprehensive way to understand and learn PM-SDLCs reported in the literature, and (d) also, the new PM-SLDC cycles—such as the ones based on agile systems development approach—still requires and uses the phases of analysis and design to avoiding the risk of returning to the pre-early methodology practice (Avison & Fitzgerald, 2003).

In turn, we can suggest the following research recommendations: (a) to study the selection features of PM-SDLCs, (b) to study the combination of well-documented models with the agile-based approaches, (c) to study the customization or adaptation of generic PM-SDLC models, and (d) under the consideration of evolution map knowledge derived in this study, and the emergent technology for service-oriented systems, we can conclude the need and relevance to study or develop service-oriented PM-SDLCs (Di Nitto et al., 2006).

REFERENCES

Aoyama, M. (1998, April 25-26). New age of software development: How component-based software engineering changes the way of foftware development? In *Proceedings of the First International Workshop on Component-based Software Engineering* (pp. 1-5). Kyoto, Japan.

Andoh-Baidoo, F., White, E., & Kasper, G. (2004). Information systems' cumulative research tradition: A review of research activities and outputs using pro forma abstracts. In *Proceedings of the Tenth Americas Conference on Information Systems* (pp. 4195-4202) New York.

Arsanjani, J., Hailpern, B., Martin, J., & Tarr, P. (2006). *Web services: Promises and compromises.* IBM Research Division, Thomas J. Watson Research Center.

Avison, D., & Fitzgerald, G. (2003). Where now for development methodologies? *Communications of the ACM, 46*(1), 78-82.

Beck, K. (1999). Embracing change with extreme programming. *IEEE Computer, October,* 77-70.

Boehm, B. (1988). A spiral model of software development and enhancement. *IEEE Computer, May,* 61-72.

Boehm, B., & Bose, P. (1994). *A collaborative spiral software process model based on theory W* (Technical Report USC-CSE-94-501). University of Southern California.

Brown, A., & Wallnau, K. (1996). Engineering of component-based systems. In *Proceedings of the Second IEEE International Conference on Engineering of Complex Computer Systems* (pp. 414-422).

Center for Software Engineering (1997). *Guidelines for Model-Based (System) Architecting and Software Engineering (MBASE).* University of Southern California.

Counelis, J. (2000). Generic research design in the study of education: a systemic typology. *Systems Research, 17,* 51-63.

Cross, S. (2006). Toward disciplined rapid application development. *Software Tech News 2,* 1.

Dickover, M., McGowan, C., & Ross, D. (1977, October 16-19). Software design using SADT. In *Proceedings of the 1977 Annual Conference of the Association for Computing Machinery (ACM)* (pp. 125-133). Seattle, Washington.

Di Nitto, E., Hall, R., Han, J., Han, Y., Polini, A., Sandkuhl et al. (2006). Report on the international workshop on service oriented software engineering (IW-SOSE06). *ACM SIGSOFT Software Engineering Notes, 31*(5), 36-38.

Egyed, A., &Boehm, B. (1998, September). Tele-cooperation experience with the winwin system. In *Proceedings of the 15th IFIP World Computer Congress.* Vienna, Austria.

Fuggetta, A. (2000, June 4-11). Software process: a roadmap. In *Proceedings of the Conference on the Future of Software Engineering* (pp. 25-34). Limerick (Ireland). New York: ACM Press.

Glass, R., Vessey, I., & Ramesh, V. (2002). Research in software engineering: an analysis of the literature. *Information and Software Technology, 44*, 491-506.

Humphrey, W. (2000). *The personal software process (PSP)* (Technical Report CMU/SEI-2000-TR-022). Software Engineering Institute, Carnegie Mellon University.

INCOSE. (2004). *Systems engineering handbook*. CA: INCOSE.

Lee A. (2004). Inaugural editor's comments. *MIS Quarterly, 23*(1), 5-11.

McAndrews, D. (2000). *The team software process (TSP): An overview and preliminary results of using disciplined practices* (Technical Report CMU/SEI-2000-TR-015). Software Engineering Institute, Carnegie Mellon University.

Mora, M. (2004). *The conceptual research approach* (Technical Internal Report). Autonomous University of Aguascalientes, Aguascalientes, Mexico (in Spanish language).

Naumann, J., & Jenkins, A (1982). Prototyping: The new paradigm for systems development. *MIS Quarterly, 6*(3), 29-44.

Oktaba, H., & Ibargüengoitia, G. (1998). Software process modeled with objects: Static view. *Computación y Sistemas CIC-IPN ISSN 1405-5546, 1*(4), 228-238.

Rational Software Corporation. (1998). *Rational unified process: Best practices for software development teams* (White Paper from Rational Software Corporation).

Rodríguez L., Mora, M., & Alvarez F. (2007, September 24-25). A descriptive/comparative Study of the evolution of process models of software development life cycles (PM-SDLCs). *SIS 07: Simposio de Ingeniería de Software, in ENC 2007: Encuentro Internacional de Computación*. Morelia, México.

Royce, W. (1970, August). Managing the development of large software systems. In *Proceedings of the IEEE WESCON* (pp.1-9).

Sage, A., & Armstrong, J. (2000). *Introduction to systems engineering*. New York: Wiley.

Scacchi, W. (2001). Process models in software engineering. In J. J. Marciniak (Ed.), *Encyclopedia of software engineering* (2nd ed.) (pp.) New York: John Wiley and Sons.

Sorensen, R. (1995). A comparison of software development methodologies. *Crosstalk Journal, January*, 1-15.

SWEBOK. (2001). *Guide to the software engineering body of knowledge*. Los Alamos, CA: IEEE Society.

Tyrrel, S. (2000). The many dimensions of the software pProcess. *ACM Crossroads Student Magazine, 6*(4), 1-7.

Yang, H. (2002). *Successful evolution of software systems*. Norwod, MA: Artech House, Incorporated.

Yourdon, E. (1993). *Modern structured analysis* (Spanish version). New York: Prentice-Hall.

KEY TERMS

CASE—Computer-Assisted Software (or systems) Engineering: Software tool for assisting the software development.

Classic PM-SDLCs: (70-90's): Waterfall, SADT—*structured analysis and design technique*, prototyping, modern structured cycle, spiral.

CMMI—Capability Maturity Model Integration: A quality model for software process assessment and improvement.

Current PM-SDLCs: (90's-2000) RAD—*rapid application development,* win-win spiral, unified process, PSP—*personal software process,* TSP—*team software process.*

Emergent PM-SDLC: (1997-present) MBASE—m*odel-based (system) architecting and software engineering,* XP—e*xtreme programming* (ASP) [6], CBSE—component-based software engineering (ASP).

Process Model of Software Development Life-Cycle = PM-SDLC: A chain of activities, transformations, events, and artifacts to guide the full process of software creation. Such models can be used to develop more precise and formal descriptions of software life-cycle activities (based in Scacchi, 2001).

Software Life-Cycle Model: *The term software life-cycle model is equivalent to term life-cycle framework model. These "frameworks models" are the definition of phases to software development, at high level. These models do not provide detail definitions but show the high-level activities and its interrelationships. The most common models are waterfall model, prototyping model, spiral model"* (based in the SWEBOK, 2000).

ENDNOTES

[1] Author considers prototyping a technique that can be used in the first phases of any SDLCs. Other authors could report prototyping as a SDLC.

[2] In MBASE, a *postmortem phase* is not explicitly reported but it is implied.

[3] In XP-based process, the concept of postmortem analysis is performed as a *retrospective analysis.*

[4] Royce (1979) reported that the classic waterfall cycle could be modified to integrate some iterations.

[5] **Waterfall** model -according to Royce's ideas (1970)—considers a preliminary design phase that could produce a pilot system or prototype. Often literature confuses **waterfall** with the **stage-wised** model.

[6] ASP—agile software process. Also know as *light methodologies*

Chapter VI
Requirements Engineering:
A Review of Processes and Techniques

Fernando Flores
Autonomous University of Aguascalientes, Mexico

Manuel Mora
Autonomous University of Aguascalientes, Mexico

Francisco Alvarez
Autonomous University of Aguascalientes, Mexico

Rory O'Connor
Dublin City University, Ireland

Jorge Macias-Luévano
Autonomous University of Aguascalientes, Mexico

ABSTRACT

Requirements engineering is the process of discovering the purpose and implicit needs of a software system that will be developed and making explicit, complete, and non ambiguous their specification. Its relevance is based in that omission or mistakes generated during this phase and corrected in later phases of a system development lifecycle, will cause cost overruns and delays to the project, as well as incomplete software. This chapter, by using a conceptual research approach, reviews the literature for developing a review of types of requirements, and the processes, activities, and techniques used. Analysis and synthesis of such findings permit to posit a generic requirements engineering process. Implications, trends, and challenges are then reported. While its execution is being mandatory in most SDLCs, it is done partially. Furthermore, the emergence of advanced services-oriented technologies suggests further research for identifying what of the present knowledge is useful and what is needed. This research is an initial effort to synthesize accumulated knowledge.

INTRODUCTION

In the field of software engineering several process models have been formulated to guide the development of software systems (e.g., software or system development life-cycle). Independent of what process model is selected by a development team, all activities conducted can be grouped into three main macro-phases: ***system definition*** (*software specification of functional and constrain requirements*), ***system development*** (*design and building*), and ***system deployment*** (*software implementation, software validation (to confirm that the new software system satisfies the users' needs) and software evolution (evolution of the users' requirements as the users' reality evolves)*) (Sage & Armstrong, 2000; Sommerville, 2002).

First, macro-phase's activities have been studied by the requirements engineering (RE) discipline, which can be defined as: "the process of discovering the purpose of the software system by identifying stakeholders and their needs, and documenting these in a form that is amenable to analysis, communication, and subsequent implementation" (Nuseibeh & Easternbrook, 2000). The overall goal of RE is to elicit valid users′ requirements because the strong impact on quality and cost of the final software product. Accordingly to Jin et al (1998): "…errors made at this stage are extremely expensive to correct when are discovered during testing or during actual working." However, even though such evidence of relevance and that RE has been identified (Sommerville, 2005) as essential for successful software development, these activities are often overlapped, uncompleted, or missed in development projects. As Sumano (1999) alerts "it is a general practice not to do it well, or do it faster and careless, because they do not have enough time or because they do not know a good methodology to do it." Consequently, it is possible multiple errors are introduced in early activities and not discovered until later phases of the lifecycle raising the project costs and exceeding the project deadlines.

In this chapter, we use a conceptual research methodology (Glass, Vessey, & Ramesh, 2002; Mora, 2004) to review the state of the art on the process and techniques used in software requirements engineering for software products to answer the following research questions: (a) How can the software requirements be classified?, (b) How can the main processes, activities, and techniques proposed by the software requirements engineering, be organized ?, and (c) Can these processes, activities, and techniques be synthesized in a theoretically-developed generic process of software requirements engineering? According to Mora (2004), despite several sources report the utilization of a conceptual research approach and its wide usage in the domain of the software engineering (43%) (Glass et al., 2002), there is little detailed literature on how to use this research method. Counelis (2000) quoted by Mora (2004) indicates that conceptual research is part of the research methods that study ideas, concepts or constructs on real objects rather than study them directly. Despite scarce literature, Mora (2004) reports that several studies consider the conceptual research method as common as the survey, experimental, and case study methods. This chapter then uses the process described in Mora (2004) that consists in the following phases: (1st) formulation of the research problem; (2nd) analysis of related studies; (3rd) development of the conceptual artifact; and (4th) validation of the conceptual artifact. The first phase and second phases are similar to other research methods. In the third phase, two activities are conducted: the development of a high-level framework/model and the development of low-level details of specific components selected from the high-level framework/model. This third phase is a creativity-intensive process guided by the findings, contributions, and limitations found in the second phase and a set of preliminary proforms that are fixed through an iterative process (Andoh-Baidoo, White, & Kasper, 2004). In the last phase, the conceptual artifact's validation is developed through: face validity from a panel of experts, logical argumentation, or proof of concept developing a prototype or pilot survey.

The objectives of this research are: (a) to develop an updated classification of software requirements,

(b) to clarify the similarities and differences among software requirements engineering methods reported in the literature, and (c) to identify a generic process for software requirements engineering trough a synthesis process. This research is strongly motivated by the lack of discussion in the requirements engineering literature about standardized (e.g., generic) software requirements engineering stages and activities. Accordingly, academics and practitioners face a myriad of process and techniques and organizational utilization is influenced rather for knowledge availability than by system's adequacy. Because every software development lifecycle starts with a software definition, this study contributes to improve our understanding and application of general software development lifecycles through identifying a generic method for software requirements engineering.

BACKGROUND

The concepts of *requirement* and *requirements engineering* are core for the software engineering discipline. From the multiple definitions of what a requirement is, two comprehensive definitions (IEEE software engineering glossary, Abbott, 1986) are reported in a relevant source (SEI Curriculum Module SEI-CM-19-1.2, 1990): (a): *(1) A condition or capability needed by a user to solve a problem or achieve an objective. (2) A condition or capability that must be met or possessed by a system or system component to satisfy a contract, standard, specification, or other formally imposed document. The set of all requirements forms the basis for subsequent development of the system or system component*; and (b) *requirements is any function, constraint, or other property that must be provided, met, or satisfied to fill the needs of the system intended user(s).*

In turn, the *requirements engineering* can be defined as a discipline or knowledge area (Zave, 1997; SWEBOK, 2004; Sawyer & Kotonya, 2000; Gonzalez, 2005) and as an abstract or specific pro-

cess (SEI Curriculum Module SEI-CM-19-1.2, 1990; SWEBOK, 2004; Nuseibeh & Easternbrook, 2000; Sawyer & Kotonya, 2001; Sommerville, 2005). As discipline, Zave (1997) defines requirements engineering as: "the branch of software engineering concerned with the real-world goals for functions and constraints on software systems." In same study, the author states that "the great difficulty in constructing such a classification scheme is the heterogeneity of the topics usually considered part of requirements engineering." These topics include the following: tasks that must be finished, problems that must be solved, solutions to problems, ways of contributing to knowledge, and types of system. In turn, in SWEBOK (2004), the requirements engineering knowledge area is "...concerned with establishing a common understanding of the requirements (e.g., study of methods for) to be addressed by the software product." In Sawyer and Kotonya (2001), requirements engineering is considered as "the knowledge area (that) is concerned with the acquisition, analysis, specification, validation and management of software requirements." For Gonzalez (2005), requirements engineering is the study of "methods for capturing, specifying, and managing requirements." Under such definitions and research effort classification, this study can be considered as a conceptual research on the tasks must be performed (capturing, specifying, communication/validation, and managing) and can be located also in the convergence of the RE and software requirements engineering research streams (SWEBOK, 2004).

As an abstract process the requirements engineering "... consists of a set of transformations that attempt to understand the exact needs of a software-intensive system and convert the statement of needs into a complete and unambiguous description of the requirements, documented according to a specified standard" and define the activities of "requirements elicitation, analysis, and specification" (SWEBOK, 2004). In similar mode, RE as a broad process can be defined as "the process of discovering the purpose of the software system by identifying stakeholders and their needs, and documenting these in a form that is amenable to analysis, communication, and subsequent implementation" and can be composed by the following activities: *eliciting requirements, modeling and analyzing requirements, communicating requirements, agreeing requirements,* and *evolving requirements* (Nuseibeth & Easterbrook, 2000).

As a specific process, the SEI curriculum module SEI-CM-19-1.2 (1990) proposes the following activities: requirements identification, identification of software development constraints, requirements analysis, requirements representation, requirements communication, and preparation for validation of software requirements. For Sawyer and Kotonya (2001), requirements engineering must have the following activities: requirements elicitation, requirements analysis, requirements specification, requirements validation, and requirements management. Sommerville (2005) defines requirements engineering as an abstract process as "... a structured set of activities that help develop this understanding and that document the system specification for the stakeholders and engineers involved in the system development," and as a specific process, as composed of the: elicitation, analysis, validation, negotiation, documentation, and management activities. Other proposal for requirements engineering activities (from the ESA Software Engineering Standards Issue 2, prepared by ESA Board for Software Standardization and Control, 1994), proposes a differentiation from user and software: user requirement (capture the user requirements, determination of operational environment, specification of user requirements, and reviews) and software requirement (construction of the logical model, specification of software requirements, and reviews).

Hence, despite the literature reporting multiple processes for requirements engineering, there is not a unique and agreed (or standardized) requirements engineering process, but some shared activities can be identified. Then, given the vast literature and myriad of definitions, process, and techniques, their understanding and final utilization by academics and practitioners is obfuscated.

MAIN FOCUS OF THE CHAPTER

The main focus of this chapter is to provide an updated and comprehensive software requirements classification, an organized view of processes, activities, and techniques for software requirements engineering and identify core activities and techniques for positing a generic process for requirements engineering. The contribution is to improve the understanding of the requirements engineering process, activities, and techniques. The conceptual analysis is realized through the development and utilization of a set of pro-forms (Andoh-Baidoo et al., 2004). Units of study are the process, activities, and techniques discussed in the main papers reported in the literature.

A requirement can be defined as a mandatory or wished attribute (as an adjective), capability (as a verb), or condition (as a logical or numerical constrain) that a product, service, process, or system must possess. While requirements are characteristics owned by artifacts or systems (in the software domain), these are demanded by human beings (e.g., all stakeholders related with the definition of the system). Then, a requirements engineering process for determining the set of valid requirements for a system can be considered a human-intensive interaction process. Furthermore, while an extensive research (Beckworth & Garner, 1994; El-Eman & Madhavjin, 1995; Nikula, Fajaniemi, & Kalviainen, 2000; Juristo, Moreno, & Silva, 2002; Neil & Laplante, 2003) has been conducted on process, techniques, and their real utilization in organizations, few studies have been focused in classifying requirements and the findings show overlaps, omissions, and mixed interpretations. Then, for achieving the research purpose implicitly established in research question (a), we believe that a comprehensive and updated requirements classification is needed. Table 1 shows such classification from several sources (Brackett, 1990; ESA PSS-05-03, 1995; SWEBOK, 2004) analyzed.

Main findings from Table 1 are: (a) the identification of the environmental requirements, few mentioned and explained in usual literature; (b) the sub-classification and focus of external requirements on social and human affairs; and (c) the re-grouping of classic functional versus non-functional requirements with emergent relevant sub-types such as: security, lifecycle, inverse, and documentation requirements. In particular, the security issues are not reviewed extensively

in this study but we recognize as the information systems are used for mission critical systems (and supported by the software systems), and deployed in ICT internet-based platforms, this issue can be critical. This new classification suggests that software requirements systems engineers should not omit the social and human influences that the external politic-power, socio-cultural, legal, and economic environmental systems perform on the organization and lately of the software systems users. While that information systems literature (Keen) has extensively alerted on such issues, the

Table 1. An updated and comprehensive software requirements classification

Main Category	Type	Sub-type	
ORGANIZATIONAL ENVIRONMENT These requirements can be derived from the internal and external environment where the software system will be deployed.	**EXTERNAL ENVIRONMENT** Requirements derived from the potential influence of the relevant social systems in the outer organizational environment for the software system	• Politic-power requirements • Legal requirements • Socio-cultural requirements • Economic requirements	
	INTERNAL ENVIRONMENT Requirements derived from the potential influence of the relevant social systems in the inner organizational environment for the software system	• Business goals requirements • Organizational interface requirements • User's expectation requirements	
FUNCTIONAL These requirements can be derived for defining the behavioral capabilities for the software system to be deployed.	SERVICES	The visible capabilities that the software system will provide to users (humans and other systems)	
	TECHNICAL INTERFACES	The characteristics that permit to the software system communicating with other systems	
	OPERATIONAL	The characteristics that define how to operate correctly the software system	
NONFUNCTIONAL These requirements can be derived for defining a complementary set of characteristics (usually required for user's system acceptance) to the behavioral capabilities for the software system to be deployed.	PERFORMANCE	The characteristics that define how well to the software system operates	
	CONSTRAINS Requirements derived to establish explicitly conditions (events that must or must not occur) to be satisfied by the software system	• Inverse	Requirements on what must not occur in the software system
		• Lifecycle	Design, Building, Testing, User Implementation, Disposal Requirements
	QUALITY Classic requirements for the software system that jointly define its objective and subjective quality (e.g. overall conformance to user's expectations)	Functionality, Reliability ,Usability Efficiency, Maintainability, Portability Requirements (based in ISO 9126)	
	SECURITY	Requirements derived to establish explicitly the security (e.g. safeness, protection, vulnerability, recoverability, survivability) characteristics for the software system	
	DOCUMENTATION These requirements found out the documentation needs.	Technical, Operative, Politics & Procedures	

Table 2. List of software requirements engineering techniques/methods analyzed

Technique/Method	Sources
Interview	Durán and Bernárdez (2000)
JAD (Join Application Development)	Satzinger et al (2000)
SADT (Structured Analysis and Design Technique)	Siltala (2004)
Structured System Analysis	ITC InfoTech (2006)
Object Oriented Modeling	Insfrans et al (2001)
Goal Oriented Modeling	Delor et al (2003); Mylopoulos et al, 1999
Prototype	Buchenau and Fulton (2000)
Walkthroughs[1]	Bias (1991)
PSL / PSA	Teichroew and Sayani (1980); Beregi (1984);
Formal Methods	FAA System Safety Handbook (2002); Vienneau (1993)
Artificial Intelligence based Techniques	Pohl et al (1994)

software engineering literature is scarce. However, some authors (Ross, 1997; referenced by Brackett, 1990; Mylopoulos, Bordiga, Jarke, & Koubarakis, 1999) have identified the relevance of considering such issues (e.g., requirements should not only answer the what and general how questions, but also the why inquiry).

Table 1 does not imply that each software system to be developed should consider all types and sub-types. Rather than, this suggests that requirements engineers should analyze what of them are relevant for such specific situations and decide jointly with stakeholders what will be considered.

For achieving the second purpose on the clarification of similarities and differences among the several software requirements engineering processes, activities, and techniques reported in the literature, several pro-forms are used. Table 2 shows the techniques/methods analyzed. In Table 6 the four processes analyzed are showed.

The pro-form in Table 3 is used to identify the inputs, phases, and results proposed by a software engineering process analyzed. In this table, the software requirements engineering process posed by SEI is conceptually dissected. A similar analysis was conducted with the remainder process reported in Table 6.

Simultaneously, for a better understanding, a detailed analysis of each technique/method was conducted. Table 4 shows the pro-form used to identify their name, description, tasks, discipline that belongs to, a classification, and the sources. In Table 4, SE stands by system engineering, IS by information systems, and SwE by software engineering.

From the analysis conducted to techniques and process, two main general findings can be reported: (a) a re-grouping of techniques/methods (Table 5) and (b) a comparative of software requirements engineering process (Table 6). Techniques can be classified into four classes: traditional, group oriented, modeling oriented, and formal logic (Table 5).

The first class (traditional) can be used to the contextual analysis and elicitation activities for its potential for managing social-politic and human affairs. The second class (group oriented) can be used in the elicitation, constraints identification, and metric parameter definition activities for its clarity of representation for physical artifacts. The third class (modeling oriented) can be used to define data and processes representations, and finally, the fourth class (formal logic) to do elicitation, modeling, and validation activities when mission critical and

Table 3. Analysis of a software requirements engineering

Software Requirements Engineering Process from SEI			
Purpose : It is concerned with the definition of software requirements –the software engineering process of determining what is to be produced- and the products generated in that definition			
Inputs	**Proposal Phases**		**Results**
	Name	**Description**	
Context analysis should answer the following questions: • Why is the software developed? • What is the environment where the software will be created and operated? • What are the technical, operational, and economic boundary conditions that an acceptable software implementation must satisfy?	Requirements Identification	The software requirements are elicited from people or derived from systems requirements.	There are three principal groups: • **Functional Requirements**: these specify the functions of the system or system component. • **Non-Functional Requirements**: these consider the performance, interface, and reliability requirements. • **Constraints on the design**: these define the operational and implementation limits.
	Identification of Software Development Constraints	Acceptable constraints (costs, the characteristics of the hardware to which the software must interface, existing software with which the new software must operate, fault tolerance objectives, and portability requirements and implemented within the restrictions imposed) are identified.	
	Requirements Analysis	Potential problems, classification of requirements and evaluation of feasibility and risk are developed.	
	Requirements Representation	The results of the requirements identification are portrayed.	
	Requirements Communication	The results of requirements definition are presented to diverse audiences for review and approval.	
	Preparation for Validation of Software Requirements	The criteria and techniques are established for ensuring that the software, when produced, meets the requirements. The customer and software developers must reach agreement on the proposed acceptance criteria and the techniques to be used during the software validation process, such as execution of a test plan to determine that the criteria have been met.	

Table 4. Technique/method analysis

Technique/Method: Formal					
Description: Formal Methods (FM) consists of a set of techniques and tools based on mathematical modeling and formal logic that are used to specify and verify requirements and designs for computer systems and software. Formal methods may be used to specified and model behavior of a system and to mathematically verify that the system design and implementation satisfy system functional and safety properties. These specifications, models, and verifications may be done using a variety of techniques and with various degrees of rigor.					
Tasks:					
Level 1: Formal specification of all or part of the system.					
Level 2: Formal specification at two or more levels of abstraction and paper and pencil proofs that the detailed specification implies the more abstract specification.					
Level 3: Formal proofs checked by a theorem prover.					
Discipline			**Classification**	**Reference:**	
SE	IS	SwE (X)	Formal Logic	[FAA2000]	FAA System Safety Handbook, Appendix D; (2000) "Appendix D Structured Analysis and Formal Methods"

Table 5. Classification of software requirements engineering techniques/methods

Class	Technique
Traditional	Interview
Group Oriented	JAD (Join Application Development)
	SADT (Structured Analysis and Design Technique)
	Walkthroughs
Modeling Oriented	PSL / PSA (Problem Statement Language / Problem Statement Analyzer)
	Structured System Analysis
	Object Oriented Modeling
	Goal Oriented Modeling
	Prototypes
Formal Logic	Formal Techniques
	Artificial Intelligence based Techniques

Table 6. Comparison of software requirements engineering processes

Documents / Generic Process Stages	Software Requirements SEI Curricula: SEI (1990)	Requirements Engineering: A Road Map: Neseibeth & Easterbrook (1990)	Software Requirements (in SWEBOK): Sawywer & Kontoya (2001)	Guide to the Software Requirements Definition Phase: ESA Board for Software Standardization and Control; European Space Agency (1990)
A.1 Social Context Analysis	Briefly mentioned	---	---	---
A.2 Operational Context Analysis	Briefly mentioned	Briefly mentioned	Briefly mentioned	Operational environment determination
A.3-4 Elicitation and Analysis	Requirements Identification	Eliciting Requirements	Requirements Elicitation	Definition of the user requirements
	Identification of software development constraints	Modeling and analysis requirements	Requirements Analysis	
	Requirements Analysis			
A.5 Requirements modeling and representation	Requirements Representation		Requirements Specification	Specification of the user requirements
A.6 Requirements Communication	Requirements Communication	Communicating Requirements		---
A.7 Requirements Validation & Specification	Preparation for validation of software requirements	Agreeing Requirements	Requirements Validation	Reviews
A.8 Changing Management	---	Evolving Requirements	Requirements Management	---

high-risk process are being modeled. Table 6 shows a comparison of the several software requirements engineering processes analyzed.

It is important to note that the term "elicitation" includes the normal "gathering information" and the "analysis of the information gathered" that requirement engineers have to perform in order to find all the issues that could be potentially useful for determining the characteristics mandatory and expected of the software system. These issues can come from real organizational or user's events or situations but the users could omit intentional or involuntary because political-power reasons or simply by daily routine. Findings from Table 7 suggest that social context as well as operational context analysis are critical activities to be pursued by software requirements engineering in order to avoid critical organizational or user's omissions. Based in such a comparison and using a well-known notation for process specification in systems engineering (IDEF0, Mayer, 1990), Figure 1 shows the posited "generic software requirements engineering process."

The process proposes three core phases. Phase 1 is "make business contextual analysis," which includes the A.1 social context analysis and A.2. pperational context analysis activities. Phase 2 is "perform elicitation," which includes: A.3 elicitation and A.4 analysis. Phase 3 is "make requirements representation," which includes: A.5 requirements modeling and representation, A.6 requirements communication, and A.7 requirements validation & specification. A "change management" activity is also required, but in this first version of the process, is not considered a full phase. Table 7 shows an initial description each phase and activity for the generic software requirements process.

This generic process was elaborated through the analysis and synthesis of all activities reported in the literature (described in the background section). A main finding that we identified in this study was the relevance played by contextual analysis (and scarcely addressed by most processes analyzed). Contextual analysis considers the environmental influences such as economics, political, business goals, and legal, that could affect the successful

Table 7. Description of phases and activities of the generic SRE process

PHASE		ACTIVITY	DESCRIPTION
MAKE BUSINESS CONTEXTUAL ANALYSIS		A.1 Social Contextual Analysis	To make sense of the social, organizational and user environment where the new software system will be deployed.
		A.2 Operational Contextual Analysis	To identify the operational settings where the new software system will be deployed...
PERFORM ELICITATION		A.3 Elicitation	To identify the explicit (visible) and implicit (non visible) stakeholders' needs that new software system to be deployed must satisfy as well as additional (optional) characteristics.
		A.4 Analysis	To organize and classify needs as well as to evaluate their real (priority and feasibility) need.
MAKE REQUIREMENTS REPRESENTATION		A.5 Modeling and Representation	To translate the needs in graphic, textual or even real system prototypes representations that help to understand the stakeholders' needs...
		A.6 Communication & Negotiation	To let stakeholders know the identified requirements and negotiate the final agreements.
		A.7 Validation and Definitive Specification	To identify potential mistakes, omissions or unfeasible requirements. This activity is conducted simultaneously with A.6. If corrections are required, then will be needed to redo some activities.
A.8	CHANGE MANAGEMENT		To establish procedures control for change management during the full requirements engineering process.

Figure 1. IDEF0 specification of the generic software requirements engineering process

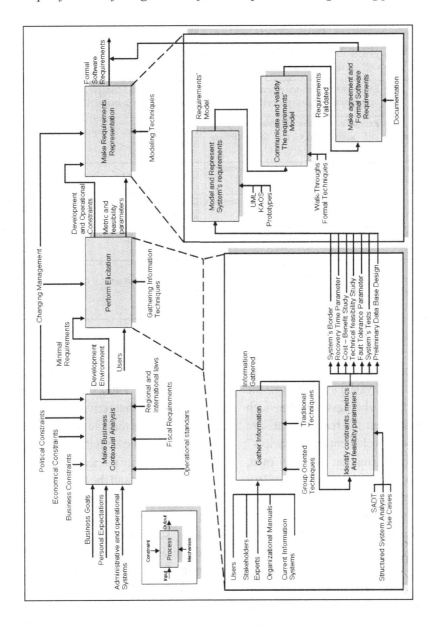

software system development. Other important aspects are those concerned with training needs and the way that the new software system will affect the current information systems and the current software systems. Then, the contextual analysis activity was added in order to identify such that aspects. A change management activity that is performed after each activity in order to record every change made is also added. With it, a history of the process is available for auditing and continuous improvement issues. All activities are rationally ordered to get the generic process.

In order to complete our generic software engineering process, we identified the actors and their

Table 8. Actors/stakeholders and their roles

Actor	Description	Roles
User	People who will operate the system or will use the information gotten from it	Final User
Expert	People who know the management and operational business processes	Implementation Manager, Process Manager, Tests Manager & Inspection Manager
Customer	People how know the business goals and usually pay for the software product	Process Manager, Customer Interfaces Manager
Business Manager	People who make the expenses control they most know the other actors	Inspection Manager, Meetings Planner
Systems Analyst	Expert personal in Information Systems Analysis and Design	Design Manager, Planning Manager, Project Leader
Development Team	Computer programmers, experts in Graphical User Interfaces	Support Manager
Project Manager	Experts in Requirement Engineering and Information Systems	Planning Manager, Quality Manager, Inspection

roles. As it was established, despite the requirements are attached to a physical system (e.g., the software system), are human beings who define such characteristics. Then, when the requirements are elicited, the most important element are the "actors" (or stakeholders), the information that they own, and their willingness to provide it. An "actor" (or stakeholder) is everyone that affects or is affected for the new system. Actors (as team) know how the system works, what information is needed, where the information comes from, what business goals are, and how to manage projects. They are usually experts doing their work, analyzing information, and making decisions. "Actors" participate in the current organizational systems and processes that an organization wants to support with information software-intensive systems. Actors can rescue a bad project or block a correct one. Actors have enforce and exercise power and politics issues. Table 8 shows the names, description, and roles. These roles were taken from Davis and McHale (2003).

The actors and their level of participation in the activities of the generic software requirements en-

gineering process can be assessed as "participant" or "chairman." "Chairman" means that the actor is responsible for that activity; on the other hand, "participant" means that the actor participates in doing satisfactorily, the activity. It is important to notice that in the activity named "validations & specification," the users (and the remainder of stakeholders) are responsible for doing it, the systems analysts and the development equipment only participate in it; we suggest that because the users have to be sure that their needs were well understood and well identified, the software specification will include them. Table 9 shows such issues.

The theoretical validity of this generic process for requirements engineering was assessed through an evaluation form (available upon request) reported in Mora (2004). According to Mora (2004): *the validation in conceptual researches could be done establishing the extent in which the conceptual model successfully accomplishes with the following criteria: (a) the conceptual model is supported on robust theories and principles; (b) the conceptual model is logically coherent, congruent with the*

Table 9. The level participation of actors/stakeholders in the generic process

Activity		Actors							
Num	Description	User	Expert	Customer	Business Manager	Systems Analyst	Development Team	Project Manager	Changing Management Influence Area
A.1	Contextual Analysis					Chairman			
A.2		Participant	Participant	Participant	Participant		Participant	Participant	
A.3	Elicitation					Chairman			
		Participant	Participant	Participant	Participant		Participant	Participant	
A.4	Analysis					Chairman			
		Participant	Participant	Participant	Participant		Participant	Participant	
A.5	Modeling and Representation					Chairman			
							Participant		
A.6	Communication & Negotiation					Chairman			
		Participant	Participant	Participant	Participant	Participant	Participant	Participant	
A.7	Validation and Specification	Chairman							
		Participant	Participant	Participant	Participant	Participant	Participant	Participant	
A.8	Change Management							Chairman	
		Participant	Participant	Participant	Participant	Participant	Participant	Participant	
		Change Management Influence Area							

Table 10. Theoretical assessment of the generic process

ITEMS	Scores					
	Expert 1	Expert 2	Expert 3	Expert 4	Expert 5	Average
1. The conceptual model is supported by strong theoretical principles.	3	3	5	5	5	**4.2**
2. The theoretical principles used are relevant to the topic under study.	NA	5	5	5	5	**5**
3. The reviewed literature does not have relevant omissions to the related topic.	NA	4	4	4	4	**4**
4. The conceptual model is logically coherent.	5	5	5	5	5	**5**
5. The conceptual model is adequate with the purpose for which was designed	4	5	5	5	5	**4.8**
6. The resultant conceptual model is congruent with the research paradigm used.	5	5	5	5	5	**5**
7. The conceptual model provides new insights and is not just a duplication of an existing model.	3	4	4	4	5	**4**
8. The form in which the model is presented is adequate to a scientific study.	4	5	5	5	5	**4.8**

reality under study, and adequate to the purpose to which is designed; and (c) the conceptual model contributes with something new and it is not a duplication of an existing model. A panel of five experts in software engineering performed the evaluation to determine if the model accomplishes with the three criterions established. The evaluation consists in a questionnaire with eight questions (available upon request). Each item uses a five-point Likert scale. The overall results achieved show that the work is considered theoretically valid for the panel of experts.

FUTURE TRENDS

According to the findings of this research, several surveys on utilization of specific techniques and a related recent study on systems development life-cycles process (SDLCs) (Rodriguez et al., 2008), it can identified that a requirements engineering process is included as a mandatory phase in most SDLCs. Another initial trend is the gradual diminishing of the analysis phase to be incorporated partially to requirements engineering and to design phases in the SDLCs. A final initial trend is that for the case of critical software systems, the security (non functional) set of requirements are mandatory while that for other kinds of systems, this category has been overlapped.

However, the surveys show that not all activities (e.g., elicitation-analysis, modeling-representation, communication-negotiation, validation-specification, and changing management) are followed and not all techniques are used. There is no evidence of a change in this situation. Furthermore, the debate between rigor-discipline versus agile-light oriented SDLCs inhibits a unique trend to deploy a full requirements engineering process. Consequently, a critical challenge for practitioners is the incorporation of such an engineering process as a routine practice. Another challenge identified in this research is the mandatory inclusion of the contextual analysis activity, originally posed by

Ross and Schoman (1997) (reference by Brackett, 1990), and extended in this research to enrich the requirement engineering process by considering social, political, legal, and economical issues that surround the external and internal environment. A requirements engineer should know the people's expectations, beliefs and norms, and should also appreciate the fears that the deployment of a new system could generate. Evidences of similar social issues impacts in the development of software have been reported (Curtis et al, 1988).

A final challenge is the updating of the requirements engineering processes to incorporate the management and technical issues that the emergent paradigm of service-oriented software/systems, ICT service management (e.g., based in ITIL), and CRM approaches are demanding. What is useful and what must be generated are core research questions worthy to be pursued. The generic requirements software engineering process posited in this chapter is an initial step towards this challenge.

CONCLUSION

In this conceptual study, a deep review of the literature related to requirements engineering from both a software engineering and information systems perspective is reported, as well as a new "generic process for requirements engineering." The main conclusion to report is that the stage of "software/system requirements engineering," independently of the systems development lifecycle selected for a development team, has been recognized as the most important stage, because the errors introduced during it and discovered in later steps will produce significant cost overruns, delays, and unsatisfied systems' requirements in the project. It is also identified that a "generic process" for the system/software requirements engineering could be used in each software development project. Its adaptation for large, medium, or small projects could also be required. Further research is suggested regarding to the "make business contextual analysis" phase, which is a primary activity that has been scarcely reported in the software engineering literature. This activity is strongly suggested to be integrated in any "generic process" in order to assist systems designers for acquiring a broader perspective of the business organizational environment in which the software is expected finally to be deployed. Finally, new types of software requirements are identified when critical mission systems are developed. As a main limitation of this study, it must be reported that the "generic process for requirements engineering" elaborated, has not been still empirically tested. However, the results of a theoretical validation from a panel of experts in software engineering suggest a positive and relevant contribution to the disciplines of information systems and software engineering.

REFERENCES

Abbott, R. J. (1986). *An integrated approach to software development*. New York: John Wiley.

Andoh-Baidoo, F., White, E., & Kasper, G. (2004, August). Information systems' cumulative research tradition: A review of research activities and outputs using pro forma abstracts. In *Proceedings of the Tenth Americas Conference on Information Systems* (pp. 4195-4202). New York.

ANSI/IEEE Standard 729-1983. (1983). *IEEE standard glossary of software engineering terminology*. IEEE.

Beckworth, G., & Garner, B. (1994) *An analysis of requirements engineering methods*. School of Computing and Mathematics. Australia: Deakin University.

Brackett, J. (1990). *Software requirements; SEI curriculum module SEI-CM-19-1.2*. Software Engineering Institute: Carnegie Mellon University.

Counelis, J. (2000). *Generic research design in the study of education: a systemic typology. Systems Research, 17*, 51-63.

El-Emam, K., & Madhavji, N. (2005, March). A field study of requirements engineering practices in information systems development. In *Proceedings of the Second IEEE Int. Symp. on Requirements Engineering* (pp. 68-80). York, UK, England.

ESA software engineering standards. ESA Board for Software Standardisation and Control. 1994

ESA PSS-05-03. (1995). *Guide to the software requirements definition phase*. Paris, France: ESA Board for Software Standardisation and Control (BSSC).

Glass, R., Vessey, I., & Ramesh, V. (2002). Research in software engineering: an analysis of the literature. *Information and Software Technology, 44*, 491-506.

González, R. (2005). Developing the requirements discipline: Software vs. systems. *IEEE Software, March-April*, 59-61.

Jin, Z., Bell, D., Wilkie, F. G. (1998). Automatically acquiring the requirements fo business information system by using business ontology. In Proceedings of Workshop on Application of Ontologies and Problem Solving Methods (pp. 1-15). Brighton, UK.

Juristo, N., Moreno, A. M., & Silva, A. (2002). Is the European industry moving toward solving requirements engineering problems? *IEEE Software, November-December*, 70-77.

Mayer, R. J. (1990). *IDEF0 functional modeling*. College Station, TX: Knowledge Based Systems, Inc.

Mora, M. (2004). *Conceptual research method description*. Aguascalientes, México: UAA. (In Spanish Language).

Mylopoulos, J., Bordiga, A., Jarkc, M., & Koubarakis, M. (1999). Telos: representing knowledge about information system. *ACM Trnas. on Information Systems, 8*(4), 325-362.

Neil, C., & Laplante, P. (2003). Requirements engineering: The state of the practice. *IEEE Software, November-December*, 40-45.

Nikula, U., Fajaniemi, J. & Kalviainen, H. (2000) Management view on current requirements engineering practices in small and medium enterprises. In *Proceedings of the Fifth Australian Workshop on Requirements Engineering* (pp. 81-89). Queensland University of Technology, Brisbane, Australia, Faculty of Information Technology, University of Sydney (UTS).

Nuseibeh, B., & Easterbrook, S. (2000). *Requirements engineering: A roadmap.* ACM Digital Library, 1/58113-253-0/00-6.

Rodríguez, L. C. (2006). *Comparative study on systems development life-cycles process.* Aguascalientes, Mexico: UAA.

Ross, D.T., & Schoman, K.E., Jr. (1997). Structured analysis for requirements definition. *IEEE Trans. Software Eng., SE-3*, (1), 6-15.

Sage, A., & Armstrong, J. (2000). *Introduction to systems engineering.* New York: Wiley.

Sawyer, P., & Kotonya, G. (2001). *Chapter 2 software requirements.* SWEBOK, IEEE-Trial Version 1.00-May.

Sommerville, I. (2005). *Software engineering.* Addison Wesley.

Sumano, M. (1999). *Stated of the art of software requirements analysis* (Technical Report No. 33). Mexico: Computer Sciences Research Center, National Politechnical Institute. (In Spanish Language).

SWEBOK. (2004). *Guide to the software engineering body of knowledge.* A project of the IEEE Computer Society Professional Practices Committee.

Viennau, R. (1993). A review of formal methods. *In A Review of Formal Methods, Kaman Science Corp.* (3-15).

Zave, P. (1997). Classification of research efforts in requirements engineering. *ACM Computing Surveys, 29*(4), 315-321.

KEY TERMS

Changing Management: Control of every change proposal made during the software specification process.

Contextual Analysis: Analysis of the social, technical, and operational environment where the system software will be developed and operated.

Generic Process: Universal process that can be used for every software development project.

Operational Context Analysis: Analysis of the operational environment where the system software will be developed and operated.

Requirements Elicitation: Process of discovering the requirements for a system by communication with customers, system users, and others who have a stake in the system development.

Requirement Engineering: Discipline that establishes the services that a software system must provide, and constrains that must satisfy.

Social Context Analysis: Analysis of the social environment where the system software will be developed and operated.

Chapter VII
Individual Improvisation in Information Systems Development

Massimo Magni
Bocconi University, Italy

Bernardino Provera
Bocconi University, Italy

Luigi Proserpio
Bocconi University, Italy

ABSTRACT

Improvisation is rapidly becoming an important issue for both scholars and practitioners. Organizations that operate in turbulent environments must learn to swiftly adapt and respond to such instability, especially in areas as innovation and new product development. In such contexts, traditional top-down, carefully-planned approaches to innovative projects may represent an obstacle to effectively dealing with environment uncertainty. Prior research on improvisation has focused considerable attention on the centrality of improvisation in individual and group outcomes, while less emphasis has been placed on how individual attitude toward improvisation is formed. In an attempt to fill this gap, we will theoretically analyze the antecedents of individual attitude toward improvisation, by looking at the information systems development (ISD) domain. In particular, the outcome of this chapter is the development of theoretical propositions which could be empirically tested in future research.

INTRODUCTION

Improvisation has become an important issue for both scholars and practitioners. Organizations operating in turbulent environments must learn to swiftly adapt and respond to them, especially in areas as innovation and new product development (Brown & Eisenhardt, 1997; Kamoche & Pina e Cunha, 2001). In such contexts, traditional top-down, carefully-planned approaches to innovative projects may represent an obstacle to effectively dealing with environment uncertainty (Kamoche & Pina e Cunha, 2001). Indeed, improvisation may enable managers to continuously adjust to change through a creative process that allows for the development of novel and useful solutions (Crossan, Pina e Cunha, Vera, & Cunha, 2005).

Improvisation has been studied in domains as different as organizational learning (Miner, Bassoff, & Moorman, 2001) technology implementation (Orlikowski & Hofman, 1997) and new product development (Kamoche & Pina e Cunha, 2001). Research has addressed the issue of improvisation at different levels of analysis: individual, group, and organization (Moorman & Miner, 1998). Similar, multi-level approaches have been applied to investigate the dynamics of improvisation-related concepts as creativity and innovation. However, differently from research on creativity and innovation, research on improvisation is still at an immature stage (Kamoche & Pina e Cunha, 2001). First, studies on improvisation suffer from an over-reliance on the use of metaphors as jazz music, theatre, sports, and public speaking (Pina e Cunha, Vieira da Cunha, & Kamoche, 1999). This view tends to obscure the notion that "improvisation is more than a metaphor" (Crossan, 1998). A key challenge for future research is to go beyond the metaphorical conceptualization of improvisation, to provide theoretical insights grounded in business organizations. Second, prior research has focused considerable attention on the centrality of improvisation in individual and group outcomes (Kamoche & Pina e Cunha, 2001), while less emphasis has been placed on how individual attitude toward improvisation is formed.

In order to address these two issues that have not been exhaustively developed by previous studies, we theoretically analyze the antecedents of individual attitude toward improvisation in the information system development (ISD) domain. In particular, following the suggestions put forward by Orlikowski (1996), we focus on open-ended, customizable technologies which are related to complex organizational changes. In our opinion, knowing what factors influence the intention to engage in improvisational behaviour is a necessary condition to support improvisation and, thus, to "(...) make sense of complex situations and put us in closer touch with human experience" (Ciborra, 1999b).

By relying on the organizational theory of improvisation, the aim of this chapter is to provide a theoretical contribution to the IS field by developing a theoretical framework on the antecedents of individual attitude to improvise in the ISD. In particular, the outcome of this chapter is the development of theoretical propositions which could be empirically tested in future researches.

The remainder of this chapter is structured as follows. The following section describes the concept of improvisation, underscoring its overall characteristics, as well as the peculiarities in the ISD domain. Building on improvisation theory, we next develop a theoretical framework and propositions that describe how the individual, social, and organizational dimensions affect individual attitude toward improvisation. Finally, we offer recommendations for future research in both the ISD and improvisation domains.

BACKGROUND

The Concept of Improvisation

Improvisation has been defined as a form of intuition which guides action in a spontaneous way (Crossan & Sorrenti, 1997) or as "the conception of action as it unfolds—acting without the benefit of elaborate prior planning" (Kamoche & Pina e Cunha, 2001), and "drawing on available cognitive, affective, social, and material resources" (Kamoche, Pina e Cunha, & Vieira da Cunha, 2003). Improvisation can be regarded as "the deliberate and substantive fusion of the design and execution of a novel production" (Miner et al., 2001). Furthermore, Moorman and Miner define it as "the degree to which composition and execution converge in time" (1998).

These definitions essentially focus on the temporal sequence of two distinct activities, planning and acting, and on the need to react to particular stimuli by relying on immediately-available resources. The latter aspect of improvisation is often refereed to as the "*bricolage*" component (Ciborra, 1996; Pina e Cunha et al., 1999). Temporal pressure, originated by either internal or external sources, is regarded as a key condition reducing the distance between planning and acting, thereby increasing the chance of improvisational activities (Pina e Cunha et al., 1999). Other significant conditions include fortuity, complexity, and uncertainty (Weick, 1998).

Characteristics of Improvisation

Organizational improvisation can be deliberate or extemporaneous (Pina e Cunha et al., 1999). Moreover, it should not necessarily be regarded as the result of stand-alone events as organizational crises (Ciborra, 1999b; Vera & Crossan, 2004). On the contrary, improvisation is thought to occur along a continuum between totally planned action and spur-of-the moment activities (Pina e Cunha et al., 1999). Accordingly, individuals and groups may improvise to incremental and radical degrees, by adjusting to current procedures as well as by swiftly responding to dramatic crisis events (Vera & Crossan, 2004).

Managerial studies suffer from a dominant bias according to which innovation and, ultimately, competitive advantages are the results of carefully-planned actions and uncertainty avoidance (Mintzberg, 1994; Weick, 1998; Kamoche & Pina e Cunha, 2001). Organizations develop routines that yield activities and solutions learned from past experience. Routines embody ordinary learning. In some occasions, though, routines perpetuate the same response to different stimuli (Weick, 1991) and organizations tend to fall into competency traps (Levitt & March, 1988). As a consequence, learning is hampered. Moreover, reliance on successful past experience leads organizations to regard improvised outcomes as misgivings to be avoided and,

if detected, punished. If improvisation is regarded as utterly unacceptable, though, organizational members will hardly engage in creative endeavours that could result in significant innovations.

On the contrary, organizations must develop their abilities to improvise to cope with tumultuous external conditions (Vera & Crossan, 2004), attempting to continuously and creatively change in order to move product and services out the door (Brown & Eisenhardt, 1997). Therefore, improvisation is a creative process that aims at developing novel and useful solutions to a particular situation (Crossan et al., 2005).

Improvisation and ISD

In the XXI century, organizations are making significant investments in highly-complex for integrating data and developing knowledge (e.g., knowledge management, peer-to-peer collaboration), as well as to cope with new problem domains (e.g., datawarehousing). Given the complexity of these projects, returns on IT investment are often constrained by poor development and implementation processes in the organizational environment (Bwusi-Mensab, 1997).

ISD refers to the "analysis, design, and implementation of IS applications/systems to support business activities in an organizational context" (Xia & Lee, 2005). As noted by Ciborra (1991) and Avison and Fitzgerald (1999), the dominant approaches to the ISD have focused on the identification of pre-defined phases, allowing for better control during the whole development project. Such approaches are based upon the principle of functional decomposition, that is, the breaking down of a complex problem into more manageable units in a disciplined way. However, the attempt to bring some discipline to the development of information systems has often brought to the failure of ISD projects (Jesitus, 1997), as well as to a negative impact on user acceptance (Agarwal, 2000) and productivity (Lewis, Agarwal, & Sambamurthy, 2003). Today's rapidly changing environment leads developers to cope with both technological issues and organizational factors which are outside the project team's realm of control (Kirsch, 1996; Schmidt & Lyytinen, 2001). Therefore, because of the complexity of designing and introducing an IS in organizations, the a priori establishment of all encompassing requirements is unfeasible (Orlikowski & Hofman., 1997). Indeed, the development of a new information system through functional decomposition methods, which implies system requirements to be closed early in the process, constrains the rise of emergent behaviours (Truex, Baskerville, & Travis, 2000).

Information systems cannot be considered as stable and discrete entities, as they belong to "information infrastructures" which constantly change and adapt (Ciborra, 1999a). Therefore, information systems require a high degree of unplanned action by organizational actors. Basic requirements are established a priori, but the success in the development of the system derives from the ability to fulfill the emergent requests for customization, also by capturing and integrating extemporaneous ideas emerging from "below," from the end user level (Ciborra & Lanzara, 1990). Indeed, according to Orlikowski and Hofman (1997) and Cooper et al. (2000) there should be a continuous process of alignment between the technological change and the organizational factors involved in the change process.

The Concept of Individual Attitude

The proliferation of articles, chapters, and books about attitudes underscores the importance growth of such concept (Ajzen, 2001 for a literature review). According to Fishbein and Ajzen (1975), individual attitude can be defined as a predisposition to respond in a consistently favourable or unfavourable manner with respect to a given psychological object. The importance of individual attitude can be traced back to its ability to predispose individual to action (Ajzen, 2001). Many models have been developed in order to explore the relationship between attitude and individual action in different domains, such

as social psychology, sociology, and organization. Besides these disciplines, the concept of attitude received significant attention within the information system domain, with particular focus on individual use of IT (i.e., Venkatesh & Davis, 2000).

Since attitude has demonstradeted its robustness for representing individual predisposition to perform a behavior, it could also be adopted to understand individual's tendency to improvise. According to the definition of attitude, and reframing it into the improvisation domain, we define attitude toward improvisation as the individual predisposition to take improvise action.

A critical issue can be traced back to the formation of individual attitude toward improvisation. Previous literature points out that the development of a person's attitude is related to the formation of a set of individual's beliefs about a particular object, action, or event. According to Ajzen (2001), "each belief associates the object with a certain attribute, and a person's overall attitude toward an object is determined by the subjective values of the object's attributes in interaction with the strength of the associations." Many studies in the information systems domain have underscored the relationship between beliefs and attitude, pointing out that beliefs are related to different aspects and psychological levels (see Lewis et al., 2003). Indeed, each belief may refer to the individual herself, to the group characteristics she belongs to, and to the organizational environment in which she is involved. Besides beliefs, other studies have pointed out that attitudes may be shaped by individual traits (Rogers, 1995).

THE ANTECEDENTS OF INDIVIDUAL ATTITUDE TOWARD IMPROVISATION: PROPOSING A MULTI-LEVEL MODEL

Extant theoretical literature points out that organizational improvisation relies on factors related to the individual, group and organizational level

(Crossan et al., 2005; Moorman & Miner, 1998; Vera & Crossan, 2005).

The focus of this research is solely on the relationship between beliefs and individual attitude toward improvisation. Starting from the widely acknowledged proposition that individual attitudes formation depends on individual beliefs and traits, we propose a model which considers how individual beliefs may affect the individual attitude to take improvised actions. To capture the formation of individual attitude toward improvisation, we specify traits and beliefs referred to individual, group, and organizational levels, proposing the following research framework of individual attitude toward improvisation in the IS development domain (Figure 1).

These facets capture individual psychological processes of individuals relative to themselves, to the team in which they are involved, and to the organization they belong to. Therefore, we are focused on those beliefs and traits which are involved in individual psychological processes of

attitude formation, rather then on other individual, group, and organizational characteristics which do not belong to traits or beliefs. Therefore, concepts that can be traced back to individual background such as, for instance, tenure and organizational position, are not comprised in this study. Moreover, characteristics are related to the nature of the task are not included in the study because they are not consistent with the multi-level model adopted in our research, since they do not insist on any of the three levels we consider. Consequently, the level of task complexity or the degree of task routinization are not included in the model. Furthermore, we do not consider the structural characteristics at the group or organization level. Indeed, constructs such as team composition (Pelled, 1996), group size (Campion, Papper, & Medsker, 1996), or evaluation criteria and reward systems (Orlikowski, 1996) cannot be considered as individual beliefs or personal traits. Altough we do not consider such elements in our model, we recognize that they may have an influence on organizational improvisation through different

Figure 1. A multilevel perspective of individual improvisation

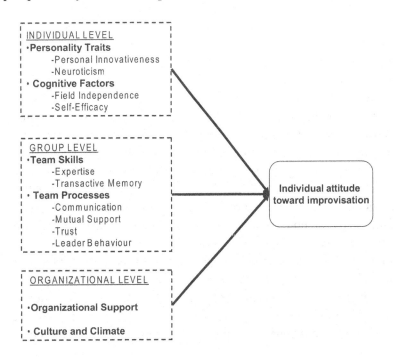

theoretical pathways than those related with individual psychological processes (i.e., Orlikowski & Hofman, 1997; Vera and Crossan, 2004).

Individual Level

Individual traits and beliefs related to the individual level of analysis may have a significant influence on improvisational behaviours (Crossan, 1998). This issue has been pointed out in different domains, ranging from theatre and jazz (Kamoche & Pina e Cunha, 2001) to management (Vera & Crossan, 2004) and surgery (King & Ranft, 2001). Literature on attitude formation points out that factors belonging to personality traits and cognitive factors have received consistent support as important predictors of individual attitude (e.g., Barrick & Mount, 1991; Judge & Bono, 2001). Togheter, these two categories refer to the degree to which an individual is comfortable in situations in which improvisation may occur, ultimately influencing attitude toward improvisation.

Personality traits. Personality traits refer to individual characteristics which are relatively stable overtime (Woodman, Sawyer, & Griffin, 1993). In the IS domain, it is possible to identify two different kinds of individual traits: broad traits and situation-specific traits. Broad traits are enduring and predispose individuals to respond consistently to stimuli across situations (Thatcher & Perrewe, 2002). On the contrary, situation-specific traits refer to enduring individual predisposition to respond to stimuli in a consistent manner within a narrowly defined context. Since our research is framed within the broad situation of ISD, we argue that broad traits may exert a more pervasive influence on individual attitudes. In particular, referring to the broad traits in the IS and improvisation domain, it is possible to underscore two concepts which may enhance or constrain attitude toward improvisation: personal innovativeness and neuroticism. Personal innovativeness refers to individual predisposition toward change ad risk-taking (Hurt et al., 1977; Bommer & Jalajas, 1999). Moreover, individuals who present

a high level of personal innovativeness are more likely to tolerate ambiguity, and to act independently from social influence. Therefore, we argue that innovative individuals are also more likely to improvise, departing from standard procedures for IS development. On the other side, we argue that neuroticism may constrain individual attitude toward improvisation. The fundamental role of neuroticism in shaping attitudes and behaviours can be traced back to the literature on individual stress, which posits its critical role in stressful contexts (Watson & Clark, 1984). Individuals with high neuroticism are more likely to experiment anxiety when faced with problems or challenges, as well as in the absence of an objective source of stress (Watson & Clark, 1984). Moreover, other studies have pointed out that individuals with high levels of neuroticism have a higher propensity to dwell on mistakes or inadequacies (Thatcher & Perrewe, 2002). Given the complexity and uncertainty associated with the ISD process, we argue that individuals with a high level of neuroticism present a lower attitude toward improvisation. Thus,

PROPOSITION 1: Personality factors are antecedents of individual's attitude toward improvisation in ISD projects.

Cognitive factors. According to Woodman et al. (1993), the ability of individuals to produce ideas is also related to the individual cognitive processes. Despite that extant literature pointed out many cognitive factors that influence individual attitudes and behavior, we argue that, in the improvisation domain, the most critical factors are those which allow individual to cope with lack of time and to face an emergent and new situation. These two aspects can be captured by looking at two main cognitive factors: field independence and self-efficacy. Field independence refers to the ability of an individual to focus on relevant aspects of a certain situation, ignoring irrelevant issues (Woodman et al., 1993). Therefore, in a situation characterized by lack of time, an individual with high field independence is more likely to take spontaneous action because he or she possesses the ability to distinguish important from less important aspects. The other central cognitive aspect which may influence individual attitude toward improvisation is self-efficacy. Self-efficacy refers to judgments of what one can do with whatever skills one possesses. Individuals with a low level of self-efficacy are more likely to follow instructions and directions more carefully (Marakas, Yi, & Johnson, 1998). Therefore, individuals with a high degree of confidence in their ability to exploit their skills will be less likely to follow standard procedures in the development of the system, thereby experimenting with new pathways and behaving in a spontaneous fashion. Thus,

PROPOSITION 2: Cognitive factors are antecedents of individual's attitude toward improvisation in ISD projects.

Group Level

Improvisation usually occurs through the social interaction among individuals and group members (Vera & Crossan, 2004). This issue is consistent with the proposition of Nemeth and Staw (1989), who state that several attitudes are socially constructed because individuals are immersed in an organizational environment which may facilitate or constrain the improvisational process (see also Vera & Crossan, 2004). In particular, according to Tannenbaum, Beard, and Salas (1992), it is possible to identify two group-level dimensions which may affect individual attitudes. The first one refers to the initial capabilities of of group members in order to reach a certain goal (the input phase in the Tannenbaum model), while the second refers to the process through which these resources are exploited (the throughput phase in the same model). Therefore, in our conceptualization we focus on individual beliefs referred to team skills, and to team processes.

Team skills. According to Vera and Crossan (2004), it is necessary for the team to possess a broad set of skills and expertise to allow individuals to feel confident enough to improvise. In the ISD, expertise represents one of the most critical resources for project effectiveness (Faraj & Sproull, 2000). Moreover, expertise has a positive impact on individual improvisational processes because "the larger the set of skills in a work team, the more numerous are the alternatives for developing new combination of ideas" (Vera & Crossan, 2004). Another important issue related to team-level knowledge refers to the notion of transactive memory, which allows team members to encode, store, and retrieve relevant information related to previous experience (Liang, Moreland, & Argote, 1995). During the development of a complex information system, access to diverse memory resources helps individuals improvise, as they can leverage on the recombination of past team experience (Vera & Crossan, 2004) in order to face the paucity of requirements that are defined a priori. Thus,

PROPOSITION 3: Team skills are antecedents of individual's attitude toward improvisation in ISD projects.

Team processes. Team processes refer to the way individuals within the group cooperate to more effectively manage their interdependences. In particular, it is possible to look at the team processes from two different perspectives: the relationship between the individual an his/her peers, and the relationship between the individual and his/her team leader. The degree of collaboration among team members can be analysed through the multifaceted concept of teamwork quality developed by Hoegl and Gemuenden (2001). Considering the six concepts which constitute the concept of teamwork quality, we argue that two of them are more likely to foster the process of resource exchanges among individuals, functioning as a facilitating condition to the improvisational process. Good quality in the communication process allows exchanging information more effectively, helping individuals obtain relevant information in a short time frame. The effect of a good information flow on ISD projects outcomes has also been empirically demonstrated (i.e., Faraj & Sproull, 2000). The second important issue concerning the cooperation among team members refers to the presence of mutual support. Indeed, mutual support is an important issue to avoid interpersonal conflict among members (Hoegl & Gemuenden, 2001). Moreover, the lack of conflict allows individuals to cooperate to achieve common goals (Tjosvold, 1984). When individuals believe that there is mutual support within the team, they are more likely to rely on one another when they are facing with an unexpected situation. Besides the aspects comprised in the teamwork quality construct, we argue, consistently with Vera and Crossan (2004), that trust among team members represents a fundamental issue in shaping individual attitude toward improvisation. Trust can be considered as "the extent to which a person is confident in, and willing to act on the basis of, the words, actions, and decisions of another" (McAllister, 1995). On the receiver side, trust allows to reduce efforts to verify the accuracy and the validity of received information. In other words, members will be more likely to accept other members' information because of the presence of trust. Therefore, a lack of trust and dysfunctional interaction among members leads individual not to have access to the material needed for improvise (Vera & Crossan, 2004), thereby decreasing their attitude to perform spontaneous actions.

Altough team members represent the main factor influencing individuals behavior, it is widely acknowledged that the leader's behaviour may affect the attitudes and behaviours of employees. We consider supervisor's behaviour as a group-level construct as we assume that members belonging to the same group are likely to be exposed to the influence of the same supervisor, thereby involving a relatively homogeneous experience that is distinct from those of other groups (Liao & Chuang, 2004). Given the complexity of ISD projects, leaders cannot rely on predefined structures, although they should be able to provide support in situations where there are no clear directions (Mumford, Scott, Gaddis, &

Strange, 2002). The importance of leader support in conditions of uncertainty has been pointed out by many studies (see Amabile, Schatzel, Moneta, & Kramer, 2004). Since the improvisation process involves trial and error and discovery, the leader's behaviour should be consistent with this approach. Accordingly, leaders should provide the necessary resources to help individuals improvise. In an ISD environment characterized by uncertainty and unclear solutions, leaders who offer a certain degree of freedom to their employees may provide a fertile ground for spontaneous actions (Mumford et al., 2002). Therefore, we hold that individuals who perceive support from their leader present a higher attitude toward improvisation in the context of complex ISD projects. Thus,

PROPOSITION 4: Team processes are antecedents of individual's attitude toward improvisation in ISD projects.

Organizational Level

Individual beliefs referred to the organizational level represent a facilitating condition for improvisational process (Vera & Crossan, 2004), thereby enhancing individual attitude toward improvisation. Recalling the theories of improvisation, many authors underscore the influence of the organizational environment on the improvisational process and outcome (Kamoche & Pina e Cunha, 2001; Vera & Crossan, 2004). Following such insights, we point out that those individual beliefs concerning the organizational context which may affect individual attitude to improvise. These factors include organizational support and organizational culture and climate.

Organizational support. The concept of organizational support can be traced back to the "employees' perception about the extent to which the organization cares about their well being" (Eisenberger, Fasolo, & Davis-LaMastro, 1990). In the IS domain, Igbaria, Guimaraes, and Davis (1995) underscore the importance of top management support, which refers to the allocation of sufficient resources and to the encouragement of employees. George and Brief (1992) suggest that organizational support is positively related to employees' efforts. In particular, employees who perceive that the organization recognizes and rewards their efforts to carry out their job effectively are more likely to engage in behaviours that go beyond their formal duties. Therefore, if individuals in ISD projects perceive that they are supported by the organization through sufficient resources, they may be more likely to break routines and to engage in improvisational behaviours. Thus,

PROPOSITION 5: Organizational support is an antecedent of individual's attitude toward improvisation in ISD projects.

Organizational culture. Hierarchical organizations permeated by authority relations and rigidly-controlled workplaces are expected to obstruct improvisational behaviour (Orlikowski, 1996). On the contrary, experimental cultures rewarding exploration and creativity, and tolerating mistakes, are expected to foster improvisation (Pina e Cunha et al., 1999; Vera & Crossan, 2005). When errors are regarded as viable sources of learning, and the ideas of others are not blocked but are encouraged and freely discussed, improvisational activities within individuals and groups are free to emerge and be evaluated. Therefore, we argue that during the development of an information system, individuals who perceive a positive climate and an experimental culture would be more likely to improvise, thereby departing from established plans. Thus,

PROPOSITION 6: Organizational culture is an antecedent of individual's attitude toward improvisation in ISD projects.

FUTURE TRENDS

The importance of carrying out thorough empirical investigation is highlighted by the consideration that improvisation is not an inherently positive or negative phenomenon (Crossan et al., 2005; Miner et al., 2001). Positive outcomes of improvisation include flexibility, learning, motivation, and affectivity (Pina e Cunha et al., 1999). Negative outcomes may comprise biased learning, opportunity traps, amplification of emergent actions, over-reliance on improvisation, and anxiety (Pina e Cunha et al., 1999). Consequently, empirical efforts are required to distinguish between descriptive features (what improvisation is) and prescriptive aspects (how to leverage improvisation to enhance organizational objectives) of improvisational processes (Crossan et al., 2005). Therefore, future research should test the validity of the theoretical model presented in the present contribution for a better understanding of descriptive features of improvisational attitude. Furthermore, research should clearly investigate the relationship between improvisational processes and performance (Vera & Crossan, 2004), for understanding the contingencies that allow a positive outcome of improvisational actions.

Moreover, future research should take into account that the concept of organizational improvisation is tightly interrelated with a variety of theoretical domains. These may include organizational learning (Moorman et al., 1998; Weick, 1991), teamwork dynamics (Moorman et al., 1998), creativity (Moorman et al., 1998), innovation (Kamoche, Pina e Cunha, & Vieira da Cunha, 2003), and organizational change (Orlikowski, 1996). Consequently, a better understanding of improvisational dynamics may contribute to strengthen extant research on management studies.

In our theoretical arguments, we did not consider group-level structural characteristics as team composition (Pelled, 1996) and geographical dispersion (Hoegl & Proserpio, 2004). Although we did not consider such elements in our model, we recognize that they may have an influence on organizational improvisation through different theoretical pathways (i.e., Orlikowski & Hofman, 1997; Vera & Crossan, 2005) and encourage further inquiry exploring such possible relationships.

CONCLUSION

Theoretical and Managerial Implications

The present study has provided a theoretical framework to be validated and tested in subsequent empirical research. By doing so, we have moved an initial step towards answering Ciborra's call to design activities, settings, and systems in a way that captures open experimentation, deviations, incongruencies, and mismatches that "(…) populate the design and implementation agenda" (Ciborra, 1991). The ability to manage improvisation is a critical determinant for organizations to control, at least to a certain extent, the emergent and unpredictable part of their everyday actions, as well as the manifestation of fortuitous events (Pina e Cunha et al., 1999). Consequently, understanding the antecedents which lead to improvisation is crucial in order to fully grasp how "emergent strategies" (Mintzberg, 1994; Weick, 1998) unfold and relate to structured planning. Increased awareness of the potential of improvisational activities may help organizations avoid dismissing improvisation as a dysfunction resulting from unintended processes and design failure (Lewin, 1998; Vera & Crossan, 2004).

Organizations should consider improvisation as a potentially effective skill and tool "(…) that complements planning efforts, but that, because of its creative and spontaneous nature, it is not necessarily tied to success, the same way planning is not necessarily associated with success" (Vera & Crossan, 2004).

Besides implication for theory building and formulation, mastering the dynamics of improvisation has direct relevance for practitioners (Vera & Crossan, 2005). At the top management level, executives may increase their capability to flexibly enact business plans, by understanding when, and how, emergent factors may cause their organization to deviate from pre-planned action and, consequently, adopt improvisational behaviours. Moreover, team leaders and project managers may benefit from understanding the micro-processes of improvisation, as they gain a better understanding of the situations in which individuals engage in un-anticipated activities. Overall, managers may learn to leverage improvisation by defining the boundaries and constraints within which organizational actors and units are free to experiment and engage in risk-taking actions (Vera & Crossan, 2005).

Recognizing and capturing the instances and outputs of improvisation, bricolage, serendipity, and tinkering can allow organizations to keep the development of IS "(…) close to the competencies of the organization and to on-going fluctuations in local practices" (Ciborra, 1991).

Moreover, if the model offered here is supported empirically, some important practical implication may rise for the ISD domain. First of all, this chapter offers a more structured perspective to guide organizations in looking at ISD through a new perspective. This aspect is consistent with the assumption made by Ciborra (1999a) when he argues that, in order to improve the effectiveness of IT in organisations, "(…) due consideration for the role played by improvisation in human affairs advises us to stay more attached to those everyday micro-practices and means developed by mankind over the centuries to survive." Connected to this perspective, the present study can offer another important trigger in order to re-focus the alignment between the requirements of an ISD project and the capabilities of individuals involved in the project team. Indeed, besides the focus on project management and technical skills, individuals should have some peculiar characteristics which allow them to improvise in an uncertain environment.

Furthermore, the ability of the group and of the firm to facilitate the emergence of improvising behaviour could also represent a critical aspect in the relationship between team members and end users. Developers who have an attitude toward improvisation may be better able to understand and grasp the emergent signals and requests from users. The ability to fulfill users' emergent requests may allow for a deeper involvement of end users, with a consequent enhancement of their satisfaction using the system (Agarwal, 2000).

REFERENCES

Agarwal, R. (2000). Individual acceptance of information technologies. In R. W. Zmud (Ed.), *Framing the domains of IT management: Projecting the future from the past* (pp. 85-104). Cincinnati: Pinnaflex Educational Resources.

Ajzen, I. (2001). Nature and operation of attitudes. *Annual Review of Psychology, 52*, 27-58.

Amabile, T. M., Schatzel, E. A., Moneta, G. B., & Kramer, S. J. (2004). Leader behaviors and the work environment for creativity: Perceived leader support. *Leadership Quarterly, 15*(1), 5-32.

Avison, D., & Fitzgerald, G. (1999). Information systems development. In W. L. Currie & B. Galliers (Eds.), *Rethinking management information systems* (pp. 250-278). Oxford University Press.

Barrick, M.R., & Mount, M. K. (1991). The big five personality dimensions and job performance: A meta-analysis. *Personnel Psychology, 44*(1), 1-26.

Bommer, M., & Jalajas, D. S. (1999). The threat of organizational downsizing on the innovative propensity of R&D professionals. *R & D Management, 29* (1), 27-34.

Brown, S. L., & Eisenhardt, K. M. (1997). The art of continuous change: linking complexity theory and time-paced evolution in relentlessly shifting organizations. *Administrative Science Quarterly, 42*(1), 1-34.

Bwusi-Mensab, K. (1997). Critical issues in abandoned infomation systems development projects. *Communications of the ACM, 40* (9), 74-80.

Campion, M. A., Papper, E. M., & Medsker, G. J. (1996). Relations between work team characteristics and effectiveness: a replication and extension. *Personnel Psychology, 49*, 429-452.

Ciborra, C. U. (1991). From thinking to tinkering: the grass roots of strategic information systems. In *Proceedings of the International Conference on Information Systems (ICIS)* (pp. 283-291).

Ciborra, C. U. (1996). The platform orgnization: recombining strategies, structures, and surprises. *Organization Science, 7*(2), 103-118.

Ciborra, C. U. (1999a). A theory of information systems based on improvisation. In W. L. Currie & B. Gallers (Eds.), *Rethinking management information systems* (pp. 136-155). Oxford: Oxford University Press.

Ciborra, C. U. (1999b). Notes on improvisation and time in organizations. *Accounting, Management and Information Technologies, 9*, 77-94.

Ciborra, C. U., & Lanzara, G. F. (1990). Designing dynamic artifacts: computer systems as formative contexts. In P. Gagliardi (Ed.), *Symbols and artefacts: views of the corporate landscape*. Berlin: De Gruyter.

Cooper, B. L., Watson, H. J., Wixom, B. H., & Goodhue, D. L. (2000). Data warehousing supports corporate strategy at first american corporation. *MIS Quarterly, 24*(4), 547.

Crossan, M. M. (1998). Improvisation in action. *Organization Science, 9*(5), 593-599.

Crossan, M. M., Pina e Cunha, M., Vera, D., & Cunha, J. (2005). Time and organizational improvisation. *Academy of Management Review, 30*, 129-145.

Crossan, M., & Sorrenti, M. (1997). Making sense of improvisation. *Advances in Strategic Management, 14*, 155-180.

Eisenberger, R., Fasolo, P., & Davis-LaMastro, V. (1990). Perceived organizational support and employee diligence, commitment, and innovation. *Journal of Applied Psychology, 75*, 51-59.

Faraj, S., & Sproull, L. (2000). Coordinating expertise in software development teams. *Management Science, 46*(12), 1554, 1515.

Fishbein, M., & Ajzen, I. (1975*). Belief, attitude, intention and behavior: An introduction to theory and research*. Reading, MA: Addison-Wesley Publishing Company.

George, J. M., & Brief, A. P. (1992). Feeling good-doing good: A conceptual analysis of the mood at work-organizational spontaneity relationship. *Psychological Bulletin, 112*, 310-329.

Hoegl, M., & Gemuenden, H. G. (2001). Teamwork quality and the success of innovative projects: A theoretical concept and empirical evidence. *Organization Science, 12*(4), 435-449.

Hurt, H. T., Joseph, K., & Cooed, C. D. (1977). Scales for the measurement of innovativeness. *Human Communication Research, 4*, 58-65.

Igbaria, M., Guimaraes, T., & Davis, G. B. (1995). Testing the determinants of microcomputer usage via a structural equation model. *Journal of Management Information Systems, 11*(4), 87.

Jesitus, J. (1997). Broken promises? FoxMeyer's project was a disaster. Was the company too aggressive or was it misled? *Industry Week, November 3*, 31-37.

Judge, T. A., & Bono, J. E. (2001). Relationship of core self-evaluations traits—self-esteem, generalized self-efficacy, locus of control, and emotional stability—with job satisfaction and job performance: A meta- analysis. *Journal of Applied Psychology, 86*, 80–92.

Kamoche, K., Cunha, M. P., & Cunha, R. C. (2003). Improvisation in organization. *International Studies of Management and Organization, 33*(1).

Kamoche, K., & Pina e Cunha, M. (2001). Minimal structures: from jazz improvisation to product innovation. *Organization Studies, 22*(5), 733-764.

Kamoche, K., Pina e Cunha, M., & Vieira da Cunha, J. (2003). Toward a theory of organizational improvisation: looking beyond the jazz metaphor. *Journal of Management Studies, 40*, 2023-2051.

Karahanna, E., Evaristo, J. R., & Srite, M. (2005). Levels of culture and individual behavior: An integrative perspective. *Journal of Global Information Management, 13*(2), 1-20.

King, A. W., & Ranft, A. L. (2001). Capturing knowledge and knowing through improvisation: what managers can learn from the thoracic surgery board certification process. *Journal of Management, 7*(3), 255-277.

Kirsch, L. J. (1996). The management of complex tasks in organizations: Controlling the systems development process. *Organization Science, 7*(1), 1.

Levitt, B., & March, J. G. (1988). Organizational learning. *Annual Review of Sociology, 14*, 319-338.

Lewin, A. Y. (1998). Jazz improvisation as a metaphor for organization theory. *Organization Science, 9*(5), 539-539.

Lewis, W., Agarwal, R., & Sambamurthy, V. (2003). Sources of influence on beliefs about information technology use: An empirical study of knowledge workers. *MIS Quarterly, 27*(4), 657.

Liang, D. W., Moreland, R., & Argote, L. (1995). Group vs. individual training and group performance: The mediating role of transactive memory. *Personality and Social Psychology Bulletin, 21*(4), 384-393.

Liao, H., & Chuang, A. (2004). A multilevel investigation of factors influencing employee service performance and customer outcomes. *Academy of Management Journal, 47*(1), 41-58.

Lovell, J., & Kluger, J. (1995). *Apollo XIII*. New York: Simon & Schuster.

Marakas, G. M., Yi, M. Y., & Johnson, R. D. (1998). The multilevel and multifaceted character of computer self-efficacy: Toward clarification of the construct and an integrative framework for research. *Information Systems Research, 9*(2), 126.

McAllister, D. J. (1995). Affect- and cognition-based trust as foundations for interpersonal cooperation in organizations. *Academy of Management Journal, 38*(1), 24-59.

Miner, A. S., Bassoff, P., & Moorman, C. (2001). Organizational improvisation and learning. *Administrative Science Quarterly, 46*, 304-337.

Mintzberg, H. (1994). *The rise and fall of strategic planning.* New York: Free Press.

Moorman, C., & Miner, A. S. (1998). Organizational improvisation and organizational memory. *Academy of Management Review, 23*, 698-723.

Mumford, M. D., Scott, G. M., Gaddis, B., & Strange, J. M. (2002). Leading creative people: Orchestrating expertise and relationships. *Leadership Quarterly, 13*, 705.

Nemeth, C. J., & Staw, B. M. (1989). The tradeoffs of social control and innovation in groups and organizations. In L. Berkowitz (Ed.), *Advances in experimental social psychology* (Vol. 22, pp. 75-210). New York: Academic Press.

Orlikowski, W. J. (1996). Improvising organizational transformation over time: A situated change perspective. *Information Systems Research, 7*(1), 63.

Orlikowski, W. J., & Hofman, J. D. (1997). An improvisational model for change management: The case of groupware technologies. *Sloan Management Review, 38*(2), 11.

Pelled, L. H. (1996). Demographic diversity, conflict, and work group outcomes: An intervening process theory. *Organization Science, 7*(6), 615-631.

Pina e Cunha, M., Vieira da Cunha, J., & Kamoche, K. (1999). Organizational improvisation: what, when, how and why. *International Journal of Management Reviews, 1*, 299-341.

Rogers, E. M. (1995). *Diffusion of innovations* (4th ed.). New York: Free Press.

Schmidt, R., Lyytinen, K., Keil, M., & Cule, P. (2001). Identifying software project risks: An international Delphi study. *Journal of Management Information Systems, 17*(4), 5-32.

Tannenbaum, S. I., Beard, R. L., & Salas, E. (1992). Team building and its influence on team effectiveness: An examination of conceptual and empirical developments. In K. Kelley, (Ed.), *Issues, theory, and research in industrial/organizational psychology* (pp. 117-153). Amsterdam, Holland: Elsevier.

Thatcher, J. B., & Perrewe, P. L. (2002). An empirical examination of individual traits as antecedents to computer anxiety and computer self-efficacy. *MIS Quarterly, 26*(4), 381-316.

Tjosvold, D. (1984). Cooperation theory and organizations. *Human Relations, 37*(9), 743-767.

Truex, D., Baskerville, R., & Travis, J. (2000). Amethodical systems development: the deferred meaning of systems development methods. *Accounting, Management & Information Technologies, 10*, 53-79.

Venkatesh, V., & Davis, F. D. (2000). A theoretical extension of the technology acceptance model for longitudinal field studies. *Management Science, 46*(2), 186-204.

Vera, D., & Crossan, M. M. (2004). Theatrical improvisation: lessons for organization. *Organization Studies, 25*, 727-749.

Vera, D., & Crossan, M. M. (2005). Improvisation and innovative performance in teams. *Organization Science, 2*, 203-224.

Watson, D., & Clark, L. (1984). Negative affectivity: The disposition to experience aversive psychological states. *Psychological Bulletin, 96*, 465-490.

Weick, K. E. (1979). *The social psychology of organizing.* Reading, MA: Addison-Wesley.

Weick, K. E. (1991). The non-traditional quality of organizational learning. *Organization Science, 2*, 116-124.

Weick, K. E. (1998). Improvisation as a mindset for organizational analysis. *Organization Science, 9*(5), 543-555.

Woodman, R. W., Sawyer, J. E., & Griffin, R. W. (1993). Toward a theory of organizational creativity. *Academy of Management Review, 18*, 293-321.

Xia, W., & Lee, G. (2005). Complexity of information systems development projects: Conceptualization and measurement development. *Journal of Management Information Systems, 22*(1), 45-83.

KEY TERMS:

Individual Improvisation: Creative and spontaneous process of managing an unexpected event.

Information Systems Development: Analysis, design, and implementation of IS applications/systems to support business activities in an organizational context.

Individual Attitude: Predisposition to respond in a consistently favourable or unfavourable manner with respect to a given psychological object.

Personality Trait: Individual characteristic which is relatively stable overtime.

Team Processes: The way individuals within the group cooperate to manage their interdependences.

Organizational Support: Employees' perception about the extent to which the organization cares about their well being.

Chapter VIII
Design and Analysis of Decision Support Systems

John Wang
Montclair State University, USA

James Yao
Montclair State University, USA

Qiyang Chen
Montclair State University, USA

Ruben Xing
Montclair State University, USA

ABSTRACT

Since their creation in the early 1960's, decision support systems (DSSs) have evolved over the past 4 decades and continue to do so today. Although DSSs have grown substantially since its inception, improvements still need to be made. New technology has emerged and will continue to do so and, consequently, DSSs need to keep pace with it. Also, knowledge needs to play a bigger role in the form of decision making. We first discuss design and analysis methods/techniques/issues related to DSSs. Then, the three possible ways to enhance DSSs will be explored.

INTRODUCTION

Over the 4 decades of its history, decision support systems (DSSs) have moved from a radical movement that changed the way information systems were perceived in business, to a mainstream commercial information technology movement that all organizations engage. This interactive, flexible, and adaptable computer based information system

derives from two main areas of research: the theoretical studies of organizational decision making done at the Carnegie Institute in the 1950's and early 1960's, as well as the technical work on interactive computer systems which was mainly performed by the Massachusetts Institute of Technology (Keen & Morton, 1978).

DSSs began due to the importance of formalizing a record of ideas, people, systems, and technologies implicated in this sector of applied information technology. But the history of this system is not precise due to the many individuals involved in different stages of DSSs and various industries while claiming to be pioneers of the system (Power, 2003; Arnott & Pervan, 2005). According to Arnott (2006), the DSS field began in the early 1970s as a radical alternative to large-scale management information systems (MIS). Over time, major changes in information technology have enabled new decision support movements. In the late 1980s and mid-1990s, multidimensional modeling, OLAP technology, and advances in storage technology and data modeling led to the deployment of large-scale executive information systems, data warehousing, and business intelligence. Now DSSs have become very sophisticated and stylish since the early pioneering research. Many new systems have expanded the frontiers established by these pioneers, yet the core and basis of the system remains the same. Today, DSSs are used in the finance, accounting, marketing, medical, as well as many other fields.

BACKGROUND

The basic ingredients of a DSS can be stated as follows: the data management system, the model management system, the knowledge engine, the user interface, and the users (Donciulescu, Filip, & Filip, 2002). The database is a collection of current or historical data from a number of application groups. Databases can range in size from storing it in a PC that contains corporate data that has been downloaded, to a massive data warehouse that is continuously updated by major organizational transaction processing systems (TPSs). When referring to the model management system, it is primarily a stand-alone system that uses some type of model to perform "what if" and other kinds of analysis. This model must be easy to use, and therefore the design of such model is based on a strong theory or model combined with a good user interface.

A major component of a DSS is the knowledge engine. To develop an expert system requires input from one or more experts, this is where the knowledge engineers go to work, who can translate the knowledge as described by the expert into a set of rules. A knowledge engineer acts like a system analyst but has special expertise in eliciting information and expertise from other professionals (Laudon & Laudon, 2005).

The user interface is the part of the information system through which the end user interacts with the system, the type of hardware, and the series of on-screen command and responses required for a user to work with the system. An information system will be considered a failure if its design is not compatible with the structure, culture, and goals of the organization. Research must be conducted to design a close organizational fit, to create comfort and reliability between the system and user. In a DSS, the user is as much a part of the system as the hardware and software. The user can also take many roles such as decision maker, intermediary, maintainer, operator, and feeder. A DSS may be the best one in its industry but it still requires a user to make the final decision.

Power (2003) introduced a conceptual level of DSSs, which contains five different categories. These categories include model-driven DSS, communication-driven DSS, data-driven DSS, document-driven DSS, and knowledge-driven DSS. Defining DSS is not always an easy task due to the many definitions available. Much of this problem is attributed to the different ways a DSS can be classified. At the user level, a DSS can be classified as passive, active, or cooperative.

Essentially, DSS is a computer-based system that provides help in the decision making process. However, this is a broad way of defining the subject. A better way of describing DSS is to say it is a flexible and interactive computer-based system that is developed for solving non-structured management problems. Basically, the system uses information inputted from the decision maker (data and parameters) to produce an output from the model that ultimately assists the decision maker in analyzing a situation. In the following sections, we first discuss design and analysis methods/techniques/issues related to DSSs. Then, the three possible ways to enhance DSSs will be explored. At the end, future trends in DSSs will be discussed.

DESIGN AND ANALYSIS METHODS/ TECHNIQUES/ISSUES RELATED TO DSSs

Design Methods

Today, DSSs hold a primary position in an organization's decision making by providing timely and relevant information to decision makers. It has become a key to the success or survival of many organizations. However, there is a high tally of failure in information systems development projects, even though they are a focal point of industrial concern (Goepp, Kiefer, & Geiskopf, 2006). Designing methods have become an important component that assures a successful information system design. This issue is in relevance to the design of a DSS.

There have been many different strategies employed for the design of a DSS, including the early decision-oriented design approach (Stabell, 1983). Current research on DDS design has witnessed the rapid expanding of object-oriented (OO) approach, which exploits object-oriented software engineering with unified modeling language (UML); knowledge management (KM) approach, which supports end-users by embedding declarative and/or procedural knowledge in software agents; structured modeling (SM) approach, which employs a hierarchically organized, partitioned, and attributed acyclic graph to represent models; and design science (DS) approach, which attempts to create artifacts that serve human purposes and solve organizational problems.

Object-oriented (OO) approach: The characteristic of OO approach is to use object-oriented software engineering with UML in the design and implementation of a DSS. OO design concepts are based on software engineering in that knowledge encapsulation present in a set of objects in an object-oriented system, where sub-classes show inheritance of the properties of the main class, is more compact and yet extensive compared to a logic-based system. Higher order logic is required to duplicate the performance of a simple object-oriented system (Pillutla & Nag, 1996). OO approach is considered a novel way of systems thinking. It provides designers and developers with easy analysis of complex systems and design of suitable software systems. It allows the developers and users to think in terms of objects and their behaviors instead of thinking about processes and process complexities. The main advantages are due to the features like data abstraction, encapsulation, inheritance, and polymorphism of OO approach (Nagarur & Kaewplan, 1999).

OO approach involves basically three major steps (Tian, Ma, Liang, Kwok, & Liu, 2005). The user's requirements are first captured by using a set of use case diagrams. These diagrams indicate all the functionalities of the system from the user's point of view. Then classes and their relationships are identified and described in class diagrams. Finally, sequence diagrams or collaboration diagrams are developed, which describe the interaction between objects (instances of classes). Tian et al. (2005) designed a DSS with the OO approach for an organization, which was implemented successfully.

Knowledge management (KM) approach: In some environments (non-preprogrammed applications), end-users, especially the less experienced end-users, need to have certain knowledge guiding them how to use the system. The KM design approach supports end-users by embedding declarative and/or procedural knowledge in software agents.

West Jr. and Hess (2002) used KM design approach to support end-users with spatially oriented decision-making by reporting on a specific spatial DSS that uses the approach. Procedural knowledge about performing spatial analysis was embedded in software agents that assist users with difficult and spatially oriented tasks. Because the system used a metadata repository, users were supported in some tasks by using the metadata repository directly and in others by using the software agents that access the metadata. According to West Jr. and Hess (2002), KM design approach provides better assistance to inexperienced users of spatial DSS, which requires a design approach that will prioritize knowledge support of the end-users' decision-making activities, and this approach, with the distribution of knowledge between metadata, agents, and end-users, has similar potential as a determinant of system success in any DSS (spatial or otherwise) where both declarative and procedural knowledge are needed to effectively accomplish the decision-making task. .

Structured modeling (SM) approach: SM (Geoffrion, 1987) approach "uses a hierarchically organized, partitioned, and attributed acyclic graph to represent models" (Srinivasan & Sundaram, 2000). It is a formal framework for describing models. SM identifies the basic components of models, the relationships among these components, and conditions under which a model may be termed structured (Lenard, 1993). It includes a language for describing a model schema and prescribes data tables for capturing the details of model instances.

SM decomposes a decision problem into genera and elements within genera in a hierarchic way, which forms a system that is sensitive to natural definitions of entities and objects in the problem (Pillutla & Nag, 1996). It consists of three levels: elemental structure, generic structure, and modular structure. The elemental structure intends to capture the definitional detail of a specific model instance. The generic structure targets at capturing the natural familial groupings of elements. The modular structure seeks to organize generic structure hierarchically according to commonality or semantic relatedness. The leveled structures allow the complexity of a model to be managed and ranked according to its hierarchies. The graph feature allows modelers and decision makers to understand the model better. A key advantage of SM is the ease with which structured models can be visualized (Srinivansan & Sundaram, 2000).

Srinivansan and Sundaram (2002) propose using SM in the design of model based DSS with

the intention of solving existing design problems, such as lack of theory or design principles and domain specific issues, in other approaches. They select object relational database environment to implement SM, to be specific, they propose using SM to provide a systematic general framework for conceptual modeling and an object relational database management system (ORDBMS) to implement it. They believe an object relational platform for implementing structured models offers a development platform that is well suited to their needs. Such a platform is uniquely capable of meeting the conceptual requirements outlined by SM while satisfying many practical design concerns such as performance, persistence, and interoperability. They trust that their proposition of using SM approach for specific problem conceptualization and such a powerful environment as ORDBMS to implement it will provide design ideas that can potentially serve a very useful class of applications (Srinivansan & Sundaram, 2000).

Design science (DS) approach: Arnott (2006) defines design science as an alternative, or complement, to the natural science approach which has been a dominant research methodology in information systems field. Natural science tries to understand reality, but design science attempts to create things that serve human purposes (March & Smith, 1995). In design science, researchers create and evaluate information technology artifacts that are intended to solve identified organizational problems (Hevner et al., 2004). Design science is especially relevant to information system research because it helps to address the role of the information technology artifact in information system research and the low professional relevance of many information system studies (Benhasat & Zmud, 1999; Orlikowski & Iacono, 2001).

The functionality of a DSS evolves over a series of development cycles where both the end-users and the systems analyst are active contributors to the shape, nature, and logic of the system (Arnott, 2004). Yet system developers have little guidance about how to proceed with evolutionary DSS development.

DSS developers are facing the fact that insufficient knowledge exists for design purpose, and designers must rely on intuition, experience, and trial-and-error methods. Design science approach, on the other hand, can facilitate developers to create and evaluate information technology artifacts that are intended to solve identified organizational problems (Hevner, March, Park, & Ram, 2004). Vaishnavi and Kuechler (as in Arnott, 2006) proposed a design science methodology with the major process steps of awareness of problem, suggestion, development, evaluation, and conclusion. Arnott (2006) proposed a five steps approach, which was adapted from Vaishnavi and Kuechler, for designing evolutionary DSS: problem recognition, suggestion, artifact development, evaluation, and reflection. A research project by Arnott indicates that design science approach can tackle problems of both theoretical and practical importance.

DSS design model: DSS design model is the most recent DSS design approach developed by Klashner and Sabet and is worthy of a discussion. According to Klashner and Sabet (2007), DSS design model differs from any other models and approaches in that it is a more comprehensive design approach to address domain and nondeterministic complexities arising from real-world decision-making requirements. Incorporating morphogenetic principles, the model reflectively and concurrently informs its own evolution and directly impacts the design of the proposed DSS under development "although this new DSS design model appears simple and straightforward" (Klashner & Sabet, 2007).

The model consists of three major components: theory and analysis, simulation, and decision/design. Within the theory and analysis component, multiple data from system domain are fed into theory and analysis. A relation between the theory and domain is maintained to continuously exchange synchronous data and update the theory. The simulation component interacts with the theoretical components to integrate the data feed. As to the decision/design component, the design decision-making process will inevitably be influenced by

the effect of theoretical analysis and simulation combined to the degree of not violating the decision-makers' shared understanding of the design goals. Then the newly integrated design decisions immediately act on the relationship between the system domain and information infrastructure, thus completing the first full iteration since the general iterative flow of data.

Klashner and Sabet (2007) argue that in the early years of DSS research, design choices were intuitively understood in most cases because of the straightforward nature of the stakeholder's requirements. But today, because stakeholder decisions have become highly subjective and complicated due to the increased problem complexity arising from various semi- to ill-structured problems (Nemati, Steiger, Iyer, & Herschel, 2002), a more comprehensive systems design approach is needed. Thus, the new DSS design model has been developed to address this issue. At present, the model application is domain specific, but it is currently being applied to another mission critical infrastructure design effort to test its generalizability to other domains where DSS plays a key role in daily operations (Klashner & Sabet, 2007).

Design Techniques

As we are advancing in information technologies, business decision makers can now have access to vast amount of information. On one hand, they may gain necessary and important information for making informed decisions, but on the other hand, they may also become overloaded by the information irrelevant to what they need. Thus, there is a pressing need for decision aiding tools that would effectively process, filter, and deliver the right information to the decision makers. Proper combination of DSSs and agent technologies could prove to be a very powerful tool for rendering decision support (Vahidov & Fazlollahi, Winter 2003-2004).

A software agent performs interactive tasks between the user and the system. The user instructs the system what he/she intends to accomplish. The software agent carries out the task. By analogy, a software agent mimics the role of an intelligent, dedicated and competent personal assistant in completing the user's tasks (Bui & Lee, 1999). In the DSS environment, software agents have been more formally described as autonomous software implementations of a task or goal that work independently, on behalf of the user or another agent (Hess, Rees, & Rakes, 2000). As the traditional, direct manipulation interface of our computing environment is much limited (Maes, 1994), software agents would seem to be a suitable and most needed solution for providing procedural assistance to end-users (West Jr. & Hess, 2002). "These 'robots of cyberspace' can be effectively utilized in automating many information processing tasks" (Vahidov & Fazlollahi, 2003-2004).

In some DSS environments, such as spatial DSS (Sikder & Gangopadhyay, 2002; West Jr. & Hess, 2002), Internet-based DSS (Bui & Lee, 1999) and Web DSS (Vahidov & Fazlollahi, 2003-2004), a multi-agent system should be designed and implemented in the DSS to facilitate the decision makers since decision making involves complex set of tasks that requires integration of supporting agents (Bui & Lee, 1999), and these agents should have behaviors to work in team (Norman & Long, 1994). Vahidov and Fazlollahi (2003-2004) developed architecture of multi-agent DSS for e-commerce (MADEC), in which intelligence team (agents), design team (agents), and choice team (agents) were composed. The multi-agent system was implemented in a prototype of MADEC, which received higher user satisfaction.

THREE POSSIBLE WAYS TO ENHANCE DSSs

Creating Knowledge Warehouses (KW)

Nemati (2002) proposed that a new generation of knowledge-enabled systems that provides the infrastructure required to capture, enhance, store, organize, leverage, analyze, and disseminate not only data and information but also knowledge (Nemati, 2002). Expanding data warehouses to encompass the knowledge needed in the decision making process is the creation of knowledge warehouses (KW). An important component of KW is a very complex process known as knowledge management. Knowledge management allows for knowledge to be converted from tacit to explicit through such processes as filtering, storing, retrieving, and so forth, thus allowing it to be utilized by decision makers.

The goal of KW is to give the decision maker an intelligent analysis standpoint that enhances all aspects of the knowledge management process. The main drawbacks of KW are the amount of time and money that need to be invested as well as some of the same problems that are found in successfully implementing DSSs. Among these factors are the users' involvement and participation, values and ethics, organization and political issues within the company, and other external issues. The development and implementation of KW still has much work to be done, however, DSSs seem to be headed toward knowledge enhancement in the future and KW looks to have a promising outlook in the upcoming years as a result.

Focusing on Decision Support

While knowledge management systems seem like a logical way to advance the shortcomings of DSSs, another view also exists. By removing the word "system" from DSSs and focusing on decision support, decision making might cause some interesting, new directions for research and practice. Decision support (DS) is the use of any plausible computerized or non-computerized means for improving sense making and/or decision making in a particular repetitive or non-repetitive business situation in a particular organization (Alter, 2004).

DS embodies a broader perspective that seems logical in environments where the user does not necessarily need the technical aspects of DSSs. This is based on the belief that most work systems of any significance include some form of computerized support for sense making and decision making (Alter, 2004). The difference between DSSs and DS is not too drastic but DS is a sensible option for many companies due to the increase in technology since the creation of DSSs; DSSs may not fit the needs of a business as it had in the past.

Integrating DSSs and KMSs

In line with Bolloju (2002), integrating decision support and knowledge management may correct some of the deficiencies of DSSs. The decision-making process itself results in improved understanding of the problem and the process, and generates new knowledge. In other words, the decision-making and knowledge creation processes are interdependent. By integrating the two processes, the potential benefits that can be reaped make the concept seem more worthwhile.

Integrating DSSs and KMSs seems to be the best choice out of the three possible ways to enhance DSS. The reasoning behind this selection is that integrating the two seems to provide a way for including both options without sacrificing one for the other. More importantly, while KW appears to have a very bright future, KW currently requires a great amount of time and money. The combination of both areas allows for a better overall utilization in the present. In time, KW may not be as time consuming and costly as it is now. However, to achieve a better balance of usefulness and efficiency, the integration of DSSs and KMSs appears to be the smartest choice.

FUTURE TRENDS

DSS in Business Analytics

The future of DSSs, Angus (2003) argued and supported by SAS (2004), is in the field of *business analytics* (BAs). BAs differ from that of the recently and previously more common business intelligence (BI). With the fast pace of business and life today it would only make sense for a shift to BA because it does focus on the many possibilities and the future outcomes for production and service.

BAs focus on the future of operations. Opposed to that of BI where it focuses on the past and what can be done to change the past if things were done wrong or repeat if things were done right. However, BAs let managers center on what future trends are developing, which allows them not to accumulate a surplus of inventory of outdated products. It also enables managers to change their prices before the market does, or introduce their new product before anyone else gets the chance to. This is known as first-to-market (Gnatovich, 2006). BAs give the companies that use it a tremendous advantage over their competitors in the market place.

Power-Hungry DSS

As everyone can see, the computing power is still accelerating. With its plan of "Itanium" processors, Intel is rushing towards its upcoming generation of 64 bit chips to support power-craving applications. Without any doubt, the power-hungry, large scale, integrated DSS application with dynamic calculation, background data mining, and high-end data visualization falls right into this end of the spectrum (Thomsen, 2003).

Web-Based DSS

The fast growing Internet and e-commerce have greatly impacted the way we conduct business. With the support of intelligent agents, DSS has been implemented for aiding decision makers in e-commerce. E-commerce combines transaction and decision support within an e-framework. Ultimately, the e-world is just another channel (Thomsen, 2003). If we can use the e-channels appropriately, integrate text engines within an overall DSS architecture, and provide for interoperability between DSS components, we may actually learn a few things about all this data we are collecting and make better decisions—without losing our humanity (Thomsen, 2003).

DSS in Retailing Business

In the retailing business sector, the competition over customers grows fierce. A customer's decision of buying from one retailer over another becomes the dividing factor in competition. Additionally, product mix between general and specialty retail is becoming homogenized. This expands the growth for more sophisticated and accurate decision support technology in the business (Rowen, 2005).

A few other trends in the retail business also call our attention. According to Rowen (2005), decision support solutions must interact with forecasting, allocation, and many other demand-chain applications from disparate vendors to increase margins. Additionally, we are being confronted with the coming onslaught of customer, events, and transactional data. Retailers are generating information at a volume that few can find significant use for today. Finally, forecasting and tracking anticipated sales has become another decision support trend within retail. Such technology enables a retailer to investigate the situation at hand, determining if a product is available.

Research in DSS

In terms of trends in DSS research, in the late 1980s and early 1990s, data warehouse and data mining was one of the focuses of research in DSS field. Since then software agents, also know as intelligent agents, emerged as an interdisciplinary area involving researchers from such fields as expert systems, DSS, cognitive science, psychology, databases, and so forth (Eom, 1999). Citations relevant to software agents in this chapter support such a proposition.

Studies of design science have shown a significant number in recent years in DSS research (Arnott & Pervan, 2005). This research stream has

been rapidly expanding with a range of new topics encouraged by technological advances, methodological innovations, and increased expectations for theory development and empirical analysis of the new artifacts (Banker & Kauffman, 2004), such as the design of auction mechanisms (Bapna, Goes, & Gupta, 2003; Kelly & Steinberg, 2000) and optimal strategies for investment in knowledge by using a market mechanism (Ba, Stallaert, & Whinstone, 2001). It is likely that it will remain as a major topic in years to come.

According to Eom's (Eom, 1999) study, Web-based DSS is another emerging topic in the DSS area. Sikder and Gangopadhyay (2002) identified research issues on the design and implementation of a Web-base collaborative spatial decision support system. Vahidov and Fazlollahi (2003-2004) proposed architecture for a multi-agent DSS for e-commerce and described a prototype system for making online investment decisions with such a Web-based multi-agent DSS. In the pre-Web era, DSS was primarily used in an "island" mode. In e-commerce applications today, DSS can be an integral part of the digital environment and directly support the actions of the involved parties (Vahidov & Fazlollahi, 2003-2004).

CONCLUSION

Since their creation in the early 1960's, DSSs have evolved over the past 4 decades and continue to do so today. Although DSSs have grown substantially since its inception, improvements still need to be made. New technology has emerged and will continue to do so and, consequently, DSSs need to keep pace with it. Also, knowledge needs to play a bigger role in the form of decision making.

Shim (2002) emphasized that DSSs researchers and developers should (i) identify areas where tools are needed to transform uncertain and incomplete data, along with qualitative insights, into useful knowledge, (ii) be more prescriptive about effective decision making by using intelligent systems and methods, (iii) exploit advancing software tools to improve the productivity of working and decision making time, and (iv) assist and guide DSSs practitioners in improving their core knowledge of effective decision support.

The prior statement sums up the courses of action that need to be taken very well. The successful integration of DSSs and KMSs could revolutionize DSSs and propel it to even greater heights in the future. In closing, DSSs have a storied history that spans the course of 4 decades; however, the greatest mark may be made in the not so distant future as DSSs continue to evolve.

REFERENCES

Alter, S. (2004). A work system view of DSS in its fourth decade. *Decision Support Systems, 38*(3), 319-327.

Angus, J. (2003). *Does BA beat BI? New, predictive business analytics tools mean business can do much more than react to the vagaries of chance.* Retrieved August 25, 2007, from http://infoworld.com/article/03/08/29/34FEbusan_2.html

Arnott, D. (2004). Decision support systems evolution: framework, case study and research agenda. *European Journal of Information Systems, 13*(4), 247-259.

Arnott, D. (2006). Cognitive biases and decision support systems development: A design science approach. *Information Systems Journal, 16*(1), 55-79.

Arnott, D., & Pervan, G. (2005). A critical analysis of decision support systems research. *Journal of Information Technology, 20*(2), 67-87.

Ba, S., Stallaert, J., & Whinstone, A. B. (2001). Optimal investment in knowledge with a firm using a market mechanism. *Management Science, 47*, 1203-1220.

Banker, R. D., & Kauffman, R. J. (2004, March). The evolution of research on information systems: A fiftieth-year survey of the literature in management science. *Management Sciences, 50*(3), 281-298.

Bapna, R., Goes, P., & Gupta, A. (2003). Analysis and design of business-to-consumer online auctions. *Management Science, 49*, 85-101.

Benbasat, I., & Zmud, R. W. (1999). Empirical research in information systems: The question of relevance. *MIS Quarterly, 23*(1), 3-16.

Bolloju, N., Khalifa, M., & Turban, E. (2002). Integrating knowledge management into enterprise environments for the next generation decision support. *Decision Support Systems, 33*(2), 163-176.

Bui, T., & Lee, J. (1999). An agent-based framework for building decision support systems. *Decision Support Systems, 25*(3), 225-237.

Donciulescu, D. A., Filip, C. I., & Filip, F. G. (2002). Towards intelligent real-time decision support systems for industrial milieu. *Studies in Informatics and Control, 11*(4).

Eom, S. (1999). Decision support research: current state and trends. *Industrial Management & Data Systems, 99*(5), 213-221.

Geoffrion, A. (1987). An introduction to structured modeling. *Management Science, 33*(5), 547-588.

Goepp, V., Kiefer, F., & Geiskopf, F. (2006). Design of information system architectures using a key-problem framework. *Computer in Industry, 57*(2), 189-200.

Gnatovich, R. (2006). *BI versus BA. Analytics is a lot more than just a dashboard.* Retrieved August 25, 2007, from http://cio.co.nz/cio.nsf/UNID/0B520925A900C4BCCC25712D005DBF5E

Hess, T. J., Rees, L. P., & Rakes, T. R. (2000). Using autonomous software agents to create the next generation of decision support systems. *Decision Sciences, 31*(1), 1-31.

Hevner, A. R., March, S. T., Park, J., & Ram, S. (2004). Design science in information systems research. *MIS Quarterly, 28*(1), 75-106.

Keen, P. G. W., & Morton, M. S. S. (1978). *Decision support systems: an organizational perspective.* Reading, MA: Addison-Wesley Pub. Co.

Kelly, F., & Steinberg, A. (2000). A combinatorial auction with multiple winners for universal service. *Management Sciences, 46*(4), 586-597.

Klashner, S., & Sabet, S. (2007). A DSS design model for complex problems: Lessons from mission critical infrastructure. *Decision Support Systems, 43*, 990-1013.

Lauden, K. C., & Lauden, J. P. (2005). *Management information systems: managing the digital firm* (6th ed.). Upper Saddle River: Pearson Prentice Hall.

Lenard, M. L. (1993). An object-oriented approach to model management. *Decision Support Systems, 9*, 67-73.

Little, J. D. C. (1970). Models and managers: the concept of a decision calculus. *Management Science, 16*(8), 466-485.

Maes, P. (1994). Agents that reduce work and information overload. *Communications of the ACM, 37*(7), 31-40.

March, S., & Smith, G. F. (1995). Design and natural science research on information technology. *Decision Support Systems, 15*, 251-266.

Nagarur, N. N., & Kaewplang, J. (1999). An object-oriented decision support system for maintenance management. *Journal of Quality in Maintenance Engineering, 5*(3), 248-258.

Nemati, H. R., Steiger, D. M., Iyer, L. S., & Herschel, R. T. (2002). Knowledge warehouse: An architectural integration of knowledge management, decision support, artificial intelligence and data warehousing. *Decision Support Systems, 33*(2), 143-161.

Orlikowski, W. J., & Iacono, C. S. (2001). Desperately seeking the "IT" in IT research—a call for theorizing the IT artifact. *Information Systems Research, 12*(2), 121-134.

Pillutla, S. N., & Nag, B. N. (1996). Object-oriented model construction in production scheduling decisions. *Decision Support Systems, 18*, 357-375.

Power, D. J. (2003, May 31). *A brief history of decision support systems.* Retrieved August 25, 2007, from http://DSSResources.com/history/dsshistory.html

Rowen, S. (2005). Decision support becomes a necessity. *Chain Store Age, 81*(2), 46.

SAS, Inc. (2004). *Software and services that give you the power to know. New business analytics report highlights SAS' leadership in scope.* Retrieved August 25, 2007, from http://www.sas.com/offices/europe/uk/press_office/press_releases/october2004/analytics.html

Shim, J. P., Warkentin, M., Courtney, J. F., Power, D. J., Sharda, R., & Carlson, C. (2002). Past, present, and future of decisions support technology. *Decision Support Systems, 33*(2), 111-126.

Sikder, I. U., & Gangopadhyay, A. (2002). Design and implementation of a web-based collaborative spatial decision support system: organizational and managerial implications. *Information Resources Management Journal, 15*(4), 33-47.

Srinivasan, A. & Sundaram, D. (2000). An object relational approach for the design of decision support systems. *European Journal of Operational Research, 127*(3), 594-610.

Stabell, C. B. (1983). A decision-oriented approach to building DSS. In J. L. Bennet (Ed.), *Building decision support systems.* Reading, MA: Addison-Wesley.

Thomsen, E. (2003). This year brought to you by the letter E. *Intelligent Enterprise, 1, 3*(1), 18-20.

Tian, Q., Ma, J., Liang, J., Kwok, R. C. W., & Liu, O. (2005). An organizational decision support system for effective R&D project selection. *Decision Support Systems, 39*, 403-413.

Vahidov, R., & Fazlollahi, R. (2003-2004, Winter). A multi-agent DSS for supporting e-commerce decisions. *The Journal of Computer Information Systems, 44*(2), 87-93.

West, L. A., Jr., & Hess, T. J. (2002). Metadata as a knowledge management tool: supporting intelligent agent and end user access to spatial data. *Decision Support Systems, 33*(2), 247-264.

KEY TERMS

Business Analytics (BA): A technological system that collects and evaluates all relevant data then scrutinizes it and puts it into different simulations to find out which one is the most appropriate.

Business Intelligence (BI): A system of technologies for collecting, reviewing, and hoarding data to assist in the decision making process.

Decision Support Systems (DSSs): An interactive, flexible, and adaptable computer-based information system, especially developed for supporting the solution of a non-structured management problem for improved decision making. It utilizes data, provides an easy-to-use interface, and allows for the decision maker's own insights

Interface (or User Interface): A component designed to allow the user to access internal component of a system, also known as the dialogue component of a DSS.

Knowledge Management: The distribution, access, and retrieval of unstructured information about human experiences between interdependent individuals or among members of a workgroup.

Sensitivity Analysis: Running a decision model several times with different inputs so a modeler can analyze the alternative results.

Software Agent: A software program that intelligently performs its duties without human inter-action.

Structured Modeling: A generic design strategy for representing complex objects that are encountered in modeling applications (Srinivasan & Sundaram, 2000).

Transaction Processing System (TPS): Computerized systems that perform and record the daily routine transactions necessary to conduct the business; they serve the organization's operational level.

Use Case: A complete sequence of related actions initiated by an actor; it represents a specific way to use the system.

Chapter IX
A Systematic Implementation of Project Management

John Wang
Montclair State University, USA

James G.S. Yang
Montclair State University, USA

Jun Xia
Montclair State University, USA

ABSTRACT

In contrast to ongoing, functional work, a project is a temporary endeavor undertaken to achieve or create a unique product or service(s). The project management knowledge and practices are best described as component processes—initiating, planning, executing, controlling, and closing. We have taken a closer look at project management by reviewing the types of methodologies and tools that exist in business today. We observed the major existing risk factors facing project management practices. We also evaluated the unique issues in delivering projects brought about by globalization. As we were extracting the information, it became apparent that there should be measures taken related to the project management process that could alleviate the some major risk factors in some way.

INTRODUCTION

A comprehensive management of employee, resources, analytics, customer relationship management (CRM), supply chain, and project management is of paramount importance for modern corporations. Businesses can plan, track, and analyze time and labor through applications for scheduling, time and attendance, leave, and labor. While companies can focus on a number of areas in their efforts to become high performance organizations, this chapter discusses the role that effective project management practices play in this process.

Project management is the discipline of defining and achieving targets while optimizing (or just allocating) the use of resources—time, money, people, materials, energy, space, and so forth, over the course of a project (a set of activities of finite duration). In contrast to ongoing, functional work, a project is a temporary endeavor undertaken to achieve or create a unique product or service(s). The project management knowledge and practices are best described as component processes—initiating, planning, executing, controlling, and closing (Westland, 2006; Jin, Koskela, & King, 2007).

We have taken a closer look at project management by reviewing the types of methodologies and tools that exist in business today. We observed the major existing risk factors facing project management practices. We also evaluated the unique issues in delivering projects brought about by globalization. As we were extracting the information, it became apparent that there should be measures taken related to the project management process that could alleviate the some major risk factors in some way. Our chapter illustrates a solution idea for the project management process, which may close the issue gap with regard to many globalization issues and other identified risks. The idea is to include a sub-process for project management as it applies to the project life cycle, that would benefit an organization internally for a parent organization, and also externally for their client's benefit.

BACKGROUND

There are various methods of project management, which differ, based on the scope and the complexity of the project undertaken. The Gantt chart is a well known standard in project management. Henry Gantt (1861-1919) studied in great detail the order of operations in work. His studies of management focused on Navy ship construction during WWI (Mintzer, 2002). His charts, complete with tasks bars and milestone markers, outlined the sequence and duration of all tasks in a process. These chart diagrams proved to be a very powerful analytical tool for managers, that they remained virtually unchanged for nearly 100 years. The chart plots a number of tasks across a horizontal time scale. It is easy to understand and it allows all team members to maintain the status of their tasks against the projected progress.

Many new techniques have been developed, which emerged from two major network systems, the program evaluation and review technique (PERT) and critical path method (CPM) (Punmia & Khandelwal, 2005). PERT is the method of project scheduling and coordination based on an integrated logic network, first developed by the U.S. Navy in 1958 to plan and control the Polaris missile project (Burgher, 1964). PERT allows for randomness in activity completion times. PERT has the potential of reducing total project lead time as well as reducing the cost of the project. CPM was developed at about the same time, by Remington Rand and DuPont and is very similar differing only in the way in which they arrive at time estimates (Dalcher, 2004; Lechler & Ronen, 2005). In the history of management methods, it would be difficult to find any other techniques which have received as much widespread attention as that of these network methods for planning, scheduling, and controlling. These methods are still very widely used today to achieve the earliest possible completion time at the least possible cost.

CPM is a planning tool developed for more complex projects, as is PERT. CPM provides a graphical view of a project (Lechler & Ronen, 2005). CPM estimates the amount of time required to complete the project and shows which activities are critical to keeping to the projects schedule and which are not. CPM models the activities and events of a project as a network. The larger CPM network may be considered a series of linked conditional statements. Activities are depicted as nodes on the network and events that signify the beginning or ending of activities are depicted as arcs or lines between the nodes. The CPM model is able to discern which activities are dependent on each other. Determining the critical path is at the heart of the CPM model. The critical path is the longest duration through the project's full network. A delay in the critical path results in a delay in the project's total completion time. Opportunities may be to "crash" or accelerate a project's completion time by reducing the allotted time for one or more activities of the project. CPM was developed for more complex projects but projects that are somewhat routine in nature with a minimal amount of uncertainty. A limitation of the CPM model is for projects with a high degree of uncertainty; this uncertainty limits the effectiveness of the deterministic CPM model (Dalcher, 2004). This model's inability to consider time variations may have a significant impact on accurately estimating a project's total completion.

An alternative to the CPM model of project management is PERT. Unlike the CPM model, PERT allows for randomness in activity completion times. PERT has the potential of reducing total project lead time as well as reducing the cost of the project. In a project, an activity is a task that must be performed and an event is a milestone marking the completion of one or more activities. Before an activity can begin, all of its predecessor activities must be completed. Project managers, now more than ever, need to posses knowledge, skill, and expertise in every aspect of project management methodology. Of the many certifications, *project management institute*'s (PMI) project management professional (PMP) is the most widely recognized of any project management credential (Carbone & Gholston, 2004).

We have explored the existing methods of project management and their effects on overall implementations. It is evident that there may be a gap with the normal process that we believe is an important factor in successful implementations. Secondly, we would like to evaluate what the prevalent risk factors are related to project management in addition to the issues brought about by globalization, a need for process training. When change is needed, either within an organization, or within a client project, it should be addressed in a consistent, procedure driven way, so the company can reduce ambiguity, and learn from its past mistakes by amicably agreeing on what is a best. With our evaluation, we will assert a commonality with the various risks and propose an idea for improvement through change control. Finally, we touch upon a future trend which may per-

haps change the landscape of project management and the overall future role of the project manager.

Risk Associated with Project Management

In today's environment, risk is associated with every aspect of life; there is healthy risk and unhealthy risk—resulting in numerous reasons for failure in project management (Peters, 1987). Failure continues to be viewed as an organizational taboo even though corporate values such as learning and active experimentation for growth and profitability are increasingly exposed in this modern economy.

However, the fear and intolerance of failure go against the tenets of organizational learning and continuous improvement (Thorne, 2000). If failure is ignored, denied, or repressed, the opportunity to learn from past mistakes is lost. So when failure is embraced as an integral part of learning and development, much deeper insights into success can be gained (Chua & Lam, 2005).

The main reasons for failures in project management are often thought to be over-cost, behind schedule, and not meeting the user's needs. It is evident that intervention is an integral part of project management and is important in the prevention of project failures. The complexity of projects should determine the types of monitoring and the frequency. It may require periodic checks. Early detection of a problem allows the project manager to escalate or de-escalate commitment to the project. In escalating, additional resources may be all that is needed to prevent a potentially catastrophic business failure. In reexamining the project, it allows an alternative course of action or the implementation of an exit strategy (Ivory & Aderman, 2005). Below are some types of risk leading to the failure of project management practices (Aiyer, Rajkumar, & Havelka, 2005):

- Problems are denied
- Denial in detection of problems

- Lack of communication to stakeholders defining the nature and magnitude

Also, organizational issues may originate from selecting team members from different areas. This sometimes results in rigid points of view, lack of collaboration, lack of trust, usually because the project is short term, and on a temporary basis resulting in minimal cooperation from participants.

In addition to these, the project manager may have difficulty communicating upstream and downstream without having sufficient authority over either group (Kuhl, Schnelle, & Tillmann, 2005). Causes of technology failures, as originally stated by Perrow (1984) and confirmed by Ivory & Alderman (2005), are:

- Multiple interactions since an nonlinear behavior can be either positive or negative in a project context
- Internal contradictions
- Multiple sites of control and influence
- Some interactions occur deep within the system and are hidden
- Low quality service from suppliers resulted from the fact that the project would not result in a long-term stream of work for the suppliers
- Contradictory demands of safety and speed need to co-exist and as such, complex systems can never be entirely coherent. This was originally stated by Law (2000) and confirmed by Ivory & Alderman (2005)

As Augustine, Payne, Sencindiver, and Woodcock (2007) discovered, leading a team by establishing a guiding vision, nurturing small, dynamic teams, setting simple rules, championing open information, and managing with a light touch is extremely challenging

An example of this is with a complex system implementation. When there are many linked tasks to complete a milestone, the impact one task has on a group might overlook some important aspects

needed for a future task that depends on it. This could have downstream effects on the usability of the final product, causing a defect not foreseen by the original resource. This could add additional costs to debug or identify the cause of original failure. These risks are generic to most projects and we agree that they still exist today.

From our observation, most employees are reluctant to share ideas to help foster needed change, due to fear that they might lose their jobs to outsourcing or outside consultants. Most improvements via technology usually result in staff reduction; as a result, many employees and some managers are very reluctant to share ideas that will eliminate their jobs and return profit to the company at their expense. On the other hand, the opposite of staff reduction sometimes could happen under certain circumstances.

Large ongoing projects may lead to failure simply because the length of time required for project development and anchoring. This increases the project's exposure to potential risk events (Miller & Hobbs, 2005). In most cases, by the time the project is completed, most of the software used is outdated or the resources are drained, or in some cases, the original vendors could be taken over by larger software house. This can result in loss of relationships between the company and their consultants; the new organization might be difficult to conduct business with or simply not supportive the old business strategy. There might be claims and counterclaims about broken promises, leading to additional cost factors with litigation and claims, and so forth.

Change Management and Project Success

"We are experiencing an acceleration of change in our generation. Project management has to be...able to change the architecture of an organization," according to Semler. "Project management has to be more strategic; it has to be able to change the architecture of an organization" (2006). Change is imminent and change is constant, especially with the technological advances happening today. The way which employees deal with change in project driven organizations is often with great hesitation or even avoidance. We believe that this could lead to inconsistencies lacking repetitiveness, lead to lost revenue, and ultimate project failure. We hope to demonstrate how change management affects the project success framework by starting with detailing the project management process, issues, and flaws.

While we can infer that standardization is important for consistency with operational project management. We can see by the issues observed that project management process steps need a closer look to help identify where the process is broken, to see if missing steps or oversight helped to generate or promote any of these risks.

Project success has many challenges. What determines success? Do we limit the definition of success to the implementation phase? Do we need to gain consensus from the stakeholders to determine success? This topic is important because it has bearings on the future direction of project management in the strategic context (Jugdev & Müller, 2005). With that said, one option is to integrate an application process flow, a change management process (strategically, for infrastructure), and then operationally (for clients), based upon the need to repress ambiguity in the organization, and to contain scope creep. We prefer to include a "change management process" as a subset of the overall project management process, regardless of what type of methodology is suited and chosen. Change management is a planned approach to deal with change in an institution. This will ensure maximized benefits for all stakeholders involved, employees, and clients alike. This will minimize the risk of project failure.

Organizations often experience difficulty when taking on new projects, especially when important work needs to be coordinated across different geographical locations. Managers can take practical steps to identify critical commitments within the organization and should locate, diagnose, and

intervene to fix them. Managing by commitment increases flexibility because managers and employees can exercise in selecting the best people to work with and negotiate terms tailored to the task. Employees see a promise as personal security and they work harder to honor that commitment (Sull & Spinosa, 2005). Organizations should establish procedures to manage these criticalities or risk events in a repetitive fashion. The organization, especially global entities, should consider becoming a *learning organization* to disseminate those procedures to all affected functional personnel, by recording and teaching the new process steps of project management. This will solidify the internal tasks necessary to bring about the required change. Commitment to instill learning/teaching to introduce the new process is key.

Project management is the result of managing people, not managing work. Up until now, it was commonly thought that valued project managers stayed within the iron triangle (cost, time, and scope) optimizing these efficiencies, eluding the function to an operational role. As Jugdev and Müller (2005) emphasized that, in fact, the project management function is really more strategic in nature. Organizations need to realize that they must adjust their infrastructure to deliver projects through the best practice tools within their organizations. Whether it be by adding dashboard reviews, risk, action item, or gap metrics reporting, stakeholder or status meetings, project managers must draw attention toward heightened awareness of the importance of presenting input from and to the customer and effectively feed back results with the clients input into the equation. The strategy and mission statement of an organization should include functionality that embraces *change* for all stakeholders, clients, and employees. Definitely, in addition to people, resources, equipment, working capital, and so forth, are also important entities of project management.

In Dewett's research, the main benefits that IT affords organizations have been considered and then applied to the requirements for creative production, the stages of the individual creative process, the process of organizational learning as related to creativity, and the creative process within large-scale project-based work. In keeping with Bromberg (2005), Thomas Edison held 1,093 patents. He guaranteed productivity by giving himself and his assistants idea quotas. In a study of 2,036 scientists throughout history, Dean Keith Simonton of the University of California at Davis found that the most respected scientists produced not only great works, but also many "bad" projects. They were not afraid to fail, or to produce mediocre in order to arrive at excellence.

In the case study of the British Library, Harris (2006) suggests that the bureaucratic context offers a more propitious environment for innovation than has been suggested by managerialist accounts of the "post-bureaucratic organization" in project management. Recently, Hodgson and Cicmil (2007) take as the focus of their analysis, a specific management model which has a significant and growing impact on many sectors of contemporary industry, that of project management. Their discovery shows that the suppression of creativity, innovation in organizations may come from the standardization of contemporary management knowledge.

Groupthink, a term coined by psychologist Irving Janis in 1972, is another barrier for a successful project management. Groupthink is a situation where people think alike and new ideas are not tolerated. Therefore, creativity, innovation, and/or individual responsibility are discouraged and critical thinking is suspended during the decision making process.

Creativity and innovation are vital to organizational success. Project management and knowledge management have increasingly become a major influence on organizational efficiency and effectiveness. We should begin to fill this gap by exploring the ways that project management might influence creativity and innovation in organizations. This is very important for organizational studies, given that knowledge and information are among the most important ingredients for creativity and innovation.

Globalization

In today's working environments, new developments often require cross-functional team members living and working on separate continents, to communicate accurately and effectively. Different languages, cultures, and time zones added complexity to the already difficult task of managing project team members with different perspectives and backgrounds (Barczak, McDonough, & Athanassiou, 2006).

In the current environment, companies have to globalize in order to achieve success in the business. Most large corporations deal with international companies directly or indirectly. No American corporation is immune from the impact of globalization. The fact is corporations must cope with diverse cross-cultural employees, customers, suppliers, competitors, and creditors if they are to become and/or remain successful. People are often not aware of the tremendous impact different cultures have on their vision and interpretation of the world.

Team members cannot fulfill their roles and responsibilities if they do not have necessary information about the project. The project leaders need to share relevant project information with all team members, even if they are not directly affected. By sharing important information with all team members, the project manager also keeps them motivated and committed to the project. This type of sharing is more important in some countries than others, because in some countries employees feel an obligatory sense of responsibility that necessitates a closer relationship with their managers.

Project management strategies are the key elements for corporations when dealing domestically or globally. The best business models and associated processes were those that were fully documented and incorporated within the company's total quality management (TQM) systems. "Good leaders do inspire confidence in themselves, but a truly great leader inspires confidence within the people they lead to exceed their normal performance level" (Prabhakar, 2005). Idealized influence is an important leadership quality that has an impact on a successful project anywhere in the world. With these combinations of global integration practices, success is imminent and measurable.

FUTURE TRENDS

Much research has been done on the methods of project management, but it is evident that more attention is needed on best practice standard methods, namely, the delivery of change control in client projects (operationally) and in project management infrastructure procedures alike. Ambiguity caused by change is probably the single-most derailing element that leads to project failure today. As Bresnen, Goussevskaia, and Swan (2005) observed, "There is a lack of research that explores the micro-processes of organizational change and their effects on the development and emergence of organizational routines."

If the organization had the vision to implement a robust change control process for all client and infrastructural work, it could tackle this ambiguity and turn it into a welcomed positive aspect for the organization and clients. The client will consider this process as a highly organized component to the business, eliminating questions, controlling scope creep, and adding overall value to new service or product offerings in the future, thus improving client and employee relationships. A change control process would not only manage ad-hoc requests by clients, but also to deal with systems and process changes within the infrastructure of the organization.

It is apparent that organizations are examining the nature and dynamics of organizational routines and their relationship to change processes today. We believe it will increase knowledge and learning across all functional teams, but not without capturing this and other processes in some type of learning vehicle, such as learning management systems (LMS). The capturing, storing, training, and then re-evaluating the best practices procedures

are key factors to project management and overall success.

There is much resistance to change and less willingness with sharing knowledge for fear of having one's position eliminated. If a procedure or uniform planning mechanism were established across all projects, there would be accountability and acceptability on all fronts. Today there exists *business practice management* (BPM) software that is an example of such a learning vehicle for intercontinental organizations willing to optimize processes. What we foresee is the software to incorporate a process evaluation for us. While this may prove to be a daunting invention, we see this as a very real possibility. BPM is different from conventional approaches in that it hinges on *continuous process improvement* (CPI) as their core competency and philosophy (Miers, 2006).

We see a future trend as similar learning software as having the capability to detect or "alert" organizations when breakthrough developments emerge, which are closely related to the current organizational process or technological application(s). The implications of an "alerting" system would be vast and great if it could be applied. Of course, our opinion is that the use of subject matter experts would still be required to evaluate how the alerts were applied. This alerting system could revolutionize project management process in that a proactive approach could be taken by applying new and better methods. This would ultimately change the role of the project manager to a less administrative role, task pusher, risk mitigator, to the people manager, with less emphasis paid to issues and risks related to "missing" steps, or overlooking the quality of a task performed. Certainly, system designers, systems analysts, administrators, and managers have a big role to play in the future.

CONCLUSION

Project management is the application of knowledge, skills, tools, and techniques to a broad range of activities in order to meet the requirements of the particular project. The methods of project management must be evaluated on a company basis to decide which method is best for its organization to implement its projects. If possible, an analysis should precede it to find what processes need improvement, if any. The new proposal of incorporating change management procedures overall, would also be useful with any project management method. Whether utilizing a Gantt chart, PERT chart, CPM network, dashboard reporting, overall team procedures with meeting schedules, and pertinent project information needs to be disseminated to all functional team members and stakeholders alike.

With the risks today, all organizations must realize the value of our mistakes. With all projects, success needs to be defined, and overall project lessons learned must be admitted and documented. Mistakes or risks in projects should be raised as soon as they are found, and in conjunction with the client involvement. This will alleviate catastrophic failure. Failure in any way should be embraced, not punished or looked upon as negative. With global knowledge database incorporation, organizations could capture these lessons and improve upon their processes to correct any future actions. This emphasis on risk identification, process documentation, and overall communication, must be emphasized from the top stakeholder down to the last functional team members, especially important with global team members. This will ensure a vehicle for organizations to always keep up with the ever-changing organization strategy and vision.

Then change management is an additional subprocess step, which might be a consideration for the project management process overall to help capture the ever-present change requests, whether it be out of scope (scope creep) items or in scope (overlooked) items needed for any client projects, or actual organizational process steps. Any of these items cause additional work and may be a root cause for not having tasks completed on time. With globalization, having people work on projects in functional roles across continents is an added constraint. To break

down restrictions with borders, it is important for organizations to relay all necessary information about a project to these global constituents, including the methods of project management and the steps necessary to complete the project. Communication and learning is the key.

The top stakeholder must make a commitment to put forth this strategy, because this will unite all team members together and motivate them to commit to the project's success. Globalization and outsourcing is an ever-increasing reality today and attention must be paid to process steps and knowledge storage. This is why it is important to have organizations seriously consider using a training tool for all team members in all areas of the world. Here is where we should document all functional procedures, including project management procedures.

We can always fix technical failures, however, it is more challenging to understand the cause of the problems and how people factors are impacted in the ultimate success of a system implementation in an organization. A careful and continuous analysis of risks, gaps, and issues will minimize problems in the future. System analysis and design managers, practitioners, researchers, instructors, and so forth, should be knowledgeable about project management.

REFERENCES

Aiyer, J., Rajkumar, M. T., & Havelka, D. (2005). A staged framework for the recovery and rehabilitation of troubled IS development projects. *Project Management Journal, 36*(4), 32-44.

Augustine, S., Payne, B., Sencindiver, F., & Woodcock, S. (2005). Agile project management: steering from the edges. *Communications of the ACM, 48*(12), 85-89. Online http://agileprojectmgt.org/docs/augustine2.pdf

Barczak, G., McDonough, E. F., & Athanassiou, N. (2006). So you want to be a global project leader? *Research Technology Management, 49*(3), 28-38.

Bresnen, M., Goussevskaia, A., & Swan, J. (2005). Organizational routines, situated learning and processes of change in project-based organizations. *Project Management Journal, 36*(3), 27-41.

Bromberg, P.A. (2005). *Developer productivity as science and art.* Retrieved on Aug. 25, 2007, from http://www.eggheadcafe.com/articles/20051218.asp

Burgher, P. H. (1964). PERT and the auditor. *Accounting Review, 39*(1), 103-104.

Carbone, T., & Gholston, S. (2004). Project manager skill development: A survey of programs and practitioners. *Engineering Management Journal, 16*(3), 10-16.

Chua, A., & Lam, W. (2005). Why KM projects fail: a multi-case analysis. *Journal of Knowledge Management, 9*(3), 6-17.

Dalcher, D. (2004). Methods—project management. *Project Management Journal, 35*(2), 51.

Dewett, T. (2003). Understanding the relationship between information technology and creativity in organizations. *Creativity Research Journal, 15*(2&3), 167-182.

Harris, M. (2006). Technology, innovation and post-bureaucracy: the case of the British Library. *Journal of Organizational Change Management, 19*(1), 80-92.

Hodgson, D., & Cicmil, S. (2007). The politics of standards in modern management: Making 'the project' a reality. *Journal of Management Studies, 44*(3), 431-450.

Ivory, C., & Alderman, N. (2005). Can project management learn anything from studies of failure in complex systems? *Project Management Journal, 36*(3), 5-17.

Jin, X. M., Koskela, L., & King, T. M. (2007). Towards an integrated enterprise model: combining product life cycle support with project management. *International Journal of Product Lifecycle Management (IJPLM), 2*(1), 50-63.

Jugdev, K., & Müller, R. (2005). A retrospective look at our evolving understanding of project success. *Project Management Journal, 36*(4), 1-19.

Kuhl, S., Schnelle, T., & Tillman, F. J. (2005). Lateral Leadership: An organizational approach to change. *Journal of Change Management, 5*(2), 177-190.

Law, J. (2000). *Ladbroke Grove, or how to think about failing systems.* Lancaster University, Lancaster LA, UK: Centre for Science Studies. Retrieved Aug. 25, 2007, from http://www.lancs.ac.uk/fss/sociology/papers/law-mol-local-entanglements-utopias-and-train-accidents.pdf

Lechler, T., & Ronen, B. (2005). Critical chain: A new project management paradigm or old wine in new bottles? *Engineering Management Journal, 17*(4), 45-59.

Miers, D. (2006). Best practice (BPM). *ACM Queue, 4*(2), 40-49.

Miller, R., & Hobbs, B. (2005). Governance regimes for large complex projects. *Project Management Journal, 36*(3), 42-51.

Mintzer, R. (2002). *The everything project management book.* Avon, Mass: Adams Media Corporation.

Perrow, C. (1984). *Normal accidents: Living with high risk technologies.* New York: Basic Books.

Peters, T. (1987). *Thriving on chaos: Handbook for management revolution.* New York: Harper-Collins.

Prabhakar, G. P. (2005). An empirical study reflecting the importance of transformational leadership on project success across twenty-eight nations. *Project Management Journal, 36*(4), 53-60.

Punmia, B. C., & Khandelwal, K. (2005). *Project planning and control PERT and CPM.* New Delhi, India: Laxmi Publications.

Semler, R. F. (2006). International project management day. *PMI Today Project Management Institute, 1*(1), 1-10.

Sull, D. N., & Spinosa, C. (2005, Fall). Using commitments to manage across units. *MIT Sloan Management Review, 47*(1), 73-82.

Thorne, M. L. (2000). Interpreting corporate transformation through failure. *Management Decision, 38*(5), 305-314.

Westland, J. (2006). *The project management life cycle: A complete step-by-step methodology for initiating, planning, executing & closing a project successfully.* Philadelphia: Kogan Page.

KEY TERMS

Business Process Management (BPM): An approach or technique that is applied to work flow models. It refers to a set of activities, which organizations can perform to either optimize their business processes or adapt them to new organizational needs. As software tools usually aid these activities, the term BPM is synonymously used to refer to the software tools themselves.

Change Control: A formal process used to ensure a product, service, or process is only modified in line with the identified necessary change. It is particularly related to development as during the early development of this engineering process it was found that many changes were introduced to software that had no obvious requirement other than the whim of the software writer. Quite often these unnecessary changes introduced faults (bugs) necessitating further change.

Critical Path Method (CPM): One of the techniques used in project planning. It is ideal for projects that are made up of numerous individual activities, some of which require other activities to finish before they can start. The activities are linked to show task relationship predecessors and successors, which then reveals a variety of paths, including the longest path, the "critical" one (hence the name!).

Learning Management Systems (LMS): Allows anyone with a personal computer and Internet access to enroll in Web-based courses and performs interim progress tracking and submits to the learning management system server for permanent storage. IBM first invented this system for the use of domestic and global learning when training was necessary for specific types of projects (i.e., privacy issues).

Program Evaluation and Review Techniques (PERT): A project management technique for determining how much time a project needs before it is completed. Each activity is assigned a best, worst, and most probable completion time estimate. These estimates are used to determine the average completion time. The average times are used to figure the critical path and the standard deviation of completion times for the entire project.

Scope Creep: It is the slow and continuous expansion of the scope of a project, such as data type or routine, resulting in a broad, unfocused, and unmanageable scope and usually leads to cost-overruns, missed deadlines, and loss of original goals.

Total Quality Management (TQM): The process that a company uses to achieve quality, where the goal is elimination of all defects. It is also a management strategy to increase awareness of quality in all organizational processes.

Chapter X
Decision Rule for Investment in Frameworks of Reuse

Roy Gelbard
Bar-Ilan University, Israel

ABSTRACT

Reuse helps to decrease development time, code errors, and code units. Therefore, it serves to improve quality and productivity frameworks in software development. The question is not HOW to make the code reusable, but WHICH amount of software components would be most beneficial, that is, cost-effective in terms of reuse, and WHAT method should be used to decide whether to make a component reusable or not. If we had unlimited time and resources, we could write any code unit in a reusable way. In other words, its reusability would be 100%. However, in real life, resources are limited and there are clear deadlines to be met. Given these constraints, decisions regarding reusability are not always straightforward. The current research focuses on decision-making rules for investing in reuse frameworks. It attempts to determine the parameters, which should be taken into account in decisions relating to degrees of reusability. Two new models are presented for decision-making relating to reusability: (i) a restricted model and (ii) a non-restricted model. Decisions made by using these models are then analyzed and discussed.

INTRODUCTION

Reuse helps decrease development time, code errors, and code units, thereby improving quality and productivity frameworks in software development. Reuse is based on the premise that educing a solution from the statement of a problem involves more effort (labor, computation, etc.) than inducing a solution from a similar problem for which such efforts have already been expended. Therefore, reuse challenges are structural, organizational, and managerial, as well as technical.

Economic considerations and cost-benefit analyses in general, must be at the center of any discussion of software reuse; hence, the cost-benefit issue is not HOW to make the code reusable, but WHICH amount of software components would be most beneficial, that is, cost-effective for reuse, and WHAT method should be used when deciding whether to make a component reusable or not.

If we had unlimited time and resources, we could write any code unit in a reusable way. In other words, its reusability would be 100% (reusability refers to the degree to which a code unit can be reused). However, in real life, resources are limited and there are clear deadlines to be met. Given these constraints, reusability decisions are not always straightforward.

A review of the relevant literature shows that there are a variety of models used for calculating-evaluating reuse effectiveness, but none apparently focus on the issue of the degree to which a code is reusable. Thus, the real question is how to make reusability pragmatic and efficient, that is, a decision rule for investment in reuse frameworks. The current study focuses on the parameters, which should be taken into account when making reusability degree decisions. Two new models are presented here for reusability decision-making:

- A non-restricted model, which does not take into account time, resources, or investment restrictions.
- A restricted model, which takes the above-mentioned restrictions into account.

The models are compared, using the same data, to test whether they lead to the same conclusions or whether a contingency approach is preferable.

BACKGROUND

Notwithstanding differences between reuse approaches, it is useful to think of software reuse research in terms of attempts to minimize the average cost of a reuse occurrence (Mili, Mili, & Mili, 1995).

*[Search + (1-p) * (ApproxSearch +q *Adaptation old + (1-q)* Development new)]*

Where:

- *Search* (*ApproxSearch*) is the average cost of formulating a search statement of a library of reusable components and either finding one that matches the requirements exactly (appreciatively), or being convinced that none exists.
- *Adaptation* old is the average cost of adapting a component returned by approximate retrieval.
- *Development* new is the average cost of developing a component that has no match, exact or approximate, in the library.

For reuse to be cost-effective, the above must be smaller than:

p *Development* exact +*(1-p)* q * *Development* approx +*(1-p)* *(1-q)´ Development* new)

Where:

- *Development* exact and *development* new represent the average cost of developing custom-tailored versions of components in the library that could be used as is, or adapted, respectively. Note that all these averages are time averages, and not averages of individual components, that is, a reusable component is counted as many times as it is used.

Developing reusable software aims at maximizing P (probability of finding an exact match) and Q (probability of finding an approximate match), that is, maximizing the coverage of the application domain and minimizing adaptation for a set of common mismatches, that is, packaging components in such a way that the most common old mismatches are handled easily. Increasing P and Q does not necessarily mean putting more components in the library; it could also mean adding components that are more frequently needed, because adding components not only has its direct expenses (adaptation costs), but also increases search costs.

There are two main approaches to **code adaptation**: (1) identifying components that are generally useful and (2) covering the same set of needs with fewer components, which involves two paradigms: (i) abstraction and (ii) composition. Composition supports the creation of a virtually unlimited number of aggregates from the same set of components, and reduces the risk of combinatorial explosion that would result from enumerating all the possible configurations. In general, the higher the level of abstraction at which composition takes place, the wider the range of systems (and behaviours) that can be obtained. The combination of abstraction and composition provides a powerful paradigm for constructing systems from reusable components (Mili et al., 1995).

Frakes and Terry describe a wide range of metrics and adaptation models for software reuse. Six types of metrics and models are reviewed: cost-benefit models, maturity assessment models, amount of reuse metrics, failure modes models, reusability assessment models, and reuse library metrics (Frakes & Terry, 1996).

Other studies (Henninger, 1999; Otso, 1995; Virtanen, 2000; Ye, Fischer, & Reeves, 2000; Ye & Fischer, 2002), present additional metrics and methods, evaluate and make comparisons, but as is typical in an emerging discipline such as systematic software reuse, many of these metrics and models still lack formal validation. Despite this, they are used and are found useful in industrial practice (Ferri et al., 1997; Chaki, Clarke, Groce, Jha, & Veith, 2004).

Empirical work (Mens & Tourwé, 2004; Paulson, Succi, & Eberlein, 2004; Tomer, Goldin, Kuflik, Kimchi, & Schach, 2004; Virtanen, 2001; Ye, 2002) has analyzed existing reuse metrics and their industrial applicability. These metrics are then applied to a collection of public domain software products and projects categories to assess the level of correlation between them and other well-known software metrics such as complexity, volume, lines of code, and so forth.

Current research is focused on decision-making rules for investment in reuse frameworks. The well-known "simple model" and "development cost model" deal with these decisions, but do not take into account restrictions and constraints such as time, budget, resources, or other kinds of investment, such as delivery time, that may impact on the decision to reuse.

ANALYZING NEW REUSE MODELS

Assume a software development project contains 3 code components: A, B, and C, and we need to determine two things: Which of these components should be reusable? What criteria should be taken into account?

There are eight combinations—choice alternatives for these 3 components, as shown in Table 1 (+ represents "make reusable," - represents "don't make reusable").

A. The Non-Restricted Model

The model contains the following parameters:

- **Ci**—cost of creating component **i** from scratch (without making it reusable).
- **Ri**—cost of making component **i** reusable (extra costs – not included in **Ci**).
- **ICi**—cost of implementing reusable component **i** into code.
- **NRi**—number of reuses of component i. (C, R, and NR are in man-hours).

Savings resulting from making component **i** reusable are represented as follows:

$$SAV_i = NR_i * (C_i - IC_i) - (C_i + R_i)$$

Therefore: If **SAVi** > 0, it is worthwhile to make component **i** reusable.

Suppose a company that employs two kinds of programmers: **M** and **N**. Programmers of type **M**

Table 1. Choice alternatives

Alternative	Component A	Component B	Component C
1	-	-	-
2	+	-	-
3	-	+	-
4	+	+	-
5	-	-	+
6	+	-	+
7	-	+	+
8	+	+	+

are permanent employees of the firm. Programmers of type **N** are highly qualified consultants who are employed by the company for specific projects. The company is going to write/create/develop a new project, and has to make a decision regarding which components should be reusable.

The following are additional parameters:

- **Cim**—hours needed for programmer M to create component **i** from scratch.
- **Rim**—hours needed for programmer M to make component **i** reusable.
- **ICim**—hours needed for programmer M to implement reusable component **i** into code.
- **Sm**—costs of programmer M, per 1 hour.

Hence:

$$Ci= Min(Cim*Sm, Cin*Sn)$$
$$Ici= Min(ICim*Sm, ICin*Sn)$$
$$Ri= Min(Rim*Sm, Rin*Sn)$$

Hence:

$$SAVi = NRi *(Min(Cim*Sm, Cin*Sn) - Min(ICim*Sm, ICin*Sn)) - (Min(Cim*Sm, Cin*Sn) + Min(Rim*Sm, Rin*Sn))$$

B. The Restricted Model

The non-restricted model has the following limitations:

- It requires absolute values
- It is quite difficult to measure parameters such as: **Ci**, **Ri**, and **Ici**
- It does not take into account the most typical situation where time and budget are restricted as well as in-house investment in reuse, that is, time and resources for reusable code developing.

In order to avoid these limitations, the restricted model is based upon the following parameters:

- **I**—maximal **investment** that can be allocated for writing a reusable code.
- **T**—maximal calendar **time** that can be allocated for writing a reusable code.
- **Ii**—percent of "**I**" needed to make component **i** reusable.
- **Ti**—percent of "**T**" needed to make component **i** reusable.
- **Ci**—relative **complexity** of creating component **i** from scratch.
- **Fi**—**frequency** (%) of future projects that are likely to reuse component **i**.
- **Pi**—relative **profit** of making component **i** reusable.
- **R$_I$**—remainder of "**I**", after some reusable components have been written.
- **R$_T$**—remainder of "**T**," after some reusable components have been written.

Assume that: $P_i = C_i * F_i$.

Hence: component **i** is the next component to be made reusable if:

$P_i = Max(P_1, P_2, ..., P_{n-1}, P_n)$
$I_i <= RI$
$T_i <= RT$

C. Illustrative Example: Non-Restricted Model

The following example (Example 1) demonstrates the decision made by the non-restricted model. Assume we want to develop 10 projects, each one containing components A, B, and C according to Table 2.

Hence: $NR_a = 10$, $NR_b = 1$, $NR_c = 4$

Table 3 presents illustrative assumptions concerning **Cim** and **Cin** (hours needed for programmer type M and N to create component **i** from scratch).
Moreover, assume programmers' costs to be: $S_m = 20$, $S_n = 40$

Hence:

$C_a = Min(300*20, 200*40) = 6,000$
$C_b = Min(20*20, 10*40) = 400$
$C_c = Min(150*20, 100*40) = 3,000$

Table 4 presents illustrative assumptions concerning **Rim** and **Rin** (hours needed for programmers type M and N to make component **i** reusable).

Hence:

$R_a = Min(650*20, 300*40) = 12,000$
$R_b = Min(15*20, 7*40) = 280$
$R_c = Min(150*20, 80*40) = 3,000$

Table 5 presents illustrative assumptions concerning **ICim** and **ICin** (hours needed for programmers type M /N to implement reusable component **i** into code).

Hence:

$IC_a = Min(60*20, 15*40) = 600$
$IC_b = Min(5*20, 3*40) = 100$
$IC_c = Min(50*20, 10*40) = 400$

Table 2. Example 1, number of components for future reuse

Project	1	2	3	4	5	6	7	8	9	10
Component A	+	+	+	+	+	+	+	+	+	+
Component B	+									
Component C	+	+	+	+						

Table 3. Example 1, Ci illustrative assumptions

Programmer type	Component A	Component B	Component C
Type M	*300*	*20*	*150*
Type N	*200*	*10*	*100*

Table 4. Example 1, Ri illustrative assumptions

Programmer type	Component A	Component B	Component C
Type M	*650*	*15*	*150*
Type N	*300*	*7*	*80*

Table 5. Example 1, ICi illustrative assumptions

Programmer type	Component A	Component B	Component C
Type M	*60*	*5*	*50*
Type N	*15*	*3*	*10*

Hence:

SAVa = 10 *(6,000 − 600) − (6,000 + 12,000) = 36000 > 0

SAVb = 1 *(400 − 100) − (400 + 280) = -380 < 0

SAVc = 4 *(3000− 400) − (3,000+ 3,000) = 4400 > 0

In light of the mentioned, the reuse decision according to the non-restricted model is to make components A and C reusable (i.e., alternative 6).

D. Illustrative Example: Restricted Model

The following example (Example 2) demonstrates the decision made by the restricted model, based on the previous example (Example 1). Assume the following:

1. **I**—10,000.
2. **T**—150. The available remaining time to make the existing code reusable.
3. **Ci**—assume component B is the easiest one to develop, and requires 10 hours. Assume component A requires 300 hours and component C requires 150 hours. Hence, complexities are: C_A=30, C_B=1, C_C=15.
4. **Fi**—component A will be reused by 100% of future projects, B by 10%, and C by 40%.

5. I_A = 12,000/10,000 = 120%, I_B = 280/10,000 = 2.8%, I_C = 3000/10,000 = 30%.
6. T_A = 300/150 = 200%, T_B = 7/150 = 4.7%, T_C = 150/150 = 100%.

Hence Example 2 parameters are shown in Table 6.

Taking time and investment restrictions into account, the reuse decision, according to the restricted model is to make only component C reusable (i.e., alternative 5).

CONCLUSION AND FUTURE TRENDS

The current study presented two new reuse decision making models: a restricted model and a non restricted model, which mainly differ in the way they take into account real-life constraints-restrictions such as time, budget, and resources repetition.

The models produced different results from the same data. The decision made by the restricted model pinpointed fewer software components for reuse. It is worth mentioning that different groups of software components were not the issue, but rather different subgroups of the same group, that is, software components selected by the restricted model were subgroups of components selected by the non-restricted model.

Table 6. Parameters used by Example 2

Component	Ci	Fi(%)	Pi	Ii(%)	Ti(100%)
A	*30*	*100*	*30*	*120*	*200*
B	*1*	*10*	*0.1*	*2.8*	*4.7*
C	*15*	*40*	*0.6*	*30*	*100*

Moreover, the parameters of the restricted model relate to relative value arguments, by contrast to the parameters of non-restricted model, which relate to absolute values. While absolute values are difficult to measure, relative values are simpler to define. There are a variety of formal methods by which relative values may be defined, methods that are used in other areas of software engineering, such as cost estimation, effort estimation, priority decision, and others.

The reusability decision made by the restricted model may be biased by the following parameters: time, resources, component complexity, and number-percent of future projects in which the component would be reused. Further research should be conducted, focusing on decision robustness in light of the mentioned parameters and their possible spectrum.

ACKNOWLEDGMENT

I would like to thank Tami Shapiro for her contribution to this work.

REFERENCES

Chaki, S., Clarke, E. M., Groce, A., Jha, S., & Veith, H. (2004). Modular verification of software components. *IEEE Transactions on Software Engineering, 30*(6), 388-402.

Desouza, K. C., Awazu, Y., & Tiwana, A. (2006). Four dynamics for bringing use back into software reuse. *Communications of the ACM, 49*(1), 96-100.

Ferri, R. N., Pratiwadi, R. N., Rivera, L. M., Shakir, M., Snyder, J. J., Thomas, D. W. et al. (1997). Software reuse: Metrics for an industrial project. In *Proceedings of the 4th International Symposium of Software Metrics* (pp.165-173).

Fischer, G., & Ye, Y. (2001). Personalizing delivered information in a software reuse environment. In *Proceedings of the 8th International Conference on User Modeling* (p. 178).

Frakes, W., & Terry, C. (1996). Software reuse: Metrics and models. *ACM Computing Surveys, 28*(2), 415-435.

Henninger, S. (1999). An evolutionary approach to constructing effective software reuse repositories. *ACM Transactions on Software Engineering and Methodology, 6*(2), 111-140.

Kirk, D., Roper, M., & Wood, M. (2006). Identifying and addressing problems in object-oriented framework reuse. *Empirical Software Engineering, 12*(3), 243-274.

Mens, T., & Tourwé, T. (2004). A survey of software refactoring. *IEEE Transactions on Software Engineering, 30*(2), 126-139.

Mili, H., Mili, F., & Mili, A. (1995). Reusing software: Issues and research directions. *IEEE Transactions on Software Engineering, 21*(6), 528–562.

Otso, K. J. (1995). *A systematic process for reusable software component selection* (Tech. Rep.). University of Maryland.

Paulson, J. W., Succi, G., & Eberlein, A. (2004). An Empirical study of open-source and closed-source software products. *IEEE Transactions on Software Engineering, 30*(4), 246-256.

Reifer, D. J. (1997). *Practical software reuse.* Wiley.

Spinellis, D. (2007). Cracking software reuse. *IEEE Software, 24*(1), 12-13.

Tomer, A., Goldin, L., Kuflik, T., Kimchi, E., & Schach, S. R. (2004). Evaluating software reuse alternatives: A model and its application to an industrial case study. *IEEE Transactions on Software Engineering, 30*(9), 601-612.

Virtanen, P. (2000). Component reuse metrics—Assessing human aspects. In *Proceedings of the ESCOM-SCOPE* (pp. 171-179).

Virtanen, P. (2001). Empirical study evaluating component reuse metrics. In *Proceedings of the ESCOM* (pp. 125-136).

William, B., Frakes, W. B. & Kang, K. (2005). Software reuse research: Status and future. *IEEE Transactions on Software Engineering, 31*(7), 529-536.

Ye, Y. (2002). An empirical user study of an active reuse repository system. In *Proceedings of the 7th International Conference on Software Reuse* (pp. 281-292).

Ye, Y., & Fischer, G. (2002). Supporting reuse by delivering task-relevant and personalized information. In *Proceedings of the International Conference on Software Engineering* (pp. 513-523).

Ye, Y., Fischer, G., & Reeves, B. (2000). Integrating active information delivery and reuse repository systems. In *Proceedings of ACM-SIGSOFT 8th International Symposium on Foundations of Software Engineering* (pp. 60-68).

KEY TERMS

Decision Rule: Either a formal or heuristic rule used to determine the final outcome of the decision problem.

Non-Restricted Reuse-Costing Model is a reuse-costing model that does not take into account real-life constraints and restrictions, such as time, budget, resources, or any other kind of investment.

Reuse: Using an item more than once. This includes conventional reuse where the item is used again for the same function and new-life reuse where it is used for a new function (wikipedia).

Reuse-Costing Model: A formal model, which takes into account the expenditure to produce a reusable software product.

Restricted Reuse-Costing Model: A reuse-costing model that takes into account real-life constraints and restrictions such as time, budget, resources, or any other kind of investment.

Software Reuse: Also called code reuse, is the use of existing software components (e.g., routines, functions, classes, objects, up to the entire module) to build new software.

Chapter XI
Strategies for Static Tables

Dean Kelley
Minnesota State University, Mankato, USA

ABSTRACT

This chapter presents three alternatives for structuring static tables—those tables in which the collection of keys remains unchanged and in which the FIND operation is optimized. Each alternative provides performance guarantees for the FIND operation which can help those who design and/or implement systems achieve performance guarantees of their own. The chapter provides clear and concise algorithms for construction and/or usage and simple guidelines for choosing among the strategies. It is intended that this presentation will help inform system design decisions. It is further intended that this chapter will assist implementation activities for systems which make use of static tables.

INTRODUCTION

System designers and implementers are frequently required to guarantee system performance. Often, performance depends on efficient interaction with tables and dictionaries of data. When table operations require communication via resources whose availability may not be guaranteed (e.g., networked communication with a database), designers/implementers may not be able to make firm guarantees of system or system component performance. Consequently, it may be necessary to incorporate tables into a system rather than rely on external support for them.

Generally, tables fall into two categories depending on the type of operations they are required to support. *Static* tables are ones which, once built, do not change. The set of keys that they contain remains unchanged throughout their lifetime (although the data associated with the keys may change). A *dynamic* table may change its set of keys by means of insertion and deletion during the time that the table is active. Both types of table support searching to determine if a specific key is present as well as to retrieve data associated with a key.

This chapter focuses on techniques for implementing static tables. The first section presents necessary technical background. The second section presents a general technique for situations in which keys can be totally ordered and searching can be accomplished by key comparisons. The third section extends that technique to a situation in which the probabilities for search operations for each key are known. The fourth section presents a technique in which, at most, a single key comparison is required and that comparison is only for equality, consequently the keys do not need to be totally ordered.

The topics of this chapter provide system designers and implementers with alternatives for static tables which can yield firm guarantees of performance.

BACKGROUND

This chapter is concerned with *static* tables, tables in which data are associated with keys and the set of keys remains unchanged throughout the life of the table. Access to a specific item of data is accomplished by searching for its key by means of a FIND operation.

Table techniques are evaluated by their consumption of time and space. Time is measured by the number of key comparisons which take place during a FIND operation. Space is measured by the size of the structure(s) necessary to contain the keys and additional supporting data necessary to make the technique work. We do not include the "user" data associated with the keys in the space cost.

Key comparisons may be for equality ("k_1 equals k_2") or order ("k_1 is before k_2"). The search techniques of the second and third sections require comparisons for order. Consequently, the comparison of any two keys in the set of keys must yield information about their relative order. When a relation equivalent to "$\leq$" holds for all elements of a set, that set is said to be *totally ordered*. Thus, the techniques of the second and third sections require that the keys be from a totally ordered set.

The study of efficient techniques for static tables owes much to the paper by Yao (1981). In this paper it was shown that if the number of keys in the table is small relative to the number of possible keys, then the number of comparisons necessary to determine if a particular key is present (and where it is) is $\Omega(\log n)$. That is, it requires at least a constant times $\log n$ comparisons. Consequently, binary search in a

sorted array (the topic of the second section) is the best approach under these circumstances.

Alternatives to array-based tables lead to tree-like structures built with links. In the third section, we present a specific type of binary tree structure, the *optimal binary search tree*, which yields a guarantee of the *average* number of key comparisons over all possible searches. Binary search trees were independently discovered by a number of people. Gilbert and Moore (1959) provided the basis for constructing optimal binary search trees when the probabilities of each key being searched for are known.

Yao (1981) also observed that by allowing one additional item to be stored, the $\Omega(\log n)$ bound can be beat and constant-time FIND performance is possible. Typically, the additional item is the name of a hash function. Fredman, Komlòs, and Szemerédi (1984) showed that there is a structuring technique which uses $n+o(n)$ space and attains $O(1)$ time for the FIND operation. The tool of the final section is based on the improved technique of Czech, Havas, and Majewski (1992) and Majewski, Wormald, Havas, and Czech (1996).

SORTED TABLES

A *comparison-based* search technique is one in which information about the location of a key is obtained by comparing it with keys in the table. Comparison-based techniques require that the keys involved be from a totally ordered set so that any key can be compared with any other key. It is known (Yao, 1981) that $\Omega(\log n)$ comparisons are required for comparison-based static tables. Binary search (presented below) attains this cost and is, therefore, an optimal approach.

Binary Search in a Sorted Array

A sorted array $A[\ ]$ can support an efficient static table. Suppose that the key x is being searched for in $A[\ ]$. Because the array is in sorted order, comparison of x with the key at $A[k]$ yields 3 possible results:

- x compares equal to the key at $A[k]$, in which case x is found.
- x compares less than the key at $A[k]$. In this case, if x is present in the table, it must be at an index less than k.
- x compares greater than the key at $A[k]$. In this case, if x is present in the table, it must be at an index greater than k.

If k is chosen as the middle index of the sorted array $A[]$, approximately half of the keys can be eliminated from consideration by the comparison of x and $A[k]$. The process is then repeated on the portion of the array which was not eliminated, again eliminating approximately half of those keys. If x is present, it will eventually be at the middle of some segment of the array that is still under consideration (in the worst case, it would be the middle element of a 1-element sub-array). If x is not present, the segment still under consideration will eventually shrink to a 0-element sub-array.

Because the problem size is approximately halved at each step and only a constant number of comparisons are performed at each step, this *binary search* algorithm requires $O(\log n)$ comparisons to determine if x is present in $A[\ ]$ and, if so, its location.

Algorithm and Implementation

The discussion above leads directly to a simple recursive algorithm. Suppose that the array $A[i...j]$ is to be searched for the key x. The initial values of i and j correspond to the first and last index of the array. Subsequently, i and j are adjusted to reflect the beginning and ending indices of the sub-array under consideration.

To search $A[i...j]$ for x:
    If $j < i$ then
        the key x is not present in the array

    Let m be the middle index of $A[i...j]$
    If x compares equal to the key at $A[m]$ then
        the key x has been found at $A[m]$
    Else, if x compares less than the key at $A[m]$
    then recursively search $A[i...(m\text{-}1)]$ for x
    Else,
        recursively search $A[(m\text{+}1)...j]$ for x

To implement this recursive algorithm, there are only two significant considerations: how to find the middle index and how to pass the appropriate sub-array to a subsequent recursive call (if one is needed). The middle index is obtained by the calculation $\left\lfloor \frac{i+j}{2} \right\rfloor$. Here, $\lfloor\ \rfloor$ is the floor function which yields the largest integer smaller than or equal to y. This calculation can be realized in many modern programming languages by allowing integer division to truncate or by using a truncation function to eliminate any fractional portion of the result of the division. Care must be taken to correctly deal with potential addition over-flow when i and j are extreme.

Care must also be taken when passing a sub-array to a subsequent recursive call. Programming languages which support call-by-reference can implement the call with the reference to the array and two indices as parameters. In programming languages which do not support call-by-reference, using a global variable for the array and passing two indices may avoid the penalty of an execution-time copy of the array being made at each recursive call.

The comparison of x and the key at $A[m]$ may cost considerably more than the trivial cost of comparing base-types. For example, comparing two character strings involves character-by-character comparison. If a key comparison involves substantial cost, it is advantageous to store the result of the key comparison and then use that result at the two points where the algorithm makes decisions based on that comparison.

Finally, it should be pointed out that the overhead incurred by recursive binary search is not likely to be significant. A binary search of a sorted array containing 700 million keys requires roughly 30 recursive calls. Moreover, since the algorithm requires few local variables, activation records associated with each invocation of the function or method are quite small.

Because the recursion in the binary search algorithm is *tail recursion*, this recursive algorithm can easily be converted into an iterative one.

To iteratively binary search $A[i...j]$ for x:
While $i \leq j$
>Let m be the middle index of $A[i...j]$
>If x compares equal to the key at $A[m]$ then
>>the key x has been found at $A[m]$
>
>Else, if x compares less than the key at $A[m]$ then
>>$j = m - 1$
>
>Else,
>>$i = m + 1$

x is not in the array

An iterative version of the algorithm may yield slightly faster execution for long searches although the asymptotic behavior of the algorithm is unchanged since $O(\log n)$ comparisons are made in both versions.

Building, Saving, and Recovering the Table

The initial construction of the table consists of loading the keys (and any associated data) into an array. If the keys can be loaded in sorted order, there is no other preparation necessary. If the keys are not available in sorted order, then the array must be sorted into key order before the table can be searched.

Sorting an array of n items can be accomplished with $O(n \log n)$ cost. Most language libraries contain sorting utilities which can efficiently sort an array. Note that sorting the array is purely a preprocessing step. It must be done before the array can be used as a table, but does not need to be done at any other time. In fact, once sorted, the table can be saved in

sorted order so that subsequent loading of it requires no sorting step.

In a static table, keys may be associated with additional data which is allowed to change. If the associated data has changed during the lifetime of the table, it may be necessary to save the table at system termination. If the array is saved in order, restoring the table consists of no more than simply re-loading the array.

TABLES OPTIMIZED BY PROBABILITY

Binary search in a sorted table assumes that each key is equally likely to be the objective of a search. Frequently, it is known (or can be determined) that some keys are more likely to be searched for than others. In this case, overall performance can be improved by organizing the table so that frequent searches require fewer comparisons than infrequent ones.

In this section, a technique is presented for optimizing tables so that the *average number of comparisons* for all keys is minimized. The underlying structure is a linked structure known as a *binary search tree*. Linked structures have the added benefit that they are less prone to memory allocation and swapping delays than contiguous arrays. On the other hand, linked structures require additional space overhead for their links. Still, the overall space requirement is directly proportional to the table size (i.e., $O(n)$) for a table containing n keys).

Binary Search Trees

A *binary search tree* is a binary tree which has the *search order property*:

For any node X in the tree, the key at X compares greater than any key in its left sub-tree and less than any key in its right sub-tree.

This property facilitates searching in the tree in much the same manner that binary search is facilitated by the order of a sorted array: a comparison of a node's key and the key being searched for will identify which sub-tree, if any, the search should move into next. The search algorithm that results is similar to binary search of a sorted array:

To search for key x in the binary search tree rooted at Y

    If Y is null then

        x is not present in the tree

    Else, if x compares less than the key at Y then

        recursively search for x in the tree rooted at Y's left child

    Else, if x compares greater than the key at Y then

        recursively search for x in the tree rooted at Y's right child

    Else,

        the key x has been found at Y

A binary search tree with n keys can be structured so that its height is $\Theta(\log n)$. Since a search begun at the root of the tree will descend one level at each recursive invocation of the search, the number of comparisons required for the longest search in a tree of height $\Theta(\log n)$ will also be $\Theta(\log n)$. Consequently, a well-structured binary search tree (known as a *balanced binary search tree*) yields the same asymptotic performance as binary search in a sorted array.

For non-static tables, insertion and deletion are considerably faster in a balanced binary search tree than they are in a sorted array. As a result, this kind of tree is very efficient for such tables. In the case of static tables, though, there is little argument for using a binary search tree rather than a sorted array except in cases where some other circumstance comes into play. One such circumstance is the *average cost* of the FIND operation when keys have different probabilities of being searched for.

The average number of comparisons performed by FIND is computed by adding up the number of comparisons necessary to FIND each of the n keys in the binary search tree and then dividing by n. By careful structuring, a binary search tree can be built so that keys with high probability of being searched for contribute smaller comparison counts to the sum than those with low probabilities. As a result, the average number of comparisons can be minimized.

The optimization process which is presented in the next subsection is expensive, requiring $O(n^3)$ time to determine the optimal binary search tree for n keys (notes at the end of the chapter indicate how to improve the time complexity to $O(n^2)$). The algorithm requires $\Theta(n^2)$ space. These costs are pre-processing costs, however. Once the tree structure has been determined (and the tree has been built), it is not necessary to repeat the process unless the keys and/or their probabilities change. This is true even if the data associated with the keys changes and it is necessary to save and reload the tree at system termination and startup.

Optimization Algorithm and the Optimal Tree

The optimization algorithm builds two arrays, C and R. The array C contains information about the smallest average number of comparisons for the optimal tree as well as its sub-trees. As C is being constructed, decisions about the values that are its entries provide information about the keys which root sub-trees in the optimal tree. The array R keeps track of the resulting roots of the sub-trees. In the end, the optimal binary search tree can be constructed by extracting information from R.

Let $k_i ... k_n$ be the n keys arranged in sorted order and let p_i be the probability that key k_i will be the objective of a search.

The arrays C and R consist of rows and columns. The entry at $C[i,j]$ will ultimately be the smallest average number of comparisons used by FIND in a binary search tree containing the keys $k_i ... k_j$. When the algorithm is finished, $C[1,n]$ will contain the minimum/optimal average number of comparisons required by FIND for the optimal binary search tree containing all of the keys. To compute the entry at $C[i,j]$, the algorithm searches for the best choice of root among the keys $k_i ... k_j$. When it finds the best choice, it sets the appropriate value into $C[i,j]$ and places the index of the best root into $R[i,j]$. That is, $R[i,j]$ contains the index of the best choice for the root of the optimal binary search tree for *keys k_i ... k_j*. In the end, $R[1,n]$ will contain the index of the root of the optimal binary search tree containing all of the keys.

The process that the algorithm performs begins with pairs of indices i and j that are a distance of 1 apart and then repeatedly increases that distance. For each pair of indices i and j, it determines the smallest average cost of FIND in a tree rooted at each possible key between k_i and k_j (inclusive). The minimum of these costs is then placed in $C[i,j]$ and the index of the corresponding key is placed in $R[i,j]$.

The algorithm is given below. For this presentation, assume that C is an array of $n+2$ rows and $n+1$ columns and that R is an array of $n+1$ rows and columns. In both arrays, the row 0 is unused—it is present so that the discussion can refer to key indices beginning at 1 rather than 0.

For each i between 1 and n
    Initialize $C[i,i] = p_i$, $C[i,i-1] = 0$ and $R[i,i] =$
    i
Initialize $C[n+1,n] = 0$
For each value of d between 1 and $n-1$
    For each index i between 1 and $n-d$
        $j = i + d$
        $min = \infty$
        For each m between i and j
            If $C[i,m-1] + C[m+1,j] < min$ then
                $min = C[i,m-1] + C[m+1,j]$
                $rmin = m$
        $R[i,j] = rmin$
        $C[i,j] = min + p_i + \cdots + p_j$

When the algorithm is finished, $R[1,n]$ contains the index of the key which is at the root of the optimal binary search tree. Suppose that $R[1,n]$ is the index t. Then, in the optimal tree, the root will have as its left sub-tree the optimal tree containing keys $k_1 ... k_{t-1}$. This sub-tree will be rooted by the key with index $R[1,t-1]$. Similarly, the right sub-tree of the root will have key $R[t+1,n]$ and contain keys $k_{t+1} ... k_n$. These relationships continue down through the tree's levels. Consequently, the optimal binary search tree may be built by processing the $R[\ ]$ array (described in the subsection Extracting the Optimal Tree).

Unsuccessful Searches

The optimization algorithm presupposes that all searches are successful. That is, it is assumed that every time the FIND operation is performed it locates the key it searches for. If this is not the case and the probabilities of unsuccessful searches are known, the following simple adjustment to the algorithm will build a binary search tree that has the minimal average cost for all searches, successful or not.

Suppose that, in addition to the keys $k_1, ... k_n$ and their probabilities $p_1, ..., p_n$, the probabilities of searches for keys not in this key set are known. Let q_0 be the probability of a search for a key that compares before k_1, let q_n be the probability of a search for a key that compares after k_n and let q_i be the probability of a search for a key that compares between k_i and k_{i+1}. In this case, the only change necessary in the algorithm is to replace the last line,

$$C[i,j] = min + p_i + \cdots + p_j$$

by this line

$$C[i,j] = min + p_i + \cdots + p_j + q_{i-1} + q_i + \cdots + q_j$$

The three nested loops of the algorithm each contribute at worst $O(n)$ cost to build the C and R arrays. Consequently, the algorithm has a worst-case cost of $O(n^3)$. Because of the two arrays, the space requirement for the algorithm is $\Theta(n^2)$.

Extracting the Optimal Tree

Once the array $R[\,]$ has been built the optimal binary search tree can be constructed by means of an $O(n)$ algorithm that uses the information in $R[\,]$ to make and link together the nodes of the tree. The arithmetic that computes the indices of $R[\,]$ at each step in an iterative version of the algorithm is cumbersome and tends to induce coding errors. For that reason, the algorithm is presented recursively.

It is assumed that a node structure is available which can contain a key (and perhaps a link for the data associated with that key) as well as links to a left child and a right child. In the general situation, the algorithm locates the key that roots the current sub-tree and makes a node for it. Then the left and right sub-trees are recursively built and linked to the node and the node is returned.

The logic of the algorithm will use $R[\,]$ to build the optimal binary search tree for keys $k_i \dots k_j$. The initial call to the algorithm asks for the optimal tree for $k_1 \dots k_n$ (that is, it is initially called with $i = 1$ and $j = n$). Each invocation of the algorithm returns the root of a tree.

Build the optimal tree for keys $\,k_i \dots k_j$.
   If $i = j$ then
      return a new node for key k_i (the node has no children)
   Else,
      Make a new node x for the key $k_{R[i,j]}$
      If $i \neq R[i,j]$ then
         Build optimal tree for keys $k_i, \dots, k_{R[i,j]-1}$
      at x's left child
      If $j \neq R[i,j]$ then
         Build optimal tree for keys $k_{R[i,j]+1} \dots k_j$ at x's right child
      Return x

Since it processes each node of the tree exactly once, this algorithm requires $O(n)$ time for a tree with n nodes. As the tree is being constructed, there are never more recursive calls active than there are nodes in the longest path in the resulting tree. Assuming the $R[\,]$ array is passed via call-by-reference (see the section on Sorted Tables), each recursive call requires only a small amount of space for its activation record. As a result, the space requirement for the algorithm is proportional to the height of the resulting tree, which is at most n.

Saving and Restoring Trees

In this subsection, techniques for saving and restoring binary trees are presented. For even relatively small table sizes, it is considerably faster to restore the saved optimal binary search tree from a file than it is to rebuild it by means of the above algorithms.

The techniques for saving and restoring, presented here, will work for *any* binary tree regardless of whether or not it is a binary search tree. The saving technique will save a binary tree so that it can be restored to exactly the same shape. This is significant for optimal binary search trees because it allows the tree to be saved and restored to its optimal shape (which optimizes the average cost of searches) without having to be rebuilt.

Saving the Tree

In order to restore a tree's node to its correct location, it is necessary to know the node's data, how many children that node had, and where they were (i.e., left child, right child). Additionally, during restoration, it is necessary to encounter a node's information at the time when it can have it's children reattached and be attached to its parent. Thus, the saving algorithm is closely tied to the restoration algorithm.

The technique for saving a binary tree so that it can be restored will save each node's data (which will usually consist of a key and its associated data) together with a code indicating the number and placement of its children (left or right). The data/code will be saved in pre-order by means of an adapted pre-order traversal beginning at the tree's root.

The following algorithm uses the codes '0,' 'L,' 'R,' and '2' to indicate 0 children, a single left child, a single right child, and two children, respectively. Its input is a node x for which it saves the tree rooted at x. Initially, it is called with the root of the entire tree. It then is recursively called on the left and right children of x.

Save tree rooted at x
    c = appropriate code for x (i.e., 0, L, R, 2)
    Store (write out) x's data and c
    If x has a left child then
      recursively save tree rooted at x's left child
    If x has a right child then
      recursively save tree rooted at x's right child

Because the algorithm is basically a simple pre-order traversal which performs a constant number of operations when it visits a node, it requires $\Theta(n)$ time on a binary tree of n nodes. It's space requirement is the space needed for the recursion which is proportional to the height of the tree (i.e., it requires $O(\text{height})$ space) which is at worst $O(n)$ for a tree with n nodes.

Restoring the Tree

During restoration, the data and codes saved from the nodes will be encountered in pre-order. Consequently, a node can be constructed for the data and then a decision may be made about how many children to attach to the node and where to attach them.

The tree-building algorithm described below also uses the codes '0,' 'L,' 'R,' and '2.' Each time it is invoked, it will return the node which roots the tree it was able to build during that invocation. It first loads the current node data (key and associated data) into a node then it makes decisions about children based on the code associated with the node's data. As it does so, it attaches sub-trees returned by recursive invocations according to the code.

BuildTree()
    Get the next node data and code in D and C
    Create a new node x with data D
    If C is 'L' or '2' then
      recursively call BuildTree() and attach the tree it builds as x's left child
    If C is 'R' or '2' then
      recursively call BuildTree() and attach the tree it builds as x's right child
    Return x

This algorithm encounters each node once and therefore requires $O(n)$ time to restore a tree of n nodes. The recursion requires $\Theta(\text{height})$ space for the recursion (referring to the height of the resulting tree). The height of a tree is at most $O(n)$ for an n-node tree.

An optimal binary search tree gives minimal *average* performance for FIND. The cost to build the tree ($O(n^3)$ time and $\Theta(n^2)$ space), save the tree ($O(n)$ time and $\Theta(\text{height})$ space for the recursion), and restore a saved tree (also $O(n)$ time and $\Theta(\text{height})$ space for the recursion) are pre-processing or post-processing costs which are not incurred during the use of the tree.

CONSTANT-TIME TABLES

This section presents an approach for tables in which searching is composed of some computation together with zero or more tests. Because the testing (if done) is for equality, the keys are not required to be from a totally ordered set.

Hashing and Perfect Hash Tables

Hash tables are based on a simple concept. Suppose that the keys are integers in the range $0, 1, \ldots n-1$. Let $A[0..n-1]$ be an array and store the data for key k at $A[k]$. (An appropriate flag can be stored in $A[j]$ in the case that there is no data in the table with key j.) The FIND operation is then trivial. To look up the key k, simply go to $A[k]$ and determine if $A[k]$

contains the key or the flag. That is, FIND is a constant-time ($O(1)$) operation in such a table.

Generalizing the above to a useful table structure encounters a number of problems. While a detailed presentation of these problems and their solutions is beyond the scope of this chapter, a general understanding of the problems is important for understanding the powerful and efficient technique of this section.

Hash Functions and Hash Tables

If the keys for the table entries are not integers or not integers in a convenient range, some process must be employed to adapt them for use as indices in an array. This is part of the role of a *hash function*.

A hash function takes a key as an argument and produces an index into the array as its output. Since the output is required to be a viable index for the array, any hash function is closely tied to the size of the array used to store the key's data. For a given key k, the value (index) that the hash function $h()$ produces for k is called the *hash value* of k, denoted $h(k)$. The data associated with k is then found at $A[h(k)]$ in the array (or $A[h(k)]$ will contain a flag indicating that no data associated with key k exists in the table).

The combination of a hash function and an array for which it generates indices is referred to as a *hash table*.

Collisions, Perfect Hashing, and Minimal Perfect Hashing

Translating non-numeric keys into integers is relatively simple (see, for example, Chapter 11 of Cormen, Leiserson, Rivest, & Stein, 2001). In the following, we will assume that the keys are integer values and focus on the problem of translating those values into usable array indices.

A problem arises when the range of *possible* hash values is large relative to the number of *actual* hash values. For example, suppose that keys are 9-digit integers but that there are only a few thousand keys

which actually correspond to items in the table. The mechanism which makes array indexing work efficiently is based on the array being allocated as a contiguous segment of memory. Creating an array of a size sufficient to accommodate all 9-digit integers as indices may cause serious runtime delays as the operating system swaps blocks of memory. Such delays are undesirable, particularly when only a relatively small number of the array slots will actually be used.

Consequently, it would be preferred that the range of hash values to be associated with keys be restricted to approximately n (the actual number of keys). It is an unfortunate fact that for any hash function, if the number of possible keys is at least the product of the number of slots in the table and n, then *some* set of n keys will all yield the same hash value—the same array index!

When two or more keys have the same hash value, a *collision* occurs and some strategy must be employed to resolve it. Resolution strategies necessarily involve some form of searching to locate the desired key and, as a result, can yield $O(n^2)$ performance for individual FIND operations.

Things are not as dismal as the previous paragraph seems to suggest. In the case of *static* tables, where all the keys are known in advance, it is possible to construct a *perfect hash function* which will map keys to indices with no collisions. Perfect hash functions which yield indices in the range $0, 1, \dots$ n-1 (where n is the number of keys) are known as *minimal perfect hash functions*. Hash tables which use minimal perfect hash functions attain theoretically optimal time and space efficiency.

The construction of a minimal perfect hash function is a search process which searches through the space of all potential minimal perfect hash functions on a given set of keys. Because the search space is large and checking an individual function to see if it is perfect may be costly, the process can be very time consuming. However, once the function is constructed, the process never need be repeated unless the set of keys changes.

All currently known techniques for generating minimal perfect hash functions make use of algorithms and representations considerably beyond the scope of this chapter. However, there are several software tools available which implement these techniques and generate minimal perfect hash functions. One of these tools is described in the next subsection and references to other tools are given in the notes at the end of this chapter.

Minimal Perfect Hash Table Tools

This section describes the MinimalPerfectHash class, a freely available software tool which generates minimal perfect hash functions. It can be used to create efficient tables for programs written in Java. At the time of this writing, it is stable and is distributed under the LGPL (Lesser Gnu Public License).

The MinimalPerfectHash Class

The MinimalPerfectHash class is a component of the MG4J Project (Managing Gigabytes for Java). This project is "aimed at providing a free Java implementation of inverted-index compression techniques" (MG4J, 2006). As a by-product, the project offers several general-purpose optimized classes including a minimal perfect hash class. The MG4J project encompasses far more than minimal perfect hash tables, but we focus only on that aspect of it here.

The MinimalPerfectHash class provides an order-preserving minimal perfect hash table constructed for a set of keys. *Order-preserving* means that the order of the keys in the table is the same as the order in which they were provided to the table's constructor. Having the same order simplifies creating any necessary additional structure to contain data associated with the keys.

Constructing and Using the Hash Table

The MinimalPerfectHash class constructors convert a sequence of unique character-based keys into a minimal perfect hash table in which the order of the keys is preserved. A number of constructors are provided. We focus on only one here.

The constructor:

public MinimalPerfectHash(String keyFile)

creates a new order-preserving minimal perfect hash table for the given file of keys. The parameter keyFile is the name of a file in the platform-default encoding containing one key on each line. It is assumed that the file does not contain duplicates. Behavior of the constructor when duplicate keys are present is undefined.

The minimal perfect hash table constructed by the constructor provides methods to look up individual keys. These methods return the *ordinal number* of a key—its position in the original order of the key sequence. We focus on only one here. The method:

public int getNumber(CharSequence key)

returns the ordinal number of the key in the original order that the constructor encountered the keys, beginning at 0. (CharSequence is a Java interface for a readable sequence of char values). This method effectively computes the hash value of the key using the minimal perfect hash function associated with the minimal perfect hash table that was built by the constructor.

For example, suppose that a collection of n records, $R_0...R_{n-1}$, each of which is identified by a unique key, is to be used as a static table. First, the n keys, $k_0...k_{n-1}$, are extracted from the records into a file (in the indicated order, i.e., k_i is the key of R_i). This file is then used as the parameter for MinimalPerfectHash's constructor, which builds a MinimalPerfectHash table for them. The records are then loaded into an array of size n putting R_i into the array at index i. To look up the data associated with key k, getNumber() is first called with parameter k to find the index of the data which is associated with key k. That index is then used to access the data.

Table construction is purely a preprocessing step. It consists of building the minimal perfect hash table for the keys and loading the data associated with the keys into an array. Once this has been done, use of the table costs $O(1)$-time for each FIND operation.

The MinimalPerfectHash class implements the Serializable interface, so the hash table may be saved and reused later. Consequently, once the hash table has been built it is not necessary to rebuild it unless the key set changes. The data associated with the keys may change during the table's use, so it may be necessary to save that data at termination, but this can be accomplished simply by looping through the array and saving the data in that order.

Other Considerations

It should be noted that in the above, the FIND operation consists of looking a given key up in the MinimalPerfectHash table via getNumber() and then using that result to index into an array. This process assumes that FIND will always be successful—that every key for which the FIND operation is performed is a key which is in the table. As a result, no actual key comparisons are required: given a key, getNumber() computes an index into the data array and the data is then retrieved from the array slot at that index.

If it is necessary to establish whether a given key is or is not in the table, a slightly different approach must be taken because the getNumber() method of MinimalPerfectHash returns a random position if it is called with a key that was not in the original collection.

The SignedMinimalPerfectHash class, which is also a component of MG4J, will always return a usable result, even for keys that are not in the table (here, "signed" refers to "signature" rather than mathematical sign). In a signed minimal perfect hash table, every key has a signature which is used to detect false positives. When getNumber() is called in SignedMinimalPerfectHash, the hash value of the given key is computed as before.

Then a comparison is made to determine if the given key has the same signature as the key in the original collection which has the same hash value. If the signatures match, the position of the key is returned as before. If the signatures do not match, getNumber() returns -1.

SignedMinimalPerfectHash provides (via subclasses) considerable flexibility in how signatures can be created and/or evaluated. The additional comparison of signatures may require significant cost at execution time depending on how the comparison takes place. Nevertheless, it is possible to perform the comparison in time proportional to the size of the largest key.

CONCLUSION

To determine which of the techniques to use for constructing a static table, one has to take into consideration the properties of the key set. In particular, if the keys are *not* from a totally ordered set, neither the technique of binary search in a sorted array nor the optimal binary search tree technique can be used because both rely on comparisons yielding order information about the keys. On the other hand, minimal perfect hashing yields an efficient table for key sets regardless of whether they are from totally ordered sets or not.

Binary search in a sorted array guarantees $O(\log n)$ performance in the worst case and is quite easy to set up. The optimal binary search tree technique guarantees minimal average performance and is only slightly harder to set up but requires at least information about the probability of each key being sought. If that information is unavailable, then the technique cannot be used. Both of these techniques are easily programmable in modern programming languages.

The minimal perfect hash table tools described in this chapter (and those referred to in the notes below) are language-specific. As a result, if development is not taking place in Java, C++, or C, extra steps will be necessary to convert the hash table into the development language after it has been built.

Notes on Static Tables

The binary search technique of the first section is nearly folklore in computer science. Knuth (1988) reports that the first published description appeared in 1946 but that the first *correct* description did not appear until 1962!

The optimal binary search tree algorithm given is essentially from Knuth (1971), although the presentation here is adapted from Levitin (2003), with the extension to failed searches adapted from Cormen, Leiserson, Rivest, and Stein (2001). Gilbert and Moore (1959) gave a similar algorithm and discussed it's relationship to other problems. Knuth (1971), in fact, showed how to speed up the algorithm by a factor of n (yielding an $O(n^2)$-time algorithm. The speedup is accomplished by altering control of the innermost loop to:

For each m between $R[i,j$-1$]$ and $R[i+1,j]$.

The justification for this is beyond the scope of this chapter. Interested readers should consult Knuth (1971), Knuth (1988), or Bein, Golin, Larmore, and Zhang (2006) for more information. Subsequently, Vaishnavi, Kriegel, and Wood (1980) and Gotlieb and Wood (1981) investigated adapting the algorithm to multi-way search trees (in which the nodes of the tree may have more than 2 children). In doing so, they showed that the "monotonicity principle," which is responsible for the speed up of Knuth, does not extend to optimal multiway search trees in general. Spuler and Gupta (1992) investigated alternatives to optimal binary search trees in which the average cost of the FIND operation is nearly optimized.

In addition to the MG4J tools described in this chapter, several others exist to generate minimal (and near-minimal) perfect hash tables. GPERF described in Schmidt (1990) and distributed under the Gnu GPL, produces a minimal perfect hash table in the form of C or C++ code. It is distributed via the Free Software Foundation. GGPERF, by Kong (1997) is similar to GPERF but written in Java (GPERF is written in C++ and is also available in C), can produce output in C/C++ and Java, and is faster than GPERF because it is based on the improved algorithm of Czech, Havas, and Majowski (1992). Botelho, Kohayakawa, and Ziviani describe the BMZ algorithm which has appeared in the development of another minimal perfect hash table generator.

REFERENCES

Bein, W., Golin, M., Larmore, L., & Zhang, Y. (2006). The Knuth-Yao quadrangle-inequality speedup is a consequence of total-monotonicity. In *Proceedings of the Seventeenth Annual ACM-SIAM Symposium on Discrete Algorithms* (pp. 31-40).

Botelho, F., Kohayakawa, Y., & Ziviani, N. (2005). *A practical minimal perfect hashing method.* Paper presented at the 4th International Workshop on Efficient and Experimental Algorithms (WEA05) (vol. 3505, pp. 488-500), Springer-Verlag Lecture Notes in Computer Science.

Cormen, T., Leiserson, C., Rivest, R., & Stein, C. (2001). *Introduction to algorithms* (2nd ed.). Cambridge, MA: MIT Press.

Czech, Z., Havas, G., & Majewski, B. (1992). An optimal algorithm for generating minimal perfect hash functions. *Information Processing Letters, 43,* 257-264.

Fredman, M. L., Komlòs, J., & Szemerédi, E. (1984). Storing a sparse table with $O(1)$ worst case access time. *Journal of the Association for Computing Machinery, 31,* 538-544.

Gilbert, E., & Moore, E. (1959). Variable-length binary encodings. *Bell System Technical Journal, 38,* 933-967.

Gotlieb, L., & Wood, D. (1981). The construction of optimal multiway search trees and the monotonicity principle. *International Journal of Computer Mathematics, 9,* 17-24.

Knuth, D. E. (1971). Optimal binary search trees. *Acta Informatica, 1,* 14-25.

Knuth, D. (1998). *The art of computer programming: Sorting and searching* (vol. 3) (3rd ed.). Reading, MA: Addison-Wesley.

Kong, J. (1997). *GGPERF: A perfect hash function generator.* Retrieved June 22, 2006, from http://www.cs.ucla.edu/ jkong/public/soft/GGPerf

Levitin, A. (2003). *Introduction to the design and analysis of algorithms.* Boston: Addison-Wesley.

Majewski, B., Wormald, N., Havas, G., & Czech, Z. (1996). A family of perfect hashing methods. *The Computer Journal, 39,* 547-554.

MG4J. (2006). *Minimal Perfect Hash documentation page.* Retrieved June 22, 2006, from http://mg4j. dsi.unimi.it/docs/it/unimi/dsi/mg4j/MinimalPerfectHash.html

Schmidt, D. C. (1990, April 9-11). GPERF: A perfect hash function generator. In *Proceedings of the 2nd C++ Conference, USENIX,* San Francisco, (pp. 87-102).

Spuler, D. A., & Gupta, G. K. (1992). *An empirical study of nearly optimal binary search trees and split trees* (Tech. Rep. 92-2). Department of Computer Science, James Cook University.

Vaishnavi, V. K., Kriegel, H. P., & Wood, D. (1980). Optimum multiway search trees. *Acta Informatica, 14,* 119-133.

Yao, A. C. (1981). Should tables be sorted? *Journal of the Association for Computing Machinery, 29,* 615-628.

KEY TERMS

Binary Search: An efficient ($O(\log n)$) search technique for sorted arrays.

Binary Search Tree: A binary tree in which the search order property holds. Binary search trees may be searched by means of a technique similar to binary search in a sorted array.

Hash Table: An indexed data structure in which the index of a key is computed by means of a function called a *hash function*.

Minimal Perfect Hash Table: A hash table in which every key hashes to a unique index in the range 0,...,(n-1) for n keys. Minimal perfect hash tables attain theoretically optimal space and time performance.

Optimal Binary Search Tree: A binary search tree in which the average number of comparisons required to search for all keys is minimized.

Pre-Order, Pre-Order Traversal: For any tree, pre-order visits, lists, or processes a node before it visits, lists, or processes the node's children.

Search Order Property: A property of binary trees which facilitates searching. The key at any node compares greater than any key in the node's left sub-tree and less than any key in the node's right sub-tree.

Static Table: A table consisting of keys and associated data for which the set of keys is static (does not change). The data associated with the keys may change, however.

Tail Recursion: A form of recursion in which the last action of a recursive function is a recursive call. Tail recursion can easily be converted to iteration.

Totally-Ordered Set: A set upon which a reflexive, transitive, antisymmetric, relation which also satisfies the trichotomy law is defined.

Chapter XII
Notes on the Emerging Science of Software Evolution

Ladislav Samuelis
Technical University of Kosice, Slovakia

ABSTRACT

This chapter introduces the irreducibility principle within the context of computer science and software engineering disciplines. It argues that the evolution, analysis, and design of the application software, which represent higher level concepts, cannot be deduced from the underlying concepts, which are valid on a lower level of abstractions. We analyze two specific sweeping statements often observed in the software engineering community and highlight the presence of the reductionism approach being treated already in the philosophy. We draw an analogy between the irreducibility principle and this approach. Furthermore, we hope that deep understanding of the reductionism approach will assist in the correct application of software design principles.

INTRODUCTION

Dealing with continuously increasing software complexity raises huge maintenance costs and rapidly slows down implementation. One of the main reasons why software is becoming more and more complex is its flexibility, which is driven by changing business rules or other volatile requirements. We note that this flexibility is rooted in the generality of the programmable John von Neumann machine. Due to these inevitable facts, which influence software development, the software systems' complexity increases continuously. Recently, soft-

ware maintenance represents 45% of software cost (Cartwright & Shepperd, 2000). This phenomenon motivates researchers and practitioners to find theories and practices in order to decrease the maintenance cost and keep the software development within reasonable managerial and financial constraints. The notion of *software evolution* (which is closely related and often interchanged with the term *maintenance*) was already introduced in the middle of the seventies when Lehman and Belady examined the growth and the evolution of a number of large software systems (Lehman & Belady, 1976). They proposed eight laws, which are often cited in software engineering literature and are considered as the first research results gained by observation during the evolution of large software systems.

The term software evolution has emerged in many research papers with roots both in computer science and software engineering disciplines (e.g., Bennett & Rajlich, 2000). Nowadays, it has become an accepted research area. In spite of the fact that the science of software evolution is in its infancy, formal theories are being developed and empirical observations are compared to the predicted results. Lehman's second law states the following: "*an evolving system increases its complexity unless work is done to reduce it*" (Lehman, 1980). Due to the consequences of this law and due to the increased computing power, the research in software and related areas is being accelerated and very often causes confusion and inconsistency in the used terminology.

This chapter aims to discuss the observations concerning evolution within the context of *computer science* and *software engineering*. In particular, it analyzes frictions in two sweeping statements, which we observe reading research papers in computer science, software engineering, and compares them with reality. We will analyze them from the reductionism point of view and argue that a design created at a higher level—its algorithm—is specific and in this sense it cannot be deduced from the laws, which are valid on more fundamental levels. We introduce a new term, the *irreducibility principle*, which is not mentioned explicitly in the expert literature within the context of *computer science* and *software engineering* (to the best of our knowledge). Finally, we summarize the ideas and possible implications from a wider perspective.

SOME HISTORICAL NOTES ON THE SOFTWARE EVOLUTION

Research on software evolution is discussed in many software related disciplines. Topics of software evolution are subjects of many conferences and workshops, too. In the following paragraphs, we will briefly characterize the scene in order to highlight the interpretation of the notion of evolution in the history of software technology.

The notions of *program synthesis* or *automated program construction* are the first forerunners of the evolution abstraction in software engineering. Papers devoted to these topics could be found in, for example, the research field of automated program synthesis. Practical results achieved in the field of programming by examples are summed up, for example, in the book edited by Lieberman (2001). The general principle of these approaches is based on the induction principle, which is analyzed in the work of Samuelis and Szabó in more details (Samuelis & Szabó, 2006). The term evolution was a synonym for *automation of the program construction* and for the discovery of *reusable code*—that is, searching for loops.

Later on, when programming technologies matured and program libraries and components were established into practice, the research field of *pattern reuse* (Fowler, 2000) and engineering *component-based systems* (Angster, 2004) drove its attention into theory and practice. In other words, slight shift to component-based aspect is observed in the course of the construction of programs. We may say that the widely used term of *customization* was stressed and this term also merged later with the notion of *evolution*. Of course, this shift was heavily supported by the object-oriented programming languages, which penetrated into the industrial practice during the 80s in the last century.

Since it was a necessity to maintain large and more complex legacy systems, the topic of *program comprehension* came into focus and became more and more important. Program comprehension is an activity drafted in the paper of Rajlich and Wilde as: Program comprehension is an essential part of software evolution and software maintenance: software that is not comprehended cannot be changed. The fields of software documentation, visualization, program design, and so forth, are driven by the need for program comprehension. Program comprehension also provides motivation for program analysis, refactoring, reengineering, and other processes. (Rajlich & Wilde, 2002). A very relevant observation concerning the comprehension is from Jazayeri who says "*Not the software itself evolves, but our understanding and the comprehension of the reality*" (Jazayeri, 2005). This is in compliance with the idea that our understanding of the domain problem incrementally evolves and learning is an indispensable part of program comprehension.

Rajlich, when dealing with the changing paradigm of software engineering, stresses the importance of the *concept location*. He argues that the volatility of the requirements is the result of the developer's learning. Thus, learning and understanding (or comprehension) are indispensably coupled with the evolution (Rajlich, 2006). We add that mental activities associated with understanding are dealt within the cognitive sciences and it is important to realize that, for example, software design concepts from certain higher level of abstractions cannot be formalized.

The scattered results from the mentioned areas lead to the attempt to establish the taxonomy of software evolution (Buckley, Mens, Zenger, Rashid, & Kniesel, 2005). Further areas of the contemporary research, which deal more or less with the evolution concept, are software merging (Mens, 2002), measurement of the flexibility and complexity of the software (Eden & Mens, 2006), and software visualization for reverse engineering (Koschke, 2000). It is also obvious that the evolution principle in the biological interpretation heavily attracted and influenced the research of the evolution in software engineering. The paper written by Nehaniv, Hewitt, Christianson, and Wernick critically warns the software engineering community about the non-obvious traps when the evolution principles valid in biology are mechanically applied to the area of software artifacts (Nehaniv et al., 2006). The analysis of these fields deserves special attention but examining them is not the aim of this chapter.

Summing up, the mentioned emerging disciplines are approaching the phenomenon of evolution from various aspects of the systems' analysis and design. These short introductory notes have glanced on the interlacing of software related disciplines and how they mutually influence each other. These approaches have their own history and theoretical roots; they are in various branches of computer science and treated from the philosophical point of view, too (King & Kimble, 2004). It is guaranteed that new techniques and research areas will emerge in the near future and further deal with the phenomenon of evolution.

SYSTEM, MODEL, AND REDUCTIONISM

Probably, the only unquestioned abstraction of the system theory is the *universe*, that is, the existing reality. This applies simultaneously and unambiguously to two things. It refers to the concept of the universe and the abstraction that our brain creates about it. We are able to deal with the things of the universe only through our abstractions about it and this is a dichotomy that we cannot solve with any argument.

Natural entities are existing units in reality, which we can select from the environment based on some *written* criteria. This unit may be for instance, an engine, a building, or a description of a complex banking system. A system is an entity when it comprises sub-entities.

The human cognition happens always through *system-models*. Modeling is always simplification and a kind of identification between two different systems. The cognitive human being creates a model in piecemeal growth. We use the model in a way that we *run* the model and this way we predict the modeled system's complex operation.

In the process of building the model, the following question rises naturally: Which features are stressed and measured in a model? In practice, this depends on the importance of a particular feature in a given context. In other words, we selectively omit features during the abstraction. We may also deliberately omit or intentionally extend specific features. This is part of the learning process when the acquisitions of new patterns are observed through experience.

New models can be created in a *revolutionary* or *evolutionary* manner. In essence, the difference between these two definitions lies in the fact that the non-incremental (revolutionary) approach is based on one-shot experience and the incremental (evolutionary) learning allows the learning process to take place over time in a continuous and progressive way, also taking into consideration the history of the training sets during building the inferred rules.

We may draw an analogy between these modes of models-creation and the definitions of the *s-type* and *e-type softwares* (Lehman & Ramil, 2001). Software evolution is only related to the *e-type* per definition. This type of software is influenced mainly with non-functional attributes as: reliability, availability, fault tolerance, testability, maintainability, performance, software safety, and software security. In other words, the e-type software has been influenced by unpredictable factors since the earliest stages of development and that is why it is continuously evolving without building it from the scratch.

We introduce the notion of *reductionism*, which frames the *irreducibility* principle. Reductionism generally says that the nature of complex things is reduced to the nature of sums of simpler or more fundamental things. In the following sections we will focus on and will clarify the two following sweeping statements that seem obvious at the first sight: (1) Theory valid within the computer science alleviates programming and (2) Programming is coding. They are often applied among the researchers and practitioners working in the field of computer science and software engineering.

STATEMENT 1: THEORY VALID WITHIN THE COMPUTER SCIENCE ALLEVIATES PROGRAMMING

It is often argued misleadingly in research papers that a specific theory valid within the computer science alleviates programming or software design. We introduce the notion of the *organizational level* or *levels of abstraction* and map the science valid within the computer to the lower level and the domain specific software to the higher level.

We argue that the sweeping statement: "*Theory valid within the computer science alleviates programming*" represents a typical reductionism approach. Actually, the analysis and design of software systems cannot be traced back, for example, to the state space of the computer's internal memory. The higher level of the abstraction has its own set of limits, which are domain specific and cannot be explained by the concepts, which are valid at lower levels. The limits of software design at higher levels cannot be reconstructed or predicted from the descriptions of abstractions, which are valid on lower levels. Naturally, we are able to follow causally the whole sequence of events, which happen on lower level, but this will not lead to solutions concerning design decisions

In other words, lower level laws equal the laws valid within a computer, and the aim of theoretical computer science is to reveal and establish the appropriate theories which describe the analyzed processes realized within the computer (e.g., automata theory). The functions valid at a higher level (the behavior and the algorithms) cannot be deduced back to a lower level. That is why it is an illusion that the paradigms valid within a computer can enhance the comprehension process and the programming of the system at the domain (higher) level. Of course, it is much better when somebody understands both levels of abstraction. The owner of such knowledge is in an advantageous position since the specific domain knowledge is definitely better underpinned.

Let us explain it through an analogy. As an example, we could mention the knowledge of the thermodynamics theory, which is valid within the cylinder of an internal-combustion engine, does not imply that we are able to construct an engine, which is produced for embedding it into a specific vehicle devoted to alleviate some work in a certain domain. It is also valid vice versa. It means that it is impossible to obtain the answer on the direction of vehicle's movement from the thermodynamic laws, which govern processes inside the cylinder. That is why we have to draw a sharp line between different abstraction (or organization) levels in order to feasibly argue and manage the relevant questions and tasks within that abstraction level (or domain). This is called the *irreducibility* concept, which is not a new idea in the theory of general evolution, as mentioned earlier.

In the context of software engineering, we can observe a similar situation; when applying the object-oriented approach to the analysis of a specific problem, we neglect the lower implementation level (the computer domain). Vice versa, when we investigate the domain of formal languages, then we neglect the application domain. Both considerations are also closely related to the pedagogical issue, which says that first we have to ponder about the domain problems and only later about the implementation details.

The mentioned sweeping statement can also be explained in philosophical terms, namely it is in accordance with the *reductionism* approach, when the nature of complex things is reduced to the nature of sums of simpler or more fundamental concepts. In the context of software, where we have several strata of the complexities (Mittermeir, 2001), it is obvious that the reductionism approach cannot be applied.

STATEMENT 2: PROGRAMMING IS CODING

This idea states that programming is a mere coding. It is far from reality that constructing programs equals coding. We are not going to summarize the historic milestones of software engineering but highlight that analyzing and designing software systems are essentially about building a model of reality, first of all. This activity is a complex set of actions and involves work of domain experts and specialists on the workflow management within the software project development.

Generally, software systems are determined by specifications or requirements, which are in fact sets of limits (barriers) on the required functionalities. We try to create a model of reality and to locate concepts. Yes, it is also valid in the opposite way. It is necessary to locate concepts in case we have a legacy code and would like to implement modifications. This includes activities related to program comprehension, which was mentioned earlier.

The core problem of the software development is getting an intellectual grasp on the complexity of the application. Software engineering is an empirical science because grasping requires experiments. Algorithms give answers and solutions for questions defined in a certain domain. These mechanisms are valid for a particular domain and they cannot be deduced from the underlying mechanisms valid within a computer. Mechanisms depend on a lot of project-specific criteria, such as the type, size, and criticality of application. It is not only the speed of running an application but, what is more important, the speed of developing reliable software functionality regardless of how fast it runs. From this point of view, almost any improvements in a piece of software could be viewed as an experimental debugging, which aims to improve the code.

We may turn back and stress that the experimental feature is inherent for the *e-type* software. The importance of the experiments or their ignorance, for example, Ariane flight failure (Lann, 1997) is underpinned with the already established experimental software engineering institutions throughout the world (Basili & Reiter, 1981). The more software is produced, the more its importance is increased on our everyday life. This fact highlights the dependency of the so-called information society on the reliable and robust software applications.

CONCLUSION

To conclude, knowledge of the laws, which govern on the level within the computer, cannot predict the aims (or outputs) of an application program, which is designed by the program (software) designer. The analysis and design of the system (on a higher organizational level) cannot be predicted from the behavior of the laws, which are valid on the lower organizational level. That is why mechanical transition of knowledge between the organizational levels is considered harmful and the knowledge transfer is *irreversible*. From another point of view, this is a kind of servicing, when a lower organizational level serves the higher organizational level. Services provided at the higher level cannot be deduced from mechanisms valid for lower levels (Bennett, 2004).

This chapter revealed rather old knowledge that was purified within the context of software related areas. We hope that the discussed ideas will focus the attention of software engineers towards reconsideration of the obviously claimed statements, which are against the facts observed in reality.

ACKNOWLEDGMENT

This work is supported by the Slovak Scientific Grant Agency: VEGA 1/0350/05—Knowledge-based software life cycle and architecture.

REFERENCES

Angster, E. (2004). SDP-city against a vicious circle! *First Monday, 9*(12). Retrieved February 28, 2004, from http://firstmonday.org

Basili, V., & Reiter, R., Jr. (1981). A controlled experiment quantitatively comparing software development approaches. *IEEE Transactions on Software Engineering, 7*(3), 299-320.

Bennett, K. (2004). Software evolution and the future for flexible software. Paper presented at the Erasmus University of Bari.

Bennett, K., & Rajlich, V. (2000). Software maintenance and evolution: A roadmap. In A. Finkelstein (Ed.), *The future of software engineering* (pp. 73-90). Limerick, Ireland: ACM.

Buckley, J., Mens, T., Zenger, M., Rashid, A., & Kniesel, G. (2005). Towards a taxonomy of software change. *Journal on Software Maintenance and Evolution: Research and Practice, 17*(5), 309-332.

Cartwright, M., & Shepperd, M. (2000). An empirical investigation of an object-oriented software system. *IEEE Transactions on Software Engineering, 26*(8), 786-796.

Eden, A. H., & Mens, T. (2006). Measuring software flexibility. *IEE Software, 153*(3), 113-126.

Fowler, M. (2000). *Analysis patterns: Reusable object models.* The Addison-Wesley Object Technology Series.

Jazayeri, M. (2005, September 5-6). *Species evolve, individuals age.* Paper presented at the International Workshop on Principles of Software Evolution, ACM, Lisbon.

King, D., & Kimble, C. (2004). Uncovering the epistemological and ontological assumptions of software designers. In *Proceedings 9e Colloque de I'AIM*, Evry, France.

Koschke, R. (2002). Software visualization for reverse engineering. In S. Diehl (Ed.), *Springer lecture notes on computer science (LNCS) 2269: Software visualization, state-of-the-art survey.*

Lehman, M. M. (1980). On understanding laws, evolution, and conservation in the large-program life cycle. *Journal of Systems and Software, 1*(3), 213-231.

Lehman, M. M., & Belady, L. A. (1976). A model of large program development. *IBM Systems Journal, 15*(3), 225-252.

Lehman, M. M., & Ramil, J. F. (2001). *Evolution in software and related areas.* Paper presented at the workshop *IWPSE* (pp. 1-16), Vienna Austria.

Le Lann, G. (1997). An analysis of the Ariane 5 flight 501 failure—a system engineering perspective. Paper presented at the 10th IEEE Intl. ECBS Workshop (pp. 339–346).

Lieberman, H. (Ed.). (2001). *Your wish is my command, programming by example.* Media Lab., MIT, Academic Press.

Mens, T. (2002). A state-of-the-art survey on software merging. *IEEE Transactions on Software Engineering, 28*(5), 449-462.

Mittermeir, R. L. (2001). Software evolution—let's sharpen the terminology before sharpening (out-of-scope) tools. Paper presented at the Workshop *IWPSE* (pp. 114-120), Vienna, Austria.

Nehaniv, L. C., Hewitt, J., Christianson, B., & Wernick, P. (2006). *What software evolution and biological evolution don't have in common?* Paper presented at the Second International IEEE Workshop on Software Evolvability, IEEE, Philadelphia, Pennsylvania, USA.

Rajlich, V. (2006). Changing the paradigm of software engineering. *Communications of the ACM, 49*(8), 67-70.

Rajlich, V., & Wilde, N. (2002). The role of concepts in program comprehension. In *Proceedings of the IEEE International Workshop on Program Comprehension* (pp. 271-278). IEEE Computer Society Press.

Samuelis, L., & Szabó, C. (2006). Notes on the role of the incrementality in software engineering. *Univ. Babes, Bolyai, Informatica, LI*(2), 11-18.

KEY TERMS

Automatic Programming: The term identifies a type of computer programming in which some mechanism generates a computer program rather than have human programmers write the code.

Induction: Induction or inductive reasoning is the process of reasoning in which the premises of an argument are believed to support the conclusion but do not ensure it. It is used to formulate laws based on limited observations of recurring phenomenal patterns.

Irreversibility: Processes in general that are not reversible are termed irreversible.

Reductionism: Is a philosophical theory that asserts that the nature of complex things is reduced to the nature of sums of simpler or more fundamental things.

Reusability: Reusability is the likelihood a segment of source code can be used again to add new functionalities with slight or no modification. Reusable modules and classes reduce implementation time, increase the likelihood that prior testing and use has eliminated bugs, and localizes code modifications when a change in implementation is required.

Software evolution: Software evolution refers to the process of developing software initially, then repeatedly updating it for various reasons.

Synthesis of Programs: Comprises a range of technologies for the automatic generation of executable computer programs from high-level specifications of their behavior.

Section II
Modeling Processes

Chapter XIII
Software Modeling Processes:
UML–xUML Review

Roy Gelbard
Bar-Ilan University, Israel

ABSTRACT

Applications require short development cycles and constant interaction with customers. Requirement gathering has become an ongoing process, reflecting continuous changes in technology and market demands. System analysis and modeling that are made at the initial project stages are quickly abandoned and become outmoded. Model driven architecture (MDA), rapid application development (RAD), adaptive development, extreme programming (XP), and others have resulted in a shift from the traditional waterfall model. These methodologies attempt to respond to the needs, but do they really fulfill their objectives, which are essential to the success of software development? Unified modeling language (UML) was created by the convergence of several well-known modeling methodologies. Despite its popularity and the investments that have been made in UML tools, UML is not yet translatable into running code. Some of the problems that have been discovered have to do with the absence of action semantics language and its size. This chapter reviews and evaluates the UML evolution (UML2, xUML), providing criteria and requirements to evaluate UML and the xUML potential to raise levels of abstraction, flexibility, and productivity enhancement. At the same time, it pinpoints its liabilities that keep it from completely fulfilling the vision of software development through a continuous exactable modeling process, considered to be the future direction for modeling and implementation.

INTRODUCTION

In his book, Evitts describes the beginnings of UML tools (Evitts, 2000). The context prompting the development of UML was the increasing complexity of software which began in the 90s, when technologies (tools) that could deal with a network

and information-driven world did not yet exist. In 1991, Malone and Rockart described expectations that would soon emerge from all quarters. They noted that whenever people work together, there is a need to communicate so as to make decisions, allocate resources, and provide and receive products and services at the right time and place. However, in the early 90s, methodologies were rarely supported, either by common modeling tools, traditional methodologies (based upon process charts, ERD, and DFD), or object oriented methodologies. The semi-standard development process, the "waterfall," was convenient, albeit unperfected, whereas object-oriented provided none of these comforts, and the general opinion was that very few of its efforts had any real advantages over mainstream approaches.

In early 90s, the rise of Java, the standardization of C++, the birth and rebirth of CORBA, and the emergence of pattern languages for software design attracted a great deal of attention and popularity to UML. In June 1996, Rational released the 0.9 revision of UML, and then later on January 1997, Rational's 1.0 spec reached the market. In September 1997, Rational's UML 1.1 was combined with the OMG's UML proposal to create the final product that was called UML 1.0.

The current chapter evaluates the extent to which the UML can be used to support the modeling process, providing not only better communication among system analysts and developers. Primarily, it examines productivity enhancement through generating capabilities of wider range of software elements based upon modeling definitions.

BACKGROUND REVIEW

A. From UML 1 to UML 2.0

The scope of the UML has recently broadened. It is no only longer used to describe software systems, but now also business processes. With the service-oriented architect (SOA) and model driven architecture (MDA) initiatives, it has evolved to describe and automate business processes (activity diagram is a UML variation of the traditional process diagram), as well as become a language for developing platform-independent systems.

Earlier versions of the UML standard did not describe what it meant to support the standard. As a result, UML tool vendors were free to support incomplete UML features, and converting models from one tool to another was often extremely difficult, if not impossible.

UML 2.0 defines 38 compliance points (Ambler, 2004; Bjorkander & Kobryn, 2003). A compliance point is an area of UML, such as use cases. All implementations are required to implement a single compliance point, the kernel. The other 37 compliance points are currently optional. Evaluating modeling tools in light of these compliance points helps clarify which model elements are supported, and to what extent. For each compliance point, there are four compliance options. A compliance option determines how compliant a given implementation is. The four options are as follows:

- **No compliance**—the implementation does not comply with the syntax, rules, and notation for a given compliance point.
- **Partial compliance**—the implementation partially complies with the syntax, rules, and notation for a given compliance point.
- **Compliant compliance**—the implementation fully complies with the syntax, rules, and notation for a given compliance point.
- **Interchange compliance**—the implementation fully complies with the syntax, rules, notation, and XMI schema for a given compliance point.

However, UML 2.0 does not address any of UML 1.x's significant deficiencies, namely the lack of **business rule** Modeling, **workflow** modelling, and **user interface** modeling, although there is a business rule working group within the OMG. Several methodologists have suggested approaches to user interface flow modeling and design modeling using UML, but no official effort to develop a common profile exists.

B. Executable UML (xUML)

xUML is a subset of the UML, incorporating action language that allows system developers to build executable domain models and then use these models to produce system source code. Hence, xUML is an executable version of the UML.

The xUML process involves action specification language (ASL) (Raistrick, Francis, Wright, Carter, & Wilkie, 2004). The resulting models can be independently executed, debugged, viewed, and tested. Multiple xUML models can be assembled together to form complex systems with their shared mappings, expressed using ASL (Raistrick et al., 2004). Executable models can then be translated into target implementations. The execution rules of the xUML formalism means that the same models can be translated into a wide variety of target architectures without introducing changes into the models.

The xUML model enables modeling independency concerning hardware and software organization; in the same way typical, a compiler offers independency concerning register allocation and stack/heap organization. Furthermore, just as a typical language, compiler makes decisions about register allocation and the like for a specific machine environment, so a xUML model compiler makes decisions about a particular hardware and software environment, deciding, for example, to use a distributed Internet model with separate threads for each user window, HTML for the user interface displays, and so on.

The xUML methodology suggests a system partitioned into domains or subject matters (Miller & Mukerji, 2003). Each domain is modelled separately. Bridges are defined between domains, with some requirements placed between one domain and another and connector points defined for their exchange of information. The various domains and their dependency relationships are commonly displayed using package diagrams.

According to the OMG MDA approach (Miller & Mukerji, 2003), each xUML model is a platform-independent model (PIM). The mappings between such models are PIM-to-PIM mappings. The translation approach makes use of PIM to platform specific model (PSM) and platform specific implementation (PSI) mappings, in order to achieve executable modeling, large-scale reuse, and pattern-based design.

The xUML does not use all of the UML diagrams and constructs, as many are thought to be redundant. The xUML is intended to precisely model a system; any construct or building blocks that could introduce ambiguity should be left out of the model (Raistrick et al., 2004).

The most fundamental modeling diagrams in xUML are the class and state chart diagrams. Classes should be modeled with some degree of precision. A state machine is attached to each class to describe its dynamic behavior and lifecycle. In other words, in xUML, each class is thought to have a state machine that responds to events. Actions that are taken in response to events or about a certain state are specified precisely using some sort of action language. The specification 1.4 of the UML includes the specification of action semantics even though no concrete syntax for these semantics is specified. Typically, the xUML tool will provide an explanation about the action language syntax or syntaxes that the tool can interpret.

Use case and activity diagrams **are not** an integral part of the xUML but they are recommended as methods for gathering requirements before the model is constructed. Activity diagrams are employed to show the sequence of use cases and branching possibilities. Collaboration and sequence diagrams can be used to gain insight into the system or in some cases for visualizing aspects of the system after it has been built. They, too, are not executable.

C. Model Driven Architecture (MDA)

Model driven architecture initiated by the object management group OMG aims to place models at the core of the software development process, that is, model driven architecture of both the system and the software. The MDA claim can be regarded as a mere recommendation for how the system should be built, with little guarantee that the system will actually be built as specified. If some design decisions have to be revised, and decisions are taken to build the system differently during the implementation phase, rarely are the design models updated to reflect the decisions that make design models ineffective in the same manner as static documents, which are all ineffective as regards future maintenance.

RAD and other agile methods are based upon the same concept. The typical situations where analysis and design models often end up serving their intended purpose rather poorly, has led to iterative methods, having short iterations that repeat all modeling steps from analysis up to implementation.

Another MDA concept is platform independency. As technology progresses at a fast rate, new platforms are quickly introduced. Software written for a certain platform has very little use when transferred to other platforms—meaning most of the software must then be rewritten from scratch. If we were able to create a platform-independent model that could be translated to fit diverse platforms, many of the problems arising from platform instability could be avoided.

The MDA approach is based upon separation between a computation independent model (CIM), which is a precise business model, stakeholder oriented, uncommitted to specific algorithms or system boundaries, also known as a domain model and platform independent model, which is created at the analysis phase of software development. The PIM therefore is a long-term asset. A platform specific model is generated from the PIM in the design phase with some degree of [automation] autonomy. The PIM and the PSM concepts are not new, but the way they are modeled is. According to the MDA, there are four levels of modeling:

- **M0**—Objects living and interacting in a real system.
- **M1**—Models that define the structure and behavior of those objects. M1 models, on the other hand, are written in a language. These language constructs have to be defined somewhere.

- **M2**—Meta-models, or models about how M1 models are built. For instance, at level M2, one can find the UML meta-model, or a model about how M1 models are written by the language. Meta-models themselves have to be written in a language—that is what the level M3 stands for.
- **M3**—Meta-meta-modeling, defines how meta-models for language modeling can be built, or a language for meta-model refinement.

Theoretically, we could continue this way until we reach an arbitrary modeling level. In other words, there could be level M4 defining a language for M3, and level M5 from which M4 models are instanced, and so on. However, the MDA initiative defined that the M3 model is written with the M3 language, so there are no higher modeling levels, and M3 language is the metadata object facility (MOF), which is one of the OMG standards. The MOF model is written in MOF itself. Meta-models or models defining modeling languages are instances of the MOF model and thus written in the language defined by it. For instance, there is a meta-model for UML and it is written according to the one specified in the MOF model.

Another OMG standard is the XML metadata interchange or XMI. XMI defines model coding and meta-models in XML format. The standard defines XML generating for any MOF compliant language or meta-models. Moreover, because the MOF meta-model is written in MOF, the MOF meta-model itself can also be coded and exchanged in XML, enabling any vendor to make built-in variations or adaptations at the core of UML or any modeling concept.

Profile (UML Profiles) is also an MDA standard. UML profiles are basically a way to define UML dialects using UML standard extensibility mechanisms (stereotypes, tags, etc.). A number of profiles have been created or are being created for some popular platforms; these profiles serve as convenient PSM language for these platforms.

xUML is essentially related to MDA. xUML can be thought of as one way of implementing the MDA concept, with one notable exception (Raistrick et al., 2004). While MDA recommends that a platform-independent model be transformed into a platform-specific one before it is translated into code, xUML skips this intermediate step. Most xUML tools will translate models straight into code without generating a platform-specific model. On the other hand, the xUML model compiler can be thought of as being analogous to a transformation definition, where the rules about the transformation are declared.

COMPARISON ANALYSIS

The current chapter reviews and evaluates UML evolution (UML2, xUML), providing criteria and requirements to evaluate UML and the xUML potential to raise levels of abstraction, flexibility, and productivity enhancement, while pointing out the disadvantages that prevent it from completely fulfilling the vision of software development through a continuous exactable modeling process.

The following table presents these requirements, noting whether a requirement is supported or not. Based on the following data, the missing pieces that still need to be resolved in the upcoming versions of UML can be determined.

The (+) and (–) symbols note the presence and the absence of the relevant required feature.

Table 1. Requirements for executable software model

#	Required Feature	UML 2	xUML
1	Visualization	+	+
2	System Specification	+	+
3	System Documentation	+	+
4	Automatic Update	-	+
5	System Construction	+ (Partial)	+
6	Code Generation	+ (Partial)	+
7	Standardization	+	+
8	Modeling of classes with attributes, operations, and relationship	+ (Enhanced)	+ (Different relationships between classes in diagrams, state machine associated to each class)
9	Modeling of states and behavior of individual classes	+	+ (though the modeling is for a higher tier)
10	Modeling of packages of classes and their dependencies	+	+ (Extended to domains)
11	Modeling of system usage scenarios	+ (Enhanced)	+ (Enhanced)
12	Modeling of object instances with actual attributes in a scenario	+ (Enhanced)	+ (Enhanced)
13	Modeling of actual behavior of interacting instances in a scenario	+ (Enhanced)	+ (Enhanced)
14	Modeling of distributed component deployment and communication	+ (Enhanced)	+ (Enhanced)
15	Modeling of exceptions	+	+
16	Extension: Stereotypes	+	+
17	Extension: Profiles	+ (Enhanced)	+ (Enhanced)

continued on following page

Table 1. continued

#	Requirements	UML 2	xUML
18	Extension: meta-model	+	+
19	Modeling test cases	+	+
20	Scalability and precision of diagrams	+ (Enhanced but still partial)	+ (Limited support by available tools)
21	Gap reduction between design and implementation	-	+ (PIM, PSM)
22	Multiple views of the system	+	+
23	Domain, platforms, and process customization	+	+ (PIM, PSM)
24	Supporting visualization of user interfaces	-	-
25	Supporting logical expressions required for business logic, detailed definition, and design	-	-
26	Supporting organization and authori-zation structures	-	-
27	Supporting processes and workflow simulation	-	-
28	Supporting technical requirements		
29	Ability to represent the relation-ship between the design and specific platform	-	+ (PSM)
30	Describing structural and behavioral issues in a way that is easier to survey than in ordinary textual programming languages	+	+ (Enhanced functionality and action specification language, i.e., ASL, support)
31	Affecting translation into code: 1. Compiler is fast and reliable 2. Generated code is fast and robust	-	+ (PIM, PSM)
32	Generating diagrams from code	+	N/a (We always work on the model itself—all updates done on model and the code is generated from the model)
33	Possibility to under-specify unwanted or unavailable properties still to be defined	-	+ (PSM)
34	Possibility to transfer UML models between models	-	+ (partial)
35	Possibility to transfer UML models from one target language to another	-	+ (PSM)

FUTURE TRENDS: CURRENT UML AND XUML HOLDBACKS

As shown in the table, there are major areas of analysis which are not yet covered by the UML, such as user interface, business logic, organization and authorization structured, and so forth. Some of these areas are not adequately supported by the object oriented methodology itself, while others are mainly technical issues not methodological ones, such as affecting translation into code (requirement 31).

The current deficiencies of UML and xUML are listed.

1. One basic deficiency is language inability to support real-life facts and components that have to be defined and established in the system. This includes supporting visualization of user interfaces, logical expressions required for business logic and its detailed definition and design, organization and authorization structures, processes and workflow simulation, and technical requirements (such as performance, response time, etc.). Until we are able to do so, no system can be fully constructed. UML 2 provided enhanced diagrams, but the language was still not fully expressive. Therefore, there are still major significant pieces of code that must be hand-written or revised. There is no doubt that ideally, the entire system should be able to be constructed at the click of a button, but this cannot happen until the language is fully expressive. Until this happens, there is not much benefit in using xUML.

    Further UML steps should address this issue and enable system analysts to define entire business functionality, interface components, and technical requirements. This is easier to state than to implement.

2. The action semantics for the UML is a semantic standard alone, not a syntactic standard. This was, presumably a marketing decision, enabling vendors to supply either AMD-CASE tools or development tools, which already contained fully-realized action languages with proprietary syntaxes. One point of view maintains that syntax does not matter; however, it is easy to see that competing syntaxes may constrain the ability of xUML to acquire growth rates. On the other hand, because action languages exist at such a high level of abstraction, they do not require such sharp learning curves as those of third generation languages. Therefore, after learning one action language syntax, modellers could easily learn another, as they would, in essence, be dealing with the same semantic set.

    Further UML steps should address this issue in order to enable language and API transparency, and put aside political interests. Again, this is easy to say, but very complicated to apply, not so much because of technical reasons, but rather as a result of "human factors."

3. The original intent of the system analyst is impaired and lost in translation, when translating the UML model to PIM and then to PSM. The resulting code is sometimes awkward. Meta-models allow for the easy addition of new concepts. However, they do not ensure that these concepts will make semantic sense or that the different meta-models, such as UML profiles, will be consistent or orthogonal, with no contradictions with the original.

    Further UML steps should be directed towards integrity validation mechanisms, as developers are "developing-oriented" not "version comparing-oriented," which is quite a cumbersome and tedious task.

4. Moreover, the modeller tends to focus not only on the properties s/he is modeling (Rumpe, 2002), but also on execution efficiency. Therefore, the resulting code must include functionality and business accuracy, as well as performance and efficiency.

    Further UML steps should be directed towards supporting optimizing models and tools.

5. When using code generators that map UML to a target language, the semantics of the target language as well as its notational capabili-

ties tend to become visible on the UML level (Rumpe, (2002). For example, missing multiple-inheritance in Java may restrict xUML to single inheritance as well. Furthermore, the language's internal concurrency concept, message passing or exception handling may impose a certain dialect on xUML. This will cause UML dialects to be semantically incompatible. In particular, it will not be easy to make it possible to transfer UML models from one target language to another.

Further UML steps should address precise model transformation.

6. Last but not least are "model debugging" and the traceability-closure problem, that is, analysis error detection and closure between requirements and model components. Although the model, at the modeling stage, is only an outline, it has to be checked, debugged, optimized, and tested. Moreover, it has to enable detailed tracing in light of all requirements (both business and technical).

Further UML steps should be directed at "model debugging" and full traceability-closure, which has a huge impact not only on each one of the development cycles, but also over the entire system's life cycle.

CONCLUSION

The vision of generating an entire system at a single click is still not a reality, as is the vision of fully expressive modelling, which is also still not available. Furthermore, current field studies have shown that UML does not fulfill the "modelling vision" we all wish for. Dobing and Parsons studied "How UML is used" (Dobing & Parsons, 2006), and Davies, Green, Rosemann, Indulska, and Gallo published "How do practitioners use conceptual modeling in practice?" (Davies et al., 2006). Both

found the same trends, namely that UML diagrams are not clear enough to users or to developers, and recommend that additional demonstrative methods should be employed. Modeling of business logic, user interfaces, requirements (such as performance, response time, etc.), and other system components are still not fully available. The same goes for "model debugging" and detailed tracing and closure, which are crucial to the modeling stage. Technical aspects are also crucial in order to ensure usability and performance, but this seems to be a temporal issue rather than a conceptual one.

In light of the mentioned, the vision of generating an entire system by a single click will take place if and only if modelling languages, theories, and methodologies can overcome their conceptual limitations. In the IT domain, technical limitations are usually temporal, whereas conceptual limitations can lead to a dead-end.

ACKNOWLEDGMENT

I would like to thank David Belostovsky and Daphna Tsur for their contribution to this work.

REFERENCES

Ambler, S. W. (2004, March). What's new in UML 2. *Software Development Online Magazine.* Retrieved December 2006, from http://www.sdmagazine.com/documents/s=815/sdm0402i/

Bjorkander, M. (2000). Graphical programming using UML and SDL. *Computer, 33*(12), 30-35.

Bjorkander, M., & Kobryn, C. (2003). Architecting dystems with UML 2.0. *IEEE Software, 20*(4), 57-61.

Davies, I., Green, P., Rosemann, M., Indulska, M., & Gallo, S. (2006). How do practitioners use conceptual modeling in practice? *Data &Knowledge Engineering, 58*(3), 358-380.

Di Nitto, E., Lavazza, L., Schiavoni, M., Tracanella, E., & Trombetta, M. (2002). Deriving executable process descriptions from UML. In *Proceedings of the 24th International Conference on Software Engineering* (pp. 155-165).

Dobing, B., & Parsons, J. (2006). How UML is used. *Communication of the ACM, 49*(5), 109-113.

Evitts, P. (2000). *A UML pattern language*. New Riders Publishing.

Fei, X., Levin, V., & Browne, J. C. (2001). Model checking for an executable subset of UML. In *Proceedings of the 16th International Conference on Automated Software Engineering* (pp. 333-336).

Fowler, M. (2003). *UML distilled: A brief guide to the standard object modeling language* (3rd ed.). Addison Wesley.

Hölscher, K., Ziemann, P., & Gogolla, M. (2006). On translating UML models into graph transformation systems. *Journal of Visual Languages & Computing, 17*(1), 78-105.

HongXing, L., YanSheng, L., & Qing, Y. (2006). XML conceptual modeling with XUML. In *Proceedings of the 28th international conference on Software engineering* (pp. 973-976).

Jia, X., Steele, A., Qin, L., Liu, H., & Jones, C. (2007). Executable visual software modeling—The ZOOM approach. *Software Quality Journal, 15*(1), 27-51.

Liu, L., & Roussev, B. (2006). *Management of the object-oriented development process*. Idea Group.

Miller, J., & Mukerji, J. (2003, May). MDA guide. *OMG Organization*. Retrieved December 2006, from http://www.omg.org/mda/mda_files/MDA_Guide_Version1-0.pdf

Raistrick, C., Francis, P., Wright, J., Carter, C., & Wilkie, I. (2004). *Model driven architecture with executable UML*. Cambridge.

Rumpe, B. (2002). *Executable modeling with UML—A vision or a nightmare?* (Tech. Rep.). Munich University of Technology. Retrieved December 2006, from http://www4.in.tum.de/~rumpe/ps/IRMA.UML.pdf

Seidewitz, E. (2003). Unified modeling language specification v1.5. *IEEE Software, 20*(5), 26-32.

Thomas, D. (2004). MDA: Revenge of the modelers or UML Utopia?. *IEEE Software, 21*(3), 15-17.

KEY TERMS

Agile Software Development: A conceptual framework for undertaking software engineering projects that embraces and promotes evolutionary change throughout the entire life cycle of the project.

Executable UML (xUML): A software engineering methodology that graphically specifies a deterministic system using UML notations. The models are testable and can be compiled, translated, or weaved into a less abstract programming language to target a specific implementation. Executable UML supports MDA through specification of platform independent models (PIM).

Model-Driven Architecture (MDA): A software design approach launched by the object management group (OMG) in 2001.

Object Management Group (OMG): A consortium, originally aimed at setting standards for distributed object-oriented systems, and is now focused on modeling (programs, systems, and business processes) and model-based standards.

Platform-Independent Model (PIM): A model of a software or business system that is independent of the specific technological platform used to implement it.

Rapid Application Development (RAD): A software development process developed initially by James Martin in the 1980s. The methodology involves iterative development, the construction of prototypes, and the use of computer-aided software engineering (CASE) tools.

Software Engineering: The application of a systematic, disciplined, quantifiable approach to the development, operation, and maintenance of software.

System Modeling: An abstraction or conceptual representation used for system illustration.

Unified Modeling Language (UML): A standardized specification language for object modeling. UML is a general-purpose modeling language that includes a graphical notation used to create an abstract model of a system,

Chapter XIV
From Business Process Model to Information Systems Model:
Integrating DEMO and UML

Peter Rittgen
University College of Borås, Sweden

ABSTRACT

The main purpose of a corporate information system is the support of the company's business processes. The development of information systems is therefore typically preceded by an analysis of the business processes it is supposed to support. The tasks of analysing business processes and designing information systems are governed by two seemingly incompatible perspectives related to the interaction between human actors or inanimate agents (objects), respectively. As a consequence, the corresponding modeling languages also differ. DEMO (dynamic essential modeling of organization) is a typical language for modeling business processes, the UML is the predominant language for information systems modeling. We challenge the assumption of incompatibility of the perspectives by providing a framework for the integration of these languages.

INTRODUCTION

In the action view, a system consists of a number of agents (people or organizational units) who interact with each other by communicating. The basic unit of communication is a speech act (Austin, 1962; Searle, 1969). A transaction (Weigand & van den Heuvel, 1998) is the smallest sequence of actions that has an effect in the social world (e.g., establishing a commitment). It typically consists of two speech acts: an utterance and the response (e.g., a request and the promise). On the third level, the workflow loop (or action workflow, Medina-Mora, Winograd, Flores,

& Flores, 1992) describes a communicative pattern consisting of two consecutive transactions that aim at reaching an agreement about (1) the execution of an action and (2) the result of that execution. The left side of Figure 1 shows three examples of workflow loops. Higher levels can be defined such as contract and scenario but the first three are sufficient for the purpose of this chapter. More details on the action view are given in the section "Dynamic Essential Modeling of Organization."

In the reaction view, object orientation prevails today. It has largely replaced the functional paradigm that characterized early approaches to software en-

Figure 1. Action view and reaction view

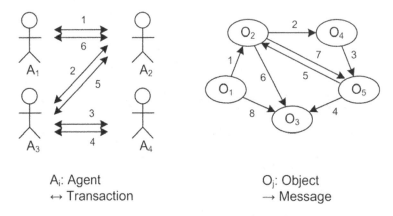

A$_i$: Agent
↔ Transaction

O$_j$: Object
→ Message

gineering (and is still used in certain areas such as databases). In object orientation, a system is seen as a collection of objects exchanging messages. Each object encapsulates data and functionality (or structure and behaviour, or attributes and operations). An object is in principal a passive (or reactive) unit that only acts if it receives a message. It will then carry out the appropriate operation which might involve sending messages to other objects. Finally, it will deliver the result as a reply to the original message but "communication" is essentially one-way (see Figure 1, right). More details on the reaction view can be found in the object-oriented literature, for example (Dori, 2002).

The major conceptual differences between the views are:

1. The action view describes social systems that consist of human beings that can both act of their own accord and react to stimuli from the environment, whereas an object can only react.

2. By performing speech acts, agents create obligations for themselves or others. Having a conscience, they are fully aware of the consequences of entering into a commitment and also of not fulfilling an obligation. An object is not equipped with a conscience so it cannot commit itself. If an object behaves in the

"desired" way, this is due to a pre-programmed automatism and not the result of an individual decision based on free will. An object cannot be responsible for its "actions."

3. Communicating is not just exchanging messages. We communicate to achieve a certain purpose for which we need the help of others. An object sends a message because its code prescribes this behaviour and the message is received, processed, and "answered" for precisely the same reason. An object has no intentions.

BACKGROUND

Regarding the reaction view, the task of finding an appropriate language is not difficult. The software engineering community has subjected itself to a rigorous standardization process that resulted in the unified modeling language (UML). It follows the object-oriented paradigm and is widely used in the design of information systems. Adhering to the reaction view, its focus is more on the technical part of the information systems than on the organizational (i.e., social) part, but the proponents of UML claim that it can also be used for the latter. As evidence for this standpoint, they mention use cases and business processes. For the former, UML provides a specific language construct: use case diagrams. The latter were originally supposed to be represented as activity diagrams (with swimlanes), but a language extension called enterprise collaboration architecture (ECA, OMG 2004) now takes care of business processes. Nevertheless, UML does not offer an action view because the concept of an actor is weakly integrated and restricted to the role of a user of the information system. Moreover, empirical research shows (Dobing & Parsons, 2006) that UML is often not applied in a use case-driven way, which suggests a need for a different front-end that provides better communication with users.

The situation regarding the action view is more complex. The approaches assuming this view cover a wide range of epistemological orientations coming from disciplines as diverse as social sciences, political science, law, linguistics, cognitive science, organizational theory, artificial intelligence, and computer science. They have in common that they are based on the speech-act theory (Austin, 1962; Searle, 1969; Habermas, 1984). Examples of such approaches are conversation-for-action (Winograd & Flores, 1986), DiaLaw (Lodder & Herczog, 1995), illocutionary logic (Dignum & Weigand 1995), dynamic essential modeling of organizations (DEMO, Dietz, 1999), action workflow (Medina-Mora, Winograd, Flores, & Flores, 1992; Denning & Medina-Mora, 1995), action-based modeling (Lehtinen & Lyytinen, 1986), business action theory & SIMM (Goldkuhl & Röstlinger, 1993; Goldkuhl, 1996), and discourse structures (Johannesson, 1995). As we aim at finding a language that is suitable for being mapped to UML, we would like it to exhibit certain external similarities with UML: on the syntactic level it should provide a diagram-like notation and on the semantic level it should possess an appropriate degree of formality. We found that dynamic essential modeling of organization (DEMO) fulfils these criteria best.

DYNAMIC ESSENTIAL MODELING OF ORGANIZATION

In the action view, the structure of an organization is understood as a network of commitments. As these commitments are the result of communication, it follows that a model of the organization is essentially a model based on purposeful, communicative acts. In DEMO, all acts that serve the same purpose are collected in a *transaction* in which two roles are engaged: the *initiator* and the *executor*. The definition of a transaction in DEMO is broader than that given in the introduction. It comes closer to that of a workflow loop but it also includes a non-communicative action, namely the agreed action that the executor performs in the object world. Hence, each transaction is assumed to follow a certain pattern which is divided into three sequential phases and three layers. The phases are: *order* (O), *execute* (E), and *result* (R). The layers are: success, discussion, and discourse. On the success layer, the phases are structured as follows. In the order phase the contract is negotiated. This involves typically a *request* being made by the initiator and a *promise* by the executor to carry out the request. In the next phase the contract is executed which involves factual changes in the object world (as opposed to the inter-subject world of communication). Finally, in the result phase the executor *states* that the agreed result has been achieved and the initiator *accepts* this *fact*. If anything goes wrong on the success layer, the participants can decide to move to the discussion or discourse layer. For details on these layers see Reijswoud (1996). The models of DEMO are: interaction model, business process model, action model, fact model, and interstriction model. The strengths of DEMO lie in its systematic and stringent ontology that provides strong guidelines for modeling and fully implements the (communicative) action perspective. On the other hand, DEMO subscribes to a particular conceptualization of the world and does not allow expressing a system from another perspective, for example, the reaction view.

It therefore needs to be complemented by another language, in our case, UML.

Figure 2 gives examples of an interaction model and a business process model. They are taken from Reijswoud and Dietz (1999) and show a part of the business process of an organization called SGC, a non-profit organization that mediates consumer complaints in the Netherlands.

The transactions of the example are as follows:

- T6: handling_complaint
- T7: defending_complaint
- T8: giving_advice
- T9: passing_judgement

A LANGUAGE-MAPPING FRAMEWORK FOR DEMO AND UML

The object management group (OMG) has suggested architecture for language integration that is called model-driven architecture (MDA, Miller & Mukerji, 2003). In it, a system is specified from three different viewpoints: computation independent, platform independent, and platform specific. Although the scope of MDA is much broader, a typical assumption is that all models (views) can be constructed

with the help of only one language, and UML is the preferred candidate for that role. But Evans, Maskeri, Sammut, and Willans (2003) argue that "a truly flexible model-driven development process should not dictate the language that practitioners should use to construct models, even an extensible one. Instead they should be free to use whichever language is appropriate for their particular domain and application, particularly as many languages cannot be shoe-horned into the UML family." We follow this argument and suggest extending the model mapping of MDA (Caplat & Sourrouille, 2003) to "language mapping."

We distinguish between the conceptual level and the instance level. On the conceptual level, we first perform concept mapping. This step involves finding for each concept of the source language a matching one in the target language. A successful match implies that a significant part of the semantics of the source concept can also be expressed by the target concept. Note that concept mapping as defined here does not relate to the one known from (empirical) social research. For example, the DEMO concept of an action maps to the UML concept of an action state. The latter is something that is performed while the system is in a certain state. As this is very general, it encompasses the meaning of action in DEMO for which the same holds, but in addition to that, an action is restricted to being

Figure 2. Examples of an interaction model and a business process model

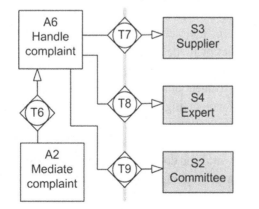
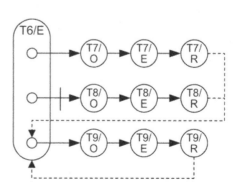

either an objective action in the object world or a communicative action in the inter-subject world. Note that such a mapping is not always possible because the target language might not have a related concept at all or the "common denominator" between both concepts is not a significant part of the semantics of the source concept (i.e., the two concepts have very little in common). This implies that language mapping cannot be done for any combination of languages, at least not in the way described here. Moreover, we cannot expect that we always succeed in establishing a one-to-one correspondence between concepts. Sometimes several source concepts jointly map to one target concept or one source concept maps to a conjunction of target concepts.

The second step consists of a notational mapping. We assume that each concept is associated with a notational element in the respective language, so with concept mapping being done, this step is straightforward. The third and last step is about establishing a relation between the diagram types of both languages. This step provides rules for carrying out the actual diagram transformation on the instance level. Typical types of transformations include:

1. One element has to be mapped to a number of elements (e.g., a sub graph). This process is called unfolding.
2. Additional elements (of a different type) have to be introduced. This process is called element introduction.
3. Nodes are transformed into arcs (called node inversion) or arcs are transformed into nodes (arc inversion).
4. A substructure of the source language is transformed into a different substructure of the target language. This is called graph conversion.

In the following subsections, we specialize this framework for DEMO as the source language and UML as the target language.

DIAGRAM TRANSFORMATION

Figure 3 shows the overall framework for the language mapping. The DEMO diagrams are represented by rounded boxes, the UML diagrams by rectangular boxes. The mapping of concepts is visualized by single-headed arrows, the transformation of diagrams by double-headed arrows. Each diagram conversion involves a transformation of the notation but will also require some more sophisticated transformation process (e.g., transaction unfolding). Concurrency explication and class association are graph conversions, signal and infolink introduction are element introductions, and transaction unfolding is an unfolding in the sense of the general integration framework.

The interaction model introduces systems, actors, and transactions that all become classes in UML. But the transactions (the most important concept of DEMO) also form states in the statechart diagram. The business process model refines transactions into phases which in turn become sub states of the respective transaction state in the statechart diagram. The basic elements of the fact model are the categories. They correspond to classes in UML. The interstriction model introduces fact and communication banks to store records of facts and communication. They also correspond to classes in UML. The action model introduces wait states which map to signal receipts in activity diagrams.

The interaction model is transformed into the collaboration diagram. Apart from a notational conversion, this requires an unfolding of the transactions, a concept which has no immediate dynamic counterpart in UML. Each transaction is split into its communicative acts which then are represented by messages in UML. An example of that is given in the next section.

The business process model is transformed into the statechart diagram. Again, this involves a change in notation but also an explication of the inherent concurrent behaviour of a phase. A phase can have many concurrent initiation points but each state has only one initial (sub) state. Dividing the

Figure 3. Framework for integrating DEMO and UML

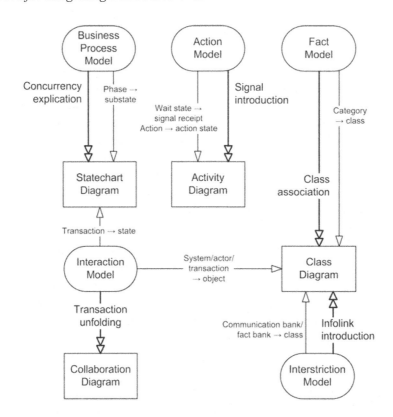

state into concurrent regions is not feasible due to the asynchronous nature of the threads triggered by the initiation points. Hence, the initial state is forked into as many threads as there are initiation points that have no arrows pointing at them (plus one that leads to the final state if no arrow points to the phase). An arrow pointing at a phase maps to one pointing at the corresponding final state. If more than one arrow points at a phase or initiation point, the respective arrows in the statechart diagram are joined by a synchronization bar. Optional relationships map to guarded transitions. An example for such a transformation is given in the next section.

The action model is transformed into the activity diagram. Apart from the usual notational conversion, this means that a signal receipt has to be introduced into the activity diagram for each wait state that is found in the action model. Likewise, a signal sending is introduced after the activity that corresponds to the action that is waited for.

The fact model is transformed into the class diagram. This involves that each fact (which is an *n*-ary relations between categories) is mapped to an association class that has associations to each of the classes corresponding to the categories. That process is called class association.

The interstriction model introduces further associations into the class diagram, one for each informational link between an actor and a transaction, fact bank, or communication bank. We call that process infolink introduction.

EXAMPLES OF DIAGRAM TRANSFORMATION

Due to the limited space, we give examples for the first two transformations only. Figure 4 shows the collaboration diagram (upper half) for the interaction model of Figure 2 (left) and also the statechart diagram (lower half) for the business process model of Figure 2 (right). Each system or actor of the interaction model becomes an object (instance) in the collaboration diagram. A transaction is represented by a (communication) link that bears the name of the transaction (i.e., its purpose). This link is bidirectional (i.e., it does not have an arrowhead that restricts the navigability) because a transaction involves communication in both directions, from initiator to executor and back. This link can now be used to exchange the messages that

correspond to the communicative acts in DEMO. Each executor has also a link to itself which means that the execution phase is self-induced. A request and an accept message are introduced along the link with arrows that point from the initiator to the executor. They represent the first and the last communicative acts of a transaction, respectively. In the same way, a promise and a state message are attached to the link. They are passed from the executor to the initiator and form the second and penultimate speech acts, respectively. Observe that a collaboration diagram does not require us to specify the order of messages, but we could do so with the help of sequence numbers in front of the message names.

The lower half of Figure 4 shows the statechart diagram that corresponds to the excerpt from the business process model of Figure 2. The execution

Figure 4. Collaboration diagram and statechart diagram

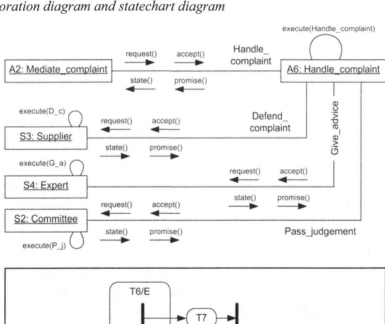

phase of T6 becomes a state (which itself is a sub state of the transaction state T6). Within T6/E, the initial state is forked into two concurrent threads to trigger transactions T7: defending_complaint and T8: giving_advice. While T7 is triggered in any case, the transition to T8 is guarded by [c], which means that the expert is asked to give advice under a condition that has not yet been specified; the business process model only indicates that T8 is optional, not under which circumstances it is carried out. On completion of T7 (and possibly T8), T9: passing_judgment is carried out. After that, we enter the terminal state of T6/E which concludes the execution phase of T6.

This and the preceding section give only an overview of the overall process. The details can be found in Rittgen (2006). The benefits of the language mapping include a smooth transition from the analysis to the design phase and an improved user-oriented front-end for UML.

FUTURE TRENDS

The work we have described can be seen as an implementation of a specific strategy of method engineering (Ralyté, Deneckère, & Rolland, 2003) called method chunks assembly, with the chunks being DEMO and UML. It is certainly worthwhile to investigate a more profound integration of language mapping and method engineering and how these fields could benefit from each other. There is some evidence that language mapping can be used in other method engineering strategies, too, and the mapping process might be supported by method engineering techniques such as the association technique.

Finally, our chapter only scratches at the surface of a fundamental research question that deserves more attention: How can we align the processes of organizational development and systems development in such a way that the information systems support the business in an optimal way? This question is studied under the heading "co-design

(or co-evolvement) of business and IT," but so far we have only seen the very beginnings of research in that area.

CONCLUSION

The ideas in this chapter were inspired by a project we carried out together with two companies: a logistics provider and a large retail chain. The objective was to model the complex interorganizational business process as a basis for its reorganization. We found that the language-action perspective was successful in that scenario. One of the reasons for this is certainly the highly interactive nature of the process we studied, where communication is vital and frequent. But LAP also facilitated understanding among people who not only came from different organizations but also worked in different domains: purchase, marketing, inbound and outbound logistics, and so forth. It made a complex process more transparent to all participants (each of whom provided only a small puzzle piece to the overall picture) and it allowed them to discuss in a constructive way possible options for reorganization. As a result, two major areas for improvement were identified: a tighter integration between the different information systems of both companies and a greater accuracy in the forecasts concerning incoming and outgoing commodity flows.

The framework that we have presented suggests an approach to solving the first problem. It allows for the mediation between two important views by providing a mapping between their associated languages, DEMO and UML. This is done by mapping their respective concepts and eventually transforming diagrams of the former into corresponding ones of the latter. These two languages represent completely different paradigms: DEMO is an approach that is deeply rooted in linguistics and the study of human communication, while UML has many of its roots in computer science and the study of software artefacts (though by far not all). It is therefore surprising that a language mapping can be undertaken at all. It should be noted, though, that we have chosen from the set of all language-action approaches the one that best facilitates integration with UML. Other languages of the action view might prove to be less suitable. Nevertheless, we hope that our work can contribute to narrowing the gap between organizational modeling and the design of information systems.

REFERENCES

Austin, J. L. (1962). *How to do things with words.* Oxford University Press.

Caplat, G., & Sourrouille, J. L. (2003, October 21). Considerations about model mapping. In J. Bezivin & M. Gogolla (Eds.), *Workshop in software model engineering (WiSME@UML '2003)* San Francisco. Online version available at http://www.metamodel. com/wisme-2003/18.pdf

Denning, P. J., & Medina-Mora, R. (1995). Completing the loops. *Interfaces, 25*(3), 42-57.

Dietz, J. L. G. (1999). Understanding and modeling business processes with DEMO. In J. Akoka, M. Bouzeghoub, I. Comyn-Wattiau, & E. Métais (Eds.), *Proceedings of Conceptual modeling—ER '99 (Lecture notes in computer science 1728)* (pp. 188-202). Berlin: Springer.

Dignum, F., & Weigand, H. (1995, June 12-16). Modelling communication between cooperative systems. In J. Iivari, K. Lyytinen, & M. Rossi (Eds.), *Advanced information systems engineering, Proceedings of the 7th International Conference, CAiSE '95,* Jyväskylä, Finland (Vol. 932, pp. 140-153). Lecture Notes in Computer Science Berlin: Springer.

Dobing, B., & Parsons, J. (2006). How UML is used. *Communications of the ACM, 49*(5), 109-113.

Dori, D. (2002). *Object-process methodology. A holistic systems paradigm.* Berlin: Springer.

Evans, A., Maskeri, G., Sammut, P., & Willans, J. S. (2003, October 21). Building families of languages for model-driven system development. In J. Bezivin & M. Gogolla (Eds.), *Workshop in Software Model Engineering (WiSME@UML'2003).* San Francisco Online version available at http://www.metamodel. com/wisme-2003/ 06.pdf

Goldkuhl, G. (1996). Generic business frameworks and action modelling. In F. Dignum, J. Dietz, E. Verharen, & H. Weigand (Eds.), *Communication Modeling—The Language/Action Perspective, Proceedings of the First International Workshop on Communication Modeling, Electronic Workshops in Computing.* Berlin: Springer.

Goldkuhl, G., & Röstlinger, A. (1993). Joint elicitation of problems: An important aspect of change analysis. In D. Avison, J. Kendall, & J. DeGross (Eds.), *Human, organizational, and social dimensions of information systems development.* Amsterdam: North-Holland.

Habermas, J. (1984). *The theory of communicative action 1, Reason and the rationalization of society.* Boston: Beacon Press.

Johannesson, P. (1995). Representation and communication: A speech act based approach to information systems design. *Information Systems, 20*(4), 291-303.

Lehtinen, E., & Lyytinen, K. (1986). An action based model of information systems. *Information Systems, 11*(4), 299-317.

Lodder, A. R., & Herczog, A. (1995). DiaLaw—A dialogical framework for modelling legal reasoning. In *Proceedings of the fifth International Conference on Artificial Intelligence and Law* (pp. 146-155). New York: ACM.

Medina-Mora, R., Winograd, T., Flores, R., & Flores, F. (1992). The action workflow approach to workflow management technology. In J. Turner & R. Kraut (Eds.), *Proceedings of the Conference on Computer-Supported Cooperative Work, CSCW'92.* New York: ACM Press.

Miller, J., & Mukerji, J. (Eds.). (2003). *MDA guide* (version 1.0.1). Needham: OMG. Online version available at http://www.omg.org/docs/omg/03-06-01.pdf

OMG (2004). *Enterprise collaboration architecture specification* (version 1.0). Needham: OMG. Online version available at http://www.uml.org

Ralyté J., Deneckère, R., & Rolland, C. (2003, June 16-18). Towards a generic model for situational method engineering. In *Proceedings of the15th International Conference on Advanced Information Systems Engineering (Caise 2003)*, Klagenfurt, Austria, (pp. 95-110). Heidelberg, Germany: Springer-Verlag.

Reijswoud, V. E. van (1996). *The structure of business communication: Theory, model and application*. PhD Thesis. Delft, The Netherlands: Delft University of Technology.

Reijswoud, V.E. van, & Dietz, J. L. G. (1999). *DEMO modelling handbook* (volume 1). TU Delft. Online version available at http://www.demo.nl/documents/handbook.pdf

Searle, J. R. (1969). *Speech acts, an essay in the philosophy of language*. London: Cambridge University Press.

Weigand, H., & van den Heuvel, W. J. (1998). Meta-patterns for electronic commerce transactions based on FLBC. In *Proceedings of the Hawaii Int. Conf on System Sciences (HICSS '98)* IEEE Press.

Winograd, T., & Flores, F. (1986). *Understanding computers and cognition: A new foundation for design*. Norwood, NJ: Ablex.

KEY TERMS

Action View: In the action view, a system consists of a number of actors that can act of their own accord motivated by internal needs and desires as well as react to stimuli from the environment or other actors.

Actor: An actor is a human being. An actor can act on his/her own behalf or on the behalf of some organization.

Agent: An agent is an artefact, that is, inanimate, but can nevertheless exhibit behaviour. This behaviour is pre-determined and follows a given set of instructions which involve suitable reactions to external stimuli.

Concept Mapping: In concept mapping, we identify concepts in the target language that match the concepts of the source language. This is not always a one-to-one correspondence and may involve complex and structured relations.

Diagram Transformation: Models are typically represented as diagrams, that is, graphs. Graph conversion rules are employed to translate the source diagram into the target diagram.

Language Mapping: In language mapping, we "translate" a model from one language to another while preserving as much as possible of the original semantics. The steps involved in this process are concept mapping, notational mapping, and diagram transformation.

Notational Mapping: Notational mapping resolves conflicts arising from different notations (symbols) used for the same or similar concepts in source and target language.

Reaction View: In the reaction view, the system consists of a number of agents that merely react to stimuli from the environment or other agents.

Chapter XV
Foundations of Business Process Modeling

Jan Mendling
Queensland University of Technology, Australia

ABSTRACT

This chapter provides an overview of business process management and business process modeling. We approach business process management by giving a historical classification of seminal work, and define it by the help of the business process management life cycle. Business process models play an important role in this life cycle, in particular, if information systems are used for executing processes. We deduct a definition for business process modeling based on a discussion of modeling from a general information systems point of view. In the following, we detail business process modeling techniques, in particular, modeling languages and modeling procedures for business process modeling. Finally, we discuss some future trends with a focus on the business process execution language for Web services (BPEL), and conclude the chapter with a summary. The chapter aims to cover business process modeling in a comprehensive way such that academics and practitioners can use it as a reference for identifying more specialized works.

INTRODUCTION

This section provides an overview of business process management. The first part elaborates on the background of business process management by giving a historical classification of seminal work. The second part defines business process management and illustrates it by the help of the business process management life cycle. Business process models play an important role in this life cycle.

HISTORY OF BUSINESS PROCESS MANAGEMENT

In the last couple of years, there has been a growing interest in business process management, from practice as well as from business administration and information systems research. In essence, business process management deals with the efficient coordination of business activities within and between companies. As such, it can be related to several seminal works on economics and business administration. Fayol (1966), as one of the founders of modern organization theory recommended a subdivision of labor in order to increase productivity. Adam Smith (1776) illustrated its potential benefits by analyzing pin production. As a drawback, subdivision of labor requires coordination between the subtasks. Business process management is concerned with coordination mechanisms, in order to leverage the efficient creation of goods and services in a production system based on such subdivision of labor. In this context, the individual tasks and the coordination between them can be subject to optimization efforts. Frederick Taylor advocated the creation of an optimal work environment based on scientific methods to leverage the most efficient way of performing individual work steps. In the optimization of each step, he proposed to "select the quickest way," to "eliminate all false movements, slow movements, and useless movements," and to "collect into one series the quickest and best movements" (Taylor, 1911). The efficient coordination of business processes is addressed by the innovation of the assembly line system. Its inventor Ford (1926), proudly praised the production cycle of only 81 hours in his company "from the mine to the finished machine" to illustrate the efficiency of the concept.

In academia, Nordsieck was one of the first to distinguish structural and process organization (Nordsieck, 1932, 1934). He described several types of workflow diagrams, for example, for subdivision and distribution of labor, sequencing of activities, or task assignment (Nordsieck, 1932). In this context, he identifies the order of work steps and the temporal relationship of tasks as the subject of process analysis with the overall goal of integrating these steps. He distinguishes between five levels of automation: free course of work, concerning the contents bound course of work, concerning the order bound course of work, temporally bound course of work, and concerning the beat bound course of work (Nordsieck, 1934).

In the decades after World War II, operations research devoted more attention to structural organization than to process organization. In the

early 1970s, it became apparent that information systems would become a new design dimension in an organizational setting (see Grochla & Szyperski, 1975). But the focus, even in this context, remained on the structure. At that time, the logic of business processes used to be hard-coded in applications such as production floor automation systems and was, therefore, difficult to change (Hsu & Kleissner, 1996; zur Muehlen, 2004). Office automation technology during the late 1970s was the starting point for a more explicit control over the flow of information and the coordination of tasks. The basic idea was to build electronic forms for clerical work that was originally handled via paper. In his doctoral thesis, Zisman (1978, 1977) used Petri nets (Petri, 1962a, 1962b) to specify the clerical work steps of an office agent and introduced a respective prototype system called SCOOP. A comparable approach was presented by Ellis (1979), who modelled office procedures as information control nets, a special kind of Petri nets consisting of activities, precedence constraints, and information repositories. An overview of further work on office automation is provided in Ellis and Nutt (1980).

Although the business importance of processes received some attention in the 1980s (see Porter, 1985) and new innovations were introduced in information system support of processes, for instance (e.g., system support for communication processes (Winograd, 1987-1988) based on speech act theory (Austin, 1962; Searle, 1969)), it was only in the early 1990s that workflow management prevailed as a new technology to support business processes. An increasing number of commercial vendors of workflow management systems benefited from new business administration concepts and ideas such as process innovation (Davenport, 1993) and business process reengineering (Hammer & Champy, 1993). On the other hand, these business programs heavily relied on information system technology, in particular workflow systems, in order to establish new and more efficient ways of doing business. In the 1990s, the application of workflow systems, in particular, those supporting information systems integration processes, profited from open communication standards and distributed systems technology that both contributed to interoperability with other systems (see Georgakopoulos, Hornick, & Sheth, 1995). The workflow management coalition (WfMC) founded in 1993 is of special importance for this improvement (Hollingsworth, 2004). The historical overview of office automation and workflow systems given in zur Muehlen (2004) nicely illustrates this breakthrough. This period also saw a growing body of scientific publications on workflow technology and process specification (see van der Aalst, 1998; Casati, Ceri, Pernici, & Pozzi, 1995; Ellis & Nutt, 1993; Georgakopoulos et al., 1995; Jablonski & Bussler, 1996; Leymann & Roller, 2000; Oberweis, 1996; Oberweis & Sander, 1996; Reichert & Dadam, 1998; Scholz-Reiter & Stickel, 1996). Up to the late 1990s, intra-enterprise processes remained the major focus of business process management (see Dayal, Hsu, & Ladin, 2001).

Since the advent of the extended markup language (XML) and Web services technology, application scenarios for business process integration have become much easier to implement in an inter-enterprise setting. Current standardization efforts mainly address interoperability issues related to such scenarios (see Mendling, Nüttgens, & Neumann, 2004; Mendling, zur Muehlen, & Price, 2005; Mendling, Neumann, & Nüttgens, 2005). The common interest of the industry to facilitate the integration of inter-organizational processes leverages the specification of standards for Web service composition, like the business process execution language for Web services (Alves et al., 2007, Andrews et al., 2003, Curbera et al., 2002), for Web service choreography, like the Web service choreography description language (WS-CDL) (Kavantzas et al., 2005), or for inter-organizational processes based on ebXML and related standards (see Hofreiter, Huemer, & Kim, 2006). The integration of composition and choreography languages is currently one of the main research topics in this area (see Mendling & Hafner, 2005; Weber, Haller, & Mülle, 2006).

Today, business process management is an important research area that combines insights from business administration, organization theory, computer science, and computer supported cooperative work. Furthermore, it is a considerable market for software vendors, IT service providers, and business consultants.

Definition of Business Process Management

Since the beginnings of organization theory, several definitions for business processes have been proposed. Nordsieck, in the early 1930s, describes a business process as a sequence of activities producing an output. In this context, an activity is the smallest separable unit of work performed by a work subject (Nordsieck, 1934). In this tradition, Becker and Kugeler (2003) propose the following definition:

A process is a completely closed, timely and logical sequence of activities which are required to work on a process-oriented business object. Such a process-oriented object can be, for example, an invoice, a purchase order or a specimen. A business process is a special process that is directed by the business objectives of a company and by the business environment. Essential features of a business process are interfaces to the business partners of the company (e.g., customers, suppliers).

As Davenport (1993) puts it, a "process is thus a specific ordering of work activities across time and place, with a beginning, an end, and clearly identified inputs and outputs: a structure for action." Van der Aalst and van Hee (2002) add that the order of the activities is determined by a set of conditions. In this context, it is important to distinguish between the business process and several individual cases. Consider a business process such as car production. This process produces cars as an output. The production of one individual car that is sold to customer John Smith is a case. Accordingly, each case can be distinguished from other cases, and a business process can be regarded as a class of similar cases (van der Aalst & van Hee, 2002).

Related to business processes and information systems support, several categorization schemes were proposed. As an extension of Porter's value chain model (see Porter, 1985), van der Aalst and van Hee (2002) distinguish between production, support, and managerial processes. Production processes create products and services of a company that are sold to customers. These processes are of paramount importance since they generate income for the company. Support processes establish an environment in which the production processes go smoothly. Therefore, they do not only include maintenance activities, but also marketing and finance. Managerial processes direct and coordinate production and support processes. They are basically concerned with defining goals, preconditions, and constraints for the other processes. Leymann and Roller (2000) provide a classification scheme[1] for processes based on their business value and their degree of repetition. They use the term production process to refer to those processes that have both a high business value and a high degree of repetition. Administrative processes are also highly repetitive, but of little business value. Furthermore, collaborative processes are highly valuable, but hardly repeatable. Finally, ad hoc processes are neither repetitive nor valuable. Leymann and Roller conclude that information systems support should focus on production processes. In particular, workflow management systems are discussed as a suitable tool. Further classifications can be found, for example, in Dumas, ter Hofstede, and van der Aalst (2005).

Business process management can be defined as the set of all management activities related to business processes. In essence, the management activities related to business processes can be idealistically arranged in a life cycle. Business process management life cycle models have been described for instance in van der Aalst and van Hee (2002), Dumas et al. (2005), and zur Muehlen (2004). In the remainder of this section, we mainly follow the life cycle proposed by zur Muehlen (2004), firstly, because it does not only include activities but also artefacts, and secondly, because it consolidates several earlier life cycle models for business process management. The life cycle shares the activities analysis, design, and implementation with the general process of information systems development identified by Wand and Weber (1990). Altogether, the life cycle comprises the management activities of analysis, design, implementation, enactment, monitoring, and evaluation. The solid arcs represent the typical order of these activities; while the dotted arcs depict atypical feedback loops (see Figure 1).

- **Analysis:** The business process management life cycle is entered with an analysis activity (see Figure 1). This analysis covers both the environment of the process and the organization structure. The output of this step is a set of requirements for the business process, such as performance goals.

- **Design:** These requirements drive the subsequent design activity. In particular, the design includes the identification of process activities, the definition of their order, the assignment of resources to activities, and the definition of the organization structure. These different aspects of process design are typically formalized as a business process model. This model can be tested in a simulation if it meets the design requirements.[2]

- **Implementation:** The process model is then taken as input for the implementation. In this phase, the infrastructure for the business process is set up. This includes (among others) training of staff, provision of a dedicated work infrastructure, or the technical implementation and configuration of software. If the process execution is to be supported by dedicated information systems, the process model is used as a blueprint for the implementation.

- **Enactment:** As soon as the implementation is completed, the actual enactment of the

Figure 1. Business process management life cycle

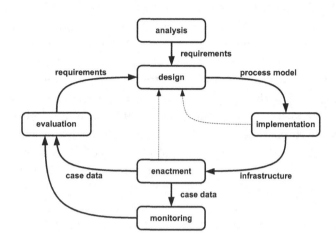

process can begin. In this phase, the dedicated infrastructure is used to handle individual cases covered by the business process. The enactment produces information such as consumption of time, resources, materials, and so forth, for each of the handled cases. This data can be used as input for two subsequent activities: monitoring and evaluation.

- **Monitoring:** A continuous activity that is performed with respect to each individual case. Depending on process metrics, as, for instance, maximum waiting time for a certain process activity, monitoring triggers respective counteractions if such a metric indicates a problematic situation.

- **Evaluation:** On the other hand, considers case data on an aggregated level. The performance results are compared with the original requirements and sources of further improvement are discussed. In this way, evaluation leads to new requirements that are taken as input in the next turn of the business process management life cycle.

The business process management life cycle reveals that business process models play an important role in the design, implementation, and enactment phase, especially when information

systems support the process enactment. Thus, they are valuable resources for continuous process improvement, quality management, knowledge management, ERP system selection, and software implementation (Rosemann, 2003). Current market research supports this relevance, since about 90% of the participating companies in a survey conducted or considered business process modeling (Palmer, 2007). In practice, software tools play a decisive role in performing the various management activities in an efficient and effective manner. There are several commercial and academic tools which support different life cycle activities (van der Aalst & van Hee, 2002). In order to link these tools, the workflow management coalition has proposed five interfaces in a reference model (Hollingsworth, 1994). In particular, the availability of tools is important to the modeling of business processes in a correct and consistent way.

BACKGROUND ON BUSINESS PROCESS MODELING

Before defining business process modeling, the term "modeling" has to be discussed in a more general setting. Nordsieck (1932) has emphasized that "the utilization of symbols enables the model not only to replace or to complement natural language for the representation of complex matters, but to reveal the notion of the subject matter often in a more comprehensive way as with any other form of representation." The most protuberant features of a model are brevity, clarity, precision, and its graphic quality (Nordsieck, 1932). In the first part, we discuss the foundations of modeling. The second part introduces concepts related to business process modeling techniques.

Foundations of Modeling

Stachowiak (1973) defines a model as the result of a simplifying mapping from reality that serves a specific purpose. According to this perception, there are three important qualities a model should possess. Firstly, there is a mapping that establishes a representation of natural or artificial originals that can be models itself. Secondly, only those attributes of the original that are considered relevant are mapped to the model; the rest is skipped. Therefore, the model provides an abstraction in terms of a homomorphism in a mathematical sense (Kühne, 2006). Thirdly, the model is used by the modeller in place of the original at a certain point in time and for a certain purpose. This means that a model always involves pragmatics.

A weakness of Stachowiak's concept of a model is that it implies an epistemological position of positivism.[3] This is, for instance, criticized in Schütte and Rotthowe, where the authors propose an alternative position based on insights from critical realism and constructivism.[4] This position regards a model as a "result of a construct done by a modeller" (Schütte & Rotthowe, 1998). As such, it is heavily influenced by the subjective perception of the modeller. This fact makes modeling a non-deterministic task (Mendling & Recker, 2007), which requires standards in order to achieve a certain level of inter-subjectivity. The guidelines of modeling (GoM) (Becker, Rosemann, & Schütte, 1995; Becker, Rosemann, & von Uthmann, 2000; Schütte & Rotthowe, 1998) define principles that serve

this standardization purpose. They are applicable for either epistemological positions or positivism and constructivism, because both the choice for a certain homomorphism (positivist position) and the perception of the modeller (constructivist position) introduce subjective elements.

Therefore, the guidelines of modeling (Becker et al., 1995; Schütte & Rotthowe, 1998) include six particular principles for achieving inter-subjectivity of models. The first three define necessary preconditions for the quality of models, that is, correctness, relevance, and economic efficiency, and the other three are optional, that is, clarity, comparability, and systematic design.

- **Correctness:** Firstly, a model has to be syntactically correct. This requirement demands the usage of allowed modeling primitives and combining them according to predefined rules. Secondly, a model must be semantically correct. Therefore, it has to be formally correct and consistent with the (perception of the) real world.

- **Relevance:** This criterion demands that only interesting parts of the universe of discourse are reflected in the model. It is, therefore, related to the notion of completeness as proposed in Batini, Lenzerini, and Navathe (1986).

- **Economic efficiency:** This guideline introduces a trade-off between benefits and costs of putting the other criteria into practice. For example, semantic correctness might be neglected to a certain extent, in case achieving it is too expensive.

- **Clarity:** This is a highly subjective guideline demanding that the model must be understood by the model user. It is primarily related to layout conventions or the complexity of the model.

- **Comparability:** Demands consistent utilization of a set of guidelines in a modeling project. Among others, it refers to naming conventions.

- **Systematic design:** This guideline demands a clear separation between models in different views (e.g., statical aspects and behavioral aspects) and defined mechanisms to integrate them.

An alternative, but more abstract framework for assessing the quality of modeling is the SEQUAL framework (Krogstie, Sindre, & Jørgensen, 2006; Lindland, Sindre, & Sølvberg, 1994). It builds on semiotic theory and defines several quality aspects based on relationships between a model, a body of knowledge, a domain, a modeling language, and the activities of learning, taking action, and modeling. In essence, syntactic quality relates to model and modeling language, semantic quality to model, domain, and knowledge, and pragmatic quality relates to model and modeling and its ability to enable learning and action. Although the framework does not provide an operational definition of how to determine the various degrees of quality, it has been found useful for business process modeling in experiments (Moody, Sindre, Brasethvik, & Sølvberg, 2002).

Beyond these quality considerations, there are several approaches that discuss different layers of modeling, and the relationship of the meta-layer towards philosophical theories. The following paragraph sketches ontology and meta-modeling as two alternative foundations. These two approaches are chosen as examples for their wide-spread application in information systems research.

Ontology is the study of being. It seeks to describe what is in the world in terms of entities, categories, and relationships. It is a prominent subdiscipline of philosophy. Wand and Weber were among the first to adopt ontology for a foundation of information systems modeling (see Wand & Weber, 1990, 1995). They make two basic assumptions. Firstly, as information systems reflect what is in the real world they should also be modelled with a language that is capable of representing real-world entities. Secondly, the ontology proposed by Bunge (1977) is a useful basis for describing the real world.

The so-called Bunge-Wand-Weber (BWW) ontology proposed by Wand and Weber includes a set of things that can be observed in the world. They should be identified in the process of modeling a specific domain and fulfill certain consistency criteria (Wand & Weber, 1995). For examples of other ontological models, refer to Guizzardi, Herre, and Wagner (2002) and Wand and Weber (2002). Recently, ontology languages, such as OWL (McGuinness & Harmelen, 2004), have become popular for defining domain ontologies to be used as a component of the semantic Web (Berners-Lee, Hendler, & Lassila, 2001).

Metamodeling frees modeling from philosophical assumptions by extending the subject of the modeling process to the general (i.e., meta) level. The philosophical theory of this level, such as, for instance, an ontology, is replaced by a metamodel. The difference to an ontological foundation is that a metamodel does not claim any epistemological validity. Essentially, the metamodel identifies the abstract entities that can be used in the process of designing models, that is, in other words, the metamodel represents the modeling language (see Atkinson & Kühne, 2001b; Karagiannis & Kühn, 2002; Kühne, 2006). The flexibility gained from this meta-principle comes at the cost of relativism: as a metamodel is meta relative to a model, it is a model itself. Therefore, a metamodel can also be defined for the metamodel and it is called metametamodel. This regression can be continued to infinity without ever reaching an epistemological ground.[5] Most modeling frameworks define three or four modeling levels, see UML's meta object facility (OMG, 2002), CASE data interchange format (CDIF) (Flatscher, 1998), or graph exchange language (GXL) (Winter, Kullbach, & Riediger, 2001). The definition of a modeling language based on a metamodel is more often used than the explicit reference to a philosophical position. Examples of metamodeling can be found in Atkinson and Kühne, Atkinson and Kühne, Atkinson and Kühne, Österle and Gutzwiller, Scheer, and Scheer. Several tools like MetaEdit (Kelly Lyytinen, & Rossi, 1996;

Smolander, Lyytinen, Tahvanainen, & Marttiin, 1991), Protegé (Noy, Fergerson, & Musen, 2000), or ADONIS (Junginger, Kühn, Strobl, & Karagiannis, 2000) support metamodeling in such a way that modeling languages can be easily defined by the user.

The meta-hierarchy provides a means to distinguish different kinds of models. Still, a model can never be a metamodel by itself, but only relative to a model for which it defines the modeling language. Models can also be distinguished depending on the mapping mechanism (Strahringer, 1996): Non-linguistic models capture some real-world aspects as material artefacts or as pictures. Linguistic models can be representational, verbal, logistic, or mathematical. Models also serve diverse purposes. Focusing on business administration, Kosiol (1961) distinguishes descriptive models, explanatory models, and decision models. In this context, descriptive models capture objects of a certain area of discourse and represent them in a structured way. Beyond that, explanatory models define dependency relationships between nomological hypotheses. These serve as general laws to explain real-world phenomena, with a claim for empirical validity. Finally, decision models support the deduction of actions. This involves the availability of a description model to formalize the setting of the decision, a set of goals that constraint the design situation, and a set of decision parameters.

Business Process Modeling Techniques

The explicit definition of a modeling technique is a useful means to address several of the quality requirements that we discussed in the previous section. A modeling technique consists of two interrelated parts: a modeling language and a modeling method[6] (see Figure 2). The modeling language consists of three parts: syntax, semantics, and optionally, at least one notation. The syntax provides a set of constructs and a set of rules how these constructs can be combined. A synonym is modeling grammar (Wand & Weber, 2002, 1990, 1995). Semantics bind the constructs defined in the syntax to a meaning. This can be done in a mathematical way, for example, by using formal ontologies or operational semantics. The notation defines a set of graphical symbols that are utilized for the visualization of models (Karagiannis & Kühn, 2002). The modeling method defines procedures by which a modeling language can be used (Wand & Weber, 2002). The result of applying the modeling method is a model that complies with a specific modeling language.[7] Consider, for example, entity-relationship diagrams (ERDs) as defined by Chen (1976). Since they define a modeling language and a respective modeling method, ERDs are a modeling technique. Entities and relationships are syntax elements of its language. They are used to capture certain semantics of a universe of discourse. The notation represents entities as rectangles and relationships as arcs connecting such rectangles carrying a diamond in the middle. Respective procedures, like looking for nouns and verbs in documents, define the modeling method. In practice, modeling tools are of crucial importance for the application of a modeling technique. Among others, they support the specification of models, the redundancy controlled administration of models, multi-user collaboration, and model reuse via interfaces to other tools (Rosemann, 2003). A recent comparison of business process modeling tools is reported by Ami and Sommer (2007).

Against this background, the terms business process model, business process modeling language, and business process modeling can be defined as follows:

- A business process model is the result of mapping a business process. This business process can be either a real-world business process as perceived by a modeller, or a business process conceptualized by a modeller.
- Business process modeling is the human activity of creating a business process model. Business process modeling involves an abstraction from the real-world business process,

Figure 2. Concepts of a modeling technique

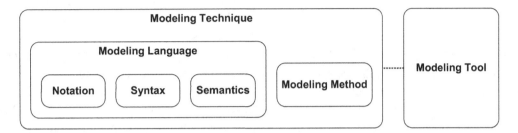

because it serves a certain modeling purpose. Therefore, only those aspects relevant to the modeling purpose are included in the process model.

- Business process modeling languages guide the procedure of business process modeling by offering a predefined set of elements and relationships for the modeling of business processes. A business process modeling language can be specified using a metamodel. In conjunction with a respective method, it establishes a business process modeling technique.

This definition requires some comments. In contrast to Stachowiak (1973), it does not claim that the business process model is an abstraction and serves a purpose. These attributions involve some problems about whether a model always has to be abstract or to serve a purpose. Instead, the procedure of business process modeling is characterized in such a way that it is guided by abstraction and a purpose in mind. This is important as a model is not just a "representation of a real-world system" as Wand and Weber (1990) put it, but a design artefact, in the sense of Hevner, March, Park, and Ram (2004), that itself becomes part of the real world as soon as it is created. Beyond that, business process models can be characterized as linguistic models that are mainly representational and mathematical. The representational aspect points to the visual notation of a business process modeling language,

while the mathematical notion refers to the formal syntax and semantics. In practice, business process models are often used for documentation purposes (Davies, Green, Rosemann, Indulska, & Gallo, 2006). Therefore, they can be regarded as descriptive models for organization and information systems engineers. Still, they also serve as explanatory and decision models for the people who are involved in the actual processing of cases. In the following section, we will utilize the concepts related to modeling techniques as illustrated in Figure 2, for the introduction of different popular business process modeling languages.

BUSINESS PROCESS MODELING LANGUAGES AND METHODS

In this section, we focus on the control flow perspective of business process models and introduce several popular business process modeling languages. In particular, we introduce Petri nets, EPCs, YAWL, UML activity diagrams, and BPMN, and compare these languages based on the semantics of their routing elements and based on the workflow patterns defined by van der Aalst, ter Hofstede, Kiepuszewski, and Barros. Furthermore, we discuss how the process of modeling can be described as a method, and which measures of quality assurance should be considered.

Modeling Languages

Petri Nets

Petri nets introduced by Petri (1962a, 1962b) are a formal language that can be used for the specification of business processes. The syntax of Petri nets is defined as a special kind of a graph with two different node types. So-called transitions typically represent activities of a business process. Furthermore, they can be used to capture routing conditions of a process. So-called places define the pre-conditions and post-conditions of these transitions. Accordingly, places and transitions have to alternate in the Petri net graph, and directed arcs are used to connect them. The notation of Petri nets symbolizes transitions as rectangles and places as circles. The behavioral semantics of Petri nets relate to the concept of a marking (or state). A marking assigns none, one, or multiple so-called tokens (represented by a dot) to each place of a Petri net. A Petri net together with a marking is called system. The behavior of a system is defined by the firing rule: a marking of a system enables a transition if and only if all its predecessor places have at least one token assigned. In this case, a new marking is reached from the current marking by firing the enabled transition such that the new marking equals the current marking minus one token in each predecessor place of the enabled transition and plus one token in each successor place of the enabled transition.

Figure 3 shows a Petri net model for a loan request process inspired by Nüttgens and Rump (2002). The net belongs to the class of workflow nets, these are Petri nets with one start and one end place. As a first transition in the net, record loan request has to be executed. After conduct risk assessment, there is a decision to either continue with negative risk assessment or with positive risk assessment: firing the transition conduct risk assessment produces a token in the subsequent place which can be consumed by one of the following transitions. In case of a negative risk assessment, there is the option to

repeat the risk assessment if check client assessment yields a positive result. If that is not the case, the reject loan request transition is executed. In case of a positive risk assessment, there is another choice depending on whether the client is a new client or not. The dot in the subsequent place indicates that the state of the system now permits to make this choice. If the client is new, the right column of transitions is executed in addition to setting up the loan contract. This behavior is provided by the requester is new client transition producing a token on both its output places which introduces parallelism. The transition without a label synchronizes the two transitions sign loan contract and offer further products which are meant to be executed for any client. This transition produces a token in the end place signalling the completion of the process.

Petri nets are often used not only for the modeling of business processes and workflows, but also for the verification of desirable behavior. The so-called soundness property (van der Aalst, 1997) defined for workflow nets is of pivotal importance in this context. It demands that a process should have (1) the option to complete, (2) that proper completion is guaranteed, and (3) that there are no dead tasks that will never be executed. Based on a Petri net and an initial marking, one can check soundness by calculating the so-called reachability graph. The reachability graph represents all states that can be reached in a Petri net as nodes and all permitted state changes as directed arcs between these nodes. If the net is large and there is a high degree of parallelism, such a verification approach might suffer from the state explosion problem (Valmari, 1998). This problem can be partially solved by applying reduction rules (see Berthelot, 1987, 1986; Esparza, 1994). Deadlocks are a prominent type of error that results in a net to be unsound. In the example process of Figure 3, there is a deadlock if the client is not a new client. In this case the requester is not a new client transition consumes the token of the current marking and forwards it to its successor place. Eventually, the loan contract is set up transition produces two tokens. The right

Figure 3. Petri net for a loan request process with a deadlock

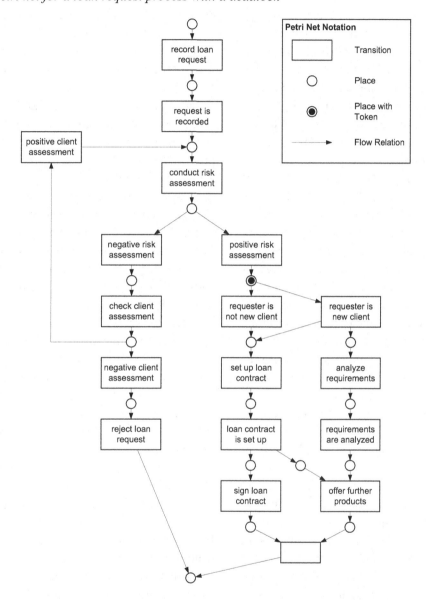

one which is an input to the offer further products transition can actually never be forwarded, since the transition will never receive a another token at its second input place. Therefore, this marking is called a deadlock, since no state change is possible even though the final state has not yet been reached. In practice, such verification analysis has to be performed by tools. An example of an open source tool for the verification of soundness

is Woflan (Verbeek et al., 2001). For an extensive introduction to Petri nets, the reader is referred to Desel and Esparza (1995), Murata (1989), and Reisig and Rozenberg (1998).

EPCs

The event-driven process chain (EPC) is a business process modeling language for the representation of temporal and logical dependencies of activities in a business process (Keller, Nüttgens, & Scheer, 1992). It is utilized in the architecture of integrated information systems (ARIS) by Scheer (1998, 2000) as the central method for the conceptual integration of the functional, organizational, data, and output perspective in information systems design. The EPC syntax offers function type elements to capture activities of a process and event type elements describing pre-conditions and post-conditions of functions. Furthermore, there are three kinds of connector types including AND (symbol ∧), OR (symbol ∨), and XOR (symbol ×) for the definition of complex routing rules. Connectors have either multiple incoming and one outgoing arc (join connectors) or one incoming and multiple outgoing arcs (split connectors). As a syntax rule, functions and events have to alternate, either directly or indirectly when they are linked via one or more connectors. Furthermore, OR- and XOR-splits after events are not allowed, since events cannot make decisions. Control flow arcs are used to link these elements. The EPC notation represents functions as rounded rectangles, events as hexagons, and connectors as circles with the respective symbol in it.

The behavioral semantics of an EPC can be described as follows. The AND-split activates all subsequent branches in concurrency. The XOR-split represents a choice between one of several alternative branches. The OR-split triggers one, two or up to all of multiple branches based on conditions. In both cases of the XOR- and OR-split, the activation conditions are given in events subsequent to the connector. Accordingly, splits from an event to multiple functions are forbidden with XOR and OR as the activation conditions do not become clear in the model. The AND-join waits for all incoming branches to complete, and then it propagates control to the subsequent EPC element. The XOR-join merges alternative branches. The OR-join synchronizes all active incoming branches. This feature is called non-locality since the state of all transitive predecessor nodes has to be considered. There are several approaches towards the formalization of

EPC semantics (see Kindler, 2006; Mendling & van der Aalst, 2007). The most recent formalization is defined by Mendling (2007).

Figure 4 shows an EPC model for the same loan request process as described in Nüttgens and Rump. The start event loan is requested and signals the start of the process and the precondition to execute the record loan request function. After the post-condition request is recorded, the process continues with the function conduct risk assessment after the XOR-join connector. The subsequent XOR-split connector indicates a decision. In case of a negative risk assessment, the function check client assessment is performed. The following second XOR-split marks another decision: in case of a negative client assessment the process ends with a rejection of the loan request; in case of a positive client assessment, the conduct risk assessment function is executed a second time under consideration of the positive client assessment. If the risk assessment is not negative, there is another decision point to distinguish new clients and existing clients. In case of an existing client, the set up loan contract function is conducted. After that, the AND-split indicates that two activities have to be executed: first, the sign loan contract function; and second, the offer further products function. If the client is new, the analyze requirements function has to be performed in addition to setting up the loan contract. The OR-join waits for both functions to be completed if necessary. Therefore, there is no deadlock here. If the analyze requirements function will not be executed in the process, it continues with offer further products immediately.

EPCs are often used for modeling business processes on a conceptual level. Originally, EPCs were introduced to offer an understandable representation of processes, and experiments confirmed that users indeed seem to understand them more easily compared to Petri nets (Sarshar & Loos, 2005). On the other hand, the introduction of the OR-join and the option to define multiple start and end events has been a considerable challenge for the verification of EPCs. Dehnert and Rittgen (2001) argue that business processes are often conceptually modelled in such a way that only the desired behavior results in a proper completion. Since such models are not used for workflow execution, non-normative behavior is resolved by the people working in the process in a cooperative and ad-hoc fashion. Accordingly, they define a process to be relaxed sound if every transition in a Petri net representation of the EPC model is included in at least one proper execution sequence. This Petri net representation of the EPC can be derived if OR-joins are mapped to a Petri net block (see Dehnert, 2002). In this case, the Petri net state space is larger than the actual state space with synchronization. Furthermore, based on the relaxed soundness criterion, it is possible to check whether a join should synchronize (Dehnert & van der Aalst, 2004). The verification of relaxed soundness has, for instance, been implemented in the open source tool ProM (see van Dongen, van der Aalst, & Verbeek, 2005) and been used for the verification of the SAP reference model (van Dongen & Jansen-Vullers, 2005; Mendling et al., 2006b). Only recently, the property of EPC soundness has been defined by Mendling and van der Aalst (2006, 2007), based on the EPC semantics formalization in Mendling (2007).

YAWL

Triggered by their analysis of control flow modeling support by existing workflow systems, van der Aalst et al. (2003) identify a set of 20 so-called workflow patterns. These patterns cover different behavioral properties of a process that one might want to express by the help of a modeling language. The analysis of both Petri nets and EPCs revealed that these languages have problems to represent certain behavior. While EPCs are not able to express state-based patterns properly, Petri nets do not support advanced synchronization semantics such as defined by the OR-join. Furthermore, both languages do not provide a mechanism to express multiple instantiation and cancellation. YAWL (yet another workflow language) has been defined to

directly support the specification of all patterns (van der Aalst & ter Hofstede, 2005).[8] As a consequence, YAWL can be considered a superset of both Petri nets and EPCs in terms of modeling elements.

The YAWL syntax includes conditions that match Petri net places and tasks that match Petri net transitions. Similar to Petri nets, conditions and tasks have to alternate, but single conditions between two tasks can be omitted. YAWL tasks optionally include a split and a join condition of type AND, XOR, or OR with basically the same semantics as the respective EPC connectors. Beyond that, a multiple instance task might be executed several times in parallel until a condition is fulfilled. Such multiple instance tasks specify four parameters: the minimum and the maximum number of instances, a threshold for continuation, and whether new instances may be created dynamically or not. Furthermore, after a task is completed a specified set of other tasks in a cancellation area may be cancelled. Using this mechanism, it is easy to expression exceptional behavioral when a process must be terminated abnormally. The YAWL notation is illustrated on the right-hand top of Figure 5.

Figure 5 also shows the loan request process as a YAWL model. The process is modelled in a similar way as the Petri net model. Still, the OR-join before offer further products resolves the deadlock problem. The condition after the first task illustrates that conditions may be explicitly modelled, but YAWL also permits to leave them out. Furthermore, this task is defined as a multiple instance task. Its parameters indicate that it has to be executed at least zero times, but at maximum three times. Offering only three products to a customer prevents the customer to become tried of offers. There is no threshold, but it is possible to create new instances dynamically, that is, if the clerk identifies demand for a further product, she can easily start offering it.

Based on the YAWL workflow language, a whole open source workflow system has been built which is called YAWL system (van der Aalst et al., 2004). There is several verification features included in the YAWL modeller (see Wynn, Edmond, van der

Figure 4. EPC for a loan request process (Nüttgens & Rump, 2002)

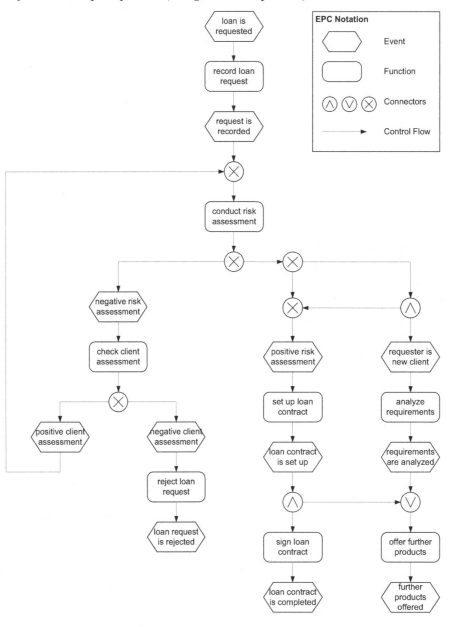

Aalst, & ter Hofstede, 2005; Wynn, Verbeek, van der Aalst, ter Hofstede, & Edmond, 2006).

UML Activity Diagrams

Activity diagrams belong to the diagram family of the unified modeling language (UML) specified by the object management group (OMG, 2004). Since UML, and also activity diagrams, cover an extensive set of notation elements, we focus only on those ones which are used in the workflow pattern analysis reported by Wohed, van der Aalst, Dumas, ter Hofstede, and Russell (2005). The basic syntax elements of UML activity diagrams are actions and control nodes. An action transforms a set of inputs into a set of outputs which implies a state change of the system. Wohed et al. (2005), in particular, focus on the action subtypes send signal action and accept event action in their discussion of control flow modeling with UML activity diagrams. The send signal action creates a signal which may be received by a matching accept event action. The initial node and the activity final representing the start and the completion of a process belong to the set of control nodes. Furthermore, a decision branches to one of alternative branches based on conditions. These alternative branches flow together at merge nodes. The folk can be used to introduce parallelism which can be synchronized with a join. The semantics of these routing elements are similar to that of the respective EPC and YAWL splits and joins. The notation of these different elements is displayed in Figure 6. There is an extensive tool support for modeling UML activity diagrams in practice. Furthermore, there is some research on adopting Petri net verification techniques for UML activity diagrams reported in Eshuis (2002) and Eshuis and Wieringa (2003).

BPMN

The business process modeling notation (BPMN) started as an working group within the business process management initiative (BPMI). Since the merge of BPMI and OMG, BPMN has also become an OMG standard (see OMG, 2006). Figure 7 shows the notation of the main BPMN syntax elements. BPMN covers tasks and events. But in contrast to EPCs, these elements do not have to alternate. The semantics of so-called gateways is similar to the respective joins and splits of EPCs and YAWL. For a complete introduction to BPMN, refer to the specification (OMG, 2006). In practice, there is a growing BPMN support by tool vendors. There are also some academic works on the verification of BPMN models (Puhlmann & Weske, 2006).

Comparison Based on Routing Elements

In this section, we consider the six different connectors of EPCs, that is, XOR-split and XOR-join, AND-split and AND-join, OR-split and OR-join, for the comparison of the different modeling languages. Table 1 takes these routing elements as a benchmark, and shows that the behavioral semantics of XOR-connectors and AND-connectors, as well as OR-split connectors, can be represented in all the considered languages. In workflow nets XOR-connectors and AND-connectors are captured by places and transitions with multiple input and output arcs, respectively. OR-split behavior can be specified as a complex sub-net that determines each possible combination of inputs. OR-join behavior cannot be modelled directly, but a relaxed soundness analysis is possible. In UML activity diagrams the XOR-split maps to a decision, the XOR-join to a merge, the AND-split to a fork, the AND-join to a join, and the OR-split to a fork with guards on its output arcs. OR-joins cannot be represented in UML activity diagrams directly. In BPMN, routing elements are called gateways. Basically, each EPC connector can be transformed to a respective gateway. In YAWL, there are also similar splits and joins matching the behavior of the EPC connectors.

Comparison Based on Workflow Patterns

The workflow patterns identified by van der Aalst et al. (2003) can be utilized to clarify semantics or to serve as a benchmark. Table 2 illustrates the result of several workflow pattern analyses of EPCs (Mendling et al., 2005b), Workflow nets (van der Aalst, 1997), UML activity diagrams (Wohed et al., 2005), BPMN (Wohed et al., 2006), and YAWL (van der Aalst & ter Hofstede, 2005). It can be seen that EPCs support the basic control flow patterns, multiple choice, and synchronizing merge. These patterns can be directly represented with the different EPC connectors. Furthermore, EPCs permit

Figure 5. YAWL model for the loan request process

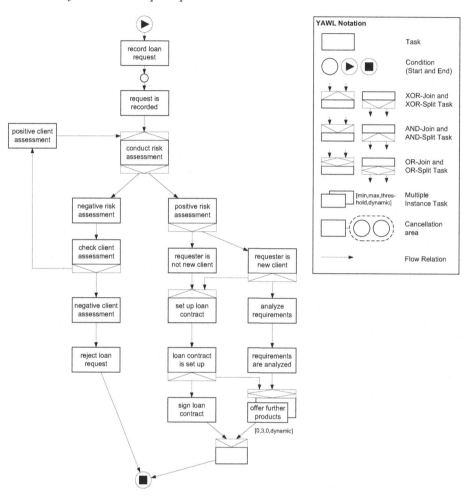

Figure 6. UML notation of important control flow elements

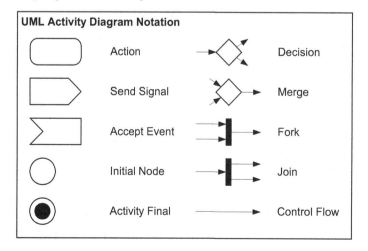

Figure 7. BPMN notation of important control flow elements

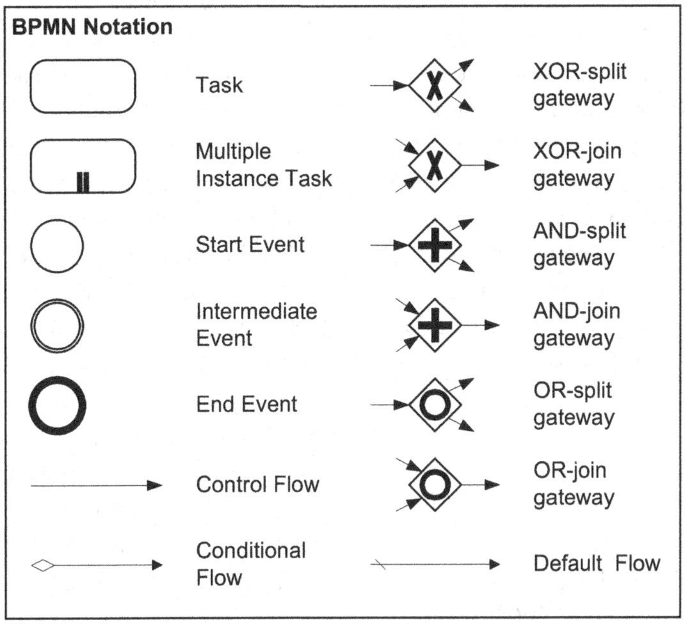

Table 1. EPC routing elements and equivalent elements in other business process modeling languages

EPC	workflow nets	UML AD	BPMN	YAWL
XOR-split	multi-out place	Decision	XOR-gateway	XOR-split task
XOR-join	multi-in place	Merge	XOR-gateway	XOR-join task
AND-split	multi-out transition	Fork	AND-gateway	AND-split task
AND-join	multi-in transition	Join	AND-gateway	AND-join task
OR-split	complex subnet	Fork	OR-gateway	OR-split task
OR-join	-	-	OR-gateway	OR-join task

arbitrary cycles and offer implicit termination. Multiple instances with a priori design time knowledge can be modelled by an AND-block, with as many instances as required of the same activity in parallel. The yEPC extension of EPCs provides support for all patterns (see Mendling et al., 2005c).

In contrast to EPCs, workflow nets support the state-based patterns, but perform weak when it comes to advanced branching and synchronization patterns. UML activity diagrams cover several patterns missing only the synchronizing merge, multiple instances without apriori runtime knowledge, and two state-based patterns. BPMN performs even better since it supports the synchronizing merge, but only in a structured block. As YAWL was defined to provide a straight-forward support for the workflow patterns, it is no surprise that it has the best score. The implicit termination pattern is not supported in order to force the designer to make the completion condition explicit. The comparison reveals that BPMN and YAWL support most of the patterns. Yet, they offer much more syntax elements than EPCs and Petri nets, which might imply that users would need more time to learn them. In practice, the choice for or against a language should be taken with care, considering also the tool support for modeling and verification. For more details on the workflow patterns, refer to van der Aalst et al. (2003).

Modeling Methods

It is a fundamental insight of software engineering that design errors should be detected as early as possible (see Boehm, 1981; Moody, 2005; Wand & Weber, 2002). The later errors are detected, the more rework has to be done, and the more design effort has been at least partially useless. This also holds for the consecutive steps of analysis, design, and implementation in the business process management life cycle (see Philippi & Hill, 2007; Rosemann, 2006). In the design phase, process models are typically created with semi-formal business process modeling languages while formal executable models are needed for the implementation. This issue is often referred to as the gap between business process design and implementation phase (see zur Muehlen & Rosemann, 2004). Therefore, the guidelines of process modeling stress correctness as the most important quality attribute of business process models (Becker et al., 2000).

In order to provide a better understanding of potential modeling errors, we consider the information modeling process as identified by Frederiks and Weide (2006) as a modeling method. This process can also serve as a framework for discussing business process modeling in the analysis and design phase of the business process management life cycle. Furthermore, it covers several steps to provide quality assurance in the modeling phase,

which is of paramount importance for the success of modeling projects (see Rosemann, 2006). Figure 8 gives a business process modeling process mainly inspired by Frederiks and Weide (2006) and consisting of eight steps. In accordance with van Hee, Sidorova, Somers, and Voorhoeve (2006), we propose to first verify the process model (step 6) before validating it (step 7-8).

The business process modeling process starts with collecting information objects relevant to the domain (step 1). Such information objects include documents, diagrams, pictures, and interview recordings. In step 2, these different inputs are verbalized to text that serves as a unifying format. This text is rearranged according to some general guideline of how to express facts (step 3) yielding an informal specification. The following step (step 4) takes this informal specification as a basis to discover modeling concepts from and to produce a normalized specification. This normal form specification is then mapped to constructs of the process modeling language (step 5) in order to create a business process model. These models have to be verified for internal correctness (step 6) before they can be paraphrased back to natural language (step 7) in order to validate them against the specification (step 8). In steps 6-8, the order of activities follows the proposal by van Hee et al. (2006). It is a good idea to first verify the internal correctness of a model before validating it against the specification, as this prevents incorrect models from being unnecessarily validated.

The business process modeling process points to two categories of potential errors based on the distinction between verification and validation. This distinction follows the terminology of different authors, including Boehm (1979), Hoppenbrouwers, Proper, and van der Weide (2005), Sommerville (2001), and Valmari (1998). Different terms for similar concepts are used by Soffer and Wand (2004).

- Verification addresses both the general properties of a model and the satisfaction

Table 2. Workflow pattern support of EPCs and other business process modeling languages. + means pattern supported, +/- partially supported, and - not supported

Workflow Pattern	EPC	Wf. nets	UML AD	BPMN	YAWL
Basic Control Flow Patterns					
1. Sequence	+	+	+	+	+
2. Parallel Split	+	+	+	+	+
3. Synchronization	+	+	+	+	+
4. Exclusive Choice	+	+	+	+	+
5. Simple Merge	+	+	+	+	+
Advanced Branching and Synchronization Patterns					
6. Multiple Choice	+	+	+	+	+
7. Synchronizing Merge	+	-	-	+/-	+
8. Multi Merge	-	+	+	+	+
9. Discriminator	-	-	+	+/-	+
Structural Patterns					
10. Arbitrary Cycles	+	+	+	+	+
11. Implicit Termination	+	-	+	+	-
Patterns involving Multiple Instantiation (MI)					
12. MI without Synchronization	-	+	+	+	+
13. MI with apriori Design Time Knowledge	+	+	+	+	+
14. MI with apriori Runtime Knowledge	-	-	+	+	+
15. MI without apriori Runtime Knowledge	-	-	-	-	+
State-based Patterns					
16. Deferred Choice	-	+	+	+	+
17. Interl. Parallel Routing	-	+	-	+/-	+
18. Milestone	-	+	-	-	+
Cancellation Patterns					
19. Cancel Activity	-	+/-	+	+	+
20. Cancel Case	-	-	+	+	+

of a given formula by a model. Related to the first aspect, formal correctness criteria play an important role in process modeling. Several criteria have been proposed including soundness for Workflow nets (van der Aalst, 1997), relaxed soundness (Dehnert & Rittgen, 2001), or well-structuredness (see Dehnert & Zimmermann, 2005). The second aspect is the subject of model checking and involves issues like separation of duty constraints, which can be verified, for example, by using linear temporal logic (see Pnueli, 1977).

- Beyond that, validation addresses the consistency of the model with the universe of discourse. As it is an external correctness criterion, it is more difficult and more ambiguous to decide. While verification typically relies on an algorithmic analysis of the process model, validation requires the consultation of the specification and discussion with business process stakeholders. SEQUAL can be used as a conceptual framework to validate different quality aspects of a model (Krogstie et al., 2006, Lindland et al., 1994).

Figure 8. Business process modeling process in detail, adapted from Frederiks and Weide (2006)

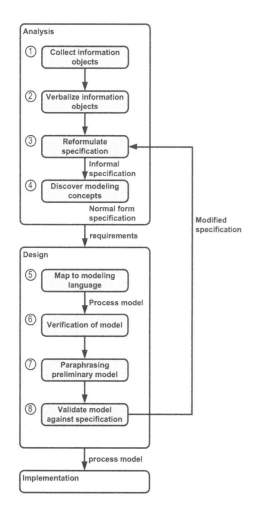

In practice, a well-structured modeling process is not always followed. Recent empirical research by Rittgen (2007) and Stirna, Persson, and Sandkuhl (2007) shows that social aspects and organizational constraints have a strong influence on how the modeling processes is actually conducted. Beyond that, verification and validation depends on respective support provided by tools for the language of choice. Several surveys stress the importance of quality assurance in process modeling. The verification of the EPC models of the SAP reference model has shown that there are several formal errors in the models (Dongen & Jansen-Vullers, 2005; Dongen et al., 2005, Mendling et al., 2006a; Zukunft & Rump, 1996). In Mendling et al. (2006a), the authors identify a lower bound for the number of errors of 34 (5.6%), using the relaxed soundness criterion. Based on EPC soundness, Mendling (2007) finds 126 models with errors (20.9%). In another survey, Gruhn and Laue (2007) analyze a collection of 285 EPCs mainly taken from master theses and scientific publications. From these 285 models, 30% had trivial errors and another 7% had non-trivial errors. Up to now, tool support for verification and validation of business process models is rather weak which might partially explain the high error rates. This makes it even more important to follow a structured modeling process to detect and correct errors as early as possible.

FUTURE TRENDS

The standardization and the seamless transformation from conceptual business process models to executable workflow models is a current trend in research and industry. BPMN was created with the ambition to provide a direct mapping to executable BPEL web service processes. BPEL, that is, business process execution language for Web service, is at the time of writing in the final phase of standardization of its second version. This section presents standardization efforts with a focus on the concepts of BPEL and its support by major software vendors.

Finally, we discuss some transformation issues that are only partially solved up to now.

Business Process Execution and Standardization

The standardization of business process management and workflow technology has been discussed for more than 10 years (see Hollingsworth, 2004). Several standardization bodies have proposed specifications for different aspects of business process management. The five bodies that have gained the most attention in this context are WfMC, OMG, BPMI, W3C, and OASIS. The WfMC (workflow management coalition) has been the first organization to promote workflow standards. Its workflow reference model distinguishes five interfaces of a workflow system (Hollingsworth, 1994). From WfMC's set of specifications,[9] the XPDL standard for process definition (interface 1) is the most prominent one (see Workflow Management Coalition, 2005). The BPMI (business process management initiative) started off in 2000 as an industry consortium to promote business process management standards. In 2002, BPMI published BPML (Arkin, 2002), an XML-based language for the specification of executable processes with Web service interaction, and in 2004, the standardization of BPMN as a visual notation started. The OMG (Object Management Group) first got involved with workflow technology as they accepted the workflow management facility specification as a standard in 1998. In 2005, OMG and BPMI agreed to merge their business process related activities. As a consequence, BPMN is now an OMG standard (see OMG, 2006). The W3C (World Wide Web Consortium) has published several standards for web service choreography. Choreography describes the interaction of distributed processes from a global point of view. WS-CDL (Kavantzas et al., 2005) is the most recent specification in this area. It is meant to be utilized in conjunction with process definition languages that define the private implementation of processes. OASIS (Organization for the Advance-ment of Structured Information Standards) is an industry group that defines XML-based standards for Web services and business integration. OASIS participates, for example, in the specification of the ebXML framework. For further details on business process related standards see (Mendling et al., 2005b).

Since 2003, OASIS is also responsible for the standardization of BPEL.[10] The work on BPEL started with a merger of IBM's WSFL process definition specification with Microsoft's XLANG which resulted in the first version of BPEL (Curbera et al., 2002). In 2003 BEA, SAP, and Siebel joined in to extend BPEL to version 1.1 (Andrews et al., 2003). Currently, the second version of BPEL is in the final phase of standardization (see Alves et al., 2007).[11]

Main Concepts of BPEL

BPEL is an XML-based language that models a business process as a composition of elementary Web services. A so-called BPEL engine is a dedicated software component that is able to execute BPEL process definitions. Each BPEL process can be accessed as a Web service of the BPEL engine, too. The BPEL specification depends on the W3C standards WSDL for Web service description, XML schema for the definition of data structures, and XPath for retrieval of XML elements. Six of BPEL's most important concepts are briefly presented in the following, that is, partner links, variables, correlation, basic activities, structured activities, and handlers. We will use the element names of BPEL 2.

- **Partner links:** A partner link provides a communication channel to remote Web services which are utilized in the BPEL process. A respective partner link type must be defined first to specify the required and provided WSDL port types.
- **Variables:** Variables are used to store both message data of Web service interactions and

control data of the process. A variable must be declared in the header of a BPEL process by referencing a WSDL or an XML Schema data type.

- **Correlation:** As BPEL supports long-running business processes, there may be several process instances waiting for Web service messages at a certain point of time. A correlation set specifies so-called properties, that is, XPath statements to retrieve message parts that are unique for a specific process instance. According to a certain property value, like, for example, ordernumber=1002006, a message is handed to the matching process instance.

- **Basic activities:** The basic steps of a BPEL process are performed by basic activities. There are activities to send and receive messages from Web services (receive, invoke, reply), to change the content of variables (assign), to wait for a certain period or up to a certain point in time (wait), or to terminate the process (exit, formally called terminate).[12] The second version of BPEL introduces an activity to check conformance to a schema (validate) and the possibility to add proprietary activities (extensionActivity).

- **Structured activities:** The control flow of basic activities can be defined in two different styles: block-oriented or graph-based. Both styles can be mixed. Block-oriented control flow can be defined with structured activities. BPEL offers activities to specify parallel execution (flow), conditional branching based on data (if-else) or on receipt of a message (pick), sequential execution (sequence), and different loops (while, repeatUntil, forEach). Structured activities can be nested. Scopes are special structured activities. They mark-off the scope of local variables and handlers. Control flow can also be defined graph-based, but without introducing cycles, using so-called links. A link represents synchronization between two activities.

- **Handlers:** BPEL provides handlers to deal with unexpected or exceptional situations. Event handlers wait for messages or time events. They can be used to specify deadlines on the process level. Fault handlers catch internal faults of the BPEL process. If the fault cannot be cured, the compensation handler can be triggered to undo the effects of already completed activities. Finally, the termination handler offers a mechanism to force a process to terminate, for example, due to external faults.

Even though BPEL supports a rich set of primitives to specify executable processes, there are still some features missing towards full-fledged business process specification. The extension activity of BPEL 2 is a useful anchor point to fill these gaps. Currently, there are several BPEL extensions in progress of development, in particular BPELJ[13] for Java inline code, BPEL4People[14] for human worklists, and BPEL-SPE[15] for sub-processes.

BPEL Support

Several major software vendors support the standardization of BPEL.[16] Several of these companies already provide BPEL support in their products. Furthermore, there are also open source implementations of BPEL including ActiveBPEL, bexee, MidOffice, and Twister. Therefore, it should be expected that BPEL will soon become not only a de-iure, but a de-facto standard for the definition of executable business processes.

For vendors, there are basically two options to align with BPEL, either to develop a BPEL engine and related tools from scratch or to implement BPEL import and export for existing systems. Oracle is one of the few vendors who offer a generic implementation of BPEL called Oracle BPEL Process Manager. Several other companies have chosen to extend their systems with import and export. In this case, the BPEL process has to be mapped to the object structure of the target system. The mapping between BPEL and graph-based control flow, in particular with unstructured loops, is an interesting challenge for both academia and practice. So-called transformation strategies (Mendling et al., 2006) can serve as a blue print for that. Van der Aalst and Lassen (2006) define a transformation from Petri nets to BPEL using reduction rules. Ouyang, van der Aalst, Dumas, and ter Hofstede (2006) propose a transformation of unstructured loops to event-condition-action rules that are implemented via BPEL event handlers. Another option, but not in the general case, is to derive structured from unstructured loops (Zhao, Hauser, Bhattacharya, Bryant, & Cao, 2006). The simplest solution to this problem for the vendors is to prohibit the definition of unstructured cycles in their process design tool. Then all import and export transformations between BPEL and internal graph-based representation can be implemented without loss of information.

CONCLUSION

This chapter provided an overview of business process management and business process modeling. In particular, we elaborated on the background of business process management by giving a historical classification of seminal work, and by discussing the business process management life cycle. In this life cycle, business process models play an important role. We approached business process modeling from a general information systems point of view and deducted a definition. Furthermore, we presented several frequently-used business process modeling languages including Petri nets, EPCs, YAWL, UML activity diagrams, and BPMN, as well as modeling methods for business process modeling. As a future trend, we identified standardization and executability of business process models. In particular, we focused on recent standardization efforts and research challenges related to the business process execution language for Web services. We expect this area to be the driver for new concepts and innovations within the next couple of years.

REFERENCES

Alves, A., Arkin, A., Askary, S., Barreto, C., Bloch, B., Curbera, F., et al. (2007). Web services business process execution language version version 2.0. Committee specification 31 January 2007, OASIS.

Ami T., & Sommer, R. (2007). Comparison and evaluation of business process modelling and management tools. *International Journal of Services and Standards*, 3(2), 249-261.

Andrews, T., Curbera, F., Dholakia, H., Goland, Y., Klein, J., Leymann, F., et al. (2003). Business process execution language for Web services, Version 1.1. Specification, BEA Systems, IBM Corp., Microsoft Corp., SAP AG, Siebel Systems.

Arkin, A. (2002). *Business process modeling language (BPML)*. Spec., BPMI.

Atkinson, C., & Kühne, T. (2001a). Processes and products in a multi-level metamodeling architecture. *International Journal of Software Engineering and Knowledge Engineering, 11*(6), 761-783.

Atkinson, C., & Kühne, T. (2001b). The essence of multilevel metamodeling. In M. Gogolla & C. Kobryn (Eds.), *UML 2001—The unified modeling language, modeling languages, concepts, and tools, Proceedings of the 4th International Conference, Toronto, Canada* (Vol. 2185, pp. 19-33). Springer.

Atkinson, C., & Kühne, T. (2003). Model-driven development: A metamodeling foundation. *IEEE Software, 20*(5), 36-41.

Austin, J. L. (1962). *How to do things with words.* Cambridge, MA: Harvard University Press.

Batini, C., Lenzerini, M., & Navathe, S. B. (1986). A comparative analysis of methodologies for database schema integration. *ACM Computing Surveys, 18*(4), 323-364.

Becker, J., & Kugeler, M. (2003). *Process management: A guide for the design of business processes.* Springer-Verlag.

Becker, J., Rosemann, M., & Schütte, R. (1995). Grundsätze ordnungsmässiger Modellierung. *Wirtschaftsinformatik, 37*(5), 435-445.

Becker, J., Rosemann, M., & von Uthmann, C. (2000). Guidelines of business process modeling. In W. M. P. van der Aalst, J. Desel, & A. Oberweis (Eds.), *Business process management. Models, techniques, and empirical studies* (pp. 30-49). Berlin: Springer.

Berners-Lee, T., Hendler, J., & Lassila, O. (2001). The semantic web. *Scientific American, May.*

Berthelot (1986). Checking properties of nets using transformations. In G. Rozenberg (Ed.), *Advances in Petri nets 1985* (Vol. 222, pp. 19-40). Berlin: Springer-Verlag.

Berthelot, G. (1987). Transformations and decompositions of nets. In W. Brauer, W. Reisig, & G. Rozenberg (Eds.), *Advances in Petri nets 1986 Part I: Petri Nets, central models and their properties* (Vol. 254, pp. 360-376). Berlin: Springer-Verlag.

Boehm, B. W. (1979). *Research directions in software technology.* MIT Press.

Boehm, B. W. (1981). *Software engineering economics.* Englewood Cliffs: Prentice-Hall.

Bunge, M. (1977). *Treatise on basic philosophy* (vol.3). *Ontology I. The furniture of the world.* New York: D. Reidel Publishing.

Casati, F., Ceri, S., Pernici, B., & Pozzi, G. (1995). Conceptual modeling of workflows. In *Proceedings of the OOER International Conference*, Gold Cost, Australia.

Chen, P. (1976). The entity-relationship model—towards a unified view of data. *ACM Transactions on Database Systems (TODS), 1*, 9-36.

Curbera, F., Goland, Y., Klein, J., Leymann, F., Roller, D., Thatte, S., et al. (2002). *Business process execution language for Web services, version 1.0. specification, BEA systems.* IBM Corp., Microsoft Corp.

Davenport, T. H. (1993). *Process innovation: Reengineering work through information technology.* Boston: Harvard Business School Press.

Davies, I., Green, P., Rosemann, M., Indulska, M., & Gallo, S. (2006). How do practitioners use conceptual modeling in practice? *Data & Knowledge Engineering, 58*(3), 358-380.

Dayal, U., Hsu, M., & Ladin, R. (2001, September). Business process coordination: State of the art, trends, and open issues. In P. M. G. Apers, P. Atzeni, S. Ceri, S. Paraboschi, K. Ramamohanarao, & R. T. Snodgrass (Eds.), *Proceedings of the 27th International Conference on Very Large Data Bases (VLDB),* Roma, Italy.

Dehnert, J. (2002). Making EPC's fit for workflow management. In M. Nüttgens & F. J. Rump (Eds.), *Proceedings of the 1st GI-Workshop on Business Process Management with Event-Driven Process Chains EPK 2002,* Trier, Germany, (pp. 51-69).

Dehnert, J., & van der Aalst, W. M. P. (2004). Bridging the gap between business models and workflow specifications. *International J. Cooperative Inf. Syst., 13*(3), 289-332.

Dehnert, J., & Rittgen, P. (2001). Relaxed soundness of business processes. In K. R. Dittrick, A. Geppert, & M. C. Norrie (Eds.), *Proceedings of the 13th International Conference on Advanced Information Systems Engineering* Vol. 2068, pp. 151-170,). Interlaken: Springer.

Dehnert, J., & Zimmermann, A. (2005, September 5-8). On the suitability of correctness criteria for business process models. In W. M. P. van der Aalst, B. Benatallah, F. Casati, & F. Curbera (Eds.), *Proceedings of the Business Process Management, 3rd International Conference, BPM 2005,* Nancy, France (Vol. 3649, pp. 386–391).

Desel, J., & Esparza, J. (1995). *Free choice Petri nets, volume 40 of Cambridge tracts in theoretical computer science.* Cambridge, UK: Cambridge Univ. Press.

Dumas, M., ter Hofstede, A., & van der Aalst, W. M. P. (2005). *Process aware information systems: Bridging people and software through process technology.* Wiley Publishing.

Ellis, C.A. (1979). Information control nets: A mathematical model of office information flow. In *Proceedings of the Conference on Simulation, Measurement and Modeling of Computer Systems* (pp. 225-240). Boulder, CO: ACM Press.

Ellis, C. A., & Nutt, G. J. (1980). Office information systems and computer science. *ACM Computing Surveys, 12*(1), 27-60.

Ellis, C. A., & Nutt, G. J. (1993). Modelling and enactment of workflow systems. In M. Ajmone Marsan (Ed.), *Application and theory of Petri nets* (Vol. 691, pp. 1-16). Berlin: Springer-Verlag.

Eshuis, H. (2002). *Semantics and verification of UML activity diagrams for workflow modelling.* PhD thesis, University of Twente, Enschede, The Netherlands.

Eshuis, H., & Wieringa, R. (2003). Comparing Petri nets and activity diagram variants for workflow modelling—a quest for reactive Petri nets. In H. Ehrig, W. Reisig, G. Rozenberg, & H. Weber (Eds.), *Petri net technology for communication based systems* (Vol. 2472). Berlin: Springer-Verlag.

Esparza, J. (1994). Reduction and synthesis of live and bounded free choice Petri nets. *Information and Computation, 114*(1), 50-87.

Fayol, H. (1966). *Administration industrielle et générale. Prévoyance, Organisation, Commandement, Coordination, Control.* Dunod.

Flatscher, R. G. (1998). *Meta-modellierung in EIA/CDIF.* ADV-Verlag, Wien.

Ford, H. (1926). *Today and tomorrow.* Doubleday, Page and Company.

Frederiks, P. J. M., & van der Weide, T. P. (2006). Information modeling: The process and the required competencies of its participants. *Data & Knowledge Engineering, 58*(1), 4-20.

Georgakopoulos, D., Hornick, M., & Sheth, A. (1995). An overview of workflow management: From process modeling to workflow automation infrastructure. *Distributed and Parallel Databases, 3,* 119-153.

Grochla, E., & Szyperski, N. (1975). *Information systems and organizational structure.* Walter de Gruyter.

Gruhn, V., & Laue, R. (2007). What business process modelers can learn from programmers. *Science of Computer Programming, 65*(1), 4-13.

Guizzardi, G., Herre, H., & Wagner, G. (2002, Octoer 7-11). On the general ontological foundations of conceptual modeling. In S. Spaccapietra, S. T. March, & Y. Kambayashi (Eds.), *Proceedings of the Conceptual Modeling—ER 2002, 21st International Conference on Conceptual Modeling,* Tampere, Finland (Vol. 2503, pp. 65-78). Springer.

Hammer, M., Champy, J. (1993). *Reengineering the corporation: A manifesto for business revolution.* New York: Harpercollins.

Hevner, A. R., March, S. T., Park, J., & Ram, S. (2004). Design science in information systems research. *MIS Quarterly, 28*(1), 75-105.

Hirschheim, R., & Klein, H. K. (1989). Four paradigms of information systems development. *Commun. ACM, 32*(10), 1199-1216.

Hofreiter, B., Huemer, C., & Kim, J.-H. (2006). Choreography of ebXML business collaborations. *Information Systems and E-Business Management.*

Hollingsworth, D. (1994). The workflow reference model. TC00-1003 Issue 1.1, Workflow Management Coalition.

Hollingsworth, D. (2004). *The workflow handbook 2004,* chapter The Workflow Reference Model: 10 Years On, pages 295–312. Workflow Management Coalition.

Hoppenbrouwers, S., Proper, H. A., & van der Weide, T. P. (2005, October 24-28). A fundamental view on the process of conceptual modeling. In L. M. L. Delcambre, C. Kop, H. C. Mayr, J. Mylopoulos, & O. Pastor (Eds.), *Proceedings of the Conceptual Modeling—ER 2005, 24th International Conference on Conceptual Modeling*, Klagenfurt, Austria, (Vol. 3716, pp. 128–143). Springer.

Hsu, M., & Kleissner, C. (1996). Objectflow: Towards a process management infrastructure. *Distributed and Parallel Databases, 4*(2), 169-194.

Jablonski, S., & Bussler, C. (1996). *Workflow management: Modeling concepts, architecture, and implementation*. London: International Thomson Computer Press.

Junginger, S., Kühn, H., Strobl, R., & Karagiannis, D. (2000). Ein Geschäftsprozessmanagementwerkzeug der nächsten Generation—Adonis: Konzeption und Anwendungen. *Wirtschaftsinformatik, 42*(5), 392-401.

Karagiannis, D., & Kühn, H. (2002). Metamodelling platforms. Invited Paper. In K. Bauknecht, A. Min Tjoa, & G. Quirchmayer (Eds.), *Proceedings of the 3rd International Conference EC-Web 2002—Dexa 2002*, Aix-en-Provence, France, (Vol. 2455, pp. 182-196).

Kavantzas, N., Burdett, D., Ritzinger, G., Fletcher, T., Lafon, Y., & Barreto, C. (2005). Web services choreography description language Version 1.0. W3C Candidate Recommendation 9 November 2005, World Wide Web Consortium, April 2005.

Keller, G., Nüttgens, M., & Scheer, A.-W. (1992). *Semantische Prozessmodellierung auf der Grundlage "Ereignisgesteuerter Prozessketten (EPK)"*. Heft 89, Institut für Wirtschaftsinformatik, Saarbrücken, Germany.

Kelly, S., Lyytinen, K., & Rossi, M. (1996, May 20-24). Metaedit+: A fully configurable multi-user and multi-tool case and came environment. In P. Constantopoulos, J. Mylopoulos, & Y. Vassiliou (Eds.), *Proceeedings of the Advances Information System Engineering, 8th International Conference,* *CAiSE'96,* Heraklion, Crete, Greece, (Vol. 1080, pp. 1-21). Springer.

Kindler, E. (2006). On the semantics of EPCs: Resolving the vicious circle. *Data & Knowledge Engineering, 56*(1), 23-40.

Kosiol, E. (1961). Modellanalyse als Grundlage unternehmerischer Entscheidungen. *Zeitschrift für betriebswirtschaftlicher Forschung*, 318–334.

Krogstie, J., Sindre, G., & Jørgensen, H. D. (2006). Process models representing knowledge for action: a revised quality framework. *European Journal of Information Systems, 15*(1), 91-102.

Kühne, T. (2006). Matters of (meta-) modeling. *Software and Systems Modeling, 5*(4), 369-385.

Leymann, F., & Roller, D. (2000). *Production workflow—concepts and techniques*. Prentice Hall.

Lindland, O. I., Sindre, G., & Sølvberg, A. (1994). Understanding quality in conceptual modeling. *IEEE Software, 11*(2), 42-49.

McGuinness, D. L., & van Harmelen, F. (2004). *OWL Web ontology language overview*. W3c recommendation, World Wide Web Consortium.

Mendling, J. (2007). *Detection and prediction of errors in EPC business process models*. PhD thesis, Vienna University of Economics and Business Administration.

Mendling, J., & van der Aalst, W. M. P. (2006). Towards EPC semantics based on state and context. In M. Nüttgens, F. J. Rump, & J. Mendling (Eds.), *Proceedings of the 5th GI Workshop on Business Process Management with Event-Driven Process Chains (EPK 2006)*, Vienna, Austria, (pp. 25-48). German Informatics Society.

Mendling, J., & van der Aalst, W. M. P. (2007). Formalization and verification of EPCs with OR-joins based on state and context. In J. Krogstie, A.L. Opdahl, & G. Sindre (Eds.), *Proceedings of the 19th Conference on Advanced Information Systems*

Engineering CAiSE 2007, Trondheim, Norway, (Vol. 4495, pp. 439-453). Springer-Verlag.

Mendling, J., & Hafner, M. (2005). From inter-organizational workflows to process execution: Generating BPEL from WS-CDL. In R. Meersman, Z. Tari, & P. Herrero (Eds.), *Proceedings of OTM 2005 Workshops*, (Vol. 3762).

Mendling, J., Lassen, K. B., & Zdun, U. (2006). Experiences in enhancing existing BPM tools with BPEL import and export. In J. L. Fiadeiro, S. Dustdar, & A. Sheth (Eds.), *Proceedings of BPM 2006,* Vienna, Austria, (Vol. 4102, pp. 348-357). Springer-Verlag.

Mendling, J., Moser, M., Neumann, G., Verbeek, H. M. W., van Dongen, B. F., & van der Aalst, W. M. P. (2006a). *A quantitative analysis of faulty EPCs in the SAP reference model*. BPM Center Report (BPM-06-08, BPMCenter.org).

Mendling, J., Moser, M., Neumann, G., Verbeek, H. M. W., van Dongen, B. F., & van der Aalst, W. M. P. (2006b). Faulty EPCs in the SAP rReference model. In J. L. Fiadeiro, S. Dustdar, & A. Sheth (Eds.), *Proceedings of BPM 2006,* Vienna, Austria, (Vol. 4102, pp. 451-457). Springer-Verlag.

Mendling, J., zur Muehlen, M., & Price, A. (2005). *Process aware information systems: Bridging people and software through process technology.* Wiley Publishing.

Mendling, J., Neumann, G., & Nüttgens, M. (2005a). *Workflow handbook 2005*. Lighthouse Point, FL, USA: Future Strategies Inc.

Mendling, J., Neumann, G., & Nüttgens, M. (2005b). Towards workflow pattern support of event-driven process chains (EPC). In M. Nüttgens & J. Mendling (Eds.), *Proceedings of the 2nd GI Workshop XML4BPM—XML for Business Process Management at the 11th GI Conference BTW 2005*, Karlsruhe, Germany, (Vol. 145, pp. 23-38).

Mendling, J., Neumann, G., & Nüttgens, M. (2005c). Yet another event-driven process chain. In *Proceedings of BPM 2005*, (Vol. 3649).

Mendling, J., Nüttgens, M., & Neumann, G. (2004). A comparison of XML interchange formats for business process modelling. In F. Feltz, A. Oberweis, & B. Otjacques (Eds.), *Proceedings of EMISA 2004—Information Systems in E-Business and E-Government* (Vol. 56).

Mendling, J., & Recker, J. (2007). Extending the discussion of model quality: Why clarity and completeness may not be enough. In *Proceedings of the CAiSE Workshops at the 19th Conference on Advanced Information Systems Engineering (CAiSE 2007).*

Moody, D. L. (2005). Theoretical and practical issues in evaluating the quality of conceptual models: current state and future directions. *Data & Knowledge Engineering, 55*(3), 243-276.

Moody, D. L., Sindre, G., Brasethvik, T., & Sølvberg, A. (2002, October 7-11). Evaluating the quality of process models: Empirical testing of a quality framework. In S. Spaccapietra, S. T. March, & Y. Kambayashi (Eds.), *Proceedings of the Conceptual Modeling—ER 2002, 21st International Conference on Conceptual Modeling,* Tampere, Finland, *Proceedings,* (Vol. 2503, pp. 380-396). Springer.

Murata, T. (1989). Petri nets: Properties, analysis and applications. *IEEE, 77*(4), 541-580.

Nordsieck, F. (1932). *Die Schaubildliche Erfassung und Untersuchung der Betriebsorganisation.* Organisation—Eine Schriftenreihe. C. E. Poeschel Verlag, Stuttgart.

Nordsieck, F. (1934). *Grundlagen der Organisationslehre.* C. E. Poeschel Verlag.

Noy, N. F., Fergerson, R. W., & Musen, M. A. (2000, October 2-6). The knowledge model of protégé-2000: Combining interoperability and flexibility. In R. Dieng & O. Corby (Eds.), *Proceedings of the Knowledge Acquisition, Modeling and Management, 12th International Conference, EKAW 2000,* Juan-les-Pins, France, (Vol. 1937, pp. 17-32). Springer.

Nüttgens, M., & Rump, F. J. (2002). Syntax und Semantik Ereignisgesteuerter Prozessketten (EPK). In J. Desel & M. Weske (Eds.), *Proceedings of Promise 2002,* Potsdam, Germany, (Vol. 21, pp. 64-77).

Oberweis, A. (1996). An integrated approach for the specification of processes and related complex structured objects in business applications. *Decision Support Systems, 17,* 31-53.

Oberweis, A., & Sander, P. (1996). Information system behavior specification by high-level Petri nets. *ACM Transactions on Information Systems, 14*(4), 380-420.

OMG. (2002). *Meta object facility. Version 1.4.* Object Management Group.

OMG. (2004). *Unified modeling language. Version 2.0.* Object Management Group.

OMG. (2006, February). Business process modeling notation (BPMN) specification. Final adopted specification (dtc/06-02-01). Object Management Group.

Österle, H., & Gutzwiller, T. (1992). *Konzepte angewandter Analyse- und Design-Methoden. Band 1: Ein Referenz-Metamodell für die Analyse und das System-Design.* Angewandte InformationsTechnik-Verl. GmbH.

Ouyang, C., van der Aalst, W. M. P., Dumas, M., & ter Hofstede, A. H. M. (2006). *Translating BPMN to BPEL.* BPMCenter Report BPM-06-02, BPMcenter.org.

Palmer, N. (2007). *A survey of business process initiatives.* BPT Report, Business Process Trends and Transformation+Innovation, January.

Petri, C. A. (1962a). *Fundamentals of a theory of asynchronous information flow.* Amsterdam: North-Holland.

Petri, C. A. (1962b). *Kommunikation mit Automaten.* Ph.D. thesis, Fakultät für Mathematik und Physik, Technische Hochschule Darmstadt, Darmstadt, Germany.

Philippi, S., & Hill, H. J. (in press). Communication support for systems engineering—process modelling and animation with April. *The Journal of Systems and Software.*

Pnueli, A. (1977). The temporal logic of programs. In *Proceedings of the 18th IEEE Annual Symposium on the Foundations of Computer Science* (pp. 46-57). Providence: IEEE Computer Society Press.

Porter, M. E. (1985). *Competitive advantage: Creating and sustaining superior performance.* New York: The Free Press.

Puhlmann, F., & Weske, M. (2006). Investigations on soundness regarding lazy activities. In S. Dustdar, J. L. Fiadeiro, & A. Sheth (Eds.), *Proceedings of the Business Process Management, 4th International Conference, BPM 2006,* (Vol. 4102, pp. 145-160). Springer-Verlag.

Reichert, M., & Dadam, P. (1998). ADEPTflex: Supporting dynamic changes of workflow without loosing control. *Journal of Intelligent Information Systems, 10*(2), 93-129.

Reisig, W., & Rozenberg, G. (Eds.). (1998). *Lectures on Petri nets I: Basic models.* Berlin: Springer-Verlag.

Rittgen, P. (2007). Negotiating models. In J. Krogstie, A. L. Opdahl, & G. Sindre (Eds.), *Proceedings of the 19th Conference on Advanced Information Systems Engineering CAiSE 2007,* Trondheim, Norway, (Vol. 4495, pp. 561-573). Springer-Verlag.

Rosemann, M. (2003). *Process management: A guide for the design of business processes.* Springer-Verlag.

Rosemann, M. (2006). Potential pitfalls of process modeling: part a. *Business Process Management Journal, 12*(2), 249-254.

Sarshar, K., & Loos, P. (2005, September 5-8). Comparing the control-flow of epc and Petri net from the end-user perspective. In W. M. P. van der Aalst, B. Benatallah, F. Casati, & F. Curbera (Eds.),

Proceedings of the Business Process Management, 3rd International Conference, BPM 2005, Nancy, France, (Vol. 3649, pp. 434-439).

Scheer, A.-W. (1998). *ARIS—business process frameworks* (2nd ed.). Berlin: Springer.

Scheer, A.-W. (2000). *ARIS—business process modeling* (3rd ed.). Berlin: Springer.

Scholz-Reiter, B., & Stickel, E. (Eds.). (1996). *Business process modelling.* Springer-Verlag.

Schütte, R. & Rotthowe. T. (1998) The guidelines of modeling—an approach to enhance the quality in information models. In T. W. Ling, S. Ram, & M-L. Lee (Eds.), *Proceedings of the 17th International Conference on Conceptual Modeling,* Singapore, (Vol. 1507, pp. 240-254). Springer.

Searle, J. (1969). *Speech acts: An essay in the philosophy of language.* Cambridge, England: Cambridge University Press.

Simon, C. (2006). *Negotiation processes. The semantic process language and applications.* University of Koblenz: Habilitationsschrift.

Smith, A. (1776). *An inquiry into the nature and causes of the wealth of nations.* London.

Smolander, K., Lyytinen, K., Tahvanainen, V.-P., & Marttiin, P. (1991, May 13-15). Metaedit—a flexible graphical environment for methodology modelling. In R. Andersen, J. A. Bubenko Jr., & A. Sølvberg (Eds.), *Proceedings of the Advanced Information Systems Engineering, CAiSE'91,* Trondheim, Norway, (Vol. 498, pp. 168-193). Springer.

Soffer, P., & Wand, Y. (2004, June 7-11). Goal-driven analysis of process model validity. In A. Persson & J. Stirna (Eds.), *Proceedings of the Advanced Information Systems Engineering, 16th International Conference, CAiSE 2004,* Riga, Latvia, (Vol. 3084, pp. 521-535). Springer.

Sommerville, I. (2001). *Software engineering* (6th ed.). Addison-Wesley.

Stachowiak, H. (1973). *Allgemeine modelltheorie.* Springer-Verlag.

Stirna, J., Persson, A., & Sandkuhl, K. (2007). Participative enterprise modeling: Experiences and recommendations. In J. Krogstie, A. L. Opdahl, & G. Sindre (Eds.), *Proceedings of the 19th Conference on Advanced Information Systems Engineering CAiSE 2007,* Trondheim, Norway, (Vol. 4495, pp. 546-560). Springer-Verlag.

Strahringer, S. (1996). *Metamodellierung als Instrument des Methodenvergleichs. Eine Evaluierung am Beispiel objektorientierter Analysemethoden.* Shaker Verlag: Aachen.

Taylor, F. W. (1911). *The principles of scientific management.* New York and London: Harper and Brothers.

Valmari, A. (1998, September). The state explosion problem. In W. Reisig & G. Rozenberg (Eds.), *Proceedings of the Lectures on Petri Nets I: Basic Models, Advances in Petri Nets, the Volumes are Based on the Advanced Course on Petri Nets,* Dagstuhl, (Vol. 1491, pp. 429-528). Springer.

van der Aalst, W. M. P. (1997). Verification of workflow nets. In P. Azéma & G. Balbo (Eds.), *Application and theory of Petri nets 1997, Lecture notes in computer science* (vol. 1248, pp. 407-426). Springer Verlag.

van der Aalst, W. M. P. (1998). The application of Petri nets to workflow management. *The Journal of Circuits, Systems and Computers, 8*(1), 21-66.

van der Aalst, W. M. P., Aldred, L., Dumas, M., & ter Hofstede, A. H. M. (2004). Design and implementation of the YAWL system. In A. Persson & J. Stirna (Eds.), *Advanced information systems engineering, Proceedings of the 16th International Conference on Advanced Information Systems Engineering (CAiSE'04)* (Vol. 3084, pp. 142-159). Berlin: Springer-Verlag.

van der Aalst, W. M. P., & and van Hee, K. (2002). *Workflow management: Models, methods, and systems.* The MIT Press.

van der Aalst, W. M. P., & ter Hofstede, A. H. M. (2005). YAWL: Yet another workflow language. *Information Systems, 30*(4), 245-275.

van der Aalst, W. M. P., ter Hofstede, A. H. M., Kiepuszewski, B., & Barros, A. P. (2003). Workflow patterns. *Distributed and Parallel Databases, 14*(1), 5-51.

van der Aalst, W. M. P., & Lassen, K. B. (in press). Translating unstructured workflow processes to readable bpel: Theory and implementation. *Information and Software Technology.*

van Dongen, B. F., & Jansen-Vullers, M. H. (2005, September 5-8). Verification of SAP reference models. In W. M. P. van der Aalst, B. Benatallah, F. Casati, & F. Curbera (Eds.), *Proceedings of the Business Process Management, 3rd International Conference, BPM 2005,* Nancy, France, , (Vol. 3649, pp. 464-469).

van Dongen, B. F., van der Aalst, W. M. P., & Verbeek, H. M. W. (2005, June 13-17). Verification of EPCs: Using reduction rules and Petri nets. In O. Pastor & J. Falcão e Cunha (Eds.), *Proceedings of the Advanced Information Systems Engineering, 17th International Conference, CAiSE 2005,* Porto, Portugal, (Vol. 3520, pp. 372-386). Springer.

van Hee, K., Sidorova, N., Somers, L., & Voorhoeve, M. (2006). Consistency in model integration. *Data & Knowledge Engineering, 56.*

Verbeek, H. M. W., Basten, T., & van der Aalst, W. M. P. (2001). Diagnosing workflow processes using Woflan. *The Computer Journal, 44*(4), 246-279.

Wand, Y., & Weber, R. (1990). *Studies in Bunge's treatise on basic philosophy.* Rodopi: The Poznan Studies in the Philosophy of the Sciences and the Humanities.

Wand, Y., & Weber, R. (1995). On the deep structure of information systems. *Information Systems Journal, 5,* 203-223.

Wand, Y., & Weber, R. (2002). Research commentary: Information systems and conceptual modeling —a research agenda. *Information Systems Research, 13*(4), 363-376.

Weber, I., Haller, J., & Mülle, J. A. (2006, February). Derivation of executable business processes from choreographies in virtual organizations. In *Proceedings of XML4BPM.*

Winograd, T. (1987-88). A language/action perspective on the design of cooperative work. *Human-Computer Interaction, 3*(1), 3-30.

Winter, A., Kullbach, B., & Riediger, V. (2001). An overview of the GXL graph exchange language. In S. Diehl (Ed.), *Proceedings of the Software Visualization—International Seminar,* Dagstuhl Castle, (Vol. 2269, pp. 324-336).

Wohed, P., van der Aalst, W. M. P., Dumas, M., ter Hofstede, A. H. M., & Russell, N. (2005). Pattern-based analysis of the control-flow perspective of UML activity diagrams. In L. Delcambre, C. Kop, H. C. Mayr, J. Mylopoulos, & O. Pastor (Eds.), *Proceedings of the 24nd International Conference on Conceptual Modeling ER 2005,* (Vol. 3716, pp. 63-78). Berlin: Springer-Verlag.

Wohed, P., van der Aalst, W. M. P., Dumas, M., ter Hofstede, A. H. M., & Russell, N. (2006). On the suitability of BPMN for business process modelling. In S. Dustdar, J. L. Fiadeiro, & A. Sheth (Eds.), *Proceedings of the Business Process Management, 4th International Conference, BPM 2006,* (Vol. 4102, pp. 161-176). Springer-Verlag.

Workflow Management Coalition. (2005, October 3). *Workflow process definition interface—XML process definition language* (Document Number WFMC-TC-1025). Version 2.00, Workflow Management Coalition.

Wynn, M. T., Edmond, D., van der Aalst, W. M. P., & ter Hofstede, A. H. M. (2005). Achieving a general, formal and decidable approach to the OR-join in workflow using reset nets. In G. Ciardo & P. Darondeau (Eds.), *Proceedings of the Applications and Theory of Petri Nets 2005,* (Vol. 3536*S,* pp. 423-443). Berlin: Springer-Verlag.

Wynn, M. T., Verbeek, H. M. W., van der Aalst, W. M. P., ter Hofstede, A. H. M., & Edmond, D. (2006). *Reduction rules for YAWL workflow nets with cancellation regions and or-joins.* BPMCenter Report BPM-06-24, BPMcenter.org.

Zhao, W., Hauser, R., Bhattacharya, K., Bryant, B. R., & Cao, F. (2006). Compiling business processes: untangling unstructured loops in irreducible flow graphs. *Int. Journal of Web and Grid Services, 2*(1), 68-91.

Zisman, M. D. (1977). *Representation, specification and automation of office procedures.* PhD thesis, University of Pennsylvania, Warton School of Business.

Zisman, M. D. (1978). Use of production systems for modeling asynchronous concurrent processes. *Pattern-Directed Inference Systems*, 53-68.

Zukunft, O., & Rump, F. J. (1996). *Business process modelling.* Springer-Verlag.

zur Muehlen, M. (2004). *Workflow-based process controlling. Foundation, design, and implementation of workflow-driven process information systems.* Logos, Berlin.

zur Muehlen, M., & Rosemann, M. (2004). Multiparadigm process management. In *Proceedings of the Fifth Workshop on Business Process Modeling, Development, and Support—CAiSE Workshops.*

KEY TERMS

BPMN: BPMN is an OMG standard for modeling business processes. It is meant to be used in conjunction of BPEL as an execution language. BPMN offers different kind of task and event nodes as well as gateways for the definition of split and join conditions.

BPEL: BPEL is an XML-based language that models a business process as a composition from a set of elementary Web services. A so-called BPEL engine is a dedicated software component that is able to execute BPEL process definitions. Six of BPEL's most important concepts are briefly presented in the following, that is, partner links, variables, correlation, basic activities, structured activities, and handlers.

Business Process: "A process is a completely closed, timely, and logical sequence of activities which are required to work on a process-oriented business object. Such a process-oriented object can be, for example, an invoice, a purchase order, or a specimen. A business process is a special process that is directed by the business objectives of a company and by the business environment. Essential features of a business process are interfaces to the business partners of the company (e.g., customers, suppliers)." (Becker and Kugeler, 2003)

Business Process Model: A business process model is the result of mapping a business process. This business process can be either a real-world business process as perceived by a modeller, or a business process conceptualized by a modeller.

Business Process Modeling: Business process modeling is the human activity of creating a business process model. Business process modelling involves an abstraction from the real-world business process, because it serves a certain modeling purpose. Therefore, only those aspects relevant to the modeling purpose are included in the process model.

Business Process Modeling Language: Business process modeling languages guide the procedure of business process modeling by offering a predefined set of elements and relationships for the modeling of business processes. A business process modeling language can be specified using a metamodel. In conjunction with a respective method, it establishes a business process modeling technique.

EPCs: EPCs are a language for conceptual modeling of business processes. EPCs have three node types: functions, events, and connectors. Connectors can be used to define split and join conditions of type AND, XOR, and OR.

Petri Nets: Petri nets are a formalism that can be used for modeling business processes. A Petri net is a special kind of graph that has two types of nodes: transitions for representing business activities and routing, and places for defining pre-conditions and post-conditions of transitions.

UML Activity Diagrams: UML activity diagrams belong to the UML family of diagrams. They are used for the description of system behavior. A UML activity diagram basically consists of actions and control nodes. There are different types of control nodes for the definition of complex routing including decision, merge, fork, and join. Furthermore, UML activity diagrams offer special actions to represent the sending of a signal and receiving an event.

YAWL: YAWL is a workflow modeling language that was defined to provide straight-forward support for the 20 workflow patterns identified by Aalst et al. (2003). In addition to Petri nets and EPCs, YAWL offers constructs for the specification of multiple instance tasks and for cancellation.

ENDNOTES

1   The authors refer to the GIGA group who originally introduced the scheme.

2   Note that zur Muehlen (2004) considers simulation as a separate activity related to evaluation, but this neglects the fact that simulation is always done to evaluate different design alternatives.

3   Positivism is the philosophical theory that establishes sensual experience as the single object of human knowledge.

4   In contrast to positivism, constructivism regards all knowledge as constructed. Therefore, there is nothing like objective knowledge or reality.

5   This negation of a theoretical foundation of a modeling language has some similarities with approaches that emphasize that models are not mappings from the real world, but products of negotiations between different stakeholders, as in Hirschheim and Klein (1989) and Simon (2006).

6   Several authors use heterogeneous terminology to refer to modeling techniques. Our concept of a modeling language is similar to grammar in Wand and Weber (2002, 1990, 1995), who also use the term method with the same meaning. In Karagiannis and Kühn (2002), a modeling method is called "procedure" while the term "method" is used to define a composition of modeling technique plus related algorithms.

7   Instead of model, Wand and Weber (2002, 1990, 1995) use the term "script."

8   Implicit termination is an exception. On purpose, this pattern is not supported in order to force the modeler to carefully consider the completion condition of the process.

9   See http:www.wfmc.orgstandardsdocsStds_diagram.pdf for an overview of WfMC workflow standards and associated documents.

10   The old acronym is *BPEL4WS* (business process execution language for Web services), the new one *WSBPEL* (Web service business process execution language). The acronym *BPEL* can be used for both.

11   The committee specification is available at http:docs.oasis-open.orgwsbpel2.0CS01wsbpel-v2.0-CS01.html.

12   Basic activities in BPEL 2 are: receive, invoke, reply, assign, validate, empty, throw, rethrow, exit, wait, compensate, compensateScope, and extensionActivity.

13   ftp:www6.software.ibm.comsoftwaredeveloperlibraryws-bpelj.pdf

14   ftp:www6.software.ibm.comsoftwaredeveloperlibraryws-bpel4people.pdf

15   https:www.sdn.sap.comirjservletprtportal-
      prtrootdocslibraryuuid5cbf3ac6-0601-0010-
      25ae-ccb3dba1ef47
16   WSBPEL technical committee participants
      at OASIS are Adobe, BEA, EDS, Hewlett-
      Packard, IBM, IONA, JBoss, Microsoft, NEC,
      Oracle, Sterling Commerce, Sun, Tibco, and
      webMethods

Section III
Agile Software Development

Chapter XVI
Some Method Fragments for Agile Software Development

Q.N.N. Tran
University of Technology, Sydney, Australia

B. Henderson-Sellers
University of Technology, Sydney, Australia

I. Hawryszkiewycz
University of Technology, Sydney, Australia

ABSTRACT

The use of a situational method engineering approach to create agile methodologies is demonstrated. Although existing method bases are shown to be deficient, we take one of these (that of the OPEN Process Framework) and propose additional method fragments specific to agile methodologies. These are derived from a study of several of the existing agile methods, each fragment being created from the relevant powertype pattern as standardized in the Australian Standard methodology metamodel of AS 4651.

INTRODUCTION

It is increasingly recognized that a universally applicable methodology (a.k.a. method) for software (and systems) development is not possible (Brooks, 1987; Avison & Wood-Harper, 1991; Fitzgerald, Russo, & O'Kane, 2003). One way to approach this is to eschew all attempts to create and promote a single methodology but instead to create a repository (or methodbase: Saeki, Iguchi, Wen-yin, & Shinohara, 1993) containing a large number of method fragments gleaned from a study of other methodologies, an evaluation of best industry practice, and so forth. Situational methods (Kumar & Welke, 1992; Odell, 1995) are then constructed by a method engineer "bottom up" from these fragments in such a way that they are "tailored" to the process requirements of the industry in question. This is the method engineering (ME) or situational method engineering (SME) approach to methodologies.

A second thread of relevance is the increasing interest, both in academe and industry, of agile methods—methodological approaches to software development that tend to the minimalistic, focus on people rather than documented processes, and react well to rapidly changing requirements (Abrahamsson, Warsta, Siponen, & Ronkainen, 2003; Turk, France, & Rumpe, 2005). However, as published and often as practiced, these agile methods themselves may be overly rigid. To make them more flexible and possess so-called "dual agility" (Henderson-Sellers & Serour, 2005), a method engineering approach can be applied to agile methods as well as more traditional software development approaches. To do so, it is incumbent upon the method engineers who provide the method bases to ensure that these repositories of method fragments contain adequate fragments from which a range of agile methods can indeed be constructed.

In this chapter, we hypothesize that an agile method can be created from method fragments, once those fragments have been identified and appropriately documented. Following an introduction to the general characteristics of agile software development, we then examine an underpinning metamodel (AS4651). We then identify and document method fragments that conform to this metamodel and that support a range of agile methods including XP, Crystal, Scrum, ASD, SDSM, and FDD. We thus propose the addition of these newly document fragments to one extensive ME repository, that of the OPEN Process Framework (OPF) (Firesmith & Henderson-Sellers, 2002; http://www.opfro.org), chosen on the basis of it having the most extensive content in its methodbase. An important part of any such research is the validation phase. This is described in the complementary chapter (Tran, Henderson-Sellers, & Hawryszkiewycz, 2007), where we (re-)create four agile methods from the fragments in the newly enhanced OPF methodbase.

GENERAL CHARACTERISTICS OF AGILE SOFTWARE DEVELOPMENT

Although each agile development methodology is distinct, they do share some common characteristics. Agile development adheres to the following fundamental values (Agile Manifesto, 2001):

- **Individuals and interactions** should be more important than processes and tools.
- **Working software** should be more important than comprehensive documentation.
- **Customer collaboration** should be more important than contract negotiation.
- **Responding to change** should be more important than following a plan.

Firstly, agile development emphasizes the relationship and communality of software developers, as opposed to institutionalized processes and development tools. Valuing people over processes allows for more creativity in solutions. In the existing agile practices, this value manifests itself in *close team relationships*, *close working environment arrangements*, and other *procedures boosting team spirit*. The importance of teamwork to agile development has been emphasized by agilists (Cockburn & Highsmith, 2001; Highsmith & Cockburn, 2001).

Secondly, an important objective of the software team is to continuously produce tested working software. It is argued that documentation, while valuable, takes time to write and maintain, and is less valuable than a working product. Some agile methodologies promote *prototyping* (e.g., ASD), while others encourage *building simple but completely functional products quickly* as possible (e.g., XP).

Thirdly, *customer involvement* is promoted in all agile methodologies. The relationship and cooperation between the developers and the clients are given the preference over strict contracts. The clients are encouraged to actively participate in the development effort.

Fourthly, the developers must be prepared to *make changes* in response to the emerging/changing needs during the development process. Any *plan must be lightweight* and easily modifiable. The "plan" might simply be a set of post-it notes on a whiteboard (e.g., as in Scrum: Schwaber, 1995).

Boehm (2002) presents a comparison (Table 1) between agile development and conventional process-oriented development (or plan-driven as he calls them). This comparison helps to highlight further characteristics of agile methodologies. While many method fragments were identified in the era of plan-driven methodologies, the atomic nature of these method fragments should mean that they are equally usable for the creation of agile methods. Indeed, this is amply demonstrated in empirical studies (Henderson-Sellers & Serour, 2005), which illustrated how several Sydney-based organizations have successfully created an agile situational method.

In our research project, we aim to identify method fragments for supporting agile development by examining:

- The characteristics of agile development described above; and
- The existing prominent agile methodologies, namely XP, Scrum, adaptive software development (ASD), dynamic systems development methodology (DSDM), Crystal methodologies, and feature driven development (FDD).

In this chapter, only method fragments extracted from the general agility characteristics and XP, Scrum, Crystal clear, and Crystal orange are listed.

THE UNDERPINNING METAMODEL AND AVAILABLE REPOSITORY

When method fragments are extracted from a methodology, they need to conform to some standard. Here, we ensure that they conform to an official Australian Standard, AS 4651 (Standards Australia, 2004)—a standard metamodel for development methodologies that has recently been "internationalized" through the normal ISO process resulting in the international standard ISO/IEC 24744 in 2007.

Both AS 4651 (as described here) and the newer ISO/IEC 24744 use two important architectural elements that are outlined here: powertypes and a multi-level architecture aligned with the information systems/business domain in which software development takes place (Note that in ISO/IEC 24744, some of the metaclass names are slightly different from those in AS 4651. Here we use the AS 4651 names).

The overall architecture is shown in Figure 1. The three layers reflect best practice and are organized to match the conceptual concerns of various subgroups within the software engineering community. People working on an endeavour (e.g., a specific software development project) (in the "endeavour layer") utilize methodologies, tools and so forth, which are all defined in the "method layer." This pair of layers is all the software development team is concerned with. However, a different pair of layers is of interest to methodologists, method engineers, and tool builders: the method layer together with

Table 1. Comparison of agile and plan-driven methods

Home-ground area	Agile methods	Plan-driven methods
Developers	Agile, knowledgeable, collocated, and collaborative	Plan-oriented; adequate skills; access to external knowledge
Customers	Dedicated, knowledgeable, collocated, collaborative, representative, and empowered	Access to knowledgeable, collaborative, representative, and empowered customers
Requirements	Largely emergent; rapid change	Knowable early; largely stable
Architecture	Designed for current requirements	Designed for current and foreseeable requirements
Refactoring	Inexpensive	Expensive
Size	Smaller teams and products	Larger teams and products
Primary objective	Rapid value	High assurance

the metamodel layer. It is this last (metamodel) layer that forms the basis and foundation for the others. This layer contains *all* the rule-focussed information necessary for creating methods, tools, and so forth.

The multilayer architecture reflects best *practice* and is no longer governed by the is-an-instance-of relationship as in the OMG's strict metamodelling hierarchy. Classes belong to the most "natural" layer as defined by the software engineering group of people most likely to be interested in their definition and usage. In particular, we wish to define (and standardize) certain abstract features of methodology elements in such a way that their subtypes can be defined in the method layer rather than the metamodel layer. We also wish to be able to allocate values to some attributes at the method layer while leaving other attributes without values until the endeavour layer, that is, for attributes to straddle *two* layers—not possible with current, traditional instantiation-based metalevel architectures (such as that employed by the OMG). To accomplish both these goals, we introduce the notion of a powertype (Odell, 1994)—the current most promising solution. A powertype is a class that has instances that are subtypes of another class (the partitioned class). Together the powertype class and the partitioned class form a *powertype pattern* (Henderson-Sellers & Gonzalez-Perez, 2005a, b).

A powertype pattern (as used in AS 4651) is shown in the metamodel layer of Figure 2. In this example, the powertype class is DocumentKind and the partitioned class is document. This means that there is a generalization relationship across layers, between (here) requirements specification document and its supertype Document as well as the more regular instantiation relationship (here between requirements specification document and the DocumentKind class in the metamodel layer). In other words, requirements specification document is concurrently an object (an instance of DocumentKind) and a class (a subtype of document). Such an entity was called by Atkinson (1998) a "clabject"—clabjects are an essential component of the powertype approach. In this example, as an instance of DocumentKind, requirements specification document has attribute values of name=requirements specification document and MustBeApproved=Yes. It also has attributes derived from its subtyping of document (title and version) that need to be given values at the endeavour level. To do this, they are first transmitted unchanged via the generalization relationship from document to requirements specification document. An object in the endeavour layer called, say, "MySystem" requirements specification, then instantiates requirements specification document (in the method layer), consequently allocating values to these attributes—here the values are shown (in Figure 2) as Title="MySystem" Requirements Specification and Version=1.1.

Figure 1. Schematic of the architecture underpinning AS 4651

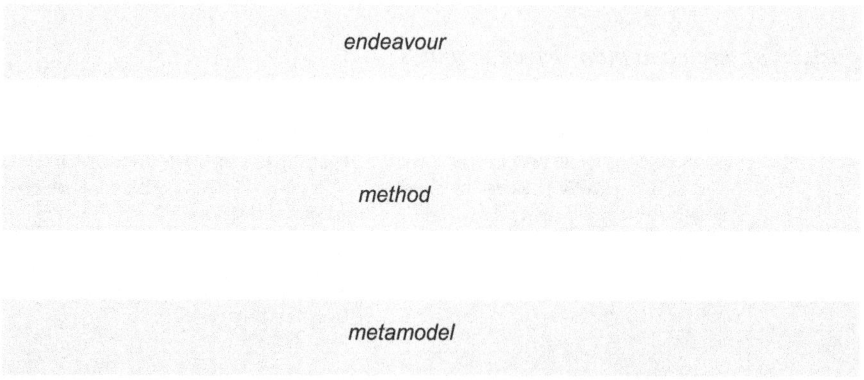

endeavour

method

metamodel

Figure 2. Powertype pattern showing how some attributes from the metamodel layer are instantiated at the model layer and others at the endeavour layer

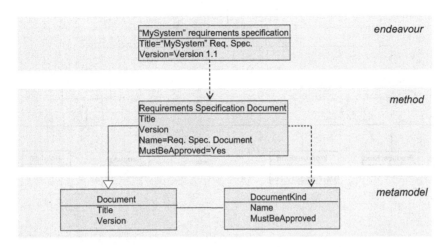

Note that the suffix "Kind" is used to represent an element belonging to a *methodology*, which needs to be distinguished from an element that belongs to a particular *endeavour*. For example, "Producer" refers to people involved in a particular systems development project, while "ProducerKind" refer to kinds of producers described by the methodology used by that project. Note that project-level elements must be instances of some methodology-level elements. In this report, we only use *kind fragments, because we focus on the methodology level, not the project level.

The overall architecture of AS 4651 (and ISO/IEC 24744) is shown in Figure 3. Most of the classes in the metamodel participate in powertype patterns (left hand side) although some do not (right hand side). The instances of these latter classes are used at the method level as endeavour-independent sources of information rather than as classes from which instances can be created for a particular endeavour, for example, a programming language. These two categories were named templates and resources, respectively in Gonzalez-Perez and Henderson-Sellers (2005).

We will now describe in more detail each of the metaclasses that are relevant to agile fragments—the focus of this chapter.

Producer-Related Metaclasses

A producer is an agent that executes work units. A ProducerKind is a specific kind of producer, characterized by its area of expertise. The ProducerKind class is specialized into TeamKind, ToolKind, and RoleKind.

A team is an organized set of producers that collectively focus on common work units. A TeamKind is a specific kind of team, characterized by its responsibilities. A role is a collection of responsibilities that a producer can take. A RoleKind is a specific kind of role, characterized by the involved responsibilities. A tool is an instrument that allows another producer to perform a work unit in an automated way. A ToolKind is a specific kind of tool, characterized by its features.

WorkProduct-Related Metaclasses

A WorkProduct is an artefact of interest for the project. A WorkProductKind is a specific kind of

Figure 3. Overall architecture of AS 4651

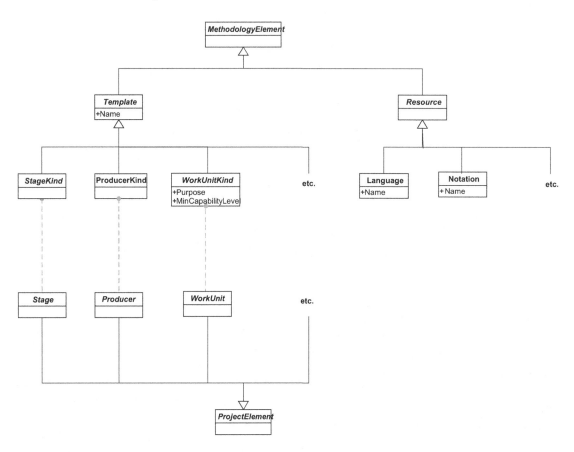

work product, characterized by the nature of its contents and the intention behind its usage. It is specialized into DocumentKind and ModelKind. A document is a durable depiction of a fragment of the observed reality. A DocumentKind is a specific kind of document, characterized by its structure, type of content and purpose. It can contain other documents, recursively. In contrast, a model is a formal representation of some subject that acts as its surrogate for some well defined purpose. A ModelKind is a specific kind of model, characterized by its focus, purpose, and level of abstraction.

Although not directly needed in our current study, it is of interest to note that a ModelUnit is an atomic component of a model, representing a cohesive fragment of information in the subject modelled. A ModelUnitKind is a specific kind

of model unit, characterized by the nature of the information it represents and the intention of using such representation. It allows a wide variety of subtypes; in particular, it supports the generation of all the metaclasses of a modeling language, assuming that modeling language definition has a "top" class equivalent to ModelUnitKind (e.g., the class element in UML Version 1.4 and 2.0)

Stage-Related Metaclasses

A Stage is a managed time frame within a project. A StageKind is a specific kind of stage, characterized by the abstraction level at which it works on the project and the result that it aims to produce.

WorkUnit- and Workflow-Related Metaclasses

There are two other groups of metaclasses of importance: WorkUnit and Workflow are the supertypes in question. Their definitions and the descriptions of agile method fragments conforming to these metaclasses will be discussed in a subsequent chapter of this book (Tran et al., 2007).

Discussion of OPF and its Repository

In order to capitalize on the use of method fragments, they need to be accumulated in a repository—here we utilize the repository of the OPEN Process Framework (OPF) (Henderson-Sellers & Graham, 1996; Firesmith & Henderson-Sellers, 2002), an example of an SME approach that uses the AS 4651 metamodelling approach. As well as the metamodel, the OPF also contains a well populated method fragment repository (see also http://www.opfro.org). The combination of the extensive methodbase content and the metamodel make OPF the best choice as the starting point for this investigation of agile method engineering.

The original work on the OPF was focussed on the necessary fragment support for object-oriented software development, although more recently it has been enhanced in order to support:

- Organizational transition (Henderson-Sellers & Serour, 2000; Serour, Henderson-Sellers, Hughes, Winder, & Chow, 2002)
- Web development (Haire, Henderson-Sellers, & Lowe, 2001; Henderson-Sellers, Haire, & Lowe, 2002)
- Component-based development (Henderson-Sellers, 2001)
- Agent-oriented development (Debenham & Henderson-Sellers, 2003; Henderson-Sellers, Giorgini, & Bresciani, 2004)
- Usage-centered design (Henderson-Sellers & Hutchison, 2003)

- Model transformations based on MDA (Pastor, Molina, & Henderson-Sellers, 2005)
- Aspect-oriented design (Henderson-Sellers, France, Georg, & Reddy, 2007)

Here, we first evaluate what current support is available for a range of agile methods. When the support is not available (in terms of a fragment held in the methodbase), we propose the addition of a new fragment, documented in the OPF standard style including alphabetical ordering (see Appendixes).

NEWLY IDENTIFIED FRAGMENTS TO SUPPORT AGILE DEVELOPMENT

This study has identified a large number of new fragments that could be considered for addition to the current OPF repository/method base. These are summarized in the following sections (and in Table 2) and are detailed in Appendices A-E in terms of the metaclass from which they are generated. Although listed in Table 2, those fragments in the context of WorkUnits and Workflows are not discussed here – details are to be found in the companion chapter (Tran et al., 2007).

Producer Fragments

There are three kinds of producer fragments: those from TeamKind, those derived from RoleKind, and those derived from ToolKind (These may also be constructed based on a set of coherent, identified responsibilities, since responsibility is an attribute of RoleKind).

TeamKind

Although there are three TeamKind fragments already in the OPF repository (peer programming team kind, XP-style team kind, and several subtypes of project team kind), our detailed analysis of XP, Scrum, and Crystal leads us to identify one further

Table 2. List of newly identified method fragments to support agile software development (N.B. There is no meaning to horizontal alignments).

ProducerKind Fragments	WorkProductKind Fragments	WorkUnitKind Fragments
Generated from TeamKind	*Generated from DocumentKind*	*Generated from TaskKind*
Scrum	Iteration plan	Design agile code
Generated from RoleKind	Product backlog	Develop release plan
Agile customer	Release plan	Explore architectural possibilities
Agile programmer	Story card	Manage shared artefacts
Coach	Team management (3 subtypes)	Mediate/monitor the performance of team's tasks
Consultant		Monitor work products
Product owner		Specify team policies
Scrum Master		Specify team structure
Tracker		Write user stories
XP tester	**StageKind Fragments**	
Generated from ToolKind	*Generated from StageWithDurationKind*	*Generated from TechniqueKind*
Groupware (6 subtypes)	Iteration/sprint	Agile team building
	Generated from InstantaneousStageKind	Collective ownership
	Iteration/sprint completed milestone	Conflict resolution
	Release completed milestone	Continuous integration
		Daily meeting
		Holistic diversity strategy
		Iteration planning game
		Methodology-tuning technique
		Monitoring by progress and stability
		Open workspace
		Pair programming
		Parallelism and flux
		Planning game
		Reflection workshop
		Role rotation
		Round-robin participation technique
		Simple design
		Small/short releases
		Sprint/iteration review meeting
		Sprint planning meeting
		System metaphor
		Team facilitation
		Team motivation
		Test driven development
		Generated from ActivityKind (subtype of WorkFlowKind)
		Team management

missing fragment. Scrum has its own definition of Team, such that we must introduce a new fragment to represent this—we call is "Scrum Team Kind." A full description of this new Scrum Team Kind fragment is to be found in Appendix A.

RoleKind

The OPF repository contains already a large number of useful RoleKind fragments: programmer, peer programmer, customer, tester, project manager/big boss, several kinds of software engineers, and stakeholders such as user, manager, vendor representative, and of course customer.

Nevertheless, our detailed analysis of these three agile methods led us to identify eight new roles pertinent only to one or more of these agile approaches. These eight new roles are described in full in Appendix B.

ToolKind

To add to the two existing OPF fragments in this group, lowerCASE tool kind and upperCASE tool kind, we propose just one new one for furthering tool support for agile methods: Groupware Tool-Kind, which describes the kind of tools that support and augment group work (Greenberg, 1991). Their goal is to assist team members in communicating, collaborating and coordinating their activities (Ellis, Gibbs, & Rein, 1991). Groupware tools are particularly important in agile projects, where team members are required to work closely together and maintain a cohesive, mutually supportive team relationship.

Six potential sub-classes of Groupware Tool kind have been identified from the literature (Saunders, 1997; Terzis & Nixon, 1999) and are summarized in Appendix C.

This study suggests that future software development teams may begin to use Groupware based on the notions of agency, where the architecture of the Groupware consists of one or more agents (Tarumi, & Mizutani et al., 1999). This is still a subject of research.

Work Product Fragments

Work products can be classified as either documents or models, that is, instances of DocumentKind or ModelKind, respectively.

DocumentKind

An extensive list of document kinds has been documented in Firesmith and Henderson-Sellers (2002). These include build plans, system requirements specifications, user's annuals, templates, standards, design-focussed document sets, test sets, and documents relating to teamwork. To add to these, for the support of agile methodologies, we recommend five new document kinds, as described in Appendix D.

ModelKind

As discussed earlier, an agile project values "working software" more than documentation. Thus, except for user requirements that are documented by story cards, no formal models are required to capture analysis and design decisions. These decisions can be captured in the code itself. In other words, the code is the main repository of design information; formal models and diagrams are only developed if necessary, for example, to summarize and highlight important design issues at the end of the project (Fowler, 2001; Jeffries, 2004).

Stage Fragments

The OPF repository (Firesmith & Henderson-Sellers, 2002) already contains four useful StageWithDurationKinds (XP lifecycle, Scrum lifecycle, phase, and release build) and one useful InstantaneousStageKind (Code Drop Milestone)—these readily map to XP and Scrum phases (Table 3). In the former category, we suggest that agile methodologies need one further fragment (Iteration/Sprint BuildKind) and in the latter category it needs two (Iteration/Sprint Completed MilestoneKind, and

Table 3. Correspondence between OPEN phases and agile methodologies' phases

OPEN PhaseKinds	XP Phases	Scrum
Initiation	Exploration Planning	Pregame
Construction	Iterations to release	Development/Game
Delivery	Productionizing	Postgame
Usage	Maintenance Death	
Retirement		

ReleaseCompleted MilestoneKind) (for details see Appendix E).

SUMMARY, CONCLUSIONS, AND FURTHER WORK

We have argued that a situational method engineering approach can be used in the context of agile software development. Existing method bases have been shown to be deficient and in need of enhancement—in terms of more method fragments—in order to completely support these new methodologies. Based on a study of several of the existing agile methods, we have taken the existing methodbase of the OPEN Process Framework, or OPF (Firesmith & Henderson-Sellers, 2002), and proposed additions to it. These additions are a set of method fragments that uniquely support agile software development, each of which is created from the relevant powertype pattern as standardized in the Australian Standard methodology metamodel of AS 4651 (Standards Australia, 2004).

ACKNOWLEDGMENT

We wish to thank Dr. Cesar Gonzalez-Perez for his useful comments on an earlier draft of this chapter. We also wish to thank the Australian Research Council for funding under Discovery Grant DP0345114.

REFERENCES

Abrahamsson, P., Warsta, J., Siponen, M. T., & Ronkainen, J. (2003). New directions on agile methods: a comparative analysis. In *Proceedings of ICSE '03* (pp. 244-254). Los Alamitos, CA, USA: IEEE Computer Society Press.

AgileManifesto. (2001). *Manifesto for agile software development*. Retrieved March 14 2005, from http://www.agilemanifesto.org/

Atkinson, C. (1998). Supporting and applying the UML conceptual framework. In J. Bézivin & P.-A. Muller (Eds.), *«UML» 1998: Beyond the notation,* (Vol. 1618, pp. 21-36). Berlin, Germany: Springer-Verlag.

Avison, D. E., & Wood-Harper, A. T. (1991). Information systems development research: an exploration of ideas in practice. *The Computer Journal, 34*(2), 98-112.

Beck, K. (2000). *Extreme programming explained: Embrace change.* Boston: Addison-Wesley.

Boehm, B. (2002). Get ready for agile methods, with care. *IEEE Computer, 35*(1), 64-69.

Brooks, F. P., Jr. (1987). No silver bullet: essence and accidents of software engineering. *IEEE Computer, 20*(4), 10-19.

Cockburn, A., & Highsmith, J. (2001). Agile software development: the people factor. *IEEE Computer, 34*(11), 131-133.

Coram, M., & Bohner, S. (2005). The impact of agile methods on software project management. In *Proceedings of the 12th IEEE International Conference and Workshops on the Engineering of Computer-Based Systems (ECBS'05).*

Debenham, J., & Henderson-Sellers, B. (2003). Designing agent-based process systems—extending the OPEN Process Framework. In V. Plekhanova (Ed.), *Intelligent agent software engineering* (pp. 160-190). Hershey, PA, USA: Idea Group Publishing.

Ellis, C. A., Gibbs, S. J., & Rein, G. (1991). Groupware: Some issues and experiences. *Communications of the ACM, 34*(1), 39-58.

Firesmith, D. G., & Henderson-Sellers, B. (2002). *The OPEN Process Framework. An introduction.* London: Addison-Wesley.

Fitzgerald, B., Russo, N. L., & O'Kane, T. (2003). Software development method tailoring at Motorola. *Communications of the ACM, 46*(4), 65-70.

Fowler, M. (2001). Is design dead? In G. Succhi & M. Marchesi (Eds.), *Extreme programming examined* (pp. 3-7). Boston: Addison-Wesley.

Gonzalez-Perez, C., & Henderson-Sellers, B. (2005). Templates and resources in software development methodologies. *Journal of Object Technology, 4*(4), 173-190.

Greenberg, S. (1991). *Computer-supported co-operative work and Groupware.* London: Academic Press Ltd.

Haire, B., Henderson-Sellers, B., & Lowe, D. (2001). Supporting web development in the OPEN process: additional tasks. In *Proceedings of the 25th Annual International Computer Software and Applications Conference. COMPSAC 2001* (pp. 383-389). Los Alamitos, CA, USA: IEEE Computer Society Press.

Henderson-Sellers, B. (2001). An OPEN process for component-based development. In G.T. Heineman, & W. Councill (Eds.), *Component-based software engineering: Putting the pieces together* (pp. 321-340). Reading, MA, USA: Addison-Wesley.

Henderson-Sellers, B. (2006, May 30-31). Method engineering: theory and practice. In D. Karagiannis & H. C. Mayr (Eds.), *Proceedings of the Information Systems Technology and its Applications. 5th International Conference ISTA 2006.* Klagenfurt, Austria, (Vol. P-84, pp. 13-23). Bonn: Gesellschaft für Informatik.

Henderson-Sellers, B., France, R., Georg, G., & Reddy, R. (2007). A method engineering approach to developing aspect-oriented modelling processes based on the OPEN Process Framework. *Information and Software Technology, 49*(7), 761-773

Henderson-Sellers, B., Giorgini, P., & Bresciani, P. (2004). Enhancing agent OPEN with concepts used in the tropos methodology. In A. Omicini, P. Pettra, & J. Pitt (Eds.), *Engineering Societies in the Agents World IV. 4th International Workshop, ESAW2003 LNAI* (Vol. 3071, pp 323-245). Berlin, Germany: Springer-Verlag.

Henderson-Sellers, B., & Gonzalez-Perez, C. (2005a). The rationale of powertype-based metamodelling to underpin software development methodologies. In S. Hartmann & M. Stumptner (Eds.), *Conferences in Research and Practice in Information Technology,* Sydney, NSW, (Vol. 43, pp. 7-16). Australia: Australian Computer Society.

Henderson-Sellers, B., & Gonzalez-Perez, C. (2005b). Connecting powertypes and stereotypes. *Journal of Object Technology, 4*(7), 83-96.

Henderson-Sellers, B., & Graham, I. M. (1996). OPEN: toward method convergence? *IEEE Computer, 29*(4), 86-89.

Henderson-Sellers, B., & Hutchison, J. (2003). Usage-centered design (UCD) and the OPEN Process Framework (OPF). In L. L. Constantine (Ed.), *Proceedings of the Performance by Design USE2003, Second International Conference on Us-*

age-Centered Design (pp. 171-196). Rowley, MA, USA: Ampersand Press.

Henderson-Sellers, B., & Serour, M. (2000). Creating a process for transitioning to object technology. In *Proceedings of the Seventh Asia--Pacific Software Engineering Conference APSEC 2000* (pp. 436-440). Los Alamitos, CA, USA: IEEE Computer Society Press.

Henderson-Sellers, B., & Serour, M. K. (2005). Creating a dual agility method - the value of method engineering. *Journal of Database Management, 16*(4), 1-24.

Highsmith, J., & Cockburn, A. (2001). Agile software development: the business of innovation. *IEEE Computer, 34*(9), 120-127.

Hogan, C. (2003). *The rules and practices of extreme programming.* Retrieved August 5, 2005, from http://www.everiware.com/cgi-bin/view/Lifecycle/ExtremeProgramming

Jeffries, R. (2004). *Where's the spec, the big picture, the design?* Retrieved on August 15, 2005, from http://www.xprogramming.com/xpmag/docBigPictureAndSpec.htm

Kumar, K., & Welke, R.J. (1992). Methodology engineering: a proposal for situation-specific methodology construction. In W. W. Cotterman, & J. A. Senn (Eds.), *Challenges and strategies for research in systems development* (pp. 257-269). Chichester, UK: John Wiley & Sons.

MountainGoatSoftware. (2005). *The Scrum development process.* Retrieved on August 23, 2005, from http://www.mountaingoatsoftware.com/Scrum/index.php

Odell, J. J. (1994). Power types. *Journal of Object-Oriented Programming, 7*(2), 8-12.

Odell, J. J. (1995). Introduction to method engineering. *Object Magazine, 5*(5).

Pastor, O., Molina, J. C., & Henderson-Sellers, B. (2005, May 27-June 1). Supporting ONME with

a method engineering framework. *Proceedings of the Software Development. Int. Conf. on Software Development, SWDC-2005,* (pp. 195-208). Reykjavik, Iceland: University of Iceland Press.

Qumer, A., & Henderson-Sellers, B. (in press). An evaluation of the degree of agility in six agile methods and its applicability for method engineering. *Information and Software Technology.*

Saeki, M., Iguchi, K., Wen-yin, K., & Shinohara, M. (1993). A meta-model for representing software specification & design methods. In *Proceedings of the IFIP WG8.1 Conference on Information Systems Development Process, Come* (pp. 149-166).

Saunders, J. H. (1997). *A manager's guide to computer supported collaborative work (also known as Groupware).* Retrieved July 1, 2005, from http://www.johnsaunders.com/papers/cscw.htm

Schwaber, K. (1995). SCRUM development process. In *Proceedings of the OOPSLA'95 Workshop on Business Object Design and Implementation.*

Schwaber, K., & Beedle, M. (2002). *Agile software development with Scrum.* New Jersey, USA: Springer-Verlag.

Serour, M., Henderson-Sellers, B., Hughes, J., Winder, D., & Chow, L. (2002). Organizational transition to object technology: theory and practice. In Z. Bellahsène, D. Patel, & C. Rolland (Eds.), *Object-oriented information systems, LNCS 2425* (pp. 229-241). Berlin, Germany: Springer-Verlag.

Standards Australia. (2004). *Standard metamodel for software development methodologies* (AS 4651-2004). Sydney, NSW, Australia: Standards Australia. Purchasable online at http://www.sai-global.com

Tarumi, H., Mizutani, S., et al. (1999). Simulation of agent-based Groupware with human factors. In *Proceedings of the 1999 International Symposium on Database Applications in non-traditional environments, Kyoto, Japan.*

Terzis, S., & Nixon, P. (1999). *Building the next generation Groupware: A survey of Groupware and its impact on the virtual enterpris* (Technical Report TCD-CS-1999-08). Dublin, Ireland: Trinity College, Computer Science Department.

Tran, Q. N. N., Henderson-Sellers, B., & Hawryszkiewycz, I. (2007). Agile method fragments and construction validation. In M. Syed (Ed.), *Handbook of research on modern systems analysis and design technologies.* Hershey, PA, USA: IGI.

Turk, D., France, R., & Rumpe, B. (2005). Assumptions underlying agile software-development processes. *Journal of Database Management, 16*(4), 62-87.

van Deursen, A. (2001). Customer involvement in extreme programming: XP2001 workshop report. *ACM SIGSOFT Software Engineering Notes, 26*(6), 70-73.

Wake, W. C. (2001). *Extreme programming explored.* Boston: Addison Wesley.

APPENDIX A. TEAM KINDS

Scrum Team Kind

This is a subclass of "Project Team Kind," which follows particular Scrum practices during the system development process. A Scrum team is different from an "XP-Style Team" in that its members can be cross-functional, including people with all of the skills necessary, for example, analysts, designers, quality control, and programmers (instead of only programmers as in an "XP-Style Team").

A Scrum team is characterized by its full authority to make any decisions and to do whatever is necessary to produce a product increment each sprint and to resolve problems/issues, being constrained only by organizational standards and conventions. The Scrum team should also self-organize to draw on its strengths and to allow everyone to contribute to the outcome. This need for self-organization implies that there should be no titles or job descriptions within a Scrum team. Each member applies his/her expertise to all of the problems. Scrum avoids people who refuse to code on the grounds that they are systems architects or designers.

APPENDIX B. ROLE KINDS

Agile Customer Role Kind

"Agile Customer RoleKind" is a subclass of "Customer RoleKind." Being a customer in an agile project requires many more responsibilities than a customer in a traditional development project. Traditional customers may only be involved at the inception of the project (e.g., helping to define requirements and contractual obligations) and at the end of the project (e.g., performing alpha, beta, and acceptance testing) (Coram & Bohner, 2005). In contrast, customers in agile projects are involved in the development process much more frequently and with more influence. In XP, at least one customer must be part of the project team and actively participate in the development process. Agile development style works best when customers operate in dedicated mode with the development team and when their tacit knowledge is sufficient for the full span of the application (Boehm, 2002). Note that merely having a customer representative available in the team is not sufficient. They must be committed, knowledgeable, collaborative, representative, and empowered (van Deursen, 2001; Boehm, 2002). An agile customer is required to be responsible for (and empowered to do) the following:

- Writing "stories" or listing "backlog items" to describe to developers the requirements of end users
- Making decisions in release planning and iteration planning (namely what requirements should be implemented in which release and which iteration, desired release date). This

involves making decisions on prioritizing and trading off the requirements

- Providing inputs (mainly opinions and decisions) into design and prototyping sessions
- Reviewing and accepting delivered releases
- Writing, organizing, and running functional tests on the delivered system. The customer will need to work closely with other project team members to learn what kind of things is helpful to test and what kind of tests are redundant
- Handling user training.

The best agile customers are those who will actually use the system being developed, but who also have a certain perspective on the problem to be solved (Beck, 2000).

Agile Programmer Role Kind

"Agile Programmer Role Kind" is a subclass of "Peer Programmer Role Kind." An agile programmer is responsible for not only the basic responsibilities of writing, unit testing, and debugging source code, but also responsible for:

- Analyzing user requirement
- Estimating how much effort and time are needed to satisfy each user requirement, thereafter letting the customer know about this estimate in order for them to make the decision on what to include in each release
- Designing the software solution
- Refactoring source code to keep the code as simple and definitive as possible
- Writing and running tests to demonstrate some vital aspect of the software
- Integrating new code to base-lined code and make sure the integrated product passes all Regression Tests
- Communicating and coordinating with other programmers and team members. If the programs run, but there is some vital component of communication left to be done, the job of the agile programmer is not yet over.

Coach Role Kind

A coach is responsible for the development process of the XP team as a whole. However, a "coach" is not to be equated with a team leader. While team leaders are often isolated geniuses making the important decisions on the project, the measure of a coach is how few technical decision he makes. A coach's job is to get everyone else in the team making good decisions. Responsibilities of a coach are:

- Understanding the practices and values of XP deeply, so as to guide other team members in following the XP approach (e.g., what alternative XP techniques might help the current set of problems, how other teams are using XP, what the ideas behind XP are, and how they relate to the current situation)
- Noticing when people are deviating from the team's process (e.g., programmers are skipping unit tests) and bringing this to the individuals' or team's attention
- Seeing long-term refactoring goals and encouraging small-scale refactorings to address parts of these goals
- Helping programmers with individual technical skills, such as testing, formatting, and refactoring
- Explaining the process to upper-level managers.

The role of coach usually diminishes as the team matures.

Consultant Role Kind

A consultant is not a part of an XP team. Rather, he/she is an external specialist whom the team seeks for technical help. Normally, an XP team does not need to consult a specialist, but from time to time the team needs deep technical knowledge. The responsibility of a consultant is to teach XP team members how to solve a particular problem that the team needs to solve. The consultant must not solve the problem by themselves. Instead, one or two team members will sit with the consultant while he/she solves the problem.

Product Owner Role Kind

A Product owner is responsible for managing and controlling the "Product Backlog" in Scrum (see DocumentKind section). Their specific responsibilities are:

- Creating the product backlog together with the "Scrum Master" and project team members
- Maintaining and sustaining the content and priority of the product backlog, including adding, removing and updating product backlog items and their priority during releases and iterations/sprints. Note that the product owner solely controls the product backlog. Any member wanting to update/add/remove an item or its priority has to convince the product owner to make the change. Without a single product owner, floundering, contention and conflicts surrounding the product backlog result
- Turning 'issues' in product backlog into specific features or technology to be developed (i.e., workable items)
- Ensuring the product backlog is visible to everyone
- Segmenting and allocating product backlog items into probable releases, thereby developing the "Release Backlog Document" (see DocumentKind section)
- Working with project team members to estimating the amount of work in days to implement each product backlog item for "Product Backlog Document" and "Release Backlog Document" (see DocumentKind section)
- Revising the "Release Backlog Document" as the project team builds the product during each iteration/sprint (e.g., revising the release date or release functionality).
- Making final decisions on the tasks related to product backlog items, thereby developing "Sprint Backlog Document"

- Reviewing the system with other stakeholders at the end of iteration/sprint.

In a Scrum project, a product owner is chosen by the "Scrum Master," customers, and management.

Scrum Master Role Kind

Scrum introduces the role of "Scrum Master," which is essentially a sub-class of both "Coach Role Kind" and "Project Manager/big Boss Role Kind" in XP. A Scrum Master is a coach in that he/she is responsible for guiding the project team members in following the Scrum practices and values, for keeping track of the progress and ensuring everyone is on track, and providing assistance to members that need help (as well as for other responsibilities of a coach; see Coach Role Kind section). A Scrum Master is also a project manager in that he/she works with management to form the project team, represents the team and management to each other, and makes decisions. An important responsibility of a Scrum Master (which is not specified for a coach or a project manager) is to ensure that any impediments to the project are promptly removed and changed in the process, so as to keep the team working as productively as possible (Schwaber & Beedle, 2002). The Scrum Master can either personally remove them, or cause them to be removed as soon as possible. When the Scrum Master does the latter, he or she needs to make visible to the team a particular procedure, structure or facility that is hurting productivity. Another responsibility is to conduct the "Daily Scrum Meeting" and "Sprint/ Iteration Review Meeting" (see TechniqueKind section in Tran et al., 2007).

Tracker Role Kind

The role kind "tracker" is introduced based on an XP tracker. A tracker is responsible for giving feedback to other members of an XP team. In particular, he/she handles the following responsibilities:

- Tracing the estimates made by the team (in release planning and iterative planning) and giving feedback on how accurate these estimates turn out, in order for the team to improve future estimations.
- Tracing the progress of each iteration and evaluating whether the team is able to achieve the desired goal if they follow the current course or if they need to change something. A couple of iterations into a release, a tracker should be able to tell the team whether they are going to make the next release without making big changes.
- Keeping a log of functional test scores, reported defects, who accepts responsibility for each of them, and what test cases were added on each defect's behalf.

XP Tester Role Kind

In an XP team, a lot of testing responsibilities actually lie with the "Agile Programmer Role Kind" (i.e., unit testing) and "Agile Customer Role Kind" (i.e., acceptance/functional testing). Thus, the responsibility of a tester role is really to help the customer write and execute functional tests. Accordingly, we introduce an "XP Tester Role Kind" as a subclass of "Tester Role Kind" who is responsible for helping the customer write and execute functional tests. An XP tester is also responsible for making sure the functional tests are run regularly and the test results are broadcasted in a prominent place.

APPENDIX C. SIX SUBTYPES OF GROUPWARE TOOLKIND

Conferencing Tool Kind

- Text-based conferencing: IRC, COW (conferencing on the Web)
- Audio/video conferencing: CUSeeMe, Sun Show Me, Intel TeamStation, PictureTel

Electronic Mail Tool Kind

- E-mail systems that support message-based collaboration and coordination: Lotus Notes, Novel Groupwise, and MS Exchange (these offer support for calendaring & scheduling, discussion groups, & notetaking)
- Newgroups systems: USENETS and GrouplLens

Group Decision Support Tool Kind

- Support for group-agenda setting, brainstorming, filtering, classifying, or prioritizing the issues at hand: GroupSystems, MS NetMeeting, Meeting Room, TeamEC, ICBWorks

Meeting Support Tool Kind

- Support for audio-video conferencing and application-data sharing: MS NetMeeting, NewStar Sound IDEAS, and GroCo
- Support for the preparation and management of team meetings: DOLPHIN

Shared Workspace Tool Kind

- Sharedspaces, GMD FIT BSCW (basic support for cooperative work), Collaborative Virtual Workspace
- Room-based systems: TeamRooms, Mushroom
- Virtual environments: Virtual Society
- Support for group coordination: Lotus Notes, IBM FlowMark, JetForm, Action Workflow

Workflow Tool Kind

- Support for group coordination: Lotus Notes, IBM FlowMark, JetForm, Action Workflow

APPENDIX D. DOCUMENTKINDS

Iteration Plan Document Kind

- *Purpose*: A subclass of "Build Plan Document Kind," which documents the plan for a particular iteration/sprint within a release.
- *Description*: An "Iteration Plan Document Kind" specifies the *requirements* to be implemented in the forthcoming iteration/sprint, the *tasks* to be performed during the iteration/sprint to implement these requirements, and the *time estimates* to complete each task.

In XP, the requirements included in "Iteration Plan Document Kind" are 'user stories' selected from "Release Plan Document." The iteration plan is to be generated by XP programmers. These programmers also need to sign up for individual tasks and this information should also be recorded in the "Iteration Plan Document Kind" (Wake, 2001).

In Scrum, the "Iteration Plan Document Kind" is referred to as "Sprint Backlog Document." Requirements listed in it are backlog items selected from "Release Backlog Document" (Schwaber & Beedle, 2002). Once a task is started, its time estimate is to be updated daily (by the developer working on the task) to show the remaining hours needed to complete that work. Sprint backlogs are produced by the developers, "Scrum Master" and "Product Owner" (see RoleKind section).

Product Backlog Document Kind

- *Purpose*: A subclass of "System Requirements Specification Document Kind" generated and used in Scrum projects. Product backlog documents can be produced by multiple stakeholders, including customers, users, project team, marketing, sales division, customer support, and management.
- *Content*: A product backlog contains a master list of all requirements that can be foreseen for a system product. Product backlog items can include, for example, features, functions, bug fixes, defects, requested enhancements, technology upgrades, and issues requiring solution before other backlog items can be done (Schwaber & Beedle, 2002). These items can be technical (e.g., "refactor the login class to throw an exception") or more user-centric (e.g., "allow undo on the setup screen"). It is possible to express each Scrum backlog item in the form of XP's user story (see "Story Card Document Kind") (MountainGoatSoftware, 2005).

The list of product backlog items should be prioritized by the "Product Owner" (see RoleKind section). Items that have high priority are the ones that are the most desired. The effort needed for each item's implementation should also be estimated by the "Product Owner". The Product backlog is to be constantly expanded or updated with new and more detailed items, new priority order and more accurate estimations, as more is learned about the product and its customers (particularly throughout sprints and releases).

Release Plan Document Kind

- *Purpose*: A subclass of "Build Plan Document Kind," which documents the overall plan for a particular release.
- *Description*: A "Release Plan Document kind" specifies which requirements are going to be implemented by a particular release, the prioritization of these stories and the estimated date of the release (Wake, 2001; Hogan, 2003). A release plan will be used to create iteration plans (see "Iteration Plan Document Kind").

In XP, the requirements listed in the release plan are user stories selected from "story card documents." The release plan is to be developed by both development and business actors. A release plan used to be called "commitment schedule" in XP. The name was changed to more accurately describe its purpose and be more consistent with "iteration plan" (Hogan, 2003).

In Scrum, the "Release Plan Document" is referred to as a "Release Backlog Document." It is to be developed by the "Product Owner" (see RoleKind section).

Story Card Document Kind

- *Purpose*: A subclass of "System Requirements Specification Document Kind" which is generated and used in XP projects. Story card documents are typically produced by customers in XP teams.
- *Content*: Each story card captures a "user story" describing a feature that the customer wants the system to provide. Each story is accompanied with a name and a short paragraph documenting the purpose of the story.

Team Management Document Kinds:

a. Team Structure Document Kind

- *Purpose*: This document kind is equivalent to the organization chart document kind, but at the team level.
- *Content*: This document kind should contain the specification of the structure of a particular team in terms of:
  - Roles (or individuals) that make up the team
  - Acquaintance relationships amongst these roles
  - Authority relationships that govern these acquaintances

The team structure document kind can be developed and updated by team leaders and distributed to newly joined team members.

b. Team Policies Document Kind

- *Purpose*: Specify team policies (or rules or conventions).

- *Content*: When working in teams, developers usually have to comply with certain policies (or rules or conventions) that govern the collaborative work within the team. These policies should be identified and documented. Example policies: each team member can only play one role at a time within the team; every team member must report to team leader; interactions/communications amongst team members are mediated by team leader.

The team structure document kind can be developed and updated by team leaders and distributed to team members.

c. Artefact Access Permissions Document Kind

- *Purpose*: Specify access permissions of particular artefact(s).
- *Content*: Different roles in a team, or different teams, may have different permissions to access the same artefact (for example, a team's message board can be read and updated by a team leader, but only read by team members). In such cases, the artefact should be accompanied by an "artefact access permission document," which specifies the permissions granted to each different role/team.

The artefact access permissions document kind can be produced and kept by the artefact manager role or team leader role (depending on which role is responsible for managing the artefact) and distributed to team members (probably only the permissions that the member is concerned).

APPENDIX E. BUILD KINDS

Iteration/Sprint Build Kind

An "Iteration/Sprint Build"[1] is a period of time from one to 4 weeks within a "Release Build" during which a new set of features/requirements are implemented and added to a release. Each "Release Build" should be broken into several "Iteration/Sprint Builds."

At the beginning of an iteration/sprint, "Develop Iteration Plan Task"[2] is performed to determine what features/requirements are to be implemented in that iteration/sprint. During the iteration/sprint, the project team designs, codes, and tests for the selected features/requirements. At the end of the iteration/sprint, various "Testing Tasks"[3] are carried out to see if the software produced by the iteration/sprint satisfies the desired requirements.

In Scrum projects, each sprint also involves "Iteration Review" and "Iteration Adjust" tasks[4] which identify any risks/issues affecting the iteration/sprint and adjust the iteration/sprint or the overall requirements (or even development direction) to reconcile these risks/issues.

Iteration/Sprint Completed Milestone Kind

This milestone marks the event when an iteration/sprint is completed. Ideally at each "Iteration Completed Milestone," the customer will have completed the functional tests on the resulting code and these tests should all pass. In XP, "Iteration Completed Milestones" occur during the XP "Iteration to First Release" phase, "Productionizing" phase, and "Maintenance" phase. The first ever iteration should put the overall system's architecture in place. In Scrum, "Sprint Completed Milestones" occur during Scrum's "Game" phase.

Release Completed Milestone Kind

This milestone marks the event when a release of the system is delivered to the customer. In Scrum, the whole Scrum's cycle (including "Pregame," "Game," and "Postgame" phases) works towards a particular release. Thus, the "Release Completed Milestone" occurs at the end of the cycle, or more specifically, the end of the "Postgame" phase. In

XP, however, the first release is produced at the end of the "Productionizing" phase, while subsequent releases are delivered during the "Maintenance" phase. This gives rise to two subtypes of "Release Completed Milestone Kind":

- "First Release Completed Milestone Kind"
- "Subsequent Release Completed Milestone Kind"

KEY TERMS

Agile Method: A method that is people focused, flexible, speedy, lean, responsive, and supports learning (based on Qumer & Henderson-Sellers, 2007).

Agility: *Agility is a persistent behaviour or ability of a sensitive entity that exhibits flexibility to accommodate expected or unexpected changes rapidly, follows the shortest time span, uses economical, simple and quality instruments in a dynamic environment and applies updated prior knowledge and experience to learn from the internal and external environment* (Qumer and Henderson-Sellers, 2007).

Metamodel: A model of models.

Method Engineering: The engineering discipline to design, construct, and adapt methods, techniques, and tools for systems development.

Method Fragment: Construction of a software development method for a specific situation.

Producer: An agent that executes work units.

ProducerKind: A specific kind of producer, characterized by its area of expertise.

Stage: A managed time frame within a project.

StageKind: A specific kind of stage, characterized by the abstraction level at which it works on the project and the result that it aims to produce.

Task: A small-grained work unit that focuses on what must be done in order to achieve a given purpose.

TaskKind: A specific kind of task, characterized by its purpose within the project.

Technique: A small-grained work unit that focuses on how the given purpose may be achieved.

TechniqueKind: A specific kind of technique, characterized by its purpose within the project

WorkProduct: An artefact of interest for the project.

WorkProductKind: A specific kind of work product, characterized by the nature of its contents and the intention behind its usage.

WorkUnit: A job performed within a project.

WorkUnitKind: A specific kind of work unit, characterized by its purpose within the project.

ENDNOTES

[1]   XP uses the term "iteration" while Scrum uses "sprint."

[2]   See TaskKind section in Tran et al. (2007)

[3]   See TaskKind section in Tran et al. (2007)

[4]   See TaskKind section in Tran et al. (2007)

Chapter XVII
Agile Method Fragments and Construction Validation

Q.N.N. Tran
University of Technology, Sydney, Australia

B. Henderson-Sellers
University of Technology, Sydney, Australia

I. Hawryszkiewycz
University of Technology, Sydney, Australia

ABSTRACT

Method fragments for work units and workflows are identified for the support of agile methodologies. Using one such situational method engineering approach, the OPEN Process Framework, we show how the full set of these newly identified agile method fragments, each created from the relevant powertype pattern as standardized in the Australian Standard methodology metamodel of AS 4651, can be used to recreate four of the currently available agile methods: XP, Scrum, and two members of the Crystal family—thus providing an initial validation of the approach and the specifically proposed method fragments for agile software development.

INTRODUCTION

Situational method engineering (Welke & Kumar, 1991) is the subdiscipline of software engineering in which methodologies (a.k.a. methods) are envisaged as being constructed from parts called method fragments. These are identified from best practice and stored in a repository (or method base). In this chapter, we identify new fragments to support the work units and work flows needed to support agile software development—a set of method fragments

that completes and complements those described in Tran, Henderson-Sellers, and Hawryszkiewycz (2007). These fragments are compliant with the metamodel of the Australian Standard AS4651 and extend the existing repository of the OPEN Process Framework (OPF: Firesmith & Henderson-Sellers, 2002; http://www.opfro.org), chosen on the basis of it having the most extensive content in its method base. Following this discussion of new fragments, we then use them to recreate a number of existing agile methods as validation of both the SME approach and the particular set of newly proposed agile method fragments.

AGILE SOFTWARE DEVELOPMENT AND THE AS4651 METAMODEL

As discussed in Tran et al. (2007), agile development adheres to the following fundamental values (Agile Manifesto, 2001):

- **Individuals and interactions** should be more important than processes and tools.
- **Working software** should be more important than comprehensive documentation.
- **Customer collaboration** should be more important than contract negotiation.
- **Responding to change** should be more important than following a plan and has a strong focus on teamwork.

Here, we use the basic understanding of agile software development to identify method fragments compatible with the OPEN Process Framework and the metamodel described in AS4651 (Standards Australia, 2004). The overall architecture of this metamodel is shown in Figure 1, using the notion of a powertype (Odell, 1994) (for full details see Tran et al., 2007).

We will now describe in more detail the metaclasses that are relevant to agile fragments but which were not covered in Tran et al. (2007), that is, work units (tasks and techniques) and workflows (a third kind of work unit)—the focus of this chapter.

WorkUnit-Related Metaclasses

A WorkUnit is a job performed within a project. A WorkUnitKind is a specific kind of work unit, characterized by its purpose within the project. It is specialized into TaskKind, TechniqueKind, and WorkFlowKind.

A task is a small-grained work unit that focuses on what must be done in order to achieve a given purpose. A TaskKind is a specific kind of task, characterized by its purpose within the project.

A technique is a small-grained work unit that focuses on how the given purpose may be achieved. A TechniqueKind is a specific kind of technique, characterized by its purpose within the project.

WorkFlow-Related Metaclasses

A WorkFlow is a large-grained work unit that operates within a given area of expertise. A WorkFlowKind is a specific kind of work flow, characterized by the area of expertise in which it occurs. It is specialized into ActivityKind and ProcessKind. An activity is a work flow that represents a continuous responsibility. An ActivityKind is a specific kind of activity, characterized by the area of expertise in which it occurs. A process is a work flow that represents a discrete job. A ProcessKind is a specific kind of process, characterized by the area of expertise in which it occurs.

Here, we first evaluate what current support is available for a range of agile methods for these two groups of metaclasses and their generated fragments. When the support is not available (in terms of a fragment held in the methodbase), we propose the addition of a new fragment, documented in the OPF standard style including alphabetical ordering (see Appendices).

NEWLY IDENTIFIED FRAGMENTS TO SUPPORT AGILE DEVELOPMENT

This study has identified a large number of new work unit fragments that could be considered for addition to the current OPF repository/methodbase. These are summarized in the following sections and are detailed in Appendixes A-C in terms of the metaclass from which they are generated.

Figure 1. Overall architecture of AS 4651

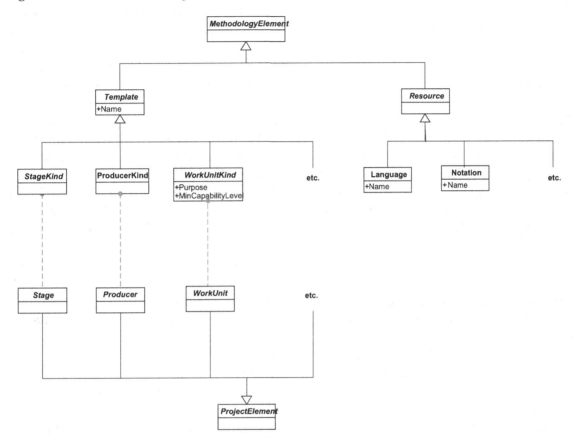

Work Unit Fragments

There are three major kinds of work unit kinds in the metamodel from which fragments have been generated. These are discussed in turn: TaskKind fragments, TechniqueKind fragments, and two sorts of WorkFlowKind fragments.

TaskKind

Existing TaskKind fragments include analyze technology, describe application, elicit requirements, prototype the architecture, develop iteration plan, code, refactor, integrate software, write manuals, and prepare other documentation, document the design as well as several risk assessment and management tasks, testing tasks, and teamwork building and management tasks.

However, there are new tasks associated with agile methods that are not encompassed by these agile-focussed tasks in the existing repository. These are documented in Appendix A for addition to the repository.

TechniqueKind

As one might anticipate, the support for agile *techniques* in the existing OPF repository is incomplete, although some minimal descriptions of pair programming, planning game, system metaphor, and refactoring were made in Henderson-Sellers (2001). In addition to those already documented (Firesmith & Henderson-Sellers, 2002)—regression testing, acceptance testing, beta testing, unit testing, team building, role assignment, group problem solving, brainstorming and workshops—the recommended new fragments to describe agile-specific techniques are found in Appendix B (those mentioned in Henderson-Sellers, 2001 are also included there in full, expanded detail for the sake of completeness).

WorkFlowKind

ActivityKind

In addition to OPF's build, evolutionary development, user review, consolidation, and project management activity kinds, we propose one additional fragment: team management activity kind (as detailed in Appendix C).

ProcessKind

The phases described in the current OPF repository appear to be sufficient to support all the agile methods studied to date.

The "build activity kind" for XP development (see ActivityKind section) can alternately be replaced by the aggregation of:

- "Requirement engineering process kind;"
- "Designing process kind;"
- "Implementation process kind;"
- "Testing process kind;"
- "Deployment process kind;" and
- "Evaluation process kind"

given that the process of each kind is repeated in short iterative cycles.

Note: Team building may be viewed as a process. However, the work involved in team building has been covered by "human resource management" sub-activity kind of "project management" activity kind of OPEN (particularly, staffing and task allocation).

RECREATING AGILE METHODS

Process construction can be undertaken in one of several ways. Three of these (maps, activity diagrams, and deontic matrices) are compared in Seidita, Ralyté, Henderson-Sellers, Cossentino, and Arni-Bloch (2007). Of these, the one recommended for use with the OPF is that of deontic matrices, first introduced in MOSES (Henderson-Sellers & Edwards, 1994) and SOMA (Graham, 1995). A deontic matrix is a two dimensional matrix of values that represent the possible or likely relationship between each pair of method fragments in the OPF. The actual values depend upon a number of factors such as project size, organizational culture, domain of the application to be developed, and the skills and preferences of the development team. Once completed, they give guidance on the most appropriate selection of method fragments. Although five levels are suggested in the literature, for a specific project often binary values are used. In addition, increasingly sophisticated teams will wish to see their process mature commensurately. Using the deontic matrix approach, new method fragments are easily added to an organization's existing methodology. In this approach, there is a deontic matrix to link activities to tasks, tasks to techniques, producers to tasks, and so forth.

In the following subsections we outline the results of the use of these deontic matrices and list the fragments selected for inclusion in each of the four respective methodologies: XP (Table 1), Scrum (Table 2), Crystal Clear (Table 3), and Crystal Orange (Table 4).

DISCUSSION OF THE RECREATED AGILE METHODS

For each of the four agile methods, we have identified all the fragments from the enhanced OPF methodbase necessary for their recreation. Each approach is seen to be different (as one might expect) supporting the application of a method engineering approach to construct *situational* methodologies. It is thus reasonable to propose that the fragments created and documented in this chapter are complete and adequate to support (at least these four) agile methodologies.

Table 1. Assembly of method fragments to reproduce XP Methodology

ACTORS			
Teams	Peer programming team XP-style team		
Roles	Agile programmer Agile customer XP tester Tracker Coach Consultant Project manager		
PROCESS			
Lifecycle	XP lifecycle		
Builds	Release Iteration		
Milestones	Code drop Iteration completed First release completed Subsequent release completed		
Documents	Story cards Release plan Iteration plan Test set of documents		
Software Items	Software components (source code, running code, test software)		
Tools			
Phases, tasks and techniques	*Initiation phase*	*Tasks:* Write user stories Explore architectural possibilities Analyze technologies Describe application Prototype the architecture Develop release plan Develop iteration plan	*Techniques:* Agile team building Small/short release System metaphor Planning game Iteration planning game Stand-up meeting
	Construction phase	*Activity:* Build *Tasks:* Design agile code Code Refactor Testing tasks Integrate software	*Techniques:* Pair programming Simple design Refactoring Continuous integration Collective ownership Open workspace Regression testing Acceptance testing Unit testing Stand-up meeting
	Delivery phase	*Activity:* Build (in shorter cycles; more focused on "user review" and "consolidation" sub-activities) *Tasks:* Design agile code Code Refactor Testing tasks	*Techniques:* Same as above (more usage of testing techniques, e.g., acceptance testing)
	Usage phase	Write manuals and prepare other documentation	

Table 2. Assembly of method fragments to reproduce Scrum Methodology

ACTORS			
Teams	Scrum team		
Roles	Scrum master Product owner Common feveloper roles Agile customer		
PROCESS			
Lifecycle	Scrum lifecycle		
Builds	Release Sprint		
Milestones	Sprint completed Release completed		
Documents	Product backlog Release plan Iteration plan (i.e., sprint backlog) Test set of documents		
Software Items	Software components (source code, running code, test software)		
Tools			
Phases, tasks and techniques	*Pregame phase*	*Tasks:* Elicit requirements Develop release plan Risk assessment and management Team building	*Techniques:* Agile team building
	Development/game phase	*Activity*: Build *Tasks*: Design agile code Code Testing tasks Integrate software	*Techniques:* Sprint planning meeting Daily Scrum meeting Sprint/iteration review meeting Testing techniques
	Postgame phase	*Tasks*: Integrate system Write manuals and prepare other documentation	*Techniques:*

Table 3. Assembly of method fragments to reproduce Crystal Clear Methodology

ACTORS		
Teams	Project team	
Roles	Designer Programmer Agile customer Sponsor Requirements engineer Project manager	
PROCESS		
Lifecycle	Iterative, incremental, parallel	
Builds	Release Iteration	
Milestones	Iteration completed Release completed Various technical milestones within each iteration, for example, start of requirements engineering, first design review, first user review, final user review, pass into test…	
Documents	System requirements specification (use case specification or feature descriptions) User's manual Templates Standards (e.g., for coding, regression testing) Design sketches Test set of documents	
Software Items	Software components (running code, migration code, test software)	
Tools	upperCASE tools (configuration management and documentation management tools) lowerCASE tools (compiler) Groupware tools (e.g., printing whiteboard)	
Phases, tasks and techniques	(For each iteration): *Activity*: Build *Tasks*: Design tasks Code Testing tasks Document the design Monitor work product	*Techniques* Small/short releases (2-3 months) Testing techniques Monitoring by progress and stability Parallelism and flux Reflection workshop Methodology tuning

Table 4. Assembly of method fragments to reproduce Crystal Orange Methodology

ACTORS		
Teams	Function team (equivalent to the composition of OPEN's software requirements team, software architecture team, and software development team) Infrastructure team (equivalent to the composition of OPEN's system development team and hardware development team) Test team System planning team (equivalent to OPEN's project initiation team or management team) Project monitoring team (equivalent to OPEN's management team) Architecture team Technology teams (one per each speciality, equivalent to OPEN's user interface team, peer programming team, database team, documentation team, or test team)	
Roles	Project manager/big boss Requirements engineer Architect Designer Programmer Tester Technical writer Tester User Business expert (equivalent to a type of stakeholder such as "manager") Technical facilitator, design mentor (equivalent to tracker, coach, or Scrum master)	
PROCESS		
Lifecycle	Iterative, incremental, parallel	
Builds	Release Iteration	
Milestones	Iteration completed Release completed Various technical milestones within each iteration, for example, start of requirements engineering, first design review, first user review, final user review, pass into test…	
Documents	System requirements specification Design set of documents (e.g., UI design, object model, database design etc.) Schedules (equivalent to release plan and iteration plan documents) Status report User's manual Templates Standards (e.g., for coding, regression testing, notation, design, and quality) Test set of documents	
Software Items	Software components (source code, running code, migration code, test software)	
Tool	upperCASE tools (configuration management, documentation management, and modeling tools) lowerCASE tools (compiler) Groupware tools (e.g., printing whiteboard, team progress tracking, team communication)	
Phases, tasks and techniques	Develop release plan Develop iteration plan (For each iteration): *Activity*: Build *Tasks*: Design tasks Code Testing tasks Document the design Monitor work product	*Techniques* Small/short release (3-4 months) Individual ownership Testing techniques Sprint/iteration review Monitoring by progress and stability Parallelism and flux Holistic diversity strategy Reflection workshop Methodology tuning

SUMMARY, CONCLUSION, AND FURTHER WORK

Using the concepts embodied in the situational method engineering approach, we have argued that existing method bases are deficient in their support for agile methodologies. Complementing and extending the set of method fragments outlined by Tran et al. (2007) in the preceding chapter, we have described fragments relevant to work units and workflows. Together, these additions comprise a set of method fragments each of which is created from the relevant powertype pattern as standardized in the Australian Standard methodology metamodel of AS 4651 (Standards Australia, 2004). Finally, we have validated this approach by recreating four agile methods: XP (Table 1), Scrum (Table 2), and two members of the Crystal family (Tables 3 and 4).

ACKNOWLEDGMENT

We wish to thank Dr. Cesar Gonzalez-Perez for his useful comments on an earlier draft of this chapter. We also wish to thank the Australian Research Council for funding under Discovery Grant DP0345114.

REFERENCES

Abrahamsson, P., Salo, O., Ronkainen, J., & Warsta, J. (2002). *Agile software development methods, reviews and analysis* (VTT Publication no 478). Espoo, Finland: VTT.

Adams, S. G. (2003). Building successful student teams in the engineering classroom. *Journal of STEM Education Innovations and Research, 4*(3&4).

AgileManifesto. (2001). *Manifesto for agile software development.* Retrieved March 14, 2005, from http://www.agilemanifesto.org/

Auer, K., & Miller, R. (2001). *XP applied.* Boston: Addison Wesley.

Barker, J., Tjosvold, D. et al. (1988). Conflict approaches of effective and ineffective project managers: a field study in a matrix organization. *Journal of Management Studies, 25*(2), 167-177.

Beck, K. (1999). Embracing change with extreme programming. *IEEE Computer, 32*(10), 70-77.

Beck, K. (2000). *Extreme programming explained: Embrace change.* Boston: Addison-Wesley.

Beck, K. (2003). *Test driven development—by example.* Boston: Addison Wesley.

Bens, I. (1997). Facilitating conflicts. In M. Goldman (Ed.), *Facilitating with ease!* (pp. 83-108). Sarasota, FL, USA: Participative Dynamics.

Bloom, P. J. (2000). *Circle of influence: Implementing shared decision making and participative management.* Lake Forest, USA: New Horizons.

Capozzoli, T. K. (1995). Conflict resolution: a key ingredient in successful teams. *Supervision, 56*(12), 3-5.

Cockburn, A. (1998). *Surviving object-oriented projects—a manager's guide.* Boston: Addison-Wesley.

Cockburn, A. (2002a). *Agile software development.* Boston: Addison-Wesley.

Cockburn, A. (2002b). Agile software development joins the "would-be crowd." *Cutter IT Journal, 15*(1), 6-12.

Cockburn, A., & Highsmith, J. (2001). Agile software development: the people factor. *IEEE Computer, 34*(11), 131-133.

Cohen, C. F., Birkin, S. J., et al. (2004). Managing conflict in software testing. *Communications of the ACM, 47*(1), 76-81.

Coram, M., & Bohner, S. (2005). The impact of agile methods on software project management.

In *Proceedings of the 12th IEEE International Conference and Workshops on the Engineering of Computer-Based Systems (ECBS'05)*.

Corn, M., & Ford, D. (2003). Introducing an agile process to an organization. *IEEE Computer, 36*(6), 74-78.

Couger, D., & Smith, D.C. (1992a). Evaluating the motivating environment in South Africa compared to the United States—Part 1. *South African Computer Journal, 6*.

Couger, D., & Smith, D. C. (1992b). Evaluating the motivating environment in South Africa compared to the United States—Part 2. *South African Computer Journal, 8*.

Firesmith, D. G., & Henderson-Sellers, B. (2002). *The OPEN Process Framework. An introduction.* London: Addison-Wesley.

Fisher, K., Rayner, S., & Belgard, W. (1995). *Tips for teams: a ready reference for solving common team problems.* New York: MacGraw-Hill, Inc.

Fowler, M. (2001). Is design dead? In G. Succhi & M. Marchesi (Eds.), *Extreme programming examined* (pp. 3-7). Boston: Addison-Wesley.

Graham, I. M. (1995). *Migrating to object technology.* Wokingham, UK: Addison-Wesley.

Grazier, P. (1998). *Team motivation: Ideas to energize any team.* TeambuildingInc.com.

Henderson-Sellers, B. (2001). Enhancing the OPF repository. *JOOP/ROAD, 14*(4), 10-12, 22.

Henderson-Sellers, B., & Edwards, J. M. (1994). *BOOKTWO of object-oriented knowledge: The working object.* Sydney, NSW, Australia: Prentice-Hall.

Highsmith, J. (2000). Extreme programming. *CUTTER Consortium's Agile Project Management Advisory Service.*

Jarboe, S. (1996). Procedures for enhancing group decision making. In B. Hirokawa and M. Poole (Eds.), *Communication and group decision making* (pp. 345-383). Thousand Oaks, CA, USA: Sage Publications.

Jeffries, R. (2004). *Where's the spec, the big picture, the design?* Retrieved on August 15, 2005, from http://www.xprogramming.com/xpmag/docBigPictureAndSpec.htm

Kearny, L. (1995). *The facilitator's toolkit: tools and techniques for generating ideas and making decisions in groups.* Amherst, USA: Human Resource Development Press.

Kezsbom, D. S. (1992). Bringing order to chaos: Pinpointing sources of conflict in the nineties. *Cost Engineering, 34*(11), 9-16.

Kim, M. O. (2002). Coping with conflict in concurrent design environment. *ACM SIGGROUP Bulletin, 23*(1), 20-23.

McDaniel, G., Littlejohn, S., et al. (1998). A team conflict mediation process that really works! In *Proceedings of the 9th International Conference on Work Teams, Dallas, USA.*

Millis, B. J., & Cottell, P. G. (1997). *Cooperative learning for higher education.* Phoenix, AZ, USA: Oryx Press.

Odell, J. J. (1994). Power types. *Journal of Object-Oriented Programming, 7*(2), 8-12.

Paulsen, D. (2004). Leadership essentials: facilitation skills for improving group effectiveness. In *Proceedings of the 32nd Annual ACM SIGUCCS Conference on User services*, Baltimore, USA.

Qumer, A., & Henderson-Sellers, B. (in press). An evaluation of the degree of agility in six agile methods and its applicability for method engineering. *Information and Software Technology.*

Rayeski, E., & Bryant, J. D. (1994). Team resolution process: a guideline for teams to manage conflict, performance and discipline. In M. Beyerlein & M. Bullock (Eds.), *Proceedings of the International Conference on Work Teams Proceedings: Anni-*

versary Collection. The Best of 1990-1994 (pp. 215-221). Denton, TX, USA: University of North Texas, Center for the Study of Work Teams.

Rees, F. (1998). *The facilitator excellence handbook: Helping people work creatively and productively together*. San Francisco: Jossey-Bass/Pfeiffer.

Rees, F. (2001). *How to lead work teams: Facilitation skills*. San Francisco: Jossey-Bass/Pfeiffer.

Seidita, V., Ralyté, J., Henderson-Sellers, B., Cossentino, M., & Arni-Bloch, N. (in press). A comparison of deontic matrices, maps and activity diagrams for the construction of situational methods. In J. Eder, S.L. Tomassen, A.L. Opdahl, & G. Sindre (Eds.), (pp. 85-88).

Serour, M. K., Henderson-Sellers, B., & Dagher, L. (2006). Augmenting an existing software development process with a team building activity: a case study. In Z. Irani, O.D. Sarikas, J. Llopis, R. Gonzalez, & J. Gasco (Eds.), *Proceedings of the European and Mediterranean Conference on Information Systems 2006 (EMCIS2006)*, CD. West London, UK: Brunel University.

Sibbet, D. (2002). *Principles of facilitation: the purpose and potential of leading group*. San Francisco: The Grove Consultants International.

Soller, A. L. (2001). Supporting social interaction in an intelligent collaborative learning system. *International Journal of Artificial Intelligence in Education 12*(1), 40-62.

Standards Australia. (2004). *Standard metamodel for software development methodologies—AS 4651-2004*, Sydney, NSW, Australia: Standards Australia.

Tran, Q. N. N., Henderson-Sellers, B., & Hawryszkiewycz, I. (2007). Some method fragments for agile software development. In M. Syed (Ed.), *Handbook of research on modern systems analysis and design technologies*. Hershey, PA, USA: IGI.

Trimmer, K. J., Collins, R. W., Will, R. P., & Blanton, J. E. (2000). Information systems development: can there be "good" conflict? In *Proceedings of the 2000 ACM SIGCPR Conference on Computer personnel research,* Chicago, USA.

Wake, W. C. (2001). *Extreme programming explored*. Boston: Addison Wesley.

Webne-Behrman, H. (2005). *Conflict resolution*. Retrieved July 31, 2005, from http://www.ohrd.wisc.edu/onlinetraining/resolution/index.asp

Welke, R., & Kumar, K. (1991). Method engineering: a proposal for situation-specific methodology construction. In W. W. Cotterman & J. A. Senn (Eds.), *Systems analysis and design: A research agenda*. Chichester, UK: Wiley.

Wikipedia. (2005). *Extreme programming*. Retrieved August 10, 2005, from http://en.wikipedia.org/wiki/Extreme_Programming

KEY TERMS

Agile Method: A method that is people focused, flexible, speedy, lean, responsive, and supports learning (based on Qumer & Henderson-Sellers, 2007).

Agility: *Agility is a persistent behaviour or ability of a sensitive entity that exhibits flexibility to accommodate expected or unexpected changes rapidly, follows the shortest time span, uses economical, simple and quality instruments in a dynamic environment, and applies updated prior knowledge and experience to learn from the internal and external environment.* (Qumer & Henderson-Sellers, 2007)

Metamodel: A model of models.

Method Engineering: The engineering discipline to design, construct, and adapt methods, techniques, and tools for systems development.

Method Fragment: Construction of a software development method for a specific situation.

Producer: An agent that executes work units.

ProducerKind: a specific kind of producer, characterized by its area of expertise.

Stage: A managed time frame within a project.

StageKind: A specific kind of stage, characterized by the abstraction level at which it works on the project and the result that it aims to produce.

Task: A small-grained work unit that focuses on what must be done in order to achieve a given purpose.

TaskKind: A specific kind of task, characterized by its purpose within the project.

Technique: A small-grained work unit that focuses on how the given purpose may be achieved.

TechniqueKind: A specific kind of technique, characterized by its purpose within the project

WorkProduct: An artefact of interest for the project.

WorkProductKind: A specific kind of work product, characterized by the nature of its contents and the intention behind its usage.

WorkUnit: A job performed within a project.

WorkUnitKind: A specific kind of work unit, characterized by its purpose within the project.

ENDNOTES

[1]   See "Simple design" technique and Technique-Kind section.

[2]   These are existing OPEN tasks fragments listed in the TaskKind section.

[3]   See TechniqueKind section.

[4]   See OPEN's technique "regression test"

APPENDIX A. TASK KINDS

Design Agile Code

•   *Purpose*: Designing is creating a structure that organizes the logic of the system, which is eventually implemented by code (Beck, 2000). The "design agile code" task refers to the designing task in an *agile* process.

It may appear that agile processes, for example, XP, involve only coding without designing (Jeffries, 2004). Actually, an agile process involves a lot of design, although it does it in a very different way from the conventional development processes (Beck, 2000; Fowler, 2001). This is because the cycle of requirements specification, designing and implementation is much more rapid in an agile project than in a conventional plan-driven process (Jeffries, 2004). Thus, the task of design in an agile process (which we name "design agile code" task) adopts the following unique practices:

1.   Do not separately document designs in formal graphical models or specifications as in the conventional processes. Instead, capture the design primarily in the code itself. Thus, design is part of the coding process: design generated are described by code and implemented by code. The team communicates the design through the code. Pictures and documents are only generated when it is deemed really necessary (Fowler, 2001; Jeffries, 2004).

2.   Follow an "evolutionary, incremental, and continuous" design approach, instead of a "planned design" approach as in an conventional process (Highsmith, 2000; Fowler, 2001). The evolutionary design approach means that the design of the system grows as the system is implemented. The design will change as the program evolves. This indicates

again that design needs to be part of the coding process. On the other hand, in planned design, agilists argue that the designers make all major design decisions in advance, generating a complete system design before handing it off to programmers to code. Agile developers are against this planned design approach because it involves high cost in dealing deal with changing requirements.

When performing the "design agile code" task, the "simple design" technique should be used (see TechniqueKind section).

The "design agile code" task must be performed in conjunction with the "refactor" task (this is an existing OPEN's TaskKind). Each time a new requirement emerges and a new piece of code needs to be designed and added to the existing program, the previous design of (the affected part of) the existing program should be revisited and improved (if necessary) to ensure that the new system (once the new code is added) will exhibit a "simple design"[1]—that is, the existing code should be refactored before newly designed code is added (Beck, 2000). The coupling between "refactor" task and "design agile code" task allow the evolutionary design mechanism to be carried out in a systematic, easy-to-manage and effective manner, rather than in an ad-hoc manner of design restructuring.

The "design agile code" task should also be coupled with testing tasks,[2] testing techniques, and "continuous integration" technique,[3] so as to ensure that the newly designed and added code still keeps the system in synchronization (Highsmith, 2000).

Develop Release Plan

- *Purpose*: Plan for a forthcoming release, including determining *what requirements/features* are included in the release and *when* it is going to be delivered.

This task generates a "release plan document" (see DocumentKind section in Tran et al., 2007). Both developers and customers and both parties need to agree on the developed plan. Release planning can be conducted using the planning game technique (see TechniqueKind section). Release planning initiates, and can be affected by, iteration planning.

Explore Architectural Possibilities

- *Purpose*: Explore the possible architectural configurations for the target system. This task is performed in the "exploration phase" of the XP development process.

The programmers in an XP team can perform this task by spending a week or two building a system similar to what they will build eventually, but doing it in three or four ways. Different programmer pairs can try the system different ways and compare them to see which one feels best, or two pairs can try the system the same way and see what differences emerge. This task may involve building a prototype for each possible architectural configuration; cross reference: task "prototype the architecture" of OPEN.

Architectural explorations are most important when the customer comes up with stories that the XP team has no idea how to implement.

Monitor Work Products

- *Purpose*: Monitor the development progress of each work product of each team. This task should be performed throughout an iteration/release of an agile development process. "monitoring by progress and stability" can be used.

Team Management Task Kinds

a. **"Manage shared artefacts" task kind:** consisting of the following sub-tasks:

- **"Identify shared artefacts"**: is the task of identifying artefacts that can be accessed mutually by different teams or different members in a team.
- **"Allocate shared artefacts":** is the task of allocating these shared artefacts to teams, roles, and/or tasks.
- **"Specify Permissions to Shared Artefacts"**: is the task of defining the permissions granted to each different role/team to access the artefact.

b. "Mediate/monitor the performance of team's tasks" task kind: consisting of the following sub-tasks:

- **"Meditate/monitor team's interactions"**: is the task of enforcing/monitoring interactions between team members during the task. Each team member's interaction protocols should depend on his/her roles.
- **"Conflict management"**: is the task of identifying and resolving conflicts between team members.
- **"Monitor members' performance"**: is the task of assessing how well a team member is performing the task and (probably) providing private/public feedback to reinforce team members' focus on task
- **"Member motivation"**: is the task of encouraging team members' participation in tasks (e.g., by initiating & facilitating round-robin participation or role switching around the team)
- **"Ensure workload balance":** is the task of detecting workload imbalance amongst team members and taking actions to balance the workload.

c. "Specify team policies" task kind:

- *Purpose*: Identify and document the policies (or rules or conventions) that govern the collaborative work within a particular team.

d. "Specify team structure" task kind:

- *Purpose*: Define the structure of a particular team in terms of:

- Roles that make up the team (both SE roles and teamwork roles)
- Acquaintance relationships amongst these roles
- Authority relationships that govern these acquaintances

Note that in agile development, the team structure can frequently change.

Write User Stories

Purpose: Allow customers (users of the system) to specify their requirements. This task should be considered as a new sub-task of the existing OPEN's task "elicit requirements." It is to be performed by customers in an XP project team (see "story card document kind" in the DocumentKind section in Tran et al., 2007).

Ideally, the feature/requirements described by each story should be able to be accomplished within 1-5 programming weeks. Stories should be testable.

Other team members (e.g., programmers) should give copious and quick feedback to the first few stories written by the customer, so that the customer can learn quickly how much ground to cover in each story and what information to include and exclude. A story should be specified in such a way that the programmers can confidently estimate the effort needed to provide the feature required by the story.

APPENDIX B. TECHNIQUE KINDS

Agile Team Building

- *Purpose*: Assist in the building of project teams for agile projects, for example, XP-style team

Table 1. Comparison of team support in four agile methods

	XP	Scrum	Crystal Clear	Crystal Orange
Number of teams	1 team per project	1-4 or more	1	1-10
Team size	3-16	5-9	1-6	1-6

(see TeamKind section in Tran et al., 2007).

- *Description*: Since agile development relies substantially on teamwork, collaboration and communication, the team is the key for success (Coram & Bohner, 2005). Consequently, special care must be given to the building of project teams (Serour, Henderson-Sellers& Dagher, 2006).

Agile project teams have various important characteristics that distinguish them from traditional OO-development teams. As such, the conventional practices for team building (e.g., OPEN's "team building" technique) are not sufficient (or inappropriate) to the building of agile teams.

The following suggestions should be considered when forming project teams, specifically for agile development:

- *Small number and size* (Coram & Bohner, 2005): There should be a small number of teams per project and a small number of members per team. This ranges from a single team of 3-16 developers on XP to up to six teams of 2-6 members on DSDM (see Table 1). Small teams are required to foster collaboration and are more likely to require less process and planning to coordinate team members' activities.

- *High competence of members*: Agile development derives much of its agility by relying on the tacit knowledge embodied in the team, rather than writing the knowledge down in plans (Cockburn, 2002a, b). In addition, the productivity difference between the best and worst programmers on a team would surface most clearly when the members are working on tasks essential to software delivery, which make up most of an agile process (note that agile processes strip non-essential activities from projects, leaving developers more tasks on software delivery) (Corn & Ford, 2003). Thus, Boehm's principle of top talent, "use better and fewer people" (Cockburn & Highsmith, 2001), is central to an agile process (Corn & Ford, 2003), and high competency of team members is a critical factor in agile projects' success (Cockburn & Highsmith, 2001). In all agile methodologies (e.g., XP, Scrum, ASD, and DSDM), the emphasis on team members' talent, skill, and knowledge is evident. Too many slow workers either slow the entire team or end up left behind by their faster teammates.

- *Good rapport amongst team members* (Coram & Bohner, 2005): Developers who do not work well together, or a single strong-willed developer, could each destroy the collaborative nature of the team. Low team rapport represents a significant risk for an agile project. A successful agile team is one which is highly cohesive and mutually supportive.

- *Low risks from high turnover* (Coram &Bohner, 2005): High turnover of team members can lead to loss of critical knowledge. The project manager should consider this risk when examining whether a team is right for an agile project. To retain relevant knowledge, appropriately skilled and knowledgeable members should be retained when building (or changing) teams.

- *Co-location of members* (Corn & Ford, 2003): Teams using agile processes tend to make decisions more quickly than plan-driven teams, relying on more frequent (and usually informal) communication to support this pace. Thus, team members should try to avoid distributed development for at least the first 2 or 3 months after initiating an agile process. If distributed developers must be combined, the team leader/project manager should bring as many people as possible together for the first week or two of the project can increase the likelihood of success. Crystal, Scrum, and ASD all advocate close and direct collaboration practices including barrier-free collocated teams.

- Minimal interaction and dependencies between different teams and maximal cohesion within each team.

Collective Ownership

- *Purpose*: Facilitate sharing of responsibilities of teams' outcomes, support sharing of knowledge amongst team members and promote the code's quality.
- *Description*: In XP, everybody takes responsibility for the whole of the system. Any team member who sees an opportunity to add value to any portion of the code is required to do so at any time. This technique is opposed to other two models of code ownership: no ownership and individual ownership. In the former model, nobody owns any particular piece of code. If someone wants to change some code, he/she can do it to suit his own purpose, whether it fits well with what is already there or now. The result is chaos. The code grows quickly but it also quickly grows unstable. With individual ownership, the only person who can change a piece of code is its official owner. Anyone else who sees that the code needs changing has to submit his request to the owner. The result is that the code diverges from the team's understanding, as people are reluctant to interrupt the code owner.

Conflict Resolution

- *Purpose*: Manage conflicts between team members in teamwork.
- *Description*: There are numerous techniques for conflict resolution in the literature. Only some are discussed here.

Webne-Behrman (2005) proposes an 8-step resolution process that can be employed by a team member to effectively managing conflict in teamwork. These steps will not guarantee an agreement, but they greatly improve the likelihood that the problems can be understood, solutions explored, and consideration of the advantages of a negotiated agreement can occur within a relatively constructive environment.

1. "Know thyself" and take care of self
2. Clarify personal needs threatened by the dispute
3. Identify a safe place for negotiation
4. Take a listening stance into the interaction
5. Assert your needs clearly and specifically
6. Approach problem-solving with flexibility
7. Manage impasse with calmness, patience, and respect
8. Build an agreement that works

Rayeski and Bryant (1994) suggest the use of the team resolution process for managing conflict in teams. The process allows the team to address conflict as it occurs, thus providing the team with self-sufficient methods for handling disagreement on their own. Rayeski and Bryant's process includes three steps:

1. Collaboration: Initially as conflict arises, it should be handled informally between the two team members in a private setting.
2. Mediation: If the situation escalates, a mediator is brought into the dispute to assist both sides in reaching an agreement (e.g., the team leader or task facilitator).

3. Team counseling: If efforts of collaboration and mediation fail, team counseling is held at a team meeting, with all members of the team present.

Other resources for team conflict resolution:

*   Generic teams (Barker, Tjosvold et al., 1988; Kezsbom, 1992; Fisher, Rayner, & Belgard, 1995; Capozzoli, 1995; Bens, 1997; McDaniel, Littlejohn et al., 1998; Rees, 1998).
*   IS teams (Trimmer, Collins, Will, & Blanton, 2000; Kim, 2002; Cohen, Birkin et al., 2004).

Continuous Integration

*   *Purpose*: Promote correctness of systems/ programs and support early discovery of errors/defects.
*   *Description*: With the "continuous integration" technique, developers integrate their new codes into a baseline system/program and run a set of regression tests[4] on it until it is 100% correct (Beck, 2000; Coram & Bohner, 2005). This should be done after every few hours or a day of development at most.

Continuous integration helps to promote quality of the developed system/program because errors caused by a change can be quickly discovered and it is also obvious who should fix the errors—the developers who produce the change. Finding defects early also reduces the effort of fixing them.

However, the downside of this technique is that developers must write a comprehensive set of tests to be used as regression tests and must take the time to integrate and test their code. This may require a shift in developer perspective if the developer is accustomed to simply writing code that is then tested by a different group (Coram & Bohner, 2005).

Daily Meeting

*   *Purpose*: Encourage frequent communication amongst team members about their work progress; Promote team-based, rapid, intense, cooperative, and courteous development; identify and remove impediments to development process.
*   *Description*: These meetings are held daily in a short period of time (15-30 min.) when all team members meet with each other in a room and each takes turn to tell the group:

    ◦   What he or she accomplished the prior day
    ◦   What he or she plans to do today
    ◦   Any obstacles or difficulties he or she is experiencing

The time and location of the daily meeting should be constant. Any team members working from remote locations can join via conference phones.

Someone should be responsible for keeping the daily meetings short (by enforcing the rules and making sure people speak briefly) and promoting the productivity of the meeting as much as possible. In XP, this person can be "coach," while in Scrum, the "Scrum master" is usually selected.

While others (such as managers and customers) may attend the daily meetings, only those directly involved the work such as developers, coach, Scrum master, and product owner can speak.

Team members should arrange themselves in a circle, generally around a focus such as a table. People not on the team should sit/stand outside the team's circle.

In XP projects, the daily meetings are referred to as "stand-up meetings," since everyone is required to stand (standing is intentional to motivate the team to keep the meeting short) (Auer & Miller, 2001). Often the pair-programming pairs are dynamically formed during the daily meeting as the tasks for the day are discussed. Two programmers that are best equipped to handle the task join together.

In Scrum projects, the daily meetings are called "daily Scrum meeting." An important activity of the Scrum master during daily Scrum meetings is to record and remove any impediment that is reported by a team member, for example, slow network/server, uncertain technology use, uncertain design decision, over-loaded individual responsibilities, and so forth. If a Scrum master cannot make a decision on how to remove an impediment during the meeting, he/she is responsible for making a decision and communicating it to the whole team within one hour after the meeting.

If there are multiple teams, a daily "Scrum of Scrums" can be organized, where "Scrum masters" from each Scrum team meet after the daily Scrums for their own daily Scrum.

Holistic Diversity Strategy (Cockburn, 1998)

- *Purpose*: Assist in the building of project teams for agile projects.
- *Description*: Holistic diversity strategy suggests that for each function (or set of functions) to be delivered, a small team consisting of 2-5 members from *mixed, different specialties* should be formed, to be responsible for delivering that function. For example, a team can include different specialists, each from requirements gathering, UI design, technical design, programming, or testing. The team should be evaluated as a unit, so there is no benefit to hiding within a specialty. The team members should be co-located so they can communicate directly, instead of by writing. There should be no documentation within the team, although the team will have documentation responsibilities to the rest of the project.

Iteration Planning Game

- *Purpose*: Assist planning for an iteration in XP (see "develop iteration plan" in TaskKind section).
- *Description*: The iteration planning game is similar to the planning game in that cards are used as the pieces. This time, though, the pieces are task cards instead of story cards. The players are all he individual programmers. The timeframe is iteration (1 to 4 weeks) instead of release. The phases and moves are similar.

- *Exploration phase*:
  ○ Write a task: Programmers take the stories for the iteration and turn them into tasks.
  ○ Split a task/combine tasks: If a task cannot be estimated at a few days, it should be broken down into smaller tasks. If several tasks each take an hour, they should be combined to form a larger task.

- *Commitment phase*:
  ○ Accept a task: A programmer accepts responsibility for a task.
  ○ Estimate a task: The responsible programmer estimates the number of ideal engineering days to implement each task.
  ○ Set load factors: Each programmer chooses their load factor for the iteration—the percentage of time they will spend actually developing.
  - Balancing: Each programmer adds up their task estimates and multiplies by their load factor. Programmers who turn out to be overcommitted must give up some tasks.

- *Steering phase*:
  ○ Implement a task: A programmer takes a task card, finds a partner (i.e., pair programmer), writes the test cases for the task, makes them all work, then integrates and releases the new code when the universal test suite runs.
  ○ Record progress: Every 2 or 3 days, one member of the team asks each programmer how long they have spent on each of their tasks and how many days they have left.

○ Recovery: A programmer who turns out to be overcommitted, asks for help by reducing the scope of some tasks, asking the customer to reduce the scope of some stories, shedding non-essential tasks, getting more or better help, and asking the customer to defer some stories to a later iteration

○ Verify story: When functional tests are ready and the tasks for a story are complete, the functional tests are run to verify that the story works.

Methodology-Tuning Technique (Cockburn, 2002a)

- *Purpose*: Facilitate on-the-fly methodology construction and tuning.

- *Description*: The technique supports methodology construction and tuning by suggesting what to do at five different times in a project: right away, at the start of the project, in the middle of the first release, after each release, and in the middle of subsequent releases.

- Right away (regardless when it is in any project): Discover the strengths and weaknesses of the development organization through short interviews. People to be interviewed may be the project manager, team leaders, designers, and/or programmers. Questions to ask include a short history of the project, work products, what should be changed next time, what should be repeated next time, and project's priorities.

- At the start of the project: Have two or more people working together on creating/selecting a base methodology for the project, for example, XP, RUP, or Crystal. Then, hold a team meeting to discuss the base methodology's workflow and conventions, and tailor it to the corporate methodological standards, producing a starter methodology.

- In the middle of the first release: Run a small interview with team members (individually or in a group), asking whether the team is going to be successful in the way that they are working. The goal is not to change the whole starter methodology if the team is not working (unless it is catastrophically broken). The aim is to get safely to the first release delivery.

- After each release: Hold a reflection workshop (see technique "reflection workshop"). The two questions to be asked are what the team learned and what can they do better. Very often the team would tighten standards, streamline the workflow, increase testing, and reorganize the team structure.

- In the middle of the subsequent increments: Hold interviews or a reflection workshop to think of new and improved ways of working.

Monitoring by Progress and Stability (Cockburn, 2002a)

- *Purpose*: Monitor each work product of each team throughout an iteration/release.

- *Description*: Each team's work product should be monitored with respect to *both* progress and stability (Cockburn, 1998). Progress is measured in milestones, which are sequential; the stability states are not necessarily sequential.

Progress milestones:

1. Start
2. Review 1
3. Review 2
4. To test
5. Deliver

Stability states:

1. Wildly fluctuating
2. Fluctuating

3. Stable enough to review

A common sequence of stability states might be 1-2-3-2-3-2-3. A deliverable rates "to test" may get re-labeled as "fluctuating" if some unexpected problem were encountered that questioned the design or the requirements.

Open Workspace

*   *Purpose*: Facilitate physical proximity in teamwork, particularly for agile teams.
*   *Description*: The project team works in a large room with small cubicles around the periphery. Pair programmers work on computers set up in the centre (Beck, 1999). With this work environment setting, it is much easier for any team member to get help if needed, just by calling across the room. In the long term the team benefits from the intense communication. The open workspace helps pair programming to work, and the communication aids all the practices.

Pair Programming

*   *Purpose*: Promote communication between team members, productivity of members, and quality of resulting products in an agile development. This technique is used in XP methodology.
*   *Description*: Pair programming is a programming technique where two people program with one computer, one keyboard, and one monitor (Beck, 2000). It should be noted that pair programming is not about one person programming while another person watches. Pair programming is a dialogue between two people trying to simultaneously program (and analyze and design and test) and understand together how to program better. It is a conversation at many levels, assisted by and focused on a computer.

In XP, pairing is dynamic. If two people pair in the morning, they might be paired with other developers at different times during the day.

Sometimes pairs contain one partner with much more experience than the other partner. If this is true, the first few sections will look a lot like tutoring. The junior partner will ask lost of questions and type very little. However, in a couple of months, typically, the gap between the partners is not nearly as noticeable as it was at first.

Pair programming is particularly suitable to agile development because it encourages communication. When an important new bit of information is learned by someone on the team, this information can be quickly disseminated throughout the team, since the pairs switch around all the time. The information actually becomes richer and more intense as it spreads and is enriched by the experience and insight of everyone on the team. Pair programming is also often more productive and results in higher quality code than if the work is divided between two developers and then the results are integrated.

Parallelism and Flux (Cockburn, 2002a)

*   *Purpose*: Maximize the parallelism in the production of an iteration/release, while permitting changes in the work products.
*   *Description*: This technique can easily be followed if the above technique, "monitoring by progress and stability" has been followed. According to the "parallelism and flux" technique, any dependent task can start as soon as all the predecessor work products are in the "stable enough to review" stability state. While the predecessor work products are still "wildly fluctuating," the performers of the successor tasks can start working out their basic needs, but should not start serious design/coding. For example, as soon as the system requirements are "stable enough to review," designs can begin parallel design. Similarly, as soon as the design reaches "stable enough

to review" status, serious programming can begin (although tentative programming may have been done earlier, to assist in creating the design).

Planning Game

- *Purpose*: Assist planning for a release in XP (see "**develop release plan**" in TaskKind section).
- *Description*: The planning game offers a set of rules that remind everyone in an XP project of how they should act during planning for a release. The rules serve as an aid for the building of a trusting and mutually respectful relationship between the customer and the XP project team. The rules of the planning game are as follows.
- *The goal*: the goal of the game is to maximize the value of software produced by the team. From the value of the software, the cost of its development and the risk incurred during development need to be determined.
- *The pieces*: The pieces in the planning game are the story cards (see "story card" in DocumentKind section in Tran et al., 2007).
- *The players*: Two players in the planning game are development and business. Development consists collectively of all the people who will be responsible for implementing the system, for example, programmers, coaches, trackers, and project managers. Business consists collectively of all the people who will make the decisions about what the system is supposed to do, for example, customers, real users of the project, and sales people.
- *The moves*: There are three phases to the game.
  - *Exploration phase*: The purpose of this phase is to give both development and business players an appreciation for what the system should eventually do. Exploration has three moves:

- Write a story: Business players write a story describing something the system needs to do (see "story card" in DocumentKind section in Tran et al., 2007).
- Estimate a story: Development players estimate how long the story will take to implement.
- Split a story: If development players cannot estimate a whole story, or if business players realize that part of a story is more important than the rest, business players can split a story into two or more stories.
  - *Commitment phase*: The purpose of this phase is for business players to choose the scope and date of the next release, and for development players to confidently commit to delivering it. The commitment phase has four moves.
    - Sort by value: Business players sort the stories into three piles: 1) those without which the system will not function, 2) those that are less essential but provide significant business value, and 3) those that would be nice to have.
    - Sort by risk: Development players sort the stories into three piles: 1) those that they can estimate precisely, 2) those that they can estimate reasonably well, and 3) those that they cannot estimate at all.
    - Set velocity: Development players tell business how fast the team can program in ideal engineering time per calendar month.
    - Choose scope: Business players choose the set of story cards in the release.
  - *Steering phase*: The purpose of this phase is to update the plan based on what is learned by development and business

263

players. The steering phase has four moves.

- Iteration: At the beginning of each iteration, business players pick one iteration worth of the most valuable stories to be implemented.
- Recovery: If development players realize that they has overestimated their velocity, they can ask business players what is the most valuable set of stories to retain in the current release based on the new velocity and estimates.
- New story: If business players realize they need a new story during the middle of the release, they can write the story. Development players estimate the story, and then business players remove stories with the equivalent estimate from the remaining plan and insert the new story.
- Re-estimate: If Development players feel that the plan no longer provides an accurate map of development, they can re-estimate all of the remaining stories and set velocity again.

Reflection Workshop (Cockburn, 2002a)

- *Purpose*: Review team practices in the past period or set desirable team practices for the upcoming period.
- *Description*: This workshop involves all team members meeting in the same room to discuss what practices are going well with the team and what practices should be improved or performed differently in the upcoming/next period. These reviews are written on a flipchart and posted in a prominently visible place so that team members are reminded about them during their work.

The flipchart may have the following columns:

1. Keep these: which lists the practices that have been used and are still desirable for the upcoming/next period (e.g., daily meetings, pair programming)
2. Problems: which lists the current problems in team practices (e.g., too many interruptions, shipping buggy code)
3. Try these: which lists the practices that have not been used but are desirable for the upcoming/next period (e.g., pair testing, fines for interruptions)

The workshop should be 1 to 2 hours long. At the start of the next workshop, the team should bring in the flipchart from the previous workshop and start by asking whether this way of writing and posting the workshop outcome was effective.

Crystal methodologies suggest that a team should hold reflection workshops at the beginning and end of each release, probably also mid-release (Cockburn, 2002a).

Role Rotation (Millis & Cottell, 1997; Soller, 2001; Adams, 2003):

- *Purpose*: Encourage participation of team members; balance workload amongst team members.
- *Description*: The roles assigned to team members can be rotated amongst these members during the course of a team's shared task or during the lifetime of the team. For example, the role of "quality controller" may be assigned to different team members in different tasks of the team.

Role rotation can form positive interdependence between team members. It discourages domination by one person—a problem common in less-structured teamwork—and gives all members an opportunity to experience and learn from the different positions.

It may be useful to give the rationale for role rotation practice to team members before they join the team.

Round-Robin Participation Technique (Jarboe, 1996)

- *Purpose*: Encourage participation of team members during a particular team's shared task (e.g., discussion, workshop, creation of a particular work product); balance workload amongst team members.
- *Description*: The round-robin technique establishes an environment in which each team member, in turn, has the opportunity to express themselves openly without their teammates interrupting or evaluating their opinions.

Simple Design

- *Purpose*: Help to produce fast, economic, easy-to-understand, and easy-to-modify designs in XP development.
- *Description*: "Simple design" technique is often known as "do the simplest thing that could possibly work" or "you are not going to need it" (YAGNI). It recommends two rules (Highsmith, 2000):

1. Only design for the functionality that is required in the forthcoming iteration, not for potential future functionality.
2. Create the simplest design that can deliver that functionality. Beck (2000) gives four criteria for a simple design:

- Run all the tests;
- Have no duplicated logic, including hidden duplication like parallel class hierarchies;
- State every intention important to the programmers (i.e., the generated code should be easy to read and understand); and

- Have the fewest possible classes and methods.

Small/Short Releases

- *Purpose*: Allow for fast delivery of products to customers, particularly in an agile development project.
- *Description*: One of the principles of agile development is to deliver working software frequently, from a couple of weeks to a couple of months, with a preference to the shorter timescale (Agile Manifesto, 2001). Accordingly, the "small release" technique suggests that every release should be as small as possible, containing the most valuable business requirements (Beck, 2000; Abrahamsson, Salo, Ronkainen, & Warsta, 2002). The initial simple system should be in production rapidly. New versions are then released on a very short cycle, even daily, but at least monthly.

Note that a release has to make sense as a whole, that is, it cannot implement half a feature just to make the release cycle short.

In order to practice the "small release" technique, the developers should (Beck, 2000):

- Determine beforehand what are the most valuable features or business requirements, so even a small system would have business value.
- Integrate continuous (see technique "**continuous integration**"), so the cost of packaging a release is minimal.

Sprint/iteration Review Meeting

- *Purpose*: Present the final product of an iteration/sprint to management, customers, users, and product owner; review past performance of the sprint.
- *Description*: On the last day of an iteration/sprint, a sprint/iteration review meeting is

held and conducted by the Scrum master. In the meeting, the development team presents the product to management, customers, users and product owner, reporting the system architecture, design, functionality, strengths, and weaknesses.

The sprint goal and "sprint backlog document" are compared to the actual product of the sprint, and reasons for any discrepancies are discussed. The sprint/iteration review meeting may uncover new backlog items to be added to the "release backlog document" (and "product backlog document") and may even change the direction of the project. Difficulties and successes of the project team during the iteration/sprint should also be reported. All stakeholders can then make an informed decision on what to do next (i.e., next sprint or release).

The sprint/iteration review meeting should be conducted in an informal manner.

Sprint Planning Meeting

- *Purpose*: Assist planning for an iteration/sprint in Scrum (see "develop iteration plan" in TaskKind section).
- *Description*: A sprint planning meeting actually consists of two consecutive meetings organized by the "Scrum master." In the first meeting, the developers, product owner, Scrum master, customers, and management meet with each other to decide upon what functionality to build during the forthcoming iteration/sprint. In the second meeting, the developers work by themselves to figure out how they are going to build this functionality during the iteration/sprint.

Inputs to the sprint planning meeting are "release backlog documents," the most recent iteration product, business conditions, and the capabilities and past performance of the project team. Output of the meeting is a "sprint backlog document."

To start the first sub-meeting of the sprint planning meeting, the product owner presents the top priority items in the "release backlog document" to everyone and leads the discussion on what everyone wants the project team to work on next and what changes to the current "release backlog document" (and "product backlog document") are appropriate. Having selected the backlog items for the iteration/sprint, a sprint goal is drafted. A sprint goal is an objective that will be met through the implementation of the selected backlog items. This goal is needed to serve as a minimum, high-level success criteria for the sprint and keep the project team focused on the big picture, rather than just on the chosen functionality. If the work turns out to be harder than the team had expected, the team might only partially implement the functionality but should still keep the sprint goal in mind.

In the second sub-meeting, the developers compile the "sprint backlog document" by identifying a list of tasks that they have to complete during the iteration/sprint in order to reach the sprint goal. These tasks are the detailed pieces of work needed to convert the selected backlog items into working software. The developers have the total freedom and autonomy in determining these tasks. Each task should take roughly 4-16 hours to finish. The sprint backlog is normally modified throughout the iteration/sprint. All developers are required to be present at the second sub-meeting. The product owner often attends.

System Metaphor

- *Purpose*: Help to establish a shared understanding between everyone in the project team about the future system, including its structure and how it works. The metaphor in XP replaces much of the system architecture, by identifying the key objects and their interactions. This technique can be used to support task "describe application" (see TaskKind section).

- *Description*: A metaphor is a story that everyone—customers, programmers, and managers—can tell about how the system works (Beck, 2000). It provides an overall view of how the future system is perceived, while the "stories" that are used to describe individual features of the system. For example, a customer service support system can be described by the following potential metaphors:

- Naïve metaphor (where the real-life objects are referred to themselves): For example, customer service representatives create problem reports on behalf of customers and assign them to technicians.
- Assembly line metaphor: Problem reports and solutions are thought of as an assembly and the technicians and customer service representatives are workers at stations.
- Subcontractors metaphor: The customer service representatives are general contractors, with control over the whole job. They can let work out to subcontractors (i.e., technicians).
- Problem-solving chalkboard metaphor: The customer service representatives and technicians are experts who put a problem on the board and solve the problem.

In XP, the most appropriate metaphor of the system should be determined during the "exploration phase," when user stories are written (Wake, 2001). It can be revised over time as the project team members learn more about the system. The whole project team should agree on the key objects in the metaphor. The metaphor can be used to help orient the developers when they are trying to understand the system functionality at the highest levels, and to guide the developers' solutions. Use the object names in the metaphor as the "uppermost" classes in code. Methods, variables, and basic responsibilities of the system can also be derived from the metaphor.

Team Facilitation

- *Purpose:* Facilitation is "the art of leading people through processes towards agreed-upon objectives in a manner that encourages participation, ownership, and creativity from all involved" (Sibbet, 2002).
- *Description:* Generally, the processes and methods of facilitation provide value to teams by enabling the following (Paulsen, 2004): 1) shared responsibility for outcomes; 2) individual accountability; 3) improved decision-making, problem-solving, and conflict resolution; 4) staff participation and empowerment; 5) efficient use of resources; 6) creative teams and projects; 7) productive meetings and teams; 8) flexible responses to changes; 9) alignment to common plans or goals; and 10) organizational learning.

Basic facilitation techniques include verbal techniques and nonverbal techniques (Bloom, 2000; Rees, 2001).

- Verbal techniques: Asking questions, redirecting, referencing back, paraphrasing, humor, positive reinforcement, obtain examples, unity and diversity, and meta-communication and skill development.
- Nonverbal techniques: test inferences, active listening, voice, facial expressions, and silence.

There are also facilitation techniques for "expanding" and "narrowing" processes. The process of expanding includes generating ideas and gathering information while the process of narrowing entails comparing and evaluating information and making decisions (Kearny, 1995). Examples of expanding facilitation techniques (Kearny, 1995; Rees, 2001) are brainstorming, nominal group process, fishbone (Ishikawa) diagram, and mapping the territory. Some narrowing facilitation techniques are sorting by category (affinity diagram), N/3 (rank order), polling the group, jury of peers, and good news/bad news.

Team Motivation

- *Purpose*: Motivate productivity and morality of team members during team's tasks.
- *Description*: A huge pool of techniques for team motivation can be found in the literature on organizational management or human resource management. Here we just list some example techniques.

Grazier (1998) suggests 54 ideas for the motivation of generic teams. Some of which are:

- Vision and mission (the team's goals and tasks should be in line with the members' wants and needs).
- Challenge (the tasks and responsibilities assigned to team members should pose a challenge to them).
- Growth (the tasks and responsibilities assigned to team members should encourage their personal growth).
- Recognition (frequent appraisal and recognition of team member's contribution).
- Communications (open, direct communications).
- Responsibility (responsibility should be assigned to members together with authority. Responsibility can be de-motivating if the consequences of error or failure are too great).

Other recommended techniques fall in the categories of fun, exercises, training, and involvement.

Couger and Smith (1992a, b) propose some motivational techniques for IS development teams in particular. According to their international surveys of different job types, IS staff have the highest growth need (i.e., the need to achieve and accomplish tasks) and lowest social need (i.e., the

need to interact with others) of all the professions surveyed. Accordingly, Couger and Smith suggest the following techniques for motivating IS team members:

- **Skill variety:** The tasks and responsibilities assigned to team members should require a number of different skills and talents from the members, thus posing a challenge to them.
- **Task identity:** The task assigned to team members should be a "whole" and identifiable piece of work.
- **Task significance:** The task assigned to team members should be clearly scoped in term of the overall project goal.
- **Autonomy:** Team members should be provided substantial freedom, independence, and discretion. The team leader/task facilitator should focus on the delivery of the products and not on the specific approach used to achieve them.
- **Feedback:** Team members should be given formal feedback on their performance and deliverable's quality.

Given that many of the team members in IS projects have high growth-need and low social-need, the above techniques can reinforce productive behaviour. Personnel with a high need for growth will readily accept the excitement of challenging work. A person with a low social need will be comfortable receiving such work and being allowed to complete it with low people interaction.

Test Driven Development

- *Purpose*: Facilitate automated unit testing of code.
- *Description*: Programmers develop code through rapid iterations of the following steps (Beck, 2003):

1. Writing automated test cases
2. Running these unit test cases to ensure they fail (since there is no code to run yet)

3. Implementing code which should allow the unit test cases to pass
4. Re-running the unit test cases to ensure they now pass with the new code
5. Refactoring the implementation or test code, as necessary
6. Periodically re-running all the test cases in the code base to ensure the new code does not break any previously running test cases.

APPENDIX C. ACTIVITY KINDS

Team Management Activity Kind: is an activity of ensuring that every team in the project functions in an effective manner. The objectives of the team management activity kind include:

- To ensure that each team member is clear of his role, responsibilities, and position within the team.
- To ensure that team members collaborate smoothly, with no intra-team or inter-teams unsolvable conflicts
- To ensure that the goals of each team are achieved or exceeded.

The team management activity kind involves team leaders (and/or team members) performing the following tasks (cf. TaskKind section):

- "Choose project teams"
- "Specify team structure"
- "Specify team policies"
- "Identify project toles and responsibilities"
- "Manage shared artefacts"
- "Mediate/monitor the performance of team's tasks"

Section IV
System Design and Considerations

Chapter XVIII
Utility–Cost Tradeoffs in the Design of Data Resources

Adir Even
Ben Gurion University of the Negev, Israel

G. Shankaranarayanan
Boston University School of Management, USA

Paul D. Berger
Bentley College, USA

ABSTRACT

This chapter introduces a novel perspective for designing and maintaining data resources. Data and the information systems that manage it, are critical organizational resources. Today the design and the maintenance of data management environments are driven primarily by technical and functional requirements. We suggest that economic considerations, such as the utility gained by the use of data resources and the costs involved in implementing and maintaining them, may significantly affect data management decisions. We propose an analytical framework for analyzing utility-cost tradeoffs and optimizing design. Its application is demonstrated for analyzing certain design decisions in a data warehouse environment. The analysis considers variability and inequality in the utility of data resources, and possible uncertainties with usage and implementation.

INTRODUCTION

Data, along with information systems and technologies (IS/IT) that manage it, is a critical organizational resource. Advances in data management technologies and the growing diversity of data sources allow firms to manage large data repositories and benefit from using them for enabling new business processes, supporting decision making, and generating revenue as a commodity. Different aspects of data management such as design, quality improvement, and integration into business processes have typically been studied from technical and functional perspectives. Economic aspects, such as the benefits gained from the use of data resources and the costs associated with managing them, have not been explored in depth. In this chapter, we suggest that economic considerations significantly affect data management decisions, hence, deserve further examination. As investments in data resources grow, it is important to better understand their contribution to economic performance and business benefits. By conceptualizing business benefits as utility, we propose a framework for assessing and maximizing the contribution of data resources to the firm's economic performance.

We specifically link economic contribution to the design of data resources. Designs that improve capacity have higher utility contribution, but are often more expensive to implement. Enhancing design may require higher investments in IT and labor, increasing costs to the point of offsetting the utility gained. To what extent can design affect economic performance? Can maximizing performance direct design? These questions highlight a gap in data management research—while functional and technical aspects of design are well addressed, economic aspects are rarely explored. In this study, we identify design characteristics that impact utility-cost tradeoffs, model their economic effects, and use the models to assess design alternatives. We refer to this approach as *economics-driven design*. Importantly, we view administration and maintenance of information systems and data resources as an integral part of the implementation lifecycle. Hence, we use the term *design* to refer not only to the efforts involved in implementing entirely new systems or data resources, but also to the formulation of data and system administration policies and the implementation of data maintenance, improvement, and enhancement solutions.

We examine economics-driven design in the context of a data warehouse (DW)—an IS environment that manages large data archives. The high implementation and maintenance costs associated with a DW have been examined, but their business-value contribution has been rarely assessed. This study contributes by examining the utility of data resources in a DW. It introduces the concept of "utility inequality"—the extent to which items within a data collection differ in their business contribution. Understanding inequality and the associated utility-cost tradeoffs can help improve data management decisions from an economic standpoint. We link these tradeoffs to DW design decisions. Understanding economic effects of these decisions can improve design outcomes and help justify associated investments.

In the rest of this chapter, we first review the relevant background. We then lay the theoretical foundations of our framework for economic assessment of design alternatives, focusing on design decisions in a DW. We introduce the concept of utility inequality and develop quantitative tools for assessing it in large datasets. Utility inequality is shown to introduce economic tradeoffs. We analyze these tradeoffs and their implications for design decisions in data management environments. Acknowledging uncertainties with the utility gained, we then frame certain high-level design strategies as real-options investments. We further model economic effects of some design decisions along these strategies, describing conditions under which a certain strategy can turn out to be superior. We conclude by highlighting contributions and limitations of this study and suggest directions for further research.

RELEVANT BACKGROUND

Design is defined as teleological and goal-driven activity, aimed at the creation of new artifacts (Simon, 1996). Design research seeks to extend the boundaries of human and organizational capabilities by creating new and innovative artifacts (March & Smith, 1995). It is particularly important to field of Information Systems (IS) management, as the success and the impact of information systems significantly depend on their design (Hevner, March, Park, & Ram, 2004). March and Smith (1995) differentiate between behavioral research as "knowledge producing" and design research as "knowledge using." While the key contribution of the former category is producing theories that explain behavior, the latter applies these theories in contexts of usage. This study offers new insights into the design of information systems, data management environments in particular, by linking design and maintenance decisions to economic tradeoffs.

Data offers benefits when used to support business operations and managerial decision making, and as a source for generating revenue. To use data effectively, organizations invest in repositories that store data resource, systems that process them, and tools that deliver data products to consumers. Today, the design and administration of data management environments are driven primarily by technical (e.g., storage space, processing speed, and monitoring capabilities) and functional requirements (e.g., the data contents, presentation format, delivery configuration). The need to address both these requirements affects the selection of information technologies, the design of data resources and the systems that manage them, as well as data management policies and procedures. Unlike technical and the functional perspectives, economic outcomes are rarely explored and addressed in the context of data management. As the volumes of data managed by organizations rapidly increase along with associated costs, we argue that understanding the economic impact of data management decisions is becoming no less important. To better understand the economic perspective of data management, we link the usage of data resources to utility and associate the implementation of systems and resources for supporting usage with costs. We suggest that certain data management decisions may influence both utility and cost and, hence, introduce significant economic tradeoffs. Importantly, we do not suggest that the economic view of design replaces the need to address technical and functional needs. However, assessing economic outcomes and tradeoffs in the design process can offer important insights for addressing these needs in the most cost-effective manner.

Research has rarely offered an explicit link between data management decisions and their economic outcomes. Design methodologies such as the entity-relationships modeling and the relational database design (Elmasri & Navathe, 2006) link functional requirement to technical design, but do not offer insights into their economic implications. Functional and technical link exists, to some extent, in data quality management (DQM) research. Data quality, at a high level, is defined as fitness for use (Redman, 1996). DQM studies offer different methodologies for improving quality such as error detection and correction and analysis of quality measurements (Redman, 1996; Pipino, Yang, & Wang, 2002). As data management environments involve multiple processing stages (e.g., data acquisition, cleansing, transformation, storage, and delivery), DQM studies often view them as data manufacturing processes that create information products (Wang, 1998). We adopt this process/product view for conceptualizing data management from an economic perspective. Our framework is influenced by a study by Ballou, Wang, Pazer, and Tayi (1998), which associates data quality targets and economic outcomes.

Information products contribute value through usage and experience (Shapiro & Varian, 1999). This value reflects benefits such as improvements in decision outcomes or willingness to pay (Ahituv, 1980). The value depends on the context of usage and requires successful integration with complementary organizational resources (Sambamurthy, Bharadwaj, & Grover, 2003), and is often subject to risk and uncertainty (Benaroch, Lichtenstein, & Robinson, 2006). The value contribution of information resources may be affected by their technical characteristics and/or by the design of the environment that manage them (Even, Shankaranarayanan, & Berger, 2007). The utility function maps the configuration of IS/IT attributes to tangible value within some specific usage (Ahituv, 1980). Utility mappings have been used for optimal configuration of quality attributes in complex data processes (Ballou et al., 1998), and for identifying an optimal design of datasets (Even, Shankaranarayanan, & Berger, 2007). In this study, we examine the extent to which utility distribution in large datasets impacts data management decisions. We specifically examine the magnitude of utility inequality—whether utility contribution is the same for each record in a dataset, or concentrated in a relatively small number of records. To support this, we adapt statistical tools that are commonly used in economic and social welfare studies for analyzing inequality in large populations.

Data management environments (and information systems in general) involve a diverse set of cost components (West, 1994). We differentiate between two high level cost categories—fixed versus variable. The former represents costs that do not vary directly with data volume and the latter represents costs that monotonically increase with the volume. We view the management of data as involving four high-level steps: acquisition, processing, storage, and delivery. Costs, both fixed and variable, can be attributed to these activities. Some costs are common to all activities. For example, fixed cost associated with investments in system infrastructure (e.g., hardware, operating systems, and networking), software design and programming efforts, and managerial overhead, or variable costs associated with on-going monitoring and troubleshooting. Other costs are more specific to certain activities. For example, fees paid to a data vendor (West, 2000) can be interpreted as variable acquisition costs. Investments in ETL (extraction, transformation, and loading) tools and business-intelligence platforms in a data warehouse environment can be viewed as fixed processing cost and fixed delivery cost, respectively. Purchasing database management software is a fixed storage cost, while investing in storage capacity (i.e., disk space and hardware for managing it) can be viewed as a variable storage cost. We assume, in general, that the variable costs are linearly proportional to the data volume.

We view the goal of data management as maximization of economic performance. The criterion evaluated is the net-benefit—the difference between the overall utility and the overall cost. Increasing data volume and system capacity improves utility,

but also involves higher costs. In certain cases, the marginal cost may more than offset the marginal utility; hence, maximizing volume and capacity may result in a sub-optimal net-benefit. We apply microeconomic modeling techniques to analyze these tradeoffs. Such models are commonly used for analyzing utility-cost tradeoffs and optimizing the benefit of products, processes, and services. Microeconomic models have been applied in IS/IT studies to a limited extent. Ballou et al. (1998) use utility-cost mapping for optimizing data quality targets and Even et al. (2007) apply microeconomic model for optimizing large datasets in a data warehouse. In this study, we develop microeconomic models that map the effect of increasing data volume and system capacity on utility and cost and use these models for evaluating tradeoffs and optimizing design decisions.

THE DESIGN OF A DATA WAREHOUSE

A data warehouse (DW) is an IS environment for managing large data repositories, aimed to support data analysis and decision making (Kimball, Reeves, Ross, & Thornthwaite, 2000). The implementation of these large complex environments involves major technical efforts and substantial managerial and organizational challenges (Wixom & Watson, 2001). Figure 1 describes the DW architecture at a high level. The key components of this architecture and the associated design challenges are further described in the following paragraphs.

- **Data acquisition:** A DW typically imports and integrates data from multiple sources. These sources are commonly other operational systems in the organization, but in certain cases they may by external (e.g., importing financial quotes from a market-data vendor).
- **Data staging:** The purpose of data staging is to prepare the data that was retrieved from a source for permanent storage. Data staging

Figure 1. A high-level data warehouse architecture

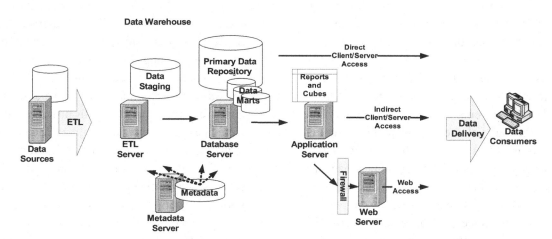

involves cleansing (i.e., detection and correction of quality defects), integration of data from multiple datasets, and transformation into new formats.

- **Primary data repository:** After staging, the data is loaded for permanent storage in the primary data repository. Datasets in a DW are often organized in star schemes. The "center of the star" is a fact table that contains measures of historical business transactions (e.g., price, quantity, and revenue). It is linked to multiple dimension tables, each representing a business dimension (or entity) that describes the transaction (e.g., client, product, location, and date). Fact tables are the largest datasets in the DW repository, and the number of records in such a table significantly affects the overall size of the repository. In this study, we demonstrate the economics-driven design principles for configuring of the number of records in a large dataset, such as a fact table.

- **Data marts:** A data mart is a dataset (or a collection of associated datasets), which contains data subsets from the main repository, restructured to address certain data usage needs. These data subsets are retrieved from the main repository and transformed into structures the permit efficient support

for decision making and data analysis. The data marts are occasionally refreshed with new data and enhanced to support new usage requirements.

- **Data delivery and consumption:** A DW needs to provide utilities for retrieving data from the data repository and the data marts, transforming data to interpretable presentation formats (e.g., tables, charts), and delivering it to consumers (end-users, or other systems). Data usage typically involves specification of content (the underlying data), presentation, and delivery configuration (e.g., recipients and schedule). It also involves management of user authentication, as some users are not authorized to view certain data elements or to use certain reports and analysis tools. In today's DW environments, data delivery is typically managed with software platforms that permit rapid development of data products and efficient management of delivery schedules and user authorizations. Such platforms, commonly known as business intelligence (B.I.) tools, offer a variety of presentation capabilities, such as tables, charts, summary statistics, and advanced analytics. Some also permit interactive use, commonly known as OLAP (online analytical processing). Data delivery platforms often support multiple access modes—two-tier client-server configuration which permits access to data within the same network, and three-tier configuration that permits remote access. In certain cases, power-users are also authorized to access the data resources directly (e.g., via SQL queries).

- **Data maintenance and enhancement:** Due to the high volume and complexity, data in a DW is vulnerable to quality defects such as missing records and attribute values, inaccuracies due to data human errors or calculation mistakes, or changes in real-life entities that have not been captured. To support effective use and the ability to gain business benefits, data in the DW has to be constantly maintained and improved (Kimball et al., 2000). Further, the DW has to be frequently enhanced with new data entities and attributes to support new types of usage. Data enhancement and maintenance often requires investment in utilities for data monitoring, error detection, and automated correction. It also requires the development of maintenance procedures and policies.

- **ETL (extraction transformation loading):** A DW involves substantial data processing, including data acquisition, data transfer between stages, transformation to different structures and formats, and loading data into designated targets. A common term for data processing in a DW is ETL—extraction, transformation, and loading. ETL is commonly managed by dedicated software packages that permit rapid development of new processes (Kimball et al., 2000). ETL platforms also manage the ongoing execution of processes—scheduling, maintaining a certain sequence, monitoring, and evaluating the results. Many ETL platforms also provide utilities for data cleansing and automated error detection and correction.

- **Metadata:** Metadata is a high-level abstraction of data. It is essential for managing the different functionalities of DW subsystems such

as data dictionary, documentation of database structure, process and delivery configuration, and user administration (Shankaranarayanan & Even, 2004). DW subsystems (e.g., database, ETL engines, and data delivery tools) may have different metadata requirements. The software platforms on which these subsystems are implemented typically provide some metadata management capabilities. Metadata requirements of different components are often inter-related—for example, mapping an ETL process, or configuring a data product, require knowledge of tables and attribute structure in the data resource layer. DW designers may therefore choose to enforce consistency between the different subsystems by centralizing metadata management and implementing a metadata repository that serves all applications.

- **Server configuration:** A DW typically requires a few servers, each addressing a different role: (a) *ETL server*: hosts the ETL engines and manages and executes back-end processing of data, (b) *database server*: manages the data resources, including the primary data repository and the derived data marts. This server requires installation of database management system (DBMS) software and sufficiently large storage space, (c) *application server*: manages utilities and tools for data retrieval, analysis and delivery, (d) *Web servers*: manages remote access via the Web, and (e) *metadata server:* manages the DW metadata layer. Each server should have sufficient storage and processing capacity to perform the role. A scalable design of these capacities is encouraged—the volumes of data that are managed in a DW are likely to grow over time, and with them processing and storage capacity needs. In DW environments that manage large-scale data resources, each of these roles is typically implemented with a different server (often, multiple servers per role). In relatively small environments, different roles can be possibly addressed initially by the same server (e.g., one server managing ETL, metadata, and data-delivery applications), and as the DW grows the roles can be managed by specialized servers.

- **Security and access management:** Managing security and authorizations in a DW is critical. User groups are allowed to view only certain subsets of the data, and most users should not be allowed to access the system infrastructure, and/or to make changes to data resources and the derived data products. Managing the authorizations typically requires differentiation between three high-level roles: (a) developers—people who develop new components of the DW such as database schemas, ETL processes, reports, and other data products, (b) administrators—people who are in charge of the on-going operation of the DW, and (c) end users—people who are authorized to use the data product outcomes, but to make changes to the system, or interfere with its ongoing operation. Utilities for managing security and user authorizations are often offered by software development platforms (e.g., DBMS, ETL engines, and business-intelligence tools). Such utilities permit definitions of new users and user groups, assigning roles to different users and groups, and defining the authorizations for each role. Managing this authorization schema typically requires substantial metadata support. Firms often choose to centralize user authorization (e.g., the "single sign-on") for the DW and other organizational applications. This is accomplished by managing the associated metadata in a central repository and developing authentication utilities that are used consistently by all applications.

A key factor that derives and affects design decisions in a DW is the volume of the data resources managed. Rich and diverse data resources enhance usability and the utility potential. On the other hand, providing large data resources increases costs, as it requires investments in powerful servers, advanced software platforms (e.g., DBMS, ETL engines, and B.I. tools), and extensive maintenance and administration efforts. Though apparent, these tradeoffs between utility and cost are insufficiently addressed by today's DW design and management approaches. Introducing an economic perspective into existing DW methodologies, and developing analytical tools to aid with economic assessment, require explicitly and systematically linking data volumes and the associated design decisions to economic outcomes. For developing a more robust economic perspective for DW design, we next introduce a methodology for modeling and measuring the inequality of the utility in large data resources.

INEQUALITY IN THE UTILITY OF DATA RESOURCES

The utility of data reflects its business value contribution. Though all records have a similar structure, they may significantly vary in their content. We assume that this variability differentiates their relative importance to data consumers and, hence, their utility contribution in certain usage contexts. Given this variability, the overall utility in certain cases depends on the entire dataset, while in other cases it is affected only by a small subset of records. We interpret this as the magnitude of *utility inequality* in datasets. In this section, we lay the foundations for the utility inequality and develop analytical tools for modeling and assessing it in large datasets. In real-life, a dataset may have multiple usages, each with a different utility allocation. For brevity, we restrict our description here to a single utility allocation. The models and the analytical methods described can be extended to address multiple-usage scenarios as well.

We consider a tabular dataset with N records maximum utility of $u^D \geq 0$. Utility reaches maximum when the entire dataset is available and may reduce to some extent if some records are missing or unfit for use. We allocate the dataset utility u^D

among the records ($u_n \geq 0$ for record *[n]*), based on their relative importance for the evaluated usage. We assume utility-additivity with no interaction effects, hence, $u^D = \Sigma_n u_n$. A simple utility allocation may assign an identical value per record (i.e., a constant $u_n = u^D/N$). However, while easy to compute, this "naïve" allocation rarely reflects real life data consumption, as dataset records often significantly differ in their importance, and hence, in their utility contribution.

For a large dataset (large *N*), we represent the distribution of utility among the records as a random variable *u* with a known probability density function (PDF) *f(u)*. From the PDF we can calculate the mean $\mu = E[u]$, the cumulative distribution function (CDF) *F(u)*, and the percent point function (PPF, the inverse of the CDF) *G(p)*. In this section, we demonstrate the computations for the continuous *Pareto distribution*, commonly used in economic, demographic, and ecological studies. However, similar computations can be applied to many other statistical distributions, continuous or discrete (e.g., uniform, exponential, or Weibull). The Pareto distribution (Figure 2) is characterized by two parameters—the highest probability is assigned to the lowest possible value of *Z>0* (Z can be arbitrarily close to 0). The probability declines as the value grows and the parameter *w≥1* defines the rate of decline:

$$f(u) = wu^{-(w+1)}/Z^{-w} \quad u \geq Z, \quad F(u) = 1 - (u/Z)^{-w} \quad u \geq Z$$
$$G(p) = Z/(1-p)^{1/w}, \quad \mu = wZ/(w-1)$$

$$(1)$$

To assess the extent to which dataset records differ in their utility contribution, we define *R*, the proportion of highest-utility records, as a *[0,1]* ratio between the N^* records of highest utility and *N*, the total number of records in the dataset (e.g., *R=0.2* for a dataset with *N=1,000,000* records is the ratio for the $N^*=200,000$ records that offer the highest utility). The *cumulative utility curve L(R)* is defined as a *[0,1]* proportion of the overall utility as a function of *R*. *L(R)* can be calculated from the percent point function *G(p)*. For a large *N*, the added utility for a small probability interval *[p, p+Δp]* can be approximated by *NG(p)Δp* (Figure 2a). Taking *Δp→0*, integrating the PPF over *[1-R, 1]* (Figure 2b), and dividing the result by the total utility (approximated by *μN*), we obtain the cumulative utility curve *L(R)* (Figure 2c):

$$L(R) = \frac{N \int_{1-R}^{1} G(p)dp}{N\mu} = \frac{1}{\mu} \int_{1-R}^{1} G(p)dp, \text{ where}$$

$$(2)$$

- *R* – the *[0,1]* proportion of highest-utility records
- *L(R)* – the cumulative utility curve of the utility variable *u*, within *[0,1]*
- *N* – the number of dataset records
- *U, μ* – the utility variable and its mean
- *G(p)* – the percent point function of the utility variable *u*

As shown in *(3)*, *L(R)* does not depend on *N* or on the unit used to measure utility, but does depend on the utility distribution. The curve is defined for *[0,1]*, where *L(0)=0* and *L(1)=1*. The percent point function *G(p)* is monotonically increasing, hence, *L(R)* which is calculated by "backwards integration" over *G(p)* is monotonically increasing and concave within the *[0,1]* range. The first derivative of *L(R)* is therefore positive and monotonically decreasing, and the second derivative is negative. The maximum point of the curve (i.e., *L(1)=1*) represents the maximum possible dataset utility u^D, and the curve reflects the maximum portion of overall utility that can be obtained by the partial dataset—that is, when only a portion *R* of the dataset is available, the utility of $u^D L(R)$ can be achieved at best.

The cumulative utility *L(R)* is equivalent to the Lorentz curve, a statistical tool for modeling inequality in value distributions. Gini's coefficient, derived from the Lorentz curve, is commonly used to measure inequality. This coefficient *(φ)* measures

Figure 2. Obtaining the cumulative utility curve from the PPF by integration

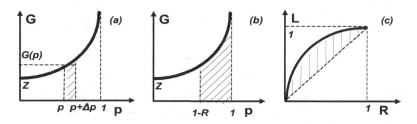

the relative area between the curve and the *45°* line (i.e., *f(R)=R*). This area is highlighted in Figure 2c, and can be calculated by:

$$\varphi = \frac{\int_0^1 L(r)dr - \int_0^1 rdr}{\int_0^1 rdr} = 2\int_0^1 L(r)dr - 1 =$$

$$2\int_0^1 \left(\frac{1}{\mu} \int_{1-R}^1 G(p)dp \right) dr - 1 = \frac{2}{\mu} \int_0^1 pG(p)dp - 1 \qquad (3)$$

The value of *φ* is within *[0,1]*, where a higher value indicates a greater utility inequality. The lower bound, *φ→0*, indicates perfect equality—dataset records with identical utility and a curve that approaches *L(R)=R*. The upper bound, *φ→1*, indicates a high degree of inequality—a small portion of records with a relatively high utility, while the utility of most other records is substantially lower. The corresponding curve in this case approaches *L(R)=1*. The curve and the coefficient can be further evaluated for specific distributions and can often be expressed using a closed analytical form. For the Pareto distribution, the curve and coefficient are:

$$L(R) = \frac{1}{\mu} \int_{1-R}^1 G(p)dp = \frac{w-1}{wZ} \int_{1-R}^1 \frac{Z}{(1-p)^{1/w}} dp = R^{1-\frac{1}{w}}$$

$$\varphi = \frac{2}{\mu} \int_0^1 pG(p)dp - 1 = \frac{1}{2w-1} \qquad (4)$$

With the Pareto distribution, the curve and coefficient do not depend on the minimum value parameter *Z*, but only on the decline rate parameter *w*.

Inequality decreases with *w*, where *w=1* indicates the highest possible inequality (*L(R)=1*, *φ=1*). Conversely, with *w→∞*, *L(R)→R*, and *φ→0*. The utility in this case is nearly identical for all records, that is, *u=~Z* with probability of *~1*.

IMPLICATIONS FOR THE DESIGN AND THE MAINTENANCE OF DATA RESOURCES

Utility inequality among records may have implications for data management decisions. This effect can be evaluated from an economic perspective by assessing the effects of inequality on utility-cost tradeoffs and the overall net-benefit. We first consider utility-cost tradeoffs and net-benefit optimization for a single system configuration, assuming a linear cost model. We then extend the analysis to include decision scenarios that evaluate multiple system configurations.

For a single configuration, we consider *u*, the aggregated utility variable with corresponding maximum utility *u^D*, cumulative utility curve *L(R)*, and inequality coefficient *φ*. We define *U(R)*, the dataset utility curve (Figure 3a), as a function of *R*, the proportion of highest-utility records:

$$U(R) = u^D L(R), \text{ where} \qquad (5)$$

- *R* – the *[0,1]* proportion of highest-utility records
- *U(R)* – the maximal possible utility for *R*

- u^D – the maximal possible utility for the entire dataset (i.e., for $R=1$)
- $L(R)$ – the cumulative utility of the utility variable u, the aggregated utility variable

The cumulative utility curve $L(R)$, hence also $U(R)$, are monotonically increasing with a declining marginal return—a critical property that supports our argument of utility-cost tradeoffs. This property is explained by our definition of the proportion variable R as reflecting the sorting of records in a descending order of utility contribution.

Managing the dataset under a certain system configuration involves costs. We assume identical variable cost per record, uncorrelated to the record's utility—records are often acquired using the same acquisition tools, purchased at the same price, processed and monitored by the same back-end applications, and stored in the same format. Accordingly, we model the cost (for a given system configuration) as a linear curve (Figure 3b) with a variable component c^v, linearly-proportional to the dataset size (hence, to R), and a fixed component c^f, independent of the dataset size (we relax this assumption later, when evaluating multiple configurations):

$$C(R)= c^f + c^v R \text{, where} \tag{6}$$

- R – the *[0, 1]* proportion of highest-utility records

- $C(R)$ – the dataset cost for R
- c^f – a positive fixed cost
- c^v – a positive unit variable cost

Assuming that utility and cost are scaled to the same units, the net-benefit contribution $B(R)$ of the dataset is the difference between utility and cost (Figure 3c):

$$B(R)= U(R)- C(R)= u^D L(R)- \left(c^f + c^v R\right) \tag{7}$$

Due to c^f, $B(R)$ is negative at $R=0$ (the entire curve may be negative if the fixed cost is higher than the utility for all values of R). It is concave, and hence, has a single maximum within *[0, 1]*. An optimum R^{OPT} can be obtained by comparing the first derivative of *(7)* to *0*:

$$dB(R)/dR = u^D \left(dL(R)/dR\right)- c^v = 0 \text{, or}$$

$$dL(R)/dR = c^v/u^D \tag{8}$$

Below R^{OPT}, the net-benefit can be improved by increasing R, since the added utility is higher than the added cost. Beyond R^{OPT}, the marginal cost exceeds the marginal utility and increasing R reduces the net-benefit. For a steep curve (i.e., a high degree of inequality, $L(R)$→*1*, φ→*1*), or when the variable cost is significantly higher than the maximal utility

Figure 3. The (a) utility, (b) cost, and (c) net-benefit curves

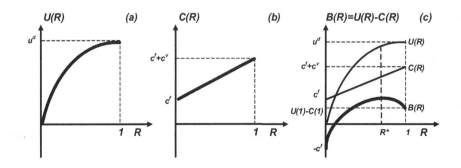

(i.e., $c^v >> u^D$), the optimum approaches a low record proportion (i.e., $R^{OPT} \rightarrow 0$). If no positive R^{OPT} exists, the dataset cannot provide a positive net-benefit due to the fixed cost c^f. Conversely, if the variable cost is relatively low (i.e., $c^v << u^D$), R^{OPT} is obtained at a high record proportion (i.e., $R^{OPT} \rightarrow 1$). When the cumulative curve approaches the 45° line (i.e., $L(R) \rightarrow R$, $\varphi \rightarrow 0$), the solution will be at one of the edges—either at $R^{OPT}=0$, or at $R^{OPT}=1$. Whether the R^{OPT} solution is within the *[0,1]* range or at the edges, a positive net benefit is not guaranteed and has to be verified.

The optimality equation *(8)* can be extended for specific utility distributions. For example, using the Pareto distribution's curve *(4)*, the optimum R^{OPT} can be obtained by:

$$dL(R)/dR = (1-1/w)R^{-1/w} - c^v/u^D, \text{ and}$$

$$R^{OPT} = \left[(1-1/w)u^D/c^v \right]^w \qquad (9)$$

For *w>1*, the optimum R^{OPT} for the Pareto distribution is always positive. It is within *[0,1]* when the utility-cost ratio is $c^v/u^D \geq 1-(1/w)$, otherwise, the optimal net-benefit is obtained at $R^{OPT}=1$. The optimum approaches *0* for a high degree of inequality *(w→1)*, that is, when the majority of the utility is obtained from a relatively small fraction of records. The dependence of R^{OPT} on the utility-cost ratio grows with equality (i.e., greater *w*). When the variable cost is relatively very small (i.e., $c^v << u^D$), the optimal net-benefit is more likely to be obtained when the entire dataset is included *(R^{OPT}=1)*. When the variable cost is substantially large, the optimal net-benefit is more likely to be at $R^{OPT}<1$. For a high a degree of inequality (i.e., *w→∞*), the expression *(1-1/w)^w* converges to a constant *1/e*. If the utility is higher than the variable cost $(u^D>c^v)$, $(u^D/c^v)^w \rightarrow \infty$, and the optimum is obtained for the entire dataset (i.e., $R^{OPT}=1$). If $u^D<c^v$, $(u^D/c^v)^w \rightarrow 0$, $R^{OPT} \rightarrow 0$, and the dataset is unlikely to yield any positive net-benefit.

Utility-cost trade-offs for Pareto-distributed utility can be also assessed at the record level. A Pareto distribution implies positive record utility: *Z>0* (Eq. 1) represents the lowest-possible utility. If the variable-cost per record $c^{v,R}$ is always lower than *Z*, the added utility will always justify the added variable cost, hence, *R* will be maximized at *1* (it is still possible that the entire dataset will not be implemented if the fixed cost is too high). On the other hand, if $c^{v,R}>Z$, for low-utility records, the variable cost will offset the benefit and we are likely to get $R^{OPT}<1$.

Managerial Implications of Utility Inequality and Utility-Cost Tradeoffs

The presence of utility-cost tradeoffs, which may turn out to be significant in some cases, demands reexamination of key data management decisions. Key insights and recommendation are summarized in Table 1.

- **Dataset configuration:** When the utility distribution creates utility-cost tradeoffs, there is a need to carefully evaluate the economic effects of the design characteristics of the dataset (such as the targeted quality level, inclusion/exclusion of attributes, time span coverage and granularity) and design the dataset accordingly. For some datasets, the decision to implement can be an "all-or-nothing" decision (i.e., implement/manage the entire dataset, or avoid implementation altogether). Such datasets will be characterized by a low degree of inequality (i.e., $L(R)$ converging to the 45° line and φ approaching *0*). Datasets with high utility inequality (i.e., $L(R) \rightarrow 1$ and $\varphi \rightarrow 1$), are likely to benefit from differentiating records based on their relative utility contribution, and managing each subset differently. Depending on utility-cost tradeoffs, the designer may exclude low-utility records or manage them separately in a cheaper storage. A typical situation in real life data management is the archiving of older data. Less recent records are assumed to be less important and, hence, administrators often exclude older records from actively used datasets. Modeling and assessing inequality by associating utility with the age of records can help configure the economically optimal time span in the dataset.

- **The design of data management environments:** The differential in utility values can possibly change the scope of data design, especially in environments that manage large datasets. The magnitude of inequality and the associated economic tradeoffs may affect the design of the entire data warehouse (DW). Large datasets require high investments in infrastructure (e.g., more powerful computers and database servers) and data delivery (e.g., data retrieval, reporting and business intelligence tools), as certain system configurations may have capacity limits on the volumes of data that they can effectively manage. Investment in powerful DW infrastructure will be harder to justify if the vast majority of the utility is obtained from a small fraction of the data, which can be effectively managed with a simple and inexpensive system configuration.

- **Data acquisition, retention, and pricing:** Utility inequality can impact data acquisition and retention policies. The value gained from purchasing and maintaining large data volumes is not always obvious. If data records can be differentiated based on utility contribution, it would make sense to acquire and maintain the records that contribute more to utility. Records with lower contribution may be archived or deleted, avoiding maintenance costs. Further, understanding the variability in utility can help define differential pricing policies by data vendors. Data vendors typically apply bulk pricing policies, based on technical characteristics such as data volume and the number of data retrieval activities required to serve the customer (West, 2000). If the utility distribution of data resources is

better understood, vendors can develop more profitable pricing policies for data, based on its potential utility to the buyer.

- **Data quality management:** Utility differentiation can help define superior assessments of data quality along quality dimensions (e.g., completeness and accuracy). Such assessments reflect quality assessment in context (Even & Shankaranarayanan, 2007). Since the relative utility of a record can vary with usage contexts, purely objective measurements of data quality are not particularly beneficial. Data quality measurements that are based on relative utility consistently reflect contextual assessment, while complementing objective quality definitions. Further, differentiating the data records based on their utility contribution can help target quality monitoring and error detection efforts on the records that offer higher utility. This can help defining monitoring procedures and policies that are economically efficient.

EXTENDING THE SCOPE: REAL-OPTION DESIGN STRATEGIES

Our model for designing a tabular dataset assumed deterministic utility. In this section, we extend the framework to address design scenarios in which the utility gained from data usage is uncertain to some extent. To assess the affect of uncertainty on design decisions we apply real-options modeling. This modeling approach addresses the optimization of investment policies under conditions of uncertain outcome, where certain investments can be deferred to future stages. It has been applied in IS research for optimizing the investments in information technologies (Benaroch et al., 2006).

Two design aspects must be considered for addressing uncertainty:

- **Capacity:** To support usage requirements, an information system has to provide certain resources and capabilities, which we refer to as its capacity. DW environments, for example, need to support different capacities in terms of data storage, processing, presentation, and delivery. These capacities are affected by design choices such as technology selection, data acquisition, and system configuration. Investing in slack capacity is a mechanism for addressing uncertainties. However, the cost of increasing capacity may be high, and when usage is relatively predictable the incentive to invest in slack capacity is low.

- **Timing:** A designer may consider deferring some investments to a later stage, until after some uncertainties are resolved. Postponing implementation can cause a delay penalty—implementing DW resources is often time-consuming and delaying the support of usage requirements might damage utility to some extent. Another drawback with deferring investments is a high switching cost. A certain system configuration can manage capacity effectively only to a certain limit. Increasing capacity beyond that limit may require switching to a new technology and discarding the old technology and writing off the associated initial investment. We link this interplay between capacity, deferred invest-

ments, delay penalties, and switching costs to design choices. Certain system configurations optimize the capacity to known needs with limited growth capability. Others allow some future growth with minimal delay penalties and switching costs, but involve a relatively high initial investment. We assume a two-stage design process. Some decisions and the associated investments are made at the initial stage. Others may be deferred, assuming that better decisions can be made after evaluating usage needs further.

- **Utility:** We represent utility as a binomial variable: U with a probability of P, or 0 with a probability of $1-P$. We consider two possible usage modes:

a. **Exploitative:** Data consumption within relatively predictable business processes. Exploitation is assumed to contribute U^A utility with high certainty (i.e., probability of $P^A \approx 1$).

b. **Explorative:** Business processes for which the utility contribution U^B has some uncertainty (i.e., $p^B < 1$). The designer may consider evaluating explorative usages further. After some evaluation time (T^E), and at some evaluation cost (C^E), the designer can assess whether

Table 1. The implications of utility-cost tradeoffs for data management

	High Inequality ($L(R) \rightarrow 1$, $\varphi \rightarrow 1$)	High Equality ($L(R) \rightarrow R$, $\varphi \rightarrow 0$)
Dataset Configuration	- Exclude or manage differently low-utility record.	- "All or nothing" decision—implement and manage the entire dataset, or avoid implementation altogether
DW Design	- Consider managing smaller, partial dataset, and reducing capacity requirements accordingly	- Invest in sufficient storage, processing, and delivery capacity to manage the entire dataset.
Data Acquisition, Retention, and Pricing	- Acquire and enrich only data subsets with high utility contribution - Consider removing lower-utility records, or archiving them separately - Consider differentiating pricing policies	- Apply similar acquire and enrichment policies to all data records - Allow equal access to the entire dataset - Charge equally for all data items
Data Quality Management	- Consider relative utility contribution when measuring data quality levels - Give higher priority to error detection and correction in higher-utility records	- Attribute equal weight to all records when measuring quality levels - Apply similar error correction and detection to the entire dataset

explorative usage will be successful (i.e., $U^B>0$), or not (i.e., $U^B=0$).

- **Delay penalty:** The utility might diminish to some extent with delay. We define the delay sensitivity $D(T)$ as a *[0,1]* decreasing function that reflects the extent to which utility is affected by delay. With no delay, there is no utility reduction (i.e., $D(T=0)=1$). As the delay increases, the utility reduces and may diminish entirely if the time delay is too large (i.e., $D(T\to\infty)=0$). Different usages may have different sensitivities to delays. Accordingly, we assume two different delay sensitivities for exploitative and explorative usages (D^A and D^B respectively).

- **Technology xelection and cost:** Costs are attributed to investments in capacity. We consider three configuration alternatives, each providing a different capacity at a different cost:

  a. *high-end solution*—provides the highest capacity, sufficient to support all usages. It is costly (C^H) and takes a long time (T^H) to implement.

  b. *low-end solution*—provides a low capacity, sufficient to satisfy exploitative usages (but not explorative) at a low cost ($C^L<C^H$) and requires a short implementation time ($T^L<T^H$). It does not permit capacity extensions, and hence, supporting explorative usages mandates switching to an entirely new solution and losing the investment on the previous solution.

  c. *upgradeable solution*—permits implementing a relatively low capacity initially and increasing it later, if needed. We assume a time T^F for implementing the foundation for such a solution that has a cost of C^F. This foundation can support exploitation, but not exploration. The foundation is costlier ($C^L<C^F$) and takes longer to implement ($T^L<T^F$) than the low-end solution, but is cheaper ($C^F<C^H$) and less time-intensive ($T^F<T^H$) than the

high-end solution. To support exploration the foundation needs upgrades, costing C^U and taking time T^U to implement. The combined cost and time of the upgradeable solution is higher than that for the high-end solution, ($C^F+C^U>C^H$, $T^F+T^U>T^H$). Hence, for a single-stage decision, the latter will be preferred.

Given these parameters, we evaluate four design strategies, show their utility-cost effects, and identify conditions under which a strategy can outperform the others. The first strategy, an investment in full-capacity made at the initial stage, is the baseline for comparison. The others, in which some investments are deferred, are viewed as real-options—the designer "buys the option" to decide later. The real-option net benefit (*RONB*) considers: *(1) real-option utility cifferential (ROUD)*—the gain (or loss) of utility due to the ability to deliver solutions earlier (or later), and *(2) real-option cost differential (ROCD)*—costs that are added or reduced by deferring the investment. A real-option strategy is preferred over the baseline if it increases the net benefit (i.e., *RONB=ROUD–ROCD>0*). We assume that the overall net benefit is positive for at least one strategy, otherwise the design initiative cannot be economically justified.

Maximize (M)

Here, the designer chooses to implement a high-end solution at the start with a cost of C^H. This solution permits gaining utility from both exploitation and exploration, but with some delay penalty due to the long implementation time (T^H). Applying (*1*), the anticipated net benefit B^M from this strategy is:

$$B^M = D^A\left(T^H\right)U^A + P^B D^B\left(T^H\right)U^B - C^H \qquad (10)$$

Switch (S)

With this strategy, the designer initially invests in a low-end solution that supports exploitative usage. After some evaluation time (T^E), the designer switches to a high-end solution if explorative usage can yield positive utility, or maintains the low-end solution otherwise. Applying (*1*), the anticipated net benefit B^S from this strategy is:

$$B^S = D^A\left(T^L\right)U^A + P^B D^B\left(T^E + T^H\right)U^B - \left(C^L + C^E + P^B C^H\right) \qquad (11)$$

When compared with "maximize," some exploitative utility is gained due to a smaller delay-penalty *(T^L<T^H)*, but some utility is lost due delaying exploration. The real-option utility differential is:

$$ROUD^S = \left[D^A\left(T^L\right) - D^A\left(T^H\right)\right]U^A - P^B\left[D^B\left(T^H\right) - D^B\left(T^E + T^H\right)\right]U^B$$

It is likely to be positive when the utility gained from exploitation is significantly higher that the utility gained from exploration ($U^A >> U^B$), when the probability of gaining utility from exploration is low ($P^B \rightarrow 0$), when the time saved by implementing a low-end solution is significant ($T^L << T^H$), and/or when the evaluation time is relatively short ($T^E << T^H$). The cost differential of this strategy is $ROCD^S = C^L + C^E - \left(1 - P^B\right)C^H$. It increases with the costs of a low-end solution (C^L) and evaluation (C^E), and decreases with a higher opportunity to save the cost of a high-end solution ($1-P^B)C^H$. This cost-saving opportunity will be significant when C^H is high, and/or when the probability P^B of gaining utility from exploration is low. However, there is a chance that the investment in a low-end solution will be wasted, and that the firm will need to reinvest in a high-end solution and suffer some delay penalty. This strategy will outperform "maximize" if its real-option net benefit ($RONB^S = ROUD^S - ROCD^S$) is positive:

$$RONB^S = \left[D^A\left(T^L\right) - D^A\left(T^H\right)\right]U^A - P^B\left[D^B\left(T^H\right) - D^B\left(T^E + T^H\right)\right]U^B - \left(C^L + C^E - \left(1 - P^B\right)C^H\right) \qquad (12)$$

Upgrade (G)

Here, the designer initially invests in a foundation that allows gradual growth in capacity. After some evaluation of explorative usage (which consumes a time of T^E and costs C^E), the designer can decide whether or not to invest in capacity upgrades. Applying (*1*), the anticipated net benefit B^G from this strategy is:

$$B^G = D^A\left(T^F\right)U^A + P^B D^B\left(T^E + T^U\right)U^B - \left(C^F + C^E + P^B C^U\right) \qquad (13)$$

Compared to "maximize," some exploitative utility is gained due to time savings and some explorative utility is lost due to delay. The corresponding real-option utility differential is:

$$ROUD^G = \left[D^A\left(T^F\right) - D^A\left(T^H\right)\right]U^A - P^B\left[D^B\left(T^H\right) - D^B\left(T^E + T^U\right)\right]U^B$$

This differential is likely to be positive when the utility gained from exploitation is significantly higher that the utility gained from exploration ($U^A >> U^B$), when the probability of gaining utility from exploration is low ($P^B \rightarrow 0$), when the time-saved by implementing the foundation solution is significant ($T^F < T^H$), and/or when the evaluation time is relatively short ($T^E << T^H$). The cost differential of this strategy is $ROCD^G = C^F + C^E + P^B C^U - C^H$. It will increase with higher costs of the evolutionary solution (C^F, C^U) and the evaluation (C^E). It will decrease when a high-end solution is expensive, or when the probability of gaining utility from exploration is low. Overall, this strategy will outperform "maximize" if its real-option net-benefit $RONB^E$ is positive:

$$RONB^G = \left[D^A\left(T^F\right) - D^A\left(T^H\right)\right]U^A - P^B\left[D^B\left(T^H\right) - D^B\left(T^E + T^U\right)\right]U^B - \left(C^F + C^E + P^B C^U - C^H\right) \qquad (14)$$

285

"Upgrade" has a similar decision structure as "switch;" however, it reduces risk to some extent. Here, the designer pays an initial "premium" by decreasing the exploitative utility ($T^F > T^L$, hence, higher delay penalty), and increasing the cost ($C^F > C^L$). The benefit, which materializes at the second stage, is a faster support for exploration ($T^U < T^H$) at a lower cost ($C^U < C^H$). Overall, the "upgrade" strategy will outperform "switch" when its net benefit is higher ($B^G > B^S$), that is, when the second-stage gain is higher than the premium paid at the first stage:

$$P^B\left[\left(D^B\left(T^E+T^U\right)-D^B\left(T^E+T^H\right)\right)U^B+\left(C^H-C^U\right)\right] > \left[D^A\left(T^L\right)-D^A\left(T^F\right)\right]U^A+\left(C^F-C^L\right)$$

The gain (the left-hand side) is higher than the premium if explorative utility (U^B) and/or the chance of gaining it (P^B) are high. It is also higher if the time saved (T^U vs. T^H) is more significant than the time added for implementing the foundation (T^F vs. T^L), and/or if the cost differential between the high-end solution and the upgrade (C^H-C^L) is more significant than the cost differential between the foundation and a low-end solution (C^H-C^L).

Postpone (P)

In this case, the designer will avoid implementation at the first stage, but prefer to evaluate usage more extensively and then decide between a high-end solution and a low-end solution. Applying (*1*), the anticipated net benefit from this strategy B^P is:

$$B^P = \left(1-P^B\right)\left(D^A\left(T^E+T^L\right)U^A-C^L\right)+ P^B\left(D^A\left(T^E+T^H\right)U^A+D^B\left(T^E+T^H\right)U^B-C^H\right)-C^E$$

(15)

This strategy has some utility loss due to time delay. The real-option utility differential is:

$$ROUD^P = -\left[\begin{array}{l}\left(1-P^B\right)\left(D^A\left(T^H\right)-D^A\left(T^E+T^L\right)U^A\right)+ \\ P^B\left(D^B\left(T^H\right)-D^B\left(T^E+T^H\right)\right)U^B\end{array}\right]$$

Depending on the evaluation time, this differential may turn out to be insignificant (if T^E is very short), or even positive (e.g., if $T^L+T^E<<T^H$). The cost differential is $ROCD^P = C^E - \left(1-P^B\right)\left(C^H-C^L\right)$. This strategy may significantly reduce the cost, compared to capacity maximization, if the evaluation cost (C^E) is relatively small, if the cost-margin between a high-end and a low-end solution (C^H-C^L) is high, and/or if the chance of gaining explorative utility is low (P^B). Under this strategy, there is no wasted investment besides the evaluation cost. This strategy will outperform "maximize" if its real-option net-benefit $RONB^P$ is positive:

$$RONB^P = -\left[\begin{array}{l}\left(1-P^B\right)\left(D^A\left(T^H\right)-D^A\left(T^E+T^L\right)U^A\right)+ \\ P^B\left(D^B\left(T^H\right)-D^B\left(T^E+T^H\right)\right)U^B\end{array}\right] - \left(C^E-\left(1-P^B\right)\left(C^H-C^L\right)\right)$$

(16)

When compared with "switch," "postpone" strategy offers the same performance with respect to explorative usage. However, for exploitation, it saves the wasted investment in a low-end solution, but at the expense of some delay penalty. It will outperform "switch" if the net benefit is higher *(B^P>B^S)*, or

$$P^B C^L > \left[\begin{array}{l}D^A\left(T^L\right)-\left(1-P^B\right)D^A\left(T^E+T^L\right)- \\ P^B D^A\left(T^E+T^H\right)\end{array}\right]U^A$$

The cost saving (the left-hand side) may be more significant than the utility reduction (the right-hand side) if exploitative utility (U^A) is relatively low, and/or if the chance of gaining explorative utility (P^B) is high and the delay penalty is insignificant. "Postpone" will outperform "upgrade" if its net benefit is higher ($B^P>B^G$), that is, if the cost saving exceeds the utility loss:

$$C^F - \left(1-P^B\right)C^L - P^B\left(C^H-C^U\right) > \left[D^A\left(T^F\right)-\left(1-P^B\right)D^A\left(T^E+T^L\right)-P^B D^A\left(T^E+T^H\right)\right]U^A + P^B\left[D^B\left(T^E+T^E\right)-D^B\left(T^E+T^H\right)\right]U^B$$

(17)

Table 2 lists conditions under which a certain strategy outperforms others. The superiority is affected by exploitative versus explorative usages, decrease in utility due to time delays, and capacity and cost differentials between technologies. To demonstrate the use of our analysis framework, we now extend it to address a specific DW design scenario.

Design Scenario: Configuring the Database Server

Purchasing, setting up, and maintaining the DW infrastructure that provides the hardware, software, and network resources needed for establishing data repositories can be very expensive. Data storage is a key factor determining capacity, as a DW often manages very large datasets. Implementing storage capacity involves the purchase of database management systems (DBMS) server software (e.g., Oracle, MS-SQL), the hardware to support it (e.g., server, disk space), and labor. Here we model the effects of establishing storage capacity and the associated selection of DBMS, considering a single large tabular dataset (e.g., a fact table in a DW). Dataset size is a key factor (among others) that influences DBMS selection, here reflected by the *[0,1]* proportion of high-utility records (*R*). We assume that the utility for usage *[i]* follows a Pareto distribution with corresponding parameters (Z_i, w_i). For brevity, we denote the sensitivity factor $\alpha_i = 1-1/w_i$. The corresponding cumulative utility curve $L_i(R) = R^{\alpha_i}$ monotonically increases with *R*. Since $w_i \geq 1$, $0 \leq \alpha_i \leq 1$ and the marginal utility added, decreases with *R*. Usage *[i]* may require some minimum record proportion coverage φ_i, defining a set of lower-bound constraints: $\{\varphi_i \leq R \leq 1\}$. The extended utility model for usage *[i]* is:

$$U_i = P_i D_i(T) U_i^{Max} R^{\alpha_i}, \text{ where} \qquad (18)$$

- U_i, U_i^{Max} – utility contribution and its upper bound, respectively
- P_i, $D_i(T)$ – the probability of gaining utility, and the delay sensitivity, respectively

- *R* – the *[0,1]* proportion of highest-utility records, $\varphi_i \leq R \leq 1$
- α_i – utility-sensitivity parameter, $0 \leq \alpha_i \leq 1$
- φ_i – lower bound on record proportion

We consider *K* possible DBMS solutions (indexed by *k*), each requiring an implementation time of T_k and has a fixed cost of C_k^F (e.g., DBMS software and hardware). A larger *R* covered implies a larger number of records and a larger storage space. Assuming an approximately fixed number of records per time unit, the dataset volume will be linearly proportional to *S*. Thus, the variable cost for adding storage space increases linearly with the record proportion—$C_k^V R$, where C_k^V is the cost for covering *R=1*. We also assume an upper limit on storage capacity A_k for configuration *[k]* ($0 \leq R \leq A_k$) as some DBMS are limited by the volume of data they can handle without performance degradation. Similar to the previous scenario, the designer may choose to evaluate usage further (evaluation time—T^E, and cost - C^E). Using *(1)*, the choice of DBMS configuration can be a design optimization—select a configuration (indexed by *k*) and record proportion *R* such that the net benefit is maximized:

$$B_k = U_k - C_k = \sum_{i=1}^{I} P_i D_i \left(T_k + ET^E\right) U_i^{Max} R^{\alpha_i} - C_k^F - C_k^V R - EC^E$$

$$\text{s.t. } 0 \leq R \leq A_k \text{ per k}, \varphi_i \leq R \leq 1 \text{ per i}, \qquad (19)$$

where

- B_k, U_k, C_k – overall net benefit, utility and cost, respectively
- T_k – implementation time
- C_k^F, C_k^V – fixed and variable implementation costs
- C^E, T^E – evaluation cost and time, respectively
- *E* – indicator of whether evaluation is performed (*=1*) or not (*=0*)
- A_k – data volume capacity *R*, $U_i^{Max}, P_i, D_i, \alpha_i,$ φ_i – same as in (18)

Table 2. Design strategies

	Maximize (M)	Switch (S)	Upgrade (G)	Postpone (P)
Investment Strategy	- Implement a high-end solution at the first stage	- Implement a low-end solution at the first stage - Switch to a high-end solution later, if required	- Implement the foundation for an upgradeable solution first - Upgrade later, if required	- Avoid implementation at first stage - Choose later between a low end and a high end solution
Superior to others when	- High utility can be gained from exploration - Small cost/time differential - Long and/or expensive evaluation	- Low level and/or low probability of explorative utility - Small delay penalty for postponing support for explorative usage - A low-end solution is significantly faster and cheaper than others	- Significant, but not high explorative utility - Foundation cost/time not significantly high compared to low-end - The overall cost/time (foundation + upgrade) margin from a high-end solution is insignificant	- Evaluation can be performed in a fast and cheap manner - The cost and time of implementing a low-end solution are significant - The probability of success with explorative usage is relatively high

This design scenario involves a discrete set of choices (DBMS selection) and a continuous variable *(R)*. Solving a mixed-integer optimization model requires repeating the optimization of the continuous component iteratively for all possible discrete configurations, and choosing the DBMS solution that yields the highest net-benefit, along with the corresponding optimal setup.

Illustrative example: A hospital evaluates a DW for analyzing treatment history (e.g., doctor visits, treatments, medications, and labs). Possible usages evaluated are: (a) exploitative—ongoing reporting and monitoring such as inventory tracking, resource utilization, and treatment history for specific patients. These usages require a minimum R of φ^A. Their utility (U^A) has sensitivity of α^A, and delay sensitivity of D^A and (b) explorative—advanced analyses such as detecting shifts in resource utilization, identifying patterns of reactions to drugs, and segmenting treatment history along demographic and socioeconomic attributes. These usages require a minimum R of φ^B ($>\varphi^A$). Their anticipated utility is U^B with a success probability $P_b<1$, sensitivity of α^B, and a delay sensitivity, D^B. Covering the entire dataset (R=1) implies a larger data volume and the designer considers two database configurations. A low-end solution can be implemented within a short time (T^L) at low fixed/variable costs ($C^{F/L}$ and $C^{V/L}$ respectively). The capacity limit of this solution (A^L) permits exploitative usage, but not explorative. A high-end configuration can be implemented within a time of T^H, and at fixed/variable costs of $C^{F/H}$ and $C^{V/H}$ respectively. Its capacity (A^H) can support all usage types.

Based on these parameters, which DBMS configuration must be chosen, and what is the optimal record proportion coverage for this choice? Using (19), we evaluate different possible configurations considering the high-level strategies:

Maximize (M): Implement a high-end solution with no further evaluation (i.e., E=0) and cover a record proportion large enough to support all usages. The corresponding net-benefit is:

$$B^M(R) = D^A\left(T^H\right)U^A R^{\alpha^A} + P^B D^B\left(T^H\right)U^B R^{\alpha^B} - \left(C^{F/H} + C^{V/H}R\right)$$

s. t. $\varphi^B \leq R \leq 1$ (20)

This strategy is preferred if advanced analysis can lead to high utility gains with a substantial level of certainty, the evaluation cost is high, and/or the delay penalty is too severe. The advantage will also depend on the maximum net-benefit obtainable by optimizing the record proportion R. Candidates for R^{OPT} can be obtained by comparing the first derivative of (20) to 0:

$$\alpha^A D^A \left(T^H\right)U^A R^{\alpha^A-1} + \alpha^B P^B D^B \left(T^H\right)U^B R^{\alpha^B-1} = C^{V/H}$$

(21)

The left-hand side of (21) represents the marginal utility as a function of R. Since α^A and α^B are within $[0,1]$, this margin is positive at $R=\varphi^B$ and decreases to $\alpha^A D^A \left(T^H\right)U^A + \alpha^B P^B D^B \left(T^H\right)U^B$ as R approaches 1. The right-hand side of (21) is a positive constant with respect to R, representing a fixed marginal cost. As the left-hand side is monotonically decreasing, (21) has a single solution at most, within $[0,1]$. To validate the optimality of the candidate solution (if it exists and lies within the $[\varphi^B,1]$ range), the second derivative of (20) must be evaluated:

$$\partial^2 B^M\left(R\right)/\partial R^2 = \left(\alpha^A-1\right)\alpha^A D^A \left(T^H\right)U^A R^{\alpha^A-2} + \left(\alpha^B-1\right)\alpha^B D^B \left(T^H\right)U^B R^{\alpha^B-2}$$

(22)

Since α^A and α^B are within $[0,1]$, the second derivative is negative and a candidate solution is a local maximum. If no solution exists within the $[\varphi^B,1]$ range, two edge conditions are possible: (a) the marginal-utility exceeds the marginal-cost, hence, $R=1$ and (b) the marginal-utility is always lower, hence, $R=\varphi^B$.

Switch (S): with this strategy, the designer first implements a low-end solution and optimizes the record proportion coverage for exploitative usage. After some evaluation, the designer may switch to a high-end solution and re-optimize R accordingly. The evaluation of net-benefit and the corresponding R has to consider two possible scenarios:

1. Keeping a low-end solution at the later stage, with a corresponding net-benefit of:

$$B^{S/1}\left(R\right)= D^A \left(T^L\right)U^A R^{\alpha^A} - \left(C^{F/L} + C^{V/L}R + C^E\right)$$
, s.t. $\varphi^A <R<A^L$

(23)

The record proportion coverage in this case $\left(R^{OPT/1}\right)$ can be calculated by following the methodology described above under the "maximize" strategy.

2. *Switching to a high-end solution at the second stage,* assuming that $R^{OPT/1}$ will be covered at the first. The net-benefit depends on a different optimal R $\left(R^{OPT/2}\right)$, obtained from:

$$B^{S/2}\left(R\right)= D^A \left(T^L\right)U^A R^{\alpha^A} + D^B \left(T^E + T^H\right)U^B R^{\alpha^B} - \left(C^{F/L} + C^{V/L}R^{Opt/1} + C^E + C^{F/H} + C^{V/H}R\right)$$
, s.t. $\varphi^B <R<1$

(24)

The former scenario has an occurrence probability of $\left(1-P^B\right)$ and the latter has an occurrence probability of P^B. The expected net-benefit from this strategy is:

$$B^S = \left(1-P^B\right)B^{S/1}\left(R^{Opt/1}\right) + P^B B^{S/2}\left(R^{Opt/2}\right)$$

(25)

This strategy is preferred if implementing a low-end DBMS solution is significantly faster and cheaper, and/or if the expected utility from advanced analysis is relatively low or has low probability of obtaining. This solution will also be advantageous when the penalty for delaying support for explorative usage is relatively small.

Upgrade (G): Here, the designer will invest in the infrastructure for a high-end DBMS, but will initially optimize S for exploitation. After evaluation, the designer may consider increasing S to support all usages. The evaluation must consider two possible scenarios:

1. Keeping R coverage at a low level ($R^{OPT/1}$) and supporting exploitative usage only:

$$B^{G/1}\left(R\right)= D^A \left(T^H\right)U^A R^{\alpha^A} - \left(C^{F/H} + C^{V/H}R + C^E\right)$$
, s.t. $\varphi^A <R<1$

(26)

2. Enlarging R coverage at the second stage to support explorative usage as well. Unlike "switch," with this strategy the investments made at stage one are not wasted. The net-benefit and the corresponding optimal $R^{OPT/2}$ can be obtained from:

$$B^{G/2}(R) = D^A\left(T^E\right)U^A R^{\alpha^A} + P^B D^A\left(T^H\right)U^B R^{\alpha^B} - \left(C^{H/L} + C^{H/L}R + C^E\right)$$

, s.t. $\varphi^B < R < 1$ (27)

Considering the occurrence probabilities of both scenarios, the expected net-benefit is:

$$B^G = \left(1 - P^B\right)B^{G/1}\left(R^{Opt/1}\right) + P^B B^{G/2}\left(R^{Opt/2}\right)$$

(28)

This strategy is advantageous if implementing the foundation is fast and inexpensive, but the marginal cost of increasing R is high. This is likely, for example, if data has to be acquired at a high cost, or if improving its quality is expensive.

Postpone (P): with this strategy, the designer first evaluates usage needs and accordingly decides on the solution. This assessment must consider two cases:

1. Implementing a low-end solution and maintaining R at a low level ($R^{OPT/1}$):

$$B^{P/1}(R) = D^A\left(T^E + T^L\right)U^A R^{\alpha^A} - \left(C^{F/L} + C^{V/L}R + C^E\right)$$

, s.t. $\varphi^A < R < A^L$ (29)

2. Implementing a high-end solution and maintain R at a high level ($R^{OPT/2}$):

$$B^{P/2}(R) = D^A\left(T^E + T^L\right)U^A R^{\alpha^A} + D^A\left(T^E + T^H\right)R^{\alpha^B} - \left(C^{F/H} + C^{V/H}R + C^E\right)$$

, s.t. $\varphi^B < R < 1$

(30)

Considering the occurrence probabilities of both scenarios, the expected net-benefit is:

$$B^P = \left(1 - P^B\right)B^{P/1}\left(R^{Opt/1}\right) + P^B B^{P/2}\left(R^{Opt/2}\right)$$

(31)

This strategy is preferred if the evaluation is fast and inexpensive. It is also likely to be better if the implementation cost and time for a low-end solution are relatively high, and/or if the probability of the explorative usage being successful is significant.

Storage capacity is a key design decision in DW environments. A large capacity might turn out to be very expensive in certain scenarios—DBMS software that supports high volume storage is expensive to license and requires considerable labor to configure and maintain. Alternately, a cheaper DBMS may be sufficient for most usages, but might limit storage capacity and consequently the ability to enhance the DW to support new information products and usages. The record proportion covered within the storage capacity limit has to be carefully evaluated, as it can significantly impact utility and the costs of data acquisition and maintenance.

CONCLUSION

The design and the maintenance of data management environments are resource-intensive. As the volumes of data managed and the associated costs increase, we advocate the need to examine data management from an economic perspective. We do not minimize the importance of satisfying technical and functional requirements in the design process but argue that design decisions must be economically justified. The perspective proposed will effectively supplement the traditional design approaches. We believe that this study is a first step in incorporating economic considerations into design of data management environments.

This study contributes to the design of a data warehouse by developing a framework for evaluating design decisions within. We explore the link between design decisions and economic benefits, suggesting that modeling the effects of these decisions on economic outcomes can enhance design processes. We link economic tradeoffs and the related data design and administration decisions to the utility distribution of datasets, and develop analytical tools for assessing utility inequality. Utility is attributed to data resource by understanding usage in different business contexts. The need to support both exploitative usages (with relatively certain outcome) and explorative (with uncertain outcomes) usages has important design implications for the data management environment that supports these. Each usage type differs significantly in its data utilization patterns, and the differences can direct design decisions. Similarly, design decisions are linked to costs, as higher capacity, faster performance, and sophisticated capabilities require larger investments. Modeling the effect of design decisions on utility and costs can help assess tradeoffs and identify economically optimal designs. We analyze these tradeoffs in the context of designing the warehouse capacities, treating certain strategies as real-option investments. Increasing DW capacity to certain layers allows timely and less expensive support for new usages, thereby enhancing utility. Our evaluation addresses common DW design tradeoffs—investing in expensive slack capacity for explorative usages that offer a larger potential for utility gains but, at a substantial risk, versus optimizing capacity for more certain exploitative usages. We demonstrate these tradeoffs for some DW design scenarios and identify conditions in which a certain design strategy will outperform others.

The framework proposed here offers several opportunities for further research. It develops inequality measurements specifically for the Pareto distribution. Other distributions (continuous or discrete) may better reflect real-life utility distributions and should be explored. The cost model assumes an equal variable cost per dataset records. However, depending on the business setting, variable costs may not be linear with number of records, and the cost model might have to be revised. The current model applies sum-additive modeling of utility and cost factors, suggesting that the factors are independent and orthogonal. Value enhancement or neutralizing relationships may exist among utilities and costs, in which case the whole is not necessarily an additive sum of the parts. The framework needs to be enhanced to model such interactions and dependencies. Estimation of utility may turn to be an even greater challenge in business settings. Data resources contribute value through usage when embedded within business processes together with complementary resources such as financial investments, physical assets, and human expertise. It is difficult to attribute a utility contribution to data in complex business settings, isolated from business processes and complementary resources, and to allocate the utility across dataset records. Further, a data resource can be used by multiple consumers, each with different, and possibly conflicting, utility assignments. Adding multiple usage contexts adds yet another dimension to the complexity. Further, some usages are unknown when the dataset is established. Considering all these difficulties, methods for estimating utility and allocating it across records certainly require a more in-depth examination in real life settings.

To conclude, we state that design for improved economic performance is important not only for data management but also for system design. Our evaluation framework and the factors examined (the expected outcome and associated uncertainty, the differences in cost and performance across alternate technologies, and the negative impact of time delays) can be applied to design scenarios in other IS/IT environments. The magnitudes of utility-cost tradeoffs associated with design decisions are often high and quantitative evaluation of design alternatives can help identify economically-optimal choices. This in turn, can guide investment decisions regarding technology solutions. Our framework, which emphasizes economic considerations as goals that direct design and impact architectural choices, assists by laying a better foundation of the economic perspective for IS design.

REFERENCES

Ahituv, N. (1980). A systematic approach towards assessing the value of information system. *MIS Quarterly, 4*(4), 61-75.

Ballou, D. P., Wang, R., Pazer, H., & Tayi, G. (1998). Modeling information manufacturing systems to determine information quality. *Management Science, 44*(4), 462-484.

Benaroch, M., Lichtenstein, Y., & Robinson, K. (2006). Real-options in information technology risk management: An empirical validation of risk-option relationships. *MIS Quarterly, 30*(4), 827-864.

Elmasri, R., & Navathe, S. B. (2006). *Fundamentals of database systems* (5th ed.). Redding, MA: Addison Wesley.

Even, A., & Shankaranarayanan, G. (2007). Assessing data quality: a value-driven approach. *The Data Base for Advances in Inf. Systems, 38*(2), 76-93.

Even, A., Shankaranarayanan, G., & Berger, P. D. (2007). Economics-driven data management: An application to the design of tabular datasets. *IEEE Transactions on Knowledge and Data Engineering, 19*(6), 818-831.

Hevner, A. R., March, S. T., Park, J., & Ram, S. (2004). Design science in information systems research. *MIS Quarterly, 28*(1), 75-105.

Kimball, R., Reeves, L., Ross, M., & Thornthwaite, W. (2000). *The data warehouse lifecycle toolkit*. New York: Wiley Computer Publishing.

March, S. T., & Smith, G. F. (1995). Design and natural science research on information technology. *Decision Support Systems, 15*, 251-266.

Pipino, L. L., Yang, W. L., & Wang, R. Y. (2002). Data quality assessment. *Communications of the ACM, 45*(4), 211-218.

Redman, T. C. (1996). *Data quality for the information age*. Boston: Artech House.

Sambamurthy, V., Bharadwaj, A., & Grover, V. (2003). Shaping agility through digital options: Reconceptualizing the role of information technology in contemporary firms. *MIS Quarterly, 27*(2), 237-263.

Shankaranarayanan, G., & Even, A. (2004). Managing metadata in a data warehouse: Pitfalls and possibilities. *Communications of the Association of Information Systems (CAIS), 14*(13), 1-49.

Shapiro, C., & Varian H. R. (1999). *Information rules*. Cambridge, MA: Harvard Business School Press.

Simon, H. A. (1996). *The science of the artificial* (3rd ed.). Boston: The MIT Press.

Wang, R. Y. (1998). A product perspective on total quality management. *Communications of the ACM, 41*(2), 58-65.

West, L. A., Jr. (1994). Researching the cost of information systems. *Journal of Management Information Systems, 11*(2), 75-107.

West, L. A., Jr. (2000). Private markets for public goods: Pricing strategies of online database vendors. *Journal of Management Information Systems, 17*(1), 59-84.

Wixom, B. H., & Watson, H. J. (2001). An empirical investigation of the factors affecting data warehousing success. *MIS Quarterly, 25*(1), 17-41.

KEY TERMS

Business Intelligence (B.I.) Tools: Software tools for reporting and data analysis in DW environments (e.g., business objects, cognos, and microstrategy). B.I. tools typically provide utilities for retrieving data, transforming in into different presentation formats (e.g., charts, tables, reports), and applying different forms of analysis (e.g., aggregation, statistics, data mining) towards decision making.

Data Structure: Data repositories follow a typical hierarchical structure. The lowermost-level of this hierarchy is the data-item, or the datum, the atomic data entity. The data-item is defined as a triplet <a,e,v>. The data value 'v' is selected from the value-domain associated with attribute 'a' of entity 'e,' which represents a physical or conceptual real-world object. The data-record is a collection of data-items that represent a set of attributes of an entity instance. A dataset is a collection of records that belong to the same instance type (e.g., a subset of records in a table), and a database is a collection of datasets with meaningful relationships among them. A data repository typically manages multiple databases, each serving different business purposes.

Data Utility, Cost, and Net-Benefit: Economic-performance measures, commonly expressed in monetary units. Utility reflects of the business value attributed to data within specific usage contexts. Cost reflects investments made in establishing data resources and the systems that manage them—for example, in acquisition, processing, storage, and delivery. The net-benefit is the difference between the overall utility and the overall cost.

Data Warehouse (DW): An IS environment that manages large data resources. The DW offers a broad and integrated view of the firm along different business functionalities, towards better support for managerial decision making. This is achieved by integrating data from multiple data sources, accumulating it over a long period of time, and providing utilities for efficient retrieval, aggregation, presentation and delivery of large amounts of data.

Extraction, Transformation, and Loading (ETL): A common name for back-end application for processing data in a DW. An ETL application provides utility for extracting and integrating data from different data sources (e.g., text files, RDBMS, on-line data feeds), transforming it to a different format, and loading it into a target data repository.

Real Options: A methodology for analyzing irrecoverable investments when outcome is uncertain. The investor may decide to make a smaller investment at current stage (perceived as "buying an option"), which permits deferring the decision on a full-scale investment to a later stage, when some of the uncertainly is resolved.

Star Schema, Facts, and Dimensions: Tabular datasets in a DW database are often organized in a "star schema." The fact table (the "center of the star") contains measures of historical business transactions (e.g., price, quantity, revenue). It is linked to multiple dimension tables, each representing a business dimension (or entity) that describes the transaction (e.g., client, product, location, and date).

Tabular Datasets, Relational Dataset Modeling, and RDBMS: The table is a commonly-used two-dimensional data model, which represents data-attributes as columns (a.k.a. fields) and entity-instances as rows (a.k.a. records). The relational database model maps data that represents business entities and the relationships between them into a collection of tabular datasets. The relational model underlies RDBMS (relational database management system) technologies for database management (e.g., Oracle, MS-SQL, and Sybase). Tabular datasets are also used in other common data-storage technologies, such as flat-files, spreadsheets, and statistical packages.

Glossary of notations

X	A vector of design characteristics
B	Net Benefit
U, u	Utility
C, c^F, c^V	Cost, Fixed Cost, Variable Cost
$I, [i]$	Number of usages, Corresponding index
$J, [j]$	Number of cost factors, Corresponding index
$N, [n]$	Number of records, Corresponding index
$f()$	Probability density function (PDF)
$F()$	Cumulative distribution function (CDF)
$G()$	Percent-Point function (PPF)
M	The mean of a random variable
Z, w	The parameters of a Pareto distribution
R	The proportion of highest-utility records
$L(R)$	The cumulative utility curve
Φ	The utility inequality coefficient
$K, [k]$	Number of databases, Corresponding index
P	Probability
T	Time, Time-delay
$D(T)$	Delay-penalty, as a function of time
$ROUD$	Real-Option Utility Differential
$ROUC$	Real-Option Cost Differential
$RONB$	Real-Option Net Benefit
$()^D$	Dataset-level variables
$()^A$	Exploitative usage variables
$()^B$	Explorative usage variables
$()^E$	Evaluation variables
$()^L$	Low-end technology variables
$()^H$	High-end technology variables
$()^F$	Foundation of upgradeable technology variables
$()^U$	Upgrade of upgradeable technology variables
$()^M$	"Maximize" strategy variables
$()^S$	"Switch" strategy variables
$()^G$	"Upgrade" strategy variables
$()^P$	"Postpone" strategy variables

Chapter XIX
Security Considerations in the Development Life Cycle

Kenneth J. Knapp
U.S.A.F. Academy, USA

ABSTRACT

To promote the development of inherently secure software, this chapter describes various strategies and techniques for integrating security requirements into the systems development life cycle (SDLC). For each major phase of the SDLC, recommendations are made to promote the development of secure information systems. In brief, developers should identify risks, document initial requirements early, and stress the importance of security during each phase of the SDLC. Security concerns are then offered for less traditional models of systems analysis and development. Before concluding, future trends are discussed. Practitioners who read this chapter will be better equipped to improve their methodological processes by addressing security requirements in their development efforts.

INTRODUCTION

A perception exists among some information system (IS) security professionals that systems developers generally do not consider security as an integral part of the development process. Instead, a perception exists that developers often treat security more as an afterthought. Considering today's high-threat cyber environment, it is essential that security requirements remain a priority throughout the systems development life cycle (SDLC). In this paper, a description of SDLC strategies and techniques is provided to promote the development of secure systems. The key to integrating security into the SDLC is by documenting security requirements early and making security considerations a priority during each phase of development. Practitioners who read this chapter will be equipped to improve their methodological processes by including security requirements in their development efforts.

BACKGROUND

The motivation to write this chapter initiated from a previous study that involved a set of interviews the author conducted with certified information security professions between 2004 and 2006. In 2004, the author conducted e-mail interviews with over 200 certified information systems security professionals (CISSP) located in over 20 countries worldwide. The interviews discussed what each participant felt were the most critical information security issues facing organizations today. A recurring perception among the participants was that security concerns are not a high priority among many system developers. One typical response stated, "It seems that unless the project is a security initiative, the involvement of a security resource to identify control requirements is an afterthought. By the time the security resource is formally involved, the project is so far ahead that insisting on changes to accommodate [security] controls is often viewed as a source of threat to the project's timelines." Another expressed frustration by stating, "Vendors are under constant pressure to meet their figures [deadlines], thus delivering the product with sacrifices in security and quality. The end customer assumes the risk when this software is delivered into the market space. This is a great concern these days and will continue to be a major security concern even 10 years from now." Another interviewee said, "Late security planning is (often) started well into the implementation phase of a project's SDLC. A current large organization is deploying a…management enterprise tool. This project has been in engineering and deployment for over a year and they are just now beginning to supply security."[1]

In 2006, the author conducted an interview with a certified information security professional with over 20 years of IT experience working for both government and Fortune 100 employers. The interviewee indicated that his own company recently cut security engineers by 50% in an effort to save costs and that top management typically does not place much priority on security unless they can be convinced that security requirements effect the financial bottom-line. Yet, demonstrating how security can bring about direct financial benefits or improve return on investment can be challenging for security professionals. Many find it difficult to quantify security in financial terms and stumble

over simple questions asked by top managers, such as, "What am I getting for my security dollars?" One study found that U.S. companies spent only an average of .047% of their revenue on security (Geer, Hoo, & Jaquity, 2003). The difficulty of quantifying security benefits in financial terms that top management can appreciate is partially to blame for these low budgets.

One of the reasons that security is perceived as a development afterthought is that modern software systems often contain serious security flaws and require frequent patch updates. Yet, evidence suggests that by focusing on building security into software during development, money can be saved by minimizing the number of flaws that require patch updates. A 1981 IBM Systems Sciences Institute study reported that the cost to fix an error found after product release can be 100 times more costly than one identified during the design phase (Geer, 2002). For security defects, late fixes often cost more because in addition to having to remediate the flaw, successful exploits may lead to data theft, sabotage, or other cyber-related attacks (Berg, 2006). Security professionals should keep these facts in mind when asked by top management, "What am I getting for my security dollars?"

To promote the development of inherently secure software, this chapter describes various strategies and techniques of integrating security requirements into the SDLC. Secure software does not happen by itself, it requires process improvement and commitment from the development team and from management. The processes discussed in this chapter do not require the creation of a separate development process; instead, the processes can be integrated into an organization's existing methodology.

SECURITY CONSIDERATIONS IN THE SYSTEM DEVELOPMENT LIFE CYCLE

This section describes important security considerations for the major phases in a representative software development life cycle model. This model emphasizes developing information systems in general stages that often overlap, but follow a progressive development toward a fielded system.[2] For the purposes of discussing security considerations during software development, the following paragraphs address strategies and techniques for incorporating security in a notional seven-phase model that is an expanded version of a model presented in Bishop (2005). The seven phases covered in this paper include: system investigation, requirements analysis, system and software design, implementation and unit testing, integration and system testing, operation and maintenance, and retirement. This section will also discuss the importance of regular reviews as well as considerations for less traditional models of system development.

System Investigation

System developers should not necessarily use all the security measures discussed in this chapter because not all systems require the same level of security. Just as an automobile owner would not install an expensive car alarm in a used automobile with little worth, system developers should not build high security into a system that poses little risk. Since a high-security system can entail additional development and administrative costs, the level of security should address the level of estimated risk. The more sensitive and valuable the data within a system, the higher the priority security should have during development. In short, the security level of the proposed system should be sensible and support the business goals of the organization. Supporting this goal, the initial security assessment serves as a guide to ensure the security level in the system is reasonable and not overly burdensome.

In this first phase, analysts investigate the feasibility of a proposed system to include an initial estimation of cost and time. To promote security, this phase can include an *initial systems risk assessment* that developers can use as a basis for future security decisions. Emerging from this assessment,

the proposed system can be generally classified as a low, medium, or high-risk system. The risk level should drive the designed level of security in the proposed system. This assessment can include an analysis of the target environment, an identification of threat vulnerabilities, as well as the potential of undesirable outcomes. This assessment can also evaluate potential countermeasures (Hansche, Berti, & Hare, 2004). The initial security assessment is a necessary step before moving to the more detailed phases of the SDLC.

Requirements Analysis

During this phase, initial requirements documented in the investigation phase are expanded to describe the intended functionality of the proposed system. These functional requirements can include a number of important security considerations. Following is a list of eight categories that developers should address during this phase:

- System management processes such as security training and policy requirements
- Application processing and data storage security requirements
- Access control and system sign-on requirements
- Transmission, communication, cryptographic, and network security requirements
- Physical and facility security requirements
- Operational and administrative security requirements
- Disaster recovery planning and system continuity requirements
- Ethical, legal, and regulatory requirements

The requirements should be collected from the functional users, system owners, and qualified experts in their respective area (e.g., a lawyer can help define the legal requirements). At this point, it is important that the output from this phase does *not* provide specific technical or engineered solutions. The problem of jumping directly into technical solutions is that the developers may not understand the essential security requirements of the proposed system. Without this knowledge, it is more likely the developed system may not have the optimum degree of security; the system may have too much or, more likely, too little security. For example, while documenting data communication needs, developers can write the functional requirements that data needs to be protected using "state of the art technology" or "strong encryption" rather than recommending a specific cryptographic solution. Recommending specific product solutions should be a part of the design phase.

Systems Security Requirements Document

For some systems and particularly higher risk systems, it might be practical to weigh the option of producing a system security requirements document (SSRD). A stand-alone SSRD has the benefit of emphasizing the importance of documenting security requirements so that security does not get lost in the primary document. However, in some development cultures, a separate SSRD may actually increase the risk that developers treat security requirements separately and not part of the overall development strategy. This can be a problem if developing a separate security document means that security is "out of sight" when important design decisions are made (Flechais, Sasse, & Hailes, 2003). Nevertheless, depending on the risk level of the proposed system and the culture of the development environment, developers should weigh the merits of writing an SSRD.

Security Requirements Traceability

It is valuable to extend the concept of requirements traceability to track security requirements throughout the SDLC. Requirements traceability is intended to ensure continued alignment between user requirements and various outputs of the systems development process (Ramesh & Jarke, 2001).

Each identified requirement should have a specific solution in the design of the system and be tested during the appropriate phase of the SDLC. Likewise, each design feature should be traceable to an identified requirement. Requirements traceability can help designers identify areas in a developing system that do not meet the documented requirements. Thus, applying requirements traceability can help developers integrate security requirements throughout the SDLC.

System and Software Design

Documentation produced during the system and software design phase includes the technical and engineering designs that are traceable to the original requirements. Here, developers specifically spell out technical solutions, such as proposing a network architectural design or a cryptographic product. It is critical that the proposed design adequately addresses security requirements. If requirements are neglected, the system may not provide adequate security resulting in costly configuration changes and redesign efforts once the system is fielded. Security should not be treated as a design afterthought; instead, each identified requirement should have a traceable solution that is built into the system design.

For higher risk systems, in addition to unit and system test plans, developers should consider writing a dedicated security test plan during this phase. A test plan involves defining the criteria by which the system will be tested and measuring the criteria against an acceptable failure rate (Ayer & Patrinostro, 1992). Such a document spells out exactly the type of tests that are necessary to demonstrate that individual program units, as well as the total system, meet the original security requirements. Such a test document is advantageous as it objectively lays out test requirements during the design phase before system implementation begins. A test document can also have benefits during certification & accreditation of the system, which is discussed shortly.

Implementation and Unit Testing

In this phase, developers implement and test the software programs built during the previous design phase. Experienced testers realize that even the best system designs and most competent developers can produce systems with security flaws. The purpose of testing is to identify and correct these flaws before system operation. During unit testing, system testers should ensure that security solutions meet the original requirements. Tests can include both manual and automated code reviews that look for common design flaws and program errors. Some of the more common security flaws include unnecessary design complexity, buffer overflows, or incomplete error handling (Murray, 2001). Some automated tools will assess a piece of code without requiring a complete and integrated application. Thus, coders and testers alike can use tools to pinpoint vulnerabilities at the precise line of code and apply a fix early in the SDLC (Berg, 2006). In higher-risk systems, consideration can be given to hiring an independent agency to objectively and thoroughly conduct unit testing. Finally, testers should take care to use fabricated and not sensitive data in testing environments. For example, using actual social security numbers should be avoided during testing.

It is important to note that during this phase, implementation and testing can be treated as separate phases or can be accomplished concurrently. Either way, cooperation and teamwork between coders and testers will best ensure the correction of identified flaws. To this end, it may be advantageous to use some type of defect reporting and tracking database. Such a tool allows the testing team to enter identified flaws for coders to correct (Jordan, 2006). The tool should identify each flaw and provide a history of the flaw until the corrected code is successfully re-tested. To be thorough, the flaw history should document all retests after each attempt to fix any particular flaw.

Integration and System Testing

During integration, the development team combines individual program units into a total system. Testers then ensure that the completed system meets its intended security requirements. Like unit testing, this process can be iterative as testers find bugs for the development team to correct. The corrected system is then re-tested. Testing can be done using automated tools as well as by manual procedures. Because some security flaws are difficult for humans to find, automated tools are available to assistant testers during the testing phases of the SDLC.

Abuse Cases

A practical approach to system testing involves a process called *abuse cases*, which is a concept derived from *use case* development. Use cases are a behaviorally related sequence of steps for the purpose of completing a single business task or case (Whitten, Bentley, & Dittman, 2000). A use case is not a functional requirement, but instead a story of how users will use the system in their day-to-day activities. An *abuse case* is similar except that developers document ways that the system can be maliciously used. Abuse cases explicitly test for security flaws. For example, the developer can create a series of abuse cases that depict how malicious users can seek to overflow input buffers, insert malicious logic, and penetrate system defenses. Once fielded, the system can be retested against these cases to see if the system is adequately protected (van Wyk & McGraw, 2005).

Certification and Accreditation (C&A)

Completed systems can go through a mandatory C&A assessment that includes a security evaluation of the system against a predetermined set of standards. Certification is the technical evaluation of compliance with security requirements for the purpose of accreditation. Security accreditation is the official management decision given by a senior agency to authorize operation and explicitly accept the risk of an IS based on agreed-upon controls. By accrediting an information system, management accepts responsibility for the system and is accountable for adverse impacts (Hansche et al., 2004). An important C&A milestone can help developers as well as management to focus and maintain a security-aware mindset throughout all phases of the SDLC.

Operation and Maintenance

Once integrated and properly tested, the system is fielded and begins production. This phase includes all of the processes needed to run the system in its operational environment. Some important security aspects include reoccurring user security training as well as user account maintenance and deletion.

Security Response Process

Operational systems still have flaws and a process to correct them should be in place. It may take several revisions before most system errors and security flaws are finally identified and fixed. Some security flaws may not show up for years until after system fielding (Beaver, 2006). Even with a fully certified and accredited information system, software that once was thought to be secure may not be as time passes. New vulnerabilities in the cyber world can introduce unanticipated security problems. For example, newer technologies such as small USB storage devices or a new Internet-based threat can introduce significant new security risks not anticipated in the initial risk assessment. Thus, an established organizational response process is essential for the rapid correction of newly identified errors and vulnerabilities. With a robust process in place, maintainers can quickly attempt to correct and test software flaws when new vulnerabilities surface. Once recertified, the corrected system can then be re-fielded.

Retirement

Some systems may still exhibit unique security risks even when entering the retirement phase. If an organization phases a system out, system administrators may relax security standards as management focuses on developing a replacement system. Yet, if the data in the retiring system is sensitive, administrators must continue to take due care in protecting data. A recent study of computer disks available on the second-hand market indicated that over 50% of the disks examined still contained significant volumes of sensitive information (Jones, Mee, Meyler, & Gooch, 2005). It remains critical that system administrators properly sanitize or dispose of sensitive data when an IS enters the retirement phase.

Dedicated Security Reviews and Audits

In addition to each of the seven phases in our notional model, a series of dedicated security reviews and audits can promote security integration throughout the SDLC. A security review can bring together the entire development team to focus on security. In addition, a security review should not just involve the security team, but all appropriate players on the project. It can be especially valuable to have the most experienced senior team members present at reviews so they can share their knowledge with the entire team. Significant gains can be realized by leveraging the experience of senior members and peers during reviews.

For lower risk systems, a dedicated review may not be necessary but security concerns should still be addressed during periodic system reviews. For higher risk systems, consideration should be given to hiring third-party professionals or consultants as they can provide a more objective review of the system under development (Howard, 2004). For example, an independent third-party team can specifically review the system security design before the implementation phase begins.

Security Considerations: Other Models of System Development

Other approaches to systems development exist that are variations, extensions, or streamlined versions of the notional "waterfall" model. Yet in each case, the same basic security challenge exists: developers can be tempted to push aside security requirements in the name of rapid development and thus fall prey to an "add security later" attitude. Following are a few security considerations for less traditional models of systems analysis and development.

Prototyping

Prototyping involves the rapid development of an early working system, often done using an iterative approach. Prototypes should include the security mechanisms appropriate for the prototype version. If developers delay putting security functionality until a later prototype version, they risk relegating security concerns to an afterthought.

Joint Application Development (JAD)

JAD is a team-based tool for gathering user requirements and creating system designs; it is often used during the earlier stages of the SDLC. With this team approach, it may be advantageous to have at least one member who understands and can articulate the security needs of the proposed system.

Rapid Application Development (RAD)

RAD is similar to a condensed version of the SDLC. RAD also uses a team approach involving users, managers, and IT professionals. The RAD methodology compresses analysis, design, implementation, and test phases into a series of shorter, iterative development cycles. With its stress on rapid, iterative development, security considerations and requirements can get lost without proper security representation on the team.

Extreme Programming (XP)

This is a team-based approach based on rapid prototyping; XP uses an evolving design, daily testing, and integration to design the system. Rather than using longer "traditional" development cycles, XP attempts to blend all SDLC phases, a little at a time, throughout a software development project (Beck, 1999). However, an evolving requirements approach does not necessarily ensure security considerations will be properly implemented into the system. Again, programmers must take care to ensure that security needs are included using this rapid approach.

Systems Assembly from Reusable Components

This process involves more of an assembly of a system from existing parts rather than the creation of a new system. It can be complex because developers need to validate that the individual components are secure before assembling the system. Insecure code with flaws can easily be placed in a reusable software library. Thus, developers should not simply copy code and assume the code is secure.

FUTURE TRENDS

Several key trends that affect the development of secure systems are worthy of mention. Following, three are briefly discussed: outsourcing, litigation, and automated tools.

Outsourcing

In many environments, increased competition has necessitated the hiring of outsourced workers to develop lower cost software. In some instances, requirements analysis and design phases are conducted in a home country while coding-intensive work is outsourced to third parties often located in foreign countries. This trend can make developing secure systems more challenging since outside players are involved in the software development team. Management should carefully evaluate the added risks of outsourcing high-security systems to third parties. If a software development project represents a high-risk to a company, hiring third parties from a foreign country where different laws apply could add unnecessary risk compared to hiring in-country sources.

Litigation

A number of recent legal mandates worldwide have affected the information security field including the Sarbanes-Oxley Act, Gramm-Leach-Bliley Act, California Senate Bill 1386, European Union Data Protection Directive, and the Basel II Accord. The trend is toward greater corporate accountability for security breaches. If insecure software is partially the reason for a costly security incident, the developers of the system may be liable for damages. Thus, due diligence must be exercised when developing systems that process sensitive data (e.g., privileged information), that supports human life (e.g., medical systems), or that protects expensive resources (e.g., climate control software).

Automated Tools

Today, tools are available to support every phase of the SDLC and are often part of a computer aided software engineering (CASE) tool suite. Tools are available for source code management, requirements analysis, requirements traceability, defect and correction tracking, test management, as well as production phases. Not all tools are the same and developers should carefully choose tools to meet the specific needs of a project. If a tool is inappropriate for the task, it can be detrimental to the effort or simply not used by the development team. Fortunately, today one can find a number of available automated tools specifically designed to support the security needs encountered during software development (e.g., Giorgini, Massacci, Mylopoulos, & Zannone, 2005).

CONCLUSION

Considering the importance of cyber security in the modern world, the need to develop secure information systems is critical. In this chapter, emphasis was placed on identifying security risks and documenting requirements as early as possible. In short, developers should document initial requirements and security considerations should remain a priority in each phase of the SDLC. In addition, attention was given toward improving security with automated tools, performing abuse cases, tracing security requirements, holding regular security reviews, conducting certification and accreditation, and developing security response processes. By following these steps, practitioners will be able to improve both the security and the overall quality of computerized information systems.

RESOURCES

Resources are available to guide the development of secure systems. Following is a list of useful documents that can aid information system developers.

1. Systems Security Engineering—Capability Maturity Model (SSE-CMM). Site: http://www.sse-cmm.org
2. NIST Special Publication 800-64—Security Considerations in the Information System Development Life Cycle. Site: http://csrc.nist.gov/publications/nistpubs/
3. NIST Special Publication 800-37—Guide to the Certification and Accreditation of Federal Information Systems. Site: http://csrc.nist.gov/publications/nistpubs/
4. ISO/IEC 17799:2005—Code of Practice for Information Security Management. Site: http://www.iso.org.
5. Microsoft's Security Developer Center and the Trustworthy Computing Security Development Lifecycle. Sites: http://msdn2.microsoft.com/en-us/security or http://msdn.microsoft.com/security/

NOTE

Opinions, conclusions, and recommendations expressed or implied within are solely those of the authors and do not necessarily represent the views of USAF Academy, USAF, the DoD, or any other government agency.

REFERENCES

Ayer, S., & Patrinostro, F. (1992). *Documenting the software development process*. New York: McGraw Hill.

Beaver, K. (2006). *Securing your software development life cycle*. Security Park.net. Retrieved July 28, 2006, from http://www.securitypark.co.uk/article. asp?articleid=25356

Beck, K. (1999). Embracing change with extreme programming. *IEEE Computer, 32*(10), 70-77.

Berg, R. (2006). *Implementing source code vulnerability testing in the software development cycle* (White Paper). Waltham, MA: Ounce Labs.

Bishop, M. (2005). *Introduction to computer security*. New York: Addison-Wesley.

Flechais, I., Sasse, M. A., & Hailes, S. M. V. (2003). *Bringing security home: A process of developing secure and usable systems*. Paper presented at the New Security Paradigms—ACM Workshop, Ascona, Switzerland.

Geer, D. (2002). *Information security: What the markets want and why?* Dartmouth College Institute for Security Technology Studies. Retrieved August 1, 2006, from http://www.ists.dartmouth. edu/speaker_series/geerslides.pdf

Geer, D., Hoo, K. S., Jr., & Jaquity, A. (2003). Information security: Why the future belongs to the quants. *IEEE Security & Privacy, 1*(4), 24-32.

Giorgini, P., Massacci, F., Mylopoulos, J., & Zan-none, N. (2005, September). *St-tool: A CASE tool for security requirements engineering*. Paper presented at the 13th IEEE International Conference on Requirements Engineering.

Hansche, S., Berti, J., & Hare, C. (2004). *Official (ISC)² guide to the CISSP exam*. New York: Auerbach.

Howard, M. (2004). Building more secure software with improved development processes. *IEEE Security & Privacy, 2*(6), 63-65.

Jones, A., Mee, V., Meyler, C., & Gooch, J. (2005). Analysis of data recovered from computer disks released for sale by organizations. *Journal of Information Warfare, 4*(2), 45-53.

Jordan, M. (2006). *Tools for securing the software development lifecycle (webcast presentation)*. Search Security. Retrieved July 27, 2006, from www.searchsecurity.com

Knapp, K. J., Marshall, T. E., Rainer, R. K., Jr., & Morrow, D. W. (2004). *Top ranked information security issues: The 2004 international information systems security certification consortium (ISC)² survey results*. Alabama: Auburn University.

Murray, W. H. (2001). Common system design flaws and security issues. In H. F. Tipton & M. Krause (Eds.), *Info. security management handbook* (Vol. 2, pp. 291-303). Boca Raton, FL: CRC Press.

Ramesh, B., & Jarke, M. (2001). Toward reference models for requirements traceability. *IEEE Transactions on Software Engineering, 27*(1), 58-93.

Royce, W. W. (1970, August). *Managing the development of large software systems*. Paper presented at the IEEE WESCON.

van Wyk, K. R., & McGraw, G. (2005). Bridging the gap between software development and information security. *IEEE Security & Privacy, 3*(5), 75-79.

Whitten, J. L., Bentley, L. D., & Dittman, K. C. (2000). *Systems analysis and design methods* (5th ed.). New York: McGraw-Hill Irwin.

KEY TERMS

Abuse Cases: Special security requirements can be documented in *abuse cases* where the system developers document and test ways that the system can be maliciously used and how it could affect the system. When fielded, the system can then be tested against these abuse cases to see if the system is adequately protected.

Certification and Accreditation (C&A): Completed systems can go through a process that evaluates the security stance of the system against a predetermined set of security standards while also testing how well the system performs its intended functional requirements. After system certification, management then accredits a system, accepts responsibility, and is accountable for adverse impacts.

Extreme Programming (XP): A team-based development approach based on rapid prototyping that uses an evolving design of often daily testing and integration to design the system. Rather than using longer development cycles, XP advocates blending all SDLC phases, a little at a time, throughout a software development project.

Initial Systems Risk Assessment: During the investigation phase of the systems development life cycle, analysts investigate the required security level of a proposed information system. This initial risk assessment should be grounded in the business needs of the system and can be used as a basis for future security decisions.

Joint Application Development (JAD): Introduced by IBM in the 1970s, JAD is an interactive, team-based approach to systems development that uses groups of individuals for collecting user requirements and creating system designs.

Rapid Application Development (RAD): RAD offers a condensed version of the entire development process while emphasizing the use of prototypes and automated tools to help speed up application development. RAD also uses a team approach composed of users, managers, and IT professionals to help complete the project.

Response Process: Once fielded, software that once was thought and even accredited to be secure may not be as secure as time passes. New threats and vulnerabilities in the cyber world can introduce unanticipated security problems. An established organizational response process can help the security team quickly address newly identified threats and vulnerabilities. The corrected system should be re-tested before re-fielded.

Security Requirements Traceability: Requirements traceability is intended to ensure continued alignment between security requirements and various outputs of systems development. Implementing security requirements traceability can help designers identify areas in a developing system that do not meet the documented requirements.

Systems Development Life Cycle (SDLC): The SDLC is a systems approach to developing information systems and is notionally made up of several phases: investigation, requirements analysis, design, implementation, integration, operations, maintenance, and retirement.

System Security Requirements Document: A stand-alone requirements document that gathers the security requirements of a proposed system.

ENDNOTES

[1] For details of the research study, see Knapp, Marshall, Rainer, and Morrow (2004).

[2] For an expanded discussion of managing the development of software systems, see Royce (1970).

Chapter XX
Cognitive Perspective on Human–Computer Interface Design

Robert Z. Zheng
University of Utah, USA

Laura B. Dahl
University of Utah, USA

Jill Flygare
University of Utah, USA

ABSTRACT

This chapter focuses on the design of human-computer interface, particularly the software interface design, by examining the relationship between the functionality and features of the interface and the cognitive factors associated with the design of such interface. A design framework is proposed followed by an empirical study to validate some of the theoretical assumptions of the framework. The findings indicate that learners become more perceptually engaged when a multiple sensory-input interface is used. Our study also shows that building affective interaction at the perceptual level could significantly enhance learners' perceptual engagement which further leads them to cognitive engagement. Guidelines for designing an effective interface are proposed. The significance of the study is discussed with some suggestions for future study.

INTRODUCTION

The advancement of new digital technologies has brought a spectrum of changes in our society, particularly in the areas of education, industry, commerce, government, and so forth. According to a recent study, use of computers and Internet access at school rose from 51% in 1998 to 93% in 2003 (National Center for Education Statistics, 2005). The U.S. Department of Labor 2002-2012 employment projections indicate that 8 of the 10 fastest growing occupations require technological fluency (Bureau of Labor Statistics, 2007). Coupled with this increasing computer technology use is the issue of human-computer interface (HCI) design. Wallace and Sinclair (1995) express their concern about the negative cognitions and attitudes towards technology caused by poorly designed human-computer interface related to both hardware and software. Preece, Rogers, and Sharp (2002) argue that the hardware may work effectively from an engineering perspective but can cause "numerous people immense grief" at the expense of "how system will be used by real people" (p. 1). They called for a systematic study of the human-computer interface that focuses on both hardware and software by examining the human factors pertaining to human-computer interaction.

While the hardware issue is worth attention with regard to the physical interactivity between the user and the computer as well as the impact of such interactivity on the user's information process (Kroemer & Kroemer, 2001; Patterson & Hennessy, 2005), studies on software design and user relations begin to emerge. Numerous studies have been conducted in screening behavior and human cognition (Kearny & Smith, 1999), mental model and computer implementation (Goodwin & Johnson-Laird, 2005), computer-related tasks and human factors (Serenko, 2006), agent-based human-computer interaction (Baylor, 2002, 2004; Moreno & Mayer, 2004), and so forth. There has been a considerable interest in understanding the relationship between human cognition and software interface design. Scholars from computer science and cognitive psychology (Mayer & Moreno, 2003; Norman, 1988; Schneiderman, 1980, 1982) concurred that an appropriately designed software interface can facilitate learners' cognitive information process. For example, Schneiderman's theory of direct manipulation and Mayer and Moreno's principles of multimedia learning design have shown that the learner's ability to process information can be affected by the mode of interactivity where human cognition is intertwined with the design of the computer interface.

So far, most research has mainly focused on the general relationship between human cognition and computer interface, few studies have been done to explore the underlying operational conditions that facilitate the cognitive information process through the computer interface which has been the key subject in the study of software ergonomics. This chapter describes the characteristics of human perceptions, and how such characteristics affect human information process both in short-term memory and long-term memory. Emphases will be made on the idiosyncratic features of the computer interface and the cognitive attributes associated with such features in human information processing.

The purposes of this chapter are:

1. Defining the software interface design by identifying its underlying concepts;
2. Discussing the issues related to software interface design;
3. Presenting related cognitive theories pertinent to effective interface design; and
4. Proposing guidelines for effective software interface design.

COGNITIVE FUNCTIONS AND SOFTWARE INTERFACE DESIGN

Oftentimes, software designers become confused about what users' needs are. Part of this is caused by a lack of understanding of the cognitive functions related to the interface. Sugar (2001) conducted a study on novices who designed hypermedia. He found that the novices had difficulty in fixing the flaws identified by the users based on a usability test. Most novice designers used Band-Aid solutions that merely answered direct, obvious problems but hardly addressed and repaired complex, indirect problems. Sugar's study addressed an important issue that has significant ramifications in human-computer interface design: What is the skill set and knowledge base that are essential for designing an effective software interface?

For many people, the interface design is about the graphics, programming, and the layout of the interface elements. For others, it means to incorporate the patterns of human behavior and cognitive functions into the design of software. A case in point is to design the interface of a calculator that matches the cognitive architectures within the program. Kozma (1994) argues that the cognitive attributes of software can expand a learner's capacity in cognitive learning. For example, the rotational function of an animated 3D program in math and science can help learners understand the abstract concepts, thus improve their learning. Understanding the cognitive functions and how they relate to a cognitive information process is important for effective interface design. Thus, knowledge about the graphics, programming, as well as cognitive functions related to the interface is essential for software designers who want to create usable interfaces that meet the needs of users.

Research shows that cognitive functions such as perception and the ability to formulate external and internal representations are related to interface design (Ziegler, Vossen, & Hoppe, 1990). Human perceptions and cognitive engagement can be affected by the way the interface is designed. For instance, the interface that is text only, or text with images, or images, only can affect the learner's information process differently depending on the cognitive and learning styles of the learner. Therefore, it is critical to examine the cognitive functions (e.g., perceptions, mental representations) in interface design. Likewise, it is important to understand the role of interface components (e.g., modality, locus of control) and how they can be optimally designed to promote cognitive functions in learning.

HUMAN PERCEPTIONS AND INTERFACE

Software interface design refers to the design of software applications with a focus on the user's experience and interaction. It involves both the external and internal representations of learning objects. The external representation includes the interface layout of a software application, the multimodal information delivery, and so forth. The internal representation refers to the cognitive architectures that simulate human cognitive process in learning. Schneiderman (1980) defines the study of software interface design as something that "applies the techniques of experimental psychology and the concepts of cognitive psychology to the problems of computer and information science" (p. 3).

It is believed that human-computer interaction is largely influenced by the user's perceptual abilities which include the range of visibility, perceptual focus, attention, and so forth. These abilities are further affected by the design elements embedded in the interface, that is, color, text size, text/graphic ratio, and others (Blake & Sekuler, 2006). Blake and Sekuler point out that perception is a biological process that "provides us with a useful view of the world, where useful means being able to interact safely and effectively within our environment" (p. 1). In a human-computer environment, this means focusing on the important information and ignoring the irrelevant. What is it that influences the choice of perception? According to Blake and Sekuler, four interfaces have critically influenced the choice of perception. They include (a) constructive, (b) contextual, (c) interpretative, and (d) synchronizing interfaces (Figure 1).

Constructive Interface

From an interface design perspective, the user's ability to construct meaning is determined by the visual elements that create "the constructive nature of visual perception" (Blake & Sekuler, 2006, p. 111). In other words, the visual interface should allow the brain to go beyond the optical information provided by the eye and generate plausible interpretations. Panel A of Figure 1 underscores the constructive nature of visual perception by providing an illusory figure (e.g., triangle) that the user is be able to construct. Studies show that constructing or making meaning via visual elements in the interface can enhance users' engagement with the software (Hyerle, 1996).

Contextual Interface

One of the key principles in software interface design is to provide meaningful context for users to engage in meaningful interaction (Preece et al., 2002). Blake and Sekuler (2006) state that the brain does not concentrate on individual features in isolation but, instead, exploits relationships among features as contextual clues about how those features ought to be knitted together. In panel B of Figure 1, the faces of the hexagon cone at the top of the panel have been embedded in the whole hexagon cone below. The user does not fully understand the use of the segment of the hexagon faces until they become part of the entire hexagon figure. Blake and Sekuler thus argue that meaningful perception occurs when the part is perceived as relevant to a whole object.

Interpretative Interface

The notion of interpretative interface originates from the concept of the relativity of human perception. Human perception can fluctuate between alternatives when an ambiguous interface is presented. For example, Panel C of Figure 1 entails multiple interpretations that the user probably has trouble deciding what the user sees. At one moment the

figure appears to be a chess trophy against a white background but then, without warning, it turns into a pair of white faces looking at each other against a mahogany background. Researchers caution that interpretative interface can lead to confusion and misinterpretation of the purpose of the interface. It is suggested that the interface design should minimize ambiguity and reduce the chance of multiple interpretations from the user.

Synthetic Interface

The synthetic interface refers to the user's ability to piece bits of information together to form a perception of what is initially considered indecipherable. Panel D of Figure 1 looks like a collection of black splotches. To make sense of this picture, your visual system must synthesize contour and texture information gathered from a large portion of the picture, and try to figure out which pieces of the image go together. The human ability to visually synthesize clues from a seemingly random collection of splotches proves that visual perception depends on more than just the pattern of light striking the retina. Perception, rather than being a mindless process of measuring how much light enters the eye, is an intelligent activity of a finely tuned brain. Understanding human ability to visually synthesize information enables the designer to design an engaging software interface that facilitates higher level thinking such as pattern recognition and information synthesis.

Figure 1. Meaningful perceptual determinants for constructive, contextual, interpretative and synthetic interfaces

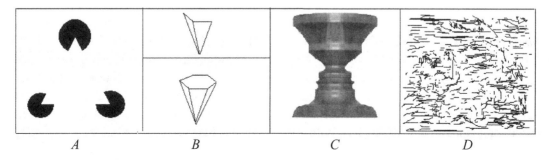

A   *B*   *C*   *D*

BEYOND THE INTERFACE: MENTAL REPRESENTATIONS

As part of the human cognitive process, perception provides critical information for cognitive information processing. However, information derived from perceptions can sometimes be insufficient in terms of deep mental operation. For example, text-based input can cause problems for visual users to form a mental representation of the external object because such users often rely on visual forms to help externalize the abstract concepts in the text. Thus, the effects of interface can be mitigated if the user's ability to create a mental representation of the external object is compromised due to the limitation to a particular type of perceptual interface. In other words, the user may not be able to process information effectively if there is a discrepancy between user's cognitive style and the interface presented. In the last two decades there has been an increasing interest in designing cognitively functional interface (Schneiderman, 2005). Two theories have played contributing roles toward designing cognitively functional human-computer interface. They are (a) dual coding theory and (b) cognitive load theory.

Dual Coding Theory

Paivio (1986) suggested that the input information is processed through multiple sensory channels. For example, the verbal information is registered through the verbal channel whereas the nonverbal information such as images is registered through the nonverbal channel. According to dual coding theory, there are three levels of processing pertaining to incoming verbal and nonverbal information: representational, associative, and referential. The representational process refers to the connections between the external object and internal representation of the object. The associative process means the activation of the information stored within the long-term memory. Depending on the input stimuli, the activation process can be either in the verbal

or nonverbal (e.g., visual) system. The referential process is the cross-reference process between the verbal and nonverbal systems. Research on dual coding practices suggests that pictures can be coded both visually and verbally, whereas words are believed to be far less likely to be coded visually (Paivio, 1991; Rieber, 1994).

Mayer and Sims (1994) examined the effects of text (monosensory mode) vs. multimedia (multiple sensory mode) on learners' ability to solve problems. They found that instructions with multimedia facilitate learners' comprehension and knowledge transfer. They concluded that multiple sensory inputs such as multimedia enable learners to construct meaning more effectively than does the monosensory input.

Cognitive Load Theory

Although dual coding theory describes the cognitive process in terms of information encoding, it fails to address a very important issue in information process, that is, the human capacity to handle incoming information. In other words, how much incoming information should be delivered at the moment of learning? What is the optimal way to deliver the information so that the learner can efficiently encode the incoming information?

Studies show that working memory is very limited in both duration and capacity. Van Merrienboer and Sweller (2005) observe that working memory stores about seven elements but normally operates on only two or three elements. They also find that working memory can deal with information "for no more than a few seconds with almost all information lost after about 20 seconds unless it is refreshed by rehearsal" (p. 148). When working memory becomes overloaded with information, learning can be adversely affected (Paas, Tuovinen, Tabbers, & Gerven, 2003; Sweller & Chandler, 1994; Marcus, Cooper, & Sweller, 1996). According to the cognitive load theory (CLT), three types of cognitive load exist: *intrinsic load*, *extraneous* or *ineffective load*, and *germane* or *effective load*.

The intrinsic cognitive load refers to a cognitive load that is induced by the structure and complexity of the instructional material. Usually, teachers or instructional designers can do little to influence the intrinsic cognitive load. The extraneous cognitive load is referred to the cognitive load caused by the format and manner in which information is presented. For example, teachers may unwittingly increase a learner's extraneous cognitive load by presenting materials that "require students to mentally integrate mutually referring, disparate sources of information" (Sweller & Chandler, 1991, p.353). Finally, the germane cognitive load refers to a cognitive load that is induced by learners' efforts to process and comprehend the material. The goal of CLT is to increase this type of cognitive load so that the learner can have more cognitive resources available to solve problems (Brunken, Plass, & Leutner, 2003; Marcus et al., 1996).

Relationship between Intrinsic and Extraneous Load

The difficulty of a subject area is determined by both the number of elements that must be learned and the extent to which they interact. According to Sweller and Chandler (1994), the cognitive load imposed by the intrinsic nature of the material is determined solely by element interactivity, not by the total number of elements that must be assimilated. For instance, in science learning the learner not only must learn the concepts but also must understand the relationship between the concepts. The cognitive load associated with learning the concepts is low because the elements of the materials to be learned do not interact with each other whereas the cognitive load involved in learning the relationship between the concepts can be high because the learning not only taxes our limited processing ability but also our ability to assimilate large amounts of information into long-term memory over relatively short periods (Lee, Plass, & Homer, 2006). Sweller and Chandler (1994) point out that materials with a high degree of interactivity that would impose high

intrinsic cognitive load are particularly susceptible to any extraneous cognitive load imposed by the manner of presentation. The extraneous cognitive load is imposed purely because of the design and organization of the learning materials rather than the intrinsic nature of the task. However, if the intrinsic element interactivity and consequent cognitive load is low, the extraneous cognitive load caused by instructional design may not be very important. In contrast, extraneous cognitive load is critical when dealing with intrinsically high element interactivity materials (Sweller & Chandler, 1991, 1994).

The cognitive load theory has been widely adopted in the design of instruction, particularly in the learner-interface design. Efforts have been made to facilitate the user's mental representation in learning by designing interfaces that would reduce the cognitive load. Opfermann, Gerjets, and Scheiter (2007) studied the media effects and cognitive load in a hypermedia environment and found that the hypermedia interactive interface provides better learner control and is conducive to prior knowledge activation, which would help reduce both intrinsic and extraneous cognitive load in learning. Opfermann et al.'s findings concurred with the study by Lee et al. (2006) who found the use of optimized visual displays promoted comprehension and transfer, especially for low prior-knowledge learners.

DESIGNING COGNITIVELY FUNCTIONAL INTERFACE

As it was discussed above, the problems with the design of perceptual interfaces is that the input information from the perceptual interfaces does not necessarily facilitate information processing at a deeper level. For example, a contextual interface with monosensory input may hinder the user's information process as the information process in contextual interface depends on multiple perspectives and clues. Likewise, the user may have difficulty constructing an external representation in mind when the information presented in Panel A of Figure 1 is delivered text only. The distributed cognition theory (Hitchins, 1995) posits that cognitive process is a sharing and interacting process that includes both external and internal representations. When the external representation is conveyed through perceptions, the executive control systems in the brain respond by activating prior knowledge, connecting it with the input information to form an internal representation of the external representation. Comprehension occurs when there is a meaningful connection between the external and internal representations. Conversely, the user's ability to comprehend can be affected if the connection between external and internal representations deteriorates due to, for example, a cognitive overload. There are several issues related to interface design that have affected the use and application of software.

Issues in Software Interface Design

A major challenge for interface designers is to design and develop applications that engage users in various tasks efficiently. A review of the relevant literature revealed that interface control, cognitive overload, poor interactivity, and lack of flexibility are among the key issues that continue to affect the design of effective interface (Dix, Roselli, & Sutinen, 2006; Laurel, Oren, & Don, 1990; Teege, Kahler, & Stiemerling, 1999).

System Control vs. Learner Control

There has been a considerable debate on whether the interface should be system-controlled or learner-controlled (Kay, 2001; Laurel et al., 1990; Sedig, Klawe, & Westrom, 2001; Teege et al., 1999). Teege et al. concluded that the system control approach, that is, the learner followed a sequence of steps defined by the system, can limit users' creative and innovative thinking. Kay (2001) cautions that the system control approach could result in low interactivity and lack of flexibility in interface design. He

argues that the design of software interface should "give the learner greater responsibility and control over all aspects of the learning" (p. 111). Sedig et al. (2001) suggest that a balanced approach should be taken. They pointed out that learner control and system control were inextricably coupled. While allowing some degree of learner control, an instructional source must be capable of certain system control, including taking learner input, assessing learner performances, providing appropriate feedback, adapting to changing needs, and advancing the learner in the right direction.

The above issue can be best understood in light of recent development in *agent-based* learning environments (Baylor, 2002, 2004; Moreno & Mayer, 2004). Agent-based design consists of dynamically interacting rule-based agents. The systems within which they interact can therefore create complexity like that which we see in the real world. Moreno and Mayer conducted a research on teaching science through an agent-based multimedia game. The subjects were self-initiated to design the roots, stem, and leaves of plants to survive in five different virtual environments. While they were given full learner control in terms of selecting a natural environment and designing trees to survive in the natural environment, the subjects were guided by a built-in control system called agent who gave advice on a range of topics from soil selection to the DNA structure of trees. Thus, Moreno and Mayer's research proposed a system control of knowledge acquisition while giving full learner control to the use of the knowledge after it has been acquired. Parallel with this effort is Baylor's (2002, 2004) multiple intelligent mentors instructing collaboratively (MIMIC) system which uses agent-based computer environments to help preservice teachers apply educational theories to their design of instruction. The agent in MIMIC system represents a particular educational theorist, such as Piaget. Preservice teachers can select one or several agents for their lessons. The agent will provide feedback based on the lesson presented and advise the preservice if his/her lesson fits well with the theory as represented by the agent. The system significantly enhanced preservice teachers' understanding of the educational theories as well as their ability to apply those theories to their teaching and learning. The MIMIC system takes an eclectic approach by allowing both learner and system controls in learning the educational theories.

The balance between system control and learner control is important in the human-computer interface design (Baylor, 2002, 2004; Sedig et al., 2001). Baylor (2004) identifies four dimensions of learner/system control in the design of agent-based computer environment: the first dimension of control involves instantiating the "instructional purpose" of the environment on a constructivist (high learner control) to instructivist (high program/*agent* control) continuum; the second dimension entails managing "feedback," involving issues of type, timing, amount, explicitness, and potential for learner choice; the third dimension involves the desired "relationship" of the learner to *agent*(s) (e.g., *agent* as learning companion, *agent* as mentor, multiple pedagogical *agents,* or *agent* as personal assistant); and the fourth dimension defines the degree of agent control in which the learner would develop "confidence" in the *agent*(s) in terms of believability, competence, and trust. Perceivably, the four dimension framework proposed by Baylor reflects a balanced approach toward human-computer design with regard to system and learner control. As the agent-based design has become increasingly prominent in computer assisted instruction (CAI), the framework provides instructional and software designers with a practical guidance that can be used to identify and drive decision-making processes that occur during the design and development of instruction.

Cognitive Overload

The issue of cognitive overload has been of much concern to both researchers and designers. Laurel et al. (1990) found that inappropriately designed interface can cause cognitive overload which would further affect the learner's comprehension, understanding, and the ability to learn or solve problems. Davis and Bostrom (1993) points out that the cognitive overload issue may be related to the interface design, such as presentation modes (i.e., monosensory vs. multiple sensory modes), the application retrieval system (i.e., recall vs. recognition), and so forth.

Factors Related to Effective Human-Computer Interface

Research has shown that factors such as direct manipulation, flexibility, cognitive architectures, and so forth are important in creating effective human-computer interface (Byrne, 2003; Schneiderman, 2005; Stiemerling, Kahler, & Wulf, 1997). In this chapter we focus on direct manipulation, flexibility, and cognitive architectures which we believe are particularly relevant to the cognitive aspects of interface design.

Direct Manipulation

Schneiderman (1982) suggests that the interface design should allow the user to directly manipulate objects presented to them, using actions that correspond at least loosely to the physical world. Schneiderman's theory of direct manipulation emphasizes manipulation through sensory perceptions including visual, auditory, haptic, and others. Direct manipulation employs real-world metaphors for objects and actions which make it easier for a user to learn and use an interface. Additionally, rapid, incremental feedback allows a user to make fewer errors and complete tasks in less time, because they can see the results of an action before completing the action (Iwata, 2003; Preece at al., 2002). Direct manipulation recognizes the role of both external and internal representations in the cognitive process. It facilitates information process through multiple sensory channels, the notion of which has been supported by several cognitive theories discussed above.

Flexibility

Flexibility in software interface design entails a broad conceptual framework that "concerns not the regular procedures and standard way of doing things but the unexpected, unprecedented, the exceptional cases, situations and events" (Stiemerling et al., 1997, p. 367). According to Stiemerling et al (1997), flexibility means (a) aligning a human cognitive profile with the cognitive architecture and (b) meeting dynamically evolving and differentiated requirements. Designing an interface that aligns a human cognitive profile with the cognitive architecture means the designer needs to take into consideration how users' cognitive and learning styles (e.g., auditory, visual, logical, etc.) can be matched with the cognitive architectures (i.e., the logical algorithm of cognitive thinking) in the software. For example, the interface design of a calculator requires a thorough understanding of the cognitive architecture within the program of the calculator, that is, the steps that simulate how humans calculate numbers, as well as an elaborative thinking on how the interface would support users with different cognitive and learning styles. That is, all users, visual or auditory, would be able to perform the calculation with the same efficiency.

Building flexibility into interface design also means to dynamically meet various requirements of the user. It requires the interface to be designed in a way that the user can, for example, select and combine multiple fields, control the level of difficulty, transfer files through multiple platforms, and so forth. Stiemerling et al (1997) note that allowing users to select levels of difficulty in tasks or providing the option of combining multiple fields in information search, for example, can enhance users' ability to engage in complex learning and promote skills in both well-structured and ill-structured problem solving.

Cognitive Architectures

The concept of cognitive architecture originates from cognitive science related to the early days of cognitive psychology and artificial intelligence, as manifested in the general problem solver (Newell & Simon, 1963), one of the first successful computational cognitive models. However, cognitive architectures differ from traditional research in psychology in that work on cognitive architecture is integrative. That is, they include attention, memory, problem solving, decision making, learning, and so on (Byrne, 2003). The notion of cognitive architecture has been widely used in the gaming, intelligent tutorials, and the like. Cognitive architectures have been identified and integrated in the design of programming. For instance, in designing a math problem solving tutorial, the cognitive algorithm related to math problem solving should be identified, followed by an analysis of the sequence of behaviors to successfully carry out the math problem solving. The computational model of math problem solving thus reflects the structure of human cognition and a specific domain of knowledge. The cognitive architectures can be integrated in programs that help users perform simple calculations, make quantitative predictions, and so on. Designing interfaces that optimize human performance with the cognitive architecture in the program is one of the endeavors pursued by aspiring interface designers.

A FRAMEWORK FOR SOFTWARE INTERFACE DESIGN

In this section of the chapter we would like to propose a framework for effective interface design. Having identified various factors related to interface and information processing, we would go further to explore the commonality among the variability in terms of interface design. Our approach would be to use Wang and Gearhart's (2006) research as a basis to develop our framework of effective interface design.

The concept of interaction has been much studied in the areas of general learning, counseling, and other fields including interface design. Wang and Gearhart (2006) identify three dimensions of interaction, namely, cognitive, affective, and social interactions.

Cognitive Interaction

The cognitive interaction means cognitive engagement through interactive approaches such as providing informative feedback to learners. Wang and Gearhart (2006) assert that informative feedback can help reveal gaps or inconsistencies in users' existing knowledge and prompt them to refine their understanding and acquire new knowledge.

Affective Interaction

The affective interaction means the user becomes motivated and engaged in what the user is doing. Research shows that motivation is influenced by several factors including the aesthetic appeal, relevance, usability, and self-efficacy related to learning and performance (Naquin & Holton, 2002; Teo, Lim, & Lai, 1999). The difference between cognitive interaction and affective interaction is that the former shows a cognitive engagement whereas the latter displays an emotional attachment.

Social Interaction

Social interaction is a continuous interaction between the user and what surrounds the user. Research shows that meaningful learning occurs where a socially organized environment is supported (Salomon, 1981; Vygotsky, 1978). Social interaction promotes both cognitive and affective development.

According to Wang and Gearhart (2006), two levels of information processes exist; they are perceptual and conceptual information processes. The perceptual information process refers to the initial interaction with the interface where the information is processed through sensory channel(s) whereas the conceptual information process refers to cognitive engagement with the content after the initial perceptual information is completed.

Wang and Gearhart's work provides a common ground for lining up various factors identified in the previous section. For example, many operational concepts related to interface design such as direct manipulation, flexibility, and cognitive architectures can be subsumed under the construct of cognitive interaction. Additionally, the cognitive factors such as cognitive load discussed above can be related to cognitive interaction as well as social interaction as we examine social and behavioral patterns in a human-computer interface environment. In short, Wang and Gearhart's categorization of human interaction and levels of information processes is relevant to the interface design. Based on their work, we propose a framework for effective interface design by crisscrossing the levels of information processes (i.e., perceptual and conceptual) with the types of access (i.e., interface and content) in terms of the interactions described in Wang and Gearhart's study. Figure 2 shows a matrix that illustrates the relationship between perceptual-conceptual and interface-content in design.

The above perceptual-conceptual and interface-content matrix presents a framework that identifies the relationship between information process and access as users engage in various interactions with the interface. A detailed description of the relationships follows.

Perceptual-Interface Relationship

The perceptual-interface relationship emphasizes a sensory information process and its relations with the interface. The perceptual-interface relationship occurs when the user first accesses the interface through sensory channels. The user's perceptions could be influenced by the aesthetic appeals of the interface and the mode presented (i.e., mono vs. multimodal interface). The affective and, in some cases, social interactions are the primary forms of interaction for the perceptual-interface relationship.

Perceptual-Content Relationship

As the initial sensory information is processed through the working memory, the user becomes cognitively engaged, trying to make sense of the new information by connecting it with prior knowledge. However, the information received through the sensory channels can become less useful if the user becomes cognitively overloaded by the input information due to an inappropriate delivery of information, such as presenting through a mono-sensory channel. Other issues such as lack of flexibility and feedback can hamper users' information process as well. The primary mode of interaction in the perceptual-content relationship is cognitive interaction between the user and the content. However, affective and perhaps social interactions are still possible and may continue to influence the user at this stage.

Conceptual-Content Relationship

The conceptual-content relationship reflects users' cognitive engagement with the content. Such engagement is marked by a high adaptation of the interface to users' learning and cognitive style. The cognitive interaction is the predominant mode of interaction with social interaction being used in some situation. The affective interaction is possible but less essential at this stage.

It should be noted that there is no conceptual-interface relationship because cognitive engagement occurs after the initial perception. The cognitive activity of conceptualization takes place where there is the content. Initial perceptions at the interface level are essentially guided by the impression that is based more on aesthetic appeals or values than cognitive conceptualization.

The above framework identified the relationship between information process and access in terms of cognitive, affective, and social interactions. It is a descriptive approach that emphasizes the components rather than the algorithm of interface design. The following study is an example of applying the framework to design an effective interface.

Figure 2. The perceptual-conceptual and interface-content matrix

Levels of info. processes Types of access	Perceptual	Conceptual
Interface	Interaction: • Affective Interaction • Social Interaction Design • Aesthetic appeals • Mode	
Content	Interaction: • Cognitive interaction • Affective Interaction • Social Interaction Design • Mode • Flexibility • Feedback	Interaction: • Cognitive Interaction • Social Interaction • Affective Interaction Design • Adapting to users' learning and cognitive styles

A STUDY: EFFECTS OF INTERFACES ON LEARNERS' PROBLEM-SOLVING ABILITIES, COGNITIVE LOAD, AND SELF-EFFICACY

The purpose of the study was to investigate whether using different interfaces would affect learners' ability to solve problems, their cognitive load, self-efficacy, and spatial ability in problem solving. The perceptual-conceptual and interface-content framework was used to identify the levels of information processes and the types of access.

Interface Design

The focus of the interface design was to help learners efficiently solve a particular type of problems: the multiple rule-based problem which is characterized by a high intrinsic cognitive load. A detailed discussion of the multiple rule-based problems is presented in the next section. According to Sweller and Chandler (1991, 1994), extraneous cognitive load is critical when dealing with intrinsically high element interactivity materials. Using Mayer's (2001) principle of contiguity in multimedia design, we made the problems and questions along with the pictures in the same screen to reduce extraneous cognitive load in learning. That is, learners did not have to mentally assimilate information from different places (i.e., separate computer screens) to solve problems. To test whether using different instructional mode would engage learners' cognitive engagement differently, two versions of interfaces were created: interactive multimedia and noninteractive multimedia with the assumption that the interactive multimedia interface would be more effective than the noninteractive multimedia interface in terms of cognitive load reduction, self-efficacy, and problem-solving skills.

The Study

The study was conducted during the fall of 2005 and the spring of 2006. Two hundred and twenty-two participants were recruited from three universities that included a large urban university and a private university in the northeastern region of the United States, and a midsize teaching university in the south. Of 222 participants, 32% ($n = 72$) were males and 68% ($n = 150$) were females. Approximately 87% ($n = 194$) were Caucasian and 13% ($n = 28$) were nonwhite. Participants varied in age from 19 to 57 years old, with a mean of 24 ($SD = 7.33$).

Instrumentation

Four instruments were used to measure (a) students' self-efficacy, (b) problem solving skills, (c) spatial ability, and (d) cognitive load involved in the problem solving. They include self-and task perception questionnaire (STPQ) scales, multimedia problem-solving tasks (MPSTs), and cognitive load questionnaire (CLQ).

Self-and task perception questionnaire (STPQ) scales. The STPQ scales was originally developed by Lodewyk et al. (2005) who reported internal consistency reliability coefficients before and after each task ranged from .72 to .92. The instrument was adapted for the study with the permission of the original authors. Changes were made to better fit the purpose of this study. For example, the statement "Knowing the difficulty of this project, the teacher, and my skills, I think I will do well on this project" was changed to "Knowing my skills and abilities, I think I will do well on problem solving." The instrument consisted of seven statements including: (a) Knowing my skills and abilities, I think I will do well on problem solving; (b) I expect to do well on problem solving; (c) I believe I will attain a high score on problem solving; (e) I'm confident I will gain the basic skills for problem solving; (f) I'm certain I have the skills necessary for problem solving; (g) I'm confident I will understand the most difficult problems; and

(h) I know which mental techniques would be the best for this problem solving. Participants reported answers on a 5-point Likert scale ranging from strongly disagree (1) to strongly agree (5). The total possible score one could obtain on the test was 35 points.

Multimedia problem-solving tasks (MPSTs). The problem solving tasks were developed by the first author using Flash MX, Adobe Photoshop, and Microsoft Active Server Page (ASP). The MPSTs were composed of six multiple-rule based problems that included: Air Traffic Control, Tower of Hanoi, Sailing Boat, Seating Arrangement, Taking Pictures, and Office Inspection. Each task consisted of two parts, that is, (a) a problem presented with text format along with a visual presentation (either interactive or noninteractive), and (b) multiple choice questions. The problem included a description of a problem situation and several mutually restricting conditions. The subject had to consider these conditions simultaneously before a solution could be reached. For example, Task 5, *Taking Pictures,* had a set of conditions that restricted the order of the individuals who could stand next to each other. The subject had to consider all the conditions and then decided the order in which individuals could take pictures without violating the conditions.

Two versions of a multimedia task interface were created: interactive and noninteractive. In the interactive multimedia interface, subjects were able to manipulate and move important components of the image (e.g., individuals). In the noninteractive multimedia interface, subjects were given a static visual representation of each problem. For each problem, subjects were asked to answer two questions that measured the subject's problem solving skills. After completing the two questions, the subject clicked the submit button. A timer recorded the start and the end of the response time for each set of two questions. The total possible score one could obtain on the test was 12 points.

Spatial orientation questionnaire (SOQ). The SOQ was developed by the first author. To meet the assumption of construct validity, the instrument was developed based on the theoretical constructs identified in the literature (e.g., Dermen, 1976; Gilford & Zimmerman, 1956; NewCombe & Huttenlocher, 2000). A three-item questionnaire was developed which consisted of (a) I have a good sense of direction, (b) I am a visual person, and (c) I am a hands-on person, with a Likert scale ranging from strongly disagree (1) to strongly agree (5). The questions were reviewed by a group of three panelists who were professors in educational psychology. The Cronbach's reliability test was conducted which reported an internal consistency reliability coefficients of .72. The total possible score one could obtain on the test was 15 points.

Cognitive load questionnaire (CLQ). The CLQ was a three item questionnaire developed by Homer, Plass, and Blake (2005). Changes were made to better fit the purpose of the study. The first item was the statement "In solving the preceding problems I invested" with a 9-point Likert scale ranging from *very low mental effort* (1) to *very high mental effort* (9). The second item included a statement of "I experienced the foregoing problem solving as" with a 9-point Likert scale ranging from *not difficult at all* (1) to *very difficult* (9). The third item was the question "How easy or difficult was the problem solving to understand?" with a 7-point Likert scale that ranged from *very easy* (1) to *very difficult* (7). The total possible score one could obtain on the test was 25 points.

Procedures

A randomization procedure was used to divide subjects into two groups: interactive and noninteractive multimedia interface applications. The subjects were given the URL to logon to the problem solving Web site. They were asked to complete a self-efficacy pretest, fill out a demographic information sheet, and then work on the MPSTs problem solving tasks. The subjects in the interactive multimedia group were able to move the figures to help solve problems whereas the subjects in the noninteractive multimedia group were provided with the same graphic except that they were not able to move the figures. None of the groups were allowed to use paper and pencil during their problem solving test. After finishing the MPSTs test, they were asked to fill out a cognitive load questionnaire and complete the self-efficacy posttest. It took about an hour and half for the subject to complete the entire experiment. Each participant was given a consent form to sign before each participant participated in the study.

Results and Analysis

The data analyses were performed with SPSS version 14. The correlation analysis and the independent samples t-test analyses were employed to analyze the relationship among the variables and determine whether the interface mode affected such variables as cognitive load, self-efficacy, spatial ability, and learners' performance in problem solving.

A correlation analysis was conducted by entering the variables of performance scores, cognitive load, spatial ability, and change in self-efficacy and interface mode. The results show that the interface modality was correlated significantly with the change in self-efficacy ($r = -.506, p < .01$), cognitive load ($r = -.581, p < .01$), and performance ($r = -.732, p < .01$). The change in self-efficacy was found to be significantly correlated with the cognitive load ($r = -.253, p < .01$) and performance ($r = .355, p < .01$). Finally, the cognitive load was significantly correlated with the performance ($r = -.466, p < .01$) (Table 1).

The independent samples t-test was performed to find out if there were differences between interactive and noninteractive interface modes with regard to learners' cognitive load, problem solving, and self-efficacy. Significant differences were found between the interactive interface mode and the noninteractive interface mode in learners' self-efficacy ($t(2, 220) = 8.701, p < .01$), cognitive load

($t(2, 220) = -10.585, p < .01$), and the performance ($t(2, 220) = 15.959, p < .01$) (Table 2).

Discussion

The results of the study indicated that the interface mode was significantly correlated with the change in self-efficacy, the cognitive load, and the performance in learning. Students who studied with the interactive multimedia interface mode had a higher self-efficacy, lower cognitive load, and better performance results than did their counterparts who learned with the noninteractive multimedia interface mode. The findings concurred with the literature that the multimodal interactive mode can reduce learners' cognitive load, thus improve their self-efficacy and performance in academic study (Mayer & Moreno, 2003; Zheng, Miller, Snelbecker, & Cohen, 2006).

The study supported the perceptual-conceptual and interface-content framework that learners' affective interaction played an important role for taking students further to cognitive interaction. The interactive multimedia interface, which has the advantage of engaging students in haptic learning and enabling them to process information through multiple sensory channels, provides the opportunity for effective student cognitive engagement by reducing learners' cognitive load, and consequently, enhances their self-efficacy in learning as well as academic performance.

GUIDELINES FOR EFFECTIVE SOFTWARE INTERFACE DESIGN

Learners' initial perception of the software interface is critical in that it can influence learners' further engagement with the software. The concept of initial perception has a broad connotation which refers to not only the aesthetical aspects of the design but also the functionality of application. For example, if an application has an appealing interface but requires considerable mental effort to process the

Table 1. Correlations among the variables

Correlations

		Change in				Interface
Change in self efficacy	Pearson Correlation	1	-.253**	.355**	-.069	-.506**
	Sig. (2-tailed)		.000	.000	.308	.000
	N	222	222	222	222	222
Cognitive load	Pearson Correlation	-.253**	1	-.466**	.053	.581**
	Sig. (2-tailed)	.000		.000	.436	.000
	N	222	222	222	222	222
Performance	Pearson Correlation	.355**	-.466**	1	-.024	-.732**
	Sig. (2-tailed)	.000	.000		.721	.000
	N	222	222	222	222	222
Spatialilty	Pearson Correlation	-.069	.053	-.024	1	-.042
	Sig. (2-tailed)	.308	.436	.721		.530
	N	222	222	222	222	222
Interface Modality	Pearson Correlation	-.506**	.581**	-.732**	-.042	1
	Sig. (2-tailed)	.000	.000	.000	.530	
	N	222	222	222	222	222

**. Correlation is significant at the 0.01 level (2-tailed).

information, then the chances are the learner will either become frustrated or turn away from the application to look for other alternatives.

As it was previously discussed, factors such as cognitive load, learner characteristics, locus of control, and so on can influence learners' information process and cognitive engagement. The perceptual-conceptual and interface-content framework was proposed here as an approach that can help improve and enhance the design of effective software interface. Although the framework cannot be expected to address all aspects of the issues in interface design, it can help designers to identify the critical elements in design by examining the cognitive, affective, and social interactions involved in human-computer interaction. Here are some general guidelines to consider:

1. The interface design should reach a balance between the beauty and the functionality of the software application. It should put in perspective such factors as the aesthetic appeal of the interface and the efficiency in information process.

2. The interface design at the perceptual level should facilitate the affective interaction in which the user feels connected and promoted to further cognitive engagement.

3. The interface design at conceptual level should allow flexibility with which the learner is able to control the levels of difficulty, range of the subject, and the mode of information process.

4. The interface design should facilitate, wherever possible, social interaction in which the cognitive process is distributed between learners and learners, and between learners and software application.

5. Following user interaction with interface design, designers should update and/or change any part of the interface that does not meet the above guidelines from user perspective.

CONCLUSION

This chapter focuses on the design of human-computer interface, particularly the software interface design, by identifying the factors that are critical to the design process. The factors can be subsumed under three categories: (1) functionality, which includes interaction dimensions, interface-content relationship, and levels of information process, and (2) cognition, which includes cognitive load, learner characteristics, and learning styles. They collectively contribute to the design of an effective interface, and (3) features which include the interface mode, such as using multiple sensory inputs, and locus of control, such as allowing learner or system control.

A design framework was proposed to examine the perceptual-conceptual and interface-content relationships in interface design. Our study suggested that the user's perceptions of an interface were influenced by the features as well as the functionality of the interface. The findings of our study indicated that learners became more perceptually engaged when they were exposed to the interface with multiple sensory inputs. Our study also showed that building affective interaction at the perceptual level can significantly enhance learners' perceptual engagement.

This study confirms research in cognitive performance and distributed cognitions that tools can influence human condition to think along a particular path (Sedig et al., 2001). The study highlights the need for understanding the cognitive engagement and the components that support the learner's cognitive interaction with the interface. The results suggested that cognitive load, spatial ability, and so forth could influence learners' self-efficacy and achievement in learning. Therefore, it is suggested that the software interface design should examine the cognitive factors and the impact it has on learners' learning to design interfaces that promote effective learning.

The chapter is significant at both practical and theoretical levels. Theoretically, it contributes to the understanding of the cognitive effects in human-computer interaction by identifying the relationship between cognitive factors and interface design. The perceptual-conceptual and interface-content framework has a theoretical significance as it delineates the relationships between interface and content, and between perceptual and conceptual information processes in terms of the three interaction dimensions. Practically, the chapter presents a new approach toward interface design by putting in perspective the cognitive and functional aspects in the design process. The framework proposed in

Table 2. Independent samples t-test

Independent Samples Test

		Levene's Test for					Mean	Std. Erro	95% Confidence Interval of the	
Change in self effi	Equal variance assumed	55.367	.000	8.701	220	.000	4.615	.530	3.570	5.660
	Equal variance not assumed			8.869	152.88	.000	4.615	.520	3.587	5.643
Cognitive load	Equal variance assumed	3.540	.061	-10.58	220	.000	-5.4278	.51277	-6.4384	-4.4173
	Equal variance not assumed			-10.51	203.12	.000	-5.4278	.51606	-6.4453	-4.4103
Performance	Equal variance assumed	.050	.823	15.959	220	.000	4.0058	.25101	3.5111	4.5005
	Equal variance not assumed			16.001	219.59	.000	4.0058	.25035	3.5124	4.4992

this chapter can help teachers, designers, and other related professionals to design and develop an effective human-computer interface.

Future research should apply the design framework to a larger population with more diverse background to validate the generalizability of the framework in other subject areas. Further research is needed to find out the impact of other cognitive traits such as field dependent vs. field independent on the use of and design in interface.

REFERENCES

Baylor, A. L. (2002). Agent-based learning environments as a research tool for investigating teaching and learning. *Journal of Educational Computing Research, 26*(3), 227-248.

Baylor, A. L. (2004). Permutations of control: Cognitive considerations for agent-based learning environments. *Journal of Interactive Learning Research, 15*(4), 403-425.

Blake, R., & Sekuler, R. (2006). *Perception* (5th ed.). Boston: McGraw Hill.

Brunken, R., Plass, J. L., & Leutner, D. (2003). Direct measurement of cognitive load in multimedia learning. *Educational Psychologist, 38*(1), 53-61.

Bureau of Labor Statistics. (2007). *Occupational outlook handbook, 2006-2007 edition*. Washington, D.C.: The U.S. Department of Labor.

Byrne, M. D. (2003). Cognitive architecture. In J. A. Jacko & A. Sears (Eds.), *The human-computer interaction handbook: Fundamentals, evolving technologies and emerging applications* (pp. 97-117). Mahwah, NJ: Lawrence Erlbaum Associates.

Davis, S. A., & Bostrom, R. P. (1993). Training end users: An experimental investigation of the roles of the computer interface and training methods. *MIS Quarterly, 17*(1), 61-85. Retrieved March 22, 2007, from http://www.jstor.org/

Dix, A., Roselli, T., & Sutinen, E. (2006). E-learning and human-computer interaction: Exploring design synergies for more effective learning experiences. *Educational Technology & Society, 9*(4), 1-2.

Goodwin, G. P., & Johnson-Laird, P. N. (2005). Reasoning about relations. *Psychological Review, 112*(2), 468-493.

Hitchins, E. (1995). *Cognition in the wild.* Cambridge, MA: MIT.

Homer, B. D., Plass, J. L., & Blake, L. (2005). *The effects of video on cognitive load and social presence in computer-based multimedia learning.* Paper presented at the Annual Meeting of the American Educational Researcher Association, Montreal, QC.

Hyerle, D. (1996).*Visual tools for constructing knowledge* (ERIC Document Reproduction Service No. ED399257). Alexandria, VA: Association for Supervision and Curriculum Development.

Iwata, H. (2003). Haptic interfaces. In J. A. Jacko & A. Sears (Eds.), *The human-computer interaction handbook: Fundamentals, evolving technologies and emerging applications* (pp. 206-219). Mahwah, NJ: Lawrence Erlbaum Associates.

Kay, J. (2001). Learner control. *User Modeling and User-Adapted Interaction, 11*(1-2), 111-27.

Kearny, L., & Smith, P. (1999). Creating workplaces where people can think: *Cognitive ergonomics. Performance Improvement, 38*(1), 10-15.

Kozma, R. (1994). Will media influence learning? Reframing the debate. *Educational Technology Research & Development, 42*(2), 7-19.

Kroemer, K., & Kroemer, A. D. (2001). *Office ergonomics.* London: CRC/Taylor & Francis.

Laurel, B., Oren, T., & Don, A. (1990). Issues in multimedia interface design: Media integration and interface agents. In *Proceedings of the Conference on Human Factors in Computing Systems: Empowering People,* Seattle (pp.133-139).

Lee, H., Plass, J. L., & Homer, B. D. (2006). Optimizing cognitive load for learning from computer-based science simulations. *Journal of Educational Psychology, 98*(4), 902-913.

Logie, R. H. (1995). *Visuo-spatial working memory.* Hove, UK: Lawrence Erlbaum Associates.

Marcus, N., Cooper, M., & Sweller, J. (1996). Understanding instructions. *Journal of Educational Psychology, 88*(1), 49-63.

Mayer, R. E. (2001). *Multimedia learning.* New York: Cambridge University Press.

Mayer, R. E., & Moreno, R. (2003). Nine ways to reduce cognitive load in multimedia learning. *Educational Psychologist, 38*(1), 43-52.

Mayer, R. E., & Sims, V. K. (1994). For whom is a picture worth a thousand words? Extensions of a dual-coding theory of multimedia learning. *Journal of Educational Psychology, 86*(3), 389-401.

Moreno, R., & Mayer, R. E. (2004). Personalized messages that promote science learning in virtual environments. *Journal of Educational Psychology, 96*(1), 165-173.

Naquin, S. S., & Holton, E. F. (2002). The effects of personality, affectivity, and work commitment on motivation to improve work through learning. *Human Resource Development Quarterly, 13*(4), 357-376.

National Center for Education Statistics. (2005). *Internet access in U.S. public schools and classrooms: 1994-2005.* Washington, D.C.: The U.S. Department of Education.

Newell, A., & Simon, A. (1963). GPS, a program that simulates human thought. In E. A. Feigenbaum & J. Feldman (Eds.), *Computers and thought* (pp. 279-293). Cambridge, MA: MIT Press.

Norman, D. (1988). *The design of everyday things.* New York: Basic Books.

Opfermann, M., Gerjets, P., & Scheiter, K. (2007). *Learning with hypermedia: The influence of representational formats and different levels of learner control.* Paper presented at 2007 American Educational Research Association, Chicago.

Paas, F., Tuovinen, J. E., Tabbers, H., & Gerven, P. W. M. (2003). Cognitive load measurement as a means to advance cognitive load theory. *Educational Psychologist, 38*(1), 63-71.

Paivio, A. (1986). *Mental representations: A dual coding approach.* Oxford, England: Oxford University Press.

Paivio, A. (1991). Dual coding theory: Retrospect and current status. *Canadian Journal of Psychology, 45*, 255-287.

Patterson, D., & Hennessy, J. (2005). *Computer organization and design: Hardware/software interface* (3rd ed.). Atlanta: MC Strategies/Elesevier.

Preece, J., Rogers, Y., & Sharp, H. (2002). *Interaction design: Beyond human-computer interaction.* New York: John Wiley & Sons.

Rieber, L. P. (1994). *Computers, graphics, and learning.* Madison, WI: Brown & Benchmark.

Salomon, G. (1981). *Communication and education: Social and psychological interactions.* London: Sage Publications.

Schneiderman, B. (1980). *Software psychology: Human factors in computer and information systems.* Cambridge, MA: Winthrop Publishers.

Schneiderman, B. (1982). The future of interactive systems and the emergence of direct manipulation. *Behavior and Information Technology, 1*(3), 237-56.

Schneiderman, B. (2005). *Designing the user interface: Strategies for effective human-computer interaction* (4th ed.). Boston: Pearson/Addison-Wesley.

Sedig, K., Klawe, M., & Westrom, M. (2001). Role of interface manipulation style and scaffolding on cognition and concept learning in learnware. *ACM*

Transitions on Computer-Human Interaction, 8(1), 34-59.

Serenko, A. (2006). The use of interface agents for email notification in critical incidents. *International Journal of Human-Computer Studies, 64*(11), 1084-1098.

Stiemerling, O., Kahler, H., & Wulf, V. (1997). How to make software softer: Designing tailorable applications. In *Proceedings of the Conference on Designing Interactive Systems: Processes, Practices, Methods, and Techniques,* Amsterdam, The Netherlands (pp. 365-376).

Sweller, J., & Chandler, P. (1991). Evidence for cognitive load theory. *Cognition and Instruction, 8*(4), 351-362.

Sweller, J., & Chandler, P. (1994). Why some material is difficult to learn. *Cognition and Instruction, 12*(3), 185-233.

Teege, G., Kahler, H., & Stiemerling, O. (1999). Implementing tailorability in groupware. *ACM SIGGROUP Bulletin, 20*(2), 57-59. Retrieved March 22, 2007, from http://portal.acm.org/

Teo, T. S. H., Lim, V. K. G., & Lai, R. Y. C. (1999). Intrinsic and extrinsic motivation in Internet usage. *Omega, 27*(1), 25-37.

Van Merrienboer, J. G., & Sweller, J. (2005). Cognitive load theory and complex learning: Recent developments and future directions. *Educational Psychology Review, 17*(2), 147-177.

Vygotsky, L. (1978). *Mind in society.* Cambridge, MA: Harvard University Press.

Wallace, A., & Sinclair, K. (1995). *Affective responses and cognitive models of the computing environment* (ERIC Document No. 389279). Paper presented at the Annual Meeting of the American Educational Research Association, San Francisco.

Wang, H., & Gearhart, D. (2006). *Designing and developing Web-based instruction.* Upper Saddle River, NJ: Pearson/Merrill

Zheng, R., Miller, S., Snelbecker, G., & Cohen, I. (2006). Use of multimedia for problem-solving tasks. *Journal of Technology, Instruction, Cognition and Learning, 3*(1-2), 135-143.

Ziegler, J. E., Vossen, P. H., & Hoppe, H. U. (1990). Cognitive complexity of human-computer interfaces: An application and evaluation of cognitive complexity theory for research on direct manipulation-style interaction. In P. Falzon (Ed.), *Cognitive ergonomics.* London: Academic Press.

KEY TERMS

Agent-Based Design Model: Agent-based design model consists of dynamically interacting rule-based agents. The systems within which they interact can therefore create complexity like that which we see in the real world. The model was developed through a simple conceptual form in the late 1940s, and it took the advent of the microcomputer to really get up to speed. The idea is to construct the computational devices (known as agents with some properties) and then simulate them in parallel to model the real phenomena. On some levels, agent-based models complement traditional analytic methods. Whereas, analytic methods enable us to diagnose and find solutions to a system, agent-based models allow us to explore the possibility of generating those solutions. This generative contribution may be the most mainstream of the potential benefits of agent-based modeling. Agent-based models also can be used to identify lever points, moments in time in which interventions have extreme consequences, and to distinguish among types of path dependency.

Cognitive Architectures: The concept of cognitive architecture originates from cognitive science related to the early days of cognitive psychology and artificial intelligence, as manifested in the general problem solver (Newell & Simon, 1963), one of the first successful computational cognitive models. However, cognitive architectures differ from traditional research in psychology in that work on cognitive architecture is integrative. That is, they include attention, memory, problem solving, decision making, learning, and so on (Byrne, 2003). The notion of cognitive architecture has been widely used in the gaming, intelligent tutorials, and the like. Cognitive architectures have been identified and integrated in the design of programming. For instance, in designing a math problem solving tutorial, the cognitive algorithm related to math problem solving should be identified, followed by an analysis of the sequence of behaviors to successfully carry out the math problem solving. The computational model of math problem solving thus reflects the structure of human cognition and a specific domain of knowledge. The cognitive architectures can be integrated in programs that help users perform simple calculations, make quantitative predictions, and so on. Designing interfaces that optimize human performance with the cognitive architecture in the program is one of the endeavors pursued by aspiring interface designers.

Cognitive Load: According to the cognitive load theory (CLT), three types of cognitive load exist: *intrinsic load*, *extraneous* or *ineffective load*, and *germane* or *effective load*. The intrinsic cognitive load refers to a cognitive load that is induced by the structure and complexity of the instructional material. Usually, teachers or instructional designers can do little to influence the intrinsic cognitive load. The extraneous cognitive load is referred to the cognitive load caused by the format and manner in which information is presented. For example, teachers may unwittingly increase a learner's extraneous cognitive load by presenting materials that "require students to mentally integrate mutually referring, disparate sources of information" (Sweller et al., 1991, p.353). Finally, the germane cognitive load refers to a cognitive load that is induced by learners' efforts to process and comprehend the material. The goal of CLT is to increase this type of cognitive load so that the learner can have more cognitive resources available to solve problems (Brunken et al., 2003; Marcus, et al., 1996).

Direct Manipulation: Schneiderman's (1982) theory of direct manipulation emphasizes manipulation through sensory perceptions including visual, auditory, haptic, and others. Direct manipulation employs real-world metaphors for objects and actions which make it easier for a user to learn and use an interface. Additionally, rapid, incremental feedback allows a user to make fewer errors and complete tasks in less time, because they can see the results of an action before completing the action (Iwata, 2003; Preece at al., 2002). Direct manipulation recognizes the role of both external and internal representations in the cognitive process. It facilitates information process through multiple sensory channels, the notion of which has been supported by several cognitive theories such as dual coding theory, cognitive load theory, and so on.

Dual Coding Theory: Paivio (1986) suggests that the input information is processed through multiple sensory channels. For example, the verbal information is registered through the verbal channel whereas the nonverbal information such as images is registered through the nonverbal channel. According to dual coding theory, there are three levels of processing pertaining to incoming verbal and nonverbal information: representational, associative, and referential. The representational process refers to the connections between an external object and internal representation of the object. The associative process means the activation of the information stored within the long-term memory. Depending on the input stimuli, the activation process can be either in the verbal or nonverbal (e.g., visual) system. The referential process is the cross-reference process between the verbal and nonverbal systems. Research on dual coding practices suggests that pictures can be coded both visually and verbally, whereas words are believed to be far less likely to be coded visually (Paivio, 1991; Rieber, 1994).

Human Perception: The human perceptual abilities include the range of visibility, perceptual focus, attention, and so forth. These abilities are further affected by the design elements embedded in the interface, that is, color, text size, text/graphic ratio, and others (Blake & Sekuler, 2006). Blake and Sekuler point out that perception is a biological process that "provides us with a useful view of the world, where useful means being able to interact safely and effectively within our environment" (p. 1). In a human-computer environment, this means focusing on the important information and ignoring the irrelevant. According to Blake and Sekuler, four interfaces have critically influenced the choice of perception. They include (a) constructive, (b) contextual, (c) interpretative, and (d) synchronizing interfaces.

Working Memory: Working memory is a theoretical framework that refers to the structures and processes used for temporarily storing and manipulating information. According to Baddeley and Hitch (1974), the working memory consists of two "slave systems" responsible for short-term maintenance of information, and a "central executive" responsible for the supervision of information integration and for coordinating the slave systems. One slave system, the articulatory loop, stores phonological information and prevents its decay by silently articulating its contents, thereby refreshing the information in a rehearsal loop. The other slave system, the visuo-spatial sketch pad, stores visual and spatial information. It can be used, for example, for constructing and manipulating visual images, and for the representation of mental maps. The sketch pad can be further broken down into a visual subsystem (dealing with, for instance, shape, color, and texture), and a spatial subsystem (dealing with location). The central executive system is, among other things, responsible for directing attention to relevant information, suppressing irrelevant information and inappropriate actions, and coordinating cognitive processes when more than one task must be done at the same time. Studies show that the working memory is very limited in both duration and capacity. The working memory typically stores about seven elements but normally operates on only two or three elements.

Chapter XXI
Frameworks for Model–Based Design of Enterprise Information Systems

Mara Nikolaidou
Harokopio University of Athens, Greece

Nancy Alexopoulou
University of Athens, Greece

ABSTRACT

System design is an important phase of system engineering, determining system architecture to satisfy specific requirements. System design focuses on analyzing performance requirements, system modeling and prototyping, defining and optimizing system architecture, and studying system design tradeoffs and risks. Modern enterprise information systems (EIS) are distributed systems usually built on multitiered client server architectures, which can be modeled using well-known frameworks, such as Zachman enterprise architecture or open distributed processing reference model (RM-ODP). Both frameworks identify different system models, named views, corresponding to discrete stakeholder's perspectives, specific viewpoints, and could serve as a basis for model-based system design. The main focus of this chapter is to explore the potential of model-based design for enterprise information systems (EIS). To this end, the basic requirements for model-based EIS design are identified, while three alternative approaches are discussed based on the above requirements, namely, rational unified process for systems engineering (RUP SE), UML4ODP and EIS design framework.

INTRODUCTION

Many different stakeholders are usually involved in the process of constructing an enterprise information system. Each of them focuses on certain concerns and considers these concerns at a certain level of detail. Therefore, various methodologies and frameworks have been developed aiming at the consistent construction of enterprise information systems. Most of them have adopted the notion of *separating concerns* by establishing different *viewpoints*, each depicting the concerns of a specific stakeholder (e.g., user, designer, implementer, etc.). Following, we focus on the *system designer* viewpoint, exploring issues related to the analysis and design of enterprise information systems (EIS).

System design is the process of analyzing system requirements, designing the desired architecture of a system, and exploring performance requirements, ensuring, thus, that all system components are identified and properly allocated and that system resources can provide the desired performance. System design is a phase of *system engineering*, defined by the International Council on System Engineering (INCOSE) as "the interdisciplinary approach and means to enable the realization of successful systems" (INCOSE, 1998). System engineering covers different phases, as the definition of customer needs and required functionality early in the development cycle, the documentation of requirements, the design synthesis, and system validation, while the overall system life cycle, performance, and even maintenance is also considered (Oliver, Kellher, & Keegan, 1997).

System design corresponds to the system designer viewpoint. Although, vendors (as IBM or Oracle) actively promote information system development based on multitiered architectures, the proposed solutions, although expensive, often fail to provide the desired performance. This is due to the fact that system designers often neglect engineering issues contributing to the overall system performance. In practice, discrete issues, as network architecture description or resource allocation, are supported by autonomous automated or semiautomated tools, each of which adopts its own metamodel for system representation. Thus, no interaction between them is supported. To effectively explore EIS design, heterogeneous tools and system models should be integrated. This integration could be accomplished by adopting *model-based system design* (MBSD). MBSD provides a central system model (tool-independent) that captures system requirements and design decisions that fulfill them at different levels of abstraction. It enables integration of system models supported by autonomous design tools and

interoperability between them without interfering with their internal implementation. When applying model-based system design, a multilevel, technology-neutral model for EIS representation should be defined, taking into account different aspects of the system, such as network architecture, resource allocation, application execution requirements, and so forth, involved in system design.

Existing well-known frameworks may be used for system modeling. The *open distributed processing reference model* (RM-ODP) is such a framework, dealing with aspects related to the distribution, interoperation, and portability of distributed information systems. Another widely referenced framework is the *enterprise architecture framework* defined by Zachman, which specifies the development process of enterprise information systems, starting from the identification of the enterprise's business objectives and resulting in a detailed system implementation. Independently of the framework used, the different system views defined from each viewpoint should be represented by graphical models enhancing the designer perspective of the system. Graphical models may be expressed using various modeling languages. However, the most popular and widely adopted modeling language is the unified modeling language (UML). System designers commonly use the extension mechanisms provided by UML to create profiles (i.e., specializations of UML diagrams) to better serve their modeling purposes.

The main focus of this chapter is to explore the potential of model-based design for enterprise information systems. To this end, the basic requirements for model-based EIS design are identified, while three alternative approaches are discussed based on the above requirements. Although they are not the only ones, they were chosen since they focus on system design, provide formal EIS models, and adopt UML as the modeling language for EIS representation. These are: a) the rational unified process (RUP) system engineering approach, b) the UML for open distributed processing (UML4ODP) proposed standard with emphasis on engineering viewpoint, and c) the EIS engineering framework proposed by the authors.

The rest of the chapter is organized as follows: In second section, background information regarding model-based system design and system viewpoints is provided. Also, the Zachman framework and RM-ODP are briefly presented and their relevance to the proposed approach is discussed. In the next section, the requirements for successful model-based design for enterprise information systems are presented. In the following sections, the three alternative approaches are analyzed and discussed based on these requirements. Future trends and conclusions reside in the last two sections.

BACKGROUND

This section describes the main principles of model-based system design (MBSD) and its advantages for enterprise information systems. System modeling is a critical issue in MBSD. The IEEE Std 1471, which provides guidelines for the description of systems from different perspectives (viewpoints), is considered as the basis for the definition of a central system model for MBSD. An overview of existing frameworks for enterprise architecture description is discussed by Goethals, Lemahieu, Snoeck, and Vandenbulcke (2006) and Leist and Zellner (2006). We discuss two of them, namely the Zachman framework and RM-ODP, since they support the designer perspective and can be used as a basis for EIS modeling. They are well-known and come from different origins. It should be noted that although defined prior to IEEE 1471 standard, they both adopt the concepts of views and viewpoints.

Model-Based System Design

System modeling constitutes an important part of system design, since it may facilitate the complete description of all aspects involved and contribute to the effectiveness of the whole process. How many different system models should be supported? Should all of them provide the same level of detail? How can the correspondences between different

models be identified and ensured? Since discrete design issues are usually resolved by different methodologies and autonomous software tools, the support of different system models cannot be avoided. In many cases, these models are not compatible, thus, design issues, although interrelated, are often solved in isolation. Even if a certain design problem, for example, a network architecture, is optimized, there is no guarantee that the overall EIS architecture will be optimized as well. To resolve such a situation, a central, tool-independent model should be adopted.

Model-driven technologies for application development, such as model driven architecture (MDA) (Brown, 2004), proposed by Object Management Group (OMG), enable the definition of *platform-independent models* (PIMs) for the specification of system functionalities and *platform-specific models* (PSMs) for the specification of the implementation of these functionalities on a particular technological platform and the definition of couplings between PIMs and PSMs. Modeling languages, methods and tools have been established to support model-driven software development. In a similar fashion, model-based system design (MBSD) provides a central system model (corresponding to a PIM) that captures, at different levels of abstraction, system requirements and design decisions that fulfill them. In addition, tool-specific models could be defined (corresponding to PSMs), while MBSD also provides for model transformation (couplings between PIM and PSMs). Thus, the interoperability between models and methods corresponding to discrete design issues is achieved, without interfering with their internal implementation in the respective software tools. The central system model serves all design activities; for example, it could be executed by a simulator to validate design decisions.

The UML is a modeling language attempting to standardize graphical language elements for modeling software systems. It is a well-known software engineering standard, since most software developers are familiar with it, while there is a lot of activity in advancing both the UML supported functionality and the UML tools. Numerous designers use the extension mechanisms provided by UML to create profiles (i.e., specializations of UML diagrams) to better serve their modeling purposes. UML 2.0 (OMG, 2007) consists of 13 diagram types used for structural, behavioral, and interaction modeling. Many diagram types, such as use-case, state, and activity, can be used for general functional requirement analysis. Evidently, UML is adopted in MBSD as well, serving as a common enterprise notation language, while UML extensions have been proposed for system design (Murray, 2003a; Nikolaidou, Alexopoulou, Tsadimas, Dais, & Anagnostopoulos, 2006).

As it will be elucidated in this chapter, MBSD is appropriate for enterprise information system analysis and design. When applying MBSD, a multilevel, technology-neutral model for EIS representation should be defined, taking into account different aspects of the system, such as network architecture, resource allocation, application execution requirements, and so forth involved in system design. Existing modeling frameworks are explored for this purpose in the following paragraphs. Independently of the framework used, we suggest that UML should be adopted for model representation.

Defining Views and Viewpoints for Enterprise Information System Architecture

An important milestone in the field of enterprise system architecture descriptions is ANSI/IEEE Std 1471 - Recommended Practice for Architectural Description of Software-Intensive Systems (IEEE1471). It defines enterprise system concepts and their relationships that are relevant for architectural description, thus providing a standard way of defining EIS architecture models. It also provides guidance on the structure of architectural descriptions.

The main concepts standardized are *architecture, architectural description, concern, stakeholder, viewpoint,* and *view.* Architecture is defined as "the

fundamental organization of a system embodied in its components, their relationships to each other, and to the environment, and the principles guiding its design and evolution." Architecture description is "a collection of artifacts documenting the architecture." Stakeholders are "people with key roles or concerns about the system," while concerns are "the key interests crucially important to the stakeholders and determine the acceptability of the system from stakeholder specific perspective." Views are "representations of the whole system from the perspective of a related set of concerns," while viewpoints define "the perspective from which a view is taken." The main concepts of IEEE 1471 standard and their interrelations are depicted in Figure 1.

A viewpoint defines: (a) how to construct and use a view; (b) the information that should appear in the view; (c) the modelling techniques for expressing and analyzing the information; and (d) a rationale for these choices (by describing the purpose and intended audience of the view). Different stakeholders with different roles in the system have different concerns, which are expressed through different viewpoints. Each view is a capture of the representation of the system architecture design, typically comprising of one or more architecture *models.* In simple words, a view is what you see, while a viewpoint is where you are looking from, that is, the vantage point or perspective which determines what you see. Viewpoints are generic, while a view is always specific to the architecture for which it is created. To successfully define an architecture description, specific characteristics should be obtained (Hilliard, 2001):

- Views should be modular. A view may consist of one or more architectural models.
- Views should be well-formed. Each view has an underlying viewpoint specifying view definition using a formal method, as languages, notations, models, and analytical techniques.

Figure 1. IEEE/ANSI Std 1471 conceptual model

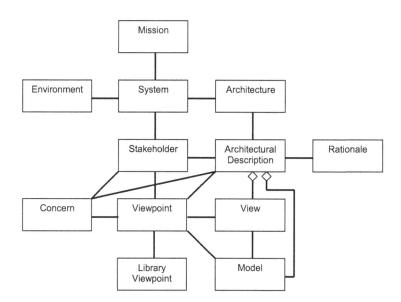

• View consistency should be ensured. Viewpoints may also include: a) any consistency or completeness checks associated with the underlying method to be applied to models within the view; b) any evaluation or analysis techniques to be applied to models within the view; and c) any heuristics, patterns, or other guidelines which aid in the synthesis of an associated view or its models.

Although not defined in IEEE 1471, additional issues should be addressed, such as (Hilliard, 2001):

• View integration and inter-view consistency. It has been long recognized that introducing multiple views into architectural descriptions leads to an integration problem. How does one keep views consistent and nonoverlapping? The introduction of viewpoint declarations, while not solving the problem, gives us a tool for detecting overlaps and inconsistencies, and potentially a substrate for solving the integration problem.

• Formalization. The conceptual framework of IEEE 1471 is an informal, qualitative model. If it is useful, which appears to be the case, it may be insightful to attempt to formalize the concepts therein. Such a formalization could have benefits in several topics, such as view checking, view integration, and inter-view analysis.

Since its publication in 2000, IEEE 1471 has received much appraisal. The concepts of stakeholders, concerns, and views are accepted as essential. The terminology proposed by IEEE 1471 is now being used by many architects. The focus on concerns of stakeholders is a good stimulus for otherwise possibly too technically-oriented IT architects. After all, it is the interests of the stakeholders that need to be served.

IEEE 1471 proposes a formal method to define system architectures, but it does not propose nor prescribe any specific viewpoint for system architects and stakeholders (Greefhorst, Koning, & Hans van, 2006). However, it can be used as a guide to define viewpoints and views for EIS model-based analysis and design, as discussed in the following sections. Inter-view consistency and formal description is the focus of our concern. As already mentioned, each view may be formally defined by a *model*, while it should also be communicated to the stakeholder by a *representation model*, which is a concrete representation of the system view on some medium (e.g., paper or computer program) (Boer, Bonsangue, Jacob, Stam, & Torre, 2004). The aforementioned definitions are adopted throughout the rest of the chapter.

The attainment of a consistent representation of the systems entails that view interrelations must be typically defined. In order to formally define a viewpoint, one should define a metamodel describing the supported views independently of the modeling language used for system representation and then define the representation model. In this way, a view may be represented using different languages, such as UML, in a common manner, facilitating thus the transformation between representation modeling languages. As indicated by Dijkman, Quartel, Pires, and Sinderen (2003), two basic relations are identified between views: *refinement* (the internal view refines the external view on a different level of detail) and *complement* (two views may complement each other by considering complementary concerns).

Zachman Framework

Enterprise information systems can be described based on the Zachman framework. The widely referenced enterprise architecture framework of Zachman (1999), simply referred as the *Zachman framework* is a logical structure for organizing and classifying the artifacts created during the development of enterprise information systems. The purpose of the framework is to ensure the establishment of enterprise information systems starting from the identification of the enterprise's business objectives. As a typical problem of modern enterprises is that in spite of time and money spent on the implementation of information systems, they often fail to meet business objectives.

The Zachman framework is deployed in two dimensions. The first dimension addresses the different perspectives of the stakeholders participating in information system development. These perspectives derive from the parallelism of information system development with the construction of a building. As such, Zachman defines the *owner's*, *designer's*, and *builder's* viewpoints. The first viewpoint, defined by the *business model*, is a description of the enterprise within which the information system will function. The second delineates how the system will satisfy the requirements ensuing from the business objectives, yielding the *system model*. The third viewpoint represents how the system will be implemented, providing the *builder model*. To produce a comprehensive framework for enterprise information system development, Zachman has added three more viewpoints, namely *scope,* which denotes the business purpose and strategy defining the context for the other viewpoints, the *out-of-context,* which includes implementation-specific details, and the *operational,* which is the functioning system. The second dimension distinguishes different focal points of the system. The *data* aspect describes what entities are involved, while the *function* aspect shows how the entities are processed. The *network* perspective indicates where the entities are located. Apart from the *what, how,* and *where*, the framework addresses also three other questions, specifically *who, when,* and *why.* As such, it defines the *people* who work with the system, when events occur (*time* aspect), and why these activities take place (*motivation* aspect). The combination of the two dimensions in a matrix, with the focal points indicated by the columns and the different perspectives by the rows, yields the Zachman framework as presented in Figure 2.

Each cell constitutes a separate view. As such, an organization should create a wide range of diagrams and documents representing the different views defined within the Zachman framework. As shown in Figure 2, the Zachman framework contains suggested specification models for each view (e.g., using ER technique for modeling the data description in the owner's viewpoint or using functional flow diagrams for modeling the process description in the owner's viewpoint). However, it does not suggest a specific methodology or technique for the description of view models. Moreover it does not typically define a metamodel to integrate the information of all cells nor does it describe a way to trace information between cells (Frankel, Harmon, & Mukerji, 2003). Its objective is to provide some basic principles that should guide the implementation of enterprise information systems. As such, it says nothing about the development of conformant views or the order that should be developed. The strength of the framework is that it provides an organized way of thinking about an enterprise, in respect to information systems. It enables the individuals involved in producing enterprise information systems to focus on selected aspects of the system without losing sight of the overall enterprise context. Moreover, it facilitates them to find out possible gaps and inconsistencies between view representations and thus modify the models appropriately to eliminate all inconsistencies.

EIS design issues are obviously addressed in the *system model* raw of Zachman's matrix. The system designer may actually work concurrently with the system developer (the builder of the model), although system design is usually performed prior to its implementation. As already stated, the Zachman framework does not specify whether these two stages must be performed sequentially or in parallel. In many cases, during system design, although system architecture is defined and the services provided by the distributed applications are identified, detail software design and implementation is considered in the builder model. In practice, system engineering issues can be dealt with independently of the status of software development process. Thus, following we will focus on the system model raw of Zachman's matrix.

Lastly, it should be noted that while a plethora of methodologies and formalisms exist, each applicable to some subset of cells, Zachman however encourages a single common language to describe the subject of all the cells as well as their interrelationships, rather than using a specialized notation for each view separately (Sowa & Zachman, 1992).

Figure 2. Overview of the Zachman framework (Sowa & Zachman, 1992)

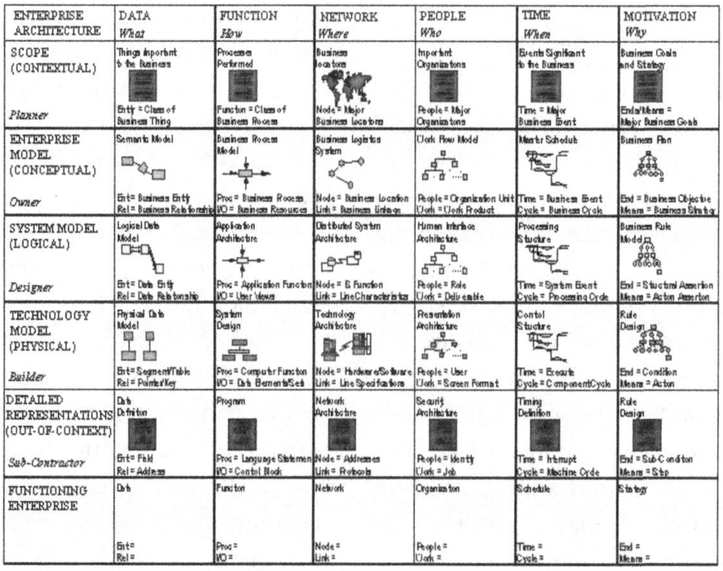

Open Distributed Processing Reference Model

As enterprise information systems are distributed, they can alternatively be described by the reference model of open distributed processing (RM-ODP). The RM-ODP is a conceptual framework established by ISO (ISO/IEC, 1998) for the specification of large-scale distributed systems. RM-ODP integrates aspects related to the distribution, interoperation, and portability of distributed systems in such a way that network/hardware infrastructure is transparent to the user. RM-ODP manages system internal complexity through the *separation of concerns*, addressing specific problems dealt with during system development from different viewpoints (ISO/IEC, 1998). It provides an object-oriented representation of the system, while it is highly technical, relatively complex, and focuses on distributed application development. RM-ODP manages system internal complexity through the identification of five generic and complementary viewpoints, which are as follows:

- *Enterprise* viewpoint, which concentrates on the business activities of the specified system.
- *Information* viewpoint, which focuses on the information that needs to be stored and processed in the system.
- *Computational* viewpoint, which describes system functionality through functional decomposition of the system into components that interact via interfaces.
- *Engineering* viewpoint, which examines the mechanisms and functions required to support distributed interactions between components.
- *Technology* viewpoint, which focuses on the choice of technology for system implementation.

For each viewpoint there is an associated viewpoint language which can be used to express a specification of the system from that viewpoint. The object modeling concepts give a common basis for the viewpoint languages and make it possible to identify relationships between the different viewpoint specifications and to assert correspondences between the representations of the system in different viewpoints. Viewpoint languages provide the means for the detailed description of systems according to viewpoint perspective. System views are formally defined based on the corresponding viewpoint languages.

System design issues are addressed in RM-ODP *engineering viewpoint*. The engineering language focuses on the way system component interaction is achieved and on the resources needed to do so. In the engineering language, the main concern is the support of interactions between computational objects, defined in the computational view to represent a service or a program operating in the distributed platform. As a consequence, there are very direct links between the viewpoint descriptions; computational objects are visible in the engineering viewpoint as *basic engineering objects (BEOs)*, representing the actual implementation of computational objects. Engineering objects are physically located and associated with processing resources by grouping them into *nodes*, which can be thought of as representing independently managed computing systems. A *cluster* is a grouping of basic engineering objects, used for resource allocation purposes (all objects in a cluster are manipulated as a singe entity). Clusters form *capsules* (a single entity for the purpose of resource allocation and protection). Capsules are associated to *nuclei* which are responsible for making communications and processing facilities available (to capture the notion of a virtual machine). When engineering objects in different clusters interact, mechanisms are needed to cope with it. The set of mechanisms needed to do this constitute a *channel* (represents client-server communication), which is made up of a number of interacting engineering objects: *Stubs* are concerned with the information conveyed in an interaction; *binders* are concerned with maintaining the association between the set of basic engineering objects linked by the channel; and *protocol objects* manage the actual communication. Basic engineering entities and their interrelations are depicted in Figure 3.

Although RM-ODP has been well-known since the late 90s, the concepts defined to describe system architecture (as clusters, capsules, or nuclei) in the engineering viewpoint are complex ones; while they are not adopted by system designers in their everyday work, they cannot be instantly related to them. Network architecture is described in great detail using client-server concepts, while the description of systems entities (e.g., communication channels) might be too detailed. Alternative architectural approaches should be easily described within engineering viewpoint to enhance its acceptance by system designers. Furthermore, the dependencies between viewpoints, although identified, are not formally enforced.

Regarding system design, within the engineering viewpoint the following aspects are clarified:

- A system-oriented view of distributed applications.
- System access points.
- The distributed platform infrastructure (e.g., network architecture and hardware configuration).
- The association of software components to network nodes (resource allocation) in order to ensure performance requirements.

However, the means of actually performing resource allocation are not provided, since performance requirements are not depicted within engineering viewpoint.

Frankel (2003) suggests separating the engineering viewpoint into two discrete subviewpoints, the *logical* and the *deployment* one. The deployment one focuses on a technology-independent description of the network architecture and hardware configuration. The logical one corresponds to the description of distributed application architecture and the policies adopted for the operation (e.g., replication policy). This separation helps in clarifying

Figure 3. Basic engineering entities and their interrelations (ISO/IEC, 1998)

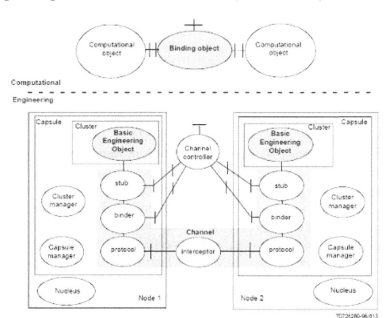

the dependencies between application requirements and distributed platform infrastructure.

MODEL-BASED EIS DESIGN

Modern enterprise information systems are based on distributed architectures, consisting of a combination of Intranet and Internet Web-based applications. They are built on multitiered client-server models (Serain, 1999), as the J2EE architecture. Such platforms distinguish application logic from the user-interface and contribute to system configurability and extendibility. Despite the fact that vendors (such as IBM and Oracle) actively promote information system development using the aforementioned architectures, the proposed solutions, although expensive, often fail to provide the desired performance (Savino-Vázquez et al., 2000). This is due to the fact that design issues, although interrelated, are solved in isolation, while the internal complexity of applications is neglected when estimating the quality of service (QoS) imposed to the network supporting them.

In practice, discrete issues, as network architecture description or resource allocation, are supported by autonomous automated or semiautomated tools (Gomaa, Menasce, & Kerschberg, 1996; Graupner, Kotov, & Trinks, 2001; Nezlek, Hemant, & Nazareth, 1999). Each of these tools supports its own representation metamodel (e.g., queuing networks, Petri-nets, and objects), while different system properties are depicted in them. The existence of a common metamodel describing all EIS properties is of great importance for the efficient requirement analysis and design of such systems, since it would facilitate the communication between autonomous design stages/tools and act as a "reference point." Thus, a model-based approach for EIS analysis and design is considered most efficient.

In order to provide an integrated framework for model-based enterprise information system design, the following requirements should be addressed:

- *Definition of a common, multilayered, platform-independent model of EIS architecture.* EIS architecture description should follow IEEE Std 1471, thus EIS model definition should consist of well defined views and viewpoints. Each view should address a discrete design issue and should be formally defined. Furthermore, view and inter-view consistency should be well-established, since the main reason for adopting model-based design is to ensure integration of discrete design issues/tools. Lastly, compatibility of the proposed model with Zachman system model or RM-ODP engineering viewpoint should also be explored to promote integration with other methodologies addressing system issues corresponding to complementary viewpoints.

- *Covering basic EIS architecture design issues* (as defined in both Zachman's system model and RM-ODP engineering viewpoint). These are: a) definition of EIS architecture (e.g., a system-oriented view of distributed applications) indicating system performance requirements; b) definition of system access points; c) description of platform-independent distributed infrastructure (e.g., network architecture and hardware configuration); and d) mapping of software components to network nodes (resource allocation) in order to ensure performance requirements.

- *Description of a methodology for EIS architecture design.* This could be part of the viewpoints defined or independent of them. Thus, it could be applied at different levels of detail, facilitating the progressive definition of system architecture.

- *Definition of a UML representation model for EIS architecture.* It should provide for an integrated, easy-to-use interface for system designer.

- *Tool integration - Model exchangeability.* Since discrete design issues may be resolved using autonomous tools, heterogeneous tool integration should be supported. Most of them employ their own internal model for EIS representation. Thus, tool coordination and internal metamodel transformation should also be supported. According to model-based design principles, consistency is ensured, since the common metamodel acts as a "reference point." Prior to using an existing tool, the partial transformation of the common metamodel (platform-independent) into the tool's internal metamodel (platform-dependent) must be facilitated. Using this transformation, the invocation and initialization of any tool can be automatically performed. Input/output parameters must be represented in the common metamodel. Their values could be either entered by the system designer or automatically computed by the tool.

Following, we discuss three alternative approaches for model-based EIS design with regard to the above requirements. All of them adopt UML as the modeling language for EIS representation. These are: a) the RUP system engineering approach (Murray, 2003a, 2003b), b) the UML4ODP proposed standard with emphasis on engineering viewpoint (ISO/IEC, 2006), and c) EIS design framework proposed by the authors (Nikolaidou & Anagnostopoulos, 2005).

RUP SYSTEM ENGINEERING

Rational unified process for systems engineering (RUP SE) is a framework developed by Rational (Murray, 2003a) to address system design issues in conjunction with RUP methodology for software engineering. RUP SE adopts all the modeling concepts and perspectives of RUP and is fully compatible with it.

The purpose of RUP SE is to support teams of system engineers as they determine the black box view of the system (e.g., the system as a whole, that is, the services it provides and the requirements it meets) and specify an optimal white box

system design (e.g., elements or parts that make up the system) that meets all stakeholder needs. In particular, RUP SE comprises:

1. An architecture framework, which describes the internals of a system (architectural elements) from multiple viewpoints;
2. A set of UML-based artifacts for system architecture modeling; and
3. A methodology, called *use-case flowdown* (Murray, 2003c), for deriving requirements for architectural elements.

RUP SE System Architecture Modeling Framework

The RUP SE system architecture framework is deployed in two dimensions (Brown & Densmore, 2005), as shown in Table 1. The first dimension defines a set of viewpoints that represent different areas of concern that must be addressed in the system architecture and design. Analytically, *worker* viewpoint expresses roles and responsibilities of system workers regarding the delivery of system services. *Logical* viewpoint concerns the logical decomposition of the system into a coherent set of UML subsystems that collaborate to provide the desired behavior. *Physical* viewpoint regards the physical decomposition of the system and specification of physical components. *Information* viewpoint focuses on the information stored and processed by the system. *Process* viewpoint examines the threads of control that carry out the computation elements. Lastly, *geometric* viewpoint denotes the spatial relationship between physical components.

In addition to viewpoints, building system architecture requires levels of specification as the architecture is being developed. There are four model levels defined in RUP SE, consistent to RUP. As shown in Table 1, these constitute the second dimension of the RUP SE architecture framework. The *context* level treats the entire system as a single entity, that is, a black box. It does not address the system's internal elements. At the *analysis* level, the system's internal elements are defined (white box approach), describing domain elements at a relatively high level. These elements vary, depending on the specific viewpoint. For example, in the logical viewpoint, *subsystems* are defined to represent abstract, high-level elements of functionality. Less abstract elements are represented as *sub-subsystems* or *classes*. In the physical viewpoint, *localities* are defined to represent the places in which functionality is distributed. The *design* level is where design decisions that will drive the implementation are captured. The *implementation* level concerns decisions about technology choices for implementation. The intersection of model level rows with the viewpoint columns yields the different views of a system lifecycle. As shown in Table 1, each view comprises different model elements. It should be noted that RUP SE does not dictate that all system development efforts require every viewpoint. The introduced viewpoints are a mechanism to address different stakeholders' concerns but also to maintain an integrated, consistent representation of the overall system design.

One could identify a correspondence between RUP SE and Zachman's viewpoints, while we consider that context, analysis, and design model level could be incorporated within the system model row

of Zachman's matrix. The context model level, in particular, may constitute the bridge to the upper Zachman row (business model) and the design model to the lower (technology model).

As presented in Figure 4, all system model aspects of the Zachman framework, except for the motivation which is not examined within RUP SE, are covered by the corresponding RUP SE viewpoints. RUP SE defines 18 different views corresponding to the system model row of the Zachman framework, which could be a bit confusing for the system designer. Furthermore, there is no formal definition of the models corresponding to each view (a formally defined metamodel), although the purpose and functionality of each of them is clearly defined, as stated in IEEE Std 1471.

UML Representation Model

RUP SE employs UML 1.4 to create system artifacts for each view specified in the architecture framework. Each viewpoint is described using specific collaborating entities through context, analysis, and design levels. The use of UML for both object and relational database modeling is a well-developed practice that RUP SE makes use of in the information viewpoint, thus no stereotypes

Table 1. The RUP SE architecture framework (Brown & Densmore, 2005; Murray, 2003b)

MODEL LEVELS	VIEWPOINTS					
	Worker	Logical	Information	Physical	Process	Geometric
Context	UML Organization diagram	UML System Context Diagram UML Use Case Diagram Specification	UML Enterprise Data View Containing Extended Product Data	UML Enterprise Locality View	UML Business Processes diagram	Domain-dependent Views
Analysis	UML Partitioning of System into Human Machine	UML System Logical Decomposition Diagram	Product Data Conceptual Schema	UML System Locality View	UML Process View	Parameterized Geometric Model Layouts
Design	UML System Worker View	UML Software Component Design	Product Data Schema	UUML Descriptor Node View	UML Detailed Process View and Timing diagrams	MCAD Design
Implementation	Hardware and Software Configuration					

Figure 4. Mapping RUP SE to the Zachman framework

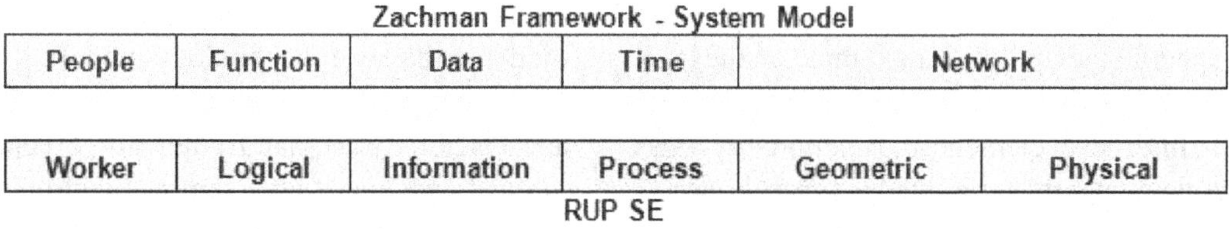

Zachman Framework - System Model

People	Function	Data	Time	Network

Worker	Logical	Information	Process	Geometric	Physical

RUP SE

were defined. The process viewpoint is represented as collaborating processes, using standard UML semantics (e.g., activity diagrams). The same is applied to geometric viewpoint as well, described as collaborating components (standard component diagrams).

Worker viewpoint mainly consists of *worker diagrams*, deriving from class diagrams containing *worker* and *machine* stereotypes. Logical viewpoint consists of *context diagrams*, used to depict logical decomposition of the system as a coherent set of UML subsystems that collaborate to provide the desired functionality. In UML 1.4, systems and subsystems inherit from classifiers and packages; there is no UML syntax that captures both the classifier and package aspects of a subsystem. In RUP and RUP SE, proxy classes are used to represent the classifier semantics. In RUP SE, systems/subsystems are stereotypes of proxy and package entities, while their distinct semantics are appropriately defined. A *system context diagram* captures a black box description of the system (*Context level*) and is further decomposed to its components in the *system logical decomposition diagram* (*analysis level*). Figure 5 presents as an example a RUP SE *system context diagram* for a retail system.

In the physical viewpoint, the system is decomposed into elements that host the logical subsystem services. *Locality diagrams* are the most abstract expression of this decomposition. They express where processing occurs without tying the processing locality to a specific geographic location, or even the realization of the processing capability to specific hardware. Locality refers to proximity of resources, not necessarily location, which is captured in the

design model. The locality diagrams show the initial partitioning, how the system's physical elements are distributed, and how they are connected. The term locality is used because locality of processing is often an issue when considering primarily nonfunctional requirements. Locality is defined as stereotype of a UML *node* element. Figure 6 presents a *locality diagram* that documents an engineering approach to a click-and-mortar enterprise that has a number of retail stores, central warehouse, and a Web presence. The rounded cube icon is used for the representation of the locality.

To support RUP SE, a RUP plug-in is provided for IBM rational tools. The currently available plug-in was released in June 2003 and can be used together with RUP v. 2003. It is based on UML 1.4, while in future versions RUP SE will move on to UML 2.0 semantics.

Use-Case Flowdown Methodology for EIS Architecture Design

Moving down model levels adds specificity to the models. As you move down the levels, each view is a more specific decision, resulting in configuration items at the implementation level. It is important to note that each model level *realizes* requirements discovered at a higher level. For example, physical viewpoint at the design level contains a descriptor node diagram, which shows a physical design that realizes each locality contained in the system locality diagram.

The context level treats the entire system as a single entity, thus the transition from the context to the analysis level is the process of adding detail

Figure 5. A system context diagram for a retail system (Murray, 2003b)

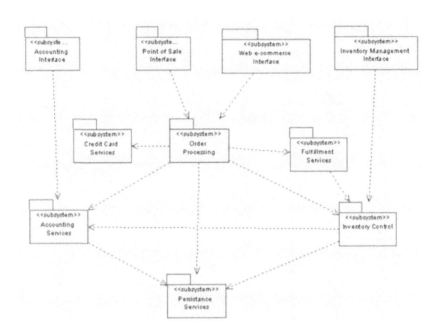

in the system model (black box to white box representation). In going from analysis to design, subsystems/classes and localities are transformed into hardware, software, and worker designs. This is not a direct mapping, since design decisions have to be made about how the functionality represented in the subsystems and classes will be allocated. Factored into these design decisions are considerations for supplementary requirements and distribution represented by the localities. The resulting design must realize all of the specifications from the analysis level. In other words, designing the system at the analysis level creates requirements that the design level must satisfy. Again, going from the design level to the implementation level is a transformation, but this time the mapping is more direct.

RUP SE use-case flowdown (Murray, 2003c) is the methodology used for the transition between model levels. Flowdown can be applied to add detail within a model level or to specify elements at a lower model level. For example, it can be used to determine system services at the context level, but similarly, it can be used at the analysis level to

identify subsystem services and to break subsystems into further subsystems. Through use-case flowdown requirements may propagate from context to analysis and to design model levels. Use-case flowdown is applied recursively. Table 2 includes the steps of a simple flowdown for constructing system context diagram, as the one described in Figure 5, and identifying system services.

Flowdown steps may be applied as a *joint realization* analyzing the way the elements of multiple viewpoints collaborate in carrying out a service. The generic procedure of joint realization flowdown for context model level is presented in Table 3.

Discussion

The plethora of views all referring to the system model, although providing the capability of detail system description, are complex to manage. The most important issue is that they should be kept aligned and consistent with respect to each other. The design activity must ensure that these views can be related to each other, either directly or

Figure 6. A locality diagram for a retail system (Murray, 2003b)

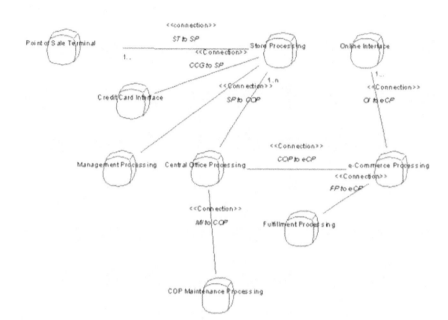

indirectly, and to the information system as well. Thus, in order to ensure consistency and avoid the loss of critical information during system design, various types of relations between different views (and corresponding models) should be enforced (e.g., equivalence or refinement relations). To this end, the formal definition of a metamodel describing views lacking in RUP SE is very important.

RUP SE addresses all issues related to EIS design, utilizing the six viewpoints defined. Furthermore, different levels of detail are supported though model levels. Although the use-case flow-down methodology is concrete, it is a complex process, which can not be easily automated. The integration of specific tools for system design is also not mentioned.

UML 1.4 diagrams are employed for the illustration of proposed views. The RUP SE framework defines appropriate stereotypes for the views and a plug-in is provided for UML 1.4. UML 2.0 will be supported in a later version.

RUP SE is best suited for EIS that are large enough to obtain internal complexity, have concurrent hardware and software development, obtain architecturally significant deployment issues, and include a redesign of the underlying information

Table 2. Simple flowdown example – system context diagram (Murray, 2003c)

1	Model an enterprise whitebox as a set of collaborating systems.
2	Model how systems collaborate to realize enterprise services, mission, and so forth.
3	Create a context diagram for the system.
4	Determine actors (i.e., entities that collaborate with the system).
5	Identify I/O entities.
6	Aggregate similar collaborations between the system and its actors into use cases.
7	Add use-case detail: performance, pre- and post-conditions, and so forth.
8	Identify system service and aggregate similar whitebox steps.
9	Add system attributes from your analysis of enterprise needs.

Table 3. Joint realization procedure (Murray, 2003c)

1	Choose the participating viewpoints. The logical viewpoint is mandatory.

2	For each white box step in realizing a black box service, you must:
	 - Specify the logical element that executes it.
	 - Model how the additional viewpoints participate. For example, you might include:
	   - *Physical viewpoint* -- Specify hosting locality; if there are two localities, then decompose into two steps.
	   - *Process viewpoint* -- Specify executing process; if there are two processes, then decompose into two steps.
	   - *Information viewpoint* -- Specify which data schema element supports handling of any information that is used.
	
	 Throughout this process, apply the following *joint realization rule*: If a given logical element white box step requires more than one element of the other viewpoints, divide that step into further steps so that each step requires exactly one.

3	Create interaction diagrams for each viewpoint: - Architecture interaction diagram - Locality interaction diagrams - Process interaction diagrams

technology infrastructure to support evolving business processes. Usually it is applied in conjunction to RUP.

UML4ODP

UML4ODP is a standard developed by ISO (ISO/IEC, 2006), which further refines the ODP systems by using UML for the expression of ODP system specification in terms of RM-ODP viewpoint specifications. Using UML concepts, as well as the lightweight extension mechanism supported by UML, it provides:

1. A set of UML 2.0 profiles (one for each RM-ODP viewpoint) and the a way to use these profiles;
2. A profile for correspondences between viewpoints; and
3. A profile for conformance of implementations to specifications.

UML4ODP is also concerned about the relationships between RM-ODP viewpoint specifications and model-driven architectures such as MDA. UML notation contributes to RM-ODP's acceptance and promotes its usage by system designers. The engineering profile of UML4ODP expresses the concepts specified in the RM-ODP engineering viewpoint and conforms to engineering language.

Engineering Viewpoint Metamodel

The basic entities of engineering viewpoint metamodel and their interrelations as defined in the UML4ODP standard are illustrated in Figure 7. Most of the entities presented in the figure are briefly introduced in the following section. The metamodel is defined using standard UML notation.

Engineering Viewpoint UML Profile

In the UML4ODP engineering profile, an *engineering object* is expressed by a UML InstanceSpecification of component (e.g., an instance of *component* UML classifier), stereotyped as *NV_Object*. Basic engineering objects are particular kinds of engineering objects. Therefore, stereotype *NV_BEO* that identifies such objects inherits from *NV_Object*. A cluster is expressed by a UML InstanceSpecification of component, stereotyped as *NV_Cluster*. This includes a configuration of basic engineering objects and has bindings to required channels for communication. Likewise, cluster manager, capsule manager, nucleous, and node are expressed by a UML InstanceSpecification of component, stereotyped as *NV_ClusterManager, NV_Capsule-Manager, NV_Nucleus,* and *NV_Node,* respectively. A *channel* is expressed by a UML package, stereotyped as *NV_Channel*. It consists of stubs, binders, protocol objects, and possibly interceptors. It is also expressed by a tag definition of Channel ID for a set of engineering objects (i.e., stub, binder, protocol object, and interceptor) comprising a channel. Also, a *binder* is expressed by a UML InstanceSpecification of component, stereotyped as *NV_Binder*. A diagrammatic representation of part of this UML profile is presented in Figure 8.

All the UML elements corresponding to the engineering language are defined within a UML model, stereotyped as *Engineering_Spec*. Such a model contains UML packages that express:

- Structure of a node, including nucleus, capsules, capsule managers, clusters, cluster managers, stubs, binders, protocol objects, interceptors, and basic engineering objects, with UML component diagram;
- Channels, with UML component diagram and packages;
- Domains, with UML packages; and
- Interactions among those engineering objects,

with UML activity diagrams, state charts, and interaction diagrams.

The stereotype definition also comprises constraints expressed in object constraint language (OCL) (OMG, 2006). Examples of the constraints include:

- Each stub to which a basic engineering object is related must be part of a channel to which the BEO is related
  context BEO **inv** SameChannel:
  self.stub->forAll (stub | self.channel->exists (channel | channel = stub.channel))
- For each channel to which a basic engineering object is related, the basic engineering object must be related to exactly one stub that is part of that *channel*
  context BEO **inv** OneStubPerChannel:
  self.channel->forAll (channel | self.stub->select (stub | stub.channel = channel)->size ( ) = 1)

Figure 7. Part of the RM-ODP engineering viewpoint metamodel (ISO/IEC, 2006)

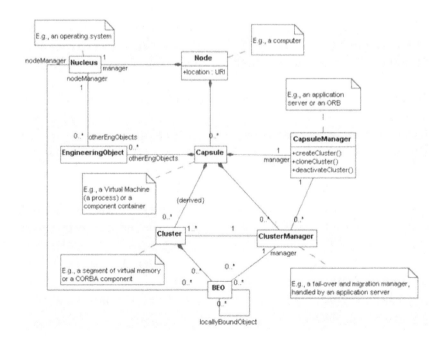

- The basic engineering objects constituting a channel's endpoints must each reside in different clusters
  context Channel **inv** EndPointsInDifferentClusters:
  self.endPoint->forAll (ep1, ep2 | ep1.cluster <> ep2.cluster)

As an example of the engineering specification, Figure 9 depicts the node structure of the enterprise server defined for the Templeman Library discussed in Annex B of ISO/IEC, 2006. As shown, in Figure 9, the enterprise server node consists of the node itself, nucleus, capsule, capsule manager, cluster, cluster manager, BEOs, stub, binder, protocol object, and interceptor. In the enterprise server node configuration, BEOs for all computational objects are hosted in different clusters. The borrowing cluster is depicted in the figure. Communication is performed using stub1 (belonging in the channel connecting enterprise server to interaction server) and stub2 (belonging in the channel connecting enterprise server to enterprise information server).

The UML profiles of the five ODP viewpoints and corresponding metamodels have been defined using MagicDraw 10.0 and are available at www.rm-odp.net.

Discussion

It is self-evident that UML4ODP engineering specification fully corresponds to RM-ODP engineering language. It proposes a well-defined metamodel including all entities described in the RM-ODP engineering viewpoint. Based on this metamodel, a complete UML 2.0 profile is defined comprising a set of stereotypes, as well as a number of relative constraints written in OCL. The profile contributes to the wider acceptance and usage of RM-ODP, although it inherits all RM-ODP expression difficulties since it adopts the same terminology.

UML4ODP, as RM-ODP itself, is mainly focused on distributed application implementation based on the business requirements the applications should fulfill. However, performance requirements (e.g., expected response time for a certain application) are not considered. In particular, in the engineering viewpoint, allocation and replication decisions are not effectively explored, since the designer may relate engineering objects to nodes, but still has

Figure 8. Part of the engineering profile of UML4ODP (ISO/IEC, 2006)

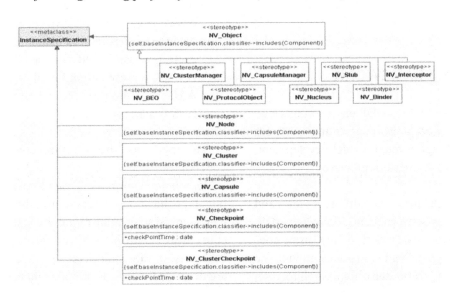

Figure 9. Part of the engineering profile of UML4ODP (ISO/IEC, 2006)

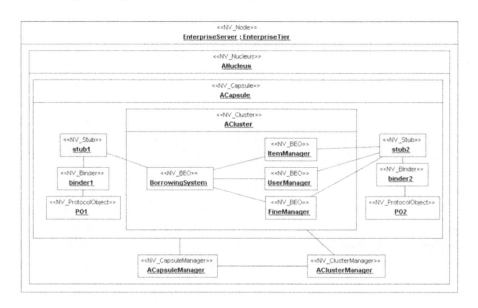

no means to explore the performance of alternative design decisions. Splitting the engineering view into two subviews, as suggested by Frankel (2003), might contribute towards this direction.

It is not within the scope of UML4ODP to define a formal methodology for EIS architecture design, though EIS architectures may be represented within engineering viewpoint specifications. Lastly, the integration of specific design tools (e.g., for resource allocation or performance evaluation) is also not mentioned.

EIS DESIGN FRAMEWORK

Like RUP SE and UML4ODP engineering viewpoint, EIS framework aims at augmenting the system analysis and design through model development. In particular, the framework provides:

1. A metamodel describing different views and the relations between them (EIS metamodel). These relations are strictly defined using constraints. The defined viewpoints provide the means to a) describe the network architecture,

b) describe application logic in terms of the service requirements imposed to the network infrastructure, and c) perform resource allocation.

2. A methodology for EIS design based on the proposed views. The methodology consists of discrete stages performed by the system designer, software tools, or a combination of both. Taking advantage of the formal definition of relations identified between views, system design stages may be invoked as a result of metamodel constraint validation, ensuring that each stage can be independently performed.

3. A UML representation for all defined views. A UML 2.0 profile is defined for this purpose (EIS design profile).

The framework is based on three complementary viewpoints:

Functional viewpoint is used to describe functional specifications (e.g., system architecture, user behavior and application requirements). System architecture refers to the architectural model adopted. In the case of EIS, multitiered client-server models are described. Services provided by each application tier (called modules) are also defined. User behavior is modeled through user profiles defining the behavior of different user groups and their performance requirements. Application requirements are described in terms of QoS requirements imposed to the network infrastructure (e.g., amount of data processed, transferred, or stored). Each service is described in a greater level of detail through the *service description* subview.

Topology viewpoint facilitates the definition of system access points and the resource allocation and replication. The term *site* is used to characterize any location (i.e., a building, an office, etc.). As such, a site is a composite entity which can be further analyzed into subsites, forming thus a hierarchical structure. Functional and topology views are interrelated. Resources (e.g., processes and files) correspond to services and data described through functional view and are located into sites.

Physical viewpoint refers to the aggregate network. Network nodes are either workstations allocated to users or server stations running server processes. Topology and physical views are interrelated. Both are decomposed to the same hierarchical levels of detail. At the lowest level, network nodes are related to processes/data replicas.

Figure 10 suggests a mapping of the proposed views to system model raw of Zachman's matrix and RM-ODP engineering viewpoint (note that Frankel suggestion is adopted).

EIS Metamodel

Following, the metamodel will be analytically described in respect to each viewpoint.

Functional Viewpoint

For each distributed application operating in the EIS framework, a discrete *functional view* is defined. Applications are conceived as sets of interacting *modules* (either server or client), such as application servers, database servers, and so forth. Modules represent a coherent unit of functionality provided by a system. Each module offers specific *services*, representing the specific set of tasks executed when a module is activated in a certain way. *Data entities* are defined to indicate portions of data used by application modules. A file server module is used in each application for managing data entities. For each data entity, the name, size, and specific characteristics (whether it is executable or data, shareable, updatable, and replicable) must be defined.

User behavior is also described in functional view through *user profiles* activating client modules. Each profile includes *user requests*, which invoke specific client services. Each *user request* acquires a *percentage* attribute, indicating how often the user activates the specific application module, and a *response time* attribute indicating the time within which the request must be served.

For each module service, the requirements imposed to the distributed platform infrastructure must be defined. Thus, the portion of data processed, stored, or transferred must be estimated. Also other services participating in its implementation must be identified. This is performed using a set of predefined *operations*, sketching service functionality, and describing its needs for *processing, storing, and transferring* (called *elementary operations*) (Nikolaidou & Anagnostopoulos, 2005). Since it is difficult for the system designer to estimate the elementary operations describing service requirements, an operation library, named *operation dictionary,* is provided. *Complex operations* are added in the dictionary, such as *request* responsible for other service activation or *write/read* for data entity management. Complex operations represent the requirements of composite functionality. All complex operations are further decomposed into others, elementary or not. The system designer may add custom complex operations in the dictionary to ease the description of a specific application. Thus, a service description subview is defined for every service appearing in the functional view (see Figure 11).

345

Figure 10. Mapping EIS designing viewpoints to the Zachman framework and RM ODP

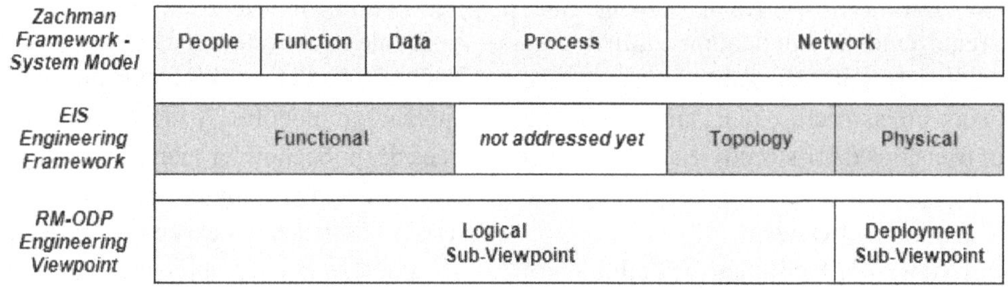

Zachman Framework - System Model	People	Function	Data	Process	Network	
EIS Engineering Framework	Functional			not addressed yet	Topology	Physical
RM-ODP Engineering Viewpoint	Logical Sub-Viewpoint					Deployment Sub-Viewpoint

Physical Viewpoint

Physical view comprises the network infrastructure. The overall *network* is decomposed to subnetworks, producing thus a hierarchical structure. Local area networks (LANs) typically form the lowest level of the decomposition. Nodes, such as servers and workstations, are associated with LANs of the lowest level. Nodes may include a *processing unit* and a *storage unit*.

Topology Viewpoint

Topology view comprises sites, processes (defined as instances of application modules), data entity replicas (stored in the corresponding file server processes), and users (defined as instances of user profiles) (see Figure 11). Two types of sites are supported: composite, composed by others, and atomic, not further decomposed, constituting therefore the lowest level of site hierarchy. Users, processes, and data replicas are associated with atomic sites. In essence, the hierarchy indicates where (in which location) each process runs and each user is placed. The site hierarchy should correspond to the network hierarchy depicted in the physical view, while processes, files, and users are related to nodes included in physical view. Each site is characterized by QoS requirements as *average and maximum network rate* regarding process communication a) within site limits (*avgWithin* and

maxWithin attributes of the site entity), b) exiting the site (*avgOut* and *maxOut*), and c) entering the site (*avgIn* and *maxIn*). These requirements must be satisfied by the *throughput* attribute of the corresponding network (see attributes of *network* entity in Figure 11). Thus, topology and physical views are interrelated. Both views can be either defined by the system designer or automatically composed by logical and physical configuration tools. The introduction of progressive site refinement, as well as the mapping of site range onto network range, enables the identification of dependencies between application configuration and network topology (Nikolaidou & Anagnostopoulos, 2005).

Consistency between these two views is accomplished using constraints embedded in the metamodel. Some of the constraints implementing the restrictions imposed between topology and physical views include:

- Network and site hierarchy must be identical, thus corresponding network and site entities must have corresponding parents. This constraint is used to initiate the respective logical or physical configuration tool, whenever the site or network hierarchy is changed.
- Topology view may only contain components (e.g., processes) related to entities (e.g., modules) belonging to existing functional views.
- Constraints are used to relate topology view entities (e.g., a server process) to the respective physical view entities (e.g., server node).

Figure 11. The proposed EIS metamodel

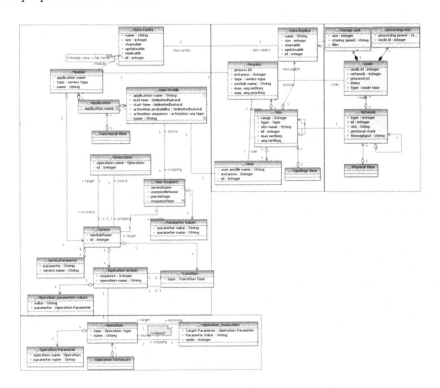

It is obvious that the definition of constraints is a powerful mechanism to represent the dependencies between topology and physical view in a similar fashion for both the system designer and software tools addressing specific design issues.

EIS Design Methodology

EIS design framework facilitates the following discrete stages of system design process:

1. System requirement definition
2. Resource (process/data) allocation and replication policy definition
3. Network architecture design
4. Performance evaluation of the proposed solution (prior to implementation); although it is not a necessity, it is certainly useful

As resource allocation and network design problems cannot be independently solved, stages (2) and (3) are repeatedly invoked for different abstraction levels until an acceptable solution is reached (Nikolaidou & Anagnostopoulos, 2005). Both resource allocation and network architecture problems are usually supported by automated or semiautomated tools using mathematics, heuristics, or a combination of both. These tools may be repeatedly invoked for different abstraction levels (Graupner et al., 2001, Nezlek et al., 1999). The system designer may perform or partially perform these tasks on the system designer's own time, thus both options must be supported. To evaluate system performance, a simulation tool as the one described by Nikolaidou and Anagnostopoulos (2003) can be used. The simulator uses as input the overall system model and produces performance results. Since each of these tools supports its own representation metamodel (e.g., queuing networks, Petri-nets, and objects), there is a need to properly create and instantiate the "internal" system model prior to invoking the tool. In order to facilitate model exchangeability, the common metamodel is realized in XML, which is a standard exchangeable format. The partial transformation of the common metamodel into tool-specific metamodel must be facilitated before using an existing tool for a specific configuration stage.

The proposed methodology stages along with the EIS model consisting of the predefined views are presented in Figure 12. Discrete stages receive/modify information from/to specific system views, as depicted by the arrows between them. The relation between views and between stages is also depicted in the figure. Requirement definition is the initial stage and corresponds to the definition of system architecture and application requirements (functional view), the system access points (topology view), and existing network architecture, if any (physical view). A metamodel is provided for the formal definition of views and the relations between them. Each view is represented by one or more UML diagrams properly extended, thus a corresponding UML 2.0 profile is defined. Relations between views must also be described in the UML profile. Specific tool invocation and coordination must also be facilitated either by the profile or the metamodel itself or by both.

The metamodel itself contains relationships and restrictions inflicted between system entities belonging to the same or different views, which may lead to a specific stage invocation (e.g., if the network hierarchy in the physical view is modified, this modification must be depicted in the topology view as well). Embedding restrictions within the metamodel facilitates EIS design process management, taking into account the overall system model and not a specific system view corresponding to a discrete stage. Thus, the overall process becomes more effective, since discrete stage (and corresponding tool) dependencies are depicted within the model as view dependencies and consequently they are easily identified. Furthermore, it becomes more efficient to integrate autonomous software tools at different levels of detail, as each of them is independently invoked without knowing the existence of others.

EIS Design UML 2.0 Profile

In order to provide a standard method to represent system views and help the designer to efficiently interact with them, a UML 2.0 profile was defined facilitating the following:

1. Representation of EIS metamodel different views. More than one UML 2.0 diagram may be used for each view. Thus a specific system entity may participate in more than one diagram represented through a different UML entity.
2. Linkage between different model views, as represented in the metamodel.
3. Representation of all relationships and restrictions included in the metamodel. This must be applied between entities participating in the same or different UML diagrams to ensure model consistency.
4. Definition of system entities, attributes, and relationships.

UML 2.0 diagrams are used for the representation of different EIS views. The relative EIS entities are depicted as UML elements, properly extended to include additional properties and constraints. This means that appropriate UML 2.0 stereotypes have been defined for each view. Essentially, the concepts of the metamodel are reflected onto the stereotype attributes and constraints. Attributes convey the information required to describe EIS metamodel entities (e.g., *throughput, activationFrequency, processingPower*, etc.). Constraints, which are extensively used within the profile, represent relationships and restrictions between metamodel entities maintaining model consistency. Constraints mainly facilitate:

•   Automatic computation of specific attribute values;
•   Limiting attribute value range;
•   Relating attribute values of specific elements to attribute values of other entities belonging

Figure 12. EIS design framework

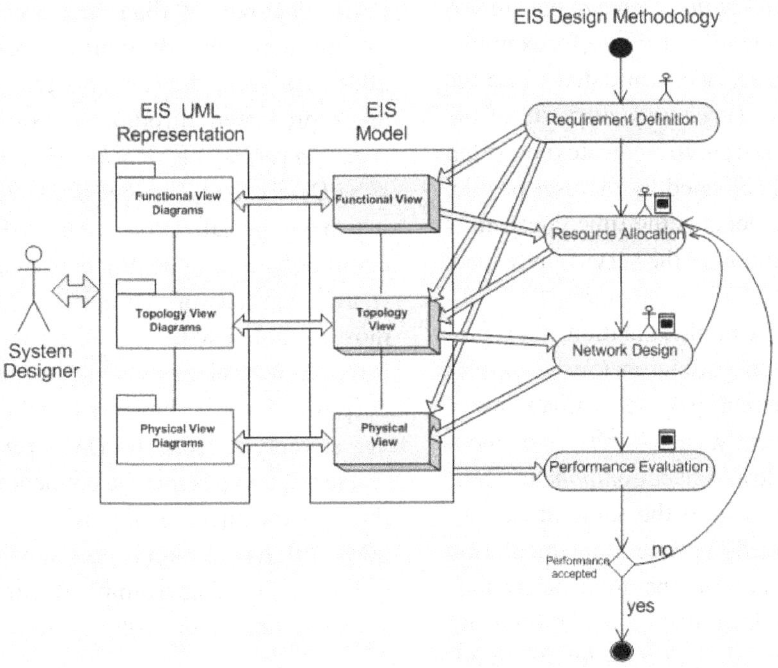

to the same or other UML diagrams (implementing thus the linkage between different models); and

- Model validation in view and overall model level.

Attributes and constraints for each stereotype are analytically introduced by Nikolaidou et al. (2006). Following, the UML diagrams employed for each view are briefly presented. Each stereotype has been named so that the first part of the name indicates the corresponding EIS metamodel entity, while the second part denotes the UML class it derives from.

Functional View

Functional views are represented as UML component diagrams, since the latter are eligible for representing system functionality at a logical level. As such, modules are defined as stereotypes of the UML *component* element (*ServerModuleComponent* and *ClientModuleComponent*). Module services are also defined as stereotypes of *component* (*ServiceComponent* stereotype) because in UML, a component has recursive properties, meaning that it may include other components. For the interactions among services, the *InvokeDependency* stereotype has been defined. *Dependency* is the relationship defined in UML between components. *FileServerModuleComponent* is the stereotype defined for the representation of a file server, which is associated with *DataEntityComponent* stereotypes used to depict data.

The *UserProfileComponent* stereotype has been defined for the representation of user profiles. Each profile may initiate client module services. Therefore, we have defined the *InitiateDependency* stereotype as a specialization again of UML *dependency*. As mentioned earlier, the interaction between user profiles and services plays a determinative role in system design, since user profiles include performance requirements imposed by users. This is indicated by attributes of the *User-ProfileComponent* and *InitiateDependency* stereotypes. *ActivationProbability* attribute, for example, denotes how often a service is initiated while the user profile is active. *Percentage* attribute of the *InitiateDependency* stereotype indicates how often a specific service is activated by the user profile, while *responseTime* denotes the time constraints imposed to the execution of the service in respect to the user profile.

Concerning service implementation, it is represented through an activity diagram (*ServiceImplementationActivity* stereotype), as it involves flow of operations. Consequently, each *ServiceImplementationActivity* maps to a *ServiceComponent*. Thus, these two stereotypes have the same attributes. As already mentioned, service implementation consists of a sequence of operation activations executed upon module activation. Operations are represented through the *OperationAction* stereotype. The operation dictionary that includes the operations is represented through communication diagrams as the latter are used to show interactions among elements.

Figure 13 presents a simple application as an example. A user (student) initiates a simple search in a library Online Public Access Catalog (OPAC), thus performing a database search through the appropriate Common Gateway Interface (CGI) in the Web server. The example involves three modules: *Web client*, *Web server*, and *External database server*, consisting of services. The Web server module, for example, includes two services, *get page* and *perform search*. Figure 13 illustrates also the implementation of the *simple search* service as well as a fraction of the operation idctionary. The dotted lines indicate the correspondences among the external part of functional view, the implementation of simple search, and the operation dictionary fraction.

Physical View

UML deployment diagrams are typically used to represent network architectures (Kaehkipuro, 2001). As such, the elements that denote devices are represented through stereotypes of *device* (i.e., *ServerDevice*, *WorkstationDevice*, *ProcessUnitDevice*, and *StorageUnitDevice* stereotypes), which is a specialization of the UML *node* element, commonly used in deployment diagrams.

As each network comprises subnetworks, the most suitable UML element for its representation is the *package* element, which is used for grouping purposes. Thus, we have created the *NetworkPackage* stereotype from the UML *package* element. These stereotypes may be connected to each other through the membership relation introduced in UML 2.0. Its notation is presented in the example of Figure 14a. This example illustrates part of the University of Athens Library network.

Topology View

Topology view is based on UML component diagrams. All entities included in topology view are represented through the corresponding stereotypes of component (i.e., *ServerProcessComponent*, *ClientProcessComponent,* and *UserProfileComponent* stereotype). Data replicas are also represented through a stereotype of component (i.e., *DataReplicaComponent* stereotype). Since each site comprises subsites, the most suitable UML element for its representation is the *package* element (as with network in physical view) Therefore, we have defined the stereotype *SitePackage* as a specialization of *package*. Interaction among process instances, as well as between user profile and client process instances, are represented through the *InvokeDependency* and *InitiateDependency* stereotypes respectively, with different constraints though, defined within the context of topology view. Sites relate to each other through the membership relationship. The topology view corresponding to the physical view of Figure 14a is presented in the Figure 14b.

As already stated, constraints are defined for the representation of relationships and restrictions between physical and topology views of the EIS metamodel and for the definition of interrelations between the corresponding stereotypes. An excerpt of the constraints defined in both views to ensure the consistency between them is included in Table 4.

Constraints 3-5 of the network package and 3-4 of site package ensure that site hierarchy of the topology view should correspond to the network hierarchy depicted in the physical view. Composite sites correspond to composite networks, while atomic sites correspond to atomic networks representing simple LANS. *Max* and *avg netReq* attributes of site package are automatically computed based on traffic flow within, in, and out of the site (constraint 5 in topology view). Instances of processes/user profiles (constraints 6-11 in physical view and constraint 9 in topology view) and data replicas (constraint 12

in physical views and 13 in topology view) located in atomic sites are allocated to nodes (servers or workstations) and storage devices included in the corresponding LAN of physical view. Note that constraints, as for example, those relating data replicas to storage devices, are applied in both views to avoid inconsistencies. Constraints are checked every time the system designer makes a change in either topology or physical view or a design tool is invoked. Changes may be either prohibited or propagated.

The proposed UML 2.0 profile has been implemented in rational software modeler in the form of a plug-in (EIS plug-in). EIS plug-in, apart from the definition of the stereotypes and constraints, also provides additional functionality that first augments usability for the system designer and second performs validation of the constraints defined within as well as between viewpoints. Through this plug-in,

Figure 13. Functional view example

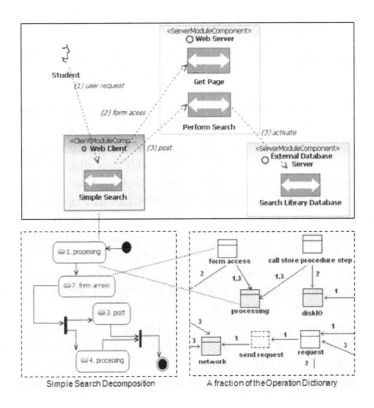

Figure 14. (a) Physical view example (b) topology view example

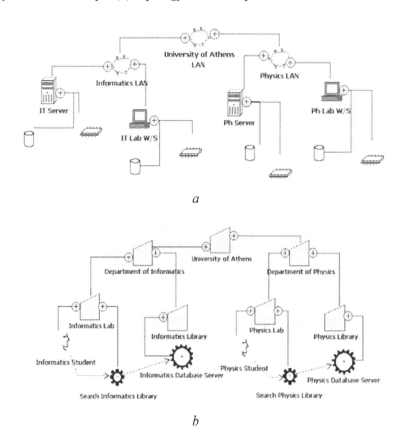

a

b

external tools can be invoked either by the system designer or automatically to enforce consistency between views.

Discussion

In the EIS design framework, a small number of viewpoints is proposed. The viewpoints as well as their interrelationships are formally defined through a metamodel. Based on this metamodel, consistency between views is ensured through the definition of constraints relating model entities belonging to the same (view consistency) or different (inter-view consistency) views. The small number of views enables their effective manipulation.

EIS framework strictly focuses on system design issues, such as resource allocation and architecture specification. The function column of Zachman's matrix is regarded as the initial view the system designer should consider, corresponding to system architecture and functionality (functional viewpoint). Data and people columns do not fall into the scope of EIS design framework as the latter deals only with data allocation and replication policies rather than data specification, while user profiles are used mainly to indicate user behavior and performance requirements affecting system modules. All views are supported by UML 2.0 stereotypes, typically defined in a UML profile. Constraints are used extensively to maintain consistency and depict all the relations defined between system entities included in the metamodel.

The methodology proposed addresses all issues related to EIS design, utilizing the viewpoints defined, through four discrete stages (i.e., requirement definition, resource allocation, network design, and

Table 4. Stereotypes and constraints for physical and topology viewpoints

	Stereotype	Notation	Constraints
Physical View	Network Package		1. The value of attribute *type* is either "atomic" or "composite". 2. Composite *NetworkPackages* contain only other *NetworkPackages* while simple *NetworkPackages* correspond to simple LANs and contain only *ServerDevices* or *WorkstationDevices*. 3. Each *NetworkPackage* corresponds to a single *SitePackage* in the Topology View. 4. Corresponding *Network* and *Site Packages* are of the same type. 5. Corresponding *Network* and *SitePackages* have corresponding parents.
	Server Device		6. Each *ServerDevice* relates to a set of *ServerProcessComponents* defined in the Topology View.
	Workstation Device		7. Each *WorkstationDevice* relates to one *userProfileComponent* defined in the Topology View. 8. Each *WorkstationDevice* relates to all *ClientProcessComponents* defined in the Topology View that are invoked by the *userProfile Component* assigned to it. 9. The *items* value is the same as the *instances* value of the corresponding *userProfileComponent* in the Topology View.
	ProcessUnit Device		10. Each *ProcessUnitDevice* relates to an existing *ServerDevice* or *WorkstationDevice*.
	StorageUnit Device		11. Each *StorageUnitDevice* relates to an existing *ServerDevice* or *WorkstationDevice*. 12. Each *StorageUnitDevice* hosts *data replicas* defined in the Topology View.
Topology View	SitePackage		1. The value of attribute *type* must be either "atomic" or "composite". 2. Composite *SitePackages* contain only other *SitePackages* while simple *SitePackages* contain only *ServerProcessComponents*, *ClientProcessComponents*, and *UserProfile Components*. 3. Each *SitePackage* corresponds to a single *NetworkPackage* in the Physical View. 4. Corresponding *Network* and *Site Packages* have corresponding parents. 5. *max* and *avg* attributes are automatically computed based on traffic flow within, in and out of the site.
	Server Process Component		6. *application* corresponds to one Functional View. 7. The *module* attribute indicates an existing *ServerModulePackage* in the selected Functional View. 8. The value of the *name* attribute is produced as a concatenation of *processId* and *module* attributes. 9. Each *ServerProcessComponent* relates to a *ServerDevice* in the Physical View. 10. *NetReq* attributes are automatically computed based on traffic flow to the *ServerProcessComponent*. 11. *ProcReq* attributes are automatically computed based on the processing requirements of the process.
	DataReplica Component		12. The names and other attribute values are extrapolated by corresponding *DataEntityComponent* attributes of relative Functional View. 13. *DataReplicaComponent* is related to an existing *StorageUnitDevice* of Physical View.
	Invoke Dependency	- - - ->	14. *Invoke* connects only *ClientProcessComponents* or *ServerProcessComponents* to *ServerProcessComponents*. 15. Every *Invoke* relationship is included in the corresponding Functional View.

performance evaluation). The last three stages may be performed by the system designer or specialized tools. Moreover, EIS framework supports model exchangeability through the transformation of the common metamodel to internal tool-specific metamodels.

FUTURE TRENDS

Model-based system design is based on the assumption that a central system model can be defined, covering all aspects related to system analysis and design, in a similar fashion as the platform-independent model serves model-based software engineering. In both cases, UML is the dominating choice for representation purposes. An important issue though is the provision of an integrated model for both software and system design. There are already endeavors initiated, such as RUP framework, working towards this direction. It is important that not only common principles are introduced, but also a formal identification and definition of model dependencies and transformations is established.

Agile systems, as described by Dove (2005), are imperative for modern enterprises operating in highly turbulent environments, since such systems are able to adjust to both expected and unpredicted

Table 5. Characteristics of RUP-SE, UML4ODP and EIS frameworks in respect to system design requirements

	RUP-SE	UML4ODP	EIS
Central system model	◉	●	●
System Engineering Design Issues	●	◉	●
Methodology	●	○	◉
UML representation	◉	●	●
Model exchangeability – Tool Integration	○	○	◉

Legend:
○ not supported
◉ supported
● fully supported

changes in a timely and cost-effective manner. Model-driven architectures, such as MDA, are working towards obtaining system agility, which can be strengthened by a common model-based approach to study all aspects regarding enterprise information system design and development. Existing enterprise architecture frameworks, such as those presented in this chapter, should be enhanced to serve agility.

CONCLUSION

This chapter discussed the model-driven design of enterprise information systems and the principle requirements for applying it to EIS analysis and design.

Three different frameworks, namely RUP SE, UML4ODP, and EIS design framework, were studied in respect to these requirements. The frameworks have different origin, and they target different system design aspects. However, they all adopt UML language for model representation and contribute to the system analysis and design process. The characteristics of each framework in respect to the system design requirements identified in the previous section are summarized in Table 5.

REFERENCES

Boer, F. S., Bonsangue, M. M., Jacob, J., Stam, A., & Torre, L. (2004). A logical viewpoint in architectures. In *Proceedings of the IEEE EDOC 2004*. IEEE Computer Press.

Brown, A. (2004). Model driven architecture: Principles and practice. *Software System Modeling, 3, 314-327.*

Brown, D., & Densmore, J. (2005). The new, improved RUP SE architecture framework. *IBM Rational Edge.* Retrieved from www.ibm.com/developerworks/rational/library/junos/brown/index.html

Dijkman, R. M., Quartel, D. A. C., Pires, L. F., & Sinderen, M. J. (2003). An approach to relate viewpoints and modeling languages. In *Proceedings of IEEE EDOC 2003.* IEEE Computer Press.

Dove, R. (2005, March). *Fundamental principles for agile systems engineering.* Paper presented at the Conference on Systems Engineering Research (CSER), Stevens Institute of Technology, Hoboken, NJ.

Frankel, D. (2003). *Applying EDOC and MDA to the RM-ODP engineering and technology viewpoints:*

An architectural perspective. INTAP - David Frankel Consulting.

Frankel, D., Harmon, P., & Mukerji, J. (2003). The Zachman framework and the OMG's model driven architecture. *Business Process Trends.* Whitepaper. Retrieved from www.omg.org/md8/mda_files/og-03-WP_Mapping_MDA_to_to_Zachman_framework1.pdf

Goethals, F., Lemahieu, W., Snoeck, M., & Vandenbulcke, J. (2006). An overview of enterprise architecture framework deliverables. In R. K. J. Banda (Ed.), *Enterprise architecture: An introduction.* ICFAI University Press.

Gomaa, H., Menasce, D., & Kerschberg, L. (1996). A software architectural design method for large-scale distributed information systems. *Distributed System Engineering Journal, 3(3).* IOP.

Graupner, S., Kotov, V., & Trinks, H. (2001). A framework for analyzing and organizing complex systems. In *Proceedings of the 7th International Conference on Engineering Complex Computer Systems.* IEEE Computer Press.

Greefhorst, D., Koning, H., & Hans van, V. (2006). The many faces of architectural descriptions. *Information Systems Frontiers, 8*(2), 103-113.

Hilliard, R. (2001, January). *IEEE Std 1471 and beyond.* Position Paper for SEI's First Architecture Representation Workshop.

IEEE. (2000). IEEE Recommended practice for architectural description of software-intensive systems. *IEEE Std 1471.*

INCOSE. (1998). *INCOSE system engineering terms glossary.*

ISO/IEC. (1998). Information technology – open distributed processing – part 1 – overview. *ISO/IEC 10746-1 | ITU-T Recommendation X.901.* Author.

ISO/IEC. (2006). Information technology – open distributed processing – use of UML for ODP system specifications. *ITU-T Recommendation X.906.*

Kaehkipuro, P. (2001). UML-based performance modeling framework for ocmponent-based distributed systems. *Performance engineering* (LNCS 2047). Springer-Verlag.

Leist, S., & Zellner, G. (2006, April 23-27). Evaluation of current architecture frameworks. In *Proceedings of SAC'06,* Dijon, France.

Murray, C. (2003a). Rational unified process for systems engineering - part 1: Introducing RUP SE version 2.0. *Rational Edge.* Retrieved from /download.boulder.ibm.com/ibmdl/pub/software/dw/rationaledge/aug03/f_rupse_mc.pdf

Murray, C. (2003b). Rational unified process for systems engineering – part II: System architecture. *Rational Edge.* /download.boulder.ibm.com/ibmdl/pub/software/dw/rationaledge/sep03/m_systemarch.pdf

Murray, C. (2003c). Rational unified process for systems engineering – part III: Requirements analysis and design. *Rational Edge.* /download.boulder.ibm.com/ibmdl/pub/software/dw/rationaledge/oct03/m_rupse_mc.pdf

Nezlek, G. S., Hemant, K. J., & Nazareth, D. L. (1999). An integrated approach to enterprise computing architectures. *Communications of the ACM, 42*(11). ACM Press.

Nikolaidou, M., Alexopoulou, N., Tsadimas, A., Dais, A., & Anagnostopoulos, D. (2006). Extending UML 2.0 to augment control over enterprise information system engineering process. In *Proceedings of International Conference on Software Engineering Advances (ICSEA 2006).* IEEE Computer Press.

Nikolaidoum, M., & Anagnostopoulos, D. (2003). A distributed system simulation modeling approach. *Simulation Practice and Theory Journal, 11*(4). Elsevier Press.

Nikolaidoum, M., & Anagnostopoulos, D. (2005). A systematic approach for configuring Web-based information systems. *Distributed and Parallel Database Journal, 17,* 267-290. Springer Science.

Oliver, W. D., Kelliher, T. P., & Keegan, J. G. (1997). *Engineering complex systems with models and objects.* McGraw-Hill Companies.

OMG Inc. (2006, June 5). *Object constraint language* (Version 2.0).

OMG Inc. (2007, March 2). *Unified modeling language: Superstructure* (Version 2.1.1).

Savino-Vázquez, N. N., et al. (2000). Predicting the behavior of three-tiered applications: Dealing with distributed-object technology and databases. *Performance Evaluation, 39*(1-4). Elsevier Press.

Serain, D. (1999). Middleware. *Practitioner series.* Springer-Verlag.

Sowa, F. J., & Zachman, A. J. (1992). Extending and formalizing the framework for information systems architecture. *IBM Systems Journal, 38*(2&3), 590-616.

Zachman, A. J. (1999). A framework for information systems architecture. *IBM Systems Journal, 31*(3), 445-470.

KEY TERMS

Central System Model: A technology-neutral multilevel model used as a basis for model-based system design.

Model-Based EIS Design Requirements: Requirements that EIS analysis and design frameworks must satisfy to effectively facilitate model-based system design.

Model-Based System Design: A system design method providing a central system model (tool-independent) that captures system requirements and design decisions that fulfill them at different levels of abstraction. It enables integration of system models supported by autonomous design tools and interoperability between them without interfering with their internal implementation.

System Design: The process of analyzing system requirements, designing the desired architecture of a system, and exploring performance requirements, ensuring, thus, that all system components are identified and properly allocated and that system resources can provide the desired performance.

System Engineering: The interdisciplinary approach and means to enable the realization of successful systems.

System Model: A set of entities and their relationships describing a system.

System Model Representation: A graphical notation for the illustration of a system model.

View: A representation of the whole system from the perspective of a related set of concerns.

Viewpoint: The perspective from which a view is taken. It serves a specific category of system stakeholders.

Chapter XXII
On the Design of Multiagent, Context–Aware, and Mobile Systems

Tagelsir Mohamed Gasmelseid
King Faisal University, Saudi Arabia

ABSTRACT

This chapter addresses the software engineering dimensions associated with the development of mobile and context-aware multiagent systems. It argues that despite the growing deployment of such systems in different application domains little has been done with regards to their analysis and design methodologies. The author argues that the introduction of mobility and context awareness raises three main challenges that deserve a paradigm shift: the challenge of information integrity, service availability on mobile devices, and the complexity of decision modeling. Because they reflect different operational and procedural dimensions, the author argues that the conventional software engineering practices used with intelligent systems that possess other agency qualities need to be "re-engineered." The chapter emphasizes that the envisioned methodology should reflect a thorough understanding of decision environments, domains representation, and organizational and decision-making structures. Furthermore, the chapter provides a description for the appropriate enablers necessary for integrated implementation.

INTRODUCTION

The significant advances exhibited in the field of mobile and wireless information systems have resulted in a rapid proliferation of mobile information devices and considerable improvement in their capabilities. Devices such as cellular or Web phones, laptop computers, and personal digital assistants (PDA) have developed from basic means of communication and simple electronic calendar management units into computing devices capable of transmitting and processing data with wireless access to the Internet. Their uses in large scale distributed networks and grids allow new distributed applications to emerge in different domains. They have been widely used in e-business, e-learning, supply chain management, virtual enterprises (Jain, Aparicio, & Singh, 1999), information retrieval (Cabri, Leonardi, & Zambonelli, 2000), Internet-based auctions (Sandholm & Huai, 2000), distributed network management (Du, Li, & Chang, 2003), resource management and broadband intelligent networks (Chatzipapadopoulos, Perdikeas, & Venieris, 2000), telecommunication services, and mobile and wireless computing *(Keng, Ee-Peng, & Zixing,* 2001). They have enhanced the functionality of such systems by improving the availability, accessibility, and management of decentralized repositories of concurrent data. In addition, the transformation of business environments and availability of mobile technology have encouraged the study of "context awareness" as a leading feature. Context awareness is directly and inexorably related to "mobility" where decision makers and users of mobile systems can use mobile networks to access data and carryout transactions using a wide range of intelligent units and applications.

MULTIAGENT MOBILE AND CONTEXT AWARE SYSTEMS

An intelligent agent is an autonomous, computational software entity that has access to one or more heterogeneous and geographically distributed information sources, and that proactively acquires, mediates, and maintains relevant information (Gasmelseid, in press). Intelligent agents are used to carry out functions on behalf of their users, other agents, or programs with some degree of autonomy using multiple information and communication platforms. While some agents have been used for information search and retrieval and the management of information overload, others perform repetitive activities and specific tasks such as scheduling and interface presentation, task delegation, users training, event monitoring, information search, matchmaking, and filtering (Wooldridge & Jennings, 1995; Gasmelseid, 2007).

Within the context of a distributed work environment, software agents can assist in facilitating coordination, cooperation, and interaction among different agencies (Gasmelseid, 2007). Their deployment in electronic commerce, traffic control, healthcare provisioning, portfolio management, and telecommunications proved their relevance to

handle complex, distributed problems involving a multiplicity of interconnected processes whose solutions demand the allocation of fusion of information and expertise from demographically distributed sources (Gasmelseid, 2006). Using an agent in the healthcare sector, for example, patients can receive remote monitoring and telemedicine services from one or more healthcare service providers (i.e., hospitals, physicians, nurses, pharmacies, laboratories, clinics, emergency centers, and consultants) in a high quality cost effective form. In a distributed healthcare setting, general practitioners, hospital specialists, nurses, and home care organizations have to work together to provide the appropriate care to a sick patient (Huang et al, 1995). Industrial applications of agent technology, on the other hand, include the application of contract net task allocation protocol in a manufacturing environment. In process control, multiagent systems have been applied in electricity transportation management, and particle accelerator control (Jennings & Wooldridge, 1998).

In response to the growing situational and business complexities and the increasing focus on resource sharing, agents are usually assembled into "multiagent organizations" and structures rather than being used as individual components. Due to the lack of an universally accepted definition for the concepts that govern and dictate "agency," multiagent systems are described in accordance with their functions based on the qualities possessed by the agents making them up.

The transformations exhibited in business environments, the growing importance of "delegation" and resource sharing as a business imperative, and the improvement of technological platforms have moved "mobility" and "context awareness" to the list of highly acknowledged agent qualities. While such qualities are not usually considered on individual bases, they are coupled with other qualities in pursuit of orchestrating and harmonizing the functionality of the entire multiagent organization. Therefore, when mobile agents are used to constitute the entire multiagent system they can jointly use knowledge and resources to solve problems in a context-dependent way (Gasmelseid, 2006a) and move interactively to realize some objectives and perform functions.

In telecommunications terms, mobility is defined as the ability to "wirelessly" access all of the services that one would normally have in a fixed wired line environment such as a home or office, from anywhere. It includes terminal mobility (provided by wireless access), personal mobility (based on personal numbers), and service portability supported by the capabilities of intelligent networks. Especially in technology-intensive and information-rich distributed environments, mobile agents interact to gather information, route processing outcomes, update a database, and read performance levels, among others. In addition to its ability to meet objectives, the efficiency of any mobile multiagent system is also based on its capacity to adapt to changing environments.

Despite the increasing deployment of mobile agent-based systems in different domains (e.g., education, medicine, airlines, commerce, etc.), their use is being constrained by the unpredictable variation in network quality, lowered trust and robustness of mobile elements, limitations on local resources imposed by weight and size constraints, and concern for battery and power consumption (Satyanarayanan, 2001). Fortunately, the unprecedented advancement exhibited in the fields of mobile networking and performance-improving techniques, consistency of mobile information access, adaptivity and location sensitivity, and energy saving are relaxing these constraints. These developments are directed, among others, towards fostering adaptability and ensuring a balance between autonomy (reliance on static servers dictated by the relative resource poverty of mobile units and their lower trust and robustness) and interdependence (self-reliance necessary to cope with unreliable and low-performance networks, and power consumption). The use of mobile agents demands unique mobile hardware and software components because the entire multiagent system exhibits considerable data management complexi-

ties originating from the mobility of devices, hosts (and connections among them), and users on the one hand and the unique way mobile components operate on a wireless network and in disconnected mode on the other hand.

In addition to mobility, issues related to context awareness are also emerging. The importance of bringing "context awareness" into the decision-making environment, especially for global enterprises, is dictated by a wide range of factors:

a. The growing level of complexity, sophistication, and downside risks associated with distributed (yet integrated) business transactions.

b. The growing emphasis on accountability, corporate responsibility, and orchestrated processing and the increasing importance of real time information. The fear of taking decisions based on incomplete information (using cost benefit analysis and institutional trade offs) increased the importance of acquiring different types of information and introduced the question of "context awareness" into the "mobile" decision-making domain.

Context awareness relates to the ability of the entire "system" to sense and use the elements of its surrounding environment. A mobile context-aware multiagent system appreciates its environment and adapts its configuration and functionalities in accordance with available context information that can be used to characterize the situation of any entity such as the location of the user, collection of nearby objects and people, hosts, accessible devices, and change to them over time. While using context information and context-aware systems in physical applications (like robots) may be simple, understanding, acquiring, and using context information in decision support domains is a complex task. The complexity stems from the difficulty of using and exploiting new classes of context-aware applications in a changing technical and operational environment in which different types of context information is generated. However, despite the production of different types of context information, what constitutes "context-relevance" of information in a decision-making domain is contingent upon:

1. The nature and magnitude of the potential change and/or improvement an information element generates about the states of decision making, for example, minimizing risk or moving to the state of "certainty."
2. The degree of information integrity to be incorporated in the decision-making environment and the variables interacting across it.

Within this context, mobile and multiagent systems are being widely used for mobility management and enhancement of context awareness. Their use tends to allow for better performance, scalability, portability, connectivity, bandwidth, energy, and robustness (*Ee-Peng & Keng,* 2001; Yu Jiao & Hurson, 2004). They assist in balancing workload because, by migrating from the mobile device to the core network, agents can take full advantage of the high bandwidth of the wired portion of the network and the high computation capability of servers and workstations. They also assist in reducing network traffic because the migration capability of mobile agents allows them to handle tasks locally instead of passing messages between the involved databases.

The ability of a multiagent context-aware system to provide decision support by sensing, extracting, interpreting, and using decision-related context information is based on the following considerations:

1. The ability of system developers to model the decision-making situation and configure it in a multiagent mobile and context-aware setup. This process demands the articulation of context-related information that relate to specific decision-making patterns (individual vs. group) and states (i.e., risk, certainty, uncertainty).
2. Modeling the magnitude of change associated with context information to improve

its candidacy of capturing; that is, modeling data to crystallize the types of context-related information can be regarded as a "perfect information" and whose inclusion in multiagent, mobile, and context-aware decision-making processes makes a difference in the states of decision making and accordingly, the patterns adopted. In general terms, contextual knowledge associated with the current focus of attention (contextual knowledge) can be extracted, assembled, and structured to form the proceduralized context that is used in the current focus as a "chunk of knowledge." The part of context information which is not relevant for current focus or operations can be regarded as external knowledge.

3. Analyzing the orientation of decision makers and the way such orientations affect the nature and magnitude of context information and its utilization.

In the absence of concrete mobile and context-aware software engineering methodologies oriented towards decision-making environments, mobility and context awareness presents three types of uncertainties. First, information held in a mobile device is likely to be incomplete or outdated and may not reliably support user's needs in critical situations. Second, the availability of services over mobile and wireless networks necessary for business transactions varies in accordance with network traffic, the change of locations of users and machines, and the type and size of mobile devices. Third, modeling the behavior of decision makers is a prerequisite for the articulation and modeling of context-aware applications, a requirement that is difficult to achieve.

AGENT ORIENTED SOFTWARE ENGINEERING (AOSE) REVISITED

The recent technological developments have been accompanied with a shift from "conventional" to "agent-oriented" software engineering methodologies that can be used for engineering the software that has the concept of agents as its core computational abstraction particularly in the context of complex, open, networked, large, and heterogeneous applications (Gerhard, 2002; Jennings, 2001; Jennings & Wooldridge, 2002; Wei, 2001). Such migration is being motivated by the requirement that any software life cycle, process, or product model must be tailored towards the needs of the application domain of the target system (Basili et al, 1994). The main purposes of AOSE are to create methodologies and tools that enable inexpensive development and maintenance of agent-based software in a flexible, easy-to-use, scalable, and quality fashion (Erol, Lang, & Levy, 2000). Another purpose is to improve the ability of developers to construct flexible systems with complex and sophisticated behavior by combining highly modular components in the form of a multiagent organization. The adoption of AOSE methodologies to emphasize the underpinning organizational context to agents' interactions is seen as a vehicle for managing "complexities" through decomposition (dividing problems into manageable chunks in order to limit the designer's scope), abstraction (defining a simplified model of the system to emphasize and supports its properties), and organization (defining and managing the interrelationships between the various problem-solving components (Jennings, 2001). Based on this understanding, adopting an agent-oriented approach, "designers" can use multiple agents to represent the decentralized nature of problems and the multiplicity of control which incorporates different perspectives and/or competing interests.

Although many object-oriented analyses view the world as a set of autonomous agents that collaborate to perform some higher level function based on localization and encapsulation considerations (Booch, 1994; Parunak, 1999), agents can follow the same trend by localizing purpose inside each agent, giving each agent its own thread of control, and encapsulating action selection to support usability and system integration. However, despite the

wide spreading and deployment of agent-oriented applications, Wooldridge and Jennings (1999) argue that agent-oriented software engineering methods may have some political, conceptual, analysis and design, agent-level, and society-level pitfalls. While political pitfalls occur when the concept of agents is oversold or sought applied as the universal solution, conceptual pitfalls occur if the understanding that agents are conceptualized as "multithreaded software" is not emphasized. Analysis and design pitfalls occur if the developer ignores related technologies. On the other hand, agent-level pitfalls may occur if the developer tries to use too much or too little artificial intelligence in the agent-system. Society-level pitfalls can occur if the developer sees agents everywhere or applies too few agents in the agent-system.

ENGINEERING MOBILE AND CONTEXT AWARE MULTIAGENT SYSTEMS

Despite the growing deployment of multiagent, mobile, and context-aware systems in different domains, little has been done with regards to the development of the methodologies that can be used to "engineer" them. While responses to complexities exhibited tend to be based on the reconfiguration of resources (hardware and software) and processes associated with tasks, models, databases, and interfaces (devices accessible for user input and display), current AOSE methodologies fall short to represent and manage the context of network processing capacity, organizational preparedness, connectivity, and cost. In addition, the proceduralization processes associated with multiagent, mobile, and context information increased the necessity of developing a consistent explanatory framework for explaining and anticipating the results of a decision or an action and therefore, deserves a paradigm shift with regards to software engineering methodologies and patterns. The proposed paradigm transformation needed (represented in Figure 1) should be reflected in the following aspects:

1. Agent modeling as well as data molding and management.
2. The spatial context and the use of integrated architectures such as service-oriented architectures.
3. Managing service push and agent pull matrix and mechanism.

Domain Analysis

Domain analysis aims at improving the understanding of problem domains and solution spaces by identifying decision-making partners and stakeholders together with their objectives, preferences, and utility matrix. Existing agent-oriented software engineering methodologies have done much emphasis on task decomposition, associating agent functionalities with assumed privileges and drawing up road maps for agent-oriented analysis of problem domains. However, despite the similarity of the tasks incorporated, the process of domain analysis is being approached differently by different methodologies. Some AOSE methodologies approach task decomposition and assignment of roles to agents by using the main object-oriented concepts in a way that allows for "encapsulation," "inheritance," and "reusability" of software modules

and components. However, the process of coupling object-oriented concepts with agent-oriented ones has been challenged by the fundamental mismatch between the two concepts when they are implemented (Wooldridge & Jennings, 1999). To overcome this limitation, other AOSE methodologies approach domain analysis by incorporating agent-oriented concepts and theories of agent-hood into their models, knowledge base, and structures (Odell, Parunak, & Bauer, 2000; Wooldridge, Jennings, & Kinny, 2000). While each methodology is claiming comprehensive coverage of the phases of system development, the lack of maturity and inability to capture and represent the autonomous and proactive behavior of agents, as well as the richness of the interactions, have limited their deployment (Zambonelli, Jennings, & Wooldridge, 2001). Each successive development either claims to make the engineering process easier or promises to extend the complexity of applications that can feasibly be built (Jennings, 2001). While the main emphasis of all AOSE methodologies tend to be on drawing a framework for agent-oriented systems' analysis and design and developing implementation tools, they do not provide straightforward connections to the implementation of agent-based systems (DeLoach, Mark, Wood, & Clint, 2001; Wooldridge et al.,

Figure 1.

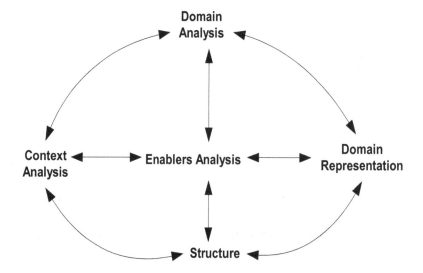

2000). The problem has been complicated by the emergence of the dimensions of context awareness and the expanding use of mobile multiagent systems for the implementation of mobile computing and other electronic transactions.

To take these variables into account, much emphasis needs to be made on domain analysis by crystallizing data access and using paths and processes associated with wireless mobile devices while they are operating in the active mode and the activities of their users when they are disconnected or using other devices. Such processes include the activities undertaken by mobile agents when they work to shift the workload from a low-capacity terminal to a server, or to filter or customize data before transfer. Incorporating these activities in domain analysis enables the development of efficient location mechanisms for mobile entities (Gasmelseid, in press). When emphasizing on decision-making environments, integrated domain analysis improves the understanding of the dynamics of using mobile agents and context-aware applications for dynamic optimization and control of decision support queries and their evaluation in a wide-area distributed domain of databases. Additional effort is needed to appropriately conceptualize a "context-aware" decision-making domain.

Context Analysis

The issue of context analysis relates to the creation of a context-rich decision-making environment that enables decision makers—while they are on move—to take decisions, monitor progress, and carry out tasks. The transformation of business enterprises and their migration to global complex operations has increased the need for real-time information and the use of intelligent Web-based "delegation" techniques on the one hand, and increased the importance of analyzing the "contextual" domains using Web technologies and the emerging data analysis and representation techniques (i.e., data mining, data warehousing, OLAP, etc.) on the other hand. While databases are currently developed as a part of

the general system development process, contextual analysis enables the appropriate development and use of "mobile multidatabases," the articulation and refinement of the methods of information retrieval and decomposition of "intelligent" tasks. It also "reshapes" the rationale of domain analysis as it significantly affects the nature of information to be acquired, the methods to be used, and the way to be represented. Thorough context analysis also affects the nature of analytical tools to be used (including Web intelligence) and the management of information representation concepts (e.g., semantics, ontologies, and acquisition).

Because they used to be occupied with "task definition" and "role assignment," current AOSE methodologies do not pay enough attention to the "context of decision-making problems." The problem will be complicated by the introduction of context awareness and mobility considerations and the inability of many developers to associate "their development efforts" with the nature and context of decision making. When decision-making domains are characterized with the lack of relevant information, the process of context analysis will differ from the situation where decision makers are faced by an "over abundance" of irrelevant information. While emphasis of context analysis of the former situation tend to be oriented towards the acquisition of information from multiple and heterogeneous data sources to be used for the development of multiple databases and "indexation," the later situation demands emphasis on "data reduction techniques," "filtering," and information organization. Despite the growing use of context-aware systems, none of the existing AOSE methodologies are providing an in-depth context-based analysis.

Structure

In addition to their ability to represent linkages, "structures" integrate different architectural considerations governing the nature and magnitude of context awareness and mobility concerns to be experienced by agents either individually or collectively. While the structure dictates and significantly affects the "processing capacity" of the entire system, it also affects the structure and fabric of wired and wireless communication infrastructure as well as the necessary "file management" tasks and the automatic reconfiguration of network components. Especially in decision support systems, the incorporation of context awareness and mobility qualities also challenge the capacity of current AOSE methodologies to adequately capture an agent's flexible, autonomous problem-solving behavior, the richness of an agent's interactions, and the complexity of an agent system's organizational structures. Most of these methods feature a technology-driven, model-oriented, and sequential approach and assumes (in advance) the suitability of multiagent technology for the development of multiagent applications which may not always be the case in different problem domains. Because model orientations of these methodologies are obvious, the process of model coupling and integration process does not explicitly reflect the links between models. Besides the main issues (known as agent qualities) to be addressed by agent-oriented software engineering methodologies (such as autonomy, reactivity, proactiveness, and social ability), the concern for mobility have been growing over time (White, 1997). In spite of the growing diffusion of mobile agent technology, little research has been done to settle "design" directions to be followed in order to determine when mobile agents are convenient to be used or not. However, the current agent-oriented software engineering methodologies used for developing multiagent systems do not provide methods to determine in which cases mobile agents should be used. Many of the existing methodologies intentionally do not support intelligent agents; rather, they aim for generality and treat agents as black boxes (Padgham & Winikoff, 2002).

Domain Representation

Domain representation relates to the selection of software platforms, spatial and visual mechanisms

necessary for the representation of contextual and noncontextual information as well as the technologies that make the acquisition, sharing, and use of such information possible. While different software platforms are being developed to support agent programming and context awareness, such efforts are still challenged by the lack of universally accepted programming languages and architectures that allow the incorporation of context awareness and mobility concerns in decision-making domains.

The process of information utilization in multiagent systems is challenged by the lack of communication languages geared towards direct machine-to-machine communication and the programming of hardware or software computer systems in accordance with a specific structure. Despite the fact that a number of agent communication languages have been proposed, notably hyper text mark up language (HTML), knowledge query and manipulation language (KQML), and Foundation for Intelligent Physical Agents (FIPA) agent communication language, so far, no standard exists to express the structure and content of messages and allow agents to understand each other. Furthermore, most of the languages do not specify syntax or semantics of the contents of the message leaving the relationship between logic and the interpreted programming language loosely defined.

Enablers' Analysis

Context awareness and mobility brings a wide range of new issues and/or increases the urgency and critical-ness of others. All concepts and issues that affect the four components shown in Figure 1 above are all called "enables." The set of enablers includes security considerations, change of user preferences and location, change of problem domains and solution spaces, authentication, and third party certification, efficiency of network, and connectivity and severity of database dependencies. Despite the variety of enablers and their situational-dependence, the focus of this chapter will be limited to the main two enablers that significantly shape software engineering efforts.

Authentication and Third Party Certification

The importance of "authentication" and third party certification stems from the interface matrix (among agents and between agents and their owners) as well as from the dynamics of "mobility and context awareness" associated with the mobility of agents to access different networks (for task handling and information acquisition), communicate with different service providers, and use multiple types of data and structures. Such considerations are associated with a wide range of agent-user (change of agent model base, knowledge engines, system infrastructure and architecture) and network-specific (change of infrastructure and architecture) considerations. While user-agent considerations reflect changes on "domains and context," network-specific ones bring load balancing and network optimization issues to the surface. Especially in decision-oriented, context-aware and mobile multiagent systems, the domain of decision making should not be left for full and absolute autonomy of agents. Because strategic decision making, for example, is oriented towards the external environment, the possibility of change is high, therefore. such consideration must be incorporated into the agent's development methodology.

On the other hand, the mobility and context-awareness of agents results in different modifications on the size of the agent and its ability (as a partner in a multiagent organization) to use load balancing mechanisms to manage context-based challenges. Throughout such movement and rooming the size of the entire agent may increase, the service provider misdirect it, other agents (absorb) it, and/or having other networks block its functionality as of change and frequent modifications of Web site addresses and/or data types. The entire agent-oriented software engineering methodology must incorporate suitable guidelines to be used for developing and mainstreaming of the necessary load balancing mechanisms and artifacts to be used by the entire agent or multiagent organization to destroy

a part of the agent's contents (which part?), to pass it to the corporate knowledge base, or to limit its rooming, mobility, and context awareness by its capacity to exercise load balancing mechanisms. While these issues are affecting the efficiency of the entire multiagent organization, their importance looms very big when mobility and context-awareness issues are incorporated. However, despite the emphasis of current AOSE methodologies on "task decomposition" and "task-functionality" coupling, little has been done to approach theses issues.

Incorporating Security Mechanisms

The development of mobile and context-aware multiagent information systems increased the importance of information security by focusing on the use of technological solutions in terms of hardware devices or computer programs (e.g., cryptographic algorithms, digital signatures and challenge response authentication techniques, hash algorithms, and hybrid encryption mechanisms and protocols). The basic aim of such "technological" intervention mechanism is to prevent, avoid, detect, or prepare for breaches of security that threaten the confidentiality, integrity, or availability of information processed by computer systems.

While the entire agent-oriented software engineering methodologies have provided alternative ways for task decomposition and description of "relationships," little, also, has been done to incorporate "information security" considerations in multiagent "mobile" and "context-aware" applications (Gasmelseid, 2006). The importance of maintaining the information security of multiagent systems originates from two basic considerations:

a. The expanding use of these systems in different life-related domains such as banking, insurance, education, medicine, tourism, airlines, entertainment, and the management of pooled natural resources, among others; and

b. The growing number and type of threats associated with the enterprise transformations and change of the qualities that constitute agent hood. Threats to multiagent systems range from uncontrolled accessibility and modification of core agent codes and services to the integrity of processes and communications, service execution, and coordination.

Incorporating information security considerations demands not only change of programs and technological solutions but also deserves a thorough "revisiting" of the way multiagent systems are being "engineering" and "developed." Accordingly, such paradigm shift necessitates increasing emphasis on the description and implementation of two basic issues of information security:

1. Linking information security with functional decomposition, message initiation, and communication in pursuit of integrated multiagent task management; and
2. Viewing security mechanisms on "layered bases" in order to enhance information flow, mainstream feed back, and use appropriate metrics and standard operating procedures to reduce threats at earlier stages.

The decision-making context reflects the entire organizational structure (through which information is exchanged), objective (to be supported by the multiagent information system), and the decision-making models (reflecting managerial styles). The importance of maintaining task-security coherence and layered information security is affected by the increase and diversity of the devices and resources to be used in heterogeneous networks and the functions to be performed in spontaneous ad hoc communications in a transparent, integrated, and extensible fashion.

Approaching information security through technological solutions is challenged by the variety of key length, computational complexity, and breach possibilities. Therefore, it is essential to "couple" technological solutions with an array of other factors (i.e., human resources, standard operating proce-

dures, structure, and system development methodologies) that should be investigated when addressing information security. The importance of analyzing and understanding "enablers" originates from the fact that multiagent, mobile, and context-aware systems use multidatabases and multi-DBMSs that may present some obstacles generated by local database heterogeneity. While the summary schemas model can be used in multidatabases as a solution that utilizes hierarchical metadata in which a parent node maintains an abstract form of its children's data semantics in intelligent systems, the analysis of enablers looms very big. For the hierarchical structure and the automated schema abstraction of the entire multiagent, mobile, and context-aware system to significantly improve the robustness and generate a dynamic expansion capability, the analysis of enablers facilitate the incorporation of security and integration dimensions in the body of software engineering methodologies and allows for early warning and prompt response.

However, revisiting AOSE methodologies to incorporate information security considerations has three reflections on the functionality of multiagent, mobile, and context-aware systems. (a) It "embodies" security in solution spaces when specifying and structuring problems in accordance with rules, behavior expectations, and authority relations particularly in open dynamic environments. (b) The emphasis on AOSE-based information security measures, rather than technological solutions only, brings "ontological and semantic" considerations to the surface at early stages. (c) Also, it significantly affects the trade off among alternative agent architectures.

FUTURE TRENDS

The migration towards Web-based, context-aware, and mobile systems warrants more understanding of the way such AOSE methodologies are used. The use of ad hoc networks and mobile components "databases and devices" to support the mobility of users incorporates some network-specific, user-oriented, and third party-based functionalities and processes that should be reflected by AOSE methodologies in use together with the appropriate metrics, standard operating procedures, and feedback mechanisms that comply with "mobility" and "contextual" requirements.

The projection of future trends shows more deployment of mobile commerce applications of the dynamics of the international economic system, organizational transformations, and changes of life styles. Within this context, more emphasis will be made on integrating features from different computing paradigms (i.e., mobile, pervasive, ubiquitous, grid, and soft) as an attempt to relax "architectural" limitations. To streamline functionalities, more focus is expected to be made on the orchestration of mobile and context-aware applications by maximizing benefits of Web technologies and managing "ontological and semantic" problems.

On the other hand, future trends can also be seen in organizational landscapes where organizations will continue to invest in improving their learning curves and turning into "learning organizations" by focusing on context awareness and mobility and maintaining linkages with decision-making domains. Future trends also show that additional R&D efforts will be directed towards relaxing the difficulties associated with context acquisition, representation, and sharing.

CONCLUSION

The focus on "responsiveness" and "coordination" in today's digital economy is being motivated by the trends of competition, market fragmentation, and shift of consumer preferences. To ensure "safe migration" from "conventional" to "electronic" business domains, enterprises have been increasingly concerned with "revisiting" their decision-making styles and decision support systems in pursuit of achieving objectives. The unprecedented technological developments (i.e., hardware, software, and

telecommunications) exhibited over the last couple of years has been accompanied by a wide range of concepts (such as context-aware systems, ubiquitous computing, wearable computing, and pervasive computing) which have significantly reflected "some fragmentation" of decision-making processes across an archipelago of geographical locations and increased the interest of decision makers in "context-related" information as a complementary for internal and external organizational repositories of information to support mobile applications.

Despite the expanding use of mobile applications and the emergence of context-aware ones little has been done to "reinvestigate" the potential of current AOSE methodologies and their potential to represent mobility and context awareness considerations. While some focus has been made on "domain analysis," additional efforts are needed with regards to "context analysis," "domain representation," "structures," and linking them with the set of enablers in an integrated way.

REFERENCES

Booch, G. (1994). *Object-oriented analysis and design* (2nd ed.). Reading, MA: Addison-Wesley.

Cabri, G., Leonardi, L., & Zambonelli, F. (2000). Mobile agent coordination models for Internet applications. *IEEE Computer, 33*(2), 82-89.

Chatzipapadopoulos, F., Perdikeas, M., & Venieris, L. (2000). Mobile agent and CORBA technologies in the broadband intelligent network. *IEEE Communication Magazine, 38*(6), 116-124.

DeLoach, S., Mark, A., Wood, F., & Clint, H. (2001). Sparkman. Multiagent systems engineering. *International Journal of Software Engineering and Knowledge Engineering, 11*(3), 231-258.

Du, T., Li, E., & Chang, A. (2003). Mobile agents in distributed network management. *Communications of the ACM, 46*(7), 127-132.

Ee-Peng, L., & Keng, S. (2001). Mobile commerce. *Journal of Database Management, 12*(3), 1-3.

Erol, K., Lang, J., & Levy, R. (2000). Designing agents from reusable components. In *Proc. of the Fourth Int. Conf. on Autonomous Agents* (pp. 76-77).

Gasmelseid, T. M. (in press). Engineering multiagent systems. *Encyclopedia of information security and ethics*. Hershey, PA: IGI Global.

Gasmelseid, T. M. (2006a, April 22-24). A multi agent negotiation framework in resource bounded environments. In *Proceedings of the ICTTA06*, Damascus Syria.

Gasmelseid, T. M. (2006b). Multiagent Web based decision support systems for global enterprises: An architectural blueprint. *Engineering Letters, 13*(2), 173-184. Hershey, PA: IGI Global.

Gasmelseid, T. M. (2007, July-September). A multiagent service-oriented modelling of e-government initiatives. *International Journal of Electronic Government Research, 3*(3), 87-105.

Gerhard, W. (2002, January). Agent orientation in software engineering. *Knowledge Engineering Review, 16*(4), 349-373.

Huang, M., John, T. Robert, S., & Towers, M. (1995). *Understanding the context of Medical Informatics*. Tokyo: Robertson Press.

Jain, A., Aparicio, M., & Singh, M. (1999). Agents for process coherence in virtual enterprises. *Communications of the ACM, 42*(3), 62-69.

Jennings, N. (2001). An agent-based approach for building complex software systems. *Communications of the ACM, 44*(4), 35-41.

Jennings, N. R., & Wooldridge, M. (1998). *Applications of intelligent agents*. Retrieved September 18, 2007, from http://agents.umbc.edu/introduction/jennings98.pdf

Jennings, N., & Wooldridge, M. (1999). Software engineering with agents: Pitfalls and pratfalls. *IEEE Internet Computing, 3*(3), 20-27.

Jennings, N., & Wooldridge, M. (2002). Agent-oriented software engineering. In J. Bradshaw (Ed.), *Handbook of agent technology*. AAAI/MIT Press.

Keng, S., Ee-Peng, L., & Zixing, S. (2001). Mobile commerce: Promises, challenges, and research agenda. *Journal of Database Management, 12*(3), 4-10.

Odell, J., Parunak, H. V., & Bauer, B. (2000). Extending UML for agents. In G. Wagner, Y. Lesperance, & E. Yu (Eds.), *Proceedings of the Agent-Oriented Information Systems Workshop at the 17th National conference on Artificial Intelligence,* Austin, TX (pp. 3-17).

Padgham, L., & Michael, W., (2002). *Prometheus: A methodology for developing intelligent agents*. Retrieved May 20, 2007, from http://www.cs.rmit.edu.au

Parunak, H. (1999). Industrial and practical applications of distributed AI. In G. Weiss, (Ed.), *Multiagent systems* (pp. 377-421). MIT Press.

Sandholm, T., & Huai, Q. (2000). Nomad: Mobile agent system for an Internet-based auction house. *IEEE Internet Computing, 4*(2), 80-86.

Satyanarayanan, M. (2001). Pervasive computing: Vision and challenges. *IEEE Personal Communications, 8*(4), 10-17.

Wei, G. (2001). Agentenorientiertes software engineering. *Informatik Spektrum, 24*(2), 98-101.

White, J. (1997). Mobile agents. In A. Bradshaw (Ed.), *Software agents* (pp. 437-472). AAAI Press.

Wooldridge, M., & Jennings, N. (1995). Agent theories, architectures and languages: A survey. *Lecture Notes in Computer Science, 890*, 1-39.

Wooldridge, M., Jennings, N., & Kinny, D. (2000). *The Gaia methodology for agent-oriented analysis and design*. Kluwer Academic Press.

Yu, J., & Hurson, A. R. (2004, October-December). Application of mobile agents in mobile data access systems: A prototype. *Journal of Database Management*, *15*(4), 1-24.

Zambonelli, F., Jennings, N., & Wooldridge, M. (2001). Organizational rules as an abstraction for the analysis and design of multi agent systems. *International Journal of Software Engineering and Knowledge Engineering*, *11*(3), 303-308.

KEY TERMS

Agent-Oriented Software Engineering: It is the process or methodology of developing and engineering software that has the concept of agents as its core computational abstraction, particularly in the context of complex, open, networked, large, and heterogeneous applications. The main purposes of agent-oriented software engineering (AOSE) are to create methodologies and tools that enable inexpensive development and maintenance of agent-based software in a flexible, easy-to-use, scalable, and quality fashion.

Context Awareness: It is the feature that reflects the ability of mobile devices to acquire and use information about the circumstances under which they operate and can react accordingly. By making assumptions about the user's current situation, context awareness assists in the design of user interfaces in ubiquitous and wearable computing environments and hybrid search engines. It reflects any task-relevant information and/or service that can be used to characterize the situation of an entity to a user.

Context Management: Denotes all activities related to the acquisition of context-related information and developing integrated frameworks that maintain linkages between the domain of decision making, architectural styles, and technological components.

Decision-Making Context: A decision-making context can refer to the "situation in which decision-making processes take place among different decision partners (denoted as objects including customers, suppliers, and governments)" with special emphasis on the change agents incorporated in the decision-making environment (i.e., those influenced by and influencing decision-making processes such as mediators and competitors) irrespective of the location at which decisions are taken.

Mobility: As a key quality of multiagent and context-aware systems, mobility is concerned with providing universal access to communication tools, networks, databases, and information repositories, as well as reliable applications, regardless of their location or type of access devices. It can be implemented through calling, conferencing management, presence, messaging management, contact and information management, and personal efficiency management and other tools that guarantee access to messages represented in different data formats.

Multiagent Systems: A multiagent system is a collection of, possibly heterogeneous, computational entities that use their own problem-solving capabilities to interact in order to reach an overall goal. Their ability to improve information availability, problem solving capabilities, corporate control, and distributed data processing gave them more importance in different domains of application. They proved to be suitable for complex, distributed problems involving a multiplicity of interconnected processes whose solutions demand the allocation of fusion of information and expertise from demographically distributed sources.

Multidatabase Systems: They represent the global (federated and nonfederated) systems on top of the existing heterogeneous local databases that generate an impression of uniform access with reasonable cost. Nonfederated database systems do not support local autonomy but federated database systems do. A federated databases system consists of component databases that are autonomous and sharable. To overcome the local schema heterogeneity problem and support global transactions, federated database systems normally adopt the layered schema architecture to orchestrate heterogeneous local-level data models with the uniform global ones (canonical or common data models). When using multidatabase systems, special attention should be paid to the management of schema redundancy that may exist between different layers, and the maintenance and manipulation of the global-level schema.

Chapter XXIII
Modern Design Dimensions of Multiagent CSCW Systems

Tagelsir Mohamed Gasmelseid
King Faisal University, Saudi Arabia

ABSTRACT

This chapter introduces and investigates the applicability of the multiagent paradigm for engineering and developing CSCW systems with the aim of advocating modern design dimensions and software engineering implications. It argues that the use of multiagent systems can significantly improve and enhance the functionalities of computer supported work systems. To meet such an objective, the chapter raises the importance of "revisiting" the context and domain of CSCW in accordance with the growing organizational transformations, situational shifts, and technological developments. While such changes are motivating group collaboration, the information systems that support them must be powerful. The author believes that because of their specific limitations and the continuous changes in the collaboration environment, there is an urgent importance of using thorough system-oriented approaches to address the way they evolve. Furthermore, the chapter draws a framework for the use of the multiagent paradigm to understand and deploy CSCW systems by adopting an integrated context of analysis that improves our general understanding about their potentials.

INTRODUCTION

The proliferation and advancement of information technology is dictating new axioms for collaborative work especially in information intensive working environments. Within such environments information technology plays an increasingly significant role by extending the back office (core and support processes) to the front office and beyond the branch. The Internet and e-business, for example, have affected enterprise-wide information availability both in terms of type and quantity. Because the adoption of Internet-based business transaction models has outpaced the development of tools and technologies to deal with information explosion, many businesses are being motivated to share information and tasks through integrated computer supported collaborative work systems. Especially for global enterprises, the use of networks is enabling collaborative work through information sharing and task accomplishment. While such collaboration allows organizations to save resources, it also improves their learning curves within a wider environment of a computer supported collaborative work.

Despite their growing deployment, little has been done to investigate the development aspects of CSCWs. Emphasis continued to be placed on understanding the role of computer systems in group work by using different theories without focusing on the way such systems are being developed. The migration of organizations towards decentralization, micro-management, delegation, networking and alliances, and customer satisfaction coupled with the growing functionality of hardware, software, and communication systems are increasing the demand for augmenting the benefits of such developments by refining the process of CSCW systems design.

The review and analysis of related work provided evidence that the use of agents' technology can improve the functionality of computer supported collaborative work systems. Their use can improve task collaboration and refinement, communication, and coordination by coupling both task identification and implementation characteristics (domain) with the capabilities of agents (agent qualities) in accordance with organizational principles (i.e., unity of command, hierarchy, structure, and decision-making styles) and technological build ups (multiagent technology). However, it is only through this approach that it becomes possible to understand the context of collaboration and the way to support it.

CSCW: BACKGROUND

The growing deployment of computer network technologies (including the Internet) has drastically changed not only the way network-based systems are designed and used but also affected the styles, methods, and environments in different application domains and dictated new axioms for interorganizational collaboration. Within such a technology-intensive environment, it is becoming increasingly possible for groups located in remote

trajectories to engage in both synchronous (where all members of the entire work group are working on the task on-line) and asynchronous (when at least some of them are off-line and working separately on the task) collaborative work processes.

The migration towards CSCW originates from the emerging pressures to reduce resources (e.g., lead time, costs, and defects), to increase client satisfaction, to improve communication with others, and to establish consistency in tools and procedures (Steve & Phebe, 2003). They are used to provide and maintain shared information resources and workspaces (David, Jenkins, & Joseph, 2006; Siriwan & Peter, 2006;).

Computer supported collaboration environments are often promoted as an open, safe, and trustable "learning" domains that allow equal opportunities—for collaborating members—to participate without the limitation of knowledge levels associated with work and individual characteristic, collaboration processes, and satisfaction with collaborative work (Silvia, Saskia, Wim, & Nick, 2007; Yan & Jacob, 2006). They have been also viewed as means for maintaining transparency for decision-making quality and trust for openness of communication (Henk, Paul, & van Doremalen, 2004). During such collaborative work, many activities, guidelines, operating procedures, and functions can be initiated, negotiated, "mainstreamed," revised, and implemented by the "collaborating members" of the entire group.

CSCW aims at understanding how collaborative activities, their coordination, productivity, and effectiveness can be supported by means of computer systems (Carstensen & Schmidt, 2002; Kevin, 2003). It is regarded as a fundamentally design-oriented concept that has two main dimensions: (a) technology-centric placing (emphasizing on devising ways to design computer technology to better support people to work together) and (b) work-centric placing (emphasizing on understanding work processes with an aim to better design computer systems so as to support group work). Such orientations reflect the role of computer systems in supporting work groups and the "technology-oriented" socially organized practices of their members (Bannon & Schmidt, 1989; Suchman, 1989; Wilson, 1999).

The operationalization of CSCW depends on the use of groupware (software and related computer networks) that facilitate interaction among collaborating members and sharing of "tasks" and "resources" through interfaces. CSCW's groupware includes, among others, software for tracking document changes, electronic mail software, application-sharing programs, videoconferencing software, instant and e-mail messaging, groupware, wikiwiki Web, computer assisted design (CAD), and software to support the collaborative viewing of Web pages. While different types of groupware can be used in different collaborative environments, they must facilitate cooperation, coordination, and communication among the collaborating members by splitting cooperative tasks into independent (yet integrated) subtasks and managing and supporting "dependencies" among tasks and activities. The functionality of the CSCW's groupware should not be limited to the provision of a sophisticated interface but it must also provide some degree of group awareness that enriches "mutual understanding" among the collaborating members. Group awareness plays an essential and integral role in group collaboration by simplifying communication, supporting coordination, and providing chances for process management and coupling in pursuit of group collaboration. In addition to groupware, perceiving and understanding the responsibilities, activities, and intentions of other members of a collaborating ensemble is a basic requirement for group interaction (Minh et al., 2006).

RELATED WORK

The development of CSCW systems continued to be guided by a wide range of theories including activity theory, conversation analysis, coordination theory, distributed cognition theory, ethno-methodology, grounded theory, situated action, and social/symbolic interactionism (Ackerman & Halverson, 1999; Engestrom, Miettinen, & Punamaki, 1999; Fitzpatrick, Kaplan, & Mansfield, 1996; Shapiro, 1994; Schiff, Van House, & Butler, 1997; Strauss & Corbin, 1998).

The emphasis of such theories tends to be oriented towards describing native cooperative phenomena and computer support for (cooperative) work in fairly abstract and stable context of organizational interaction. The basic assumption is that collaborating members (actors) are interrelated as parts of communities (in which the principles of division of labor applies) to contribute different kinds of "interactive expertise." Based on this understanding, the design of CSCW systems is regarded as a joint activity crossing borders of different communities of practice engaged in interdependent activities. Corporate organizational memory has also been used to approach CSCW systems by using it as a way for capturing accumulated knowledge and making it available and accessible to collaborating members in pursuit of improving their efficiency and effectiveness in a knowledge-intensive environment. Even when using the concept of "active remembering" to improve the potential of "organizational memory" by incorporating organizational, technical, and process-specific constraints, emphasis continued to be made on "tasks" and "processes" rather than on "the way" to develop necessary collaborative work information systems.

Most of the theories are used to study and describe CSCW settings and systems but few of them have explicitly and thoroughly approached their design process and the appropriate support tools. While the development of CSCW systems has witnessed a shift from a system-centered view of information systems to a user-centered paradigm by focusing on contextual enquiry, participatory design, and end user development (Beyer & Holtzblatt 1998; Greenbaum & Kyng, 1991), little has been done to use "reliable" software engineering methodologies to investigate the nature and magnitude of collaboration, the "socio-behavioral" styles of collaborating members, the sophistication of the entire collaborative work, and the "envisioned" support to be provided by computer technologies in a "shared" environment.

Previous studies reveal that CSCW did not seem to be achieving the influence it promised. Because of the lack of integrated design dimensions that address the dynamics of individual and group interactions and the context of information exchanged, the majority of theories used to conceptualize CSCW did not display a sophisticated level of integration. There has been more emphasis on "multidisciplinary" working and less "interdisciplinary" working (Steve & Mann, 2003).

Because CSCW systems are characterized by a high degree of user-user and user-system interaction and hence generate and huge amount of information, it is important to adopt systematic measures to understand information acquisition and utilization domains, explain and predict patterns of group behavior, and detect collaboration breakdowns and support group activity with adequate feedback (Thanasis, Alejandra, & Fatos, 2006). This demands a paradigm shift that incorporates the growing organizational, institutional, technological, and structural transformations. This chapter suggests the use of multiagent systems and "agency" concepts for the development of CSCW systems and the articulation of relevant new design dimensions.

MULTIAGENT SUPPORTED COLLABORATIVE WORK

"Agents," as software entities, can carry out some of the tasks on behalf of their users, other agents or programs with some degree of autonomy using the appropriate information and communication platforms (Bradshaw, 1997; Hyacinth, 1996). Accordingly, they can play different roles including task delegation, users training, event monitoring, information search, matchmaking, and filtering. Despite the differences regarding "what constitutes agency," attributes such as autonomy, reactivity, collaboration, mobility, goal orientation rationality,

and socialability are widely cited in agent publications. However, the topology of agents included a wide spectrum of agent types, such as collaborative, interface, information, task, mobile, and reaction agents. Based on the complexity of the agent representation style (individual vs. multiagent), additional agent qualities can be crystallized (Gasmelseid, in press).

A multiagent system is a system consisting of agents that communicate and cooperate to carry out work on the bases of intelligence, communication, cooperation, and massive parallel processing. In a multiagent system, agents jointly use knowledge and resources to solve problems in a context-dependent way. Multiagent systems are deployed to a wide range of applications such as electronic commerce, traffic control, healthcare provisioning, portfolio management, and telecommunications. They proved to be suitable for complex, distributed problems involving a multiplicity of interconnected processes whose solutions demand the allocation of fusion of information and expertise from demographically distributed sources (Sycara, 1998).

The potential and applicability of multiagent paradigm to support collaborative work is driven by the following considerations:

1. Within the context of the knowledge economy multiagent systems can facilitate collaboration by reducing the entry requirements of collaborating groups by shifting work burden to "agents" especially in sophisticated tasks using some integrated "delegation" parameters.
2. Its use enhances coordination and communication through the use of "specialized agents" like task, information, and interface agents linked within the same organizational chains of command by viewing them across a spectrum of superior-subordinate landscape of "agency."
3. The use of multiagent concepts facilitates negotiation, cooperative work, and information sharing in support of the growing institutional migrating to decentralized scales and the

use of cooperative distributed applications. Therefore, the nature and context of CSCW and its growing emphasis on communication, configuration, negotiation, coordination, usability, and information access improves the candidacy of using multiagent systems in CSCW.

The multiagent supported collaborative systems (MASCWS) is driven by the concepts derived from organizational theory, theory of decision making, theory of delegation, as well as agency and information system engineering and development theories. Because members are operating in a socio-organizational context, their "objective" functions and utility matrices can be represented by sets of "collaborating" specialized agents. Based on the principles of division of labor, agents have hierarchal task assignments that coincide with their hierarchy of command and goal congruence mechanisms. Therefore, as shown in Figure 1 below, task, superior, and high level agents are supported by "staff" ones acting in an advisory capacity. Privileges and coordination rights are preserved based on an integrated understanding of the collaboration environment.

The entire MASCWS supports communication across two layers: participants' layer (a.k.a interactions and understanding domain) and agents' layer (a.k.a cooperation and collaboration domain) in the form of computer mediated communication. Computerized artifacts are activated in environments where information sharing is a focus for communication and cooperation. They also support coordination, cooperation, and negotiation through the automation of feedback, feed through, control mechanisms, and computerized artifacts vs. noncomputerized ones. Artifacts are regarded as tools for the achievement of objectives or ends. This demands that agents should understand the work itself as well as necessary linkages with other agents dictated by soft artifacts.

Interactions in the MASCWSs are based on the following main components:

a. **Processing and functional artifacts**
The functionality of agents interacting in the context of the MASCWS environment depends on two levels of artifacts:

1. **Agent-specific artifacts:** These artifacts are agent-based, context-related, and are usually incorporated and represented into the agent's knowledge base and interface engine in order to guide its agent-user interaction and maintain conviviality across its specific and corporate domain of interaction.

2. **Shared artifacts:** These artifacts reflect the dynamics and functionality of not only interagent interaction and cooperation but also the nature and magnitude of tasks, changes of agents' behavior, expectations, and actions to be undertaken within a shared environment.

Artifacts (both individual and shared) are created and transformed incrementally across the entire multiagent CSCW environment until a detailed work is achieved. Shared and individual soft artifacts (databases, plans methods) are controlled and acted upon by all participating agents to improve collaborative practices and benefit from the outstanding processing, integration, communication, and negotiation capabilities of agent-oriented systems. Accordingly, the behavior of agents can be automatically adjusted to enhance mutual understanding among participants. For agents to control artifacts they must be able to perceive the state of the artifacts themselves because different agents and participants have different levels of control over them.

The use of artifacts and their orchestration in a collaborative processing environment brings two issues to the surface: (a) ontological and semantic considerations and (b) functionality orchestration. Ontology refers to the process of sharing and agreeing on a common definition of process-related concepts (e.g., structure of messages, instructions, requests to be supported, semantics, and the list of terms to be used in the content of messages). The explicit definition of (all) concepts to be represented

Figure 1. MASCWS's interaction framework

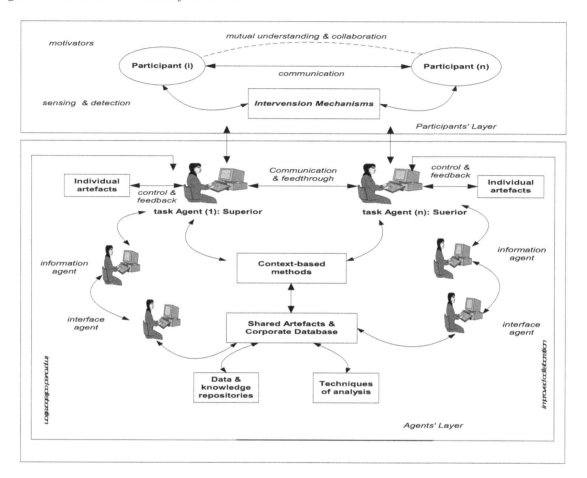

is not limited to the definition of the concepts themselves, but also expands to include attributes' meaning, constraints on attributes' values, and the relations between the attributes of different concepts. However, despite the use of general purpose ontologies and the provision of editors for creating domain specific ontologies and converters for translating between ontologies, the context and magnitude of the problem of ontology have not been yet appreciated (Gasmelseid, 2007a).

While significant degree of ontological sophistication of agents is necessary for knowledge sharing, cooperation, and interoperability, the interaction between "domain" and "task" ontologies is cumbersome. When designing a MASCWS, knowledge of the task for which the ontology will

be used is a prerequisite for the definition of the domain ontology.

The importance of maintaining an appropriate level of (both agent-based and institutional) functionality orchestration stems from the imperativeness of using coherent sets of shared rules, behaviors, expectations, and authority relationships. Particularly in open dynamic environments, negotiation, criteria assignment, partial global planning, assumption surfacing, argumentation, and evidential reasoning techniques, among others, can be developed and deployed to build coherence, orchestrate functionality, and mainstream coordination in the multiagent CSCW environments (Cammatara, McArthur, & Steeb, 1983; Durfee, 1987; Huhns &

Bridgeland, 1991; Steeb, Cammarata, Hayes-Roth, Thorndyke, & Wesson, 1988; Sycara, 1998).

Associated with the use of individual and shared artifacts is the development and activation of appropriate feedback mechanisms. It is paramountly important that all agents must be capable of perceiving and controlling artifacts and states of objects directly not through other agents or participants and be capable also of gaining feedback. Feedback is associated with the capability to control artifacts. Within this context, all agents must have equal (or layered) access to shared and individual artifacts and should be in a position to control the interactions associated with these artifacts. This is because shared artifacts are usually used as the subject and medium of communication between agents with regards to actions to be implemented based on such artifacts in a way that significantly affects the actions of other agents, the work itself, and the overall collaborative system.

The ability of other agents to observe the reactions of an entire agent or participant is called a "feed through." While feedback denotes the information an agent receives about its entire performance and actions, feed through provides information about the actions of their fellow agents, other programs, or users (collaborative members). Because of this feed through agents are able to communicate through the artifact where they, collaboratively, feel the effects of each other depending on the nature and magnitude of the tasks implemented and shared through shared artifacts. Accordingly, agents became able to indicate different objects or reactions by moving, sending information, or doing any other action which may be accompanied with phrases. Such a process becomes more complicated when multiple means are used because that will result into some semantic and ontological complications.

b. Context-based methods and models

The question of models and methods assumes high importance in MASCWSs. The development of the model base of such collaborative system is guided by two basic considerations:

1. **Model congruence and methods' consistency:** The model base of a MASCWS incorporates two modeling layers: agent-specific and system-oriented. Agent specific models reflect the nature and magnitude of objectives of its owner, the degree of task stability, and the set of expectations. However, the efficiency of such models is contingent upon its conviviality with the operating environment shaped by the interactions between agents and their owners and interfacing with different knowledge and data repositories or context. System-oriented models reflect the dynamics of the entire collaborative work across the processing landscape managed by different agents representing and serving collaborating members. The modeling of the entire MASCWS depends exclusively upon

    i.   The ability of system developers to, thoroughly, understand the context of collaborative work and, accordingly, model individual and collaborating members' practices, processes, and expectations. Such a consideration reflects the degree of model congruence and coupling needed.

    ii. The nature of the work to be collaborated, that is, whether members are collaborating on work that can be achieved in both synchronous and asynchronous work patterns or does the existence of all collaborating members' constitutes a prerequisite for task implementation. Another dimension is that the work to be achieved may have some decision-making dimensions which significantly affect not only the entire model base of each collaborating member and the entire CSCW system but also calls for developing the appropriate mechanisms necessary for the management of privileges, decision-prioritization, negotiation, and model-method-modification matrix techniques.

2. **Context orientation of models and methods:** The term "context" reflects different dimensions. It is usually used to denote "a domain for data collection, processing, information generation, and use." It has also been associated with the ability of different CSCW systems to "be aware about the objects in their surrounding environments." The orientation of the models incorporated into the entire CSCW system is known to be context-oriented when they reflect both the functionality and objectives of the collaborating members while they interact with their respective agents as well as when they interact in the open space of the multiagent SCW and its environment. However, based on the nature of the task to be achieved as well as the nature and type of agents (and accordingly models) to be involved it is possible to decide upon the importance of incorporating different levels of "context awareness" to account for the mobility of members, machines, and database and understand their affects on the process of agent and system modeling.

c. **Data and knowledge repositories** The MASCWS includes a corporate database that represents different types of data based on the functionality of agents and collaborating members. The degree of sophistication to be exhibited in such database reflects the degree of work complications and the nature of agent and system interface matrix. Therefore, the design of such database as shown in Figure 1 above brings the following issues to the frontline agenda of system developers:

   i. The importance of focusing on data refinement, integration, and management to ensure that all data elements can be incorporated as "usable" components into the agent's database and the corporate database of the SCW system. While such consideration may affect the overall functionality of the system and collaboration practices, it also increases the need for developing and using appropriate mechanisms for the discovery and management of database dependencies.

   ii. The need to place emphasis on knowledge mainstreaming, management of privileges, and accessibility control. Such consideration is driven by the fact that the process of database design will be complicated with the variety, unpredictability, and instability of the "qualities" of collaborating agents and the growing importance of incorporating "mobility" and "context-awareness" dimensions.

d. **Analytical techniques** The set of analytical methods includes all possible data analysis tools that are needed for the achievement of the entire task. They include data analysis tools such as data mining, OLAP (multidimensional data analysis, etc.), task scheduling and prioritizing, information acquisition and sending, dialogue enablers, and user-agent interventions, among others. For a comprehensive functioning of the MASCWS the applications that run such tools must be orchestrated to enable agents to switch from synchronous to asynchronous modes of work and migrate across applications and networks. While such techniques can be a part of the shared artifacts of the system, they must be incorporated into the knowledge and interface engine of the collaborating agents. However, it should be noted that the development and the implementation of such tools for cooperative work may result in unpredictable changes not only in the work to be shared but also in the communication, resource use, and coordination matrix of the overall system.

DESIGN-ORIENTED CHALLENGES

The growing organizational and operational shifts are dictating some transformations that significantly affect the process of designing CSCW systems as shown below:

Information Integration and Model Coupling

CSCW systems usually run on a WAN or LAN or separated independent application-oriented and functional processing systems. Therefore, the central concern is how to allow for interconnection and interoperation of multiple existing legacy systems to facilitate information sharing. Such a requirement calls for the adoption of an integrated approach for conceptualizing such legacy systems by maintaining an integrated view that accommodates a wide range of system specific and task-oriented issues. The basic challenge is how to acquire and integrate relevant information to support distributed problem solving and processing. The acquisition, communication, sharing, and use of relevant integrated information aims at improving the capacity of collaborating parties to model relevant phenomenon based on the majority (if not all) interdependencies, using multidimensional decision data. The failure to adopt an integrated approach that enables collaborating parties (and their applications) to interact with databases, application servers, content management systems, data warehouses, workflow systems, search engines, message queues, Web crawlers, mining and analysis packages, and other enterprise integration applications, challenges the efficiency of the entire MASCWS.

The development and appreciation of enterprise and system models is a complex task that deserves the mobilization of different resources particularly in legacy systems encompassing a wide range of complex infrastructures. While enterprise and business models are concerned with promoting understanding of business deliverables, functionalities, and utilization of resources, system models address design issues that fulfill both technical and functional specifications. Coupling such models is constrained by a wide range of organizational and policy limitations that shape information requirements to be gathered and the extent of flexibility

of data retrieval and response times. On the other hand, the process of model integration is also constrained by the thoroughness of understanding the technological infrastructure in terms of database, programming languages, operating systems, CASE tools and compliers, and so forth, and the way they can be used to produce the relevant system.

System and Network Optimization

Because CSCW systems operate as industrial networks they need to be optimized at two layers: the system layer and the network layer. Unless, under careful monitoring, the functional aspects of the legacy systems are optimized at the expense of the data and the network for implementation expediency, that is, the data and hardware/systems software were tailored to the application and therefore disintegrated with regard to the enterprise.

Related to the optimization of system and network processes is the management of flexibility issues. The banking system, for example, operates as a "legacy system," and is simply organized around existing applications which were built under the assumption that nothing would ever change. If anything changes, particularly in models, they have to be "reverse engineered" from available information in a very costly domain with significantly questionable confidence in its accuracy and "do-ability."

MODERN DESIGN DIMENSIONS AND SOFTWARE ENGINEERING IMPLICATIONS

The above mentioned complexities and challenges motivate the inclusion of some system design dimensions such as the following.

Dynamic Knowledge Streamlining

Determining relationships such as functional and inclusion dependencies within and across databases is important for information integration in MAS-CWSs. When such information is not available as explicit metadata, it is impossible to discover potential dependencies from "distributed" source databases, to manage redundancy of space and time and to minimize complexity. The discovery of inclusion dependencies will be beneficial in any effort to integrate or compare unknown databases particularly with applications in which data about similar real world objects is collected independently. The inclusion dependency discovery problem is loosely related to the problem of association rule mining (Agrawal & Ramakrishnan, 1995).

Generally speaking, an inclusion dependency (IND) over a database schema $\mathbf{R}$ is a statement of the form $R_1[X] \subseteq R_2[Y]$, where R_1, $R_2 \subseteq \mathbf{R}$ and X, Y are sequences of attributes such that $X \subseteq$ schema (R_1), $Y \subseteq$ schema (R_2) and $|X| = |Y|$. Let d be a database over a database schema $\mathbf{R}$, where r_1, $r_2 \subseteq$ d are relations over relation schemas R_1, $R_2 \subseteq \mathbf{R}$. An IND $R_1[X] \subseteq R_2[Y]$ is satisfied in a database d over $\mathbf{R}$, denoted by $d \models R_1[X] \subseteq R_2[Y]$, if for all $t1 \subseteq r_1$, there exists $t_2 \subseteq r_2$, such that $t_1[X] = t_2[X]$.

As shown in Figure 2 below, it is possible to articulate and manage at least six interconnected schemas together with their relations and dependencies in a collaborative work system. Such a system is designed and basically dedicated for collaborative assessment and approval of credit requests placed by farmers to different bank branches. These schemas include a banker information schema, a branch schema, a loan schema, a customer's schema, a credit card schema, and an accounts' schema as a base for articulating relevant database inclusion dependencies.

The problems associated with the discovery and management of database (especially) inclusion dependencies affect the semantics of databases, relational database design and maintenance, database reverse engineering, semantics query optimization, and efficient view maintenance in data warehouses. The discovery of suitable inclusion dependencies is a complex process because it is impractical to discover all nontrivial inclusion dependencies satis-

fied by a particular instance especially when testing multiple relational schemas. Inclusion dependency should not be regarded as a process of "duplicating attributes that are used to link together the relational schemas in a database schema" but instead, it should reflect processes at a single functional system (such as investment) as well as cross-system linkages in a way that promotes information sharing and the development of learning-oriented value-adding networks (Gasmelseid, 2007a, 2007b).

One of the main design dimensions of multiagent CSCW systems is to streamline the process of database dependencies through dynamic streamlining of agents' knowledge and interface engine. The basic aim of such design dimension is to account for the nonlinearity associated with the shift in the context of data processing and interface capabilities on the one hand and the paramount importance of maintaining sustained database orchestration domains on the other hand.

While the discovery of such dependencies may be simple in a computer supported collaborative loan approval process as shown in Figure 2 above because of the limited number of schemas, the change of the context of data processing may affect the whole process significantly. The simplicity of articulating these six schemas stems from the possibility of developing and managing "associations." However, under the situation of mobility (i.e., user, application, or service), creating that association is not a simple task.

Based on Figure 2, the entire database processing can be done online where finance seekers can interact with an investment information agent and place a query. The information agent actually is a task agent that uses other information and interface agents to retrieve information from a database or knowledge base that includes not only string and numeric data but also a repository of maps, sounds, multimedia and so forth, a feature that no human can handle over time. Information included in maps is difficult to update and needs much more expertise and a complex interface.

The dynamics of database dependencies become more complicated (especially in global enterprises) because of "task re-engineering," the migration from centralized decision making towards "micro management" and "delegation," and the engagement in international coalition systems or multinational mergers and acquisitions. While such shifts are complicating the management of database dependencies and generating modified management styles they are also being accompanied with a considerable migration towards distributed database and file management systems, mobility and context awareness considerations and incorporation of advanced ubiquitous pervasive features to maintain "reliable" management information ensure operational and outstanding reach and integrate processing among remote trajectories of operating units. Because the movement from the "mainframe era" through the PC era to the "ubiquitous computing era" is shaping business environment and dictating new axioms for doing business, the dynamic knowledge streamlining appears as an emergent design consideration through which not only task orchestration can be handled but also the interface, model base, and knowledge engine of the entire collaborative multiagent organization can be reengineered.

"Good Practices" Oriented Accumulation and use of Integration-Design Knowledge

Because of the uniqueness of applications and hence system design mechanisms, the development of multiagent collaborative systems should be based on the use of multiple methodologies. In addition to generally accepted agent-oriented software engineering theories, there is a growing importance to use the principles of "good practices" and "lessons learned" as complementary design techniques. While previous research has advocated some "agent qualities" and characteristics based on the existing business and industrial functionalities, additional features may be acknowledged as a result of future shifts. Therefore, the use of the principles of good practices and lessons learned can provide more

process-oriented emphasis on clear specification and communication of problems and constitute a base for a new deign dimension with regards to the development of knowledge-based models (domain-specific and domain-independent), and enhanced capturing of the (formal) semantics of different application domains. When we adopt the principles of good practices and lessons learned for the development of multiagent CSCW systems the functionality of the domain-specific approach to self-integrating systems may be enhanced with regards to the management of operational complexities. Because good practices and lessons learned may result into new agent qualities, the design of the entire multiagent CSCW system may significantly be affected due to the possible change of designer's "perception" with regards to agent (and collaborating members') intentions, goals, plans, beliefs, and "prioritization" of experience models on top of knowledge-based models to share domain-specific concepts. Integrating good practices and lessons learned as design dimensions also affects "machine learning" strategies and automated adaptation methods that provide for an efficient means of self-integration.

The adoption of good practices and lessons learned from different application domains enhances knowledge acquisition and use and facilitates the development and refinement of a set of "implementation" metrics supported by theoretical foundations necessary for gauging semantic equivalence. While coordination, collaboration, and negotiation theories and technologies may allow for flexible integration of systems at the level of task and process definitions, incorporating good practices and lessons learned allows for the development of smart human-computer interfaces and enables the development of usable semantic-based ontological descriptions.

INSTITUTIONAL IMPLICATIONS

There are some institutional and organizational implications associated with CSCW systems and

Figure 2. Schema representation

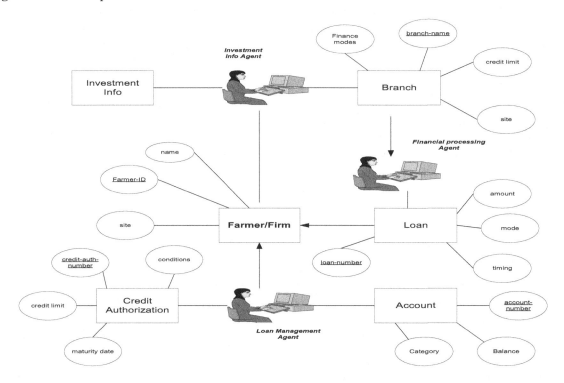

their development. This is because "information systems development" is usually viewed as an "organizational development" process through which foundations can be set for the resolution of different potential "conflicts" across organizational landscapes. Accordingly, CSCW systems can be used as means for managing (primary, secondary, tertiary, and quaternary) contradictions and mainstreaming processes as described by the activity theory.

The deployment of multiagent systems to support task handling, information sharing, and decision making in a multiagent SCW environment differs from their use to enable a robot to move (as it is the case of engineering applications), a customer buys a commodity through on line platforms (transaction processing as it is the case of electronic commerce), or researcher acquires and filters information. In contrast to other areas, the use of multiagent systems to support collaborative work is signifi-

cantly affected by the domain and environment of such collaboration which significantly dictates their architectures, models, and frameworks. The style of task integration and coordination adopted determines the type of "agents" to be included in an agent organization, the function-capability matrix, and the framework to be adopted to design the appropriate architecture. On the other hand, because the dynamics of collective work as well as their environments are complex, the deployment of multiagent systems should encompass a wide range of hierarchical, organizational, and institutional considerations.

Within this context, significant efforts are required to streamline technological as well as organizational concepts of division of labor (which guides the articulation of agents and their capabilities), hierarchy (which establishes linkage among agents and guides the distribution of control and supervision), goal congruence, and unity of command (which shape the extent of coordination needed). The orientations to be followed to conceptualize and develop "decision-oriented" multiagent organizations to support collaborative work must emphasize these concepts to maintain a considerable degree of decision-technology feasibility.

The complexities associated with collaborative work have been related to the various organizational transformation exhibited in organizations which originate from competitiveness, resource scarcity, and technological development. Such transformation has been accompanied with the need for maintaining competitive advantage, curtailing conflicts, and emphasizing the involvement of stakeholders. Within this context, the incorporation of the concepts derived from the context of multiagents systems can improve the capacity of decision support systems to provide the appropriate aid in complex decision-making environments. However, particularly under conditions of scarcity where the potentials of conflicts are high, multiagent decision support systems can play a significant role in the process of involvement and negotiation.

However, the feasibility and effectiveness of using multiagent systems to enhance collaborative work in a complex decision making environments has some institutional considerations depending on:

a. The level of information accessibility available for the collaborating parties and whether any sort of information asymmetry exists.

b. The degree of flexibility and resource modifications affecting the context of collaboration through improved capabilities on the part of the provider of resources.

These two basic variables indicate the degree of independence an agent exhibits during the collaborative process and the level of "collaborative" involvement. The level of such involvement is governed by the nature of problems faced by the collaborating members, the basic contributions of

agents and the degree of agent-user delegation. Especially in collaborative works that take place in uncertain situations, agents cannot be provided full autonomy to carry on all processes and functions in a fully-delegated fashion. The intervention of the collaborating members is paramountly essential to manage exceptional situations arising from societal, political, and economic considerations that cannot be a part of the corporate model.

CONCLUSION

The technological advancements experienced in the areas related to computer-based information systems such as telecommunication, databases, and software together with the expanding mobility, parallel processing, and enabled human-computer interaction functionalities have set the foundation for the growing deployment of software agents' technology in different areas. The approaches used to conceptualize "agents" ranges from the attempts oriented towards stating definitions to the focus on "the qualities that constitute agency." On the other hand, the variety of the "solutions" envisioned from the use of agents in different applications reflects the diversity and multiplicity of such technology. The deployment and use of multiagent CSCW should rather help not only "mediate" between collaborating groups but also reduce differences in a wider context of organizational learning in which collaboration takes place.

While the use multiagent technology to support collaborative work practices may provide outstanding advantages that improve interorganizational operations and cooperation, their success warrants considerable degree of system monitoring, network administration, infrastructure reconfiguration, and, most importantly, wider involvement of the collaborating groups.

REFERENCES

Ackerman, M., & Halverson, C. (1999). *Organizational memory: Processes, boundary objects, and trajectories.* Paper presented at the 32nd Hawaiian International Conference on Systems Science, Maui, HI. IEEE. Retrieved December 26, 2005, from www.eecs.umich.edu/~ackerm/pub/99b26/hicss99.pdf

Agrawal, R., & Ramakrishnan, S. (1995). *Mining sequential patterns.* Retrieved November 2006, from http://citeseer.ist.psu.edu/agrawal95mining.html

Bannon, L., & Schmidt, L. (1989). CSCW: Four characters in search of a context. In *Proceedings of the First European Conference on Computer Supported Cooperative Work*, Amsterdam. Retrieved November 2006 from http://www.it-c.dk/~schmidt/papers/cscw4chart.pdf

Beyer, H., & Holtzblatt, K. (1998). *Contextual design: Defining customer-centered systems.* San Francisco: Morgan Kaufmann.

Bradshaw, J. (1997). An introduction to software agents. In J. Bradshaw (Ed.), *Software agents* (pp. 3-46). Menlo Park, CA: AAAI Press.

Cammarata, S., McArthur, D., & Steeb, R. (1983). Strategies of cooperation in distributed problem solving. In *Proceedings of the Eighth International Joint Conference on Artificial Intelligence (IJCAI-83)* (pp. 67-770).

Carstensen, P., & Schmidt, K. (2002). Computer supported cooperative work: New challenges to systems design. In K. Itoh (Ed.), *Handbook of human factors.* Tokyo. Retrieved July 2006, from http://www.it-c.dk/people/schmidt/papers/cscw_intro.pdf

David, G., Jenkins, J., & Joseph, F. (2006). Collaborative bibliography. *Information Processing & Management, 42*(3), 805-825.

Durfee, E. (1987). *A unified approach to dynamic coordination: Planning actions and interactions in a distributed problem solving network.* Unpublished doctoral dissertation, University of Massachusetts, Department of Computer and Information Science.

Engeström, Y., Miettinen, R., & Punamaki, R. (1999). *Perspectives on activity theory.* Cambridge University Press.

Fitzpatrick, G., Kaplan, S., & Mansfield, T. (1996). Physical spaces, virtual places and social worlds: A study of work in the virtual. In *Proceedings of the Conference on Computer Supported Cooperative Work, ACM* (pp. 334-343).

Gamelseid, T. (in press). *Engineering multiagent systems: An information security perspective. Encyclopedia of information security and ethics.* Hershey, PA: IGI Global.

Gamelseid, T. (2007a). Multiagent Web-based DSS for global enterprises: An architectural blueprint. *Engineering Letters, 13*(2), 173-184.

Gamelseid, T. (2007b, July-September). From operational dashboards to effective e-business: Multiagent formulation and negotiation of electronic contracts. *International Journal of E-Business Research, 3*(3), 77-97.

Greenbaum, J., & Kyng, M. (1991). *Design at work: Cooperative design of computer systems.* Hillsdale, NJ: Lawrence Erlbaum.

Henk, A., Paul, B., & van Doremalen, J. (2004). Travail, transparency and trust: A case study of computer-supported collaborative supply chain planning in high-tech electronics. *European Journal of Operational Research, 153*(2), 445-456.

Huhns, M., & Bridgeland, D. (1991). Multiagent truth maintenance. *IEEE Transactions on Systems, Man, and Cybernetics, 216*(6), 1437-1445.

Hyacinth, S. (1996). Software agents: An overview. *Knowledge Engineering Review, 11*(3), 1-40.

Kevin, L. M. (2003). Computer-supported cooperative work. *Encyclopedia of Library and Information Science*, 666-677.

Minh, H., Tran, G., Raikundalia, K., & Yun Yang, S. (2006). An experimental study to develop group awareness support for real-time distributed collaborative writing. *Information and Software Technology, 48*, 1006-1024.

Schiff, L., Van House, N., & Butler, M. (1997). Understanding complex information environments: A social analysis of watershed planning. In *Proceedings of the Conference on Digital Libraries* (pp. 161-168).

Shapiro, D. (1994). The limits of ethnography: Combining social sciences for CSCW. *Computer supported cooperative work.* Chapel Hill, NC: ACM.

Silvia, D., Saskia, B., Wim J., & Nick, J. (2007). Students' experiences with collaborative learning in asynchronous computer-supported collaborative learning environments. *Computers in Human Behavior, 23*(1), 496-514.

Siriwan, S., & Peter, H. (2006). A Bayesian approach to generating tutorial hints in a collaborative medical problem-based learning system. *Artificial Intelligence in Medicine, 38*(1), 5-24.

Steeb, R., Cammarata, S., Hayes-Roth, F., Thorndyke, P., & Wesson, R. (1988). Distributed intelligence for air fleet control. In A. H. Bond & L. Gasser (Eds.), *Readings in distributed artificial intelligence* (pp. 90-101). San Francisco: Morgan Kaufmann.

Steve, G., & Phebe, M. (2003). Interdisciplinary: Perceptions of the value of computer-supported collaborative work in design for the built environment. *Automation in Construction, 12*(5), 495-499.

Strauss, A. L., & Corbin, J. M. (1998). *Basics of qualitative research: Techniques and procedures for developing grounded theory.* Sage Publications.

Suchman, L. A. (1989). *Notes on computer support for cooperative work.* Jyvaskyla, Finland: University of Jyvaskyla, Department of Computer Science.

Sycara, K. P. (1998). Multiagent systems. *AI Magazine, 19*(2), 79-92.

Thanasis, D., Alejandra, M., & Fatos, X. (2006). A layered framework for evaluating on-line collaborative learning interactions. *International Journal of Human-Computer Studies, 64*(7), 622-635.

Wilson, P. (1999). *Computer supported cooperative work: An introduction.* Kluwer Academic Publishers.

Yan, X., & Jacob, F. S. (2007). Emergent CSCW systems: The resolution and bandwidth of workplaces. *International Journal of Medical Informatics.* Corrected Proof, doi:10.1016/j.ijmedinf.2006.05.037, Available online 5 July 2006.

KEY TERMS

Collaborative Systems Engineering: It describes the integrated process of using (collaborative) software engineering methodologies to develop collaborative systems by addressing their contexts, functionalities, interface qualities, and implementation parameters.

Computer Supported Collaborative Work Systems: The group of computer-based systems that facilitate collaboration among people through enhanced information availability and sharing, task accomplishment, and consensus building. Their functionality is based on the use of a mix of groupware components.

Context Orientation: It denotes the ability of the collaborative work system to benefit from the qualities of computer systems to sense and understand the characteristics of its work-related and function-based attributes to use them for group collaboration.

Data Mining: Describes the process used to collect and analyze large amounts of data in order to understand patterns of behavior. Data analysis techniques such as OLAP, OLTP, and multidimensional analysis, among others, are commonly used for data mining to produce reports and generate functional data marts.

Groupware: Groupware includes all components (i.e., hardware, software, and data communication processes) that facilitate group collaboration through task accomplishment and information sharing. Based on the nature of the work to be done collaboratively, the appropriate mix of groupware technologies (e.g., e-mail, GDSS, digital voice mail systems, text conferencing, and video teleconferencing) can be selected.

Ontological Representation: Refers to the systematic representation of a shared (and agreed upon) common definition of the concepts that derive the functionality of the entire MASCW such as the structure of messages to be exchanged among collaborative members, semantics, and the list of terms to be used in the content of messages, instructions, individual, and joint requests.

Software Agents: They are the software components that use resources to perform activities on behalf of their owners and/or other agents or programs. They possess qualities of reactivity, autonomy, collaboration, mobility, and conviviality, among others, that increase their deployment in the form of multiagent organizations to support distributed problem solving and collaborative work.

Section V
Object Oriented Development

Chapter XXIV
Class Patterns and Templates in Software Design

Julio Sanchez
Minnesota State University, Mankato, USA

Maria P. Canton
South Central College, USA

ABSTRACT

This chapter describes the use of design patterns as reusable components in program design. The discussion includes the two core elements: the class diagram and examples implemented in code. The authors believe that although precanned patterns have been popular in the literature, it is the patterns that we personally create or adapt that are most useful. Only after gaining intimate familiarity with a particular class structure will we be able to use it in an application. In addition to the conventional treatment of class patterns, the discussion includes the notion of a class template. A template describes functionality and object relations within a single class, while patterns refer to structures of communicating and interacting classes. The class template fosters reusability by providing a guide in solving a specific implementation problem. The chapter includes several class templates that could be useful to the software developer.

DESIGN PATTERNS

Engineers and architects have reused design elements for many years (Alexander, Ishikawa, Silverstein, Jacobson, Fiksdahl-King, & Angel, 1977); however, the notion of reusing elements of software design dates back only to the early 1990s. The work of Anderson (1990), Coplien (1992), and Beck and Johnson (1994) set the background for the book *Design Patterns* by Gamma, Helm, Johnson, and Vlissides (1995), which many considered the first comprehensive work on the subject.

The main justification for reusing program design components is based on the fact that the design stage is one of the most laborious and time-consuming phases of program development. Design reuse is founded in the assumption that once a programmer or programming group has found a class or object structure that solves a particular design problem, this pattern can then be reused in other projects, with considerable savings in the design effort. Anyone who has participated in the development of a substantial software project appreciates the advantages of reusing program design components.

The present-day approach to design reuse is based on a model of class associations and relationships called a class pattern or an object model. In this sense, a pattern is a solution to a design problem. Therefore, a programming problem is at the origin of every pattern. From this assumption we deduce that a pattern must offer a viable solution; it must represent a class structure that can be readily coded in the language of choice.

The fact that a programming problem is at the root of every design pattern, and the assumption that the solution offered by a particular pattern must be readily implementable in code, are the premises on which we base our approach to this topic. In the context of this chapter we see a design pattern as consisting of two core elements: a class diagram and a coded example or template, fully implemented in code. Every working programmer knows how to take a piece of existing code and reengineer it to solve the problem at hand. However, snippets of code that may or may not compile correctly are more a tease than a real aide.

Although we consider that design patterns are a reasonable and practical methodology, we must also add that it is the patterns that we ourselves create, refine, or adapt that are the most useful. It is difficult to believe that we can design and code a program based on someone else's class diagrams. Program design and coding is a task too elaborate and complicated to be done by imitation or by proxy. A programmer must gain intimate familiarity with a particular class and object structure before committing to its adoption in a project. These thoughts lead to the conclusion that it is more important to explain how we can develop our own design patterns than to offer an extensive catalog of someone's class diagrams, which can be difficult to understand, and even more difficult to apply.

CLASS TEMPLATES

Occasionally, a programmer or program designer's need is not for a structure of communicating and interacting classes but for a description of the implementation of a specific functionality within a single class. In this case we can speak of a class template rather than of a pattern. The purpose of a class template is also to foster reusability by providing a specific guide for solving a particular implementation problem. In the following sections we include several class templates that could be useful to the practicing developer.

A Pattern is Born

We begin our discussion by following through the development of a design pattern, from the original problem, through a possible solution, to its implementation in code, and concluding in a general-purpose class diagram.

One of the most obvious and frequent uses of dynamic polymorphism is in the implementation of class libraries. The simplest usable architecture is by means of an abstract class and several modules in the form of derived classes that provide the specific implementations of the library's functionality. Client code accesses a polymorphic method in the base class and the corresponding implementation is selected according to the object referenced. But in the real world a library usually consists of more than one method. Since many languages allow mixing virtual and nonvirtual functions in an abstract class, it is possible to include nonvirtual methods along with virtual and pure virtual ones. The problem in this case is that abstract classes cannot be instantiated; therefore, client code cannot create an object through which it can access the nonvirtual methods in the base class. A possible but not very effective solution is to use one of the derived classes to access the nonvirtual methods in the base class. Figure 1 depicts this situation.

The first problem of the class diagram in Figure 1 is that the client code accesses the nonvirtual

Figure 1. A class library implemented through dynamic polymorphism

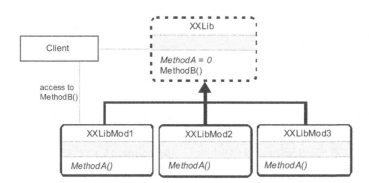

MethodB() in the base class by means of a pointer to one of the derived classes. A second, and perhaps more important one, is that method selection must take place in the client's code. Both of these characteristics expose the class structure and add a substantial processing burden to the client.

There are several possible solutions to the first problem. We could make the base class a concrete class with MethodA() as a simple virtual function, with no real implementation. In this case MethodB() becomes immediately accessible. Another solution would be to create a new class to hold the nonvirtual methods originally in the base class and have this new class inherit abstractly. However, neither of these solutions addresses the most important problem, which is that client code must perform method selection. It is this characteristic of inheritance that breaks encapsulation.

Encapsulation can be preserved by using object composition instead of inheritance. Also, combining object composition and inheritance achieves dynamic binding of polymorphic methods while preserving encapsulation. Figure 2 is a possible class diagram for implementing the library by means of object composition and inheritance.

Design of a VESA True Color Library

The design of a VESA true color graphics library can be based on combining object composition and class inheritance. The minimal functionality of this library can be stated as follows:

1. A way of setting the desired VESA true color mode.
2. A way of obtaining the current VESA mode as well as the vertical and horizontal resolution.
3. A way of drawing a screen pixel defined in terms of its x and y screen coordinates and its color attribute.
4. A way of reading the color attribute of a screen pixel located at given screen coordinates.

Figure 3 is a diagram of the library classes.

Observing the class diagram in Figure 3 we detect some features of the class structure:

1. The nonvirtual methods are located in the class named VesaTCLib.
2. VesaTCLib is a concrete class and can be instantiated by the client.
3. The mode-dependent, polymorphic methods for setting and reading pixels, named Draw-Pixel() and ReadPixel(), respectively, are located in an inheritance structure.
4. The methods named GetPixel() and SetPixel() in the class VesaTCLib provide access by means of a pointer to the polymorphic methods DrawPixel() and ReadPixel().

Figure 2. An alternative implementation of the class library

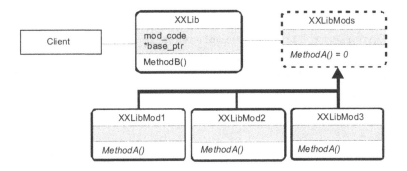

The result of this class design is that the implementation is now transparent to the client, as shown by the gray shaded background in Figure 3. The following program (Box 1) contains the schematic implementation of the class and inheritance structure in Figure 3.

The previous code sample, named SAMP-01.CPP, deserves a few additional comments. The constructor receives a coded signature that defines the VESA true color mode requested by the caller. A switch construct stores the VESA mode number, vertical and horizontal resolution, and the address of the library methods used in setting and reading

a pixel in this mode. Therefore, the contingency code executes only once, when the object is created. Thereafter, each object of the class VesaTCLib is associated with a particular mode and keeps the address of the method to be used in its own pixel setting and reading operations. The methods Get-Pixel() and ReadPixel() of the class VesaTCLib are the client's interface to the pixel-level primitives in the library. The actual setting and reading of a screen pixel is performed as follows:

Figure 3. Class diagram for a VESA true color graphics library

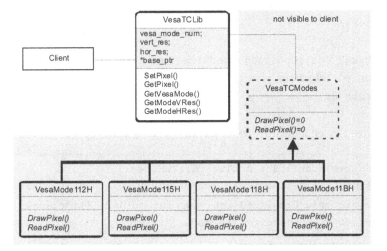

Box 1.

```
//*****************************************************************
// C++ program to illustrate implementation of a VESA true
// color graphics library using object composition and class
// inheritance
// Filename: SAMP-01.CPP
//*****************************************************************


#include <iostream.h>


//*****************************************************************
//               classes
//*****************************************************************
// Abstract base class
class VesaTCModes {
public:
// Pure virtual functions
 virtual void DrawPixel(int, int, int) = 0;
 virtual unsigned long ReadPixel(int, int) = 0;
};
//*****************************
//   Polymorphic classes
//*****************************
// Note: methods have stub implementations in this demo
//    program

class VesaMode112H : public VesaTCModes {
public:
 virtual void DrawPixel(int row, int column, int color) {
 cout << "Setting pixel in Mode 112H\n";
 return;
 }
 virtual unsigned long ReadPixel(int row, int column) {
 cout << "Reading pixel in Mode 112H\n" ;
 return 0;
 }
};

class VesaMode115H : public VesaTCModes {
public:
 virtual void DrawPixel(int row, int column, int color) {
 cout << "Setting pixel in Mode 115H\n";
```

continued on following page

Box 1. continued

```
  return;
  }
 virtual unsigned long ReadPixel(int row, int column) {
 cout << "Reading pixel in Mode 115H\n" ;
 return 0;
  }
};
class VesaMode118H : public VesaTCModes {
public:
 virtual void DrawPixel(int row, int column, int color) {
 cout << "Setting pixel in Mode 118H\n";
 return;
  }
 virtual unsigned long ReadPixel(int row, int column) {
 cout << "Reading pixel in Mode 118H\n";
 return 0;
  }
};

class VesaMode11BH : public VesaTCModes {
public:
 virtual void DrawPixel(int row, int column, int color) {
 cout << "Setting pixel in Mode 11BH\n";
 return;
  }
 virtual unsigned long ReadPixel(int row, int column) {
 cout << "Reading pixel in Mode 11BH\n";
 return 0;
  }
};
//***********************
// non-virtual classes
//***********************
class VesaTCLib {
private:
 int vesa_mode_num;      // Object data
 int vert_res;
 int hor_res;

 VesaMode112H obj_112H;   // Objects of derived classes
 VesaMode115H obj_115H;   // required for filling pointer
 VesaMode118H obj_118H;
```

continued on following page

Box 1. continued

```
 VesaModel1BH obj _ 11BH;

 VesaTCModes *base _ ptr;  // Base class pointer
public:
 VesaTCLib (int);      // Constructor
// Other methods
 int GetVesaMode();
 int GetModeVRes();
 int GetModeHRes();
 void SetPixel(int, int, int);
 void GetPixel(int, int);
};
//*****************************
// Methods for class VesaTCLib
//*****************************
// Constructor
VesaTCLib::VesaTCLib(int vesa _ mode) {
/* The constructor is passed a mode code as follows:
   1 = VESA mode 112H
   2 = VESA mode 115H
   3 = VESA mode 118H
   4 = VESA mode 11BH
According to the mode selected, code sets the definition,
VESA mode number, and a pointer to the corresponding
object of the library module.
*/
 switch (vesa _ mode) {
 case (1):
  vesa _ mode _ num = 0x112;
  hor _ res = 640;
  vert _ res = 480;
  base _ ptr = &obj _ 112H;
  break;
 case (2):
  vesa _ mode _ num = 0x115;
  hor _ res = 800;
  vert _ res = 600;
  base _ ptr = &obj _ 115H;
  break;
 case (3):
  vesa _ mode _ num = 0x118;
  hor _ res = 1024;
```

continued on following page

Box 1. continued

```
  vert_res = 768;
  base_ptr = &obj_118H;
  break;
 case (4):
  vesa_mode_num = 0x11b;
  hor_res = 1280;
  vert_res = 1024;
  base_ptr = &obj_11BH;
  break;
 default:
  vesa_mode_num = 0x0;
  hor_res = 0;
  vert_res = 0;
  base_ptr = &obj_112H;
 }
}
// Methods for reading and setting a screen pixel
void VesaTCLib::SetPixel(int row, int col, int attribute) {
 base_ptr->DrawPixel(row, col, attribute);
};
void VesaTCLib::GetPixel(int row, int col) {
 base_ptr->ReadPixel(row, col);
};


// Methods that return the mode information
int VesaTCLib::GetVesaMode() {
 return vesa_mode_num;
}

int VesaTCLib::GetModeVRes() {
 return vert_res;
}

int VesaTCLib::GetModeHRes() {
 return hor_res;
}

//************************************************************
//           client code
//************************************************************

main() {
```

continued on following page

Box 1. continued

```
// Objects of class VesaTCLib
 VesaTCLib obj_1(1);     // Object and mode code
 VesaTCLib obj_2(2);
 VesaTCLib obj_3(3);
 VesaTCLib obj_4(4);

// Operations on obj_1, mode code 1
 cout << "\nVESA mode: " << hex << obj_1.GetVesaMode();
 cout << "\nHorizontal Res: " << dec << obj_1.GetModeHRes();
 cout << "\nVertical Res: " << obj_1.GetModeVRes() << "\n";
 obj_1.SetPixel(12, 18, 0xff00);
 obj_1.GetPixel(122, 133);
 cout << "\n";

// Operations on obj_2, mode code 2
 cout << "VESA mode: " << hex << obj_2.GetVesaMode();
 cout << "\nHorizontal Res: " << dec << obj_2.GetModeHRes();
 cout << "\nVertical Res: " << obj_2.GetModeVRes() << "\n";
 obj_2.SetPixel(12, 18, 0xff00);
 obj_2.GetPixel(122, 133);
 cout << "\n";

// Operations on obj_3, mode code 3
 cout << "VESA mode: " << hex << obj_3.GetVesaMode();
 cout << "\nHorizontal Res: " << dec << obj_3.GetModeHRes();
 cout << "\nVertical Res: " << obj_3.GetModeVRes() << "\n";
 obj_3.SetPixel(12, 18, 0xff00);
 obj_3.GetPixel(122, 133);
 cout << "\n";

// Operations on obj_4, mode code 4
 cout << "VESA mode: " << hex << obj_4.GetVesaMode();
 cout << "\nHorizontal Res: " << dec << obj_4.GetModeHRes();
 cout << "\nVertical Res: " << obj_4.GetModeVRes() << "\n";
 obj_4.SetPixel(12, 18, 0xff00);
 obj_4.GetPixel(122, 133);
 cout << "\n";

 return 0;
}
```

```
void VesaTCLib::SetPixel(int row, int col,
int atts) {
  base _ ptr->DrawPixel(row,  col,  attri-
bute);
};

void VesaTCLib::GetPixel(int row, int col)
{
 base _ ptr->ReadPixel(row, col);
};
```

The processing in this case is done with a smaller processing overhead. The principal advantage of the new class design and implementation can be summarized as follows:

1. Contingency code to select the corresponding mode-dependant, pixel-level primitives is now located in the constructor; therefore, it executes only when the object is created.
2. Client code does not need to perform the mode selection operations, which have been transferred to the library classes.
3. Client code does not see or access the class inheritance structure since the pixel-level operations are handled transparently.

Developing the Pattern

In the previous sections we addressed a programming problem and found one possible solution that could be implemented in code. We also constructed a class diagram that reflects the relationships and associations of this solution in object-oriented terms. In order to make this solution easier to reuse we can eliminate all the case-specific elements from both the pattern and the coded example. Furthermore, the resulting abstraction can be given a name that provides an easy reference to the particular case.

In selecting a name for a design pattern we must carefully consider its purpose and applicability. Observe that the class structure for constructing the VESA true color library is probably applicable to many programming problems that are not related

to computer graphics, or even to libraries. Its fundamental purpose is to provide an interface to an inheritance structure so that its operational details are hidden from client code. Since interface is too general a term, we could think of the word concealer in this context. For the lack of a better term we call this pattern a concealer, since its purpose is to conceal an inheritance structure so that its existence and operation are made transparent to the client. Figure 4 shows the concealer pattern in a more abstract form.

Unifying Dissimilar Interfaces

A simple but frequent design problem is to present a unified and friendly interface to a set of classes that perform different operations, for example, a set of classes that calculates the area of different geometrical figures, such as a parallelogram, a circle, a rectangle, and a square. The formula for the area of a parallelogram requires three parameters: the base, the side, and the included angle. The area of the circle and the square require a single parameter, in one case the radius and in the other one the side. The area of a rectangle requires two: the length and the width. Our task is to provide the client with a single interface to the calculation of the area of any one of these four geometrical figures. This class structure is known as a unifier pattern.

In the previous example the implementation could be based on the client passing four parameters. The first one is a signature code indicating the geometrical figure, the other three parameters hold the pertinent dimensional information. By convention, we agree that unnecessary parameters are set to NULL. The class diagram in Figure 5 represents one possible solution.

In the case of Figure 5 the method selection is based on an object of the corresponding class, therefore, it is a case of object composition. An alternative implementation could easily be based on pointers instead of object instances. Program SAMP-02.CPP shows the necessary processing in the first case (Box 2).

Figure 4. A Concealer pattern

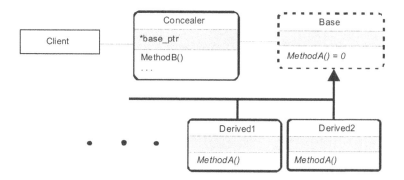

Note that in program SAMP-02.CPP the objects are instantiated inside the switch construct in the GetArea() method. This ensures that only the necessary object is created in each iteration of GetArea(). Since the objects have local scope their lifetime expires when GetArea() returns. Therefore, only the necessary memory is used.

Unifier patterns have found frequent use in modeling object-oriented frameworks. InterViews 2.6 defined a similar construct for modeling interface elements such as buttons, scrollbars, and menus (Vlissides, 1988).

An Interface Pattern

By generalizing the class diagram in Figure 5 we can develop an interface pattern in which a class provides access to other classes that implement certain functionality. Figure 6 shows this generalization.

Aggregated Class Hierarchies

On occasions we may need to implement a set of classes related hierarchically. For example, a pro-

Figure 5. Implementing an interface class

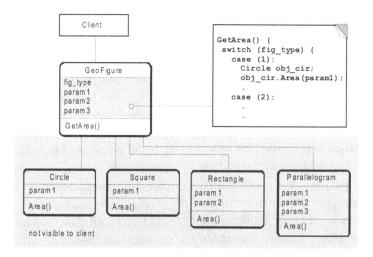

Box 2.

```
//****************************************************************
// C++ program to illustrate implementation of an interface
// class
// Filename: SAMP-02.CPP
//****************************************************************

#include <iostream.h>
#include <math.h>
#define PI 3.1415


//***************************
//     classes
//***************************
//
class Circle {
public:
 float Area(float radius) {
   return (radius * radius * PI);
 }
};

class Rectangle {
public:
 float Area(float height, float width) {
   return (height * width);
 }
};

class Parallelogram {
public:
  float Area(float base, float side, float angle) {
    return (base * side * sin (angle) );
  }
};

class Square {
public:
  float Area(float side) {
    return (side * side);
  }
};
```

continued on following page

Box 2. continued

```
// Interface class
class GeoFigure {
private:
 int fig_type;
 float param1;
 float param2;
 float param3;
public:
 GeoFigure(int, float, float, float);
 void GetArea();
};
// Constructor
GeoFigure::GeoFigure(int type, float data1, float data2,
       float data3) {
 param1 = data1;
 param2 = data2;
 param3 = data3;
 fig_type = type;
};

// Implementation of GetArea() method
void GeoFigure::GetArea() {
float area;
 switch (fig_type) {
  case (1):         // Circle
   Circle obj_cir;
   area = obj_cir.Area(param1);
   break;
  case (2):         // Rectangle
   Rectangle obj_rec;
   area = obj_rec.Area(param1, param2);
   break;
  case (3):         // Parallelogram
   Parallelogram obj_par;
   area = obj_par.Area(param1, param2, param3);
   break;
  case (4):         // Square
   Square obj_sqr;
   area = obj_sqr.Area(param1);
   break;
  }
```

continued on following page

Box 2. continued

```
    cout << "The area is of this object is: "
    << area << "\n";
};


//***************************
//      main()
//***************************
main() {
 GeoFigure obj1(1, 3, NULL, NULL);  // A circle object
 GeoFigure obj2(2, 12, 4, NULL);    // A rectangle object
 GeoFigure obj3(3, 12, 4, 0.7);     // A parallelogram object
 GeoFigure obj4(4, 3, NULL, NULL);  // A square object

 cout << "\nCalculating areas of objects...\n";
// Calculate areas
 obj1.GetArea();     // Area of circle object
 obj2.GetArea();     // Area of rectangle object
 obj3.GetArea();     // Area of parallelogram object
 obj4.GetArea();     // Area of square

 return 0;
}
```

gram can draw geometrical figures, such as circles, squares, and triangles, where each of the figures is contained in an invisible, rectangular frame. Also assume that in this case the figure and its containing frame are so related that the creating of a figure (i.e., a circle, rectangle, or triangle) mandates the creation of its container frame.

A library of figure-drawing primitives could be provided by means of four classes: three to create the circle, square, and triangle figures, and one to generate the containing frame. The client would create an object of the corresponding figure and then one of the frame. Alternatively, figure-drawing classes could be linked to the frame generation class so that for each figure a corresponding frame object would be automatically created. With this approach, the frame generation operation is transparent to the client and programming is simplified.

We can add complications to the preceding example without altering its validity. For instance, we can assume that each frame implies the creation of another element called a border, and that the border must be contained in still another one called a window. Therefore, the resulting hierarchy is a geometrical figure, contained in a frame, requiring a border, which, in turn, must exist inside a window. In this example the object structure is mandated by the problem description since all the classes in the hierarchy are obligatory.

A class hierarchy can be implemented in C++ by inheritance, because the creation of an object of a derived class forces the creation of one of its parent class. If the inheritance hierarchy consists of more than one class, then the constructor of the classes higher in the hierarchy are called in order

Figure 6. An interface pattern

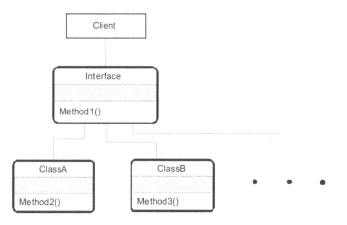

of derivation. Destructors are called in reverse order. The program SAMP-03.CPP demonstrates constructors and destructors in an inheritance hierarchy (Box 3).

When program SAM12-03.CPP executes the following messages are displayed:

```
Constructing a BaseA object
Constructing a Derived1 object
Constructing a Derived2 object
Destroying a Derived2 object
Destroying a Derived1 object
Destroying a BaseA object
```

A Class Hierarchy by Object Composition

One way of solving the problem described at the beginning of this section is to use inheritance. For example, we could implement a class hierarchy in which Circle, Square, and Rectangle were derived from a base class called Figure. The Figure class could contain polymorphic methods for calculating and drawing the geometrical object, as well as methods for creating the frame, the border, and the window. In this case the client would have the responsibility of calling all of the required methods. This is an example of how inheritance

often constraints programming and exposes the underlying class structure.

Although in some cases a solution based on class inheritance may be acceptable, it often happens that the hierarchy of super classes is related to a particular method of a derived class, or to several related methods, but not to all of them (Gamma et al., 1995). Consider the case of several types of geometrical figures, all of which must be part of a window, contain a border, and be enclosed in a frame as described previously. In this case the figure-drawing methods could be made part of an inheritance structure; however, the methods that produce the window, border, and frame need not be part of the inheritance construct since these elements are required for any of the geometrical figures. One possible solution is to implement a class structure in which some methods form part of an inheritance association while others are implemented by means of object composition. Figure 7 shows a possible class diagram for this case.

In Figure 7 there are two mechanisms collaborating within the class structure. An inheritance element provides polymorphic methods that can be selected at run time in the conventional manner. Simultaneously, another class hierarchy is based on object composition. Note that the method Draw() of the classes Circle, Square, and Triangle, contains

Box 3.

```
//****************************************************************
// C++ program to illustrate constructors and destructors in
// a class inheritance hierarchy
// Filename: SAMP-03.CPP
//****************************************************************

#include <iostream.h>

//***************************
//    classes
//***************************
class BaseA {
public:
 BaseA() {
  cout << "Constructing a BaseA object\n";
 }
 ~BaseA() {
  cout << "Destroying a BaseA object\n";
 }
};

class Derived1 : public BaseA {
public:
 Derived1() {
 cout << "Constructing a Derived1 object\n";
 }
 ~Derived1() {
 cout << "Destroying a Derived1 object\n";
 }

};
class Derived2 : public Derived1 {
public:
 Derived2() {
 cout << "Constructing a Derived2 object\n";
 }
 ~Derived2() {
 cout << "Destroying a Derived2 object\n";
 }
};
```

continued on following page

Box 3. continued

```
//***************************
//     main()
//***************************
main() {

// Program creates a single object of the lower class in the
// hierarchy. Constructors and destructors of the class higher
// in the hierarchy are automatically executed.

  Derived2 obj _ d;
  return 0;
}
```

Figure 7. Class hierarchy by object composition

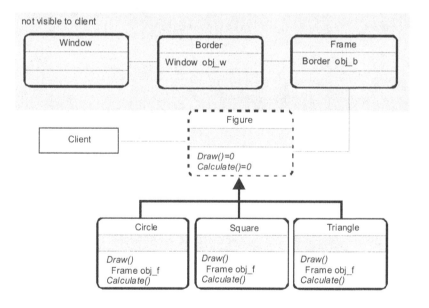

an object of the class Frame. Also note that the class Frame contains an object of Border, which contains an object of Window. Therefore, we can say that a circle, a square, and a triangle are a kind of figure and that all of them have a frame, a border, and a window. The program SAMP-04.CPP is an implementation of the class diagram in Figure 7 (Box 4).

Note in the program SAMP-04.CPP, as well as in Figure 7, that it is the method named Draw() in the concrete classes of the inheritance structure that instantiates the object of the class higher in the hierarchy, in this case the class named Frame. Once this object is referenced, the remainder of the hierarchy is produced automatically by means of the member object mechanism. The purpose of this construct is that the object hierarchy is generated when the method named Draw() executes, not when an object of the lower classes is instantiated. We can certify this operation when the program executes.

There may be cases in which we prefer that the hierarchy of super classes be instantiated at the time that the object of the lower class is created. In the example in Figure 7 this could be achieved by having a member object of the Frame class in the base class named Figure.

A Chain Reaction Pattern

In the class diagram of Figure 7 we note that when the lower classes (Circle, Square, and Triangle) instantiate an object of the class higher in the hierarchy, they start a chain reaction that produces objects of the entire hierarchy. We can abstract this operation by means of a class diagram that focuses exclusively on the chain reaction element, as is the case in Figure 8.

In Figure 8 we have implemented chaining by referencing the first chained object within a method

Box 4.

```
//****************************************************************
// C++ program to illustrate a class hierarchy by object
// composition
// Filename: SAMP-04.CPP
//****************************************************************


#include <iostream.h>


//***************************
//    classes
//***************************
class Window {
public:
Window() {
 cout << "Creating a window\n";
 }
};


class Border {
private:
 Window obj _ w;      // Border class contains Window object
public:
 Border() {
  cout << "Drawing a border\n";
```

continued on following page

Box 4. continued

```
    }
  };

  class Frame {
  private:
   Border obj _ b;        // Frame class contains Border object
  public:
   Frame() {
     cout << "Drawing a frame\n";
    }
   virtual void Draw() { return; };
  };

  // Abstract class
  class Figure {
  public:
   virtual void Draw() = 0;
   virtual void Calculate() = 0;
  };

  // Circle, Triangle and Square are at the bottom of the class
  // hierarchy
  class Circle : public Figure {
  public:
   virtual void Draw() {
   Frame obj _ f;
   cout << "Drawing a circle\n";
    }
   virtual void Calculate() {
   cout << "Calculating a circle\n";
    }
  };

  class Square : public Figure {
  public:
   virtual void Draw() {
   Frame obj _ f;
   cout << "Drawing a square\n";
    }
   virtual void Calculate() {
   cout << "Calculating a square\n";
    }
```

continued on following page

Box 4. continued

```
};

class Triangle : public Figure {
public:
 virtual void Draw() {
 Frame obj_f;
 cout << "Drawing a triangle\n";
 }
 virtual void Calculate() {
 cout << "Calculating a triangle\n";
 }
};


//****************************
//     main()
//****************************
main() {


  Figure *base_ptr;   // Pointer to base class
  Circle  obj_c;   // Circle, Square, and Triangle
  Square  obj_s;   // objects
  Triangle obj_t;

  cout << "\n\n";
  base_ptr = &obj_c;  // Draw a circle and its hierarchical
  base_ptr->Draw();   // super classes

  cout << "\n";
  base_ptr = &obj_s;  // Draw a square and its hierarchical
  base_ptr->Draw();   // super classes

  cout << "\n";
  base_ptr = &obj_t;  // Draw a triangle and its hierarchical
  base_ptr->Draw();   // super classes

  cout << "\n";
  base_ptr->Calculate(); // Calculate() method does not generate
           // an object hierarchy
  return 0;
}
```

of the Chainer class, and then by member objects of the chained classes. There are many other ways of implementing a chain reaction effect.

Object Chaining

A programming problem often encountered consists of determining which, if any, among a possible set of actions has taken place. For example, an error handling routine posts the corresponding messages and directs execution according to the value of an error code. A common way of performing the method selection is by contingency code that examines the error code and determines the corresponding action. In C++ this type of selection is usually based on a switch construct or on a series of nested if statements. Alternatively, we can use object composition to create a chain in which each object examines a code operand passed to it. If it corresponds to the one mapped to its own action, then the object performs the corresponding operation, if not, it passes along the request to the next object in a chain. The last object in the chain returns a special value if no valid handler is found.

One of the advantages of using an object chain is that it can be expanded simply by inserting new object handlers anywhere along its members. To expand a selection mechanism based on contingency code we usually have to modify the selecting method by recoding the switch or nested if statements.

An Object Chain Example

A slightly more complicated case is one in which the selected object must return a value back to the original caller. For example, we define a series of classes that perform arithmetic operations which take two operands. The classes are called Addition, Subtraction, Multiplication, and Division. An operation code is furnished as a third parameter to a class called Operation, containing a method called SelectOp() that calls the Add method in the first object in the chain. In this case the object is of the Addition class. Add() examines the opcode operand; if it corresponds to the add operation, add executes and returns the sum to the caller. If not, it passes the object to Subtract, which proceeds in a similar fashion. Figure 9 shows the class structure for this example.

The program SAMP-05.CPP shows the processing details for implementing an object chain (Box 5).

An Object Chain Pattern

We can generalize the example of an object chain in Figure 9 and abstract its basic components. In this case the fundamental characteristic of the class structure is a series of related methods, each one of which inspects a program condition that determines whether the method is to respond with a processing

Figure 8. A chain reaction pattern

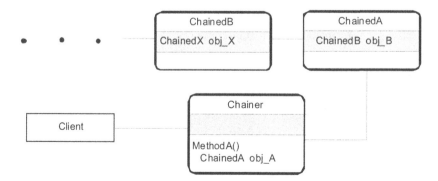

Figure 9. Class diagram for an object chain

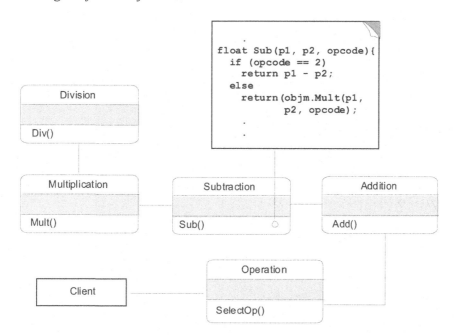

```
    .
float Sub(p1, p2, opcode){
  if (opcode == 2)
    return p1 - p2;
  else
    return(objm.Mult(p1,
           p2, opcode);
    .
    .
```

Division
Div()

Multiplication
Mult()

Subtraction
Sub()

Addition
Add()

Client

Operation
SelectOp()

action or pass the request along to the next object in the chain. Figure 10 is a class diagram for an object chain pattern.

STRING HANDLING CLASS TEMPLATE

The solution of some program development problems is based on patterns of interacting classes and objects, while others simply require a description of the internal structure of a single class. In this case we speak of a class template. For example, programs that deal with strings or that perform substantial string manipulations could profit from a particular class design that is optimized for string handling.

String Operations

A string that is defined at run time is sometimes difficult to store as an array since its length may not be known beforehand. The C++ new and delete operators can be used to allocate memory in the free store area, but it is easier to implement a class that performs all string-handling operations consistently and efficiently, rather than to create and delete each string individually. Implementing a string-handling class is possible because the new and delete operators can be used from within member functions and pointers are valid class members.

String operations often require knowing the string's length. The strlen() function defined in the string.h header file returns this value. Alternatively, we can implement a string as an object that contains a pointer to a buffer that holds the string itself and a variable that represents its length. A parameterized constructor can take care of initializing the string object storage using the new operator as well as its length parameter. The contents of the string passed by the caller are then copied into its allocated storage. This operation determines that the two data members associated with each string object are stored independently, however, they remain associated to the object and can be readily accessed as a pair.

In addition to the parameterized constructor, the proposed class could have a default constructor that

Box 5.

```
//******************************************************************
// C++ program to illustrate an object chain
// Filename: SAMP-05.CPP
//******************************************************************


#include <iostream.h>


//****************************
//     classes
//****************************
class Division {
public:
 float Div(float param1, float param2, int opcode) {
 if (opcode == 4)
  return (param1 / param2);
 else
   return 0;
 }
};


class Multiplication {
private:
 Division obj _ div;
public:
 float Mult(float param1, float param2, int opcode) {
 if (opcode == 3)
  return (param1 * param2);
 else
  return (obj _ div.Div(param1, param2, opcode));
 }
};


class Subtraction {
private:
 Multiplication obj _ mult;
public:
 float Sub(float param1, float param2, int opcode) {
 if (opcode == 2)
  return (param1 - param2);
 else
```

continued on following page

Box 5. continued

```
    return (obj_mult.Mult(param1, param2, opcode));
  }
};


class Addition {
private:
Subtraction obj_sub;
public:
 float Add(float param1, float param2, int opcode) {
 if (opcode == 1)
  return (param1 + param2);
 else
  return (obj_sub.Sub(param1, param2, opcode));
 }
};


class Operation{
private:
 float param1;
 float param2;
 int opcode;
 Addition obj_add;
public:
 Operation(float val1, float val2, int op) {
  param1 = val1;
  param2 = val2;
  opcode = op;
 }
 float SelectOp() {
 return (obj_add.Add(param1, param2, opcode));
 }
};


//***************************
//     main()
//***************************
main() {
 Operation obj_1(12, 6, 1); // Declaring objects of the
 Operation obj_2(12, 6, 2); // four established opcodes
 Operation obj_3(12, 6, 3);
 Operation obj_4(12, 6, 4);
```

continued on following page

Box 5. continued

```
   cout << "\n";
  // Performing operation on objects
   cout << "Operation on obj _ 1: " << obj _ 1.SelectOp() << "\n";
   cout << "Operation on obj _ 2: " << obj _ 2.SelectOp() << "\n";
   cout << "Operation on obj _ 3: " << obj _ 3.SelectOp() << "\n";
   cout << "Operation on obj _ 4: " << obj _ 4.SelectOp() << "\n";

   return 0;
  }
```

Figure 10. Object chain pattern

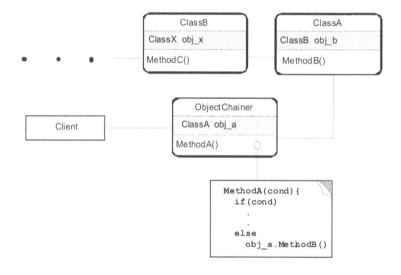

initializes both data members to zero whenever it is necessary. An explicit destructor method is also required in this case. The fact that the new operator is used to allocate space for the string buffer implies that the delete operator must be used to free the allocated memory. Other useful methods would be to get the length of the string and to insert a character in a string, to read a string character by specifying its index, and to append a new string to an existing one. Additional functionalities can be added by editing the class or by inheriting its methods. Figure 11 class diagram can serve as a template in this case.

The following program (Box 6) implements the string handling class template of Figure 11.

COMBINING FUNCTIONALITIES

In the implementation of libraries, toolkits, and application frameworks (Deutsch, 1989) we often come across a situation in which a given functionality is scattered among several classes. Rather than giving a client access to each one of these individual classes it is often a reasonable alternative to combine several methods into a single class

Figure 11. String handler class template

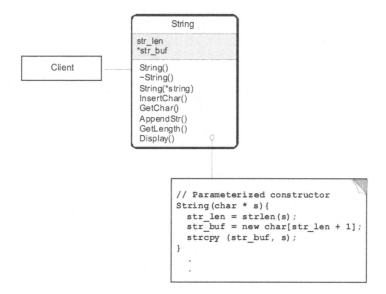

which can then be presented and documented as standard interface.

A Mixer Pattern

One of the practical uses of multiple inheritance is in combining functionalities by creating a class that inherits from two or more classes. The inheriting class serves to mix and unify the methods of the participating base classes. The class in Figure 12 shows a pattern based on multiple inheritance into a mixer class.

The following code fragment shows how to implement multiple inheritance in the case of the mixer class in Figure 12:

```
// Multiple inheritance
class Mixer : public ClassA, public ClassB,
public ClassC {
 // Implementation
};
```

When implementing multiple inheritance we must be careful to avoid situations which could lead to resolution conflicts; for example, inheriting a method that has the same name and interface in the parent classes, or inheriting multiple copies of the same method.

AN OBJECT-CLASSIFIER TEMPLATE

The objects in a class need not have identical signatures. A class can contain several parameterized constructors that create objects with different numbers or types of parameters. In this sense the constructors serve as object classifiers since each constructor executes according to the object's signature. The constructor can also store the object's type in a variable so that the object can be declassified during processing. For example, we wish to provide a class that calculates the area of various types of geometrical figures. Some figures such as the square require a single parameter, other figures such as the rectangle, have two parameters, and still others like the parallelogram have three parameters. If there is a parameterized constructor for each ob-

Figure 12. Mixer pattern for combining disperse functionalities

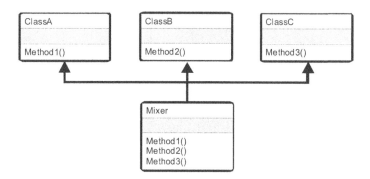

Box 6.

```
//**************************************************************
// C++ program template for string operations
// Filename: SAMP-06.CPP
//**************************************************************


#include <iostream.h>
#include <string.h>


//***************************
//    classes
//***************************
// String-handling class template
class String {
private:
 int str_length;      // Length of string
 char *str_buf;       // Pointer to string buffer
public:
// Declared constructors
 String();            // Default constructor
 String(const char *str);  // Parameterized constructor
// String processing methods
 void InsertChar(int index, char new_char);
 char GetChar(int index) const;
 void AppendStr( const char *sub_str);
 ~String();           // Explicit destructor
// Methods expanded in line
```

continued on following page

Box 6. continued

```
  int GetLength() const { return str_length; }
  void Display() const { cout << str_buf; }
};


// Implementation of the default constructor
String :: String() {
 str_buf = 0;
 str_length = 0;
}


// Implementation of the parameterized constructor
String :: String (const char *s) {
 str_length = strlen(s);
 str_buf = new char[str_length + 1];
 strcpy( str_buf, s);
}


// Implementation of operational methods
void String :: InsertChar(int index, char new_char) {
 if ((index > 0) && (index <= str_length))
  str_buf[index - 1] = new_char;
}
char String :: GetChar(int index) const {
 if ((index >= 0) && (index <= str_length))
  return str_buf[index];
 else
  return 0;
}


void String :: AppendStr( const char *sub_str) {
 char *temp_str;
 str_length = str_length + strlen( sub_str);
 temp_str = new char[str_length + 1]; // Allocate buffer
 strcpy (temp_str, str_buf);       // Copy old buffer
 strcat(temp_str, sub_str);       // Concatenate both strings
 delete [] str_buf;
 str_buf = temp_str;
}


// Implementation of destructor
String :: ~String() {
 delete [] str_buf;
```

continued on following page

Box 6. continued

```
    }


//**************************
//     main()
//**************************
main() {

// Object of type String
 String string1( "Montana State University" );

// Operations using String class
 cout << "\nstring is: ";
 string1.Display();
 cout << "\nlength of string: " << string1.GetLength();
 cout << "\nfirst string character: "
 << string1.GetChar(0) << "\n";
// Appending a substring
 cout << "appending the sub-string: - Northern\n"
 << "string now is: ";
 string1.AppendStr( " - Northern\n\n");
 string1.Display();

 return 0;

}
```

ject signature, then the processing is automatically directed to the corresponding constructor, which can also preserve the object's type by storing an associated code. This action of the constructor is consistent with the notion of function overloading. Processing routines can dereference the object type and proceed accordingly.

Implementing the Object Classifier

The following program (Box 7) shows the processing for implementing a class named GeoFigure with four constructors: a default constructor that zeroes all the variables, and three parameterized constructors, one for each object signature. The constructors of the GeoFigure class perform object classification as the objects are created.

Observe in the program SAMP-07.CPP that processing operations that are often the client's burden are now handled by the class. The classifier class encapsulates knowledge about each object type, which is encoded and preserved with its signature. Thereafter, client code need not classify objects into squares, rectangles, or parallelograms, since this information is held in the class and handled transparently by its methods. The objects created by the classifier class know not only their dimensions but also their geometrical type, which in turn defines the processing operations necessary for performing calculations such as the area.

A classifier class is appropriate whenever there are objects with different signatures and their signatures determine the applicable processing operations or methods. Figure 13 is a generalized diagram for a classifier class; it can serve as a template for implementing this type of processing.

COMPOSING MIXED OBJECTS

Libraries, toolkits, and frameworks often provide two types of services to a client. A first level service performs the more elementary operations. A second-level service, called an aggregate or composite, allows combining several primitives to achieve a joint result. The pattern is referred to as a composite pattern. The composite is based on the notion of a Glyph, which is a class that encompasses all objects in

a document (Calder, 1990). Composite patterns are found in most object-oriented systems, including the original View class of Smalltalk (Krasner & Pope, 1988). Also in financial applications, aggregation of assets in a portfolio have been modeled using a Composite class (Birrer & Eggenschwiler, 1993).

Box 7.

```
//**************************************************************
// C++ class template for an object classifier class
// Filename: SAMP-07.CPP
//**************************************************************


#include <iostream.h>
#include <math.h>


//***************************
//     classes
//***************************
class GeoFigure {
private:
 float dim1;
 float dim2;
 float dim3;
 int fig _ type;
public:
// Declaration of four constructors for GeoFigure class
 GeoFigure();
 GeoFigure(float);
 GeoFigure(float, float);
 GeoFigure(float, float, float);
// Area() method uses object signature
 float Area();
```

continued on following page

Box 7. continued

```
};

// Parameterless constructor
GeoFigure::GeoFigure() {
 dim1 = 0;
 dim2 = 0;
 dim3 = 0;
 fig _ type = 0;
}
// Constructor with a single parameter
GeoFigure :: GeoFigure(float x){
 dim1 = x;
 fig _ type = 1;
}
// Constructor with two parameters
GeoFigure :: GeoFigure(float x, float y){
 dim1 = x;
 dim2 = y;
 fig _ type = 2;
}
// Constructor with three parameters
GeoFigure :: GeoFigure(float x, float y, float z){
 dim1 = x;
 dim2 = y;
 dim3 = z;
 fig _ type = 3;
}

float GeoFigure::Area() {
 switch (fig _ type) {
  case (0):
   return 0;
  case (1):
   return dim1 * dim1;
  case (2):
   return dim1 * dim2;
  case (3):
   return dim1 * (dim2 * sin(dim3));
  }
 return 0;
 }
```

continued on following page

Box 7. continued

```
//***************************
//      main()
//***************************
main() {
  GeoFigure fig0;          // Objects with different signatures
  GeoFigure fig1(12);
  GeoFigure fig2(12, 6);
  GeoFigure fig3(12, 6, 0.6);

  // Calculating areas according to object signatures
  cout << "\nArea of fig1: " << fig1.Area();
  cout << "\nArea of fig2: " << fig2.Area();
  cout << "\nArea of fig3: " << fig3.Area();
  cout << "\nArea of fig0: " << fig0.Area() << "\n";

  return 0;
}
```

A Graphics Toolkit

For example, a drawing program provides primitives for drawing geometrical figures such as lines, rectangles, and ellipses, for displaying bitmaps, and for showing text messages. A second-level function (the composite) allows combining of the primitive elements into a single unit that is handled as an individual program component. In the context of graphics programming, the term "descriptor" is often used to represent a drawing primitive and the term "segment" to represent a composite that contains one or more primitives.

Often a toolkit designer gives access to both the primitive and composite functions. In other words, the programmer using the drawing toolkit mentioned in the preceding paragraph would be able to create drawings that contained any combination of primitive and composite objects using a single, uniform, interface. In this example it may be useful to think of a composite as a list of instructions that includes the methods of one or more primi-

tives. Figure 14 shows an image that contains both primitive and composite objects. The composite objects consist of a rectangle, a bitmap, an ellipse, and a text message. The primitive objects are text, a rectangle, and an ellipse.

The class structure for the sample toolkit could consist of a class for every one of the primitive operations and a composite class for combining several primitives into a drawing segment. An abstract class at the top of the hierarchy can serve to define an interface. Figure 15 shows the class structure for the graphics toolkit.

Note in Figure15 that the abstract class Image provides a general interface to the toolkit. The class Segment contains the implementation of the segment-level operations, the methods CreateSegment(), DeleteSegment(), and DrawSegment(). The drawing primitives are the leaves of the tree structure. Program SAMP-08.CPP (Box 8) is a partial implementation of the class diagram in Figure 15. Note that the classes Bitmap and Text were omitted in the sample code.

Figure 13. Object classifier class template

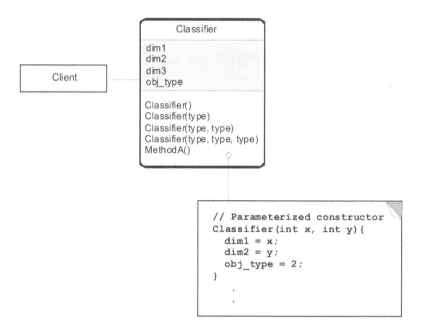

In the program SAMP-08.CPP the segment operation is based on an array of pointers. For this mechanism to work we need to implement run-time polymorphism since the composite (each instance of the Segment class) is created during program execution. In C++ run-time polymorphism can be achieved by inheritance and virtual functions. In this case the function Draw() is a pure virtual function in the abstract class Image, a virtual function in the class Segment, and is implemented in the leaf elements of the tree, which are the classes Line, Rectangle, and Ellipse. By making Draw() a simple virtual function we avoid making Segment into an abstract class. Therefore we can instantiate objects of Segment and still access the polymorphic methods in the leaf classes.

The actual code for implementing an array of pointers to objects has several interesting points. The array is defined in the private group of the Segment class, as follows:

```
Segment *ptr _ ar[100];
```

This creates an array of pointers to the class Segment, and assigns up to 100 possible entries

for each instantiation. The actual pointers are inserted in the array when the user selects one of the menu options offered during the execution of CreateSegment(). At this time a pointer to the Segment base class is reset to one of the derived classes, one of the Draw() methods at the leaves of the inheritance structure. The selected method is then placed in the pointer array named ptr_ar[]. For example, if the user selected the r (rectangle) menu option the following lines would instantiate and insert the pointer:

```
case ('r'):
  ptr _ ss = &obj _ rr; // Base pointer set
to derived object
  ptr _ ar[n] = ptr _ ss; // Pointer placed
in array
  n++; // Array index is bumped
  break;
```

Although it may appear that the same effect could be achieved by using a pointer to the method in the derived class, this is not the case. In this application a pointer to a derived class will be unstable and unreliable.

Figure 14. Primitive and composite objects in a graphics toolkit

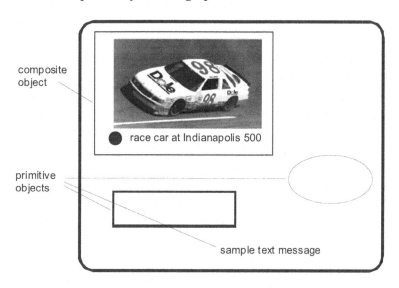

Figure 15. Tree structure for creating simple and composite objects

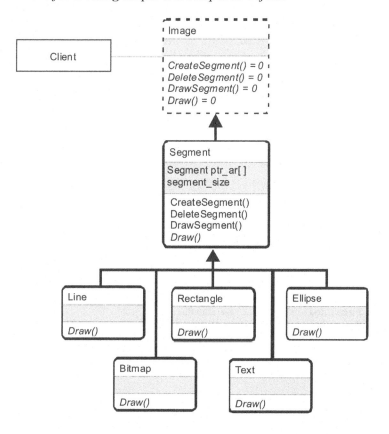

Box 8.

```
//**************************************************************
// C++ program to illustrate the creation of simple and
// composite objects
// Filename: SAMP-08.CPP
//**************************************************************


#include <iostream.h>
#include <stdlib.h>
#include <conio.h>


//***************************
//     classes
//***************************
// Image class provides a general interface
class Image {
public:
 void virtual CreateSegment() = 0;
 void virtual DrawSegment() = 0;
 void virtual Draw() = 0;
};

class Segment : public Image {
private:
 Segment *ptr_ar[100];        // Array of pointers
 int seg_size;            // Entries in array
public:
 void CreateSegment();
 void DrawSegment();
 void DeleteSegment();
 void virtual Draw() { return; };
};



class Rectangle : public Segment {
public:
 void Draw() { cout << "\ndrawing a rectangle"; }
};

class Ellipse : public Segment {
public:
 void Draw() { cout << "\ndrawing an ellipse"; }
```

continued on following page

Box 8. continued

```
};

class Line : public Segment {
public:
 void Draw() { cout << "\ndrawing a line"; }
};

// Implementation of methods in Segment class
void Segment::CreateSegment() {
 char select;
 int n = 0;          // Entries in the array
// Objects and pointers
 Segment obj_ss;
 Segment *ptr_ss;
 Line    obj_ll;
 Rectangle obj_rr;
 Ellipse obj_ee;

 cout << "\n opening a segment...\n";
  cout << "Select primitive or end segment: "
 << "\n l = line"
 << "\n r = rectangle"
 << "\n e = ellipse"
 << "\n x = end segment"
 << "\n SELECT: ";
 do {
  select = getche();
  switch(select) {
  case ('l'):
   ptr_ss = &obj_ll;
   ptr_ar[n] = ptr_ss;
   n++;
   break;
  case ('r'):
   ptr_ss = &obj_rr;
   ptr_ar[n] = ptr_ss;
   n++;
   break;
  case ('e'):
   ptr_ss = &obj_ee;
   ptr_ar[n] = ptr_ss;
   n++;
```

continued on following page

423

Box 8. continued

```
      break;
   case ('x'):
     break;
   default:
     cout << "\nInvalid selection - program terminated\n";
     exit(0);
  }
  }
 while( select != 'x');
   seg _ size = n;
   cout << "\n closing a segment...";
 }

 void Segment::DrawSegment() {
  cout << "\n  displaying a segment...";
  for(int x = 0; x < seg _ size; x++)
   ptr _ ar[x]->Draw();
  cout << "\n  end of segment display ...";
  return;
 }
//***************************
//     main()
//***************************
main() {
 Segment  obj _ s;
 Line   obj _ l;
 Rectangle obj _ r;
 Ellipse  obj _ e;

// Creating and drawing a segment
 cout << "\n\nCalling CreateSegment() method";
 obj _ s.CreateSegment();
 obj _ s.DrawSegment();
// Drawing individual objects
 obj _ l.Draw();
 obj _ r.Draw();
 obj _ e.Draw();

 return 0;
}
```

At the conclusion of the CreateSegment() method it is necessary to preserve with each object a count of the number of points that it contains. The seg_size variable is initialized to the number of pointers in the array in the statement:

```
seg _ size = n;
```

At the conclusion of the CreateSegment() method, the array of pointers has been created and initialized for each object of the Segment class, and the number of pointers is preserved in the variable seg_size. Executing the segment is a matter of recovering each of the pointers in a loop and executing the corresponding methods in the conventional manner. The following loop shows the implementation:

```
for(int x = 0; x < seg _ size; x++)
  ptr _ ar[x]->Draw();
```

PATTERN FOR AN OBJECT FACTORY

By eliminating all the unnecessary elements in the class structure of Figure 15 we can construct a general class pattern for creating simple and composite objects. This version of the Composite class can be considered as a simple object factory which uses an array to store one or more pointers to objects. In addition, each object of the Composite class keeps count of the number of pointers in the array. This count is used in dereferencing the pointer array.

Alternatively, the pointer array can be implemented without keeping a pointer counter by inserting a NULL pointer to mark the end of the array. This NULL pointer then serves as a marker during dereferencing. In either case, the corresponding methods in the leaf classes are accessed by means of the pointers in the array. Method selection must be implemented by dynamic binding. In C++ the polymorphic method must be virtual in the composite class. The pattern is shown in Figure 16.

A Simplified Implementation

We can simplify the concept of primitive and composite objects, as well as their implementation in code, by allowing a composite that consists of a single primitive object. For example, if in Figure 15 we permit a segment that consists of a single primitive, then the client needs never to access the primitives directly. This makes the interface less complicated. In many cases this option should be examined at design time.

RECURSIVE COMPOSITION

In previous sections we considered the case of a composite class that contains simple or composite objects. We also looked at the alternative of a composite object that consists of a single primitive as a way of simplifying the interface. However, we have not yet considered the possibility of a composite object containing another composite (Gamma et al., 1995). Based on the class structure shown in Figure 15 we can construct an object diagram in which a Segment can contain another Segment as shown in Figure 17. Note that in this case we have preserved the distinction between primitives and composites.

Implementation Considerations

In the previous example recursive composition is based on a nested reference to the CreateSegment() method of the Segment class. However, recursion is often accompanied by a new set of problems; this case is no exception. The first consideration is to access the CreateSegment() method. Three possibilities are immediately evident:

1. Since CreateSegment() is called from within the class, it can be referenced without instantiating a specific object.
2. We can access the CreateSegment() method by means of a this pointer. In fact, this is a

Figure 16. Pattern for an object factory class

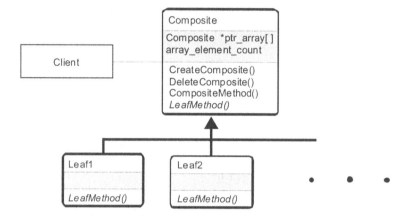

different syntax but has the same result as the previous case. In both instances the current object is used.

3.   We can create a new object and use it to access the CreateSegment() method.

Which method is suitable depends on the problem to be solved. Figure 18 shows a class diagram for recursively accessing the CreateSegment() method using the original object.

The program SAMP-09.CPP (Box 9) shows the implementation of the class diagram in Figure 18.

Several points in the code merit comment. In the first place notice that recursion occurs on the same object originally referenced at call time. This is accomplished by means of the C++ this pointer, in the following statement:

```
this->CreateSegment();
```

The CreateSegment() method could have been accessed without the this pointer since it is allowed, within the same class, to access methods directly. When CreateSegment() is accessed recursively, all the local variables are automatically reinitialized. Since the program requires a count of the number of pointers in the pointer array, we made the iteration counter (variable n) a global variable

Figure 17. Object diagram for recursive composition

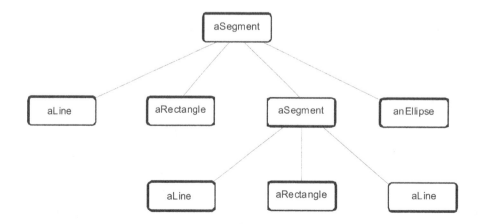

Figure 18. Class diagram for recursive composition

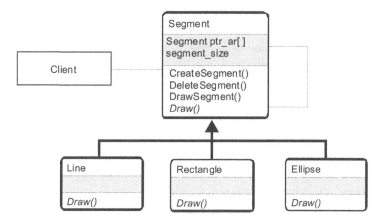

and created a switch variable named instance. This variable is set to 1 when CreateSegment() is called recursively, determining that counter variable n is not cleared on entry to the method. The result is that n holds the number of pointers inserted in the pointer array, whether they were entered directly or recursively.

A Recursion Pattern

The pattern for recursive composition is similar to the one in Figure 16, except that in recursion there is an arrow pointing to the same composite class. This is shown in Figure 19.

CONCLUSION

Software design is one of the most laborious and time-consuming phases of program development. In object-oriented systems design reuse is based on classes and object structures that solve a particular design problem and on the assumption that these class structures can be applied to other similar problems. The most recent approach to design reuse is based on class associations and relationships called patterns or object models. In this sense a programming problem is at the origin of every pattern.

We have described the use of design patterns and template classes as reusable components in program design. The discussion has been complemented with class diagrams and examples implemented in code. The chapter introduces the notion of a class template as a structure that describes functionality and object relations within a single class, while patterns refer to structures of communicating and interacting classes.

REFERENCES

Alexander, C., Ishikawa, S., Silverstein, M., Jacobson, M., Fiksdahl-King, I., & Angel, S. (1977). *A pattern language.* New York: Oxford University Press.

Beck, K., & Johnson, R. (1994, July). *Patterns generate architectures.* Paper presented at the European Conference on Object-Oriented Programming, Bologna, Italy (pp. 139-149). Springer-Verlag.

Birrer, A., & Eggenschwiler, T. (1993, July). *Frameworks in the financial engineering domain: An experience report.* Paper presented at the European Conference on Object-Oriented Programming, Kaiserslautern, Germany (pp. 21-35). Springer-Verlag.

Box 9.

```
//****************************************************************
// C++ program to illustrate recursive composition
// Filename: SAMP-09.CPP
//****************************************************************

#include <iostream.h>
#include <stdlib.h>
#include <conio.h>

//***************************
//     classes
//***************************
class Segment {
private:
 Segment *ptr_ar[100];
 int seg_size;                // Entries in array
public:
 void CreateSegment();
 void DrawSegment();
 void DeleteSegment();
 void virtual Draw() { return; };
};

class Rectangle : public Segment {
public:
 void Draw() { cout << "\ndrawing a rectangle"; }
};

class Ellipse : public Segment {
public:
 void Draw() { cout << "\ndrawing an ellipse"; }
};

class Line : public Segment {
public:
 void Draw() { cout << "\ndrawing a line"; }
};
// Global variable for controlling recursive implementation
// of the CreateSegment() method
 int n;
 int instance = 0;
```

continued on following page

Box 9. continued

```
// Implementation of methods in Segment class
void Segment::CreateSegment() {
 char select;
// Entries in the array
// Objects and pointers
 Segment obj_ss;      // An object
 Segment *ptr_ss;     // Pointer to object
 Line   obj_ll;       // Object list
 Rectangle obj_rr;
 Ellipse obj_ee;

 if(instance == 0)
  n = 0;

  cout << "\n opening a segment...\n";
  cout << "Select primitive or end segment: "
 << "\n l = line"
 << "\n r = rectangle"
 << "\n e = ellipse"
 << "\n n = nested segment"
 << "\n x = end segment"
 << "\n SELECT: ";
 do {
  select = getche();
  switch(select) {
  case ('l'):
   ptr_ss = &obj_ll;    // Pointer to object initialized
   ptr_ar[n] = ptr_ss;  // and stored in array
   n++;
   break;
  case ('r'):
   ptr_ss = &obj_rr;
   ptr_ar[n] = ptr_ss;
   n++;
   break;
  case ('e'):
   ptr_ss = &obj_ee;
   ptr_ar[n] = ptr_ss;
   n++;
   break;
  case ('n'):
```

continued on following page

Box 9. continued

```
    cout << "\n   nested segment...";
    instance = 1;
    this->CreateSegment();
    cout << "\n   nested segment closed ...";
    cout << "\n SELECT: ";
    continue;

  case ('x'):
   break;
  default:
   cout << "\nInvalid selection - program terminated\n";
   exit(0);
 }
 }
 while( select != 'x');
  seg_size = n;
  cout << "\n closing a segment...";
  instance = 0;          // Reset instance control
 }


void Segment::DrawSegment() {
 cout << "\n  displaying a segment...";
 for(int x = 0; x < seg_size; x++)
  ptr_ar[x]->Draw();
 cout << "\n  end of segment display ...";
 return;
}
//**************************
//     main()
//**************************
main() {
 Segment  obj_s;

// Creating and drawing a segment with possible nested
// segments
 cout << "\n\nCalling CreateSegment() method";
 obj_s.CreateSegment();
 obj_s.DrawSegment();

 return 0;
}
```

Figure 19. Pattern for recursive composition

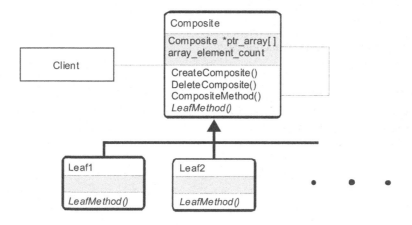

Calder, P. R., & Linton, M. A. (1992, October). *The object-oriented implementation of a document editor.* Paper presented at the Object-Oriented Programming Systems, Languages, and Applications Conference Proceedings, Vancouver, British Columbia, Canada (pp. 1-15). ACM Press.

Coplien, J. O. (1992). *Advanced C++ programming styles and idioms.* Reading, MA: Addison-Wesley.

Deutsch, L. P. (1989). Design reuse and frameworks in the Smalltalk-80 system. *Software reusability, Volume II: Applications and experience* (pp 57-71). Reading, MA: Addison-Wesley.

Gamma, E., Helm, R., Johnson, R., & Vlissides, J. (1995). *Design patterns: Elements of reusable object-oriented software.* Reading, MA: Addison-Wesley.

Krasner, G. E., & Pope, S. T. (1988, August/September). A cookbook for using the model-view controller user interface paradigm in Smalltalk 80. *Journal of Object-Oriented Programming, 1*(3)26-49.

Vlissides, J. M., & Linton, M. A. (1990, July). Unidraw: A framework for building domain-specific graphical editors. *ACM Transactions on Information Systems, 8*(3), 237-269.

KEY TERMS

Concealer Pattern: A class pattern designed to hide an inheritance structure so that its existence and operation becomes transparent to client code.

Chain Reaction Pattern: A class pattern that focuses on the property of classes that instantiate objects of other classes higher in the class hierarchy, thus starting a chain reaction in the production of objects.

Class Template: A structure of interactive objects that implements a particular functionality within a single class.

Design Pattern: A structure of interactive classes and communicating objects that provide a solution to a software design problem.

Interface Pattern: A pattern that provides access to other classes that implement a desired functionality.

Mixer Pattern: A class that inherits from two or more classes, thus providing a unified interface to the methods and objects in these classes.

Object Chaining: A chain of objects that successively examines an operand pass to them and makes some decision based on the result of this examination.

Object Classifier: A template for a class with constructors that create objects with different numbers and types of parameters.

Object Factory: A composite class that creates both simple and composite objects.

Unifier Pattern: A class pattern designed to present a unified and friendly interface to a set of classes that perform different operations.

Chapter XXV
Hibernate:
A Full Object Relational Mapping Service

Allan M. Hart
Minnesota State University, Mankato, USA

ABSTRACT

This chapter presents a brief overview of the object/relational mapping service known as Hibernate. Based on work provided in the book Java Persistence with Hibernate, it is argued that the paradigm mismatch problem consists of five problems: the problem of granularity, the problem of subtypes, the problem of identity, the problem of associations, and the problem of data navigation. It is argued that Hibernate, if it is to be considered a successful object/relational mapping service, must solve the paradigm mismatch problem and, hence, each of the five problems noted above. A simplified version of an order entry system is presented together with the mapping files required to store persistent objects to a database. Examples are given for one-to-one, one-to-many, and many-to-many mappings. The distinction between value and entity types is explained and the mapping technique required for value types is introduced into the order entry system application. The n+1 selects problem is explained and a strategy for solving that problem using Hibernate's support for lazy, batch, and eager fetching strategies is discussed.

INTRODUCTION

The purpose of this chapter is to provide the reader with an introduction to Hibernate. Hibernate, as described at its Web site, is "a powerful, high performance object/relational persistencee and query service" (Hibernate, 2008).

Hibernate is one among a number of so-called persistence frameworks. Other notables include TopLink, iBATIS, and Java data objects (JDO) (Oracle TopLink, 2008; IBATis, 2008; JDO, 2008). The basic responsibility of any persistence frame-work is to manage persistent data, that is, data that needs to be saved to persistent storage (usually a relational database) from one invocation of the application to the next. Not all objects created by a given application constitute persistent data but many of them do. For example, in an ecommerce application, information regarding the customer's name, address, and credit card information as well as the particular products the customer has ordered (and the quantity of each), constitutes data that needs to be saved to persistent storage.

Persistence frameworks can generally be divided into those that are based on an approach known as object/relational mapping (ORM) and those that are not. Both Hibernate and TopLink, for example, are correctly classified as ORM services. iBATIS, on the other hand, though often listed as an ORM service, is, strictly speaking, not an ORM service at all, but rather a data mapping service. With an ORM service like Hibernate, what are mapped, *very* roughly speaking, are classes to tables. Instances of classes become rows in a database table and associations between classes become foreign key constraints between database tables. What are mapped with iBATIS's data mapping services, on the other hand, are not tables to classes, but rather the parameters and results of SQL statements to classes.[1]

The need for ORM services grew out of the realization over the last several decades that a paradigm mismatch problem exists between the world of object-oriented programming languages and relational databases. In this chapter we will explore some of the details of this problem as well as the ways in which an ORM service like Hibernate attempts to solve the problem.

BACKGROUND

The evolution of programming languages over the last 50 years has seen a large growth not only in the *number* of different programming languages but also in the number of different *types* of programming languages. During the 60s procedural languages such as FORTRAN, BASIC, and Pascal were the rage. While object-oriented programming (OOP) was in its infancy in the 60s, its first implementation language, Smalltalk, appeared. During the 70s and 80s SmallTalk continued to evolve and newer OOP languages such as Object Pascal and C++ appeared. The appearance of Java during the mid 90s solidified OOP's position as the predominant programming language paradigm. During this same period, changes in the database world were also afoot. Edgar F. Codd's seminal paper "A Relational Model of Data for Large Shared Data Banks" was published in 1970. This paper triggered much work in the 70s and, during this time, implementations of the relational model began to appear. Soon, thereafter, relational databases had largely replaced their hierarchical and network predecessors.

As the development of OOP languages and relational database management systems proceeded, it soon became clear that there was a paradigm mismatch problem.[2] The details of the problem will be presented in the next section. For now, suffice it to say that there were primarily two responses to this problem. Some have argued that the relational model should be abandoned and that object-oriented databases should be embraced. Others have argued that relational databases should instead be expanded to include at least some of the features found in object-oriented programming languages, for example, user-defined types and inheritance. This bifurcation in the historical road down which database development has gone, constitutes, one might say, a fork in that road. During the 90s, one saw much development being done in the area of pure object-oriented databases. However, while this work deserves much praise, the effort did not bear much fruit. While pure object-oriented database management systems were developed, none of them caught on in the marketplace and much of that effort has now been abandoned. During roughly the same time period, much effort was also expended toward the other fork. The notion of a user defined type (UDT) was brought into the database world with implementations being provided for both Oracle and SQL server. While this has served to alleviate the paradigm mismatch problem to some degree (at least for those platforms), it has not successfully overcome the problem in all of its detail. Moreover, the solutions provided are not portable among those platforms.

PARADIGM MISMATCH PROBLEM

In order to gain an understanding of the way in which an ORM service like Hibernate solves the paradigm mismatch problem, we need first to gain a better understanding of just what the problem is. Christian Bauer and Gavin King (2007, pp. 12-18) break down the paradigm mismatch problem into five essential parts. The first part is the problem of granularity. Here, we reuse their example of an address to illustrate this part of the problem. Suppose, for example, that in our domain model we have Customer and Orders classes as outlined in Listing 1.

Listing 1 Customer and Orders

```
public class Customer {
  private String customerName;
  private String address;
  private Set orders;

  //other stuff
  …
}

public class Orders {
  private int orderNum;
  private Date orderDate
  private Customer customer;

  //other stuff
  …
}
```

The database tables that we might design to store persistent instances of the above classes can be defined as in Listing 2.

Listing 2 CUSTOMER and ORDERS tables

```
create table CUSTOMER (
CUSTOMERNAME VARCHAR(20) PRIMARY KEY,
ADDRESS VARCHAR(110)
);
```

```
create table ORDERS (
ORDERNUM INT PRIMARY KEY,
ORDERDATE DATE NOT NULL,
CUSTOMER VARCHAR(20) FOREIGN KEY REFER-
ENCES CUSTOMER
)
```

While this simple design seems quite benign, there is a problem with the representation of the address field. Realistically, this should be broken down into street, city, state, country, and ZIP code fields. Those fields *could* simply be added to the Customer class as a replacement for the address field but, because it is likely that *other* classes (e.g., Employee, Shipper, Vendor, etc.) will require an address field as well, it makes more sense, from an object-oriented (OO) point of view, to simply create another class named address and to include those fields in that class. The address field in the customer class then becomes a reference to an instance of the Address class. The Address and (modified) Customer class appear in Listing 3.

Listing 3 Address Class

```
public class Address {
  String street;
  String city;
  String state;
  String country;
  String zip;

  //maybe other stuff
  …
}

public class Customer {
  private String customerName;
  private Address; // this might be a set
of Addresses
  private Set orders;

  //other stuff
  …
}
```

What changes need to be made to the relational schemata to accommodate the above change to the object domain model? Should we create a separate ADDRESS table with a foreign key reference from the CUSTOMER table? Doing so might *seem* appropriate but it is not the norm in the *relational* model. Rather, the norm is to modify the CUSTOMER table as in Listing 4.

Listing 4 CUSTOMER Table

```
create table CUSTOMER(
CUSTOMERNAME VARCHAR(20) PRIMARY KEY,
STREET VARCHAR(50),
CITY VARCHAR(20),
STATE CHAR(2),
ZIP VARCHAR(10),
COUNTRY VARCHAR(20)
)
```

By not creating a separate ADDRESS table we avoid the cost involved in joining the CUSTOMER table to the ADDRESS table every time we want to look up a user's address.

As Bauer and King note (2007, p. 12), some database management systems include a facility for creating user defined types (UDTs). For such systems, it might be possible to define an ADDRESS UDT and to include it as a single column in the USER table. Doing so would restore, to some extent, the symmetry between our object domain model and our relational model (the Address class would map to a *single* column in the CUSTOMER table). However, UDT support in the database industry is neither uniform nor portable.

The above example illustrates the problem of granularity. Granularity concerns the relative size of our objects (Bauer & King, 2007, p. 12). On the object domain side, our classes come in different levels of granularity. On the one hand, we have a coarse grained class named Customer and, on the other hand, we have a finer grained class named Address. In a more realistic object domain model we might have many classes each exhibiting different

levels of granularity. By contrast, on the relational side, we have a very limited amount of granularity. This contrast is the inevitable result of two very different type systems. Java's type system is quite flexible and rich; every new class represents a new data type. The type system found in RDBMSs is, on the other hand, much less flexible. Since it is obviously impossible to impose the more flexible system on the less flexible, too often the reverse is true, that is, the less flexible is imposed on the more flexible. The net result is that the object domain model becomes bound by the relational model. In other words, the object domain model becomes a mere reflection of the relational model. Inevitably, the application developer loses much of the advantage of working in an OOP language environment.

The second part of the paradigm mismatch problem noted by Bauer and King (2007, pp. 13-14) is the problem of subtypes. As is well known, one of the biggest advantages of OOP languages over procedural languages is inheritance. Given a preexisting class, one can define a class (called a subclass) that inherits the properties and methods of the preexisting class along with new properties and methods unique to the subclass. Doing so goes a long way toward preventing us from "reinventing the wheel." Instead of starting from scratch for each new application, we can reuse classes designed originally for other applications. These new classes are not "second rate" classes somehow detached from the language. They are first rate classes that are effectively part of the language itself. To illustrate the idea, suppose that we want to countenance in our object domain model two different kinds of orders: corporate customer orders and ordinary customer orders. Corporate orders come from corporations, may be eligible for special discounts (perhaps because corporate orders are usually large volume orders), can be paid by a purchase order, require information regarding a particular corporation office, and so forth. Ordinary customer orders are not eligible for special discounts, can be paid only by cash, check, or credit card, and require no special information beyond what is already available in the CUSTOMER table. Because of inheritance, the required adjustment to our object domain model is quite simple. Perhaps we make the Orders class an abstract base class and develop concrete Corporate and Ordinary subclasses from it. Listing 5 shows the required changes.

Listing 5

```
public abstract class Orders {
 private int orderNum;
 private int Date orderDate;
 private Customer customer;

 //other stuff
 ...
}


public class Corporate extends Orders {
 private float discount;
 private String po;
 private String office;

 //other fields and methods unique to a
corporate order

 ...
}


public class Ordinary extends Orders {
 //fields and methods unique to ordinary
orders

 ...
}
```

Subclassing in this way is quite usual in an object domain model. Our customer class has an association to our (now) abstract orders class. Because our Orders class is subclassed by the Corporate and Ordinary classes, the association is *polymorphic*. During runtime, a given instance of Customer might be associated with instances of either or both of Corporate and Ordinary. So how do we make the adjustments on the relational model side to accom-

modate our new object domain model? Bauer and King (2007) answer this question as follows:

We can take the short route here and observe that SQL database products do not generally implement type or table inheritance, and if they do implement it, they do not follow a standard syntax and usually expose you to data integrity problems (limited integrity rules for updatable views).
SQL databases also lack an obvious way (or at least a standardized way) to represent a polymorphic association. A foreign key constraint refers to exactly one target table; it isn't straightforward to define a foreign key that refers to multiple tables. We'd have to write a procedural constraint to enforce this kind of integrity rule.
The result of this mismatch of subtypes is that the inheritance structure in your model must be persisted in an SQL database that doesn't offer an inheritance strategy. (p. 14)

The third part of the paradigm mismatch problem noted by Bauer and King (2007, pp. 14-16) is the problem of identity. In an OOP language like Java, there are two different notions of sameness for objects. These are provided by the == operator on the one hand and by the implementation of the equals() method on the other hand. Scores of beginning Java programmers have had their programs slashed to pieces by their instructors because they checked for the equality of two objects using == instead of equals(). The == operator, when used to compare objects, returns true if there is exactly one object and the references (as in A == B where A and B are references) involved refer to one and the same object. The equals() method, on the other hand, returns true if the implementation contract of the equals() method is satisfied. The following code snippet gives the idea.

```
String A = new String("Now is the time");
String B = A;
System.out.println(A==B); // prints true
since these is only one object
```

...

```
String C = new String("Now is the time");
System.out.println(A==C); // prints false
System.out.println(A.equals(C)); // prints
true since the contract of
                // the equals() method
for String is
                // satisfied
```

Database identity, in contrast to the above, is rather simple. The primary key value of a row in a database table governs the identity of that row. So the question becomes how does *database* identity relate to Java *object* identity? Neither the == operator nor the equals() method equates well to the notion of a primary key.

The fourth part of the paradigm mismatch problem noted by Bauer and King (2007, pp. 16-17) is a collection of problems relating to associations. There are large differences between the ways in which classes in an object domain are associated with one another and the ways in which tables in a relational database are associated with one another. Relationships between classes in an object model are represented by references and collections of references to objects. Consider the following class snippets:

```
public class A {
 private B referenceToB;
 // other stuff omitted
 ...
}


public class B {
 private A referenceToA;
 //other stuff omitted
 ...
}
```

The relationship between A and B in this example is bidirectional. Given an A object, we can get to the associated B object (assuming there is one) via the referenceToB variable. Conversely, given a B object, we can get to the associated A object (assuming there is one) via the referenceToA variable. If the referenceToA variable is eliminated from class B, then there is no way to get to an A from a B. On the other hand, in the relational model, navigation between tables is handled by foreign key associations and is inherently *non*directional. Given a foreign key association between table A and table B, one can get to table A from table B and vice versa simply by performing a join between table A and table B. The relationship between class A and class B depicted above represents a one-to-one association between As and Bs; a given instance of A is associated with at most a single instance of B (and vice versa). However, there is nothing to prevent us from depicting a many-to-many association between As and Bs. The following code snippet demonstrates how:

```
public class A {
 private Set referencesToBs;
 //other stuff omitted
 ...
}


public class B {
 private Set referencesToAs;
 //other stuff omitted
 ...
}
```

As every beginning database student soon learns, while we often have many-to-many associations represented in an entity-relation or UML diagram, the actual *implementation*

of many-to-many associations (using SQL) are handled via link or association tables. Given tables A and B, implementing a many-to-many association between them requires that we introduce a table C having separate many-to-one associations to tables A and B (via separate foreign keys linking to table A and table B).

Given the differences between how associations are represented in the object model and how they are represented in the relational model, the question becomes how do we relate the two models when it comes to associations? Do we create a link *class* even though, from the point of view of the object model, it is unnecessary? If we do so, are we not just letting our relational model dominate our object model? On the other hand, if we do not do so, just what *is* the connection between our object model and our relational model when many-to-many relationships are involved?

The fifth and last part of the paradigm mismatch problem noted by Bauer and King (2007, pp. 18-19) is the problem of data navigation. This problem is probably one of the most serious problems facing any purported persistence solution. In Java, if we want to access the data in an instance of a class B that has an association to a class A where, currently, we have only a handle to A (handleToA), we might call handleToA.getB().getMyData(). Navigation through an object graph is accomplished by simply following associations between the objects in the graph. In SQL, on the other hand, if we are interested in the data in the A table, we issue a query like this:

```
select * from A
where condition _ to _ satisfy
```

If, later, we are interested in the data in table B as well as data in table A that is related to B, we might issue this query:

```
select * from A
left outer join B on A.id = B.id
where condition _ to _ satisfy
```

Let us assume that our application is constructed using an object model and, thus, is written using an OOP language like Java. Let us assume also that we want the appropriate SQL SELECTs to be issued as we traverse the available object graph at some point in the execution of our application. The problem then is this: we may end up issuing a different SQL SELECT for each node in the graph. This "node at a time" approach to accessing the data in the database will clearly result in a performance problem for any application attempting to support concurrency.[3] Indeed, this problem (or a variant of it) has been labeled the *n+1 selects problem* (Bauer & King, 2007, pp. 18-19). On the other hand, using an approach in which the object graph contains every possible persistent object, fetched in a single access to the database, generates a complementary performance problem. One aspect of the problem is simply that, in a given scenario, one might load the *entire* database into memory when only a small portion of it is required. Another aspect of the problem is that, in so doing, it is quite likely that locks will be issued on the tables and, so, concurrency will be negatively affected. So the problem of data navigation summarizes to: How do we find a "middle ground" between acquiring too little of the data in the database (n+1 selects problem) and acquiring too much of the data in the database? A persistence solution that does not find this middle ground is going to perform extremely poorly.

Having obtained an overview of the paradigm mismatch problem, we now look at the ways in which an ORM service, such as Hibernate, overcomes the problem.

HIBERNATE

As early as 1997 Mark Fussel laid the foundations for ORM services. Scott Ambler (2002) in a well known paper provided further developments. Perhaps the best known ORM service in use today is Hibernate (Relational Persistence, 2008). While it is beyond the scope of this chapter to provide a complete explanation of how Hibernate works or even how it is used, we can say that Hibernate attempts to provide a full object to relational mapping service. Bauer and King (2007), following Fussel, define this as follows:

Full object mapping supports sophisticated object modeling: composition, inheritance, polymorphism and 'persistence by reachability.' The persistence layer implements transparent persistence; persistent classes do *not* inherit any special base class or have to implement a special interface. Efficient fetching strategies (lazy, eager and prefetching) and caching strategies are implemented transparently to the application. (p. 27)

Hibernate provides full object mapping via a number of avenues. In its original form, Hibernate utilized XML metadata as the medium by which persistent classes are stored in a database. For those who prefer not to use XML, the emergence of annotations with Java 5.0 and the completions of the Java Persistence API (JPA) and the EJB 3.0 specifications provide an alternative (Persistence, 2008; EJB 3.0, 2008).

In this section we examine the pieces that comprise Hibernate and develop some Hibernate code along the way. It is far beyond the scope of this chapter to provide a full exposition of all of Hibernate's features. Instead, we initially focus on a simplified model of an order entry system and utilize but one of several ways that Hibernate employs to enforce persistence. Our goal is to evaluate Hibernate. We will hold Hibernate to the standards developed in the previous section. In particular, we will judge Hibernate's ability to function as a "full object mapping" solution to the problem of persistence and as a solution to the paradigm mismatch problem.

FIRST CONTACT

The sample code in Listing 6 shows a Customer class that might be used in an order entry system application for an online store[4]. There is nothing special about this class. Indeed, it is simply a plain old Java object (POJO) (POJO, 2008).

Listing 6 A Customer Class

```
package org.mnsu.edu.oes;
public class Customer {
   private int id;
```

```
   private String fname;
   private String lname

   ...

   // other fields such as street, city,
state, zip,
   // balance, creditCardNum, etc. left
out for
   // the sake of brevity

   private Customer() {}
   public Customer(String fname, String
lname) {
      this.fname = fname;
      this.lname = lname;
   }
   public int getId() {
      return id;
   }
   public void setId(int id) {
      this.id = id;
   }
   public String getFname() {
      return fname;
   }
   public void setFname(String fname) {
      this.fname = fname;
   }
   public String getLname() {
      return lname;
   }
   public void setLname(String lname) {
      this.lname = lname;
   }
}
```

As it stands, the Customer class is simply a POJO and could easily be instantiated in an application and its fields accessed with calls such as:

```
Customer customer = newCustomer("Gavin",
"King");
Sytem.out.println(customer.getFname() + "
" + customer.getLname());
```

As a POJO, this class has no claims to persistence. However, because this class would be central to an order entry system application, we will definitely require that it *be* a persistent class. One Hibernate mechanism for enforcing object persistence is a metadata mapping file with a ".hbm.xml" suffix.[5] This file maps the instantiated class to a relational database table. Typically, this file's prefix is the same as the class file's name.[6] For our current version of the Customer class, the following Customer.hbm.xml file (Listing 7) will do.

Listing 7 Customer.hbm.xml

```xml
<?xml version="1.0"?>
<!DOCTYPE hibernate-mapping PUBLIC
    "-//Hibernate/Hibernate Mapping DTD//
EN"
   http://hibernate-sourceforge.net/hiber-
nate-mapping-3.0.dtd>
<hibernate-mapping>
 <class
   name="org.mnsu.edu.oes.Customer"
   table="CUSTOMERS">
   <id
     name="id"
     type="int"
     unsaved-value="0"
     <column name="CUST _ ID"
     sql-type="int"
     not-null="true"/>
     <generator class="hilo"/>
   /id>
   <property
    name="fname"
    column="FNAME"/>
   <property
     name="lname"
     column="LNAME"/>
 </class>
</hibernate-mapping>
```

Our mapping file specifies that the Customer class will be persisted to a relational database table named CUSTOMERS. The properties of the Customer class, namely "id," "fname," and "lname" will be mapped to columns in the CUSTOMERS table named "CUST_ID," "FNAME," and "LNAME," respectively.

While the mapping file specifies what *will* be done, it still remains to see how that will be accomplished in the application itself. The following code fragment gives the idea:

```
...
Session session = getSessionFactory().openSes-
sion();
Transaction tx = session.beginTransac-
tion();
Customer customer = new Customer("Gavin",
"King");
session.save(customer);
tx.commit();
session.close();
...
```

This short piece of code fulfills the promise of the mapping file. The result of executing this fragment results in this SQL code being executed against the database:

```
insert into CUSTOMER (CUST _ ID, FNAME,
LNAME) values(1, "Gavin", "King")
```

It is important to note that the value for the id property of the Customer class was not set during the creation of the customer object. So one might wonder why the above SQL command contains a value, namely 1, for the CUST_ID attribute of the CUSTOMERS table. The answer is that the id property of the Customer class is an *identifier property*, that is, it is a specially generated unique value that is assigned to the instance of the Customer class, not when that class's constructor is called, but, rather, when the call to "session. save(customer)" is made[7]. It is important to note also that, while this call makes the customer object a *persistent object*, it does *not* thereby *persist* the object to the database, that is, the generated SQL insert command is not necessarily executed at this point.[8] In the code fragment above, the execution of the generated SQL is guaranteed only *after* the call to "tx.commit()."[9] The actual point at which the generated SQL is executed can be controlled, in several ways. Each of the following, for example, will each cause immediate execution:

Certain calls to Session.find() or Sesson.iterate()
net.sf.hibernate.Transaction.commit()
net.sf.hibernate.Session.flush()

Not every persistent object is persisted to the database when these calls are made. Hibernate employs a strategy known as *automatic dirty checking* to decide which persistent objects require a database update or insert. In short, Hibernate keeps track of persistent objects that are either updated in the persistence context (session) or are new to the persistent context. Only these require an update or insert.

The delayed execution of the generated SQL and the order in which they are executed can cause problems when triggers are used in the database. By using Session.flush(), the developer can ensure that, in such circumstances, the generated SQL is executed at the proper time and in the proper order.

Note the "unsaved-value="0"" attribute in the mapping file. The inclusion of this attributes is but one of the mechanisms that Hibernate uses to distinguish between a new transient instance of a class and a *detached* instance. For our present purposes, suffice it to say that this attribute enables transitive persistence for our Customer class and, later, for our Orders class. The idea is simply that, given a persistent Customer instance and a set of Orders instances owned by the Customer instance, the Orders instances in the set will become persistent as soon as they are added to the set without a call to session.save() being required.

SECOND CONTACT: ASSOCIATIONS AND COLLECTIONS

Let us enhance our model a bit and add an Order class. The idea, of course, is that a given customer might submit many orders while a given order should be submitted by, at most, one customer. Thus, there should be a one-to-many association between the Customer class and the Order class and a one-to-many relationship between the CUSTOMERS table and the ORDERS table. The Orders class might be defined as in Listing 8.

Listing 8 Order.java

```java
package org.mnsu.edu.oes;

import java.util.date;

public class Order {
  private int id;
  private java.util.Date date;
  private Customer customer;

  public Order {}

 public Order(java.util.Date date, Customer
customer) {
    this.date = date;
    this.customer = customer;
  }
  public int getId() {
    return id;
  }
  public void setId(int id) {
    this.id = id;
  }
  public String getDate() {
    return date;
  }
  public void setDate(java.util.Date date)
{
    this.date = date;
  }
```

```
   public String getCustomer() {
      return customer;
   }
   public void setCustomer(Customer cus-
tomer) {
      this.customer = customer;
   }
}
```

The mapping file for this class appears in List-ing 9.

Listing 9 Order.hbm.xml

```
<?xml version="1.0"?>
<!DOCTYPE hibernate-mapping PUBLIC
    "-//Hibernate/Hibernate Mapping DTD//
EN"
    http://hibernate-sourceforge.net/hiber-
nate-mapping-3.0.dtd>
<hibernate-mapping>
 <class
    name="org.mnsu.edu.oes.Order"
    table="ORDERS">
    <id
      name="id"
      type="int"
      unsaved-value="0">
      column name="ORDER _ ID"
      sql-type="int"
      not-null="true"/>
      <generator class="hilo"/>
    /id>
    <property
      name="date"
      column="ORDER _ DATE"/>
    <many-to-one
      name="customer"
      column="CUST _ ID"
      class="org.mnsu.edu.Customer"
      not-null="true"/>
 </class>
</hibernate-mapping>
```

This is an example of an *unidirectional* many-to-one association. CUST_ID in the ORDERS table is a foreign key referencing the CUST_ID primary key attribute of the CUSTOMERS table. The not-null attribute is set to "true" because you cannot have an order without a customer.

As was noted earlier, associations between classes in an OO model are unidirectional while relationships between tables in the relational model are nondirectional.[10] Since, in an order entry application, we often need to traverse from an order to its associated customer and from a customer to the associated order, we need to modify the Customer class to make the association between the two classes bidirectional. Listing 10 shows the necessary modifications.

Listing 10 Modified Customer Class

```
package org.mnsu.edu.oes;
public class Customer {
   private int id;
   private String fname;
   private String lname;
   private Set orders = new HashSet();

   …
   // other fields such as street, city,
state, zip, balance,
   // creditCardNum, etc. left out for
   // the sake of brevity

   private Customer() {}
   public Customer(String fname, String
lname, Set orders) {
      this.fname = fname;
      this.lname = lname;
      this.orders = orders;
   }
   public int getId() {
      return id;
   }
   public void setId(int id) {
      this.id = id;
```

```
    }
    public String getFname() {
        return fname;
    }
    public void setFname(String fname) {
        this.fname = fname;
    }
    public String getLname() {
        return lname;
    }
    public void setLname(String lname) {
        this.lname = lname;
    }
    public Set getOrders() {
        return orders;
    }
    public void setOrders(Set orders) {
        this.orders = orders;
    }
}
```

Not surprisingly, the mapping file for the Customer class requires modification as well.

Listing 11 Modified Customer.hbm.xml

```
<?xml version="1.0"?>
<!DOCTYPE hibernate-mapping PUBLIC
    "-//Hibernate/Hibernate Mapping DTD//
EN"
    http://hibernate-sourceforge.net/hiber-
nate-mapping-3.0.dtd>
<hibernate-mapping>
 <class
   name="org.mnsu.edu.oes.Customer"
   table="CUSTOMERS">
 <id
   name="id"
   type="int"
   unsaved-value="0">
   <column name="CUST _ ID"
     sql-type="int"
     not-null="true"/>
   <generator class="hilo"/>
```

```
 /id>
 <property
   name="fname"
   column="FNAME"/>
 <property
   name="lname"
   column="LNAME"/>
 <set name="Orders"
   inverse="true"
   cascade="all-delete-orphan">
   <key column="ORDER _ ID"/>
   <one-to-many class="org.mnsu.edu.oes.
Order"/>
 </set>
 </class>
</hibernate-mapping>
```

There are a couple of things in this modified Customer.hbm.xml file that require our attention.

First, notice the inverse attribute. This tells Hibernate that the one-to-many association between the Customer class and the Order class is just a many-to-one association from the Orders class to the Customer class as seen from the Order side of the association. Without this attribute, Hibernate would see the one-to-many association and the many-to-one association as two *different* associations!

Second, notice the "cascade= ..." attribute. This attribute controls the nature of the association between the Customer class and the Order class. There are a number of XML options that can be used with this attribute, and they are:

- None (Default)
- Save-update
- Persist
- Merge
- Delete
- Remove
- Lock
- Replicate
- Evict
- Refresh
- All
- Delete-orphan

Since exploring all of these options would take us too far from our goal of providing an overview, we instead explain a few of the more commonly used options.

The "cacade=save-update" attribute relieves the developer of the need to make a call to save() in the application code every time an object referenced by a separate persistent object is created or updated. In our application, for example, had we used this attribute, as soon as a new Order instance is created, it would be automatically made persistent if it is referenced by a persistent Customer instance. Without the use of this attribute, creating and persisting Customer and Order instances would be accomplished by code such as the following:

```
...

Session session = getSessionFactory().
openSession();
Transaction tx = session.beginTransac-
tion();

Customer customer = new Customer("Gavin",
"King");
Order order = new Order(new java.util.Date,
customer);
Customer.getOrders().add(order);
Session.save(order);
session.save(customer);

tx.commit();
session.close();

...
```

By having this attribute enabled, the code reduces to the following:

```
...

Session session = getSessionFactory().
openSession();
```

```
Transaction tx = session.beginTransac-
tion();

Customer customer = new Customer("Gavin",
"King");
Order order = new Order(new java.util.Date,
customer);
Customer.getOrders().add(order);

session.save(customer);

tx.commit();
session.close();

...
```

While it is true that, in this example, the developer is saved from writing only a single line, it is also clear that, in a more substantial application, the savings can be considerable.

Like the "cascade=save-update" attribute, the "cascade=delete" attribute can save the developer a considerable amount of work. Instead of having to manually delete associated objects when a given persistent object is deleted, if "cascade=delete" is enabled, associated objects are automatically deleted. Suppose, for example, that we want to delete a Customer instance and all of the customer's related Order instances. Without "cascade=delete" enabled, our code might appear as follows:

```
Session session = getSessionFactory().
openSession();
Transaction tx = session.beginTransac-
tion();

customer = // load a Customer from the
database;

for (Iterator<Order> iter = customer.
getOrders().iterator(); iter.hasNext();) {
  Order order = iter.next();
    iter.remove();      // remove a single or-
```

```
der from the
// collection of orders
  session.delete(order);    // remove the
order from the database
}
session.delete(customer);  // remove the
customer from the database

tx.commit();
session.close();
```

With "cascade=delete" enabled, our code simplifies to this:

```
Session session = getSessionFactory().
openSession();
Transaction tx = session.beginTransac-
tion();

customer = // load a Customer from the
database;

session.delete(customer);  // remove the
customer from the database

tx.commit();
session.close();
```

The various "cascade=…" attributes can be combined so that, for example, "cascade=save-update, delete" can be used to enable both "cascade=save-update" and "cascade=delete." One can even enable all of them (save the last) by using "cascade=all."

The "cascade=delete-orphan" attribute needs to be considered separately from the other attributes since it is *not* enabled by "cascade=all." To understand its purpose we need to consider first the difference between entity and value types. As noted by Bauer and King (2007),

An object of entity type has its own database identity (primary key value). An object reference to an entity instance is persisted as a reference in the database (a foreign key value). An entity has its own lifecycle; it may exist independently of any other entity.

An object of value type has no database identity; it belongs to an entity instance and its persistent state is embedded in the table row of the owning entity. Value types don't have identifiers or identifier properties. The lifespan of a value type instance is bounded by the lifespan of the owning entity instance. A value type doesn't support shared references. (pp. 159-60)

Earlier we noted that creating an Address class separate from a Customer class has its utility from an object-oriented point of view. After all, it is likely that we will require not only customer addresses but also shipper addresses, vendor addresses, supplier addresses, and so forth. Not having a separate Address class can result in massive amounts of code duplication. On the other hand, creating a separate Address *table* in the database is possibly not something that we want to do. For example, it might be the case that most, if not all, of our queries for the tables corresponding to customers, shippers, vendors, and suppliers require the address value(s) in question. Not having a separate Address table increases performance because we are not required to perform any joins to such an Address table. Given this roughly sketched scenario, a Customer class is an entity type and an Address class is a value type.

The reader may have noticed that we left out any address attribute in the Customer class so far developed. This, of course, was deliberate. Suppose now that we want to enhance our Customer class so that it contains a reference to an Address class. We will not here include any code for an Address class. Suffice it to say that such a class would likely contain string properties such as street, city, state, and zip code together with appropriate constructors, getters, and setters. It would *not* contain an id attribute. Note that, because it is a value type, with no persistent identity of its own, there is no Address.hbm.xml file corresponding to it. Instead, Hibernate's mechanism for persisting the data in an Address instance to a Customer table is the notion of a component. By including a reference to an Address object in our Customer class, providing getters and setters for that reference, adjusting our constructors appropriately ,and including the following code in our Customer.hbm.xml file, we effectively map both the Customer and Address classes to the same database table:

```
<component name="address" class="org.mnsu.
edu.oes.Address">
  <property name="street" type="string"
    column="STREET" not-null="true"/>
  <property name="city" type="string"
    column="CITY" not-null="true"/>
  <property name="state" type="string"
    column="STATE" not-null="true"/>
  <property name="zipcode" type="string"
    column="ZIPCODE" no-null="true"/>
</component>
```

With the distinction between entity and value (component) types in mind, we can return to our discussion of "cascade=delete-orphan." Suppose that instead of mapping our Order class as an entity, we mapped it as a component. Suppose also that we wanted to delete an order for a particular customer. This can be accomplished by:

```
order =  //load a particular order
customer = //load a particular customer
customer.getOrders().remove(order);
```

Because order is a value type, no other object holds a reference to it and it can safely be removed. On the other hand, if, as we have done, the Order class is mapped as an entity type, the code to remove an order becomes slightly more complex as in:

```
order =  //load a particular order
customer = //load a particular customer
customer.getOrders().remove(order);
session.delete(order)
```

Because order is here an entity it can exist independently of the collection from which it is removed.

Thus, we must also delete it from the *session* to guarantee that no other references to it are held. By enabling the "cascade=delete-orphan" attribute in our mapping file, we are telling Hibernate that order can be safely removed from the collection in which it resides because order is the only reference to the instance it references. The code we used to remove order when it is mapped as a component will now work when it is mapped as an entity. Failure to enable the "cascade=delete-orphan" will result in a foreign key constraint exception in the following code:

```
order =  //load a particular order
customer = //load a particular customer
customer.getOrders().remove(order);
session.remove(customer);
```

It is common in OO design circles to make a distinction between association, aggregation, and composition. Associations between classes are very loose and simply represent the ability of one class to "talk" to another. This is typically implemented in a given class with a simple reference variable to another class or, perhaps, as a method argument or local variable. Aggregation, on the other hand, while an association, represents a somewhat tighter coupling between the classes involved and typifies a "part-whole" relationship. Composition, like aggregation, is also an association but represents a situation in which the class representing the "whole" is responsible for the creation and destruction of the "part." We can suppose that our business rules dictate that the association between our Customer and Orders classes is a composition. If a given instance of the Customer class is deleted, so also should any instances of the Orders class initiated by the customer in question. By using "cascade=all-delete-orphan" we have not only enabled all of the "cascade=…" attributes including "cascade=save-update" and "cascade=delete" but enforce the semantics of composition even when the associated object is an entity type.

ONE-TO-ONE ASSOCIATIONS

Let us suppose for the moment that our order entry system is for a store that offers its customers large discounts. It is able to do so because it deals in large volumes of the products that it offers for sale. However, each customer is required to fill out a membership application after which, if they qualify (and have paid the appropriate fee), they are issued a membership card. The code for a MemberCard class could appear as in Listing 12.

Listing 12 MemberCard

```java
package sales;
import java.util.Date;

public class MemberCard {
  private Long id;
  private int cardNumber;
  private Date start;
  private Date end;
  private Customer customer;

  public MemberCard() {}

  public MemberCard(int cardNumber, Date
start, Date end, Customer
    customer) {
    this.cardNumber = cardNumber;
    this.start = start;
    this.end = end;
    this.customer=customer;
  }

  public Long getId() {
    return id;
  }

  public void setId(long id) {
    this.id = id;
  }

  public int getCardNumber() {
```

```java
    return cardNumber;
  }

  public void setCardNumber(int cardNum-
ber) {
    this.cardNumber = cardNumber;
  }

  public Date getStart() {
    return start;
  }

  public void setStart(Date start) {
    this.start = start;
  }

  public Date getEnd() {
    return end;
  }

  public void setEnd(Date end) {
    this.end = end;
  }

  public Customer getCustomer() {
    return customer;
  }

  public void setCustomer(Customer cus-
tomer) {
    this.customer = customer;
  }
}
```

A given card is issued to exactly one customer and a given customer is allowed to have exactly one membership card. Thus, the association between out Customer class and our new MemberCard class is a one-to-one. To incorporate the Member-Card into our model, the Customer class needs, of course, to be augmented with an attribute of type MemberCard called memberCard, changes to the constructor for Customer need to be made, and getter and setter methods need to be included. We do not include here these changes to the Customer class for reasons of obviousness.

Hibernate offers two strategies for mapping a one-to-one association. The first strategy is based on identical primary keys for the CUSTOMERS and MEMBERCARDS tables. The MemberCard.hbm.xml file needs to include the following:

```
<hibernate-mapping package="sales">
    <class name="MemberCard"
table="MEMBERCARDS">
    <id name="id" column="MEMBERCARD _ ID"
type="long">
        <generator class="foreign">
          <param name="property">customer</
param>
        </generator>
    </id>
    <property name="cardNumber"/>
    <property name="start"/>
    <property name="end"/>
      <one-to-one name="customer"
class="Customer"
        constrained="true"/>
  </class>
</hibernate-mapping>
```

Our Customer.hbm.xml file also needs to include the following:

```
<one-to-one name="memberCard"
class="MemberCard" cascade="all"/>
```

There are two things to notice in the Member-Card.hbm.xml mapping file. First, the key generation strategy is designated as "foreign." Second, note the use of the one-to-one and constrained="true" mapping elements. The net result of these changes is that the database schema for the MEMBERCARD table contains a primary key (MEMBERCARD_ID) that is also a foreign key referencing the primary key (ID) of the CUSTOMERS table.

The second strategy offered by Hibernate for mapping a one-to-one association is based on a foreign key mapped, in our case, from the CUS-TOMERS table to the MEMBERCARDS table. The mapping element in Customer.hbm.xml now becomes:

```
<many-to-one name="memberCard"
class="MemberCard" column="MEMBERCARD _
ID" cascade="all" unique="true"/>
```

The reader may wonder why the "many-to-one" element is used since this is supposed to be a one-to-one association. The answer is that we have also set the "unique" element to "true." By doing so we guarantee that the association is actually one-to-one.

Using this strategy, if we want the association between the Customer class and the MemberCard class to be bidirectional, the mapping element in MemberCard.hbm.xml changes to:

```
<one-to-one name="customer"
class="Customer" property-
ref="memberCard"/>
```

MANY-TO-MANY ASSOCIATIONS

As noted above, the association between our Customer and Orders classes is a one-to-many association. Since our application is an order entry system, we clearly need some products for our customers to order. For the sake of argument, let us suppose that we are selling woodworking equipment. We have the usual machinery for sale, namely table saws, band saws, jointers, planers, routers, drills, and so forth. A given customer can order a table saw, and a band saw and a jointer all in the same order. Clearly we need a Product class. The question is: What kind of association is there between our Product class and our Order class? Given that a customer can order a table saw, and a band saw, and a jointer all in the same order and that table saws can be present in orders from many customers, the association is clearly a many-to-many. Now the question becomes:

How do we implement such an association? On the relational database side, the answer is clear: since only one-to-one and one-to-many relationships are countenanced in a relational database, we must introduce an intermediary table (ORDERLINE) called a *junction table* that stands in two separate many-to-one relationships to the PRODUCT table and the ORDERS table.[11] The attributes of this ORDERLINE table will include, as a minimum, the primary key attributes of the ORDERS and PRODUCT tables. It is important to note that we have no choice about this. What about the object model side; must we introduce an Orderline class? The short answer is "No." The Hibernate mapping system is more than robust enough to handle many-to-many class associations without the introduction of "junction classes."[12] The long answer is a bit more involved. In the real world, a many-to-many association not only associate entities but usually conveys information about the *association* as well. For example, in the association between the Product class and the Orders class, we would usually want to include information such as the quantity of a given product involved in the order and perhaps the quoted price for that particular product.[13] A little thought quickly reveals that this information does *not* belong in either the Product or Orders classes. As Bauer and King (2007) put it:

Our experience is that there is almost always other information that must be attached to the link between associated instances (such as the date and time when an item was added to a category) and that the best way to represent this information is via an intermediate association class. (pp. 297-298)

Before we implement our Product and Orderline classes and their mapping files, one other issue deserves our attention, namely composite keys. In an introductory database class, students are often told that the ORDERLINE schema should contain the primary key attributes of the PRODUCT and ORDERS tables as foreign keys and that, jointly, they should form a composite primary key for the ORDERLINE table. An alternative, not often taught, is to have a separate noncomposite primary key for the ORDERLINE table. This has certain advantages from Hibernate's point of view; indeed, the Hibernate team discourages the use of both composite keys and natural keys. We will follow their advice and not use a composite key for our implementation of the ORDERLINE table.[14] The following represents an acceptable schema for the ORDERLINE and PRODUCT tables:

ORDERLINE(ORDERL_ID, PROD_ID, ORDER_ID, QUANTITY)

PRODUCT(PROD_ID, DESCRIPTION, UNIT_PRICE, QOH)[15]

Our Product and Orderline classes can now be implemented as in Listings 13 and 14.

Listing 13 The Product Class

```
package org.mnsu.edu.oes;
public class Product {
  private int id;
  private String description;
  private float unitPrice;
  private int qoh;
  private Set orderline = new HashSet();

  public Product {}
  public Product(String description, float
unitPrice, int
    qoh, Set orderline) {
    this.description = description;
    this.unitPrice = unitPrice;
    this.qoh = qoh;
    this.orderline = orderline;
  }
  …


  //getters and setters for description,
etc.

  …

}
```

Listing 14 The Orderline Class

```
package org.mnsu.edu.oes;
public class Orderline {
  private int id;
  private int orderid;
  private int productid;
  private int quantity;

  public Orderline {}
  public Orderline(int orderid, int pro-
ductid, int quantity) {
    this.orderid = orderid;
    this.prodid = prodid;
    this.quantity = quantity;
  }
  ...

  // getters and setters for orderid,
etc.

  ...
}
```

Listing 15 and 16 shows the mapping files for our new classes.

Listing 15 Product.hbm.xml

```
<?xml version="1.0"?>
<!DOCTYPE hibernate-mapping PUBLIC
    "-//Hibernate/Hibernate Mapping DTD//
EN"
  "http://hibernate.sourceforge.net/hiber-
nate-mapping-3.0.dtd">

<hibernate-mapping>

  <class  name="org.mnsu.edu.oes.Product"
table="PRODUCT">

  <id name="id" type="int" unsaved-val-
ue="0">
    <column name="PROD_ID"
```

```
sql-type="int"
not-null="true"/>
  <generator class="hilo"/>
  </id>

    <property    name="description"
type="string">
      <column    name="DESCRIPTION"
length="50"/>
  </property>

    <property    name="unitPrice"
type="double">
      <column  name="UNIT_PRICE"  sql-
type="double"/>
  </property>

  <property name="qoh" type="int">
   <column name="QOH" sql-type="int"/>
  </property>

  <set name="Orderline"
  table="ORDERLINE"
  lazy="true"
  inverse="true"
  cascade="all"
  sort="unsorted">
    <key column="PROD_ID"/>
    <one-to-many class="org.mnsu.edu.oes.
Orderline"/>
  </set>
 </class>
</hibernate-mapping>
```

Listing 16 Orderline.hbm.xml

```
<?xml version="1.0"?>
<!DOCTYPE hibernate-mapping PUBLIC
    "-//Hibernate/Hibernate Mapping DTD//
EN"
  "http://hibernate.sourceforge.net/hiber-
nate-mapping-3.0.dtd">

<hibernate-mapping>
```

```
<class name="org.mnsu.edu.oes.Orderline"
table="ORDERLINE">

  <id name="id" type="int" unsaved-val-
ue="0">
     <column name="ORDERLINE _ ID" sql-
type="int" not-null="true"/>
     <generator class="hilo"/>
  </id>

  <property
   name="quantity"
   column="QUANTITY"/>

  <many-to-one
   name="Orders"
   column="ORDER _ ID"
   class="org.mnsu.edu.oes.Orders"
   not-null="true"/>

  <many-to-one
   name="Product"
   column="PROD _ ID"
   class="org.mnsu.edu.oes.Product"
    not-null="true"/>
 </class>
</hibernate-mapping>
```

Since we must connect our Orders class with our Orderline class in a one-to-many association we need to modify the mapping file for the Orders class as in Listing 17.

Listing 17 Orders.hbm.xml

```
<?xml version="1.0"?>
<!DOCTYPE hibernate-mapping PUBLIC
    "-//Hibernate/Hibernate Mapping DTD//
EN"
   "http://hibernate.sourceforge.net/hiber-
nate-mapping-3.0.dtd">

<hibernate-mapping>
```

```
<class  name="org.mnsu.edu.oes.Orders"
table="ORDERS">
   <id name="id"  type="long"  unsaved-
value="null">
  <column name="ORDER _ ID" sql-type="bigint"
not-null="true"/>
    <generator class="hilo"/>
  </id>

  <property name="date" type="date">
   <column name="ORDER _ DATE" />
  </property>

  <many-to-one
   name="customer"
   column="CUST _ ID"
   class="org.mnsu.edu.oes.Customer"
   not-null="true"/>
  <set name="Orderline" table="ORDERLINE"
lazy="true"
    inverse="true"
    cascade="all" sort="unsorted">
     <key column="ORDER _ ID"/>
     <one-to-many class="org.mnsu.edu.oes.
Orderline"/>
  </set>
 </class>
</hibernate-mapping>
```

With the above class and mapping files in place, the following code (Listing 18) can be used to create Customer, Product, Order, and Orderline instances.

Listing 18 Driver Code

```
...
// configuration code omitted
try {
   session = app.sessionFactory.openSes-
sion();
  tx = session.beginTransaction();
  // Create and make persistent a Customer
and a Product
```

```
    // The Product and possibly the Customer
objects
    // would normally be read from the da-
tabase using
    // a HQL query
    Customer cust1 = new Customer("Gavin",
"King");
    session.save(cust1);
    Product prod1 = new Product("Delta DJ20",
1400.00,
    20);
    session.save(prod1);
    prod1.setQoh(prod1.getQoh()-5);
    // Create an Order object
    Orders order1 = new Orders(new java.util.
Date(),
    cust1);
    // It is initially a transient object
    cust1.getOrders().add(order1);
    // Now it is a persistent object be-
cause
    // it is referenced by a persistent Cus-
tomer object
    // Create an Orderline object
    Orderline ordline1 = new Orderline(order1,
prod1, 5);
    // It is initially a transient object
    order1.getOrderline().add(ordline1);
    prod1.getOrderline().add(ordline1);
    // Now it is a persistent object be-
cause
    // it is referenced by persistent Order
and Product
    // objects
    tx.commit(); // cust2, prod1, order1,and
ordline1
    // are now garanteed to be in the da-
tabase
  } catch (HibernateException e) {
   tx.rollback();
   e.printStackTrace();
  } finally {
   if (session != null)
    session.close();
```

```
  }
  ...
  // other code
```

The above code creates Customer and Product instances, makes them persistent via the calls to session.save(), creates Orders and Orderline instances, adds them to the set collections in Customer and Product, and then commits all of these instances to the database. Note that there was no need to call session.save() on the Orders and Orderline instances. This is the result of the fact that we enabled transitive persistence for those instances.

INHERITANCE STRUCTURES

It is no secret, of course, that one of the hallmarks of any OOP language worthy of the name is inheritance. A given class can be a subclass of one or more superclasses. The subclass inherits the fields and methods of the superclass(es) and can add its own new fields and methods. In this way, the superclass can be used over and over again and the OO developer is relieved of the need to start from scratch and reinvent the wheel. If a class inherits from more than one superclass, we have *multiple* inheritance. If only one superclass is involved, we have *single* inheritance. In practice, multiple inheritance has led to problems and, as a result, the folks who developed Java opted for a single inheritance model but, in deference to the usefulness of multiple inheritance, included the notion of an *interface*. An interface is rather similar to an abstract class but allows no implementation whatsoever. While a Java class can extend at most one other Java class, it can implement as many Java interfaces as needed (Arnold, Gosling, & Holmes, 2006, Chapter 4).

Hibernate's strategy for inheritance support comes in four forms, namely table per concrete class with implicit polymorphism, table per concrete class, table per class hierarchy, and table per subclass. The names describe the strategies. The Hibernate team prefers the table per class hierarchy strategy for reasons of performance and simplicity (Bauer & King, 2007, p. 199). Using this strategy, the table created for a particular class hierarchy contains columns for all of the properties of all classes in the hierarchy. Additionally, the table contains a discriminator column. This column is responsible for identifying which rows in the table correspond to instances of which class in the hierarchy. The downside of this strategy is that the table columns mapped by the properties of the subclasses involved must be nullable.

We illustrate the table per class hierarchy strategy by subclassing the Customer class with CorpCustomer (corporate customer) and PrivateCustomer. Though a corporate customer is a customer, it needs to be distinguished from a private customer by virtue of the fact that corporate customers have tax-id numbers while private customers have social security numbers. There would be other differences, of course, but this will suffice for our purposes. The code for CorpCustomer and Private Customer appears as in Listing 19 and 20.

Listing 19 CorpCustomer

```
package org.mnsu.edu.oes;
public class CorpCustomer extends Cus-
tomer {
  private String taxId;
  public CorpCustomer() {}
  public CorpCustomer(String fname, String
lname, String taxId) {
    super(fname,lname);
    this.taxId = taxId;
  }
  public void setTaxId(String taxId) {
    this.taxId = taxId;
  }
  public String getTaxId() {
    return taxId;
  }
}
```

Listing 20 PrivateCustomer

```
package org.mnsu.edu.oes;

public class PrivateCustomer extends Cus-
tomer {
  private String ssnum;

  public PrivateCustomer() {}
    public PrivateCustomer(String  fname,
String lname, String ssnum) {
    super(fname, lname);
    this.ssnum = ssnum;
  }

  public void setSsnum(String ssnum) {
    this.ssnum = ssnum;
  }
  public String getSsnum() {
    return ssnum;
  }
}
```

The necessary modifications for the Customer.hbm.xml file are included in Listing 21.

Listing 21 Customer.hbm.xml

```
<?xml version="1.0"?>
<!DOCTYPE hibernate-mapping PUBLIC
    "-//Hibernate/Hibernate Mapping DTD//
EN"
    "http://hibernate.sourceforge.net/hiber-
nate-mapping-3.0.dtd">

<hibernate-mapping>
  <class
    name="org.mnsu.edu.oes.Customer"
        table="CUSTOMERS"  discriminator-
value="CT">

    <id
      name="id"
      type="long"
```

```
  unsaved-value="null">
  <column name="CUST _ ID"
    sql-type="bigint"
    not-null="true"/>
    <generator class="hilo"/>
 </id>


<discriminator
  column="CUSTOMER _ TYPE"
  type="string"/>


<property
   name="fname"
   column="FNAME"/>
<property
   name="lname"
   column="LNAME"/>
<set name="Orders"
  table="ORDERS"
  lazy="true"
  inverse="true"
  cascade="all"
  sort="unsorted">
  <key column="ORDER _ ID"/>
     <one-to-many class="org.mnsu.edu.
oes.Orders"/>
  </set>
  <subclass
  name="org.mnsu.edu.oes.CorpCustomer"
  discriminator-value="TXID">
  <property
    name="taxId"
    column="TAX _ ID"/>
</subclass>
  <subclass
    name="org.mnsu.edu.oes.PrivateCus-
tomer"
    discriminator-value="SS">
  <property
  name="ssnum"
  column="SS _ NUM"/>
  </subclass>
  </class>
</hibernate-mapping>
```

The following code snippet instantiates and makes persistent CorpCustomer and PrivateCustomer objects.

```
PrivateCustomer   cust1   =   new
PrivateCustomer("Gavin", "King", "555-55-
5555");
CorpCustomer cust2 = new CorpCustomer("Steve",
"Ebersole", "41-1234567");
session.save(cust1);
session.save(cust2);
```

When the transaction commits, we have the following in the database (Box 1).

mysql> select * from customers;

HIBERNATE QUERIES

Though not specifically mentioned in our earlier discussion of full object mapping, most ORM services, purporting to implement full object mapping, include an object-oriented query language. Note that this is in contrast to a *data* mapping service like iBATIS. The query language for iBATIS is SQL itself. Hibernate supports three different query "languages": hibernate query language (HQL), the criteria API, and native SQL. HQL is a full object-oriented query language that is deliberately designed to resemble SQL. Indeed, new Hibernate users are often confused by this and wonder just what the difference is between HQL and SQL. The criteria API allows one to express query by criteria (QBC) and query by example (QBE) queries (Bauer & King, 2007, p. 615). Native (direct) SQL queries are also supported (Bauer & King, 2007, p. 615). In this chapter, we will focus on HQL.

A HQL query is created by instantiating the query interface. This can be done as simply as follows:

```
Query query = session.createQuery("from
Customer");
List<Customer> queryResult = query.
list();
```

Or, more simply, using method chaining:

```
List<Customer> queryResult = session.
createQuery("from Customer").list();
```

In this code, queryResult is a list of available Customer instances and we can, for example, iterate through queryResult and print out customer names as in this code:

```
for (Customer customer: queryResult) {
  System.out.println(customer.getFname() +
" " + customer.getLname();
}
```

Hibernate also supports parameter binding in the form of positional parameters and named parameters. The following is an example using positional parameters:

```
String qString = "from Customer c where
c.fName like ?";
Query query = session.createQuery(qString).
setString(0, "Gavin King");
```

The named parameter(s) equivalent of this is:

```
String qString = "from Customer c where
c.fName like :fName";
Query query = session.createQuery(qString).
setString("fName", "Gavin King");
```

Note that in the above queries, we are using "c" as an alias for Customer. A HQL alias is a shorthand name and functions in HQL much like its SQL counterpart.

Hibernate supports a number of different join types, including all of the following:

- Inner join
- Left (outer join)
- Right (outer join)
- Full join
- Join fetch

Each of these, save the last, should be familiar to readers already familiar with SQL. We will examine join fetches in a later section.

As an example of a left outer join in HQL, consider the following code snippet:

```
Query query = session.createQuery("from
Customer c left join c.orders o");
```

This query returns a list of customers together with their associated orders. The list contains customers who have orders together with those who do not. The list actually consists of a collection of Object[] arrays with customer values at index 0 and order values at index 1.

To obtain a list of only those customers who have placed orders, use this query:

Box 1.

```
+---------+---------------+-------+----------+------------+-------------+--------+----------------+
| CUST_ID | CUSTOMER_TYPE | FNAME | LNAME    | TAX_ID     | SS_NUM      |
+---------+---------------+-------+----------+------------+-------------+--------+----------------+
| 1       | SS            | Gavin | King     | NULL       | 555-55-5555 |
| 2       | TXID          | Steve | Ebersole | 41-1234567 | NULL        |
+---------+---------------+-------+----------+------------+-------------+--------+----------------+

2 rows in set (0.00 sec)
```

```
Query query = session.createQuery("from
Customer c join c.orders o");
```

Just as in SQL, one can use a select clause in HQL to restrict the values returned by a query. In the last two queries we did not use a select clause and, as a result, we would incur the additional overhead of manipulating Object[] arrays if we only wanted, for example, to print out the customer names of customers who have placed orders. We can avoid this overhead with a select clause as in this code:

```
Query query = session.createQuery("select
c from Customer c join c.orders o");
```

Earlier we noted that HQL is an *object-oriented* query language. As such, we expect that polymorphic queries should be possible. HQL does not disappoint us in this regard. Assuming that we have subclassed both CorpCustomer and PrivateCustomer from Customer (as in the section on inheritance strategies), the following query will return instances of all three classes:

```
Query query = session.createQuery("from
Customer c");
```

To underscore the fact that HQL is truly object-oriented and truly supports polymorphic queries, note that all of the following are valid, if somewhat pointless, HQL queries:

```
Query query = session.createQuery("from
java.lang.Object");
Query query = session.createQuery("from
java.util.Set");
Query query = session.createQuery("from
java.util.List");
```

As might be expected, in addition to supporting logical operators such as and, any, between, exists, in, like, not, or, some and comparison operators such as =, >, <, >=, <=, and <>, HQL also supports the use of aggregate functions. In particular, it supports the following five:

- count()
- min()
- max()
- sum()
- avg()

The following is thus a valid HQL:

```
Query query = session.createQuery("select
count(serialNumber) from
Product");
```

SQL students soon learn that the use of an aggregate function needs to be qualified with a "group by" expression if the SELECT clause contains a normal column reference in addition to the aggregate function. The same is true in HQL. For example, suppose our Product class contained a productDescription property of type String. If we wanted to retrieve productDescription(s) as well as a count of the serialNumber(s), we would need to issue the following query:

```
Query query = session.createQuery("select
productDescription, count(serialNumber)
from    Product    p    group    by
p.productDescription");
```

As might be expected, Hibernate also supports the use of a HAVING clause to qualify the results obtained from the use of a GROUP BY clause:

```
Query query = session.createQuery("select
productDescription, count(serialNumber)
from Product p group by p.productDescription
having p.description like 'Bandsaw%');
```

Correlated and uncorrelated subqueries are often used in SQL to achieve an economy of expression and power not easily obtained without them. Not surprisingly, HQL supports them as well. HQL supports subqueries in the WHERE clause (Bauer & King, 2007, p. 659). The following are each valid HQL:

```
//correlated - gets customers who have
placed more than 5 orders
from Customer c where 5 < (select count(o)
from c.orders o)
//uncorrelated - gets customers who have
placed an order
from Customer c where c.id in (select
o.customer from Order o)
```

FETCHING STRATEGIES

The astute reader will have noticed that a new attribute appeared in Listings 15, 17, and 21 for the Products.hbm.xml, Orders.hbm.xml, and Customer.hbm.xml files, namely lazy="true." There is in fact no real need to include this in our mapping files since the default for this attribute is "true" as of version 3.x of Hibernate. However, there *is* a definite need to understand what this attribute is and why we want "true" to be the default in most cases. To help in our understanding of this, we need to consider a problem that plagues *any* ORM implementation, namely, the *n+1 selects problem* mentioned in the Paradigm Mismatch Problem section.

Suppose we want a list of Order objects using data stored in the ORDERS table in the database. Each Customer object is associated with a set of Order objects. Does this mean that when we instantiate an Order object, we must also instantiate any associated Customers? If so, then we are likely to generate an object graph that includes much data from the Customer table when all we wanted was a list of Orders objects. By having the lazy attribute set to "true," we are enabling lazy fetching, that is, we are telling Hibernate that, for example, when we obtain an Orders object from the database, we do *not* want the customer attribute of that class to be loaded until we really need it. Instead, a proxy object is created as a stand in for the customer attribute and we thereby avoid the problem of loading customer data into the object graph when we only wanted data from the ORDERS table (see work by Gamma, Helm, Johnson, and Vlissides [1995,

pp. 207-217] for a discussion of the proxy design pattern). If later, we decide to "examine" the customer attribute, then a new database select will be issued and the proxy will be replaced by the "real thing." Conversely, if we obtain a Customer object from the database, we may not necessarily want to obtain the list of Orders objects associated with that customer. Instead, with lazy fetching enabled, an uninitialized collection wrapper will be obtained that does not generate a database hit[16].

While having lazy fetching enabled solves one aspect of the n+1 selects problem, it can generate another problem if we are not careful. Suppose we want to obtain some information about a particular customer in our database. Suppose also that the desired information is held in the customer table. We can accomplish this in any number of ways and the particular method chosen is not important so long as it results in a single select query being issued against the customer table in the database.

If now we wish to iterate through our graph of customer objects and examine their orders, the formerly noninitialized collection wrapper will get replaced by the "real thing."

However, when we start to "walk the object graph" and examine a customer's orders, several more selects will be issued, one for each of the customer's orders. Our problem now is not one of having obtained an object graph much larger than needed. The problem is that our application is issuing too many selects against the database. In a highly concurrent application, performance will suffer greatly as a result.

Hibernate's solution to this dilemma comes in the form of programmer controlled fetching strategies. We have already seen part of the solution in the use of the lazy fetching attribute at the level of the mapping files. Hibernate also allows two other modes of fetch control. The first of these is called *batch fetching*. Along with having lazy set to "true," a developer can enable batch fetching in the mapping file. That is, we can modify our Customer.hbm.xml file thusly:

```
<set name="Orders" table="ORDERS"
lazy="true" inverse="true" batch-size="10"
cascade="all"
 sort="unsorted">
 <key column="ORDER _ ID"/>
 <one-to-many class="org.mnsu.edu.oes.Or-
ders"/>
</set>
```

Note the inclusion of batch-size="10" in the above. This tells Hibernate to fetch 10 sets when the first set is accessed. While this reduces the size of our n+1 selects problem somewhat, it clearly is not a solution to the problem in general. It is probably impossible for most applications to "know" at the level of the mapping file what the "correct" choice is for the batch size. For some transactions carried out by the application, a particular batch size might be just fine, while for others it might be too large or too small. The third mode of fetch control supported by Hibernate is *eager fetching*. Eager fetching is a bit like batch fetching with a batch size of "all." Using eager fetching at the mapping file level is likely to produce the problem, noted above, of loading the entire database into the object graph when only a small portion is required. Instead, Hibernate recommends that eager fetching be used when needed not in the mapping files, but rather in the application code itself. Since Hibernate supports runtime declarations of association fetching strategies, this turns out to be quite easy to do. Consider an object domain somewhat simpler than our current one. In this scenario, we have associations between courses (in a school) and exams. Each course can have one or more exams. Figure 1 depicts the situation.

Suppose that the course data consists of four courses with the following names:

* CS1
* CS2
* Data Structures
* Design Patterns

Suppose further that each course has associated with it two exams with the following descriptions:

* Midterm CS1
* Final CS1
* Midterm CS2
* Final CS2
* Midterm Data Structures
* Final Data Structures
* Midterm Design Patterns
* Final Design Patterns

The java code for creating these classes, their associated mapping files, and the scripts necessary to create the database tables is quite easy to construct and is not included here for the sake of brevity. What *is* included here is some driver code (and output from it) that shows what happens when we utilize only Hibernate's default lazy loading fetch plan. Suppose, for example, that we want to retrieve the course names from the database and also the exam descriptions associated with each course. The code in Listing 22 shows one way to do this.

Listing 22 (Lazy Loading Only and a Join)

```
//other stuff omitted
List<Course> courseList = session.
createQuery("select c from Course c left
join c.exams").list();
System.out.println();
for (Course courses : courseList) {
 System.out.println(course.getCourseName()
+ " exams: ");
    for (Exam examination : (Set<Exam>)
courses.getExams()) {
    System.out.println("\t" + examination.
getExamDescription());
 }
System.out.println();
}
```

This code first retrieves a list of courses from the database using lazy fetching. Thus, there are no exams retrieved thus far. It then iterates through the list and prints out the course names. Next, in the inner for-loop, the set of exams associated with the course in question is retrieved via the call to "courses.getExams()" and the exam description for each exam is printed out. The following output shows the SQL code generated by Hibernate during this process:

```
[java] Hibernate: select distinct course0_
.COURSE_ID as COURSE1_0_, course0_
.COURSENAME as COURSENAME0_ from COURSE
course0_ left outer join EXAM exams1_ on
course0_.COURSE_ID=exams1_.COURSE_ID
    [java]
    [java] CS1 exams:
    [java] Hibernate: select exams0_.COURSE_
ID as COURSE4_1_, exams0_.EXAM_ID as
EXAM1_1_, exams0_.EXAM_ID as EXAM1_
1_0_, exams0_.EXAMDESCRIPTION as EX-
AMDESC2_1_0_, exams0_.EXAMNUMBER as
EXAMNUMBER1_0_, exams0_.COURSE_ID as
COURSE4_1_0_ from EXAM exams0_ where
exams0_.COURSE_ID=?
    [java]    Final CS1
    [java]    Midterm CS1
    [java]
    [java] CS2 exams:
    [java] Hibernate: select exams0_.COURSE_
```

```
ID as COURSE4_1_, exams0_.EXAM_ID as
EXAM1_1_, exams0_.EXAM_ID as EXAM1_
1_0_, exams0_.EXAMDESCRIPTION as EX-
AMDESC2_1_0_, exams0_.EXAMNUMBER as
EXAMNUMBER1_0_, exams0_.COURSE_ID as
COURSE4_1_0_ from EXAM exams0_ where
exams0_.COURSE_ID=?
    [java]    Midterm CS2
    [java]    Final CS2
    [java]
    [java] Data Structures exams:
    [java] Hibernate: select exams0_.COURSE_
ID as COURSE4_1_, exams0_.EXAM_ID as
EXAM1_1_, exams0_.EXAM_ID as EXAM1_
1_0_, exams0_.EXAMDESCRIPTION as EX-
AMDESC2_1_0_, exams0_.EXAMNUMBER as
EXAMNUMBER1_0_, exams0_.COURSE_ID as
COURSE4_1_0_ from EXAM exams0_ where
exams0_.COURSE_ID=?
    [java]    Final Data Structures
    [java]    Midterm Data Structures
    [java]
    [java] Design Patterns exams:
    [java] Hibernate: select exams0_.COURSE_
ID as COURSE4_1_, exams0_.EXAM_ID as
EXAM1_1_, exams0_.EXAM_ID as EXAM1_
1_0_, exams0_.EXAMDESCRIPTION as EX-
AMDESC2_1_0_, exams0_.EXAMNUMBER as
EXAMNUMBER1_0_, exams0_.COURSE_ID as
COURSE4_1_0_ from EXAM exams0_ where
exams0_.COURSE_ID=?
```

Figure 1. UML diagram for Course and Exam

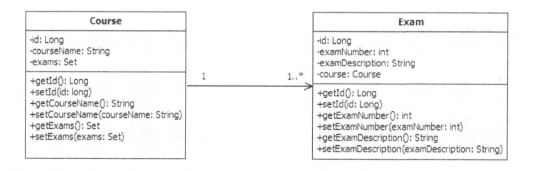

```
[java]    Final Design Patterns
[java]    Midterm Design Patterns
[java]
```

Note that there are five SQL SELECTS generated. What we have here is the n+1 selects problem. The "1" in this case refers to the first SQL SELECT where the list of courses is retrieved. The "n" in this case refers to the next four SQL SELECTs required to retrieve the exams (two per course) associated with each of the four courses. Because lazy fetching was utilized to retrieve the list of courses, the set of exams associated with each is not retrieved in the first SQL SELECT but, as noted earlier, an uninitialized collection wrapper (in effect a collection proxy) is retrieved instead. When we iterate through the course list and print the list of exam descriptions, the collection is initialized via additional SQL SELECTs.

There are a number of ways to avoid the n+1 selects in the scenario outline above. One of the simplest ways is to employ a dynamic fetching strategy as in Listing 23.

Listing 23 (Using Join Fetch)[17]

```
List<Course> courseList = session.
createQuery("select distinct c from Course
c left join fetch c.exams").list();
System.out.println();
for (Course courses : courseList) {
 System.out.println(courses.getCourseName()
+ " exams: ");
   for (Exam examination : (Set<Exam>)
courses.getExams()) {
    System.out.println("\t" + examination.
getExamDescription());
  }
 System.out.println();
}

Output:
```

```
[java] Hibernate: select distinct course0 _
.COURSE _ ID as COURSE1 _ 0 _ 0 _ , exams1_
.EXAM _ ID as EXAM1 _ 1 _ 1 _ , course0 _
.COURSENAME as COURSENAME0 _ 0 _ , exams1_
.EXAMDESCRIPTION as EXAMDESC2 _ 1 _ 1 _ ,
exams1 _ .EXAMNUMBER as EXAMNUMBER1 _ 1 _ ,
exams1 _ .COURSE _ ID as COURSE4 _ 1 _ 1 _ ,
exams1 _ .COURSE _ ID as COURSE4 _ 0 _ _ , ex-
ams1 _ .EXAM _ ID as EXAM1 _ 0 _ _ from COURSE
course0 _ left outer join EXAM exams1 _ on
course0 _ .COURSE _ ID=exams1 _ .COURSE _ ID
[java]
[java] CS1 exams:
[java]    Final CS1
[java]    Midterm CS1
[java]
[java] CS2 exams:
[java]    Final CS2
[java]    Midterm CS2
[java]
[java] Data Structures exams:
[java]    Midterm Data Structures
[java]    Final Data Structures
[java]
[java] Design Patterns exams:
[java]    Midterm Design Patterns
[java]    Final Design Patterns
[java]
```

Note that in this case there is only one SQL SELECT generated.

In the example above, we provided an example of the n+1 selects problem and one way of overcoming that problem (using join fetch). The example was from the perspective of the one side of a one-to-many association. We now demonstrate the problem again but from the perspective of the many side.

Suppose that we want to retrieve and print the exam descriptions data from the database and, for each such description, the course name associated with that description. The code in Listing 24 shows one way to do this.

Listing 24 (Lazy Loading Only and a Join)

```
List<Exam> examsList = session.
createQuery("select e from Exam e left
join e.course").list();
System.out.println();

for (Exam examinations : examsList) {
 System.out.println(examinations.getExam-
Description() + " is a ");
  System.out.println("\t" + examinations.
getCourse().getCourseName()
  + " exam: ");
}
```

Output:

```
 [java] Hibernate: select exam0 _ .EXAM _ ID
as  EXAM1 _ 1 _ ,  exam0 _ .EXAMDESCRIPTION
as  EXAMDESC2 _ 1 _ ,  exam0 _ .EXAMNUMBER
as  EXAMNUMBER1 _ ,  exam0 _ .COURSE _ ID as
COURSE4 _ 1 _  from EXAM exam0 _  left outer
join COURSE course1 _  on exam0 _ .COURSE _
ID=course1 _ .COURSE _ ID
  [java]
  [java] Final CS1 is a
 [java] Hibernate: select course0 _ .COURSE _
ID as COURSE1 _ 0 _ 0 _ , course0 _ .COURSENAME
as COURSENAME0 _ 0 _ from COURSE course0 _
where course0 _ .COURSE _ ID=?
  [java]  CS1 exam
  [java]  Midterm CS1 is a
  [java]  CS1 exam
  [java]  Final CS2 is a
 [java] Hibernate: select course0 _ .COURSE _
ID as COURSE1 _ 0 _ 0 _ , course0 _ .COURSENAME
as COURSENAME0 _ 0 _ from COURSE course0 _
where course0 _ .COURSE _ ID=?
  [java]  CS2 exam
  [java]  Midterm CS2 is a
  [java]  CS2 exam
  [java]  Final Data Structures is a
 [java] Hibernate: select course0 _ .COURSE _
ID as COURSE1 _ 0 _ 0 _ , course0 _ .COURSENAME
```

```
as COURSENAME0 _ 0 _  from COURSE course0 _
where course0 _ .COURSE _ ID=?
  [java]  Data Structures exam
  [java]  Midterm Data Structures is a
  [java]  Data Structures exam
  [java]  Final Design Patterns is a
 [java] Hibernate: select course0 _ .COURSE _
ID as COURSE1 _ 0 _ 0 _ , course0 _ .COURSENAME
as COURSENAME0 _ 0 _  from COURSE course0 _
where course0 _ .COURSE _ ID=?
  [java]  Design Patterns exam
  [java]  Midterm Design Patterns is a
  [java]  Design Patterns exam
```

Again, notice that there are five SQL SELECTS generated. In this case, instead of providing an uninitialized collection wrapper for a set of exams, a proxy for the course associated with a given set of exams is provided. The reader may wonder why there are only four SQL SELECTS for the course names. After all there are eight exams involved and the call to

```
"System.out.println("\t" + examinations.
getCourse().getCourseName()"
```

is, therefore, executed eight times. The answer is that, for a given set of exam descriptions, the *first* call does generate a SQL SELECT but, since the *second* call "retrieves" the very same Course instance as the first call, no additional SQL SELECT is required because the appropriate Course instance is already available. In any case, the cure for this version of the n+1 selects problem is similar to that in the first example. Again, we use dynamic fetching as in Listing 25.

Listing 25 (Using Join Fetch)

```
List<Exam> examsList = session.
createQuery("select e from Exam e left
join fetch e.course").list();
System.out.println();
```

```
for (Exam examinations : examsList) {
  System.out.println(examinations.getExam-
Description() + " is a ");
    System.out.println("\t" + examinations.
getCourse().getCourseName()
    + " exam ");
}
```

```
Output:
```

```
  [java] Hibernate: select exam0 _ .EXAM _ ID
as EXAM1 _ 1 _ 0 _ , course1 _ .COURSE _ ID as
COURSE1 _ 0 _ 1 _ , exam0 _ .EXAMDESCRIPTION
as EXAMDESC2 _ 1 _ 0 _ , exam0 _ .EXAMNUMBER
as EXAMNUMBER1 _ 0 _ , exam0 _ .COURSE _ ID
as COURSE4 _ 1 _ 0 _ , course1 _ .COURSENAME
as COURSENAME0 _ 1 _ from EXAM exam0 _ left
outer join COURSE course1 _ on exam0 _
.COURSE _ ID=course1 _ .COURSE _ ID
  [java]
  [java] Final CS1 is a
  [java]   CS1 exam
  [java] Midterm CS1 is a
  [java]   CS1 exam
  [java] Final CS2 is a
  [java]   CS2 exam
  [java] Midterm CS2 is a
  [java]   CS2 exam
  [java] Final Data Structures is a
  [java]   Data Structures exam
  [java] Midterm Data Structures is a
  [java]   Data Structures exam
  [java] Final Design Patterns is a
  [java]   Design Patterns exam
  [java] Midterm Design Patterns is a
  [java]   Design Patterns exam
```

Notice, as in the first example, that a single SQL SELECT is generated.

There are many more options that can be used in setting up a fetching plan appropriate for a given application than can be show here. The reader is urged to turn to Bauer and King (2007), Chapters 13-15.

PERSISTENT OBJECTS

In Hibernate, an object instantiated from a class (e.g., using the new operator) may be in one of three states, namely transient, persistent, or detached. The state of an object is *transient* if it is not yet tied to a database table row. As soon as a transient object is dereferenced in its application, it becomes available for garbage collection just as any ordinary Java object would. A transient object has no database identity. The state of an object is *persistent* if it has been saved to the session using either save() or saveOrUpdate(). A persistent object is an object with a database identity and has a primary key value as its database identifier. The state of a persistent object is guaranteed to be synchronized with the database. A persistent object can become a transient object by using delete(). The state of an object is *detached* if it was once a persistent object but the session with which it was previously associated is now closed. The state of a detached object is *not* guaranteed to be synchronized with the database. Additionally, a persistent object can become detached via a call to evict(), close(), or clear() and a detached object can become a persistent object via a call to update(), saveOrUpdate(), or lock().[18] While this discussion suggests a seemingly simple API for manipulating objects between transient, persistent, and detached states, it is, in fact, too simple. Consider the following code (Listing 26) which *appears* to load a Customer object into a session, close the session (thereby transitioning the Customer object from persistent to detached), change the first name of the Customer object, create a new session, and transition the Customer object from detached to persistent via a call to update().

Listing 26

```
Session session =???//get a session - can
be done in lots of ways
Transaction  tx  =  session.beginTransac-
tion();
```

```
Customer customer = (Customer) session.
load(Customer.class,customerId);

tx.commit();
session.close();//customer is now detached

customer.setName("Jill");
```

However, this code will usually generate an error when run. The specific error reads as follows:

"could not initialize proxy – the owning Session was closed"

This error is actually quite instructive and illustrates one of the mechanisms that Hibernate uses to avoid unnecessary hits to the database and thereby increases performance. Because lazy fetching is enabled for the Customer class, the call to session.load() in the above listing, contrary to appearances, does not generate a database hit that loads the customer whose id is customerId. Instead, a proxy is generated that serves as a stand-in for the "real" customer object. Ordinarily, the "real" customer object would be loaded (and a database hit thereby generated) by the call to customer.setName(). However, that call is not made until *after* the session is closed. Since the session is closed, the proxied customer object is detached and cannot be initialized. Since it cannot be initialized, the call to customer.setName() generates the above error.

There are a variety of ways in which the above problem can be fixed. One *could* enable eager fetching for the Customer class. While this would solve the problem, it would reintroduce the problem of loading too many Customer objects for queries involving customers. What we want, of course, is some way of initializing a proxy *without* having to enable eager fetching. Luckily, Hibernate provides the static initialize() method from the Hibernate API. The solution now becomes very simple. Just insert the following line immediately after the call to session.load():

```
Hibernate.initialize(customer);
```

This line will cause a database hit and the proxied Customer object, with an id of customerId, will be initialized with the proper values. The subsequent call to customer.setName() on the detached customer object can now succeed and will no longer generate the error noted above.

CONCLUSION

We began our overview of Hibernate with the goal of evaluating its success in overcoming the impedance mismatch problem. Specifically, we noted that there are five aspects to this problem. The first aspect—the problem of granularity—is handled by Hibernate's support for fine-grained domain models and its ability to naturally distinguish between entity and value types (Bauer & King, 2007, Sections 4.1 and 4.2). The second aspect—the problem of subtypes—is handled by Hibernate's support for at least four different class mapping strategies and by its support for custom types (Bauer & King, 2007, Chapter 5). The third aspect—the problem of identity—is handled by Hibernate's distinction between entity and value types, its use of identifiers, and its support for transactions and caching (Bauer & King, 2007, Chapters 10 and 13). The fourth aspect—problems relating to associations—is handled by Hibernates ability to handle sets, bags, lists, and maps quite transparently (Bauer & King, 2007, Chapter 6). The fifth aspect—the problem of object network navigation and the associated n+1 selects problem—is handled by Hibernate's ability to utilize a variety of different fetching strategies (including lazy loading, batch fetching, and eager fetching), each of which can be utilized at the metadata mapping level or at the application code level (Bauer & King, 2007, Chapter 13).

In the last several years Hibernate has enjoyed a considerable amount of success and growth. Evidence for this can be seen on a number of fronts. Consider, for example, these facts: the revised EJB specification provides a Java Persistence API that is largely based on Hibernate (EJB 3.0, 2008); highly regarded Java/EE application frameworks such as Spring include facilities for integrating with Hibernate (Spring Framework, 2008); while Hibernate is aimed toward the Java developer, a .net port of Hibernate (NHibernate) is also available (NHibernate, 2008); Hibernate can be used with virtually any database for which a decent jdbc driver is available; and Hibernate is quite flexible and allows a developer to utilize either XML metadata or annotations to fulfill the persistence requirements of their applications.

The above is not to suggest that Hibernate is a "silver bullet." Indeed, for some applications Hibernate is definitely overkill and a simpler data mapping solution such as iBATIS might well be more appropriate. Hibernate is a complex ORM service with a steep learning curve that is not for those looking for a quick and dirty solution to the paradigm mismatch problem. However, for those who are looking for a full ORM service that solves virtually all aspects of the paradigm mismatch problem and who are willing to invest the time required to master it, Hibernate provides rewards in the form of increased productivity, increased maintainability, increased performance, decreased time to deployment, and vendor independence.

REFERENCES

Ambler, S. (2002). Mapping objects to relational databases (white paper).

AmbySoft Inc. Retrieved April 15, 2008, from www. ambysoft.com/mappingObjects.html

Arnold, K., Gosling, J., & Holmes, D. (2006). *The java programming language* (4th ed.). Addison Wesley.

Bauer, C., & King, G. (2007). *Java persistence with hibernate.* Manning

Begin, C., Goodin, B., & Meadors, L. (2007). *iBATIS in action.* Manning.

Codd, E. F. (1970, June). A relational model of data for large shared data banks. *Communications of the ACM, 13*(6), 377-387.

EJB 3.0. Retrieved April 15, 2008, from http://java. sun.com/products/ejb

Fussel, M. L. (1997). Foundations of object relational mapping. *Chimu Corporation.* Retrieved April 15, 2008, from www.chimu.com/publications/objectRelational/

Gamma, E., Helm, R., Johnson, R., & Vlissides, J. (1995). *Design patterns elements of reusable object-oriented software.* Addison Wesley.

Hibernate. Retrieved April 15, 2008, from http:// www.hibernate.org

iBATIS. Retrieved April 15, 2008, from http://ibatis. apache.org/

Java data objects (JDO). Retrieved April 15, 2008, from http://java.sun.com/javaee/technologies/jdo/index.jsp

Oracle TopLink. Retrieved April 15, 2008, from http://www.oracle.com/technology/products/ias/toplink/index.html

NHibernate for .net. Retrieved April 15, 2008, from www.nhibernate.org

Persistence. Retrieved April 15, 2008, from http:// java.sun.com/technologies/persistence.jsp

POJO. Retrieved April 15, 2008, from http://www. martinfowler.com/bliki/POJO.html

Relational persistence for Java and .Net. Retrieved April 15, 2008, from http://www.hibernate.org

Spring framework. Retrieved April 15, 2008, from http://www.springframework.org/

KEY TERMS

Automatic Dirty Checking: A strategy for detecting which persistent objects have been modified by an application.

Entity Type: A class whose instances have their own persistent identity.

Many-to-Many Association: An association between class in which instances of the first class are associated with possibly many instances of the second class. Instances of the second class are associated with possibly many instances of the first class.

N+1 Selects Problem: The problem that occurs when an application retrieves an object from a database and then "visits" an object or collection of objects to which the original object has an association. A single SQL SELECT is issued for retrieving the original object but additional SQL SELECTs are required for the visitations.

Object/Relational Mapping Service: A service for mapping instances of classes in a domain model to tables and foreign key constraints in a relational database.

One-to-Many Association: An association between classes in which instances of the first class are associated with possibly many instances of the second class. Instances of the second class are associated with at most one instance of the second class.

One-to-One Association: An association between classes in which instances of the first class are associated with exactly one instance of the second class and vice versa. The association may be between a single object and itself.

Paradigm Mismatch Problem: A set of problems encountered by applications written in an object-oriented programming language when the application needs to store (retrieve) objects in (from) a relational database.

POJO: Plain old Java object.

Transitive Persistence: A technique that allows for the automatic propagation of persistence to objects associated with a given persistent object.

Value Type: A class whose instances do not have their own persistent identity.

ENDNOTES

[1] (Begin, Goodin, & Meadors, 2007 p. 34)

[2] Also known as the *object/relational impedance mismatch* problem.

[3] Minimizing the number of required calls to the database is clearly a performance goal for an application supporting concurrency.

[4] We chose an order entry system example because it is one that many readers will be familiar with. Our particular example is overly simplified of course and differs in a number of respects from the example given on p. 213 of the Hibernate reference manual.

[5] As noted earlier, for those who eschew XML, another mechanism that can be used with Hibernate to enforce object persistence is the use of annotations. For reasons of space, we will not explore that approach in this chapter.

[6] While it is possible to include the mapping information for several classes in a single .hbm.xml file, best practices dictates that each persistent class have its own .hbm.xml file.

[7] This is not to say that the id property of customer has no value immediately after its creation. It certainly does. Since ints in Java default to 0, the value of id is 0. However, this value will more than likely change after customer becomes a *persistent* object.

[8] To those whose linguistic sensibilities rebel against the idea of using "persists" in this way, that is, as a transitive verb, I apologize. However, as is very often the case in computer circles, jargon is pervasive in ORM circles and

9   in Hibernate's circle in particular. So I will persist in using "persists" in this way. ;-)

9   This delayed execution of the generated SQL has its merits in terms of performance.

10   or automatically bidirectional if you prefer

11   These are sometimes also called *link tables* or *association tables*.

12   Actually, the idea here is quite simple. If we have a many-to-many association between classes A and B, make a set of Bs an instance variable of A and a set of As an instance variable of B. The mapping documents (A.hbm.xml and B.hbm.xml) for A and B still need to ensure that the associations between A and B are bidirectional and that the cascade attributes are properly set. Bauer and King (2007 pp. 297-303) include a discussion of how to implement the mapping classes for a many-to-many association

13   The quoted price may well be different from the unit price. The unit price property belongs in the Product class. The quoted price might be the result of a special discount (perhaps a special "deal" between the employee who took the order and the customer who submitted the order), or the result of any number of other things. Ultimately, the quoted price is the price that will affect the total cost of the order.

14   Admittedly we are operating under the luxury of implementing our database from scratch. Were we dealing with a legacy database containing junction tables with composite primary keys and tables with natural keys, our approach would have to change. Be that as it may, Hibernate *does* contain support for both composite and natural primary keys. See Section 8.1 by Bauer and King (2007) for details.

15   QOH represents quantity on hand. We have left out the schemata for the CUSTOMER and ORDERS tables for reasons of obviousness.

16   Hibernate contains a set of its own collection wrappers for most of the usual Java collection classes like Set, List and Map. Notably, it also contains a collection wrapper for Bag.

17   The use of the "distinct" keyword in this query reflects the fact that eager-fetching a collection may return duplicates. Though the keyword is maintained in the generated SQL, it has no effect at that level for this example. See the discussion by Bauer and King (2007, p. 651) for details.

18   close() and clear() transition all persistent objects in the session to detached. evict() only affects the instance on which it is called.

Section VI
Design Applications

Chapter XXVI
Pattern Based Video Coding

Manoranjan Paul
Monash University, Australia

Manzur Murshed
Monash University, Australia

ABSTRACT

People's demands are escalating with technology advances. Now, people are not happy with only text or voice messages, they like to see video as well. Video transmission through limited bandwidth, for example, an existing telephone line, requires an efficient video coding technique. Unfortunately, existing video coding standards have some limitations due to this demand. Recently, a pattern-based video coding technique has established its potentiality to improve the coding compared to the recent standard H.264 in the range of low bit rates. This chapter describes this technique with its background, features, recent developments, and future trends.

INTRODUCTION

Video conferencing, video telephony, teleteaching, telemedicine, surveillance, and monitoring systems are some of the video coding applications that have attracted considerable interest in recent years. The burgeoning Internet has increased the need for transmitting (nonreal-time) and/or streaming (real-time) video over a wide variety of different transmission channels connecting devices of varying storage and processing capacity. Stored movies or animations can now be downloaded and many reality-type interactive applications are also available via Web-cams.

The video itself is a series of still images (or frames) taken at some specific frame rate. Considering that the frame rate has to be fast enough to exploit the persistence of vision in creating the illusion of smooth motion as well as natural colour, the digital information content of a video can pose a significant challenge in the areas of efficient digital storage and transmission. For example, a 30 *frames per second* (fps) video with 24-bit per pixel true colour frames of moderate resolution (352×288 pixels) generates more than 70 mega bits per second. In order to cater to devices with limited power and storage with stringent transmission bandwidth requirements, these raw digital video data need to be compressed in the order of 10 to 10,000 times depending on the applications.

One way for video coding technology to facilitate the amount of video data compression needed is by eliminating redundant and visually insignificant data. Intraframe spatial redundancy is usually eliminated by run length encoding, while interframe temporal redundancy is eliminated by skipping a block of data. Insignificant data are usually eliminated by applying spatial subsampling by dropping some intermediate pixels from each frame, temporal subsampling by dropping some intermediate frames, and quantisation. The efficiency of these elimination processes is usually significantly improved by using block-based *motion estimation* (ME) and *motion compensation* (MC), and transforming pixel-level information to energy (frequency) domain.

Another problem which also effects the video data compression is the limited transmission bandwidth. For example, the low cost common networks like *public switched telephone network* (PSTN), *integrated services digital networks* (ISDN), and many computer networks normally allow for only several *kilo bits per second* (kbps) transmission. Even wireless transmission systems using cellular phones or *personal digital assistants* (PDA) operate under similar bandwidth restrictions. *Very low bit rate* (VLBR) video coding mandates bit rates between 8 and 64 kbps to facilitate video communications over these kinds of transmission media. Therefore, an efficient encoder is indispensable to enable the transmission of video. In this chapter we like to emphasise those video coding schemes which enable limited battery power and processing capacity devices, such as mobile phones and PDAs, to encode live video data in real-time and achieve significant improvement in coding efficiency so that

the encoded steams could be transmitted cost-effectively at a much lower bit rate.

BACKGROUND

Reducing the bit rate by maintaining acceptable image quality has been a continuing effort for researchers over a long period of time. Block-based very low bit rate video coding addresses this trend at the extreme level where sacrificing quality to meet a more stringent bit rate is inevitable. A graceful degradation of quality while attaining the highest possible quality for the operating bit rate remains a challenge for the research community. There are two ways to reduce the video data. One is a trivial and simple way which can be applied with any other modern video coding technology with sacrificing video quality; another is a standard way which must be used for any professional or commercial purpose.

Simple Way of Compression

The simple ways to reduce the bit rate for a video sequence in generic coding paradigm are by extending the group of picture, down sampling the image size, skipping frames, nonmotion compensated blocks, residual-error-compensation, and by increasing quantisation values. These bit reduction techniques will be presented in the rest of the section.

- During the video coding, a video sequence is divided into a group of picture (GOP) 0. A GOP consists of one intracoded frame (I-frame), one or more predicted coded frame (P- frame), and one or more bidirectional coded frames (B- frame). This classification depends on what reference frames are used for encoding. No reference frame is used for I-frame, previous I- or P-frames are used as reference frames for P-frame, and previous and next I- or P-frames are used as reference frame for B-frames. The length of a group can only be increased by introducing more P- and/or B-frames. Although the image quality of a frame coded as an I-frame is the best, considerably fewer bits would be required if the frame were coded as a P- or B-frame. This leads to a natural trade-off between compression efficiency and image quality in that a small group exhibits better image quality with less compression; by contrast, a large GOP exhibits more compression with poorer quality. In low bit rate video coding a large GOP is preferable

- Down sampling of an image size reduces the bit rate quite significantly. A large size image format, naturally, needs more bits compared to a small size one. In low bit rate video coding applications, a small size video is preferable as it requires a small number of bits.

- Besides spatial resolution subsampling of an image, temporal subsampling can also be used to reduce the bit rate for transmitting video through limited bandwidth channels. Temporal subsampling means dropping certain intermediate frames in a video sequence. For very low bit rate applications, instead of 30, 15 or 10 or 7.5 frames may be transmitted per second. Reducing the temporal frequency by two however does not halve the bit rate, because temporal decimation introduces longer motion vectors and higher residual errors and as a consequence, the bit requirement increases.

- Sometimes transmission bits can be reduced by skipping the residual-error-compensation information if it has no significant components.

- A large quantisation value reduces the magnitude of transform coefficients so that only relatively small bits are needed to represent them. This ensures better bit compression.

- Fractional motion estimation and compensation is the another way to reduce the effective bit rates and improve the image quality.

Standard Coding

The above mentioned procedures are the basic ways to reduce the video data. Besides this there are encoder technologies which enable the video data reduction significantly. Most video encoders comprise of the basic functionalities of prediction, transformation, quantisation, and entropy coding. There still exist considerable variations in the structure of the encoder and decoder (CODEC) arrangement. An arbitrary input frame is firstly subdivided into *macroblocks* (MBs), which generally correspond to a group of 16×16 nonoverlapping pixels in the original image. Each MB is then coded in either intra- or intermode determined by the block predictor with the help of the previously coded frames (i.e., frame memory). In intramode, no motion vector is generated, and thus the original (sometimes there are differences between the original and the neighbouring MB in the same frame) MB is transformed by *discrete cosine transformation* (DCT) 0. The DCT coefficients are then quantised (Q), reordered (zigzag scanned), and entropy-encoded using any efficient *variable length coding* (VLC) technique. Sometimes a *coding control* mechanism is used to control the bit rate by adjusting the quantisation value. In intermode, an MB is formed by MC prediction from one or more reference frames using ME; however, the prediction for each MB may be formed from one or two previous or forward frames (in time order) that have already been encoded and reconstructed. The prediction MB is subtracted from the current MB to produce a residual error MB which is then transformed using DCT and quantised to give a set of coefficients which are reordered (zigzag scanned) and entropy-encoded, using any VLC algorithm. The entropy-encoded coefficients, together with the side information required to decode the MB (such as the MB prediction mode, motion vector, and quantisation step size), form the compressed bit stream. Inverse quantisation and *inverse DCT* (IDCT) are used to form the reference frames which are stored in the *frame memory* for the encoder.

The decoder path uses the quantised MB coefficients in order to reconstruct a frame for encoding further MBs. At the decoder, the incoming compressed bit stream is disassembled and the data elements are entropy-decoded and reordered to produce quantised coefficients. These are rescaled and inverse-transformed to form the residual error of MB. The decoder then creates a prediction MB from the reference frame by incorporating the motion vector to its original MB (in current frame) position. Predicted MB is added to residual error to create the decoded MB.

While for special applications, some functional elements are modified or additional blocks are included, the basic structure of a video CODEC remains the same. Examples of some of the additional components include a preprocessing filter (to reduce the noise introduced in capturing images from low-quality sources, or camera shake) and a postprocessing filter (to reduce the blocking and/or ringing effects) 0. These additional components enhance the performance in certain cases at the expense of increased hardware complexity.

H.264

The most recently advanced video coding standard, H.264/AVC 0, has been recently finalised to support a wide range of applications by including new flexible features to merge the concepts of MPEG-X and H.26X. The applications of H.264/AVC include: i) broadcast over cable, satellite, and cable modem; ii) interactive or serial storage on optical or magnetic storage; iii) conversational services over ISDN, LAN, and wireless mobile networks; and iv) video-on-demand.

A profile is defined as a set of coding functions and specifications that is required by an encoder or decoder which complies with that profile. H.264 supports three profiles: *baseline, main,* and *extended.* The baseline profile is used in low bit rate video coding applications such as telemedicine, video telephony, videoconferencing, and wireless communication. The baseline profile of H.264 sup-

ports two types of frame, namely intraframes and predicted frames.

The overall steps of H.264 video coding can be divided into several steps, such as motion estimation and compensation 0, transform, quantisation, and entropy coding. Intermacroblock prediction creates a predicted macroblock of the current block from one or more previously encoded video pictures through motion estimation. H.264 considers each MB as either skipped or nonskipped MB. The MB with no motion or little motion is considered as skipped MB and no motion vectors or residual errors are needed as it will be copied from the reference frame directly. Each nonskipped MB (16×16) may be divided four ways, and motion estimation and compensation are carried out either as one 16×16 block, two 16×8, two 8×16, or four 8×8 blocks. If the 8×8 mode is selected, each of the four 8×8 sub-MBs within the MB may be further divided four ways, either as one 8×8 sub-MB, two 8×4 sub-MBs, two 4×8 sub-MBs, or four 4×4 sub-MBs. The motion estimation mode is selected based on the minimum value of the Langragian cost function. The Langrangian cost function is defined by the total bits needed to encode the MB and the sum of square differences between the original MB and the reconstructed MB multiplied by the Langrangian multiplier 00. After motion estimation, DCT is applied on the difference between the original MB and best matched MB (based on the motion) in reference frame. Unlike H.263, H.264 used 4×4 integer transformation 0 instead of 8×8 noninteger DCT transformation. Transform coefficients are quantised for more compression. H.264 used 52 levels of quantisation where H.263 used only 31 levels. Transform coefficients are entropy-coded using a context-based adaptive variable length coding (CAVLC) 0 but not context-adaptive-based arithmetic coding (CABAC) 0. CABAC improves coding efficiency by about 10% over that obtained from the CAVLC, but it requires a larger circuit scale and more power. In applications like mobile phones and digital cameras where minimising power consumption is a prime consideration, the baseline profile is used. All other syntax elements are coded using fixed-length or Exp-Golomb 0 variable length codes.

Up to the H.263 standard, all intra-MBs are transformed by DCT and then entropy-coded, in the case of H.264, however, intramode prediction is introduced which forms a prediction block from the differences between the current block and the previously encoded and reconstructed blocks. Although this strategy involves a huge amount of computational time, it improves the performance in terms of bit rate. There are nine selection modes for an intrablock of size 4×4 and four selection modes for an intrablock of size 16×16.

Existing VLBR Schemes

Since 1980, when the VLBR concept first emerged, vector quantisation 00000 has been a serious competitor among the VLBR video coding techniques. Vector quantisation (VQ) is a nonstandard video coding technique, but is very effective for data compression as it seeks to exploit the correlation between components within a vector. Optimum coding efficiency can be achievable if the vector dimension is infinite so the correlation between all components is exploited. VQ is comprised of i) vector formation, ii) training set generation, iii) codebook generation, and iv) quantisation. Vector formation is the decomposition of images into a set of 2-D vectors like the MB, which can be considered as a set of 2-D vectors. Coding efficiency of VQ is highly dependent on choosing the best training set, which is selected from either the image, or statistically similar images. Codebook generation is the most important process in VQ, since coding efficiency will be optimal when the interrelations between the codewords in a codebook are minimised. Different criteria can be applied such that the input vector source is classified into a predefined number of regions by the minimum distance rule between intracodewords and the maximum distance rule between intercodewords. Quantisation selects the most appropriate codeword in the codebook for each input vector using some prescribed metric such as mean square error. An exhaustive search process over the entire codebook provides the optimal result, but is time-consuming. There are alternative search algorithms such as tree-search, which although suboptimal, are much faster.

To achieve high video data compression, quantisation becomes the pivotal element in the CODEC process. An ideal VQ approach based on a combination of variable vector size, multistages, dynamic codebook updating using locality, and parallel computing structures together with small codebook size, could theoretically prove a very strong competitor for any contemporary digital video coding standard. Pragmatically, however, it is not feasible to incorporate all the aforementioned properties because many have individual trade-offs. One major problem with VQ is that it does not reconstruct edge vectors efficiently as the codebook is unable to reproduce all possible patterns. VQ with a dynamically updated codebook based upon locality provides a good approximation of subimages but often requires a large number of bits due to high codebook transmission frequency to the decoder. Generally a VQ coding system requires preprocessing for vector and codebook formation as well as the codebook transmission overhead. Codebook searching time also takes a significant amount of time and these limitations ultimately restrict the range of applications of VQ.

Content-based coding for VLBR is a fundamental component of the MPEG-4 0 video-coding standard, although the concept is not exactly new. *Model-based coding* (MBC), for example, was first introduced in 1981 by Wallis, Pratt, and Plotkin 0 and represents a special kind of object-based coding. Applications of MBC 0–0, however, have tended to be restricted to video telephony and conferencing, where only one or two objects are considered and some *a priori* knowledge about a scene's content exists. In contrast to the conventional digital video coding standards that are based on eliminating spatial and temporal redundancies in a sequence, MBC treats images as two-dimensional

(2-D) projections of a 3-D world involving *a priori* knowledge of a scene's contents. One or more moving objects in a video sequence is analysed using computer vision techniques to create a parametric model incorporating key information concerning the size, location, and motion of these objects. At the decoder, the model synthesises each object, by using computer-graphical methods, with automatic tracking techniques enabling the model to mimic the respective objects' movements. The parameters needed to animate the model are then coded and transmitted to the receiver, which reconstructs the model. For low quality images, the animation data are sufficient to give a good approximation to the original image sequence, but for higher image quality, an additional residual error signal is required that typically comprises the coded frame differences between the original video sequence and the animated model. The bit rate performance of MBC is very good because only the model parameters are transmitted, and this has attracted attention as it provides high-quality images at VLBR applications. As a consequence, the MBC has been viewed as a potential competitor for MPEG-4 and H.264, though major practical problems remain to be solved, namely the difficulty in modelling unknown objects and the inevitable presence of analysis errors.

In the context of low bit rate, the video coding wavelet theory has demonstrated an ability to not only provide high coding efficiency, but also spatial and quality scalability features. Grossman and Morlet first introduced the wavelet transform in 1984 0 by mapping a time or spatial function into a two-dimensional function. The main advantages of the discrete wavelet transformation (DWT)-based video coding 00 are: i) DWT has high decorrelation and energy compaction efficiency; ii) the wavelet basis functions match well with the human visual system (HVS) characteristics; iii) blocking artefacts and perceptual distortion are far less visible in wavelet filters due to the spatially global decomposition, resulting in subjectively better reconstructed images; iv) the DWT allows multiple resolution

analysis that supports high scalability since wavelet coefficient data structures are spatially self-similar across subbands; and v) the number of image pixels and DWT coefficients are the same, so there is no information is lost. On the other hand, due to the following limitation, it is included in recent video coding standards. The limitations are: i) DWT requires more memory and processing time because global decomposition requires the whole image to be considered as a large size block; ii) computational complexity is relatively high compared to discrete cosine transformation; iii) due to the large block size, efficient coding specially in VLBR is often impossible because it cannot differentiate active from static regions; and iv) there is no standard ways to incorporate the motion information using large block size.

Though the above mentioned techniques are good competitors for the standard video coding technique, they have their own limitation in real-time video coding. Moreover, they cannot work under the existing video coding standard frameworks.

MAIN FOCUS OF THE CHAPTER

Block-based H.261/3/4 000 and block-/content-based MPEG-4 0, standards have already the VLBR video coding option. The H.261 and H.263 standards are, however, unable to efficiently encode the boundary-adjoined part of a moving object within a 16×16 pixel *macroblock* (MB) during motion estimation, resulting in all 256 residual error values being transmitted for motion compensation regardless of whether there are moving objects or not. Efficient encoding of these blocks needs to eliminate the *intrablock temporal redundancy* (ITR), because they are almost static in the successive frames. None of the block-based standards, however, are able to exploit the ITR in the form of static background within the MB. To remove this inefficiency, the MPEG-4 video standard first introduced the concept of content-based coding by dividing video frames into separate segments (instead of MBs), comprising a background and one or more arbitrary-shaped moving objects that are coded separately. As this process requires expensive segmentation and shape coding, and is also ineffective for real-world video objects, it is not suitable for low processing devices using VLBR applications.

One solution in exploiting ITR is to subdivide the MB and then apply ME and MC to each subblock. With sufficient numbers of subblocks, the shape of a moving object can be more accurately represented. This solution has been implemented in the recent H.264 standard using the *variable block size* (VBS) mode. It, however, requires not only bits overhead for the motion vector and VBS mode for each partition, but also higher computational complexity in order to identify the best partitioning. Obviously, the smaller the subblocks, the higher these overheads will be and that could potentially offset all the coding efficiency resulting from better moving object shape approximation. As a result, VLBR coding using H.264 avoids smaller subblocks, and thus makes its VBS mode ineffective.

The MPEG-4 video standard exploits intrablock temporal redundancy by dividing video frames into separate segments comprising of a background and one or more moving objects. Paradoxically, it also depends on computationally expensive segmentation and shape coding and is not suitable for low processing devices, especially nonsynthetic real-world objects.

An alternative approach was proposed by Fukuhara, Asai, and Murakami 0 who used four MB-partitioning patterns each comprising of 128-pixels. ME and MC was carried out on all eight possible 128-pixel partitions of an MB and the pattern with the lowest prediction error was selected. While this approach gives better performance compared to H.263, the computational complexity of the motion-based processing is too high for real-time applications and having only four patterns means that it is insufficient to represent moving objects 0. As well, treating each MB, irrespective of its motion content, also resulted in a higher bit-rate being incurred for those MBs which contained only static

background or had moving object(s), with little static background. In such cases, the motion vectors for both partitions were almost the same and so only one could be represented.

To address the limitations of Fukuhara et al.'s approach, Wong, Lam, and Siu 0 and Paul and Murshed 000 exploited the idea of partitioning the MBs via a simplified segmentation process that again avoided handling the exact shape of the moving objects, so that popular MB-based motion estimation techniques could be applied. This *pattern-based video coding* (PVC) algorithm focused on the moving regions of the MBs, through the use of a set of regular n ($n < 256$) pixel pattern templates, from a pattern codebook (PC). If in using some *similarity* measure, the *moving region* (MR) of an MB is well covered by a particular pattern, then the MB can be coded by considering only the n pixels of that pattern, with the remaining $256-n$ pixels being skipped as *static background*. Successful pattern matching can therefore, theoretically, have a maximum compression ratio of $256/n$:1 for any MB. The actual achievable compression ratio will be lower due to object occlusion and the computing overheads for handling an additional MB type, pattern identification numbering, and pattern matching errors. This approach is radically different from H.264 subblocking as ME and MC are carried out only for the selected patterns, thus keeping the computational complexity in check.

FUTURE TRENDS

The future trend is to contribute to the acceptance of the concept of pattern based coding (PBC) as a potential additional mode for future VLBR video coding standards through a series of innovations in the form of pattern codebook construction, real time pattern selection, pattern matching criteria, coding scalability, and optimality issues so that the overall compression gain will be achieved in relation to the conventional block-based coding techniques as well as the existing PBC. The future research, thus, focuses on the following major areas:

To extend the regular-shaped pattern codebook for better shape approximation of the moving region; to improve moving region definition in a quantitative manner for adaptability; to enhance pattern matching criterion to reduce computational complexity and ensure better coding efficiency; and to develop a variable length pattern identification coding scheme to reduce side information overhead.

To develop a real time pattern selection algorithm by intuitively engaging a low-complexity low-accuracy pattern matching criterion to restrict the amount of high-complexity accurate pattern matching per MB within a user-selectable bounded subset of the pattern codebook, and to modify the calculation strategy of the accurate pattern matching criteria to reject patterns at intermediate steps resulting in further computational complexity improvement.

To develop a feasible-sized pattern set selection technique in order to limit pattern identification overhead by pruning the universal set of all possible patterns through some content-based analysis within the regularity constraints for maximising the efficiency of the moving regions representation using the selected set as the pattern codebook.

To extend the concept of PBC to the content-based coding paradigm by developing an efficient heuristic to generate arbitrary-shaped patterns from the video content, and to investigate whether a variable pattern size mode, similar to the VBS mode in H.264, can be introduced with PBC to address its scalability issue.

Pattern Codebook

In this approach, a number of regular/irregular shaped n-pixel patterns are used. Patterns are used as an intermediate processing tool to get the moving regions from a binary matrix created from the current and reference frames based on their relative pixel intensity changes. Each pattern is defined as a 16×16 block where the white region represents '1' (i.e., motion) and the black region represents '0' (i.e., background). These patterns are selected intuitively based on the following two features: i)

as a moving region covers part of an object, the region must start from the edge of the boundary, and ii) the moving region must be a convex polygon so that it is simple and regular.

Using a small number of patterns cannot approximate the shape of the MR in MB for all kinds of moving objects, resulting in many active-region MBs (RMBs) potentially being neglected, as moving regions vary widely between objects. If the codebook size is extended, however, the number of RMBs will increase and the image quality will improve as the residual error is reduced, although, there will be a corresponding increase in the number of pattern identification bits for each RMB. Any improvement in managing the pattern identification bits will accommodate more patterns in code book. So far 8 to 32 patterns are used in pattern-based video coding. To extend the PC size certain features were assumed for each n-pixel patterns. Each would be *regular* (bounded by straight lines), *clustered* (the pixels would be connected), and *boundary-adjoined*. Since the MR of an MB is normally a part of a rigid object, assuming clustered and boundary-adjoined features for a pattern is quite justifiable. The regularity feature is added to limit the pattern codebook size.

When applied to 16×16 pixels MBs and n-pixel patterns, an astronomically high number of $^{256}C_n$ possible patterns can result. However, it is possible to select a feasible size of codebook from the universal set in the following extremes. At one extreme, arbitrary-shaped patterns can be generated through video content analysis. At the other extreme, the universal set can be pruned to obtain a set of regular-shaped patterns of a feasible size. A two-stage pruning mechanism where the universal set is first reduced to a size, say α, by using regularity constraints on the pattern shape, and then the set is further reduced using an iterative greedy approach to attain a subset of the $\lambda\,(<\alpha)$ best-matched pattern set based on the video content. A *content-based pattern generation* algorithm may be developed which does not assume any specific feature among the generated patterns. Obviously, such generated patterns would not only exhibit close conformation to the moving-region-defining *clustered* and *boundary-adjoined* features but would also approximate the shape of the region more closely. This would then lead to improved rate-distortion performance of *pattern-based video coding*. This approach also allows for the introduction of a *variable pattern size* (VPZ) mode similar to the *variable block size* (VBS) mode of H.264. This is because the additional rate-distortion improvement resulting from arbitrary-shaped pattern generation can outweigh the coding overhead required to accommodate the pattern size identifiers.

Pattern identification code (PIC) is a vital issue especially when the PC size is large, as mentioned in the earlier section. Fixed length 3-bit PICs to distinguish eight patterns is the obvious choice. Using an efficient variable length coding scheme, for example, the Huffman and arithmetic coding schemes, can reduce the effective number of bits used per PIC. VLC for all the patterns are calculated using the Huffman coding from the average RMB frequency captured by each pattern over a large number of standard and nonstandard video sequences. In this way 04.62 bits are required instead of five bits for 32 patterns. Using the co-occurrence matrix of patterns can reduce PIC up to 0.85 bits per patterns. Further research is necessary to reduce PIC bits.

MB Classification

The MB classification is also a crucial to find the MBs which would be presented by pattern templates. In implementing the RMB category, an MB is considered a *candidate* RMB (CRMB) if at least one of the four 8×8 quadrants does not contain moving pixels. This classification may, in certain instances, reduce the number of RMBs by misclassifying a possible CRMB as an active MB (AMB), where only a few moving pixels exist in another quadrant. Conversely, it may also increase computational complexity by misclassifying an AMB as a CRMB where all but one quadrant has

many moving pixels. Ultimately, a CRMB is classified as an RMB depending on a *similarity measure* based on the patterns in the codebook.

A new and more efficient parametric ($64 < \delta < 256$) MB classification may be used 0, where δ is the maximum total number of moving pixels in a MB to be a RMB, without regard to any 8×8 quadrant. The justification of the lower and upper limit is that the pattern size is 64 and total maximum moving pixels are 256. The experimental results show that the actual value of δ is within ($64 < \delta < T_S + 64$)under a similarity threshold. If δ is greater than $T_S + 64$, then no CRMBs will be classified as RMBs; on the other hand, if δ is less than 64, then some CRMBs will not be classified as RMBs although they are good candidates. This definition considers the number of '1's in an MB irrespective of their position in any specific quadrant. Moreover, this definition introduces a parameter, δ, which controls the number of RMBs. The corollary is that parameter δ directly contributes to both overall quality and compression.

Similarity Measure

Empirical results confirmed that between 6% and 29% of the total MBs are classified as RMBs in smooth motion video sequences for any PBC. The similarity metric, however, is applied much more often as the number of CRMBs will always be higher than the RMBs. Motion estimation, irrespective of a scene's complexity, typically comprises more than 60% of the processing overhead required to encode a predicted-frame with a software codec using the DCT, when a full search is used. Similarity metric calculation is also an expensive part of ME in any PBC algorithm. The corollary of this is that the computational efficiency of a similarity metric for a CRMB is critical to the overall complexity, since, for example, for a 32 PC size, the metric represents about 55% of the ME time of a RMB. Hence, any strategy that improves the computational efficiency of the metric concomitantly reduces the overall encoding complexity.

A similarity measure can be defined in two ways. Pattern-included approach considers both the mismatch areas between a pattern template and moving region. Pattern-excluded approach 0 considers only the mismatched area of moving regions. In both approaches a pattern is selected as the best-matched pattern for a given moving region if this measure is minimum. The advantage of the later approach is that it has better control in rate-distortion curves using the similarity threshold. Moreover, it reduces the computational time because it only requires calculating the mismatched area of moving regions instead of both. Obviously a large similarity threshold will select more numbers of RMBs and as a result reduce the bit rate with decreasing the image quality.

Relevant Measure

Measuring the similarity between a CRMB and all the patterns in the codebook on a piecewise-pixel basis can be very computationally expensive, especially when the PC size is large, which is always desirable for better coding efficiency. However, it can be easily observed that not all patterns are *relevant* for consideration when using the similarity measure. A gravitational centre proximity-based *pattern relevance* measure is proposed in 0 to dynamically create a smaller-sized *customised PC* (CPC) for each CRMB, by eliminating irrelevant patterns from the original codebook. This algorithm selects the best pattern for a CRMB from the CPC, using a piecewise-pixel similarity measure. The rationale in using both relevance and similarity metrics to select the best pattern for a CRMB is that it provides a facility to trade off between computational complexity and picture quality. In selecting the best pattern, the relevance metric uses only one point, say, *gravitational centre* (GC), to represent all moving pixels in a CRMB, whereas the similarity metric uses all pixels; so there will be an error between the two metrics. However, the relevance metric requires 18 times less add-equivalent operations compared with the similarity metric.

The algorithm uses a novel mechanism to control the size of the CPC within predefined bounds to adapt the computational complexity of the pattern selection process, ensuring real time operation without compromising image quality. Furthermore, the computational overhead of the similarity metric is reduced significantly by performing the processing on a quadrant-by-quadrant basis with the option to terminate whenever the measure exceeds a predefined threshold value.

This arrangement ensures the algorithm always uses the complete codebook at some stage of the pattern selection process and still manages to keep the computational complexity within real-time constraints. This principal can be easily extended to arbitrarily sized pattern codebooks. The computational efficiency of the similarity measure is significantly improved by using a predefined threshold and computing the metric on a quadrant-by-quadrant basis.

Embedding Issues with Existing H.264

To analysis the performance of pattern-based video coding, we cab easily observe that the moving region covered by the best-matched pattern template provides relatively less bits with better image quality; on the contrary, an uncovered moving region provides poor image quality. At a very low bit rate, a large scale distortion occurs, thus image distortion due to the uncovered moving region is negligible compared to the high distortion in overall image. As a result, pattern-based video coding algorithm outperforms the H.264 standard for very low bit rate range. When the target bit rate is high, the distortion in an uncovered moving region is relatively high compared to overall image distortion. As a result the rate-distortion performance of pattern-based coding diminishes with bit rates compared to the H.264.

To address this problem Paul et al. 0 proposed two ways. It considers pattern-based coding as a mode, that is, selected MB will be processed using pattern and other variable block size modes, then it will pick

Figure 1. Rate-distortion performance using H.264 standard and after embedding PVC as an extra mode in H.264 for three standard video sequences

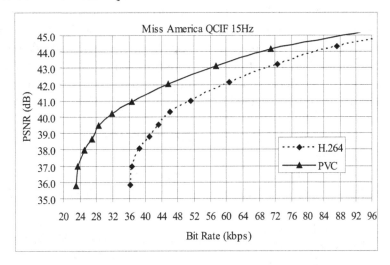

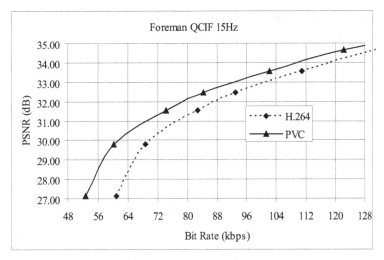

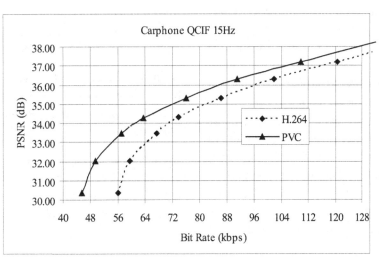

that mode which provides the best rate-distortion performance. The reason behind this approach is that when a pattern can not provide the best rate-distortion performance, the encoder automatically selects the best mode among the variable blocks so that it ensures the performance better or at least the same as the H.264 does. It considers two large pattern sets with larger variable block size modes and one small size pattern set with small modes to ensure the approximation of the variable size moving regions more accurately.

The experimental results (see Figure 1) confirmed that this new scheme improves as high as 1.5dB image quality compared to the H.264 standard at the same bit rates. There is still a scope to generate a best pattern set which can further improve the rate-distortion performance. Since pattern-based video coder as an extra mode has improved image quality significantly, less effort will be needed to include this in the existing framework of H.264; we are hopeful about the inclusion of patter-based video coder in future H.264 video coder versions.

CONCLUSION

Pattern-based video coding with efficient MB classification, optimal pattern codebook, novel similarity and relevant measurement, and successful inclusion in H.264 as a mode, has outperformed the existing H.264 video coding standard by 0.5dB to 2dB in low to mid range bit rates. Moreover, it also outperformed the H.264 in terms of computational complexity. Still it has some scopes to improve further. There is no optimal pattern set for all kind of video sequences. Arbitrary shape pattern templates may be a solution but it can not work in true real time. Further research is needed to make an arbitrary shaped pattern-based video coding in real time application. Pattern identification code is another interesting area. The bits for pattern identification code will help to retrieve the exact pattern in decoder but increase the bit rates. If we can retrieve the exact pattern in decoder from the

side information without those bits, eventually this reduction of bits will improve the rate-distortion performance. Applications of pattern-based video coding in distributed video coding concepts and application of distributed video coding concepts in pattern-based video coding approaches may be two other potential areas for future research.

REFERENCES

Ahmed, N., Nararajan, T., & Rao, K. R. (1974). Discrete cosine transform. *IEEE Transaction on Computer,* 90-93.

Ardre, T., Antonini, M., & Barlaud, M. (2005). *Puzzle temporal lifting for wavelet-based video coding.* Paper presented at the IEEE International Conference on Image Processing (Vol. 3, pp. 213-216).

Aron, A., & Girod, B. (2003). Towards practical wyner ziv coding of video. In *Proceedings of the IEEE International Conference on Image Processing.*

Asif, A., & Kouras, M. (2006). Scalable video codec by noncausal prediction, cascaded vector quantization, and conditional replenishment. *IEEE Transaction on Multimedia, 8*(1), 19-31.

Balter, R., Gioia, P., Morin, L., & Galpin, F. (2004). *Scalable and efficient coding of 3D model extracted from a video.* Paper presented at the International Symposium on 3D Data Processing, Visualization and Transmission (pp. 836-843).

Bashshur, R., & Lovett, J. (1977). Assessment of telemedicine: Results of the initial experience. *Aviation Space and Environmental Medicine, 48*(1), 65-70.

Bjontegaard, G., & Lillevoid, K. (2002). *Context-adaptive VLC coding of coefficients.* Paper presented at the 3rd Meeting of the JVT document JVT-028, JVT of ISO MPEG & ITU VCEG, Rairfax, VA.

Docef, A., Kossentini, F., Nguuyen-Phi, K., & Ismail, I. R. (2002). The quantized DCT and its application to DCT-based video coding. *IEEE Transaction on Image Processing, 11*(3), 177-187.

Fukuhara, T., Asai, K., & Murakami, T. (1997). Very low bit-rate video coding with block partitioning and adaptive selection of two time-differential frame memories. *IEEE Transaction on Circuits and Systems for Video Technology, 7*, 212-220.

Golomb, S. W. (1966). Run-length encoding. *IEEE Transactions on Information Theory, 12*, 399-401.

Grossman, A., & Morlet, J. (1984). Decompositions of hard functions into square integrable wavelets of constant shape. *SIAM J. Math. Anal, 15*(4), 723-736.

Halsall, F. (2001). *Multimedia communications: Applications, networks, protocols and standards.* Addison-Wesley.

Hu, M., Worrall, S., Sadka, A. H., & Kondoz, A. M. (2002). Model design for scalable two-dimensional model-based video coding. *Electronics Letter, 38*(24), 1513-1515.

Isechi, A., Oda, C., Shinkura, R., Akiba, S., Fujikawa, H., & Yamazaki, K. (2004). *Experiment of Internet-based tele-medicine in Amami Rural Islands.* Paper presented at the IEEE International Symposium on Applications and the Internet Workshops.

ISO/IEC 14496. MPEG-4. (1998). *Information technology-coding of audio-visual objects.*

ITU-T Rec. H.264/ISO/IEC 14496-10 AVC. Joint Video Team (JVT) of ISO MPEG and ITU-T VCEG, JVT-G050 (2003).

ITU-T Recommendation H.261. (1993). *Video CO-DEC for audiovisual services at p× 64kbits/s.*

ITU-T Recommendation H.263. (2000). *Video coding for low bit-rate communication* (version 3).

Jun, S., & Yu, S. (2001). Efficient method for early detection of all-zero DCT coefficients. *Electronics Letters, 37*(3), 160-161.

Karayiannis, N. B., & Li, Y. (2001). A replenishment technique for low bit-rate video compression based on wavelets and vector quantization. *IEEE Transaction on Circuits and Systems for Video Technology, 11*(5), 658-663.

Liu, B. (2005). Detection of region of interest in neurosurgical video used for telemedicine. In *Proceedings of IEEE International Conference of Information Acquisition.*

Lin, C-H., & Wu, J.-L. (1997). Content-based rate control scheme for very low bit-rate video coding. *IEEE Transaction on Consumer Electronics, 43*(2), 123-133.

Man, H., Queiroz, R. L., & Smith, M. J. T. (2002). Three-dimensional sub-band coding techniques for wireless video communications. *IEEE Transaction on Circuits and Systems for Video Technology, 12*(6), 386-397.

Marpe, D., Schwarz, H., & Weigand, T. (2003). Context-based adaptive binary arithmetic coding in the H.264/AVC video compression standard. *IEEE Transaction on Circuits and Systems for Video Technology, 13*(7), 620-636.

Pan, J. S., Lu, Z. M., & Sun, S. H. (2003). An efficient encoding algorithm for vector quantization based sub-vector technique. *IEEE Transaction on Image Processing, 12*(3), 265-270.

Paul, M., Frater, M., & Arnold, J. (2006). *Efficient mode selection algorithm using image distortion for H.264 video encoder.* Paper presented at the IEEE International Conference on Signal Processing (Vol. 2, pp. 16-20).

Paul, M., & Murshed, M. (2005a). Advanced very low bit rate video coding using preferential pattern selection algorithms. *Journal of Research and Practice in Information Technology, 37*(2), 89-99.

Paul, M., & Murshed, M. (2005b). An efficient similarity metric for pattern-based very low bit-rate video coding. *Journal of Internet Technology,* 6(3), 337-344.

Paul, M., & Murshed, M. (2007). *Efficient H.264/ AVC video encoder where pattern is used as extra mode for wide range of video coding.* Paper presented at the International Multimedia Modeling Conference, Lecture Notes in Computer Science, Springer-Verlag, Heidelberg (Vol. 4352, pp. 353-362).

Paul, M., Murshed, M., & Dooley, L. (2002). *Impact of macroblock classification on low bit rate video coding focusing on moving region.* Paper presented at the International Conference on Computer and Information Technology (pp. 465-470).

Paul, M., Murshed, M., & Dooley, L. (2005). A real-time pattern selection algorithm for very low bit-rate video coding using relevance and similarity metrics. *IEEE Transaction on Circuits and Systems for Video Technology,* 15(6), 753-761.

Puri, R., & Ramchandran, K. (2002). PRISM: A new robust video coding based on distributed compression principles. In *Proc. of the Conf. on Comm., Control, and Computing,* Allenton, IL.

Richardson, I. E. G. (2002). *Video codec design.* John Willey & Sons, Ltd Press.

Richardson, I. E. G. (2003). *H.264 and MPEG-4 video compression.* Wiley Press.

Shen, G., Zeng, B., & Liou, M. L. (2003). Adaptive vector quantization with codebook updating based on locality and history. *IEEE Transaction on Image Processing,* 12(3), 283-293.

Siu, M., Chan, Y. H., & Siu, W. C. (2001). A robust model generation technique for model-based video coding. *IEEE Transaction Circuits Systems for Video Technology,* 11(11), 1188-1192.

Slepian, J. D., & Wolf, J. K. (1973). Noiseless coding of correlated information sources. *IEEE Transaction on Information Theory,* 19, 471-490.

Sorwar, G., Murshed, M., & Dooley, L. (2003). *A fully adaptive performance-scalable distance-dependent thresholding search algorithm for video coding.* Paper presented at the IEEE International Conference on Speech, Acoustics, and Signal Processing (Vol. 3, pp. 649-652).

Sun, M., Lie, Q., Xu, J., Liu, B., Hu, C., Kassam, A., et al. (2004). A multimedia system for remote neurosurgical monitoring. In *Proceedings of International Symposium on Intelligent Signal Processing and Communication System* (pp. 379-383).

Wallis, R. K. Pratt, W. K., & Plotkin, M. (1981). Video conferencing at 9600 bps. In *Proceedings of the Picture Coding Symposium* (pp. 104-105).

Wang, D., Zhang, L., & Vincent, A., (2006). New method for reducing GOP-boundary artifacts in wavelet-based video coding. *IEEE Transaction on Broadcasting,* 52(3), 350-355.

Weigrand, T., Schwarz, H., Joch, A., & Kossentini, F. (2003). Rate-contrained coder control and comparison of video coding standards. *IEEE Transaction on Circuits and Systems for Video Technology,* 13(7), 688-702.

×Wiegand, T., Sullivan, G. J., Bjontegaard, G., & Luthra, A. (2003). Overview of the H.264/AVC video coding standard. *IEEE Trans. Circuits Syst. Video Technol,* 13(7), 560-576.

Wong, K.-W., Lam, K.-M., & Siu, W.-C. (2001). An efficient low bit-rate video-coding algorithm focusing on moving regions. *IEEE Transaction on Circuits and Systems for Video Technology,* 11(10), 1128-1134.

Wyner, D., & Ziv, J. (1976). The rate-distortion functions for source coding with side information at the decoder. *IEEE Transaction on Information Theory,* 22, 1-10.

Xu, J., Sclabassi, R. J., Liu, Q., Hu, C., Chaparro, L. F., & Sun, M. (2005). A region-based video coding method for remote monitoring of neurosurgery. In *Proceedings of the IEEE 31st Annual Northeast Bioengineering Conference* (pp. 89-91).

Xuan, Z., Henghua, Y., & Songyu, Y. (1998). Method for detecting all-zero DCT coefficients ahead of discrete cosine transformation and quantization. *Electronics Letters, 34*(19), 1839-1840.

Yokoyama, Y., Miyamoto, Y., & Ohta, M. (1995). Very low bit-rate video coding using arbitrarily shaped region-based motion compensation. *IEEE Transaction on Circuits and Systems for Video Technology, 5*(6), 500-507.

Zach, S. (1996). *Telemedicine overview and summary*. Paper presented at the 19th Convention of Electrical and Electronics Engineers in Israel (pp. 409-412).

KEY TERMS

Context Adaptive Based Arithmetic Coding (CABAC): This variable length coding technique is used to compress the data using arithmetic variable length coding.

Context-Based Adaptive Variable Length Coding (CAVLC): This variable length coding technique is used to compress the data using relevant context side information.

Discrete Cosine Transformation (DCT): DCT compresses the spatial image data, such that the total energy in the image becomes concentrated into a relatively small number of components, that is, the pixel data are decorrelated so compression can be achieved.

Discrete Wavelet Transformation (DWT): DWT compresses the spatial image data, such that the total energy in the image becomes concentrated into a relatively small number of components, that is, the pixel data are decorrelated so compression can be achieved.

Group of Picture (GOP): A collection of frames which are processed at a time to reduce the temporal redundancy. For more compression and low image quality a relatively large GOP size is used and for low compression and better image quality a relatively small GOP is used in video coding.

Macroblock (MB): Nonoverlapping 16×16 pixels in an image which normally is used as a processing unit in video coding.

Motion Estimation and Motion Compensation (ME and MC): ME involves identifying the translational displacement vectors (popularly called *motion vectors*) of objects based on the changes between two successive frames in a video sequence. MC involves calculating the differential signal (residual error) between the intensity value of the pixels in the moving areas and their counterparts in the reference frame, translated by the estimated motion vector.

Variable Length Coding (VLC): A reversible procedure for entropy coding that assigns shorter bit strings to symbols expected to be more frequent and longer bit strings to symbols expected to be less frequent.

Vector Quantisation (VQ): A vector quantisation matrix typically has small values in top-left elements of the matrix and larger values in the bottom-right, retaining low frequency information at the expense of higher frequencies.

Very Low bit Rate Video Coding (VLBR): VLBR broadly encompasses video coding which mandates a temporal frequency of 10 frames per second (fps) or less, and bit rates between 8 and 64 Kilo bit rate per second, facilitating video communications over mobile and fixed telephone channel transmissions as well as the Internet.

Chapter XXVII
Digital Watermarking for Digital Rights Management

Farid Ahmed
The Catholic University of America, USA

Cecilia Gomes
The Catholic University of America, USA

ABSTRACT

With the remarkable growth of Internet and multimedia applications, production and distribution of digital media has become exceedingly easy and affordable. Applications such as distance education, e-commerce, telemedicine, digital library, and live audio/video broadcast activities require distribution and sharing of digital multimedia contents. Consequently, maintaining the quality of service of the applications and the rights of the content owner as well as enforcing a viable business model among the producer, consumer, and distributor of digital contents has become an increasingly challenging task, leading to a contentious area called digital rights management (DRM). This chapter presents how digital watermarking (DWM) technology can addresses part of this DRM problem of secure distribution of digital contents

INTRODUCTION

The spectacular development in communication and network infrastructures coupled with exponential growth on digital contents and applications have placed enormous challenges on the storage, distribution, and use of these contents. The dissemination and sharing of information in this digital age consequently gives rise to a number of legal, ethical, and economic questions that need to be appropriately addressed by policy makers, consumers, developers, and technologists. We particularly address the technological aspect of the rights management of this digital distribution scenario in this chapter.

An analysis of the threat model, risks, and vulnerabilities associated with the storage and distribution of digital multimedia is first provided. Then we identify the requirements of enforcing the digital rights of different players, like the owner, distributor, and users involved in the transaction management of the digital contents. This leads to the design issues of different digital rights management (DRM) applications. Next, we specifically present a paradigm of technological solutions using the digital watermarking (DWM) technology. A fairly moderate technical know-how of the digital watermarking technology will be presented to show how it can address the DRM problems in terms of copyright protection, copy protection, owner identification, content authentication, and transaction tracking. The effectiveness of the technology will be analyzed by defining a set of metrics derived from the requirements of multimedia distribution. Finally the limitations of DWM and interoperability with other technological solutions will be presented.

THE PROBLEM: THREATS AND VULNERABILITIES OF DIGITAL MULTIMEDIA DISTRIBUTION

Digital multimedia data are easy to share and copy. Most importantly the sharing and copying can be done without any distortion done to the contents. If some distortions occur, data can be reconstructed by various algorithms well-studied in the areas of digital communications and signal processing. Interestingly, this property of digital data that facilitates the easy distribution is also responsible for its misuse.

Digital representation of text, audio, speech, image, video, graphics, and animation fall in the general umbrella of digital multimedia. The continuation of the chapter will primarily focus on the rights management of digital images. Figure

1 shows the typical distribution of digital images. Data acquisition is performed using imaging sensors such as camera, radiography, ultrasonogram, electron microscope, and so forth.

Depending upon the use of the image, it can be processed thereafter for enhancement or filtering out sensor noises. It may then be consumed for its intended use, or it may leave the digital world to enter into the analog/print world. The image may go through some wear and tear processes in the print media, and after that it may be scanned back to digital form and eventually reconstructed back to its original quality. While in the digital form the images may be copied, shared, or distributed through digital media, networks, or Internet. In this life-cycle of a digital image, different players such as the creator, owner, distributor, buyer, seller, consumer, and user have different models of ownership rights. The ease of distribution coupled with different attack models has made the rights enforcement of digital data vulnerable. The vulnerabilities are manifested through copyright thefts, identity thefts, data piracy, unauthorized access, and counterfeiting (Stallings, 2003). In a networked environment, the threats and vulnerabilities to data are even more evident. Essentially, all sorts of digital data are at risk.

The Computer Security Institute (CSI) and the Federal Bureau of Investigation (FBI) have jointly been conducting an annual survey of cyber-crimes for the last couple of years (CSI/FBI, 2007). It is

Figure 1. Life cycle of digital images

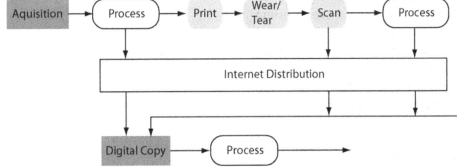

interesting to see that one of the leading financial losses is done by digital proprietary theft. It is to be noted that U.S. Copyright Industry is more than $700 billion, which is more than 5% of US GDP. According to the Federal Trade Commission (FTC) more than an estimated 10 million Americans are victims of identity theft each year. Many leading companies, such as Citigroup, ChoicePoint, Bank of America, and Lexis Nexis have experienced different forms of data/identity theft over last couple of years (http://www.consumer.gov/idtheft/). Recording Industry Association of America (RIAA) reports Piracy problems in more than 60 countries (http://www.riaa.com/default.asp). Motion Picture Association of America (MPAA) estimates that the U.S. motion picture industry loses more than $3 billion annually in potential worldwide revenue due to piracy; for example, copies of prerelease versions of *The Last Samurai* were illegally distributed. Hollywood traced the pirated version and the distribution chain back to one of the screeners (http://msnbc.msn.com/id/4037016/).

THE SOLUTION: DIGITAL RIGHTS MANAGEMENT (DRM)

Requirement Analysis of DRM

Simply said, DRM is about "digital" information, it is about "rights," and finally it is about "management." Digital asset management is sometimes used interchangeably with digital rights management. So, what is digital asset? There are some *born* digital and most of the others are *converted* digital. Born digitals are produced in a digital incubator using digital hatching. We see examples of converted digitals when large archives of analog or print media are transferred to their digital counterparts. Another form of digital data is called *induced* digital. The recent research and deployment of *sensor networks* effectively result in huge *induced* digital data. Question is: Do these different types of digital data need to be treated differently? Do they imply

different sorts of associated "rights"? Or do they require different types of "management"?

While some rights are intrinsic (governed by law of physics) most other rights are governed by laws and policies adopted by policymakers. Can policy law dictate the law of physics of bits? This has long been a debate in the digital world. The question, "Who owns the right?" is also very confusing because of the fuzzy nature of ownership. "*Born*," "*converted*," and "*induced*" entities may have different catalysts resulting in different sorts of ownership models.

The third word "management" is even more subtle. The term "management" in this context has mostly been used in a regulatory sense to imply limiting or controlling rights. But recent use of digital assets has pointed to many other implications of "management," like "facilitation of use," "enhancement of rights," and "classification of use."

Example Requirements of Content Owner/Provider

- Protection of intellectual property. The content owner has the right to exchange/disavow the ownership within the framework of an adopted business model. Technological solutions should be able to enforce this.
- Integrity and authenticity of dissemination of digital contents.
  - Is the multimedia authentic or has it been tampered with?
  - Can tampering be prevented?
  - Can the tampering be detected/localized?
  - Can the tampered part be recovered?
  - How well the traitor tracing can be done?
- Access control of digital contents: Only duly registered clients can access the data.

Example Requirements of End-User/Consumer

- Anonymity/privacy of communication
- Nonrepudiation in information exchange: The sender may not repudiate the sending, or the receiver may not deny the reception of the information.
- Access control: The buyer/consumer should have due access to the contents.

DRM TECHNOLOGIES

The primary technologies used for digital rights management are the following:

- Cryptography: Cryptographic techniques and protocols are by far the most widely used mechanisms to implement DRM systems. Both the network level and the data level solutions are provided by a host of protocols based on the public-key cryptography and the symmetric key cryptography. Pretty good privacy (PGP), secure socket layer (SSL)/TLS, IPsec, and Kerberos are just a few of the example protocols.
- Digital watermarking/steganographic solutions. The next details this technology.
- Hybrid solutions employing cryptography, watermark, and biometric technology.

DIGITAL WATERMARKING

Digital watermarking is the process of embedding a digital code (watermark) into a digital content such as image, audio, or video (Cox et al., 2001). The embedded information, sometimes called *watermark*, is dependent on the DRM requirements mentioned above. For example, if it is a copyright application, the embedded information could be the copyright notice. Figure 2 shows a block diagram of such a digital watermarking process.

To embed a message m in an image I_o (referred to as original image), the message is first encoded using source coding and optionally with the help of error correction and detection coding, represented in the figure as $e(m)$, where $W_m = e(m)$.

The encoded message W_m is then combined with the key-based reference pattern W_k, in addition to the scaling factor α, to result in W_a, which is the signal that is actually added to the original image.

$$W_a = \alpha \left(I_o \right)\left[W_M \otimes W_K \right] \qquad (1)$$

$$I_w = I_o + W_a \qquad (2)$$

The result of this process is the watermarked image I_w. When the scaling factor is dependent on the original image, informed embedding is possible which may result in more perceptually adaptive watermarking (Cox et al., 2001).

Figure 3 shows the original image, watermarked image, and the difference image using a correlation-based watermarking algorithm (Ahmed & Moskowitz, 2004). As evident from Figure 3(b), the hidden message is imperceptible as well as the change in the original image. This is one of the primary criteria of digital watermarking.

In addition to imperceptibility, DWM must make a trade off among a number of different criteria. It can thus be considered as a multidimensional problem optimizing among the criteria of imperceptibility, unobtrusiveness, capacity, robustness, security, and detectability. The message being hidden should be imperceptible as well as the changes made in the original image. This also implies that the inserted watermark should not be obtrusive to the intended use of the original image. For example, while watermarking a medical image for patient privacy or security, it should not degrade the diagnostic quality of the image. Since the watermarking process does not increase the size of the original image, it may be desirable to add as much information as possible. Generally the increase in information will severely impact on the perceptual quality of the image. From the detection point of view, a watermark should be

Figure 2. A simple watermarking process

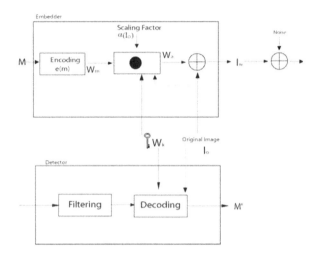

robust enough to tolerate a range of image postprocessing and degradation. In addition, the embedded watermark must be secure to prevent its removal. Finally, delectability of the embedded watermark is an important criterion that places some constraints on the embedding algorithm.

DWM FOR DRM: FINDING THE NATURAL MATCH

With this brief introduction to watermarking technology, let us turn our attention to its applicability towards DRM. In this regard, following is a list of DRM applications that the watermarking technology can help in managing (Hartun, 2000; Wu, 2002).

A. Security Enhancement
    a. Copyright Protection
    b. Copy Control
    c. Access Control
B. Enabling Technologies
    a. Bridging the Print and Digital World
    b. Device Control
    c. Intelligent Multimedia

Figure 3. (a) Original image I_0, (b) watermarked image I_w, and (c) the difference image, W_a (enhanced for visual discernment)

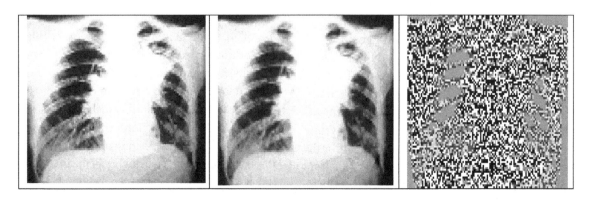

C.   Identification
  a.   Annotation
  b.   Data Mining
  c.   Digital Preservation
D.   Forensic Analysis
  a.   Transaction Tracking/Fingerprinting
  b.   Tamper Detection

Digital watermarking has demonstrated significant potential in implementing copyright protection and access control (Arnold, 2003). Copy control technology allows the media owner to monitor and control copies made, that is, DVD "copy once," "copy twice," and "no copy" mechanism. Digital watermarking can enforce this dynamic control of digital media usage.

The second category of techniques pertains to enabling digital medium. Digital libraries and archives are increasingly being populated by "*converted*" digital from their analog counterpart. One of the amazing features of digital watermarking is authentication or integrity verification across this boundary of print and digital medium. Digimarc Corporation (Digimarc Corp.) has deployed a product called MediaBridge, which effectively bridges the print and digital world. A similar application, intelligent multimedia, embeds "intelligence" information into a digital multimedia content, which can then be used for many device control applications. A third category is identification, which is becoming increasingly challenging due to the exponential growth of digital data on networks and Internet. Identification and recognition of patterns are key operations required in data mining applications in digital archives and libraries. Digital watermarking technology can hide imperceptible digital identification inside a digital content that can be used for searching through a database and data mining applications (Wu, 2002). This identification tag may be generated from the features or signatures of the media concerned. This can facilitate indexing in the digital preservation application. A variant of this application, named Marc Spider from Digimarc Corporation, searches like a Web crawler to find

registered copies of digital media content.

The fourth category relates to digital forensic analysis (Naumovich, 2003; Chai, 2001). In the continuous (re)distribution of digital content through the Internet and other digital media (e.g., CD, camera, etc.), it is important to track the distribution points to detect possible illegal distribution of contents. Tracking the usage of digital media is important to implement any legal and economic model of digital rights management as well as to track down forged and unlawful usage of digital data. A related application is tamper detection or integrity verification. This is particularly relevant in digital archival applications where data will sometimes need to be transferred from one storage medium to another and replicated in a number of places. Integrity of the digital content and authentication of the source and destination of the distribution chain is therefore of utmost importance. Tamper detection applications embed some hash of the original content into the digital media using watermarking technology. The detector then extracts this embedded hash and compares with the computed hash. If there is a discrepancy then, it is said to have been tampered with.

DWM FOR DRM: DESIGN AND IMPLEMENTATION ISSUES

While different DRM problems can be addressed by using different classes of watermarking technique, the primary design issue revolves around making an optimization in each case of the perceptuality, capacity, detectability, robustness, and security of the systems. Some of the key design questions then are:

a.   What type of DWM is used for a specific DRM problem?
b.   Which specific DRM requirements are met by a class of DWM?
c.   What type of error does the watermarking process introduce in embedding the informa-

tion? What is the impact on the quality of the media due to the embedding error? How to enhance quality by minimizing the embedding error?

d. How to increase robustness of the system, which is useful for applications like copyright protection?

e. How much information can be embedded in a digital media? How to increase the embedding capacity?

f. How to increase detectability?

g. Is there a way to prevent and/or identify any sort of tampering done to the digital multimedia?

Based on these questions, we hereby elaborate on the following four DWM-based DRM design issues:

• Determination of a specific watermarking technique
• Minimization of embedding error for better perceptual quality
• Robustness, capacity, and detectability tradeoffs
• Authentication/tamper detection issues
• Integration with encryption and compression

Determination of Specific Watermarking Technique

In order to fully appreciate the use of watermarking for secure digital rights management, it is instructive to look at different classes of watermark (Cox et al., 2001; Petitcolas, 2000; Hartung, 1999), which is (delineated) depicted in Figure 4.

Figure 4 shows watermark classifications based on different criteria. For example, depending on the robustness criteria of watermarking, they can be classified into three categories: robust, fragile, and semifragile. While the robustness of a watermark is important, it is not always equally desirable in all applications. Let us take the authentication as an

example. If an owner of a digital content embeds some authentication information into the content using watermarking. The owner might want to see the authentication fail, if the image is stolen. This a type of nonrobust watermark where the fragility of the embedded watermark is required to detect any forging done on the original digital content.

The cover document is the unwatermarked digital media in which it embeds or hides the watermark; for example, of such digital media are hardware/software, video, image, text, and audio. Based on the use of key in detection, watermarking can be public or private. In public watermarking applications, the watermark can be detected by everyone and they would not have access to the original work. In private applications, the watermark can be detected only by a selected group of people who have access to the original unwatermarked work. If the fact that "some information is hidden" in a media is kept secret, the application is steganographic, otherwise it is nonsteganographic.

The watermark detector might either have access to the original media or not have it. In the blind detector, the original media is not needed for the extraction or detection of the watermark. For the nonblind detector, the original content is needed for extraction, also called informed detector.

Invertible or reversible watermark is a distortion free data embedding scheme, used for applications which cannot tolerate the slightest amount of degradation done to the host images. For example, medical images require invertible or semiinvertible watermark. In the noninvertible case, the watermark cannot be extracted without possible alteration of the original.

The actual signal which is embedded during watermarking could be another image like a logo, or it could be a spread spectrum noise signal of a bit sequence.

A watermark signal can be embedded either directly in the spatial domain or in the transform domain. Spatial domain is useful for embedding a fragile watermark where the selected pixel values are modified by the watermark bits thereby *chang-*

Figure 4. Watermark classifications

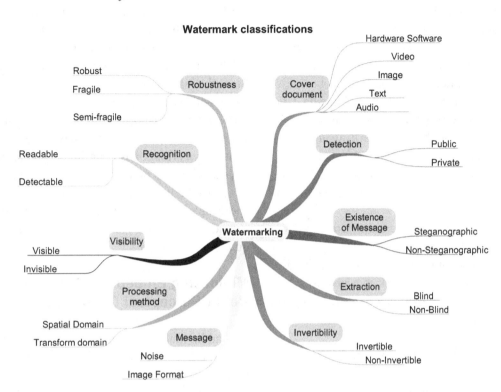

ing some of the color information of the original image. Although the embedding method is relatively easy, there is trade off in the way the embedding locations are selected. If a less significant location is selected, the watermark would be invisible but not robust because they are removed by compression. To make it robust it has to embed in the more significant locations, but that would degrade the visible quality of the image.

Transform domain, a frequency domain watermarking method, is usually more robust to attacks and compression. Discrete cosine transform (DCT), discrete fourier transform (DFT), and wavelet domain transform (DWT) are some of the domains.

The types of watermarking we are interested in are invisible watermarking, since they are imperceptible and are not intrusive to the host image. However, visible watermark that can be seen with bare eyes may also be used, which is outside the scope of this chapter.

Finally, based on the recognition of a watermark signal, in some applications such as copyright, the embedded information needs to be readable. However in an authentication application, it may only suffice to know whether some information is hidden or not.

With this understanding, as an example, let us look at a rapidly emerging application, which is the digital rights management of wireless multimedia networking (Hartung, 2000). This typically includes video streaming, teleconferencing, voice over IP, and so forth. The following considerations should be made for watermarking digital contents for these applications.

- A progressive watermark is required so that receiver can make a progressive decision about the authenticity of a received streaming multimedia, just from a handful of packets, instead of waiting for the whole stream of packets. This requires a watermark whose energy is distributed throughout the content and across the entire spectrum.

- A transform domain watermark, like a DWT domain watermark (Meerwald, 2001) may be better suited due to its better robustness against compression, which multimedia data inevitably go through while in transmission.
- Robustness of the watermark against random packet loss is desirable. Alternatively, a forward error correction mechanism may be necessary to reconstruct the watermark from packet loss.
- A fast watermarking algorithm is required for real-time communication.
- For authentication application, a semifragile or semirobust watermark is a necessity, so that its authentication decision can be made on degradation levels.

As for a second example, we turn to the electronic health record (EHR) to be used in telemedicine applications. Figure 5 shows how a specific patient clinical image, like the X-ray, can be accessed by different players with different access privileges.

This also shows that multiple different watermarks are required to enforce all the rights management of all the players, as shown in Figure 6. For example, the patient ID or demographic information can be embedded for the purpose of identification. Since the information is always attached to the image, it will result in less error in processing the data. To find out whether there has been any tampering done on a medical image, we may use an authentication watermark based on image signatures. A physician's notes on a specific image, which may be revisited later, can be embedded. Generally speaking any form of watermark used in this case should be invertible, not to degrade the diagnostic quality of the image.

Minimizing Embedding Error for Better Perceptual Quality

The additional information that a watermarking system embeds in a host image essentially leads to a distortion of the host image, as evident from Equation (2). At the same time, because of the finite depth of image pixel values there may be rounding error, clamping error, and clipping error (Cox et al.,

Figure 5. User community accessing patient data

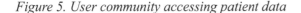
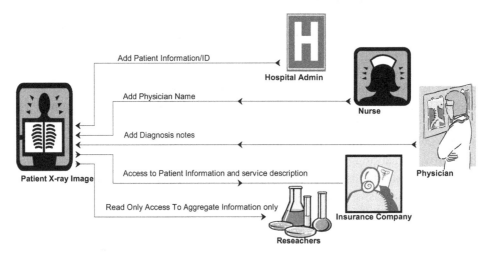

User Community Accessing Patient Data

2001). Rounding error occurs because the pixel values are represented by 8-bit integer numbers, while the watermarked signal I_w could be real-valued. Any value of I_w greater than 255, is truncated to 255, resulting in a clamping error, while any value of I_w smaller than 0, is truncated to 0, resulting in clipping error. As a result of these three types of errors, the embedding efficiency may not be completely accurate and consequently the embedded signal, W_a, may not be reconstructed perfectly by the detector. Therefore one of the design aspects of the watermarking is to reduce this error. A number of ways to achieve this are as follows:

a. Reversible watermarking (Fridrich, 2002) to ensure that the distortions done during embedding can be retrieved
b. Avoiding clipping and clamping error by selective embedding
c. Encrypting the embedded signal

The following example depicts an authentication watermark for the analysis of embedding error and ways to mitigate this.

Figure 7 shows the use of a watermark for image authentication, which has some similarities with the cryptographic authentication using digital signature (Stallings, 2003). Unlike cryptography though, watermarking gives both in-storage and in-transit authentication. Watermarking is also faster compared to encryption, which is very important in Internet-based image distribution. By comparing a watermark against a known reference, it might be possible to infer not just that an alteration occurred, but what, when, and where changes happened. As shown in Figure 7, first some features are identified from the digital content, next the digital signature is computed, which is then embedded into the content. The detector takes a test data, computes the signature and extracts the embedded signature, and then compares the two. If they match, the image is authenticated. If they do not then the image may have gone through some forging/tampering effects and the algorithm may optionally detect the tamper area as well.

As an example of an authentication watermark, let us look at the Fourier transform-based method reported in (Ahmed & Moskowitz, 2004). The original image is transformed from the spatial domain to the frequency domain via the DFT. Consider an MxN host image $h(m,n)$, where (m,n) are the spatial indices (pixel locations). The DFT of $h(m,n)$ is written as $H(u,v)$ where (u,v) represent the frequency coordinates.

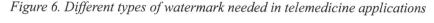

Figure 6. Different types of watermark needed in telemedicine applications

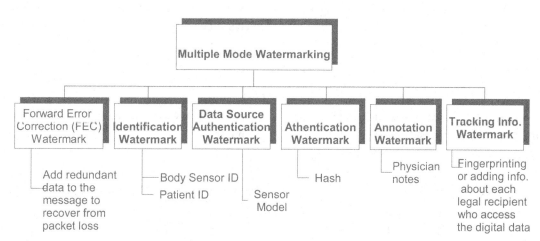

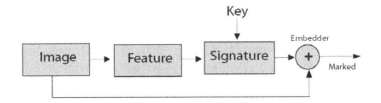

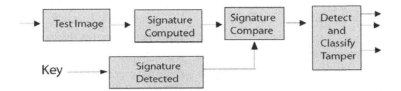

$$H(u,v) = \sum_{n=0}^{N-1}\sum_{m=0}^{M-1} h(m,n)\exp(-j2\pi(\frac{um}{M}+\frac{vn}{N}))$$

(3)

Switching to polar coordinates, the Fourier transform of the image can equivalently be expressed as:

$$H(u,v) = X(u,v)\exp(j\phi(u,v))$$

(4)

where, $X(u,v)$ is the *magnitude* $|H(u,v)|$ of the frequency component, and $\varphi(u,v)$ is the *phase* part of the (u,v) frequency given by:

$$\phi(u,v) = \arg(\frac{\text{Re}(H(u,v))}{\text{Im}(H(u,v))})$$

(5)

We then compute a signature, which is (nothing but) simply the binary phase-only filter of the image and given by:

$$S(u,v) = +1, \text{if } \cos(\phi(u,v)) \geq 0$$
$$= 0, \text{ otherwise}$$

(6)

In the embedding process, the phase is kept unchanged and the magnitude $X(u,v)$ is modulated. The real-valued $X(u,v)$ is first transformed to integer-valued as follows.

$$R(u,v) = round[X(u,v)]$$

(7)

where the *round*() function rounds the operand to the nearest integer value. That makes it able to be represented by a fixed number of q bit planes. Hence we have $R=R_{q-1},R_{q-2}, ..., R_1,R_0$ where R_i is the *i*-th bit plane of the rounded magnitude.

After the bit-plane embedding, where the *i*-th bit-plane is substituted by the signature, the Fourier spectrum becomes

$$\widetilde{H}(u,v) = \widetilde{R}(u,v)\exp(j\phi(u,v))$$

(8)

To the above we apply the inverse DFT. The watermarked image (in the spatial domain) is then given by:

$$\widetilde{h}(m,n) = \frac{1}{MN}\sum_{u=0}^{M-1}\sum_{v=0}^{N-1}\widetilde{H}(u,v)\exp(j2\pi(\frac{um}{M}+\frac{vn}{N}))$$

(9)

This will result in a real-valued image which is converted to an actual grayscale bitmap in the spatial domain, by the clamping and clipping operator *uint8* (converts to 8-bit unsigned integer to represent 0 to 255).

$$\tilde{h}_w(m,n) = uint8(\tilde{h}(m,n)) \qquad (10)$$

Now let us look at how much error is introduced because of the watermarking process itself. Keep in mind that the values of $\tilde{h}(m,n)$ have not been clipped, clamped, or rounded into integers between 0 and 255.

$$e(m,n) = \tilde{h}(m,n) - h(m,n)$$
$$= \frac{1}{MN}\sum_{u=0}^{M-1}\sum_{v=0}^{N-1}(\tilde{H}(u,v) - H(u,v))\exp(j2\pi(\frac{um}{M}+\frac{vn}{N}))$$
$$= \frac{1}{MN}\sum_{u=0}^{M-1}\sum_{v=0}^{N-1}(\tilde{R}(u,v) - R(u,v))\exp(j\phi(u,v))\exp(j2\pi(\frac{um}{M}+\frac{vn}{N}))$$
$$= \frac{2^{i-1}}{MN}\sum_{u=0}^{M-1}\sum_{v=0}^{N-1}(\tilde{R}_i(u,v) - R_i(u,v))\exp(j\phi(u,v))\exp(j2\pi(\frac{um}{M}+\frac{vn}{N}))$$

$$(11)$$

The total difference between is given by:

$$\sum_{m=0}^{M-1}\sum_{n=0}^{N-1}e(m,n) =$$

$$\frac{2^{i-1}}{MN}\sum_{m=0}^{M-1}\sum_{n=0}^{N-1}\sum_{u=0}^{M-1}\sum_{v=0}^{N-1}(\tilde{R}_i(u,v) - R_i(u,v))\exp(j\phi(u,v))\exp(j2\pi(\frac{um}{M}+\frac{vn}{N}))$$

which is shown [20] to be equal to

$$\sum_{m=0}^{M-1}\sum_{n=0}^{N-1}e(m,n) = 2^{i-1}(\tilde{R}_i(0,0) - R_i(0,0)) \qquad (12)$$

This is a very obvious result. In order to minimize the error, *i* should be small which indicates a low significant bit-plane is needed to be selected in the Fourier magnitude domain. But this error minimization comes at a cost (Farid, 2007), which is shown in Figure 8. In the following chart watermark strength is given by the value of *i*. The detectability decreases with the decrease in the strength of the watermark, but sure quality increases.

For a good trade-off between the detectability and perceptuality in this bit-plane embedding method, redistributing the embedded information in different bit planes is found to improve the quality of the image for a given bit error rate (Ahmed & Moskowitz, 2006).

In the pursuit of further improvement on minimizing the embedding error, one can have a disjoint space for embedding and signature. If the signature space and the embedding space are not disjointed, it has the undesirable effect of changing the signature domain, so that even in absence of any kind of degradation, the computed signature and the extracted signature will not be the same. In Farid (2007) that problem is partly eliminated by using wavelet decomposition for utilizing different subbands for the signature and embedding space.

Increasing the Robustness and Security of Watermarking Algorithm

Robustness is a desirable feature of a watermarking system which describes how well the embedded information can survive different sort of distortions such as compression, signal processing, and so forth. On the other hand, security is a measure of the resilience of a watermarking system against some attacks, such as tampering, forging, and so forth. There are some measures that can be taken to improve both the robustness and security of a system. Of course robustness alone does not mean much unless it is associated with something to describe against what the system has to be robust against. For example, in a video streaming of copyrighted materials the embedded copyright watermark should be robust against compression.

Figure 9 shows the authentication value and the bit error rate as a function of compression of the watermark detector of the authentication system described in the previous section. This shows that with higher strength both the compression tolerance and the authentication value improve.

Each of the different algorithms will have its built-in robustness against a specific processing.

Figure 8. Perceptability/detectability metric with watermark strength

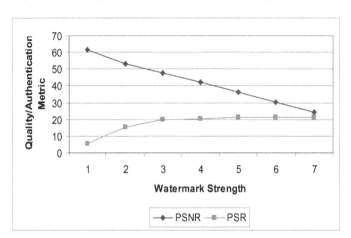

The following are a few general approaches that can be taken to enhance the robustness and security of a system. They include (Cox et al., 2001)

- Redundant embedding
- Spread spectrum coding of messages
- Embedding in a perceptually significant coefficients
- Embedding in coefficients of known robustness
- Inverting distortions in the detector
- Using error correction coding
  ◦ repetition code
  ◦ block code
  ◦ convolution code

Integration with Encryption and Compression

One of the practical concerns in DRM applications is the interoperability of watermarking with already existing protocols of encryption and compression (Merhav, 2006; Lian et al. 2007; Dittman et al., 2001), which are prevalent in multimedia communication. One design issue is the relative order of encryption, watermarking, and compression. There are a number of schemes where watermarking is performed in compressed domain using the

modulation of bits in the JPEG bit streams. The robustness of these algorithms is not very good. On the other hand, if compression is to be done after the image is watermarked, the watermarking algorithm must be robust against compression. Generally, watermarking performed in a frequency domain have better leverage in this regard. Liang, Liu, Ren, and Wang (2007) propose a commutative watermark with encryption where the order of operations can commutate. Watermarking the encrypted information has some advantages and disadvantages. On one hand, it can hide any sort of existence of hidden data; on the other hand, the capacity of the watermark may be limited due to the noisy nature of encrypted image. The success of this of course depends on an emerging area of "signal processing in the encrypted domain." An example of the interoperability of these three technologies is discussed by Mehrav (2006), where the author studies the problem of joint coding for three objectives: information embedding, compression, and encryption.

PERFORMANCE ANALYSIS OF DWM ALGORITHMS

Without a proper validation suite, the performance of the watermark-based DRM systems cannot be

Figure 9. Compression tolerance of the example authentication system

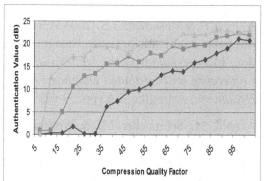

trusted. There are a number of metrics used by researchers to evaluate the perceptual quality, detectability, robustness, and the capacity of a watermarking system. A widely used objective metric to discern the perceptual quality in image processing is the Peak-signal-to-noise-ratio, defined as follows:

$$PSNR = 10\log_{10}\left(\frac{255^2}{\left[\frac{1}{MN}\sum_{m=0}^{M-1}\sum_{n=0}^{N-1}((h(m,n)-\widetilde{h}_w(m,n))^2\right]}\right)$$

(13)

Robustness of the embedded message is often represented by the ratio of the number of bits correctly detected by the total number of bits embedded, which is called *bit error rate* (BER). Most of the watermarking detectors use a correlation-based detection strategy. The performance of correlation is often given by a normalized correlation coefficient.

The performance of a watermarking algorithm against a possible attack is even more important for digital rights management under different types of attacks and vulnerabilities.

Taxonomy of attacks can be summarized as follows:

- Removal Attacks – removes the mark
  - Denoising
  - Quantization/compression attack
  - Remodulation/rewatermarking
  - Collusion attacks
  - Signal processing attack
- Filtering, cropping, print/scan
- Geometric attack- distorts the mark
  - Rotation, scale, translation, shear
- Cryptographic attacks
  - Brute force search for embedded information
  - Oracle attack (possible if detector is available)
- Protocol attacks
  - Invertibility of watermark
  - Copy attack
  - Forgery

Based on these different types of attacks and the different evaluation metrics, a number of evaluation suites have been developed, including the Stirmark, CheckMark, Optimark (Macq et al., 2004; CERTIMARK; StirMark). Finally, in order to facilitate the Web-based evaluation of DRM management capability an open watermarking open source community has also been developed (OpenWatermark).

CONCLUSION

We reported a design and analysis approach of digital watermarking technique for the enforcement of digital rights management. The design issues should always be factored in carefully for a successful DWM-based DRM application. In addition, just like cryptographic measures are subject to different types of attacks and vulnerabilities, digital watermarking is also subject to a number of attacks. In an ill-designed watermark, attackers can tamper with the mark, forge, and even remove the watermark. Cryptographic attacks on key-based watermarking systems are also possible. Another major limitation is that the watermarking process cannot be made sufficiently robust to arbitrary types of different attacks. Some watermarking algorithms are more resistant to these attacks than others. It is possible to make it more robust in the cat-and-mouse game between the attackers and designers of the watermark.

The quality degradation of media after the watermarking may be a reason of concern. With technology one can always make a tradeoff among different parameters like quality, security, and robustness. Another limitation is that the watermarking technology is not yet widely deployed, and nor is the protocol satisfactorily standardized. Therefore, the hybrid combination of cryptography and watermarking is expected to improve the secure distribution of digital content across the unreliable Internet.

REFERENCES

Ahmed, F., & Moskowitz, I. S. (2004). A correlation-based watermarking method for image authentication applications. *Optical Engineering, 43*(8), 1833-1838.

Ahmed, F., & Moskowitz, I .S. (2005, October). Phase-signature based watermarking for multimedia authentication: Analysis and design. In *Proceedings of the SPIE Multimedia Systems and Applications VIII* (Vol. 6015, pp. 97-107).

Ahmed, F., & Moskowitz, I. S. (2006, April). A semi-reversible watermark for medical image authentication. In *Proceedings of the 1st Transdisciplinary Conference on Distributed Diagnosis and Home Healthcare,* Arlington, VA (pp. 59-62).

Arnold, M., Schmucker, M., & Wolthusen, S. D. (2003). *Techniques and applications of digital watermarking and content protection.* Artech House. ISBN 1-58053-111-3.

CERTIMARK. Retrieved April 2, 2008, from http://vision.unige.ch/certimark/ public/CMK_D22.pdf

Chai, W. W. (2001). *On the design of content-based multimedia authentication systems* (IBM Research Report RC 22018 [98875]).

Cox, I., Bloom, J., & Miller, M. (2001). *Digital watermarking: Principles & practice.* Morgan Kauffman Publishers. ISBN 1-55860-714-5.

CSI/FBI computer crime and security survey. Retrieved April 2, 2008, from http://www.gocsi.com/forms/fbi/csi_fbi_survey.jhtml

Digimarc Corporation. Retrieved April 2, 2008, from http://www.digimarc.com/

Dittmann, J., Wohlmacher, P., & Nahrstedt, K. (2001, October). Using cryptographic and watermarking algorithms. *IEEE Multimedia and Security,* 54-65.

Farid, A. (2007, April). A dual Fourier-wavelet domain authentication-identification watermark. *Optics Express, 15*(8), 4804-4813.

Fridrich, J., Goljan, M., & Du, R. (2002, February). Lossless data embedding: New paradigm in digital watermarking. *EURASIP Journal on Applied Signal Processing, 2002*(2), 185-196.

Hartung, F., & Kutter, M. (1999). Multimedia watermarking techniques. *Proceedings of the IEEE, 87*(7), 1079-1107.

Hartung, F., & Ramme, F. (2000). Digital rights management and watermarking of multimedia content for m-commerce applications. *Communications Magazine, IEEE, 38*(11), 78-84.

Lian, S., Liu, Z., Ren, Z., & Wang, H. (2007, June). Commutative encryption and watermarking in video compression. *IEEE Transactions on Circuits and Systems for Video Technology, 17*(6), 774-778.

Macq, B., Dittmann, J., & Delp, E. J. (2004, June). Benchmarking of image watermarking algorithms for digital rights management. *Proceedings of the IEEE, 92*(6), 971-984.

Meerwald, P., & Uhl, A. (2001). A survey of wavelet domain watermarking algorithms. In *Proceedings of the SPIE on Security and Watermarking of Multimedia Contents* (Vol. 4314, pp. 505-516).

Merhav, N. (2006, January). On joint coding for watermarking and encryption. *IEEE Transactions on Information Theory, 52*(1), 190-205.

Naumovich, G., & Memon, N. (2003, July). Preventing piracy, reverse engineering, and tampering. *IEEE Computer*, 64-71.

OpenWatermark. Retrieved April 2, 2008, from http://www.openwatermark.org/

Petitcolas, A. P. (2002, September). Watermarking schemes evaluation. *IEEE Signal Processing Magazine, 17*, 58-64.

Petitcolas, F., & Katzenbeisser, S. (2000). *Information hiding techniques for steganography and digital watermarking*. Artech House.

Stallings, W. (2003). *Cryptography and network security: Principles and* practices (3rd ed.). Prentice-Hall. ISBN 0-13-091429-0.

StirMark. Retrieved April 2, 2008, from http://www.petitcolas.net/fabien/watermarking/ stirmark/index.html

Wu, M., & Liu, B. (2002). *Multimedia data hiding*. Springer. ISBN 0-387-95426-0.

KEY TERMS

Authentication: The process of verifying the digital identity of the sender and receiver of a communication. Usually a cryptographic hash is used for this purpose. Content authentication is used for verification of the content.

Cryptography: The technique of concealing the intended meaning of information. And it does so by encrypting a plain text into an unintelligible format, called cipher text. Only those who possess a secret key can decipher (or decrypt) the message into plain text.

Data Compression: The technique of representing the data in a format that requires fewer storage locations. Typically, lossy compression employs quantization and some sort of entropy coding, whereas lossless compression does not need quantization.

Digital Rights Management (DRM): An umbrella term that refers to access control or management technologies used by publishers and other copyright holders to limit or facilitate the usage of digital content or devices.

Digital Watermark: The process of embedding a digital code into a digital content like image, audio, or video. As an example, the digital code representing the creator/owner of a digital image can be embedded into the image for copyright protection. The embedded information, sometimes called watermark, is dependent on the intended application.

Fingerprinting: Fingerprinting is used for distribution and piracy detection of various types of digital content. It embeds in the delivered data some unique information related to the transaction, so that if any copy of this data is found later on the Internet, the leak can be traced back to the person who obtained it first.

Multimedia: Deals with multiple forms of information content and processing for example, text, audio, graphics, animation, image, and video. It can also extend to analog domain such as print media.

Reversible Watermarking: Reversible watermarking, or invertible watermark, is a distortion-free data embedding scheme, where the embedded information can be totally extracted without any distortion done to the host media. This is used for applications which cannot tolerate any degradation done to the host data, such as medical image protection.

Chapter XXVIII
Support Vector Machine:
Itself an Intelligent Systems

A. B. M. Shawkat Ali
Central Queensland University, Australia

ABSTRACT

From the beginning, machine learning methodology, which is the origin of artificial intelligence, has been rapidly spreading in the different research communities with successful outcomes. This chapter aims to introduce for system analysers and designers a comparatively new statistical supervised machine learning algorithm called support vector machine (SVM). We explain two useful areas of SVM, that is, classification and regression, with basic mathematical formulation and simple demonstration to make easy the understanding of SVM. Prospects and challenges of future research in this emerging area are also described. Future research of SVM will provide improved and quality access to the users. Therefore, developing an automated SVM system with state-of-the-art technologies is of paramount importance, and hence, this chapter will link up an important step in the system analysis and design perspective to this evolving research arena.

INTRODUCTION

Since the end of the last century, support vector machines (SVMs) have been introduced for classification and regression in the machine learning community. SVMs have a solid theoretical foundation rooted in statistical learning theory. SVMs work step by step. First, it maps the data into a high dimensional space via a nonlinear map, and in this high dimensional space it constructs an optimal separating hyperplane or linear regression function. This hyperplane or linear regression function obtained in the feature space couple with significant data points for prediction called support vectors (SVs). Therefore SVM do prediction based on SVs' information only. This process will involve a quadratic programming problem, and this will get a global optimal solution. This chapter formulates the statistical method of SVM based on classification and regression architecture. We explained both SVM classification methods: binary and muticlass classification. In each section we included a demonstration to easily understand SVM classification and regression methodology. Finally we give attention on how system analysers and designers can contribute to the construction of a full automated support vector learning algorithm.

BACKGROUND

The popular statistical learning algorithm, SVM, is an advanced version of the generalised portrait algorithm, which was developed in Russia in the late 60s (Smola & Schölkopf, 1998). After a large gap, Vapnik (1995) and his group simplified this theory and introduced SVM as an effective learning algorithm. Although SVM does not have a long history, it has already been successfully applied with significant outcomes in business, engineering, science, medicine, and many more.

SVM was introduced first to solve binary class pattern recognition problems, and then multiclass classification, regression estimation, and so many others. We can divide SVM literature into two parts: SVM classification and SVM regression. The following sections will cover both parts following the basic explanation with example.

SVM CLASSIFICATION

Let us consider a dataset D of l independently identically distributed (i.i.d) samples: $(\mathbf{x}_1, y_1), \cdots, (\mathbf{x}_l, y_l)$. Each sample is a set of feature vectors of length m, $\mathbf{x}_i = \langle x_1, \cdots, x_m \rangle$ and the target value $y_i \in \{1, -1\}$ that represents the binary class membership. Now, the pattern recognition problem or machine learning task is to learn the classes for each pattern by finding a classifier with decision functions $f(\mathbf{x}_i, \alpha_i)$, where, $f(\mathbf{x}_i, \alpha_i) = y_i, \alpha_i \in \Lambda, \forall \langle \mathbf{x}_i, y_i \rangle \in D$ and Λ is a set of abstract parameters.

Linear Hard Margin SVM

Now-a-days the general nonlinear SVM is quite popular to solve pattern recognition problems, but the root of this method is linear SVM. The original linear SVM was introduced to separate the binary class problem only.

Let us consider the above pattern recognition problem. Our aim is to find out the optimal hyperplane (OH) in the training phase with proper estimation of a weight vector $\mathbf{w}$ and the scalar bias factor b. All the training patterns are said to be linearly separable if there exists $\mathbf{w}$ and b such that the inequalities

$$(\omega \cdot \mathbf{x}_i) + b \geq 1 \qquad \text{if } y_i = 1 \text{ or } \bullet \qquad (1)$$

$$(\omega \cdot \mathbf{x}_i) + b \leq -1 \qquad \text{if } y_i = -1 \text{ or } \mathbb{C} \qquad (2)$$

These two sets of inequalities we can present into a single set such as

$$y_i = sign(\omega \cdot \mathbf{x}_i + b), \qquad i = 1, \ldots, \ell \qquad (3)$$

After extracting the OH, the whole set of vectors $\{\mathbf{w}\}$ will satisfy the Equation (3) as described in Figure 1.

The margin could be found by measuring the distance d between the binary classes' data points as shown in Figure 1 as follows:

$$d = d_{+1} + d_{-1} = \min_{i:(y_i=+1)} d(\omega, b; \mathbf{x}_i) - \min_{i:(y_i=-1)} d(\omega, b; \mathbf{x}_i)$$

$$m = \min_{i:(y_i=+1)} \frac{|\langle \omega, \mathbf{x}_i \rangle + b|}{\|\omega\|} - \min_{i:(y_i=-1)} \frac{|\langle \omega, \mathbf{x}_i \rangle + b|}{\|\omega\|}$$

$$m = \frac{1}{\|\omega\|} \left(\min_{i:(y_i=+1)} |\langle \omega, \mathbf{x}_i \rangle + b| - \min_{i:(y_i=-1)} |\langle \omega, \mathbf{x}_i \rangle + b| \right)$$

$$= \frac{2}{\|\omega\|}$$

$$(4)$$

where d_{+1} and d_{-1} are the distance of the closest positive and negative class data points from the OH.

Now the OH can be obtained through the minimisation:

$$\Phi(\omega) = \frac{1}{2} \|\omega\|^2 \qquad (5)$$

subject to: $y_i[(\omega \cdot \mathbf{x}_i) + b] \geq 1$.

It is important to mention that the OH solution is independent with the scalar quantity bias b. The OH will shift up or down due to any changing of b, but the maximum margin will remain same.

Figure 1. The hard margin linear classification. The margin is the distance between the two dashed lines.

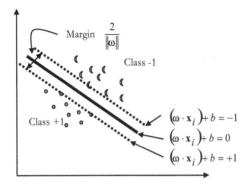

The above optimisation problem in Equation (5) can be solved using standard quadratic optimisation techniques. We construct the Lagrangian function as follows:

$$L(\omega, b, \alpha) = \frac{1}{2}\|\omega\|^2 - \sum_{i=1}^{\ell} \alpha_i \left\{ y_i \left(\omega \cdot \mathbf{x}_i + b \right) - 1 \right\}$$

$$(6)$$

where $\alpha_i = (\alpha_1, ..., \alpha_l)$ are the Lagrange multipliers.

The solution of the Lagrangian optimisation problem can be determined by a saddle point of this Lagrangian, which is to be minimised with respect to ω and b and maximised with respect to non-negative α. By getting a differentiation of Equation (6) and setting the equality with zero we can obtain:

$$\frac{\partial L(\omega, b, \alpha)}{\partial \omega} = \omega - \sum_{i=1}^{l} \alpha_i y_i \mathbf{x}_i = 0 \qquad (7)$$

$$\frac{\partial L(\omega, b, \alpha)}{\partial b} = \sum_{i=1}^{l} \alpha_i y_i = 0 \qquad (8)$$

Now, using the upper score symbol (ω^o) to identify the optimal values of the cost function, we can obtain from Equation (7)

$$\omega^o = \sum_{i=1}^{l} \alpha_i^o \mathbf{x}_i y_i, \qquad \alpha_i^o \geq 0 \qquad (9)$$

which shows the OH solution is a linear combination of the vectors of the training data points. It is noted that the training vectors $\mathbf{x}_i$ with $\alpha_O \geq 0$ only contribute to construct the OH. This fact follows the classical Karush-Kuhn-Tucker (KKT) conditions. Now substituting Equations (8) and (9) in Equation (6) and considering the KKT condition we can write

$$\alpha_i^o = \frac{1}{2}\omega.\omega - \omega.\omega - 0 + \sum_{i=1}^{l}\alpha_i$$

$$= \sum_{i=1}^{l}\alpha_i - \frac{1}{2}\sum_{i=1}^{l}\sum_{j=1}^{l}\alpha_i \alpha_j y_i y_j \left(\mathbf{x}_i \cdot \mathbf{x}_j \right)$$

$$(10)$$

From this above expansion those training vectors that have nonzero coefficient α_i^o in the expansion of ω^o (Equation 9) are called *support vectors*, which play a significant role in constructing the OH.

The scalar bias (threshold) factor b can be obtained

$$b^o = \frac{1}{2}\left[\left(\omega^o \cdot \mathbf{x}_{+1} + \omega^o \cdot \mathbf{x}_{-1} \right) \right] \qquad (11)$$

where $\mathbf{x}_{+1}$ and $\mathbf{x}_{-1}$ and $\mathbf{x}_{-1}$ are indicating the SVs belonging to the +1 and -1 classes.

Finally, the linearity of the dot product is the outcome of Equations (9) and (11), and then we can write the decision function for the hard margin classifier as follows:

$$\hat{f}(\mathbf{x}) = sign(\omega^o \cdot \mathbf{x} + b) = sign\left(\sum_{SVs} \alpha_i^o y_i \left(\mathbf{x}_i \cdot \mathbf{x} \right) + b^o \right)$$

$$(12)$$

The hard margin classifier can not handle linearly nonseparable patterns though. Therefore we consider the soft margin classifier to improve the performance on linearly nonseparable patterns.

Linear Hard to Soft Margin SVM

The hard margin classifier fails to classify the linearly nonseparable patterns. Due to this, a soft margin classifier is introduced to classify linearly nonseparable patterns (Cortes & Vapnik, 1995). The soft margin hyperplane will not be able to classify with zero errors but the generalisation performance is expected to be better than the hard margin classifier. The soft margin hyperplane can be constructed by the vector w that minimises the function

$$\Phi(\omega,\xi) = \frac{1}{2}\|\omega\|^2 + C\left(\sum_{i=1}^{l}\xi_i\right) \tag{13}$$

subject to: $y_i[(\omega \cdot \mathbf{x}_i)+b] \geq 1-\xi_i$

$\xi_i \geq 0$ where $i = 1,\cdots,l$

where C is called hyperparameter and ξ is called slack variable. The maximum value of C could be up to infinity. The value of C is the boundary for finding α_i in the quadratic programming (QP) solution. Chapelle, Vapnik, Bousquet, and Mukherjee (2002) suggest a method for choosing the value of optimal C. The slack variable is determined by optimisation to minimise the violation of constraints.

In order to solve the problem we can construct the Lagrangian optimisation function as follows:

Figure 2. Problem of non separable patterns representation due to overlapping distributions

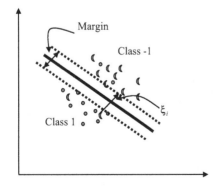

$$L(\omega,b,\xi,\alpha) =$$
$$\frac{1}{2}\|\omega\|^2 - \sum_{i=1}^{\ell}\alpha_i[y_i(\omega \cdot \mathbf{x}_i+b)-1+\xi_i] - \sum_{i=1}^{l}\alpha_i\xi_i + C\left(\sum_{i=1}^{l}\xi_i\right) \tag{14}$$

One can find the OH by following the hard margin Lagrangian quadratic solving procedure with the slightly different constraints such that:

$$0 \leq \alpha_i \leq C$$
$$\sum_{i=1}^{l}\alpha_i y_i = 0 \tag{15}$$

By following these procedures we can extract the SVs and then the decision function as follows:

$$\hat{f}(\mathbf{x}) = sign(\omega^O \cdot \mathbf{x}+b) = sign\left(\sum_{SVs}\alpha_i^o y_i(\mathbf{x}_i \cdot \mathbf{x})+b^o\right) \tag{16}$$

Unfortunately, real world pattern recognition problems are almost always nonlinear. It is a difficult task to accurately classify nonlinear problems even by soft margin SVM because the margin construction procedure is linear. Therefore we need to construct the nonlinear margin for SVM. So we consider nonlinear SVM to handle nonlinear patterns.

Nonlinear SVM

In the previous sections we have explained the hard and soft margin-based linear hyperplane methodology, which is not suitable for most real world classification problems. Now we shall introduce the nonlinear SVM. We shall see that SVM can construct a nonlinear decision boundary in the nonlinear separable data space. The decision boundary for nonlinear patterns is conceptually quite simple and is done by mapping the input vectors x into a higher dimensional space, namely *feature space*, where a linear classification boundary can be constructed easily. One can transform the input vectors $\mathbf{x}$ into a high dimensional feature space as follows:

$$\mathbf{x} \to \Phi(\mathbf{x}) = \left(a_1 \Phi(\mathbf{x}), a_2 \Phi_2(\mathbf{x}), \cdots, a_n \Phi_n(\mathbf{x}), \cdots \right) \tag{17}$$

where $\{a_n\}_{n=1}^{\infty}$ are the real numbers, which are the coefficients of the real functions $\{\Phi_n\}_{n=1}^{\infty}$. Now we can apply the soft margin construction procedure in the feature space. The solution of Equation (16) could be extended by considering the mapping as follows:

$$\hat{f}(\mathbf{x}) = sign\left(\omega^O \cdot \Phi(\mathbf{x}) + b \right) =$$
$$sign\left(\sum_{i=1}^{l} \alpha_i^O y_i \Phi\left(\mathbf{x}_i \right) \Phi(\mathbf{x}) + b^O \right) \tag{18}$$

The product of $\Phi\left(\mathbf{x}_i\right)\Phi\left(\mathbf{x}_j\right)$ is a scalar quantity. Now it is wise to introduce the so called *kernel function K:*

$$K(\mathbf{x}_i, \mathbf{x}_j) = \Phi(\mathbf{x}_i) \cdot \Phi(\mathbf{x}_j) \tag{19}$$

Finally we can construct the decision function by following the soft margin Lagrangian function for nonlinear SVM with the additional kernel property as follows:

$$\hat{f}(x) = sign\left(\sum_{i=1}^{l} \alpha_i^O y_i K(\mathbf{x}_i, \mathbf{x}_j) + b^O \right) \tag{20}$$

Therefore, the key property of nonlinear SVM is the kernel function that will be demonstrated in the next section.

KERNEL THEORY

To find an OH in a higher dimensional feature space is a complicated and computationally expensive task. Kernel theory has made it easier for the machine to extract the OH in higher dimensional feature space. The concept of the kernel method is older, but Vapnik reintroduced this method as a significant part of the statistical learning machine by combining it with SVM (Boser, Guyon, & Vapnik, 1992). Apart form SVM, kernel methods have been successfully implemented in kernel Fisher discriminant (KFD) (Baudat & Anouar, 2000), kernel principal component analysis (KPCA) (Schölkopf, Mika, Burges, Knirsch, Müller, Rätsch, et al., 1999), multiple additive regression kernel (MARK) (Bennett, Momma, & Embrechts, 2002), and many others. Like supervised learning methods, kernel functions have also been given similar attention in the unsupervised learning area (Schölkopf, Platt, Shawe-Taylor, Smola, & Williamson, 2001). Due to wide application and quite good performance, kernel-based algorithms have been renamed *kernel machines* (Schölkopf & Smola, 2000).

A simple kernel function is demonstrated on a binary class problem in Figure 3. The +1 and -1 classes are denoted by cross and rectangular symbols. The middle line in Figure 3 is indicated as an OH. Figure 3 (b) and (c) illustrate the linear and nonlinear functions of the kernel.

By implementing the kernel function, one can map the input data into a high dimensional feature space. The feature space could be of infinite dimension. After kernel transformation, it is straight forward to construct the OH in the feature space by minimising the error. One important advantage of the kernel machine is that it does not need any explicit parameter, for instance, *b*. For any continuous kernel function that satisfies the Mercer's condition of symmetry (Mercer, 1909), which is $K(\mathbf{x}_i, \mathbf{x}_j) = K(\mathbf{x}_j, \mathbf{x}_i)$, there exists a Hilbert space H, a map $\Phi : \Re^n \to H$, and positive numbers of α_i such as:

$$K(\mathbf{x}_i, \mathbf{x}_j) = \sum_{i=1}^{\infty} \alpha_i \Phi(\mathbf{x}_i) \cdot \Phi(\mathbf{x}_j) \tag{21}$$

where $\mathbf{x}_i, \mathbf{x}_j \in \Re^n$. Mercer's condition require that

$$\int K(\mathbf{x}_i, \mathbf{x}_j) g(\mathbf{x}_i) g(\mathbf{x}_j) d\mathbf{x}_i d\mathbf{x}_j \geq 0 \qquad (22)$$

is satisfied for all g such that

$$\int g^2(\mathbf{x}) d\mathbf{x} < \infty. \qquad (23)$$

The integral is considered here over a compact subset of $\mathfrak{R}^n$. Finally the kernel function K can be represented as an inner product as follows:

$$K(\mathbf{x}_i, \mathbf{x}_j) = \Phi(\mathbf{x}_i)^T \Phi(\mathbf{x}_j). \qquad (24)$$

The linear, polynomial, radial basis function (RBF), and sigmoidal are the most commonly used kernels for SVM. We formulate the SVM classical kernel as follows (Vapnik, 1999, 2000):

The linear kernel function is:

$$K\left(\mathbf{x}_i, \mathbf{x}_j\right) = \left\langle \mathbf{x}_i^T \mathbf{x}_j \right\rangle. \qquad (25)$$

The dth order polynomial kernel function is:

$$K\left(\mathbf{x}_i, \mathbf{x}_j\right) = \left\langle \mathbf{x}_i^T \mathbf{x}_j \right\rangle^d \quad \text{or} \qquad (26)$$

$$K\left(\mathbf{x}_i, \mathbf{x}_j\right) = \left(\left\langle \mathbf{x}_i^T \mathbf{x}_j \right\rangle + 1\right)^d \qquad (27)$$

Vapnik suggests choosing the second polynomial kernel function, which avoids the problems of the hessian matrix becoming zero (Boser et al., 1992).

Radial basis function has received significant attention in SVM implementation. The RBF kernel function is:

$$K\left(\mathbf{x}_i, \mathbf{x}_j\right) = \exp\{-\left|\mathbf{x}_i - \mathbf{x}_j\right|^2\} \qquad (28)$$

Boser et al. (Navarrete & Ruiz-del-Solar, 2003; Vapnik, 1998; McLachlan, 1992) modified the classical function by introducing a smoothing parameter σ as follows:

$$K\left(\mathbf{x}_i, \mathbf{x}_j\right) = \exp\left(-\frac{\left\|\mathbf{x}_i - \mathbf{x}_j\right\|^2}{2\sigma^2}\right), \quad \text{where } \sigma > 0.$$

$$(29)$$

From the beginning of the nonlinear SVM, researchers have used these linear, polynomial, and RBF kernel for classification as well as regression problems. Therefore, these kernels are called SVM classical kernels.

The sigmoidal kernel (Vapnik, 1998) function is:

Figure 3. The kernel function: (a) The input space, (b) The linear OH construction with errors, and (c) The nonlinear OH construction without error by using kernel mapping to a 256 dimensional space

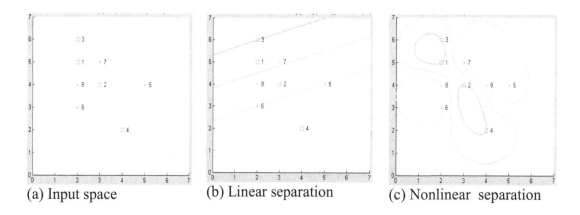

   (a) Input space   (b) Linear separation   (c) Nonlinear separation

$$K\left(\mathbf{x}_i, \mathbf{x}_j\right) = \tanh(\eta\left(\mathbf{x}_i^T \mathbf{x}_j\right) + \theta) \qquad (30)$$

This kernel requires selection of two parameters, that is, η and θ.

Another two kernels, spline and multiquadratic, are also quite popular for some specific problems. The finite spline kernel (Gunn, 1998) can be described as follows:

$$K\left(\mathbf{x}_i, \mathbf{x}_j\right) = 1 + \left(\mathbf{x}_i^T \mathbf{x}_j\right) + \frac{1}{2}\left(\mathbf{x}_i^T \mathbf{x}_j\right) \min\left(\mathbf{x}_i^T \mathbf{x}_j\right)^2 - \frac{1}{6}\min\left(\mathbf{x}_i^T \mathbf{x}_j\right)^3$$

$$(31)$$

The multiquadratic positive semi definite kernel is (Evgeniou, Pontil, & Poggio, 2000)

$$K\left(\mathbf{x}_i, \mathbf{x}_j\right) = \left(\left\|\mathbf{x}_i - \mathbf{x}_j\right\|^2 + \tau^2\right)^{\frac{1}{2}}, \text{ where } \tau > 0$$

$$(32)$$

A graphical view of these kernels is shown in Figure 4 for an artificial dataset. The example shows the differences between the kernels and their functional behaviors. The linear kernel constructs the linear boundary for SVM, which is not suitable to classify nonlinearly separable patterns. The polynomial and RBF kernels construct the nonlinear boundary for SVM to classify the patterns. Both kernels showed better performance than the others. The RBF kernel produced zero classification errors. On the other hand spline, sigmoidal, and multiquadratic kernels are constructed with a near linear boundary for SVM to classify the patterns. So the classification error is higher than the RBF and polynomial kernels.

Some other suitable kernels include engineering kernel (Zien, Rätsch, Mika, Schölkopf, Lengauer, & Müller, 2000), ANOVA kernel (Stitson, Gammerman, Vapnik, Vovk, Watkins, & Weston, 1997), wavelet kernel (Strauss, Delb, Plinkert, & Jens, 2003), kernal with moderate decreasing (KMOD)

(Ayat, Cheriet, Remaki, & Suen, 2001), semantic kernel (Siolas & d'Alche-Buc, 2000), scaling kernels (Zhang, Zhou, & Jiao, 2002), adaptive kernel (Zhao & Kuh, 2002), and tangent distance kernels (Haasdonk & Keysers, 2002), and have showed better performance based on specific problems than classical SVM kernels.

Like the evolution of SVM from hard margin to soft margin, linear to nonlinear, the SVM method has been also extended effectively from binary class to multiclass classification solver.

MULTICLASS SVM

SVM was first introduced as a binary classification solver. After that researchers extended it from binary to multiclass SVM in different ways, but still it is a research issue for an effective multiclass SVM. There are two types of multiclass SVM available in the literature. The first directly constructs a multiclass solver by considering all data points in one optimisation formulation (Crammer & Singer, 2000; Vapnik, 1998; Weston & Watkins, 1999) and the second constructs and combines several binary classifiers into a multiclass solver (Chih-Wei & Chih-Jen, 2000). There are three methods that have been developed for the second category of multiclass SVM: *one-against-one* (Kreßel, 1999; Friedman, 1996), *one-against-all* (Schölkopf, Burges, & Vapnik, 1995; Vapnik, 2000) and *directed acyclic graph* (DAG) SVM (Platt, Cristianini, & Shawe-Taylor, 2000). Weston and Watkins (1999) argue that direct multiclass SVM performs better than the second category multiclass SVM. Therefore, in this chapter we have summarised the direct method as follows (Weston, 1999):

Let us consider the same dataset as described above with extended class values $y_i \in \{1, \cdots, k\}$ and the optimisation problem is:

$$\min_{\omega, \xi} \phi\left(\omega, \xi\right) = \frac{1}{2}\sum_{m=1}^{k}\left(\omega_m \cdot \omega_m\right) + C\sum_{i=1}^{l}\sum_{m \neq y_i}\xi_i^m$$

$$(33)$$

Figure 4. A pictorial view of the linear, polynomial, rbf, spline, sigmoidal and multiquadratic kernel on an artificial dataset. The cross and rectangular sign indicates the two classes of data. The middle lines (except sigmoidal) of the above graphs represent the OH for classification. Those data points placed on the hyperplane are called SVs [Ali, S. 2005]

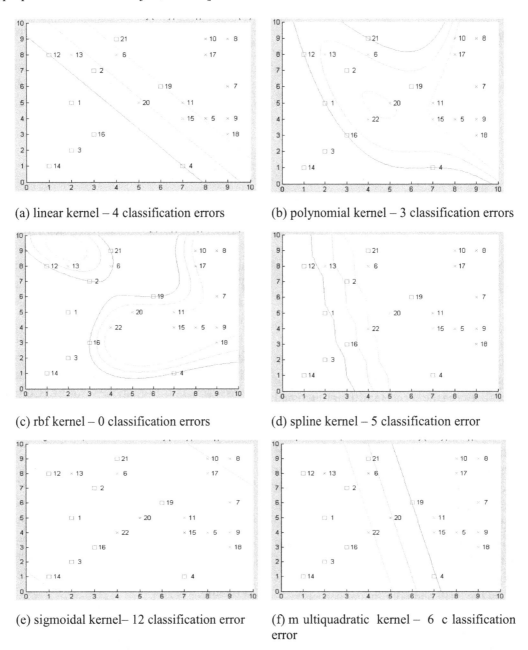

(a) linear kernel – 4 classification errors

(b) polynomial kernel – 3 classification errors

(c) rbf kernel – 0 classification errors

(d) spline kernel – 5 classification error

(e) sigmoidal kernel– 12 classification error

(f) m ultiquadratic kernel – 6 c lassification error

subject to: $\left(\omega_{y_i} \cdot \mathbf{x}_i\right) + b_{y_i} \geq \left(\omega_m \cdot \mathbf{x}_i\right) + b_m + 2 - \xi_i^m$

$\xi_i^m \geq 0, i = 1, \cdots, l \quad m \in \{1, \cdots, k\} \backslash y_i$

Now we can solve this optimisation problem by constructing the similar quadratic approach to find the saddle point of the Lagrangian:

$$L(\omega, b, \xi, \alpha, \beta) = \frac{1}{2} \sum_{m=1}^{k} (\omega_m \cdot \omega_m) + C \sum_{i=1}^{\ell} \sum_{m=1}^{k} \xi_i^m -$$

$$\sum_{i=1}^{\ell} \sum_{m=1}^{k} \alpha_i^m \left[\left(\left(\omega_{y_i} - \omega_m \right) \cdot \mathbf{x}_i \right) + b_{y_i} - b_m - 2 + \xi_i^m \right] - \sum_{i=1}^{\ell} \sum_{m=1}^{k} \beta_i^m \xi_i^m$$

(34)

with the dummy variables:

$\alpha_i^{y_i} = 0, \qquad \beta_i^{y_i} = 0, \quad \xi_i^{y_i} = 0$

subject to:

$\alpha_i^m \geq 0, \beta_i^m \geq 0, \xi_i^m \geq 0, i = 1, \cdots, \ell$ and $c \in \{1, \cdots, k\} \backslash y_i$

which is maximised with respect to α and β minimised with respect to ω by ξ considering the notation:

$$c_i^n = \begin{cases} 1 & if \ y_i = n \\ 0 & if \ y_i \neq n \end{cases} \quad and \quad A_i = \sum_{m=1}^{k} \alpha_i^m$$

(35)

After getting the differentiation, the optimal α is obtained as follows:

$$\alpha_i^o = 2 \sum_{i,m} \alpha_i^m +$$

(36)

$$\sum_{i,j,m} \left[-\frac{1}{2} c_j^{y_i} A_i A_j + \alpha_i^m \alpha_j^{y_i} - \frac{1}{2} \alpha_i^m \alpha_j^{y_i} \right] \left(\mathbf{x}_i \cdot \mathbf{x}_j \right)$$

Finally the decision function for multiclass SVM is:

$$\hat{f}(\mathbf{x}) = \arg \max_n \left[\sum_{i: y_i = n} A_i \left(\mathbf{x}_i \cdot \mathbf{x} \right) - \sum_{i: y_i \neq n} \alpha_i^n (\mathbf{x}_i \cdot \mathbf{x}) + b_n \right]$$

(37)

The inner product $(\mathbf{x}_i \cdot \mathbf{x})$ can be replaced by the convolution inner product $K(\mathbf{x}_i, \mathbf{x}_j)$, also known as the kernel function.

A SIMPLE EXAMPLE FOR SVM CLASSIFICATION

In this section, the simple Boolean exclusive-OR (XOR) problem is solved by SVM second degree polynomial kernel to illustrate the approach. This is a nonlinear classification problem. The following XOR problem (Smith, 1999; Duda, Hart, & Stork, 2001) is described in Table 1.

We choose the polynomial kernel (as described in Equation [27]) with second degree. The solution does not consider any explicit bias. First, we transform the dataset by polynomial kernel as:

$K(\mathbf{x}_i, \mathbf{x}_j) = (1 + \mathbf{x}_i \cdot \mathbf{x}_j^T)^2$

Here, $\mathbf{x}_i . \mathbf{x}_j^T = \begin{bmatrix} -1 & -1 \\ -1 & 1 \\ 1 & -1 \\ 1 & 1 \end{bmatrix} \times \begin{bmatrix} -1 & -1 & 1 & 1 \\ -1 & 1 & -1 & 1 \end{bmatrix}$,

Now we can construct the kernel matrix as follows:

$K(\mathbf{x}_i, \mathbf{x}_j) = \begin{bmatrix} 9 & 1 & 1 & 1 \\ 1 & 9 & 1 & 1 \\ 1 & 1 & 9 & 1 \\ 1 & 1 & 1 & 9 \end{bmatrix}$

We can write the maximisation term following Equation (10) as:

$$\alpha_i^o = \sum_{i=1}^{4} \alpha_i - \frac{1}{2} \sum_{i=1}^{4} \sum_{j=1}^{4} \alpha_i \alpha_j y_i y_j K(\mathbf{x}_i \cdot \mathbf{x}_j)$$

$$(= \alpha_1 + \alpha_2 + \alpha_3 + \alpha_4 - \frac{1}{2} 9\alpha_1^2 - 2\alpha_1\alpha_2 - 2\alpha_1\alpha_3 + 2\alpha_1\alpha_4 + 9\alpha_2^2 + 2\alpha_2\alpha_3 - 2\alpha_2\alpha_4 + 9\alpha_3^2 - 2\alpha_3\alpha_4 + 9\alpha_4^2)$$

subject to

$$\sum_{i=1}^{4} y_i \alpha_i = \alpha_1 - \alpha_2 + \alpha_3 - \alpha_4 = 0$$

$$0 \le \alpha_1$$
$$0 \le \alpha_2$$
$$0 \le \alpha_3$$
$$0 \le \alpha_4$$

Differentiation with respect to the Lagrangian parameters $\{\alpha_1,...,\alpha_4\}$, the following sets of simultaneous equations are

$$\begin{cases} 9\alpha_1 - \alpha_2 - \alpha_3 + \alpha_4 = 1 \\ -\alpha_1 + 9\alpha_2 + \alpha_3 - \alpha_4 = 1 \\ -\alpha_1 + \alpha_2 + 9\alpha_3 - \alpha_4 = 1 \\ \alpha_1 - \alpha_2 - \alpha_3 + 9\alpha_4 = 1 \end{cases}$$

By solving these above equations we can write the solution to this optimisation problem as $\alpha_1 = \alpha_2 = \alpha_3 = \alpha_4 = \frac{1}{8}$.

The decision function in the inner product representation is

$$D(\mathbf{x}) = \sum_{i=1}^{n} \alpha_i^* y_i H(\mathbf{x}_i, \mathbf{x}) = (0.125) \sum_{i=1}^{4} y_i \left[(\mathbf{x}_i \cdot \mathbf{x}) + 1 \right]^2$$

Table 1. Boolean XOR Problem

Input data $\mathbf{x}$	Output class y
(-1,-1)	-1
(-1,+1)	+1
(+1,-1)	+1
(+1,+1)	-1

This decision function separates the data with a maximum margin that will be demonstrated later in Figure 5.

Since the kernel considers the inner product of the input vectors, we can write the second degree polynomial kernel function as:

$$K(\mathbf{x}_i, \mathbf{x}_j) = ((\mathbf{x}_i, \mathbf{x}_j) + 1)^2$$
$$(= x_{i1}x_{j1} + x_{i2}x_{j2})^2 + 2(x_{i1}x_{j1} + x_{i2}x_{j2}) + 1$$
$$= 1 + (x_{i1}x_{j1})^2 + 2(x_{i1}x_{j1})(x_{i2}x_{j2}) + (x_{i2}x_{j2})^2 + 2(x_{i1}x_{j1}) + 2(x_{i2}x_{j2})$$
$$= \Phi(\mathbf{x}_i)^T(\mathbf{x}_j)$$

Now we can write the second degree polynomial transformation function as:

$$\Phi(\mathbf{x}_i) = [1, x_{i1}^2, \sqrt{2}x_{i1}x_{i2}, x_{i2}^2, \sqrt{2}x_{i1}, \sqrt{2}x_{i2}]^T$$

The six-dimensional feature space, where the decision function is linear with maximum margin, can be represented in Table 2.

By substituting the value of α and $\Phi(x_i)$ in Equation (9), we can construct the optimum weight vector as:

$$\omega^o = \sum_{i=1}^{4} \alpha_i y_i \Phi(\mathbf{x}_i)$$

$$\frac{1}{8}[-\Phi(\mathbf{x}_1) + \Phi(\mathbf{x}_2) + \Phi(\mathbf{x}_3) - \Phi(\mathbf{x}_4)]$$

$$\frac{1}{8} \left[-\begin{bmatrix} 1 \\ 1 \\ \sqrt{2} \\ 1 \\ -\sqrt{2} \\ -\sqrt{2} \end{bmatrix} + \begin{bmatrix} 1 \\ 1 \\ -\sqrt{2} \\ 1 \\ -\sqrt{2} \\ \sqrt{2} \end{bmatrix} + \begin{bmatrix} 1 \\ 1 \\ -\sqrt{2} \\ 1 \\ \sqrt{2} \\ -\sqrt{2} \end{bmatrix} - \begin{bmatrix} 1 \\ 1 \\ \sqrt{2} \\ 1 \\ \sqrt{2} \\ \sqrt{2} \end{bmatrix} \right] = \begin{bmatrix} 0 \\ 0 \\ -1/\sqrt{2} \\ 0 \\ 0 \\ 0 \end{bmatrix}$$

Finally the optimal hyperplane can be defined (without any external bias) as $\left(\omega^o \right)^T \Phi(\mathbf{x}) = 0$

So,

$$\left[0,0,\frac{-1}{\sqrt{2}},0,0,0\right]\begin{bmatrix} 1 \\ x_1^2 \\ \sqrt{2}x_1x_2 \\ x_2^2 \\ \sqrt{2}x_1 \\ \sqrt{2}x_2 \end{bmatrix} = 0$$

Therefore the optimal hyperplane function for this XOR problem is:

$$\hat{f}(\mathbf{x}) = -x_1x_2$$

This is the SVM 2nd degree polynomial solution for XOR problem shown in Figure 4. Due to the nonlinear nature of this data, the linear kernel is unable to separate the classes like a polynomial kernel.

In Figure 4, the polynomial, RBF, and sigmoidal kernels are capable of classifying all patterns. But the other kernels fail to classify all patterns correctly.

EXPERIMENTAL RESULTS: CLASSIFIER PERFORMANCE

We consider all the algorithms from Waikato environment for knowledge analysis (WEKA) release 3.1.8 with default parameter settings. We considered in our experiment the 100 classification problems. We choose eight popular classifiers namely IBK, C4.5, partial tree (PART), kernel density (KD), naive Bayes (NB), OneR, SVM, and finally neural network (NN). The machine configuration is

Pentium IV, CPU 2.66 GHz and 1 GB RAM. The average accuracy is the combination of true positive rate (TPR), true negative rate (TNR), percentage of correct classification, and weighted F-measure. The computational complexity considers both the model train time as well as the test set evaluation time (Ali, 2005).

From this experiment we observed that the SVM performed better in terms of accuracy. On the other hand the computational performance is average for the SVM. But it is faster than popular classifier NN.

SVM Regression

SVM has been introduced for the first time for binary class pattern recognition problems, but the application of SVM to regression problems has shown many breakthroughs and plausible performance. Moreover, applications of support vector regression (SVR) (Gunn, 1998), such as forecasting of financial market (Yang, Chan, & King, 2002), estimation of power consumption (Chen, Chang, & Lin, 2001), reconstruction of chaotic systems (Matterra & Haykin, 1999), and prediction of highway traffic flow (Ding, Zhao, & Jiao, 2002), are also under development. The time-varying properties of SVR applications resemble the time-dependency of traffic forecasting, combined with many successful results of SVR predictions encouraged also in many regression-based modeling.

Let us consider a set of training data $\{(x_1,y_1),....,(x_\ell,y_\ell)\}$, where each $x_i \subset R^n$ de-

Table 2. 2nd degree polynomial kernel feature space

Input space	Feature space						Target
(x_1,x_2)	1	x_1	x_2	x_1x_2	x_1^2	x_2^2	y
(1,1)	1	1	1	1	1	1	1
(1,-1)	1	1	-1	-1	1	1	-1
(-1,-1)	1	-1	-1	1	1	1	1
(-1,1)	1	-1	1	-1	1	1	-1

Figure 4. Pictorial view of the XOR problem classification with SVM. The polynomial kernel function is $\hat{f}(\mathbf{x}) = -(x_1 x_2)$

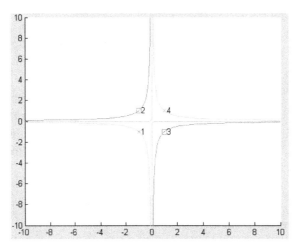

notes the input space of the sample and has a corresponding target value $y_i \subset R$ for $i = 1,..., l$ where l corresponds to the size of the training data (Vapnik, 2000). The goal for the regression problem is to determine a function that can approximate future values accurately.

The generic SVR estimating function is as follows:

$$f(x) = (w \cdot \Phi(x) + b \qquad (38)$$

where $w \subset R^n$, $b \subset R$, and Φ denotes a nonlinear transformation from R^n to high dimensional space. Our aim is to find the value of w and b such that

values of x can be determined by minimising the regression risk:

$$R_{reg}(f) = C \sum_{i=0}^{\ell} \Gamma(f(xi) - yi) + \frac{1}{2} \|w\|^2$$

(39)

where $\Gamma(\cdot)$ is a cost function, C is a constant, and vector w can be written in terms of data points as:

$$w = \sum_{i=1}^{\ell} (\alpha_i - \alpha_i^*) \Phi(x_i) \qquad (40)$$

Table 3. Formulated ranking averaged across test set classification problems based on a variety of measures (where a rank of 1 means best performing algorithm, and 0 means worst performing algorithm)

Classifier	IBK	C4.5	PART	KD	NB	OneR	SVM	NN
TPR	0.595	0.595	0.595	0.61	0.495	0.365	0.565	**0.645**
TNR	0.54	0.6	0.6	0.6	0.44	0.385	0.595	**0.605**
% of correct classification	0.505	0.615	0.55	0.565	0.385	0.325	**0.62**	0.615
F-measure	0.565	**0.625**	**0.625**	0.575	0.48	0.365	0.56	0.62
Average accuracy	0.551	0.609	0.593	0.588	0.45	0.36	0.585	**0.621**

Table 4. Average ranking of computational performance

Classifier	IBK	C4.5	PART	KD	NB	OneR	SVM	NN
Execution Time	0.535	0.535	0.52	0.51	0.705	**0.995**	0.5	0.015

By substituting Equation (40) into Equation (38), the generic equation can be rewritten as:

$$f(x) = \sum_{i=1}^{\ell} (\alpha_i - \alpha_i^*)(\Phi(x_i) \cdot \Phi(x)) + b$$
$$= \sum_{i=1}^{\ell} (\alpha_i - \alpha_i^*) k(x_i, x) + b \qquad (41)$$

In Equation (41) the dot product can be replaced by the kernel function as described early in this chapter.

In SVM literature the quality of estimation is measured by the loss function $L(y, f(\mathbf{x}, \omega))$. We use a new type of loss function called e-insensitive loss function SVM regression proposed by Vapnik (1998, 1999):

$$\Gamma(f(x) - y) = \begin{cases} |f(x) - y| - \varepsilon, & for \quad |f(x) - y| \geq \varepsilon \\ 0 & otherwise \end{cases} \qquad (42)$$

The empirical risk is:

$$R_{emp}(\omega) = \frac{1}{n} \sum_{i=1}^{n} L_{\varepsilon}(y_i, f(\mathbf{x}_i, \omega)) \qquad (43)$$

It is important that ε-insensitive loss coincides with least-modulus loss and with a special case of Huber's robust loss function (Vapnik, 1995, 1999) when ε =0. Now we can compare prediction performance of SVM (with proposed chosen ε) with regression estimates obtained using least-modulus loss(ε =0) for various noise densities.

By solving the quadratic optimisation problem in Equation (44), the regression risk in Equation

(39) and the ε -insensitive loss function in Equation (42) can be minimised:

$$\frac{1}{2} \sum_{i,j=1}^{\ell} (\alpha_i^* - \alpha_i)(\alpha_j^* - \alpha_j) k(x_i, x_j) -$$
$$\sum_{i=1}^{\ell} \alpha_i^* (y_i - \varepsilon) - \alpha_i (y_i + \varepsilon) \qquad (44)$$

subject to

$$\sum_{i=1}^{\ell} \alpha_i - \alpha_i^* = 0, \quad \alpha_i, \alpha_i^* \in [0, C]$$

The Lagrange multipliers, α_i and α_i^*, represent solutions to the above optimisation problem that act as forces pushing predictions towards target value y_i. Among these values only the nonzero values of the Lagrange multipliers in Equation (44) are useful in forecasting the regression line and are known as support vectors. For all points inside the ε-tube as presented in Figure 5 the Lagrange multipliers equal to zero do not contribute to the regression function.

The basic regression line fitting of the SVM method in the training data points are explained in Figure 5.

The constant C introduced in Equation (39) always determines penalties to estimation errors. A large C assigns higher penalties to errors so that the regression is trained to minimise error with lower generalisation while a small C assigns fewer penalties to errors; this allows the minimisation of margin with errors, thus higher generalisation ability. If C goes to infinitely large, SVR would not allow the occurrence of any error and result in a complex model. Whereas when C goes to zero, the result would tolerate a large amount of errors and the model would be less complex.

A Simple Example for SVM Regression

This is a simple problem, solving a simple regression task using LS-SVMlab (Suykens, Gestel, Brabanter, Moor, & Vandewalle, 2002). A dataset is constructed in the correct formatting. The data are represented as matrices where each row contains one data point (Box 1).

The first two variables (X and Y) we use to construct a SVM regression model and the next two variables (Xt and Yt) we will use to evaluate the model.

In order to make an LS-SVM model with RBF kernel fitting we need to initialize two extra parameters: γ (gama) (described as C in Equation 39) is the regularisation parameter, which determines the trade-off between the fitting error minimisation, and the RBF kernel function smoothness of the estimated function σ^2 (sigma^2). We initialised gama = 10 and sigma = 0.3 for this above problem. After completing the model generation we found the two parameter values for Equation (41). The

optimisation parameter α has been summerised in the above table and the bias factor b = -0.1394.

Now the LS-SVM performance can be displayed if the dimension of the input data is 1 or 2 as described in Figure 6.

Prediction Performance

We present a comparison for the best prediction performance of SVM, back-propagation neural network (BNN), multiple discriminant analysis (MDA), and logistic regression analysis (logit) in training and holdout data, and show that SVM outperforms BPN, MDA, and Logit by 0.5, 4.8, and 3.9%, respectively, for the holdout data (Min & Lee, 2005) in Table 5.

FUTURE TRENDS

It is well known that SVM generalisation performance (estimation accuracy) depends on a good setting of metaparameters C, ε, and the automated kernel and its parameters selection. Ali and Smith (in press, 2005) already published some solutions about parameter and automatics kernel selection

Figure 5. Support vector regression to fit a tube with radius ε to the data and positive slack variables ζ measuring the points lying outside of the tube

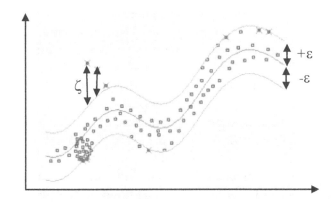

Box 1.

X =	Y =	α	Xt=	Yt
-3.0000	0.0986	0.7225	-3.0000	0.1488
-2.8000	0.0150	-2.5448	-2.9000	-0.0207
-2.6000	0.1492	0.6324	-2.8000	-0.0179
-2.4000	0.1495	1.2348	-2.7000	0.0707
-2.2000	0.0872	1.4470	-2.6000	0.1827
-2.0000	-0.1004	-0.7677	-2.5000	0.0419
-1.8000	-0.1987	-0.4472	-2.4000	0.0060
-1.6000	-0.2266	0.7385	-2.3000	0.1000
-1.4000	-0.3348	-2.2723	-2.2000	0.0785
-1.2000	-0.2615	-2.7375	-2.1000	0.0954
-1.0000	0.1472	3.8079	-2.0000	-0.0595
-0.8000	0.2394	0.3383	-1.9000	-0.0667
-0.6000	0.3828	-2.1291	-1.8000	-0.1474
-0.4000	0.7527	2.1717	-1.7000	-0.1594
-0.2000	0.8227	-0.2337	-1.6000	-0.0357
0	0.8651	-1.1451	-1.5000	-0.2729
0.2000	0.9094	0.7907	-1.4000	-0.3510
0.4000	0.8522	2.8846	-1.3000	-0.1512
0.6000	0.5174	-0.1629	-1.2000	-0.2463
0.8000	0.2995	1.2449	-1.1000	-0.0858
1.0000	-0.1168	-3.0861	-1.0000	-0.0628
1.2000	-0.2020	-0.2473	-0.9000	0.1628
1.4000	-0.2425	0.9768	-0.8000	0.2892
1.6000	-0.3105	-1.4638	-0.7000	0.3475
1.8000	-0.2359	-2.1312	-0.6000	0.2991
2.0000	0.0931	3.3496	-0.5000	0.6499
2.2000	0.0862	0.2270	-0.4000	0.9161
2.4000	0.0616	-1.8873	-0.3000	0.9602
2.6000	0.1970	2.0950	-0.2000	0.7774
2.8000	0.0900	0.7937	-0.1000	0.9758
3.0000	-0.0990	-2.1995	0	0.9318
			0.1000	0.8812
			0.2000	0.8121
			0.3000	0.8873
			0.4000	0.7139
			0.5000	0.6422
			0.6000	0.4678
			0.7000	0.3214
			0.8000	0.2710
			0.9000	0.1821
			1.0000	0.2112
			1.1000	-0.2252
			1.2000	-0.2582
			1.3000	-0.0943
			1.4000	-0.2552
			1.5000	-0.3503
			1.6000	-0.1577
			1.7000	0.0038
			1.8000	-0.0332
			1.9000	0.1440
			2.0000	0.0505
			2.1000	0.2333
			2.2000	0.0511
			2.3000	-0.0020
			2.4000	0.1050
			2.5000	0.2463
			2.6000	0.0048
			2.7000	0.1589
			2.8000	0.0067
			2.9000	0.0890
			3.0000	-0.1100

Figure 6. A simple regression problem is solved by LS-SVM. The solid line indicates the estimated output. The dotted line represents the true underline function. The star indicates the support vectors for the above line fit.

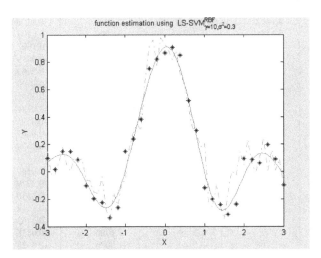

Table 5. The best prediction accuracy of SVM, BPN, MDA, and Logit (hit ratio: %)

	SVM	BNN	MDA	Logit
Training data	88.0132	85.2474	78.8079	79.8676
Holdout data	83.0688	82.5397	79.1391	78.3069

for SVM. They propose data dependent solutions for kernel and its parameter selection.

Each dataset can be described by simple, distance, and distribution-based statistical measures. They explained $X_{k,j}^i$ to be the value of the jth variable (column) in the kth example (row) of dataset i. These three types of measures characterise the dataset matrix in different ways. First, the simple classical statistical measures identify the data characteristics based on variable-to-variable comparisons (i.e., comparisons between columns of the dataset). Then, the distance-based measures identify the data characteristics based on sample-to-sample comparisons (i.e., between rows of the dataset). Finally, the density-based measures consider the relationships between single data points and the statistical properties of the entire data matrix to identify the datasets characteristics. The simple statistical measures are calculated within each column, and then averaged over all columns to obtain global measures of the dataset. Likewise, the distance measures are averaged over all pairwise comparisons, and the density-based measures are averaged across the entire matrix.

For each dataset *i,* a total of 29 measures are calculated (11 statistical, 3 distance-based, and 15 density-based). The dataset characteristics matrix is then assembled with the columns comprising the 29 measures, and the rows comprising the 112 datasets. Finally, by combining the dataset characteristics with the experimental results they generated rules with the help of decision tree algorithm C5.0 (Quinlan, 1993) for automatic kernel and its parameter selection.

This is not a state-way solution for automatic kernel and its parameter selection. More research is required for an optimal solution for SVM parameter selection. The new research can bring SVM into a fully more efficient automated system for predictions. SVM has a wide spectrum of applications including search engines, medical diagnosis, bioinformatics and cheminformatics, detecting credit card fraud, stock market analysis, market promotion identification, classifying DNA sequences, speech and handwriting recognition, object recognition in computer vision, game playing, and robot locomotion. For more information, please visit http://www.clopinet.com/isabelle/Projects/SVM/applist.html. There are a number of complex problems in medical sciences, which are really hard to carry out the acceptable solutions. For instance, the tumor node and metastasis (TNM) classification is an internationally agreed benchmark for assessing cancer severity, treatment options, and prognostic outcomes of patients with cancer. The TNM benchmark method has been used for over 50 years with various revisions made by American Joint Committee on Cancer (AJCC) (Burke, 2004). The TNM classification is derived mainly from two major sources: clinical, includes examination, imaging, endoscopy, biopsy, and surgical exploration, and pathological resection or biopsy of the primary tumor (Gospodarowicz, Miller, Groome, Greene, Logan, & Sobin, 2003). However, Burke (2004) raises concerns on the current ability of predicting survival rate using TNM classification. For instances, the five year disease-specific survival for newly diagnosed cancer patient is predicted to be the same as the mean survival of all those patients who are diagnosed with cancer before five years. Further, the TNM classification system is also unable to provide information regarding a natural history of the cancer progression, for instances, what happens after a certain period of time such spread, recurrence, or metastasis of a primary tumor.

CONCLUSION

The material covered in this chapter is an elaborate explanation of the SVM theory. SVMs have been formulated for supervised classification (both binary and multi-class) and regression. For simplicity, we demonstrated a binary classification scenario with a well known XOR problem. In the regression section we just used synthetic data to demonstrate how SVM regression methodology works. Both demonstrations made it easy to understand SVM. Moreover, the basic explanation of SVM classification included hyperplane construction procedure and the heart of SVM kernel activity. It is easily explained that, when it is possible to linearly separate two classes, an optimum separating hyperplane can be found by minimising the squared norm of the separating hyperplane. The minimisation has been done by QP problem, in which the training data are represented as a matrix of inner products between feature vectors. Once the optimum separating hyperplane is found, the machine opens the support vector points at the same time and the solution is an expansion on these points only. Other data points may be ignored for SVM prediction. There have been many benefits of the SVM method. The solution to the optimisation problem is a global minimum, whereas other machine learning methods, such as neural networks, can often terminate in local minima, therefore there is a chance of modelling the training data inaccurately. The SVM solution is an expansion on a subset of the original training data, resulting in a sparser model and comparatively less computation time required for subsequent classification. Finally, SVM always minimises the expected generalisation error, rather than just the empirical error, on the training data. The kernel method and the empirical risk analysis made SVM more attractive in the different research community. Thus, it can be proven that SVMs should generalise better than many of their counterparts. Some challenges of SVM have been explained with sufficient help text towards the end of this chapter. Therefore this research could be very useful for an efficient machine learning-based system analysis and design.

REFERENCES

Ali, S. (2005). *Automated support vector learning algorithms*. Unpublished doctoral thesis, Monash University, Australia.

Ali, S., & Smith, K. A. (in press). Automatic kernel selection for support vector machine. *Neurocomputing*. Elsevier Science.

Ali, S., & Smith, K. A. (in press). On optimal degree selection for polynomial kernel with support vector machines: Theoretical and empirical investigations. *International Journal of Knowledge-Based and Intelligent Engineering Systems*.

Ali, S., & Smith, K. A. (2005). Kernel width selection for SVM classification: A meta-learning approach. *International Journal of Data Warehousing and Mining*, 78-97. Hershey, PA: Idea Group.

Ayat, N. E., Cheriet, M., Remaki, L., & Suen, C. Y. (2001). KMOD: A new support vector machine kernel with moderate decreasing for pattern recognition. Application to digit image recognition. In *Proceedings of the 6th International Conference on Document Analysis and Recognition* (pp. 1215-1219).

Baudat, G., & Anouar, F. (2000). Generalized discriminant analysis using a kernel approach. *Neural Computation*, *12*(10), 2385-2404.

Bennett, K., Momma, M., & Embrechts, J. (2002). MARK: A boosting algorithm for heterogeneous kernel models. In *Proceedings of the SIGKDD International Conference on Knowledge Discovery and Data Mining*, Canada.

Boser, B. E., Guyon, I., & Vapnik, V. N. (1992). A training algorithm for optimal margin classifiers. In *Proceedings of the 5th Annual Workshop of Computational Learning Theory* (Vol. 5, pp. 144-152). Pittsburgh: ACM Press.

Burke, H. (2004). Outcome prediction and the future of the TNM staging system. *Journal of the National Cancer Institute, 96*(19), 1408-1409.

Chapelle, O., Vapnik, V., Bousquet, O., & Mukherjee, S. (2002). Choosing multiple parameters for support vector machines. *Machine Learning, 46*(1), 31-159.

Chen, B. J., Chang, M. W., & Lin, C. J. (2001). *Load forecasting using support vector machines: A study on EUNITE Competition 2001. Report for EUNITE competition for Smart Adaptive System.* Retrieved April 3, 2008, from http://www.eunite.org

Chih-Wei, H., & Chih-Jen, L. (2002). A comparison of methods for multiclass support vector machines, *IEEE Transactions on Neural Networks, 13*(2), 415-425.

Cortes, C., & Vapnik, V. (1995). Support vector networks. *Machine Learning, 20*, 273-297.

Crammer, K., & Singer, Y. (2001). On the algorithmic implementation of multiclass kernel-based vector machines. *Journal of Machine Learning Research, 2*, 265-292.

Ding, A., Zhao, X., & Jiao, L. (2003). *Traffic flow time series prediction based on statistics learning theory.* Paper presented at the IEEE 5th International Conference on Intelligent Transportation Systems (pp. 727-730).

Duda, R. O., Hart, P. E., & Stork, D. G. (2001). *Pattern classification*. John Wiley & Sons, Inc.

Evgeniou, T., Pontil, M., & Poggio, T. (2000). Regularization networks and support vector machines. *Advances in Computational Mathematics, 13*(1), 1-50.

Friedman, J. (1996). *Another approach to polychotomous classification* (Tech. Rep.). Stanford University Department of Statistics, Stanford, CA.

Gospodarowicz, M. K., Miller, D., Groome, P. A., Greene, F. G., Logan, P. A., & Sobin, L. H. (2003). The process of continuous improvement of the TNM classification. *American Cancer Society*, 1-5.

Gunn, S. R. (1998). *Support vector machine for classification and regression* (Tech. Rep.) University of Shouthampton, UK.

Haasdonk, B., & Keysers, D. (2002). Tangent distance kernels for support vector machines. In *IEEE Proceedings of the 16th International Conference on Pattern Recognition* (Vol. 2, pp. 864-868).

Kreßel, U. (1999). Pairwise classification and support vector machines. In B. Schölkopf et al., (Eds.), *Advances in kernel methods-support vector learning* (pp. 255-268). Cambridge: MIT Press.

Matterra, D., & Haykin, S. (1999). Support vector machines for dynamic reconstruction of a chaotic system. In B. Schölkopf, C. J. C. Burges, & A. J. Smola (Eds.), *Advances in kernel methods* (pp. 211-241). MIT Press. ISBN 0-262-19416-3.

McLachlan, G. (1992). *Discriminate analysis and statistical pattern recognition*. New York: John Wiley and Sons, Inc.

Mercer, J. (1909). Functions of positive and negative type and their connection with the theory of integral equations. *Philos. Trans. Roy. Soc. London, A*(209), 415-446.

Min, J. H., & Lee, Y.-C. (2005). Bankruptcy prediction using support vector machine with optimal choice of kernel function parameters. *Expert Systems with Applications, 28*(4), 603-614.

Navarrete, P., & Ruiz-del-Solar, J. (2003). Kernel-based face recognition by a reformulation of kernel machines. In J. Benitez & F. Hoffmann (Eds.), *Advances in soft computing: Engineering, design and manufacturing* (pp. 183-196). Springer-Verlag.

Platt, J. C., Cristianini, N., & Shawe-Taylor, J. (2000). Large margin DAG's for multiclass classification. *Advances in Neural Information Processing Systems, 12*, 547-553. Cambridge: MIT Press.

Quinlan, R. (1993). *C4.5: Programs for machine learning*. San Mateo, CA: Morgan Kaufman Publishers.

Schölkopf, B., Burges, C., & Vapnik, V. (1995). Extracting support data for a given task. In *Proceedings of the 1st International Conference on Knowledge Discovery and Data Mining* (pp. 252-257). Menlo Park: AAAI Press.

Schölkopf, B., Mika, S., Burges, C. J. C., Knirsch, P., Müller, K.-R., Rätsch, G., et al. (1999). Input space versus feature space in kernel based methods. *IEEE Transaction on Neural Networks, 10*, 1000-1017.

Schölkopf, B., Platt, J., Shawe-Taylor, J., Smola, A. J., & Williamson, R. C. (2001). Estimating the support of a high-dimensional distribution. *Neural Computation, 13*(7), 1443-1472.

Schölkopf, B., & Smola, A. (2000). *Kernel machines*. Retrieved April 3, 2008, from http://www.kernel-machines.org

Siolas, G., & d'Alche-Buc, F. (2000). Support vector machines based on a semantic kernel for text categorization. In *IEEE-INNS-ENNS Proceedings of International Joint Conference on Neural Networks* (Vol. 5, pp. 205-209).

Smith, K. A. (1999). *Introduction to neural networks and data mining for business applications*. Australia: Eruditions Publishing.

Smola, A., & Schölkopf, B. (1998). *A tutorial on support vector regression* (Tech. Rep.). Neuro-COLT2.

Stitson, M., Gammerman, A., Vapnik, V. N., Vovk, V., Watkins, C., & Weston, J. (1997). *Support vector regression with ANOVA decomposition kernels* (Tech. Rep. CSD-97-22). University of London, Royal Holloway.

Strauss, D. J., Delb, W., Plinkert, P. K., & Jens, J. (2003). Hybrid wavelet-kernel based classifiers and novelty detectors in biosignal processing. In *IEEE Proceedings of the 25th Annual International Conference of the Engineering in Medicine and Biology Society* (Vol. 3, pp. 2865- 2868).

Suykens, J. A. K., Gestel, T.V., Brabanter, J. D., Moor, B. D., & Vandewalle, J. (2002). *Least squares support vector machines*. Singapore: World Scientific. ISBN 981-238-151-1.

Vapnik, V. (1995). *The nature of statistical learning theory* (1st ed.). New York: Springer-Verlag.

Vapnik, V. (1998). *Statistical learning theory.* John Wiley and Sons.

Vapnik, V. N. (1999). An overview of statistical learning theory. *IEEE Transaction on Neural Networks, 10*(5), 988-999.

Vapnik, V. (2000). *The nature of statistical learning theory* (2nd ed.). New York: Springer-Verlag.

Weston, J. A. E. (1999). *Extensions to the support vector machine.* Unpublished doctoral thesis, University of London, Royal Holloway, England.

Weston, J., & Watkins, C. (1999). Multi-class support vector machines. In M. Verleysen (Ed.), *Proceedings of the 7th European Symposium on Artificial Neural Networks.* Belgium: Bruges.

Yang, H., Chan, L., & King, I. (2002). Support vector machine regression for volatile stock market prediction. In *Proceedings of the Third International Conference on Intelligent Data Engineering and Automated Learning* (Vol. 2412, pp. 391-396). Springer

Zhang, L., Zhou, W., & Jiao, L. (2004). Wavelet support vector machine. *IEEE Transactions on Systems, Man and Cybernetics, 34*(1), 34-39.

Zhao, X., & Kuh, A. (2002). Adaptive kernel least square support vector machines applied to recover DS-CDMA signals. In *IEEE Proceedings of the 36th Asilomar Conference on Signals, Systems and Computers* (Vol. 1, pp. 943-947).

Zien, A., Rätsch, G., Mika, S., Schölkopf, B., Lengauer, T., & Müller, K.-R. (2000). Engineering support vector machine kernels that recognize translation initiation sites in DNA. *Bioinformatics, 16,* 799-807.

KEY TERMS

Classification: This is a task of a machine learning algorithm, which labels training data into a finite number of output classes. A model that classifies training examples is sometimes referred to as a classifier. Generally a classifier's performance is measured by its ability to correctly label unseen test cases with *accuracy.* The alternative name of accuracy is called *error rate.*

Data Mining: The applied branch of machine learning that can automatically detect the trends and associations of data, which are always hidden in the data base. This hidden information is useful in making an expert decision.

Kernel: It is the heart of SVM, which is used to transform the data. After kernel transformation, nonlinear data always become a linear shape. Then, it is easy to learn the data for the SVM method.

Neural Network: It is a well established machine learning method. Neural network is a complex nonlinear modeling technique based on a model of a human neuron. It is a useful learning method for classification as well as regression tasks.

Optimisation: Optimisation is a mathematical method that always offers a best, or optimal, solution for a model.

Polynomial Kernel: This is one of the classical kernels adopted in SVM methodology. This kernel follows the polynomial transformation rule during the kernel feature space construction.

RBF Kernel: One of the popular classical kernel in SVM. The RBF kernel nonlinearly maps the example into a higher dimensional space so it can handle the example better when the relation between class labels and attributes is nonlinear.

Regression: As like classification, regression is another popular applied branch of machine learning. The prediction of regression is always a continuous value. A model or algorithm that estimates a continuous value is sometimes referred to as a regressor. Generally a regressor's performance is measured by its ability to predict a value that is near to the actual value, such as with a correlation coefficient.

Supervised Learning: Machine learning techniques used to learn the relationship between independent attributes and a dependent attribute. Most popular learning algorithms fall into the supervised learning category.

SVM: Support vector machine (SVM) is a statistical-based learning algorithm that has been widely used by researchers in various fields including business, text categorisation, pattern recognition, to protein function prediction. Recently researches added a new dimension for SVM in the cancer classification ability to deal with high dimensional data. Moreover, SVM can handle any classification, clustering, regression, and even novelty detection problems.

Section VII
Medical Applications

Chapter XXIX
Hybrid Data Mining for Medical Applications

Syed Zahid Hassan
Central Queensland University, Australia

Brijesh Verma
Central Queensland University, Australia

ABSTRACT

This chapter focuses on hybrid data mining algorithms and their use in medical applications. It reviews existing data mining algorithms and presents a novel hybrid data mining approach, which takes advantage of intelligent and statistical modeling of data mining algorithms to extract meaningful patterns from medical data repositories. Various hybrid combinations of data mining algorithms are formulated and tested on a benchmark medical database. The chapter includes the experimental results with existing and new hybrid approaches to demonstrate the superiority of hybrid data mining algorithms over standard algorithms.

INTRODUCTION

In the last few decades, medical disciplines have become increasingly data-intensive. The advances in digital technology have led to an unprecedented growth in the size, complexity, and quantity of collected data, that is, medical reports and associated images. According to Damien McAullay (Damien, Graham, Jie, & Huidong, 2005), "there are 5.7 million hospitals admissions, 210 million doctor's visits, and a similar number of prescribed medicines dispensed in Australia annually" (p. 381). All records are captured electronically. There are billions of healthcare records transaction that occur world wide every year.

On the other hand, patient-centered medical applications (e.g., electronic patient records, personal health record, electronic medical records, etc.) are also on the verge of becoming practical, further increasing data growth and leading to a data-rich but information-poor healthcare system. Thus, it has become crucial for data mining researchers to investigate and propose a novel approach that can appropriately utilize such valuable data to provide useful evidence as a basis for future medical practice. The paramount important factor is to utilize the collected data that suit specific and useful purposes which leads to enable the discovery of new "knowledge" that provides insights to assists healthcare analyst and policy makers to make strategic decisions and predict future consequences by taking into account the actual outcomes of current operative values.

In addition, the world health organization (Gulbinat, 1997) identifies some possible needs for the discovery of knowledge from medical data repositories; this includes, but is not limited to, medical diagnosis and prognosis, patient health planning and development, healthcare system monitoring and evaluation, health planning and resource allocation, hospital and health services management, epidemiological and clinical research, and disease prevention.

Lately, this abundance of healthcare data has resulted in a large number of concerted efforts to inductively discover "useful" knowledge from the collected data, and indeed interesting results have been reported by many researchers. However, despite the noted efficacy of the knowledge discovery method—known as data mining (DM) algorithm—the challenge facing healthcare practitioners today is about data usability and impact, that is, the use of "appropriate" data mining algorithms with the right data to discover value-added "action-oriented" knowledge in terms of data-mediated decision-support services.

Notably, recent advances in data mining algorithms such as neural networks (NN), statistical modeling, evolutionary algorithms, and visualization tools have made it possible to transform any kind of raw data into high level knowledge. However, the main problem is that each method has its own approach to deal with data structure, shape, and validity. This limitation affects the performance of classification systems. Consequently, the need of a hybrid data mining approach is widely recognized by the data mining community (George, & Derek, 2004, p. 151). The number of hybrid data mining endeavours has been initiated all over the globe. The limitations associated with many existing hybrid approaches are: (1) most of the existing approaches either heavily dependant on intelligent methods or statistical methods, barely ensembled to take the

advantage of both computations, that is, intelligent and statistical; and most importantly (2), existing approaches generally do not utilize the data for "secondary purposes," such as organisation planning, decision making, forecasting, outcomes and trending, and so forth.

To this end, we argue that there is a need for a hybrid DM approach which is an effective combination of various DM techniques, in order to utilize the strengths of each individual technique and compensate for each other's weaknesses. The aim of this chapter is to present current state-of-art data mining algorithms and their applications and propose a new hybrid data mining approach for clustering and classification of medical data. This chapter aims to further explore the data mining intelligent and statistical machine learning techniques, including supervised and unsupervised learning techniques as well as some effective conventional techniques and systems commonly used in the medical domain.

REVIEW OF EXISTING DATA MINING ALGORITHMS

In this section we discuss the theoretical and technical aspects of data mining and machine learning techniques, data mining algorithms, hybrid approaches, and their applications in medical domain.

Data Mining and Machine Learning

There is some confusion about the terms data mining and knowledge discovery in databases (KDD). Often these two terms are used interchangeably (Fayyad, Piatetsky-Shapiro, Smyth, & Uthurusamy, 1997, p. 154). The term KDD can be denoted to overall process of turning low-level data into high-level knowledge, whereas data mining can be defined as the extraction of useful patterns from the raw data.

The data mining step usually takes a small part of overall KDD process. More specifically, data mining is not a single technique; it deploys various machine learning algorithms and any technique that can help to procure information out of the massive data is useful. Different algorithms serve different purposes; each algorithm offers its own advantages and disadvantages. However, the most commonly used methods for data mining are based on neural networks, decision trees, a-priori, regressions, k-means, Bayesian networks, and so forth.

Before analyzing which machine learning (ML) technique works best for which problem domain and situations, it is important to have a good understanding of what machine learning is all about. ML is one of the disciplines of the AI research that deploys a variety of probability, statistical, and optimizations tools to learn from past data/examples and use that prior learning to classify new data and identify new trends in data (Fayyad et al., 1997, p. 154). Beside heavily dependent on statistics, ML techniques also employ Boolean logic (AND, OR, NOT), absolute conditional (IF, THEN, ELSE), conditional probabilities (the probability of X given Y), and unconventional optimization strategies to model data or classify patterns. This provides ML with inference and decision making capabilities which cannot be achieved by using conventional statistical methods.

There are generally three types of machine learning techniques (Fayyad et al., 1997): 1) supervised learning, 2) unsupervised learning, and 3) reinforcement learning. In supervised learning, a ML algorithm is provided with a labeled set of training data/example. These labeled data assist the algorithm to map the input data with the desired output data. In unsupervised learning, a ML algorithm is provided with set of training data/example only (without classes) and leaves the algorithm to learn and discover the similar patterns. Reinforcement learning (RL) is learning from interaction with an environment, from the consequence of actions, rather than from explicit supervision.

ML algorithms have been incorporated in DM systems for knowledge discovery and decision-making purposes. The choice and success of any

particular algorithm is heavily dependent on the good understanding of the problem domain, quality of data sets, and the properly designed experiments. However, not all ML algorithms are created equal, some are better for certain kinds of problems while others are better for other kind of problems. Thus, it is always recommended to try more than one ML algorithm on any given training set. A common problem associated with the failure of any ML algorithm is called "curse of dimensionality" (Fayyad et al., 1997), which occurs when too many variables and too few data sets are used to train the algorithm. A general rule is to reduce the number of variables (features) and increase the number of training samples. The sample-per-feature ratio should always exceed 5:1 (Fayyad et al., 1997). Over training is also an important issue as over trained algorithm tends to produce ambiguous classification (poor results).

Data Mining Tasks

The overall data mining process can roughly be classified into five mains tasks (Fayyad, & Shapiro, 1996): clustering, classification, association, prediction, and visualization.

Given a set of data items, the clustering algorithms partition this set into a set of classes such that items with similar characteristics are grouped together. Clustering is best suited for finding groups of items that are similar in properties. For example, a doctor chain could mine patient diagnostic data to determine how often the patient has been smoking cigarettes and what treatment should be given to the patient.

Given a set of predefined classes, classifier algorithms determine to which of these classes a specific data item belongs to. For example, given classes of patients that correspond to medical treatment responses, the algorithms identify the form of treatment to which a new patient is most likely to respond.

Given a set of data items, the association algorithms identify relationships between attributes and items such that the presence of one pattern implies the presence of another pattern. These relations may be associations between attributes within the same data item (e.g., out of the patients who has heart problem, 90% also has cholesterol disease) or associations between different data items (e.g., every time a certain budget drops 5%, a certain other budget raises 13% between 6 and 12 months later). One may discover the set of symptoms often occurring together with certain kinds of diseases and this can lead to further study on the reason behinds them.

Given a data item and a predictive model, the prediction algorithms predict the value for a specific attribute of the data item. For example, patient billing information can be predicted by the length of the patient stay in the hospital and treatment provided to the patient or vice versa. Prediction can also be used to validate a discovered hypothesis.

The visualization model plays an important role in making the discovered knowledge understandable by humans. The visualization techniques may range from simple scatter plots to histogram plots over parallel to two dimension coordinates. DM algorithm can be coupled with a visualization tool that aids users in understanding the discovered knowledge. These coupling of DM algorithms and visualization algorithms provides added value. For instance, the result of the neural network classifier can be displayed using a network visualizer. A simple decision tree model can be displayed and manipulated using a tree visualizer.

Intelligent (Neural Network-Based) Data Mining Algorithms

The intelligent data mining algorithms based on neural networks, also known as symbolic machine learning techniques, provide a different approach of data analysis and knowledge discovery from pure statistical methods. These algorithms, which are different in computation and behaviors, have shown promising capabilities for analyzing qualitative, symbolic, quantitative, and numeric data.

The most commonly used intelligent data mining algorithms are discussed below with their strengths and limitations.

Data Mining Using Back Propagation Neural Network (BPNN)

Early development of neural networks gathered prominent attraction in the past decade (Maria-Luiza, Zaïane, & Coman, 2001, p. 94). Neural networks were originally designed to model the way the brain works with multiple neurons being interconnected to each other through multiple axon junctions. Neural networks use multiple layers (i.e., input, hidden, and output layers) to process their inputs and generate outputs. The inputs can be continuous/discrete, numerical/categorical values. The information learned by a neural network is stored in the form of a weight matrix (Andreeva, Dimitrova, & Radeva, 2004, p. 148). The information stored inside the weights consists of real-valued numbers and therefore neural network computing can be classified as a symbolic type of processing. The various types of neural networks such as feed forward, multilayer perceptron, and so forth have been proposed. The neural networks based on back propagation algorithm are the most popular and widely used neural networks for their unique learning capability (Michael, Patrick, Kamal, & David, 1994, p. 106). Back propagation neural networks are fully connected, layered, feed-forward models. Activations flow from the input layer through the hidden layer, then to the output layer.

The strength of back propagation neural networks for data mining lies on its ability to perform a range of statistical (i.e., linear, logistic, and non-linear regression) and logical operations or inferences (i.e., AND, OR, XOR, NOT, IF-THEN) as part of the classification process. Other dominant strengths of NN include (Michael et al., 1994, p. 106): they are capable of handling a wide range of classification or pattern recognition problems and they represent compact knowledge in the form of weights and threshold values. They can also operate with noisy or missing data and can generalize quite well to similar unseen data.

The main challenge in using neural networks is its input-output mapping, that is, how the real-world input/output (for instance image, a physical characteristic, a list of medical problems, and a prognosis) can be mapped to a numeric vector. There are other common limitations (Michael et al., 1994, p. 106). They are considered as a "black-box" technology; the network structure can only be determined by experimentation which requires lengthy training times and may not necessarily reach to an optimal solution. The use of random weights initializations may lead to unwanted solutions. Neural network topology design is empirical, and that several attempts to develop an acceptable model may be necessary. NN have limited explanation facility which may prevent their use in certain applications. They are also difficult to understand as comprising of complex structure. Moreover, too many attributes can result in over fitting.

Some of the applications of BPNN with their performances in medical domain are listed in Chart 1.

Data Mining Using Self Organization Map (SOM)

SOM is an unsupervised learning algorithm which includes such methods as self-organizing feature maps (SOFMs), hierarchical clustering, and k-means data mining algorithms to create clusters from raw, unlabeled, or unclassified data (Thiemjarus, Lo, Laerhoven, & Yang, 2004, p. 52). These clusters

can be used later to develop classification schemes or classifiers.

SOM is generally used to represent (visualize) high-dimensional unsupervised data (feature space) into low-dimensional data (feature space), yet preserving the graphical properties of the input patterns. In SOM, each input unit is connected to the each output (in a feed forward manner) through weight values. A SOM begins with a set of input units (neurons), random weights matrix, nearest neighborhood radius, output units, and map dimension (width and heights). The patterns are presented to each input nodes and are calculated (generally using Euclidean distance) with the weighted values of the output unit. The output node whose weights vector closest to the input pattern is considered as the winner (Husin-Chuan, Ching-Hsue, & Jing-Rong, 2007, p. 499). When this node wins a competition, all the output units who fall in the region of defined neighborhood radius are considered as the neighbors of the wining unit. The entire neighbors unit modifies their weight with respect to wining unit weights values to form a cluster. The process repeats for each input pattern for a large number of repetitions until the SOM is capable of associating output nodes with specific groups or patterns in the input data set.

There are major advantages of SOM (Sakthiaseelan, Cheah, & Selvakumar, 2005, p. 336). They are very simple in operation and easy to understand. They not only classify data accurately but are also easy to evaluate and analyze how good the maps are and how strong the similarities among the features. The basic limitation associated with SOM is getting

Chart 1. The performance of BPNN in medical domain

Reference	Application	Performance
BPNN (Maria-Luiza, Zaïane, & Coman, 2001)	Tumor Detection	81% Accuracy
BPNN (Andreeva, Dimitrova, & Radeva, 2004)	Breast Cancer	97.89% Accuracy
BPNN (Michael, Patrick, Kamal, & David, 1994)	Breast Cancer	74% Accuracy

the right data, that is, a value for each feature from the training set is required in order to generate a map. Sometimes this problem leads towards highly misclassified data; this problem is also referred as missing data.

Some of the applications of self-organizing map with their performances in medical domain are listed in Chart 2.

Statistical Data Mining Algorithms

A number of statistical data mining algorithms has been developed and used in solving many real world data mining problems. These algorithms are used to examine quantitative data for the purposes of classification, clustering/association, hypothesis testing, trend analysis, and correlation between variables. These analysis techniques often rely on probabilistic assumptions and conditions, and complex mathematical functions. In the following subsections we provide an overview of some of the existing, yet advanced and widely used, data mining algorithms in detail.

Support Vector Machine (SVM)

A SVM is somewhat a new emerging machine learning technique and received prominent attention in the recent years (Zheng & Kazunobu, 2006, p. 389). They use supervised learning techniques for the classification and regression problems. The SVM algorithm creates a hyperplane, which is a subset of the points of the two classes, which is referred to as a support vector. This hyperplane separates the data into two classes with the maximum geometry margin, meaning that the distance between the hyperplane and the closest data sample is maximized; this helps to minimize the empirical classification errors. SVMs can be used to perform nonlinear classification using what is called a nonlinear kernel. A nonlinear kernel is a mathematical function that transforms the data from a linear feature space to a nonlinear feature space. Like NNs, a SVM can be used in a wide range of pattern recognition and classification problems, spanning from handwriting analysis, speech and text recognition, and protein function prediction to medical diagnosis problem (Zheng, & Kazunobu, 2006, p. 389).

The benefits of a SVM include (Zheng, & Kazunobu, 2006, p. 389) the models' nonlinear class boundaries, computational complexity reduced to quadratic optimization problem, over fitting is unlikely to occur, and easy to control complexity of decision rule and frequency of error. On the other hand, the major limitations associated with a SVM include: training is slow compared to Bayes classifier and decision trees, it is difficult to determine optimal parameters when training data are not linearly separable, and the difficult to understand structure of an algorithm.

Some of the applications of support vector machine with their performances in medical domain are listed below.

Decision Trees (DT)

Decision tree is a special form of tree structure (flow chart or graphical diagram) that is generated

Chart 2. The performance of SOM in medical domain

Reference	Application	Performance
SOM (Thiemjarus, Lo, Laerhoven, & Yang, 2004)	Body Sensor Network	71-88% Accuracy
SOM (Husin-Chuan, Ching-Hsue, & Jing-Rong, 2007)	Cardiovascular Disease	98% Accuracy
SOM (Sakthiaseelan, Cheah, & Selvakumar, 2005)	Breast Cancer	98.89% Accuracy

by a classifier system in order to evaluate associated patterns (Lim, Loh, & Shih, 1997). The tree is structured in a way that represents sequence of problems or tasks. The solution associated to each problem is represented along the path down the tree, whereby the root of the tree determines the classification or prediction made by the classifier. The tree can be used to represent all sorts of complex problems and patterns relation in the data sets. The decision trees can either be designed through consultation with experts or can automatically be generated by providing labeled data sets (Lim et al., 1997). A decision tree generally learns by randomly splitting the data into subsets based on a numerical or logical test. This process repeats in recursive manner until splitting stops and final classification is achieved.

The strengths of DTs are that they are simple to understand and interpret and require little data preparation (Lim et al., 1997). They can also deal with many kinds of data including numeric, nominal (named), and categorical data. DT-generated models are easy to learn and can be validated using various statistical tests. However, DTs do not generally perform as well as NN in more complex classification problems.

A disadvantage of this approach is that there will always be information loss, because a decision tree selects one specific attribute for partitioning at each stage with a single starting point. The decision tree can present one set of outcomes, but not more than one set, as there is a single starting point. Therefore, decision trees are suited for data sets where there is one clear attribute to start with. Small errors in a training data set can also lead to very complex decision trees.

The decision tree model can be designed by using various data mining analytical tools such as CHi-squared automatic interaction detector (CHAID), C4.5, ID3, and classification and regression trees (CART) (Lim et al., 1997). Bearing both classification and regression processing methods, CART is recognized as one of the most powerful approaches to design, test, and use advanced mathematically-based decision trees. The hierarchical representation of CART models also enable users to understand and interact with tree-based finding easily. The main advantage of CART over other above-mentioned models is that it offers superior speed and ease-of-use and automatically provides insight into data and produces highly accurate, intelligible predictive models. The application for a CART algorithm in designing a healthcare predictive model is ranging from healthcare to nursing domain, such as CART used as a technique to recognize critical situations derived from specific laboratory results, quality, and safety issues of healthcare delivery and identification of nursing diagnosis.

Some of the applications of decision trees with their performances in medical domain are listed in Chart 3.

k-Means

k-Means is an unsupervised machine learning algorithm that partitions the data based on maximum interclass distance and minimum intraclass distance among the data/object (Abidi & Hoe, 2002, p. 50). More specifically, a k-means algorithm clusters the data based on attributes into k partitions, where k is a predefined number of clusters (Abidi & Hoe, 2002, p. 50). The algorithm starts by portioning (either randomly or heuristically) the input points into k initial sets and then calculates the mean point of each set. It constructs a new partition by associating data-entities to one of the K clusters. Then the means are recalculated for the new clusters, for each data-record compares the distance-measure to each of the K cluster-centers and associates the record to the closest cluster. The algorithm is repeated until convergence is achieved, which is obtained when the mean points are no longer changed (Abidi & Hoe, 2002, p. 50).

A basic variation of the k-means algorithm are the "K-modes" algorithms (Derek, Alexey, Nadia, & Cunningham, 2004, p. 576), the choice of which variant should be used depends on the nature of data. If the distance function is defined based on

Chart 3. The performance of SVM in medical domain

Reference	Application	Performance
SVM (Andreeva, Dimitrova, & Radeva, 2004)	Breast Cancer	98.74% Accuracy
SVM (Andreeva, Dimitrova, & Radeva, 2004)	Diabetics	76.34% Accuracy
SVM (Zheng, & Kazunobu, 2006)	Brain Tumor	88-95% Accuracy

continuous data, the k-means algorithm is sufficient whereas for nominal distance function, the *k*-mode is a better choice.

There are advantages of using k-means (Derek et al., 2004, p. 576). It is the fastest clustering algorithm and consumes the least memory and the algorithm can be run several times to achieve the best clustering.

The main drawback of the algorithm is that it requires predefined information regarding the number of clusters (i.e., k) to be found prior to start processing (Derek et al., 2004, p. 576). If the data are not naturally clustered or the data size is quite large, the classification accuracy is always a question.

Some of the applications of K-means with their performances in medical domain are listed in Chart 4.

K-Nearest Neighbor (k-NN)

The working of K-NN is quite similar as SOM as the input patterns are mapped into multidimensional output feature space (Zeng, Tu, Liu, Huang, Pianfetti, Roth, et al., 2007, p. 424). This output space is partitioned into regions with respect to class labels of the data patterns. When new data

are presented for prediction, the distance (usually uses Euclidean distance) between K and similar records in the data set is found and the most similar neighbors are identified. The nearest neighbor method matches patterns between different samples of data with the given class. The class is identified as the nearest neighbor of *k* when it is predicted to be the class of the closest training sample (Zeng et al., 2007, p. 424).

In terms of strength, the algorithm is easy to implement, but it is computationally intensive, especially when the size of the training set grows. The main advantages of k-NN includes (Zeng et al., 2007, p. 424) fast classification of instances, it useful for nonlinear classification problems, it is robust with respect to irrelevant or novel attributes, it is tolerant of noisy instances or instances with missing attribute values, and it can be used for both regression and classification.

This method sometimes retains a small portion of the complete data sets to compare with the given class. This not only causes memory wastage but also sometimes leads to inaccuracies in the final result (Zeng et al., 2007, p. 424). The nearest neighbor approach is also more suited to numeric values rather than non-numeric data. The accuracy of the k-NN algorithm is also subject to the dimension/scale

Chart 4. The performance of k-Means in medical domain

Reference	Application	Performance
k-Means (Abidi & Hoe, 2002)	Breast Cancer	96.1% Accuracy
k-Means (Derek et al, 2004)	Diabetics	67.5 Accuracy
k-Means (Derek et al, 2004)	Thyroid	79% Accuracy

of the features and noisy or irrelevant features. Other limitations include (Zizhen & Walter, 2006, p. 11): it is slower to update a concept description neighbor and it makes the wrong assumption that instances with similar attributes will have similar classifications and attributes and will be equally relevant and too computationally complex as the number of attributes increases.

Some of the applications of k-NN with their performances in medical domain are listed in Chart 5.

Naive Bayes

The naive bayes (NB) is a probabilistic classifier (Langley, Iba, & Thompson, 1992, p. 223). The Bayes classifier greatly simplifies learning by assuming that features are independent to a given class. Although, independence is generally a poor assumption which often has no bearing in realities, hence, it is deliberately naive. However, in practice, naive Bayes often competes well with more sophisticated classifiers.

Bayes classifiers are based on probability models which can be derived by using Bayes theorem, maximum likehood method (for parameters estimations), or Bayesian inference (Langley et al., 1992, p. 223). In a supervised learning environment and depending on the nature of its probability model, a Bayes classifier can be trained very efficiently. Naive Bayes reaches its best performance in two opposite cases: completely independent features and functionally dependent features. Naive Bayes has its worst performance between these extremes. The

accuracy of naive Bayes is not directly correlated with the degree of feature dependencies measured as the class conditional mutual information between the features. Instead, a better predictor of naive Bayes accuracy is the amount of information about the class that is lost because of the independence assumption (Langley et al., 1992, p. 223).

There are some main advantages of the naive Bayes classifiers (Langley et al., 1992, p. 223). Their foundation is based on statistical modeling. They are easy to understand and are efficient training algorithms. The order of training instances has no effect on training which make them useful across multiple domains. In terms of limitations (Langley et al., 1992, p. 223), NB assumptions that are attributes are statistically independent and numeric attributes are distributed normally. In NB, redundant attributes and class frequencies can mislead classification and affect accuracy

Some of the applications of naive bayes with their performances in medical domain are listed Chart 6.

Hybrid Data Mining Systems

Various hybrid approaches have been proposed, implemented, and tested for different application domains (Dounias, 2003). Neural network and fuzzy logic-based hybrid models have been widely reported in the literature (Dounias, 2003). The model presented by Clarke and Wei (1998, p. 3384) focuses on an integration of the merits of neural and fuzzy approaches to build intelligent decision-making systems. It has the benefits of both "neural networks" like massive parallelism, robustness, and learning

Chart 5. The performance of K-NN in medical domain

Reference	Application	Performance
K-NN (Zeng et al, 2007)	Predicting Protein Structure	75.53% Accuracy
K-NN(Zizhen, et al, 2006)	Gene Function Prediction	52% Accuracy
K-NN (Rajkumar, Ognen, & Dong, 2005)	Audio-Video Emotion Recognition	95.57% Accuracy

in data-rich environments, and "fuzzy logic," which deals with the modeling of imprecise and qualitative knowledge in natural/linguistic terms as well as the transmission of uncertainty. This hybrid approach has shown a high rate of success when applied in various complex domains of medical applications. For example, Clark and Wei (1998, p. 3384) present a neural fuzzy approach to measure radiotracers in vivo. In this application, fuzzy logic is the core part of the system, which deals with the modeling of imprecise knowledge (image degradation) due to the photon scattering through the collimated gamma rays.

The neural networks and evolutionary algorithms (NN-EA) hybrid approach has also received prominent attention in the medical domain (Dounias, 2003). In general, EA is used to determine the NN weights and architecture. In most cases NN are tuned (not generated) by the EA, but there are also appreciation when NN are tuned as well as generated by EA. Hussein and Abbas (2002, p. 265), present an EA-NN hybrid approach to diagnose breast cancer, both benign and malignant. The other hybrid combination, fuzzy logic and genetic algorithms (FL-GA) has also been deployed successfully in various control engineering applications and complex optimisation problems. GA is used for solving fuzzy logical equations in medical diagnostic expert systems (Hussein & Abbas, 2002, p. 265).

The another interesting hybrid combination examined in the literature is a decision trees and fuzzy logic (DT-FL) combination, where fuzzy logic is used to model uncertainty and missing decision attributes before these attributes are subjected to decision trees for classification and diagnosis tasks (Jzau-Sheng, Kuo-Sheng, & Chi-Wu, 1996, p. 314). With regards to medical applications, this approach showed some great accuracy in diagnosing coronary stenosis and segmentation of multispectral magnetic resonance images (MRI) (Jzau-Sheng et al., 1996, p. 314). Some authors have also proposed the combination of decision trees and evolutionary algorithms (DT-EA). In this hybrid approach, decision trees are generally used to extract relevant features from large datasets whereas EA algorithms are used to generalize the data (Jzau-Sheng et al., 1996, p. 314). This approach overcomes the limitation of the EA which requires more time to process complex tasks. Pabitra and Sushmita (2001, p. 67) combine an evolutionary modular multilayer perceptron (MLP) with the ID3 decision tree algorithm for the staging of cervical cancer.

The hybridization of fuzzy decision tree (FDT) and neural network has also been investigated (Tsang, Wang, & Yeung, 2000, p. 601). With the induction of fuzzy decision trees, they happened to perform well and generate comprehensive results, but learning accuracy was not very good. A new hybrid methodology with neural networks-based FDT weights training was proposed by Tsang et al. (2000, p. 601), which lead to the development of hybrid intelligent systems with higher learning accuracy. This approach has been successfully tested on various databases and interesting results have been reported (Tsang et al., 2000, p. 601).

Chart 7 lists of some of the proposed hybrid approaches and their performances in medical diagnosis.

Chart 6. The performance of Naive Bayes in medical domain

Reference	Application	Performance
Naive Bayes (Andreeva et al., 2004)	Breast Cancer	97.05% Accuracy
Simple naive bayes (Andreeva et al., 2004)	Diabetics	79.95% Accuracy
Bayesian (Michael et al., 1994)	Breast Cancer	84% Accuracy

Chart 7. The performance of hybrid data mining in medical domain

Reference	Application	Performance
Neural-Fuzzy Combination (Wang, Palade, & Xu, 2006)	Leukemia Cancer	95.85 % Accuracy
Neural-Fuzzy Combination (Wang et al., 2006)	Lymphomia Cancer	95.65 % Accuracy
Neural Network Combination-Evolutionary Algorithm (Xin & Yong, 1996)	Diabetics	76.80 % Accuracy
Neural Network-Evolutionary Algorithm Combination (Xin & Yong, 1996)	Heart Disease	84.60 % Accuracy
Evolutionary Algorithm-Fuzzy Logic Combination (Xin & Yong, 1996)	Breast Cancer	94 % Accuracy
Decision Tree-Evolutionary Algorithm (Spela, Peter, Vili, Milan, Matej, & Milojka, 2000)	Metabolic Acidosis Classification	83.33 % Accuracy

PROPOSED HYBRID DATA MINING APPROACH

In this section, we present the architectural and functional overview of our proposed hybrid data mining methodology, as depicted in Figures 1 and 2. The proposed approach formulates a methodology whereby a number of data mining algorithms can be fused together to provide data mining decision-making services to healthcare practitioners. The concept of combining various clustering algorithms is an attempt to enhance the performance of learning classifiers.

Functionally, we implement a computer process comprising of two functionally distinct layers. Each layer comprises a number of modules; each module is responsible to perform certain tasks. Figure 1 shows the functional architecture and the workflow of the proposed methodology. The following sections explain the basic steps/phases involved in formulating the proposed approach.

Step 1: Procurement and Transformation of a Patient-Centered Data from Medical Repositories

We emphasized on the "context of data" stored in medical repositories. The word context can be defined as the extract definition of a concept and its parameters associated with it, such as measure value, the unit value, and the precision of measure. More specifically, this phase is responsible for (i) procurement of patient-centered data from distributed repositories, (ii) cleansing and transformation of legacy data into XML-based structured database, and (iii) creation of medical data warehouses:

i. This step involves the procurement of health data from multiple distributed data repositories such as electronic medical record (EMR), electronic patient record (EPR), and patient health record (PHR).

ii. The procured health record are next cleansed by way of removing undesirable information and transformed into a XML-structured database (intermediate database).

iii. Finally a data warehouse is created. The main reason for the creation of these data warehouses is that they are useful for quality improvement and decision making. Most importantly, it is also easier to query a data warehouse compare to electronic medical records because of its complex structure. The creation of these data warehouses is heavily dependant on the understanding of what constitutes medical data repositories. The features stored in EMR can be basic (e.g., text-based display of lab results) to a very advanced (e.g., dynamic graphs of lab trends). Different EMRs have different functionality domains and features. The main concern here is to identify what EMR features will be used in our domain to enable knowledge discovery.

When the data are preprocessed, they are fed into a data mining inductive learning unit, which is comprised of sets of machine learning algorithms (both intelligent and statistical), as shown in Figure 1. To elaborate it further, Figure 2 provides the detail overview and workflow of a data mining inductive learning unit.

Step2: Designing of a DM Inductive Learning Unit (ILU)

The proposed inductive learning unit deploys the variety of clustering algorithms, which varies in their methods of search and representation to ensure diversity in the errors of the learned models. The entire amount of medical data (i.e., data, text, and images features) is introduced to each clustering algorithm in the ILU. The soft clusters produced

by each algorithm are recorded, combined, and fused into MLP in both serial and parallel fashion, as depicted in Figures 3 and 4. The parallel fusion incorporates a multilayer perceptron for learning of soft clusters and classification into appropriate classes, as demonstrated in Figure 3. In the serial approach, we first monitor the individual classifier performance and then train each classifier with the classified patterns of other classifiers and note its affect on overall system performance. The deployed algorithms vary in their methods of search and representation, which ensures diversity in the errors of the learned models. More specifically, the two types of hybrid combinations are investigated in this chapter, that is, parallel hybrid data mining and serial hybrid data mining, whereby each hybrid combination consists of four parts: 1) input data, 2) hybrid clustering, 3) fusion of clusters, and 4) data visualization.

Input Data

The input data contain raw data as well as extracted features which are used as an input to the data mining algorithms. The input data are normalized between 0-1.

Figure 1. Demonstrates the functional overview of proposed methodology

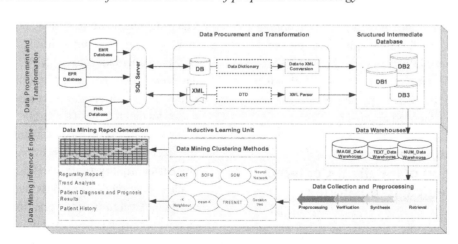

Figure 2. Work flow of data mining inductive learning unit

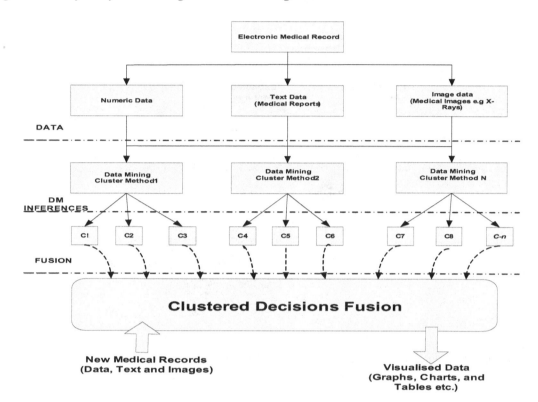

Data Mining Algorithms

Three data mining algorithms, that is, SOM, k-means, and naive Bayes have been combined in conjunction with multilayer perceptron. SOM is self-organizing, map-based on Kohonen neural network. SOM consisted of 16 neurons partitioned in a single layer in a 2-D grid of 4x4 neurons. We construed and assigned the random reference input vectors (neuron weights) to each partition. For each input, the Euclidean distance between the input and each neuron was calculated.

The reference vector with minimum distance is identified. After the most similar case is determined, all the neighbourhood neurons, connected with the same link, adjust their weights with respect to the reference vector to form a group in two dimensional grids. The whole process is repeated several times, decreasing the amount of learning rate to increase the reference vector, until the convergence is achieved. The SOM visualization offers the clear partition of data into discernable clusters.

In the k-means algorithm, we randomly partitioned the input data into k-cluster centers along with its all closest features. With each input feature, it calculates the mean point of each feature and constructs a new partition by associating data-entities to one of the k clusters. Cluster features are moved iteratively between k-clusters and intra and intercluster similarity. Distances are measured at each move. Features remained in the same cluster if they were closer to it, or they otherwise moved into a new cluster. The centers for each cluster are recalculated after every move. The convergence achieved when moving the object increases intracluster distances and decreases intercluster dissimilarity.

Figure 3. Parallel hybrid data mining approach

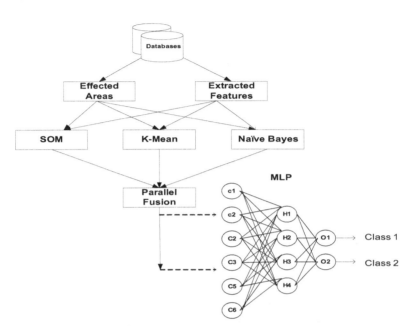

Figure 4. Serial hybrid data mining approach

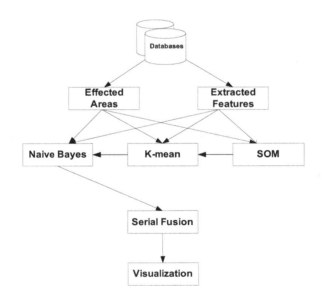

Naive Bayes clustering is based on probability distribution. It accepts raw data or features as input and creates soft clusters which are later combined with the results generated by other data mining algorithms and passed into the fusion module.

Data Fusion

The workings of a data fusion model can be understood by its fusion hypothesis, which assumes that the more similar data a cluster contains, the more reliable the cluster is for decision making. The outputs of data mining algorithms are combined using serial fusion and parallel fusion. The parallel fusion is based on a MLP as shown in Figure 3. A simple majority voting method is also used and compared with MLP.

Step 3: Data Visualization

This process involves the designing of a data mining visualization model, coupled with all data mining methods to generate the knowledge, which is derived by the data mining inference engine, in the form of charts, graphs, and maps. These coupling of DM algorithms and visualization algorithms provide added value. The visualization techniques may range from simple scatter plots to histogram plots over parallel to two dimensions coordinates.

IMPLEMENTATION AND EXPERIMENTAL RESULTS

The proposed data mining approach has been implemented in order to evaluate the performance and accuracy. The experiments were conducted on a benchmark dataset. The dataset and experimental results are described below.

Benchmark Database

The dataset of digital mammograms is used in this chapter and it is adopted from digital database for screening mammography (DDSM) established by University of South Florida. The main reason to choose DDSM for the experiment purposes is that it is a benchmark dataset so the final results can be compared with published results by other researchers. The DDSM database contains approximately 2,500 case studies, whereby each study includes two images of each breast, along with some associated patient information (ie., age at time of study, breast density rating, subtlety rating for abnormalities, and keyword description of abnormalities) and image information (e.g., scanner, spatial resolution, etc.). The database contains a mixture of normal, benign, benign without call-back, and cancer volumes selected and digitized. Images containing suspicious areas have associated pixel-level information about the locations and types of suspicious regions.

The dataset consists of six features (measurements) from 200 mammograms cases: 100 benign and 100 malignant. The features include patients' age, density, shape, margin, assessment rank, and subtlety.

Results and Discussion

The experimental results are presented below in Tables 1 and 2. From the comparative results shown in Table 1, it is observed that the proposed hybrid approach, a combination of statistical and intelligent techniques, provides better results than the stand alone individual technique. It is also noticed that the proposed approach outperforms all individual approaches in all main output categories (see Table 1), that is, classification accuracy, misclassification accuracy, and error rates. Out of the total of 100 digital mammogram cases of the test dataset, SOM made 12% misclassifications, k-means made 16% misclassifications, naive Bayes misclassified 10% cases, and proposed approach made 7.6923% misclassifications. This corresponds to classification accuracies achieved by SOM, K-means, naive Bayes, and the proposed approach, which are, 88%, 84%, 90% and 92.3%, respectively.

The experiments were also performed to compare the accuracies of algorithms by considering individual classes, both benign and malignant. For each class, the receiver operating characteristic (ROC) analysis attributes, such as true positive (TP) rate, false positive (FP) rate, and F-measure, are measured with particular algorithm as shown in Table 2. It is noticeable that the attributes frequency measures for both benign and malignant are quite high with the proposed hybrid approach.

We created a confusion matrix to evaluate individual classifier performance by displaying the correct and incorrect pattern classifications. Typical confusion matrix can be represented as:

Confusion Matrix
a   b <-------- Classified as
x1   x2 | a = Malignant

y1   y2 | b = Benign

Where row x1 and x2 represents the actual patterns and column x1 and y1 represents the classified patterns for class a (malignant). The difference between the actual patterns and the classified patterns can be used to determine the performance of a classifier. To explicate it further, we draw the confusion matrix for each classifier to evaluate how many patterns in a given class are classified correctly/incorrectly. Note the 200 mammogram cases were used, 200 cases for training purposes and 100 for testing purposes.

SOM Confusion Matrix
a   b <-------- Classified as
48   2 | a = Malignant

10   40 | b = Benign

This SOM classifier successfully classified 88 cases out of 100 cases presented. The row values (48, 2) are the actual cases for the class malignant, and row values (10, 40) represent the actual class benign. However, the classified outputs are represented by column a (48, 10) and column b (2, 40). The comparison of these rows and columns, between actual pattern and classified patterns, can provide interesting insights. For instance, for the malignant class accuracy, we notice that the original malignant patterns were (48, 2) and the classifier indicates (48, 10). Thus, it classified 48% cases correctly as a malignant class and misclassified 2 cases. It is also noticeable that those two patients will be cleared when they were supposed to be treated like a cancer patients. Similarly, for the benign class accuracy, the actual cases are (10, 40) whereas the classifier indicates (2, 40). The 40% cases were classified correctly as a class benign and 10% cases were misclassified. In this scenario, those 10 patients who are not the victim of cancers will

Table 1. Results showing the improvement in classification accuracies

Algorithms	Classification Error [%]	Root Mean Square Error	Classification Accuracy [%]
SOM	12	0.2777	88
k-Means	16	0.2433	84
Naive Bayes	10	0.3022	90
Proposed Parallel Hybrid Approach	7.6	0.2572	92.3

Table 2. Detailed accuracy by classes

	Classes	TP Rate	FP Rate	F-Measure
Individual Algorithms	Benign (SOM)	0.8	0.04	0.87
	Malignant (SOM)	0.96	0.2	0.889
	Benign (Naïve Bayes)	0.94	0.14	0.904
	Malignant (Naïve Bayes)	0.86	0.06	0.896
Proposed Parallel Hybrid Approach	Benign	0.885	0.038	0.923
	Malignant	0.962	0.115	0.926

TP = true positive rate; FP = false positive rate; F-Measure= frequency measure over class accuracy

be treated like a cancer patient despite it being the opposite scenario. However, the overall outcome is much more favourable: 48% classified correctly as a malignant class and 40% classified correctly as a benign class.

k-Means Confusion Matrix
a   b <-------- Classified as
38 11 | a = Malignant

5   46 | b = Benign

By applying the above-mentioned confusion matrix method on the k-means classifiers, the 38% cases that were classified correctly as a class malignant (11 cases were misclassified) and 46% cases that were classified correctly as a class benign (misclassified 5 cases) overall achieved 84% classification accuracy.

Naive Bayes Confusion Matrix
a   b <-------- Classified as
43 7 | a = Malignant

3   47 | b = Benign

The naive bayes classified 43% and 47% cases correctly as a class malignant and benign, respectively, with the ratio of 2 misclassified cases of a class malignant and 3 cases for a class benign, an overall computed 90% accuracy.

From the decision-making perspective, it is also noticeable that by fusing the outputs of all data mining algorithms, based on a simple voting method, we can get the final clusters which are more accurately classified. In this voting approach, the winner cluster is the one with the most votes from the classifiers. The experiments show that the proposed hybrid data mining approach is useful for the analysis of digital mammography data for the cancer diagnosis.

Clustered Visualization

Figures 5(a) and 5(b); demonstrate the visualization of the SOM of mammography data.

From the above Figure 5(a), the U-matrix, which shows the overall clustering structure of the SOM, is shown along with all six component planes. The clear separation of two classes, benign and malignant, cannot really be accessed by what U-matrix shows, but from the labels it seems that they correspond to two different parts of the cluster.

By looking at the labels, it is easy to interpret that the first two rows of the SOM form a very clear cluster; it is immediately seen that this corresponds to the benign class. The other class, malignant, forms the other clear clusters which can be seen in last two rows. The rest of the middle layers are the combination of both clusters. The empty cluster indicates some missing information in the sample data. From the component planes in Figure 5(b), it can be seen that the patient age, assessment rank, and subtlety features are very closely related to each other. Also some correlation exists between them and feature shape, margin, and density.

The variation in the colors of map units shows the similarities between the data vector. The grid scale used to measure these similarities is the normalized values of the variables used to represent one feature.

SIGNIFICANCE AND FUTURE TRENDS

With the need for advance decision-support systems in the medical domain, this research on hybrid data mining system will set the new directions. The healthcare community is being overwhelmed with an influx of data that are stored in distributed repositories. Accessing data and extracting meaningful information requires a system with powerful analytical tools rather than traditional information retrieval methods.

In this chapter, we introduced a new hybrid approach, that is, clusters of various data mining algorithms that form the predictive model to generate effective knowledge which can assist healthcare practitioners to make future decisions about the patient treatments and organization policies. For instance, outcome measurement—a data mining technique to search previously unknown valuable information from distributed databases—can help healthcare parishioners by showing statistically—in the form of graph, charts, tables, and so forth—which treatments have been most effective to the patient.

The procurement of data mining-specific knowledge (i.e., features extracted from data, text, and images) from routinely collected information will enhance the practicability of data mining systems in real-life applications, in particular for healthcare applications where a large corpus of medical data is routinely collected for clinical tasks. Thus, it is argued that the research on hybrid data mining system is very effective and significant. This research will impact both the fields of health informatics and data mining.

Figure 5(a). Data clustering based on similarities

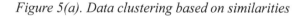

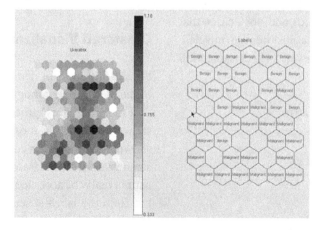

Figure 5(b). Visualizing individual feature strength

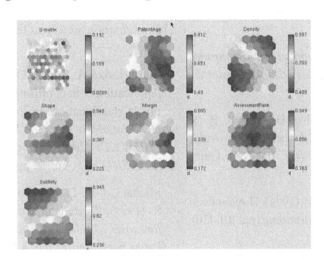

CONCLUSION

In this chapter, we presented a critical review of existing intelligent (neural network-based) and statistical-based data mining algorithms. The advantages and disadvantages of each algorithm and comparative performances have been substantiated. We also proposed a novel hybrid data mining approach, an approach that combines intelligent and statistical data mining algorithms such as SOM, k-means, and naive Bayes in conjunction with a serial fusion and a multilayer perceptron-based parallel fusion. The approach was implemented and tested on a DDSM benchmark database. The proposed hybrid approach achieved over 92% classification accuracy on a test set, which is very promising. The proposed approach is also able to visualize the data which helps in interpretation of the results.

REFERENCES

Abidi, S. S. R., & Hoe, K. M. (2002). Symbolic exposition of medical data-sets: A data mining workbench to inductively derive data-defining symbolic rules. In *Proceeding of the 15th IEEE Symposium on Computer Based Medical Systems (CBMS 2002)* (Vol. 7, pp. 50-55).

Andreeva, P., Dimitrova, M., & Radeva, P. (2004). *Data mining learning models and algorithms for medical applications.* Paper presented at the 18th International Conference on Systems for Automation of Engineering and Research (SAER-2004) (Vol. 24, pp. 148-152).

Clarke, L. P., & Wei, Q. (1998). Fuzzy-logic adaptive neural networks for nuclear medicine image restorations. In *Proceedings of the 20th Annual International Conference of the IEEE Engineering in Medicine and Biology Society. Biomedical Engineering Towards the Year 2000 and Beyond, IEEE,* Piscataway NJ (Vol. 20, pp. 3384-3390).

Damien, M., Graham, J. W., Jie, C., & Huidong, J. (2005) A delivery framework for health data mining and analytics. In *Proceedings of the Twenty-eighth Australasian Conference on Computer Science 38* (pp. 381-387).

Derek, G., Alexey, T., Nadia, B., & Cunningham, P. (2004). Ensemble clustering in medical diagnostics. In *Proceedings of the 17th IEEE Symposium on Computer-Based Medical Systems* (Vol. 2, pp. 576-580).

Dounias, G. (2003). *Hybrid and adaptive computational intelligence in medicine and bio-informatics.* ISBN 960-7475-23-2.

Fayyad, U., Piatetsky-Shapiro, G., Smyth, P., & Uthurusamy, R., E. (1997). *Advances in knowledge discovery and data mining* (pp. 154-164). Cambridge, MA: MIT Press.

Fayyad, U. M., & Shapiro, P. (1996). *Advances in knowledge discovery and data mining* (pp. 101-110). CA: AAAI Press.

George, D., & Derek, A. (2004). Linkens: Adaptive systems and hybrid computational intelligence in medicine. *Artificial Intelligence in Medicine, 32,* 151-155.

Gulbinat, W. (1997). What is the role of WHO as an intergovernmental Organisation in the Coordination of Telematics in Healthcare? *World Health Organisation.* Geneva, Switzerland. Retrieved April 8, 2008, from at http://www.hon.ch/libraray/papers/gulbinat.html

Husin-Chuan, C., Ching-Hsue, & Jing-Rong, C. (2007). Extracting drug utilization knowledge using self-organizing map and rough set theory. *Expert Systems with Applications: An International Journal, 33,* 499-508.

Hussein, A. (2002). An evolutionary artificial neural networks approach for breast cancer diagnosis. *Artificial Intelligence in Medicine, 25,* 265-28.

Jzau-Sheng, L., Kuo-Sheng, C., & Chi-Wu, M. (1996). Segmentation of multispectral magnetic resonance image using penalized fuzzy competitive learning. *Neural Computational and Biomedical Resources, 29,* 314-326.

Langley, P., Iba, W., & Thompson, K. (1992). An analysis of baysian classifiers. In W. Swartout (Ed.), *Proceeding of the Tenth National Conference on Artificial Intelligence* (Vol. 6, pp. 223-228).

Lim, T. S., Loh, W. Y., & Shih, Y. S. (1997). *An empirical comparison of decision trees and other classification methods* (Tech. Rep. 979). Madison, WI.

Maria-Luiza, A., Zaïane, O. R., & Coman, A. (2001). Application of data mining techniques for medical image classification. In *Proceeding of Second International Workshop on Multimedia Data Mining (MDM/KDD'2001,) in conjunction with the Seventh ACM SIGKDD* (Vol. 2, pp. 94-101).

Michael, J. P., Patrick, M., Kamal, A., & David, S. (1994). *Trading off coverage for accuracy in forecasts: Applications to clinical data analysis.* Paper presented at the AAAI Symposium on AI in Medicine (Vol. 2, pp. 106-110).

Pabitra, M., & Sushmita, M. (2001). Evolutionary modular MLP with rough sets and id3 algorithm for staging of cervical cancer. *Neural Computation and Application, 10,* 67-76.

Rajkumar, B., Ognen, D., & Dong, X. (2005). Profiles and fuzzy k-nearest neighbor algorithm for protein secondary structure prediction. In *Proceedings of 3rd Asia-Pacific Bioinformatics Conference (APBC 2005)* (pp. 85-94).

Sakthiaseelan, K., Cheah, Y., & Selvakumar, M. (2005). A knowledge discovery pipeline for medical decision support using clustering ensemble and neural network ensemble. *International Association for Development of the Information Society (IADIS), 9,* 336-343.

Spela, H. B., Peter, K., Vili, P., Milan, Z., Matej, S., & Milojka, M. S. (2000). The art of building decision trees. *Journal of Medical Systems, 24,* 43-52.

Thiemjarus, S., Lo, B. P. L., Laerhoven, K. V., & Yang, G. Z. (2004). Feature selection for wireless sensor networks. In *Proceeding of the 1st International Workshop on Wearable and Implantable Body Sensor Networks* (Vol. 5, pp. 52-57).

Tsang, X. Z., Wang, D. S., & Yeung, D. S. (2000). Improving learning-accuracy of fuzzy decision trees by hybrid neural networks. *In IEEE Transactions on Fuzzy Systems, 8,* 601-614.

Wang, Z., Palade, V., & Xu, Y. (2006). Neuro-Fuzzy ensemble approach for microarray cancer gene expression data analysis. In *Proceedings of the Second International Symposium on Evolving Fuzzy System (EFS'06), IEEE Computational Intelligence Society,* Lancaster, UK (pp. 82-86).

Xin, Y., & Yong, L. (1996). Evolutionary artificial neural networks that learn and generalise well. In *Proceedings of the IEEE International Conference on Neural Networks (ICNN'96), On Plenary Panel and Special Sessions* (pp. 25-29).

Zeng, Z., Tu, J., Liu, M., Huang, T. S., Pianfetti, B., Roth, D., et al. (2007). Audio-visual affect recognition. *IEEE Transactions on Multimedia, 9,* 424-428.

Zheng, J., & Kazunobu, Y. (2006). Support vector machine-based feature selection for classification of liver fibrosis grade in chronic hepatitis C. *Journal of Medical Systems, 30,* 389-394.

Zizhen, Y., & Walter, L. R. (2006). A regression-based k nearest neighbor algorithm for gene function prediction from heterogeneous data. *BMC Bioinformatics, 7,* 11-15.

KEY TERMS

Data Mining: The process of extracting useful patterns from massive amount of data.

Electronic Medical Records: A database consists of a patient's examination and treatment records in the form of data, text, and images. This includes patient's demographical and medical records and complaints, the physician's physical findings, the results of diagnostic tests and procedures, and medications and therapeutic procedures.

Hybrid Data Mining: It can be defined as any effective combination of two or more machine learning methods (algorithms) that performs in a superior or competitive way to a simple individual machine learning method.

Machine Learning (ML): ML is one of the disciplines of the AI research that deploys a variety of probability, statistical, and optimizations tools to learn from past data/examples and use that prior learning to classify new data and identify new trends in data.

Neural Networks: Neural networks were originally designed to model the way a brain works, with multiple neurons being interconnected to each other through multiple axon junctions. Neural networks use multiple layers (i.e., input, hidden, and output layers) to process their inputs and generate outputs.

Supervised Learning: A machine learning algorithm is provided with a labeled set of training data/example to learn the object. This labeled data assist the algorithm to map the input data with the desired output data.

Unsupervised Learning: A machine learning algorithm is provided with a set of training data/example only (without labeled) and leaves the algorithm to learn and discover the similar patterns.

Chapter XXX
Machine Learning for Designing an Automated Medical Diagnostic System

Ahsan H. Khandoker
The University of Melbourne, Australia

Rezaul K. Begg
Victoria University, Australia

ABSTRACT

This chapter describes the application of machine learning techniques to solve biomedical problems in a variety of clinical domains. First, the concept of development and the main elements of a basic machine learning system for medical diagnostics are presented. This is followed by an introduction to the design of a diagnostic model for the identification of balance impairments in the elderly using human gait pattern, as well as a diagnostic model for predicating sleep apnoea syndrome from electrocardiogram recordings. Examples are presented using support vector machines (a machine learning technique) to build a reliable model that utilizes key indices of physiological measurements (gait/electrocardiography [ECG] signals). A number of recommendations have been proposed for choosing the right classifier model in designing a successful medical diagnostic system. The chapter concludes with a discussion of the importance of signal processing techniques and other future trends in enhancing the performance of a diagnostic system.

INTRODUCTION

Machine learning is the study of algorithms and techniques that allow computers to "learn." It refers to an intelligent system that makes decision based on the autonomous acquisition and integration of knowledge from accumulated experience contained in successfully solved cases, analytical observation, and other means. A machine learning system uses many different mathematical methods for exploiting the computational power of a computer. In many professional fields, good tests and measurements may be available, but methods of applying this information to solve a problem may be poorly understood. Physicians, for instance, are always searching for the best possible measures to make a particular diagnosis at a very early stage. From a medical diagnostic system design perspective, there are several reasons why there has been a considerable interest in machine learning systems. The argument in favour of learning systems is that they have the potential to discover new relationships among concepts and hypotheses by examining the record of successfully solved cases. In biology and medicine, where expertise in understanding the complex physiological functions is limited, these learning systems may aggregate knowledge that has yet to be formalized. In this chapter, we confine our attention to the most prominent and basic learning task, that is, *classification*.

As illustrated in Figure 1, the fundamental goal of the machine learning system is to extract the generalized decision rules from sample data that will be applicable to new data. Then the learning system can be viewed as a classifier that produces a decision for new data to be classified. A typical learning system is designed to work with a classifier model such as a neural network, support vector machines, or a discriminant function. Learning helps to choose or adapt parameters within the model structure that work best on the samples at hand. For example, in medical diagnosis, the physician has observations and test results, and the objective is to pick the correct diagnosis. The objective of the machine learning algorithm is to customize

the classifier structure to the specific diagnosis by finding a general way of relating any particular pattern of symptoms to one of the specified diseases or conditions.

Machine learning systems have found many valuable applications in early diagnosis of diseases so that appropriate intervention can be exercised to achieve better outcomes (Begg & Palaniswami, 2006a; Ifeachor, Sperduti, & Starita, 1998; Teodorrescu, Kandel, & Jain, 1998). As biomedical diagnostic systems are becoming more specialized and complex, they adapt to new methods, instrumentation, and assay technologies that were originally developed for other applications; for example, defense, energy, and aerospace have found applications in the medical industry/environment. In this chapter, we will focus on two applications of machine learning approach in designing: (1) a diagnostic system for balance impairments based on human gait signals and (2) a diagnostic system for sleep apnoea syndrome based on electrocardiography (ECG) signals. Needless to say, such systems do not mean to replace the physician from being the decision maker but, rather, they attempt to enhance the physician's abilities to reach a correct decision.

Figure 1. A General overview of a machine learning system for classification

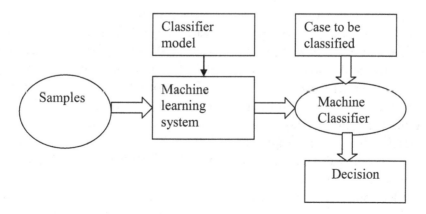

BACKGROUND

Case1: Modelling Human Gait

Gait analysis refers to the systematic recording and analysis of human walking patterns. This analysis is frequently undertaken in clinics and rehab centres to gauge the extent of abnormality in the lower limbs and also to evaluate overall walking capability. Besides disease, gait patterns change with age. There have been numerous studies undertaken in recent years focused on identifying gait measures that are affected as a result of the aging process and also that would indicate declines in the gait performance. Such declines threaten the balance control mechanisms of the locomotor system and have been reported in many gait measures (Begg, Sparrow, & Lythgo, 1998; Winter, 1991), and might be linked to reasons for falls in the older adults. Falls in the older population have been identified as a major health issue in Australia, costing the community $2.4 billion per annum (Fildes, 1994). While some research in aging gait has investigated time-distance variables (e.g., walking speed, stance/swing times, and step length) (Ostrosky, VanSwearingen, Burdett, & Gee, 1994) to identify key variables of gait degeneration in the elderly, it has been suggested that more sensitive gait variables such as minimum foot clearance (MFC) during walking over the walking surface should be used to describe age-related declines in gait in an effort to find predictors of falls risk (Karst, Hageman, Jones, & Bunner, 1999).

Minimum foot clearance during walking, which occurs during the mid-swing phase of the gait cycle, is defined as the minimum vertical distance between the lowest point on the shoe and the ground. This has been regarded as an important gait gauge as this will allow successful negotiation of the environment in which we walk. At this event, the foot travels very close to the walking surface (mean MFC height has been reported to be ~1.29 cm) with a considerably high forward velocity (4.6 m/s) (Winter, 1991). This small mean MFC value combined with the vari-ability in MFC data (0.5-0.62cm) can potentially cause tripping during walking, especially for unseen obstacles or obstructions. The literature also suggests a decrease in MFC height (1.11 cm) with aging (Winter, 1991), thereby providing a strong rationale for MFC being associated with tripping during walking, and implications for trip-related falls in older population. A model is therefore necessary that would associate MFC information with falls-risk individuals so that MFC features could be utilized to diagnose potential falls-prone individuals.

Neural networks as a machine learning method have found widespread applications for gait pattern recognition and clustering of gait types, for example, to classify simulated gait patterns (Barton & Lees, 1997) or to identify normal and pathological gait patterns (Holzreiter & Kohle, 1993; Wu, Su, & Chou, 1998). Neural networks have also been useful in the automated recognition of aging individuals with balance disorders using gait measures (Begg, Kamruzzaman, & Sarker, 2006b). Further applications in gait and in other clinical biomechanical areas are found by Chau (2001) and Schollhorn (2004). Recently, support vector machines (SVMs), a machine learning technique, have been shown to be a powerful tool for learning from data and for solving classification and regression problems with superior classification performance (Chappelle, Haffner, & Vapnik, 1999; Vapnik, 1995). Recently, we have shown that MFC gait kinematics is useful in discriminating young/elderly adults as well as healthy/falls-risk elderly adults using SVMs (Begg, Palaniswami, & Owen, 2005a; Khandoker, Karmakar, & Palaniswami, 2007). These research outcomes also highlight that gait features carry useful information regarding the quality of gait and information relating to its functional status so that these characteristics can be used to detect declines in gait performance due to aging or pathology.

Case2: Sleep Apnoea Syndrome

Sleep apnoea syndrome is a medical condition caused by sleep apnoea which is defined as the cessation of breathing for short periods during sleep. It is a common sleep related problem with a reported prevalence of 4% in adult men and 2% in adult women (Young, Palta, Dempsey, Skatrud, Weber, & Badr, 1993). When breathing does not stop but the volume of air entering the lungs with each breath is significantly reduced, then the respiratory event is called a hypopnea. Obstructive sleep apnoea (OSA) is characterized by intermittent pauses in breathing during sleep caused by the obstruction of the upper airway. The airway is blocked at the level of the tongue or soft palate, so that air cannot enter the lungs in spite of continued efforts to breathe. This is typically accompanied by a reduction in blood oxygen saturation and leads to wakening from sleep in order to breathe. Each apnoea event is defined as a respiratory pause lasting for at least 10 seconds.

Excessive day-time sleepiness is the most common complaint. An increased risk of accidents and a link between sleep apnoea and arterial hypertension have been proven in recent large-cohort studies (Nieto, Young, Lind, Shahar, Samet, Redline, et al., 2000). Sleep apnoea is now regarded as an important risk factor for the development of cardiovascular diseases (e.g. hypertension, stroke, congestive heart failure, and acute coronary syndromes) (Young, Peppard, Palta, Hla, Finn, Morgan, et al., 1997). It is successfully treated with continuous positive airway pressure (CPAP). If patients are treated at an early stage of the disease, their night-time and day-time blood pressure can be lowered, and the adverse health effects can be reduced (Dimsdale, Loredo, & Profant, 2000).

The traditional methods for the assessment of sleep-related breathing disorders are sleep studies (polysomnography), with the recording of electro-encephalography (EEG), electro-oculography (EOG), electromyography (EMG), ECG, oronasal airflow, respiratory effort, and oxygen saturation (AASM, 1999). Accurate identification of an apnoea or hypopnoea event requires direct measurement of upper airway airflow and of respiratory effort. Currently, a definitive diagnosis of sleep apnoea is made by counting the number of apnoea and hypopnoea events over a given period of time (e.g., a night's sleep). Averaging these counts on a per-hour basis leads to commonly used standards such as the apnoea/hypopnoea index (AHI) or the respiratory disturbance index (RDI) (AASM, 1999). An AHI up to 5 is regarded as normal, an AHI of 5 to 15 events per hour as mild sleep apnoea syndrome (SAS), an AHI of 15 to 30 events per hour as moderate SAS, and an AHI above 30 events per hour as severe SAS (AASM, 1999).

Sleep studies are expensive for patients, because they require overnight evaluation in sleep laboratories, with dedicated systems and attending personnel. Due to the scarcity of sleep laboratories, the vast majority of patients remain undiagnosed. Moreover, there is intra and interobserver difference in the identification of apnoea events from polysomnogram. Therefore, if SAS could be diagnosed using only ECG recordings, it would allow us to diagnose SAS simply and inexpensively from the patient's ECG recordings acquired, for example, in the patient's home.

Early in the investigation of obstructive sleep apnoea (Guilleminault, Connolly, Winkle, Melvin, & Tilkian, 1984) it was recognized that the events of apnoea and hypopnoea are accompanied by concomitant cyclic variations in heart rate (R-R intervals of ECG signals). Until now, this ordered variation in heart rate has been applied to the detection of sleep apnoea by only a few groups (Hilton, Bates, Godfrey, Chappell, & Cayton, 1999; Penzel, Amend, Meinzer, Peter, & Von Wichert, 1990; Roche, Gaspoz, Court-Fortune, Minni, Pichot, Duverney, et al., 1999). Thus, it seems possible to apply simplified ECG recording techniques combined with machine learning techniques to detect SAS because a machine learning technique has the ability to map dynamic measures like heart rate variability indexes nonlinearly onto resulting output as apnoea or no apnoea.

A number of studies during the past 15 years were accomplished for detecting SAS using features extracted from the electrocardiogram. Such approaches are minimally intrusive, relatively inexpensive, and may be particularly well-suited for medical screening tasks. Therefore, a challenge was offered to the biomedical research community to demonstrate the efficacy of ECG-based methods for apnoea detection using a large, well-characterized, and representative set of data (Penzel, Moody, Mark, Goldberger, & Peter, 2000). That competition was jointly conducted, between February and September 2000, by Computers in Cardiology (CINC) and PhysioNet. Computers in Cardiology is an annual IEEE sponsored conference that provides publicity for the event and a venue for meetings and discussion of the competition entries (Moody, Mark, Goldberger, & Penzel, 2000; Penzel et al., 2000). PhysioNet is a Web-based library of physiological data and analytic software sponsored by the US National Institutes of Health's National Center for Research Resources (NIH NCRR) (Goldberger, Amaral, Glass, Hausdorff, Ivanov, Mark, et al., 2000; Moody, Mark, & Goldberger, 2001). PhysioNet provides free access to the database of ECG recordings. The data for that challenge was provided by Dr Thomas Penzel and is made publicly available through the PhysioNet database (Penzel et al., 2000). The dataset consists of a training and a test set, each of which contains the ECG for a full night from 35 subjects. Of the 35 subjects, 20 suffered from apnoea, 10 were normal, and 5 were borderline. Borderline subjects were excluded for classification. In the challenge event, eight participants provided fully automatic analysis (De Chazal, Heneghan, Sheridan, Reilly, Nolan, & O'Malley, 2000; Jarvis & Mitra, 2000; Maier, Bauch, & Dickhaus, 2000; Marchesi, Paoletti, & Digaetano, 2000; Mietus, Peng, Ivanov, & Goldberger, 2000; Ng, Garcia, Gomis, La Cruz, Passariello, & Mora, 2000; Schrader, Zywietz, Voneinem, Widiger, & Joseph, 2000; Shinar, Baharav, & Akselrod, 2000), and five provided a visual classification stage (Ballora, 2000; Drinnan, 2000; McNames, 2000; Raymond, 2000; Stein & Domitrovich, 2000). Thirteen algorithms were compared for the apnoea recording identification. Four algorithms (De Chazal et al., 2000; Jarvis &

Mitra, 2000; McNames & Fraser, 2000; Raymond, Cayton, Bates, & Chappell, 2000) achieved the maximum possible score for the apnoea screening (30 out of 30). Only two of them (De Chazal et al., 2000; Jarvis & Mitra, 2000) were able to utilize the automatic analysis. Correctly classified test subjects scored one point each and the borderline test subjects were not scored so the maximum score obtainable was 30.

DESIGN OF AUTOMATED MEDICAL DIAGNOSTIC SYSTEM

Case1: Detection of Balance Impairments in the Elderly

We applied SVMs, for automated diagnosis of gait patterns due to balance impairments from MFC gait features, and compare their suitability as a gait classifier.

There are four main steps, as shown in Figure 2, in designing a diagnostic system for automated diagnosis of balance impairments:

1. **Signal recording:** Foot clearance (FC) data for these subjects were collected during their steady state, self-selected walking on a treadmill using a PEAK MOTUS 2D motion analysis system (Peak Technologies Inc, USA). MFC was calculated by subtracting ground reference from the minimum vertical coordinate during the swing phase through a 2D geometric model (Begg, Best, Taylor, & Dell'Oro, 2007).

2. **Feature extraction:** Each subject's MFC data was plotted as histograms showing individual MFC data and their respective frequencies (Begg, Palaniswami, & Owen, 2005a). Features included mean, median, min, max, standard deviation (SD), skewness, and so forth. In young/old gait pattern recognition, the geometry of Poincaré plot of MFC data was used to extract the reliable features

Figure 2. Schematic diagram of SVM-based gait diagnostic model

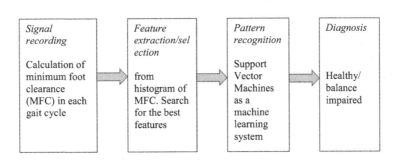

(Begg, Palaniswami, & Owen 2005a; Begg, Lai, Taylor, & Palaniswami, 2005b). A feature selection can be subsequently included in this process, by which feature vector is reduced in dimension, which includes only the most relevant features necessary for discrimination and sometimes assisted by a priori knowledge or rules. In this regard, a hill-climbing feature selection algorithm was found to be useful to identify features that provide the most contribution in separating the two gait classes (Begg, Palaniswami, & Owen, 2005a).

3. **Pattern recognition:** SVMs as a machine learning tool were used to realize an input-output mapping of the exact relationship between MFC features and falls/no-falls category. For classification, SVMs operate by finding a hypersurface in the space of possible inputs. As shown in Figure 3, this hypersurface attempts to split the positive examples from the negative examples. The split is chosen to have the largest distance from the hypersurface to the nearest of the positive and negative examples. The most important characteristic of SVMs is to condense information from a large training set into a very small number of points (i.e., the support vectors). These support vectors contain all the necessary information to define the decision hypersurface. The detailed theory behind SVM has appeared in many textbooks and journal articles (e.g., Kecman, 2002;

Vapnik, 1995). Performance of the classifier can be evaluated using accuracy rates and measures of receiver operating characteristics (ROC) curves (Chan, Lee, Sample, Goldbaum, Weinreb, & Sejnowski, 2002). The area under the ROC curve provides a measure of overall performance of the classifier, that is, the larger the ROC area the better is the classification accuracy over a range of thresholds. Many studies (e.g., Begg, Palaniswami, & Owen, 2005a; Chan et al., 2002) have used a ROC plot and its area as an index for evaluating classifier performance. Cross validation procedure is used to determine the region of optimal SVM parameters (Begg, Palaniswami, & Owen, 2005a). First a subset is used to train the SVM model while the remaining data examples are used for testing. The process is repeated for the other subsets so that in the end each example had been tested. Results of each test are combined to obtain an average result for the measure of accuracy.

4. **Diagnosis:** After the classifier is trained to set up an optimized model structure during the pattern recognition step, this step detects the balance-impaired subjects from the test samples to be detected. Our SVM model trained using a Gaussian kernel gave a high accuracy of 95% in classifying healthy and balance-impaired elderly subjects (Begg, Lai, Taylor, & Palaniswami, 2005b).

Figure 3. 2D-SVM decision surface for Polynomial kernel (d=4) plotted for Feature 1 (first-quartile) against Feature 9 (kurtosis) (Begg, 2005b)

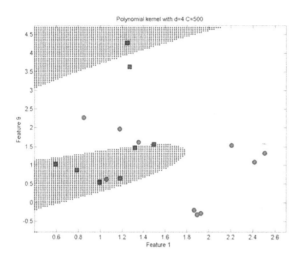

The following paragraph describes steps for designing a diagnostic system for sleep apnoea prediction.

Case 2: Automated Prediction of Sleep Apnoea Syndrome

There are five main steps as shown in Figure 4 for designing a diagnostic system for predicting sleep apnoea syndrome from ECG signals.

1. **Signal recording:** In which patient's ECG signals are recorded and filtered. A commercially available ECG recording system is always used.
2. **Signal processing:** This step processes the acquired signals to produce a relevant description of the signals. QRS complex of ECG signal detection times are calculated and the length between each QRS (R to R peak interval time) are then calculated (Engelse & Zeelenberg, 1979). Heart rate is the reciprocal of RR interval. Due to poor signal quality and errors in the automatically generated QRS detections, the RR-interval sequences generated from both sets of QRS detection times contained physiologically unreasonable time (De Chazal, Heneghan, Sheridan, Reilly, Nolan, & O'Malley, 2003).

3. **Feature extraction:** Heart rate variability indexes (Task force, 1996) are used as features. Morphology of ECG can also be used. Among all participants in the Apena challenge, six participants used spectral analysis of heart rate variability (De Chazal et al., 2000; Drinnan, Allen, Langley, & Murray, 2000; Jarvis & Mitra, 2000; McNames & Fraser, 2000; Schrader et al., 2000; Shinar et al., 2000). Two studies used the Hilbert transform to extract frequency information from the heart rate signal (Mietus et al., 2000; Schrader et al., 2000). Three algorithms used time-frequency maps for the presentation of the heart rate variability (Jarvis & Mitra, 2000; McNames & Fraser, 2000; Schrader et al., 2000). One of the participants used a threshold for the ratio of the spectral power of the heart rate in two fixed frequency bands (0.01–0.05 cycles per beat and 0.005–0.010 cycles per beat) (Drinnan et al., 2000). Another participant combined spectral analysis, Hilbert transform frequencies, and discrete wavelet analysis to use more

parameters for a subsequent feature selection (Schrader et al., 2000). Several studies used different ECG-derived parameters in addition to heart rate variability, that is, ECG pulse energy (McNames & Fraser, 2000), R-wave duration (Shinar et al., 2000), and amplitude of the S component of each QRS complex (McNames & Fraser, 2000), and two used the ECG-derived respiration (EDR) technique (Moody, Mark, Zoccola, & Mantero, 1985) to measure the amplitude modulation of the ECG signal to estimate respiratory activity. These were based on spectral analysis of the R-wave amplitude using power spectral density (PSD) (De Chazal et al., 2000) and of the T-wave amplitude using the discrete harmonic wavelet transform (Raymond et al., 2000). The algorithms that performed best used frequency-domain parameters of heart rate variability or the ECG-derived respiration signal with R-wave morphology (De Chazal et al., 2000; McNames & Fraser, 2000; Raymond et al., 2000; Shinar et al., 2000).

4. **Pattern recognition:** This step involves the development of intelligent machine learning systems dealing with the extracted and selected information in the previous step. Several machine learning techniques have been used to recognize sleep apnoea syndrome based

on the selected heart rate variability (HRV) indexes. De Chazal et al. (2003) used linear and quadratic discrimant models. Roche, Pichot, Sforza, et al. (2003) used the classification and regression tree (CART) method. Gracia, Gomis, La Cruz, Passeriello, and Mora (2000) used the Bayesian hierarchical model. We used SVM. All SVM architectures were trained and tested on the D2CSVM software (Lai, Palaniswami, & Mani, 2003, 2005).

5. **Diagnosis:** It consists of detecting potential disorders and characterizing the case by means of a pattern recognition step. This step exploits the classification provided by the pattern recognition step. Our SVM trained model showed 100% accuracy over apnoea/healthy classification of 30 ECG data sets from Physionet (see Figure 5). The novelty we introduced is the estimation of relative degree of apnoea in all subjects. As a result, the borderline group can easily be isolated (Khandoker, Lai, Palaniswami, & Begg, in press).

Some Remarks on Selecting Machine Learning Techniques for Medical Diagnostics

Machine learning techniques can be viewed as an attempt to automate parts of the diagnostic system.

Figure 4. Schematic representation of a diagnostic system for predicting sleep apnoea syndrome based on ECG signals

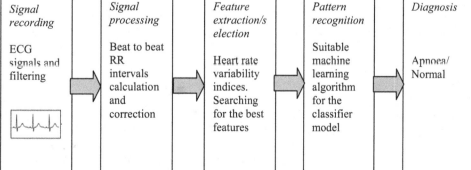

The goal of machine learning in designing a medical diagnostic system is that it can be successful in diagnosing a disease or a medical condition. We should design a diagnostic system to minimize the misdiagnosis. While much attention is often paid to the classification method, the evaluation of the performance of the system deserves equal importance. The most important question for the designer of a learning system is: Which of the well-known methods will work best on a real problem? For most problems, where the characteristics of the data are not well-known, it is impossible to answer such a question without actually trying out a variety of methods on the available samples and empirically comparing the results. There are two criteria in choosing a right classifier. First, the accuracy of diagnosis will always remain the primary criterion in choosing a classifier. Independent of any particular learning method, general principles for applying a learning method are to yield the best performance in terms of the best or smallest predictive error rate. Second, the speed of computation, which can

have a strong influence on the choice of learning method, should be considered.

The problems of the true error rate estimation arise with smaller sample sizes. Typical real-world samples run in the hundreds, not the thousands. In general, 10-fold cross-validation is adequate and sufficient for obtaining reliable error rate estimators. When the sample size is small (less than 100) and particularly when the sample is less than 50, leave-one-out or possibly bootstrapping and 2-fold cross-validation should be used (Weiss & Kulikowski, 1991). For medical diagnosis, distinctions among different types of errors turn out to be important. For example, the error committed in tentatively diagnosing someone as healthy when one has life-threatening illness (known as a false negative decision) is usually considered far more serious than the opposite type of error, that is, of diagnosing someone as ill when one is in fact healthy (known as a false positive).

Figure 5. Posterior class (Apnic) probability estimate P(Apnic|SVM_{output}), for 20 subjects with apnoea (1-20), 5 subjects with borderline apnoea (21-25) and 10 subjects with no apnoea (26-35), calculated from SVM output values for each class (Platt, 2000, pp. 1-10). ECG data were collected from Computers in Cardiology Challenge 2000. (http://www.physionet.org/physiobank/database/apnea-ecg/)

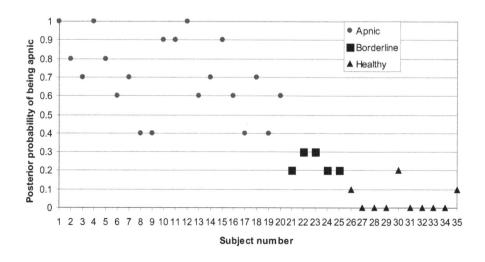

Some Remarks on Extracting and Selecting the Best Features for Machine Learning Technique in Medical Diagnostics

We hope to learn from samples that good predictions can be made for new cases. To a large extent, we are at the mercy of the features. These are the fundamental measurements or tests that we are given, and upon which we have to make decisions. In attempting to learn from the data, if all methods do badly, we may eventually just have to conclude that better features are needed to make reliable predictions. However, in some instances, it may be possible to combine and transform (mathematically and logically) the original features so that we obtain new features which enhance the maximum discriminatory information from the available data. Wavelet analysis as a sophisticated signal processing and feature enhancement technique was applied in clinical diagnosis (Ivanov, Rosenblum, Peng, Mietus, Havlin, Eugene, et al., 1996). The integration of a number of additional approaches has also been proposed for the further improvement in the reliability of the diagnostic performance. While interscale dependencies in the signal characteristics of healthy subjects has been observed (Ivanov et al., 1996), the identification of a similar multiscale relationship in the HRV data for SAS patients can be achieved by multiscale signal enhancement applied in the wavelet domain (Sendur & Selesnick, 2002). Wavelet-based signal enhancement can be customized for the HRV data in order to exploit relevant signal features, while seeking to incorporate the shift invariant properties of a family of complex wavelet transforms (Kingsbury, 2001). A shift invariant signal decomposition approach will greatly aid in the identification of the time and frequency dependent signal features upon which the diagnosis is ultimately based.

If the features have all good predictive capabilities, any classification method should do well. Otherwise, the situation is much less predictable. In practice, many features in an application are often poor, noisy, and redundant. Adding new information, in the form of weak features, can actually degrade performance (Begg, Lai, Taylor, & Palaniswami, 2005b; Begg, Palaniswami, & Owen, 2005a). That is why the primary approach to minimize the effects of feature noise and redundancy is feature selection. There are several techniques for feature selection available in the literature (e.g., Aha & Bankert, 1996; Begg, Palaniswami, & Owen, 2005a; Chang, 1990).

FUTURE TRENDS

- **Case 1:** For the diagnosis of pathological gait, like balance impairments, processing, and extraction of gait features that correlate with that particular pathology can be thought of as an important step in designing a diagnostic model of such category. Investigation into combining MFC data with other types of gait features (e.g., stride-to-stride time and distance, footground reaction forces, joint/muscle moments, and electrical activity of lower limb muscular contractions) is particularly important (Begg & Palaniswami, 2006a, pp. 259-260). Furthermore, other machine learning techniques (e.g., neural networks, fuzzy logic, Bayesian approach, or genetic algorithms) can be tried to work in cascade with the SVM technique in a hybrid design mode to further improve the performance of the classification. A further benefit that could be obtained from the diagnostic system is through the categorization of the classification outcome results in various falls risk scales (e.g., high-risk, medium-risk, low/no-risk).

- **Case 2:** The posterior class probability outputs of a classifier can be calculated to recognize the borderline subjects by estimating a relative degree of sleep apnoea on individual subjects. The estimated values can easily be validated by investigating the effect of CPAP therapy on probability outputs of a classifier. A sleep apnoea syndrome patient undergoing CPAP therapy was reported to improve (Belozeroff, Berry, Sassoon, & Khoo, 2002). Surrogate parameters such as the HRV indexes can never replace the target variables (nasal airflow with oxygen saturation) that are derived from the direct recording of respiration. As a consequence, the recognition of sleep apnoea syndrome based on HRV indexes or parameters should always be named differently to make the derived nature clear. Penzel et al. (2002) suggests that when disordered breathing in sleep is determined based on surrogate parameter such as heart rate and ECG, it would be more appropriate to make the derived nature clear. Therefore, classification labels with recommendations have the potential to make the diagnostic system more informative (Table 1).

CONCLUSION

In this chapter, we described the step-by-step methodology of designing the automated medical diagnostic system for two pathological conditions: (1) detection of balance impairments in the elderly based on gait signals and (2) prediction of sleep apnoea syndrome based on ECG signals. General illustration of applying machine learning approach in the perspective of diagnostic system design may help readers understand how a classifier model can be used to make decision. Our emphasis is on practical methods that have proven successful in building a machine learning system providing useful information to the end user. The design strategies in Case 1 can help build a SVM gait recognition model in the detection of gait changes in older adults due to balance impairments and falling behaviour. The proposed improvements in machine learning techniques and feature extraction could be encouraging not only in the falls risk diagnostic applications but also for evaluating the need for referral for fall prevention/intervention programs (e.g., exercise prescriptions to improve balance and rehabilitation).

The design strategies (described in Case 2) for predicting sleep apnoea syndrome (SAS) from ECG recording may provide essential information for introducing a novel screening device that can aid sleep specialist or other physicians in the initial assessment of patients with suspected SAS and estimate the relative risk of a sleep related breathing disorder, thereby indicating the need for referral for overnight sleep studies (i.e., polysomnogram [PSG] recording). This in turn may help prioritize patients, so that those in greatest need of treatment will undergo full PSG recordings in a timely man-

Table 1. Proposed apnoea classification labels based on HRV

Class label	Recommendation
Healthy	*Not significant SAS_{HRV}*
Healthy (borderline)	*Very slight symptom of SAS_{HRV}. Sleep physician consultation recommended*
Apnic (borderline)	Potential symptom of SAS_{HRV}. Overnight sleep studies recommended
Apnic	*Typical SAS_{HRV}. Treatment by CPAP recommended (otherwise wait for possible heart failure in a couple of years!!)*

ner, while those without apnoea will be able to avoid this tedious procedure.

REFERENCES

Aha, D.W., & Bankert, R. L. (1996). A comparative evaluation of sequential feature selection algorithms. In D. Fisher & J.-H. Lenz (Eds.), *Artificial intelligence and statistics V.* New York: Springer-Verlag.

American Academy of Sleep Medicine (AASM) Task Force. (1999). Sleep-related breathing disorders in adults: recommendations for syndrome definition and measurement techniques in clinical research. *Sleep*, 22, 667-689.

Ballora, M., Pennycook, B., Ivanov, P. C., Goldberger, A., & Glass, L. (2000). Detection of obstructive sleep apnea through auditory display of heart rate variability. *Comput. Cardiol.*, *27*, 739-740.

Barton, J. G., & Lees, A. (1997). An application of neural networks for distinguishing gait patterns on the basis of hip-knee joint angle diagrams. *Gait and Posture*, *5*, 28-33.

Begg R.K., Best R.J., Taylor S., & Dell'Oro L. (2007). Minimum foot clearance during walking: Strategies for the minimization of trip-related falls. *Gait and Posture, 25*(2), 191-8.

Begg R. K., & Palaniswami M. (Eds.) (2006a). *Computational intelligence for movement sciences: Neural networks and other emerging techniques.* IGI Publishing. ISBN: 1-59140-836-9.

Begg R. K., Kamruzzaman J., & Sarker R. (Eds.) (2006b). *Neural networks in healthcare: Potentials and challenges.* IGI Publishing. ISBN: 1-59140-848-2.

Begg R. K., Palaniswami M., & Owen B. (2005a). Support vector machines for automated gait classification. *IEEE Trans Biomed Eng*, *52*, 828-838.

Begg R.K., Lai D., Taylor S., & Palaniswami M. (2005b). SVM-based models in the assessment of balance impairments. *The Third International Conference on Intelligent Sensing and Information Processing* (pp. 248-253). Banglore, India. IEEE Press.

Begg R.K., Sparrow W.A., Lythgo N.D. (1998). Time-domain analysis of foot-ground reaction forces in negotiating obstacles. Gait Posture ;7:99-109.

Belozeroff, V., Berry, R. B., Sassoon, C. S. H, & Khoo, M. C. K. (2002). Effects of CPAP therapy on cardiovascular variability in obstructive sleep apnea: A closed-loop analysis. *AJP – Heart, 282*, 110-121.

Chan, K., Lee, T. W., Sample, P. A., Goldbaum, M. H., Weinreb, R. N., & Sejnowski, T. J. (2002). Comparison of machine learning and traditional classifiers in glaucoma diagnosis. *IEEE Trans Biomed Eng*, *49*, 963-74.

Chang, E. I. (1990). *Using genetic algorithms to select and create features for pattern classification.* Unpublished master's thesis, Massachusetts Institute of Technology, Cambridge, MA.

Chapelle, O, Haffner, P., & Vapnik, V. N. (1999). Support vector machines for histogram-based classification. *IEEE Trans. Neural Net.*, *10*(5),1055-1064.

Chau, T. (2001). A review of analytical techniques for gait data. Part 2: Neural network and wavelet methods. *Gait and Posture*, *13*, 102-120.

De Chazal, P., Heneghan, C., Sheridan, E., Reilly, R., Nolan, P., & O'Malley, M. (2000). Automatic classification of sleep apnea epochs using the electrocardiogram. *Comput. Cardiol.*, *27*, 745-748.

De Chazal, P., Heneghan, C., Sheridan, E., Reilly, R., Nolan, P., & O'Malley, M. (2003). Automated processing of the single lead electrocardiogram for the detection of obstructive sleep apnoea. *IEEE Trans. of Biomedical Engineering*, *50*(6) 686 -696.

Dimsdale, J. E., Loredo, J. S., & Profant, J. (2000). Effect of continuous airway pressure on blood pressure. *Hypertension, 35,* 144-147.

Drinnan, M. J., Allen, J., Langley, P., & Murray, A. (2000). Detection of sleep apnoea from frequency analysis of heart rate variability. *Comput. Cardiol., 27,* 259-262.

Engelse, W. A. H., & Zeelenberg, C. (1979). A single scan algorithm for QRS detection and feature extraction. *Computers in Cardiology, 6,* 37-42.

Fildes, B. (1994). *Injuries among older people: Falls at home and pedestrian accidents.* Melbourne, FL: Dove Publications.

Garcia, N. F. I., Gomis, P., La Cruz, A., Passeriello, G., & Mora, F. (2000). Bayesian hierarchical model with wavelet transform coefficients of the ECG in obstructive sleep apnea screening. *Comput. Cardiol., 27,* 275-278.

Goldberger, A. L., Amaral, A. N., Glass, L., Hausdorff, J. M., Ivanov, P. C., Mark, R. G., et al. (2000). Physiobank, physiotoolkit, and physionet. *Circulation, 101,* 215-220.

Guillemiault, C., Connolly, S. J., Winkle, R., Melvin, K., & Tilkian, A. (1984). Cyclical variation of the heart rate in sleep apnoea syndrome. Mechanisms and usefulness of 24 h electrocardiography as a screening technique. *The Lancet, I,* 126-131.

Hilton, M. F., Bates, R. A., Godfrey, K. R., Chappell, M. J., & Cayton, R. M. (1999). Evaluation of frequency and time–frequency spectral analysis of heart rate variability as a diagnostic marker or the sleep apnoea syndrome. *Med. Biol. Eng. Comput., 37,* 760-769.

Holzreiter, S. H., & Kohle, M. E. (1993). Assessment of gait pattern using neural networks. *Journal of Biomechanics, 26,* 645-651.

Ifeachor, E. C. Sperduti, A., & Starita, A. (1998). *Neural networks and expert system in medicine and health care.* Singapore: World Scientific Publishing.

Ivanov, P. C., Rosenblum, M. G., Peng, C.-K., Mietus, J., Havlin, S. Eugene, H., et al. (1996).

Scaling behaviour of heartbeat intervals obtained by wavelet-based time-series analysis. *Nature, 383,* 323-32.

Jarvis, M. R., & Mitra, P. P. (2000). Apnea patients characterized by 0.02 Hz peak in the multitaper spectrogram of electrocardiogram signals. *Comput. Cardiol., 27,* 769-772.

Karst, M. G., Hageman, A. P., Jones, F. T., & Bunner, S. H. (1999). Reliability of foot trajectory measures within and between testing sessions. *J. Gerontol.: Med. Sci., 54,* 343-347.

Kecman, V. (2002). *Learning and soft computing: Support vector machines, neural networks and fuzzy logic models.* Cambridge, MA: MIT Press.

Khandoker, A. H., Karmakar, C. K., & Palaniswami, M. (2007, October 1-3). *Screening obstructive sleep apnoea syndrome from electrocardiogram recordings using support vector machines.* Paper presented at the 34th Annual Conference on Computers in Cardiology, Durham, USA.

Khandoker, A. H., Lai, DTH, Palaniswami, M., & Begg, R. K. (2007). Wavelet-based feature extraction for support vector machines for screening balance impairments in the elderly. *IEEE transaction of Neural and Rehabilitation Engg. 15*(4), 587-597.

Kingsbury, N. G. (2001). Complex wavelets for shift invariant analysis and filtering of signals. *Applied and Computational Harmonic Analysis, 10*(3), 234-253.

Lai, D., Palaniswami, M., & Mani, N. (2003). *A new method to select working sets for decomposition methods solving support vector machines* (Tech. Rep. MECE-30-2003). Monash University, Australia.

Lai, D., Palaniswami, M., & Mani, N. (2005). *A basic heuristic decomposition framework for training Support Vector Machines* (Tech. Rep. MECSE-26-2005). Monash University, Australia.

Maier, C., Bauch, M., & Dickhaus, H. (2000). Recognition and quantification of sleep apnea by analysis of heart rate variability parameters. *Comput. Cardiol., 27,* 741-744.

Marchesi, C., Paoletti, M., & Digaetano, S. (2000). Global waveform delineation for RR series estimation: Detecting the sleep apnea pattern. *Comput. Cardiol., 27,* 71-74.

Mcnames, J. N., & Fraser, A. M. (2000). Obstructive sleep apnea classification based on spectrogram patterns in the electrocardiogram. *Comput. Cardiol., 27,* 749-752.

Mietus, J. E., Peng, C. K., Ivanov, P. C., & Goldberger, A. L. (2000). Detection of obstructive sleep apnea from cardiac interbeat interval time series. *Comput. Cardiol., 27,* 753-756.

Moody, G. B., Mark, R. G., & Goldberger, A. L. (2001). PhysioNet: A Web-based resource for the study of physiologic signals. *IEEE Eng. Med. Biol., 20,* 70-75.

Moody, G. B., Mark, R. G., Goldberger, A. L., & Penzel, T. (2000). Stimulating rapid research advances via focused competition: The computers in cardiology challenge 2000. *Comput. Cardiol., 27,* 207-210.

Moody, G. B., Mark, R. G., Zoccola, A., & Mantero, S. (1985). Derivation of respiratory signals from multi-lead ECGs. *Comput. Cardiol., 12,* 113-116.

Ng, F., Garcia, I., Gomis, P., La Cruz, A., Passariello, G., & Mora, F. (2000). Bayesian hierarchical model with wavelet transform coefficients of the ECG in obstructive sleep apnea screening. *Comput. Cardiol., 27,* 275-278.

Nieto, F. J., Young, T. B., Lind, B. K., Shahar, E., Samet, J. M., Redline, S., et al. (2000). Association of sleep disordered breathing, sleep apnea, and hypertension in a large community-based study. *J. Am. Med. Assoc., 283,* 1829-1836.

Ostrosky, K. M., VanSwearingen, J. M., Burdett, R. G., & Gee, Z. (1994). A comparison of gait characteristics in young and old subjects. *Phys. Ther., 74,* 637-646.

Penzel, T., Amend, G., Meinzer, K., Peter, J. H., & Von Wichert, P. (1990). Mesam: A heart rate and snoring recorder for detection of obstructive sleep apnea. *Sleep, 13,* 175-182.

Penzel, T., Moody, G. B., Mark, R. G., Goldberger, A. L., & Peter, J. H. (2000). The Apnea-ECG database. *Comput. Cardiol., 27,* 255-258.

Platt, J. C. (1999). Probabilistic outputs for support vector machines and comparisons to regularized likelihood methods. In A.J. Smola, P. Bartlett, B. Schölkopf, & D. Schuurmans (Eds.), *Advances in Large Marg in Classifiers* (pp. 61-74). Cambridge, MA: MIT Press.

Raymond, B., Cayton, R. M., Bates, R. A., & Chappell, M. J. (2000). Screening for obstructive sleep apnoea based on the electrocardiogram. Computers in cardiology challenge. *Comput. Cardiol., 27,* 267-270.

Roche, F., Gaspoz, J. M., Court-Fortune, I., Minni, P., Pichot, V., Duverney, D., et al. (1999). Screening of obstructive sleep apnea syndrome by heart rate variability analysis. *Circulation, 100,* 1411-1415.

Roche, F., Pichot, V., Sforza, E., et al. (2003). Predicting sleep apnoea syndrome from heart period: A time-frequency wavelet analysis. *Eur Respir J, 22,* 937-942.

Schollohorn, W. I. (2004). Applications of arificial neural nets in clinical biomechanics. *Clinical Biomechanics, 19,* 876-98.

Schrader, M., Zywietz, C., Voneinem, V., Widiger, B., & Joseph, G. (2000). Detection of sleep apnea in single channel ECGs from the PhysioNet data base. *Comput. Cardiol., 27,* 263-266.

Sendur, L., & Selesnick, I. W. (2001). Bivariate shrinkage with local variance estimation. *IEEE Signal Processing Letters, 9*(12), 438-441.

Shinar, Z., Baharav, A., & Akselrod, S. (2000). Obstructive sleep apnea detection based on electrocardiogram analysis. *Comput. Cardiol., 27,* 757-760.

Stein, P. K., & Domitrovich, P. P. (2000). Detecting OSAHS from patterns seen on heart-rate tachograms. *Comput. Cardiol., 27,* 271-274.

Task force of the European Society of Cardiology and the North American Society of Pacing and Electrophysiology. (1996). Heart rate variability. Standards of measurement, physiological interpretation, and clinical use. *Circulation, 93,* 1043-1065.

Teodorrescu, T., Kandel, A., & Jain L.C (1998). *Fuzzy and neuro-fuzzy systems in medicine.* Boca Raton, FL: CRC Press.

Vapnik, V. N. (1995). *The nature of statistical learning theory.* New York: Springer.

Weiss, S. M., & Kulikowski, C. A. (1991). *Computer systems that learn.* San Mateo, CA: Morgan Kaufmann Publishers, Inc.

Winter, D. A. (1991). *The biomechanics and motor control of human gait: Normal, elderly and pathological.* Waterloo, Canada: University of Waterloo Press.

Wu, W. L., Su, F. C., & Chou, C. K. (1998). Potential of the back propagation neural networks in the assessment of gait pattern in ankle arthrodesis. In E. C. Ifeachor, A. Sperduit, & A. Starita (Eds.), *Neural networks and expert systems in medicine and health care* (pp. 92-100). Singapore: World Scientific Publishing.

Young, T., Palta, M., Dempsey, J., Skatrud, J., Weber, S., & Badr, S. (1993). The occurence of sleep-disordered breathing among middle-aged adults. *New Engl. J. Med., 328,* 1230-1235.

Young, T., Peppard, P., Palta, M., Hla, K. M., Finn, L., Morgan, B., et al. (1997). Population-based study of sleep-disordered breathing as a risk factor for hypertension. *Arch. Intern. Med., 157,* 1746-1752.

KEY TERMS

Beat to Beat Heart Rate: It is calculated from the time interval between R to R peaks of ECG signals. Fluctuations in beat to beat heart rate indicate the activities of the autonomous nervous system or cardiovascular system.

Electrocardiogram (ECG): The ECG signal is a representation of the bioelectrical activity of the heart's pumping action. This signal is recorded via electrodes placed on the patient's chest. The physician routinely uses ECG time history plots and the associated characteristic features of P, QRS, and T waveforms to study and diagnose the heart's overall function.

Gait: Walking or running pattern. Gait analysis is routinely used to diagnose musculoskeletal problems in the lower limb and also for evaluation of treatment outcomes.

Gait Diagnostics: A process that uses objective methods to describe a patient's walking function with a view to understand the underlying pathomechanisms and to inform the clinical decision-making process which aims to improve the patient's gait through various form of interventions.

Heart Rate Variability (HRV): HRV has become the conventionally accepted term to describe variations of both beat-to-beat heart rate and RR intervals

Minimum Foot Clearance: It is defined as the minimum vertical distance between the lowest point under the front part of the shoe/foot and the ground during the mid-swing phase of the gait cycle. It has been identified as a potential gait parameter associated with especially trip-related falls in the older population.

Sleep Apnoea: It is defined as the cessation of breathing for short periods during sleep. It is successfully treated with home ventilation using nasal continuous positive airway pressure (CPAP).

Support Vector Machines (SVM): A new generation supervisor learning system based on recent advances in statistical learning theory. SVM maps input vectors to a higher dimensional space where a maximal separating hyperplane is constructed.

Wavelet Transform: Signal transformation that transforms the time signal to the frequency domain. The wavelet transform is based on a decomposition of a signal using an orthogonal family of basis functions derived from the so-called mother wavelet function.

Chapter XXXI
Achieving Effective Health Information Systems

Jim Warren
University of Auckland, New Zealand

Karen Day
University of Auckland, New Zealand

Martin Orr
University of Auckland, New Zealand

ABSTRACT

In this chapter we aim to promote an understanding of the complexity of healthcare as a setting for information systems and how this complexity influences the achievement of successful implementations. We define health informatics and examine its role as an enabler in the delivery of healthcare. Then we look at the knowledge commodity culture of healthcare, with the gold standard of systematic reviews and its hierarchy of evidence. We examine the different forms of quantitative and qualitative research that are most commonly found in healthcare and how they influence the requirements for health information systems. We also examine some domain-specific issues that must be considered by health information systems developers, including those around clinical decision support systems and clinical classification and coding systems. We conclude with a discussion of the challenges that must be balanced by the health systems implementer in delivering robust systems that support evidence-based healthcare processes.

INTRODUCTION

Effective health information systems are ones that improve health outcomes and/or reduce healthcare delivery costs. To implement these health information systems successfully we must have some understanding of the healthcare domain and adopt techniques that are attuned to managing the innate complexity of health information and healthcare in general.

Health can be viewed as a complex adaptive system (Dooley, 1997), in which many parts of the system interact interdependently in varying and unpredictable degrees with one another and their environment (Plesk & Greenhalgh, 2001a; Plesk & Wilson, 2001b; Tan, Wen, & Awad, 2005). We usually function well when most of our world is reasonably certain and predictable, fairly unambiguous, familiar, mostly known and knowable, and where interdependencies and relationships are fairly simple (Plesk et al., 2001a). Once we move out of this apparently less complex environment, we find ourselves in the zone of complexity as described by Langdon (as cited by Plesk et al., 2001a). Decisions are no longer straight forward and we are in a situation that is somewhere between simple and chaotic. Our natural tendency is to reduce ambiguity and uncertainty by attempting to create firm plans from which to work, or to strip some of the paradoxes around us by simply ignoring them. Others have found that it may be more productive to work with ambiguity and uncertainty by being reflective, learning from the consequences of our actions as we go, or creating a cycle of plan, act, review and modify as used in action research and in quality improvement practice (Waterman, Tillen, Dickson, & de Koning, 2001).

We tend to move in and out of the zone of complexity as we work through the day, acting out agreements between ourselves and others, working according to habits and pre-existing accepted patterns of activity. In healthcare we spend a high proportion of our time in the zone of complexity. For example, when a doctor calls the IS support service about a problem he is calling from a complex situation in which patient care is demanding his attention, his IT skills are limited and his capacity to describe his computer problem is not as efficient as his medical skills. Although for the most part the IT person who takes the call is able to wade through the ambiguous descriptions given by the doctor, there is still a high degree of complexity where the two worlds of medicine and IT meet, where jargon and terminology are dissimilar, and the demands of their respective worlds differ greatly. It is in this context that health informatics plays a role in supporting the delivery of safe, effective healthcare.

WHAT IS HEALTH INFORMATICS?

Health information systems stand apart from the mainstream of endeavour in computer-based infor-

mation systems. To some extent, it is just an issue of a large sector with its own specific demands—in this sense defence information systems equally stand apart from business information systems. However, with health, things have gone a step farther. A field known as *Health Informatics*, has emerged. It is also called *Medical Informatics*, and one will find frequent reference to significant sub-domains such as *Nursing Informatics, Primary Care Informatics* and *Public Health Informatics*. For the purpose of this chapter we will refer to *Health Informatics*.

The field can be defined, as "the science of using system-analytic tools... to develop procedures (algorithms) for management, process control, decision making and scientific analysis of medical knowledge" (Shortliffe, 1984, p. 185). Alternatively, van Bemmel (1984, p. 175) defines the field as comprising "the theoretical and practical aspects of information processing and communication, based on knowledge and experience derived from processes in medicine and health care." This second definition appears to be less specifically clinical; each definition reflects a key aspect of the field in practice. The unusual term 'informatics' itself derives from the French 'informatique médicale', and provides a useful reminder that the field is not just IT for health. The name *Medical Informatics* is historically entrenched, but *Health Informatics* is the preferred term to indicate:

a. That professions alongside of medicine (e.g., nurses, pharmacists, dieticians) are equally relevant, and
b. The somewhat broader goal of health, inclusive of the well members of populations.

Degrees in *Health Informatics* are available from many universities around the world, with the programmes at Stanford, Columbia and Oregon Health & Science University being some of the most historically prominent in the US. There are numerous journals and conferences in the field, with *Journal of the American Medical Informatics Association* having the highest impact factor, while the International Medical Informatics Association (IMIA) lists 48 member nations (as at April 2007). Interestingly, while there is broad agreement that there are too few formally-trained health informaticians, there is far less agreement on just who should be trained, and in what (Hersh, 2006). The field has a long tradition of involvement in technical computer science topics, e.g., the development of the MUMPs operating system, which had leading edge features for its time (1960s); medical expert systems being at the forefront of artificial intelligence in the 1970s; and the ongoing importance of advances in medical imaging technologies. However, the field is increasingly driven by the recognition of the importance of human and organizational topics, and by a broadened view of the user base, incorporating topics such as *Consumer Health Informatics.*

There are two significant motivations for IT professionals and academics to pay particular attention to the health domain.

1. **Health is big (and growing and *changing*).** At the population level, we have a seemingly endless appetite for healthcare. In the US, healthcare costs were 15.3% of GDP in 2003, significantly outpacing income growth (Gutierrez & Ranji, 2005). Moreover, the healthcare system is challenged by the need to adapt to the changing profile of patients and illness. Populations are ageing (which in part represents the **success** of medicine, after all), aided by the baby boomer generation. This demographic shift is accompanied by a preponderance of chronic illnesses, either as presenting complaints or as underlying and/or complicating factors. Moreover, choices to consume energy-dense diets (like a hamburger and cola) with reduced physical activity have set in motion the emergence of new, and combinations of, chronic conditions such as obesity and diabetes.

2. **To take lessons learned in health into other complex domains.** In healthcare, the richest and most complex possible data and knowledge

(of the human body) is integrated by a diversity of professionals. Levels of preparation vary by role, but are on average extremely high, and extend to the most intensive and lengthy levels, e.g., the apocryphal 'brain surgeon'. The disciplines are often quite difficult with, and even dismissive of, one another! The interplay of these professionals and their complex equipment is undertaken 24x7 on a vast scale, under constant time pressure, with the stakes no less than 'life and limb.'

It should be noted that our focus is on the health sector, as chiefly characterized by those who directly provide health care and their support infrastructure. We distinguish this from the biomedical research community (although, in practice, the boundary can be very blurry). There are separate lessons to be learned from biomedical research, especially in areas related to genomics and modelling of proteins and other key molecules. However, that is not the subject of the present chapter.

FACTORS INFLUENCING HEALTH INFORMATION SYSTEMS

Effective health Information system design must embrace the unique developmental nature and complexity of the health system it is aiming to enhance. There are and will continue to be different and changing views on what effective healthcare might look like, or how the components should interact (Glouberman & Mintzberg, 1996). However we can identify a number of core principles or features of an effective electronic health information system that may be independent of technology, time or place. The mnemonic C.A.R.E. G.A.P.S. F.I.R.S.T. attempts to encapsulate some of these core features. An effective health information system should seek to enhance every stakeholder's 'capacity to C.A.R.E.' or 'motivation to C.A.R.E.'. In other words, to carry out in an integrated fashion the core clinical, administrative, research and educational functions of healthcare (Orr & Day, 2004).

An electronic information system that is developed to support these functions, should embrace the power of leveraging the whole healthcare network, engaging and empowering all the key stakeholders. These stakeholders include general practitioners, allied health services, patients and their community of supports. The system design should appreciate, embrace and enhance the complex environment in which it exists and be Fast, Intuitive, Robust, Stable and Trustworthy within this complex environment (Orr, 2004; Plesk et al., 2001a; Sveiby, 1996).

Historically, the design and implementation of electronic health information systems have too often been associated with failure or limited effectiveness. Clinical, administrative, research and educational systems have not been integrated or shared common drivers. Major stakeholders have been neglected particularly patients and their supports and the large contribution they play in attaining effective health outcomes. Systems have not been fast, intuitive, robust, stable or trustworthy enough, to integrate seamlessly and enhance the complex environment in which they exist. (Ash, Berg, & Coiera, 2004; Heeks, Mundy, & Salazar, 1999; Littlejohns, Wyatt, & Garvican, 2003).

Patient Safety First

An additional complexity factor is the low tolerance for failure and error in the healthcare system (Institute of Medicine (U.S.), 2000). Errors in the delivery of healthcare as well as problems with IT in this context can end up with adverse events for patients, sometimes resulting in death or serious illness that could have been avoided. There is an imperative for health IT projects to succeed (Orr et al., 2004). A central tenet of the ethical practice of medicine is *primum non nocere* or 'first do no harm'. It is recognised that almost all interventions in healthcare have both risks and benefits. It is the role of an individual clinician, or service, to work with a consumer and their supporting community to come to an understanding and agreed balance or accommodation of these risks and benefits, as-

sociated costs and opportunity costs. Although an intervention may appear attractive on its perceived benefits, in decision making it is usually at least as important to consider the capacity to manage the perceived risks. Central to healthcare is the weighing of risks and benefits, costs and opportunity costs and making judgements in situations of ambiguity, limited time, information and resource (Protti, 2003; R. Smith, 1996). The planning decisions for health information systems are in no way immune from these factors.

Electronic systems may play a role in decreasing medical error, and increasing the efficiency and quality of workflow (Leape & Berwick, 2005). However, poorly designed or integrated systems could lead to inefficient and unsafe care (Sidorov, 2006). In healthcare every second and every click counts. Every non-essential or inefficient task has a cumulative opportunity cost on a typically highly limited clinical resource. As we strive to attain the potential benefits that can be derived from health information systems, we cannot ignore or neglect our responsibilities to consider our capacity to afford and manage the risks of such systems.

The Imperative for Security and Privacy

Bearing in mind the exhortation to do no harm, we are confronted by the problems of confidentiality (privacy) and security. In order to make good decisions and to manage risks, benefits, costs and opportunity costs, we need information (Wyatt, 2001). Multiple clinical processes, within and between healthcare services, are becoming increasingly critically dependent on system interoperability and security. However, as the number of systems and diversity of users, uses and interactions continues to rapidly increase, there has been an exponential increase in complexity and the potential for insecurity as illustrated by the examples in Box 1. Although different people are using the same patient's information, they use this information for different reasons (like clinical care, planning, evaluating, or for billing purposes), but experience different problems with the same information (Wiener, Gress, Theimannn, Jenckes, Reel, Mandell, & Bass, 1999). Multiple pieces of data may be drawn from multiple systems to produce the screen display or decision presented to the clinician. This capacity to facilitate the aggregation and analysis of clinical data is of great potential benefit to safe, timely cost effective quality care (Ash et al., 2004; Institute of Medicine (U.S.). Committee on Quality of Health Care in America, 2001). However just one error in the system interoperability, standards, data entry, sourcing, aggregation or display could lead to a fatal error.

Safe, effective healthcare is dependent upon secure, trustworthy information (Health Informa-tion Steering Committee (NZ), 2005; Institute of Medicine (U.S.). Committee on Quality of Health Care in America, 2001). The confidentiality, evi-dential integrity and availability of our informa-tion systems are core to clinician and public trust as well as business continuity. If the information stops, safe effective healthcare stops. If the quality of the information is corrupted, the quality of the associated healthcare will be corrupted (Ash et al., 2004). Some of the problems that could occur are technical as much as they are related to the people who use the information systems. A possible il-lustrative scenario would be a large metropolitan healthcare service that supports a complex array of electronic clinical information systems. The system servers all operate out of the one room. The clinical

Box 1. Same record, different views and different problems

A clinical applications portal utilises a web browser. Clinicians start to notice that when they call up a patient's lab results a different patient's lab results appear. The fault appears intermittently. The fault is later traced to a configuration error in the browser where a previ-ous patient's cached results are brought through into the new patient view.

A mental health service uses a computerised patient record both in the community and hospital settings. A clinician is carrying out an assessment in a patient's home using a laptop with a VPN connection. The VPN connection is suddenly lost and will not reconnect. The clinician cannot access nor record any further information on the patient.

A messaging standard sets a text field length at a maximum of 50 characters for trans-mission. The electronic discharge summary application a clinician is using allows them to type as many characters as they want into a text field. The copy on the clinician's screen and stored in the local system displays all the information typed in by the doctor. The copy printed for the patient is also complete and intact. However once the message is transmitted electronically, it is truncated in transition to 50 characters. Only the first 50 characters of the text field appearing on the receiving doctor's screen

In another healthcare region transmission issues with the same standard (as described above) results in multiple electronic discharge summaries being rejected and not being delivered to primary care clinicians. However, as with the truncation error, the sending clinician is not aware that any problem has occurred

In another region, the patient's current primary care clinician details have not been updated in a hospital's electronic record. The electronic discharge summary is sent to a former primary care clinician of the patient, delaying the initiation of urgently required follow up treatment.

processes in this health service are now critically dependent on the clinical information systems. A small fire starts in the server room. The server room has sprinklers which are activated. There is data backup but no operational server backup or fallover system in place to facilitate business continuity. There is severe clinical impact for five days until the clinical systems are rebuilt from the backup data tapes.

Through proactive risk management we can seek to minimise the frequency, imminence, likelihood and magnitude of security risk (Buchanan & Connor, 2001). However, when using risk management processes we have to recognise that seeking to identify and control all potential variables that may lead to an adverse outcome, is of limited efficacy in a complex environment. Adverse health outcomes may arise from variables interacting in a specific way in a specific context which may be difficult to predict at the time of deployment (Garg, Adhikari, McDonald, Rosas-Arellano, Devereaux, Beyene, Sam, & Haynes, 2005; Leape et al., 2005). In a complex environment, while not neglecting the need to identify and limit bad factors that may lead to bad outcomes, we should also focus on increasing the frequency of good factors that we know, or at least suspect, are associated with good outcomes. Creating a network that makes it easier for users to do the right thing and rapidly feed back any problems or opportunities for improvement, for analysis, resolution and deployment, should improve the frequency of good outcomes (Protti, 2003; Southon, Perkins, & Galler, 2005).

The risks to patients vary along a number of related spectrums from intermittent to continuous, localised to systematic. Traditionally the impact of a security deficit was restricted by the limited reach of the individual components of the related system. The impact of a security deficit with one record was limited to one patient, or deficits in the processes of individuals or services were limited in impact to the span of the related individuals or services (Littlejohns et al., 2003; Lorenzi et al., 1997). The impact of one patient's paper notes

being mixed up with another's is limited to two patients. A deficit in one clinician's or support staff's practice (from confidentiality breaches to failures of integrity), even if repetitive, will be limited to all the patients with whom they come into contact. However, a single security deficit in a widely diffused electronic system could impact on thousands of individuals, depending on the nature of the deficit and the delay before it is detected and resolved. The inefficiency and duplication of our current mixed paper and electronic systems may actually afford some protection in terms of limiting the impact of a security deficit. For a negative impact to actually occur, often multiple system deficits need to line up. If a record in one system states one thing and a record in another states something different there is at least the potential that this discrepancy will alert the user that there is a potential error. If one part of a mixed system goes down, other parts of the system may afford at least some backup.

In developed countries, the IS implementer will find that aspects of security and integrity requirements will be formulated within legislation and/or standards that must be adhered to as a matter of duty of care. The most prominent piece of legislation in the area of health information systems is the Health Insurance Portability and Accountability Act (HIPAA), which provides standards for electronic healthcare transactions and the handling of health data (see http://www.hhs.gov/ocr/hipaa/).

The Need for Business and Healthcare Continuity

While most healthcare services are in the process of developing electronic information systems, many activities are still dependent upon a combination of paper and IT. Good information is only as good as the workflows in which it can be used, and the complexity of these workflows adds to the difficulty in delivering relevant information appropriately to the users (Ash, 1997). This is illustrated in the example of laboratory results in a hospital setting. Laboratory tests are ordered using a paper system.

The results are provided electronically and signed off electronically. The paper ordering system does not have the granularity to always identify the specific individual who ordered a test and return the result of that test to that specific individual for sign off and action (where appropriate). The levels of specificity as to where and who ordered a test may only be at a service or clinical consultant team level. Patients may also be transferred between teams or services (within the hospital) while a result is being processed. Unless there are very clear and agreed work flow processes between the paper ordering and electronic sign off system, there can be potentially significant clinical delays in results being viewed, signed off and actioned. On a different level, these processes also have to cope with staff moves, sickness and leave. The introduction of a health practitioner index and moves towards electronic ordering should help minimise the concerns of unviewed, unsigned, and unactioned abnormal results, due to a result not being directed to the right person and that person not being prompted to act on it. Even so, there will still be significant safety issues around electronic and human process interoperability.

There is an argument for local, regional, national and indeed international backup systems to facilitate business continuity (Wyatt & Keen, 2005). This will stimulate debate around whether we build national data centres to facilitate disaster recovery and business continuity or whether these functions should be outsourced to multinationals who have a specific focus and expertise and can bring significant economies of scale to bear. Ownership and ethical control of the data, particularly if it is moved overseas, will become a significant component of this debate.

Healthcare is complex and the analysis, design, implementation and evaluation of health information systems must reflect and work with this complexity in order to support the closing of the CARE GAPS FIRST in the delivery of safe, private and secure healthcare. The complexity is exacerbated by the vast amounts of knowledge available for the delivery of healthcare and the need to harness it for quality care. Knowledge becomes a commodity.

THE KNOWLEDGE COMMODITY

Various features and fashions of health care have collided to create an environment where knowledge is treated as a commodity. There is a tendency for the results and character of individual research studies to become buried in the vastness of available medical evidence, such that the whole is managed more as a fluid rather than as a set of discrete contributions. The vast number of clinical concepts and terms has become the subject of extensive systems to support standardization and interchange. The combination of the problem of too much information, the imperative for evidence based care and the different ways in which we generate and use research evidence, results in the tension between the need for knowledge management and a tendency to treat knowledge as a commodity.

The Problem of Too Much Information

The first force for commoditization of health knowledge is the problem of 'information overload' as it pertains to any healthcare professional, to the physician in particular and most acutely to the primary care physician who deals with initial presentations of complaints. It is often quoted (although rarely with citation) that medical knowledge doubles every 19 years (Wyatt, 1991). One can build various cases to illustrate the hopelessness of the physician's attempts to keep up with all relevant information. For instance, Hanka et al (1999) assert that, not even counting basic or specialist clinical knowledge, a primary care physician in the UK is expected to know the contents of numerous health authority policies, referral protocols, governmental circulars, warnings of adverse effects of drugs, and other material sufficient to form a column 18 inches (46cm) tall. The problem of keeping up in medicine is such that providing evidence of formalized continuing medical education is a requirement for continuing to practice in many countries. Moreover, the challenge creates an emphasis on learning in the work place – looking up answers quickly, to answer immediate needs (Wyatt & Sullivan, 2005). Tools such as Quick Clinical, which federates search results over a number of online resources with a mean search time of 4.9s, have emerged to support exactly this sort of practice (Coiera, Walther, Nguyen, & Lovell, 2005). Even in the face of too much information there is a need for evidence based medicine in order to provide safe and effective healthcare.

The Imperative for Evidence Based Care

The second force for commoditization of health knowledge is evidence based medicine (EBM). EBM connects scientific evidence with patient needs in an appropriate setting by means of making judicious decisions based on conscientious and explicit use of the available evidence (Mayer, 2006). The EBM movement introduced critical thinking into clinical care, shifting clinicians away from 'expert doctrine' that was at risk of setting us up for clinical error and risking the safety of our patients (Guyatt, Cook, & Haynes, 2004; Mayer, 2006). Evidence is available in great volumes but requires critical appraisal because of varying levels of quality, validity, impact and applicability. Each publication requires critical appraisal prior to being used at the point of care in order to avoid inappropriate use of evidence or use of poor quality or inappropriate evidence. Because of the plethora of evidence and the difficulty in assessing all relevant information at the point of care, a hierarchy of evidence has been developed to assist us in identifying believable, safe and useful knowledge. This hierarchy is outlined in Figure 1. What we take from the evidence and how we interpret it in everyday clinical practice remains the clinician's responsibility.

The Mixed Blessing of Systematic Reviews

Since health information is so plentiful and clinicians are encouraged to practice on the basis of the evidence that is available, systematic reviews have become the panacea for those who need and desire the evidence but are unable to process it all themselves. A systematic review is a summary of the available evidence, which in turn is the outcome of a distinctive process (Khan, Kunz, Kleijnen, & Antes, 2003; Petticrew & Roberts, 2006). The process involves five steps and applies equally to qualitative and quantitative research. The steps include formulating a question; searching, assessing and summarising the evidence; and interpreting the the review and disseminating the outcomes. These steps are inter-related and follow preceding steps logically, making use of judgements of quality, validity and applicability in terms of the content of the literature under review. Initially, in healthcare, these reviews were limited to RCTs, but systematic reviews are growing in popularity in all forms of quantitative and qualitative research, and in different arenas such as healthcare, social sciences and business. The systematic review is becoming the evidence *du jour*, a new form of knowledge as a commodity. It makes health knowledge more accessible in what is considered to be a trustworthy format for rapid, simple, structured access to healthcare evidence at the point of care and under the demands of general practice.

As with any commodity, there are different versions of systematic review, such as the Cochrane Reviews (see http://www.cochrane.org/reviews/) and the use of systematic reviews in the development of clinical guidelines (Rousseau, McColl, Newton, Grimshaw, & Eccles, 2003). Once the review results are presented in publications, they reinforce the evidence in ways that limit interpretation at the point of care, aiming at reducing the risk of misinterpretation and information overload, thus supporting safer delivery of care. It is therefore essential to ensure the use of quality, reliable and valid research to inform these reviews.

Figure 1. Commonly-used hierarchy of evidence for healthcare interventions (after Petticrew & Roberts, 2003)

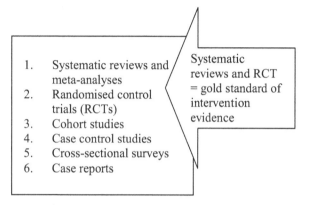

While the systematic review offers accessibility to vast amounts of information about interventions, it simultaneously removes the user from direct access to the richness of the 'raw evidence' of individual research projects reported in the literature. Such raw evidence is available in RCTs to those practitioners who require more granularity in knowledge and/or have the capacity to do their own critical appraisal of the evidence.

Tracking Down Clinical Knowledge with RCTs

RCTs are considered the gold standard to accessing good clinical treatment or intervention evidence (Stanley, 2007). A randomised control trial (RCT) is a quantitative form of medical research that follows a specific design in order to reveal the effectiveness of a treatment (Mayer, 2006). The research design allows for comparison between the effect of a treatment, (positive effect for treatment or intervention purposes, side effects, and adverse effects), and the absence of such a treatment, e.g., the therapeutic effect of antihypertensive drugs and their side effects compared against those who take a placebo or a different drug. The structure of the design narrows the focus of the research as closely

as possible onto the treatment being researched, with every effort being made to exclude confounding or contributing factors and any possible bias. In this way new knowledge about treatments is stripped of extraneous information. The published report reflects this economy in its clarity of the study objective, and component of the research design such as randomization, selection of population to be studied and its control population, statistical power (sample size), blinding, the specific nature of the clinical trial and how the participants were monitored for safety (Stanley, 2007).

Structured, Compact and Indexed Literature: The Impact of Positivism on Health Research

Perhaps as a response to the high volume of medical literature and the influence of EBM-thinking, publications themselves are becoming increasingly structured, compact and systematically indexed.

In the health and medical domain, the properties of a good abstract have been formalized. Many journals require structured abstracts. In the IT domain, we are accustomed to encountering abstracts to preface articles, especially those in peer-reviewed academic literature. A good abstract should provide, in perhaps 150 to 300 words, a brief picture of the whole message of the paper. In this way it is distinct from, say, an editor's introduction to a work of fiction, wherein you might not want to give away the ending. Especially where empirical findings are concerned, the abstract should give an indication of the population that was studied, sample size, measures taken, and the results found. Guidelines used by the *Medical Journal of Australia* are typical (Medical Journal of Australia, 2002) of those encountered in the medical literature. The abstract is divided into sections including: objective, design, setting, patients/participants, intervention, main outcome measure, results and conclusions. Even the most respected business information systems journals, such as *Information Systems Research* or *Management Science*, while certainly exhibiting high quality research with good abstracts, have not yet taken this structuring step.

The compactness of modern medical literature is striking. There is little tolerance for unsupported statements. The page and word counts of medical journals and conference proceedings are short by IT standards. A minor, but telling, facet of the compactness (and uniformity) of the medical literature is in its preference for the International Committee of Medical Journal Editors style, notably its reference style, also known as Vancouver (National Library of Medicine, 2006). Consider the following reference in the Vancouver style:

Gadzhanova S, Iankov I, Warren J, Stanek J, Misan G, Baig Z, Ponte, L. Developing high-specificity anti-hypertensive alerts by therapeutic state analysis of electronic prescribing records. *J Amer Med Inform Assoc* 2007; 14(1):100-9.

The style strives to save each and every possible character through compact presentation of the author name list, use of standardized journal name abbreviations, and by indicating the page range as '100-9' since a span from pages 100 to 109 can logically be inferred.

Another notable characteristic of the medical literature is the dominance of the systematic literature review as a means of generating evidence about what is already known. While the use of systematic reviews is not unknown in the IS literature, it is the norm in medical and health sciences. In a systematic literature review, the exact criteria, tools and results of the literature search are reported. Most typically this entails reporting the set of index terms used, the search engines interrogated, the number of results returned initially, any exclusion criteria used to narrow those results and a complete identification (sometimes in an appendix) of all remaining papers. The resemblance of systematic literature reviews to methods for knowledge discovery and data mining is striking.

An interesting thing about the systematic literature review is that the Health Informatics community

has applied this technique to IT. That is, systematic literature reviews have been undertaken on articles reporting evaluations of health information systems. Box 2 summarises results of some major systematic literature reviews that are illustrative of the power (and limitations) of this technique when applied to IT. The findings from such reviews are highly influential in the field. With respect to those reported in Box 2, each concludes with a call for even more systematic reporting of evaluation findings in the health informatics literature.

One of the most commonly used tools in health-related systematic literature reviews is PubMed, a service for online retrieval of biomedical literature citations provided by the National Center for Biotechnology Information within the US National Library of Medicine (NLM). In fact, PubMed is just one of the major database services provided by NLM; other major databases include Nucleotide and Protein Sequences, Protein Structures, and Complete Genomes. PubMed accesses over 15 million references, and is regularly updated from some 5000 journals in 37 languages. MeSH is a hierarchical structure of terms used to index PubMed. Although the MeSH terms have been designed to simplify searches and deliver comprehensive results, the relative newness and the hybrid nature of health informatics means that the best way to search this database is by means of a combination of MeSH terms and free text. The EBM culture encourages healthcare providers to issue queries to online resources regularly (i.e. to get a practical answer to the clinical problem at hand, not merely as an academic exercise). The NLM promotes access to PubMed through a variety of interfaces to facilitate use at the point-of-care – there's even an SMS txt interface to PubMed.

The structured nature of the medical literature is conducive to extensive IT processing for integration of EBM queries into point-of-care health information systems. In fact, the NLM encourages this and provides E-Utilities that facilitate programmatic access and can provide responses to PubMed queries as XML. There is a high awareness of online resources in the healthcare (especially medical) community. Health information system implementers are increasingly expected to integrate access to online resources with point-of-care systems, such as those used for Computerized Physician Order Entry (CPOE, ordering tests and procedures via the computer). Box 3 describes the case of a substantial evaluation of a widely-deployed tool for computerized decision support in primary care. The case is illustrative for identifying ways in which an IT based tool can fail to have a positive impact in healthcare. However, it also demonstrates the subtle, and to some extent fundamental, challenges in applying the RCT approach to information systems.

The insistence of evidence from RCTs as the basis for medical decision making regarding treatments has seen its detractors in the medical community. In their article 'Parachute use to prevent death and major trauma related to gravitational challenge: systematic review of randomised controlled trials' Smith and Pell (2003, p. 1459) parody the structure of many modern medical journal articles and lament the lack of willingness to rely on other forms of reasoning to justify decisions. They conclude that "everyone might benefit if the most radical protagonists of evidence based medicine organised and participated in a double blind, randomised, placebo controlled, crossover trial of the parachute."

There is too much information in healthcare as evidenced by the drive to be clear and straightforward in the literature that reflects and supports evidence based care. Knowledge becomes a commodity for use in providing evidence based care, the hierarchy of evidence indicating that systematic reviews and RCTs are the most rigorous and acceptable forms of medical research. The clinical treatment slant towards the use of specific quantitative research methods such as clinical trials presents problems when different questions are asked in search of knowledge that is not directly related to clinical treatments of healthcare interventions.

Prevailing Research Approaches and Methods in IS

Since management of information systems (MIS) is a relatively new discipline, having emerged in the last 40 years, no particular research discipline can be said to represent it (Palvia, Mao, Salam, & Soliman, 2003), in the same way as positivism represents medical research (Malterud, 2001). There does appear to be certain patterns in how MIS research is conducted and the common themes under examination (Palvia et al., 2003). According to Culnan's categorisation of MIS research topics (as outlined by Orlikowski & Baroudi, 1991), the types of MIS research include

- Individual, management and organisational approaches to IS,
- Research foundations, and
- IS curriculum.

Roughly 30 topics fit these categories, such as MIS theory, artificial intelligence and global information technology as the top three topics, with BPR and organisational impact of MIS, innovation, IS planning, implementation and usage somewhere in the middle of the list (Palvia et al., 2003). Surveys, conceptual frameworks and case studies are the most popular study design with literature analysis, mathematical modelling and interviews in the middle of the list (Orlikowski et al., 1991; Palvia et al., 2003) and action research as a form of qualitative[1] research at the end of the list of choices for research design. Action research features in 0.6 - 0.8% of MIS research and does not appear (in the literature) to be growing in popularity in terms of IS research (Orlikowski et al., 1991; Palvia et al., 2003).

To help understand the choices made in MIS research, research is broken down into empirical or positivist, and non-empirical or interpretive and critical research (Orlikowski et al., 1991; Palvia et al., 2003). Positivism is an objective form of research in which the researcher remains distanced from

Box 2. Some results from systematic literature reviews on health information systems

EPR quality. Thiru et al. (2003) reviewed scope and quality of electronic patient record (EPR) data in primary care. To be included in the review the papers had to have a 'reference standard' for judging the EPR quality (e.g. comparison to patient interview findings), and the papers had to have the objective of measuring EPR quality or to have used EPRs and commented on their quality. They found 37 studies measuring EPR data quality and 15 studies that made scoping comments. They found that prescribing data were generally of better quality than diagnostic or lifestyle data. The finding is not entirely surprising since electronic prescribing is widely used in the UK (the source of many of the accepted studies) and hence has a functional relationship to clinical workflow (the doctor enters the prescription into the EPR, not purely as an act of recordkeeping, but in order to actually prescribe).

There is a strong methodological component to the conclusions of this paper. The focus of the conclusions is on limitations in the current reporting of EPR quality. Moreover, Thiru et al. list providing a framework for categorizing and selecting papers reporting data quality in primary care as a contribution of the paper. Thiru et al. noted that most of the select research had been published since 1995 (although they searched back to 1980), indicating the growth and movement toward evidence generation in the field.

Improving clinical practice using decision support systems. Kawamoto et al. (2005) used a systematic review to assess the success factors for clinical decision support based on review of only those papers that assessed outcome with a randomized controlled trial. They found 70 appropriate studies and identified four independently significant factors: (1) automatic provision of decision support as part of clinician workflow; (2) provision of recommendations rather than just assessments; (3) provision of decision support at the time and location of decision making; and (4) computer based decision support. While only 68% of the selected systems improved clinical practice, of the 32 systems possessing all four features, 94% significantly improved clinical practice.

It is notable that Kawamoto et al. did not limit their search to computer-based decision support interventions, but instead allowed this to emerge as a success factor.

Impact of health IT on outcomes. Chaudhry et al. (2006) undertook a systematic literature review of studies that evaluate the impact of health information technology on the quality, efficiency and cost of healthcare. They found 257 studies that met their inclusion criteria. They found evidence of three major quality benefits: increased adherence to practice guidelines, improved surveillance, and decreased medication errors. They found the major efficiency benefit to be decreased utilization of care, with mixed results on time utilization.

The interesting thing about the results is that four benchmark institutions accounted for 25% of the studies found, and were the only institutions each accounting for 5% or more of the studies. Each of these four institutions demonstrated their results with internally-developed systems related to decades-long sustained initiatives. Only nine studies evaluated commercially developed, multi-functional systems of the type that most healthcare organizations would be considering; and the limited evidence from these studies does not support the guideline adherence benefit. Thus the authors are forced to conclude that it is in fact unclear whether other institutions can achieve the benefits from health IT that have been demonstrated by the benchmark institutions. They call for more evaluation of commercially developed systems in the community setting and more uniform standards for reporting research of health IT implementations.

phenomena under examination. Interpretivism and critical research are seen as being subjective, where the researcher's participation in the research itself is acknowledged, and their experience is part and parcel of understanding the phenomenon being examined. It appears that non-empirical research is favoured when researching management and organisational topics while empirical research methods are preferred in the more technical topics (Alavi & Carlson, 1992). The salient difference between the two non-empirical forms of research is the outcome – for critical research it is social change while interpretive research aims at understanding the meaning people attach to social action.

When MIS and healthcare intersect there is no way of determining which approach will be used.

Box 3. Case Study – The system that had no effect

Eccles et al. (2002) evaluated the effect of computerised evidence based guidelines on management of asthma and angina in adults in primary care. This study was significant for being a methodologically-sound, substantial, RCT-type investigation of the benefits of IT to support chronic disease management in the primary care setting, involving 60 general practices in north east England. This is important because of the trend for chronic, rather than acute, illness to dominate healthcare budgets (and the burden of disease). The study was also significant for coinciding with a large-scale primary healthcare decision support development project sponsored by the UK's National Health Service (NHS), known as PRODIGY (Prescribing RatiOnally with Decision-support In General-practice studY). The director of the Centre responsible for PRODIGY was listed as an author on the paper, and the system being studied, appeared to be an implementation of PRODIGY decision support.

The study provided a resoundingly negative assessment of computerized decision support for chronic conditions in primary care. No effect was found either on the process of care (i.e., guideline adherence) nor on disease-specific patient outcomes. Levels of system use were low. And the study called into question the feasibility of integrating computerized decision support into the complex setting of chronic disease management. Moreover, Rousseau et al. (2003) reported a qualitative interview-based study conducted in parallel to the RCT that provided additional insight on the trial findings. Rousseau et al. found that the clinical users had three major areas of concern: (a) timing of the decision support; (b) ease of use; and (c) helpfulness of the content (which is a fairly comprehensive set of concerns!). These concerns stemmed in part from limitations in the integration of the decision support to the electronic medical record, requiring the user to switch between systems. Ease of use was further exacerbated by an inadequate training and support plan. Notably, there was perceived to be an excessive gap between the training and the opportunity to use the system, and an over-extension of the 'train the trainers' concept wherein only a couple of professionals per site were sent for training. The difficulty of using the system was compounded by opinion that use of 'on demand' resources (including PubMed) provided better decision support than that embedded in the system.

The messages from this study are more complex than they may at first seem. Ten 'rapid response' letters (including an author's reply) were posted within three weeks of the initial study's publications. The letters are interesting for illustrating the tensions between different stakeholders and professional perspectives, but also demonstrate the subtle, but fundamental, difficulties in what the study attempted.

The *identity* of the system is a key challenge in evaluation of an advanced system, such as the decision support tool examined by Eccles et al. and Rousseau et al. The response letters indicate that the system was not exactly the latest-generation PRODIGY decision support tool, but rather was software that stemmed from an earlier version of PRODIGY. The letters provide conflicting (or at least complex to interpret) descriptions of when the software was evaluated, ranging from 1997-98 (several years before the publication date) to a more timely 1999-2000. At any rate, the intervention and its data collection spanned a significant period of time. During an experimental intervention, one would like conditions to remain constant, but it is natural for new and innovative software to be updated regularly. The letter from Eccles indicates that the software was in fact updated to fix problems. Over the span of an evaluation, features of the broader environment will also change, such as the availability and quality of other decision support tools.

The response letters also point out the relevance of the broader context of use of a decision support tool, including such issues as financial incentives. One cannot make an isolated change in the workflow of healthcare professionals. Time spent working with a decision support tool, and enacting its recommendations where appropriate, is time not spent on other forms of care provision.

In light of the challenges, it is perhaps not surprising that only limited evidence for benefits of health IT is available. And we are reminded to always remain critical to the context (in time, technology, policy and procedures) of any given evaluation.

Clinical medical research defaults to positivism in the form of randomised clinical trials because the circumstances of searching for evidence to support clinical decisions require rapid evidence retrieval for the purpose of appropriate clinical care (Hamilton, 2005). However, there is a growing need to match the research design to the question to be answered. Because of this, health research no longer adheres strictly to the traditional hierarchy of evidence: it is more appropriate to use qualitative research methods for asking questions about how and why (Petticrew et al., 2003), such as questions about organisational change linked to health IT projects. Action research is most prevalent in healthcare when nurses conduct research - it appears to resonate well with the way in which they normally work (Waterman et al., 2001). Action research is becoming more widely used in healthcare because of the growing variety of opportunities to use it, especially with more patient empowerment and consumer participation in the delivery of healthcare.

Action Research for Pragmatic Knowledge Development

Action research (AR) has waxed and waned in popularity over the last century, depending on what researchers wanted from it, and the situation in which it was used. The concept 'action-research' was first used by Lewin who combined research, practice and change, when he referred to change resulting from research based on social action (Waterman et al., 2001). In this way AR emerged as a tool for social change: research and practice are conducted simultaneously and the research subject is a participant in the research and in the application of new knowledge (Brydon-Miller et al., 2003). There is usually an emphasis on the development of knowledge in the practical situation where a researcher and the researched (both acting as participants, partners and collaborators of change, research and new practice) participate holistically in the achievement of shared goals (Day, Orr, Sankaran, & Norris, 2006; Waterman et al., 2001) as can be seen in Figure 2.

AR as a research methodology has two key elements: a cyclic process, and partnership with the research subjects, respondents or participants (Waterman et al., 2001). With such a strong people focus, the most appropriate definition of action research has been presented by Rapoport (1970, p. 499), as aiming to "...contribute **both** to the practical concerns of people in an immediate problematic situation and to the goals of social science by joint collaboration within a mutually acceptable ethical framework". This definition presents the idea that action research is not only a methodology, or simply a research process – it is a way of life, of working, that plays out in a mutually desired manner for all participants (researcher and researched) in a social research project.

Action research emerged in information systems in the latter half of the 20th century and echoed the early action researchers' challenge that positivism and quantitative research were not the only form of appropriate research in information systems. According to Avison et al. (2001, pp. 94 - 95) several information systems contributions have been made in the form of the Multiview contingent systems development framework, soft systems methodology, the Tavistock School sociotechnical design, Scandinavian trade union research regarding user bargaining power in systems development, and the Effective Technical and Human Implementation of Computer-based Systems (ETHICS) approach to participative systems development. Action research can be used to link the people in their complex healthcare services to the information systems they use in much more pragmatic ways than by other means (Avison et al., 2001).

Because of the broad scope of health IT research and the wide range of areas of healthcare that information systems affect, we need to carefully match the research question with an appropriate way of accessing the associated knowledge. On the flipside, the nature of health research determines to some extent the ways in which we represent, and support the use of, knowledge in health information systems.

Figure 2. The relationships of people, goals and AR cycle in action research (Day et al., 2006)

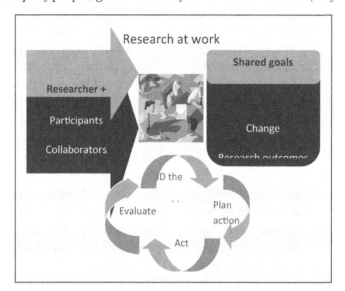

USING HEALTH KNOWLEDGE EFFECTIVELY

Different forms of health knowledge are used in a variety of settings, and for reasons that differ according to the user. Clinical information is made available at the point of care and also later classified and categorised for purposes of planning, policy making, and evaluating of healthcare service delivery. Clinical decision support systems present clinical guidelines in a format that aims at making evidence-based care more achievable, another form of knowledge commodity.

Clinical Information Systems: Recording, Accessing and Using Clinical Information

There is a range of 'workhorse' information systems components that are likely to already be in place in most developed countries, at least in the more centralized healthcare delivery facilities e.g., a classic metropolitan hospital or large clinic. In many countries – notably Denmark, the UK, the Netherlands, Australia and New Zealand, and to a lesser extent Canada and most of the rest of the EU

– these systems will also extend in large part to all but the smallest or most remote local care providers. Table 1 provides a summary based in large part of van Bemmel and Musen (1997).

The challenge for the modern health information system implementer often revolves around working with the existing *legacy* systems, those systems already in place. These challenges can include enhancement of the existing functions to meet higher requirements for reporting, security and integrity, automated decision support or timely data exchange, as well as to provide gateways for integration with larger regional or national networks, and mobile and remote access.

Guidelines and Clinical Decision Support Systems (CDSS)

The American Institute of Medicine defines clinical practice guidelines as "systematically developed statements to assist practitioner and patient decisions about appropriate health care for specific clinical circumstances" (Field & Lohr, 1992, p. 27). Such guidelines are developed and distributed on paper, but of course also increasingly find distribution channels in electronic formats. In a loose sense, any material on computer or paper that provides information to aid a decision can be considered 'decision support.' However, when the guidelines are automated to the point of automatically computing patient-specific advice, then the resultant technology is rightly termed a *clinical decision support system* (CDSS).

As per Box 2, there are a number of factors now to influence the success of decision support for clinicians; notably, making it electronic, providing recommendations specific to the patient at hand, and providing a good fit to current workflow. There is a vast range of decision technologies that can provide the underlying mathematical models for such support, including production rule expert systems, artificial neural networks, fuzzy logic, case-based reasoning systems and Bayesian reasoning systems (see Warren & Stanek, 2006 for a more complete discussion). Such systems can provide an array of 'artificial intelligence' type functions, such as suggesting diagnoses in relation to symptoms, advising on treatment strategies, including computation of recommended dosage, or calculating risks. CDSS technology can be deployed in a consultative role (where it is invoked by the clinician) or can serve as a 'critic' and provide pop-up advice or an alert for a dangerous or sub-optimal situation, such as an attempt to order a drug that may cause an adverse interaction with one already prescribed or to which the patient has a recorded an allergy. The systems may provide an explanation of reasoning, and, ideally, will provide pointers to the medical literature that supports the system recommendation. This latter aspect is extremely useful since it directs the user back to the humans that undertook the supporting clinical research, rather than advising the human user (generally a doctor) to accept the recommendation of a machine per se.

There is a growing demand for the use of CDSS to promote (if not enforce) guideline adherence, both to promote EBM for optimal patient outcome and to control costs associated with testing and procedures beyond those indicated in guidelines. The demand for CDSS is further enhanced by the desire to pro-

vide patient safety through the ability of machines to integrate tirelessly all available information, thus avoiding certain classes of adverse events.

An essential enabler for CDSS that integrates with clinician workflow is the systematic use of terminology and coding in the clinical practice, which allows the system to accurately associate the data in the health information system with key decision concepts.

Coding, Classification and Terminology Systems for Usable Knowledge

The rise of coding, classification and terminology systems is a response to the volume and complexity of information associated with the delivery of healthcare, and the different groups of people who need to use such information (like clinicians, managers and researchers). A particular feature of health information processing is the use of formalized coding and classification schemes to represent clinical concept. Table 2 provides a summary of some of the most commonly used and important schemes.

Many of the schemes are tightly tied to billing and reimbursement processes, and as such take on a life of their own. A key example is the DRG (Diagnosis-Related Group) process, as used by the US government's Medicare and, with variation, many other health funders around the world. The International Classification of Disease (ICD) codes (in variations of version 9 in the US, or version 10 in most other places) are used as the basis for assigning a patient to one of some 500 DRGs, where each DRG is meant to represent a category of approximately uniform resource consumption for the patient's care. DRG coding is functionally the mediator through which a significant proportion of hospital funding is obtained, and hence, naturally, involves specialized software and staff to optimize the claims process.

Coding and classification schemes also serve as key roles in statistical reporting, including com-

Table 1. Types of 'workhorse' (foundational) health information systems at the point of care

Type of System	Description
ADT – Admission, Discharge and Transfer	System for registering and tracking the presence of a patient in a facility, and creating clinical and administrative reports upon service completion – often tied to billing
Ordering	Systems to order tests and procedures to be performed on a patient
Results reporting	Systems to view the results of tests for ongoing patient diagnosis and treatment
Radiology	Systems to manage orders and reports of medical imaging; often integrated with a PACS function
PACS – Picture archiving communications systems	Systems to manage storage, retrieval and distribution of high-resolution medical images
Pharmacy	Systems for drug inventory and administration management, including support for preparations made onsite (as with many intravenous solutions)
Nursing	Systems supporting records of nursing care procedures delivered and patient status
Departmental systems	Systems specialized to the needs of a given department due to the nature of its business, e.g., Emergency Department, surgical facility or Intensive Care Unit, and/or providing discipline-specific features in data collection or decision support.

pliance to government regulation and support for research and management reporting. To illustrate the latter usage, if management wanted to know the average length of stay of all patients who had suffered a stroke, then a look-up of all patients with ICD9 codes in the range 430-438 is a good start. Of course, for this to be effective, procedures must be in place to achieve collection of all relevant codes. And one should not underestimate the complexity of some of these coding schemes and the opportunities available for coding a particular event in any of multiple ways.

Achieving an agreed formalized *terminology,* i.e., a set of natural-language strings that map to underlying concept codes, is considered an essential step in preparing a clinical sub-domain for extensive use of IT. An obvious advantage of an agreed term set for any concept is the ability to put it on a menu or, when the domain is very large, implement some form of structure look-up control. For large and complex domains (such as diagnosis coding in an Emergency Department), the clinical users

providing care will not have an active understanding of the entire coding/classification system, and thus will record terms at the point of care. The ideal user interface allows clinicians to record terms that match the standardized terminology and hence readily match to concept codes. This point-of-care input may be later mediated by a clinical coding specialist (as in the process of DRG coding for reimbursement). The SNOMED CT scheme is particularly complete in its representation of clinical terminology (with a one-to-many mapping of natural language terms to underlying concepts). While SNOMED has a sophisticated ability to represent clinical concepts, the scheme is large and complex. SNOMED is gaining increasing acceptance, with the US and UK, and more recently Australia, taking out national licences.

Coding and classification underpins *systems interoperability,* that is, the ability for distinct computer systems, particularly those provided by different vendors, to exchange information. Health Level 7 (HL7) is the most important set of electronic messaging standards in healthcare. Within a given message between two healthcare information systems the agreed clinical codes allow specific fields to be interpreted correctly by the receiving system. For example, Logical Observation Identifiers Names and Codes (LOINC) has since 1999 been the preferred terminology for laboratory test orders and results in HL7 messages.

Coding and classification systems are constantly being updated, and often diverge into local variations. Any health information system implementation must include a mechanism for achieving regular updates to its terminology and underlying coding and classification schemes. Moreover, there are numerous other relevant standards outside of the schemes we have discussed, such as Digital Imaging and Communications in Medicine (DICOM), a popular standard for storage and transmission of medical imaging.

LESSON/CONCLUSION

Healthcare is a complex domain that demands fast, intuitive, robust, stable and trustworthy systems that can address the needs of a range of distinct classes of users and the diverse functions they perform. Systems must be designed to support patient safety first, and to protect confidentiality of patient data. Implementers must aggressively and proactively undertake risk management to minimize the frequency and impact of system failures.

The commodity approach to health knowledge has powerful implications for health information systems analysis and design. These implications come in two general varieties:

1. The pressure for systems to manage health knowledge as a commodity, and
2. The pressure to justify design decisions and system success in the terms of the knowledge commodity culture.

The first of these implications can be, in a sense, relatively easy to manage. This is just a question of good user interface design - to speak the user's language (in accordance with Nielsen's (1994) second usability heuristic, 'match between system and the real world'). Any application that provides clinical decision support must reflect a savvy approach to EBM. Clinical input will be required not just in the functional aspects of the system specification,

Table 2. Commonly-used clinical classification and coding schemes

Scheme	Main Use	Approximate Size	Owner
ICD9 / ICD10 – International Classification of Disease	Discharge diagnosis; statistical classification	200,000 classes	World Health Organization (WHO)
SNOMED CT - Systematized Nomenclature of Medicine – Clinical Terms	Comprehensive and precise clinical terminology	350,000 concepts (>1M terms)	International Health Terminology Standards Development Organisation
LOINC - Logical Observation Identifiers Names and Codes	Laboratory test orders and results	>30,000 distinct observations	Regenstreif Institute
CPT - Current Procedural Terminology	Billing codes for services rendered	8600 codes and descriptors	American Medical Association
ICPC-2 – International Classification of Primary Care	Reason for encounter (RFE) and other General Practice Medicine concepts	750 codes	World Organization of Family Doctors (WONCA)
UMLS – Unified Medical Language System	Facilitate development of automated reasoning systems in biomedicine and health	>1M concepts (>5M concept names)	US National Library of Medicine

but in every stage of formulating the user interface presentation. Clinical coding and classification schemes, standardized terminology and other standards (such as those for medical imaging and interoperability of health messages) must be carefully considered at every stage.

The second implication is more demanding on the structure of health information systems projects. There will be a pressure to justify design decisions in a manner that is symmetric to evidence-based clinical decisions – by weight of high-quality evidence, collected via systematic literature review and critical appraisal. And there is a pressure to measure a project's success to the standard of success for clinical interventions—via an RCT. As we have seen with the Eccles et al. case study (Box 2), this path is fraught with impracticalities in terms of time-scale and constraints on the natural evolution of systems. Awareness of the broader spectrum of research approaches, notably the action research paradigm, which integrates action and reflection, will help the IS implementer to proceed on a credible basis without being hamstrung by expectations that are not feasible.

These pressures for evidence-based practice will be minimal where the system is at some distance from the clinical (notably physician) culture, such as in support for the logistics of medical supplies. In operational terms, significant pressure will be for system integrity—reliability, robustness and security. As the system moves closer to the clinical interface, however—and especially where the system is directly involved in clinical decision support—there will come the expectation to keep to the norms of the clinical domain.

The rising expectations for clinical systems can be seen with respect to CPOE systems. Ash, Berg & Coiera (2004) provide a taxonomy of the types of errors *caused* by health information systems, including such categories as: (a) cognitive overload by overemphasizing structured information; (b) human-computer interfaces not suitable to interruptions; and (c) misrepresenting clinical work as a predictable workflow. In many settings, health IT

systems are no longer optional – they are often the only way to work within a given healthcare setting. Health information systems designers will be under increasing pressure to deliver systems that truly fit with clinical work and can be demonstrated to have a net positive contribution to health outcomes.

One of the most amazing things about health information systems is that, despite the enormous barriers to their implementation, people get on with doing it anyway. It is worth noting that the US, while home to some islands of excellence in healthcare IT, is not on the aggregate a world leader in its deployment. This probably owes in part to the decentralized nature of its healthcare system, wherein the sector is not as prone to responding to a central government directive as, say, the UK with its National Health Service (NHS). However, the past couple of years have seen a major top-down push for health IT in the US with resulting major initiatives in the Department of Health and Human Services (see http://www.hhs.gov/healthit/initiatives/).

Even in environments that are heavily or fully electronic, the effort continues to achieve higher levels of integration and greater benefits from health IT. For example, in New Zealand, where virtually all primary care physicians use computers, and paperless practices are not rare, the implementation of both national and local health strategies shows nothing but acceleration in the level of health information systems implementation activity. The methods and challenges of this area are both instructive and, equally, in need of further study. Moreover, the diversity of approaches taken in healthcare can inform our choice of techniques to achieve an effective implementation in other multidisciplinary and complex domains.

The drive to achieve effective interoperability of health information systems is increasing in momentum through the 'connectathon' process as promoted by IHE (http://www.ihe.net/Connectathon/index.cfm). A connectathon is a venue for vendors to prove their implementation by exchanging information with complementary systems from other vendors, and performing all of the required transactions their system's roles in a selected profile of use cases. This process is driving ahead health information systems practice by putting vendor claims of standards adherence to the test.

On the research side, what is needed is more evaluation of the effectiveness of healthcare implementations. As per Box 2, Chaudhry et al. (2006) find rather limited evidence to support the notion that organisations can expect to achieve benefits related to health outcome from health IT deployment. This is not to say that outcomes are failing to be achieved – just that the process has not been adequately articulated. In this regard there is a particular need to understand the implementation pathways and outcomes associated with deployment of off-the-shelf systems (as compared to 'home grown' software solutions).

While we have provided some insights into the complexities of information management and systems success in health care, it is impossible to address the entire domain of Health Informatics in a single chapter. The interested reader is recommended to investigate the textbooks by Shortliffe (2006) and Coiera (2003) listed below.

REFERENCES

Alavi, M., & Carlson, P. (1992). A review of MIS research and disciplinary development. *Journal of Management Information Systems, 8*(4), 45-62.

Ash, J. (1997). Organisational factors that influence information technology diffusion [EP in Academic Health Sciences Centres]. *Journal of the American Medical Informatics Association, 4*(2), 102-111.

Ash, J., Berg, M., & Coiera, E. (2004). Some unintended consequences of information technology in health care: the nature of patient care information system-related errors. . *Journal of the American Informatics Association, 11*, 104-112.

Avison, D., Baskerville, R., & Myers, M. D. (2001). Controlling action research projects. *Information Technology & People, 14*(1), 28.

Brydon-Miller, M., Greenwood, D., & Maguire, P. (2003). Why action research? *Action Research, 1*(1), 9-28.

Buchanan, D., & Connor, M. (2001). Managing process risk: Planning for the booby traps ahead. *Strategy & Leadership, 29*(3), 23-28.

Chaudhry, B., Wang, J., Wu, S., Maglione, M., Mojica, W., Roth, E., et al. (2006). Systematic review: impact of health information technology on quality, efficiency, and costs of medical care. *Annals of Internal Medicine, 144*(10), 724-752.

Coiera, E. (2003). *Guide to Health Informatics* (2nd ed.). Hodder: Arnold.

Coiera, E., Walther, M., Nguyen, K., & Lovell, N. (2005). Architecture for knowledge-based and federated search of online clinical evidence. *Journal of Medical Internet Research, 7*(5), e52.

Day, K., Orr, M., Sankaran, S., & Norris, T. (2006). The reflexive employee: action research immortalised? *Action Learning and Action Research Journal, 11*(2).

Dooley, K. (1997). A complex adaptive systems model of organization change. *Nonlinear Dynamics, Psychology, and Life Sciences, 1*(1).

Eccles, M., McColl, E., Steen, N., Rousseau, N., Grimshaw, J., Parkin, D., et al. (2002). Effect of computerised evidence based guidelines of asthma and angina in adults in primary care: cluster randomised controlled trial. *British Medical Journal, 325*(7370), 941-948.

Field, M. J., & Lohr, K. N. (1992). *Guidelines for clinical practice: from development to use.* Washington, DC: Institute of Medicine, National Academy Press.

Garg, A. X., Adhikari, N. K. J., McDonald, H., Rosas-Arellano, M. P., Devereaux, P. J., Beyene, J., et al. (2005). Effects of computerized clinical decision support systems on practitioner performance and patient outcomes. *Journal of the American Medical Association, 293*(10), 1223-1238.

Glouberman, S., & Mintzberg, H. (1996). Managing the care of health and the cure of disease. Part 1: differentiation. *Healthcare Management Review, 26*(1), 56-59.

Gutierrez, C., & Ranji, U. (2005). US Health Care Costs: Background Brief. Henry J. Kaiser Family Foundation. Retrieved 16 April 2007, from http://www.kaiseredu.org/topics_im.asdp?imID=1&parentID=61&id=358

Guyatt, G., Cook, D., & Haynes, B. (2004). Evidence based medicine has come a long way. *British Medical Journal, 329*, 990-991.

Hamilton, J. (2005). The answerable question and a hierarchy of evidence. *Journal of the American Academy of Child and Adolescent Psychiatry, 44*(6), 596-601.

Hanka, R., O'Brien, C., Heathfield, H., & Buchan, I. (1999). *WAX ActiveLibrary; a tool to manage information overload.* Paper presented at the 32nd Hawaii International Conference on System Sciences, IEEE Computer Society Press.

Health Information Steering Committee (NZ). (2005). *Health Information Strategy for New Zealand.* Wellington: New Zealand Ministry of Health.

Heeks, R., Mundy, D., & Salazar, A. (1999). *Why health care information systems succeed or fail. Information systems for public sector management. Working paper series 9.* Manchester: Institute for Development Policy Management.

Hersh, W. (2006). Who are the informaticians? What we know and should know. *Journal of the American Medical Informatics Association, 13*, 166 - 170.

Institute of Medicine (U.S.). (2000). *To err is human: Building a safer health system.* Washington, DC: National Academy Press.

Institute of Medicine (U.S.). Committee on Quality of Health Care in America. (2001). *Crossing the quality chasm: a new health system for the 21st century.* Washington, D.C.: National Academy Press.

Kawamoto, K., Houlihan, C., Balas, E., & Lobach, D. (2005). Improving clinical practice using clinical decision support systems: a systematic review of trials to identify features critical to success. *British Medical Journal, 330*(7494), 765.

Khan, K. S., Kunz, R., Kleijnen, J., & Antes, G. (2003). Five steps to conducting a systematic review. *Journal of the Royal Society of Medicine, 96*, 118-121.

Klein, H. K., & Myers, M. D. (1999). A set of principles for conducting and evaluating interpretive field studies in information systems. *MIS Quarterly, 23*(1), 67-94.

Leape, L. L., & Berwick, D. M. (2005). Five years after *To Err is Human.* What have we learned? *Journal of the American Medical Association, 293*(19), 2384-2390.

Littlejohns, P., Wyatt, J. C., & Garvican, L. (2003). Evaluating computerised health information systems: hard lessons still to be learned. *British Medical Journal, 326*, 860-853.

Lorenzi, N. M., Riley, R. T., Blyth A. J. C., Southon, G., & Dixon, B. J. (1997). Antecedents of the people and organisational aspects of medical informatics: Review of the literature. *Journal of the American Medical Informatics Association, 4*(2), 79-93.

Malterud, K. (2001). Qualitative research: standards, challenges, and guidelines. *The Lancet, 358*(August 11), 483-488.

Mayer, D. (2006). Evidence-based medicine. *Epilepsia, 47*(Suppl. 1), 3-5.

Medical Journal of Australia. (2002). *MJA structured abstracts.* Retrieved 14 April 2007, from http://www.mja.com.au/public/information/abstract.html

National Library of Medicine. (2006). *International Committee of Medical Journal Editors Uniform*

Requirements for Manuscripts Submitted to Biomedical Journals: Sample References. Retrieved 14 April 2007, from http://www.nlm.nih.gov/bsd/uniform_requirements.html

Nielsen, J. (1994). Heuristic evaluation. In J. Nielsen & R. L. Mack (Eds.), *Usability Inspection Methods.* New York: John Wiley & Sons.

Orlikowski, W. J., & Baroudi, J. J. (1991). Studying information technology in organizations: research approaches and assumptions. *Information Systems Research, 2*(1), 1-28.

Orr, M. (2004). Evolution of New Zealand's health knowledge management system. *British Journal of Healthcare Computing and Information Management, 21*(10), 28-30.

Orr, M., & Day, K. (2004). Knowledge and learning in 'successful' IT projects: a case study [Electronic Version]. *Health Care and Informatics Review Online* from http://www.enigma.co.nz/hcro/website/index.cfm?fuseaction=articledisplay&Feature.

Palvia, P., Mao, E., Salam, A. F., & Soliman, K. S. (2003). Management information systems research: what's there in a methodology? *Communications of the Association for Information Systems, 11,* 289-309.

Petticrew, M., & Roberts, H. (2003). Evidence, hierarchies, and typologies: horses for courses. *Journal of Epidemiology & Community Health, 57*(7), 527-529.

Petticrew, M., & Roberts, H. (2006). *Systematic reviews in the social sciences. A practical guide.* Malden, MA: Blackwell Publishing.

Plesk, P. E., & Greenhalgh, T. (2001a). The challenge of complexity in health care. *British Medical Journal, 323,* 625-628.

Plesk, P. E., & Wilson, T. (2001b). Complexity science: complexity, leadership, and management in healthcare organisations. *British Medical Journal, 323,* 746-749.

Protti, D. (2003). Local clinician involvement in clinical information systems: luxury or necessity? A review of two international experiences. *British Journal of Healthcare Computing and Information Management, 20*(10), 28-30.

Rapoport, R. N. (1970). Three dilemmas in action research. *Human Relations, 23*(6), 499-513.

Rousseau, N., McColl, E., Newton, J., Grimshaw, J., & Eccles, M. (2003). Practice based, longitudinal, qualitative interview study of computerised evidence based guidelines in primary care. *British Medical Journal, 326*(7384), 314.

Shortliffe, E. (1984). The science of biomedical computing. *Medical Informatics, 9,* 185-193.

Shortliffe, E. (2006). *Biomedical Informatics: Computer Application in Health Care and Biomedicine* (3rd ed.): Springer.

Sidorov, J. (2006). It ain't necessarily so: the electronic health record and the unlikely prospect of reducing health care costs. *Health Affairs, 25*(4), 1079-1085.

Smith, G., & Pell, J. (2003). Parachute use to prevent death and major trauma related to gravitational challenge: systematic review of randomised controlled trials. *British Medical Journal, 327,* 1459-1461.

Smith, R. (1996). What clinical information do doctors need? *British Medical Journal, 313,* 1062-1068.

Southon, G., Perkins, R., & Galler, K. (2005). Networks: a key to the future of health services. *Journal of the Australian Healthcare Association, 29*(3), 317-326.

Stanley, K. (2007). Design of randomized controlled trials. *Circulation, 115,* 1164 - 1169.

Sveiby, K. (1996). Tacit knowledge. Transfer of knowledge and the information processing professions. *European Management Journal, 14*(4), 379.

Tan, J., Wen, H. J., & Awad, N. (2005). Health care and services delivery systems as complex adaptive systems. Examining chaos theory in action. *Communications of the ACM, 48*(5), 37-44.

Thiru, K., Hassey, A., & Sullivan, F. (2003). Systematic review of scope and quality of electronic patient record data in primary care. *British Medical Journal, 326,* 1070.

Van Bemmel, J. (1984). The structure of medical informatics. *Med Inform, 9,* 175 - 180.

Van Bemmel, J. H., & Musen, M. A. (Eds.). (1997). *Handbook of Medical Informatics.* Netherlands: AW Houten.

Warren, J., & Stanek, J. (2006). Decision support systems. In M. Cornick (Ed.), *Health Informatics: Transforming Healthcare with Technology* (pp. 248 - 261): Thomson Learning.

Waterman, H., Tillen, D., Dickson, R., & de Koning, K. (2001). *Action research: a systematic review and guidance for assessment.* Norwich: Queen's Printer and Controller of HMSO 2001.

Wiener, M., Gress, T., Theimannn, D. R., Jenckes, M., Reel, S. L., Mandell, S. F., et al. (1999). Contrasting views of physicians and nurses about an inpatient computer-based provider order-entry system. *Journal of the American Medical Informatics Association, 6*(3), 234 - 244.

Wyatt, J. (1991). Uses and sources of medical knowledge. *Lancet, 338,* 1368 - 1372.

Wyatt, J. (2001). Top tips in knowledge management. *Clinical Governance Bulletin, 2*(3), 8.

Wyatt, J., & Keen, J. (2005). The NHS's new information strategy. *British Medical Journal, 317*(7163), 900.

Wyatt, J., & Sullivan, F. (2005). Keeping up: learning in the workplace. *British Medical Journal, 331,* 1129-1132.

KEY TERMS

Action Research: The use of the cycle of act and reflect to solve problems in the workplace while simultaneously conducting research, within mutually agreed upon ethical parameters (Rapoport, 1970). Although AR is usually used for qualitative research it is increasingly becoming a mixed methods research tool, using both qualitative and quantitative research methods in a single study.

Clinical Decision Support Systems (CDSS): Electronic tools (usually) that have been developed from clinical guidelines in order to present clinical information appropriately, quickly and effectively at the point of care. They aim to support the delivery of evidence-based medicine.

Complex Adaptive System: Health is a complex adaptive system in that many parts of the system interact interdependently and mostly unpredictably with one another and their environment. These systems are sensitive to initial conditions, support the emergence of the unexpected, and result in unanticipated consequences.

Evidence-Based Medicine: The use of clinical evidence derived from research, best practice and experience to provide healthcare aimed at quality, cost-effective outcomes.

Health Informatics: The theoretical and practical science of using information systems, tools and processes to support and enable healthcare delivery from a range of perspectives and to achieve a broad scope of healthcare goals and objectives.

Health Information Systems: These consist of IT infrastructures and applications that support the delivery of healthcare by means of acquiring, storing and reusing electronic information.

Health Knowledge Management: The acquisition, storage, use and reuse of information as it merges with the experience of healthcare practitioners and service providers, e.g. clinicians and managers (knowledge workers). Tacit and explicit knowledge are exploited for improved health outcomes in applications such as clinical decision support systems, randomised control trials, and other components of the hierarchy of evidence.

ENDNOTE

[1] Although the literature outlining IS research categories and themes classes action research as a form of qualitative research, recent practice patterns present action research as a framework that enables both qualitative and quantitative forms of research (Brydon-Miller, Greenwood, & Maguire, 2003; Klein & Myers, 1999).

Chapter XXXII
Trends and Prospects of Telemedicine

A.H.M. Razibul Islam
Macquarie University, Australia

Rashida Begum
Eminence Associates, Bangladesh

A. B. M. Shawkat Ali
Central Queensland University, Australia

ABSTRACT

Recent development in telecommunication and information technologies came up with several technology options for telemedicine applications in hospitals and for medics for quality healthcare to patients. The research trends therefore need to be addressed for the proper deployment of technologies in a clinical setting or in a telemedicine environment with the adaptive compromise of technology and suitability. In this chapter, along with a description of the research trends and system design issues concerned with telemedicine, a mobile telemedicine system architecture and design have been proposed. Other current telemedicine technology options and prospects and challenges of future research in this emerging area are also described to indicate the possible future research challenges. Research in telemedicine is a future to provide improved and quality access to the healthcare professionals and patients. Therefore, developing telemedicine systems with state-of-the-art technologies is of paramount importance and hence, this chapter would link up an important step in system analysis and design perspective to this evolving research arena.

INTRODUCTION

Telemedicine has been defined as the use of telecommunication to provide diagnostic and therapeutic medical information and to provide healthcare services between patient and doctor without either of them having to travel across geographic, time, social, and cultural barriers. In other words, telemedicine is the delivery of healthcare services, where distance is a critical factor, by all healthcare professionals using information and communication technologies for the exchange of valid information for diagnosis, treatment, and prevention of disease and injuries, research and evaluation, and for the continuing education of healthcare providers, all in the interests of advancing the health of individuals and their communities. The ongoing advancement of the sensors, low-power integrated circuits, and wired or wireless high data-rate broadband communication services under the umbrella of the telecommunication technology recently flickered renewed research trends and prospects for the efficient and cost-effective deployment of state-of-the-art technologies in telemedicine. It is therefore worthwhile to evaluate the technologies involved in telemedicine applications and establish a relationship between telemedicine system analysis and design to efficiently deliver services in a wider geographic area depending on the bandwidth and user requirements. This chapter therefore describes the trends and prospects of research in telemedicine in this emerging world of broadband convergence with a view to review and establish system design issues in this area. First we will review the definitions of telemedicine with some background information on the development of telemedicine. Subsequent sections of this chapter explore the different applications and design issues of telemedicine in different settings of technologies. As a part of telemedicine system development using current wireless technologies, the system architecture of a mobile telemedicine application is detailed thereafter. Later on, we narrate the other research issues in telemedicine and finally summarize the possibilities and future directions in a technical perspective.

BACKGROUND

The term "telemedicine" derives from the Greek "tele" meaning "at a distance" and the present word "medicine," which itself derives from the Latin "mederi" meaning "healing" (Feliciani, 2003, p. 114). A 1999 definition adopted for a Congressional briefing on telemedicine in the USA produces a statement as follows:

Telemedicine utilizes information and telecommunication technology to transfer medical information for diagnosis, therapy and education.

The World Health Organization (WHO) describes the definition of telemedicine as follows:

The practice of medical care using interactive audiovisual and data communications including medical care delivery, diagnosis, consultation and treatment, as well as education and the transfer of medical data.

In addition to patient records, medical professionals can obtain vital signs and other reference data through telemedicine applications. Depending on the need and availability of communications infrastructure, telemedicine uses a variety of transmission modes including integrated services digital network (ISDN), local area network (LAN), asynchronous transfer mode (ATM), digital subscriber line, satellite, microwave, digital wireless, and the Internet. With all these ranges of technology deployment, telemedicine works have paved the right impetus for a cost-effective telemedicine network.

Telemedicine can be divided into two modes of operations: real-time mode (synchronous), in which patient data are available at the remote terminal immediately after acquisition, and store-and-forward mode (asynchronous), which involves accessing the data at a later time (Craig, 1999, p. 5).

In the store-and-forward mode, a digital image is taken, stored, and then forwarded to another location to a medical specialist for consultation and avoids the simultaneous communication between both parties in real time. Teleradiology, where radiographic images are needed to be transferred or in dermatology, where visually skin lesions are examined, are very good examples of this kind of mode. Store-and-forward also includes the asynchronous transmission of clinical data, such as blood glucose levels and electrocardiogram (ECG) measurements, from one site (e.g., patient's home) to another site (e.g., home, health agency, hospital, or clinic).

In the real-time mode, both locations need to have the necessary equipments like cameras or monitors to complete the interaction. Real-time mode can use something as simple as telephone calls or as sophisticated as virtual reality robotic surgery or telesurgery. The patients and providers in this mode can communicate in between themselves using audiovisual and wireless or microwave signals. It is particularly useful for monitoring of long-term care patients or patients at their home. Applications of this type of mode can be in cardiology, neurology, and gynecology.

Therefore, telemedicine unit basically consists of the following modules:

- Biosignal acquisition module through sensors and peripheral devices.
- Digital camera for image or video capturing.
- Processing unit: computers.
- Communication module: Global system for mobile communication (GSM), general packet radio services (GPRS), third generation (3G), satellite, plain old telephone system (POTS), modem, Internet, WAN, metropolitan area networks (MAN), personal area networks (PAN), and so forth.

To date back to history, telemedicine was not developed as a segregated well-defined discipline with specialized protocols. With the advent of technologies, clinicians began to adopt the new technology for other purposes depending on availability. In the 1920s, radio-linked public health physicians watched at the sea stations to ships at sea with medical emergencies because sea-voyages were the principle means of international travel at that time. The most celebrated example is the Italian International Radio Medicine Centre, which began in 1935 and had assisted over 42,000 patients, mainly seafarers, by 1996 (Stanberry, 1998).

Widespread availability of black and white television in the 1950s greatly enabled the option to visualize the patients' condition for diagnosis. At the same year, Robert Ledley pioneered the use of digital computers in the U.S. for medical purposes for dental projects at the National Bureau of Standards. For education and consultations between consultants and general practitioners (GP), the Nebraska Psychiatric Institute developed a two-way link with Norfolk State Hospital, 112 miles away, in 1964 using the closed-circuit television service (Benschoter, 1971). The link was used by doctors who consulted with each other on patient cases and also gave psychiatric consultations to patients on the other end of the link. In the late 1950s, the US Public Health Service and the National Aeronautics and Space Administration (NASA), sought to provide medical care to rural communities of Papago Indians in Arizona via the transmission of electrocardiographs and X-rays to centers staffed by specialists by the project Space Technology Applied to Rural Papago Indians Advanced Health Care (STARPAHC) (Bashshur, 1980). Another significant early implementation of telemedicine was a microwave video link set up in April of 1968 between the Massachusetts General Hospital (MGH) and Boston's Logan airport. The link was established to provide immediate health services to airport employees and passengers. It eliminated the need to have physicians permanently assigned to the clinical facilities at the airport, while avoiding the delays associated with patient transportation. Examinations at Logan included radiology, dermatology, and cardiology (Bashshur, 1975).

Later in the 1970s, the large-scale demonstrations involving the ATS-6 satellite projects took place. The paramedics in remote Alaskan and Canadian villages were linked with hospitals in distant towns or cities. In Japan, telemedicine dates back to the 1970s. In 1971, the first telemedical experiment took place in the Wakayama prefecture. The experiment involved closed-circuit television (CCTV) and the telephone circuit. CCTV was temporarily installed to provide medical care to rural mountain areas that had limited technology. Direct images and sounds were transmitted; documents were also transmitted by facsimile (called copying transmission then). Also, the North-West telemedicine project in Queensland, Australia was the only major telemedicine project outside North America until 1990 which used the satellite links to serve rural communities, including aborigine populations (Watson, 1989, p. 68). In December 1988, NASA established SpaceBridge to Armenia due to the terrible earthquake. Video, voice, and facsimile applications were used in this project for the consultations between specialist centers in USA and a medical center in Yerevan, Armenia to provide the first truly international telemedicine program. Another groundbreaking use of telemedicine (in a completely different setting) occurred in 1998, when a team of researchers from Yale and MIT collaborated with several of their research sponsors on the Everest Extreme Expedition (E3) to monitor climbers' physiological and performance parameters using "bio-packs" as they scaled the highest mountain on Earth (Lau, 1998). The system used on Mount Everest provided audio and video communications to a medical unit at the base camp via satellite and to experts at MIT, Yale Medical, and Walter Reed Army Hospital.

In USA, Allen and Grigsby reported that nearly 40,000 teleconsultations were performed in 1998 in more than 35 different specialties (Allen & Grigsby, 1998), which showed clear invasion of telemedicine. The transition from analog to digital communications and the advent of mobile communication technologies with the Internet have dramatically increased the research impetus in this telemedicine area since the late 1980s. Due to the initial lead in telemedicine research, 50% of the primary research is now conducted in USA compared with the 40% in the whole of Europe and around 10% in Australasia (Wootton & Craig, 1999).

Wireless/mobile telecommunication solutions play a key role in providing telemedicine services, due to their flexibility in installation, portability, and mobility, among other advantages. Existing systems are mostly based on wireless local area network (WLAN), WiFi, and wireless personal area network (WPAN) (e.g., Bluetooth) technologies, in indoor

applications, and on 2.5-generation cellular mobile services (mostly GPRS) in wide area applications. But in terms of coverage and/or data area, 3G wireless technology offers better services and is attractive for certain high bandwidth applications in recent days. Mobile telemedicine therefore is a new research area that exploits recent advances in next generation cellular communications networks, which provide the potential for highly flexible medical services that are not possible with standard telephony. In 1996, Garner et al. assembled a mobile demonstration terminal with a PC and a GSM modem. Image files of simulated wounds were transmitted over the system as e-mail attachments. Reponen at al. (1998) performed computerized tomography (CT) examinations at a remote portable computer that wirelessly connected to a computer network also via GSM cellular phone in 1998. The group later did similar tests with wireless personal digital assistants (PDA) (Reponen et al., 2000). The design of a prototype integrated mobile telemedicine system that is compatible with existing public mobile telecommunication network, code division multiple access (CDMA) 1xEVDO, was demonstrated in 2005 (Jung, 2005). The mobile telemedicine system consists of two parts. One is the physiological signal measuring part, and the other is a PC system for the signal processing and telecommunication. The system uses NetMeeting to transmit video, audio, and patient biosignals from a moving ambulance to a hospital and delivers the information to the personal computer of the doctor. The development of a mobile telemedicine system with multicommunication links was proposed (Ibrahim et al., 2006). The system design goal is to provide patient monitoring during the prehospital transport and to offer health services for people who live in underserved areas. Therefore, medical information transmission becomes very crucial, since there is no transmission link stability guarantee. To deal with this issue, multicommunication links, including very high frequency (VHF) radio, Internet, GSM/CDMA mobile phones, and GPRS, are applied for the system. Selection of the communication links depends on the availability of the local communication infrastructure in their work.

With the deployment of a combination of technologies in telemedicine area, the security and management of data have been considered as prime importance. Health Level 7 (HL7) is such an organization whose mission is to provide standards for the exchange, management, and integration of data that support clinical patient care and the management, delivery, and evaluation of healthcare services.

Most recently, telemedicine is currently in practice at sites such as the University of Kansas, where telemedicine has been used to care for patients in rural jails and hospice care, and at Johns Hopkins, where surgery was performed remotely on a man in Bangkok, Thailand.

The diversified technologies involved in telemedicine research are therefore key accelerators in the growth of this area. The next section encompasses the technological developments, design issues, and research trends of this demanding sector. Along with other current research trends in this area, a mobile telemedicine system analysis and design are also described in the following section as a possible solution for a telemedicine applied networked environment to provide best healthcare with wireless connectivity.

RESEARCH TRENDS IN TELEMEDICINE WITH DESIGN ISSUES AND A SYSTEM ANALYSIS

In a telemedicine system, generally four types of data are required to be transferred which are text and data, audio, still images, and video. Table 1 shows the file size requirements of these different types of data. Hence, depending on the file size, choice and performance of the telemedicine equipments are decided according to the clinical needs.

There are lots of factors that affect the performance of the types of data that are intended to be transferred in a telemedicine environment from one place to other locations without face-to-face consultation between the patients and physicians. The availability of different telecommunications technologies in telemedicine applications has also opened the enormous options of choosing a particular one according to requirements in a specific clinical setting. The alternative telecommunication options with the performance criteria for telemedicine applications are henceforth discussed briefly. And later in the following subsection, the research trends in this area will also be discussed with a description of a proposed system architecture of a mobile telemedicine system as mentioned earlier in this chapter. Thus, the main focus of this section will encompass the current research inclinations and system design issues among the ranges of technology options available in telemedicine research and to provide a system analysis and design of a mobile telemedicine system to wirelessly provide telemedicine services.

Public Switched Telephone Network (PSTN)

Also known as POTS, the early version of analog PSTN telephony was inadequate for telemedicine applications due to the low quality and low band-

Table 1. Examples of telemedicine data types (Wootton & Craig, 1999)

Source of data	Type	Typical File Size
Patient Notes	Text	< 10 KB
Electronic Stethoscope	Audio	100 KB
Chest X-ray	Still Image	1 MB
Foetal Ultrasound	Video	10 MB

width problems and was limited to only transmit audio sounds (e.g., speech) for remote diagnosis. With the advent of digital PSTN applications, limited audio, video, and data sharing are possible through the low bandwidth of 56 Kbps. But using high speed processors, encoding techniques, compression algorithms, and video display software can sustain this technology option because PSTN technology is generally available throughout the world.

Integrated Services Digital Network (ISDN)

In this purely digital service, there are two categories, which are basic rate interface (BRI) and primary rate interface (PRI). BRI comprises two 64 Kbps (B) channels and a 16 Kbps data signal (D) channel. In another word, this is an ISDN interface that provides 128k of bandwidth for videoconferencing or simultaneous voice and data services. Multiple BRI lines can be linked together using a multiplexer to achieve higher bandwidth levels. For instance, a popular choice among telehealth networks is to combine three BRI lines to provide 384k of bandwidth for video-conferencing. It should be noted that BRI services are not available in some rural locations. The advantages of BRI ISDN are immediate availability in most areas, inexpensive telecommunications equipment and line rates, and greater protocol support among existing computing hardware and software (Akselsen et al., 1993, pp. 46-51). But, BRI ISDN does not provide the bandwidth necessary for a large number of telemedicine applications which require simultaneous multimedia bit-streams, especially diagnostic-quality, full-motion video. The PRI has up to 30 B channels with a single 64 Kbps D channel. Channels can be coupled together so that a two-channel BRI system can work at 128 Kbps and a six-channel PRI set-up can function at 384 Kbps, which is fast enough to provide smooth video under most circumstances (Brebner et al., 2000). The community healthcare centers, located in major Indian cities, are connected via ISDN, with a redundant backup very small aperture terminal (VSAT) channel open.

The accepted international standard for video-conferencing is H.320 which includes support for video (H.261) and audio (G.722, G.728) compression/decompression, multiplexing, and synchronization, as well as document sharing (T.120). H.320 is designed to work over the range of ISDN connections (from 64 Kbps to 1.92 Mbps). In locations where ISDN is not available, POTS could be used to support H.324 videoconferencing, a derivative of H.320 which includes support for communications at up to 64 Kbps. Without compression, a large image transfer of 250 Mb over ISDN would require more than 2,000 seconds at 128 Kbps or 130 seconds at 1.92 Mbps where with 20:1 compression, this transfer would require 100 seconds at 128 Kbps or 6.5 seconds at 1.92 Mbps.

Asynchronous Transfer Mode (ATM)

ATM is a network technology based on transferring data in *cells* or *packets* of a fixed size. The cell used with ATM is relatively small compared to units used with older technologies. The small, constant cell size allows ATM equipment to transmit video, audio, and computer data over the same network, and assure that no single type of data hogs the line. ATM creates a fixed channel, or route, between two points whenever data transfer begins. This differs from TCP/IP, in which messages are divided into packets and each packet can take a different route from source to destination.

The advantages of ATM are higher bandwidths and statistical multiplexing of small packets (cells) with guaranteed bandwidth and minimal latency and jitter (Handel et al., 1993). Unlike ISDN, the range of bandwidths supported by ATM is sufficient for the entire range of telemedicine applications, including moving pictures expert group (MPEG) 2 video streams. A large image transfer of 250 Mb would require 1.6 seconds at 155 Mbps without compression, ignoring network overhead. With 20:1 compression and ignoring the time necessary to compress and decompress the images, this transfer would require only 0.08 seconds at 155 Mbps. In addition, because ATM connections sharing physical links are logically separate, excess traffic from one connection would not impact other connections, including connections between the same source and destination.

ATM also offers "bandwidth on demand," which allows a connection to deliver a higher bandwidth only when it is needed. The disadvantages of using ATM for telemedicine are the high costs and nonavailability of ATM equipment and telecommunications lines, especially to rural areas. However, ATM equipment and line availability have been increasing steadily and are expected to improve considerably in the future, and costs are expected to decrease as the size of the ATM market and user acceptance increases. It should be noted that ATM is one of the technologies being evaluated by telecommunications and interactive television companies for providing video dial tone services to the home. Besides contributing to the ATM infrastructure, ATM to the home would have major implications for telemedicine, including emergency services, remote monitoring of vital signs, and home patient education, thus providing a communications infrastructure to realize an ultimate goal in telemedicine, the "electronic house call," limited to the first three only. Also, when coupled with the resilient synchronous optical Network (SONET) configurations, ATM systems offer high-quality and low-delay conditions.

Microwave Links

The term microwave generally refers to alternating current signals with frequencies between 300 MHz (3×10^8 Hz) and 300 GHz (3×10^{11} Hz). For wide area network telemedicine applications, microwave connections can be a good option. Wireless LAN protocols, such as Bluetooth and the IEEE 802.11g and b specifications, also use microwaves in the 2.4 GHz industry, science and medicine (ISM) band, although 802.11a uses an ISM band in the 5 GHz range. Licensed long-range (up to about 25 km) wireless Internet access services can be found in

many countries (but not the USA) in the 3.5–4.0 GHz range. MAN protocols, such as worldwide interoperability for microwave access (WiMAX), are based in the IEEE 802.16 specification. The IEEE 802.16 specification was designed to operate between 2 to 11 GHz. The commercial implementations are in the 2.5 GHz, 3.5 GHz, and 5.8 GHz ranges. Cable TV and Internet access on coax cable as well as broadcast television use some of the lower microwave frequencies. Some mobile phone networks, like GSM, also use the lower microwave frequencies.

It is of a higher frequency than a radio and is totally dependent on line of sight from transmitter to receiver. It is usually used on a point-to-point basis over distances up to 50 kilometers. Quite high bandwidths can be achieved if used in telemedicine applications. Hence, one disadvantage of the microwave link setup is that it requires line-of-sight between antennas in order to operate without interference, a requirement that is not always easy to satisfy in highly mountainous regions.

Satellite Technology

Satellites are able to receive radio signals from Earth and then retransmit them back. The device which does this is a satellite transponder. The geographic area covered by the satellite signal is known as the satellite's footprint. Most communications satellites are in geostationary orbit over 40,000 kilometers above the equator and have footprints covering very large regions. The equipment required to transmit a signal to a satellite in geostationary orbit is expensive. The equipment required to receive the signal from the satellite is much less expensive. For this reason, satellite technology is often used to broadcast signals, for example, television or as a means of "trunking" an aggregated signal between telecommunications hubs. Satellite charges have been falling as their numbers and overall capacity have increased.

The advantages that satellite communications can bring to telemedicine include instant access to broadband services, particularly in remote areas where telecommunications are poor or nonexistent, and swift response in disaster situations where speed is vital. Satellites also provide a powerful and relatively inexpensive tool, particularly for video links between multiple users. Plus, costs are constantly decreasing and satellites are a tried, tested, and extremely reliable means of telecommunication. Many existing mobile medical systems for disaster situations use satellites to establish communication between the disaster area and remote base hospitals (Garshnek & Burkle, 1999).

Wireless Technologies

In a telemedicine environment, the physicians and healthcare workers need to be mobile most of the time due to their respective duties in a clinic or hospital. Therefore, there is an obvious necessity to provide ubiquitous connectivity to the physicians or health workers so that they can access to the central database of clinical records of patients in a computer from a remote mobile terminal whenever needed. Also, light and smaller size with longer battery life, lower costs, and better user interfaces of mobile devices have strengthen the applicability of wireless technologies in telemedicine applications. So, the term mobile telemedicine is the fastest changing term in telemedicine applications since the wireless technology is moving towards third generation to fourth generation and therefore the transmission rates of different wireless techniques vary from one to another.

GSM offers 9.6 Kbps bandwidth and therefore restricts potential mobile telemedical services and the type, speed, and quantity of medical information to be transmitted. But the advent of GPRS promises data rates from 56 up to 114 Kbps and continuous connection to the Internet for mobile phone and computer users. Also, enhanced data rates for global evolution (EDGE) is a radio-based high-speed mobile data standard. It allows data transmission speeds of 384 Kbps to be achieved when all eight timeslots are used. EDGE was ini-

tially developed for mobile network operators who fail to win the universal mobile telephone system (UMTS) spectrum. EDGE gives incumbent GSM operators the opportunity to offer data services at speeds that are near to those available on UMTS networks. With EDGE, the operators and service providers can offer more wireless data application, including wireless multimedia, e-mail (Web-based), Web infotainment, and above all, the technology of video conferencing which has certainly alleviate the limitations faced by GSM in telemedicine applications.

Emergence of 3G mobile phone networks created and increased a number of systems which use mobile phones to transfer vital signs such as ECG and heart rate rather than early mobile medical system using satellites to establish communications between remote sites and base hospitals. 3G mobile phone is a digital mobile phone based on the International Telecommunication Union (ITU) IMT-2000 standard. In 3G communication networks, basically a CDMA system is used and provides a lot of services using the high bandwidth and multimedia transmission capabilities. Since the 3G mobile phone adopts the CDMA system, noise and cut-off in communication is reduced, and high-speed data transmission can be done at the rate of 384 Kbps at the most which was not acquired in 2G mobile phones. For example, Chu and Ganz (2004) report use of 3G networks for simultaneous transmission of video, medical images, and ECG signals. They describe a portable teletrauma system that assists healthcare centers by providing simultaneous transmission of a patient's video, medical images, and ECG signals required throughout the prehospital procedure. The performance of the system is evaluated over commercially available 3G wireless cellular data service and real network conditions. With the commercially available 3G wireless links, their system can simultaneously transmit video, still-ultrasound images, and vital signs. System designs with 3G links require special considerations on managing the data to ensure smooth transmissions through low-speed and fluctuant 3G link as the actual throughput of such cellular links is fluctuant. Also, different types of streams such as real time video, images, vital signs, or other readings from medical sensors have different transmission requirements. Therefore, it is also needed to coordinate, prioritize, and compress the diverse media streams to eliminate distortion of multimedia content in cellular networks which are also essential criteria in design issues of telemedicine system involving cellular networks.

A collection of intelligent, physiological, and wearable sensor nodes capable of sensing, processing, and communicating one or more vital signs can be seamlessly integrated into wireless personal or body networks (WPANs) for health monitoring. The most important features of a wearable health monitor are long battery life, lightweight, and small size. If integrated into a telemedical system, these systems can even alert medical personnel when life-threatening changes occur. In addition, patients can benefit from continuous long-term monitoring as a part of a diagnostic procedure, can achieve optimal maintenance of a chronic condition, or can be supervised during recovery from an acute event or surgical procedure. Long-term health monitoring can capture the diurnal and circadian variations in physiological signals. These variations, for example, are a very good recovery indicator in cardiac patients after myocardial infarction (Binkley, 2003). In addition, long-term monitoring can confirm adherence to treatment guidelines (e.g., regular cardiovascular exercise) or help monitor effects of drug therapy. Other patients can also benefit from these systems; for example, the monitors can be used during physical rehabilitation after hip or knee surgeries, stroke rehabilitation, or brain trauma rehabilitation. During the last few years there has been a significant increase in the number of various wearable health monitoring devices, ranging from simple pulse monitors, activity monitors, and portable Holter monitors (Holter Systems, 2007), to sophisticated and expensive implantable sensors. However, wider acceptance of the existing systems is still limited by the following important restrictions.

Traditionally, personal medical monitoring systems, such as Holter monitors, have been used only to collect data. Data processing and analysis are performed off-line, making such devices impractical for continual monitoring and early detection of medical disorders. Systems with multiple sensors for physical rehabilitation often feature unwieldy wires between the sensors and the monitoring system. These wires may limit the patient's activity and level of comfort and thus negatively influence the measured results (Martin et al., 2000). In addition, individual sensors often operate as stand-alone systems and usually do not offer flexibility and integration with third-party devices. Finally, the existing systems are rarely made affordable. Recent technology advances in integration and miniaturization of physical sensors, embedded microcontrollers, and radio interfaces on a single chip, wireless networking, and microfabrication have enabled a new generation of wireless sensor networks suitable for many applications. A number of physiological sensors that monitor vital signs, environmental sensors (e.g., temperature, humidity, and light), and a location sensor can all be integrated into a wearable wireless body/personal area network (WWBAN) (Jovanov et al., 2005). When integrated into a broader telemedical system with patients' medical records, the WWBAN promises a revolution in medical research through data mining of all gathered information. The large amount of collected physiological data will allow quantitative analysis of various conditions and patterns.

A LAN is used to connect digital devices such as personal computers and mainframe computers over a localized area such as a building or campus of a hospital, university, or factory. In a hospital they are often used to access a patient master index, medical record tracking, appointment booking systems, and pathology test results. Distances are small, 1-2 kilometers at the most, and this allows high data transmission rates. A wide area network (WAN) is a network which covers a greater geographic area than a LAN. In health applications, a typical WAN would connect the LANs from all the hospitals in a city or region. A wireless LAN or WLAN is a wireless local area network, which is the linking of two or more computers without using wires. Thus, now-a-days, WLAN systems capable of transmitting at high speeds are being developed and installed around the world. They possess a number of advantages ranging from installation flexibility and mobility to increased scalability. Hospitals are in need of such technology as it will ensure faster and more accurate addressing of patient needs, allowing for delivery of services to the point of care, even though the treating staff could be in a different place at the time.

Originally WLAN hardware was so expensive that it was only used as an alternative to cabled LAN in places where cabling was difficult or impossible. Early development included industry-specific solutions and proprietary protocols, but at the end of the 1990s these were replaced by standards, primarily the various versions of IEEE 802.11 (Wi-Fi) and HomeRF (2 Mbit/s, intended for home use, unknown in the UK). An alternative ATM-like 5 GHz standardized technology, high performance local area network (HIPERLAN), has so far not succeeded in the market, as with the release of the faster 54 Mbit/s 802.11a (5 GHz) and 802.11g (2.4 GHz) standards. Table 2 represents the lists of the available WLAN protocols for the application in telemedicine.

Among the available protocols, Bluetooth is a low cost, low power, short-range radio technique introduced by Ericsson and others. Bluetooth was originally and essentially a replacement for physical cables. The goal of eliminating cables has lead to the creation of the notion of PAN, a close range network surrounding a person carrying several heterogeneous devices equipped with wireless communication techniques. It has the capability to allow mobile devices to communicate with computers within a 10 m distance which can be helpful in patient monitoring and emergency alarms to remote locations.

The merging of Internet and mobile computing is promoting the developments of handheld devices, wireless infrastructures, application programming languages, and protocols, all aiming to provide mobile Internet access. Among these is the wireless application protocol (WAP), a communication protocol and application environment for the deployment of the information resources, advanced telephony services, and Internet access from mobile devices. So WAP can be a possible option for telemedicine applications. Hung et al. (2003) utilize WAP devices as mobile access terminals for general enquiry and patient-monitoring services. In this experiment, an authorized user, may it be doctor or the patient's relatives, can browse the patient's general data, monitored blood pressure, and electrocardiogram in store-and-forward mode.

From the aforementioned technology options, it is now vivid that more and more investigations relating the mobile telemedicine area need to be explored because of tremendous data transmission capabilities of the future ubiquitous next generation wireless networks. Therefore, a system architecture based on the WLAN system to utilize in a mobile telemedicine environment is described in the following sub-section.

System Design Architecture of a Mobile Telemedicine System

Mobile telemedicine involves more than just communicating via a mobile phone or PDA that sends and receives some medical data. It involves some swiftly moving vehicles that are equipped with high quality, broadband wireless systems to assist patients in undeserved regions or in disaster areas. Ambulances with wireless systems provide links between the hospital physician and the paramedic in the ambulance while a patient is being transported to the hospital. Real time patient signals like ECG and spot oxygen saturation (SpO_2) can be monitored even before the patient reaches the hospital. On the other hand, conventional home care basically involves a fixed and limited number of visits by a trained nurse to a patient's home. All activities during these visits are controlled by the nurse; they may include vital signals recording, general assessment of the patient's therapy progress, medication, and patient's instruction on particular needs observed during the visit (Guillén et al., 2002). By using mobile phones, a telehomecare system is possible where the phones can interact with electromedic devices (EMDs)—like patient monitors, for example—and transmit vital signals through Internet protocols, such as transmission control protocol (TCP/IP) and user datagram protocol (UDP).

In this subsection, a design and system architecture of a mobile telemedicine system using 3G mobile communications technology with the application of orthogonal frequency division multiplexing (OFDM) scheme in a wireless LAN environment to provide an enhanced, seamless and ubiquitous healthcare information exchange is presented. The telemedicine system will include videoconferencing as well as communication of patient signals including data, images, and videos. The proposed wireless LANs for this system are IEEE 802.11a and IEEE 802.11b depending on the application area and the requirement of speed and bandwidth needed. A telehomecare system will be also included to exploit maximum benefits of the proposed model.

The most widely used wireless protocol today is the IEEE 802.11b. In the market since 2000, it usually uses complementary code keying (CCK) and direct signal spread spectrum (DSSS) techniques to spread its signal over a frequency range and avoid interference while achieving a top speed of 11 Mbps an advertised range of about 300 m which is 20-30 m in practice (Flickenger, 2003). As sophisticated as this technique is, it behaves relatively poorly in multipath environments when compared with newer modulation schemes like OFDM.

As mentioned before, IEEE 802.11b operates in the 2.4 GHz frequency band (a band also known as ISM). It is one of the least favorite frequency bands, as at 2.44 GHz water molecules resonate and microwave ovens operate. To cope with this problem, WLANs usually use some kind of spread spectrum technique, either frequency hopping spread spectrum (FHSS) or DSSS to spread their signal over a frequency range so they can avoid interference at a specific frequency. DSSS is the most widely used method and is considered slightly better than FHSS.

Regardless of the spreading technique used, the wireless transmission signal will still suffer from attenuation, especially when the mobile terminal

Table 2. WLAN protocols

Protocol	Release Date	Frequency	Bandwidth
IEEE 802.11	1997	2.4 GHz	1, 2 Mbps
IEEE 802.11a	1999	5 GHz	6, 9, 12, 18, 24, 36, 48, 54 Mbps
IEEE 802.11b	1999	2.4 GHz	5.5, 11 Mbps
IEEE 802.11g	2003	2.4 GHz	6, 9, 12, 18, 24, 36, 48, 54 Mbps
IEEE 802.11n	expected mid-2007	2.4 GHz	540 Mbps
IEEE 802.15 (Bluetooth)	1999	2.4 GHz	1 Mbps
IEEE 802.16 (Wi-MAX)	December 2005	6-66 GHz	up to 75 Mbps
HomeRF	IEEE 802.16 December 2005 6 - 66 GHz up to 75 Mbps	<5 GHz	10 Mbps

(MT) is moving away from the access point (AP). For this reason, 802.11b is designed to fall back on its speed in order to maintain signal integrity. This means that as the received signal is deteriorating, the connection speed will automatically fall from 11 Mbps to 5.5, 2, and finally to 1 Mbps. Keeping in mind that real-time applications (like telemedicine) are bandwidth demanding, the reduced bandwidth is rarely capable of accommodating the needs of real-time applications.

An attempt to increase the available bandwidth is the IEEE protocol, 802.11a, capable of operating at speeds of as high as 54 Mbps. Although suggested and standardized first, 802.11a was released after 802.11b and up until recently was only operating in the USA. This is because 802.11a operates in the 5 GHz band that is reserved in most European countries. This band is called universal networking information infrastructure (UNII) and consists of three separate bands: UNII-1 for indoor use, UNII-2 for either indoor or outdoor use, and UNII-3 for outdoor bridging only. Reflections are much more apparent in the 5 GHz spectrum, so any kind of reflective surface can have devastating effects on signal quality. The most visible consequence is when trying to cover a space with AP, a lot more are needed if 802.11a is used compared to 802.11b.

A new protocol, high performance local area network (HIPERLAN/2), also operating in the 5 GHz band, has been developed by the European Technical Standards Institute (ETSI) and promises true quality of service (QoS) and speeds of 54 Mbps. Unfortunately, despite its development for over 4 years, hardware supporting this protocol is not yet commercially available. Both HIPERLAN/2 and 802.11a share almost the same characteristics with the exception of the intermediate fallback speeds: 6, 9, 12, 18, 24, 36, 48, and 54 Mbps for IEEE 802.11a and 6, 9, 12, 18, 27, 36, and 54 for HIPERLAN/2. Since the modulation is practically the same, one can conclude that the issues discussed here concerning 802.11a apply to HIPERLAN/2 (Doufexi & Armour, 2002).

In most wireless communications, the signal does not travel from transmitter to receiver through a straight line. Mountains, buildings, floors, ceilings, furniture, and even people reflect the signal depending on the operating frequency. The lower the frequency, the more it can penetrate through objects and not get reflected. The higher the frequency, the more reflections take place and a multipath effect is more dominant.

During the multipath effect the receiver not only receives the signal directly from the transmitter, but also receives all the reflections of that signal. What makes this an undesirable effect is that since the straight-line transmission arrives the earliest, all other packet transmissions arrive with a time delay and collide with next-frame data. Depending on the distance between receiver and transmitter and the number of reflected paths, the signal can be rendered useless, even though its power would be sufficient in the absence of this effect.

The above discussion indicates that IEEE 802.11a would suffer from a much higher multipath loss than 802.11b since it is using a higher frequency band. However, a different kind of modulation from that used in 802.11b can be used in both 802.11a and HIPERLAN/2 to address this problem; OFDM rather than using CCK.

Thus the proposed OFDM system in the mobile telemedicine system can offer improvement which would mean that more data can safely go through the communication channel and, for the specific telemedical application, a better video quality can be transmitted and consequently the doctors can make a more accurate diagnosis. For the telehomecare system, the system takes advantage of the serial port available in new mobile phones using OFDM to implement a generic interface for patient monitors. The vital signals are acquired from the EMD using the RS232 interface and transmitted through the Internet.

In the proposed mobile telemedicine system, one central server and a mobile server is required. The mobile server will have a high-end laptop computer with a WLAN personal computer memory card international association (PCMCIA) card using the IEEE 802.11a/b protocol depending on the distance requirement and it will permit total mobility within the emergency department of the hospital and beyond. An AP within the emergency department acts as a wireless bridge for the network data to be transmitted to and received from the rest of the network. A high-quality digital camcorder is connected to the laptop and high-quality video and audio and still pictures can be transmitted. Medical instruments like otoscopes and dermascopes can also be connected to the system. The central server will have a fixed computer within the existing hospital network or a mobile computer. Expert consultants and doctors will be sitting there. It can be in the same hospital or a remote hospital. The central server will have the facility to provide teleconferencing and it should be able to transmit video to a PDA. Existing 3G and also future 4G mobile devices will also be used as the terminals in the central server.

The telehomecare will be provided by the interface RS232 of the mobile phones of the patients staying home. The patient's vital signals, such as ECG, heart rate, blood pressure, SpO2, respiration rate, and temperature will be taken by the patient monitor, that is, EMD, and sent by the mobile phone through RS232 interface. The signals are converted in packets and transmitted to the server using TCP/IP and/or UDP protocols. The central server settled in hospital stores data in a relational database. Then, healthcare providers or consultants monitor their patients using the server application. Videoconferencing arrangement in the patient's home can further improve the diagnosis.

Incoming emergency patients can be dealt with by the mobile server which can communicate to the central server depending on needs. The patients on the way to hospital in the ambulance can be communicated by the mobile device—with the 3G/4G technique having video options—and treated according to the advice provided by doctors. In the disaster areas or remote areas, the similar advantage of 3G/4G mobile technology with high data rate applications, that is, video or teleconferencing, can be applied. Figure 1 shows the block diagram

representation of the whole system architecture.

In the model, from the 802.11b, it will be good to use the extended range it has, its increased compatibility with radio regulatory committees all over the world, and its relatively cheap hardware. From the 802.11a, use its higher tolerance to multipath noise, a factor that affects extensively the signal quality and speed of the WLAN. Using OFDM modulation instead of CCK in the system will provide two advantages at the same time.

Fortunately, most wireless hardware (APs and client cards) in the market today give the user the ability to upgrade the firmware (software inside ROM) of the system in order to support different technologies. Also, today's hardware has embedded microprocessors that can perform a wide variety of tasks, including inverse fast Fourier transform (IFFT) and fast Fourier transform (FFT), necessary for OFDM modulation.

It is obvious that in these kinds of systems, QoS plays a critical role. It would be useless if the system could not guarantee the level of service necessary for accurate diagnosis. Despite the fact that none of the IEEE 802.11 protocols have guaranteed QoS, there are several parameters that a developer can optimize in order to keep a high operational level of the wireless network. Some of these include connection establishment delay, throughput, transit delay, residual error rate, protection, priority, and resilience. While protection refers to the security that the system applies to the transmitted data (Owens et al., 2001), throughput and resilience are definitely some of the most important QoS parameters in a WLAN. In order to maximize the throughput one has to minimize the number of errors that appear in the communication channel. One of these erroneous factors is the multipath phenomenon and that is why the OFDM modulation scheme in the IEEE 802.11 will provide better performance. Newer technology like IPv6 can also be used to provide broadband wireless network services.

Figure 1. Block diagram representation of the proposed system

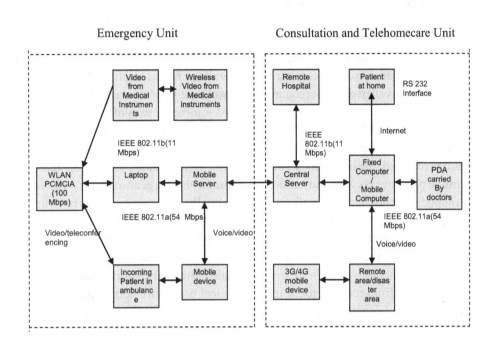

OTHER CURRENT RESEARCH IN TELEMEDICINE

Telemedicine can be divided into three areas: aids to decision making, remote sensing, and collaborative arrangements for the real-time management of patients at a distance. As an aid to decision making, telemedicine includes areas such as remote expert systems that contribute to patient diagnosis or the use of online databases in the actual practice of medicine. This aspect of telemedicine is the oldest in concept. Remote sensing consists of the transmittal of patient information, such as electrocardiographic signals, x-rays, or patient records, from a remote site to a collaborator in a distant site. It can also include transmittal of grand rounds for medical education purposes or teleconferences for continuing education. Collaborative arrangements consist of using technology to actually allow one practitioner to observe and discuss symptoms with another practitioner whose patients are far away. This raises important issues of referral and payment arrangements, staff credentialing, liability, and

licensure potentially crossing state lines. Two-way work stations which provide smooth digital motion pictures have been integral to the long distance, real-time treatment of patients. As new technology is found, collaborative arrangements are the future of telemedicine.

Perhaps the greatest impact of telemedicine may be in fulfilling its promise to improve the quality, increase the efficiency, and expand the access of the healthcare delivery system to the rural population and developing countries. As wireless technology becomes more ubiquitous and affordable, applications such as video-telephony over POTS will gradually migrate towards 3G and 4G wireless systems. This will certainly improve the quality of telemedicine applications.

The holomer (HOLO-graphic M-edical E-lec-tronic R-epresentation) (see Figure 2) is a three dimensional holographic digital image of a specific person, derived from a CT scan, MRI, ultrasound, or other modality. Physicians will be able to interact with the holomer as if it were the patients themselves. Soon, every patient will have their own unique holomer, containing not only anatomically precise information, but also physiologic, biologic, genetic, demographic, and other information contained within the image. Physicians will interact with these holomer as if they were the patients themselves. They are a human surrogate in cyberspace, an informational equivalent of the person in bits and bytes. For diagnosis, all the relevant data about the patient can be retrieved in the form of a visual medical record. In therapeutics, if a complex surgical procedure is required, the holomer can be used for preoperative planning (as is already used for complex orthopedic, neuo- and craniofacial surgery), selecting the best surgical approach for that patient. Using surgical simulation, the surgeon can practice the procedure on the holomer, until a "perfect" operation is obtained.

Now-a-days, robots roll from room to room in hospital, displaying the face of a doctor or nurse (see Figure 3) who can videoconference with patients via a wireless net connection. Science-fiction moved a step closer to reality when robots nicknamed "Sister Mary" and "Doctor Robbie" started work at a London hospital on May 18, 2005. The pair allows doctors to visually examine and communicate with patients, whether they are in another part of the hospital or even another part of the world.

Minimally invasive surgery (MIS) is a revolutionary approach in surgery. In MIS, the operation is performed with instruments and viewing equipment inserted into the body through small incisions created by the surgeon, in contrast to open surgery with large incisions. This minimizes surgical trauma and damage to healthy tissue, resulting in shorter patient recovery time. Unfortunately, there are disadvantages due to the reduced dexterity, workspace, and sensory input to the surgeon which is only available through a single video image. The "robotics lab" of University of California at Berkeley has developed (see Figure 4) a prototype glove-like device that senses the positions of the surgeon's fingers and wrist with its index, thumb, and wrist flex sensors and wrist rotation sensor. The glove provides a more natural means of control than cur-

rent minimally invasive tools. It could be used as a master to drive the miniature slave robotic hand, if force feedback is not needed.

While research into telesurgery helps to jump-start robotics in the operating room, distant operations have remained an elusive application. However, it may eventually prove to be one of the most significant uses of robotic surgery.

For the discipline of surgery, the surgical console is the interface between the real and information world; virtual reality meets real reality. From the console, the surgeon can perform open surgery, minimally invasive surgery, remote telesurgery, surgical preplanning, surgical procedure rehearsal, intraoperative image guided surgery, and surgical simulation. All these actions are possible from the single point of the surgical console. The first telesurgical procedure upon a patient was performed by Prof Jacques Marescaux in September 1991. He made a set up at his surgical console in New York City and performed a laparoscopic cholecystectomy on his patient who was in Strassbourg, France, over 4,000 km away.

Battle-field casualty care now-a-days can be totally monitored using state-of-the-art technologies in remote sensing and medical informatics. The keys are: remote monitoring of every soldier's location and vital signs with personal status monitor

Figure 2. Holomer in virtual soldier project in US (source: Virtual Soldier Project, http://www.virtualsoldier.us/showcase.htm)

(PSM) assistance at the casualty side to the medic from a remote physician with telementoring; providing immediate surgical care on the battlefield with telepresence surgery; monitoring en route therapeutics and transportation of casualties in a trauma pod; simulation of battle wounds for surgical practice; and medical forces planning and training with virtual reality.

Now-a-days, military medics carry an electronic device with an antenna to read data recorded on the tag of an injured soldier. Using the device, medics can upload the information on the soldier's medical history and add new information on medical condition, triage code, and eye and motor response into a miniature, handheld computer. In addition, once the wounded soldier is placed upon the life support for trauma and transport (LSTAT) (see Figure 6), which is a portable intensive care unit (ICU), the surgeon back in the mobile advanced support hospital (MASH) can receive by telemedicine the vital

signs, change the respirator settings, and control the flow of the intra-venous fluids and medications. The LSTAT has been used since 2000 in the conflict in Bosnia and Kosovo. From the time of wounding when the soldier is placed on the LSTAT, to the helicopter evacuation, to the ambulance transfer to the MASH, to the emergency triage, to the operating room, and finally in the post-operative ICU, the casualty is continuously monitored and the medical record is automatically recorded. In the Afghanistan and Iraq Wars, the LSTAT was recalled for servicing; however, the medics would not send them back because they were so valuable.

However, defense services place particular emphasis on encryption and other security measures for telemedicine. Computer-based telemedicine systems for military or commercial customers can offer strong safeguards to keep unauthorized eyes and ears from sensitive information.

Surgical simulators have become a leading edge technology. One of the most sophisticated systems is the endoscopic sinus surgery simulator (ES3) (see Figure 7).

Starting from the beginning level to expert level, this simulator has multiple levels of training. In the expert level, the procedures must be accomplished realistically. The student's performance is recorded, errors are counted, and the student is given an objective score of their performance. Lockheed Martin delivered the first ES3 simula-

Figure 3. Medical robot at St Mary's NHS Trust and Imperial College London ("Take two aspirin and call the robot in the morning?" 2005)

Figure 4. Prototype dextrous master (source: Robotics lab, University of California, Berkeley)

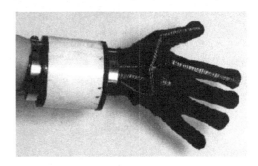

Figure 5. Surgical console using the da Vinci Surgical System (What is robotic surgery, http://www.drslawin.com/ robotic_prostatectomy.html)

tor to the Madigan Army Hospital in Tacoma, Washington for training surgeons in sinus surgery procedures. New devices such as the Blue Dragon (Blake Hannaford and Jacob Rosen, University of Washington, Seattle WA) and the Imperial College Surgical Assessment Device (Prof. Sir Ara Darzi, Imperial College, London, England) actually record the hand motions so a quantitative assessment of time, path length (economy of motion), dwell time (indecision), and other parameters can be accurately measured and reported.

Advances in robotics also enabled changes in the operating room environment. Dr. Michael Treat (Columbia University, New York City) has developed Penelope, a robot to replace a scrub nurse. Using robotics, automatic target recognition, voice activation, intelligent decision support, and other common methods from other industries, Dr. Treat is able to use the robot to hand and pick-up and hand off surgical instruments during a surgical procedure. The United States military has a new program called "Trauma Pod" (see Figure 8) in which it is envisioned that they will build an "operating room without people."

The Trauma Pod will not require human medical personnel on-site to conduct the surgery, and will be small enough to be carried by a medical ground or air vehicle. A human surgeon will conduct all the required surgical procedures from a remote location using a system of surgical manipulators. The system's actions are then communicated wirelessly to the surgery site. All phases of the operation will be conducted by the surgeon with the necessary support from the automated robotic systems.

The Israeli based company "Given Technologies" has miniaturized a camera and transmitter and placed it into a capsule that can be swallowed; an image is taken two times a minute and sends to a

Figure 6. The United States Army's new critical care transport platform the LSTAT (Johnson et al., 2002)

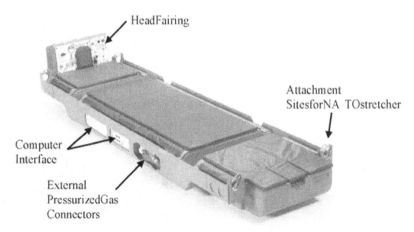

belt-worn video cassette recorder. After the camera passes, the video tape is given to the gastroenterologist to review instead of doing an endoscopic procedure.

There are number of types of disasters such as earthquakes, nuclear/hazardous chemical accidents, civil disorder/riots, bomb threats/terrorist attacks, bio-wars, and so forth. In such situations, the existing terrestrial infrastructure could be damaged. The space systems then suitably complement partly destroyed terrestrial infrastructure to answer the requirements of emergency healthcare services such as fast deployment of the management of logistic and medical means or remote medical expertise. Appropriate new telemedicine applications can improve future disaster medicine outcomes, based on lessons learned from a decade of civilian and military disaster (wide-area) telemedicine deployments. Emergency care providers must begin to plan effectively to utilize disaster-specific telemedicine applications to improve future outcomes.

Ever since September 11, 2001, with terrorist attacks in the USA and the spate of anthrax outbreaks there and elsewhere, the specter of global terrorism has become more real. In recent times, the increasing threats to use biological weapons of mass destruc-

tion have triggered off an urgent need to review current methods of disease surveillance. Some of the existing (or in the process of being developed) disease surveillance systems are as follows:

a.   Electronic Disease Reporting & Management System (EDRMS).
b.   Real-time Outbreak and Disease Surveillance (RODS).
c.   Lightweight Epidemiological Advanced Detection & Emergency Response system (LEADERS).

A number of micro sensors and other MEMS technologies are being embedded into insects to act as living sensors. Bumble bees with microsensors for anthrax and a small transmitter have been used to identify simulated biologic agents during military exercises and transmit the information back to the soldiers so they can avoid the biologic agent.

The medical informatics and technology applications consortium (MITAC) is a unique NASA research partnership center (RPC), established to develop, evaluate, and promote information and medical technologies for space flight and ground applications. It is comprised of partners from government, academic institutions, and industry that have a commercial interest in products and technology related to telemedicine, medical informatics, and medical technology.

For the discussions above, it can be well inferred that research directions in telemedicine area involve lots of technologies and their successful implementations. The current research scenario in telemedicine therefore confronts some research challenges as well for the proper implementation of a myriad of technologies available. The following section details some of the research challenges to meet.

Figure 7. Using endoscopic sinus surgery simulator (Advanced Nasal Operations, http://www.memagazine.org/backissues/feb01 /features/nasal/nasal. html)

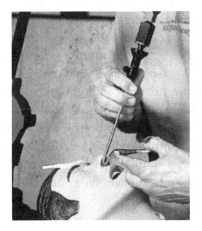

FUTURE TRENDS

Telemedicine is going to be an attractive solution for the future of healthcare. The future research trends and challenges in this area are described below.

Figure 8. Robotic surgery is being performed by Trauma Pod ("Trauma pod unmanned medical-surgical system," 2005)

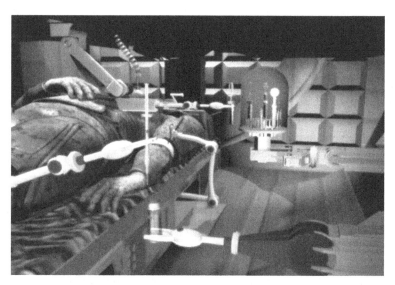

Standardization

Generally, standards are developed to provide security and integrity of information that is sent effectively through the telecommunications. Currently, inadequate standardization of procedures, terminology, equipment requirements, health service identifiers, service identifiers, and data transfer are substantial barriers to the successful implementation of telemedicine. The department of Health and Human Services (DHHS) estimates that 400 formats are used in the United States today for healthcare-related transactions. Due to the lack of standardization, vendors find it difficult to develop software and thus cost also increases for the healthcare providers. Efficient and effective use of telemedicine requires the development of proper standards in respective applications of telemedicine for remote healthcare and the healthcare industry can thus exploit the capabilities of the systems developed. Medical files, such as X-ray images, must be presented in formats that physicians are used

to seeing, but there are not many standards yet for digitizing the hardcopy images and sending them over the Internet; like a radiological image interpretation apparatus and method where a radiology healthcare network provides high quality, timely medical interpretations of radiological images on a national (e.g., across the U.S.) and regional basis.

Interoperability

The collaboration of software and hardware requires a platform to render incompatible telemedicine standards compatible, called middleware. Therefore, it requires a set of rules or policies to drive the technology so that the development in hardware and software can proceed in this area. H.320 and HL7 are some examples in this regard which have set some rules in their respective fields mentioned previously to provide interoperability. Newer technologies need similar types of interoperability to enhance the utilization of the systems.

Medical Sensors

Sensor networks are emerging as one of the emerging fields of telemedicine. Sensor networks consist of small sensing areas and typically reside in homes or in a patient. When they reside so, they are called the patient's body area network (PAN). PAN helps to monitor many facets of a patient's physical health through means of "conventional sensors" based on piezo-electrical material for pressure measurements to infrared sensors for body temperature estimation and optoelectronic sensors monitoring SpO2, heart rate, HRV, and blood pressure (Istepanian et al., 2004, p. 407). In this research, Robert et al. confirm that using existing technology such as mobile medical sensors for communication in healthcare along with prospective ideas for 4G wireless communications is the future of healthcare. Therefore, smart medical sensor design requires special attention.

Medical Robots

Intelligent medical robots, though not a new concept, will expand their functionalities in the future telemedicine research. It is expected that each person's personal health record with intelligent avatar will exist in Internet and a medical robot would be able to interact with Internet for enquiry of the medical history of a person. In this process, medical robots will play an important role in improved healthcare, timely clinical decision making, and so forth.

Human-Machine Interface

Natural language is the most natural human-machine interface now-a-days and hence development in this area requires designing sophisticated natural language depending on the needs on both sides of patient and doctor. Adding intelligence with natural language processing hence requires special attention.

Micro-Electro-Mechanical Systems (MEMS)

MEMS can offer future research opportunities in telemedicine. Application of MEMS in 3G mobile technologies can allow users to use sensors for data processing and communication components. And thus it can be possible to use this technology to consistently monitor patients. MEMS can take different forms, including MEMS robots in noninvasive arthroscopic surgery, MEMS-encapsulated cameras that can be swallowed to provide detailed images of the digestive tract, and so on. Therefore, extensive research is required in this promising area both from the academic and industry point of view.

Cellular Technology

According to ITU specification, 3G systems will offer 384 Kbps when a device is at a pedestrian speed, 128 Kbps in a car and 2 Mb in fixed applications. But the disappointing fact is, though data rates will increase, there is not enough bandwidth to transfer large e-mail attachments quickly, let alone the audio or video stream at the broadcast quality the cell phone vendors first claimed. With the natural progression of epoch-making development of technologies in cellular communication, the need for multirate services and broadband convergence have been obvious to piggyback voice, data, videos, and automated applications in a single mobile device (Razibul et al., 2005). 4G promises integrated modes of wireless communications from indoor networks, such as Bluetooth and WLAN, to cellular systems, to radio and TV broadcasting, to satellite communication. It has an expectation of supporting at least 100 Mbps in full mobility wide area coverage and 1 Gbps in low mobility local area coverage. Therefore, using 4G technologies will also reduce transmission errors and high resolution imaging and processing will also be possible. Therefore, research in adoption of 4G technologies in telemedicine area should also continue.

Security of Data

Telemedicine heavily depends on the transmission of data, video, and audio in telecommunication networks and so secure network access and data transmission are necessary for the confidentiality and privacy of patients' personal data. Research in network-level firewall and application-level firewall is important to prevent unauthorized access to computer data across the Internet. Secret key encryption and public key encryption mechanisms are also necessary to develop secure data transmission. Therefore it is important for telemedicine applications to employ end-to-end encryption mechanisms securing the data channel from unauthorized access of modification. Adaptability of newer technologies with the secure network access and data transmission capability therefore requires research.

CONCLUSION

Telemedicine is the indispensable future road of providing healthcare. Developed and developing countries both have prospects using telemedicine. Cost-adaptive, in terms of money and time deployment of telemedicine, will become acceptable in the developing and rural communities as well as developed countries. Research trends and challenges discussed above unveil the application areas of telemedicine with the existing research outcomes and represent the areas of research to be explored to exploit the maximum benefits respectively. As mentioned, the OFDM-based mobile telemedicine model discussed will provide high data rate patient monitoring systems both in emergency and homecare situations along with remote and disaster-prone areas. As telemedicine technologies and processes gradually mature, the extent and breadth of medical specialties where telemedicine technologies could prove clinically useful should expand. Indeed, reports of telemedicine implementations are appearing in orthopedics, dermatology, psychiatry, oncology, neurology, pediatrics, internal medicine, ophthalmology, and surgery. Apart from the development of standards and adoption of technologies, ethical and legal aspects of telemedicine need to be considered for successful implementation of telemedicine technologies which was not covered in this chapter. Finally, for the greater needs of mankind, telemedicine research should maximize eradicating the impossibilities of healing the patients into possible from any part of the world with the wand of state-of-the art technology deployment in all respect.

REFERENCES

Akselsen, S., et al. (1993). Telemedicine and ISDN. *IEEE Communication Magazine, 31*(1), 46-51.

Allen, A., & Grigsby, J. (1998). Fifth annual programme survey, part 2: Consultation activity in 35 specialties. *Telemedicine Today, 6*(5), 8-19.

Bashshur, R. L. (1980). *Technology serves the people: The story of a cooperative telemedicine project by NASA, the Indian Health Service and the Papago People.* US Government Printing Office.

Bashshur, R. L., et al. (1975). *Telemedicine: Explorations in the use of telecommunications in health care.* Springfield, IL: Charles C. Thomas.

Benschoter, R. (1971). *CCTV-pioneering Nebraska Medical Centre.* Educational Broadcasting.

Binkley, P. (2003). Predicting the potential of wearable technology. *IEEE Engineering in Medicine and Biology Magazine, 22*(3), 23-24.

Brebner, J. A., et al. (2000). The diagnostic acceptability of low-bandwidth transmission for tele-ultrasound. *Journal of Telemedicine and Telecare, 6*, 335-338.

Chu, Y., & Ganz, A. (2004). A mobile teletrauma system using 3G networks. *IEEE Transactions on Information Technology on Biomedicine, 8*(4), 456-462.

Craig, J. (1999). Introduction. *Introduction to telemedicine* (p. 5). U.K.: Royal Soc. Med. Press.

Doufexi, A., & Armour, S. (2002, May). A comparison of the Hiperlan/2 and IEEE 802.11a wireless LAN standards. *IEEE Communications Magazine, 40*(5), 172-180.

Feliciani, F. (2003). Medical care from space: Telemedicine. *ESA Bull, 54*(9), 114.

Flickenger, R. (2003). *Performance test: 802.11b.* Retrieved October 20, 2007 from http://www.oreillynet.com/lpt/a/713

Garner, P., et al. (1996). Mobile telecare: A mobile support system to aid the provision of community-based care. *Journal of Telemedicine & Telecare, 2*, 39-42.

Garshnek, V., & Burkle, F. (1999) Telemedicine applied to disaster medicine and humanitarian response: history and future. In *Proceedings of the 32nd Hawaii International Conference on System Sciences* (Vol. 4, p. 9).

Guillén, S., et al. (2002). Multimedia telehomecare system using standard TV set. *IEEE Transactions on Biomedical Engineering, 49*(12), 1431-1437.

Handel, R., et al. (1993). *ATM networks: Concepts, protocols, applications.* Reading, MA: Addison-Wesley.

Holter Systems. (2007). *Med-electronics Inc.* Retrieved October 10, 2007 from http://med-electronics.com/

Hung, K., et al. (2003). Implementation of a WAP-based telemedicine system for patient monitoring. *IEEE Transactions on Information Technology in Biomedicine, 7*(2), 101-107.

Ibrahim, et al. (2006). *Development of a mobile telemedicine system with multi communication links for urban and rural areas in Indonesia.* Paper presented at the 3rd Kuala Lumpur International Conference on Biomedical Engineering 2006 (Vol. 15. pp. 660-663). Springer Berlin Heidelberg.

Istepanian, R. S. H., et al. (2004). Guest editorial introduction to the special section: M-Health: Beyond seamless mobility and global wireless health-care connectivity. *IEEE Transaction on Information Technology in Biomedicine, 8*(4), 405-13.

Johnson, K., et al. (2002). Clinical evaluation of the life support for trauma and transport (LSTAT) platform. *Journal of Critical Care, 6*, 439-446.

Jovanov, E., et al. (2005). A wireless body area network of intelligent motion sensors for computer assisted physical rehabilitation. *Journal of Neuro Engineering and Rehabilitation, 2*(6). Retrieved October 15 from http://www.jneuroengrehab.com/content/2/1/6

Jung, D. K. (2005). Biosignal monitoring system for mobile telemedicine. In *Proceedings of 7th International Workshop on Enterprise Networking and Computing in Healthcare Industry* (pp. 31-36).

Lau, M. (1998). *GeoPak: Monitoring climbers and climate on Mount Everest.* Unpublished masters of engineering thesis, MIT, Department of Electrical Engineering and Computer Science.

Martin, T., et al. (2000). *Issues in wearable computing for medical monitoring applications: A case study of a wearable ECG monitoring device.* Paper presented at the International Symposium on Wearable Computers ISWC 2000 (pp. 43-49).

Owens, T., et al. (2001). *Securing a medical wireless LAN System.* Paper presented at the IEEE EMBC, Istanbul.

Razibul Islam, A. H. M., et al. (2005). Vision, framework and responsibilities for 4G wireless: A comparative approach. *Journal of Laser Engineering, 16*, 39-49.

Reponen, J., et al. (1998). Digital wireless radiology consultations with a portable computer. *Journal of Telemedicine & Telecare, 4*(4), 201-205.

Reponen, J., et al. (2000). Initial experience with a wireless personal digital assistant as a teleradiology terminal for reporting emergency computerized tomography scans. *Journal of Telemedicine & Telecare*, *6*(1), 45-49.

Stanberry, B. A. (1998). *The legal and ethical aspects of telemedicine.* Royal Society of Medicine.

Take two aspirin and call the robot in the morning? (2005, May). *What's next in science & technology.* Retrieved August 15, 2006 from http://www.whatsnextnetwork.com/technology/index.php/2005/05/

Trauma pod unmanned medical-surgical system. (2005, May). *SRI International News.* Retrieved August 15, 2006 from http://www.sri.com/news/storykits/

Watson, D. S. (1989). Telemedicine. *Medical Journal of Australia*, *151*(2), 68.

Wootton, R., & Craig, J. (1999). *Introduction to telemedicine.* Royal Society of Medicine.

KEY TERMS

Broadband: Communications (e.g., broadcast television, microwave, and satellite) capable of carrying a wide range of frequencies; refers to the transmission of signals in a frequency-modulated fashion, over a segment of the total bandwidth available, thereby permitting simultaneous transmission of several messages.

Cholecystectomy: A cholecystectomy is the surgical removal of the gallbladder. In a laparoscopic cholecystectomy, four small incisions are made in the abdomen. The abdomen is filled with carbon dioxide, and the surgeon views internal structures with a video monitor. The gallbladder is located and cut with laparoscopic scissors. It is then removed through an incision.

Encryption: The rearrangement of the "bit" stream of a previously digitally encoded signal is a systematic fashion to make it unrecognizable

until restored by the necessary authorization key. This technique is used for securing information transmitted over a communication channel with the intent of excluding all others than the authorized receivers from interpreting the message.

Endoscopy: Endoscopy allows the doctor to look at the interior lining of the esophagus, stomach, and first part of the small intestine through a thin, flexible viewing instrument called an endoscope. The tip of the endoscope is inserted through the mouth and then gently advanced down the throat into the esophagus, stomach, and upper small intestine (duodenum). Endoscopy can reveal problems that do not show up on X-ray tests, and it can sometimes eliminate the need for exploratory surgery.

Firewall: A system designed to prevent unauthorized access to or from a private network. Firewalls can be implemented in both hardware and software, or a combination of both. Firewalls are frequently used to prevent unauthorized Internet users from accessing private networks connected to the Internet, especially *Intranets*. All messages entering or leaving the Intranet pass through the firewall, which examines each message and blocks those that do not meet the specified security criteria.

H.320: This is the technical standard for videoconferencing compression standards that allows different equipment to interoperate via T1 or ISDN connections.

H.324: This is the technical standard for videoconferencing compression standards that allows different equipment to interoperate via plain old telephone service (POTS).

Moving Pictures Expert Group (MPEG): The term refers to the family of digital video compression standards and file formats developed by the group. MPEG achieves high compression rate by storing only the changes from one frame to another, instead of each entire frame. MPEG uses a type of *lossy compression* since some data are removed. But the diminishment of data is generally imperceptible to the human eye. There are three major MPEG standards: MPEG-1, MPEG-2, and MPEG-4. *MPEG-2* offers resolutions of 720x480 and 1280x720 at 60 frames per second, with full CD-quality audio. This is sufficient for all the major TV standards, including NTSC, and even HDTV. MPEG-2 is used by DVD-ROMs. MPEG-2 can compress a 2 hour video into a few gigabytes.

Personal Digital Assistant (PDA): It is a handheld device that combines computing, telephone/fax, Internet, and networking features. A typical PDA can function as a cellular phone, fax sender, Web browser, and personal organizer. Some PDAs can also react to voice input by using voice recognition technologies. PDAs of today are available in either a stylus or keyboard version.

RS-232: It is a well established interface device. Short for *recommended standard-232C,* it is a standard interface approved by the Electronic Industries Alliance (EIA) for connecting serial devices.

Synchronous Optical Networks (SONET): It is a standard for connecting fiber-optic transmission systems. With the implementation of SONET, communication carriers throughout the world can interconnect their existing digital carrier and fiber optic systems.

Telecare: Telecare is the use of information and communication technologies to transfer medical information for the diagnosis and therapy of patients in their place of domicile.

Telehealth: Telehealth is the latest hybrid approach of information and communication technologies to transfer healthcare information for the delivery of clinical, administrative, and educational services.

Telemonitoring: The use of information and communications technologies to enable the monitoring of patient health status between geographically separated individuals.

Transmission control protocol/Internet protocol (TCP/IP): It is a suite of standard protocols for connecting computers across networks over the world.

Very Small Aperture Terminal (VSAT): An earthbound station used in satellite communications of data, voice, and video signals, excluding broadcast television. A VSAT consists of two parts: a transceiver that is placed outdoors in direct line of sight to the satellite and a device that is placed indoors to interface the transceiver with the end user's communications device, such as a PC. The transceiver receives or sends a signal to a satellite transponder in the sky. The satellite sends and receives signals from a ground station computer that acts as a hub for the system. Each end user is interconnected with the hub station via the satellite, forming a star topology.

Section VIII
Educational Applications

Chapter XXXIII
Knowledge–Based Characterization of Test Questions

Javed Khan
Kent State University, USA

Manas Hardas
Kent State University, USA

ABSTRACT

The recent advances in knowledge engineering entail us to represent knowledge associated with a course in an expressive yet computable format as a hierarchical prerequisite relation-based weighted ontology. A schema called the course concept dependency schema written in Web ontology language (OWL) is designed to represent the prerequisite concept dependency. The knowledge associated with educational resources, like the knowledge required for answering a particular test question correctly, can be mapped to subgraphs in the course ontology. A novel approach for selectively extracting these subgraphs is given and some interesting inferences are made by observing the clustering of knowledge associated with test questions. We argue that the difficulty of a question is not only dependent on the knowledge it tests but also the structure of the knowledge it tests. Some assessment parameters are defined to quantify these properties of the knowledge associated with a test question. It is observed that the parameters are very good indicators of question difficulty.

INTRODUCTION AND BACKGROUND

Traditionally, concepts maps are used to represent the backend context for the course knowledge. Many efforts (Edmondson, 1993; Lee & Heyworth, 2000; Li & Sambasivam, 2003; Heinze-Fry & Novak, 1990) have gone into representing course knowledge using concept maps and using them to evaluate educational resources. In the recent past ontologies were being used to represent structured information in a hierarchical format. Concept maps offer a means to represent hierarchical knowledge; however, they are too expressive and consequently contain more information and semantic relationships than necessary for effective computation.

Ontologies provide a means to effectively map this knowledge into concept hierarchies. Course ontology, particularly, can be roughly defined as a hierarchical representation of the topics involved in the course, connected by relationships with specific semantic significance. Using ontologies for course concept hierarchies in the domain of education is only obvious. It seems such entailment can lead to several important pedagogical applications.

Testing is an integral part of any teaching and learning process. The main pedagogical focus of this research is to objectify the process of testing by estimating the difficulty of a test question based on the depth, breadth, and the amount of conceptual knowledge it tests. Consequently effective testing is possible by subjectively designing the test using these parameter values. A problem/question is one type of educational resource. The commonly observed properties of testware are difficulty or simplicity, breadth and depth of knowledge required to answer, relevance of the question to the root topic, the semantic distance between the concepts tested, ability of the question to test varying groups of students, applicability of the topics taught to a problem, and so forth. While designing a test an educator always tries to come up with questions which have maximum coverage of desired topics, diversity among the topics, good testing capabilities with respect to student knowledge, relevance to the material taught, and so forth. It is important to understand these properties for better design and reengineering of test problems. In this research, we attempt to visualize and understand these properties of test problems by qualitative knowledge-based evaluation. Currently the process of designing of test problems is completely manual, based on human experience and cognition. Design of test problems also follows the basic principles of any engineering design process. The primary elements of design in this case are the information objects. Much effort has been put in the creation and reusability of these information objects called the learning objects, for example, learning object metadata (LOM). Semantic representation standards like RDF and OWL allow

the concept knowledge space symbolized by ontologies to be represented consistently.

The main hypothesis for this work is that "*test questions*" can be qualitatively analyzed for their perceived difficulty, using a purely knowledge-based approach given a background course knowledge base. The main contributing factor to the difficulty of a question is the knowledge associated with the question, that is, the knowledge required to answer the question. Furthermore, the observed difficulty of a question is in positive correlation with the structural properties of the knowledge associated. We propose an assessment system which attempts to evaluate an educational resource like test problem for its "difficulty" based on its knowledge content. We define some parameters which are able to quantify these structural properties associated with the knowledge and observe that they are indeed very good indicators of question difficulty. These parameters can give guidelines for setting up a standard for test problem assessment. We also present an approach to course knowledge representation using ontology in an expressible and computable format using *has-prerequisite* relationships where concepts involved in teaching a course are arranged in a hierarchical order of learning. Another original method for specifically pointing out areas in ontologies of maximum relevance called *CSG extraction* is given.

Alternate educational approaches that exist do not have a concrete knowledge representation and depend too much on external psychological, cognitive, and syntactical parameters for calculating the perceived difficulty. We analyze test questions objectively from the point of view of the knowledge it tests rather than subjective external parameters. Some researches in cognition (e.g., Apted & Kay, 2002; Gruber, 1993; [18]) have identified other extrinsic parameters, like perceived number of difficult steps, steps required to finish the problem, number of operations in the problems expression, number of unknowns, and so forth which attribute difficulty to a question, but none of them are knowledge-based. The few knowledge-based approaches (Dean &

Schreiber, 2004; Lien, Chang, & Heh, 2003; Li & Sambasivam, 2003; Shrobe & Szolovits, 1993) are limited due to their lack of a solid representation technique which is often rigid, incomplete, and incomputable and disregarded for the structure of the knowledge.

The experimental set up was that of graduate level courses of operating systems and Internet engineering. Ontologies of around 1,500 and 1,000 concepts respectively were created referring to standardized text books and the help of the related instructor. A random set of 40-60 test questions was selected from the question bank relating to the course. The questions were answered by approximately 50 graduates and under graduate students and were graded by two graders. The scores from these were used for the experiments. It was observed that almost 60-70% of the time the performance parameters were in inverse correlation with the average score for a particular question, meaning the parameters were good indicators of the perceived difficulty of the question. From the experiments we were able to conclude: 1. Difficulty and knowledge associated with a question are closely correlated; 2. Knowledge associated with a test question tends to cluster in and around specific portions in the course ontology; and 3. Clustering of knowledge can provide information about which areas need to be developed, which areas are taught, and so forth, and can be used as a tool in guided tutoring. The chapter is structured as follows: in section 2 we present a method for representing the course knowledge more formally; in section 3 we quantify the semantics of the relationships and present a method for extraction; in section 4 we present the assessment parameters; and in sections 5 and 6 we observe the performance of the parameters and make inferences from the observed results.

COURSE KNOWLEDGE REPRESENTATION

Any design and evaluation system, like cognition-based models in humans, needs a back end knowl-edge base. Knowledge representation techniques like semantic networks and ontologies make this possible. The corpus of course knowledge can be hypothetically divided into two tiered description framework namely, *concept space* and *resource space*. The course ontology is the graphical abstraction of the concept space, wherein concepts are linked to each other using semantic relations. The resource space gives the description of actual resources for the corresponding concepts from the concept space. In this section we discuss the definition, specification, and constructs for course ontologies.

Granularity of Representation

Davis, Shrobe, and Szolovits (1993) define knowledge representation as a "set of ontological commitments" and "a medium of pragmatically efficient computation" (Jaakkola & Nihamo, 2003). It is important for the knowledge representation to be expressible and computable. This in turn brings us to the problem of granularity of information in course ontology. The granularity of the ontology is an important factor to consider while building the course ontology. The ontology can range from being fine grained to coarse grained. A finer grained ontology will contain more concepts in detail and more implicit relationships between concepts are also represented. The finer the ontology, the application will have more knowledge to work with giving better results. But defining a finely grained expressive ontology is costly in terms of computation. On the other hand, although coarse grained ontologies are computable, they do not have enough information. The depth of the knowledge to be represented is therefore an important question in representing any kind of knowledge. Most available finished materials today are coarse granular. Unfortunately, this is not suitable for machine processing.

Course Ontology

In computer science, ontology is generally defined as "a specification of a conceptualization" (Heffernan

& Koedinger, 1998). Ontology is a data model that represents a domain and is used to reason about the objects in the domain and the relations between them. In the context of this research the domain is that of a *course*, the objects are *concepts* in the course, and the relations between the concepts are that of *has-prerequisite*. Ontologies are increasingly being used to represent information in various domains like biological sciences, accounting and banking, intelligence and military information, geographical systems, language-based corpus, cognitive sciences, common sense systems, and so forth.

Relationships are the way the concepts in the ontology are structured with respect to each other. In the context of course ontology, the "part-of" semantics refers to the prerequisite understanding of the child node needed to understand the parent node. On the whole the course ontology is constructed in such a hierarchical fashion that the children node represent the knowledge required to understand the parent node, and their children represent the knowledge required to understand them, so on and so forth. The ontology is created using the principle of "constructivism" borrowed from the learning theory. The theory states that any new learning occurs in the context of and on the basis of already acquired knowledge. We use this theory to practically implement the has-prerequisite relationship-based course ontology (see Figure 1). Process management is the prerequisite of OS.

A node is characterized by two values, namely *self-weight* and *prerequisite weight*. The self-weight of a concept node is the value or the knowledge which is inherent to that node itself. It means that the self-weight is the amount of knowledge required to understand the concept. To understand the concept entirely, however, knowledge of the prerequisite concepts is also required, which is given by the prerequisite weight of the node. It gives the numerical realization of the importance of the understanding of the prerequisite concepts in the complete understanding of a parent concept. Another value which characterizes the course ontology is the *link weight*. The link weight is the numerical value for the semantic importance of the child concept to the parent concept. Child concepts imperative in the understanding of parent concepts will have greater link weights than the others. Thus the course ontology representation is a collection of concepts nodes with self-weights and prerequisite weights and has-prerequisite relationships linking these nodes with a value attribute given by the link weight.

Concept Mapping

Most of the educational resources today are not accompanied with metadata which makes it very difficult for machine processing. For educational resources to be machine processable, they have to be presented in the proper context (Khan, Hardas, & Ma, 2005). The mapping between the resource space and the concept space is called the *concept mapping*. All educational resources are based on a few selected concepts from the ontology. When an educator designs courseware, the educator has a mental map of the concepts taught in the course. We define a rudimentary version of this mental map in the form of the course ontology. The research problem of automatically mapping a resource to concepts from ontology is an extremely nontrivial problem which is addressed extensively in research of natural language processing, knowledge representation, and so forth. We limit our research to using the concept mapping idea.

Course Concept Dependency Schema (CCDS)

The schema for the course ontology is mostly written in OWL Lite. OWL Lite supports basic classification hierarchy and simple constraint features. The schema is shown in Appendix A. The elements of schema are header, class, property definitions, and individuals. The language is designed to harness maximum computability at the cost of reduced expressive power.

Figure 1. Operating systems CSG 2-level deep

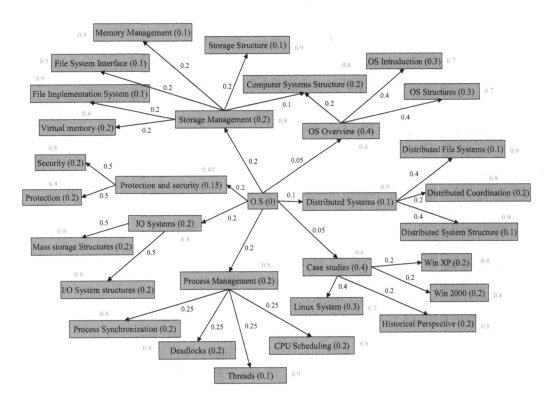

The ontology header *owl: Ontology* is a collection of assertions about the course ontology. This section can contain comments, version information, and imports for inclusion of other ontologies. Versioning can effectively be done to different levels of granularity of the ontology. All the individuals in the OWL representation are the instantiations of the class *Concept*. The object of the *subclass* axiom is a property restriction on *hasPrerequisiteWeight*, which describes an anonymous class, all of whose instances satisfy the restriction. The property restriction states that for all instances of class *Concept*, if they have a prerequisite then it must belong to extension of *Relation*. The extension of class means the set of all the members of that class. The class *Relation* is used to define all relations between concepts and give values to the *hasLinkWeight* property of the relation. It links two individuals of the class *Concept* with a data value. We first link instance of the class *Concept* to an instance of *Relation*, and then link that instance again to instance of *Concept*. The object property *connectsTo* is used to link instance of *Relation* to instance of *Concept*. Link weight is a characteristic of a relation, therefore, *hasLinkWeight* data type property applies to instances of class *Relation*. The range of the property is set by the resource *xsd:float*. For the purpose of computational convenience we set the values for all the concept and link properties between 0 and 1. The other two data *type* properties are *hasSelfWeight* and *hasPrerequisiteWeight,* which are used to assign the self-weight and prerequisite weights of a node, respectively.

Individuals are facts about their class membership and their property values. In the example the concept instance, *MemoryManagement* is a prerequisite for *OS*. Individual member *OS* is a member of class *Concept* and has the property values for *hasLinkWeight* as 0.2, *hasSelfWeight* as 0.39, and *hasPrerequisiteWeight* as 0.61. The most important part of the course ontology structure is the semantics between parent and child concepts. The tool which uses CCDS defined course ontology should be able to infer that, since *connectsTo* links *relation1* and *MemoryManagement* and *hasPrerequisite* link *OS* to *relation1*, *MemoryManagement* is prerequisite of *OS*.

Symbolic Representation

The course ontology is mathematically defined in the form of a concept space graph (CSG). A CSG is a view of the concepts space distribution in the domain of a particular course.

A concept space graph $T(C, L)$ *is* a projection of a semantic net with vertices C and links L where each vertex represents a concept and each link with weight $l(i, j)$ represents the semantics that concept c_j is a prerequisite for learning c_i, where $(c_i, c_j) \in C$ and the relative importance of learning c_j for learning c_i is given by the weight. Each vertex in T is further labeled with self-weight value $W_s(i)$ cumulative prerequisite set weight $W_p(i)$.

A CSG with root A is represented as $T(A)$ in Figure 2. For any node in the CSG, the sum of self-weight and prerequisite weights and the sum of the link weights for all children is 1.

Prerequisite Effect of a Node

The notion of node path weight is introduced to compute the effect that a prerequisite node has on the understanding of a parent node through a specific path. A single node can have different prerequisite effects on a parent through different paths.

When two concepts x_0 and x_t are connected through a path consisting of nodes given by the set $[x_0, x_1 ..., x_m, x_{m+1}, ..., x_t]$ then the node path weight between these two nodes is given by:

$$\eta(x_0, x_t) = W_s(x_t) \prod_{m=t}^{1} l(x_{m-1}, x_m) * W_p(x_{m-1}) \qquad (3)$$

The node path weight for a node to itself is its self-weight.

$$\eta(x_1, x_1) = W_s(x_1) \qquad (4)$$

In the Figure 3, concept L is connected to B through E and F. Therefore, the prerequisite effect it has on B is dependent on the prerequisite effect both E and F have on B, respectively. From the node path weight calculations we can see that L has a stronger prerequisite effect on B through F rather than E. This is because L is more important to F (0.5) than

Figure 2. Example of concept space graph, T(A)

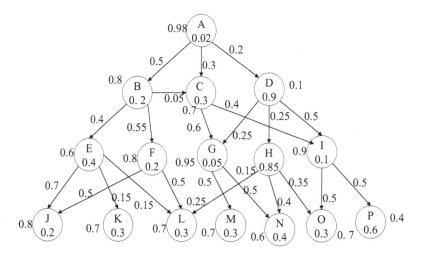

E (0.15), prerequisite importance of L is more to F (0.8) than E (0.6), and subsequently F (0.55) is more important to B than E (0.4). Thus node path weights take into consideration not only the singular effect a node has on its immediate parent but also the combined prerequisite effect a node would have on a parent (B), along a specific path.

CSG Extraction

A generalized CSG can be vast and processing a huge ontology becomes almost impossible and a gargantuan computation task. There needs to be a way to efficiently process the relevant information in these ontologies to give optimum results in minimum time and complexity of computation. Therefore we define a pruned subgraph called a *projection graph* which cuts the computation based on a limit on propagated semantic significance. The process of selecting projection graph nodes from the concept space graph is called *CSG extraction*. There are quite a few reasons to apply CSG extraction to ontology. It is computationally very expensive to work on big ontologies. Nowadays ontologies used range from thousands to millions of concepts. Therefore processing the whole ontology is very expensive and also does not logically make sense. The concepts which the question maps to are relatively very less as compared to the total number of concepts in the whole ontology. Moreover,

say if the mapped concepts are very distant from each other in the ontology. This implies that the knowledge required to understand these concepts is very diverse in the concept space. Therefore it would be a squandering of computational resources to process the whole ontology instead of just the relevant portions. The concept space graph gives the layout of the course in the concept space with a view of course organization, involved concepts, and the relations between the concepts. Examples of large CSGs include WordNet (150,000), which is an English language ontology, LinKBase (1 million in English, 3 million in other languages), which is a comprehensive medical/clinical ontology, Gene Ontology (now known as GO, with over 19,000 concepts), the genome mapping project, and so on. Thus defining a workable area of ontology is of the utmost importance from the perspective of semantic relevance and computability and it is achieved by pruning the ontology by introducing a variable called the threshold coefficient (λ).

Threshold Coefficient (λ)

By varying the threshold coefficient the size of the computable projection graph can be varied and thus the semantic significance. Since the projection graph is a subgraph of the concept space graph, it is necessary to have prerequisite weights for the leaf nodes too, although most times the prerequisite weight

Figure 3. Calculating prerequisite effect of a node along a path; node path weight

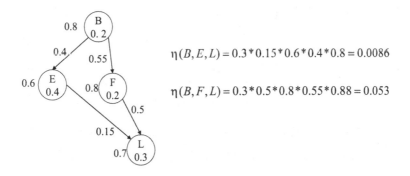

$$\eta(B, E, L) = 0.3 * 0.15 * 0.6 * 0.4 * 0.8 = 0.0086$$

$$\eta(B, F, L) = 0.3 * 0.5 * 0.8 * 0.55 * 0.88 = 0.053$$

for the leaf nodes is zero. Flexibility for optional prerequisite weights for the leaf nodes allows the CSG to be extensible and easily extractable for the projection. Threshold coefficient is a kind of virtual limit by which the size of the projection can be controlled. The greater the coefficient, more is the screening for the nodes to be added to the projection and thus smaller is the graph. Less coefficient value means more concepts will be included in the projection. In the context of education the threshold coefficient can be thought of as a parameter which can set the depth to which the topic has been taught. If a topic is not taught in detail, a greater coefficient is assigned so that the depth of the projection graph will be less. Conversely, if a topic is covered in great detail, the value assigned to the threshold coefficient is low, so that the projection graph for the concept is large, encompassing more prerequisite concepts. Threshold coefficient determines the limit to the quality of understanding of a particular concept.

Projection Graph

Given a CSG $T(C, L)$, with local root concept x_0, and projection threshold coefficient λ, a projection graph $P(x_0, \lambda)$ is defined as a subgraph of T with root x_0 and all nodes x_t where there is at least one path from x_0 to x_t in T such that node path weights $\eta(x_0, x_t)$ satisfies the condition $\eta(x_0, x_t) \geq \lambda$.

The projection set consisting of nodes $[x_0, x_1, x_2...x_n]$ for a root concept x_0 is represented as $P(x_0, \lambda) = P^{x_0} = \left[x_0^{x_0}, x_1^{x_0}, x_2^{x_0}...x_n^{x_0}\right]$, where x_i^j represents

the ith element of the projection set of node j.

Consider an example CSG from Figure 2. We find the projection of the local root concepts B and D given the threshold coefficient of $\lambda=0.001$. The projections and calculations are shown in Figures 4 and 5 and Table 1 and 2. All nodes that satisfy the condition of node path weights greater than the threshold coefficient are included in the projection. Nodes can have multiple paths to the root (J, L, and O). For node J and L, both the paths (J-E-B, J-F-B and L-E-B, L-F-B, respectively) satisfy the condition, whereas for O only one path satisfies the condition (O-I-D). Even then, O is considered in the projection of D, because it still wields some prerequisite effect on D through one of the paths. If the condition for the threshold coefficient is satisfied then the node is included in the projection. Thus by finding the projection graphs of the concepts which map to a resource, we can precisely extract parts from the course ontology which are relevant to the document and have a desired semantic significance.

ASSESSMENT PARAMETERS

In the previous sections we saw that educational resources map to a set of concepts from the course ontology. For the purpose of demonstration, in this chapter, we consider a special type of educational resource, that is, a *test question*. A test question is any random question asked in a random test for a random course. Test questions were chosen as re-

Figure 4. Projection, P(B, 0.001)

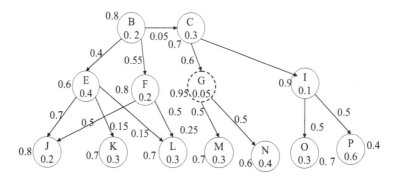

Figure 5. Projection, P(D, 0.001)

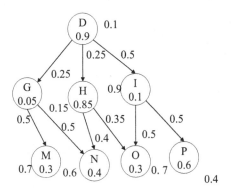

Table 1. P(B)

$P(B, \lambda = 0.001)$			
Local root "r"	Node "n"	$\eta(r,n)$	$\eta(r,n) \geq \lambda$?
B	E	0.128	✓
	F	0.088	✓
	C	0.012	✓
	J	0.027/0.035	✓
	K	0.00864	✓
	L	0.0086/0.053	✓
	G	0.00084	✗
	I	0.00112	✓
	M	0.0024	✓
	N	0.003192	✓
	O	0.001512	✓
	P	0.003024	✓

Table 2. P(D)

$P(D, \lambda = 0.001)$			
Local root "r"	Node "n"	$\eta(r,n)$	$\eta(r,n) \geq \lambda$?
D	G	0.00125	✓
	H	0.02125	✓
	I	0.005	✓
	M	0.00357	✓
	N	0.00475	✓
	L	0.00028	✗
	O	0.00034 (H)	✗
		0.00675 (I)	✓
	P	0.0135	✓

which are discussed are *coverage* of the question, that is, the amount of knowledge required to answer the question, the *diversity* of the question, that is, the amount "difference" between the knowledge, and the *conceptual distance,* that is, the amount of closeness or remoteness of the knowledge.

For the experimental setup we created a course ontology comprising of around 1.500 concepts for the graduate level course of operating systems. The ontology was created for the course by consulting with the related instructor and referring to standardized textbooks. Although there are methods for automatic ontology construction (Kay & Holden, 2002; Lee & Heyworth, 2000; Li & Sambasivam, 2003), we hand coded the ontology for accuracy and consistency. The node weights and link weights, which form an important constituent of the ontology, were assigned by guidance from the course instructor. Concepts with more intrinsic importance for understanding were assigned more self-weight and those which depended on many other prerequisite concepts were assigned more prerequisite weights. Consequently it was observed that concepts higher up in the ontology had lower self-weights, and self-weight values went on increasing further down the

sources because their concept mapping can be easily identified by the resource creator. Also, answering the question correctly is nothing but identifying the concept mapping and therefore the concept mapping for answers can also be easily identified. In this section we define some parameters which will enable us to *quantify* certain properties of the knowledge associated with test questions or any other resource for that matter. The specific properties ontology, reaching the maximum for leaf nodes. However, for the CSG to be extensible, the leaf nodes were also allowed to have prerequisite weights in case more prerequisite concepts were added later on. Keeping the ontology extensible allows for inclusion of newer concepts, results, researches, and so forth, adding to the inherent knowledge base, making the course ontology an ever changing and improving repository of course knowledge. The link weights were assigned based on the semantic importance and contribution of the child topic to the understanding of the parent topic. If the understanding of the child concept is detrimental to the understanding of parent concept, then it was assigned a greater link weight. Although by definition, the summation of the link weights for a node should add up to 1, it is generally not observed consistently. Most of the times, some space is left for the inclusion of newer links for prerequisite concepts which are newly added or already existing in the ontology. Again it is seen that higher up in the ontology there is no need to actually leave this space, as the probability of addition of newer links to higher level concepts (implying fundamental changes to the subject area) is less than that to the concepts lower in the ontology. The concept mapping for the "test question" resource was provided by the instructor. These test questions were administered by undergraduate and graduate students, the scores from which were used for the performance analysis. The answers were graded by a minimum of three graders per question, and the averages of the scores were considered to remove any anomalies.

Coverage

The coverage of a question gives a cumulative prerequisite effect of the projection graph on the knowledge required to answer a particular question. Coverage of a concept is a direct indicator to the scope of the question in context of the concept space of the course. Formally, "*coverage of a node x_0 with respect to the root node r is defined as, the product of the sum of the node path weights of all*

nodes in the projection set $P(x_0, \lambda)$ for the concept x_0, and the incident path weight γ (r, x_0) from the root r."

If the projection set for concept node x_0, $P(x_0, \lambda)$ is given by $[x_0, x_1, x_2 ... x_n]$ then the coverage for node x_0 about the ontology root r is defined as:

$$\alpha(x_0) = \gamma(r, x_0) * \sum_{m=0}^{n} \eta(x_0, x_m) \qquad (5)$$

where $\gamma(r, x_0)$ is called the *incident path weight* and

$$\gamma(x_0, x_n) = \frac{\eta(x_0, x_n)}{W_s(x_n)} = \frac{\eta(x_0, x_n)}{\eta(x_n, x_n)} \qquad (6)$$

Total coverage of multiple concepts in a problem given by set $[C_1, C_2 ... C_n]$ is

$$\alpha(T) = \alpha(C_1) + \alpha(C_2) + ... + \alpha(C_n) \qquad (7)$$

The node path weight defines the prerequisite effect of a node to its designated root. Therefore the summation of the node path weights of all the nodes in the projection set gives the cumulative prerequisite effect of the nodes in the projection graph on their respective mapped concept roots. The concepts in the projection graph in turn are the concepts which are required to understand a particular concept, controlled by the threshold coefficient. The *coverage* is thus the amount of knowledge required to answer or rather understand a particular concept.

$$\alpha(B) = \gamma(A, B) * \sum_i \eta(B, P_i^B) = (0.5 * 0.98) * (0.335882) = 0.16458218$$

$$\alpha(D) = \gamma(A, D) * \sum_i \eta(D, P_i^D) = (0.2 * 0.98) * (0.0560625) = 0.01098825$$

$$\alpha(total) = \alpha(B) + \alpha(D) = 0.16458218 + 0.01098825 = 0.17557043$$

Diversity

Diversity is calculated by measuring the effect of common and uncommon prerequisite concepts from the projections of the mapped concepts. Diversity is formally defined as "*the ratio of summation of node path weights of all nodes in the non-overlap-*

ping set to their respective roots, and the sum of the summation of node path weights of all nodes in the overlap set and summation of node path weights of all nodes in the non-overlap set."

Consider a question that asks a set of concepts, $C = [C_0, C_1, C_2 ... C_n]$. The respective projection sets are given by

$$P(C_0, \lambda) = [x_1^{C_0}, x_2^{C_0}, ..., x_a^{C_0}], \quad P(C_1, \lambda) = [x_1^{C_1}, x_2^{C_1}, ..., x_b^{C_1}]$$
$$...P(C_n, \lambda) = [x_1^{C_n}, x_2^{C_n}, ..., x_c^{C_n}]$$

The nonoverlapping and overlapping sets are $N = [N_0, N_1, N_2 ... N_p]^i$ and $O = [O_0, O_1, O_2 ... O_q]^j$, where i and j are the local root parents of any element from N and O, respectively, and $\forall \ i, j \in C$.

Cardinality restriction:

$$\forall \ [O_0, O_1 ... O_q] \in [P(C_0, \lambda) \cap P(C_1, \lambda) .. \cap P(C_n, \lambda)] \text{ and}$$

$$\forall \ [N_0, N_1 ... N_p] \in \left\{ \begin{array}{l} [P(C_0, \lambda) \cup P(C_1, \lambda) .. P(C_n, \lambda)] \\ -[P(C_0, \lambda) \cap P(C_1, \lambda) .. \cap P(C_n, \lambda)] \end{array} \right\}$$

Diversity is given by

$$\Delta = \frac{\sum_{m=1}^{p} \eta(i, N_m^i)}{\sum_{m=1}^{q} \eta(j, O_m^j) + \sum_{m=1}^{p} \eta(i, N_m^i)} \quad where \ \forall \ i, j \in C \tag{8}$$

The diversity calculated comes to 97%, which means that the concepts are very diverse in their concept space.

Conceptual Distance

Conceptual distance is a measure of distance between two concepts with respect to the ontology root. Alternatively conceptual distance measures the similarity between two concepts by quantifying the distance of the concepts from the ontology root. Formally it is defined as *"the log of inverse of the minimum value of incident path weight (maximum value of threshold coefficient) which is required to encompass all the mapped concepts from the root concept."*

The conceptual distance parameter is designed in such a way that it should be sensitive to the depth of the concepts. Hence it is a function of maximum threshold coefficient required to cover all the nodes from the ontology root. Incident path weight (γ) of a concept to the root is equivalent to the threshold coefficient (λ) required to encompass the node. If question asks concept set $C = [C_0, C_1, C_2 ... C_n]$, then the conceptual distance from the root concept r is

$$\delta(C_0, C_1 ... C_n) = \log_2 \left(\frac{1}{\min[\gamma(r, C_0)\gamma(r, C_1) .. \gamma(r, C_n)]} \right) \tag{9}$$

Figure 6. Diversity calculation example

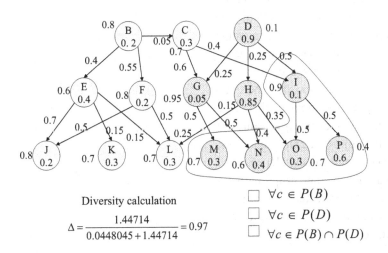

Calculation of conceptual distance for concept set [E, M, F] is shown in Figure 7. Each different type of arrow represents the different paths for a particular concept to the root. In case of multiple paths, like M, the path with the lowest value of incident path weight is considered.

OBSERVING PARAMETER PERFORMANCE

To observe the goodness of the parameters for measuring the properties of coverage, diversity, and conceptual distance for a test question, we plot the calculated values of the parameters for a question against the average score for that question. The values for coverage and diversity change according to varying threshold coefficients. Therefore, for these two parameters the values are calculated over a range of λ. In the following analysis we assume that knowledge required to answer a particular question is the major factor attributing difficulty to the question without considering external psychological and physiological parameters. The familiarity of the student with the concepts (or how well the concepts have been taught) is a factor of the threshold coefficient. By varying the threshold coefficient the size of the projection graphs can be varied, thus varying the student's familiarity with the concepts.

The coverage analysis for each question with varying threshold coefficient can be explained by the graph shown in Figure 8. It is observed that the coverage has an inverse relationship with the average score. As the average score increases the coverage for that particular question decreases and vice versa. For all values of λ the coverage has the same relationship; however, this relationship becomes more and more evident with decreasing values of λ. As λ decreases, the projection graph increases, thus increasing the coverage values. Hence if the inverse correlation of the coverage graph with average score graph is more for decreasing values of λ, we can infer that more concepts are required to answer that particular question. Coverage gives an

approximation to the knowledge required to answer a particular question. From the graph it is seen that most of the times, coverage is inversely correlated to average score.

Diversity graph characteristics are similar to coverage graph (see Figure 9). In the case of diversity it is observed that as the threshold coefficient ë decreases, the diversity values for all the questions also go on decreasing. This is because as λ decreases the projection set for each concept in the concept set increases. As the projection set increases the probability of having more common concepts increases, thus increasing the coverage of overlap set and decreasing the diversity. In some cases, however, the diversity increases with decrease in λ. This happens because sometimes when the threshold coefficient decreases, the projection obviously increases; however, instead of having more overlapping nodes, the nonoverlapping node set increases, consequently increasing the diversity.

Figure 7. Conceptual distance calculation

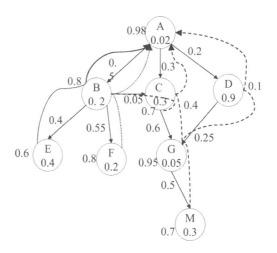

$$\delta(E,F,M) = \log_2\left(\frac{1}{\min\{\gamma(A,E)\gamma(A,F)\gamma(A,M)\}}\right)$$

$$\delta(E,F,M) = \log_2\left(\frac{1}{\min\{0.1568, 0.2156, 0.0023275\}}\right)$$

$$\delta(E,F,M) = \log_2(429.65) = 2.63$$

Figure 8. Coverage vs. average score

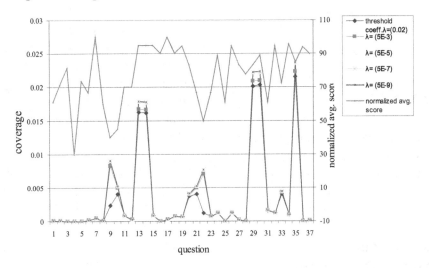

The performance of conceptual distance vs. average score is observed in Figure 10. Although not directly dependent on a projection graph, distance is also inversely correlated to average score. This means that distance is a very good indicator of the similarity between concepts. As the distance between two nodes decreases, the similarity increases. As the similarity increases, the *dissimilarity* between knowledge required to answer the concepts decreases, consequently increasing the average points scored. As conceptual distance is not a factor of a projection graph, behavior in the graph is constant for all threshold coefficient values. Distance is a logarithmic function as *log* gives the inverse behavior of an exponential function, which is observed here. Similar to coverage and diversity the conceptual distance is also inversely correlated to average score with good correlation. As seen from the behavior of all three assessment parameters, the average score has an inverse correlation with

Figure 9. Diversity vs. average score

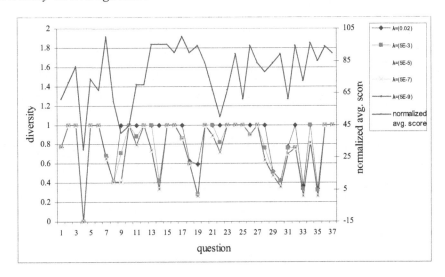

the parameters. This means that the parameters are pretty good indicators of the perceived difficulty of test problems.

OBSERVING CLUSTERING IN THE COURSE ONTOLOGY

In this section we try to make interesting intuitive inferences by observing the clustering of concepts in the ontology because of the projection graphs of several test questions spread out among several different tests.

Clustering of Concepts for Questions with Respect to High and Low Average Scores

In this analysis, we separate out the questions with high and low average scores and observe if their concept mapping results in clustering in the ontology. On observing the set of concepts to which these questions map to, it is seen that there are surprisingly high numbers of common concepts in their respective projection graphs. It is important to note here that, rather than just considering the mapped concepts, the projections of the mapped concepts were considered as they would give a better understanding of the whole set of prerequisite concepts required to answer the question. Figure 11 shows the question-concept distribution separated for the questions with high and low average scores.

Observations:

1. For concepts between 750-1,000, density of questions with high scores is more than questions with low scores. From this we can infer that students understand the concepts well, or the problems based on these concepts were fairly easy to answer, and so forth. For the same concepts though, problems 36 and 37 have low scores. This means that these problems were harder because of factors other than the understanding of the concepts. If similar clustering behavior is observed exclusively in questions with low scores, then it can conclusively be said that those concepts or that part of the ontology needs more explanation from an educator's perspective.

Figure 10. Conceptual distance vs. average score

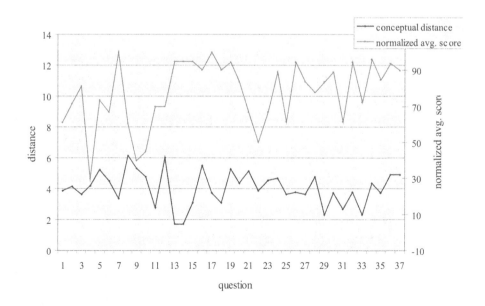

Figure 11. Concept mapping with respect to average score per question

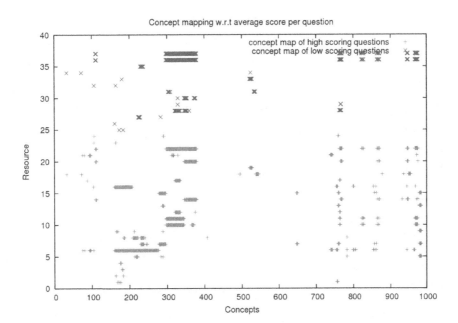

2. It is observed that in questions with low scores, concepts are more dispersed (not clustered) around the ontology as compared to those with high inverse correlation.

3. The small clustering signifies a projection of a concept. It means that questions usually ask concepts near and around a primary concept. These small clustered concepts mostly are those concepts which come in the primary concepts projection itself. Two small clusters near each other mean two primary concepts projections which are very near to each other.

4. Concepts around 200-400 and 750-1,000 are frequently asked among the questions with high and low scores equally. This means that the tests were based on those concepts and the concepts which appear scattered around the plot are those which are needed to answer the specific question. The concepts which do not form the part of the cluster are most definitely concepts which are distant from the primary concept but necessary to answer the particular problem completely.

Figure 12 shows the distribution of concepts according to the concept mapping of the questions according to their test distribution. Questions 1-6 are in Test 1, and 7-12, 13-18, 19-37 are in Tests 2, 3, and 4, respectively.

Observations:

1. Questions 13, 14, and 29, 30, 33, and 35 ask almost similar concepts. Out of these it was observed that 13, 14, 33, and 35 had high scores, and 29 and 30 had low scores. This implies that the correct answering of these questions needs some factors other than understanding the mapped concepts.

2. Most questions are based on or relate to concepts from 100-400 and 750-1,000. That means that most of the tests were based on that part of the ontology. This inference has a very interesting implication. It means that the instructor chose to set the questions only on select topics from the course ontology maybe because those were the only topics covered in the course from the ontology. The exact portions of the ontology which were taught and tested can be pointed out using this.

Figure 12. Concept mapping scatter plot with respect to tests

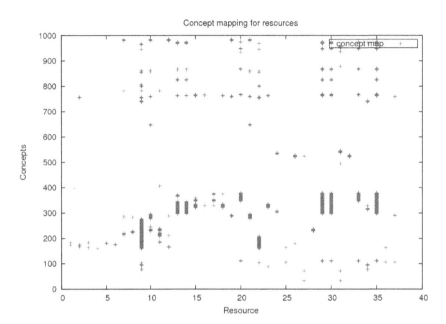

3. As more and more topics are taught from the ontology, tests are increasingly based on more concepts than the previous.

4. There are a lot of small clusters of concepts between concepts 50-400. Since the concepts were numbered "in order" it means that the small clusters are the mapped concepts, while the bigger ones are the projections of the mapped concepts. Clustering following smaller clustering usually means projections of mapped concepts.

All the observations made are specific to the domain of *course knowledge* and experimental setup for *test questions*. The observations and inferences will change in case of different domains. We present an approach to enable making *interesting* observations and inferences about the clustering and behavior of knowledge in different domains.

TEST DESIGN

This research leads to an obvious interesting question: Can such characterization be used in learning activity design, such as a *test*? Creative design is nontrivial because a composite design is not only the simple sum of the characteristics of the individual elements used in the design; painting and music compositions are few examples. The characteristics of the elements (i.e., color, shape, and lines) in the design interplay in a very complex ways. Rigorous objective knowledge about the elements is absolutely necessary to be a master. Yet it further requires sophisticated additional senses such as aesthetics about the interplays and the ability to judge specific composition. In engineering design the detail characteristics of the elements are needed as essential design data to meet various design constraints (i.e., maximum allowable weight, size, etc.) and optimization objectives (i.e., weight/power ratio, efficiency, etc.). However, engineering design too has a functional objective which requires holistic metaknowledge about the overall interplay of the elements not in the elements.

Test is an important tool in all forms of learning activity. Here we have discussed a potential method for knowledge-based characterization of test problems. This is a critical step towards the design of tests. One of the main objectives of testing in education is to gauge the student level of understanding of a topic [19]. The unit of a test is a test problem. By estimating the amount, breadth, and depth of the knowledge required to answer a test question in some quantifiable way—as this research suggested—can provide intelligent design guidance to compose better tests, perhaps with specific coverage of topics, breadth of topics, and even the difficulty. Test design also has additional goals such that a test would gauge certain concepts and are generic enough to test a varied group of students. Certain aspects of a test design problem can probably be framed as a multiobjective constraint satisfactory/optimization problem in a knowledge space. A test also is designed with some formative constraints, such as time and space. Armed, with the knowledge-based assessment technique suggested in this research, it seems many of the content-oriented measurements involved, such as completeness of coverage of all the concepts in a test and if a test is within a certain range of a difficulty value, such a process formulation of test design can be assisted. The challenge of good test design is nevertheless a whole new interesting area ripe for future investigation.

CONCLUSION AND FUTURE WORK

We propose a technique for representing hierarchical structured knowledge using weighted ontologies and demonstrate it in the domain of courses (education). A representation schema called the *course concept dependency schema* written in OWL is also given for the formal description of the course ontology. The schema is independent of the domain and can be used to represent other concept hierarchies with similar properties. The relationships in the course ontology are kept to a minimum making them expressive and computable. Another novel approach called *CSG extraction* to extract relevant information from course ontology depending upon the desired semantic significance is given. Using this approach we observe the clustering of knowl-

edge associated with test questions in the course ontology and make some interesting inferences. We also define some parameters, namely coverage, diversity, and conceptual distance, which can be used to quantify the properties of knowledge associated with test questions and aid intelligent design of test questions. The applicability of this method is not limited to the domain of education and can be extended to any domain in which knowledge can be represented as a structured hierarchy. As future work we are trying to access the ways in which this method of representation and extraction can be applied to classical learning theories which require knowledge to be represented as prerequisite concept structures.

REFERENCES

2004 MIT OCW Program Evaluation Findings Report. (June 2006). Retrieved April 6, 2008, from http://ocw.mit.edu/NR/rdonlyres/FA49E066-B838-4985-B548-F85C40B538B8/0/05_Prog_Eval_Report_Final.pdf$

Apted, T., & Kay, J. (2002). *Automatic construction of learning ontologies.* Paper presented at the 2002 International Conference on Computers in Education (ICCE '02) (p. 1563).

Croteau, E., Heffernan, N. T., & Koedinger, K. R. (2004). *Why are algebra word problems difficult? Using tutorial log files and the power law of learning to select the best fitting cognitive model.* Paper presented at the 7th Annual Intelligent Tutoring Systems Conference, Maceio, Brazil.

Cummins, D. D., Kintsch, W., Reusser, K., & Weimer, R. (1988). The role of understanding in solving word problems. *Cognitive Psychology, 20*, 405-438.

Davis, R., Shrobe, H., & Szolovits, P. (1993). What is a knowledge representation? *AI Magazine, 14*(1), 17-33.

Dean, M., & Schreiber, G. (Eds.). (2004, February 10). OWL Web ontology language reference. *W3C recommendation.* Retrieved April 6, 2008, from http://www.w3.org/TR/2004/REC-owlref-20040210/

Fortuna, B., Grobelnik, M., & Mladenic, D. (2006, May 23-26). Background knowledge for ontology construction. In *Proceedings of the 15th International Conference on World Wide Web, WWW '06,* Edinburgh, Scotland (pp. 949-950). New York: ACM Press.

Gipps, C. (1994). *Beyond testing: Towards a theory of educational assessment by V.* London: Falmer Press.

Gruber, T. R. (1993). A translation approach to portable ontologies. *Knowledge Acquisition, 5*(2), 199-220.

Heffernan, N. T., & Koedinger, K. R. (1998). A developmental model for algebra symbolization: The results of a difficulty factors assessment. In *Proceedings of the Twentieth Annual Conference of the Cognitive Science Society* (pp. 484-489). Hillsdale, NJ: Erlbaum.

Jaakkola, T., & Nihamo, L. (2003). *Digital learning materials do not possess knowledge: Making critical distinction between information and knowledge when designing digital learning materials for education.* Versailles: International Standards Organization.

Kay, J., & Holden, S. (2002). *Automatic extraction of ontologies from teaching document metadata.* Paper presented at the 2002 International Conference on Computers in Education (ICCE '02) (p. 1555).

Khan, J. I., Hardas, M., & Ma, Y. (2005). *A study of problem difficulty evaluation for semantic network ontology based intelligent courseware sharing.* Paper presented at the 2005 IEEE/WIC/ACM International Conference on Web Intelligence (WI '05) (pp. 426-429).

Kuo, R., Lien, W.-P., Chang, M., & Heh, J.-S. (2003). *Difficulty analysis for learners in problem solving process based on the knowledge map.* Paper presented at the International Conference on Advanced Learning Technologies (pp. 386-387).

Kuo, R., Lien, W.-P., Chang, M., & Heh, J.-S. (2004). Analyzing problem difficulty based on neural networks and knowledge maps. *International Conference on Advanced Learning Technologies, Education Technology and Society, 7*(20), 42-50.

Lee, F.-L., & Heyworth, R. (2000) Problem complexity: A measure of problem difficulty in algebra by using computer. *Education Journal, 28*(1).

Li, T., & Sambasivam, S. E. (2003). Question difficulty assessment in intelligent tutor systems for computer architecture. In *Proceedings of the ISECON 2003,* San Diego (Vol. 20, p. 4112). ISSN 1542-7382. *Information Systems Education Journal, 1*(51). ISSN: 1545-679X.

APPENDIX

```xml
<?xml version="1.0"?>
<rdf:RDF
  xmlns:owl = "http://www.w3.org/2002/07/owl#"
  xmlns:rdf = "http://www.w3.org/1999/02/22-rdf-syntax-ns#"
  xmlns:rdfs= "http://www.w3.org/2000/01/rdf-schema#"
  xmlns:xsd = "http://www.w3.org/2001/XMLSchema#">
<owl:Ontology rdf:about="###">
      <rdfs:comment>A schema for describing Course Ontologies</rdfs:comment>
      <rdfs:label>Course Ontology</rdfs:label>
</owl:Ontology>
<owl:Class rdf:ID="Concept">
      <rdf:comment>Course ontology concept</rdfs:comment>
      <rdfs:subClassOf rdf:resource="http://www.w3.org/2002/07/owl#Class"/>
      <rdfs:subClassOf>
            <owl:Restriction>
                  <owl:onProperty rdf:resource="#hasPrerequisite"/>
                  <owl:allValuesFrom rdf:resource="#Relation"/>
            </owl:Restriction>
      </rdfs:subClassOf>
</owl:Class>
<owl:Class rdf:ID="Relation">
      <rdfs:subClassOf>
            <owl:Restriction>
                  <owl:onProperty rdf:resource="#connectsTo"/>
                  <owl:allValuesFrom rdf:resource="#Concept">
            </owl:Restriction>
      </rdfs:subClassOf>
</owl:Class>
<owl:ObjectProperty rdf:ID="hasPrerequisite">
      <rdfs:range rdf:resource="#Relation"/>
</owl:ObjectProperty>
<owl:ObjectProperty rdf:ID="connectsTo">
      <rdfs:range rdf:resource="#Concept">
</owl:ObjectProperty>
<owl:DatatypeProperty rdf:ID="hasLinkWeight">
      <rdfs:domain rdf:resource="#Relation"/>
      <rdfs:range rdf:resource="xsd:float"/>
</owl:ObjectProperty>
<owl:DatatypeProperty rdf:ID="hasSelfWeight">
      <rdfs:domain rdf:resource="#Concept"/>
      <rdfs:range rdf:resource="xsd:float"/>
</owl:DatatypeProperty>
<owl:DatatypeProperty rdf:ID="hasPrerequisiteWeight">
      <rdfs:domain rdf:resource="#Concept"/>
      <rdfs:range rdf:resource="xsd:float"/>
</owl:DatatypeProperty>

<Concept rdf:ID="MemoryManagement"/>
<Concept rdf:ID="OS">
      <hasPrerequisite>
            <Relation rdf:ID="relation1">
                  <connectsTo rdf:resource="#MemoryManagement"/>
                  <hasLinkWeight rdf:resource="#0.2"/>
            </Relation>
      </hasPrerequisite>
      <hasSelfWeight rdf:resource="0.39"/>
      <hasPrerequisiteWeight rdf:resource="0.61"/>
</Concept>
</rdf:RDF>
```

Chapter XXXIV
Information Systems
Curriculum Design Processes

Paulette Alexander
University of North Alabama, USA

Carol Gossett
University of North Alabama, USA

ABSTRACT

The process of designing a university curriculum in the information systems discipline needs to follow many of the same processes that professional systems analysts use. Of concern are the product, the stakeholders, the drivers, and the methods; indeed, an information systems curriculum is an information system. This chapter presents a case study of one small regional university's efforts to create an updated information systems curriculum addressing the challenges of curriculum development using the framework of the very systems analysis and design course content that the students are expected to learn. The chapter identifies each component of the information system curriculum and details the processes supporting each development step along the way, from problem identification to system operation and support. This case study presents a cohesive approach to dealing with the many pressures associated with information systems curriculum development and might be instructive for curriculum development in other disciplines as well.

INTRODUCTION

The University of North Alabama has offered undergraduate courses leading to a baccalaureate degree in information systems fields since 1978. The programs were first called management information systems, then computer information systems (CIS). During the first couple of decades, these programs were part of the Department of Management and Marketing within the College of Business. In the mid-1990s a separate Department of Computer Information Systems was formed within the College of Business, incorporating the CIS programs and courses and those associated with the former Administrative Systems Management Department. During the first two decades of information systems programs, the curriculum was revised and updated numerous times, sometimes by adding courses and sometimes by totally recasting the degree requirements of the program. Attention was given to the latest technologies and to issues involving the application of technologies. Curriculum guidelines from the Association for Computing Machinery (ACM, 2005) were consulted, and faculty attended conferences and workshops dealing with curriculum matters. Faculty also maintained contact with many alumni and local employers in an effort to maintain a program which would properly train students to take their place in the ever-changing world of technology.

Since 2000, the enrollment of CIS majors has hovered somewhat above 200, fluctuating slightly from year to year, but not experiencing the precipitous drop reported by many universities. The number of full time faculty grew from 8 in 2000 to 10 at present and from two doctorally-qualified members to six. In addition to teaching courses in the CIS undergraduate major, CIS faculty members teach a basic computer applications service course required by most majors in the university, enrolling approximately 1,500 students per year. The graduate information systems program, part of the Master of Business Administration, new in 2004, now has over 50 students enrolled. The CIS department is also the subject-area home to the program responsible for preparing high school teachers of business and marketing education at both the bachelor and master of education level.

In the fall of 2004, it became clear to the faculty of the CIS department at the University of North Alabama (UNA) that a problem existed with its current curriculum. The courses being taught were not meeting the needs of the students as they prepared to enter the job market. The department's faculty needed to solve the problem by designing a curriculum to meet the needs of a CIS graduate entering the work force. How would they solve this problem? As information systems people, the faculty decided to use a problem-solving technique familiar to all the faculty members: the principles found in systems analysis and design.

When a university faculty undertakes a major curriculum revision, there are many issues to address and many procedural hurdles to cross. These are in many ways similar to the various types of constraints generally faced by information systems

developers and systems analysts. All too often, it is difficult to admit to deficiencies in an existing system (curriculum) because there are stakeholders with interests in preserving the status quo, pressures that are resistant to change, decision makers who are not fully informed of all relevant facts, outside evaluators who have established standards which must be upheld, and the list goes on. But in short, the curriculum development process requires the buy-in of a wide variety of stakeholders, including faculty, university administration, curriculum committees, alumni, potential employers of graduates, and, of course, students. The extent to which each stakeholder group accepts and embraces a curriculum is an important element of how successful the overall project is and in the case of curriculum development, how successful the program will become.

Maintaining a program with high standards, such as those required by accrediting agencies, was important to the faculty. "Accreditation focuses on the quality of education...A high quality degree program is created when students interact with a cadre of faculty in a systematic program supported by an institution" (SACS, 2007). The university holds the regional accreditation. The College of Business holds accreditation by the Association of Collegiate Business Schools and Programs (ACBSP, 2007). The college and department faculty and administration are committed to seeking additional accreditations as appropriate.

Inasmuch as the ultimate objective of curriculum revision is educating students to achieve their objectives, usually employment objectives, the product can be assessed in terms of the types of employment objectives being targeted and the knowledge base and skills sets required to achieve those objectives. Accrediting organizations have, in recent years, come to emphasize learning outcomes as a primary element for educational institution and program evaluations. The notion of measurement of learning outcomes is also fundamental to concepts of continuous improvement and quality enhancement.

Historically, curriculum revisions have been course and credit hour-centric. In some professional programs which require licensure before a student goes into professional practice, there has been some coordination of the content within course sets constituting a program of study or a major. In most other curricula, there has been wide latitude to use teaching methods and to include content based on the individual professor's preferences within a course. Indeed, this is one of the tenets of academic freedom. Because there could be a conflict between concepts of academic freedom and the prescriptive nature of courses with prescribed learning outcomes and assessment standards, it is especially incumbent upon programs developing curricula which seek to accommodate these competing priorities to seek full, fair, and open participation by all faculty who will in effect be subscribing to a "system" of courses to meet a prescribed and agreed upon set of learning outcomes.

This case study documents in considerable detail the process of a rigorous, comprehensive, time consuming, and apparently successful curriculum revision meant to address the multitude of pressures concerning what constitutes a quality information systems program, what types of employment opportunities the graduates would or should be prepared for, how to fit the needed course material together, and how to fit that material into existing degree structures within a college of business and a university, with constraints and expectations completely outside the control of the CIS faculty. In addition, many external pressures and issues must be addressed in completing such a curriculum revision. Demonstrated in this case study are many of the concepts associated with competing priorities, allocation of scarce resources, establishing requirements, iterative decision making, user involvement, a desire to short cut important parts of the development process, and issues of implementation and transition. This case study's objective is to present an application of concepts which are at the heart of information systems education and apply those concepts to the betterment of information systems education.

The systems development life cycle (SDLC) is used to plan and manage the systems development process. The SDLC model is considered a waterfall model as the result of each phase flows sequentially into the next phase. A typical SDLC model will include the following steps or phases:

- Systems Planning
- Systems Analysis
- Systems Design
- Systems Implementation
- Systems Operation and Support

When the time arrived for the faculty to revamp the curriculum to meet the needs of the current job market, the same concepts found in the SDLC model were the obvious methods to reach the goal efficiently.

SYSTEMS PLANNING

In an SDLC model, the purpose of the initial step is to complete a preliminary investigation to identify the nature and scope of the problem. In this step, the analysts evaluate the problem and initiate the process of discovering the details, sometimes referred to as fact-finding. Whitten and Bentley (2007) state that "the problem analysis phase provides the analyst with a more thorough understanding of the problems, opportunities, and/or directives that triggered the project" (p. 174).

Students pursuing a CIS major had 3 alternatives: Option I: Application Programming and Design; Option II: Micro Systems Design; or Option III: Business Technology Management. The first option provided the student with a strong background in a mainframe programming environment using COBOL. The second option supplied the student with a diverse background in programming in a Microsoft Windows environment using C++, Java, and Oracle. The third option offered the student an opportunity to enter the information technology (IT) arena for a career but yet avoid the programming and technical aspects of the other major options. This option allowed the student to focus on Web design, desktop publishing, and multimedia reporting.

Upon entering the systems planning phase, a strengths, weaknesses, opportunities, threats (SWOT) analysis was undertaken identifying the strengths, weaknesses, opportunities, and threats of the CIS program. The SWOT analysis focused on the areas of faculty, technology infrastructure, students, and curriculum.

The faculty's strengths were in being dynamic, dedicated, competent, and multicultural professors. However, their weaknesses included teaching too many overload classes and preparing for multiple classes.

The state-of-the-art classroom hardware and software were found to be strengths for the technology infrastructure while a lack of technical support and a lack of an examination laboratory were listed as weaknesses.

The students' participation in department sponsored clubs and organizations and their high success in national and state business school competitions were definite strengths. The students were found to be lacking in mathematical logic skills and verbal skills.

Strengths of the curriculum centered on a finding that the current curriculum built strong collaborative skills as well as communication and presentation skills. The curriculum was reviewed frequently and Option II was perceived to meet the core competencies for Accreditation Board for Engineering and Technology (ABET) accreditation. The curriculum being Microsoft-centric and lacking real world projects were listed as weaknesses as was the fact that the curriculum did not meet the core competencies for ABET accreditation in the Option III area. *Criteria for Accrediting Computing Programs* (ABET, 2007) lists the curriculum standards for information systems programs as:

- All students must take a broad-based core of fundamental information systems material consisting of at least 12 semester hours.

- The core materials must provide basic coverage of the hardware and software, a modern programming language, data management, networking and communications, analysis and design, and role of IS in organizations.
- Theoretical foundations, analysis, and design must be stressed throughout the program.
- Students must be exposed to a variety of information and computing systems and must become proficient in one modern programming language.
- All students must take at least 12 semester hours of advanced course work in information systems that provides breadth and builds on the IS core to provide depth. (p. 9)

Many threats were identified. First, the department was too focused on Microsoft products to the exclusion of other vendors' software. The Option III degree was perceived to be more of an office administration degree and less of a CIS degree. There was a keen awareness of the potential for loss of faculty to better paying jobs in industry and the need to continuously upgrade skills and proficiencies due to the rapid change in technology.

Several opportunities and challenges were identified for the department. Saying the words "opportunities and challenges" in the same sentence invokes visions of changes in the future. The ultimate goal of these changes was to better the program and therefore the student. "The philosophy of technology helps us understand how IT can be designed to enhance and/or transform social actors' experiences of their organizational life-world and to improve the ways in which they interpret or relate to such technologies" (Butler & Murphy, 2007, p. 197, referencing a 1979 work of Don Ihde). The faculty felt a Web-based development option should be added to the curriculum to meet the needs of the job market. The CIS Club and Programming Club were being utilized in projects around campus and town and could be employed more with the proper dissemination of information. Recruiting seminars at local community colleges and high schools have always been a strong point for this department. Continuing this policy should allow the department to build a strong relationship with potential freshmen or transfer students.

The SWOT analysis was an educational tool for the members of the CIS faculty. After verbalizing and visualizing the strengths, weaknesses, opportunities, and threats of the CIS program, the information collected in this phase was prepared and summarized for use it in the next step of building a new curriculum to meet the needs of students entering the current job market.

SYSTEMS ANALYSIS

The purpose of this step in the traditional SDLC is to build a logical model of the new system. In this step, the requirements of the new system are investigated, agreed upon, and documented. The analysts use various team-based methods to visualize and document the new system. The discovery of details (fact-finding) continues in this phase as the analysts begin to research the requirements for the new system by using tools such as documentation review, sampling, and research.

The first step in the systems analysis phase of the curriculum revisions project was to describe the problems found in the current curriculum and to outline desired changes for the new curriculum. Baltzan and Phillips (2008) state that "systems are successful only when they solve the right problem or take advantage of the right opportunity" (p. 350).

The investigation began with a hard look at the current curriculum. Which classes are requested most by the students? Which classes are in the curriculum but are not being taught on a regular basis?

As evaluations began, the faculty was aware of the lack of interest in the Option 1 major. In fact, the COBOL programming classes were not even being taught. The strongest interests of the students lay in the Option II and Option III choices.

In another exercise, the faculty examined five case projects typical for senior level information

systems students. An evaluation was completed to see what percentage of Option II students and Option III students should be able to perform these tasks as opposed to what percentage of students could actually complete the projects.

Considering this information coupled with the results of the SWOT analysis, the faculty went through an exercise utilizing joint application development (JAD) techniques to determine the path of the new curriculum. According to Shelly, Cashman, and Rosenblatt (2008), "a JAD team usually meets over a period of days or weeks in a special conference room or at an off-site location" (p. 96). Meeting in classrooms, conference rooms, and the local country club, JAD participants (faculty members) formed focus groups and participated in exercises to clearly define the new curriculum. In the first step of this exercise, faculty members wrote the job titles held by CIS alumni on yellow sticky notes. The next step was to write the names of careers desired by current students nearing graduation on yellow sticky notes. Next, the faculty identified which courses in the current curriculum supported the skills needed to do the jobs found on the sticky notes. In the final step, the faculty suggested additional courses that would be needed to properly prepare the students for these careers. This exercise allowed the faculty to see which career areas were absent from our teaching and where opportunities for supplementary courses existed.

Armed with the information of courses that were not being utilized, courses that were not quite fulfilling a need, and additional courses that were needed, the faculty progressed to the next phase of the development of the new curriculum, the design phase.

SYSTEMS DESIGN

The purpose of this phase of the SDLC is to develop a plan that will satisfy all the requirements for the new system that were discovered during the analysis phase. In this step, a physical model of the system is built to determine how the requirements will be met. Attempting to satisfy *all* the requirements was a lofty goal. The faculty understood this could be a process of many iterations. According to Alexander and Stevens (2002),

Getting started with anything is proverbially harder than doing it. It is perfectly acceptable to make some mistakes when you first try to organize any set of requirements. As long as you know that it is only a rough cut of the final structure, you can ask users to help you improve it. (62)

After discovering the requirements needed for the new curriculum, it was clear to the faculty members that two paths should be considered: end user computing systems (EUCS) and enterprise information systems (EIS). The EUCS option was designed for students who were interested in working in a support role for end users of smaller organizations which have less complex information systems demands, use more commercial software, and have more one-of-a-kind requests. The EIS option was intended for students who were interested in positions in a larger organization. These positions will most likely be dealing with larger, more complex projects to support the enterprise. The student would be part of a team composed of representatives from various departments within the company creating solutions for the organization. The student's ability to create appropriate solutions will involve applying the knowledge gained from the CIS curriculum as well as knowledge gleaned from core business courses taken in route to a Bachelor of Business Administration degree. According to the Association to Advance Collegiate Schools of Business (AACSB International, 2007)

Undergraduate degree programs in business educate students in a broad range of knowledge and skills as a basis for careers in business. Learning expectations build on the students' pre-collegiate educations to prepare students to enter and sustain careers in the business world and to contribute positively in the larger society. Students achieve knowledge and skills for successful performance in a complex environment requiring intellectual ability

to organize work, make and communicate sound decisions, and react successfully to unanticipated events. Students develop learning abilities suitable to continue higher-level intellectual development.

In order to meet the requirements of these options, the faculty looked very carefully at the objectives of each course. Many exercises were performed to verify that course objectives and outcomes were meeting computer information systems departmental goals and College of Business goals. The course objectives and outcomes were also analyzed pursuant to ABET and AACSB accreditation. In *Criteria for Accrediting Computing Programs* (ABET, 2007), the following statement is made concerning objectives, outcomes, and assessments:

The program enables students to achieve the following attributes by the time of graduation:

a. An ability to apply knowledge of computing and mathematics appropriate to the discipline;

b. An ability to analyze a problem, and identify and define the computing requirements appropriate to its solution;

c. An ability to design, implement and evaluate a computer-based system, process, component, or program to meet desired needs;

d. An ability to function effectively on teams to accomplish a common goal;

e. An understanding of professional, ethical, legal, security, and social issues and responsibilities;

f. An ability to communicate effectively with a range of audiences;

g. An ability to analyze the local and global impact of computing on individuals, organizations and society;

h. Recognition of the need for, and an ability to engage in, continuing professional development;

i. An ability to use current techniques, skills, and tools necessary for computing practice;

j. An understanding of processes that support the delivery and management of information systems within a specific application environment. (p. 15, 26)

As the faculty considered the objectives of each course, it became apparent that some of the courses currently in the curriculum should be redesigned to meet objectives set forth by the new options. The faculty discovered a need for an introductory level management information systems course which was added to the curriculum. A course used as an introduction to theory and practice of database design and processing was added for the curriculum of EUCS students and will be used to prepare EIS students for the advanced database management systems course. As a result of the analysis step, faculty members became aware of the need for a course in electronic business. A class was included in the curriculum for EIS students to study the standards, tools, and techniques associated with the development of systems to support electronic business. Another void discovered in the analysis step was the absence of a capstone course for seniors. A projects-based course was added to both curriculums to integrate theoretical concepts and practical skills gained in other information systems courses.

The faculty members examined each course in the CIS curriculum to determine if the course should be considered introductory, intermediate, or advanced. As each course was evaluated, the faculty decided two introductory courses should be completed with a grade of C or higher before any intermediate or advanced classes could be attempted. The introductory courses identified were introduction to programming with visual BASIC. NET and the new introductory management information systems class, information systems in organizations.

As new courses were added and current courses were redesigned, the semantics of keeping up with new course numbers was quickly becoming difficult. Under the previous curriculum containing Options

I, II, and III, all course numbers ended in a zero or a five (e.g., CIS 330, CIS 315). A numbering system was developed to have numbers of courses which had been redesigned or added to the new curriculum end in a six (e.g., CIS 366, CIS 406) making it easier to recognize courses which had been changed from the previous curriculum.

With the course objectives and outcomes carefully researched, the faculty was ready to present the curriculum to the students in the fall of 2006.

SYSTEMS IMPLEMENTATION

The purpose of this phase of the SDLC is to build the new system. In the development of a computer system this phase would include the coding, testing, and documentation of the programs in the system. For the faculty of UNA, this phase included submitting the new courses and redesigned courses to the College of Business Curriculum Committee and then to the university's Undergraduate Curriculum Committee for approval and inclusion in the course catalog for the 2006-2007 academic year. The transition plans were formalized and submitted with the curriculum proposals. Approval was unanimous at each step of the approval process.

SYSTEMS OPERATION AND SUPPORT

The purpose of this phase of the traditional SDLC is to actually use the system designed in the previous steps. In this step it will be determined if the new system is actually meeting the user expectations. The system is continuously maintained and enhanced to meet the needs of the user throughout the useful life of the system.

In this final step of the problem-solving process, the new curriculum was made available to students in the 2006 fall semester. All entering freshmen were placed in either the EIS or the EUCS option. Students entering the CIS program prior to the fall of 2006 were given the opportunity to switch their declared major from the previous Option I, II, or III program to the current EIS or EUCS program.

Hoffer, George, and Valacich (2008) say that "users must be provided with 'point-of-need support' – specific answers to specific questions at the time the answers are needed" (p. 541). To assist the students and advisors in beginning the new curriculum, many tools were provided to ease the process. A four-year plan sheet was developed to give the student an idea of which courses to take in their freshman, sophomore, junior, and senior years. A flowchart was developed to show a natural flow of progression for a CIS degree including prerequisites. A "transition map" was provided to the faculty advisors and students showing the previous course number and prerequisites for a course as well as the new course number and prerequisites. A document was provided to students and advisors showing all the CIS courses in the curriculum. The course information was color-coded in highlighting to reflect if it was a course required solely for EIS majors, solely for EUCS majors, or required by both programs. Appendix A contains samples of each of these documents.

CONCLUSION

The premise of this chapter and case study is that an information system curriculum is an information system. This chapter is also constructed on the assumption that there is or should be a strong resemblance in the processes associated with developing information systems and with developing information systems curricula. The faculty of the subject university department worked for 2 years on this basis to redesign its major requirements and the courses leading to the major, providing a systematic, complete, and efficient sequence of courses and options. The entire departmental faculty participated in over 60 hours of meetings, workshops, and focus group sessions during the two-year period. Student input and alumni was sought by faculty members

preparing for these sessions and faculty members consulted with their many and varied contacts in the employer community concerning issues of importance.

The transitional phase included numerous processes to accommodate the needs of students having made program of study plans passed on old curricula and requirements. Many other academic and support departments of the University were also impacted by the changes and the department has worked tirelessly to manage those impacts and assure a smooth transition for all.

As the new curriculum entered its second semester of use, students were monitored closely by their advisors to ensure a successful completion of the prescribed study. Faculty members are monitoring the courses to see that they are teaching the skills needed by today's graduate. In the ever-changing field of information technology, it is clear that eventually the curriculum developed in this process will become obsolete and a new curriculum will need to be developed. When that day arrives, following the steps of the SDLC, the faculty will begin again at the systems planning phase and complete the cycle until the new curriculum is operational. Meanwhile, incremental changes will be managed through assessment processes encouraged by the various accrediting bodies and driven by the faculty and its interactions with the other stakeholders in the education process.

REFERENCES

AACSB International—The Association to Advance Collegiate Schools of Business. (2007). *Eligibility procedures and accreditation standards for business accreditation* (Vol. 4). Retrieved May 15, 2007, from http://www.aacsb.edu/accreditation/process/documents/AACSB_STANDARDS_Revised_Jan07.pdf

ABET Computing Accreditation Commission. (2007). *Criteria for Accrediting Computing Pro-*

grams, 9(15), 26. Retrieved May 15, 2007, from http://www.abet.org/Linked%20Documents-UPDATE/Criteria%20and%20PP/C001%2007-08%20CAC%20Criteria%202-21-07.pdf

Alexander, I. F., & Stevens, R. (2002). *Writing better requirements*. Boston: Addison-Wesley.

Association of Collegiate Business Schools and Programs (ACBSP). (2007). Retrieved May 15, 2007, from http://www.acbsp.org/index.php?module=sthtml&op=load&sid=s1_001

Association for Computing Machinery (ACM). (2005). *Education*. Retrieved May 15, 2007, from http://www.acm.org/education/

Baltzan, P., & Phillips, A. (2008). *Business driven information systems*. New York: McGraw-Hill.

Butler, T., & Murphy, C. (2007). Understanding the design of information technologies for knowledge management in organizations: A pragmatic perspective. *Information Systems Journal, 17,* 143-163. Oxford.

Hoffer, J. A., George, J. F., & Valacich, J. S. (2008). *Modern systems analysis and design*. Upper Saddle River, NJ: Pearson Prentice Hall.

Shelly, G. B., Cashman, T. J., & Rosenblatt, H. J. (2008). *Systems analysis and design*. Boston: Thomson Course Technology.

Southern Association of Colleges and Schools (SACS). (2007) *Principles of accreditation: Foundations for quality enhancement (2007 interim edition)* (Vol. 12). Retrieved May 15, 2007, from http://www.sacscoc.org/pdf/2007%20Interim%20Principles%20complete.pdf

Whitten, J. L., & Bentley, L. D. (2007). *Systems analysis and design methods*. New York: McGraw-Hill.

KEY TERMS

Curriculum: The prescribed course of study to receive an educational degree.

Preliminary Investigation: Performed by systems analysts to identify the scope and nature of the problem.

Systems Planning Phase: The first phase of the systems development life cycle (SDLC) in which a preliminary investigation will be completed.

Systems Analysis Phase: The second phase of the SDLC where a logical model of the new system is built based upon agreed upon requirements.

Systems Design Phase: The third phase of the SDLC where a plan is developed that will satisfy all the requirements for the new system that were discovered during the analysis phase.

Systems Implementation Phase: The fourth phase of the SDLC where the new system is built by coding, testing and documenting the programs in the system.

Systems Operation and Support Phase: The fifth and final phase of the SDLC where the system designed in the prior phases is continuously maintained and enhanced to meet the needs of the user.

SWOT Analysis: An analytical tool used to identify strengths, weaknesses, opportunities and threats.

UNIVERSITY OF NORTH ALABAMA

Computer Information Systems Major Options

Enterprise Information Systems and End User Computing Systems

2006-2007 Catalog Course Descriptions

CIS 225. (3) **Introduction to Programming with Visual BASIC.NET**. A study of programming syntax and logic and the fundamental features of current programming languages. Using Visual Basic.Net, students will learn to analyze, program, test, document, and maintain a variety of information systems solutions to business problems. Prerequisite: CIS 125, MA 112.

CIS 236. (3) **Information Systems in Organizations.** A survey of information systems applications to support business processes, including operational, tactical, and strategic applications. Emerging and pervasive hardware, software, telecommunications, and data resource management technologies are emphasized. Security, ethics, global/international aspects, and systems integration issues are considered using the information systems (IS) framework. Corequisite: CIS 225.

APPENDIX

Table A1.

UNIVERSITY OF NORTH ALABAMA

College of Business

2006 - 2007

COMPUTER INFORMATION SYSTEMS MAJOR OPTIONS
Enterprise Information Systems or End User Computing Systems
Four Year Plan

	First Semester		Grade	Quality Points	*Second Semester*		Grade	Quality Points
FRESHMAN	EN 111 or EN 121	3 hrs.			EN 112 or EN 122	3 hrs.		
	MA 100 OR MA 112*	3 hrs.			MA 112 OR QM 295*	3 hrs.		
	*Natural Science w/lab***	4 hrs.			*Natural Science w/lab***	4 hrs.		
	HI 101 or HI 101-H or HI 201	3 hrs.			HI 102 or HI 102-H or HI 202	3 hrs.		
	*Fine Arts Elective****	3 hrs.			CIS 125	3 hrs.		
	TOTAL	**16 hrs.**			**TOTAL**	**16 hrs.**		
SOPHOMORE	EN 231 or EN 233	3 hrs.			EN 232 or EN 234	3 hrs.		
	COM 201 or COM 210	3 hrs.			QM 292	3 hrs.		
	QM 291	3 hrs.			AC 292	3 hrs.		
	AC 291	3 hrs.			BL 240	3 hrs.		
	MG 330	3 hrs.			CIS 236	3 hrs.		
	CIS 225	3 hrs.			CAAP	0 hrs.		
	TOTAL	**18 hrs.**			**TOTAL**	**15 hrs.**		

continued on following page

Table A1. continued

JUNIOR	EC 251	3 hrs.			EC 252	3 hrs.		
	QM 295 OR *General Elective**	3 hrs.			*300/400 Level Elective*	3 hrs.		
	MK 360	3 hrs.			MG 482W	3 hrs.		
	CIS 315 or CIS 350	3 hrs.			*CIS 366*	3 hrs.		
	CIS 330	3 hrs.			*CIS 376*	3 hrs.		
	General Elective	3 hrs.			**Apply for Graduation**			
	TOTAL	*18 hrs.*			**TOTAL**	*15 hrs.*		
SENIOR	FI 393	3 hrs.			MG 498	3 hrs.		
	MG 420	3 hrs.			*300/400 Level Elective*	3 hrs.		
	CIS 406	3 hrs.			*Non-business Elective*	3 hrs.		
	CIS 445 or CIS 446	3 hrs.			*CIS 466 or CIS 456*	3 hrs.		
	*International Elective*****	3 hrs.			*CIS 486*	3 hrs.		
	TOTAL	*15 hrs.*			**TOTAL**	*15 hrs.*		

*as appropriate, based on SAT or ACT score and high school courses. Subsequent courses chosen, based on whether MA 100 is included in the student's program of study.

**FROM PRESCRIBED LIST

***FROM PRESCRIBED LIST; foreign language if pursuing B.A.

****BL 455 OR EC 463 OR FI 463 OR MG491 OR MK 491

*CIS 315. (3) **Advanced Object Oriented Programming.** An advanced programming course with emphasis on object-oriented methodologies and concepts for solving complex business problems. This in-depth study of program control structures and best practices in software development includes advanced elements from object-oriented languages such as JAVA, C++, C#, and Visual BASIC.NET, . Prerequisite: CIS 225, 236 (with a grade of C or higher in both).

CIS 330. (3) **Systems Analysis and Design.** An introduction to the strategies and technologies for developing information systems (IS) within organizations. Emphasis is placed on the concepts, methodologies, and tools associated with the analysis, design, and implementation of successful systems. Prerequisite: CIS 225, 236 (with a grade of C or higher in both).

*CIS 350. (3) **Multimedia in Business Reports and Meetings.** A study of the media formats and access technologies necessary to prepare and deliver business presentations enhanced by data from digital media sources. Emphasis is placed on the theoretical and practical aspects of design and implementation of digital multimedia presentations. Exposure to interactive multimedia and virtual meeting formats is included. Prerequisite: CIS 225, 236 (with a grade of C or higher in both).

CIS 366. (3) **Database Development and Management.** An introduction to the theory and practice of database design and processing within the information systems (IS) framework. This includes fundamental design concepts, technical aspects, and components of relational databases and database management systems (DBMS), and use of specific DBMS software. Also covered is the automation of tasks by writing Visual Basic for Applications

(VBA) code for databases. Emphasis is placed on the importance of the management and effective use of the data resource within an organization. Prerequisite: CIS 225, 236 (with a grade of C or higher in both).

CIS 376. (3) **Web Development.** Introduction to Web development (design and creation) using current standards for client-side content delivery (e.g., XHTML and CSS). Students will learn to create and publish a multi-page, static-content Web site using associated applications. Special focus is given to user interface design, data presentation, and data organization. Prerequisite: CIS 225, 236 (with a grade of C or higher in both).

CIS 406. (3) **Data Communications.** A study of data communications and networking including terminology, components, and models. Communication protocols, network architectures, network security, and network operating systems are included. The management of communications networks is examined. Prerequisite: CIS 330.

*CIS 445. (3) **Advanced Database Management Systems.** An intensive examination of organizational databases, including data validity, reliability, security, and privacy. Structured query languages and report generators, will be emphasized. Distributed databases, data mining, and data warehousing are introduced. The roles of database administrator and data administrator will be explored. A current enterprise DBMS like ORACLE will be used. Prerequisites: CIS 330, 366.

*CIS 446. (3) **Decision Support Using Spreadsheets**. A study of the use of spreadsheet software to analyze and summarize business data. The integration of spreadsheets with other business software and Internet applications is explored. Also includes automation of tasks by writing Visual Basic for Applications (VBA) code for spreadsheets. Emphasis is placed on the importance of the management and effective use of the data resource within organizations. Prerequisite: CIS 225, 236 (with a grade of C or higher in both).

*CIS 456. (3) **Desktop and Web Publishing for Business.** Applications course concentrating on the use of advanced applications for preparing promotional, periodical, informational, and specialty publications with a business emphasis, including desktop publishing concepts. Study of Web site creation and management, using current technologies, and the integration of databases. Includes sound, photo editing, animation, digital cameras, digital video and scanning techniques as they relate to business. Prerequisites: CIS 350, 376.

*CIS 466. (3) **E-Business Technologies and Applications.** A study of the standards, tools, and techniques associated with the development of systems to support electronic business. Various aspects of security, ethics, trans-border data flows, and interoperability will be studied. Included will be technologies, such as PHP, J2EE, and other languages, data management and data communications in an e-commerce environment. Prerequisite: CIS 376, 406, 445.

CIS 486. (3) **Projects in Information Systems.** This course integrates theoretical concepts and practical skills gained in previous information systems courses into a capstone information systems project. This course presents real-world problems through case studies and projects while emphasizing the student's communication, collaboration, technical, and problem solving skills. Prerequisite: CIS 330, 366, 406, Senior Standing

---

*Option-specific courses.

Figure A1.

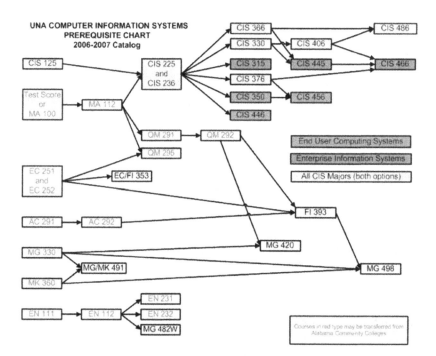

Table A2.

Fall 2005 Course Names and Section Numbers, if different from 2006	Fall 2005 Course Name	Catalog Prerequisites 2005	Catalog Prerequisites 2006	Fall 2006 Computer Prerequisite Enforcement	Fall 2006 Class	Fall 2006 Title
CIS 125-08	Bus Apl Microcomp		Honors or permit	Honors or permit	CIS 125 H-01	Honors Bus Apl Microcomp
		Permit	Permit	Permit	CIS 125- INT	Bus Apl Microcomp (PERMIT)
CIS 125-06			LC or permit	LC or permit	CIS 125- LC	Bus Apl Microcomp
CIS 125-07					CIS 125-06	Bus Apl Microcomp
	Visual Basic	125	125, MA 112	125	CIS 225-01	Intro to Prog w/Visual Basic.net
CIS 492-01	Mgmt Information Sys	330	225 (co)	330	CIS 236-01	Information Systems in Organizations
		125 or CS 110	225, 236, C	225	CIS 315-01	Advanced Obj Orient Prog
	Intro Sys Anal/DSGN	125 or CS 110	225, 236, C	225	CIS 330-01	Systems Analysis and Design
		125 or CS 110	225, 236, C	125	CIS 350-01	MMedia BN reports & Meetings
CIS 435-01	Database Records Management	125 or CS 110	225, 236, C	225	CIS 366-01	Database Development and Management
CIS 375-01	Internet & WWW	125 or CS 110	225, 236, C	125	CIS 376-01	Web Development
CIS 485-01	Data Comm & Networking	330	330	330	CIS 406-01	Data Communications
	Database Management Systems	125 or CS 110	330, 366	330	CIS 445-01	Advanced Database Management Systems
CIS 365-01	Electronic Spreadsheet Appl	125 or CS 110	225, 236, C	125	CIS 446-01	Decision Support Using Spreadsheets
CIS 495-01		375	350, 376	375	CIS 456-01	Desktop & Web Pub for Bus
			376, 406, 445	375, 485, 445	CIS-466-01	E-Business Tech & Applications
					CIS-475-01	Teach Career-Tech Bus & Mkt Ed
			330, 366, 406, Sr.	330, 485, and 435 or 445, Sr.	CIS-486-01	Projects in Information Systems
					CIS-575-01	Teach Career-Tech Bus & Mkt Ed
					CIS 602-01	Visual Basic
					CIS 625-I03	Enterprise Systems Analysis and Design
					CIS 627-I03	Research and Report Writing

Chapter XXXV
Redesigning a SAD Course to Promote Problem–Based Learning

Ann M. Quade
Minnesota State University, Mankato, USA

ABSTRACT

This chapter reports on the design, development, and implementation of a hybrid introductory systems analysis and design (SAD) semester long course taught at the junior/senior level. Five online instructional modules that focus on student-centered, problem-based learning (PBL) were developed. Each module parallels and reinforces the classroom session content. The classroom "seat-time" saved by having students study and complete online materials provides the instructor and students with additional time for face-to-face and electronic discussions. To further encourage PBL throughout the semester, students use an iterative approach to the SAD life cycle to analyze, design, and implement a prototypic solution to a real world problem presented by the authentic client. The use of a learning management system allows the client to participate in the course throughout the semester regardless of the physical distance between the students and the client. Instructor experiences, hybrid module development strategies, and a summary of student and client feedback are included.

INTRODUCTION

Systems analysis and design (SAD) courses typically introduce students to the fundamental principles used in this disciple area and provide students with an opportunity to demonstrate their understanding of these principles through a project that requires the development of a software product. This allows students to examine, practice, and demonstrate understanding of each phase in the system development life cycle.

The 15 week introductory junior/senior level SAD course discussed herein is required for all computer and information science, computer engineering, and computer management information science majors. Two sections are typically taught during the year with 20-25 students enrolled in each section. In the past, it has been taught in a traditional, face-to-face environment with instructor-centered lectures. Students worked in groups, composed of four to five students each during the semester and used systems analysis and design theory presented in the classroom to develop a prototypic software product for an instructor-selected fictitious problem. The instructor's role in this environment was one of knowledge dissemination rather than a facilitator of learning.

While it was clear that students benefited from instructor feedback throughout the semester, it is apparent that the time available using this paradigm for in-depth discussions between the instructor and individual groups was at a premium. Scheduling conflicts were a perennial problem when attempting to determine suitable student, group, and instructor meeting times outside of the assigned classroom periods. Interestingly, instructor, student, and group time conflicts, as well as difficulty evaluating individual work done within a group, are often sited as the main reasons why computer science instructors shy away from group projects (Brown & Dobie, 1999).

From the students' course evaluations, it was evident that this SAD course format was less than ideal for reaching the course's cognitive goals which focus on developing and using problem solving methodologies and social goals which stress team work and communication. Although Hazzan (2003) reports success in addressing and meeting these goals by greatly limiting the course enrollment, which allowed more time for interactions and reflection, the decrease in credit hour production is not a realistic option for many programs.

The redesign of this course focused on shifting to a student-centered, problem-based learning (PBL) environment. Edens (2000) identifies several characteristic threads of a successful PBL which, in turn, were woven in the framework of this course. These include: 1) learning is student-centered rather than instructor-centered; 2) students consistently work in small groups; 3) the instructor serves as a facilitator rather than a lecturer; and 4) problems are the focus, the stimulation for learning, and serve as the tools by which students develop problem solving skills.

It is evident that the PBL model signals a radical paradigm shift from the traditional instructor-centered classrooms to a classroom that is group-centered and stresses the development, implementation, and demonstration of higher level cognitive domain skills. The importance of infusing PBL into course design is succinctly summarized by Gibson and O'Kelly (2005) in this way: 1) Students are encouraged to think critically when analyzing and solving complex, real-world problems; and 2) Team work serves to develop and enhance participants' group skills including effective oral and written communication. While PBL and cooperative group work (Johnson & Johnson, 1989) are employed in numerous mathematics and science and engineering programs as tools to promote higher order cognitive skill development (Mehrens & Lehmann, 1984), Chinn and Martin (2005) indicate these techniques have not been readily been promoted in computer science classrooms.

At the core of this SAD course redesign are two complementary components that utilize our Web-based learning management system (LMS), Desire 2 Learn. First, a series of online course modules were developed to support learning through student participation in activities that encourage problem analysis and synthesis and interactions between classmates, group members, and the instructor. These modules parallel and reinforce a related classroom component and the phases within the SAD project development cycle. This approach shifts the responsibility of learning from one that is dependent on the instructor to that of being a shared commitment between student and instructor. The online modules are designed to be completed outside of a classroom setting. The "seat time" saved by delivering almost half of the course content online is used by groups for project-related meetings and by the instructor to provide more in-depth feedback and one-to-one interactions, both electronically and face-to-face, with students and groups.

During the course's more traditional classroom component, which encompasses approximately one half of the course, emphasis is placed on establishing a foundation for the three phases (i.e., requirements and analysis, design modeling, and prototype implementation and testing) of the system development life cycle and group presentations that summarizes their progress at the end of each phase. Calongne (2002) reports that while effective teams and interaction between team members in an online software engineering classroom is highly desirable, many students dislike team projects where there is no face-to-face interactions. The hybrid course pedagogy discussed above, where half of the course content is delivered online and the other half in the classroom, provides ample opportunity for the development and practice of successful online and off-line group communication.

Besides providing the student with access to the online modules, the LMS discussion forum and document repository area are designed to give students, groups, and the instructor additional communication routes throughout the course (Sheard, 2004).

The second component of the course redesign involved the incorporation of a virtual, authentic client who provides the class with a "real world" problem from the student's business environment. The problem, in turn, requires each group to develop, using SAD principles, a prototypic software product which evolves throughout the semester. The integration of an authentic client and problem adds a very powerful learning dimension to the course, that is, a real problem that requires a real solution. Polack-Wahl (1999) reports that prior to the advent of the Web and its resources, providing students with such real world experiences was a daunting task and often not worth the effort. With the help of a LMS, the virtual client can actively participate in the class through online discussions and participating in FAQ forums. Since students and their respective groups are required throughout the course to store course-related documents in their LMS document repository, the client may also observe and comment on work throughout the project development process (Polack-Wahl, 2001).

To some faculty, the idea of persuading an actual client to virtually join a course may seem like a daunting task. Alumni, advisory board members, and interested business partners who actively recruit and hire our program's students as interns or for full time employment have proven to be excellent resources.

Three overarching benefits are derived by delivering almost one-half of the course online and incorporating a virtual authentic client/real world problem. First, the reduced seat time allows the instructor additional time to engage in more and deeper student/group interactions throughout the semester. Second, the student groups formed early in the semester are able to use available class time to meet online or face-to-face to discuss and plan their project development. Third, active engagement in PBL provides students and the instructor with a powerful environment for learning.

Student course assessments indicate the implementation of a hybrid course which embeds PBL principles, coupled with an authentic client/problem, greatly enhances the student's understanding of: the software analysis, design, and development process; the bridge that exists between theory and practice; and the need for developing individual as well as group communication skills. Overwhelming support for this type of course has been obtained from all participating clients.

RATIONALE FOR DEVELOPING A HYBRID COURSE

Systems analysis and design courses, whether taught in a face-to-face or hybrid environment, typically address both cognitive and social aspects of learning. Cognitive course goals focus on students' understanding of the key principles behind the system development process and their ability to use this knowledge to guide the development of a solution for a given problem.

Because large problems may require a great deal of time to produce a viable solution, student groups or teams are often formed. Teams, which attempt to emulate an authentic work environment, provide a means to address social aspects of the course, thus concentrating on developing cooperative group and project management skills.

Having taught this course for several years in a traditional environment, it became clear that an effective course pedagogy, which addressed both and social goals, could be successfully developed within a hybrid course and yield a significant gain in overall student learning.

Using Smith and Tillman (1999) and Ko and Rossen (2004) as references, this author identified aspects of the traditional course that could be delivered online as well as incorporate a high degree of student-centered, problem-based learning. The class time saved by having students complete these modules outside of class provides the faculty with increased opportunities to:

- Frequently meet face-to-face with individuals and groups to assess progress and offer suggestions in team building and project development process
- Engage students in active discussions outside of physical classroom through the use of online discussion boards and postings
- Promote increased student-to-student group interactions
- Provide rapid instructor electronic feedback to questions, documents, and assignments stored within the LMS's individual and group accounts
- Electronically address and comment on problematic areas in assignments and project development prior to submission, thereby supporting learning and reducing the need for significant revisions later
- Develop a forum for the virtual, authentic client to present the project, respond to questions, and observe student work throughout the semester
- Examine frequently the electronically stored, team reports generated by a team project man-

ager to help monitor and encourage individual participation and contributions to the team project-building process
- Simulate a virtual work environment scenario where team members in diverse locations work together to solve a problem
- Exploit audio and video digital technologies for creating and posting ancillary course material
- Establish and meet virtual office hours

SAD HYBRID COURSE REDESIGN

Net generation students expect instructors to link learning with technology. While five years ago the use of a Web site for posting of assignments and grades seemed adequate, the proliferation of LMS applications on campuses makes it the obvious first choice for course deployment. It has been the experience of this author that the time required for initial LMS proficiency is 30-40 hours. Although there are several LMS vendors, many products have similar components thus less time is often required to reach a proficient usage level on subsequent LMS implementations.

Students also expect the LMS to distribute quality instructional materials. Many universities recognize the importance of excellent online components and support instructional designers to work side-by-side with faculty who, in turn, serve as the subject matter expert throughout the process. Without access to an instructional designer, the burden of course design and development falls entirely on the faculty.

Teaching a face-to-face SAD course several times prior to developing online materials helped this author build a solid understanding of active learning, depth of processing theory, student-centered learning, and group dynamics. As this author gained more experience in the design and development of online material and how students access, process, and learn in an online mode, the online instruction became more diverse and creative.

An instructional designer was not used in the development of the five online course modules. The design, development, and implementation of each module, on average, took 25 hours. This time commitment could be significantly reduced by involving an instructional designer early on and one or more graduate students to identify references and deploy materials to the LMS.

Identifying Modules for Online Delivery

By definition, a hybrid or blended course provides students with both traditional and online instruction. Determining an appropriate amount of time allocated to instruction in each setting is a determination that should be made by the faculty. A practical strategy may include the initial development of a limited amount of materials for online learning. This would facilitate rapid assessment and revision, as needed. Rosbottom and Crelling (2000) observe that with more practice, faculty expertise in designing online modules rapidly increases. As a result, additional online components can be added. These guidelines may help determine what aspects of a course are best suited for online presentation:

- Identify the activities/events that are currently part of the face-to-face class sessions that could be implemented in an online course component. This may include: discussions and lectures in audio, video, or textual formats; problems, case studies, or other scenarios that form foundations for class discussions; cooperative group experiences that encourage and develop team building among individuals in virtual space; and assignments that require the use of software engineering principles, software applications, or project management tools.
- Determine the learning objectives for each identified course component. The more objectives per component, the more complex the activities within the component.

- Assess the amount of class time that could be potentially saved by each identified online component and what the time savings could be used for.
- Establish an assessment strategy for each potential online component.
- Determine the extent of online coursework and face-to-face/virtual team experiences that students possess.
- Identify the type of Internet access most students use.
- Identify the features, file types, and the size of the allocated storage class space that the potential delivery system supports.
- Establish a comfortable balance between student-centered and instructor-led online activities.
- Identify the instructor time and technological resources available for course development.

SAD Hybrid Course Structure

The hybrid course discussed herein is divided into three phases: requirements and specifications, design and modeling, and testing and implementation. Each phase is further subdivided in topic areas that span the 15 week course as shown in Table 1. All topics have supporting online modules except for the group presentations conducted in a classroom setting at the conclusion of each phase. While Jones (2007) suggests that: as academic latency increases, traditional approaches to software development education become increasing irrelevant and as a result IT majors graduate with the theoretical knowledge of the phases and activities in the system development lifecycle but lack the skills required to build useful applications for today's marketplace the pedagogical approach to these modules is simply "doing" systems development from the very start.

Online Module Components and Student Activities

Each online supporting module has four integrated components: advanced organizers, instruction and

Table 1. Overview of the SAD hybrid course

Wk	Phase	Topic
1	Phase I: Requirements and Specifications	Course introduction Significance of project management Introduction of authentic problem and client
2		Team selection Identify requirements and specifications
3		Identify requirements and specifications
4		Project presentation I Refine requirements, specifications for semester problem as needed
5	Phase II: Design Modeling	Process/data modeling
6		Process/data modeling
7		Interface, input, output modeling
8		Project presentation II Refine process, data, interface, IO as needed
9	Phase III: Prototype Implementation and Testing	Develop testing plan
10		Prototype implementation
11		Prototype implementation
12		Prototype implementation
13		Prototype implementation
14		Cross-team testing, refine as needed
15		Project presentation III

examples, student practice, and instructor feedback. The Phase I Requirements and Specifications online module completed during week three of the course is shown in Table 2.

Rather than attending class for up to 4 hours during week three, students complete this module outside of class. Instead of preparing for and delivering four lectures during this week, the instructor may use this time to provide detailed electronic feedback to groups and conduct face-to-face meetings with groups or individuals who appear to have difficulty with the module (Sheard, 2004).

Examples of Phase I Week 3 Requirements and Specifications Module Components and Associated Student Activities

Five examples that illustrate the advanced organizers, instruction and examples, and student practice module components for this phase are presented below.

Phase I Week 3 Advanced Organizer - Learning Objectives

At the end of this phase, each group will be able to:

1. Read the Phase I Case Study and answer the questions below.
    a. *Who* are involved in this problem, opportunity, or directive and what is the role or title of each person?
    b. *What* appears to be the specific issue(s) at the core of this case study?
    c. *Why* does this problem, opportunity, or directive exist?
    d. *Where* is/are the location(s) that is/are impacted?

Table 2. Phase I week 3 requirements and specifications online module components and associated activities

Module Component	Associated Student Activity
Advance organizers	Self-test to determine mastery of concepts needed prior to beginning the activity
	Review learning objectives
	Review a course map that illustrates the relationship of this module to the course
	Module assessment rubric
Instruction and examples	Review techniques used to determine requirements and specifications
	Provide URLs, textbook references, or other sources for examples
	Use sample problem scenario to identify system requirements and specifications
Student practice	Provide document template for identifying system requirements and specifications
	Students identify requirements, specifications in problem
	Each student uploads to the group's allotted area within the LMS the student's completed sample problem document template
	Phase group project manager provides comments to individual group members on the group member's submission, prepares a final summary of the requirements and specifications, and submits it to the appropriate LMS drop box
Feedback	Instructor uses rubric to assess material and provides group text and audio feedback; if necessary, instructor initiates meeting with entire group or approves group to begin identifying requirements and specifications for the semester project

e. *When* (hour, day, week, month) does the problem, opportunity, or directive peak?

Use a table format to summarize your responses. Place the question (who, what, why, etc.) in the first column and the responses to the questions in the second column. Each question may have multiple responses.

2. Complete a table like the one described above by answering the same type of questions above the semester problem presented our business client.

3. Prepare for both the case study and the semester problem:

    a. Additional questions and identify types of documents, files, databases, or other materials that may prove useful to better understand the opportunity or directive.

    b. Sample questionnaires, interview questions and strategies, and sampling techniques that could be used.

c. Three potential solutions for the given opportunity or directive and conduct a cost benefit analysis for each solution. Submit as part of our group's written summary.

d. A final written summary of this phase using the Phase I template located in the LMS as a guide.

Phase I Week 3 Advanced Organizer - Course Map

Assume that this semester long course is divided into four equal quarters or periods. Table 3 indicates the iterative, overlapping nature of the system development process. The cell under Q1 or Quarter 1 column filled with ****** indicates where the tasks associated with the requirements and specification phase are in relation to the course and the entire system development process.

Phase I Week 3 Advanced Organizer – Assessment Rubric

Understanding the Problem Domain

3. The author provides a clear understanding of the current system as well as the problem, opportunity, or directive that drives the development of the new system. The user requirements are succinctly defined.
2. The author provides a limited view of the current system and/or the problem, opportunity, or directive that drives the development of the new system. Some user requirements are not included.
1. The author provides very little vision of the current system and/or the problem, opportunity, or directive that drives the development of the new system. Many user requirements are missing.

Fact-Gathering Tools

3. The interview questions and questionnaire or observation form demonstrate substantial thought and understanding of what information is vital for system development. Because of its design, the questionnaire or observation form is easy to follow and use.
2. The interview questions and questionnaire or observation form demonstrate some thought and understanding of what information is important to system development. Use of the questionnaire or observation form may be impeded by its limited scope.
1. The interview questions and questionnaire or observation form indicate the author does not

know what information is important to system development.

Clarity of the Alternate and Proposed Solutions

3. Creative and innovative solutions are noted. Alternative and proposed solutions demonstrate an in-depth understanding and perspective of the problem. The proposed solution addresses the issues detailed in the problem statement and user requirements.
2. Alternative and proposed solutions demonstrate an understanding of the problem. The proposed solution addresses some of the issues detailed in the problem statement and user requirements.
1. The alternative and proposed solutions demonstrate little if any understanding of the problem. The proposed solution addresses few or none of the issues detailed in the problem statement and user requirements.

Feasibility Studies

3. The authors demonstrate a clear understanding of the terms technical, operational, and economic feasibility as they apply to their project. The costs and benefits of the proposed system are well developed, thought out, and detailed. Using the costs and benefits as a foundation, the break even analysis, return on investment, and net present value calculations are realistic. Charts that are easy to read and convey a message are used to summarize important points.
2. The authors show some understanding of the terms technical, operational, and economic

Table 3.

Phase	Q 1	Q2	Q3	Q4
Requirements and Specifications	******			
Design and Modeling				
Implement Prototype, Testing				

feasibility as they apply to their project. The costs and benefits of the proposed system should contain more detail. As a result, the break even analysis, return on investment, and net present value calculations could be more realistic. Charts are used to summarize important points.

1. Little if any understanding of the terms technical, operational, and economic feasibility as they apply to their project is noted. The costs and benefits of the proposed system are weak resulting in poor break even analysis, return on investment, and net present value calculations. Charts are difficult to follow.

Organization

3. The order, structure, and overall presentation of the written final summary of the phase are compelling and move the user through section by section.
2. The organizational structure is strong enough to move the reader through the work with undo confusion.
1. The writer lacks a clear sense of direction. The sections seem unrelated.

Mechanics/Conventions

3. The same format (i.e., font, margins, headings, etc.) are used consistently throughout the final summary document. The headings and subheadings are meaningful and provide solid visual clues to the reader as to the content following them. Text is free of misspellings and/or grammatical errors.
2. The format (i.e., font, margins, headings, etc.) is somewhat the same throughout the document. Most of the subheadings are meaningful and provide visual clues to the reader as to the content following them. Text has less than three misspellings and/or grammatical errors.

1. The format (i.e., font, margins, headings, etc.) is not the same throughout the document. Most of the subheadings provide little if any visual clues to the reader as to the content following them. Text has numerous misspellings and/or grammatical errors.

Scoring:
Advanced = 17-18 Proficient = 16-14 Basic = 13-12 Minimal = 11-9 Poor = 8 or less

Phase I Week 3 Instruction and Examples - Development of Effective System Requirements and Specifications

Examples that demonstrate effective use of system analysis and design techniques can be found in many trade and business publications as well as newspapers. Often such publications are available online or through individual college or university library database providers. The most effective examples are often ones that students can relate to and/or have experience with. The redesign of United Parcel Service (UPS) to include more technology as an approach for expanding the efficiency the package delivery system is appealing because the students' experiences with delivery services and varied uses of technology (Dade, 2006).

Phase I Week 3 Student Practice - Case Study for Student Practice

Examples selected for student practice are often projects that have not followed several overriding principles of the systems analysis and design process. The Denver International Airport (DIA) baggage transport system fiasco is a classic case study that illustrates every aspect of what can go wrong and what happens as a result. It is interesting to observe students as they discern how effective analysis and design tend to encourage the development of effective and efficient systems. An online search will generate numerous reviews of the DIA baggage system blues.

COURSE OUTCOMES

While individual and group submissions, presentations, and traditional testing are used by the instructor to assess student learning throughout the semester, the course itself is assessed each semester by participating students and the authentic client. Three weeks prior to the end of the semester, students anonymously complete an institutional course assessment form that is composed of 15 Liker-type questions that seek to provide general course and instructor evaluations and four general, opened-ended questions related to the course. The same type of assessment form has been used by this instructor with both the traditional and hybrid SAD classes for the past 8 years. Although no significant difference is noted on the responses to the Liker-type questions by the traditional and hybrid classes, the responses to the opened-ended questions by the hybrid classes were most insightful.

Student Responses

Anonymous comments have been solicited from students enrolled in this hybrid course for the past 3 years. The feedback has captured the essence of team work and individual responsibility, strengths and weaknesses of the hybrid course design, and use of authentic client and project. Some of the more salient responses include:

Team work and individual responsibility
- *"In other courses you are always told what to do. Here you have to be focused and take personal responsibility for getting the job done."*
- *"Although I realize being able to work as part of a team is important, the move to a team project work was very difficult for me. Up to this time, every computer science instructor preached and published a code of ethics that included a thou shall not share your work, code, or anything with anybody. It's just the opposite here."*

- *"This was the first time I worked on team project in college. My team members worked well together. I liked the rotation of each team member having a chance to take on the role of project manager for several weeks during the course."*

Strengths and weaknesses of the hybrid course design
- *"The course appeared organized because all materials were available online 24/7. The examples from other projects were very useful. Because of the up-front grading rubrics, there were no issues as to how me or my team would be graded."*
- *"At first, the idea of online work to replace class time bothered me. As the course moved forward, I began to really get into it. I realized what the instructor was doing, freeing up more of her time so she could help us with our work online and in person."*

Use of authentic client and project
- *"I'm very impressed with the time commitment and effort put forth by client. He made the course more meaningful and gave insights that I don't think our instructor could have provided."*
- *"This was the most challenging course I have taken and I am a senior! I worked hard but learned more than in any other class in the program."*

Client Responses

From the first time this course was offered utilizing an authentic client and project to the present, there has been no shortage of volunteers to assume the role of client. This involvement provides a win-win situation for the client, students, and institution. Participant provides a mechanism for businesses and institutions to establish and cultivate relationships that support internships, employment, and scholarships. It offers an opportunity for businesses and their employees to give back to the community and provide students and departments with a window to cutting edge ideas, trends, and technologies. Selected comments from clients are listed below.

Strengths and weaknesses of the hybrid course design

- *"Over time, the problems I present to the class have become more sophisticated and therefore require more detailed and intricate solutions. Otherwise the students have solutions in a matter of days instead of weeks. I attribute this to the additional time the instructor spends working with the students."*

- *"The experience brought back memories of my own college days. Using the LMS was very easy and it allowed me to keep in close contact with students."*

- *"I liked to see the improvements in the project each time a milestone required work submitted. The online discussions keep students on track. You could easily see from their responses how the solutions were derived."*

- *"As first I was a bit hesitant about serving as client. Once I became familiar with the LMS, my time commitment averaged two hours/week. Our organization has benefited greatly form this experience because it allowed to observe students and help identify those that, upon graduation, would be solid contributors to our organization."*

CONCLUSION

The process of developing a problem-based hybrid course is time intensive and requires an intricate understanding of the subject matter, team building dynamics, and learning. Learning the structure of an LMS, developing and revising materials, encouraging student in interactions both online and face-to-face, maintaining online threaded discussions, and establishing and building relationships with authentic clients, can initially seem overwhelming.

It is realistic to begin building a hybrid course by developing and assessing a limited amount of online material at any given time. Once developed, these materials can be reused in subsequent courses. A LMS tool greatly enhances the opportunity to implement online modules and the authentic client/project model. This virtual environment allows frequent, fluid interchange ideas and thoughts between the client, students, and faculty that would be difficult to develop without such support.

Both the student and client levels of satisfaction identified through use of a course assessment instrument indicate that this type of course creates a unique environment for active, project-based learning. The student feedback obtained from this course parallel that of Woodworth and Applin (2007), whose hybrid introductory computers and information course engaged students in team-based problem solving activities using application software. Although there has been much written about the pros and cons of e-learning in computing, Zhang, Zhao, Zhou, and Nunamaker (2004) concisely summarize its merits in this way: "In an e-learning environment that emphasizes learner-centered activity and interactivity, remote learners can outperform traditional classroom students."

REFERENCES

Brown, J., & Dobie, G. (1999). Supporting and evaluating team dynamics in group projects. *Proceedings of 30ᵗʰ SIGCSE Technical Symposium on Computer Science Education, 31*(1), 281-285.

Calongne, C. (2002). Promoting team interaction in the online classroom. *Journal for Computing Sciences in Colleges, 18*(1), 218-227.

Chinn, D., & Martin, K. (2005). Collaborative, problem-based learning in compute science. *Journal of Computing Sciences in Colleges, 21*(1), 239-245.

Dade, C. (2006, July, 24). Moving ahead: How UPS went from low-tech to an IT power-and where it is headed next. *The Wall Street Journal*, p. R4

Edens, K. M. (2000). Preparing problem solvers for the 21st century through problem-based learning. *College Teaching, 48*(2), 55-61.

Gibson, P. J., & O'Kelley, J. (2005). Software engineering as a model of understanding for learning and problem solving. In *Proceedings of the 2005 Workshop on Computing Education Research* (pp. 87-97).

Hazzan, O. (2003). Cognitive and social aspects of software engineering: A course framework. In *Proceedings of the 8th Annual Conference on Innovation and Technology in Computer Science Education* (pp. 3-6).

Johnson, D. W., & Johnson, R. T. (1989). *Cooperation and competition: Theory and research*. Edina, MN: Interaction Book Company.

Jones, C. G. (2007). Bringing the systems analysis and design course into the 21st century: A case study in implementing modern software engineering principles. In *Proceeding of the IEEE 29th International Conference on Software Engineering (ICSE'07)* (pp. 744-747).

Ko, S., & Rossen, S. (2004). *Teaching online: A practical guide (2nd ed.)*. Boston: Houghton Mifflin Company.

Mehrens, W., & Lehmann, I. (1984). *Measurement and evaluation in education and psychology*. New York: Holt, Rinehart and Winston.

Polack-Wahl, J. (1999). Incorporating the client's role in a software engineering course. In *Proceedings of 30th SIGCSE Technical Symposium on Computer Science Education* (Vol. 31, pp. 73-77).

Polack-Wahl, J. (2001). Enhancing group projects in software engineering. *Journal of Computing Sciences in Colleges, 16*(4), 111-121.

Rosbottom, J., & Crelling, J. (2000). A generic model for on-line learning. *ACM SIGCSE Bulletin, 32*(3), 108-111.

Sheard, J. (2004). Electronic learning communities: Strategies for establishment and management. *ACM SIGCSE Bulletin, 36*(3), 37-41.

Smith, P., & Tillman, R. (1999). *Instructional design*. New York: John Wiley and Sons.

Woodworth, P., & Applin, A. (2007). A hybrid structure of the introductory computers and information technology course. *Journal of Computing Sciences in Colleges, 22*(3), 136-144.

Zhang, D., Zhao, L. J., Zhou, L., & Nunamaker, J., Jr. (2004). Can e-learning replace classroom learning? *Communications of the ACM, 47*(5), 75-79.

KEY TERMS

Active Learning: Encourages student participation in knowledge construction through reading, writing, discussing, and engagement in higher-order thinking tasks like analysis, synthesis, and evaluation.

Depth of Processing: A theory that posits that learners will recall information better if they learn it in a way that enables them to draw understandings from material studied, not just a superficial understanding gained through memorization.

Hybrid Course: A course with both an online and traditional face-to-face component.

Instructional Designer: A specialist that has extensive experience in learning theory, communication theory, psychology, and pedagogy and uses expertise to design and develop learning materials.

Learning Management System: A software package that enables the management and delivery of online content to learners. Most LMSs are Web-based to facilitate "anytime, any place, any pace" access to learning content and administration. Examples include WebCt, BlackBoard, and Desire 2 Learn.

Rubric: A guide used to score performance assessments in a reliable, fair, and valid manner and is generally composed of dimensions for judging student performance, a scale for rating performances on each dimension, and standards of excellence for specified performance levels.

Virtual, Authentic Client: This phrase refers to an alumnus, advisory board member, or other interested business partners who provides students with a real-life problem that requires the development of a prototypic software product. The client actively participates and interacts with students via the LMS throughout the semester.

About the Contributors

Farid Ahmed is an associate professor of electrical engineering and computer science at the Catholic University of America (CUA), Washington, DC. He directs the Multimedia Security Lab at CUA, where he is currently performing research in information hiding. Ahmed's background include information security, digital watermarking, steganography, cryptography, computer networks, and signal/image processing. He has published over 45 technical papers in refereed international journals and conferences in these areas and holds four US patents in watermarking. Ahmed is a member of SPIE, Computer Security Institute, IEEE, and ACM.

Paulette Alexander has been a member of the UNA Computer Information Systems Faculty since 1981, serving as chair since 2002. Her PhD is in information systems from The University of Memphis. Alexander also holds a Master of Public Affairs degree from The University of Texas and a Master of Arts degree in business statistics and a Bachelor of Science degree from The University of Alabama. Her primary current research centers on internet privacy issues with previous research topics including economic development, technology and its management, public education accountability and finance, and distance education issues and strategies.

Nancy Alexopoulou is a research associate at Harokopio University of Athens. She holds an MSc in advanced information systems and a bachelors degree in informatics from the Department of Informatics and Telecommunication of the University of Athens. Currently, she works on her PhD in agile business process execution. Her research interests include business process modeling, agile process-aware information systems and enterprise architectures.

A.B.M. Shawkat Ali is a senior lecturer in the School of Computing Sciences at Central Queensland University, Australia. He holds a BSc (Hons.) and MSc in applied physics and electronics Eegineering, and MPhil in computer science and engineering from University of Rajshahi, Bangladesh and a PhD in information technology from the Monash University, Australia. Ali has published a quite good number of refereed journal and international conference papers in the areas of support vector machine, data mining and telecommunication. Recently he published a text book, *Data Mining: Methods and Techniques*.

Francisco Alvarez-Rodríguez is an associate professor of software engineering and the dean of the Basic Sciences Center in the Autonomous University of Aguascalientes. He holds a BA in informatics (1994) and a MA (1997) from the Autonomous University of Aguascalientes and a EdD degree from the Education Institute of Tamaulipas, México and he is Ph(c) from the National Autonomous University of México. He has published research papers in several international conferences in the topics of software engineering and e-learning process. His research interests are software engineering lifecycles for small and medium sized enterprises and software engineering process for e-learning.

Rezaul Begg received his BSc and MSc Eng degrees in electrical and electronic engineering from Bangladesh University of Engineering and Technology, Dhaka, Bangladesh, and his PhD degree in biomedical engineering from the University of Aberdeen, UK. Currently, he is an associate professor of biomedical engineering at Victoria University, Melbourne, Australia where he researches in biomedical engineering, biomechanics and machine learning areas. His current research focuses on gait and movement analysis, sensor networks for ageing healthcare and computational intelligence techniques and their applications in various biomedical domains.

Rashida Begum worked as a research assistant in Eminence Associates (a private humanitarian organization to develop a sustainable and appropriate health care system in Bangladesh) from August 2005 to August 2007. She completed her Bachelor of Medicine and Bachelor of Surgery (MBBS) from Shahid Ziaur Rahman Medical College, Bangladesh in 2004. She is also a member of Bangladesh Medical and Dental Council since 2004. Her research interests include health implications of wireless technologies, use of telemedicine in rural communities of the world and reproductive health care status in developing communities etc.

Paul D. Berger is professor of mathematical sciences (visiting) at Bentley College. He was formerly professor of marketing and quantitative methods at the School of Management, Boston University. He earned his SB, SM, and PhD degrees from the Massachusetts Institute of Technology Sloan School of Management. He has co-authored several books, including *Experimental Design with Applications in Management, Engineering, and the Sciences* (2002), and *e-Marketing and e-Commerce: Theory, Practice, and Application*, forthcoming in early 2008. He has authored over 120 refereed-journal articles, including in such journals as *Management Science, American Statistician, Technometrics*, and *IEEE Transactions on Knowledge and Data Engineering*.

Sjaak Brinkkemper is a professor of organization and information at the Institute of Information and Computing Sciences at Utrecht University, The Netherlands. Before that, he was a consultant at the Vanenburg Group and a chief architect at Baan. He has held academic positions at the University of Twente and the University of Nijmegen. He holds an MSc and a PhD from the University of Nijmegen. His research interests are software product development, information systems methodology, meta-modeling and method engineering.

Maria P. Canton is the author of over 20 books in the field of computer programming and system hardware. She holds a PhD in computer science and teaches mathematics at South Central College, North Mankato, Minnesota.

Qiyang Chen is an associate professor of MIS in the School of Business at Montclair State University. He received his PhD in information systems from the University of Maryland, Baltimore. Chen's research interests, publications, and consulting activities are in the areas of strategic issues in MIS, database design and data modeling, human-computer interaction and soft computing. Chen is a member of the editorial boards of several academic journals. He also serves regularly in program committees for international conferences and is included in the Millennium Edition of International *Who's Who of Information Technology*.

Alan Cole is employed at the IBM T.J. Watson Research Center in Hawthorne, New York, where he is a member of the User Technologies Group. His work over the past few years has been in the area of pervasive and wireless computing, specifically involved with position determination technologies and location-based services. He is currently part of a team working on mobile collaboration. He received his bachelor's degree from Hope College and master's degrees in mathematics and computer science from the University of Michigan, joining IBM in 1976.

Laura Dahl is a faculty member in the College of Continuing Education at the University of Utah. Her research interests are multimedia and cognition, human-computer interaction, and educational technology. Laura worked as a software and Web developer, and has spent years designing and teaching technology courses. She frequently conducts workshops on technology integration to faculty at higher education institute.

Karen Day has a special interest in health informatics, change in health organisations and how we adapt to change when it is linked to health IT projects. Her concern about the application of theory in the workplace as well as our capacity to learn and adapt as we develop professionally resulted in her discovery of action research. Her experience in nursing, health service management, health insurance, managed care, and health IT project management is now being used in her role as health informatics co-ordinator at the University of Auckland. Karen teaches health informatics principles, knowledge management, and qualitative research. She is also involved, with professor Jim Warren, Martin Orr and others, in the establishment of the National Institute for Health Innovation associated with the University of Auckland.

Adir Even received the MS degree in electrical and computer engineering from the Technion of Israel (1991) and the MBA degree from Tel-Aviv University (1996). He is a doctoral student in Boston University School of Management, specializing in information systems management. His research focuses on the economic perspectives of the design and the implementation of data resources and the system that manage them. His articles have appeared in *Communications of the ACM, Communications of the AIS, IEEE Transactions on Data and Knowledge Engineering*, and *Database for Advances in Information Systems*.

Jill Flygare is currently a faculty member in the Department of Teaching and Learning as well as a PhD candidate in the Department of Educational Psychology at the University of Utah. She holds a BA in secondary social sciences and a MEd in instructional design and educational technology. Her research interests are in the area of effective online design and online social communication.

Tagelsir Mohamed Gasmelseid holds BSc, MSc, Postgraduate Diploma, Mphil and PhD degrees in information systems. He is affiliated to King Faisal University (Saudi Arabia) and the University of Medical Sciences and Technology (Sudan). He published some articles in referred journals and contributed some presentations for international conferences. His research interests include multiagent systems, mobile and context aware applications, agent oriented simulation, AOSE, MIS and DSS.

Roy Gelbard is a faculty member of the Information System Program at the Graduate School of Business Administration, Bar-Ilan University. He received his PhD and MSc degrees in information systems from Tel-Aviv University. His work involves software engineering, software project management, knowledge representation and data mining.

Cecilia Gomes is an assistant professor teaching programming languages and application softwares at the Information Technology Department, Northern Virginia Community College, Annandale Campus. She is also a student at the Catholic University of America (CUA), Washington, DC, studying towards her PhD degree in computer science, researching in digital watermarking and information hiding.

Carol Gossett has taught at the University of North Alabama located in Florence, Alabama, for 11 years. Gossett has obtained certification as a certified computing professional (CCP) in the areas of systems analysis and design and programming. Prior to teaching, Gossett's career included experiences as a programmer and a systems analyst. Gossett currently teaches courses in systems analysis and design, decision support for business, and microcomputer applications.

Manas Hardas is a graduate student pursuing his doctoral degree in computer science at the Kent State University. He obtained his master's degree from Kent State University and bachelor's degree from Mumbai University, India. His research interests include cognition, learning theory, computational and machine learning, knowledge representation, e-learning and automatic pedagogy.

Allan M. Hart (PhD) is an assistant professor in the Information Systems and Technology Department, Minnesota State University, Mankato. His interests include database, design patterns, object relational mapping (ORM), aspect-oriented programming (AOP) and Java EE 5 technologies

Syed Zahid Hassan is currently undertaking his PhD research at Central Queensland University (CQU), Australia. He successfully completed BS in electronics and communication systems and research-based masters in computer sciences. During his master's, the core of his research was agent-based data mining system. Zahid's research interest includes: hybrid data mining systems, data clustering, machine learning algorithms and multi-agents systems. Before joining CQU as a PhD research fellow in 2005, he has served as a research officer at health informatics research group at the Science University of Malaysia from 2001-2005. He has published over 25 research papers in various reputable international conferences and journals. Zahid has recently been awarded an ARC (Australian Research Council) ISSNIP (Intelligent Sensors, Sensor Networks and Information Processing) postgraduate grant for 2007.

He is the recipient of IPRS (international postgraduate research scholarship) PhD fellowship from the Australian government: department of education, science and training (DEST). He also received IRPA (intensified research priorities areas) scholarship from the Science University of Malaysia (Malaysia); towards his masters' studies. He was selected for the SSUET Merit Scholarship from Sir Syed University of Engineering and Technology (Pakistan); for his undergraduate studies (1997). Zahid is a member of the technical program committee of Artificial Intelligence Research Group, Cambridge University, UK. He served as a chair person in one parallel session of the international symposium on information technology (ITSim2003), Kuala Lumpur, Malaysia, 30th September-02nd October 2003.

Igor Hawryszkiewycz is currently professor of computing sciences at the University of Technology, Sydney. He has held several visiting positions in Europe in both academe and industry. Since 1988, his work has concentrated on designing systems that support focused teams and communities using Internet and groupware technologies. It has concentrated on developing methods for analyzing knowledge needs within distributed systems and choosing the best technologies to satisfy these needs.

Brian Henderson-Sellers is director of the Centre for Object Technology Applications and Research and professor of information systems at the University of Technology, Sydney. He is author or editor of 28 books and is well-known for his work in object-oriented and agent-oriented methodologies, OO metrics and metamodelling. He is co-editor of the ISO/IEC International Standard 24744 ("SE Metamodel for Development Methodologies") and eitor of the *International Journal of Agent-Oriented Software Engineering*. In July 2001, Henderson-Sellers was awarded a Doctor of Science (DSc) from the University of London for his research contributions in object-oriented methodologies.

Winnie Hua is a principal consultant in CTS Inc. She has more than 15-year project and consulting experience on a broad range of leading-edge technologies. She holds a master's degree in computer science. As a solution architect/lead, she has led lifecycle design and development of large-scale e-commerce systems on diverse platforms using a variety of cutting-edge technologies and unified/agile methodologies. She has initiated/participated in advanced research on various emerging web technologies. She is a member of numerous professional associations, a regular speaker in conferences/seminars, and also a co-founder of Charlotte Architecture and Technology Symposium (CATS).

A.H.M. Razibul Islam is currently a PhD student and a member of Guided Wave & Photonics Research Group at Macquarie University, Australia. He completed his Master of Engineering in radio communications from Kyung Hee University, South Korea in 2007 and Bachelor of Science in electrical and electronic engineering from Islamic University of Technology (IUT), Bangladesh in 2002. He is also a lecturer (on leave) of Department of Electrical and Electronic Engineering, Islamic University of Technology (IUT), Bangladesh since 2002. His research interests include optical and wireless access networks, use of wireless and wired technologies in developing countries, Radio over Fibre links, and their performance analyses, telemedicine applications etc.

Robert B. Johnston (BSc (Hons), MSc, PhD) is an associate professor in the Department of Information systems. His research areas are electronic commerce, supply chain management and theoretical foundations of information systems. He has over 100 refereed publications, many in leading international journals including *Management Science*, *Journal of the Operational Research Society*, *OMEGA*, *International Journal of Production Economics*, and *European Journal of Information Systems*. Before becoming an academic he was an IT consultant, designing and implementing about 25 large computer systems in Australian manufacturing companies.

Dean Kelley (PhD) is associate professor of computer science at Minnesota State University, Mankato.

Javed I. Khan is currently a professor at Kent State University, Ohio. He has received his PhD from the University of Hawaii and BSc from Bangladesh University of Engineering & Technology (BUET). His research interest includes complex networked systems, extreme networking, cross-layer optimization, and digital divide. His research has been funded by U.S. Defense Advanced Research Project Agency and National Science Foundation. He has also worked at NASA for Space Communication Team. As a Fulbright senior specialist he also studies the issues for high performance higher education networking. He is member of ACM, IEEE and Internet Society. More information about Khan's research can be found at medianet.kent.edu.

Ahsan Khandoker received the BSc in electrical and electronic engineering from Bangladesh University of Engineering and Technology, Dhaka, Bangladesh in 1996, M. EngSc in 1999 from Multimedia University, Malaysia and M. Engg in 2001 & Doctor of Engineering in physiological engineering from Muroran Institute of Technology, Japan in 2004. Currently, he is an Australian Research Council Research Fellow at University of Melbourne, Australia, where he researches in the area of mathematical processing and machine classification of physiological signals. His research interests focus on the diagnosis of sleep disordered breathing, gait analysis and its pattern recognition.

Kenneth J. Knapp (PhD) is an assistant professor of management at the U.S. Air Force Academy. He received his PhD in 2005 from Auburn University. His research focuses on information security effectiveness issues and has been published in numerous practitioner and academic outlets including *Information Systems Management, Information Systems Security, Communications of the AIS, Information Management & Computer Security, International Journal of Information Security and Privacy, Journal of Digital Forensics, Security, and Law*, as well as multiple articles in editions of the *Information Security Management Handbook* edited by Tipton & Krause.

Jorge Eduardo Macías Luévano is an associate professor of information systems in the Autonomous University of Aguascalientes (UAA), México, since 1986. Macías holds a BS in computer systems engineering (1985) from Monterrey Tech (ITESM) and an MSc in information systems (1997) from the Autonomous University of Aguascalientes (UAA). He has worked as information systems consultant for many organizations in México.

Massimo Magni is assistant professor of organization and information systems at Bocconi University. He has been a visiting scholar at the R.H. Smith School of Business, University of Maryland. His area of expertise revolves around organizational change during information systems implementation, with a particular focus on individual and group behaviors related to technology acceptance and exploration.

Fernando Flores Mejía is a lecturer in software engineering, Program of Software Engineering for Industry and a PhD student in the Autonomous University of Aguascalientes, México. He holds a BS in informatics from the National Polytechnic Institute (IPN), Mexico (1980), and titled by professional experience in 1996), and a MSc in computer sciences from Autonomous University of Aguascalientes (2007). He has worked as a Software Engineer in Mexican and international private enterprises from 1980. His current research interest is the specification and evaluation of requirements engineering processes for service-oriented software-intensive and information systems.

Jan Mendling is a postdoctoral fellow at the Business Process Management (BPM) Group at Queensland University of Technology, Brisbane, Australia. He holds a PhD from the Vienna University of Economics and Business Administration, Austria, and diplomas in business administration and in business information systems from the University of Trier, Germany. Mendling is the author of more than 50 refereed papers and co-organizer of the XML4BPM workshop series and member of programme committees for several international workshops and conferences. He is co-author of the EPC Markup Language (EPML), an XML-based language for exchanging EPC process models.

Simon Milton received his PhD from the University of Tasmania in 2000 in which he reported the first comprehensive analysis of data modelling languages using a common-sense realistic ontology. Milton continues his interests in the ontological foundations of data modeling languages and the implications of top-level ontological commitments in information systems modelling. He holds a senior lectureship in the Department of Information Systems at The University of Melbourne.

Manuel Mora-Tavarez is an associate professor of information systems in the Autonomous University of Aguascalientes (UAA), Mexico, since 1994. Mora holds a BS in computer systems engineering (1984) and a MSc in artificial intelligence (1989) from Monterrey Tech (ITESM), and an EngD in systems engineering (2003) from the National Autonomous University of Mexico (UNAM). He has published several research papers in international conferences and journals. His main research interest is the development of a common management and engineering body of knowledge for software engineering, systems engineering and information systems underpinned in the systems approach.

Jonathan Munson received his PhD in computer science from the University of North Carolina in 1997. At UNC he worked in the field of collaboration systems and developed the Sync replicated data framework. He joined the IBM T.J. Watson Research Center in 1998 and has worked on virtual-reality-based collaboration systems, systems for distributing and protecting digital content, and location- based services for wireless networks. He is currently working in the areas of automotive telematics and spatial collaboration systems.

Manzur Murshed received his BSc Engg (Hons) degree in computer science and engineering from Bangladesh University of Engineering and Technology (BUET), Bangladesh (1994) and PhD degree in computer science from the Australian National University, Australia (1999). He is an associate professor and the head of the Gippsland School of Information Technology at Monash University, Australia, where his major research interests are in the fields of multimedia signal processing and communications, parallel and distributed computing, simulations, and multilingual systems development. He received many research grants including a prestigious Australian Research Council (ARC) Discovery Projects grant. He has published more than 100 peer-reviewed journal articles, book chapters, and conference papers. Murshed is the recipient of numerous academic awards including the University Gold Medal by BUET. He recently received the inaugural Faculty of Information Technology Award for Excellence in Research for Early Career Researchers and was one of the nominees for the Vice Chancellor's Award for Excellence in Research for Early Career Researchers.

Mara Nikolaidou is an assistant professor of IT at Harokopio University of Athens. She holds a PhD and a bachelor's degree in computer science from the Department of Informatics and Telecommunication of the University of Athens. She is a member of IEEE and ISCA. Her research interests include software and information system engineering, e-government and digital libraries.

Rory O'Connor is a senior lecturer in software engineering at Dublin City University and a senior researcher with Lero, The Irish Software Engineering Research Centre. He has previously held research positions at both the National Centre for Software Engineering and the Centre for Teaching Computing, and has also worked as a software engineer and consultant for several European technology organizations. His research interests are centered on the processes whereby software intensive systems are designed, implemented and managed.

Martin Orr is a psychiatrist, a senior lecturer at Auckland University School of Population Health and clinical director of information services for the Waitemata District Health Board (Auckland, New Zealand). Orr is involved on a daily basis in the pragmatics of meeting the 'opportunities and challenges' of developing health knowledge systems. His key research interests lie in working with the dedicated professionals who, through the development, implementation and utilization of health knowledge systems, strive to 'make a healthy difference' for their communities. He has an interest in change, action research, reflective practice, innovation diffusion, individual and group dynamics, and information privacy and security within the complex health sector, particularly with relationship to health knowledge management systems. He is also involved in the establishment of the National Institute for Health Innovation.

Manoranjan Paul received his BSc (Hons) in computer science and engineering from Bangladesh University of Engineering and Technology (BUET) in 1997 and PhD degree in computing and IT from Monash University, Australia in 2005. He is currently working as research fellow at Gippsland School of Information Technology, Monash University, Australia. His major research interests are in the fields of image/video coding, multimedia communication, surveillance, video on demand, and image segmentation. He has published more than 25 refereed international journals, book chapters, and conference publications. He received ARC grant $25,000 for organizing workshop on Video Signal Processing and Communication 2006/2007. He was a main coordinator of Video Signal Processing & Communication Workshop 2007 (www.eiii.com.au/vspc). Dr Paul is a full member of the IEEE, ACS, and ARC ECR.

Luigi Proserpio is assistant professor of organization and management at Bocconi University. His main research interests are focused on geographically-dispersed teams, e-learning and technology adoption. He has published several articles on the topic in a variety of journals, including *Research Policy, Journal od Product innovation Management, Academy of Management Learning & Education.*

Bernardino Provera holds a post-doctoral scholarship at at the Institute of Organisation and Information Systems, Bocconi University. He has been a visiting scholar at the Management Learning Department of Lancaster University Management School. He is an associate of the Advanced Institute of Management Research (AIM). His research interests lie in the field of improvisation and knowledge management in high-reliability organizations and creative industries.

Ann Quade is a professor in the Department of Computer and Information Sciences at Minnesota State University, Mankato (MSU). She received her PhD from the University of Minnesota. Throughout her career, she has published research in several areas related to computer science education including: attracting and retaining women in computer science; classroom models that promote undergraduate research; assessing the merits of student online notetaking; the syntax and semantics of learning object meta-data; and the development and assessment of active, problem-based hybrid online courses. Since becoming a MSU faculty member in 1984, Quade has represented her University through participation in: numerous national and international conferences; the Computing Research Association mentoring program; and the 2002 International Grace Hopper Celebration of Women in Computing Conference steering committee. In 1998, she presented both oral and written testimony before the U.S. House of Representatives, Committee on Science in support of H.R. 3007, The Advancement of Women in Science, Engineering, and Technology Development Act. She works diligently to build partnerships between industry and education. At MSU she has been recognized as a: Teaching Scholar; William Flies fellow; recipient of the Minnesota State Student Association Dr. Duane Orr teaching award; and six year member of the MSU Foundation Board of Directors.

Peter Rittgen received an MSc in computer science and computational linguistics from University Koblenz-Landau, Germany, and a PhD in economics and business administration from Frankfurt University, Germany. He is currently a senior lecturer at the School of Business and Informatics of the University College of Borås, Sweden. He has been doing research on business processes and the development of information systems since 1997 and published many articles in these areas. For further details the reader is referred to http://www.adm.hb.se/~PRI/.

Laura C. Rodríguez-Martínez is a lecturer in software engineering in the Technology Institute of Aguascalientes, and a PhD student in the Autonomous University of Aguascalientes, both located in Aguascalientes, México. She holds a BS in computer systems engineering from the Technology Institute of the Laguna, Torreón, México (1991) and a MSc in computer sciences from Autonomous University of Aguascalientes (2006). She has worked as a software engineer in Mexican private enterprises from 1998. Her current research interest is the specification and evaluation of lifecycle processes for service-oriented software-intensive and information systems.

Ladislav Samuelis (assistant professor), obtained MSc in electrical engineering at Prague Technical University (1975), and PhD in informatics at Budapest University of Technology (1990). He has been engaged in research into the automatic program synthesis at the Institute of Computer Technology at the Technical University of Košice, Slovakia. Since 1998 he affiliated with the Dept. of Computers and Informatics, Faculty of Electrical Engineering and Informatics at the same university. He taught operating systems, database systems, computer networks and Java. Currently, he is involved in research of intelligent tutoring systems and software evolution

Julio Sanchez is the author of 24 books in the field of computer architecture, programming, and software engineering. He holds doctoral degrees in physics and law. He is presently an associate professor of Computer Science at Minnesota State University, Mankato, Minnesota, where he teaches courses in programming and computer architecture.

Tony Shan is a renowned expert working in the computing field for 20+ years with extensive experience on architecture engineering, technology strategies, and system designs in a number of multi-million dollar IT projects in a broad range of industries. Having been involved in web technologies since the earliest Html, Java and .Net versions, he has, as an enterprise/solutions/chief architect, directed the lifecycle design and development of large-scale award-winning distributed systems on diverse platforms using a variety of cutting-edge technologies and unified/agile methodologies. He has initiated advanced research on emerging computing technologies, resulting in an invention patent and several patent-pending initiatives as well as many unified methodologies and platform models for adaptive enterprise system development.

G. Shankaranarayanan received the PhD degree in management information systems from The University of Arizona Eller School of Management (1998). His research interests include data modeling and design, database schema evolution, metadata modeling and management, data quality management, and the economics of data management. His research has appeared in journals such as the *Journal of Database Management, Decision Support Systems, Communications of the ACM, Database for Advances in Information Systems*, and *IEEE TKDE*. He serves on the editorial board of the *International Journal of Information Quality*. He is a member of the IEEE and a member of the ACM.

Quynh Nhu Numi Tran completed her PhD in the area of intelligent agent systems at the University of New South Wales, Australia in 2005. In her dissertation, she proposed a methodology for developing multi-agent systems using an ontology-based approach. She later worked as a research fellow at the University of Technology, Sydney, with research interests including method engineering, agile methodologies and collaborative systems. She is currently working at IBM Australia as a data-warehouse developer and business intelligence specialist.

Miguel Vargas-Martin is an assistant professor of the University of Ontario Institute of Technology (Oshawa, Canada). He obtained a BSc (computer science) from the Autonomous University of Aguascalientes (1996), a MEng (electrical) from CINVESTAV of IPN (1998), and a PhD in computer science from Carleton University (2002). Before joining UOIT, Vargas-Martin was a postdoctoral researcher for Alcatel Canada Inc. His main research interests include network security through defense systems against malicious software attacks and abusive use of network services. He is CTO and co-founder of Hoper Inc., a software company that develops innovative web tools.

Brijesh Verma is an associate professor of IT in the School of Computing Sciences at Central Queensland University in Australia. His research interests include computational intelligence, hybrid algorithms, pattern recognition, data mining and Web information retrieval. He has published twelve books, five book chapters and over hundred papers and supervised 29 research students in the above mentioned areas. He has served as a chief/co-chief investigator on twelve competitive research grants including ARC (Australian Research Council) LIEF, ARC research network and industry linkage grants. He is a co-editor in chief of *International Journal of Computational Intelligence and Applications* published by World Scientific and editorial board member/associate editor of four international journals. He has served as general chair, program chair, advisory chair, steering committee chair and program committee member on organizing, program and advisory committees of over 35 national and international conferences. He is a senior member of IEEE, IEEE Computational Intelligence Society and a member of International Neural Network Society. He is a chair of IEEE Computational Intelligence Society's Queensland Chapter.

Vivienne Waller (BA, BSc, Grad Dip Pub Ec Pol, PhD) was involved in the project of developing situated systems while working in the Department of Information Systems, University of Melbourne. She is particularly interested in socio-technical systems and is currently at the Institute for Social Research, Swinburne University of Technology, investigating how people search for information.

John Wang is a professor of information and decision sciences at Montclair State University. Having received a scholarship award, he came to the USA and completed his PhD in operations research from Temple University in 1990. He has published over 100 refereed papers and four books. He has also developed several computer software programs based on his research findings.

Jim Warren is professor of health informatics at the University of Auckland, holding a joint appointment between the Department of Computer Science and the School of Population Health. He is a member of the Executive of Health Informatics New Zealand and co-editor of the recent proceedings of the International Medical Informatics Association's 12th World Congress. He has been consulting and researching on health information systems since 1989. He holds a Bachelor of Science in computer science and PhD in information systems from UMBC in Baltimore. From 1993 to 2005 (up until joining the University of Auckland) he worked for the University of South Australia in Adelaide. He is also involved, with Karen Day, Martin Orr and others, in the establishment of the National Institute for Health Innovation associated with the University of Auckland.

Inge van de Weerd is a PhD student at the Institute of Information and Computing Sciences at Utrecht University, The Netherlands. She holds an MSc in information science from Utrecht University. Her research interests comprise method engineering, meta-modeling, product management, information systems development and knowledge management. Her PhD research focuses on the development of a knowledge infrastructure for software product management methods that enable situational capability evolution.

David Wood is a member of IBM's T.J. Watson Research Center, where he manages a group of projects in the area of pervasive computing. He has been with IBM since 1992 working in areas including parallel computing, data visualization, visual and spoken user interfaces, and location-based services and architectures. His department is currently focused on solutions and middleware for Telematics service providers, location-based services and middleware for client devices. He obtained a BA in physics from UC San Diego in 1985 and a master's degree in computer science from New York University in 1989.

Jun Xia is an assistant professor of international management in the Department of International Business at Montclair State University. He received a PhD in management with a concentration in strategic management and international business management from Texas Tech University. His current research interests include international expansion strategies, transition economies, trade and foreign direction investment, organizational learning, and corporate social responsibility.

Yuni Xia is an assistant professor of computer and information science at Indiana University Purdue University – Indianapolis. Her research includes databases, moving object databases, sensor databases, data mining, data uncertainty management, data stream management and ubiquitous/pervasive computing. She holds a bachelor degree from the Huazhong University of Science and Technology of China, an MS and a PhD degree from Purdue University. She has served on the program committee of a number of conferences in databases and pervasive computing.

Ruben Xing received his Doctor of Global Information Development (PhD) in 1992, Master of Computer Science (MS) in 1989, and Master of Math & Science Education (MA) in 1987 from Columbia University. Xing has worked as a vice president of the E-business Group at Citicorp, assistant vice president of the Global Information Technology group at Merrill Lynch and some other large financial conglomerates in metropolitan New York for more than 15 years. His current research interests include Broadband, Wireless Communications, the Internet security, Disaster Recover/Business Continui

James G.S. Yang (MPh MBA, CPA, CMA) is a professor of accounting at Montclair State University. He specializes in individual and corporate income tax and international taxation. He has published thirty-seven articles in peer-reviewed academic journals and presented 21 papers to academic conferences. In his profession, he is also a CPA practitioner and served as a consultant to many CPA firms in the areas of taxation and accounting standards.

James E. Yao is a full professor of MIS in the Department of Management and Information Systems, School of Business, Montclair State University, New Jersey. Yao teaches management information systems, database, programming, and other MIS courses. His research interests are in the areas of IT innovation adoption, diffusion, and infusion in organizations, e-business, e-commerce, and m-commerce. Yao's research papers have been published in journals on information technology and information systems.

Robert Z. Zheng is a faculty member and director of instructional design and educational technology (IDET) program in the Department of Educational Psychology at the University of Utah. His research interests include online instructional design, cognition and multimedia learning, and human-computer interaction. He edited *Cognitive Effects on Multimedia Learning* and co-edited *Online Instructional Modeling: Theories and Practices*. He has published numerous book chapters and research papers in the areas of multimedia, online learning, and cognition. He has presented extensively at national and international conferences.

Index

A

action research (AR) 573
ActivityKind 246
activity types 37
adaptive software development (ASD) 2
agent oriented software engineering (AOSE) 360
aggregated class hierarchies 398
agile development support, new fragments 229
agile method fragments 243–270
agile software development 223–242
agile software development, characteristics 224
architecting method 5
architecture development method (ADM 2
architecture readiness maturity (ARM) 5, 15
architecture stack and perspectives (ASAP) 10
AS4651 metamodel 244
asynchronous transfer mode (ATM) 589
automated medical diagnostic system 544–559
automated medical diagnostic system, design 548

B

back propagation neural network (BPNN) 526
binary search trees 151
BPEL, main concepts 209
BPEL support 210
Business Process Management xxvii
business process management, definition 191
business process management, history 189
business process management initiative (BPMI) 203
business process modeling, foundations 189–222
business process modeling languages and methods 197
business process modeling notation (BPMN) 203
business process modeling techniques 196

C

cellular technology 603
certification and accreditation (C&A) 299
chain reaction pattern 405
change management 133
class templates 389
clinical decision support systems (CDSS) 574
clinical knowledge with RCTs 568

clustering in course ontology 622
cognitive functions 306
cognitive load theory 309
cognitive overload 312
cognitive perspective on human-computer interface design 305–325
composing mixed objects 417
concept mapping 612
concept types 40
conceptual-content relationship 315
conceptual distance 619
concurrent activities 38
conditional activities 39
constant-time tables 155
constructive interface 307
context analysis 363
context aware systems 358
contextual interface 308
course concept dependency schema (CCDS) 612
course knowledge representation 611
course ontology 611
CSCW systems, modern design dimensions 371–387
CSG extraction 615
customer relationship management (CRM) 130

D

data acquisition 274
database server configuring 287
data maintenance and enhancement 276
data marts 275
data mining tasks 525
data resources design, utility-cost tradeoffs 271
data staging 274
data warehouse (DW) 272
data warehouse design 274
decision support (DS) 124
decision support systems (DSSs), design and analysis xv–xxv, 119–129
decision trees (DT) 528
design patterns 388
design philosophy 3
design science (DS) approach 122
design techniques 123